for GCSE mathematics **Intermediate**

CAMBRIDGE UNIVERSITY PRESS
Cambridge, New York, Melbourne, Madrid, Cape Town, Singapore, São Paulo

Cambridge University Press
The Edinburgh Building, Cambridge CB2 2RU, UK

www.cambridge.org
Information on this title: www.cambridge.org/9780521890267

First published 2003
4th printing 2006

Printed in Italy by G. Canale & C. S.p.A., Borgaro T.se, (Turin)

A catalogue record for this publication is available from the British Library

ISBN-13 978-0-521-89026-7 paperback
ISBN-10 0-521-89026-8 paperback

Typesetting and technical illustrations by The School Mathematics Project
Other illustrations by Robert Calow and Steve Lach at Eikon Illustration
Photographs by Graham Portlock
Cover image © Getty Images/Nick Koudis
Cover design by Angela Ashton

Acknowledgements

The authors and publishers are grateful to the following Examination Boards for permission to reproduce questions from past examination papers:

AQA (NEAB)	Assessment and Qualifications Alliance
AQA (SEG)	Assessment and Qualifications Alliance
Edexcel	Edexcel Foundation
OCR	Oxford, Cambridge and RSA Examinations
WJEC	Welsh Joint Education Committee

This product includes mapping data licensed from Ordnance Survey mapping with the permission of the Controller of Her Majesty's Stationery Office, © Crown copyright. All rights reserved. Licence no. 100001679

The authors and publishers would like to thank Evan Sedgwick-Jell for his help with the production of this book.

Contents

1 Pythagoras's theorem

You will revise square roots.

This work will help you

- find the length of one side of a right-angled triangle if you know the lengths of the other two sides
- solve problems involving the lengths of sides of right-angled triangles

A Areas of tilted squares

To get the area of a tilted square …

… find the area of a surrounding square, then subtract the area of the triangles ...

… **or** divide the square up like this and find the area of the parts.

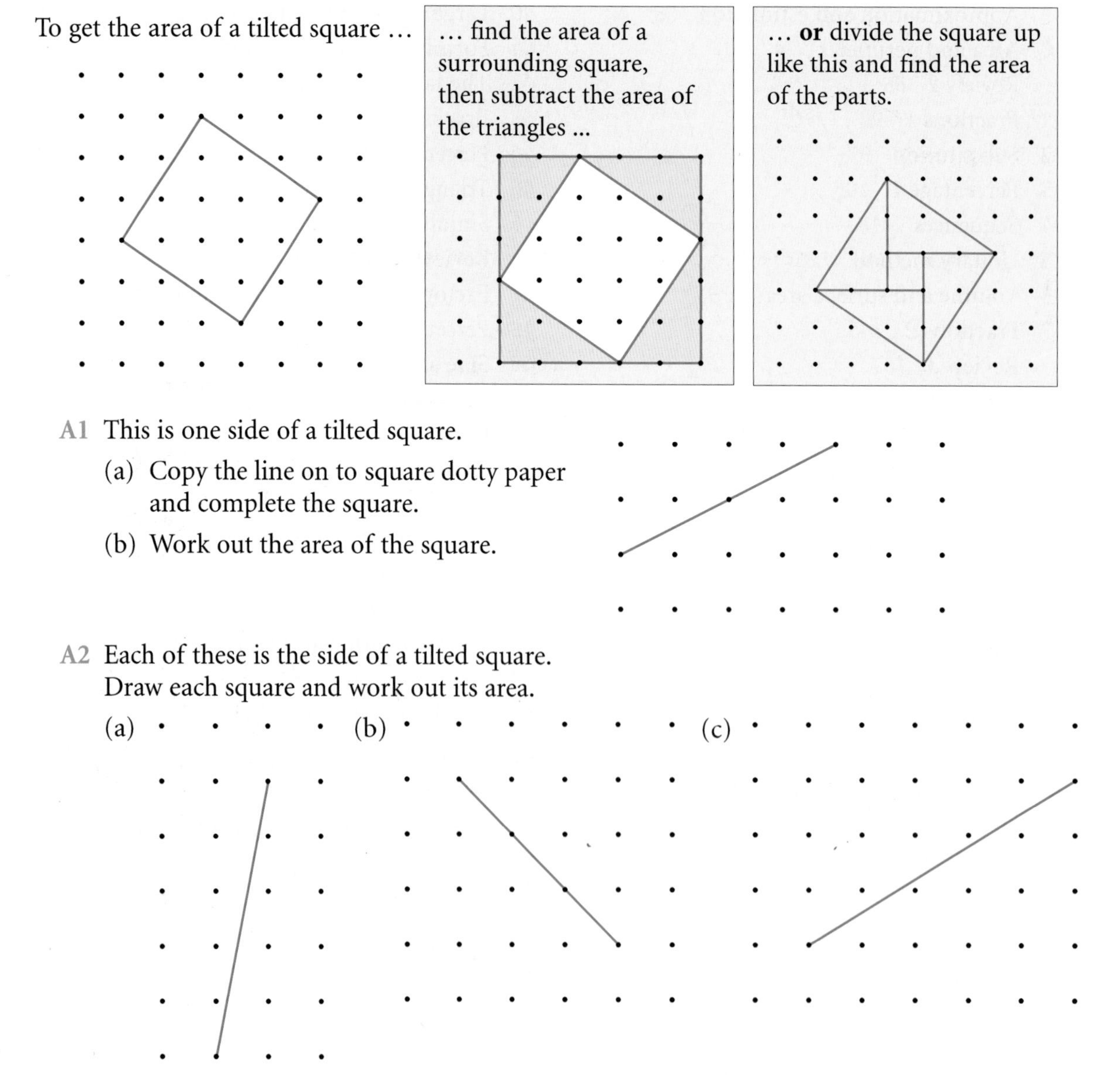

A1 This is one side of a tilted square.

(a) Copy the line on to square dotty paper and complete the square.

(b) Work out the area of the square.

A2 Each of these is the side of a tilted square. Draw each square and work out its area.

(a) (b) (c)

B *Squares on right-angled triangles*

The three squares Q, R and S are drawn on the sides of a right-angled triangle.

Copy the drawing on to dotty paper.
Find and record the area of each square.
Repeat this process for different right-angled triangles.
Square S must be on the side opposite the right angle.
Record your results in a table.

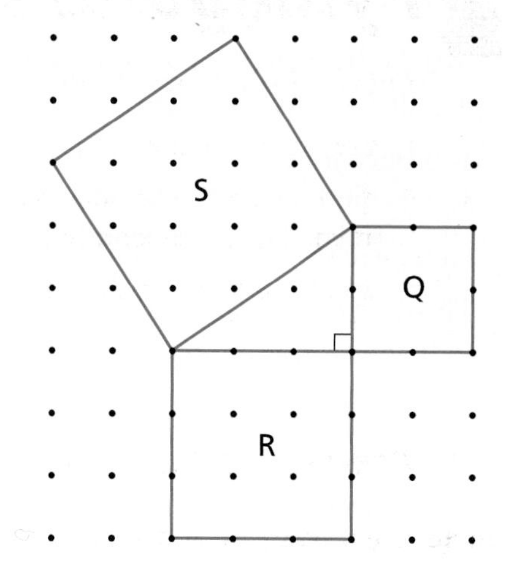

Area of square Q	Area of square R	Area of square S

What happens?

B1 Find the missing areas of the squares on these right-angled triangles.

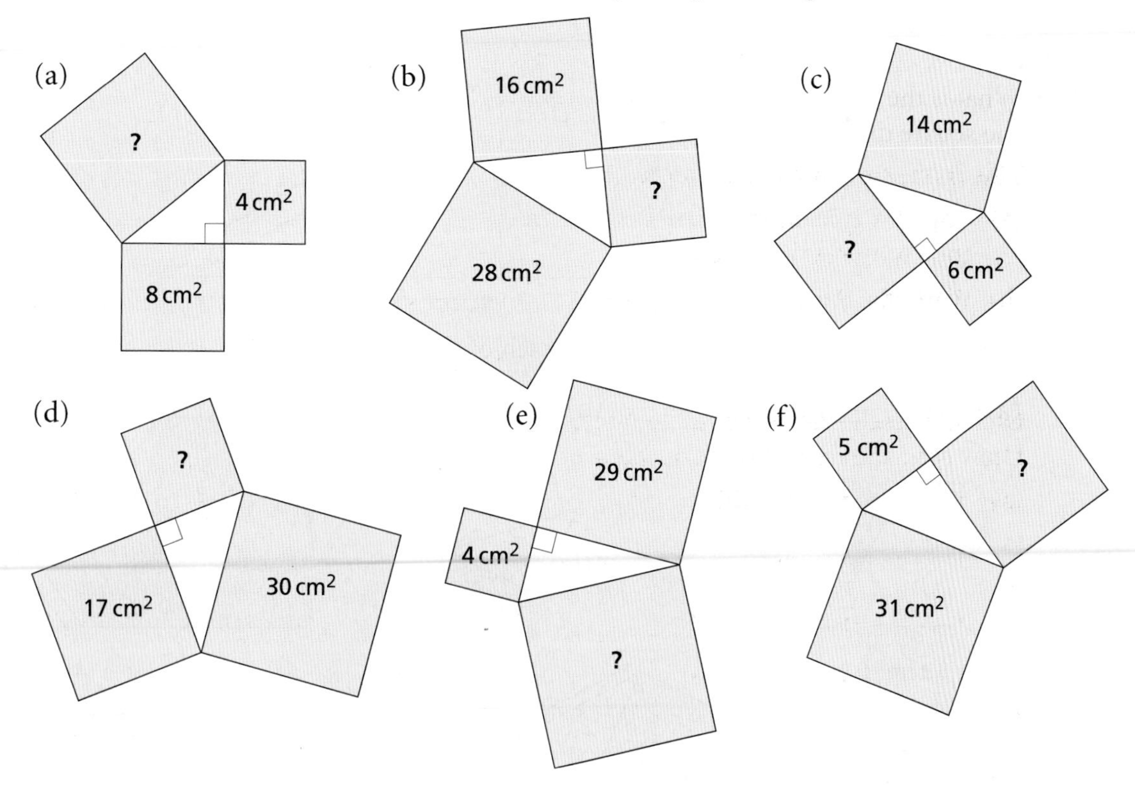

TG

Pythagoras's theorem

In a right-angled triangle the side opposite the right angle is called the **hypotenuse.**

You have found that the area of the square on the hypotenuse equals the total of the areas of the squares on the other two sides.

Here, Area C = Area A + Area B

This is known as Pythagoras's theorem.
Pythagoras was a Greek mathematician and mystic.
A theorem is a statement that can be proved true.

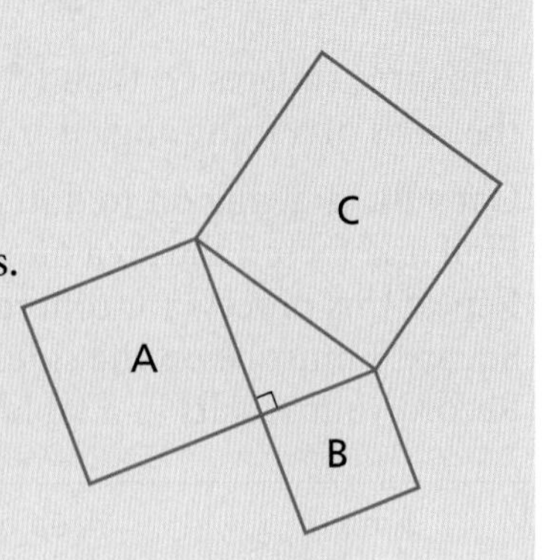

Using Pythagoras's theorem you can work with the lengths of sides as well as the areas of squares on them.

B2 (a) What is the area of the square drawn on side XY?

(b) What is the length of side XY?

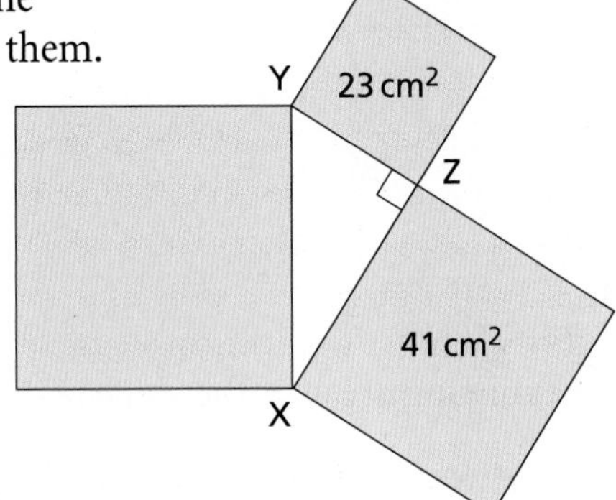

B3 What is the area of the square drawn here?

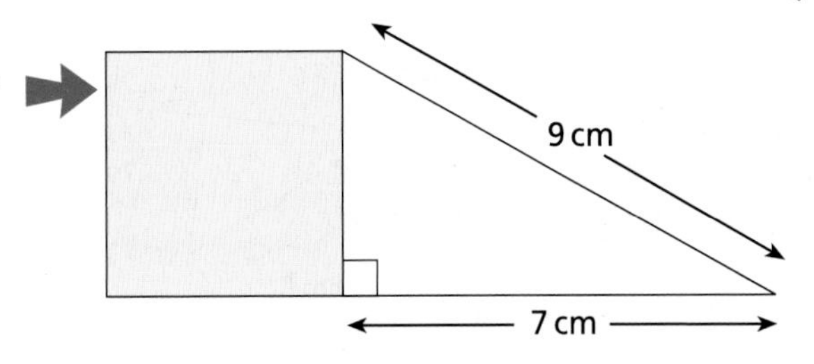

B4 Work out the missing area or length in each of these.

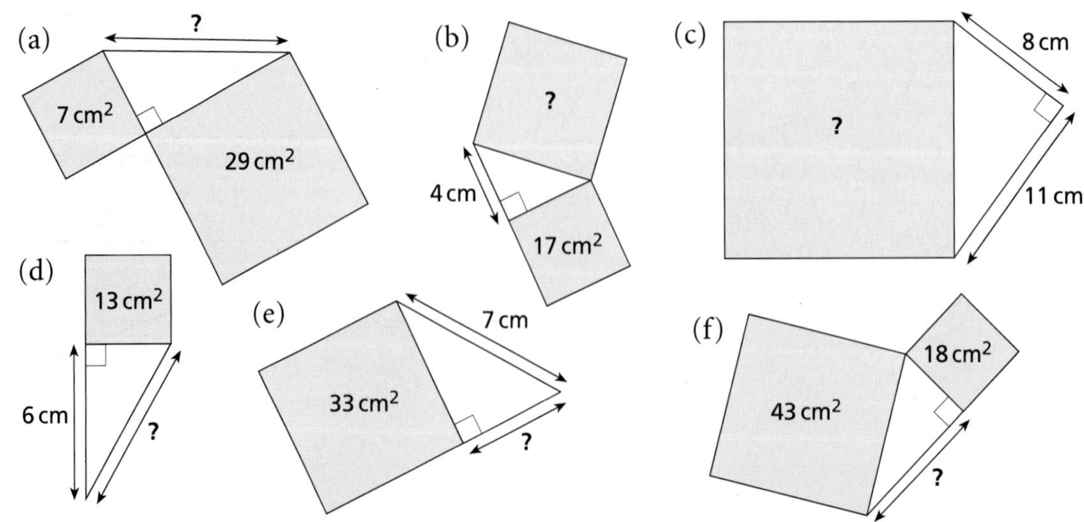

B5 Work out the missing area or length in each of these.

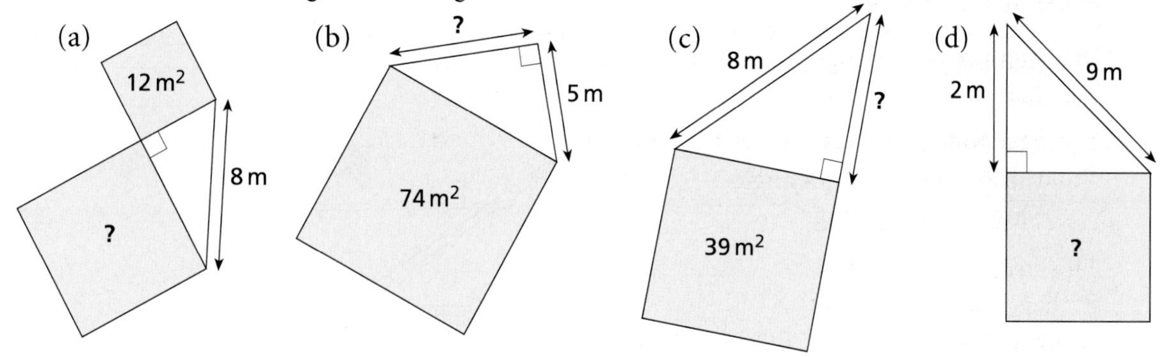

Pythagoras in practice

Pythagoras is useful for working out lengths when designing and constructing things.

You don't have to draw squares on the sides of the right-angled triangle you are using. You can think of Pythagoras just in terms of the lengths of the sides, as shown here.

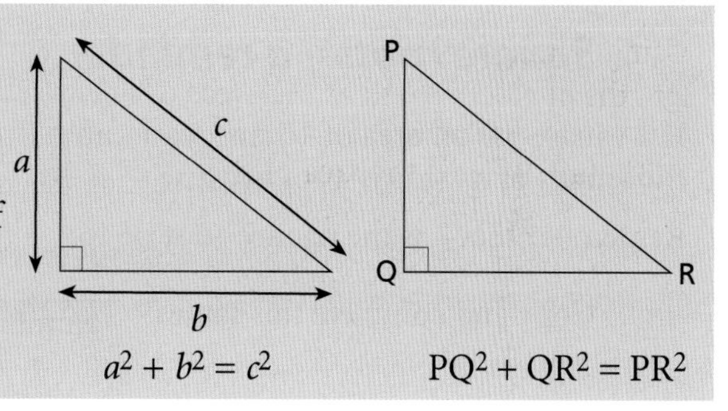

$a^2 + b^2 = c^2$ $\qquad$ $PQ^2 + QR^2 = PR^2$

B6 (a) Use Pythagoras to find out what length side LN should be.

(b) Now draw the triangle accurately with a ruler and set square. Measure the length of LN and see if it agrees with the length you calculated.

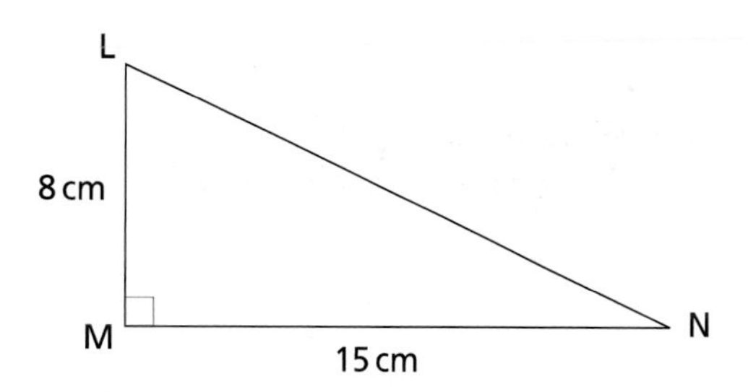

B7 Work out the missing lengths here.

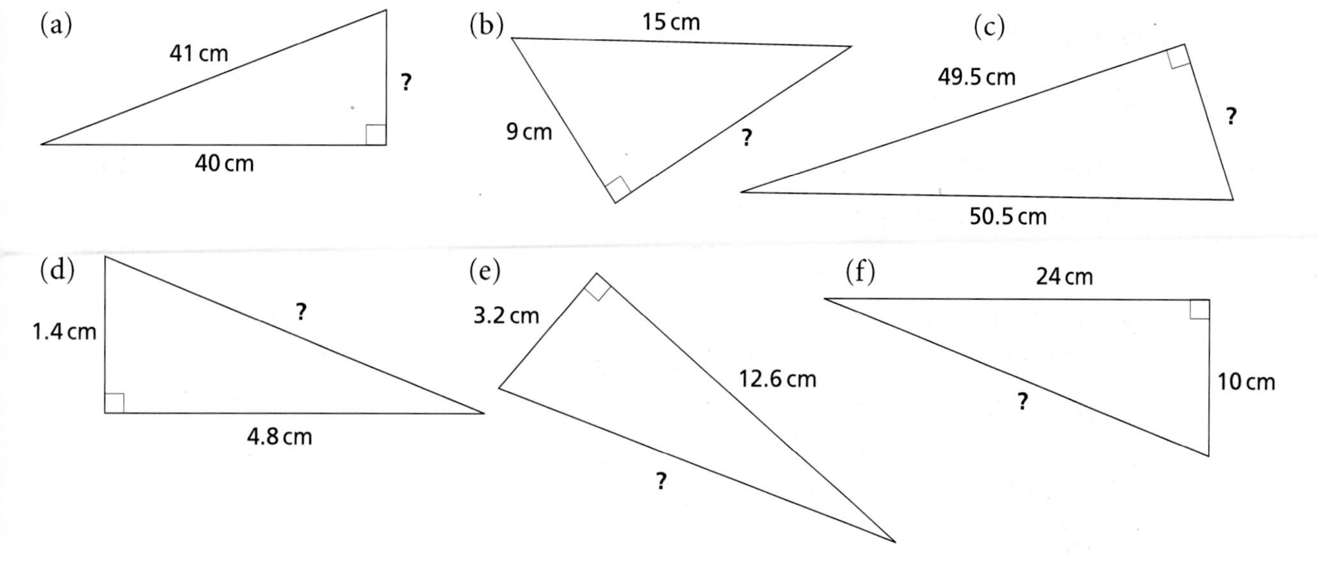

B8 People marking out sports pitches need to mark lines at right angles.

They sometimes use a rope divided into 12 equal spaces to form a 3, 4, 5 triangle.

Use Pythagoras to check that this produces a right angle. Show your working.

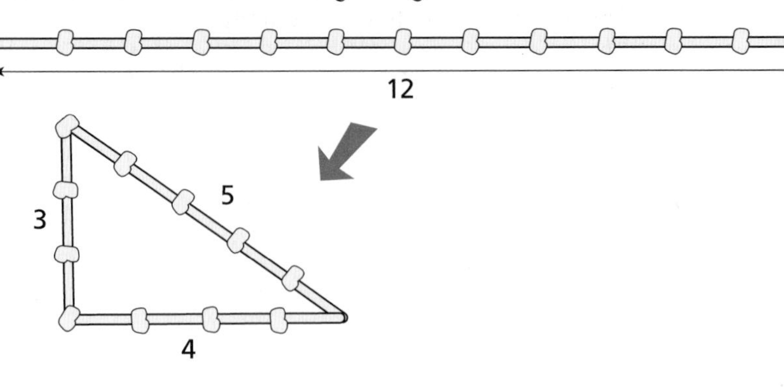

C Square roots – a reminder

If a square has an area of $16\,\text{cm}^2$, you know the length of its side is 4 cm because 4^2 is 16.

Remember that 4 is the **square root** of 16.

C1 Copy and complete this table.

Number	Square root
1	
4	
	3
	4
25	
36	
	7

C2 What is the square root of each of these numbers?

(a) 81 (b) 100 (c) 121 (d) 400

We use the symbol $\sqrt{\ }$ to mean square root.

So $\sqrt{16}$ means the square root of 16.

C3 Work out the value of these.

(a) $\sqrt{49}$ (b) $\sqrt{9}$ (c) $\sqrt{144}$ (d) $\sqrt{169}$

C4 For each of these square roots,

(i) first write down a rough answer

(ii) find the value to two decimal places on a calculator

(a) $\sqrt{10}$ (b) $\sqrt{2.5}$ (c) $\sqrt{150}$ (d) $\sqrt{15}$

(e) $\sqrt{200}$ (f) $\sqrt{20}$ (g) $\sqrt{42}$ (h) $\sqrt{420}$

(i) $\sqrt{85}$ (j) $\sqrt{8.5}$ (k) $\sqrt{805}$ (l) $\sqrt{50}$

(m) $\sqrt{500}$ (n) $\sqrt{5}$ (o) $\sqrt{0.5}$ (p) $\sqrt{5000}$

C5 Use the square root key on your calculator to work out the missing lengths here.
Give your answers to one decimal place.

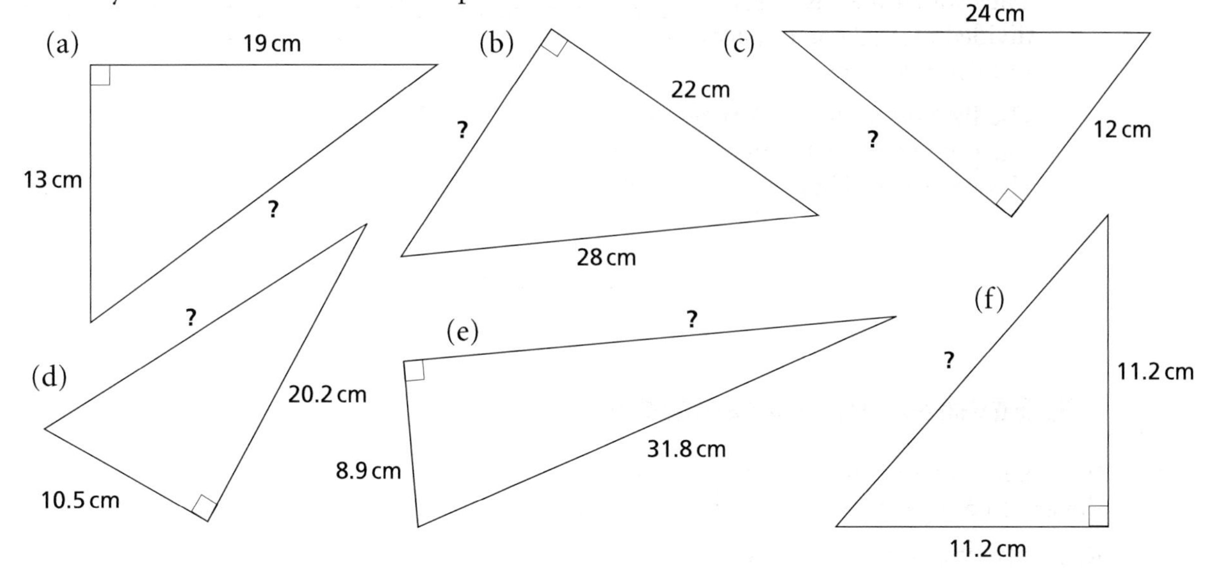

C6 (a) Use Pythagoras to work out side PQ to the nearest 0.1 cm.

(b) Now draw the triangle accurately with a ruler and set square.
Measure the length of PQ and see if it agrees with the length you calculated.

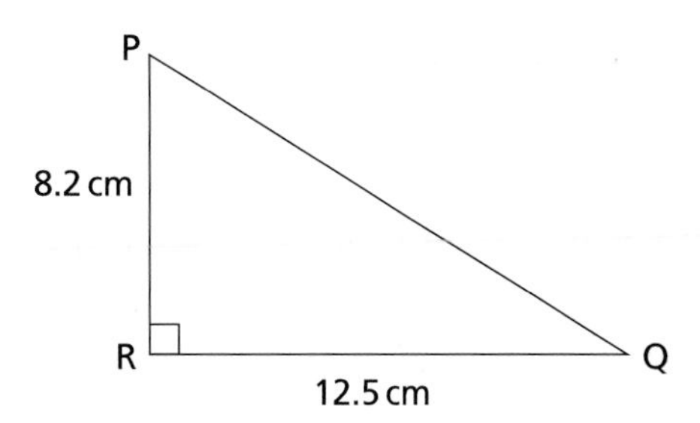

D *Using Pythagoras*

D1 A certain exercise book is 14.0 cm wide by 20.0 cm high.

(a) How long is the longest straight line you can draw on a single page of the book?

(b) How long is the longest straight line you can draw on a double page?

D2 Measure the height and width of your own exercise book.
Repeat the calculations in D1 for your own book.
Measure to check your answers.

D3 This is the plan of a rectangular field.
There is a footpath across the field from A to C.

How much shorter is it to use the footpath than to walk from A to B and then to C?

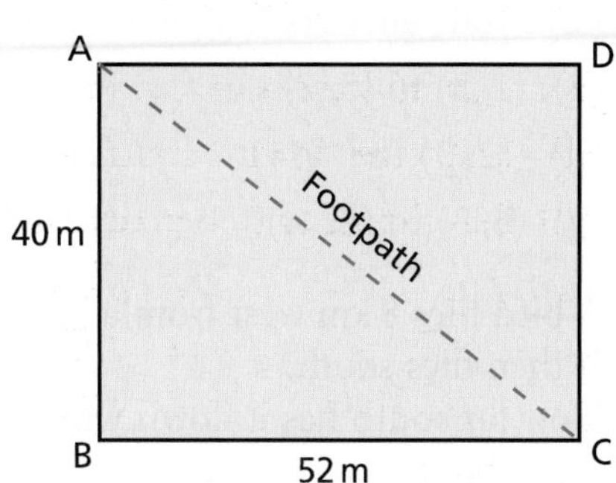

D4 Points A and B are plotted on a grid on centimetre squared paper.

(a) How far is it in a straight line from A to B?

(b) How long would a straight line from (2, 2) to (14, 7) be? (Draw them on a grid or make a sketch if you need to.)

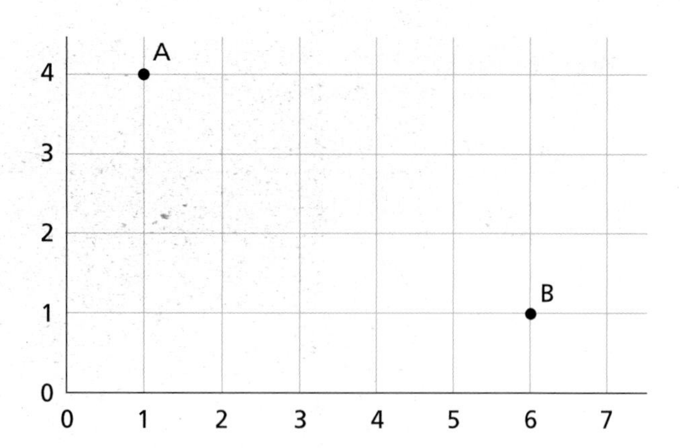

D5 (a) Calculate the lengths of the sides of this quadrilateral.

(b) Use your working to say whether it is exactly a rhombus.

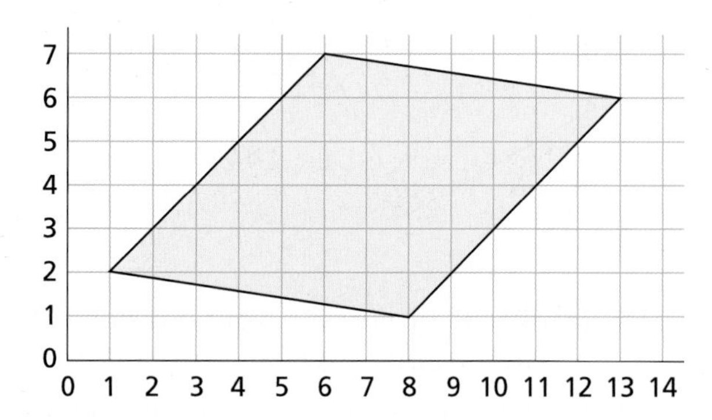

D6 A helicopter flies 26 km north from a heliport, then 19 km west.

How far is it from the heliport now?

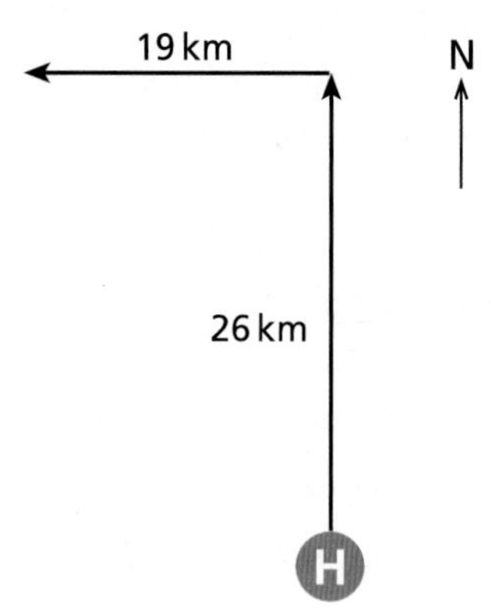

D7 How long is a straight line joining each pair of points if they are plotted on a centimetre squared grid? Give your answers to one decimal place.

(a) $(1, 3)$ to $(5, 7)$ (b) $(2, 4)$ to $(8, 1)$ (c) $(5, 0)$ to $(7, {}^{-}3)$

(d) $({}^{-}2, 3)$ to $({}^{-}4, 1)$ (e) $({}^{-}2, 6)$ to $(2, 8)$ (f) $(3, 1)$ to $({}^{-}6, 4)$

(g) $(6, 3)$ to $(2, {}^{-}4)$ (h) $(11, {}^{-}1)$ to $(8, 3)$ (i) $({}^{-}7, 5)$ to $({}^{-}4, {}^{-}5)$

D8 A bird flies 8 km west from a lighthouse.
It then flies south.
How far south has it flown when it is 22 km from the lighthouse?

Test yourself

T1 Find the missing areas.

(a)

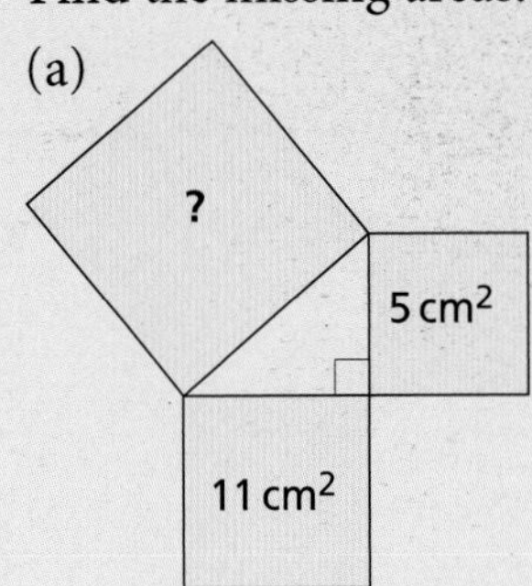

(b)

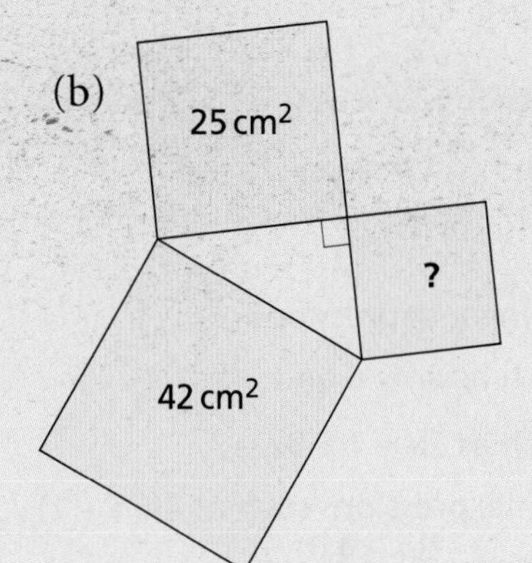

(c)

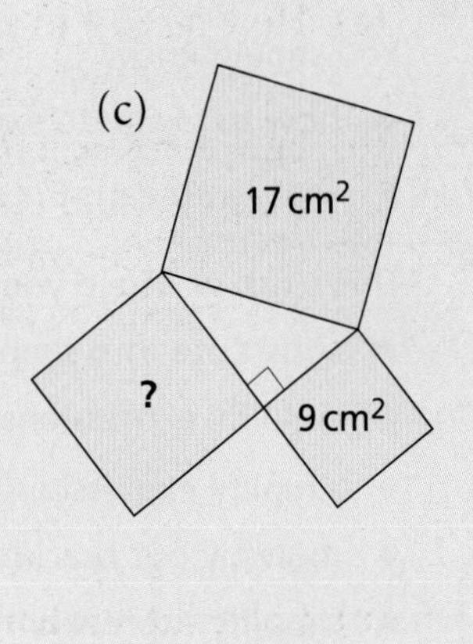

T2 Find the missing lengths (to 1 d.p.).

(a)

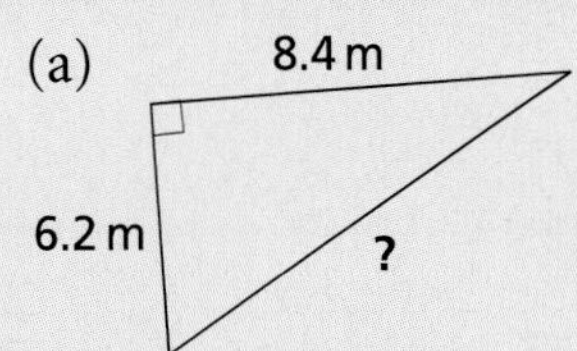

(b)

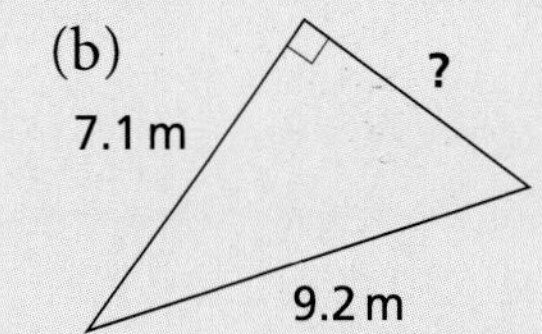

(c)

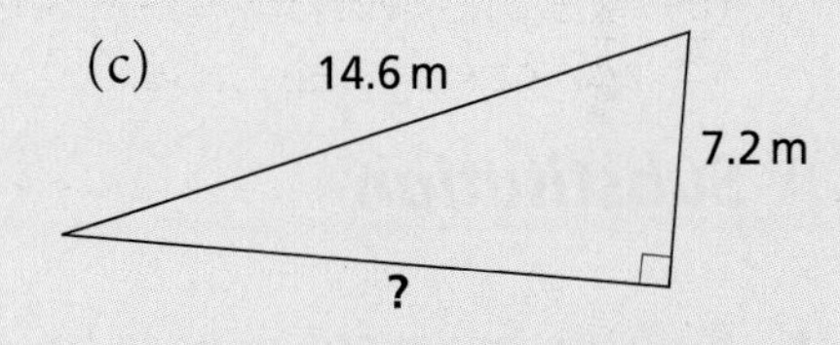

T3 A lifeboat travels 24 km east from its station and then 11 km south.
It then travels in a straight line back to its station.
How far has it gone altogether?

T4 A ladder 3.0 m long rests against a vertical wall.
The foot of the ladder is 0.9 m away from the bottom of the wall, on horizontal ground.

(a) Draw a sketch and label it with these measurements.

(b) Calculate the distance from the top of the ladder to the bottom of the wall.

T5 This trapezium has two right angles.
Calculate (to 1 d.p.)

(a) the length of the fourth side

(b) the length of each of its diagonals

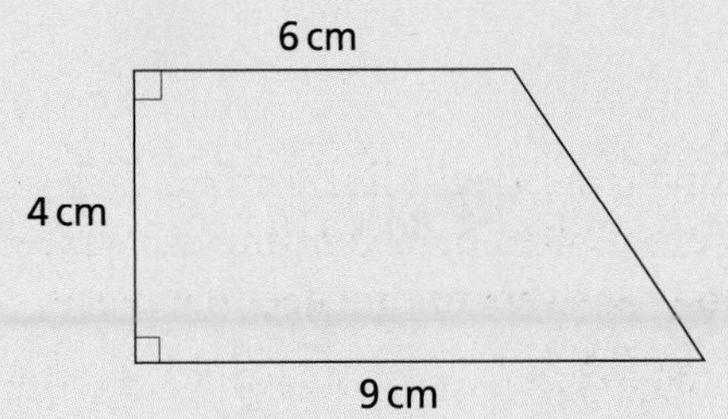

2 Working with expressions

You should know

- how to evaluate expressions such as $2 - 7 + 3$ and $7 - 2 \times 3$
- that $6n$ means $6 \times n$ and $\frac{12a}{4}$ means $12a \div 4$

This work will help you

- substitute into simple linear expressions
- simplify expressions such as $4n \times 6$ and $\frac{8n}{2}$
- simplify expressions such as $2x + 1 + 3x - 7$
- multiply out brackets in expressions such as $4(6n + 1)$
- simplify expressions such as $\frac{8n - 4}{2}$
- use algebra to prove general statements like 'The result for this puzzle will always be 2.'

A *Substitution*

- Evaluate any expressions in brackets first.
- Then work out any multiplications and divisions.
- Then work out any additions and subtractions.

Examples

Find the value of $2x + 5$ when $x = 3$.

$$\begin{aligned} 2x + 5 &= 2 \times 3 + 5 \\ &= 6 + 5 \\ &= 11 \end{aligned}$$

Find the value of $3(x - 1)$ when $x = 5$.

$$\begin{aligned} 3(x - 1) &= 3 \times (5 - 1) \\ &= 3 \times 4 \\ &= 12 \end{aligned}$$

Find the value of $\frac{14 - 3h}{2}$ when $h = 2$.

$$\begin{aligned} \frac{14 - 3h}{2} &= \frac{14 - 3 \times 2}{2} \\ &= \frac{14 - 6}{2} \\ &= \frac{8}{2} = 4 \end{aligned}$$

A1 **P** $2(n + 1)$ **Q** $3n + 1$ **R** $12 - n$ **S** $3(5 - n)$ **T** $10 - \frac{n}{2}$

U $\frac{n + 1}{2}$ **V** $\frac{n}{2} + 1$ **W** $10 - 2n$

(a) Find the value of each expression when $n = 4$.

(b) Which expressions have a value of 0 when $n = 5$?

(c) Which expression has the greatest value when $n = 3$?

(d) Which expression has the lowest value when $n = 1$?

A2 Find the value of the following expressions when $a = 10$.

(a) $2a - 3$ (b) $15 - a$ (c) $30 - 2a$ (d) $2(a + 7)$

(e) $3(2a - 5)$ (f) $\frac{2a - 5}{3}$ (g) $\frac{2a + 4}{6}$ (h) $10 - \frac{3a}{5}$

A3 Each expression in the diagram stands for the length of a side in centimetres.

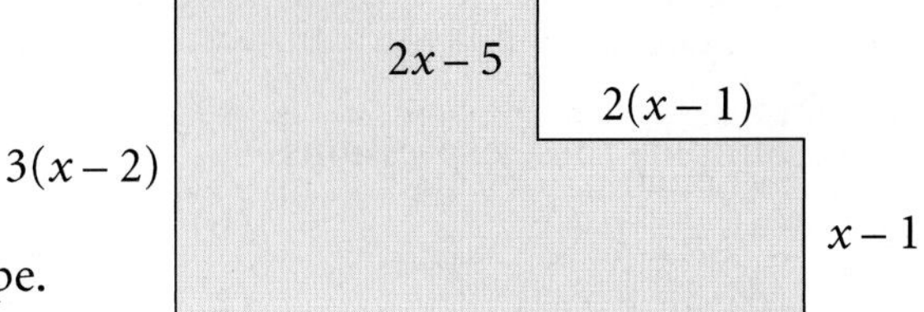

(a) What is the length of the longest side when $x = 3$?

(b) (i) Work out the length of each side when $x = 3$ and draw the shape.

(ii) What is the perimeter of your shape?

(c) What is the perimeter of the shape when $x = 5$?

B *Simplifying*

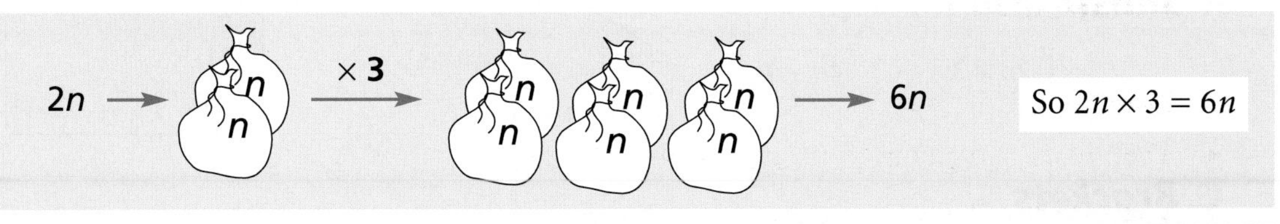

So $2n \times 3 = 6n$

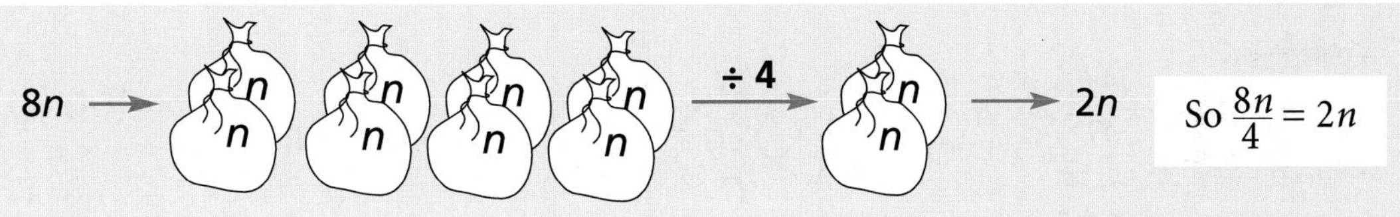

So $\frac{8n}{4} = 2n$

B1 Simplify these expressions.

(a) $2 \times 5n$ (b) $3 \times 2y$ (c) $6a \times 5$ (d) $4 \times 7b$ (e) $4x \times 9$

(f) $\frac{4n}{2}$ (g) $\frac{6a}{3}$ (h) $\frac{15y}{5}$ (i) $\frac{20x}{4}$ (j) $\frac{36b}{9}$

B2 Which of these is an expression for the area of this rectangle?

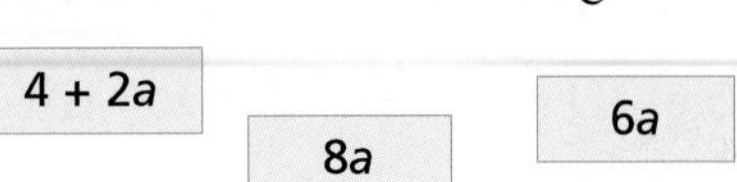

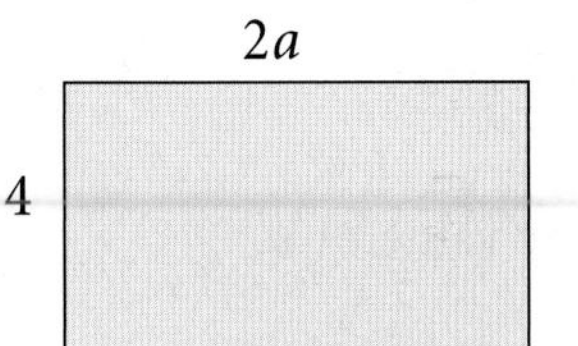

B3 Write an expression for the area of each of these rectangles.

(a)

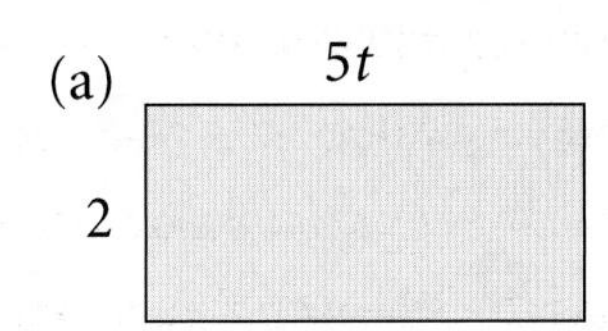

(b)

3b

3

Simplifying by collecting like terms

Examples

$6 + a - 5$
$= a + 6 - 5$
$= a + 1$

$7b - 3b + b$
$= 5b$

$7 - 2p - 3 + 2p$
$= 7 - 3 - 2p + 2p$
$= 4$

$3n - 5 - n - 6$
$= 3n - n - 5 - 6$
$= 2n - 11$

B4 Simplify these expressions.

(a) $2 + p + 5$ (b) $6q + 5q - 3q$ (c) $3 + w - 1 + w$

(d) $3k + 5 - k$ (e) $2h - 3 - 5$ (f) $3m - 5 - m + 5$

(g) $6n + 3 + n - 7$ (h) $6 - 7x + 7x$ (i) $5y + 1 - y - 4y$

B5 Which of these expressions gives the perimeter of

(a) the triangle (b) the rectangle

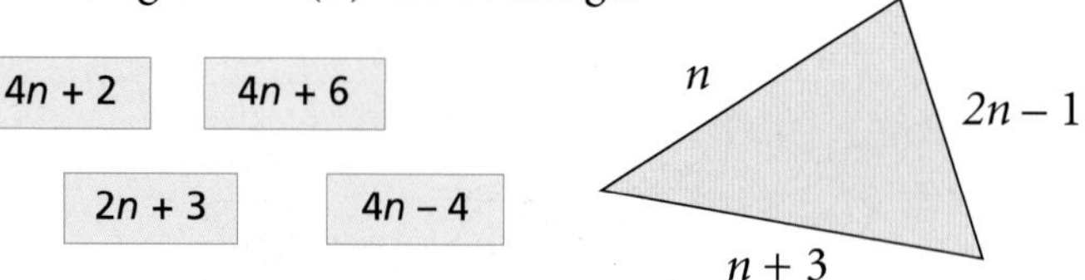

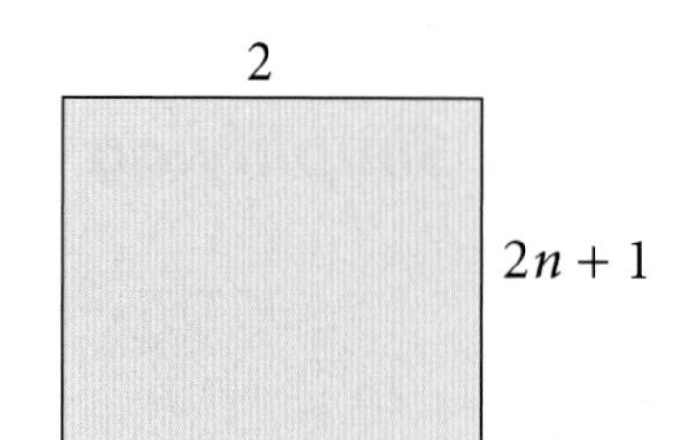

C *Brackets*

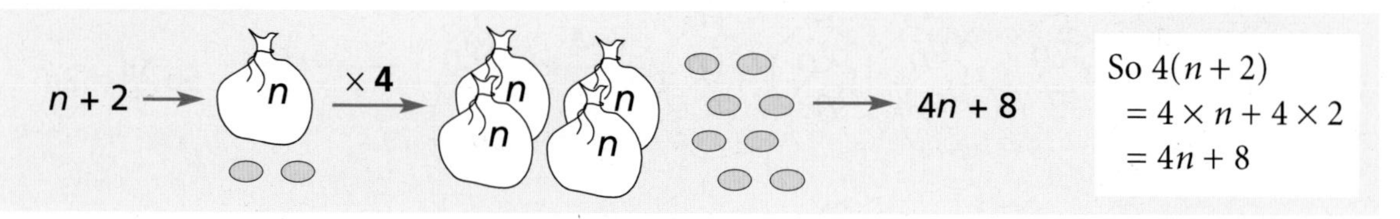

$4(n + 2)$ and $4n + 8$ are **equivalent expressions.**

For example when $n = 3$,

$4(n + 2)$
$= 4(3 + 2)$
$= 4 \times 5$

$4n + 8$
$= 4 \times 3 + 8$
$= 12 + 8$

↘ 20 ↙

This works for any value of n.

Examples

$8(p - 3) = 8 \times p - 8 \times 3 = 8p - 24$

$3(5 + 2n) = 3 \times 5 + 3 \times 2n = 15 + 6n$

$2(5x - 1) = 2 \times 5x - 2 \times 1 = 10x - 2$

C1 Find four pairs of equivalent expressions.

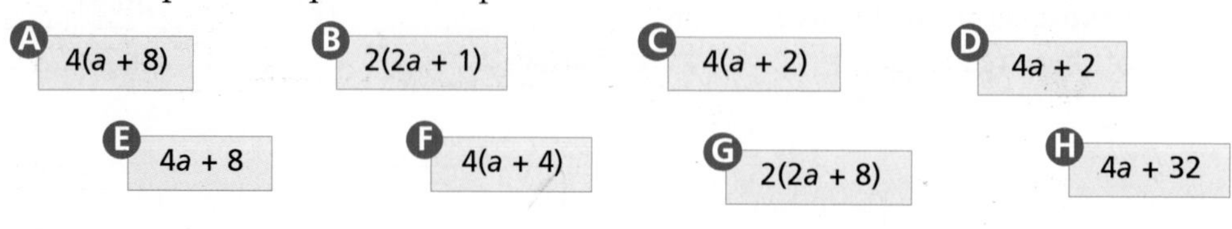

C2 Multiply out the brackets from these.

(a) $6(n + 1)$ (b) $5(m - 4)$ (c) $3(5 + k)$ (d) $5(2c + 1)$ (e) $4(3h - 2)$

(f) $2(5a + 3)$ (g) $6(2w - 3)$ (h) $5(3 - p)$ (i) $4(3 - 8x)$ (j) $7(3c + 4)$

C3 (a) Which of these expressions gives the area of rectangle A?

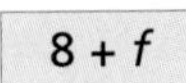

8 + 4f

2 + 4f

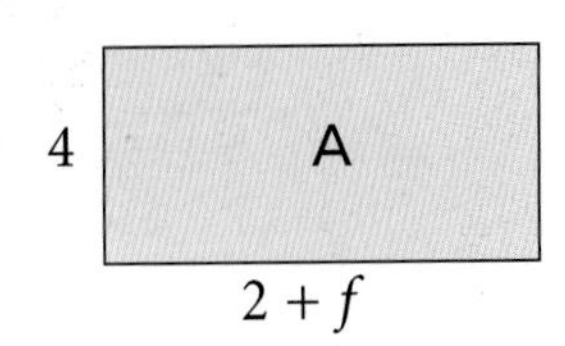

(b) Which of these expressions gives the area of rectangle B?

14x – 3

2x – 21

14x – 21

2x – 3

B

7

C4 For each shape, write expressions for the missing lengths.

(a)

2p + 1

Rectangle

?

Area = 6p + 3

(b)

?

Rectangle

2

Area = 10b – 4

C5 Copy and complete these.

(a) $3(■ + 5) = 6n + 15$ (b) $4(■ - p) = 8 - 4p$

(c) $5(■ - 3) = 20m - ■$ (d) $2(■ + ■) = 10x + 20$

C6 Ken and Fiona have £x each. They are each given £5.
Which expressions tell you the amount of money they have altogether?

$5 + x$	$2x + 5$	$2(x + 10)$	$2(x + 5)$	$2x + 10$

C7 Jo has three orchards, each with n apple trees.
Two trees in each field are blown down.
Find an expression for the total number of trees left.

C8 Sketch each shape and write expressions for the missing lengths.

(a)

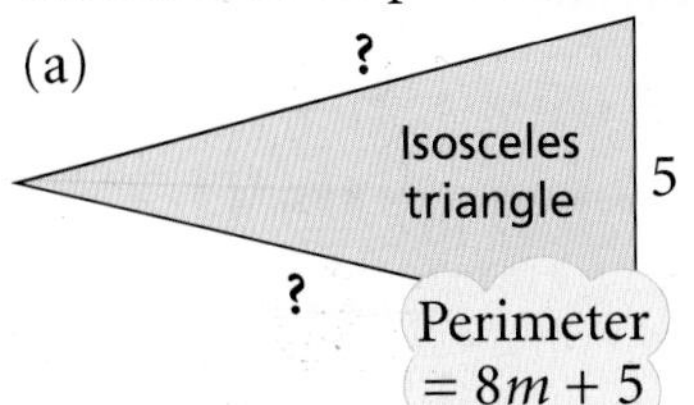

(b)

?

a

Perimeter = 6a + 6

?

Rectangle

?

(c)

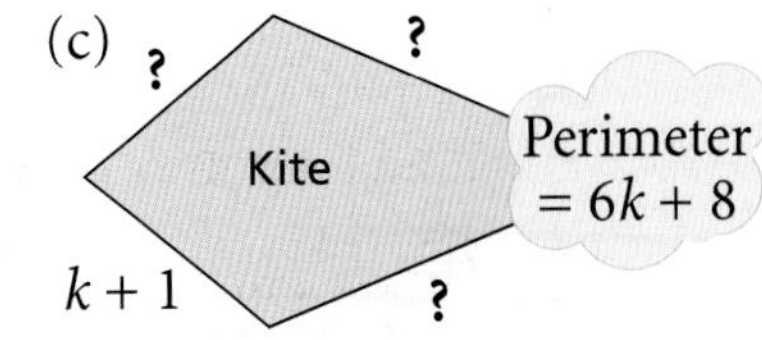

D Dividing

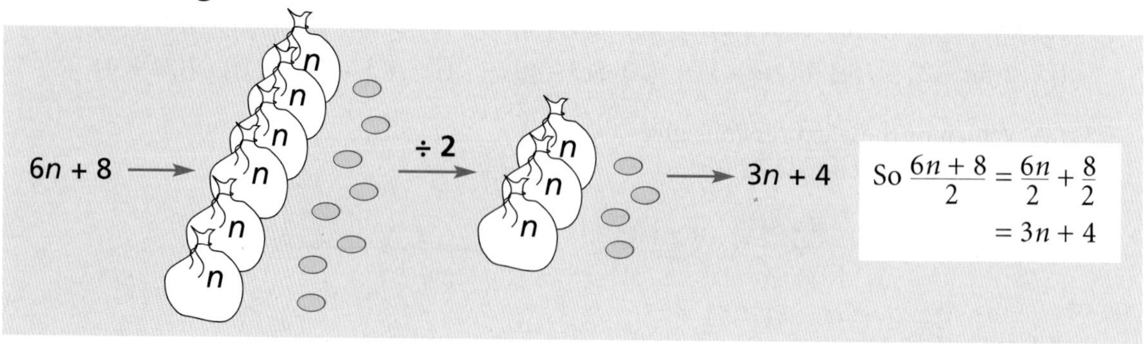

So $\frac{6n+8}{2} = \frac{6n}{2} + \frac{8}{2}$
$= 3n + 4$

Examples

$\frac{10n+5}{5}$

$= \frac{10n}{5} + \frac{5}{5}$

$= 2n + 1$

$\frac{8x}{4} + 7$

$= 2x + 7$

$\frac{15n-9}{3}$

$= \frac{15n}{3} - \frac{9}{3}$

$= 5n - 3$

$\frac{1}{5}(10k - 25)$

$= \frac{10k-25}{5}$

$= \frac{10k}{5} - \frac{25}{5}$

$= 2k - 5$

D1 I have four bags of sweets, each with n sweets in them. I also have 10 loose sweets.

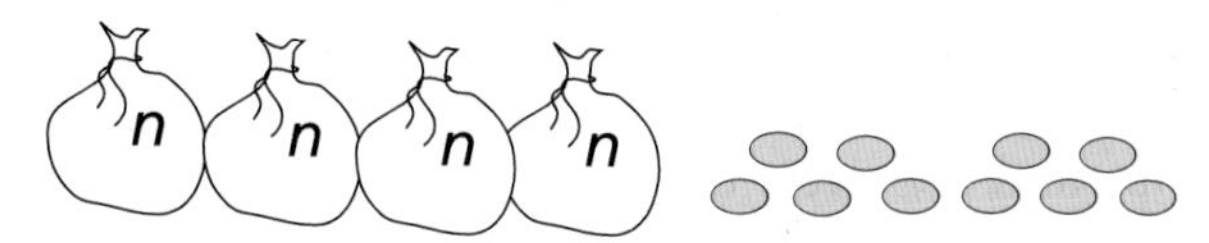

I share these sweets between two people.
Write an expression for the number of sweets each person has.

D2 Simplify these.

(a) $\frac{15n+10}{5}$ (b) $\frac{7m}{7} + 3$ (c) $4 + \frac{18k}{6}$ (d) $\frac{12h}{3} + 2$

(e) $\frac{5p+10}{5}$ (f) $\frac{4c+6}{2}$ (g) $\frac{21y}{7} + 7$ (h) $\frac{18+12w}{3}$

D3 I have six bags of sweets, each with n sweets in them. I eat 18 sweets.
I share the remaining sweets between three people.
Write an expression for the number of sweets each person has.

D4 Simplify these.

(a) $\frac{3a-6}{3}$ (b) $\frac{12b-16}{4}$ (c) $\frac{5k}{5} - 10$ (d) $\frac{8h-4}{4}$

(e) $\frac{12d-18}{6}$ (f) $\frac{20g-30}{10}$ (g) $\frac{15-5m}{5}$ (h) $12 - \frac{20n}{4}$

D5 Copy and complete these.

(a) $\frac{2m + ■}{2} = m + 7$ (b) $\frac{■ - 9}{3} = 2c - 3$ (c) $\frac{24 + 18y}{■} = 4 + 3y$

D6 Copy and complete this. $\frac{1}{3}(6n + 12) = \frac{6n + 12}{3} = 2n + ■$

D7 Simplify these.

(a) $\frac{1}{2}(6n + 12)$ (b) $\frac{1}{3}(9x - 6)$ (c) $\frac{1}{4}(8k + 20)$ (d) $\frac{1}{5}(5p - 10)$

D8 Solve the puzzle on sheet G109.

***D9** Find an expression for the area of each triangle.

(a)

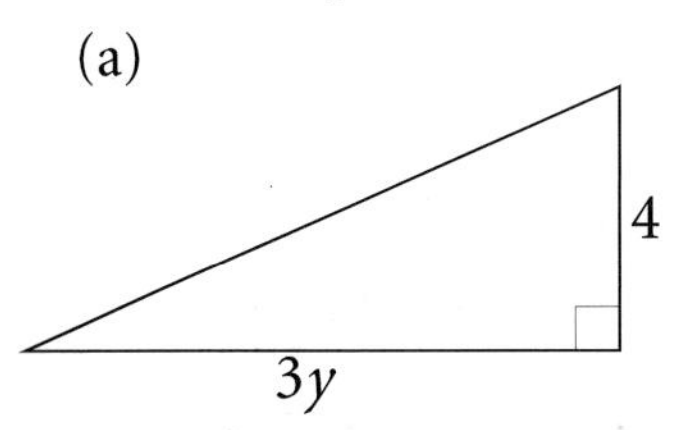

(b)

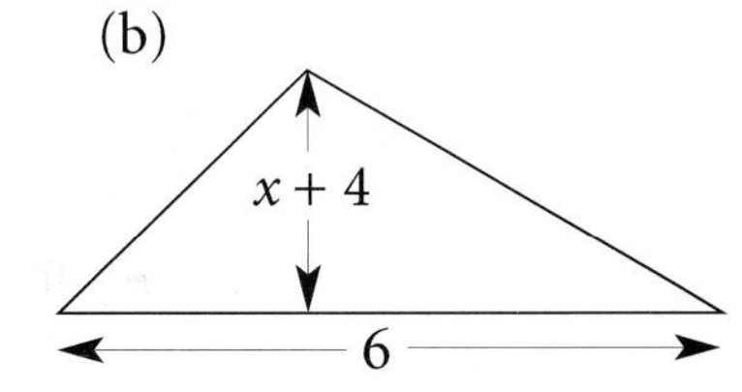

(c)

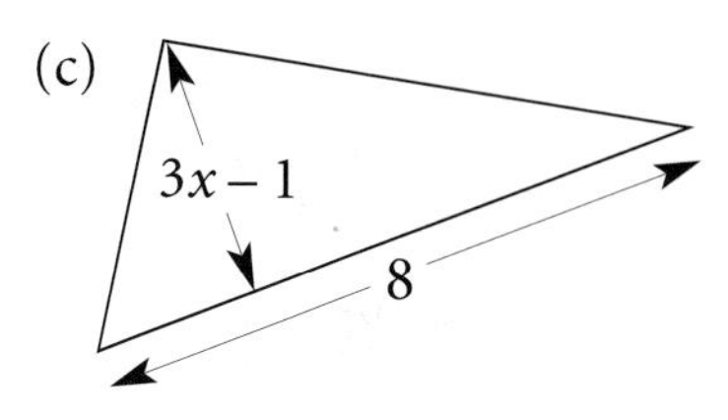

***D10** Find an expression for the **perimeter** of each rectangle.

(a)

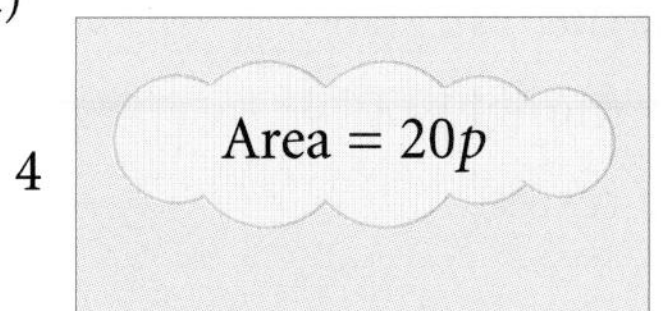

(b)

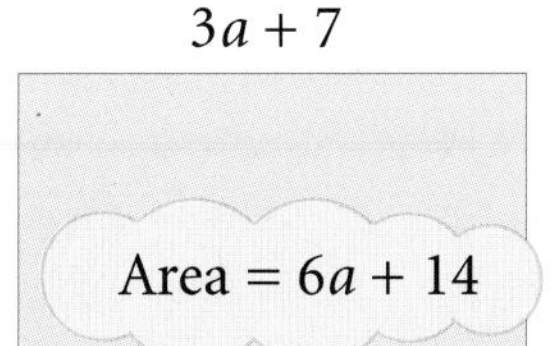

(c)

3

Area = $15n - 9$

E *Tricky business*

Think of a number
- Add 5
- Multiply by 2
- Subtract 7
- Subtract the number you first thought of
- Subtract 3

What is your final result?

Think of a number
- Add 4
- Multiply by 3
- Subtract 9
- Divide by 3
- Add 3
- Subtract the number you first thought of

What is your final result?

Think of a number
- Multiply by 4
- Subtract 2
- Multiply by 3
- Divide by 6
- Add 1
- Divide by 2

What is your final result?

- What happens with each puzzle?
- Can you use algebra to explain this?

TG

E1 (a) Try some numbers for this puzzle and describe what happens.

(b) Copy and complete the algebra box to explain how the puzzle works.

Puzzle

Think of a number
- Multiply by 6
- Add 3
- Divide by 3
- Subtract 1
- Divide by 2

What is the result?

Algebra

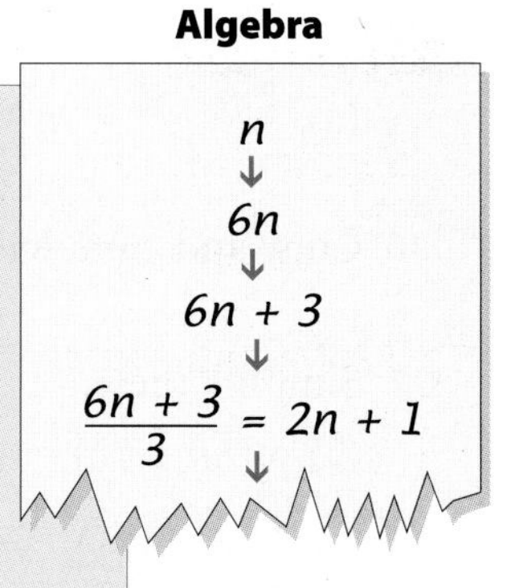

E2 (a) Try some numbers for this puzzle and describe what happens.

(b) Copy and complete the algebra box to explain how the puzzle works.

Puzzle

Think of a number
- Add 6
- Multiply by 3
- Subtract 12
- Divide by 3
- Subtract the number you first thought of

What is the result?

Algebra

n

↓

$n + 6$

↓

$3(n + 6) = 3n + 18$

↓

E3 Follow these steps for each puzzle below.

(a) Try some numbers and describe what happens.

(b) Use algebra to explain how the puzzle works.

A

Think of a number
- Add 1
- Multiply by 3
- Subtract 9
- Divide by 3
- Add 2

What is the result?

B

Think of a number
- Subtract 2
- Multiply by 4
- Add 8
- Divide by 4
- Subtract the number you first thought of

What is the result?

C

Think of a number
- Multiply by 6
- Add 15
- Subtract 3
- Divide by 3
- Add 6
- Divide by 2
- Subtract the number you first thought of

What is the result?

***E4** Try to make up your own puzzles like these.

Test yourself

T1 Find the value of the following expressions when $n = 6$.

(a) $4n - 5$ (b) $5(n - 2)$ (c) $3(2n + 1)$ (d) $\frac{2n + 3}{5}$ (e) $10 - \frac{n}{2}$

T2 Multiply out the brackets from these expressions.

(a) $3(b + 6)$ (b) $2(5 - h)$ (c) $5(2a - 3)$ (d) $4(3x + 10)$

T3 Hal and Dwayne have n sweets each. They are each given 3 sweets.
Which expressions give the number of sweets they have altogether?

$3 + n$ $2n + 3$ $2(n + 3)$ $2(n + 6)$ $2n + 6$

T4 Find an expression for the missing length in the rectangle.

?

4

Area = $12p + 28$

T5 I have six bags of marbles, each with x marbles in them.
I also have 12 loose marbles.
I share these marbles between three people.
Write an expression for the number of marbles each person has.

T6 Simplify the following expressions.

(a) $\frac{16n}{8}$ (b) $\frac{12m + 20}{4}$ (c) $\frac{1}{2}(8k - 10)$ (d) $\frac{14m}{7} - 7$

T7 (a) Try some numbers for this puzzle and describe what happens.

(b) Use algebra to explain how the puzzle works.

Think of a number
- Subtract 3
- Multiply by 6
- Add 6
- Divide by 6
- Add 2

What is the result?

T8 The perimeter of a regular hexagon is $12x - 18$.
What is an expression for the length of one edge?

T9 An expression for the length of one edge of a regular octagon is $3x + 5$.
What is the perimeter of this octagon?

3 *Mental and written calculation*

This work will help you

- do multiplications like 20×30 and divisions like $300 \div 20$ without a calculator
- multiply and divide decimals by integers without a calculator
- do multiplications like 26×34 and divisions like $476 \div 28$ without a calculator
- multiply and divide by decimals without a calculator

A *Multiplying and dividing multiples of 10, 100, ...*

Starting with $\mathbf{2 \times 4 = 8}$, we can get other multiplications.

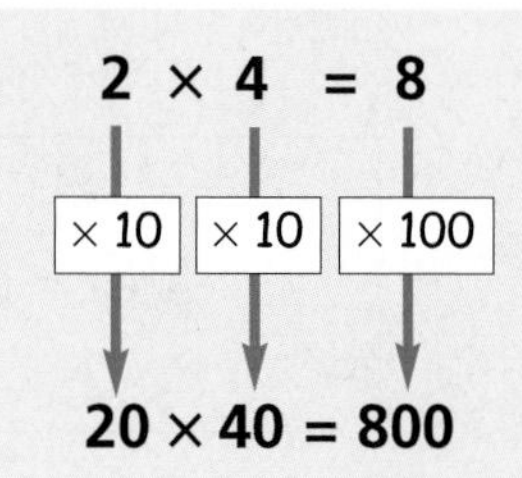

Multiply both numbers by 10. The result will be multiplied by $10 \times 10 = 100$.

A1 Calculate these.

(a) 20×3 (b) 20×30 (c) 200×300 (d) 20×300

A2 Find four matching pairs.

50×80 80×5 400 400 000

800×5000 500×800 4 million 4 thousand

A3 A box measures 20 cm by 30 cm by 40 cm.
What is the volume of the box in cubic centimetres?

This is one way to work out $\mathbf{8000 \div 20}$.

$$\frac{8000}{20} = \frac{800}{2} = 400$$

(÷ 10 applied to numerator and denominator)

A4 Calculate these.

(a) $600 \div 20$ (b) $90\,000 \div 30$ (c) $8000 \div 400$ (d) $500 \div 20$

(e) $1600 \div 40$ (f) $7200 \div 90$ (g) $120\,000 \div 200$ (h) $4\,200\,000 \div 300$

A5 Calculate these.

(a) 40×600 (b) $3200 \div 80$ (c) 600×500 (d) $7000 \div 20$

B *Decimals and place value*

B1 The '5' in 6.35 represents $\frac{5}{100}$.
What does the 5 represent in each of these numbers?

(a) 1524.9 (b) 13.52 (c) 5 200 000 (d) 0.015

B2 Put these decimals in order, smallest first.

0.18 1.27 0.3 1.09 2.1

B3 Calculate these.

(a) 1.2×3 (b) 4.1×2 (c) 5.7×4 (d) 1.93×7
(e) 0.9×6 (f) 0.16×3 (g) 1.03×9 (h) 42.15×8

B4 Jane buys 6 sandwiches.
Each sandwich costs £1.52 and she pays with a £10 note.
How much change does she receive?

B5 Eight cars are placed in a line, end to end.
Each car is 3.25 metres long.
How long is the line of cars?

B6 Calculate these.

(a) $8.2 \div 2$ (b) $6.9 \div 3$ (c) $12.4 \div 4$ (d) $4.5 \div 3$
(e) $24.5 \div 5$ (f) $40.56 \div 6$ (g) $6.37 \div 7$ (h) $17.2 \div 5$

B7 A piece of cheese that weighs 5.22 kg is cut into six equal pieces.
How heavy is each piece?

B8 A metal bar 5.8 metres long is cut into 4 equal pieces.
How long is each piece?

> When a number is multiplied by 10, the digits all move one place to the left.
> For example, $35.72 \times 10 = 357.2$.
> When a number is multiplied by 100, the digits all move two places to the left and so on.

B9 (a) Copy and complete this chain.

Input (1.24) —× 10→ ( ) —× 10→ ( ) —× 10→ ( ) —× 10→ ( ) Output

(b) Write the answers to these.

(i) 1.24×1000 (ii) 1.24×100 (iii) $1.24 \times 10\,000$

B10 Write the answers to these.

(a) 6.29×10 (b) 4.851×100 (c) 15.74×100 (d) 2.96×1000

When a number is divided by 10, the digits all move one place to the right.
For example, $35.72 \div 10 = 3.572$.

When a number is divided by 100, the digits all move two places to the right and so on.

B11 (a) Copy and complete this chain.

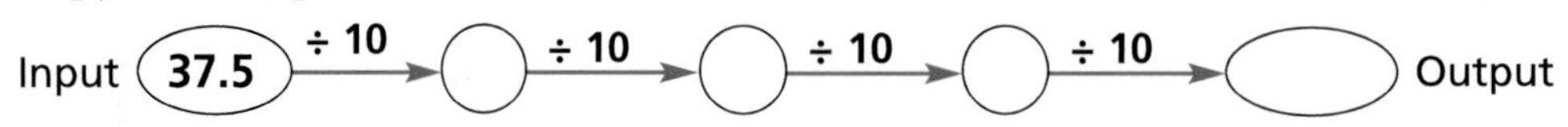

(b) Write the answers to these.

(i) $37.5 \div 100$ (ii) $37.5 \div 10\,000$ (iii) $37.5 \div 1000$

B12 Write the answers to these.

(a) $56.1 \div 10$ (b) $72.31 \div 100$ (c) $6.4 \div 100$ (d) $39.87 \div 1000$

B13 Write the answers to these.

(a) 3.91×10 (b) $42.5 \div 10$ (c) 8.69×100 (d) $52.63 \div 100$
(e) 5.9×100 (f) $0.3 \div 10$ (g) $1.56 \div 100$ (h) $2.1 \times 10\,000$

B14 A rectangular field measures 800 m by 900 m.

(a) What is the area of the field in square metres?

(b) There are 10 000 square metres in a hectare.
What is the area of the field in hectares?

C *Multiplying by a decimal 1*

For 0.3×50 you could start with 3×50.

$3 \times 50 = 150$

÷ 10 ÷ 10

$0.3 \times 50 = 15$

Divide one number by 10. The result will be divided by 10.

For 30×0.05 you could start with 30×5.

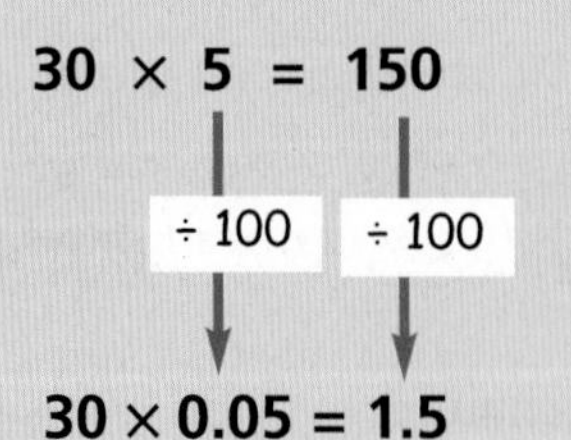

Divide one number by 100. The result will be divided by 100.

For 0.3×0.5 you could start with 3×5.

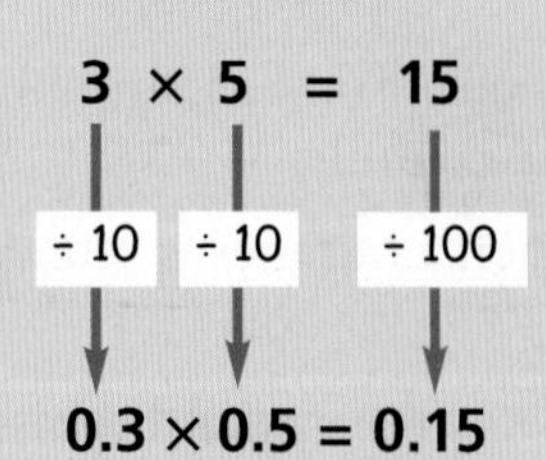

Divide **both** numbers by 10. The result will be divided by 100.

C1 Work these out.

(a) 3×0.4 (b) 0.3×0.4 (c) 30×0.4 (d) 3×0.04 (e) 30×0.04
(f) 30×0.3 (g) 3×0.03 (h) 0.3×0.3 (i) 300×0.3 (j) 0.03×30

C2 Work these out.

(a) 80×5 (b) 80×0.5 (c) 0.8×50 (d) 0.08×5 (e) 800×0.5

(f) 0.8×0.5 (g) 80×0.05 (h) 0.08×0.5 (i) 800×0.05 (j) 0.08×50

C3 These six cards can be arranged to make two correct multiplications.
Show how to do it.

0.6 | = 24 | 6 | × 40 | × 0.4 | = 2.4

C4 Show how to arrange these nine cards to make three correct multiplications.

50 | × 400 | = 200 | × 50 | 0.4 | = 2000 | 0.5 | × 40 | = 20

C5 Arrange these cards to make four correct multiplications.

30 | × 0.3 | × 0.2 | = 0.06 | × 30 | = 1.2 | = 12

0.3 | 0.2 | 0.4 | = 6 | × 4

C6 Here is a set of numbers.

0.5 5 50 500
0.6 6 60 600

You can use the same number twice.

From this set, find as many pairs as possible whose product is

(a) 30 (b) 3 (c) 300 (d) 0.3 (e) 2.5 (f) 0.36

C7 The number 50 is fed into this chain of number machines.

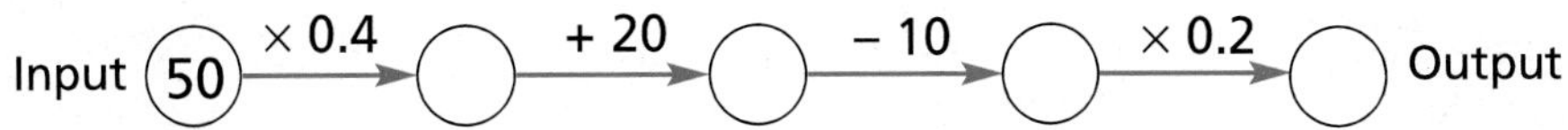

(a) What is the output?

(b) What is the output if the machines are arranged in this order:

Input (50) → + 20 → ○ → × 0.2 → ○ → – 10 → ○ → × 0.4 → ○ Output

(c) What is the largest output you can get by changing the order of the machines?
(The starting number is still 50.)

C8 The number 40 is fed into this chain of machines.

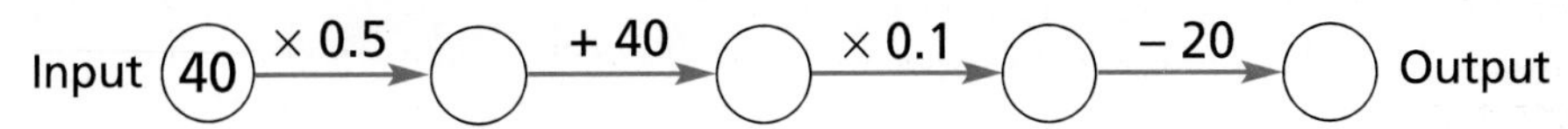

What is the largest output you can get by changing the order of the machines?

C9 Do the calculation in each box.
Arrange the answers in order of size, smallest first.
The letters will spell a word.

N	H	F	S
0.3×0.3	0.02×30	0.2×0.2	3×0.1

I	D	I	E
0.3×0.4	200×0.04	0.2×0.4	0.1×8

D *Dividing by a decimal 1*

You can change division by a decimal to division by a whole number by multiplying 'top and bottom' by 10 or 100 or ....

Examples

$$\frac{8}{0.2} = \frac{80}{2} = 40 \quad (\times 10 \text{ top and bottom})$$

$$\frac{1.5}{0.03} = \frac{150}{3} = 50 \quad (\times 100 \text{ top and bottom})$$

D1 Work these out.

(a) $\frac{6}{0.3}$ (b) $\frac{12}{0.2}$ (c) $\frac{2.4}{0.3}$ (d) $\frac{1.4}{0.2}$ (e) $\frac{120}{0.4}$

D2 Work these out.

(a) $\frac{1.2}{0.03}$ (b) $\frac{8}{0.04}$ (c) $\frac{16}{0.08}$ (d) $\frac{0.15}{0.03}$ (e) $\frac{0.8}{0.02}$

D3 Work these out.

(a) $\frac{4}{0.2}$ (b) $\frac{2}{0.05}$ (c) $\frac{2.8}{0.7}$ (d) $\frac{3.2}{0.04}$ (e) $\frac{0.36}{0.09}$

D4 These three cards **0.5** **= 8** **4** can make a division.

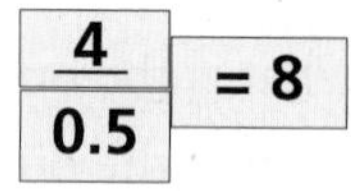

Arrange these six cards to make two correct divisions.

0.3 **= 0.5** **1.5** **30** **15** **= 5**

D5 Arrange these six cards to make two correct divisions.

0.8 **24** **2.4** **0.08** **= 3** **= 300**

D6 Choose two of the four numbers in the loop to go in the boxes to make a correct division.

4 0.4 0.8 8

$$\frac{\square}{\square} = 5$$

D7 Do the same as in D6 for each of these.

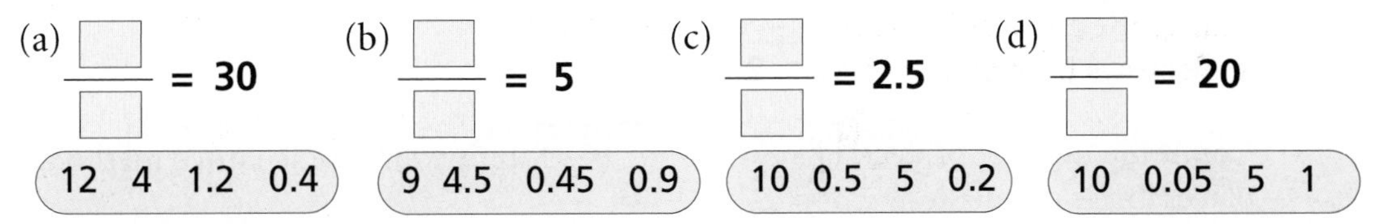

D8 Work these out.

(a) $\frac{4.68}{0.2}$ (b) $\frac{0.42}{0.3}$ (c) $\frac{0.18}{0.6}$ (d) $\frac{0.06}{0.3}$ (e) $\frac{0.86}{0.05}$

E *Long multiplication and division*

Here are two ways to work out **27 × 43**.
You may know some other methods.

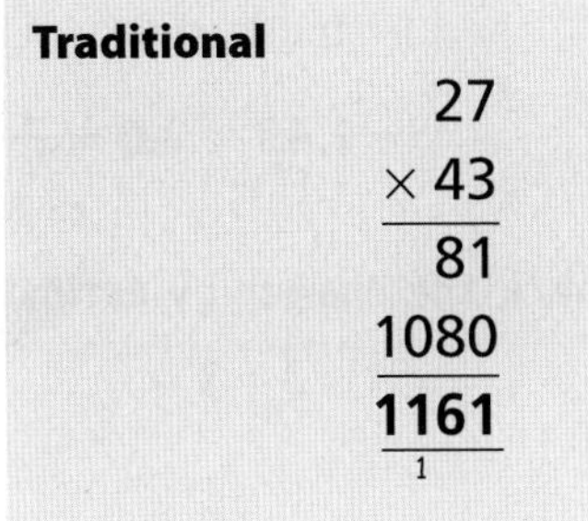

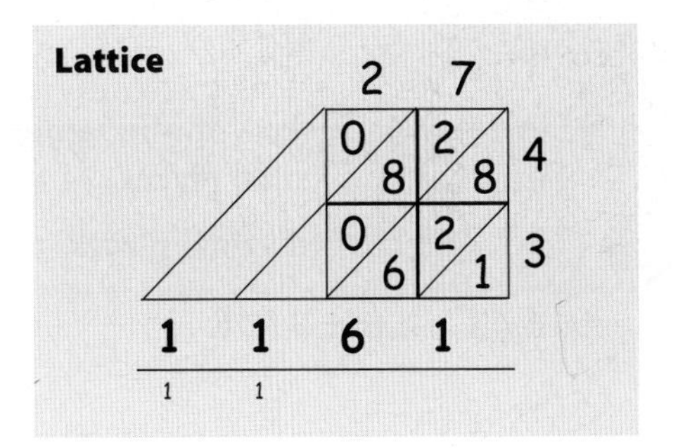

E1 Work these out.

(a) 13 × 17 (b) 12 × 41 (c) 26 × 21 (d) 31 × 47
(e) 53 × 65 (f) 98 × 27 (g) 143 × 28 (h) 208 × 13

E2 Each day in July, Tom swam 15 lengths in the local swimming pool.
How many lengths did he swim in total?

Here is one way to work out **1026 ÷ 19**.
You may know some other methods.

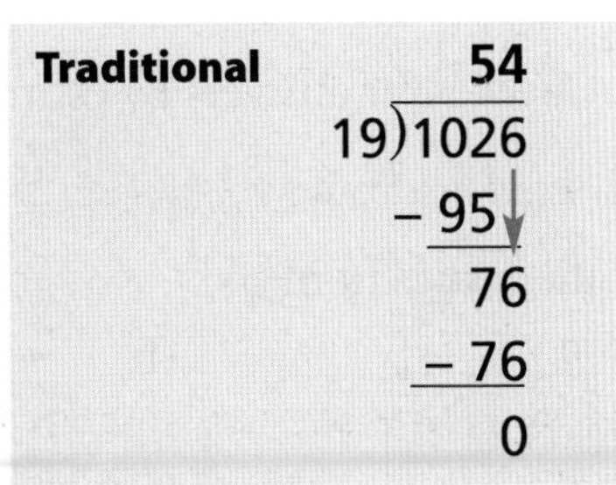

E3 Work these out.

(a) 182 ÷ 13 (b) 336 ÷ 16 (c) 480 ÷ 15 (d) 612 ÷ 18
(e) 1022 ÷ 14 (f) 2142 ÷ 17 (g) 1344 ÷ 21 (h) 5350 ÷ 25

E4 Jill is packing daffodils in bunches of 24.
How many bunches will she make with a total of 1104 daffodils?

F *Multiplying by a decimal 2*

Here are two ways to work out **1.43 × 2.6**.

- Count the number of decimal places in the calculation.

  1.<u>43</u> × 2.<u>6</u> has 3 decimal places.

- Ignore decimal points and multiply.

```
  143
×  26
  858
 2860
 3718
```

- Write the answer with the same number of decimal places.

  3.<u>718</u> has 3 decimal places.

So **1.43 × 2.6 = 3.718**

- Multiply using the lattice method.

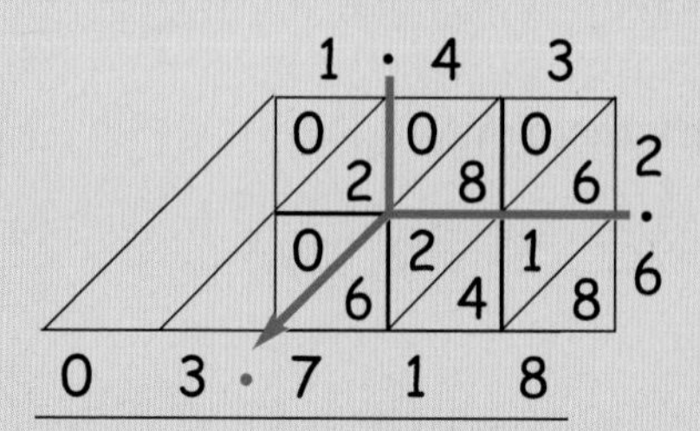

- Place the decimal point using the method shown above.

So **1.43 × 2.6 = 3.718**

Check the answer by estimating.
$1 \times 3 = 3$ ✔

F1 Use the fact that $26 \times 34 = 884$ to write down the answer to each of these.

(a) 2.6×3.4 (b) 2.6×34 (c) 0.26×3.4 (d) 0.26×0.34

F2 Use the fact that $156 \times 48 = 7488$ to write down the answer to each of these.

(a) 1.56×48 (b) 15.6×4.8 (c) 0.156×0.48 (d) 1.56×0.48

F3 (a) Write down an estimate for 2.8×5.1.

(b) Calculate 2.8×5.1.

F4 Work these out. Check your answers by estimating.

(a) 1.7×2.7 (b) 42×3.8 (c) 2.1×3.49 (d) 0.13×5.6

F5 Find the area of these rugs in m².

(a)

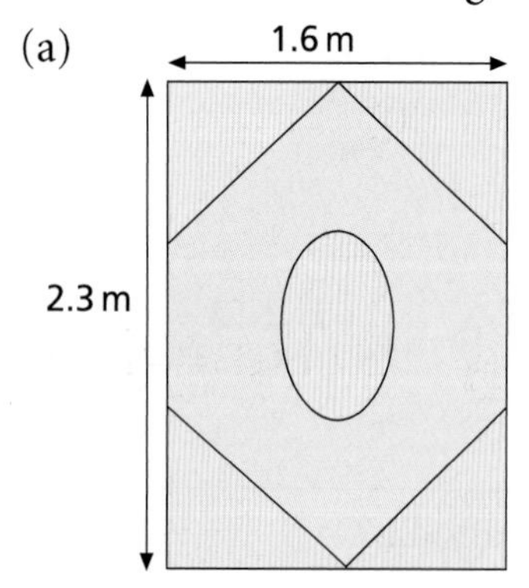

(b)

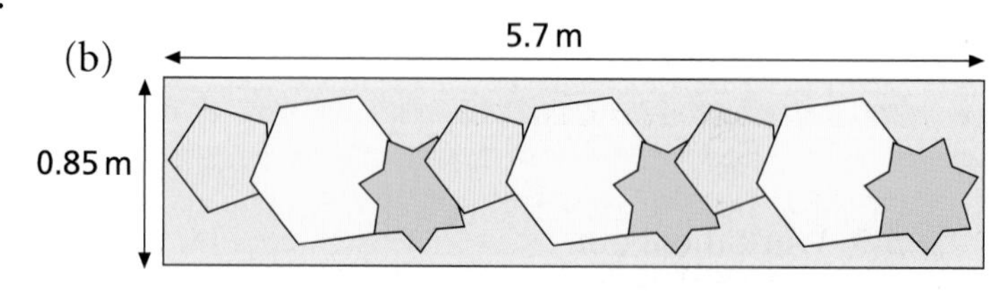

G *Dividing by a decimal 2*

Here is one way to work out **59.8 ÷ 0.26**.

Multiply top and bottom by 100 to get an equivalent whole number division.

$$\frac{59.8}{0.26} = \frac{5980}{26} \quad (\times 100 \text{ top and bottom})$$

Divide 5980 by 26.

$$\begin{array}{r} 230 \\ 26\overline{)5980} \\ -52 \\ \hline 78 \\ -78 \\ \hline 0 \end{array}$$

So **59.8 ÷ 0.26 = 230**.

Check the answer by estimating.

$$\frac{6000}{30} = 200 \checkmark$$

G1 Find three matching pairs of divisions.

$\frac{32.2}{1.4}$ $\frac{322}{0.14}$ $\frac{32.2}{0.14}$ $\frac{32200}{14}$ $\frac{3220}{14}$ $\frac{322}{14}$

G2 Given that 612 ÷ 36 = 17, work these out.

(a) $\frac{61.2}{3.6}$ (b) $\frac{6.12}{0.36}$ (c) $\frac{612}{3.6}$ (d) $\frac{612}{0.36}$ (e) $\frac{61.2}{0.36}$

G3 Work these out.

(a) $\frac{32.2}{1.4}$ (b) $\frac{4.68}{0.36}$ (c) $\frac{44.2}{0.26}$ (d) $\frac{1.69}{0.13}$ (e) $\frac{5.2}{0.65}$

G4 A Smart car is 2.5 metres long.
Bumper to bumper, a line of these cars is 40 metres long.

How many cars are in the line?

G5 You are told that 13 × 19 = 247.
Work these out.

(a) $\frac{247}{19}$ (b) $\frac{24.7}{1.3}$ (c) $\frac{24.7}{1.9}$ (d) $\frac{247}{1.3}$ (e) $\frac{247}{0.19}$

H *Mixed questions*

H1 You are told that 364 ÷ 14 = 26.

Write down the answers to these.

(a) $\frac{36.4}{1.4}$ (b) $\frac{3.64}{0.14}$ (c) $\frac{36400}{14}$ (d) $\frac{364}{1.4}$ (e) $\frac{3640}{0.14}$

H2 You are told that $18 \times 55 = 990$.
Put these calculations into groups, so that the calculations in each group have the same answer.

1.8×55 $\quad 18 \times 550$ $\quad 0.18 \times 550$ $\quad 180 \times 55$ $\quad 0.18 \times 0.55$

18×0.55 $\quad 0.18 \times 55$ $\quad 1.8 \times 5.5$ $\quad 180 \times 0.55$ $\quad 1.8 \times 0.055$

H3 Given that $17 \times 14 = 238$, write down the answers to these.

(a) 1.7×1.4 (b) 170×1.4 (c) 17×0.14 (d) $238 \div 14$

(e) $2380 \div 14$ (f) $238 \div 17$ (g) $23.8 \div 1.7$ (h) $23.8 \div 0.14$

H4 Given that $29 \times 43 = 1247$, write down the answers to these.

(a) 290×430 (b) 2.9×0.43 (c) 0.29×43 (d) 0.29×0.43

(e) $124.7 \div 4.3$ (f) $1247 \div 2.9$ (g) $124.7 \div 2.9$ (h) $12\,470 \div 4.3$

H5 Work these out.

(a) 3.9×0.17 (b) $45 \div 0.15$ (c) $35.2 \div 3.2$ (d) $66.7 \div 0.23$

H6 Given that $15 \times 73 = 1095$, write down the answers to these.

(a) $\frac{10.95}{0.15}$ (b) $\frac{109.5}{73}$ (c) $\frac{1.095}{1.5}$ (d) $\frac{0.1095}{0.73}$ (e) $\frac{0.1095}{73}$

Test yourself

T1 Work these out.

(a) 200×80 (b) $36\,000 \div 60$ (c) 0.4×100 (d) $0.4 \div 100$

T2 Work these out.

(a) 0.4×80 (b) 0.4×0.8 (c) 0.4×0.2 (d) 400×0.6 (e) 30×0.07

T3 Work these out.

(a) $\frac{2.4}{0.4}$ (b) $\frac{9}{0.3}$ (c) $\frac{16}{0.02}$ (d) $\frac{5}{0.02}$ (e) $\frac{1.8}{0.03}$

T4 Work these out.

(a) 1.4×23 (b) 1.4×0.23 (c) 2.6×1.8 (d) 260×0.18 (e) 45×0.32

T5 Work these out.

(a) $\frac{20.8}{1.3}$ (b) $\frac{64.8}{0.27}$ (c) $\frac{5.44}{0.34}$ (d) $\frac{364}{1.3}$ (e) $\frac{11.2}{0.35}$

T6 Given that $63 \times 82 = 5166$, write down the answers to these.

(a) 6.3×0.82 (b) 0.63×8.2 (c) 0.63×820 (d) 0.63×0.82

(e) $51.66 \div 0.63$ (f) $516.6 \div 8.2$ (g) $5166 \div 6.3$ (h) $5166 \div 0.82$

4 *Linear equations*

You should know that, for example, $3(x + 4) = 3x + 12$

$$\frac{3x + 6}{3} = x + 2$$

This work will help you

- simplify expressions such as $3 - 6x + 4x$
- solve a variety of linear equations, including those where you need to simplify first
- form equations to solve problems

A *Solving simple equations*

Examples

Each expression in brackets shows what is done to **both** sides to get the next line.

$$\begin{aligned} 3x - 1 &= x + 13 && [+1] \\ 3x &= x + 14 && [-x] \\ 2x &= 14 && [\div 2] \\ x &= 7 \end{aligned}$$

$$\begin{aligned} \frac{x}{3} + 5 &= 9 && [-5] \\ \frac{x}{3} &= 4 && [\times 3] \\ x &= 12 \end{aligned}$$

$$\begin{aligned} 5x - 8 &= 20 - 2x && [+2x] \\ 7x - 8 &= 20 && [+8] \\ 7x &= 28 && [\div 7] \\ x &= 4 \end{aligned}$$

A1 Solve these equations.

(a) $5x = 35$ (b) $\frac{y}{6} = 5$ (c) $4z + 9 = 21$

(d) $\frac{k}{4} + 8 = 13$ (e) $10h - 3 = 47$ (f) $\frac{m}{2} - 1 = 19$

(g) $40 - y = 30$ (h) $10 - 3g = 4$ (i) $20 - 6n = 2$

A2 Solve these equations.

(a) $2n = 3$ (b) $4n = 5$ (c) $2n + 3 = 4$

(d) $6n - 4 = 5$ (e) $5n - 3 = 3$ (f) $10n - 1 = 5$

(g) $9 - 4n = 3$ (h) $3 - 2n = 0$ (i) $6 - 10n = 2$

A3 Solve these equations.

(a) $x + 9 = 4x$ (b) $x + 5 = 2x + 4$ (c) $4x + 3 = 2x + 13$

(d) $3x + 5 = 7x - 3$ (e) $4x + 6 = 8x - 6$ (f) $5x - 9 = 3x - 1$

(g) $2x + 5 = 6x - 1$ (h) $6x + 5 = 2x + 7$ (i) $2x - 1 = 4x - 6$

A4 Solve these equations.

(a) $3n + 6 = 10 - n$ (b) $12 - 2n = 3n + 2$ (c) $15 - 3n = 4n - 6$

(d) $2n - 5 = 15 - 3n$ (e) $8 - n = 15 - 2n$ (f) $15 - 2n = 20 - 3n$

(g) $3n + 1 = 7 - n$ (h) $6n - 13 = 12 - 4n$ (i) $3 - n = 5 - 5n$

B Simplifying

Examples

$9 + 2a - 3 - 7a$	$1 - 9n + 10 + 4n$	$8 - 3n - 5 - 4n - 1$
$= 9 - 3 + 2a - 7a$	$= 1 + 10 - 9n + 4n$	$= 8 - 5 - 1 - 3n - 4n$
$= 6 - 5a$	$= 11 - 5n$	$= 2 - 7n$

B1 Simplify these expressions.

(a) $5 + 3m + 2 - 5m$ (b) $7n - 1 - 4n - 3$ (c) $12 + 4p + 2 - 9p$

(d) $3q + 10 - 7q + 2$ (e) $2 - 8v + 3v - 1$ (f) $8 + w - 3 - 3w - w$

(g) $6 - 3g + 3 - 8g - 2$ (h) $4 - 2h - 3 - h$ (i) $4 - 7k + 5 - 4k + 2k$

B2 Find and simplify expressions for the perimeters of these shapes.

(a)

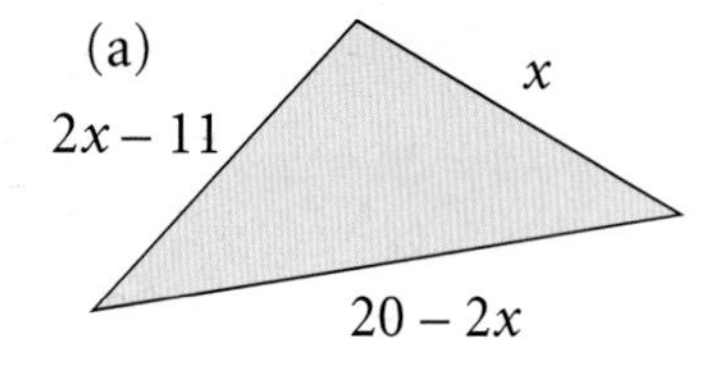

(b)

50 – 3x

x x

50 – 3x

(c)

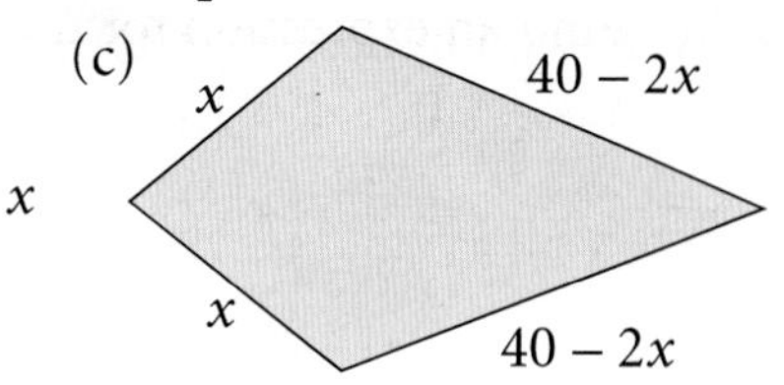

C Shape up

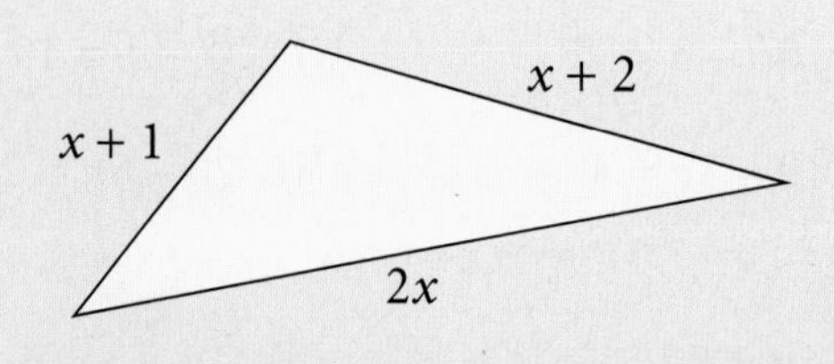

30 – 2x

x x

30 – 2x

What value of x

- gives a triangle with a perimeter of 63?
- gives a triangle and rectangle with equal perimeters?
- makes the rectangle into a square?

C1 (a) (i) Make a sketch of the triangle for $x = 3$.

(ii) Work out its perimeter.

(b) Find an expression for the perimeter of the triangle.

(c) What value of x gives a perimeter of 50?

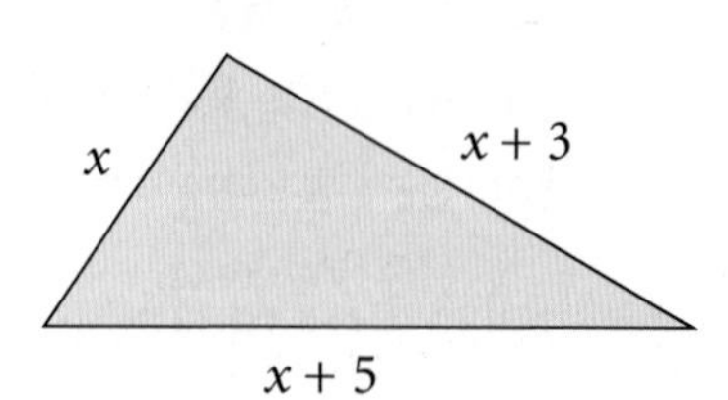

C2 (a) (i) Make a sketch of the triangle for $x = 1$.

(ii) What is the special name for your triangle?

(iii) Work out its perimeter.

(b) Find an expression for the perimeter of the triangle.

(c) What value of x gives a perimeter of 55?

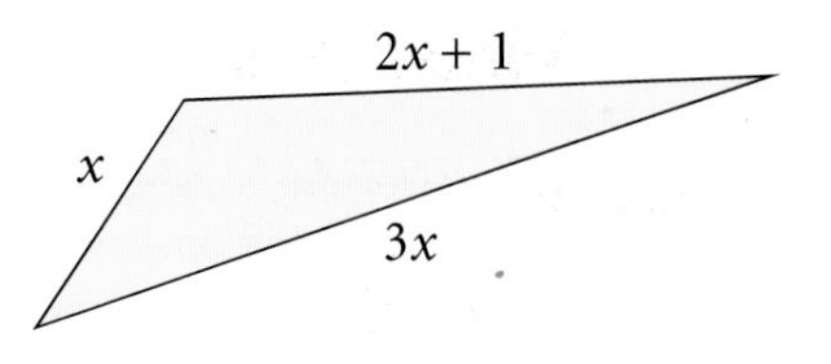

C3 (a) Find the length and width of the rectangle when $x = 5$.

(b) Find an expression for the perimeter of the rectangle.

(c) What value of x gives a perimeter of 10?

(d) What value of x gives a square?

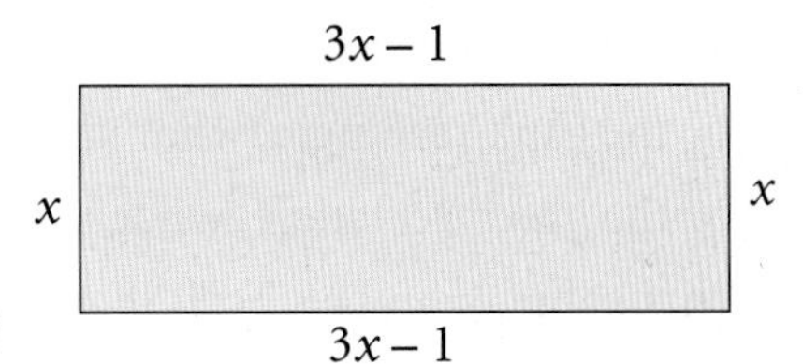

C4 (a) Find an expression for the perimeter of the rectangle.

(b) What value of x gives a perimeter of 48?

(c) What value of x gives a square?

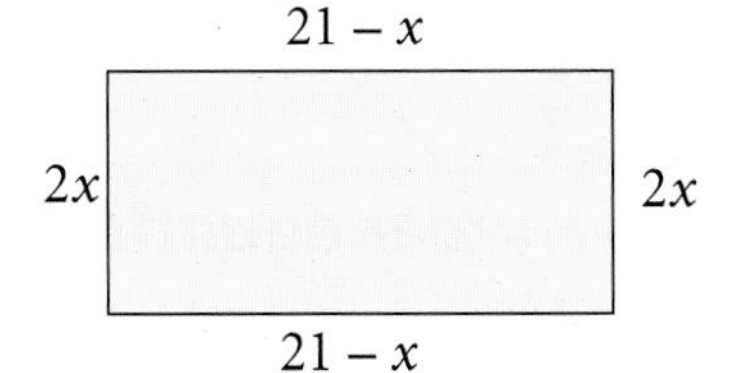

C5 (a) Find an expression for the perimeter of the kite.

(b) What value of x gives a perimeter of 68?

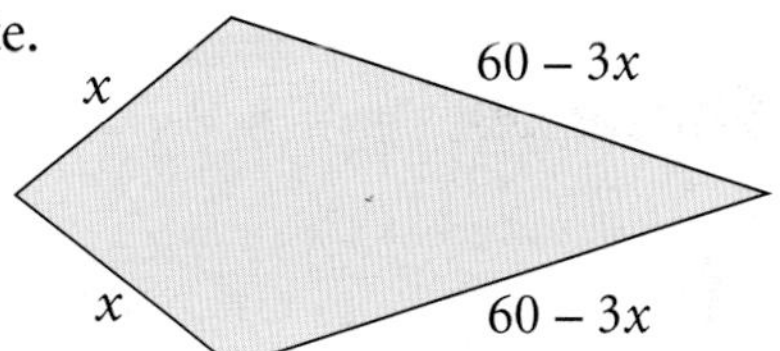

C6 (a) Find the perimeter of each triangle below when $x = 3$.

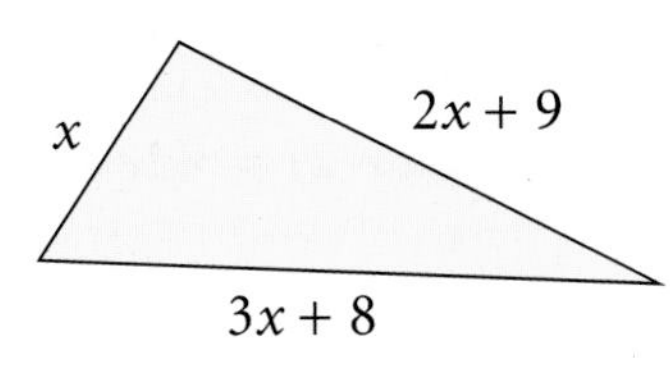

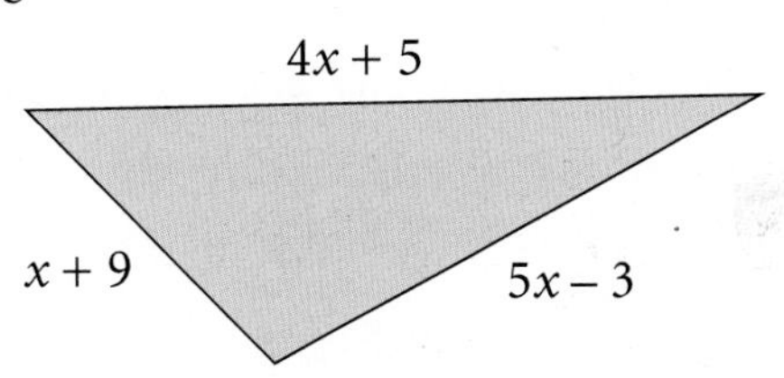

(b) (i) Find an expression for the perimeter of the yellow triangle.

(ii) What value of x gives a yellow triangle with a perimeter of 143?

(c) (i) Find an expression for the perimeter of the blue triangle.

(ii) What value of x gives a blue triangle with a perimeter of 50?

(d) What value of x gives both triangles the same perimeter?

C7 The shapes below are rectangles.

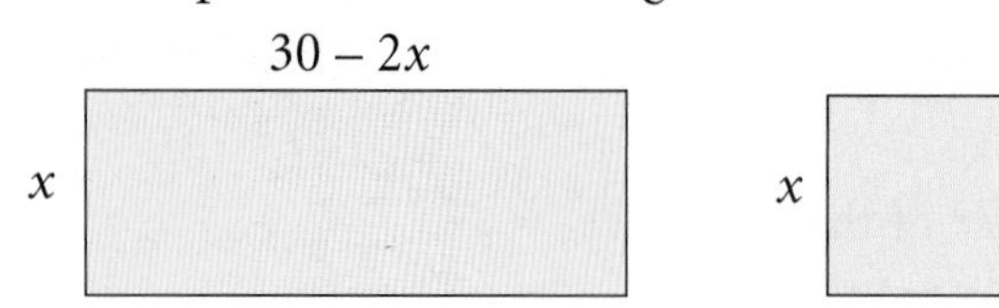

(a) Find the length and width of each rectangle when $x = 13$.

(b) Explain why it is not possible to sketch a green rectangle for $x = 14$.

(c) For the pink rectangle, what value of x gives a perimeter of 44?

(d) For the green rectangle, what value of x gives a perimeter of 60?

(e) What value of x gives both rectangles the same perimeter?

(f) What value of x gives a pink square?

(g) What value of x gives a green square?

*(h) Explain why it is not possible to sketch a pink rectangle with a perimeter of 100.

D *Harder equations*

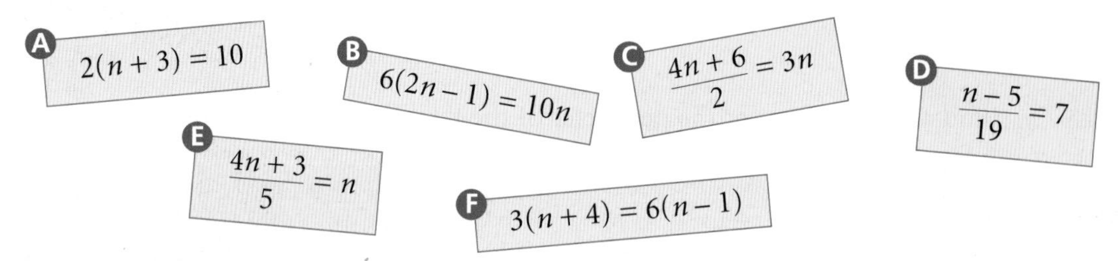

D1 Solve these equations.

(a) $2(m + 3) = 40$ (b) $3(n + 10) = 9n$ (c) $4(p + 9) = 10p$

(d) $3(2g - 1) = 24$ (e) $5(2h - 3) = 5h + 10$ (f) $4(3k - 7) = 2(3k - 2)$

(g) $2(x + 15) = 3(x + 1)$ (h) $4(y + 9) = 12y - 4$ (i) $5(z - 3) = 7(z - 5)$

(j) $2(a + 5) = 4a + 7$ (k) $3(2b - 2) = 2(b + 2)$ (l) $4(c - 2) = 5(2c - 7)$

D2 Solve these equations.

(a) $\frac{n - 1}{5} = 4$ (b) $\frac{3n + 6}{3} = 10$ (c) $\frac{n + 5}{6} = 11$ (d) $\frac{4n}{7} - 1 = 7$

(e) $\frac{n + 12}{4} = n$ (f) $\frac{2n + 132}{13} = n$ (g) $\frac{8n - 3}{7} = n$ (h) $\frac{n + 18}{2} = 5n$

D3 Solve these equations.

(a) $4(10 - n) = 24$ (b) $3(2 - p) = p - 14$ (c) $5(20 - 3q) = 10$

(d) $6(8 - u) = 3(2u - 4)$ (e) $5(10 - 3a) = 4(2a + 1)$ (f) $10(w + 3) = 18(4 - w)$

(g) $3(5 - 2v) = 9(2 - v)$ (h) $4(10 - z) = 3(11 - z)$ (i) $2(11 - 2h) = 3(14 - 3h)$

D4 Solve these equations.

(a) $\frac{10-n}{4}=2$ (b) $\frac{24-n}{9}=2$ (c) $\frac{15-3n}{2}=3$ (d) $\frac{39-2n}{8}=4$

D5 Solve these equations.

(a) $6(5-k)=8(k+2)$ (b) $\frac{8-4k}{2}=1$ (c) $4(k+2)=6(5-3k)$

(d) $\frac{20-k}{3}=6$ (e) $8(k-2)=17-3k$ (f) $\frac{18+k}{3}=k$

(g) $2(11-4k)=7-2k$ (h) $3-2k=6-4k$ (i) $3(6-k)=4(11-4k)$

Solving harder equations

Examples

It is often a good idea to multiply to get rid of brackets as soon as you can.

$6(x+2)=3(13-x)$	[multiply out brackets]
$6x+12=39-3x$	[+ 3x]
$9x+12=39$	[− 12]
$9x=27$	[÷ 9]
$x=3$	

It is often a good idea to multiply to get rid of divisions as soon as you can.

$\frac{4n-5}{2}=n$	[× 2]
$4n-5=2n$	[+ 5]
$4n=2n+5$	[− 2n]
$2n=5$	[÷ 2]
$n=2.5$	

Test yourself

T1 Solve these equations.

(a) $4x-1=39$ (b) $3x+14=5x$ (c) $5x+1=7x-3$

(d) $4x+1=10-2x$ (e) $16-x=10+2x$ (f) $10-2x=16-5x$

T2 This shape is a rectangle.

15 − n

2n

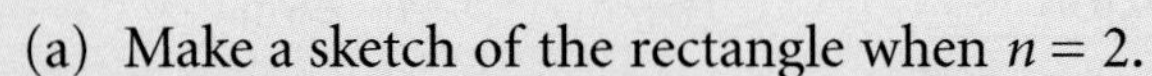

(a) Make a sketch of the rectangle when $n = 2$.

(b) (i) Find an expression for the perimeter of the rectangle.

(ii) What value of n gives a perimeter of 41?

T3 Solve these equations.

(a) $6(k+5)=33$ (b) $3(2k-5)=k$ (c) $2(k+1)=10(k-1)$

(d) $\frac{k+5}{3}=4$ (e) $\frac{2k+9}{5}=k$ (f) $5(3-k)=2(7-2k)$

Review 1

1 50 rows of chairs are set out in a school hall.
There are 30 chairs in each row.
How many chairs are there altogether in the hall?

2 Find the missing lengths in these triangles.

(a)

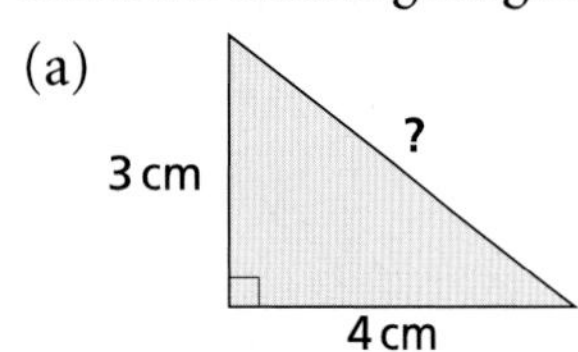

(b)

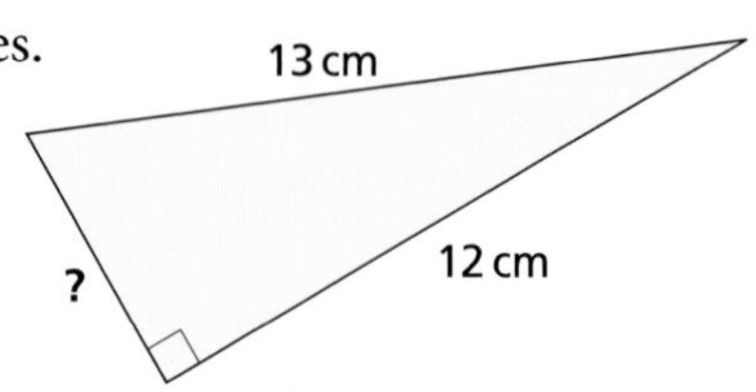

3 **P** $3(n-2)$ **Q** $2(3n-5)$ **R** $\frac{n+5}{2}$ **S** $13-2n$

(a) Find the value of each expression when (i) $n = 3$ (ii) $n = 2$

(b) Which expression has the smallest value when $n = 6$?

4 A rectangle has an area of $1600\,\text{cm}^2$.
The length is 80 cm.
Work out the width of the rectangle.

5 Simplify these expressions.

(a) $4x \times 5$ (b) $5 + 3p - 1 - 5p$ (c) $\frac{1}{4}(8y - 20)$

(d) $\frac{10b}{5} + 1$ (e) $\frac{6w + 15}{3}$ (f) $\frac{12 - 18k}{6}$

6 A ribbon that is 2.6 metres long is cut into 5 equal pieces.
How long is each piece?

7 Multiply out the brackets from these.

(a) $2(n + 5)$ (b) $3(5 - 2m)$ (c) $7(3p - 5)$

8 Find the area of each rectangle in m^2.

(a)

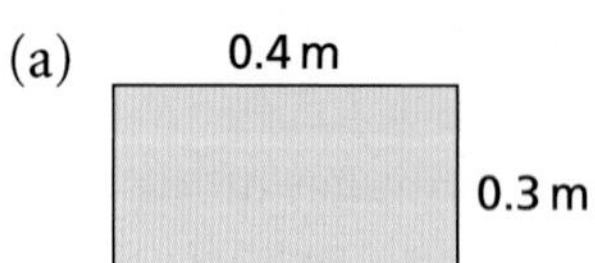

(b) 35 m, 23 m

9 Jane and Ayse have n sweets each. They are each given 2 sweets.
Which expressions give the number of sweets they have altogether?

$n + 2$ $2n + 2$ $2n + 4$ $2(n + 4)$ $2(n + 2)$

10 How many pieces of ribbon 0.7 m long could be cut from a roll of ribbon 28 m long?

11 Work out the missing lengths, giving your answers to one decimal place.

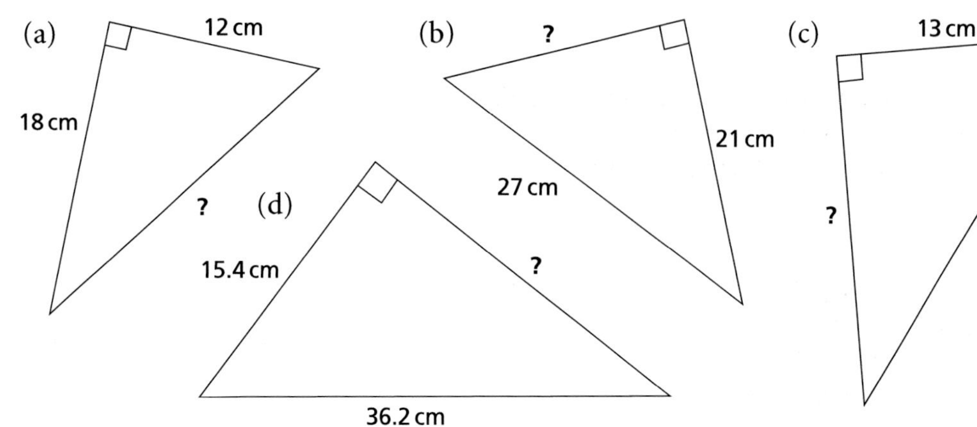

12 (a) Find an expression for the perimeter of
(i) the triangle (ii) the square

(b) What value of x gives both shapes the same perimeter?

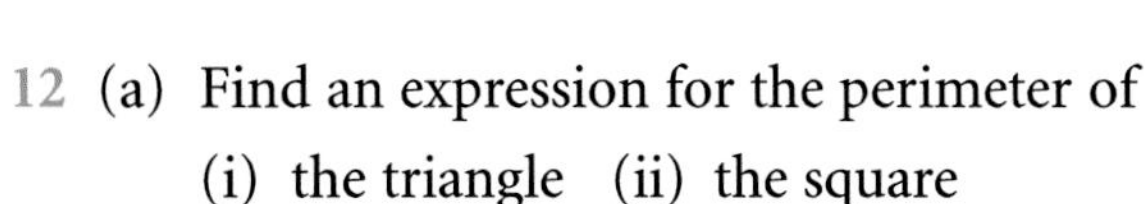

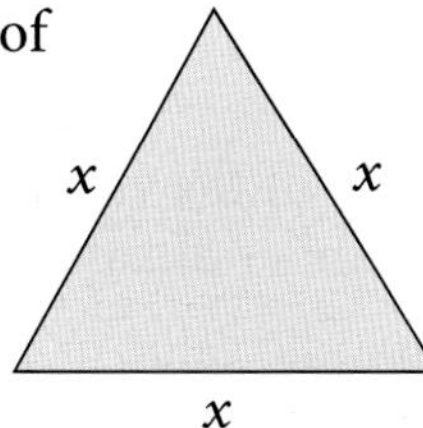

$x - 5$ $x - 5$ $x - 5$ $x - 5$

13 Calculate 2.3×0.15

14 Solve these equations.

(a) $7x + 1 = 3x + 9$ (b) $3x + 5 = 5x - 6$ (c) $5x - 18 = 3 - 2x$

15 Calculate (a) $\frac{0.21}{0.07}$ (b) $\frac{2.85}{0.19}$ (c) $\frac{8.4}{0.24}$ (d) $\frac{0.92}{2.3}$

16 Solve these equations.

(a) $5(n - 1) = 2n + 4$ (b) $5n + 11 = 3(3n - 5)$

(c) $6(2n + 1) = 9(3 - n)$ (d) $\frac{10 - 3n}{2} = n$

17 (a) Find an expression for the perimeter of this rectangle.

(b) What is the perimeter when $n = 10$?

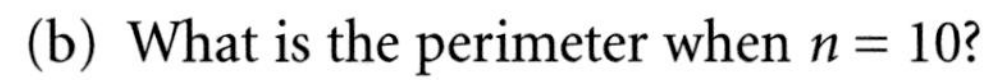

(c) What value of n gives a perimeter of 59?

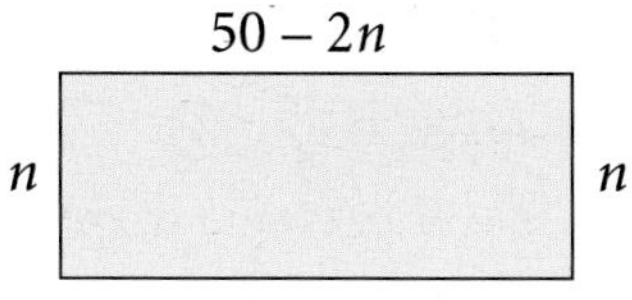

18 Find the missing length.

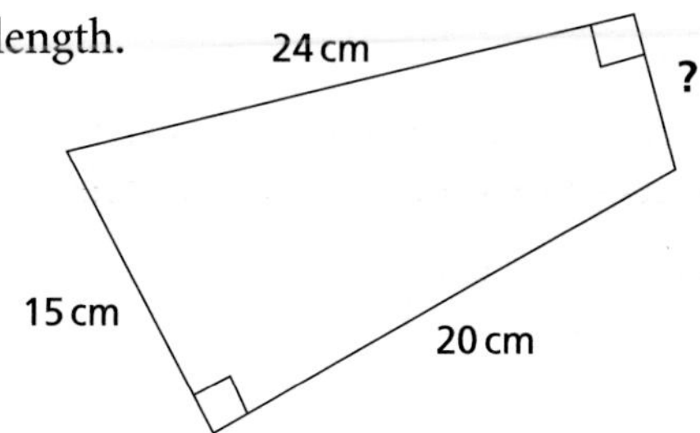

5 Distributions

You will revise how to

- find the mean, median, mode and range of sets of data
- put data into frequency tables

This work will help you

- use stem-and-leaf tables
- use grouped frequency tables
- estimate the mean from a grouped frequency table

A Review

For a set of data,

- the **mean** is $\frac{\text{the sum of the values}}{\text{the number of values}}$
- the **median** is the middle value or the mean of the two middle values when the values are put in order of size
- the **range** is the highest value minus the lowest value
- the **mode** is the value that occurs most often

Susan swims twenty lengths each weekday at her local pool.
She records her times each day.

29 minutes 30 minutes 28 minutes 35 minutes 30 minutes

The mean time is $\frac{29 + 30 + 28 + 35 + 30}{5} = \frac{152}{5} = 30.4$ minutes.

In order, the times are 28 29 **30** 30 35

The median time is 30 minutes.

The range is $35 - 28 = 7$ minutes.

A1 One year, students in Helen's class are given six French tests, each marked out of 50.
Helen's marks are

40 36 42 38 48 46

(a) Work out the mean of her marks, correct to 1 d.p.

(b) Put Helen's marks in order and calculate her median mark.

(c) What is the range of her test marks?

A2 Gina and Grace play an electronic game called 'Snake'.
One day, they write down all their scores.

Gina	236	103	65	126	198	
Grace	132	138	141	160	152	140

(a) Work out the mean, median and range of Gina's scores.

(b) Work out the mean, median and range of Grace's scores.

(c) On this evidence, who would you say is better at 'Snake'?
Give reasons for your decision.

This table shows the number of people in some cars passing a particular set of traffic lights one morning.

Number of people in a car	Number of cars
1	29
2	12
3	7
4	2

The total number of cars in the survey is 29 + 12 + 7 + 2 = 50

The number of people that occurs most often is 1 so the mode is 1 person.

The mean number of people in a car is $\frac{(1 \times 29) + (2 \times 12) + (3 \times 7) + (4 \times 2)}{50} = \frac{82}{50} = 1.64$

The median number of people is the mean of the numbers of people in the 25th and 26th cars which is $\frac{1+1}{2} = 1$.

A3 Greg surveys some people to find out how many television sets are in their homes.

Number of TV sets	Number of homes
0	8
1	20
2	37
3	29
4	6

(a) How many homes were surveyed in total?

(b) Work out the mean number of television sets in a home.

(c) Write down the mode.

(d) What is the median number of TV sets?

A4 A survey asked people to estimate how many eggs they had eaten in the previous week.

Number of eggs	Number of people
0	3
1	16
2	28
3	25
4	18
5	11
6	4
7	2

(a) What is the modal number of eggs?

(b) Work out the mean number of eggs eaten per person.

(c) What is the median number of eggs?

B *Stem-and-leaf tables*

Put your finger on the pulse

First aiders take a person's pulse from the carotid artery which is in the neck.

The pulse rate is recorded as the number of beats per minute (b.p.m.).

What is your pulse rate now?

Is your pulse faster at the beginning of the lesson or at the end?

Here are the pulse rates of a class of year 10 students taken at the beginning of a lesson.

Pulses (beats per minute) 77, 74, 85, 77, 72, 73, 55, 60, 91, 85, 80, 83, 68, 71, 60, 77, 77, 86, 97, 47, 71, 72, 63, 68, 84, 87, 77, 61

A useful way to record this data is a stem-and-leaf table.

Pulse rates (beats per minute)

Stem	Leaf
4	7
5	5
6	0 8 0 3 8 1
7	7 4 7 2 3 1 7 7 1 2 7
8	5 5 0 3 6 4 (7)
9	1 7

Stem = 10 beats 28 items

Stem *Leaf* *This is 87*

By putting the leaves in order in each row the table is even more useful.

Pulse rates (beats per minute)

Stem	Leaf
4	7
5	5
6	0 0 1 3 8 8
7	1 1 2 2 3 (4 7) 7 7 7 7
8	0 3 4 5 5 6 7
9	1 7

Since there are 28 items of data the median is between the 14th and 15th. It is easy to count from the table that it is between 74 and 77. So the median is 75.5 b.p.m.

Can you find the range easily from this table?

Can you find the mode or modal group easily from this table?

B1 A class measured how long they could hold their breath.
Here are their results.

Breath holding (seconds) *40, 41, 69, 55, 48, 28, 18, 43, 45, 63, 50, 57, 80, 38, 14, 40, 40, 58, 60, 41, 65, 48, 41, 32*

(a) Put this data into a stem-and-leaf table.
Make another copy of the table putting the data in order.

(b) Use your table to find the median time the students in this class could hold their breath for.

(c) Write down the range of the times.

B2 The data below shows the average male life expectancy of the main countries in Africa.

Life expectancy (years) in 2000	
Algeria	68
Angola	45
Ethiopia	48
Ghana	56
Kenya	52
Madagascar	57
Mauritius	68
Nigeria	51
Rwanda	41
Sierra Leone	36
South Africa	62
Sudan	54
Tunisia	68
Uganda	40

(a) Put this data into a stem-and-leaf table with the data in order.

This is the data for females in the same African countries.

Female life expectancy (years)	
3	9
4	2 3 8
5	2 4 6 6
6	0 0 8
7	0 1 5
Stem = 10 years	14 items

(b) Compare the life expectancies of males and females in these African countries.

B3 This data shows the hours of sunshine recorded in London every day one September.

Sunshine (hours)															
	10.1	9.6	9.6	6.8	7.4	10.0	11.8	10.6	8.9	5.8	0.0	8.7	9.4	5.5	6.1
	0.1	8.1	1.7	8.3	10.2	7.8	9.1	0.1	0.1	3.6	3.4	0.1	0.7	0.2	9.3

(a) Put this information into an ordered stem-and-leaf table with a stem of 1 hour units.

(b) Use your table to find the median and range of the hours of sunshine in September.

B4 Stem-and-leaf tables can be useful for showing two sets of data side by side.
This data shows the pulse rates of a class at the beginning and end of a PE lesson.

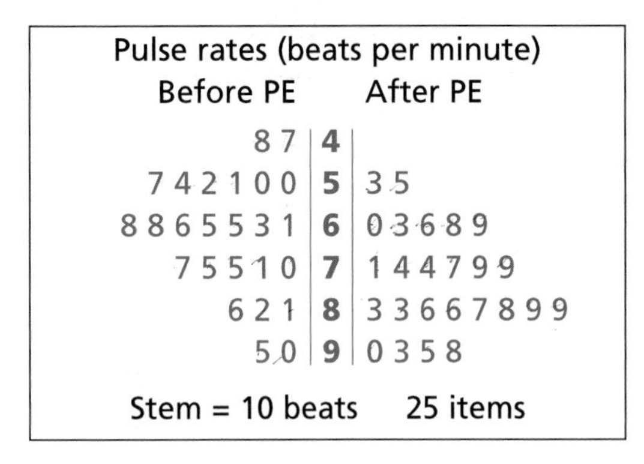

Pulse rates (beats per minute)

Before PE		After PE
8 7	**4**	
7 4 2 1 0 0	**5**	3 5
8 8 6 5 5 3 1	**6**	0 3 6 8 9
7 5 5 1 0	**7**	1 4 4 7 9 9
6 2 1	**8**	3 3 6 6 7 8 9 9
5 0	**9**	0 3 5 8

Stem = 10 beats   25 items

(a) Find the median and range of the pulse rates
  (i) before the PE lesson
  (ii) after the PE lesson

(b) Use the table and your answer to (a) to write a brief statement about the pulse rates of the class before and after their PE lesson.

B5 This data shows the pulse rates of three different groups of people in Southbury.

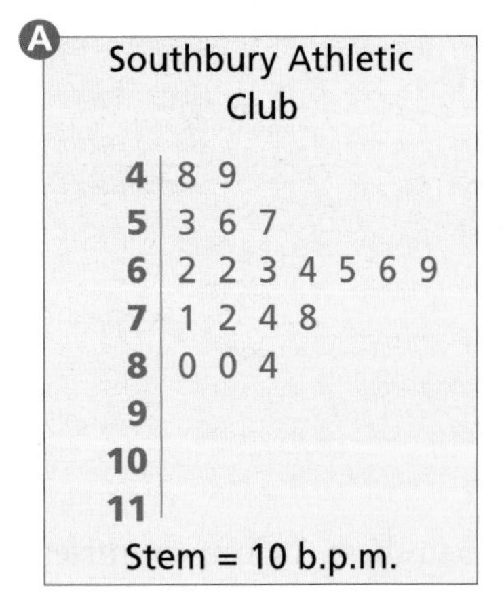

A Southbury Athletic Club

Stem	Leaf
4	8 9
5	3 6 7
6	2 2 3 4 5 6 9
7	1 2 4 8
8	0 0 4
9	
10	
11	

Stem = 10 b.p.m.

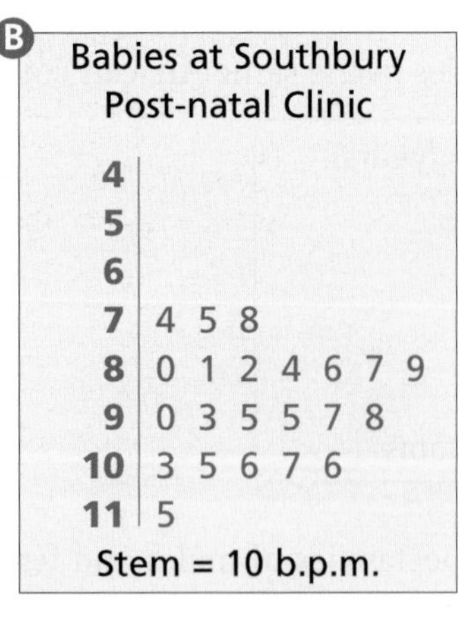

B Babies at Southbury Post-natal Clinic

Stem	Leaf
4	
5	
6	
7	4 5 8
8	0 1 2 4 6 7 9
9	0 3 5 5 7 8
10	3 5 6 7 6
11	5

Stem = 10 b.p.m.

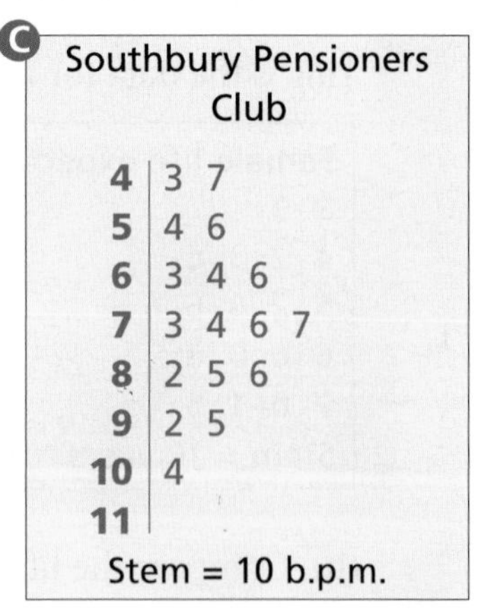

C Southbury Pensioners Club

Stem	Leaf
4	3 7
5	4 6
6	3 4 6
7	3 4 6 7
8	2 5 6
9	2 5
10	4
11	

Stem = 10 b.p.m.

Compare the pulse rates of the three groups.
Calculate any figures which help you to make comparisons.

C Grouped frequencies

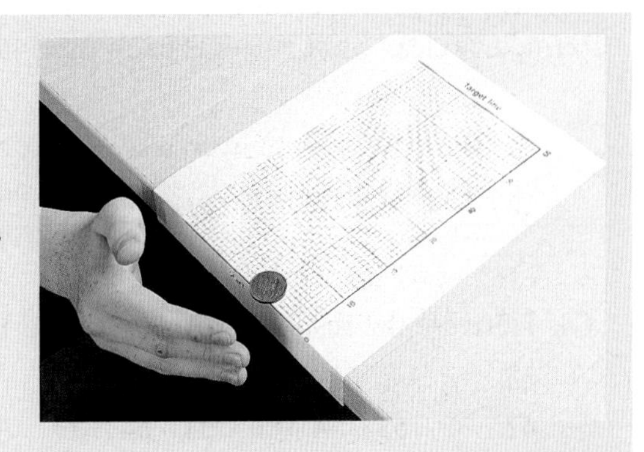

Two friends are playing 'Shove coin'.

The idea is to tap with the palm of their hand to get the coin as close to the target line as possible.

If the coin goes over the line, the player goes again. Each player records their shove by making a small mark on the next grid line between the front edge of the coin and the target line.

Each player has 50 shoves.

Amy's results are shown here.

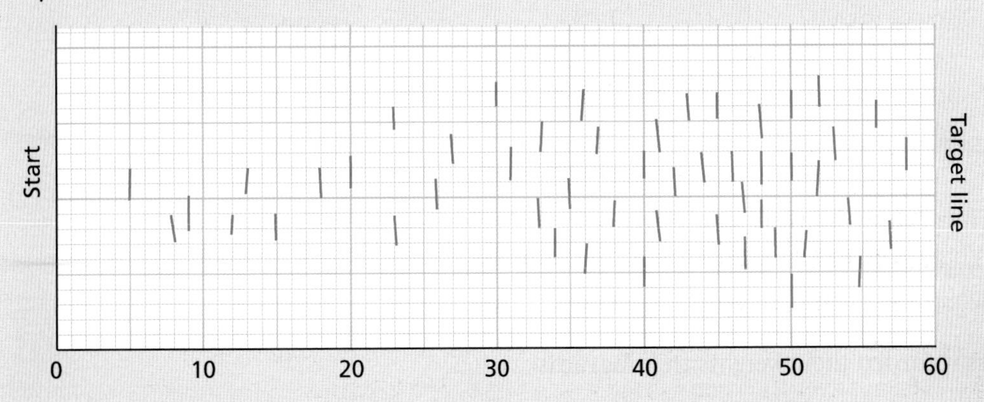

One way to record Amy's results is in a grouped frequency table.

Distance from start (cm)	Frequency
0–10	3
10–20	4
20–30	5
30–40	10
40–50	16
50–60	12
Total	50

- Which group did the 20 mark go into?
- Which group did the three 50 marks go into?
- How can you make it clear which group marks at the ends of groups go into?

It does not matter whether marks go in the group above or below provided the same rule is used with every group.
To make it clear what rule has been used here one way the **intervals** can be described is:

$0 \leq d < 10$
$10 \leq d < 20$
$20 \leq d < 30$ ← *So 20 goes in this group*
....

... where d is the distance from the start.
The ≤ sign shows that all the numbers in that group are greater than or equal to the first number.

C1 Here are the results for Amy's friend Baljit.

44 5 30 44 49 29 56 21 12 56 24 57 14 54 7 48 17 18
47 32 53 54 19 54 54 39 26 12 10 22 41 52 58 49 23 40
58 46 18 45 38 50 52 39 37 28 39 43 51 36

(a) Copy and complete this table for Baljit's results.

Distance (d cm)	Tally	Frequency
$0 \leq d < 10$		
$10 \leq d < 20$		
$20 \leq d < 30$		

(b) The group with the greatest frequency is called the **modal group** or **class**. What is the modal group for Baljit's shoves?

(c) What was the modal group for Amy's shoves?

C2 A class recorded their weights in kilograms.

Weight (kg) 46 45 52 61 57 47 61 52 47 47 42 59 51 35 48
62 62 47 52 39 72 69 57 43 50 38 61 47 54 40

The teacher asks the students to record this data in a grouped frequency table with these groupings.

Weight (w kg)	Frequency
$30 < w \leq 40$	
$40 < w \leq 50$	
$50 < w \leq 60$	
$60 < w \leq 70$	
$70 < w \leq 80$	
Total	

(a) Which group will the weight 50 kg go into?

(b) Which group will the weight 40 kg go into?

(c) Copy and complete a table showing these students' weights using these groupings. Check that you have recorded the correct number of weights.

(d) Write down the modal group of weights.

(e) Use your table to copy and complete this frequency diagram for the weights of students.

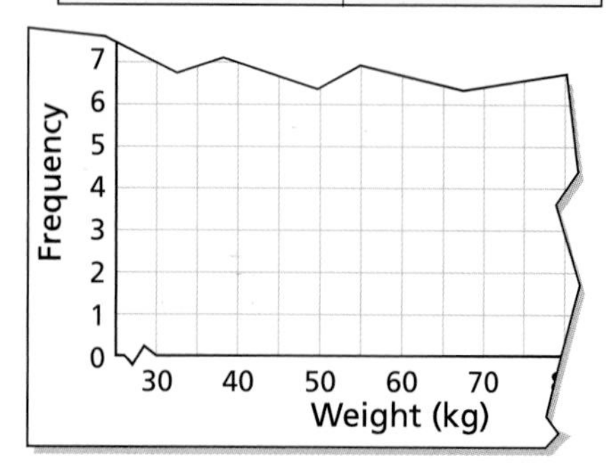

C3 The following is a record of the heights, in centimetres, of 40 guinea pigs.

21 22 11 16 22 13 11 25 9 17 21 24 27 25 12 14 8 12 6 17
23 7 12 26 14 8 12 26 17 19 23 29 21 19 26 26 18 21 13 9

(a) Copy and complete this frequency table.

Height (h cm)	Tally	Frequency
$5 \le h < 10$		
$10 \le h < 15$		
$15 \le h < 20$		
$20 \le h < 25$		
$25 \le h < 30$		

(b) Draw a frequency diagram for this information on squared paper.

(c) How many guinea pigs were under 15 cm in height?

(d) Write down the modal class interval of the heights. Edexcel

C4 The maximum daily temperature for the month of October was recorded at a Sussex weather station.

Max. temp. (°C)	16.7	13.9	15.4	14.6	14.1	14.2	12.5	14.6	12.2	12.9	12.2	13.1	14.7
	12.7	13.9	12.7	13.9	14.4	13.9	14.5	14.7	14.1	14.7	12.9	14.4	13.1
	13.6	14.6	12.8	13.3	12.4								

(a) Copy and complete this grouped frequency table to record the temperatures.

Max. temp. (°C)	Frequency
$12.0 \le t < 13.0$	
$13.0 \le t < 14.0$	
$14.0 \le t < 15.0$	
$15.0 \le t < 16.0$	
$16.0 \le t < 17.0$	
Total	

(b) What is the modal group of temperatures in Sussex during October?

(c) On how many days in October did the temperature not reach 14°C?

D *In the interval*

This data shows the heights in cm of 44 male African elephants.

272	273	287	84	95	153	165	161	168	257	262	293	194	193	204	218	218
227	186	181	182	224	231	236	237	256	260	238	235	247	200	207	201	215
245	290	317	108	124	270	287	121	135	142							

These frequency tables and diagrams show this data grouped in different intervals.

Height (h cm)	Frequency
$80 \le h < 100$	2
$100 \le h < 120$	1
$120 \le h < 140$	3
$140 \le h < 160$	2
$160 \le h < 180$	3
$180 \le h < 200$	5
$200 \le h < 220$	7
$220 \le h < 240$	7
$240 \le h < 260$	4
$260 \le h < 280$	5
$280 \le h < 300$	4
$300 \le h < 320$	1
Total	44

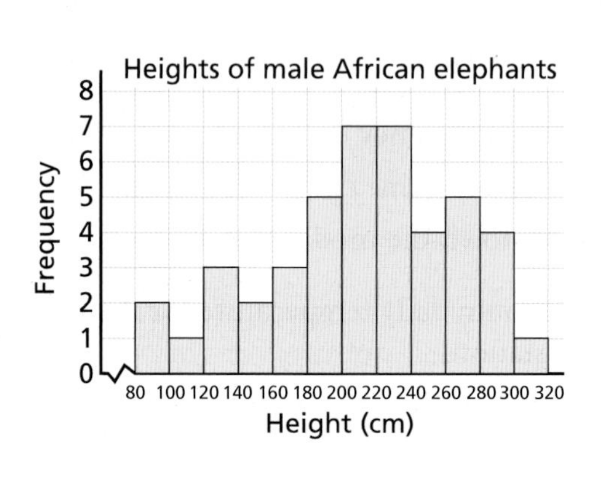

Height (h cm)	Frequency
$50 \le h < 100$	2
$100 \le h < 150$	5
$150 \le h < 200$	9
$200 \le h < 250$	16
$250 \le h < 300$	11
$300 \le h < 350$	1
Total	44

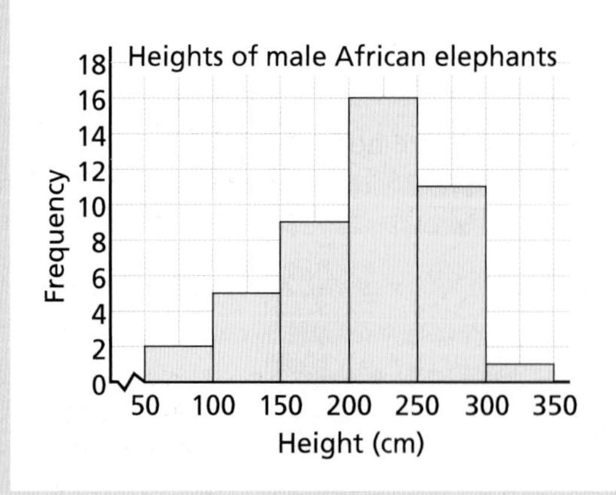

Height (h cm)	Frequency
$0 \le h < 100$	2
$100 \le h < 200$	14
$200 \le h < 300$	27
$300 \le h < 400$	1
Total	44

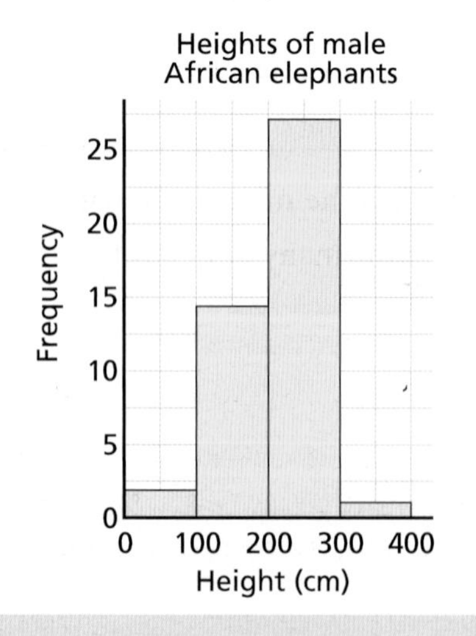

- Which way of grouping gives the clearest picture of the pattern of the data?
- Which way gives the most useful value for a modal class?
- Would using intervals of 5 cm give a clearer picture?
  Would intervals of 200 cm give you more information?
- Would using intervals of 35 cm be a useful grouping?

D1 This data shows the foot length (f) in centimetres of the 44 male African elephants.

49 49 51 17 18 28 30 30 31 46 47 52 35 35 37 40 40 41 34 33 33 41
42 43 43 46 47 43 42 45 36 38 37 39 44 52 57 21 23 48 51 23 25 26

(a) Record this data in a frequency table with intervals
$15 \le f < 20$, $20 \le f < 25$, $25 \le f < 30$, ...
What is the modal group?

(b) Write out another table with intervals $10 \le f < 20$, $20 \le f < 30$, $30 \le f < 40$, ...
What is the modal group now?

(c) Which of these two sets of intervals gives the clearer picture of the data?

D2 For each of these sets of data decide on a suitable set of intervals.
Put the data into a frequency table using these intervals.
Draw a frequency diagram from your table.

(a)

Reaction times (thousandths of a second)
20 18 18 13 18 15 16 17 17 18 22 27 17 15 11 12 12 12 13
17 18 21 19 15 16 10 11 16 15 20 16 22 15 14 14

(b)

Weights (kg)
62.5 63.1 62.9 63.8 62.4 65.7 65.3 66.9 64.7 66.1 65.0 65.2 67.6 66.3 67.3
68.1 69.0 68.4 69.6 68.9 68.5 69.2 70.5 71.3 70.4 71.8 70.0 70.8 70.3 70.7
71.2 70.1 72.4 73.6 72.7 72.9 74.5 75.1

Open-ended

This data records the time in seconds between eruptions at the Kiama Blowhole near Sydney, Australia.

83 51 87 60 28 95 8 27 15 10 18 16 29 54 91 8 17 55 10 35 47 77
36 17 21 36 18 40 10 7 34 27 28 56 8 25 68 146 89 18 73 69 9 37
10 82 29 8 60 61 61 18 169 25 8 26 11 83 11 42 17 14 9 12

- What would be a suitable set of intervals to record this data?

When there are just a few 'extreme' pieces of data, open-ended groups are often used.
The data above could be recorded in these groups.

Time (s seconds)
$0 \le s < 20$
$20 \le s < 40$
$40 \le s < 60$
$60 \le s < 80$
$80 \le s < 100$
$100 \le s$

This group includes any times greater than 100 seconds.

Can you easily draw a frequency diagram from this table?

E *Estimating means*

TG

This frequency diagram and table summarise the amount collected in a day for a charity.

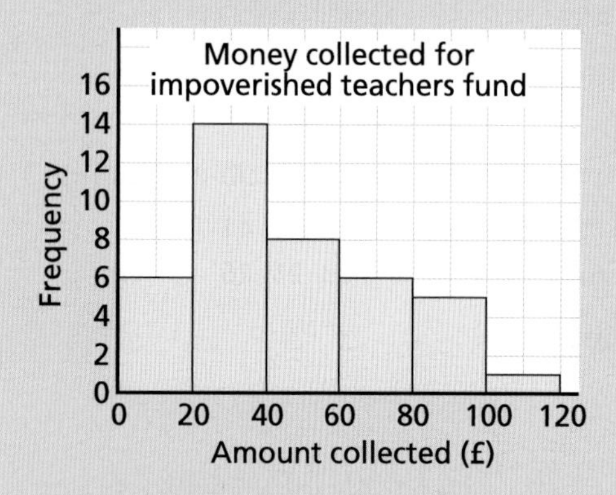

Money (£m)	Frequency
$0 \le m < 20$	6
$20 \le m < 40$	14
$40 \le m < 60$	8
$60 \le m < 80$	6
$80 \le m < 100$	5
$100 \le m < 120$	1
Total	40

To find the mean amount collected per person the total amount collected is needed.

The 6 people in the $0 \le m < 20$ interval all collected between 0 and £20.
As the average amount collected by this group was probably around £10 a reasonable estimate of the amount collected by this is group is $6 \times £10 = £60$.

A reasonable estimate of the total amount collected would be

$$(6 \times 10) + (14 \times 30) + (8 \times 50) + (6 \times 70) + (5 \times 90) + (1 \times 110) = £1860$$

So an estimate of the mean amount collected per person is $1860 \div 40 = £46.50$

Since this is only an estimate it would be sensible to quote the mean as £47 or even £50.

E1 A local police force want to estimate the mean speed of cars along a particular stretch of road which has a 40 m.p.h. speed limit.
This table shows the speeds recorded one morning and some unfinished working to estimate the mean speed.

Speed (s m.p.h.)	Frequency	Mid-interval value	Group total estimate
$20 < s \le 30$	7	25	$7 \times 25 = 175$
$30 < s \le 40$	21	35	$21 \times 35 = 735$
$40 < s \le 50$	8		
$50 < s \le 60$	3		
$60 < s \le 70$	1		
Total	40		

(a) How many people were breaking the speed limit?

(b) Copy and complete the table above.

(c) Use your table to estimate the mean speed of the cars.

E2 This bar chart gives information about the temperatures of a group of patients with a particular illness.

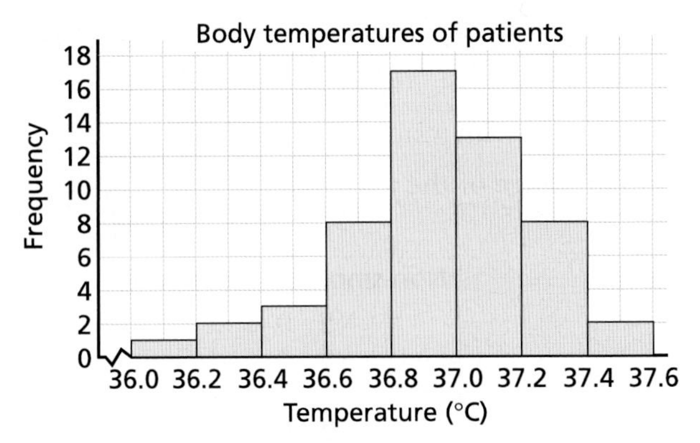

(a) How many patients were in the group altogether?

(b) Use the chart to write out a grouped frequency table with groups $36.0 < t \le 36.2$, ...

(c) Use your table to find an estimate of the mean temperature of these patients.

E3 On holiday Val records the length, of time people stay in the pool. The results are shown in the table.

Calculate an estimate of the mean time spent in the pool.

Give your answer to an appropriate degree of accuracy.

Time (t mins)	Number of people
$0 < t \le 10$	4
$10 < t \le 20$	7
$20 < t \le 30$	3
$30 < t \le 40$	2
	16

AQA 1999

E4 This grouped frequency table shows the marks in a test.

Mark	Frequency
1–5	2
6–10	5
11–15	19
16–20	4
21–25	3

(a) Meg says that the mid-interval value for the first group is 2.5.
Noel says that it must be 3.
Which is correct and why?

(b) Copy the table and add appropriate columns to find an estimate of the mean mark in the test.

Test yourself

T1 This data shows the pulse rates of a group of university students who smoked.

Pulse (b.p.m.)	70	92	75	68	88	86	65	80	90	76	69	83	70	76	88

(a) Record this data in a stem-and-leaf table with a stem of 10 b.p.m.

(b) Use the table to find the median and range of the pulse rates of these students who smoked.

(c) These are the pulse rates of some students at the same university who were non-smokers.

Find the median and range of the pulse rates of the non-smokers.

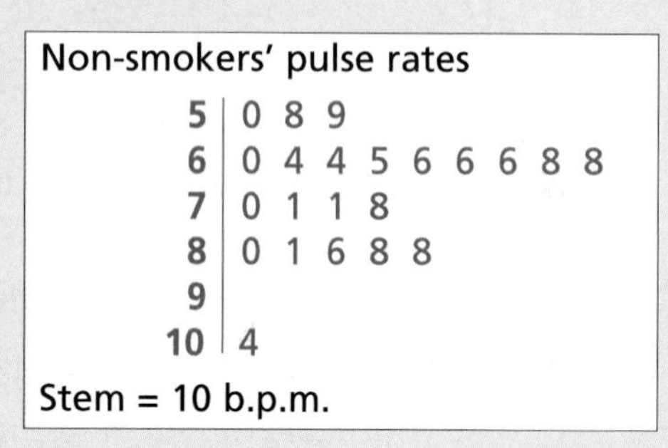

Non-smokers' pulse rates

Stem	Leaves
5	0 8 9
6	0 4 4 5 6 6 6 8 8
7	0 1 1 8
8	0 1 6 8 8
9	
10	4

Stem = 10 b.p.m.

(d) Make two statements about the difference in pulse rates between the students who smoked and those who were non-smokers.

T2 A set of 25 times in seconds is recorded.

12.9 10.0 4.2 16.0 5.6 18.1 8.3 14.0 11.5 21.7 22.2 6.0 13.6
3.1 11.5 10.8 15.7 3.7 9.4 8.0 6.4 17.0 7.3 12.8 13.5

(a) Copy and complete the table below, using intervals of 5 seconds.

Time (t seconds)	Tally	Frequency
$0 \leq t < 5$		

(b) Write down the modal class interval. Edexcel

T3 Draw a frequency diagram from the table in T2.

T4 Some women walked one mile. The time taken by each was recorded. The results are as follows.

Time (t minutes)	$12 \leq t < 16$	$16 \leq t < 20$	$20 \leq t < 24$	$24 \leq t < 28$	$28 \leq t < 32$
Number of women	1	9	43	22	5

(a) What is the modal class of the time taken?

(b) Calculate an estimate of the mean time taken.

One mile is approximately 1.6 km.

(c) Use the data to calculate an estimate of the mean time taken by these women to walk one kilometre. AQA 1998

6 Multiples, factors and powers

This work will help you

- work out factors, multiples, prime numbers and powers
- use index notation and the rules for multiplying powers of the same number
- find and use prime factorisations, for example to work out lowest common multiples and highest common factors

A Multiples, factors and primes

Lock up

A prison has 25 prisoners (one in each cell) and 25 jailers.
The cells are numbered 1 to 25.

The jailers all go to a party one night and return very merry!

- The first jailer unlocks every cell.
- The second jailer locks every cell whose number is a multiple of 2.
- The third jailer turns his key in the lock for cells whose numbers are multiples of 3. (He locks or unlocks these cells).
- The fourth jailer turns his key in the lock for cells whose numbers are multiples of 4 … and so on till the twenty-fifth jailer.

All the jailers then fall asleep and the prison is silent.

The prisoners all try their doors – which ones escape?

TG

Multiples

Multiples of 7 are numbers that can be divided exactly by 7.
Examples are 42, 84, 14, 21 and 7 itself.
Multiples of 3 are numbers that can be divided exactly by 3. Examples are 6, 21, 30, 63.

Common multiples of 3 and 7 are numbers that can be divided exactly by 3 **and** by 7.
Some common multiples of 3 and 7 are 42, 21, 63 and 105.

21 is the **lowest common multiple** of 3 and 7.

A1 Which numbers in this list are multiples of 6?
36, 6, 3, 16, 12, 60, 600, 80

A2 (a) Write down five multiples of 4.
(b) Write down five multiples of 3.
(c) Write down a common multiple of 4 and 3.

Factors

Factors of 20 are numbers that divide exactly into 20.
They can be found in pairs.

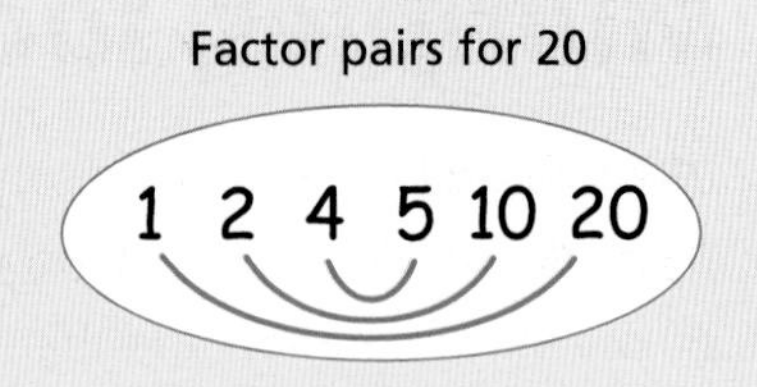

For example, $5 \times 4 = 20$ so $20 \div 5 = 4$ and $20 \div 4 = 5$
So 4 and 5 are factors of 20.

Factors of 20 are 1, 2, 4, 5, 10 and 20.
Factors of 8 are 1, 2, 4 and 8.

Common factors of 8 and 20 are numbers that divide exactly into 8 **and** 20.
They are 1, 2 and 4.

4 is the **highest common factor** of 8 and 20.

A3 One factor of 32 is missing from this list. Which is it?

16, 4, 2, 1, 32

A4 Which of these numbers are factors of 36?

5, 8, 2, 3, 4, 10, 9, 12

A5 Write down all the factors of 60.

A6 Decide whether each statement is true or false.

(a) 5 is a factor of 10 (b) 6 is a multiple of 12 (c) 14 is a multiple of 7
(d) 8 is a factor of 4 (e) 28 is a multiple of 4 (f) 4 is a factor of 28

A7 (a) Write down three different factors of 10.
(b) List three different multiples of 10.

A8 Which numbers in the loop are

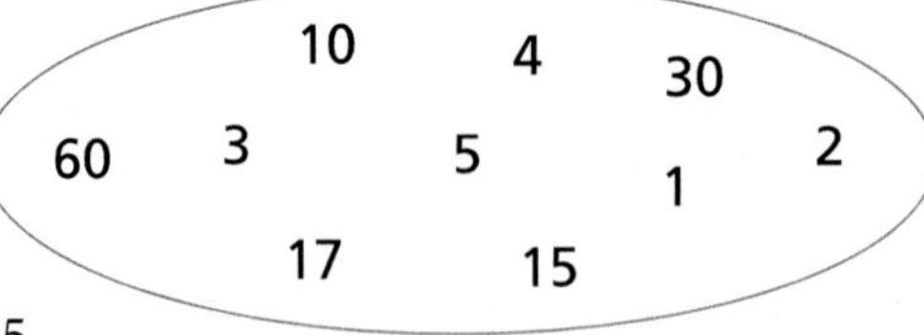

(a) multiples of 5
(b) factors of 10
(c) multiples of 3
(d) common multiples of 3 and 5
(e) common factors of 12 and 20
(f) common factors of 5 and 12

A9 (a) Write down three common multiples of 2 and 8.
(b) Write down a common multiple of 6 and 9.

A10 (a) Find all the common factors of 18 and 45.
(b) What is the highest common factor of 18 and 45?

A11 What is the lowest common multiple of

(a) 5 and 2 (b) 4 and 8 (c) 12 and 8 (d) 4 and 9

A12 What is the highest common factor of

(a) 35 and 20 (b) 5 and 9 (c) 10 and 20 (d) 24 and 54

Primes

Prime numbers are numbers with **exactly two** factors.

For example,
17 is a prime number as it has two factors (1 and 17).

Factor pairs for 17

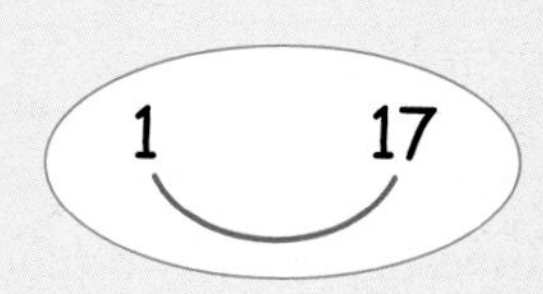

8 is not a prime number as it has more than two factors (1, 2, 4 and 8).
1 is not a prime number as it only has one factor (1).

A13 Which of the following numbers are not prime?

2, 6, 14, 19, 11, 9, 13, 21, 10, 15, 5

A14 List all the prime numbers between 20 and 40.

A15 Each set of clues gives a number.
Find these five numbers.

(a)
- A factor of 16
- An odd number

(b)
- Less than 30
- A multiple of 7
- An even number
- A number with six factors

(c)
- A common factor of 10 and 35
- A prime number

(d)
- A common multiple of 4 and 6
- A multiple of 10
- Less than 100

(e)
- A common factor of 40 and 60
- An even number
- A prime number

A16 Both 3 and 11 are prime numbers.

Find the highest common factor of 3 and 11.
Find the lowest common multiple of 3 and 11.

Repeat for some other pairs of prime numbers.
Comment on your results.

B *Powers*

TG

Ice cream

Toni sells two flavours of ice cream, strawberry and vanilla.

Here are some different ice creams that each have three scoops.

- How many different ice creams can Toni make with three scoops?
- Investigate for two scoops, one scoop, four scoops, …

Rosa sells three flavours of ice cream, strawberry, vanilla and chocolate.

- How many different ice creams can Rosa make with one scoop, two scoops, … ?

In an expression like 2^5, the raised number '5' is called the index.

Indices (more than one index) are used as a mathematical shorthand.

Examples

$2 \times 2 \times 2 \times 2 \times 2 = 2^5$ $3 \times 3 \times 3 \times 3 = 3^4$ The value of 5^3 is $5 \times 5 \times 5 = 125$

We say 3^4 as 'three to the power four'.

Powers of three can be written as 3^1, 3^2, 3^3, 3^4, …
or 3, 9, 27, 81, …

B1 Write these in shorthand form using indices.

(a) $2 \times 2 \times 2 \times 2 \times 2 \times 2 \times 2 \times 2$ (b) $4 \times 4 \times 4 \times 4 \times 4 \times 4 \times 4 \times 4 \times 4 \times 4 \times 4$

B2 Find the value of these.

(a) 2^4 (b) 4^3 (c) 3^5 (d) 7^2 (e) 5^3

B3 (a) List all the powers of two between 10 and 50.

(b) What is the value of 'three to the power two'?

B4 There is one cell in a flask in a laboratory.
The number of cells doubles every 15 minutes.

(a) How many cells are there after 2 hours?

(b) How long does it take the number of cells to increase to 2^{10}?

B5 Decide if the following statements are true or false.

(a) $5^2 = 5 \times 2$ (b) $3^2 > 2^3$ (c) $2^6 < 5^2$ (d) $3^4 < 6^2$

B6 Choose the correct symbol, <, > or =, for each box below.

(a) 4^3 ■ 3^4 (b) 7^2 ■ 2^7 (c) 2^5 ■ 5^2 (d) 9^1 ■ 1^9

B7 Find the missing numbers in these statements

(a) $2^{■} = 64$ (b) $8^{■} = 8$ (c) $9^{■} = 81$ (d) $■^3 = 1$

B8 Most calculators have a special key for working out powers.
Find this key on your calculator.
(It might look like one of these: x^y or y^x or ^)
Use this key on your calculator to work these out.

(a) 2^3 (b) 10^4 (c) 3^6

Check your answers are correct without using this key.

B9 Find the value of these.

(a) 13^4 (b) 2^{12} (c) 1^{23} (d) 5^9 (e) 9^5

B10 Arrange the following numbers in order of size, smallest first.
2^{31}, 7^{10}, 3^{20}, 16^6, 100^2

B11 Which do you think will be larger, 2^{25} or 25^4?
Check with your calculator.

B12 Copy and complete this cross number puzzle.

Across

1 3^8

5 21^2

6 A factor of 24

8 A common factor of 45 and 105

9 A power of 3

10 A power of 7

Down

2 A power of 2

3 A common multiple of 11 and 13

4 5^5

6 A power of 4

7 A multiple of 11

8 A multiple of 100

1	2		3	■	4
■		■	5		
6		■		■	
	■	7	■	8	
9			■		■
	■	10			

C *Multiplying*

C1 Find the missing numbers in these calculations.

(a) $2^3 \times 2^2 = (2 \times 2 \times 2) \times (2 \times 2) = 2^{\blacksquare}$

(b) $5^3 \times 5^6 = (5 \times 5 \times 5) \times (5 \times 5 \times 5 \times 5 \times 5 \times 5) = 5^{\blacksquare}$

(c) $7^5 \times 7^4 = (7 \times 7 \times 7 \times 7 \times 7) \times (7 \times 7 \times 7 \times 7) = 7^{\blacksquare}$

(d) $3^5 \times 3 = 3 \times 3 \times 3 \times 3 \times 3 \times 3 = 3^{\blacksquare}$

C2 Write down the numbers missing from these calculations.

(a) $3^2 \times 3^3 = 3^{\blacksquare}$ (b) $4^2 \times 4^4 = 4^{\blacksquare}$ (c) $8 \times 8^7 = 8^{\blacksquare}$

(d) $6^3 \times 6^9 = 6^{\blacksquare}$ (e) $2^{\blacksquare} \times 2^5 = 2^{11}$ (f) $7^5 \times 7^{\blacksquare} = 7^6$

C3 (a) Write down a rule for multiplying powers of the same number. Explain why your rule works.

(b) Using your rule, copy and complete $2^{12} \times 2^5 = 2^{\blacksquare}$

C4 Find three pairs of equivalent expressions.

A $2^5 \times 2^2$ B 2^9  C $2^9 \times 2$ D 2^7 E 2^{10} F $2^5 \times 2^4$

C5 Write the answers to these using indices.

(a) $3^4 \times 3^3$ (b) $10^5 \times 10^6$ (c) $4^8 \times 4^4$ (d) $8^4 \times 8$

(e) $2^4 \times 2^2 \times 2^3$ (f) $7 \times 7^9 \times 7^2$ (g) $10 \times 10^9 \times 10$ (h) $9^{20} \times 9^{10}$

C6 Copy and complete these.

(a) $2^{\blacksquare} \times 2^4 = 2^{12}$ (b) $5^2 \times 5^{\blacksquare} = 5^8$ (c) $3^{\blacksquare} \times 3 = 3^{10}$ (d) $4^3 \times 4^{\blacksquare} \times 4^5 = 4^{10}$

C7 Which two of these statements are false?

A $2^5 \times 3^4 \times 2^2 = 2^7 \times 3^4$

B $2^2 \times 3^5 = 6^7$

C $5^2 \times 6^3 \times 5^4 \times 6 = 5^6 \times 6^4$

D $5^4 \times 3^2 \times 5^5 = 15^{11}$

C8 Copy and complete these.

(a) $3^2 \times 5^3 \times 5^4 \times 3^6 = 3^{\blacksquare} \times 5^{\blacksquare}$ (b) $2 \times 9^2 \times 2^5 \times 9^3 = 2^{\blacksquare} \times 9^{\blacksquare}$

(c) $4^7 \times 3^{\blacksquare} \times 4 \times 3^2 = 3^{10} \times 4^{\blacksquare}$ (d) $3^4 \times 11^{\blacksquare} \times 3^{\blacksquare} \times 11^5 = 3^5 \times 11^8$

C9 Simplify these.

(a) $10^2 \times 3^4 \times 10^3 \times 3^5$ (b) $2^2 \times 5^3 \times 2^9$ (c) $5^9 \times 7 \times 7^6 \times 5$

To **multiply** powers of the same number, **add** the indices ($a^m \times a^n = a^{m+n}$).

Example

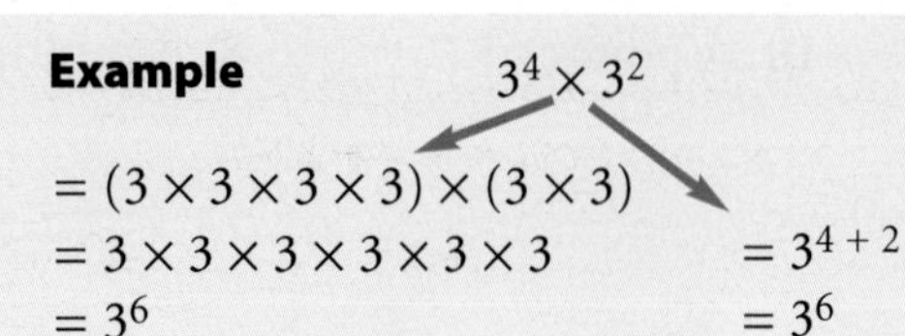

$3^4 \times 3^2$

$= (3 \times 3 \times 3 \times 3) \times (3 \times 3)$

$= 3 \times 3 \times 3 \times 3 \times 3 \times 3$

$= 3^6$

$= 3^{4+2}$

$= 3^6$

D *Prime factorisation*

There are many ways to write 84 as a product of factors.

For example, $84 = 4 \times 21$

$84 = 12 \times 7$

$84 = 2 \times 6 \times 7$

$84 = 2 \times 2 \times 3 \times 7$

$2 \times 2 \times 3 \times 7$ is called the **product of prime factors** or **prime factorisation** of 84.
We can use index notation to write it as $2^2 \times 3 \times 7$.

We can work out that 96 is $2 \times 2 \times 2 \times 2 \times 2 \times 3$ (or $2^5 \times 3$) in different ways.

Factor trees

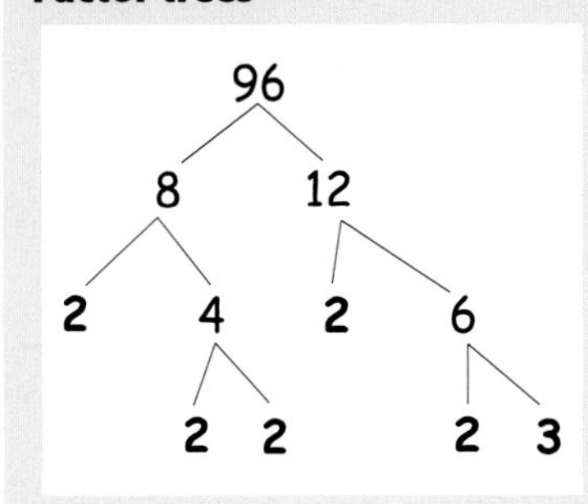

Repeated division

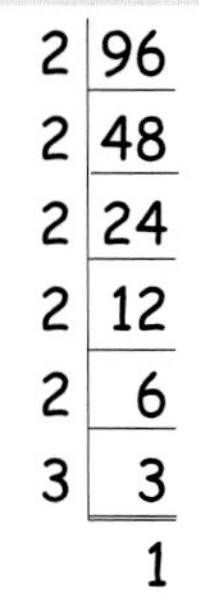

Factor products

96 = 4 x 24

= 2 x 2 x 4 x 6

= 2 x 2 x 2 x 2 x 2 x 3

D1 Match each number to its prime factorisation.

B 990 **C** 240 **D** 7425

E $3^3 \times 5^2 \times 11$ **F** $2 \times 3^2 \times 5 \times 11$ **G** $2^4 \times 3 \times 5$ **H** $2^3 \times 3 \times 5$

D2 Find the prime factorisation of each of these numbers and write it using index notation.

(a) 45 (b) 150 (c) 48 (d) 126 (e) 243

D3 The prime factorisation of 462 is $2 \times 3 \times 7 \times 11$.

(a) Without doing any calculating, decide which of these are factors of 462.
Explain how you decided.

2 | 3 | 13 | 7 | 4 | 6 | 10 | 14 | 55

(b) Check your answers by calculating.

D4 The prime factorisation of 875 is $5 \times 5 \times 5 \times 7$.

(a) Without doing any calculating, decide which of these are factors of 875.
Explain how you decided.

2 | 3 | 5 | 7 | 20 | 25 | 35 | 45 | 125

(b) Check your answers by calculating.

D5 The prime factorisation of 315 is $3 \times 3 \times 5 \times 7$.
The prime factorisation of 3465 is $3 \times 3 \times 5 \times 7 \times 11$.

Without doing any calculating, decide if 3465 is a multiple of 315.
Explain how you decided.

D6 The prime factorisation of 1155 is $3 \times 5 \times 7 \times 11$.
The prime factorisation of 5005 is $5 \times 7 \times 11 \times 13$.

Without doing any calculating, decide if 5005 is a multiple of 1155.
Explain how you decided.

D7 The prime factorisation of 24 is $2^3 \times 3$.

(a) Without doing any calculating, decide which of these are multiples of 24.

$2^3 \times 3 \times 5$ $\quad 2^3 \times 3 \times 7^2$ $\quad 2^3 \times 5$ $\quad 2^4 \times 3$ $\quad 2^3 \times 3^2$ $\quad 2^2 \times 3 \times 5$

(b) Check your answers by calculating.

D8 The prime factorisation of 189 is $3^3 \times 7$.

(a) Without doing any calculating, decide which of these are factors of 189.

5 $\quad 7$ $\quad 3^3 \times 7^2$ $\quad 3 \times 7$ $\quad 3 \times 7^3$ $\quad 3^2 \times 7$

(b) Check your answers by calculating.

E *Highest common factors and lowest common multiples*

Example

Find the HCF (highest common factor) of 84 and 120.

- Write each number as a product of prime factors.

$$84 = \underline{2} \times \underline{2} \times \underline{3} \times 7$$
$$120 = \underline{2} \times \underline{2} \times 2 \times \underline{3} \times 5$$

- Look for common prime factors.

The factors 2, 2 and 3 are common to both products (underlined).

So the highest number which is a factor of 84 **and** a factor of 120 is $2 \times 2 \times 3$ which is **12**.

E1 (a) (i) Write 64 as a product of prime factors.

(ii) Write 168 as a product of prime factors.

(b) Use your prime factorisations to find the HCF of 64 and 168.

E2 Use prime factorisation to find the HCF of these.

(a) 72 and 180 (b) 90 and 525 (c) 165 and 154 (d) 104 and 234

Example

Find the LCM (lowest common multiple) of 84 and 105.

- Write each number as a product of primes and look for common factors.

$$84 = 2 \times 2 \times \underline{3} \times \underline{7}$$
$$105 = \underline{3} \times 5 \times \underline{7}$$

- Look for common factors (underlined) and write down the product of the common factors.

3×7

- Multiply this product by all of the remaining (non-common) factors.

$3 \times 7 \times 2 \times 2 \times 5$

So the lowest number which is a multiple of 84 **and** a multiple of 105 is
$3 \times 7 \times 2 \times 2 \times 5$ which is **420**.

E3 (a) Find the prime factorisations of 18 and 42.

(b) Use your prime factorisations to find the LCM of 18 and 42.

E4 Use prime factorisation to find the LCM of these.

(a) 12 and 20 (b) 14 and 15 (c) 45 and 165 (d) 42 and 350

*E5 Di wants to make a patchwork quilt 204 cm by 374 cm.
She is going to use red and white square patches.
The width of each patch is to be a whole number of centimetres.

What is the largest size she can use for the patches?

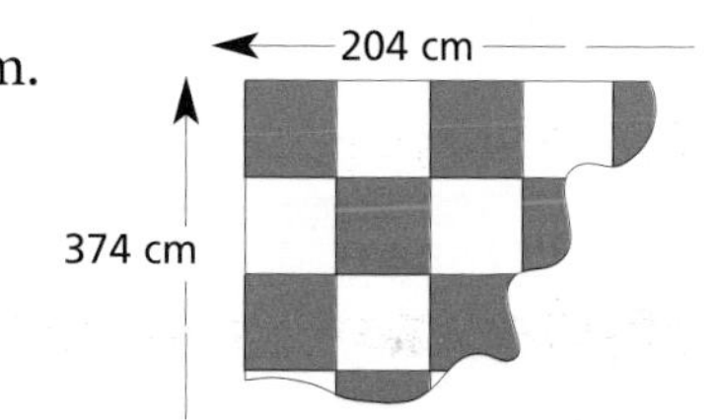

*E6 Ten friends swim at the local pool on 1 January and make a New Year's resolution.

The first person is going to swim every day, the second person every second day, the third every third day and so on.

How many days later do ten people again swim on the same day?

Test yourself

T1 (a) Find all the factors of 90.

(b) Write down the prime numbers between 10 and 30.

(c) Write down all the powers of 3 between 20 and 100.

T2 Evaluate these. (a) 3^7 (b) 13^2 (c) 10^1

T3 Write the answers to these using indices.

(a) $2^5 \times 2^9$ (b) 3×3^8 (c) $5^2 \times 5^3 \times 5^2$

T4 Find the prime factorisation of 234 and write it using index notation.

T5 Use prime factorisation to find the (a) LCM of 12 and 15 (b) HCF of 84 and 126.

7 Negative numbers

You should know how to substitute in expressions such as $x^2 + 1$, $3(x + 4)$, $\frac{x}{3} - 1$, the rules about the order of calculating with +, –, ×, ÷ and brackets, and how to solve equations.

This work will help you calculate with positive and negative numbers and substitute into a variety of expressions.

A Calculating

Calculating with positive and negative numbers	**Examples**
• To add a negative, subtract the corresponding positive	$6 + {}^-9 = 6 - 9 = {}^-3$ $^-7 + {}^-1 = {}^-7 - 1 = {}^-8$
• To subtract a negative, add the corresponding positive	$6 - {}^-9 = 6 + 9 = 15$ $^-7 - {}^-1 = {}^-7 + 1 = {}^-6$
• Multiplying or dividing two negatives gives a positive	$^-8 \times {}^-2 = 16$ $^-14 \div {}^-7 = 2$
• Multiplying or dividing a negative and a positive gives a negative	$5 \times {}^-3 = {}^-15$ $^-12 \div 4 = {}^-3$

A1 (a) Copy and complete the addition below using three different numbers from the loop.

□ + □ = □

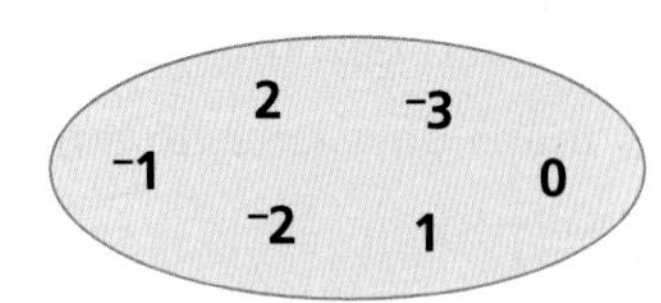

(b) Make as many different additions like this as you can.

(c) Copy and complete the subtraction here using three different numbers from the loop.

□ – □ = □

(d) Make eight different subtractions like this.

A2 Copy and complete each multiplication table.

(a)

×		$^-2$
$^-5$		
4	12	

(b)

×		
$^-1$	$^-5$	
6		$^-18$

(c)

×		$^-7$
	8	28
6		

A3 This is a 'division triangle'.

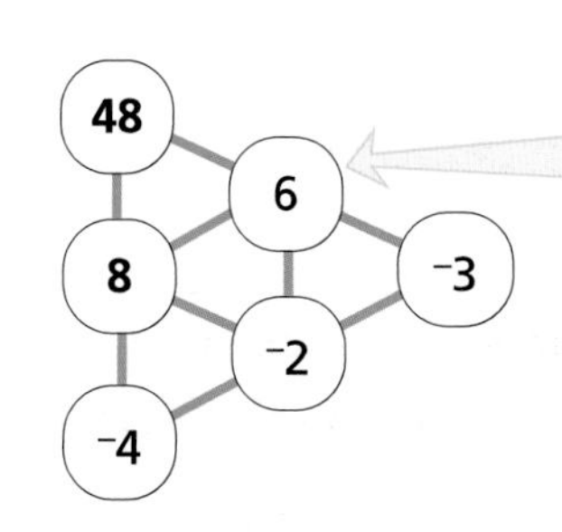

To find each number, divide the left hand pair of numbers: top number ÷ bottom number

(48 ÷ 8 = 6)

Copy and complete each division triangle.

(a)

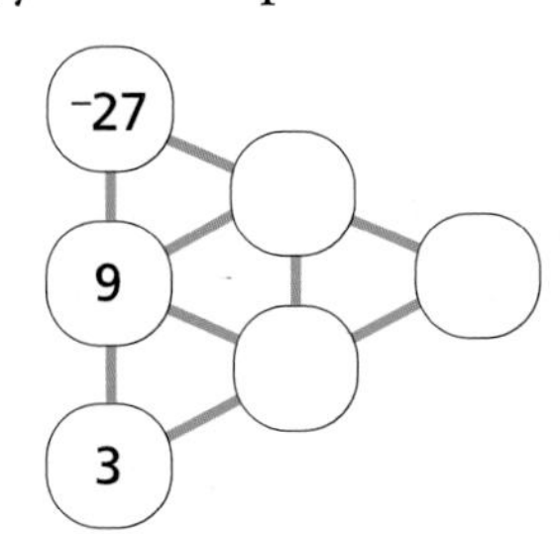

(b)

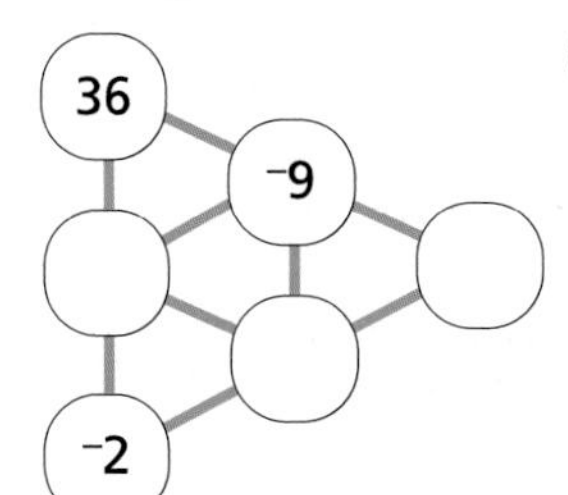

(c)

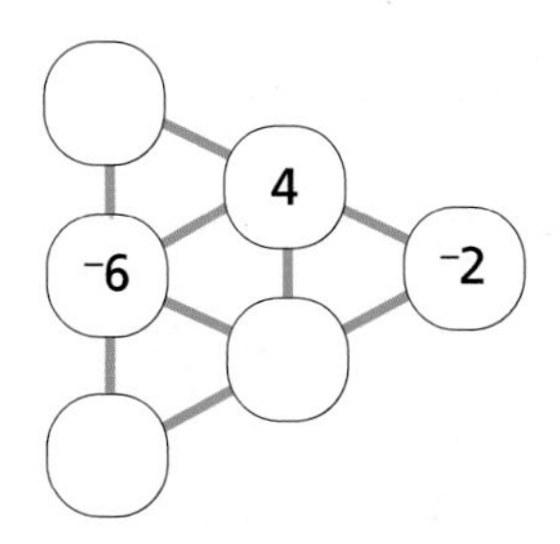

A4 Copy and complete each magic square, so that each row, column and diagonal adds to give the same total.

(a)

		0
	1	
2	$^-3$	

(b)

$^-4$	1	0
$^-2$	$^-3$	

(c)

	5	
	$^-3$	
3	$^-11$	

A5 Find the next two numbers in each sequence.

(a) 11, 9, 7, 5, 3, …

(b) $^-11$, $^-8$, $^-5$, $^-2$, …

(c) 5, 3.5, 2, 0.5, …

(d) 1, $^-2$, 4, $^-8$, 16, …

A6 Work these out.

(a) $10 + (^-3 \times 2)$

(b) $^-3 \times (^-2 + {}^-5)$

(c) $2 \times (1 - 9)$

(d) $^-2 \times 5 - 3$

(e) $6 - {}^-4 \times {}^-2$

(f) $7 - (1 - 5)$

(g) $\frac{^-12}{3} + 1$

(h) $^-5 + \frac{^-16}{^-4}$

(i) $\frac{^-8 - 2}{5}$

(j) $\frac{^-10 - {}^-8}{^-2}$

(k) $\frac{20}{^-5} - {}^-3$

(l) $^-2 - \frac{^-15}{5}$

***A7** Find the missing number in each of these calculations.

(a) $^-5 \times 3 \times$ ■ $= 30$

(b) $6 + 2 \times$ ■ $= 4$

(c) (■ $- 5) \times 3 = {}^-9$

(d) $4 - {}^-2 \times$ ■ $= 14$

(e) ■ $- {}^-3 \times {}^-2 = {}^-4$

(f) $10 +$ ■ $\times {}^-5 = 0$

(g) $\frac{10 - ■}{^-4} = {}^-3$

(h) $\frac{■}{^-3} - 9 = {}^-1$

(i) $^-1 - \frac{10}{■} = 4$

B *Substitution*

Examples

Find the value of $4x - 7$ when $x = 1$.

$$4x - 7 = 4 \times 1 - 7 = 4 - 7 = {}^{-}3$$

Find the value of $\frac{6 - a}{9}$ when $a = {}^{-}3$.

$$\frac{6 - a}{9} = \frac{6 - {}^{-}3}{9} = \frac{9}{9} = 1$$

Find the value of ${}^{-}5(n - 7)$ when $n = 2$.

$${}^{-}5(n - 7) = {}^{-}5 \times (2 - 7) = {}^{-}5 \times {}^{-}5 = 25$$

B1 What is the value of each expression when $x = 4$?

(a) $2x - 9$ (b) $19 - 6x$ (c) $10 - x^2$ (d) $\frac{x}{{}^{-}2} + 8$

B2 Find the value of each expression when $y = {}^{-}3$.

(a) $2y + 1$ (b) $y^2 + 5$ (c) $8 - y$ (d) $\frac{y}{{}^{-}3}$

B3 What is the value of each expression when $p = {}^{-}6$?

(a) $3p - 2$ (b) $2(p + 5)$ (c) $1 - 2p$ (d) $p^2 - 9$

(e) $\frac{p}{3} - 1$ (f) $(p + 3)^2$ (g) $5 - \frac{p^2}{4}$ (h) p^3

Examples

Find the value of $4(x^2 - 7)$ when $x = 2$.

$$4(x^2 - 7) = 4 \times (2^2 - 7) = 4 \times (4 - 7) = 4 \times {}^{-}3 = {}^{-}12$$

Find the value of $\frac{6 - 3h}{{}^{-}2}$ when $h = {}^{-}4$.

$$\frac{6 - 3h}{{}^{-}2} = \frac{6 - 3 \times {}^{-}4}{{}^{-}2} = \frac{6 - {}^{-}12}{{}^{-}2} = \frac{18}{{}^{-}2} = {}^{-}9$$

Find the value of $4a^2 - 38$ when $a = {}^{-}3$.

$$4a^2 - 38 = 4 \times ({}^{-}3)^2 - 38 = 4 \times 9 - 38 = 36 - 38 = {}^{-}2$$

B4 What is the value of each expression when $h = 5$?

(a) $5(2h - 11)$ (b) $\frac{10 - 6h}{5}$ (c) $3(10 - h^2)$ (d) $\frac{4h}{{}^{-}2} + 3$

B5 What is the value of each expression when $k = {}^{-}4$?

(a) $2k^2 + 1$ (b) $3(2k + 5)$ (c) $5(2 - 3k)$ (d) $\frac{1}{2}k^2 - 1$

(e) $\dfrac{8 - k^2}{{}^{-}4}$ (f) $\dfrac{k^2}{8} - 10$ (g) $\dfrac{(k - 2)^2}{9}$ (h) $5 - \dfrac{k^2}{2}$

B6

$\dfrac{3n - 17}{2}$	$5 - n^2$	$3n^2 - 11$	$\dfrac{4n + 3}{{}^{-}5}$	$2(n - 5)$	$2(n^2 - 7)$

(a) When $n = 3$, three expressions above have a value of ${}^{-}4$. Find these expressions.

(b) When $n = {}^{-}2$, three expressions above have the same value. Find these expressions.

B7 Sixteen expressions are arranged in a square grid giving four horizontal, four vertical and two diagonal sets of expressions.

For example, a set of expressions is shaded on the grid.

$\dfrac{n - 3}{2}$	$2n$	$n^2 - 3$	$n - 1$
$\dfrac{2n^2}{{}^{-}6}$	$4(12 - n)$	$\dfrac{6 - n}{4}$	$3n + 11$
$4n + 9$	$\dfrac{n^2}{4}$	$\dfrac{5 - n}{7}$	$2n + 5$
$\dfrac{4n - 3}{5}$	$n + 8$	$3n^2$	$\dfrac{n^2}{2} - 25$

(a) What is the value of each expression on a shaded square when $n = 8$? What do you notice?

(b) When $n = 2$, find a set of expressions (in a row, column or diagonal) that each have a value of 1.

(c) When $n = {}^{-}1$, which set of expressions each have a value of ${}^{-}2$?

(d) Find sets where each expression has the same value when

(i) $n = {}^{-}2$ (ii) $n = {}^{-}3$ (iii) $n = {}^{-}6$

B8 (a) Find the value of the expression $4n - 3$ when

(i) $n = 1$ (ii) $n = 0$ (iii) $n = {}^{-}2$

(b) Find the value of the expression $3n - 18$ when

(i) $n = 1$ (ii) $n = 0$ (iii) $n = {}^{-}2$

(c) There is one value of n for which both expressions have the same value.

(i) By putting $4n - 3$ equal to $3n - 18$ and solving the equation, find this value of n.

(ii) Check that the value is correct by substituting it in both expressions.

C *Equations with negative numbers*

C1 (a) Solve the equation $2n + 10 = 4$.

(b) Check that your answer fits the original equation.

C2 Solve each of these equations. Check each of your answers.

(a) $3k + 5 = 2$ (b) $\frac{m}{4} + 7 = 5$ (c) $4n + 1 = {}^{-}7$

C3 Solve the equation $4m + 21 = 3m + 16$. Check your answer works.

C4 Solve and check each of these.

(a) $3k + 14 = 2k + 10$ (b) $5g + 3 = 4g + 1$ (c) $6n + 7 = 4n + 1$

(d) $7b + 2 = 3b - 10$ (e) $2t + 5 = 5t + 8$ (f) $2x - 6 = 6x + 2$

C5 Solve and check each of these.

(a) $12 + n = 8 - n$ (b) $4t + 28 = 10 - 2t$ (c) $12 - 3b = 8 - 4b$

C6 Write equations for each of these number puzzles and solve them.

(a) I think of a number and double it.

I then add 11.

My answer is 3.

(b) I think of a number and multiply it by 3.

I then add 20.

My answer is the same as the number I started with.

(c) I think of a number and double it.

I then take my answer away from 10.

My answer is 19 more than the number I started with.

Test yourself

T1 Evaluate these.

(a) ${}^{-}3 - 6$ (b) ${}^{-}3 \times {}^{-}4$ (c) $4 + {}^{-}8$

(d) ${}^{-}3 \times (2 - 9)$ (e) $\frac{{}^{-}7 + {}^{-}8}{{}^{-}5}$ (f) $7 - \frac{{}^{-}8}{4}$

T2 What is the value of each expression when $n = {}^{-}8$?

(a) $2n - 10$ (b) $5(n + 1)$ (c) $\frac{3n}{4} + 12$ (d) $\frac{n^2 + 1}{5}$

(e) ${}^{-}3(n - 7)$ (f) $2n^2 - 100$ (g) $\frac{20 - 2n}{{}^{-}9}$ (h) $3 - \frac{n}{4}$

T3 Solve each of these equations and check that your answers work.

(a) $3x + 8 = 2$ (b) $\frac{n}{2} + 5 = 2$ (c) $2m + 3 = {}^{-}7$

(d) $5w + 11 = 2w + 5$ (e) $7n + 3 = 4n - 6$ (f) $3d + 25 = 5 - d$

8 Changing the subject 1

You should know

- how to solve equations like $3a + 2 = 17$ or $4a - 2 = 10$
- an expression like $\frac{b-6}{10}$ means 'take 6 off b and divide the result by 10'

This work will help you change the subject of a formula with letters and numbers in it, for example $a = 4d + 5$ and $h = 2k - 3$

A *Planting*

Stella is a garden designer who plants ornamental vegetable beds.
To keep away pests, she plants rows of artichokes, with marigolds by them in this pattern.

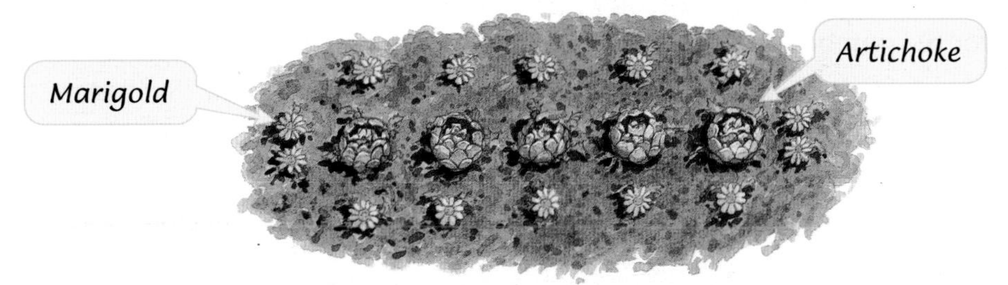

This table shows the number of marigolds for rows of artichokes of various lengths.

Number of artichokes (a)	1	2	3	4	5
Number of marigolds (m)	6	8	10	12	14

A rule for finding the number of marigolds needed is

number of marigolds = number of artichokes × 2 + 4

If a stands for the number of artichokes and m stands for the number of marigolds we can write this rule as a **formula** using letters:

$m = a \times 2 + 4$ or even shorter as $m = 2a + 4$.

A1 Use the formula to complete these shopping lists. Each is for one row of artichokes.

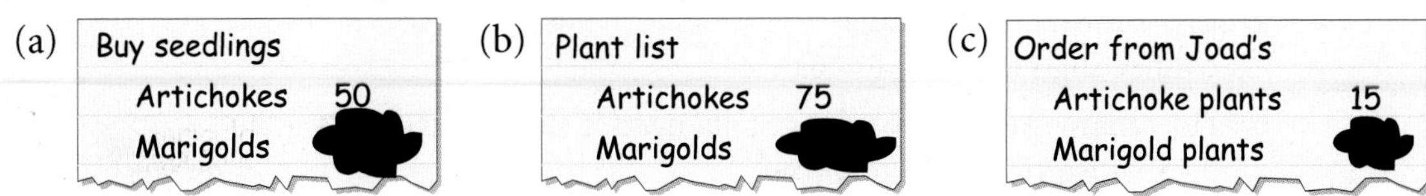

(a) Buy seedlings
Artichokes 50
Marigolds

(b) Plant list
Artichokes 75
Marigolds

(c) Order from Joad's
Artichoke plants 15
Marigold plants

A2 This is another order for one row of artichokes. We know the number of marigolds it needs, but we need to find the number of artichokes.

Put $m = 80$ in the formula $m = 2a + 4$.
Solve the equation you get to find a.

How many artichoke plants are needed?

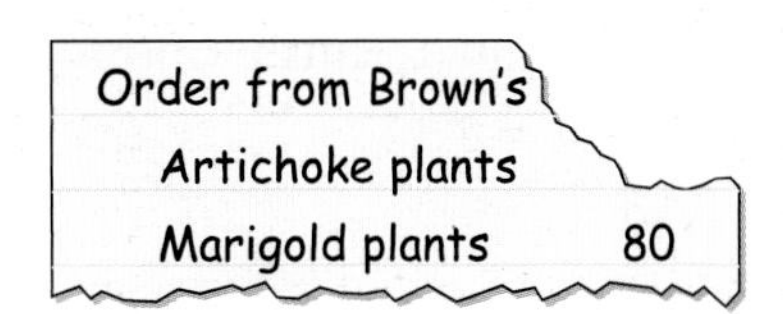

Order from Brown's
Artichoke plants
Marigold plants 80

A3 

Stella also plants rows of broccoli.
She puts ornamental cabbages above and below each row of broccoli and at the ends in the pattern shown above.

(a) Copy and complete this table for her broccoli and cabbage rows.

Number of broccoli plants (b)	1	2	3	4	5	10	100
Number of cabbage plants (c)					22		

(b) If b stands for the number of broccoli plants and c stands for the number of cabbage plants, write a formula connecting b and c.

(c) Use your formula to say how many cabbage plants she needs in a row that has
(i) 15 broccoli plants (ii) 25 broccoli plants

This is an order for one row of broccoli plants.
We need to find the number of broccoli plants to order.

Order from Brown's	
Broccoli plants	
Cabbage plants	90

(d) Put $c = 90$ in your formula.
Solve the equation you get to find b.

(e) How many broccoli plants does Stella need?

A4 Stella grows Spanish onions and garlic in patterns like this.

Suppose s stands for the number of Spanish onions in a row and g stands for the number of garlic bulbs.

(a) Explain why the formula connecting s and g is $g = 6s + 4$.

(b) How many garlic bulbs does Stella need if she plants 50 Spanish onions in one row?

(c) For one row of onions, Stella plants 100 garlic bulbs.
How many Spanish onions are in the row?

B *New formulas from old*

For Stella's onion and garlic rows, the formula $g = 6s + 4$ connects the letters g and s.

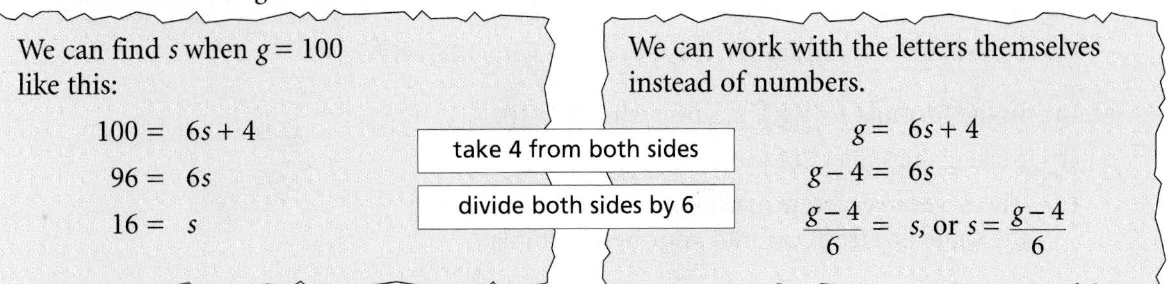

Each time, we do the same thing to both sides of the formula. We call this 'rearranging the formula to make s the subject' or 'making s the subject of the formula'.

Now we can find the value of s easily for different values of g.

We can check the rearrangement by using values of g and s.
For example, when $s = 10$ in the original formula, $g = 6 \times 10 + 4 = 64$.
Now check this in the rearranged formula.

When $g = 64$, $s = \frac{64-4}{6} = \frac{60}{6} = 10$ which checks.

B1 For Stella's onion and garlic pattern, a formula is $s = \frac{g-4}{6}$
s stands for the number of Spanish onions in a row and g stands for the number of garlic bulbs.

(a) If $g = 160$, what is s?

(b) When $g = 400$, what is s?

(c) There are 82 garlic bulbs in one row.
How many onions are there in this row?

B2 Stella plants red and white onions in rows like this.

Suppose r stands for the number of red onions and w stands for the number of white onions.

(a) Explain why $w = 3r + 2$ in this pattern.

(b) What is the value of w when $r = 20$?

(c) Copy and complete this working to make r the subject of the formula.

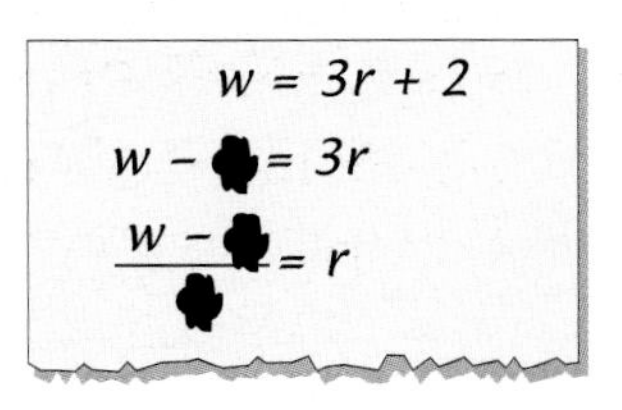

(d) What is the value of r when $w = 50$?

(e) How many red onions are there in a row that has 68 white onions in it?
Check your answer works in the formula for w.

B3 For this pattern of red and white onions $w = 2r + 4$.

(a) Rearrange the formula $w = 2r + 4$ to make r the subject.

(b) Work out r when $w = 88$.

(c) How many red onions are there in a row with 128 white?

B4 (a) In the formula $f = 3g + 2$, find f when $g = 10$.

(b) Make g the subject of the formula $f = 3g + 2$.

(c) Check your rearrangement is correct by substituting the value of f from (a) into your new formula.

B5 (a) Rearrange the formula $s = 5t + 1$ to make t the subject.

(b) Find a pair of values of s and t that fit the original formula, $s = 5t + 1$. Use this pair of values to check that your rearrangement is correct.

B6 Make the bold letter the subject of each of these formulas.
For each one, check your rearrangement by using a pair of values that fit the original formula.

(a) $b = 8\mathbf{w} + 7$ (b) $u = 5\mathbf{v} + 2$ (c) $g = 6\mathbf{d}$ (d) $y = 12 + 3\mathbf{x}$

(e) $t = 3\mathbf{b} + 5$ (f) $f = 8 + 3\mathbf{d}$ (g) $h = \mathbf{k} + 5$ (h) $w = 7\mathbf{d} + 1$

B7 (a) Copy and complete this working to make x the subject of the formula $y = 5x - 6$.

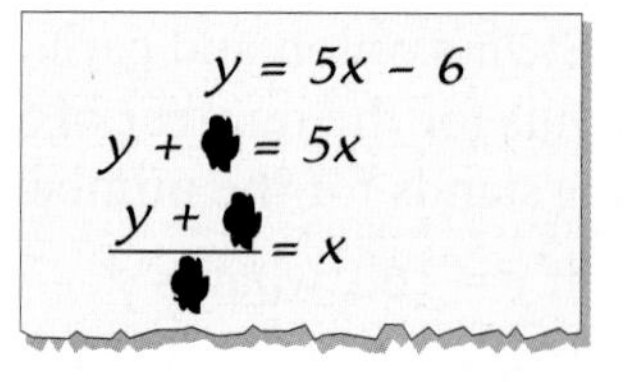

(b) Use your new formula to find x when $y = 129$.

(c) Substitute $y = 129$ and the value of x you found in (b) in the original formula to check that your rearrangement is correct.

B8 Which of the following are correct rearrangements of $a = 2b - 10$?

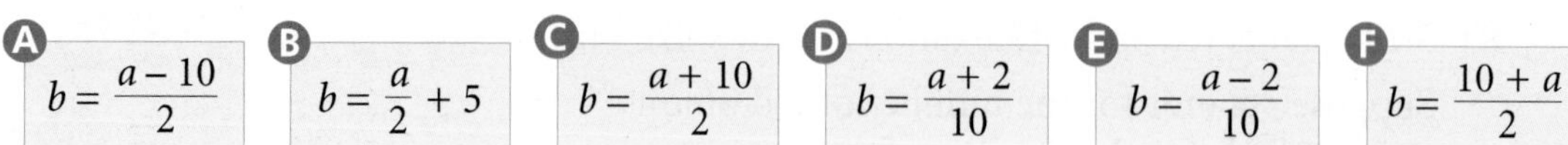

A 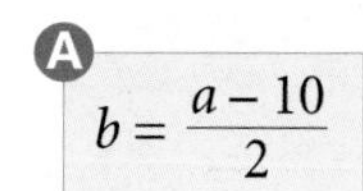 $b = \frac{a - 10}{2}$

B 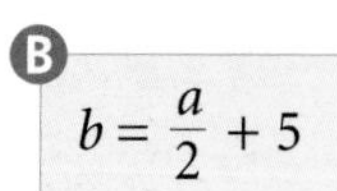 $b = \frac{a}{2} + 5$

C 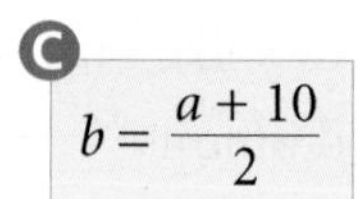 $b = \frac{a + 10}{2}$

D 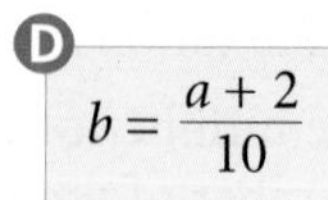 $b = \frac{a + 2}{10}$

E $b = \frac{a - 2}{10}$

F 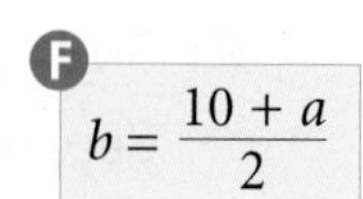 $b = \frac{10 + a}{2}$

B9 Make the bold letter the subject of each of these formulas.

(a) $a = 8\mathbf{w} - 6$ (b) $b = 4\mathbf{h} - 1$ (c) $h = 2\mathbf{f} - 2$ (d) $y = \mathbf{x} - 15$

(e) $z = 2\mathbf{r} - 15$ (f) $k = 2\mathbf{d} - 3$ (g) $b = \mathbf{g} - 5$ (h) $l = 2\mathbf{m} - 1$

B10 Here are eight formulas. Find four matching pairs of equivalent formulas.

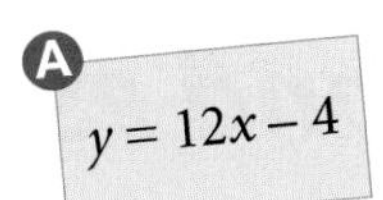

A: $y = 12x - 4$

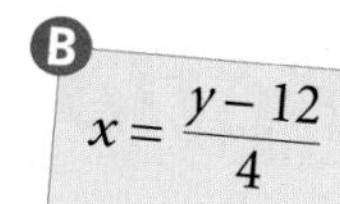

B: $x = \frac{y - 12}{4}$

C: $y = 4x - 12$

D: $x = \frac{y - 4}{12}$

E: $y = 4x + 12$

F: $x = \frac{y + 4}{12}$

G: $y = 12x + 4$

H: $x = \frac{y + 12}{4}$

B11 Rearrange each of these formulas to make the bold letter the subject.

(a) $a = 30 + 3\boldsymbol{b}$ (b) $s = 2\boldsymbol{t} - 40$ (c) $t = 12\boldsymbol{g} - 60$ (d) $f = 3\boldsymbol{b} + 12$

(e) $y = 12 + 8\boldsymbol{x}$ (f) $r = 5\boldsymbol{s} - 20$ (g) $a = 3\boldsymbol{b}$ (h) $v = 7\boldsymbol{u} - 10$

(i) $y = 35 + \boldsymbol{x}$ (j) $8 + 4\boldsymbol{j} = d$ (k) $k = 8\boldsymbol{j} - 45$ (l) $7\boldsymbol{z} - 1 = w$

Test yourself

T1 Make the bold letter the subject of each of these formulas.

(a) $a = 6\boldsymbol{r} + 8$ (b) $b = 4\boldsymbol{s} + 6$ (c) $c = 12 + 5\boldsymbol{t}$ (d) $d = 8 + 4\boldsymbol{u}$

T2 (a) Copy and complete this working to make m the subject of the formula $n = 3m - 2$.

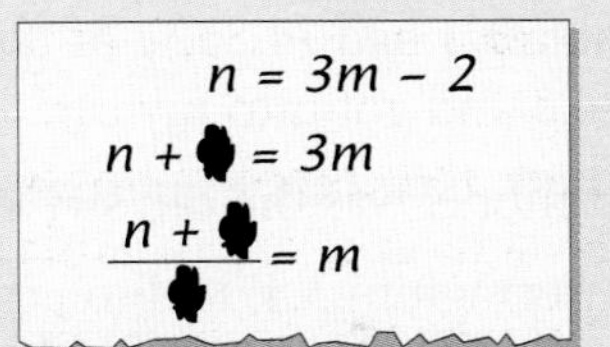

$n = 3m - 2$

$n + ● = 3m$

$\frac{n + ●}{●} = m$

(b) Find a pair of values of n and m that fit the formula $n = 3m - 2$.

(c) Use this pair of values to check your rearrangement.

T3 Which of these rearrangements of $y = 2x - 3$ are correct?

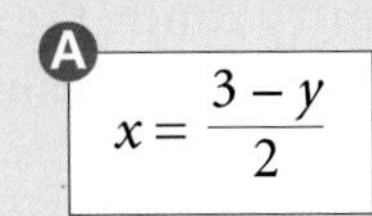

A: $x = \frac{3 - y}{2}$

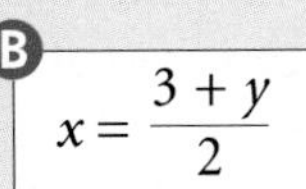

B: $x = \frac{3 + y}{2}$

C: $x = \frac{y - 3}{2}$

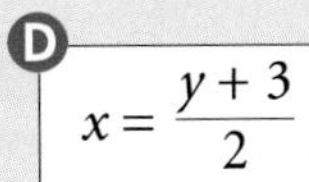

D: $x = \frac{y + 3}{2}$

E: $x = \frac{y - 2}{3}$

F: $x = \frac{y + 2}{3}$

T4 Rearrange each of these formulas to make the bold letter the subject.

(a) $e = 4\boldsymbol{v} - 12$ (b) $f = 2\boldsymbol{w} - 15$ (c) $g = \boldsymbol{x} - 12$ (d) $h = 5\boldsymbol{y} - 10$

T5 Make the bold letter the subject of each formula.

(a) $n = 8 + 5\boldsymbol{t}$ (b) $s = 4\boldsymbol{t} - 7$ (c) $y = 2\boldsymbol{x} + 12$ (d) $m = 3\boldsymbol{u} - 5$

(e) $j = 5\boldsymbol{v} + 12$ (f) $f = 15 + 5\boldsymbol{w}$ (g) $k = 3\boldsymbol{x}$ (h) $8\boldsymbol{y} + 4 = b$

9 *Approximation and estimation*

This work will help you

- round numbers to the nearest hundred, thousand, and so on
- round to a given number of decimal places
- round to a given number of significant figures
- estimate the result of a calculation by rounding

A *Rounding numbers*

TG

'This has to be the worst day of my life,' said Colin as he emerged from the wreckage of his car.

'I can understand you feeling like that,' said the police officer. 'Could you please give me as accurate an account as you can of the events leading up to the accident.'

'Well,' said Colin, 'I woke up at 32 minutes 43.8 seconds past 6. As always, I weighed myself and found that I was 72.451 kg, that's 0.078 kg more than yesterday. I put on my shirt, collar size 31.3264 cm, and trousers, waist size 71.5093 cm. I went down and had breakfast. I had 74.832 g of cornflakes with 0.327 62 litres of milk. I left the house at 7:14:26.3 and got into my car.'

'What model was the car, sir?' asked the officer. 'It's hard to tell from what's left of it.'

'It's a Ferraghini 3.4782 litre, capable of a top speed of 163.629 m.p.h.'

'Thank you, sir,' said the policeman. 'Now I did ask you to be accurate, but you are rather overdoing it, sir. Perhaps you could round off the numbers from now on.'

'Very well, officer,' said Colin. 'I'll do my best. Anyway, I usually drive to work on the A382 – sorry, A400. This time as the weather was fine I went by the country route, the B2864 – sorry, B3000. I passed a number 148 bus – sorry, 150 bus – and suddenly realised that I had left my case at my friend's house yesterday. He lives at 318 – sorry, 300 – Elm Road, but I didn't have time to go there. So I stopped at a phone box and rang him up. His number is 347 2846 – sorry, 350 0000.

'He wasn't in. So I got back into the car. I've only had the car for 4 days – sorry, 0 days – and I wasn't familiar with the gears. I accidentally put it in reverse and collided at full speed with the 150 bus as it came round the corner.'

A1 Round 4386 to the nearest (a) thousand (b) hundred (c) ten

A2 Round 2396 to the nearest (a) thousand (b) hundred (c) ten

A3 Round 40 789 to the nearest (a) ten (b) hundred (c) thousand

A4 Round (a) 32 096 to the nearest ten (b) 48 607 to the nearest hundred

B *Large numbers*

This table shows the population of Greater London at each census in the early part of the 20th century.

Greater London

Year	Population
1901	6 586 269
1911	7 225 946
1921	7 488 382
1931	8 215 673

B1 Round the 1901 population to the nearest

(a) hundred thousand (b) ten thousand
(c) thousand (d) hundred

B2 Round the 1911 population to the nearest

(a) hundred thousand (b) thousand

B3 Round the 1921 population to the nearest

(a) ten thousand (b) hundred

B4 Round the 1931 population to the nearest

(a) hundred thousand (b) thousand

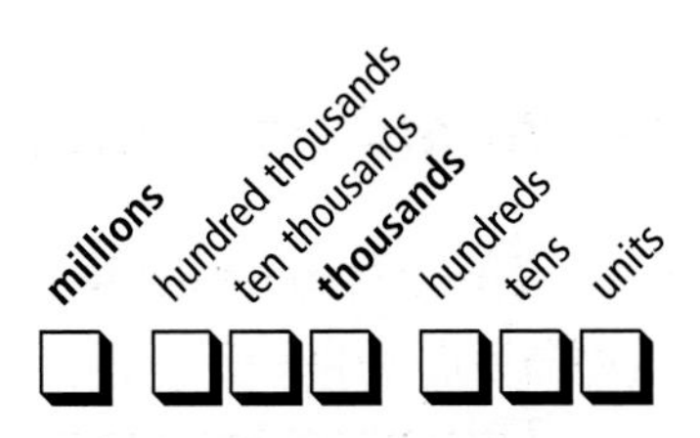

This diagram may help you.

B5 Round each of the 1901, 1911, and 1921 populations to the nearest million.
Why is it not a good idea to round them like this?

C *Rounding decimals*

Worked example

Round 4.2763 to two decimal places.

4.2763 is between 4.27 and 4.28.
Round up if the digit in the next decimal place is 5 or more.
Here it is 6, so round up to **4.28**

C1 Round each of these numbers to one decimal place (1 d.p.).

(a) 48.32 (b) 8.754 (c) 0.4503 (d) 23.962 (e) 70.0413

C2 Round each of these numbers to two decimal places.

(a) 3.9563 (b) 0.087 32 (c) 0.1659 (d) 3.5031 (e) 143.6395

C3 Round (a) 3.4783 to 1 d.p. (b) 4.083 12 to 2 d.p. (c) 8.057 23 to 3 d.p.
(d) 0.796 21 to 2 d.p. (e) 0.067 843 to 3 d.p. (f) 10.8956 to 1 d.p.

C4 Do these on a calculator and round each answer to two decimal places.

(a) $2.65 \div 3.47$ (b) $4.818 \div 0.357$ (c) 0.159×0.357 (d) 16.77×0.167
(e) 4.87×0.913 (f) $3.007 \div 27.55$ (g) $0.2619 \div 0.125$ (h) $1.169 \div 0.3894$

C5 (a) Calculate $2.467 \div 6.123$, giving the answer to 3 d.p.
(b) Calculate 3.348×4.17, giving the answer to 1 d.p.
(c) Calculate 0.5913^2, giving the answer to 3 d.p.

D Rounding to one significant figure – whole numbers

The first significant figure in a number is the figure with the highest value.

	34 168	286	5 876 672
We can round to **one significant figure**:	30 000	300	6 000 000

D1 Round these numbers to one significant figure.

(a) 278 (b) 11 328 (c) 5418 (d) 863 (e) 304 657
(f) 5842 (g) 421 987 (h) 27 083 (i) 800 264 (j) 961

D2 A coach has 57 seats.
This is how Jack estimates the number of seats in 32 coaches.

Complete his estimate.

Round the numbers to one significant figure:
57 becomes 60 32 becomes 30
So 57 x 32 is roughly

D3 Work out a rough estimate for each of these.

(a) 78×21 (b) 42×39 (c) 63×22 (d) 48×19 (e) 27×44
(f) 291×33 (g) 58×188 (h) 37×487 (i) 81×77 (j) 196×207

D4 Tickets for a concert cost £29.50 each.
Estimate the total amount taken if 403 tickets are sold.

E Rounding to one significant figure – decimals

The first significant figure is the first non-zero figure you come to working along from left to right.

	2.346	0.004 83	0.000 029 3
Rounding to one significant figure, we get:	2	0.005	0.000 03

E1 Round these numbers to one significant figure.

(a) 7.537 (b) 0.8851 (c) 0.042 87 (d) 0.067 63 (e) 0.003 196
(f) 0.088 53 (g) 0.000 475 (h) 26.46 (i) 0.003 64 (j) 4.0075

E2 Round these numbers to one significant figure.

(a) 17.507 (b) 0.0334 (c) 0.004 636 (d) 0.010 05 (e) 0.008 089
(f) 347.07 (g) 0.688 46 (h) 2.0775 (i) 0.000 767 (j) 0.9858

Worked example

Estimate the answer to 0.364×516.

0.364 x 516

Round to one significant figure: 0.4 x 500 = **200**

4 x 5 = 20
4 x 50 = 200
4 x 500 = 2000
0.4 x 500 = 200

E3 Estimate the answer to each of these.

(a) 7.2×0.23 (b) 0.48×3.13 (c) 0.27×0.41 (d) 0.186×176 (e) 68.2×0.27

(f) 2.84×0.32 (g) 378×1.77 (h) 0.471×42.7 (i) 8.71×0.031 (j) 53.2×0.97

E4 Estimate the cost of these.

(a) 0.475 kg of Stilton

(b) 0.856 kg of Brie

(c) 32.5 kg of Cheddar

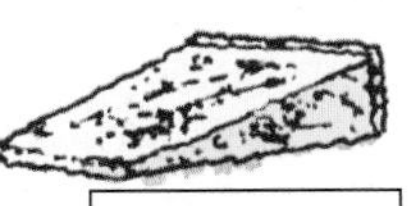

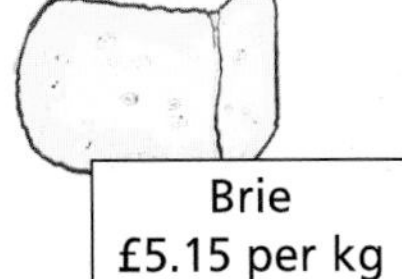

F *Rounding to two or more significant figures*

To round to two significant figures, pick out the first two significant figures.

2372 0.006 81 4.028

Then round to two significant figures: 2400 0.0068 4.0

F1 Round these numbers to two significant figures.

(a) 4628 (b) 13 752 (c) 20 984 (d) 378 (e) 341 543

(f) 29 741 (g) 5381 (h) 638 102 (i) 5 328 613 (j) 9642

F2 Round these numbers to three significant figures.

(a) 7126 (b) 43 209 (c) 60 573 (d) 3328 (e) 28 031

(f) 159 762 (g) 3612 (h) 600 813 (i) 4 136 442 (j) 10 527

F3 Round these numbers to two significant figures.

(a) 0.053 14 (b) 2.387 (c) 3.075 (d) 0.004 284 (e) 0.6696

(f) 0.000 485 1 (g) 51.852 (h) 0.067 52 (i) 6.0238 (j) 0.000 974

F4 Round these numbers to three significant figures.

(a) 0.023 74 (b) 8.189 (c) 41.023 (d) 0.006 414 (e) 0.7791

(f) 0.000 155 8 (g) 254.756 (h) 0.080 284 (i) 12.1238 (j) 0.006 918

G *Mixed questions*

G1 Round 346 718 to

(a) the nearest thousand (b) the nearest hundred (c) one significant figure

G2 Round 2 886 032 to

(a) the nearest million (b) the nearest ten thousand (c) one significant figure

G3 Round 7356.087 to

(a) the nearest hundred (b) one decimal place (c) one significant figure

G4 Round 2.4692 to

(a) the nearest whole number (b) one decimal place (c) two decimal places

G5 Round 0.058 21 to

(a) two decimal places (b) two significant figures (c) three significant figures

G6 Estimate the answer to each of these by rounding the numbers to one significant figure.

(a) 38×51 (b) 62×29 (c) 83×42 (d) 78×59 (e) 67×84

(f) 495×53 (g) 78×387 (h) 47×567 (i) 91×86 (j) 493×603

G7 (a) Estimate the answer to 28×59 by rounding the numbers to one significant figure.

(b) Explain why your estimate must be bigger than the exact answer.

(c) Work out 28×59.

G8 Pam works 28 hours a week. She is paid £6.85 per hour.

(a) Estimate how much she earns in a week.

(b) Estimate how much she earns in 31 weeks.

G9 Steve worked for 48 hours and was paid £290.40 altogether.
Estimate how much he was paid for each hour.

G10 Estimate the answer to each of these.

(a) 5.2×0.83 (b) 0.38×7.23 (c) 0.57×0.82 (d) 0.384×478 (e) 98.2×0.37

(f) 4.74×0.12 (g) 528×2.97 (h) 0.361×23.7 (i) 7.81×0.061 (j) 43.2×0.851

G11 Do these on a calculator and round each answer as shown.

(a) 4.375×0.853 Round the answer to two decimal places.

(b) $12.9 \div 0.0624$ Round the answer to two decimal places.

(c) $0.871 \div 4.271$ Round the answer to three decimal places.

G12 Round each answer to three significant figures.

(a) $4.65 \div 3.27$ (b) $6.873 \div 0.552$ (c) 0.349×0.254 (d) 36.27×0.368

(e) 2.47×0.814 (f) $7.052 \div 37.45$ (g) $0.2832 \div 0.168$ (h) $1.069 \div 0.3291$

G13 Round each answer to three significant figures.

(a) $(2.845 + 0.487) \times 0.864$ (b) $\dfrac{11.875 - 2.608}{0.427}$

(c) $0.425 + \dfrac{2.653}{5.175}$ (d) $\dfrac{5.375 + 2.634}{9.304 - 1.668}$

G14 A rectangular room measures 31.2 m by 42.3 m.

(a) Estimate the area of the room by rounding the measurements to one significant figure.

(b) Is your estimate bigger or smaller than the actual area? Explain how you can tell.

(c) Calculate the actual area, giving your answer to three significant figures.

Test yourself

T1 Round 2085.19 to

(a) the nearest hundred (b) one decimal place

(c) one significant figure (d) three significant figures

T2 Estimate the answer to each of these.

(a) 27.8×0.93 (b) 0.084×61.1 (c) 0.47×0.31 (d) 8.387×218 (e) 0.962×0.48

☒ **T3** In this question you must NOT use a calculator.
You must show all your working.

Tom buys 67 cameras at £312 each.

(a) Work out the total cost.

(b) Write down two numbers you could use to get an approximate answer to your calculation.

Edexcel

T4 Sally estimates the value of $\dfrac{42.8 \times 63.7}{285}$ to be 8.

Write down three numbers Sally could use to get her estimate: $\dfrac{\ldots\ldots \times \ldots\ldots}{\ldots\ldots}$

Edexcel

T5 (a) Write down 45.3476 correct to 3 significant figures.

(b) Write down 7462 correct to 2 significant figures.

WJEC

10 Area and perimeter

You will revise

- finding the area of a parallelogram, triangle and trapezium
- finding the area and circumference of a circle

This work will help you

- deal with shapes that are made up of simpler shapes
- solve area and perimeter problems, including some that use Pythagoras's theorem

A Parallelograms

The area of a parallelogram is **base × height** .

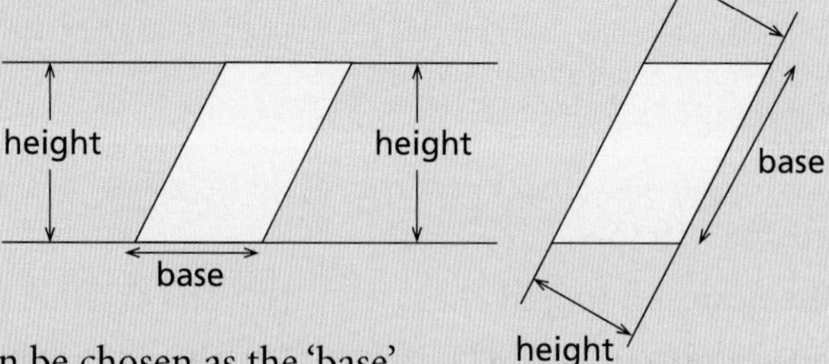

Any side of the parallelogram can be chosen as the 'base'.
But the height must be measured perpendicular (at right angles) to the base.

A1 Which measurement is a perpendicular height in each of these parallelograms?

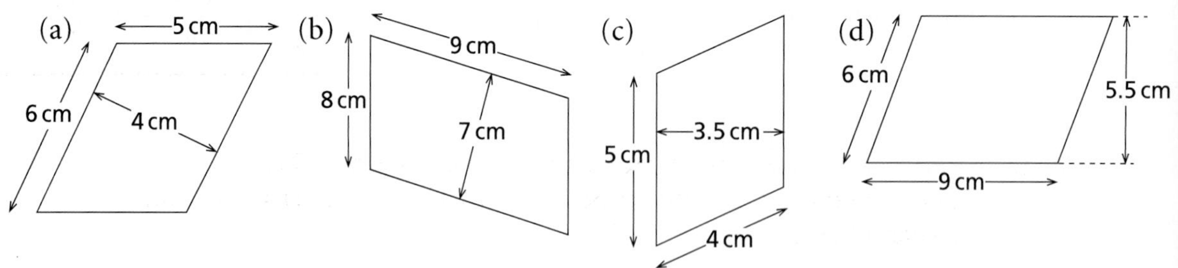

A2 Find the area of these parallelograms. They are not drawn to scale.

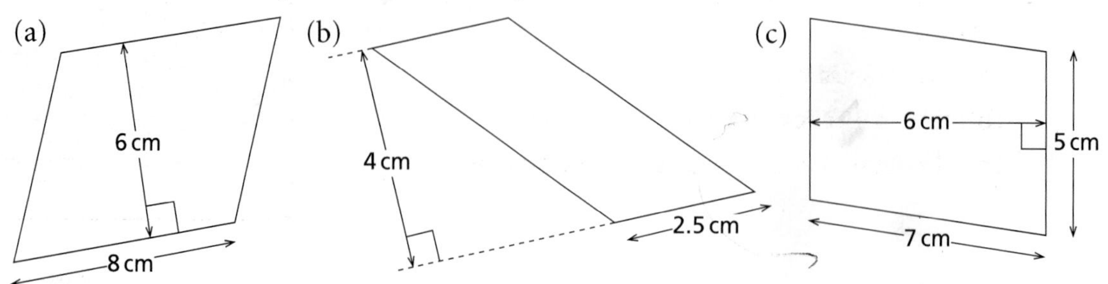

A3 Find the areas of these parallelograms, giving your answers to one decimal place.

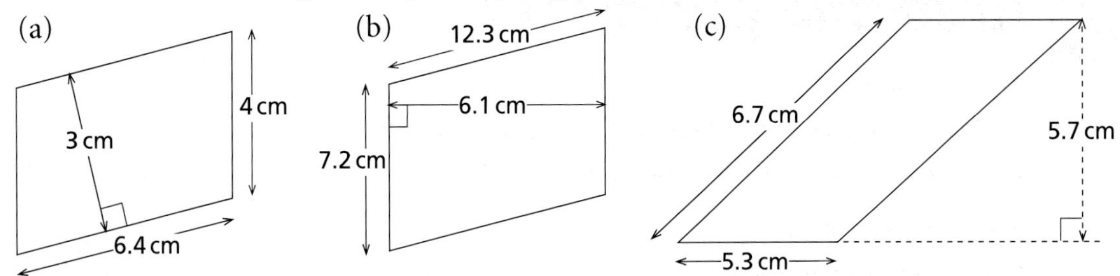

A4 Find the perimeter of each parallelogram in A3.

A5 (a) Measure, then calculate the area of this parallelogram.

(b) Find the area again measuring a different base and height.

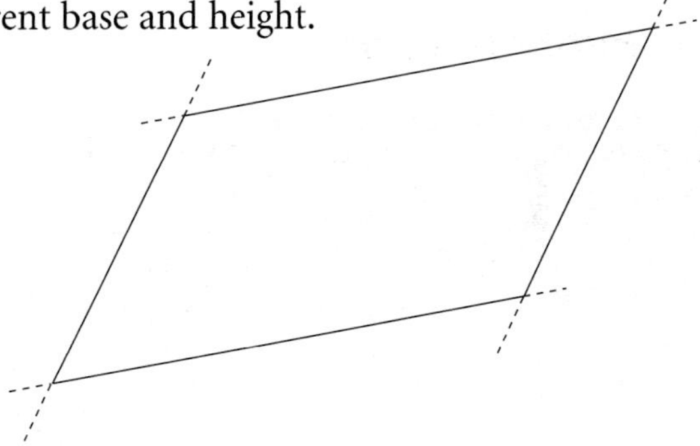

A6 This design has been drawn on centimetre squared paper. What fraction of the rectangle's area has been taken up by the parallelogram?

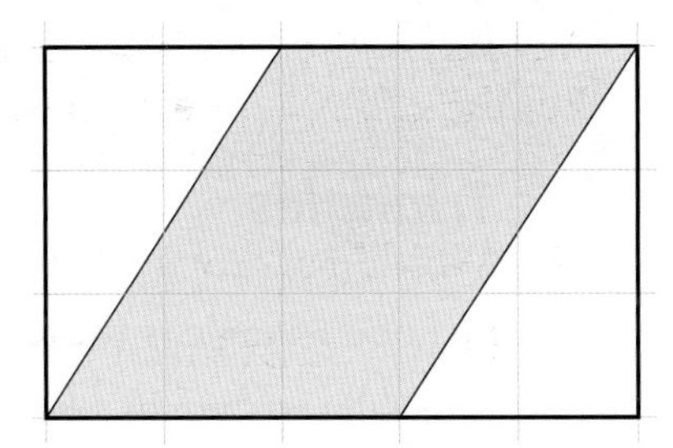

A7 (a) Draw a pair of axes on squared paper, both going from $^{-}5$ to 5. Draw a parallelogram with vertices at (3, 2), (3, $^{-}1$), ($^{-}2$, 2) and ($^{-}2$, 5). Calculate its area in square units.

(b) On the same pair of axes draw a parallelogram with area 16 square units.

A8 This design has been drawn on centimetre squared paper. Calculate

(a) the total blue area

(b) the total yellow area

(c) the ratio of the blue area to the yellow area

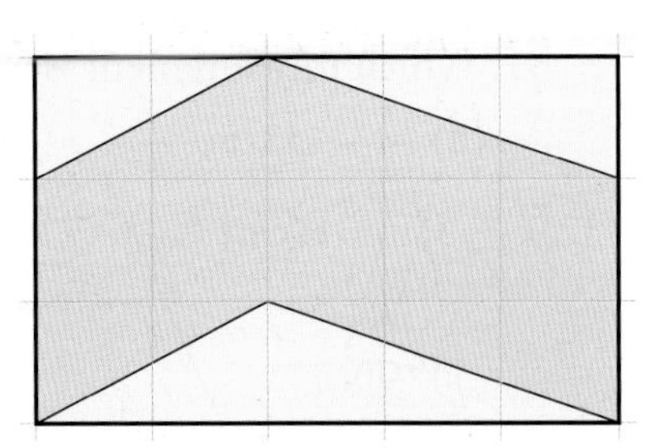

A9 Write, as simply as possible, an expression for the area of each parallelogram.

(a)

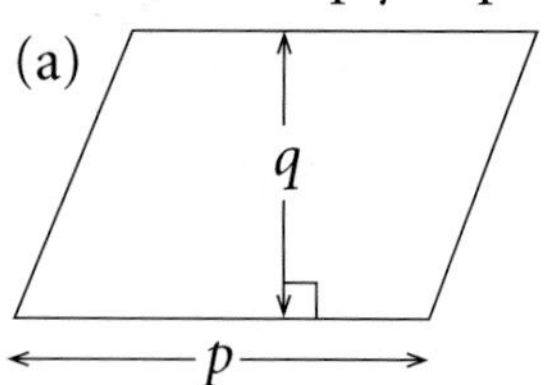

(b)

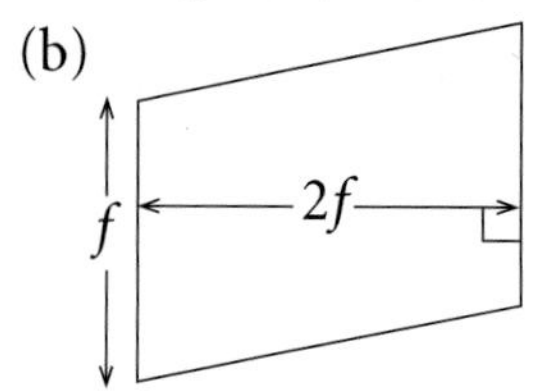

(c)

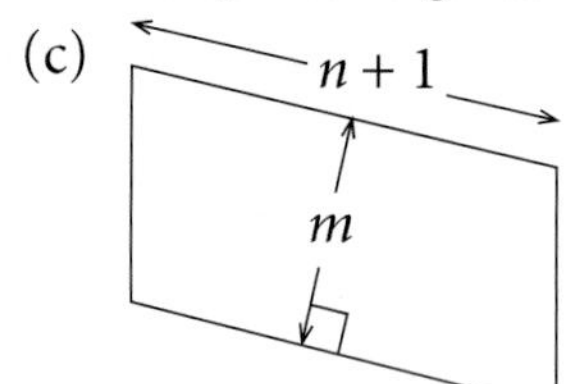

A10 Calculate the missing length in each parallelogram.

(a)

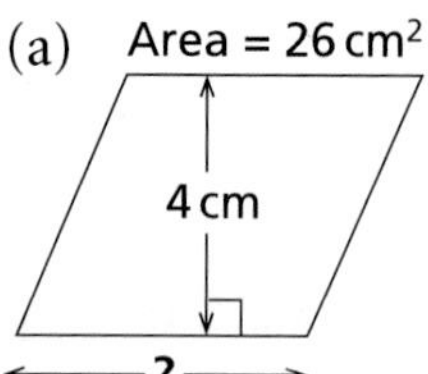

(b)

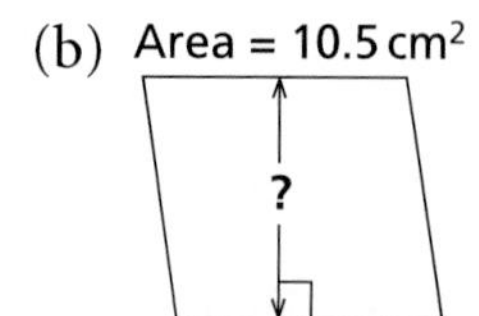

(c)

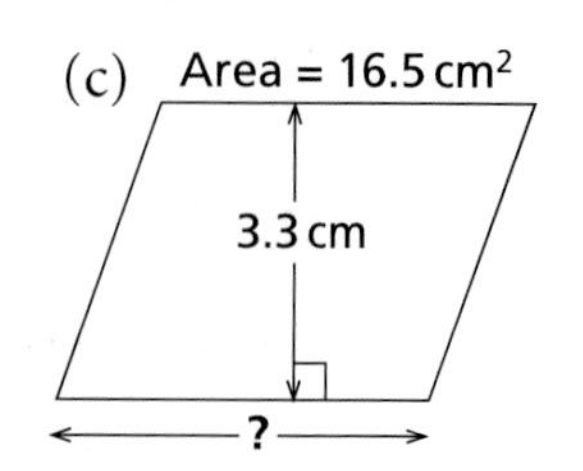

A11 A parallelogram has an area of 12 cm². One of its sides is 3 cm long. Is it possible to calculate its perimeter? Give a reason.

***A12** Calculate the missing length in each parallelogram.

(a)

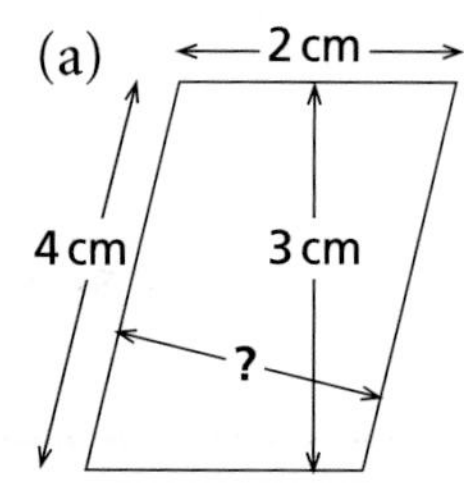

(b)

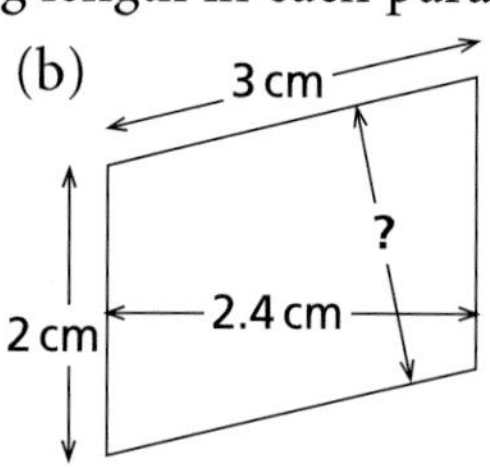

(c)

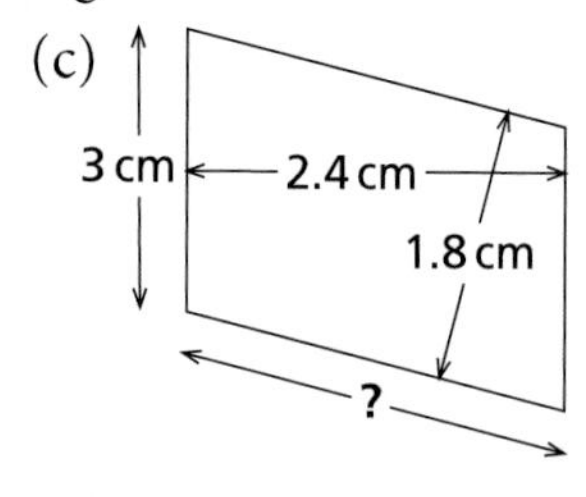

(d)

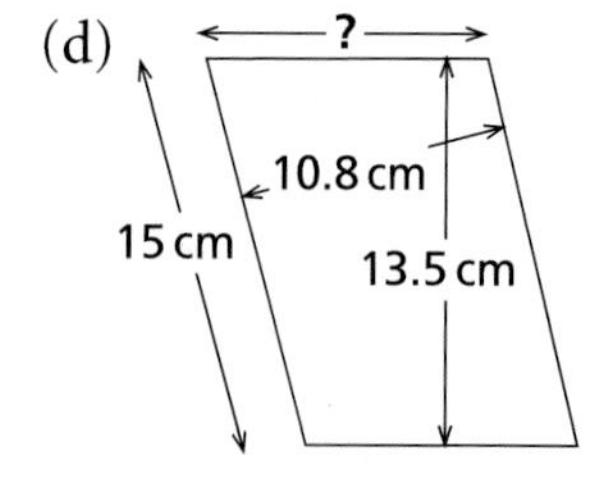

B *Triangles*

The area of a triangle is (**base** × **height**) ÷ **2**.
This is usually written as $\frac{1}{2}bh$ or $\frac{bh}{2}$.

Any side of the triangle can be chosen as the base.
But the height must be measured perpendicular to the base.

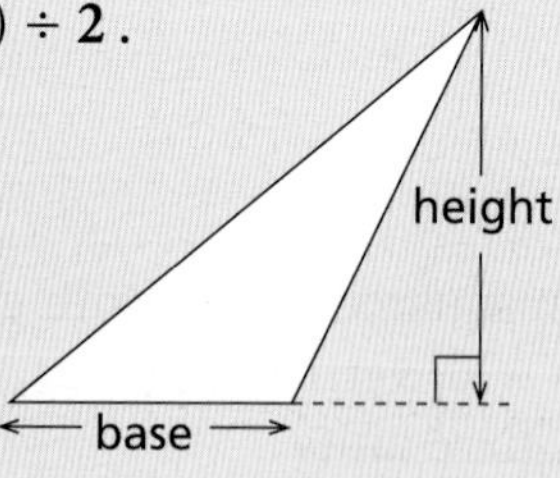

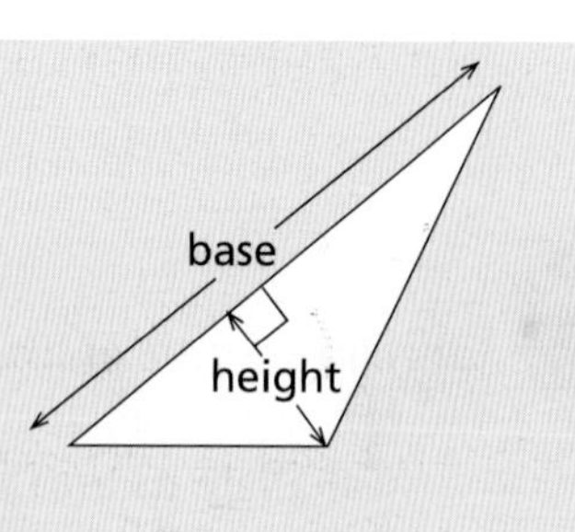

B1 Which measurement is a perpendicular height in each of these triangles?

(a)

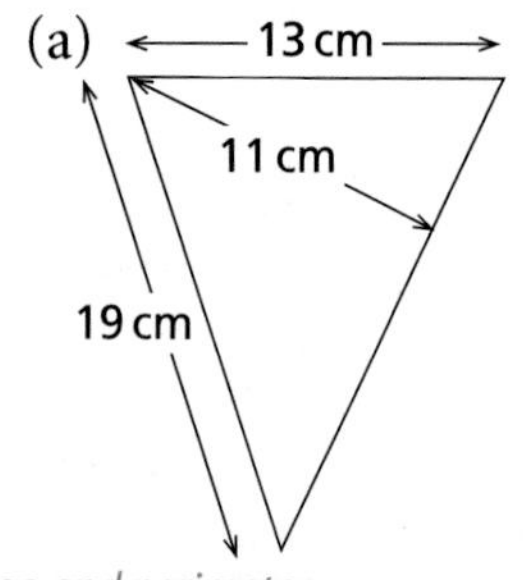

(b)

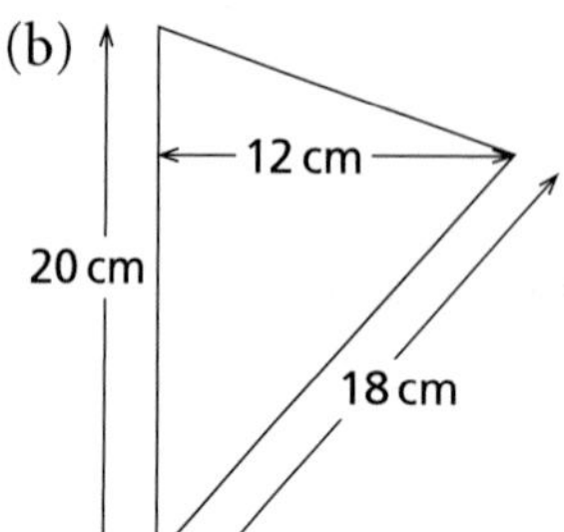

(c)

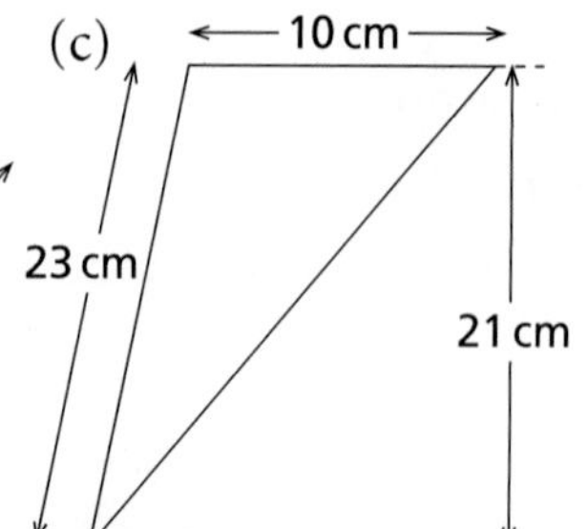

(d)

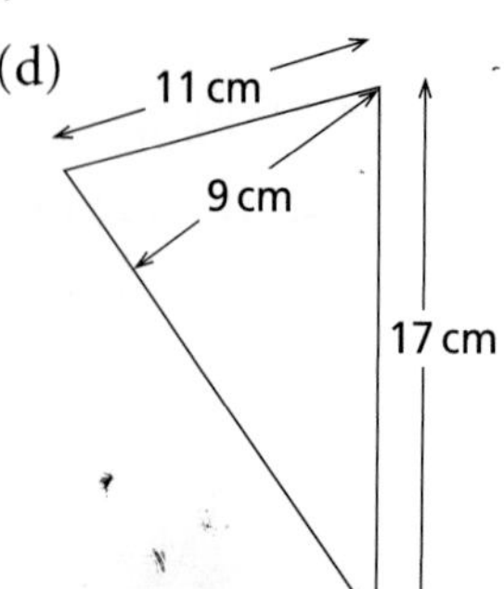

B2 Find the areas of these triangles. They are not drawn to scale.

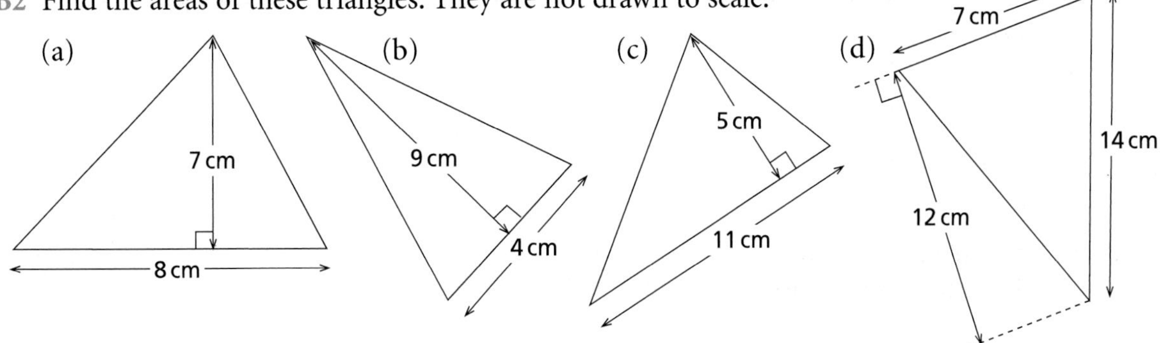

B3 Find the areas of these triangles, giving your answers to one decimal place.

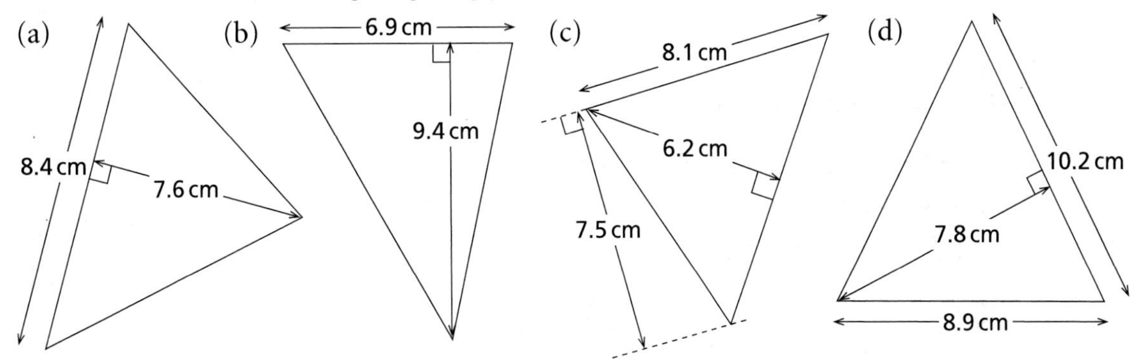

B4 This design is on centimetre squared paper.

(a) What fraction of the rectangle's area has been taken up by the blue triangle?

(b) What is the ratio of the blue area to the yellow area?

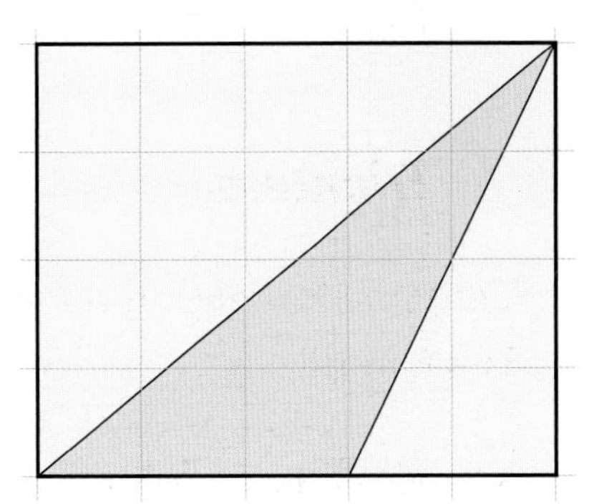

B5 (a) Measure, then calculate the area of this triangle.

(b) Find the area again, measuring a different base and height.

B6 Write, as simply as possible, an expression for the area of each triangle.

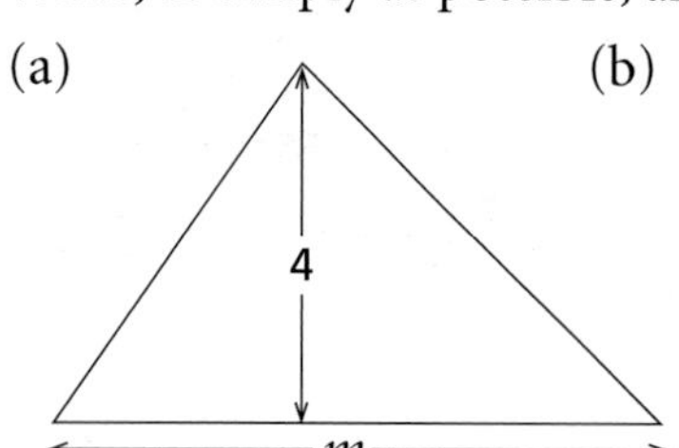

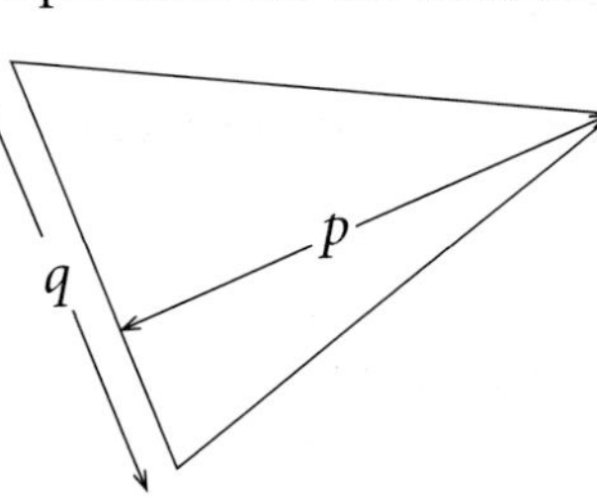

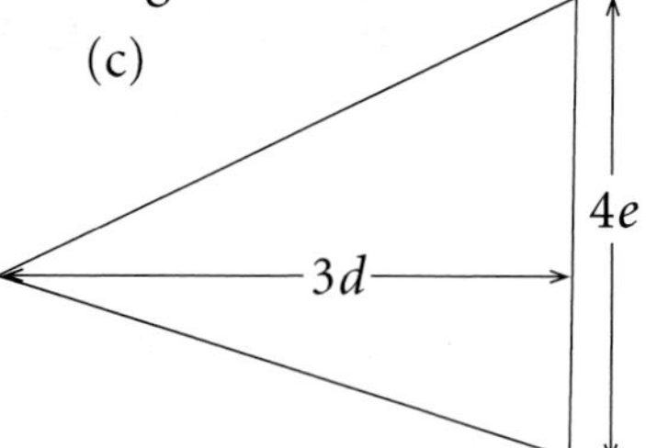

B7 These shapes are drawn on a centimetre squared grid.
Find the area of each shape.

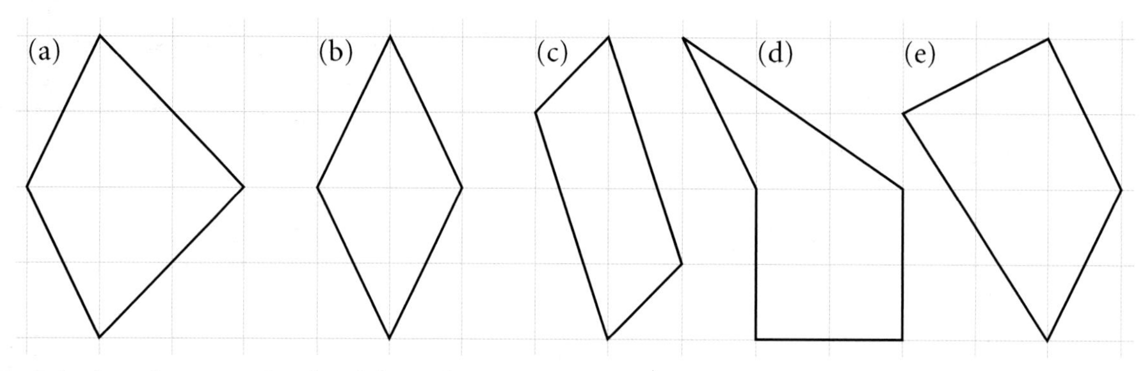

B8 Calculate the area of each of these shapes.

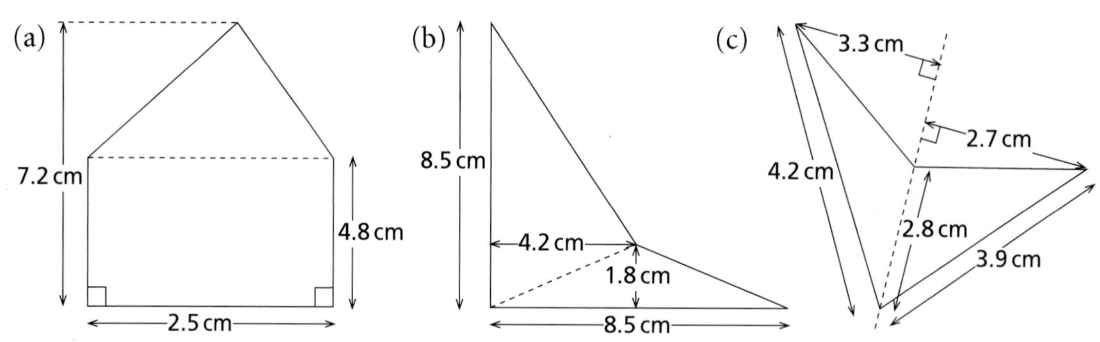

B9 Write, as simply as possible, an expression for the area of each shape.

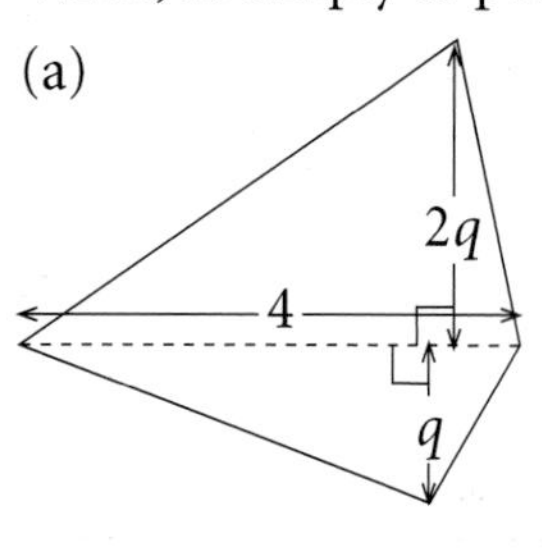

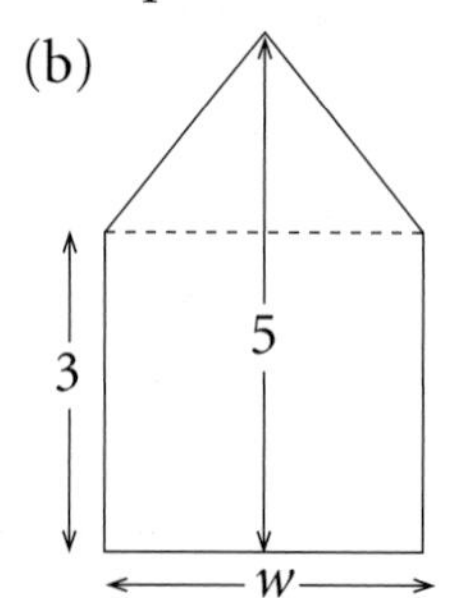

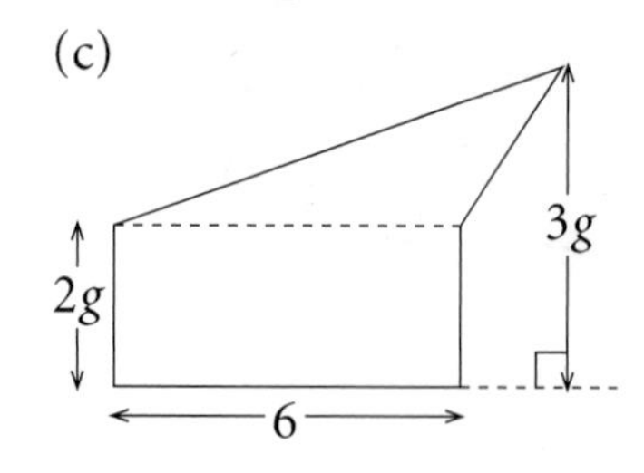

B10 (a) Substitute the values given in this diagram into the formula $A = \frac{1}{2}bh$.

(b) Solve the equation you get to find the height.

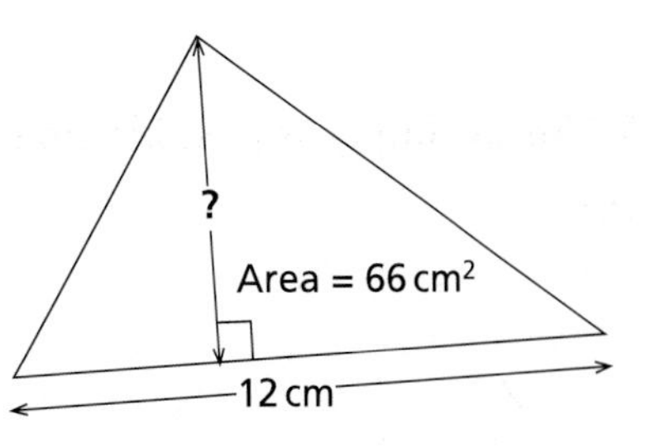

B11 Find the missing length in each of these.

(a)

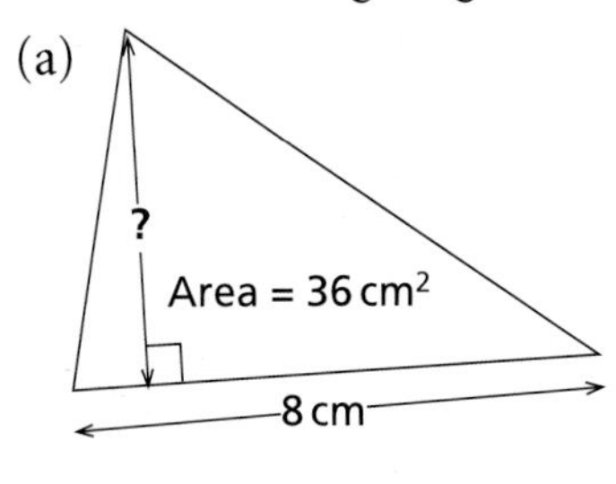

(b)

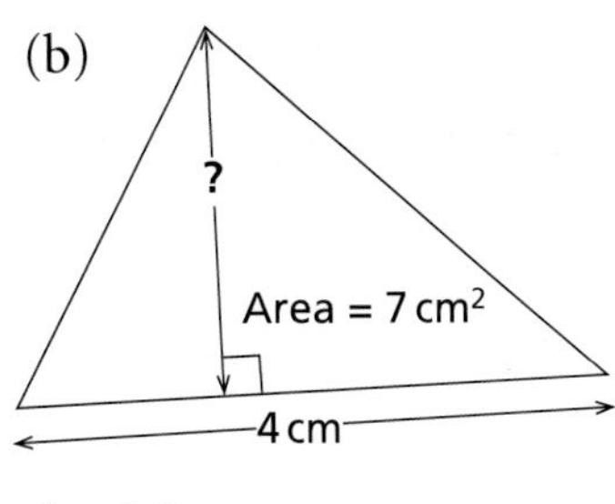

(c)

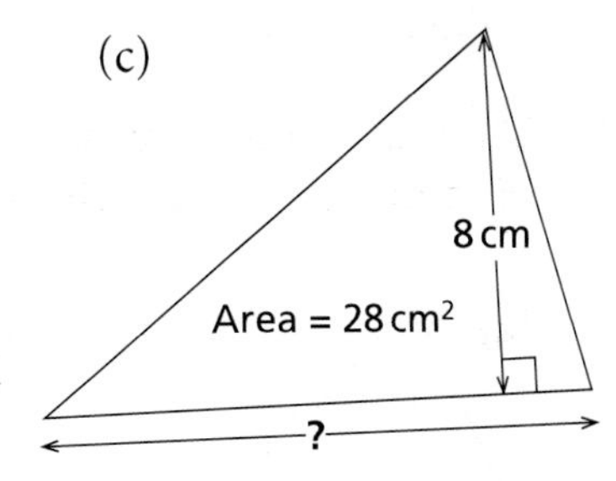

***B12** Find the missing length in each of these.

(a)

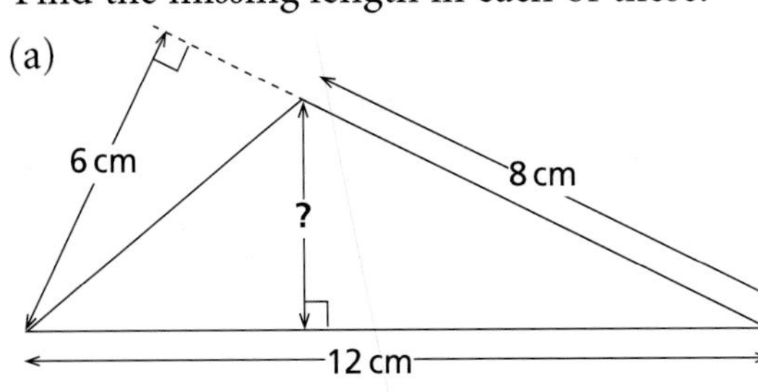

(b)

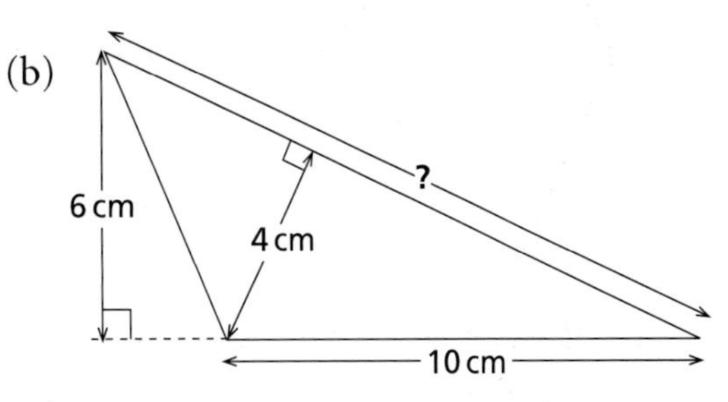

***B13** (a) Write down the areas of these three triangles. What do you notice?

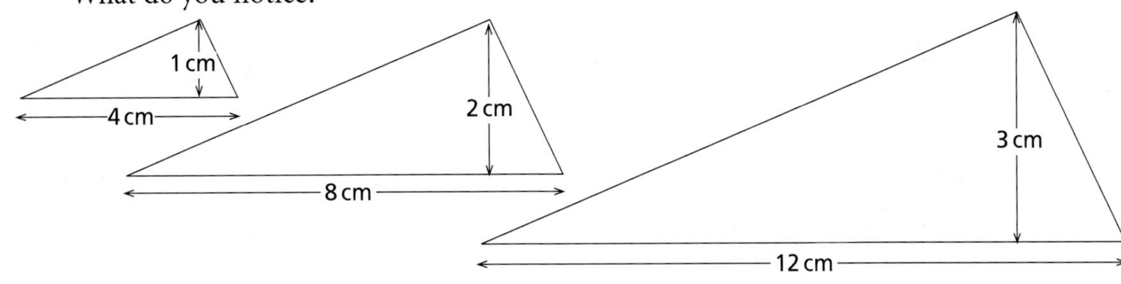

(b) Write an expression for the area of each of these triangles.

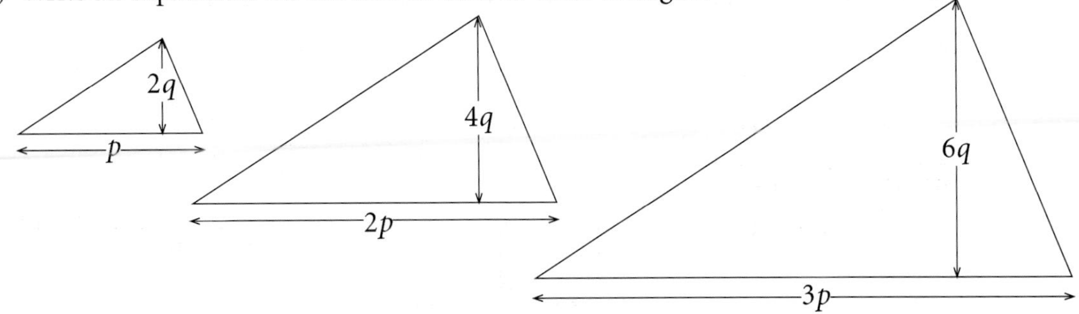

(c) What happens to the area of a triangle when its height and base are doubled?

(d) What happens to the area of a triangle when it is enlarged by scale factor 3?

C *Trapeziums*

A trapezium is a quadrilateral with two parallel sides.

The formula for finding the area of a trapezium, where a and b are the lengths of the two sides which are parallel is:

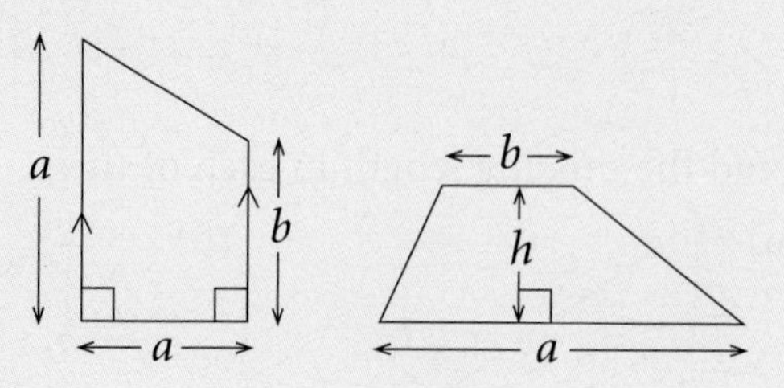

$$A = \frac{h \times (a + b)}{2} = \tfrac{1}{2}h(a + b)$$

C1 This diagram shows two identical trapeziums placed together.

(a) What shape is made from these two trapeziums?

(b) What is the area of the shape that is made?

(c) Explain how this proves the formula for the area of a trapezium.

C2 Work out the area of these trapeziums.
Round to one decimal place where you need to.

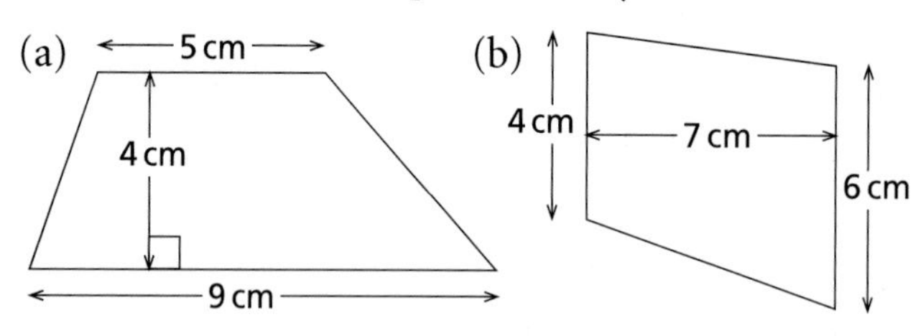

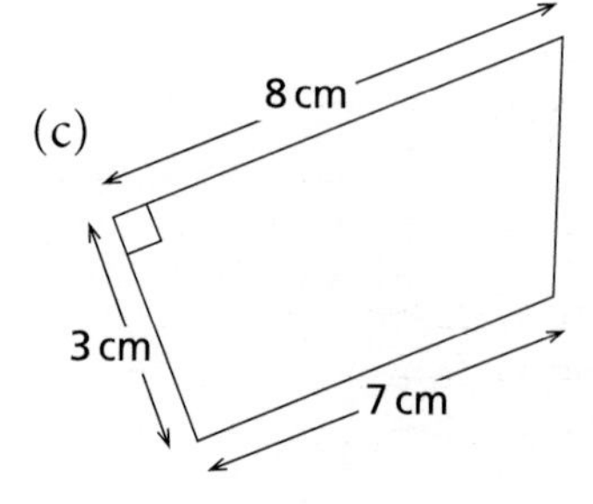

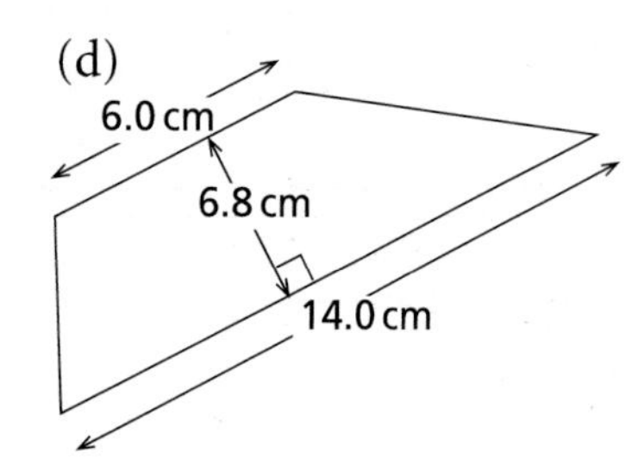

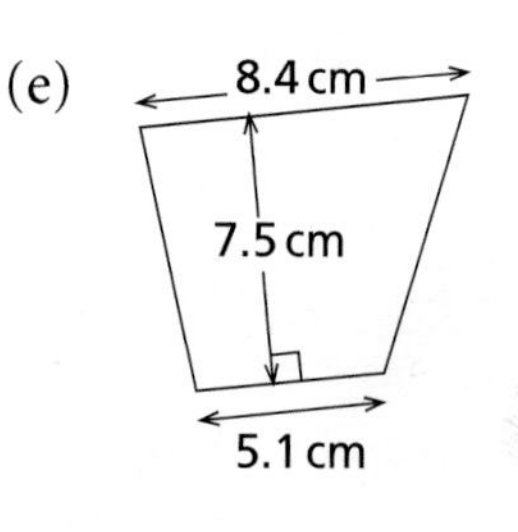

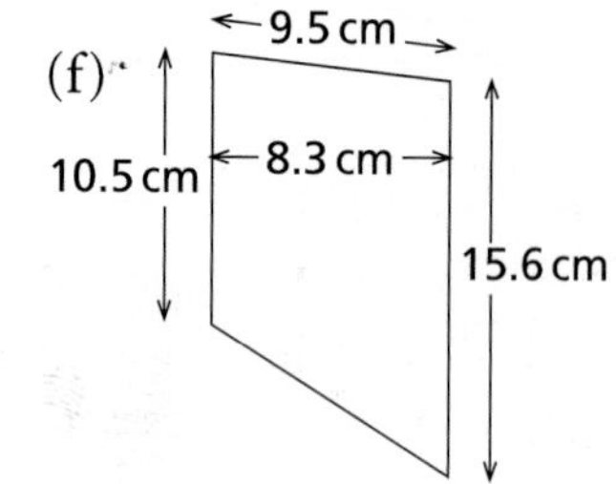

C3 ABCD is a trapezium.

(a) Find the area of ABCD.

(b) Find the area of triangle BCD.
Remember to state the units in your answer.

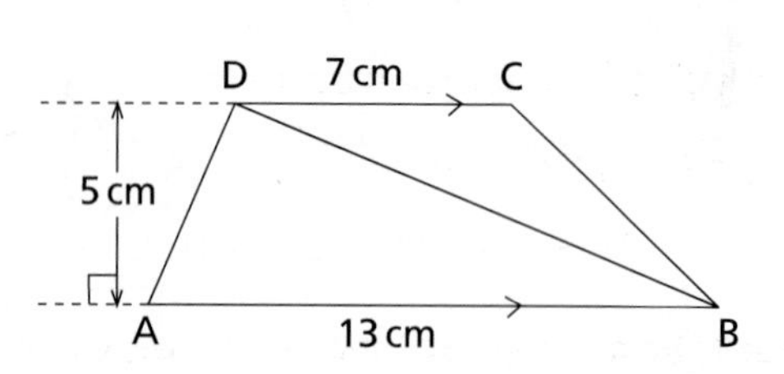

AQA (NEAB) 1997

C4 This diagram shows the end wall of a factory.

(a) Work out the area of the wall.

(b) Heat insulation costs £18 per square metre. How much would it cost to insulate this wall?

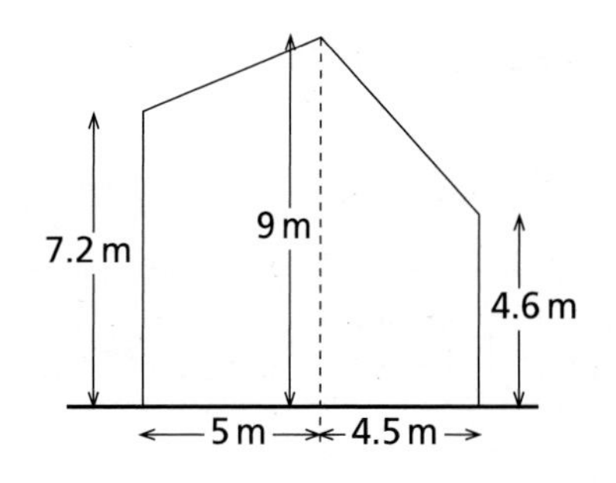

C5 The diagram shows two shapes, a parallelogram and a trapezium. They both have the same area.

Find the height of the parallelogram, marked h on the diagram.

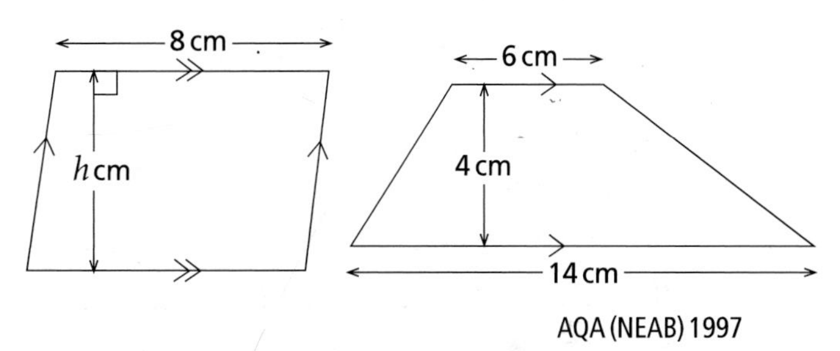

AQA (NEAB) 1997

Areas under curves

Trapeziums can be used to find an approximation to an 'area under a curve' where the other sides are straight lines such as axes on a graph.

The approximate area under this curve can be found by finding the area of trapeziums A, B, C, and D.

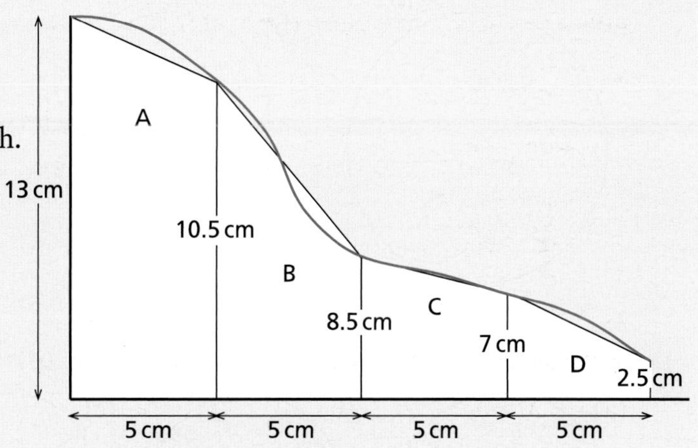

As all the trapeziums are given width 5 cm,

Area = $[\frac{1}{2}(13 + 10.5) \times 5] + [\frac{1}{2}(10.5 + 8.5) \times 5] + [\frac{1}{2}(8.5 + 7) \times 5] + [\frac{1}{2}(7 + 2.5) \times 5]$

or more simply

$= \frac{1}{2} \times 5 \times [13 + 10.5 + 10.5 + 8.5 + 8.5 + 7 + 7 + 2.5] = 168.75 \text{ cm}^2$

How good an approximation do you think this is?

The **trapezium rule** for an approximation to the area under a curve is:

Area = $\frac{1}{2}$(width of strip) × (1st height + (2 × each middle height) + last height)

Find the areas under the curves on sheet G110.

- make all your trapeziums 2 cm wide
- round all the heights to the nearest half centimetre.

D *Circles*

The circumference of a circle is the diameter (twice the radius) times π. $C = \pi d = 2\pi r$

The area of a circle is the radius squared times π. $A = \pi r^2 = \pi \times r \times r$

π is a number whose decimal value goes on forever: $\pi = 3.141\,592\,654\ \ldots$

In these questions use the π key on your calculator. Round your answers to one decimal place.

D1 For each of these circles calculate (i) the circumference (ii) the area

(a)

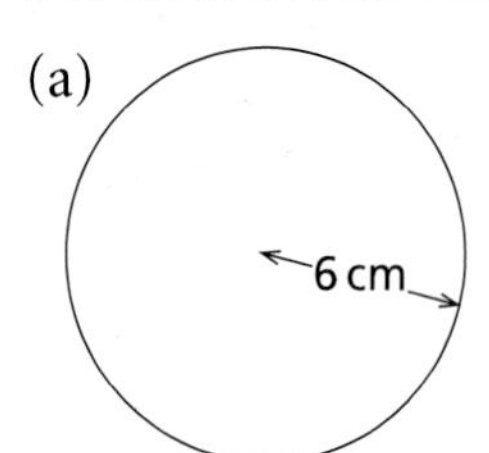

(b)

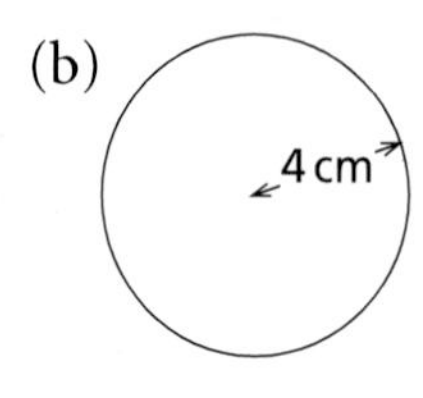

(c)

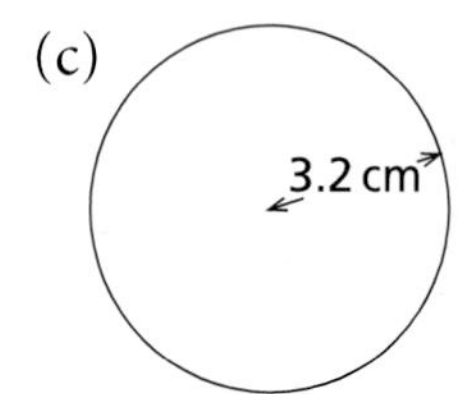

(d)

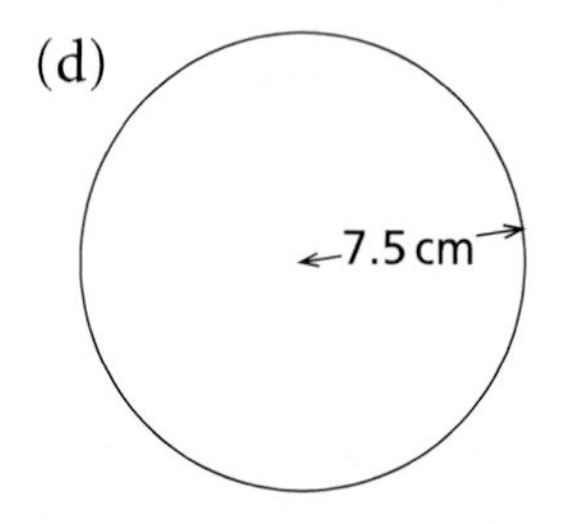

D2 For each circle, measure and calculate to find (i) the circumference (ii) the area

(a)

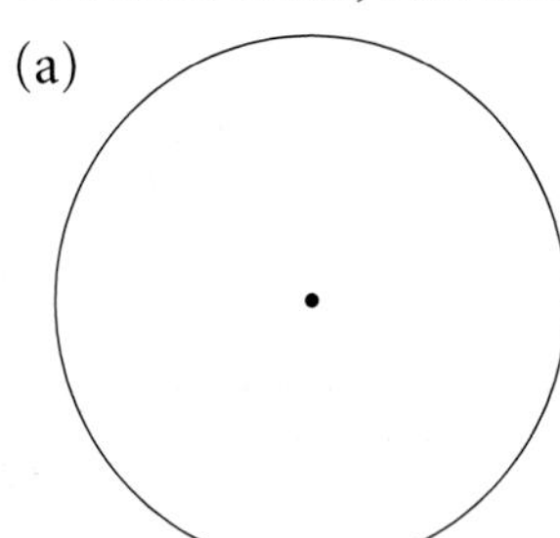

(b)

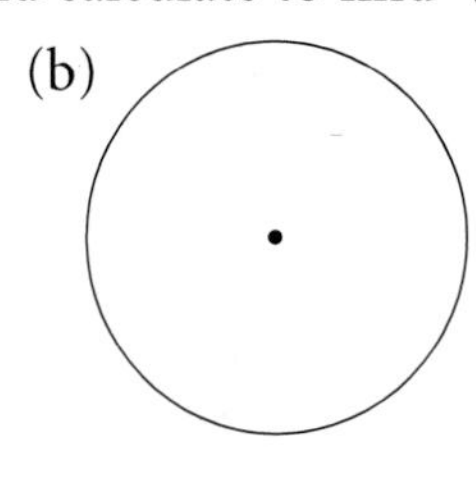

(c)

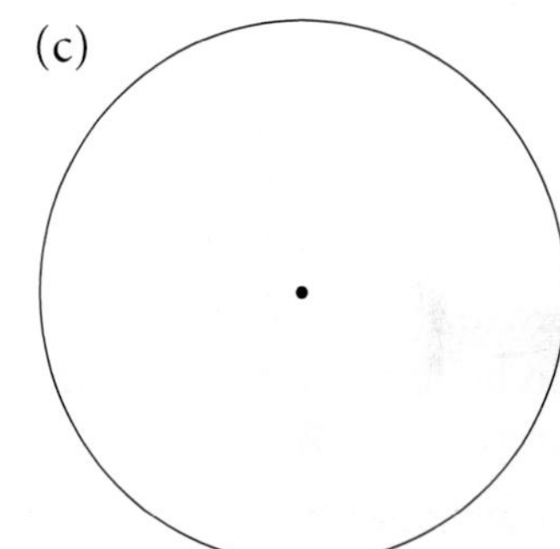

D3 For each circle calculate (i) the circumference (ii) the area

(a)

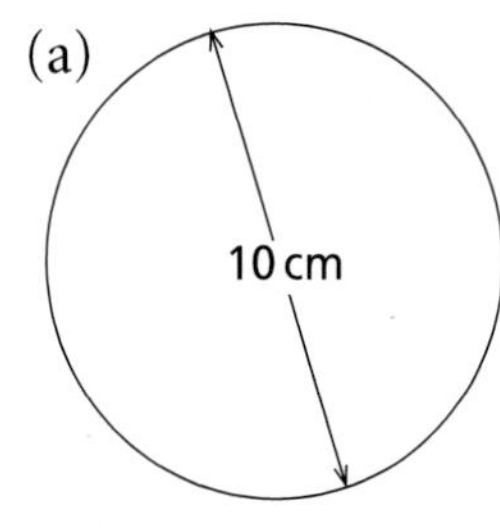

(b)

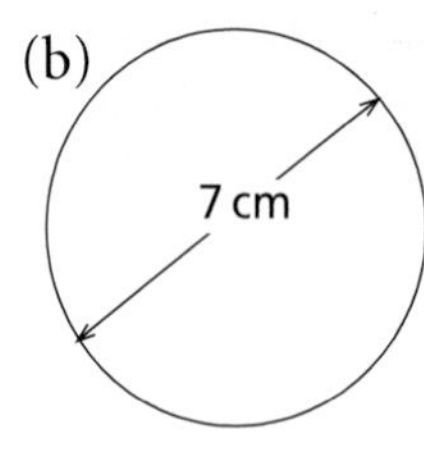

(c)

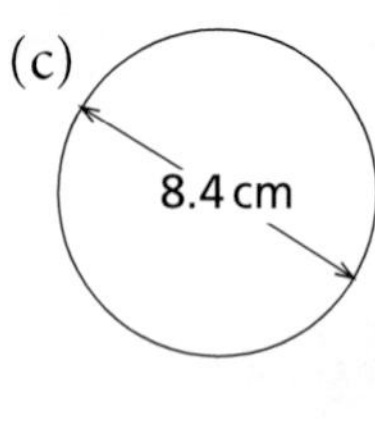

(d)

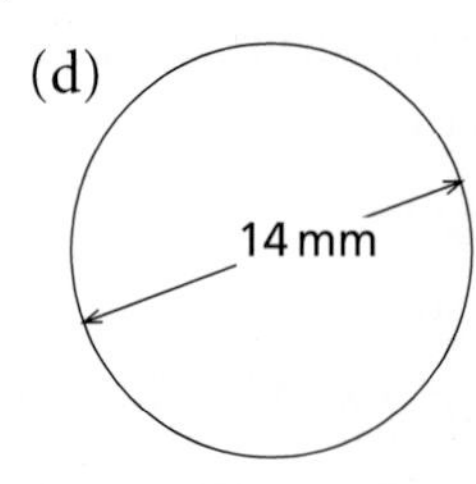

D4 For each coin, measure and calculate to find

(i) the circumference (ii) the area you can see

(a) Hong Kong (b) Tunisia (c) Canada (d) Indonesia (e) Hungary

D5 (a) A circular pond has a radius of 3 metres.
Calculate the circumference of the pond.

(b) Calculate the area of the pond.

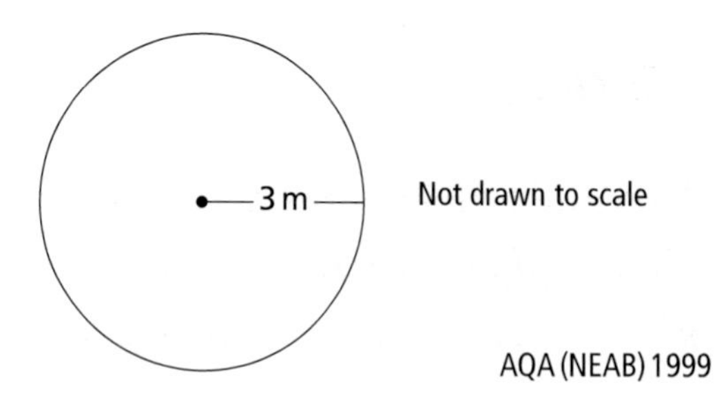

AQA (NEAB) 1999

D6 Calculate each area.
They are either a semicircle, a quarter circle or three-quarters of a circle.

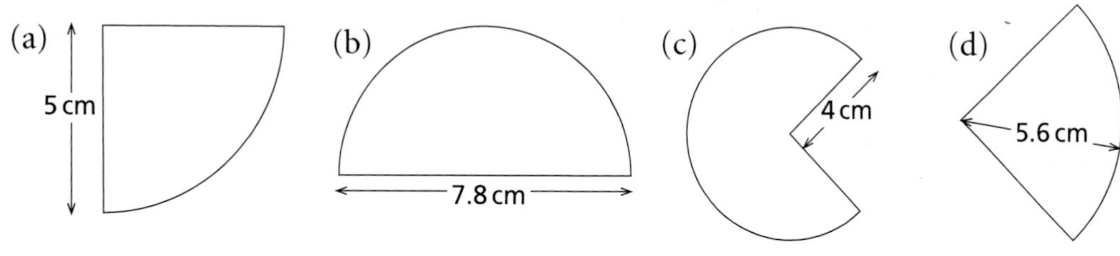

D7 The diagram shows the plan of a room.
the plan consists of a rectangle and a semicircle.
Calculate the total area of the floor.

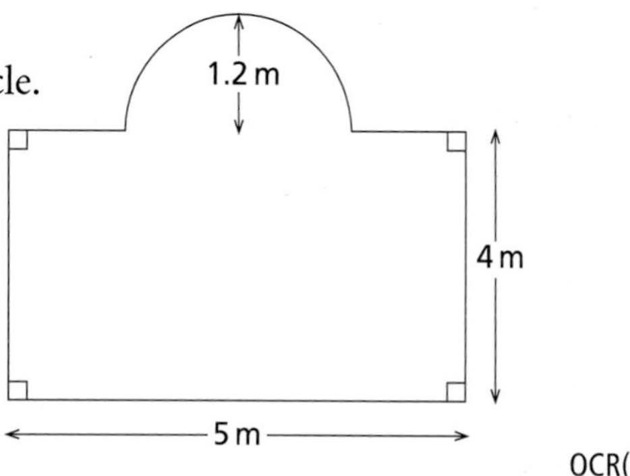

OCR(MEG)

D8 These shapes are on a centimetre squared grid.
Calculate the area of each one.

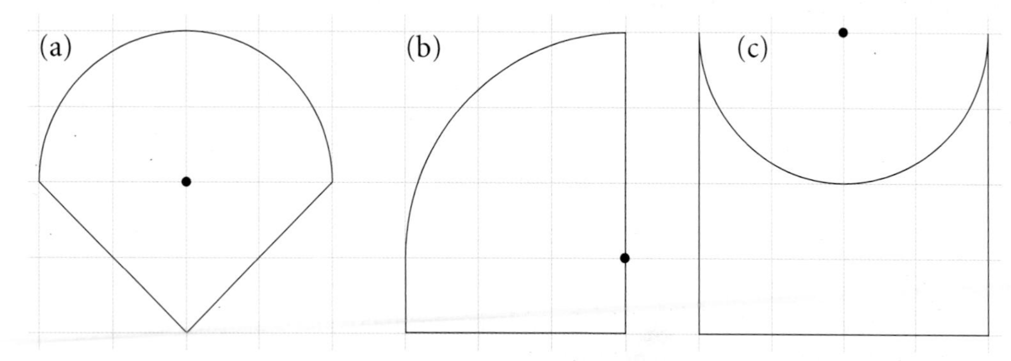

D9 Calculate the area coloured blue.

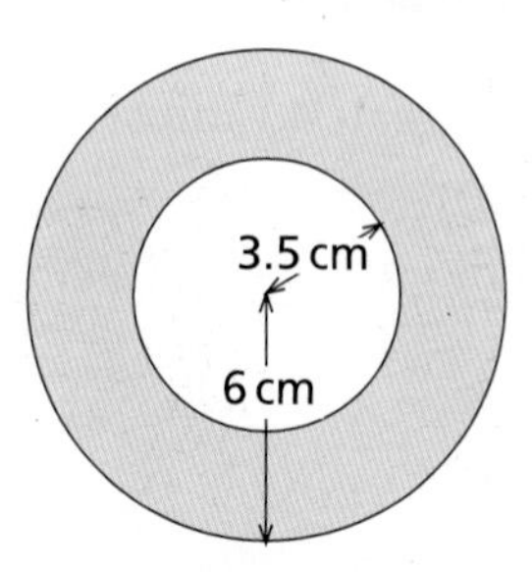

E *Finding the radius*

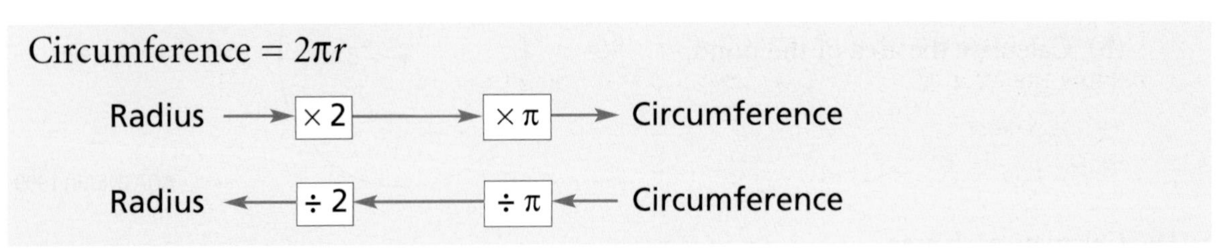

Area = πr^2

Radius → Square → $\times \pi$ → Area

Radius ← Square root ← $\div \pi$ ← Area

Give all your answers in this section to one decimal place.

E1 A bicycle wheel has a circumference of 200 cm.
What is the radius of the wheel?

E2 A rectangular piece of metal is curved to make a tube.

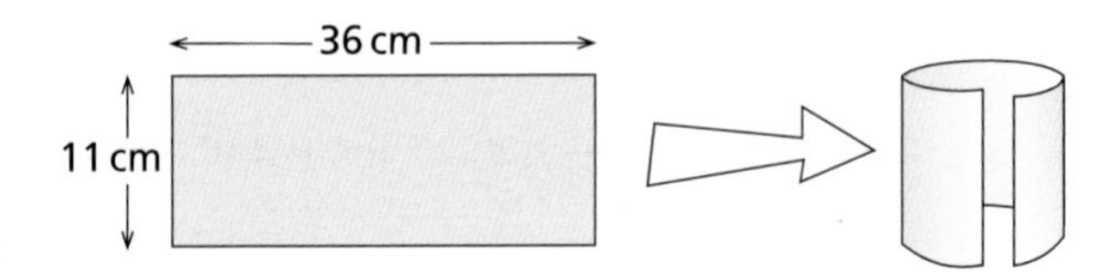

(a) What is the radius of the tube?

(b) What is the diameter of the tube?

E3 What would be the radius of circles with these areas?

(a) $50\,cm^2$ (b) $100\,cm^2$ (c) $25\,m^2$

E4 The roughly circular crater Copernicus on the moon has an area of $3200\,km^2$.
What is the diameter of the crater to the nearest kilometre?

E5 (a) A farmer wants to make a circular pen which contains an area of $200\,m^2$.
What would be the radius of the circle needed?

(b) How long a piece of fencing would she need to go round this circle?

E6 A piece of land is a square of side length 50 m.

(a) What radius would a circular piece of land need in order to cover the same area?

(b) How much fence would the square and circular fields need around the edge?
Which shape needs more fencing?

E7 Which of these circles has the greatest radius?

Circle A: diameter 12.5 cm
Circle B: circumference 40 cm
Circle C: area $105\,cm^2$

F *Mixed questions*

F1 A farmer has a length of fence 240 m long.
How big an area would this surround if it was set out as

(a) a square

(b) a rectangle which is twice as long as it is wide

(c) a circle

(d) a right-angled triangle with sides 60 m, 80 m and 100 m long?

F2 This parallelogram is on centimetre squared paper.

(a) Calculate its area.

(b) Use Pythagoras's theorem to find the length AB.

(c) Calculate the perimeter of the parallelogram.

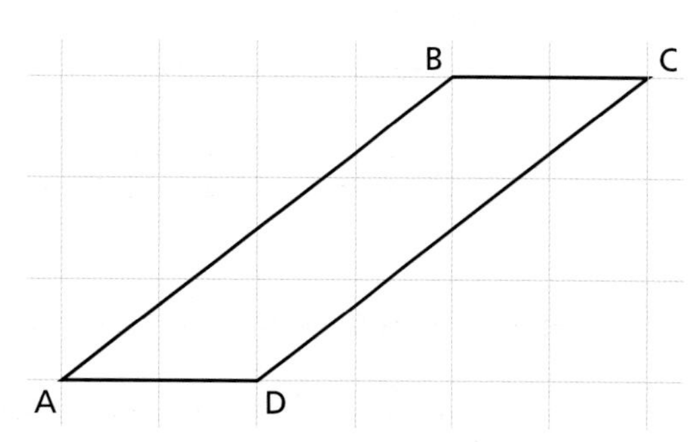

F3 This is a parallelogram.
The lengths marked are in centimetres.

(a) Work out the area of the parallelogram.
State the units of your answer.

(b) Work out the perimeter of the parallelogram.
State the units of your answer.

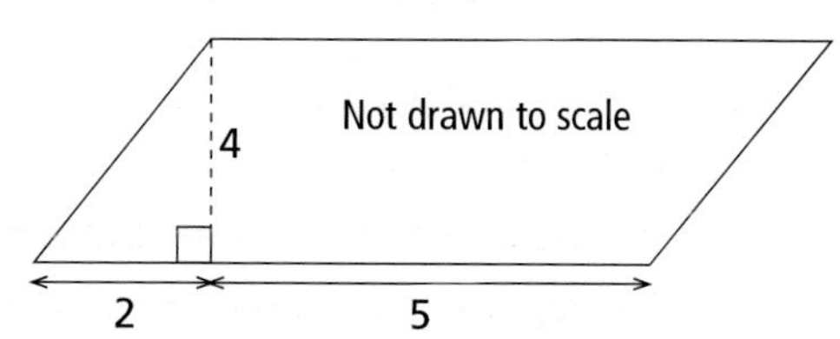

OCR

F4 The circumference of this circle has been divided into 5 arcs of equal length.

Calculate the length of one of these arcs, to 1 d.p.

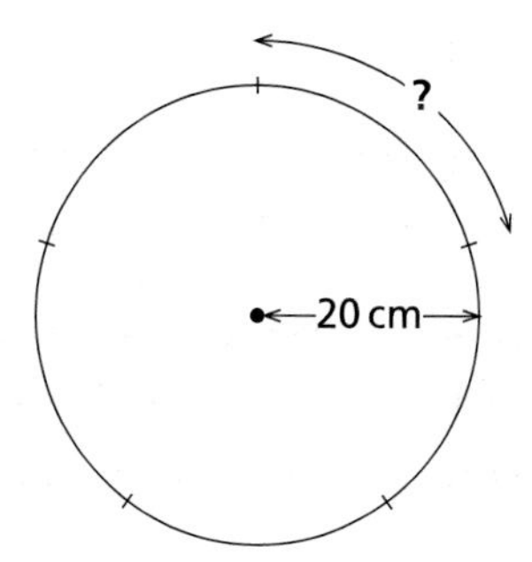

F5 The diagram shows a kite ABCD.

(a) Calculate the area of the kite ABCD.
Show all your working.
Remember to state the units in your answer.

(b) Calculate the length of AC.
Remember to state the units in your answer.

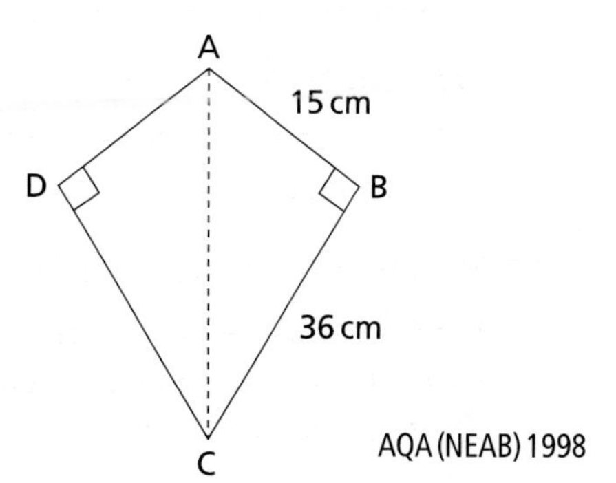

AQA (NEAB) 1998

F6 This circle has been divided into 6 equal sectors. Calculate the area of one of these sectors, to 1 d.p.

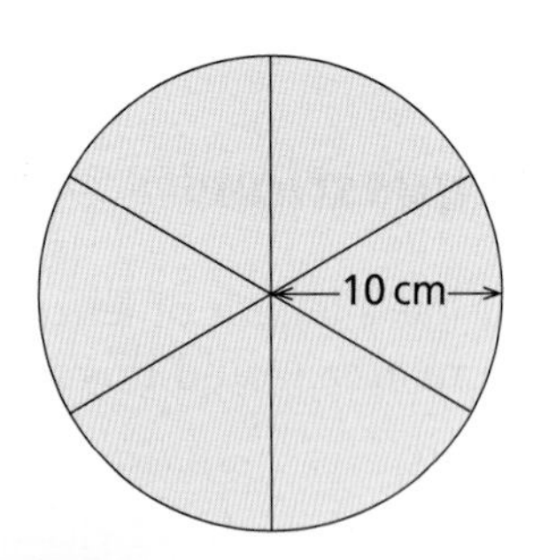

F7 The circle in this pattern has radius 2.3 cm. Find the area of

(a) one of the blue triangles

(b) the square

(c) one of the black segments

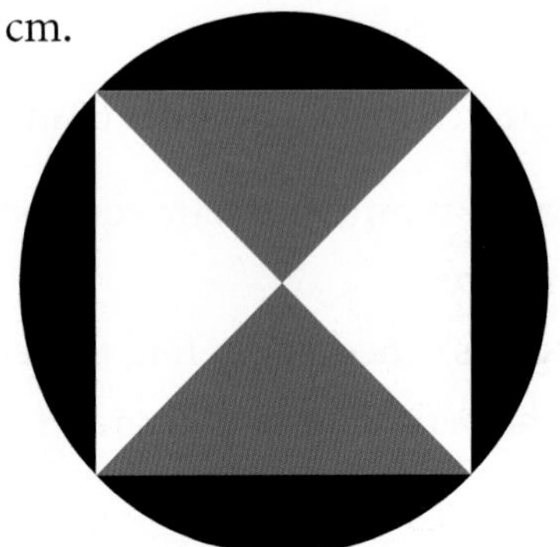

***F8** This running track has semicircles at each end.

(a) How much further would someone running around the outside of the track run compared with someone running around the inside? (Give your answer to the nearest metre)

(b) What is the area of the track (coloured)? (Give your answer to the nearest square metre.)

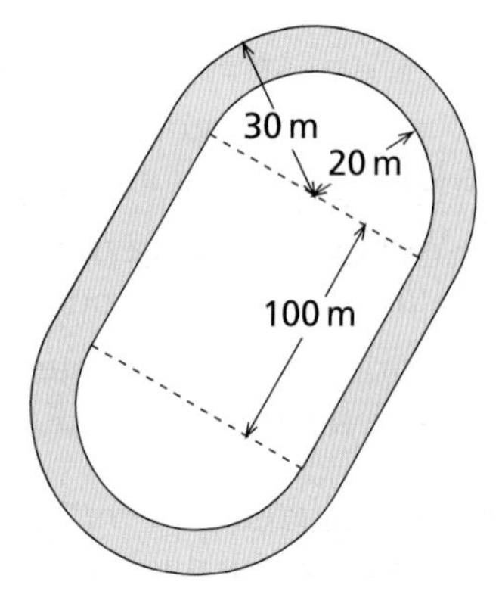

***F9** The three parallelograms in this diagram all have the same area.

Find the missing lengths.

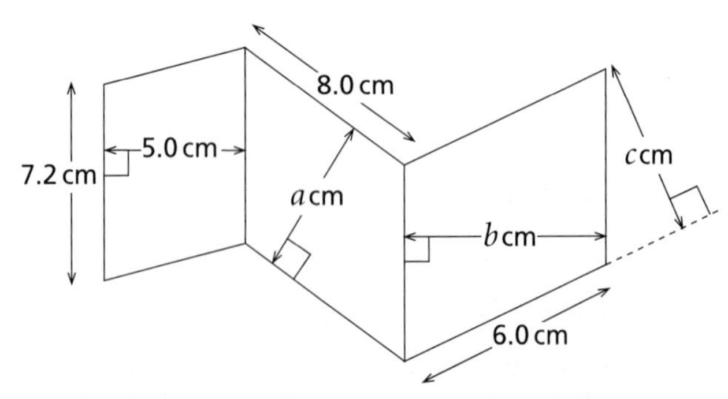

***F10** (a) This shape is a trapezium. Substitute the values given in the diagram into the formula $A = \frac{1}{2}h(a + b)$.

(b) Solve the equation you get to find the height.

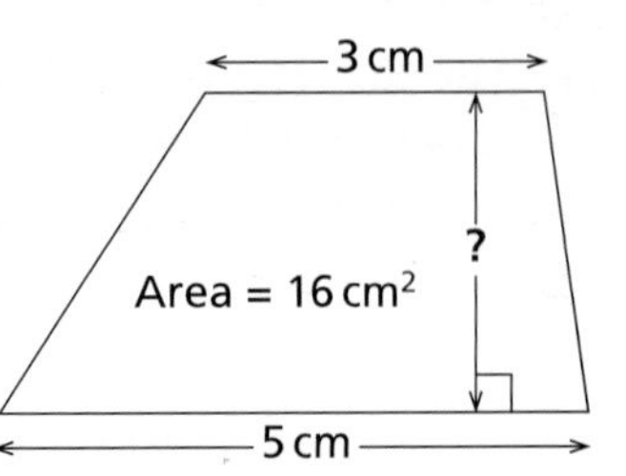

*F11 Find the missing length in each of these.

(a)

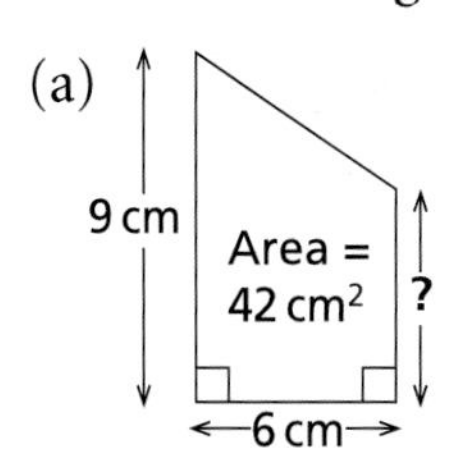

(b)

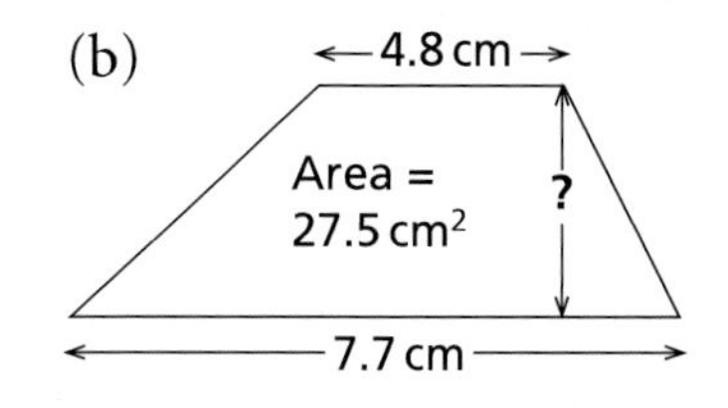

(c)

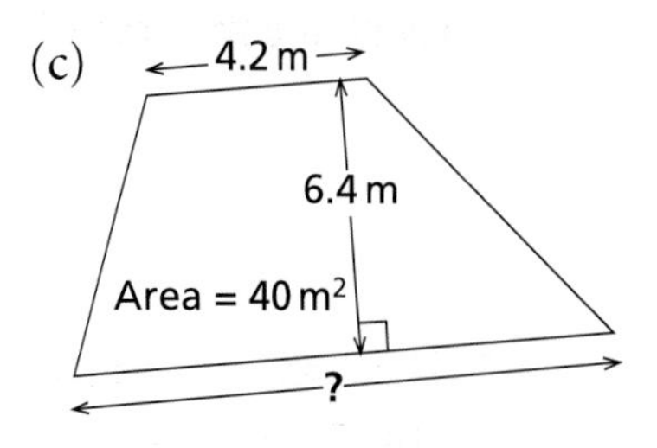

Test yourself

T1 (a) Find the area of this parallelogram.

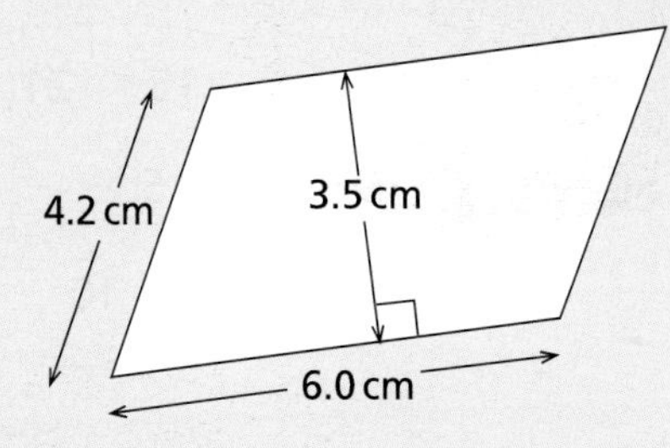

(b) Find the area of this trapezium to 1 d.p.

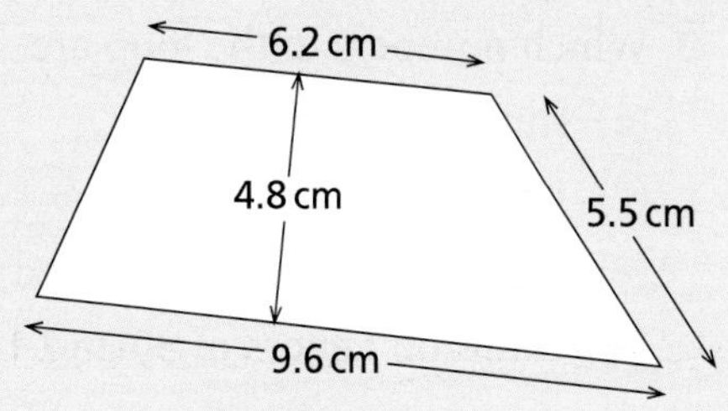

T2 (a) The base of a triangle is 8 cm. The height is 6 cm.
What is the area of the triangle?

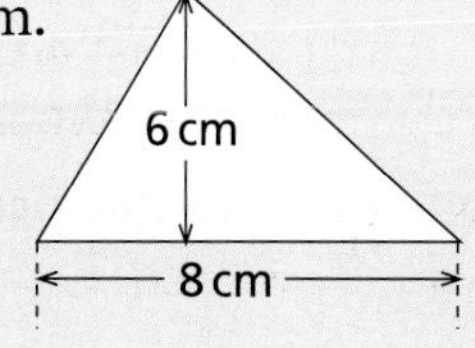

(b) The area of a rectangle is 24 cm^2.
Write down a possible pair of values for the length and the width of the rectangle.

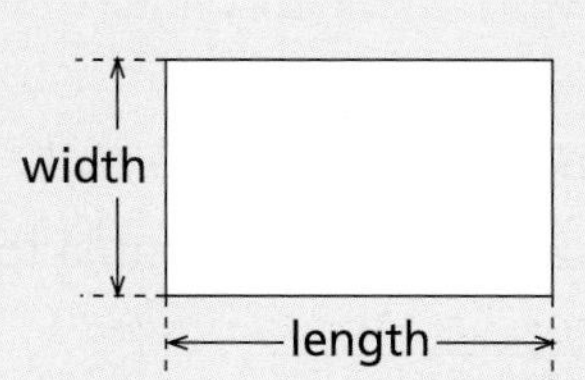

Not drawn to scale

(c) The radius of a semicircle is 2.5 cm.
Calculate the area of the semicircle.

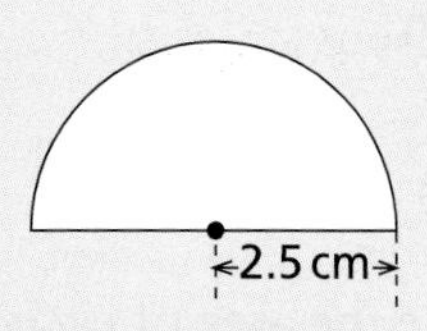

AQA (SEG) 1998

T3 A large clock face on a building is a circle with radius 2.91 metres.

(a) The minute hand reaches to the perimeter of the clock face.
How far does the tip of a minute hand travel in an hour?

(b) What is the area of the clock face?

T4 The distance round a circular running track is 1000 m.
What is its diameter?

Review 2

1 Here are the weights of some new-born baby boys.

3.81 kg   4.22 kg   2.96 kg   3.26 kg   3.85 kg

(a) What is the mean weight of these baby boys?

(b) The mean birth weight of a baby boy in the UK is about 3.4 kg. Which of these weights are less than this?

(c) What is the range of these weights?

2 Which numbers in the loop are

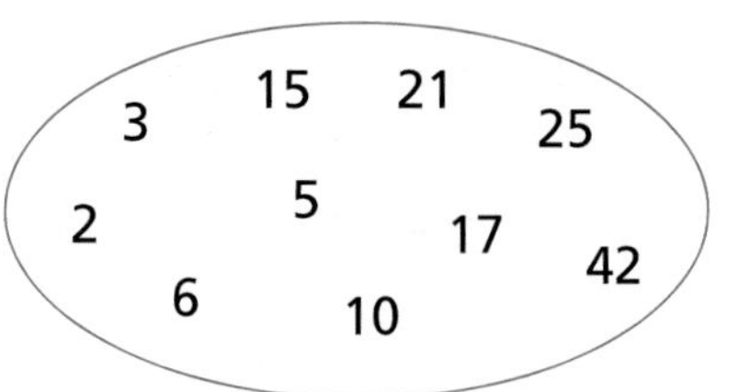

(a) multiples of 6   (b) factors of 10

(c) prime numbers   (d) powers of 5

(e) common multiples of 3 and 7

(f) common factors of 30 and 12

3 Work these out.

(a) $(^{-}6)^2$ (b) $3 \times (1 - 7)$ (c) $5 - \frac{^{-}16}{8}$ (d) $\frac{^{-}3 - 9}{^{-}4}$

4 (a) Write a formula for the perimeter of this rectangle.

$P = \ldots$

3

s s

3

(b) Rearrange the formula to make s the subject.

(c) Use your rearranged formula to find the length s when the perimeter is 15 units.

5

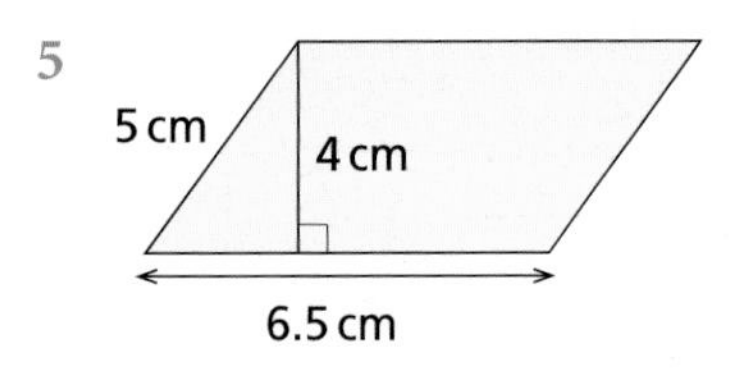

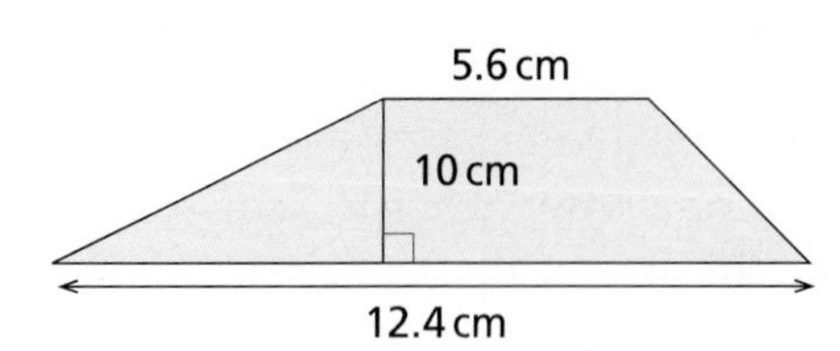

(a) Calculate the area of each shape.

(b) What is the perimeter of the parallelogram?

6 What is the value of each expression when $k = {}^{-}5$?

(a) $3k + 1$ (b) $(k - 3)^2$ (c) $\frac{1 - 3k}{^{-}2}$ (d) $\frac{k}{5} - 3$

7 Write down the numbers missing from these statements.

(a) $2^5 = ■$ (b) $3^{■} \times 2^3 = 72$ (c) $2^4 \times 2^5 = 2^{■}$ (d) $7^6 \times 7^{■} = 7^{10}$

8 Solve these equations.

(a) $3k + 11 = 2$ (b) $5x + 9 = 3x + 1$ (c) $h - 5 = 9h + 19$

9 Round the number 4 961 527 to the nearest thousand.

10 The table shows the results of a survey into the number of TV sets in people's homes.

(a) How many of these homes contain more than two TV sets?

(b) Calculate the mean number of sets in each home, correct to one decimal place.

(c) Find the median number of sets.

(d) What is the mode?

Number of sets	Number of homes
0	1
1	5
2	10
3	12
4	3

11 (a) Find the prime factorisation of 300 and write it using index notation.

(b) Find the prime factorisation of 198 and write it using index notation.

(c) Find the highest common factor of 198 and 300.

12 (a) Find the area of a circle that has a radius of 5.2 cm, correct to two significant figures.

(b) Find the radius of a circle with area 100 cm^2, correct to one decimal place.

13 This stem-and-leaf table shows the typing speeds in words per minute of some people who took an audio-typing test.

Stem	Leaves
2	9
3	2 2 4 7 8
4	0 1 1 3 4 5 5 9
5	1 3 4 4 6 7
6	2

Stem = 10 words per minute

(a) How many people took the test?

(b) What was the range of the typing speeds?

(c) What was the median speed?

(d) People with speeds of 38 words per minute or more had their work checked for accuracy. How many people was this?

14 Rearrange the formula $v = 7h - 9$ to make h the subject.

15 The table shows the times, in minutes, that some children spent on a computer game.

Time (minutes)	$0 \le t < 10$	$10 \le t < 20$	$20 \le t < 30$	$30 \le t < 40$
Frequency	6	12	15	7

(a) What is the modal class of the time spent?

(b) Calculate an estimate of the mean time spent on this computer game.

16 Round these numbers to three significant figures.

(a) 25 638 (b) 1 087 342 (c) 3.483 561 (d) 0.004 869 12

11 Fractions 1

You should know

- what is meant by equivalent fractions
- how to put decimals, for example 0.7, 0.62, 0.09, 0.115, in order of size
- how to rearrange simple formulas

This work will help you

- put fractions in order of size
- work with mixed numbers, for example $4\frac{2}{3}$
- add and subtract fractions
- express one quantity as a fraction of another
- change decimals to fractions and fractions to decimals

A Equivalent fractions

A1 Use these diagrams to help you write down three fractions equivalent to $\frac{2}{3}$.

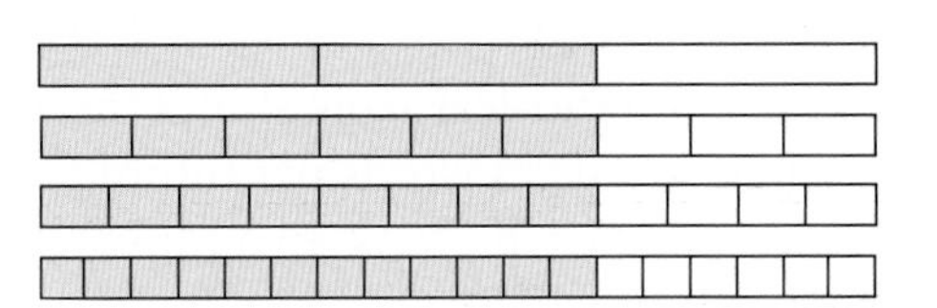

To find a fraction equivalent to $\frac{2}{3}$,
multiply numerator (top) and denominator (bottom) by the same number.

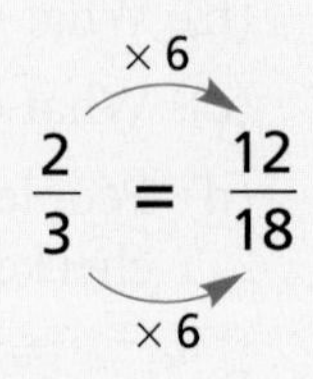

A2 (a) What is the multiplier here?

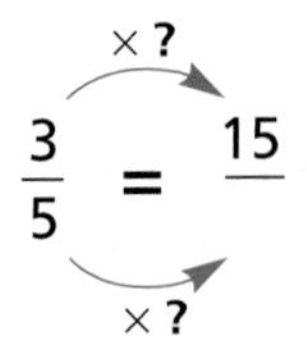

(b) Complete the second fraction.

A3 Copy these and find the missing numbers.

(a) $\frac{2}{3} = \frac{10}{}$ (b) $\frac{5}{6} = \frac{20}{}$ (c) $\frac{3}{4} = \frac{9}{}$ (d) $\frac{2}{5} = \frac{12}{}$ (e) $\frac{3}{7} = \frac{21}{}$

A4 Copy these and find the missing numbers.

(a) $\frac{3}{8} = \frac{}{32}$ (b) $\frac{5}{7} = \frac{}{35}$ (c) $\frac{4}{9} = \frac{}{36}$ (d) $\frac{5}{8} = \frac{}{24}$ (e) $\frac{7}{12} = \frac{}{60}$

Cancelling

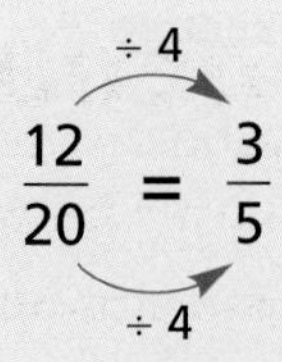

Sometimes a fraction can be **simplified** by dividing numerator and denominator by the same number.

This is called **cancelling** the **common factor** 4.

If the fraction can't be simplified any more, it is in its **lowest terms**, or **simplest form**.

A5 Write each of these fractions in its lowest terms.

(a) $\frac{20}{30}$ (b) $\frac{3}{9}$ (c) $\frac{12}{16}$ (d) $\frac{20}{25}$ (e) $\frac{30}{36}$

(f) $\frac{21}{28}$ (g) $\frac{36}{60}$ (h) $\frac{26}{39}$ (i) $\frac{22}{55}$ (j) $\frac{72}{96}$

A6 Sort these into pairs of equivalent fractions.

$\frac{7}{28}$ $\frac{5}{8}$ $\frac{2}{5}$ $\frac{3}{4}$ $\frac{20}{24}$ $\frac{12}{16}$ $\frac{1}{4}$ $\frac{9}{21}$ $\frac{3}{7}$ $\frac{15}{24}$ $\frac{8}{20}$ $\frac{5}{6}$

B *Ordering fractions*

It is easy to see from these diagrams that $\frac{2}{3}$ is greater than $\frac{7}{12}$.

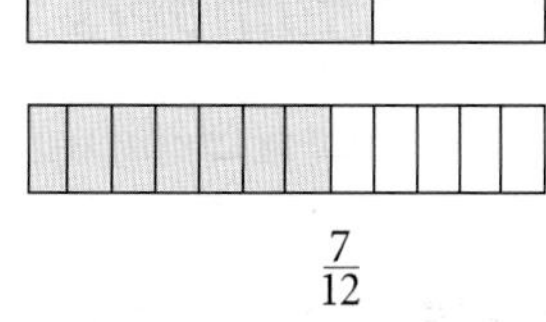

We can tell which fraction is greater, without diagrams, by changing $\frac{2}{3}$ into twelfths:

$$\frac{2}{3} \overset{\times 4}{=} \frac{8}{12}$$

B1 Which fraction is greater, $\frac{3}{4}$ or $\frac{17}{20}$? (Change $\frac{3}{4}$ to twentieths.)

B2 Which fraction is greater, $\frac{4}{5}$ or $\frac{11}{15}$?

B3 Work out which fraction in each pair is greater.

(a) $\frac{1}{3}$, $\frac{5}{12}$ (b) $\frac{11}{16}$, $\frac{3}{4}$ (c) $\frac{19}{30}$, $\frac{7}{10}$ (d) $\frac{2}{5}$, $\frac{7}{20}$ (e) $\frac{3}{8}$, $\frac{11}{24}$

B4 Pat wants to know whether $\frac{3}{5}$ is greater or less than $\frac{2}{3}$.

He makes a list of fractions equivalent to $\frac{3}{5}$, …

$\frac{3}{5} = \frac{6}{10} = \frac{9}{15} = \frac{12}{20} = \frac{15}{25} =$

and a list of fractions equivalent to $\frac{2}{3}$.

$\frac{2}{3} = \frac{4}{6} = \frac{6}{9} = \frac{8}{12} = \frac{10}{15} =$

How can you tell from the lists whether $\frac{3}{5}$ is greater or less than $\frac{2}{3}$?

Worked example

Which fraction is greater, $\frac{5}{8}$ or $\frac{7}{12}$?

We need to change $\frac{5}{8}$ and $\frac{7}{12}$ into equivalent fractions with the **same denominator**. The denominator must be a multiple of 8 and also a multiple of 12. So **24** will do.

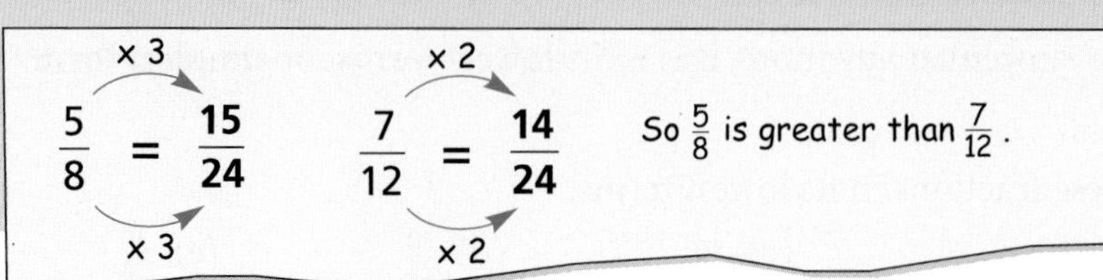

B5 Work out which fraction is greater, $\frac{3}{8}$ or $\frac{2}{5}$.

B6 Work out which fraction in each pair is greater.

(a) $\frac{1}{3}, \frac{2}{5}$ (b) $\frac{3}{5}, \frac{5}{8}$ (c) $\frac{5}{6}, \frac{7}{8}$ (d) $\frac{7}{8}, \frac{4}{5}$ (e) $\frac{5}{8}, \frac{7}{10}$

B7 Work out which fraction in each pair is greater.

(a) $\frac{5}{9}, \frac{3}{5}$ (b) $\frac{4}{7}, \frac{5}{8}$ (c) $\frac{3}{10}, \frac{1}{3}$ (d) $\frac{2}{5}, \frac{3}{7}$ (e) $\frac{3}{8}, \frac{5}{12}$

C *Mixed numbers*

A **mixed number** is made up of a whole number and a fraction, for example $2\frac{3}{4}$.

A mixed number can be changed to an **improper** ('top heavy') fraction.

For example, $2\frac{3}{4} = 1 + 1 + \frac{3}{4} = \frac{4}{4} + \frac{4}{4} + \frac{3}{4} = \frac{11}{4}$.

C1 Change these mixed numbers to improper fractions.

(a) $1\frac{1}{4}$ (b) $2\frac{1}{3}$ (c) $1\frac{2}{3}$ (d) $4\frac{1}{2}$ (e) $3\frac{2}{5}$

(f) $2\frac{2}{3}$ (g) $3\frac{1}{5}$ (h) $1\frac{5}{8}$ (i) $2\frac{1}{10}$ (j) $4\frac{7}{8}$

Worked example

Change $\frac{14}{3}$ to a mixed number.

Think of $\frac{14}{3}$ as 14 lots of $\frac{1}{3}$.

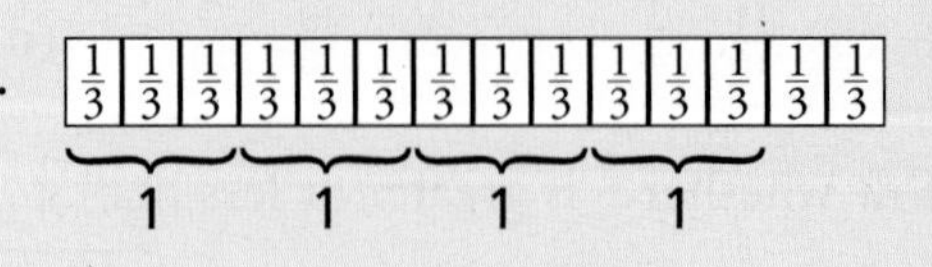

C2 Change these improper fractions to mixed numbers.

(a) $\frac{7}{2}$ (b) $\frac{13}{4}$ (c) $\frac{13}{5}$ (d) $\frac{11}{6}$ (e) $\frac{15}{4}$

C3 Change these improper fractions to mixed numbers.

(a) $\frac{22}{4}$ (b) $\frac{13}{6}$ (c) $\frac{20}{7}$ (d) $\frac{14}{5}$ (e) $\frac{29}{10}$

D Addition and subtraction

It is easy to add and subtract fractions with the same denominator.

$\frac{3}{5} + \frac{1}{5} = \frac{4}{5}$ $\frac{5}{8} + \frac{7}{8} = \frac{12}{8} = 1\frac{4}{8} = 1\frac{1}{2}$ $1\frac{1}{3} - \frac{2}{3} = \frac{4}{3} - \frac{2}{3} = \frac{2}{3}$

D1 Work these out. Simplify the result where possible.

(a) $\frac{2}{7} + \frac{3}{7}$ (b) $\frac{1}{8} + \frac{5}{8}$ (c) $\frac{3}{5} + \frac{4}{5}$ (d) $\frac{3}{10} + \frac{9}{10}$ (e) $\frac{5}{6} + \frac{5}{6}$

D2 Work these out. Simplify the result where possible.

(a) $1\frac{1}{5} + \frac{3}{5}$ (b) $2\frac{3}{4} + \frac{3}{4}$ (c) $1\frac{2}{3} + \frac{2}{3}$ (d) $\frac{5}{6} + 1\frac{1}{6}$ (e) $1\frac{3}{8} + 1\frac{1}{8}$

D3 Work out these subtractions. Simplify where possible.

(a) $\frac{4}{5} - \frac{1}{5}$ (b) $\frac{7}{8} - \frac{3}{8}$ (c) $\frac{9}{10} - \frac{3}{10}$ (d) $1\frac{5}{8} - \frac{1}{8}$ (e) $2\frac{1}{4} - \frac{3}{4}$

Worked example

Work out $\frac{3}{4} + \frac{1}{6}$.

We need to change $\frac{3}{4}$ and $\frac{1}{6}$ into equivalent fractions with the **same denominator.** The denominator must be a multiple of 4 and also a multiple of 6. So **12** will do.

$\frac{3}{4} = \frac{9}{12}$ (× 3 top and bottom) $\frac{1}{6} = \frac{2}{12}$ (× 2 top and bottom)

So $\frac{3}{4} + \frac{1}{6}$

$= \frac{9}{12} + \frac{2}{12} = \frac{11}{12}$

D4 Work these out.

(a) $\frac{1}{4} + \frac{1}{3}$ (b) $\frac{2}{3} + \frac{1}{4}$ (c) $\frac{1}{6} + \frac{1}{4}$ (d) $\frac{1}{5} + \frac{2}{3}$ (e) $\frac{2}{5} + \frac{1}{4}$

D5 Work these out.

(a) $\frac{2}{5} - \frac{1}{4}$ (b) $\frac{3}{4} - \frac{1}{6}$ (c) $\frac{2}{3} - \frac{1}{4}$ (d) $\frac{3}{4} - \frac{2}{3}$ (e) $\frac{1}{2} - \frac{2}{5}$

D6 Work these out.

(a) $\frac{2}{5} + \frac{1}{3}$ (b) $\frac{3}{5} - \frac{1}{4}$ (c) $\frac{3}{4} - \frac{2}{5}$ (d) $\frac{1}{8} + \frac{5}{6}$ (e) $\frac{1}{12} + \frac{2}{5}$

D7 Work these out. The results will be mixed numbers.

(a) $\frac{3}{8} + \frac{2}{3}$ (b) $\frac{5}{6} + \frac{1}{4}$ (c) $\frac{2}{3} + \frac{2}{5}$ (d) $\frac{5}{8} + \frac{2}{3}$ (e) $1\frac{3}{4} + \frac{2}{5}$

D8 Work these out.

(a) $\frac{3}{8} - \frac{1}{5}$ (b) $\frac{5}{8} + \frac{1}{3}$ (c) $1\frac{2}{3} + \frac{5}{6}$ (d) $1\frac{1}{3} - \frac{1}{8}$ (e) $\frac{7}{8} + \frac{2}{3}$

(f) $\frac{4}{5} - \frac{1}{8}$ (g) $\frac{7}{8} - \frac{1}{3}$ (h) $\frac{5}{6} + \frac{1}{8}$ (i) $\frac{7}{8} - \frac{5}{6}$ (j) $1\frac{2}{5} - \frac{2}{3}$

E *Expressing one quantity as a fraction of another*

Worked example

In a class of 36 children, 15 were absent with flu.
What fraction of the class were absent?

Each child is $\frac{1}{36}$ of the class.
So $\frac{15}{36}$ of the class were absent.
This simplifies to $\frac{5}{12}$ (by dividing top and bottom by 3).

E1 In a typical 24-hour period, Karl spends 6 hours working, 8 hours sleeping, 3 hours eating and the rest of the time doing other things.
Write, in its simplest form, the fraction of the time Karl spends

(a) working (b) sleeping (c) eating (d) doing other things

E2 Write each of these as a fraction in its simplest form.

(a) 12 out of 20 (b) 8 out of 30 (c) 12 out of 16 (d) 25 out of 40

E3 Gert owns 30 acres of land: 12 acres are woodland, 15 are grass and the rest is marsh.
Write, in its simplest form, the fraction of Gert's land that is

(a) woodland (b) grass (c) marsh

E4 There are 15 boys and 12 girls in a class.
What fraction of the class (in its simplest form) are boys?

E5 Last season Brockleton United won 18 matches, drew 8 and lost 10.
What fraction, in its simplest form, of the matches were

(a) won (b) drawn (c) lost

E6 Write each of these fractions in its simplest form.

(a) The fraction of the circle that is red
(b) The fraction that is blue
(c) The fraction that is green
(d) The fraction that is yellow

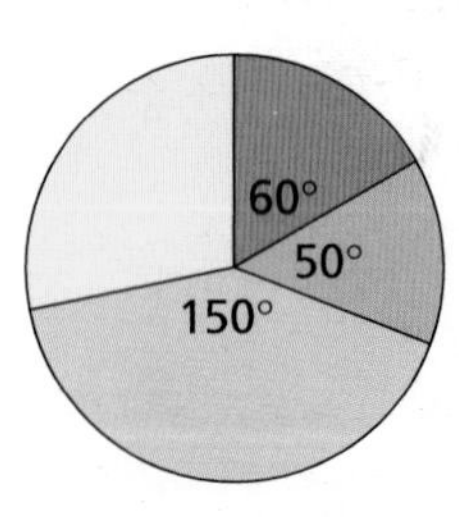

E7 Joe had £4 pocket money. He spent £1.50 on sweets.
What fraction of his pocket money did he spend on sweets?

E8 Write each of these as a fraction in its lowest terms.

(a) £2.00 out of £2.50 (b) £2.50 out of £7.50 (c) £2.40 out of £3.00

F *Changing between fractions and decimals*

Worked examples

Change each of these decimals to a fraction, in its lowest terms. (a) 0.32 (b) 0.275

(a) 0.32 means the same as $\frac{32}{100}$.

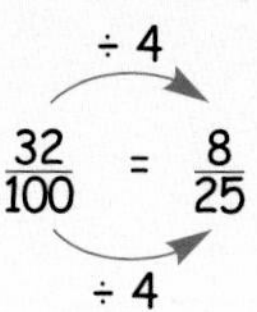

(b) 0.275 means the same as $\frac{275}{1000}$.

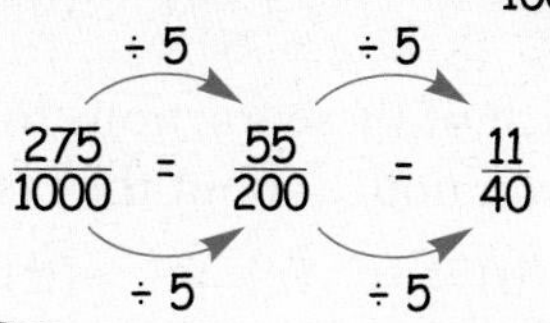

F1 Change each of these decimals to a fraction, in its lowest terms.

(a) 0.6 (b) 0.64 (c) 0.625 (d) 0.35 (e) 0.08
(f) 0.825 (g) 0.035 (h) 0.72 (i) 0.004 (j) 0.152

Worked example

Change $\frac{3}{8}$ to a decimal.

You need to divide 3 by 8.
To allow for decimal places, write 3 as 3.00…

$8\overline{)3.0^60^40}$ = 0.375 $\frac{3}{8} = 0.375$

F2 Change each of these fractions to a decimal.

(a) $\frac{1}{8}$ (b) $\frac{5}{8}$ (c) $\frac{7}{8}$ (d) $\frac{1}{16}$ (e) $\frac{5}{16}$

Fractions with denominator 50, 20 or 25 can be changed to decimals using equivalent fractions.

$\frac{9}{50} = \frac{18}{100} = 0.18$ $\frac{7}{20} = \frac{35}{100} = 0.35$ $\frac{6}{25} = \frac{24}{100} = 0.24$

F3 Write each of these lists in order, smallest first.

(a) 0.6, $\frac{5}{8}$, $\frac{13}{20}$, 0.59 (b) $\frac{37}{50}$, 0.7, $\frac{4}{5}$, 0.77 (c) $\frac{3}{10}$, 0.35, $\frac{9}{20}$, 0.4
(d) 0.25, $\frac{3}{8}$, 0.3, $\frac{7}{20}$ (e) 0.4, 0.405, $\frac{9}{20}$, 0.5 (f) $\frac{7}{8}$, $\frac{3}{4}$, 0.85, 0.8

F4 Decode this message. Rewrite the letters in the order of the numbers, smallest first.

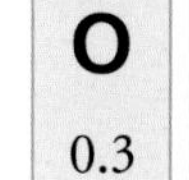

O	F	T	E	N	T	O	S	I	L	E	N	C	E
0.3	$\frac{9}{20}$	$\frac{1}{2}$	$\frac{1}{10}$	$\frac{3}{8}$	$\frac{1}{5}$	0.085	0.12	$\frac{1}{4}$	$\frac{2}{5}$	0.408	0.09	0.13	$\frac{1}{8}$

G Recurring decimals

$\frac{1}{3} = ?$ $\frac{1}{6} = ?$ $\frac{1}{11} = ?$ $\frac{1}{7} = ?$

TG

G1 Change these fractions to decimals.

(a) $\frac{2}{3}$ (b) $\frac{1}{9}$ (c) $\frac{2}{9}$ (d) $\frac{4}{9}$ (e) $\frac{7}{9}$

G2 Change each of these fractions to recurring decimals.
What do you notice about the results?

(a) $\frac{1}{7}$ (b) $\frac{2}{7}$ (c) $\frac{3}{7}$ (d) $\frac{4}{7}$ (e) $\frac{5}{7}$ (f) $\frac{6}{7}$

G3 Change each of these fractions to decimals.

(a) $\frac{5}{6}$ (b) $\frac{2}{11}$ (c) $\frac{3}{11}$ (d) $\frac{1}{12}$ (e) $\frac{1}{13}$

Investigation How can you tell when a fraction will give a recurring decimal?
Which of these fractions will be recurring? $\frac{1}{15}$ $\frac{1}{16}$ $\frac{1}{17}$ $\frac{1}{30}$ $\frac{1}{40}$

Test yourself

T1 Find the missing numbers a, b, c and d.

$\frac{2}{5} = \frac{12}{a}$ $\frac{3}{8} = \frac{b}{40}$ $\frac{5}{c} = \frac{20}{36}$ $\frac{d}{4} = \frac{24}{32}$

T2 Write each list in order, starting with the smallest.

(a) 0.04, $\frac{3}{20}$, 0.1, $\frac{1}{50}$ (b) $\frac{7}{8}$, 0.9, $\frac{17}{20}$, 0.86

T3 Work these out.

(a) $\frac{1}{5} + \frac{2}{3}$ (b) $\frac{2}{3} - \frac{1}{4}$ (c) $\frac{3}{8} + \frac{4}{5}$ (d) $3\frac{1}{4} - \frac{5}{8}$

T4 Fabia planted 80 lettuce seeds but only 25 of them grew into plants.
What fraction of the seeds grew? Write it in its lowest terms.

T5 A landowner died. In his will the land was to be shared between his three children.
The eldest inherited $\frac{2}{5}$ of the land and the second child inherited $\frac{1}{3}$.
What fraction did the youngest inherit?

T6 On a computer keyboard there are 104 keys.
26 of the keys have letters on them.
What fraction of the keys have letters on them?
(Give your answer in its simplest form.) AQA(NEAB) 1998

T7 (a) Change $\frac{3}{8}$ to a decimal.
(b) Use your answer to part (a) to write $\frac{3}{80}$ as a decimal. OCR

12 Substitution

You should know how to work out expressions such as $\frac{h-6}{10}$, $35 - 2h$, $4h^2 - 40$, $\frac{h^2}{10}$ and $200 - h^2$ when you know the value of h.

This work will help you

- substitute into expressions involving cubes
- substitute into more complex expressions, and those involving units
- substitute numbers into expressions involving several letters

A Review

A1 Work out the value of each of these expressions when $h = 4$.

(a) $2h^2$ (b) $100 - h^2$ (c) $\frac{100}{5h}$ (d) $\frac{64}{h^2}$ (e) $\frac{1 - h^2}{5}$

A2 Use a calculator to work out the value of these expressions.

(a) $8a^2$ when $a = 2.5$ (b) $7.2 - 2b^2$ when $b = 1.1$ (c) $4.5c - 2.7$ when $c = 1.5$

(d) $\frac{9}{2d - 3}$ when $d = 2.4$ (e) $1.5(2.2e + 1)$ when $e = 2$ (f) $\frac{f^2}{5} - 3f$ when $f = 4.5$

A3 The circumference of a circle is given by the formula $C = 2\pi r$.
C stands for the circumference and r for the radius.

Work out the circumference, in centimetres, of each of these circles.
Give your answers to one decimal place.

(a) (b) (c)

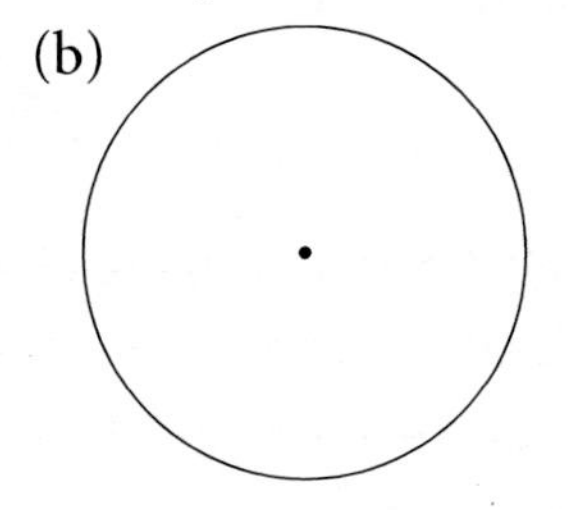

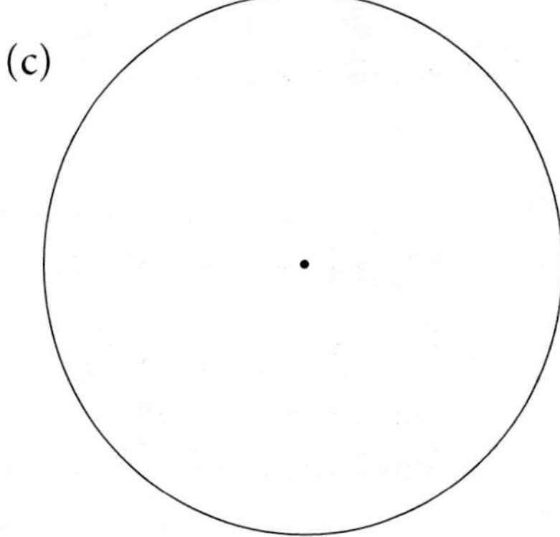

A4 The area of a circle is given by the formula $A = \pi r^2$.
Work out the areas of the circles in A3. Give each answer to the nearest 0.1 cm^2.

A5 (a) Which of the expressions in the boxes has the highest value when $x = 5$?

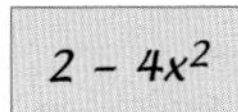

$2 - 4x^2$ $10(x + 3)$ $2(10 - x)$ $\frac{x^2}{2}$ $\frac{25}{x - 4}$

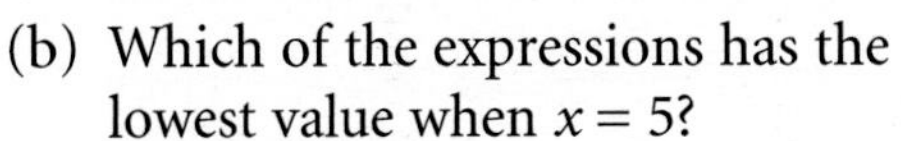

(b) Which of the expressions has the lowest value when $x = 5$?

A6 Which numbers in this list fit each equation below?
More than one number may fit an equation.

$^-5$	$^-1$	1	3.5	4	5

(a) $5x - 20 = 0$ (b) $2x^2 - 50 = 0$ (c) $4(2x - 5) = 8$ (d) $\frac{1}{x^2} = 1$

B More letters

When you have several letters in an expression, you treat them just like numbers.

Evaluate $a - bc$ when $a = 5, b = 2, c = 8$.

$a - bc$
$= 5 - 2 \times 8$
$= 5 - 16 = ^-11$

bc means b × c

Evaluate $a(b - c)^2$ when $a = 5, b = 2, c = 8$.

$a(b - c)^2$
$= 5 \times (2 - 8)^2$
$= 5 \times (^-6)^2 = 5 \times 36 = 180$

$a(b - c)^2$ means $a \times (b - c)^2$

B1 Calculate the values of each of the following expressions when $p = 2, q = 3, r = 6$.

(a) $r(p + q)$ (b) $rp + q$ (c) $\frac{r}{pq}$ (d) $\frac{q + r}{p}$ (e) $5r^2$

Check that you can make your calculator agree with you.

B2 Calculate the values of each of the following expressions when $f = 2, g = ^-6, h = 4$.

(a) $f + gh$ (b) $\frac{f}{g - h}$ (c) $(f + g)^2$ (d) $10g^2$ (e) $f^2 + h^2$

Check that you can make your calculator agree with you.

B3 Evaluate each of the expressions in B2 when $f = 7.9, g = 5.7, h = 3.8$.
Give your answers accurate to one decimal place.

B4 If $u = 2.1$, $v = 3.1$ and $w = 5.9$, evaluate each of these expressions giving answers accurate to two decimal places.

(a) $\frac{u}{v + w}$ (b) $w - \frac{u}{v}$ (c) $u + vw$ (d) $\frac{u + v}{v + w}$ (e) uv^2

B5 Evaluate each of these expressions when $a = ^-4.5$, $b = 0.5$ and $c = ^-2.5$.
Round to 2 d.p. if necessary.

(a) $\frac{a^2}{b^2 + c^2}$ (b) $(c - 2b)^2$ (c) $3b^2$ (d) $(3b)^2$ (e) $ab + bc + ca$

B6 Evaluate each of the following expressions when $w = \frac{1}{2}, x = \frac{1}{3}$ and $y = \frac{3}{4}$.

(a) $2w$ (b) $2w - y$ (c) $w + x$ (d) $w + x + y$ (e) $w + x - y$

B7 If $a = 2$ and $b = 3$, calculate the values of these.

(a) a^2b (b) ab^2 (c) $(ab)^2$

If any of your answers are the same, you have made a mistake. In that case, find it!

C Units

When using a formula for a real problem, you must be careful about the units.

To find the area of this triangle we must work entirely in either centimetres or millimetres.

The area of a triangle is given by $A = \frac{1}{2}bh$ or $\frac{bh}{2}$ where b is the base and h is the height.

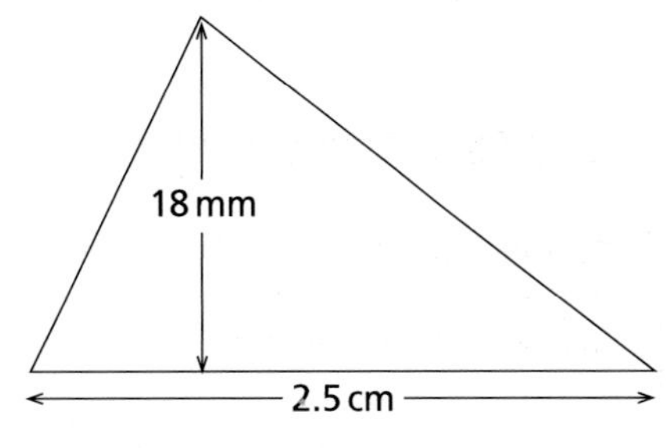

Working in centimetres, $A = \frac{bh}{2} = \frac{2.5 \times 1.8}{2}$

$= \frac{4.5}{2} = 2.25$

So the area is 2.25 cm^2.

When using formulas

- it must be clear what each letter stands for
- think carefully about the units of any quantities
- give any answers complete with units

C1 The area of a triangle is given by the formula $A = \frac{bh}{2}$.

Work out the areas of triangles where

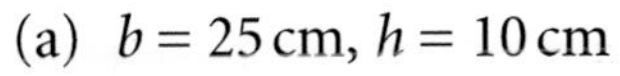

(a) $b = 25$ cm, $h = 10$ cm

(b) $b = 1.2$ m, $h = 90$ cm

C2 The area, A square units, of a trapezium is given by the formula $A = \frac{1}{2}(a + b)h$.
(a, b and h are shown on the diagram.)

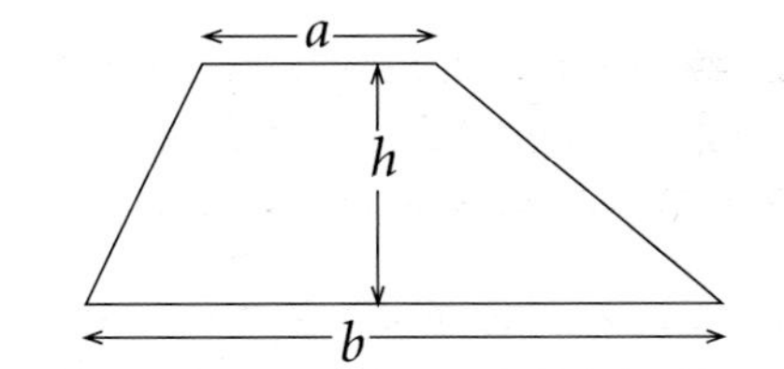

Use the formula to calculate the areas of trapeziums for which

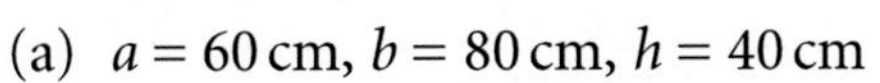

(a) $a = 60$ cm, $b = 80$ cm, $h = 40$ cm

(b) $a = 50$ cm, $b = 1.8$ m, $h = 80$ cm

C3 The power, W, used by an electrical appliance is measured in watts.
The current, A, the appliance needs in amps is given by the formula $A = \frac{W}{220}$.

(a) Work out the current needed by these.

(i) A 250 watt television (ii) An 80 watt computer

(iii) A 60 watt light bulb (iv) A 7 kilowatt cooker

1 kilowatt = 1000 watts

(Give your answers to one significant figure.)

(b) A shower needs a current of 30 amps.
How many kilowatts does it use?

C4 Calculate the area of each of these trapeziums.
Make sure you include units in your answers.

(a)

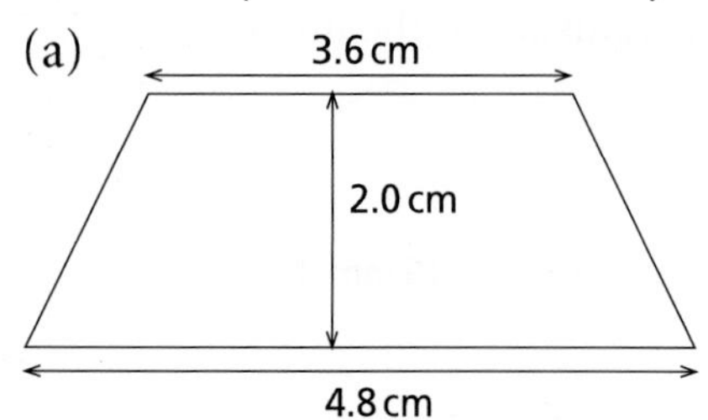

(b)

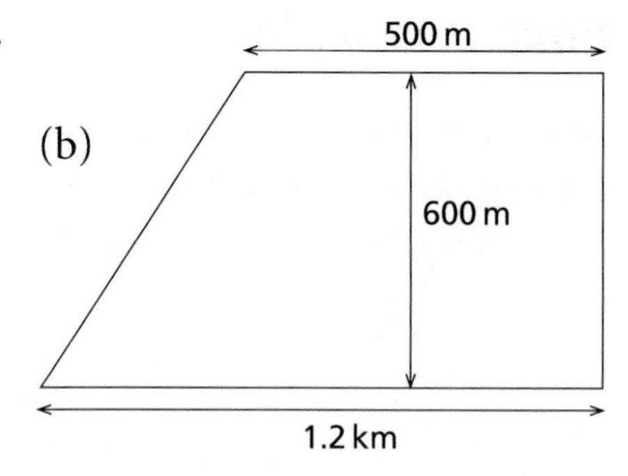

C5 A rectangle has length L and width W.
Its perimeter, P (the total distance round the edge), can be found using the formula $P = 2(L + W)$.

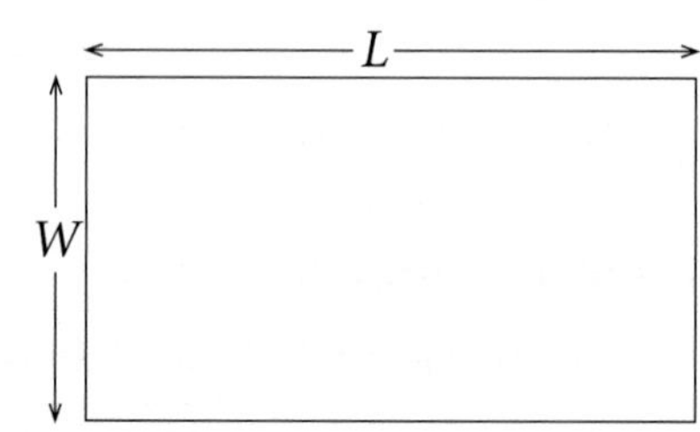

Use this formula to find the perimeters of the following rectangles.

(a) A field 120 m long and 200 m across

(b) A poster 40 cm wide and 65 cm high

(c) A postage stamp measuring 18 mm across and 2.5 cm from top to bottom

(d) A doormat measuring 1.2 m by 75 cm

C6 This cuboid has square ends.
Its volume, V, is given by the formula $V = ab^2$.

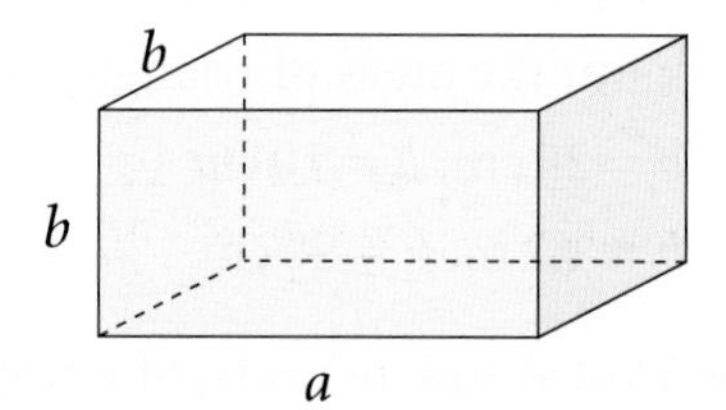

Calculate the volume of each of these cuboids with square ends.

(a)

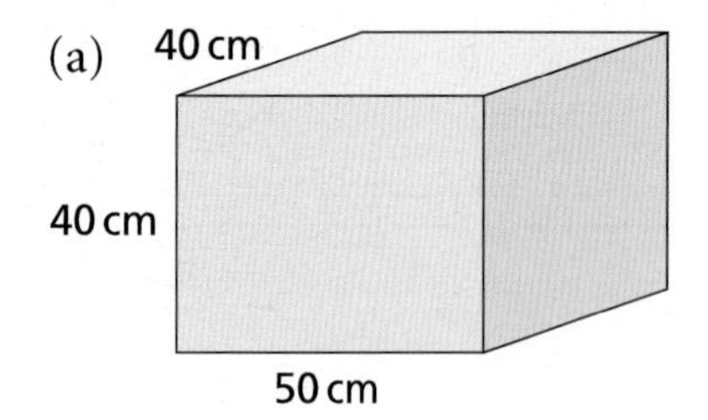

(b)

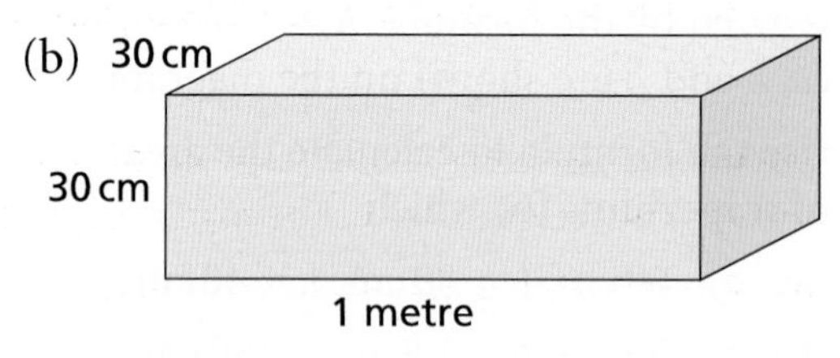

C7 A cuboid with square ends, as in C6, has a surface area, A, given by the formula $A = 4ab + 2b^2$.

Calculate the surface area of these.

(a) A cuboid that is 10 cm long, with ends 4 cm by 4 cm

(b) A cuboid that is 1.2 metres long, with ends 75 centimetres square

D *Mixed examples*

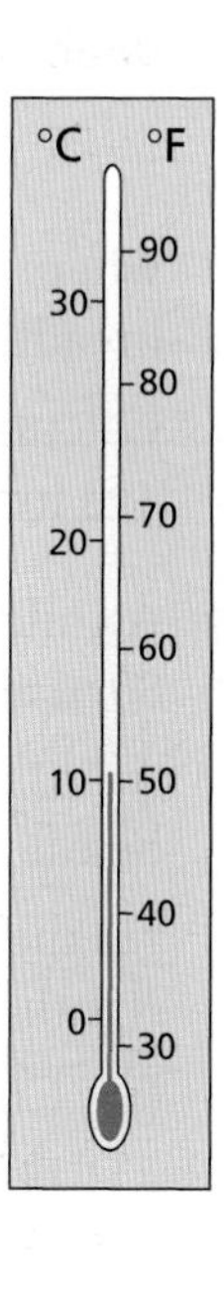

D1 To convert temperatures between Celsius and Fahrenheit you can use one of these formulas.

$$C = \frac{5(F - 32)}{9} \qquad F = \frac{9C}{5} + 32$$

C stands for the temperature in °C, F stands for the temperature in °F.

(a) The freezing point of water is 0°C. What is it in Fahrenheit?

(b) The boiling point of water is 100°C. What is it in Fahrenheit?

(c) A comfortable room temperature is about 72°F. What is it in Celsius?

(d) The temperature in a domestic fridge should be about 36°F. What is this in Celsius?

(e) The melting point of iron is about 2800°F. What is this in Celsius?

(f) The temperature at the centre of the Sun may be about 27 000 000°F. What is it in Celsius?

(g) In 1895 a temperature of $^{-}17$°F was recorded in Scotland. What is this in Celsius?

(h) In 1983 a temperature of $^{-}128$°F was recorded in Antarctica. What is this in Celsius?

(i) The freezing point of mercury is $^{-}38.86$°C. What is it in Fahrenheit?

(j) At what temperature are the measurements in degrees Celsius and degrees Fahrenheit exactly the same?

D2 Building bricks are supplied in cube-shaped packs on a pallet. The weight of a pack can be worked out using the formula

$$w = 2000l^3$$

where w is the weight of a pack in kilograms and l is the length of the side of the pack in metres.

Work out the weights of packs of bricks with these side lengths.

(a) 1.0 metres (b) 1.5 metres (c) 50 centimetres

D3 ProPlanters make large cubical lead planters. The weight of a planter, filled with earth, is given by the formula $w = 0.6S^2 + 2.2S^3$.

w is the weight of the full planter in tonnes and S is the length of the side of the planter in metres.

(a) Work out the weight of a full planter with a side of 1.1 metres.

(b) Work out the weight of a full planter that has a side of 1 m 50 cm.

(c) Four gardeners can lift about 300 kg between them. Could they lift a full 50 cm planter?

D4 The weight in kilograms that can be supported at the middle of an oak beam is given by the formula

$$w = \frac{60bd^2}{l}$$

where w stands for the weight in kilograms, and b, d and l for the breadth, depth and length of the beam in centimetres.

Calculate the load which can be supported by an oak beam 4 m long, 20 cm broad and 30 cm deep.

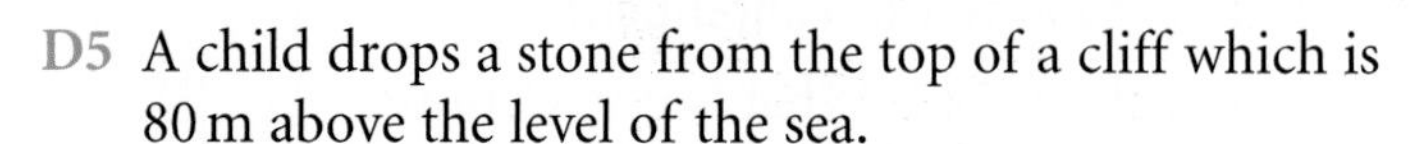

D5 A child drops a stone from the top of a cliff which is 80 m above the level of the sea.

As it falls, the height of the stone above the sea can be calculated using the formula $h = 80 - 5t^2$.

t is the time in seconds since the stone was dropped.
h is the height of the stone in metres above sea level.

(a) Copy and complete this working to find the value of h when $t = 3$.

> When $t = 3$, $h = 80 - 5 \times 3^2$
> $= 80 - 5 \times 9 = 80 - 45 =$ ●

(b) Calculate the values of h when t is 0, 1, 2, and 4. Make a table of the results, like this.

t	0	1	2	3	4
h					

(c) Describe where the stone is when $t = 0$.

(d) Does the stone fall at the same speed all the time, or does it speed up, or does it slow down?

(e) After how many seconds does the stone hit the sea?

D6 Copy this number grid puzzle onto squared paper.
To solve the puzzle, first work out the value of each of the expressions below.

Then fit the values you worked out into the grid puzzle.

To help you, the value of one of the expressions has been fitted into the grid for you.

1	2	3	0	■
	■		■	
		■		
			■	
■				

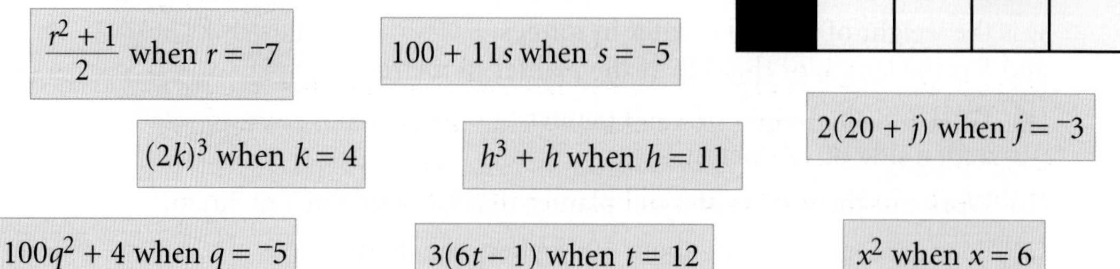

$m^3 - 20m$ when $m = 14$

$12a^2 + 3a$ when $a = 10$

$\frac{r^2 + 1}{2}$ when $r = {}^-7$

$100 + 11s$ when $s = {}^-5$

$(2k)^3$ when $k = 4$

$h^3 + h$ when $h = 11$

$2(20 + j)$ when $j = {}^-3$

$100q^2 + 4$ when $q = {}^-5$

$3(6t - 1)$ when $t = 12$

x^2 when $x = 6$

E *Using a spreadsheet*

A spreadsheet is ideal when you have a lot of calculations to do using a formula.
For example, this spreadsheet is set up to work out the areas of trapeziums.

Trapezium spreadsheet

	A	B	C	D	E
1	Length of first parallel side (a)	Length of second parallel side (b)	Height (h)	Area	
2					
3	8	12	4	=0.5*(A3+B3)*C3	
4					

The area of a trapezium is usually written as $\frac{1}{2}(a+b)h$.
Notice that we have to write the formula so that the spreadsheet understands it.

E1 Set up your spreadsheet to work out the areas of trapeziums where

(a) $a = 6, b = 5, h = 10$ (b) $a = 7.6, b = 12.2, h = 9.8$

E2 This trapezium has an area of $100\,\text{cm}^2$.
Use your spreadsheet to find the value of x to one decimal place.

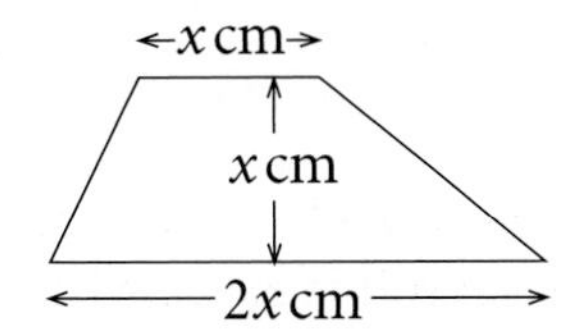

E3 Another trapezium has one parallel side 3 cm longer than the other.
The height of the trapezium is the same as the shorter side and its area is $50\,\text{cm}^2$.
Use a spreadsheet to work out the height of the trapezium to one decimal place.

E4 The area of a semicircle is given by the expression $\frac{1}{2}\pi r^2$.
Set up a spreadsheet to work out the areas of semicircles.
(You may be able to enter π as PI(); if not use 3.14159.)

Work out the areas of semicircles with these radii.

(a) 6.5 cm (b) 8.8 cm (c) 0.2 km (d) 100 m

E5 This shape is made from a square and a semicircle.
The area of the shape is $200\,\text{cm}^2$.
Use a spreadsheet to work out the length of the side of the square to one decimal place.

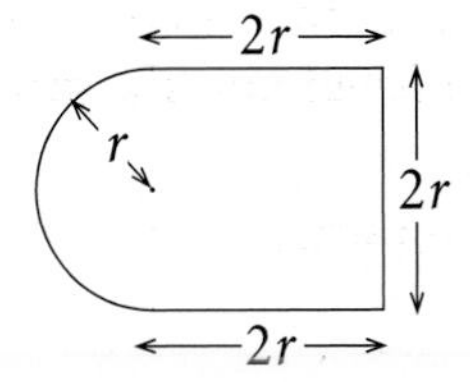

E6 This running track is made up of a square and two semicircles.
The distance round the outside of the track must be 400 metres.
Use your spreadsheet to work out what the radius of the semicircles must be to the nearest centimetre.

Test yourself

T1 Calculate the values of each of the following expressions when $a = 2$, $b = 4$, $c = {}^-1$.

(a) $a(b + c)$ (b) $ab - c$ (c) $\frac{ab}{c}$ (d) $\frac{b - 2c}{a}$ (e) ab^2

T2 Work out the value of the following expressions when $p = \frac{1}{3}$, $q = \frac{1}{4}$ and $r = \frac{7}{8}$.

(a) $p + q$ (b) $3q$ (c) $3q - p$ (d) $p + q + r$ (e) $r - 2q$

T3 The area, A, of a trapezium can be written as $A = \frac{1}{2}(a + b)h$.
Work out the areas of each of these.

(a)

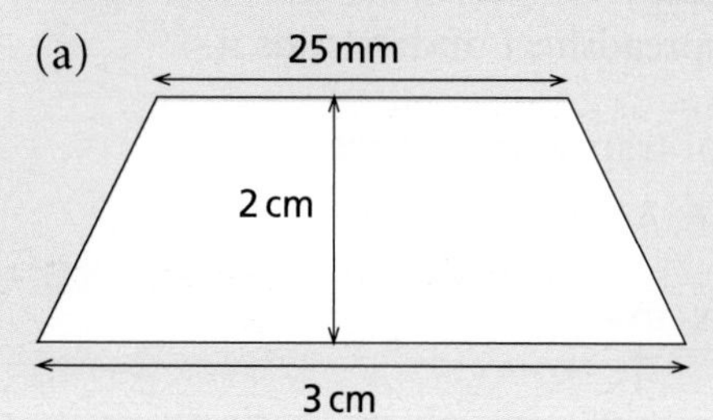

(b)

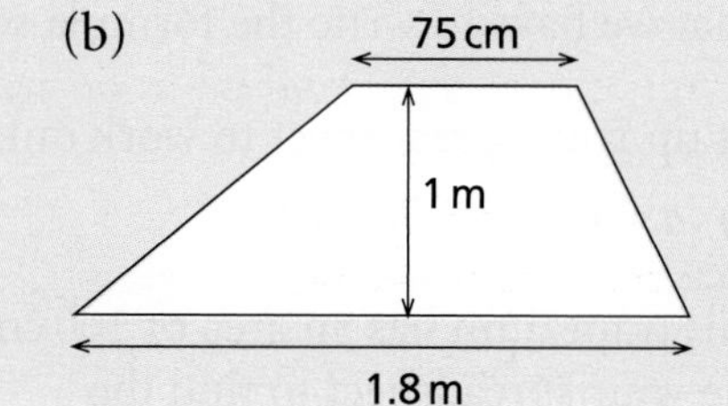

T4 The length of this metal rod is exactly 1 metre at 0°C.

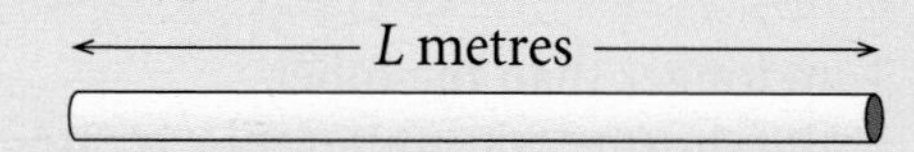

When the temperature is T°C, its length, L metres, is given by the formula $L = 1 + \frac{T}{30000}$.

Find the length of the rod at these temperatures.

(a) 150°C (b) 600°C (c) ⁻90°C (d) ⁻200°C

T5 Quattro ponds are made up of a square and four semicircles.
The radius of each semicircle is r.

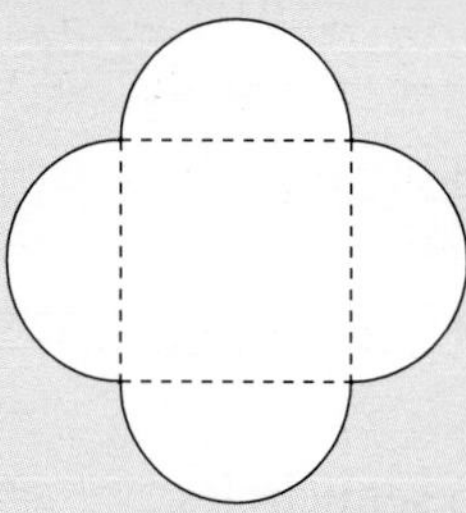

The area of a pond can be written as $2\pi r^2 + 4r^2$.
Work out the area of a Quattro pond when

(a) $r = 1$ (b) $r = 10$ (c) $r = 0.75$

13 Percentage 1

You should know how to find equivalent fractions.

This work will help you, with and without a calculator, to

- change between fractions, decimals and percentages
- find a percentage of a quantity
- write one quantity as a percentage of another

A Percentages, decimals and fractions

A scale can help you find equivalent decimals, fractions and percentages.
The scale is on sheet G111.

Some facts you need to know

$50\% = \frac{1}{2} = 0.5$

$25\% = \frac{1}{4} = 0.25$

$75\% = \frac{3}{4} = 0.75$

$1\% = \frac{1}{100} = 0.01$

$10\% = \frac{1}{10} = 0.1$

$20\% = \frac{1}{5} = 0.2$

$33\frac{1}{3}\% = \frac{1}{3} = 0.333\ldots = 0.\dot{3}$

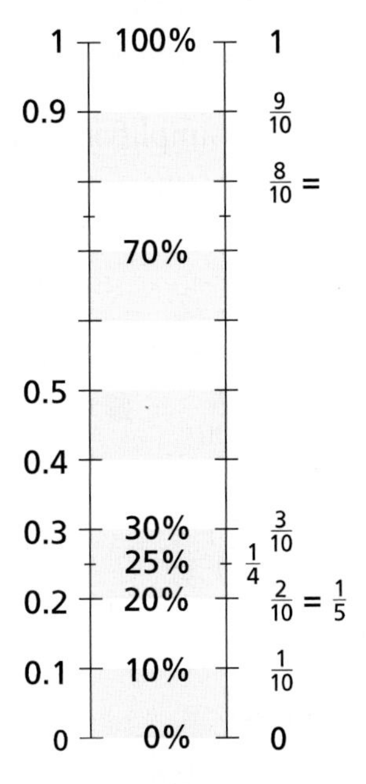

Other facts you can work out

$5\% = \frac{5}{100} = \frac{1}{20}$

$40\% = \frac{40}{100} = \frac{4}{10} = 0.4$

$\frac{4}{5} = \frac{80}{100} = 80\%$

$\frac{7}{20} = \frac{35}{100} = 0.35$

$\frac{56}{80} = \frac{7}{10} = \frac{70}{100} = 70\%$

$0.41 = \frac{41}{100} = 41\%$

$0.04 = \frac{4}{100} = \frac{1}{25}$

$16\frac{1}{2}\% = \frac{16.5}{100} = 0.165$

$0.745 = \frac{745}{1000} = \frac{74.5}{100} = 74.5\%$

A1

A	C	D	E	G	H	I	M	N	O	P	R
$\frac{3}{4}$	5%	0.01	10%	$\frac{2}{5}$	80%	$33\frac{1}{3}\%$	0.5	25%	$\frac{1}{5}$	$\frac{3}{10}$	0.9

Use this code to find a letter for each fraction, decimal or percentage below.
Rearrange each set of letters to spell a city.

(a) $\frac{1}{2}$ $\frac{10}{100}$ $\frac{9}{10}$ 0.2

(b) $\frac{1}{100}$ 1% $\frac{1}{3}$ 0.75 90% 50%

(c) $\frac{75}{100}$ 0.4 $\frac{5}{100}$ $\frac{1}{20}$ 0.333… $\frac{80}{100}$ $\frac{2}{10}$

(d) 30% $\frac{8}{10}$ 40% $\frac{25}{100}$ 20% $\frac{1}{10}$ $\frac{1}{4}$ 0.05 75% 0.1

A2 Try this without looking at the information on the previous page.

A	D	E	I	J	K	L	M	N	O	R	S	T	V	W
$\frac{1}{2}$	$\frac{4}{100}$	40%	0.75	45%	$\frac{1}{5}$	6%	0.01	0.8	$\frac{5}{100}$	$\frac{1}{3}$	$\frac{1}{4}$	60%	0.3	10%

Use this code to find a letter for each fraction, decimal or percentage below. Rearrange each set of letters to spell a mountain.

(a) 25% $\frac{4}{10}$ $\frac{2}{5}$ 0.4 0.6 $0.\dot{3}$ 30%

(b) 80% 0.1 $\frac{8}{10}$ 4% 0.25 5% $\frac{1}{20}$

(c) $\frac{4}{5}$ 1% 75% 20% 50% $\frac{3}{4}$ 0.06 0.45 0.5 $33\frac{1}{3}$% 0.05

A3 Write these percentages as decimals.

(a) 99% (b) 3% (c) 16% (d) 7% (e) 70%
(f) 30% (g) 49.5% (h) 12.6% (i) 2.5% (j) $12\frac{1}{2}$%

A4 Write these percentages as fractions, simplifying where possible.

(a) 60% (b) 35% (c) 48% (d) 8% (e) 33%

A5 Write these fractions as percentages.

(a) $\frac{7}{10}$ (b) $\frac{42}{50}$ (c) $\frac{7}{25}$ (d) $\frac{3}{5}$ (e) $\frac{9}{20}$

A6 Copy and complete $\frac{6}{40} = \frac{\blacksquare}{20} = \frac{\blacksquare}{100} = \blacksquare\,\%$

A7 Write these fractions as percentages.

(a) $\frac{18}{40}$ (b) $\frac{48}{80}$ (c) $\frac{27}{30}$ (d) $\frac{64}{200}$ (e) $\frac{9}{12}$

A8 Write $\frac{1}{8}$ as a percentage.

A9 Write these decimals as percentages.

(a) 0.55 (b) 0.07 (c) 0.8 (d) 0.375 (e) 0.015

A10 Find six matching pairs. Which card is left unmatched?

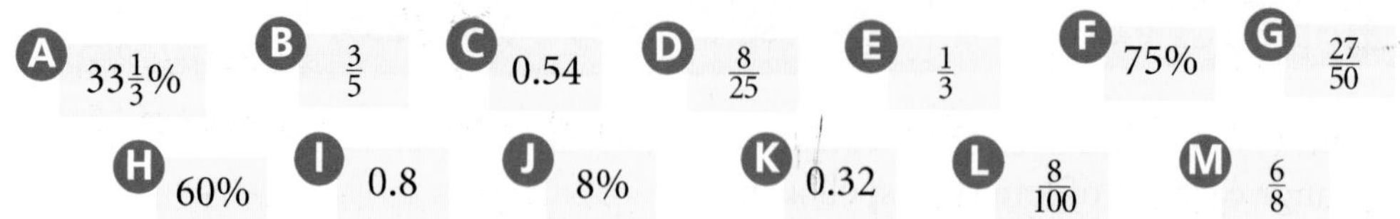

A11 Match these cards in groups of three.

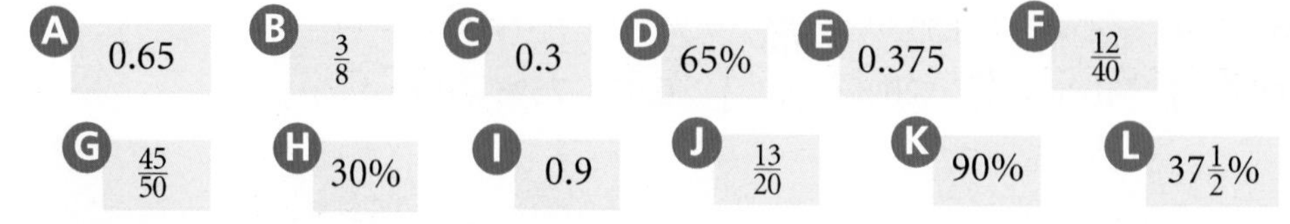

A12 For each set of decimals, percentages and fractions, put them in order, smallest first.

(a) 0.5 $\frac{1}{10}$ 49% $\frac{1}{4}$ 20%
(b) $\frac{4}{5}$ 76% 0.9 0.08 5%
(c) $\frac{1}{3}$ $\frac{2}{5}$ 45% 33% 0.03
(d) $\frac{1}{5}$ 5% 0.4 4% 51%

B *Percentage of a quantity*

100% is 84

50% is **?** 25% is **?** 75% is **?** 10% is **?** 5% is **?** 60% is **?** 15% is **?** 45% is **?**

B1 Pete has 32 apple trees.
25% of them are diseased.
How many of Pete's apple trees are diseased?

B2 In a class of 30 students, 10% have a weekend job.
How many students is this?

B3 75% of workers in a factory are full-time.
There are 120 workers. How many work full-time?

B4 A farmer has 60 sheep.
One year 40% of them have lambs.
How many have lambs?

B5 Sarah spent 10% of her £3.50 allowance on sweets. How much was this?

B6 Pete had £18 and spent 5% of his money. How much was this?

B7 Rasha saved 25% of her weekly allowance of £5. How much did she save?

B8 Work these out.

(a) 50% of £45
(b) 75% of £24
(c) 5% of 40p
(d) 25% of 60p
(e) 10% of £4.10
(f) 20% of £3
(g) 30% of £8
(h) 60% of £5

B9 Which of these is greater, and by how much? 10% of £20 or 15% of £12

B10 Which of these is smaller, and by how much? 30% of £18 or 40% of £15

B11 A cheesecake weighs 420 grams and 35% of the cheesecake is fat.
How many grams of fat are in the cheesecake?

B12 Pair up these amounts. Which amount is unmatched?

A 20% of £15 | **B** 10% of £18 | **C** 5% of £60 | **D** 30% of £6

E 15% of £40 | **F** 25% of £16 | **G** 80% of £5

B13 Work these out.

(a) 15% of 60 grams (b) 5% of 50 kg (c) 35% of 70 m

B14 (a) Work out 5% of £45.

(b) How could you use your answer to (a) to find 95% of £45?

B15 Work these out. (a) 95% of £38 (b) 90% of £10.40

B16 Work out $33\frac{1}{3}$% of these.

(a) £12 (b) 21 kg (c) 450 m (d) 213 cm

VAT (Value Added Tax) is added to many things before you buy them.
The rate of VAT is $17\frac{1}{2}$%.

Here is one method of working out the VAT for £60.

> Find $17\frac{1}{2}$% of £60.
>
> 10% of £60 = £6
>
> 5% of £60 = £3
>
> $2\frac{1}{2}$% of £60 = £1.50
>
> So $17\frac{1}{2}$% of £60 = £10.50

B17 Find the VAT at $17\frac{1}{2}$% on £40.

B18 Find $17\frac{1}{2}$% of these.

(a) £300 (b) £28 (c) £130 (d) £12.80

1% of £1

1% of £1 = 1p
13% of £1 = 13p

1% of £4 = 4p
23% of £4 = 23 × 4p = 92p

B19 Find these.

(a) 1% of £7 (b) 6% of £7 (c) 32% of £7 (d) 8% of £8 (e) 4% of £15

B20 (a) Find 1% of £24. (b) Find 99% of £24. (c) Find 2% of £5.

(d) Find 98% of £5. (e) Find 99% of £75. (f) Find 98% of £120.

***B21** Are these statements true?
Can you explain why?

3% of £8 = 8% of £3

5% of £13 = 13% of £5

When finding percentages without a calculator, it is often easiest to find 10% first.

Examples

Find 30% of £12.

10% of £12 = £12 ÷ 10 = £1.20
So 30% of £12 = £1.20 × 3 = £3.60

Find 45% of 60.

10% of 60 = 60 ÷ 10 = 6

40% of 60 = 6 × 4 = 24
5% of 60 = 6 ÷ 2 = 3

So 45% of 60 = 24 + 3 = 27

C *One number as a percentage of another*

To find one number as a percentage of another, you can start with a fraction and try to make the denominator 100.

Examples

Out of a class of 20 students, 13 of them watch *Eastenders*. What percentage watch it?

$$\frac{13}{20} \overset{\times 5}{=} \frac{65}{100} = 65\%$$

Out of a class of 30 students, 6 of them don't eat breakfast. What percentage don't eat breakfast?

$$\frac{6}{30} \overset{\div 6}{=} \frac{1}{5} \overset{\times 20}{=} \frac{20}{100} = 20\%$$

C1 Out of a total of 20 people, 18 of them said they felt happier in the summer than in the winter. What percentage is this?

C2 In a survey, 24 out of 40 people chose chicken tikka massala as their favourite meal. What percentage is this?

C3 Ibrar sat three tests. These were his results.

Geography	35 out of 50
French	32 out of 40
Science	17 out of 25

(a) Find his percentage mark for each test.

(b) In which test did he get the highest percentage?

C4 Write the following as percentages and put them in order of size, smallest first.

A 36 out of 60

B 200 out of 250

C 18 out of 45

D 14 out of 56

E 9 out of 12

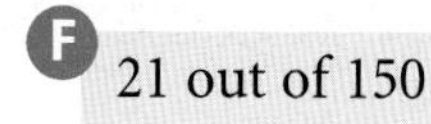
F 21 out of 150

C5 This bag contains some different sweets.

(a) What percentage of the sweets are

(i) Mintos (ii) Toffees (iii) Humbugs

(b) The Toffees and Choccos are wrapped in red paper. What percentage of the sweets are wrapped in red?

(c) Freda doesn't like Munchos. What percentage of the sweets does she like?

(d) Dean only likes Mintos and Munchos. What percentage does he like?

D *A canoe club*

Come to the Carolina Canoe Club.

We offer a range of exciting activities every Saturday.

Open to all ages.
We have 240 members.

D1 50% of the members are juniors.
How many members is this?

D2 60 members are aged 16 to 21.
What percentage are in this age group?

D3 10% of the members go canoeing every Monday evening.
How many is this?

D4 36 of the members have a life-saving certificate.
What percentage is this?

D5 55% of the club members are male.
How many males are in the canoe club?

D6 80% attend the summer barbecue.
How many come to the barbecue?

D7 One fifth of the members can do an 'Eskimo roll'.

(a) What percentage is this?

(b) How many can do an 'Eskimo roll'?

D8 84 took part on the last marathon race.
What percentage took part in this race?

D9 Two thirds attend the Annual General Meeting of the club.
How many of the members go to the meeting?

D10 Three fifths have their own canoes.

(a) What percentage is this?

(b) How many have their own canoes?

E *Percentage of a quantity (with a calculator)*

To find a percentage of a quantity, you can change the percentage into a decimal and then multiply.

$23\% = \frac{23}{100} = 0.23$

Find 23% of £140.

0.23 x 140 = 32.2

So 23% of £140 = £32.20

E1 35% of Kim's bar of chocolate is fat.
The bar weighs 120 grams.
How much fat is in this bar of chocolate?

E2 85% of the 9700 households in a village own a car.
To the nearest hundred, how many households own a car?

E3 In a town of 15 400 people, 32% own a bicycle but only 7% regularly cycle.
Find to the nearest hundred,

(a) how many people own a bicycle in this town

(b) how many people regularly cycle

E4 Work these out.

(a) 34% of 86 (b) 62% of 140 (c) 57% of 230

(d) 8% of 4500 (e) 12% of 32.5 (f) 90% of 3725

E5 82% of UK teenagers are worried about exams.
52% of UK teenagers worry about skin problems.

Out of a year group of 180, how many would you expect to

(a) worry about exams (b) worry about skin problems

E6 In a town with a population of 56 000, it is estimated that 19% live on their own.
About how many people in this town live on their own?

E7 In many countries cattle or donkeys are used in harness for pulling ploughs or carts. This table shows the number of cattle and donkeys and the percentage used for work in harness, in various African countries.

Country	Cattle		Donkeys	
	Total number	% used in harness	Total number	% used in harness
Angola	3 100 000	10%	5000	100%
Botswana	2 616 000	14%	152 000	92%
Mali	5 000 000	5%	550 000	27%
Senegal	2 740 000	5%	310 000	50%

(a) How many cattle work in harness in Mali?

(b) Which country uses the largest number of cattle in harness? Show how you decided on your answer.

(c) Which country uses the largest number of donkeys in harness?

(d) Which country uses in harness more donkeys than cattle?

E8 In a town of 15 000 only 1.4% of the population cycle to work.

(a) Write 1.4% as a decimal.

(b) How many people in this town cycle to work?

E9 Work these out.

(a) 17.6% of £850 (b) 60.8% of 600 kg (c) $3\frac{1}{2}$% of £5000

E10 Amanda has to pay a deposit of 2.25% on a car costing £13 500. How much deposit does she have to pay?

F *One number as a percentage of another (with a calculator)*

Example

Rose earns £320 each week.
One week, she spent £65 on food.
What percentage of her earnings went on food?

Write the value as a fraction and change it to a decimal by dividing.

$\frac{65}{320} = 65 \div 320 = 0.203\,125$

Multiply by 100 to change the decimal to a percentage.

$0.203\,125 \times 100 = 20.3125$

Round your answer to one decimal place if necessary.

So 20.3% of Rose's earnings went on food.

F1 In a school 115 of the 250 pupils in year 10 own a bicycle. What percentage is this?

F2 The table shows how 1560 students travel to their school in the morning.

Copy and complete the table to show the percentage of pupils in each category.

Method of transport	Number of students	% of students
Bus	313	20.1%
Car	216	
Bicycle	377	
Walk	654	
Total	1560	

F3 In Kenya there are 420 000 motor vehicles and 32 000 of these are motorbikes. What percentage of the motor vehicles in Kenya are motorbikes?

F4 In 1996, there were the following motor vehicles in the UK.

- 21 172 000 passenger vehicles
- 3 011 000 commercial vehicles
- 609 000 motorbikes

(a) How many motor vehicles were there in total in the UK in 1996?

(b) What percentage were passenger vehicles?

F5 This table shows the estimated number of donkeys in North Africa in 1996.

North African country	Number of donkeys (thousands)
Algeria	230
Egypt	1690
Libya	55
Morocco	880
Tunisia	230
Total	3085

(a) How many donkeys are there in Egypt?

(b) What percentage of North African donkeys are found in Egypt?

(c) What percentage are found in Tunisia?

(d) Is it true that about 18% of North African donkeys are found in Libya?

G *Mixed questions*

G1 This pie chart shows information about how often adults used a motor vehicle in Great Britain in 1995.

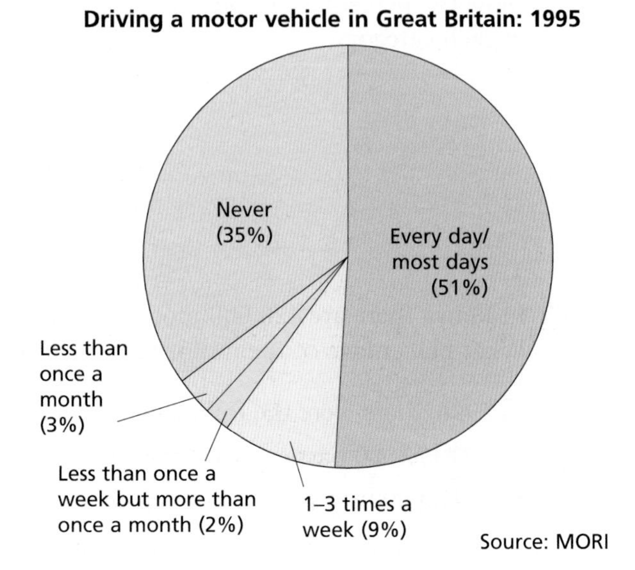

(a) What percentage of people drove at least once in 1995?

(b) A town had a population of 17 600 adults in 1995.

Find an estimate for these.

(i) The number of these adults who drove most days in 1995

(ii) The number who drove less than once a month

(iii) The number who drove once a week or more

G2 This table shows data on the use of the Channel Tunnel in 1996.

Use of the Channel Tunnel in 1996

Purpose	UK residents (thousands)	Non-residents (thousands)
Holiday	1910	1458
Business	666	481
Visiting friends and relatives	299	498
Other	583	271
Total	3458	2708

(a) How many UK residents used the Channel Tunnel in 1996?

(b) What percentage of UK residents using the tunnel were going on holiday?

(c) What percentage of people not resident in the UK used the tunnel for a business trip?

(d) What percentage of all users of the tunnel were visiting friends and relatives?

G3 France has a total road network of 805 070 kilometres.
Motorways make up a total of 6570 km.
90.0% of the total network is paved.

(a) What percentage of French roads are motorways?

(b) How many kilometres of French roads are unpaved?

Test yourself

T1 In a school council election, a total of 360 pupils voted.
90 pupils voted for Tanya Filton. What percentage voted for Tanya?

T2 A group of 40 women applied to go on an art trip.
Only 80% of all the women who applied went on the trip.
How many women went on the trip?

T3 A pupil carries out a survey in her town centre.
She chooses 200 people at random.
70 of these people say they use local swimming pool.
What percentage is 70 out of 200?

T4 400 members of a Sports Club are asked, 'What is your favourite sport?'
The pie chart shows the results.

(a) What percentage chose tennis?

(b) How many members chose volleyball?

(c) Calculate the size of the angle for football.
Show all your working.

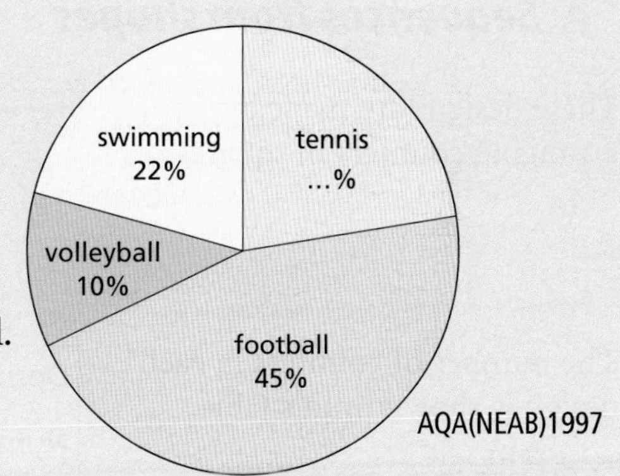

AQA(NEAB)1997

T5 There are 3270 students at a university.
At this university 1962 students have a part-time job.
What percentage of the students have a part-time job?

T6 In a survey it was found that 165 out of 440 people had been to France on holiday that year. What percentage of the people took a holiday in France?

T7 At Roughwood School there are 186 students in year 11.
101 are boys. What percentage of the students are boys?

T8 One year, a garage sells 560 cars.
$62\frac{1}{2}$% of these cars were a shade of red.
How many of these cars were red?

T9 A carriage in a train has 60 seats.
Only one of these is reserved for disabled passengers.
What percentage of seats are reserved for disabled passengers?

T10 In 1995 police carried out a total of 702.7 thousand breath tests.
13% of them were positive. How many was this, correct to the nearest thousand?

14 Sequences

You should know how to find the value of simple expressions such as 10 – 2n, n2 + 3.

This work will help you

- form sequences of numbers such as odds, evens, squares and triangle numbers
- find and use rules to continue a variety of sequences
- find and use rules for the *n*th term of linear and simple non-linear sequences
- find a sequence from a context, find a rule for the *n*th term and explain how you found it

A *Sequences from shapes*

These designs are made by arranging counters in squares.

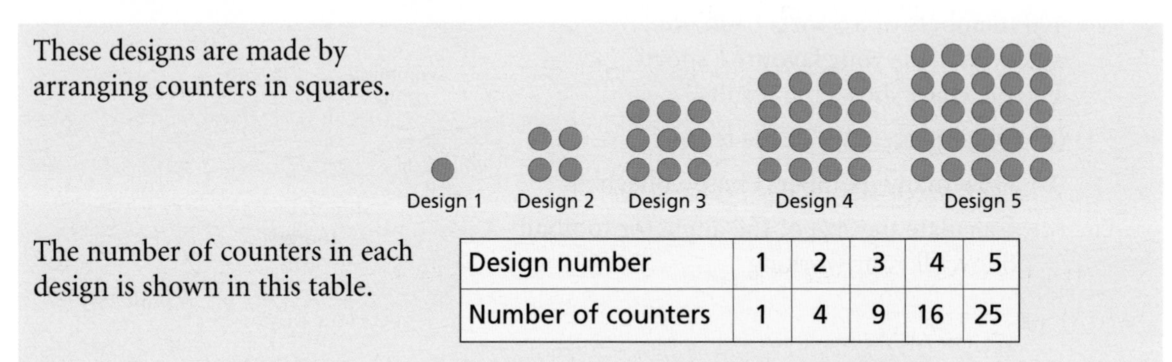

The number of counters in each design is shown in this table.

Design number	1	2	3	4	5
Number of counters	1	4	9	16	25

The numbers in the sequence 1, 4, 9, 16, 25, … are called **square numbers.**

A1 (a) Find the 6th square number.

(b) What is the 20th square number?

A2 These designs are made by arranging counters in L-shapes.

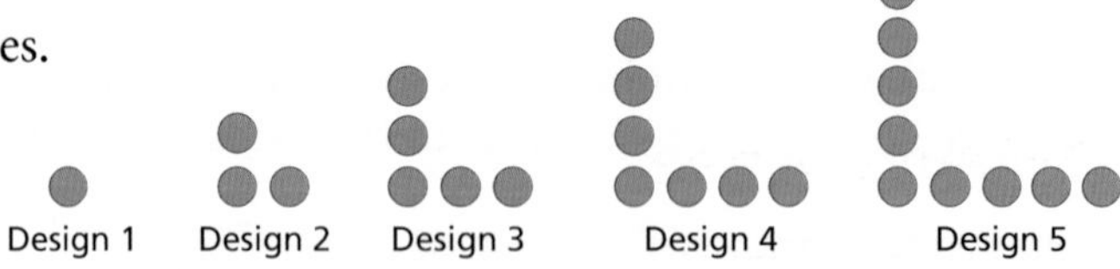

(a) Copy and complete this table for these designs.

Design number	1	2	3	4	5
Number of counters	1				

(b) How many counters are in the 6th design?

(c) How many counters are needed to make the 15th design?
Explain how you worked out your answer.

(d) Which design uses 99 counters?

(e) Is it possible to make one of these designs with 40 counters? Explain your answer.

A3 These designs are made by arranging counters in triangles.

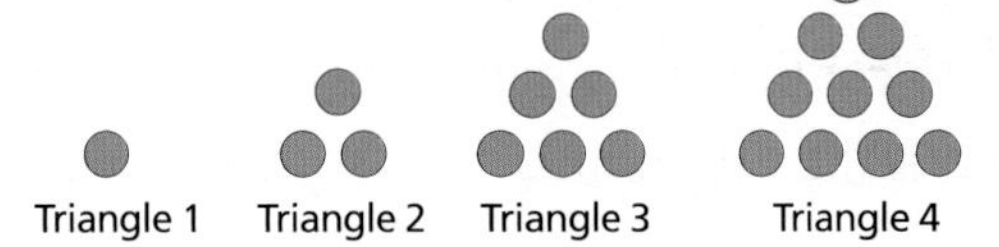

(a) Draw the next two designs.

(b) Copy and complete this table.

Design number	1	2	3	4	5	6
Number of counters			6			

(c) The numbers of counters are called **triangle numbers**.
So, for example, the third triangle number is 6.

List the first ten triangle numbers.

A4 These lattice designs are all models of salt crystals.
They are cube-shaped.

(a) Work out the number of ions in crystal 3 without counting them all.

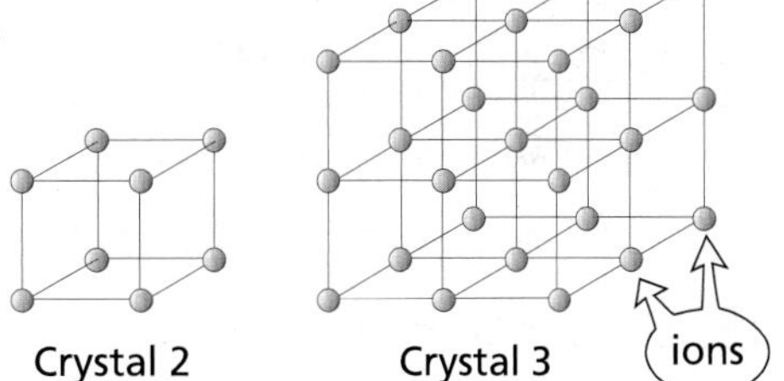

(b) Copy and complete this table.

Crystal number	1	2	3
Number of ions		8	

(c) Without drawing, work out how many ions will be in crystal 4.

(d) The numbers of ions are called **cubic numbers** or cubes.
So, for example, the second cubic number is 8.

What is the 10th cubic number?

B *Following a rule*

In sequences of numbers, there is often a rule to go from one term to the next.
Some examples are

Sequence	**Rule**
8, 16, 24, 32, 40, …	Add 8 to the previous term
8, 16, 32, 64, 128, …	Multiply the previous term by 2
4, 5, 7, 10, 14, …	Add 1, then add 2, then add 3 and so on
4, 5, 9, 14, 23, …	Add the previous two terms together

Sequences where the rule is to **add or subtract the same amount** each time are **linear.**

B1 A sequence of numbers begins 5, 9, 13, …

The rule to continue this sequence is 'add 4 to the previous term'.

(a) What is the next term? (b) What is the 8th term?

(c) Is the sequence linear?

B2 A sequence of numbers begins 5, 9, 17, …

The rule to continue this sequence is 'multiply the previous term by 2 and subtract 1'.

(a) What is the next term? (b) What is the 6th term?

(c) Is the sequence linear?

B3 (a) Write down the next two numbers in this sequence 4, 7, 10, 13, 16, …

(b) Write down a rule to find the next two numbers.

B4 Write down the next two terms in the sequence 0, 2, 6, 14, …

B5 A sequence of numbers begins 3, 4, 6, 9, 13, 18, ...

(a) Describe a rule to go from one term to the next.

(b) Using your rule, what is the 7th term of this sequence?

(c) Is the sequence linear?

B6 For each of the following sequences

- describe a rule to go from one term to the next
- find the 8th term

(a) 1, 8, 15, 22, 29, … (b) 35, 30, 25, 20, 15, … (c) 1.5, 3, 6, 12, 24, …

(d) 800, 400, 200, 100, … (e) $\frac{1}{9}$, $\frac{1}{3}$, 1, 3, 9, … (f) 1, 4, 13, 40, 121, …

B7 The first four terms of a sequence are 1, 4, 7, 10, …
For this sequence, explain how you can work out the value of the 30th term.

B8 Copy each sequence and fill in the missing numbers.

(a) 5, 7, 9, __ , 13, __ , 17, 19, … (b) 1, 3, 7, 13, 21, 31, __ , 57, __ , …

(c) __ , 0.5, 1, 2, 4, 8, __ , 32, … (d) 1, 1, 2, 3, 5, 8, 13, __ , 34, 55, __ , …

(e) 1, 5, 13, 29, __ , 125, __ , …

B9 Each sequence below is linear.
Copy each sequence and fill in the missing numbers.

(a) 4, 6, __ , __ , __ , 14, … (b) 25, __ , 19, __ , 13, 10, …

(c) 1, __ , 11, __ , 21, __ , … (d) __ , 10, __ , __ , 19, __ , …

***B10** Find the missing expression in each linear sequence below.

(a) x, $x + 4$, ______ , $x + 12$, … (b) a, $a + b$, $a + 2b$, ______ , …

(c) $n - 5$, $n - 3$, $n - 1$, ______ , … (d) x, $x - y$, ______ , $x - 3y$, …

C The nth term

We can work out any term of a sequence if we have an expression for its nth term.

Example

The nth term of a sequence is $2n + 5$. Find the first six terms.

The **1**st term is $2 \times \mathbf{1} + 5 = \mathbf{7}$
The **2**nd term is $2 \times \mathbf{2} + 5 = \mathbf{9}$
The **3**rd term is $2 \times \mathbf{3} + 5 = \mathbf{11}$ … and so on.

We can show our results in a table.

Term numbers (n)	1	2	3	4	5	6	...
Terms of the sequence ($2n + 5$)	7	9	11	13	15	17	...

C1 Linear sequences can be found on this grid. Two are shown on the diagram.

(a) Find seven more linear sequences that have four terms or more.

Write down each sequence as an **increasing** sequence and find its next term.

(b) The expressions below give the nth terms of these sequences. Match each expression to its sequence.

44	34	24	14	4	3	6	9	12
40	30	5	20	10	11	5	8	1
44	37	30	23	16	9	2	7	3
4	11	23	21	22	12	1	6	9
1	7	26	20	28	9	8	5	0
3	31	10	15	34	30	12	4	8
36	6	11	13	40	0	1	3	2

$3n$ $6n - 2$ $10n - 6$ $2n + 1$ $4n$

$3n + 1$ $n + 2$ $5n + 1$ $7n - 5$

C2 An expression for the nth term of a sequence is $4n - 3$. Work out the fourth and fifth terms of the sequence.

C3 The nth term of a sequence is $2n + 3$.

(a) Write down the first six terms of the sequence.

(b) Calculate the 100th term.

C4 The nth terms of six different sequences are:

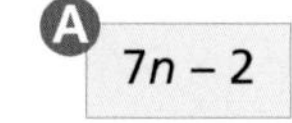

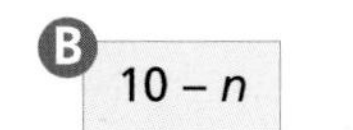

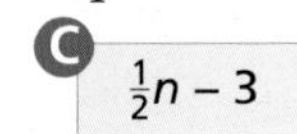

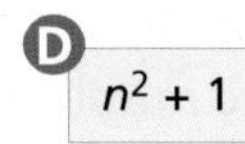

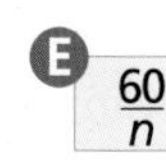

(a) Calculate the first five terms of each sequence.

(b) Calculate the 20th term of each sequence.

(c) Which of these sequences are linear?

D *The nth term of a linear sequence*

Find the nth term of the linear sequence 3, 7, 11, 15, 19, …

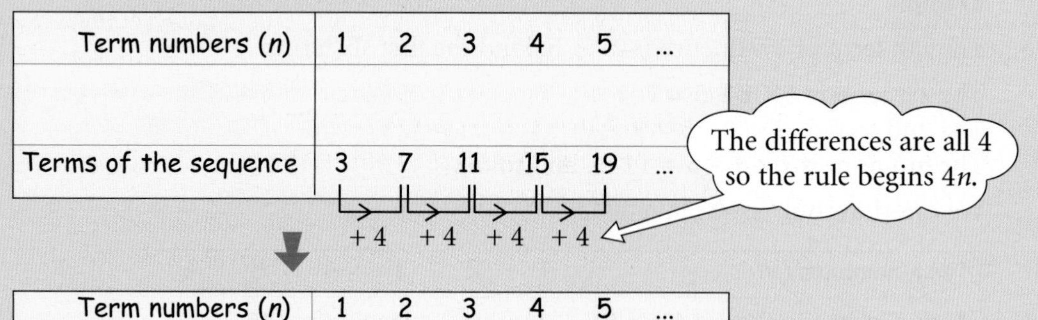

Term numbers (n)	1	2	3	4	5	…
Terms of the sequence	3	7	11	15	19	…

Term numbers (n)	1	2	3	4	5	…
$4n$	4	8	12	16	20	
Terms of the sequence	3	7	11	15	19	…

− 1

To get from 4 to 3 you can subtract 1. This works for all terms.

So a rule for the nth term of the linear sequence 3, 7, 11, 15, 19, … is $4n - 1$.

D1 For each of the following sequences

- find an expression for the nth term
- use your expression to work out the 50th term

(a) 4, 7, 10, 13, 16, … (b) 1, 10, 19, 28, 37, … (c) 2, 7, 12, 17, 22, …
(d) 4, 9, 14, 19, 24, … (e) 3, 5, 7, 9, 11, …

D2 This diagram shows house numbers on North Street.

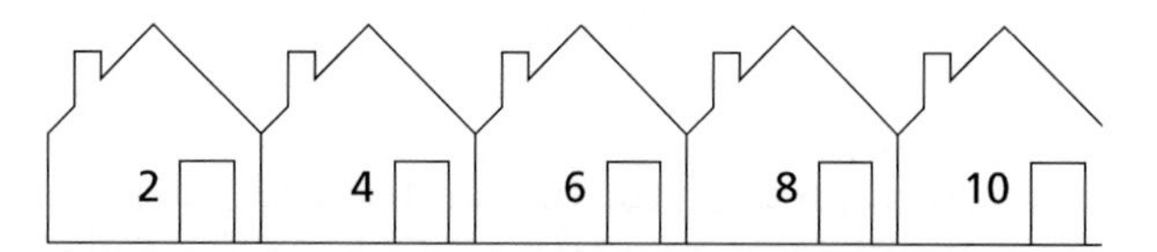

(a) What is the number of the 15th house ?

(b) Find an expression for the number of the nth house on North Street.

This diagram shows house numbers on South Street.

1 3 5 7 9

(c) What is the number of the 10th house?

(d) Find an expression for the number of the nth house on South Street.

(e) What are the house numbers of the 50th house in each street?

D3 (a) Copy and complete this table for the linear sequence 40, 38, 36, 34, 32, … .

Term numbers (n)	1	2	3	4	5	…
^-2n	$^-2$	$^-4$	?	?	?	
Terms of the sequence	40	38	36	34	32	…

(? from $^-2$ to 40)

The differences are all $^-2$ so look at ^-2n.

(b) What is an expression for the nth term of the sequence?

(c) Calculate the 20th term in the sequence.

D4 For each of the following sequences, find an expression for the nth term.

(a) 30, 28, 26, 24, 22, …
(b) 40, 37, 34, 31, 28, …
(c) 33, 28, 23, 18, 13, …
(d) 60, 54, 48, 42, 36, …

E *Not just linear sequences*

Each of the expressions below gives the nth term of a sequence.

- Investigate these sequences.

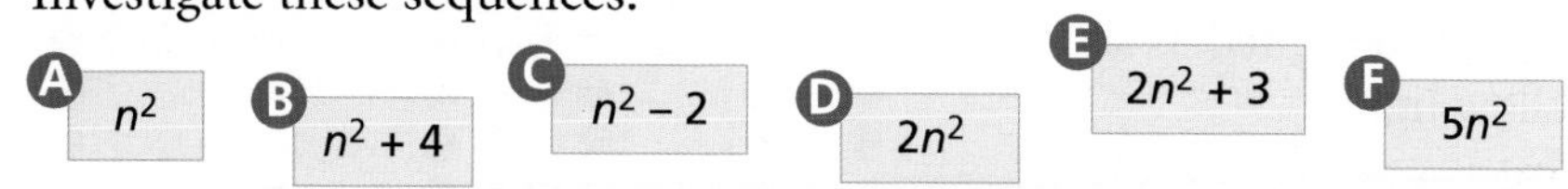

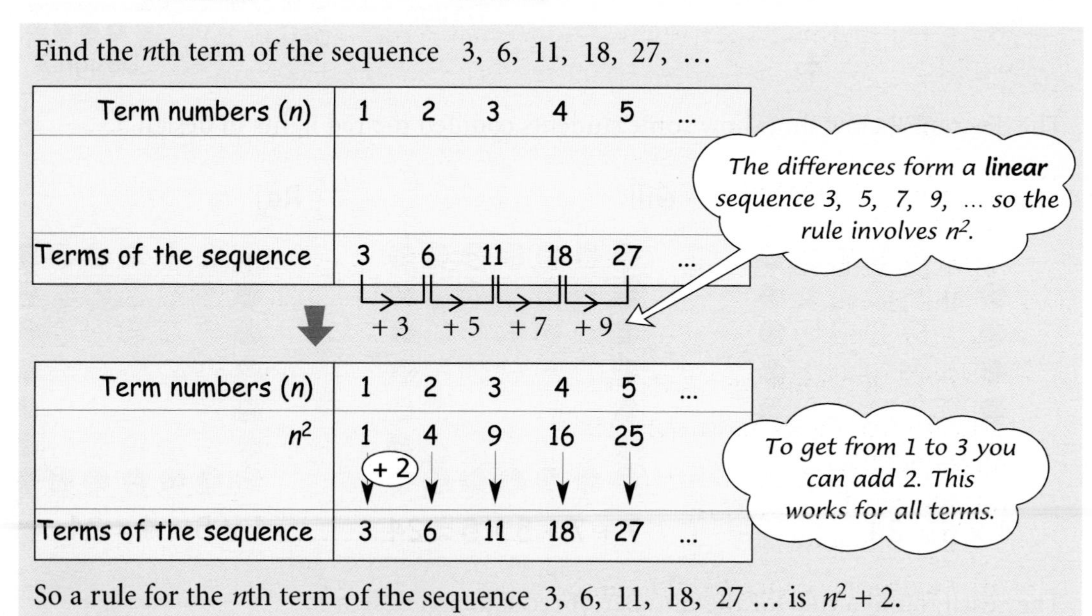

Find the nth term of the sequence 3, 6, 11, 18, 27, …

Term numbers (n)	1	2	3	4	5	…
Terms of the sequence	3	6	11	18	27	…

+3 +5 +7 +9

The differences form a **linear** sequence 3, 5, 7, 9, … so the rule involves n^2.

Term numbers (n)	1	2	3	4	5	…
n^2	1	4	9	16	25	
Terms of the sequence	3	6	11	18	27	…

(+ 2)

To get from 1 to 3 you can add 2. This works for all terms.

So a rule for the nth term of the sequence 3, 6, 11, 18, 27 … is $n^2 + 2$.

E1 A sequence of numbers begins 2, 5, 10, 17, 26, 37, …

(a) What is the next term in the sequence?

(b) Explain how you can tell that the sequence is not linear.

(c) What is an expression for the nth term of this sequence?

E2 (a) A sequence of numbers begins 4, 7, 12, 19, 28, …
What is an expression for the nth term of this sequence?

(b) Calculate the 15th term.

E3 (a) A sequence of numbers begins 3, 12, 27, 48, 75, …
What is an expression for the nth term of this sequence?

(b) Calculate the 10th term.

E4 (a) A sequence of numbers begins 2, 8, 18, 32, 50, 72, …
What is an expression for the nth term of this sequence?

(b) What is the nth term of the sequence 3, 9, 19, 33, 51, 73, … ?

E5 For each of the following sequences, find an expression for the nth term.

(a) 0, 3, 8, 15, 24, … (b) 11, 14, 19, 26, 35, …

(c) 4, 16, 36, 64, … (d) 5, 17, 37, 65, …

F *Ways of seeing*

TG

Some disco light units are designed as shown.
They use red and yellow lights.

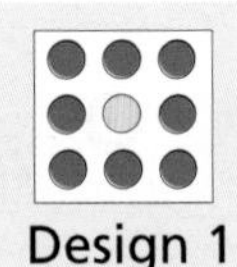
Design 1

Design 2

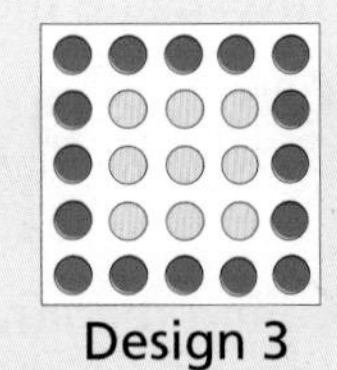
Design 3

The diagrams below show how some students counted the red lights in design 5.

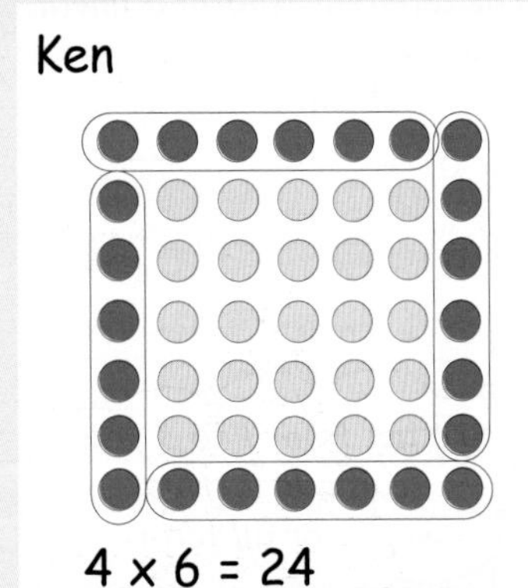

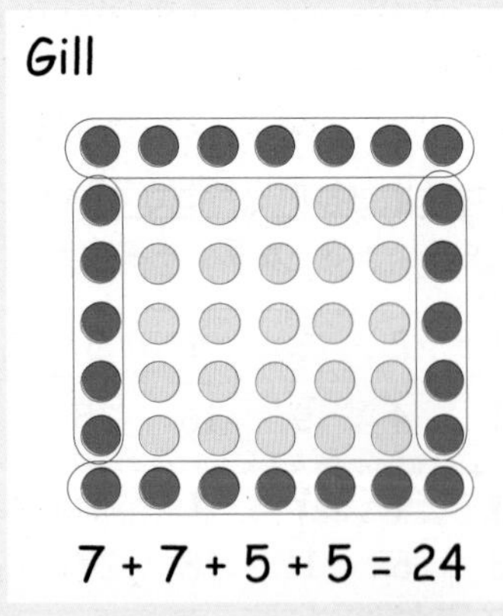

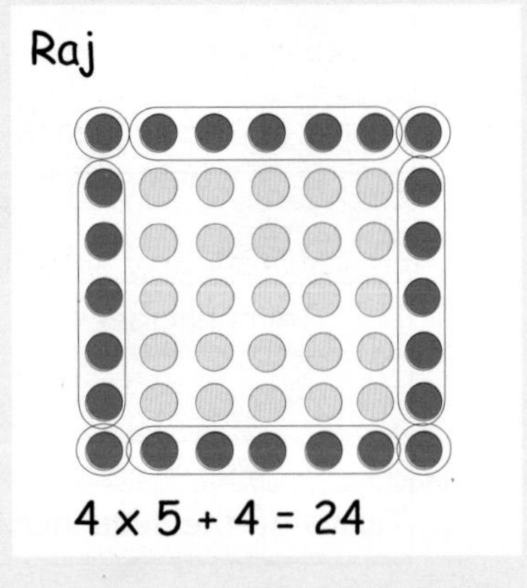

They each found a rule for the number of red lights in design n.

$r = (n + 2) + (n + 2) + n + n$

$r = 4n + 4$

$r = 4(n + 1)$

Who do you think found each rule?

F1 Here is another design for square light units.

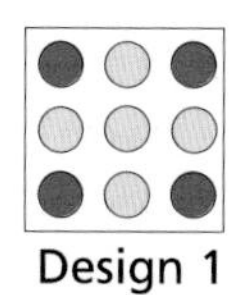
Design 1

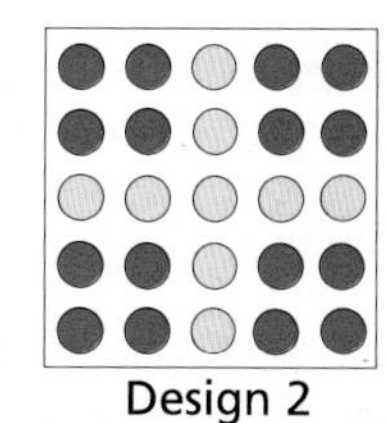
Design 2

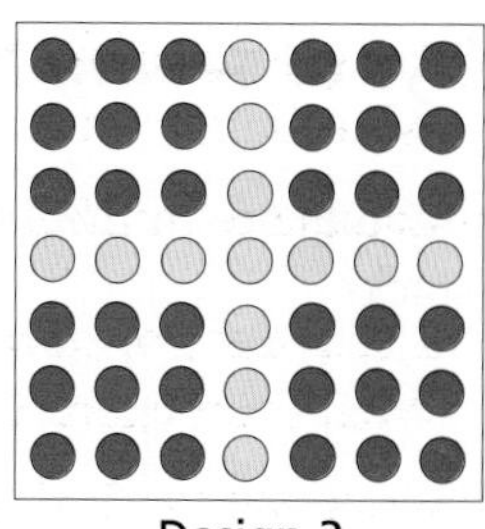
Design 3

(a) Draw a diagram to show design 4.

(b) For design 4, what is the number of yellow lights?

(c) How many yellow lights would you need for design 10?

(d) Find a rule for the number of yellow lights in design n.
Explain how you found your rule.

(e) How many yellow lights would you need for design 50?

(f) Find a rule for the number of red lights in design n.

F2 Here are some rectangular units.

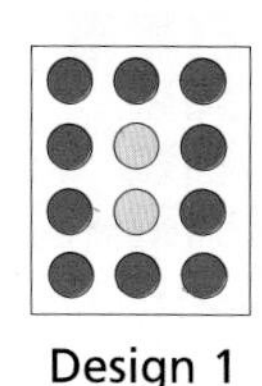
Design 1

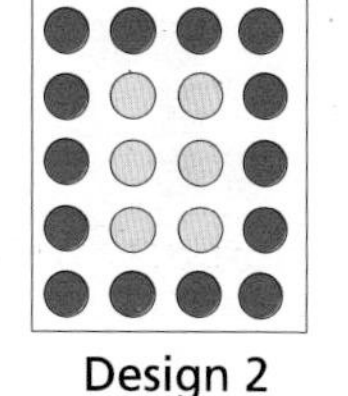
Design 2

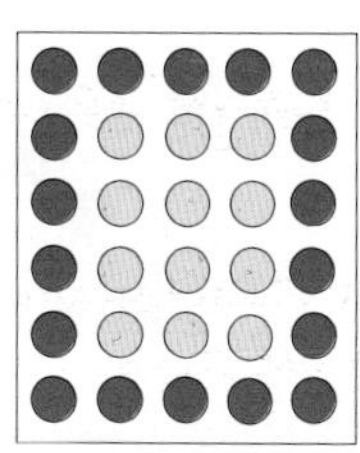
Design 3

(a) For design 3, what is the number of red lights?

(b) How many red lights would you need for design 8?

(c) Find a rule for the number of red lights in design n.
Explain how you found your rule.

(d) How many red lights would you need for design 100?

(e) Find a rule for the number of yellow lights in design n.

*F3 Here are some triangular units.

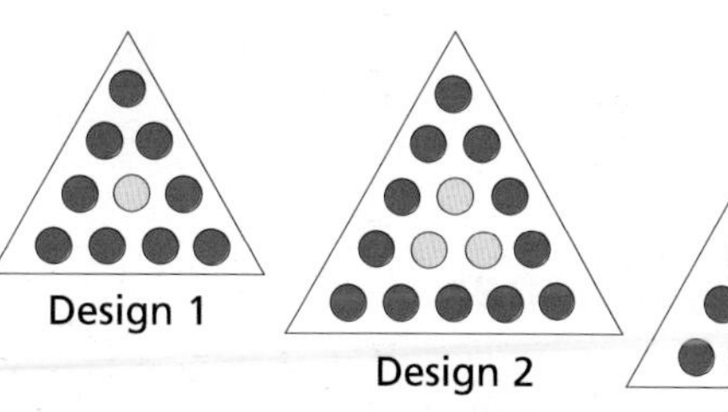

(a) Find a rule for the number of red lights in design n.
Explain how you found your rule.

(b) How many red lights would you need for design 100?

G *Ways of seeing further*

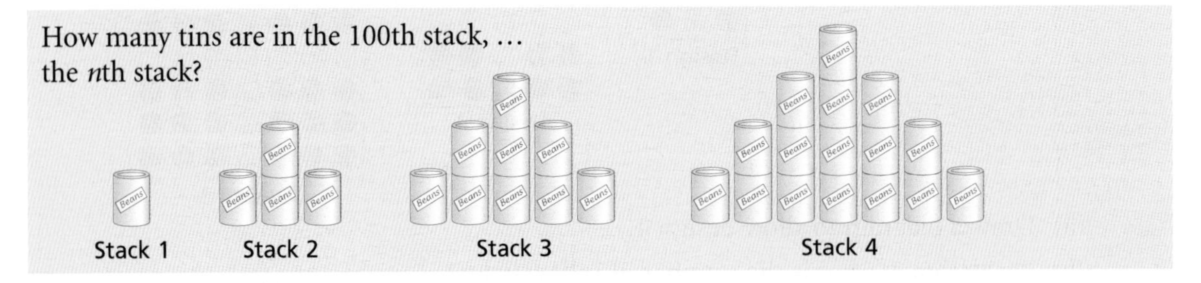

How many tins are in the 100th stack, …
the *n*th stack?

*G1 For each set of patterns below

- draw pattern 5
- find a rule for the number of black tiles in the *n*th pattern
- find a rule for the number of white tiles in the *n*th pattern

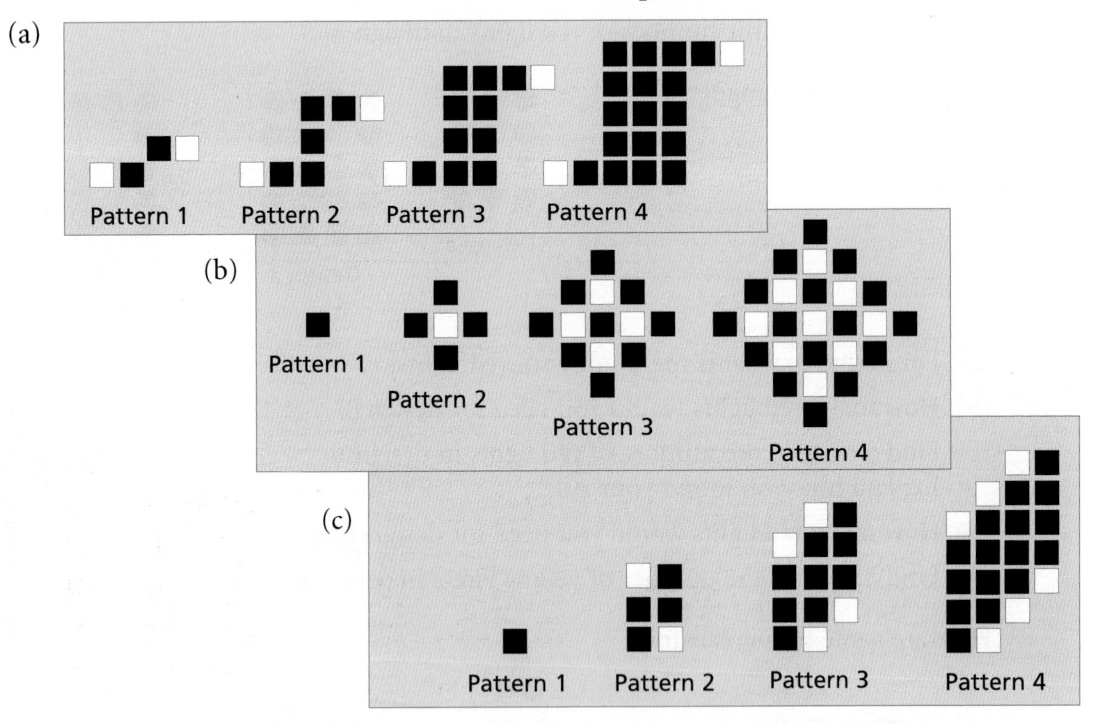

H *Seeing even further*

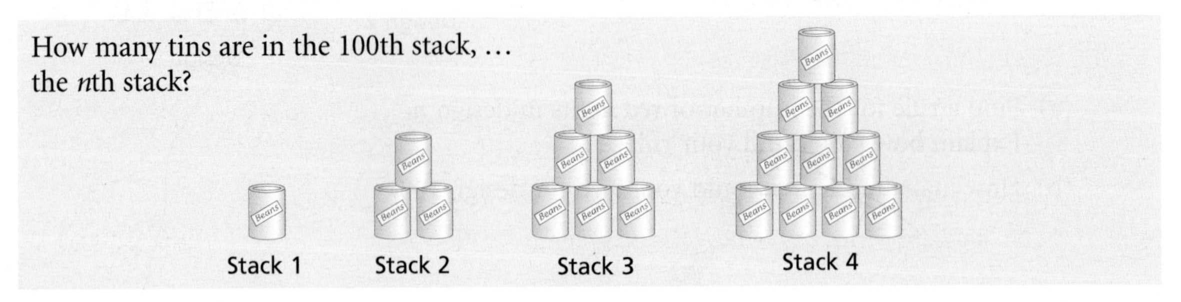

How many tins are in the 100th stack, …
the *n*th stack?

*H1 The diagrams below show how to draw a 'mystic rose'.

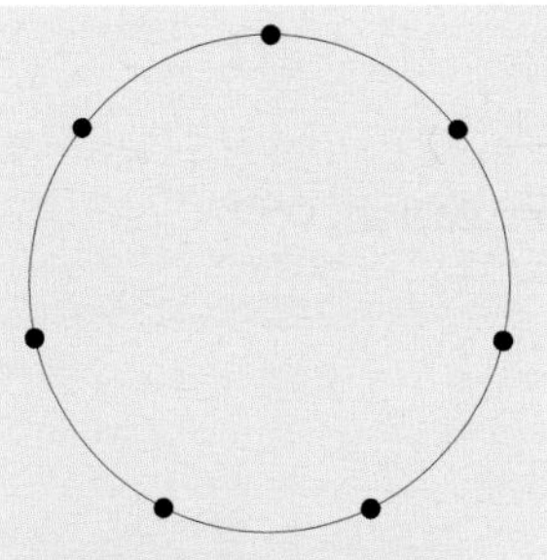
Mark equally spaced points round a circle.

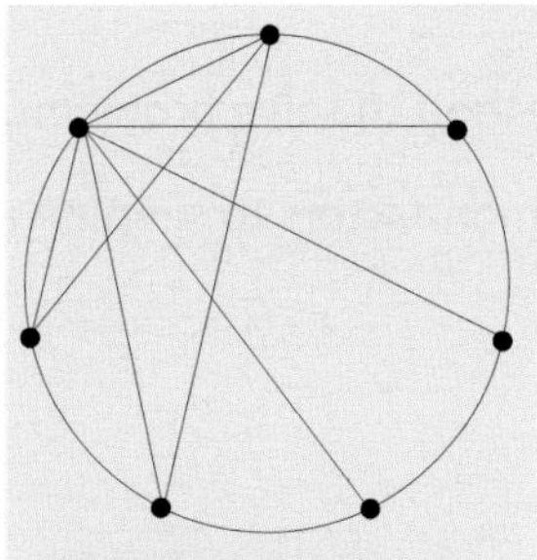
Join the points with straight lines.

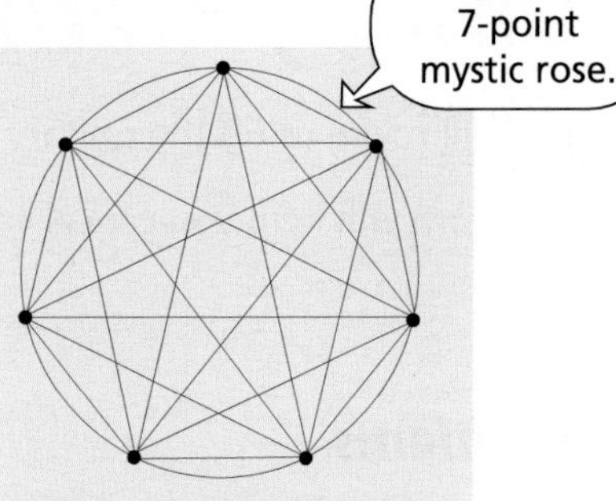

Continue until no more lines are possible.

(a) Draw three different mystic roses.
How many straight lines are in each of your designs?

(b) How many lines would be in a 20-point mystic rose?

(c) Find a rule for the number of lines in a n-point mystic rose.

Test yourself

T1 Write down the next two terms in the sequence 10, 11, 13, 16, 20, …

T2 (a) Find the eighth term of the sequence whose nth term is $4n - 1$.

(b) Find the nth term of the sequence whose first four terms are

2 8 14 20

OCR

T3 Each of these patterns uses black tiles.

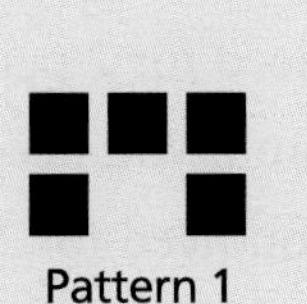
Pattern 1

Pattern 2

Pattern 3

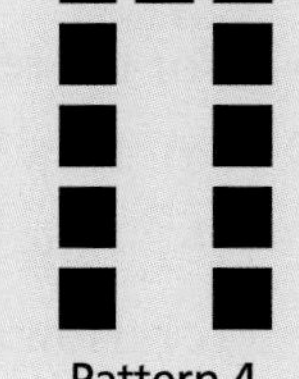
Pattern 4

(a) How many black tiles will be in pattern 5?

(b) How many black tiles will be in pattern 10?

(c) What is an expression for the number of black tiles in pattern n?
Explain how you found your expression.

(d) How many black tiles will be in pattern 100?

T4 A sequence of numbers is shown below.

4 7 12 19 28 39

(a) Write down the next term in the sequence.

(b) Find an expression for the nth term of this sequence.

(c) Calculate the 30th term of the sequence.

AQA(SEG)1999

15 Unitary method

You will revise using the unitary method to solve problems.

This work will help you cancel common factors to simplify a calculation.

A Problems

TG

Prawns with feta cheese

Serves 4

- 2 onions
- 2 large cans chopped tomatoes
- 360 g large peeled prawns
- 100 g feta cheese
- 3 tbsp chopped fresh parsley

What weight of prawns do you need for 6 people?

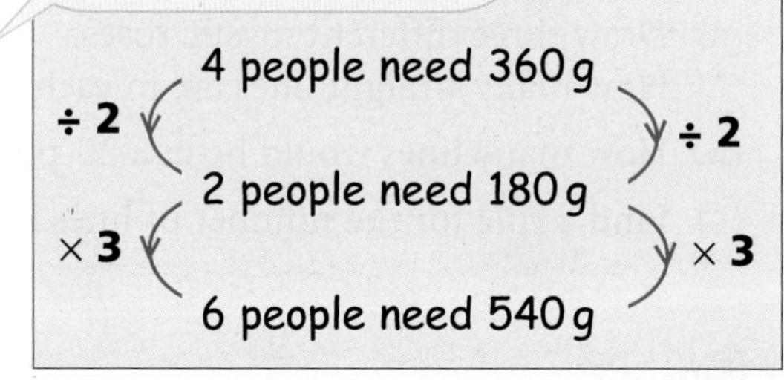

What weight of prawns do you need for 7 people?

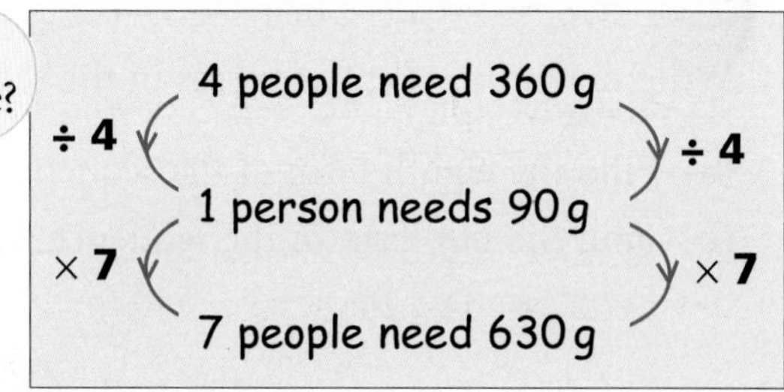

A1 For the recipe above, work these out in your head.

(a) How many onions would you need for 2 people?

(b) How many cans of tomatoes would you need for 6 people?

(c) How much feta cheese would you need for 3 people?

(d) How much parsley would you need for 2 people?

A2 Work these out in your head.

(a) The cost of 3 fruit chews is 12p.
Work out the cost of 5 fruit chews.

(b) The cost of 5 metres of ribbon is £1.50.
Find the cost of 3 metres of the same ribbon.

(c) You need 6 slices of bread for marmalade pudding for 4 people.
How many slices would you need for 6 people?

A3 Here are the ingredients for poached apricots.

(a) What weight of apricots would you need to make poached apricots for 2 people?

(b) How many cardamom pods would you need for 7 people?

(c) How much sugar would you need for 8 people?

(d) What weight of pistachios would you need for 5 people?

Poached apricots

Serves 6

- 300 g dried apricots
- 60 ml water
- 60 g sugar
- 6 cardamom pods
- 2 teaspoons of lemon juice
- 90 g pistachios

A4 Altogether, 3 identical packing cases weigh 240 kg. What will 7 of these packing cases weigh?

A5 Jim lays 8 identical drainage pipes end to end.
The total length is 32 m.
Work out the total length of 5 of these pipes.

A6 The weight of 7 identical bolts is 140 g.
What would 11 of these bolts weigh?

A7 In a recipe for buns, 600 ml of milk is needed to make 20 buns.
How much milk would be needed to make 25 of these buns?

A8 The total cost of 3 identical jars of marmalade is £2.94.
How much would I pay for 5 jars?

A9 100 g of sugar is needed to make blackberry fool for 5 people.
How much sugar would be needed for 12 people?

B *Cancelling common factors*

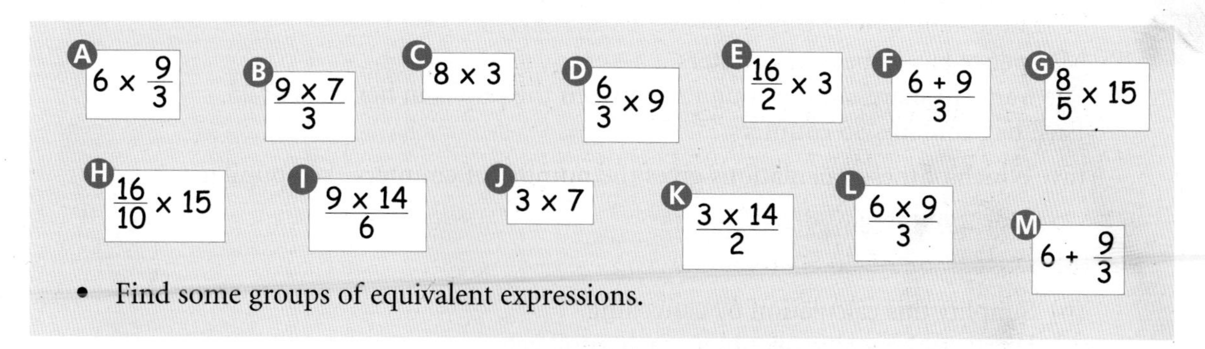

- Find some groups of equivalent expressions.

B1 For each calculation, simplify by cancelling common factors and then evaluate it.

(a) $\frac{12 \times 31}{2}$ (b) $\frac{25 \times 9}{3}$ (c) $\frac{16 \times 27}{4}$

(d) $\frac{8 \times 22}{2}$ (e) $\frac{21 \times 15}{3}$ (f) $\frac{25 \times 15}{5}$

Examples of cancelling common factors

$\frac{16}{7} \times 14 = \frac{16}{\cancel{7}_1} \times \cancel{14}^2$
$= 16 \times 2$
$= 32$

$4 \times \frac{13}{8} = {}^1\cancel{4} \times \frac{13}{\cancel{8}_2}$
$= \frac{13}{2}$
$= 6.5$

$\frac{93 \times 25}{15} = \frac{93 \times \cancel{25}^5}{\cancel{15}_3}$
$= \frac{{}^{31}\cancel{93} \times \cancel{25}^5}{\cancel{15}\,\cancel{3}_1}$
$= 31 \times 5$
$= 153$

B2 For each calculation, simplify by cancelling common factors and then evaluate it.

(a) $\frac{24}{5} \times 10$ (b) $\frac{13}{3} \times 9$ (c) $30 \times \frac{13}{6}$

(d) $45 \times \frac{8}{15}$ (e) $\frac{36}{14} \times 7$ (f) $12 \times \frac{7}{24}$

B3 For each calculation, simplify by cancelling common factors and then evaluate it.

(a) $\frac{15 \times 26}{6}$ (b) $\frac{25 \times 14}{10}$ (c) $\frac{22}{4} \times 14$

(d) $25 \times \frac{12}{15}$ (e) $\frac{21}{12} \times 6$ (f) $\frac{27}{18} \times 3$

B4 Joe has 12 bags of sweets, each holding 36 sweets.
He wants to share the sweets equally between 16 children.

(a) Which of these calculations gives the number of sweets each child gets?

$\frac{36 \times 16}{12}$ $\frac{12 \times 36}{16}$ $\frac{12 \times 16}{36}$

(b) Simplify this calculation by cancelling.
Work out how many sweets each child gets.

B5 Ms Spence has 15 bags of counters.
She wants to share out the counters between the pupils in her class of 25.
Each bag contains 45 counters.

(a) Which of these calculations gives the number of counters each pupil gets?

$\frac{25 \times 45}{15}$ $\frac{15 \times 25}{45}$ $\frac{45 \times 15}{25}$

(b) Simplify this calculation by cancelling.
Work out how many counters each pupil gets.

B6 Dee has 14 packs of humbugs, each holding 32 humbugs.
She shares the humbugs equally between 28 children.

How many humbugs does each child get?

B7 These toy bricks weigh 30 grams altogether.

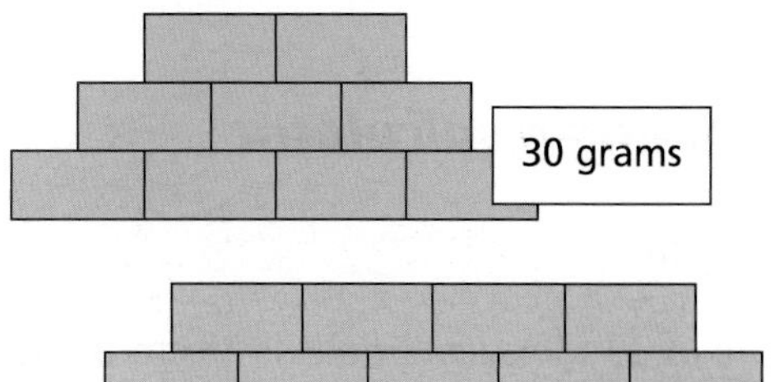

(a) Which calculation gives the total weight of the toy bricks on the right?

$\frac{30}{9} \times 15$ $\frac{30}{15} \times 9$ $\frac{15}{9} \times 30$

(b) Simplify this calculation by cancelling. Work out the weight of these bricks.

C *Using cancelling*

Example

It takes 130 g of self raising flour to make 15 chocolate cookies.

How much self raising flour would you need for 27 chocolate cookies?

15 cookies need 130 g flour

1 cookie needs $\frac{130}{15}$ g flour

27 cookies need $\frac{130}{15} \times 27 = \frac{\cancel{130}^{26}}{\cancel{15}_{3}} \times 27$

$= \frac{\cancel{130}^{26}}{\cancel{15}\cancel{3}_{1}} \times \cancel{27}^{9}$

$= 26 \times 9$

$= 234$ g flour

C1 12 bolts weigh 40 grams.
How much will 15 of these bolts weigh?

C2 21 nails weigh 28 grams.
How much will 27 of these nails weigh?

C3 It takes 150 ml of milk to make 12 scones.
How much milk would you need for 20 scones?

C4 15 sweets weigh 100 grams.
Find the weight of 21 of these sweets.

C5 It takes 450 g of caster sugar to make 36 marbled fudge bars.
How much caster sugar would you need to make 28 fudge bars?

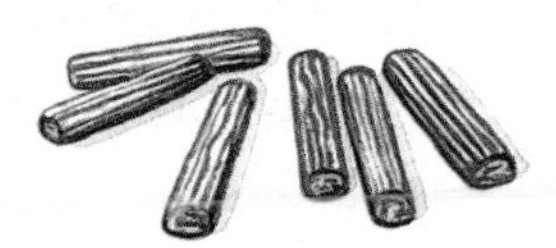

C6 A tray of 24 cookie twists can be made with 100 g of butter.
How much butter would you need for 42 cookie twists?

C7 You need 90 g of sugar to make 64 Neapolitan cookies.
How much sugar would you need for 48 cookies?

D *Using a calculator*

Example

A pile of 15 identical books is 38 cm high.

How high will a pile of 35 of these books be? Give your answer to the nearest cm.

Height of 15 books is 38 cm

Height of 1 book is $\frac{38}{15}$ cm

Height of 35 books is $\frac{38}{15} \times 35$

= 88.666 666 ...

= 89 cm (nearest cm)

D1 For 14 hours' work, Lucy was paid £67.06.
At this rate, what should she be paid for 38 hours' work?

D2 A small aircraft flies 275 km on 110 litres of fuel.
How much fuel is needed for a journey of 400 km?

D3 50 ml of milk contains 60 mg of fat.
How much fat is in 568 ml of milk?
Give your answer correct to the nearest mg.

D4 260 sheets of paper have a total thickness of 3.1 cm.
What would be the thickness of 550 of these sheets of paper, to the nearest 0.1 cm?

D5 A Caesar salad recipe for 6 uses 250 g of diced potatoes.
How much diced potato would you need for a Caesar salad for 11 people?
Give your answer correct to the nearest 5 g.

D6 Hayley bought 250 g of olives for £1.89.
What would 160 g of these olives cost?

D7 A shop charges £4.80 for 3.5 m of wire.
At this rate, what would be the cost of 8.2 m of this wire?

D8

BUY **£20 000** WORTH OF PREMIUM BONDS AND ON AVERAGE YOU'LL WIN **13** PRIZES A YEAR.

On average, someone with £20 000 in Premium Bonds should win 13 prizes each year.

Flora has £7700 in Premium Bonds.

(a) Work out the number of prizes she should win, on average, each year.

Premium Bonds are sold in multiples of £10.
Rajesh works out that he is likely to win 9 prizes next year.

(b) Work out an estimate for the amount of money Rajesh has in Premium Bonds.

Edexcel

*D9 A 1 kg block of gold is worth £5780 and has a volume of $52\,cm^3$.

(a) What is the weight of a $65\,cm^3$ block of gold?

(b) What weight of gold, to the nearest kilogram, would be worth £1 million?

(c) What is the volume of this £1 million block, to the nearest cm^3?

$52\,cm^3$ is about the size of a medium bar of chocolate.

E *Rates*

Example

There are 4.546 litres in one gallon.
Work out the number of gallons in 40 litres, correct to 1 d.p.

4.546 litres is 1 gallon

1 litre is $\frac{1}{4.546}$ gallons

40 litres is $\frac{1}{4.546} \times 40$

= 8.8 gallons (to 1 d.p.)

4.546 litres is 1 gallon

40 litres is $\frac{40}{4.546}$

= 8.8 gallons (to 1 d.p.)

TG

E1 The exchange rate to change Norwegian kroners into pounds is

12.74 Norwegian kroners = £1

Work out the number of pence in 5.50 Norwegian kroners.
Give your answer to the nearest penny.

E2 1 kilogram is equivalent to about 2.205 pounds.
What is the weight in kilograms of 5 pounds of flour?
Give your answer correct to two decimal places.

E3 One pint is equivalent to about 0.568 litres.
How many pints are equivalent to 3.6 litres?
Give your answer correct to one decimal place.

E4 On average a car travels 100 km on fuel costing £4.40.

(a) Calculate the cost of fuel for a journey of 720 km.

(b) The fuel for another journey cost £14.30.
Calculate the length of this journey. OCR

E5 A litre is about 0.220 gallons.
A litre of fuel costs 85.9p.
Calculate the cost of 800 gallons of this fuel.

E6 The table shows the amount of foreign currency that can be bought with £1.

Dave has just returned from Hong Kong.
He has 940 Hong Kong dollars.

His next trip is to South Korea.
He changes his Hong Kong dollars into South Korean won.

Calculate, to the nearest thousand, how many South Korean won he will get.

Far-east currencies £1 will buy	
India	66.65 rupees
Hong Kong	11.03 Hong Kong dollars
Indonesia	13 192.2 rupiahs
South Korea	1816.9 won

Test yourself

T1 The cost of 3 pencils is 72p.
What is the cost of 5 pencils? Edexcel

T2 It takes 100 g of flour to make 15 shortbread biscuits.

(a) How many shortbread biscuits can be made from 1 kg of flour?

(b) Calculate the weight of flour needed to make 24 biscuits. OCR

T3 Recipe for bread and butter pudding

6 slices of bread
2 eggs
1 pint of milk
150 g raisins
10 g margarine

This recipe is enough for 4 people.

(a) Work out the amounts needed so that there will be enough for 6 people.

There are 450 g in 1 pound. There are 16 ounces in 1 pound.

(b) Change 150 g into ounces. Give your answer correct to the nearest ounce.

Edexcel

T4 A pile of 12 identical coins is 3.8 cm high.

How high will a pile of 25 of these coins be, correct to the nearest mm?

T5 Asra goes on holiday to Hungary.
The exchange rate is £1 = 397.6 forints.

She changes £250 into forints.

(a) How many forints should Asra get?

She changes 1450 forints back into pounds.
The exchange rate is the same.

(b) How much money should she get?
Give your answer to the nearest penny.

16 *Volume and surface area*

You should know how to find the volume of a cuboid.

This work will help you

- find the volume of a prism
- find the surface area of three-dimensional shapes
- change between metric units in volume and area
- use density

A *Volumes of cuboids*

Volumes are measured in cubic centimetres (cm^3) or for larger volumes cubic metres (m^3).

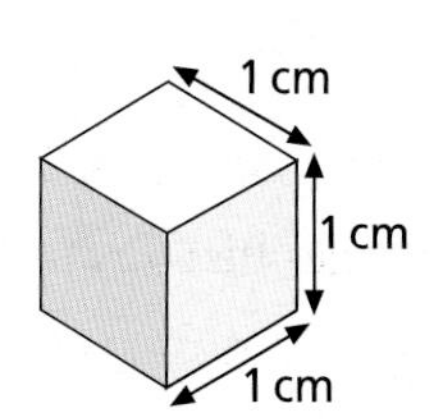

This cube has volume 1 cm^3.

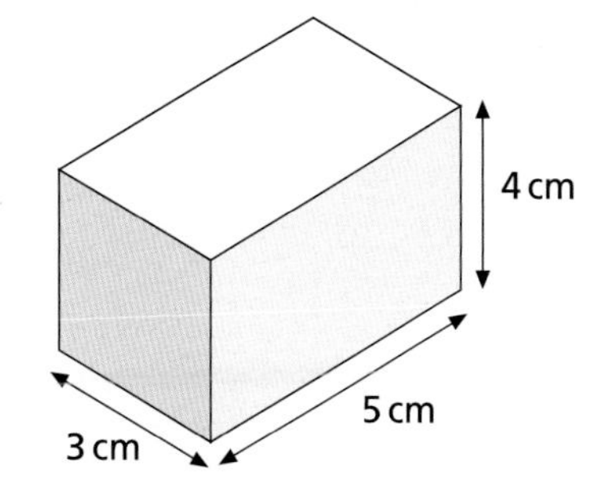

To find the volume of a cuboid use the formula

$$\text{volume} = \text{length} \times \text{width} \times \text{height}$$

This cuboid has volume

$$5 \times 3 \times 4 = 60 \text{ cm}^3$$

A1 Find the volume of each of these cuboids.

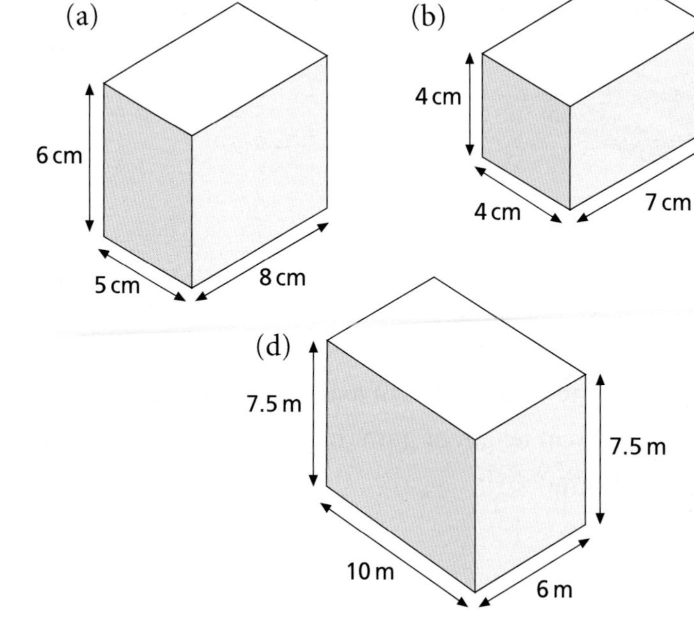

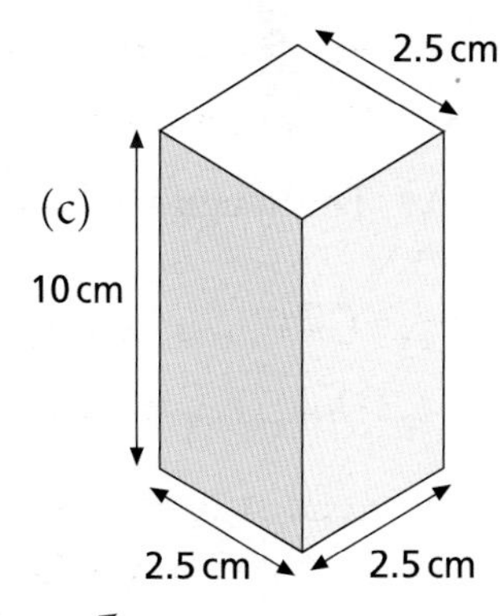

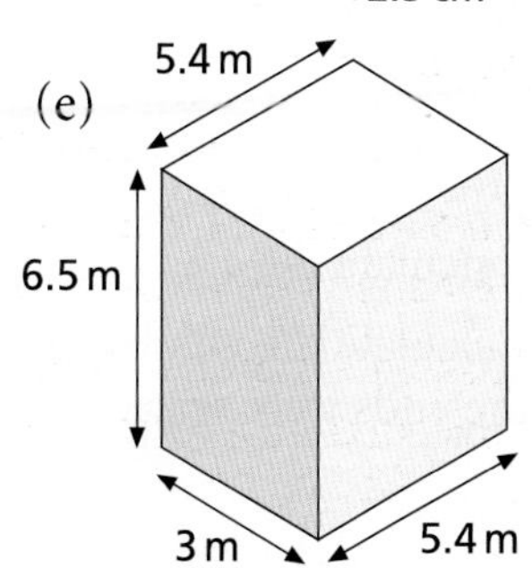

A2 These cuboids all have the same volume.
Find the missing measurements. (They are not drawn to scale.)

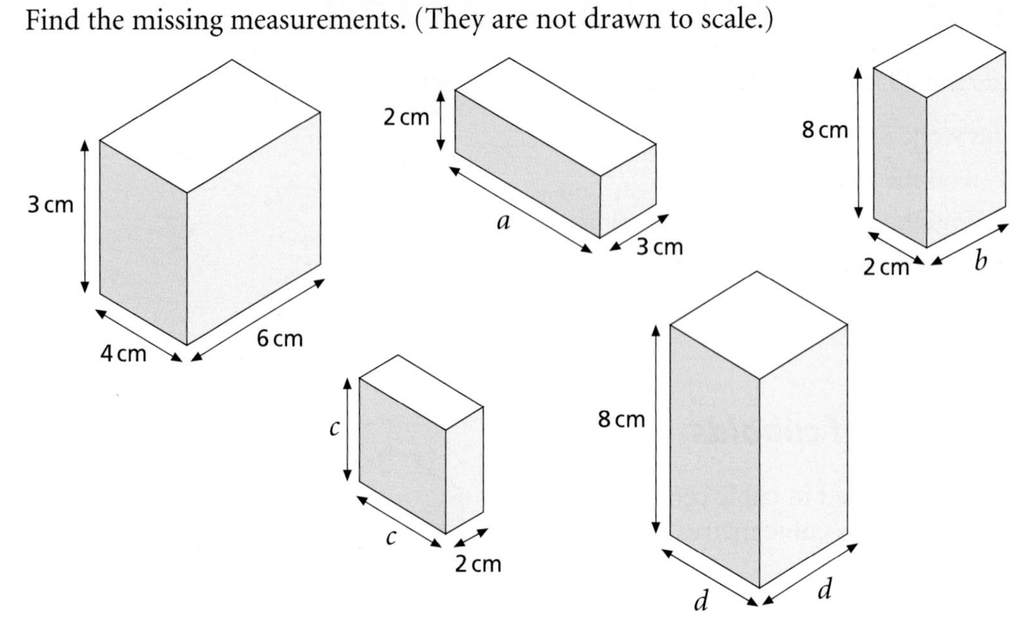

A3 The diagram shows a cuboid which is just big enough to hold six tennis balls.

Each tennis ball has a diameter of 6.8 cm.

Calculate the volume of the cuboid.

AQA(SEG) 1998

A4 This diagram shows a length of plastic guttering.

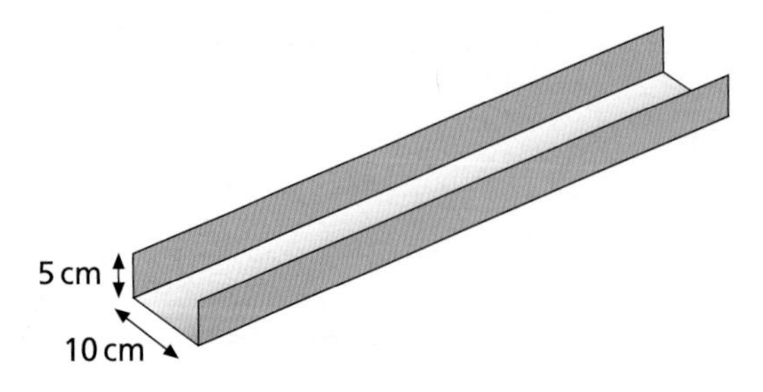

The cross-section of the guttering is a rectangle measuring 10 cm by 5 cm.

(a) Calculate the area of plastic needed to make a 200 cm length of guttering.

(b) Calculate the volume of water a 200 cm length of guttering could contain if the ends were sealed and it was full of water.

AQA(SEG) 1999

B *Prisms*

This solid is made up of 20 cuboids of size 1 cm by 1 cm by 6 cm.

- What is its volume?

The prisms below are all made from similar pieces, 6 cm long.

- Find their volumes.

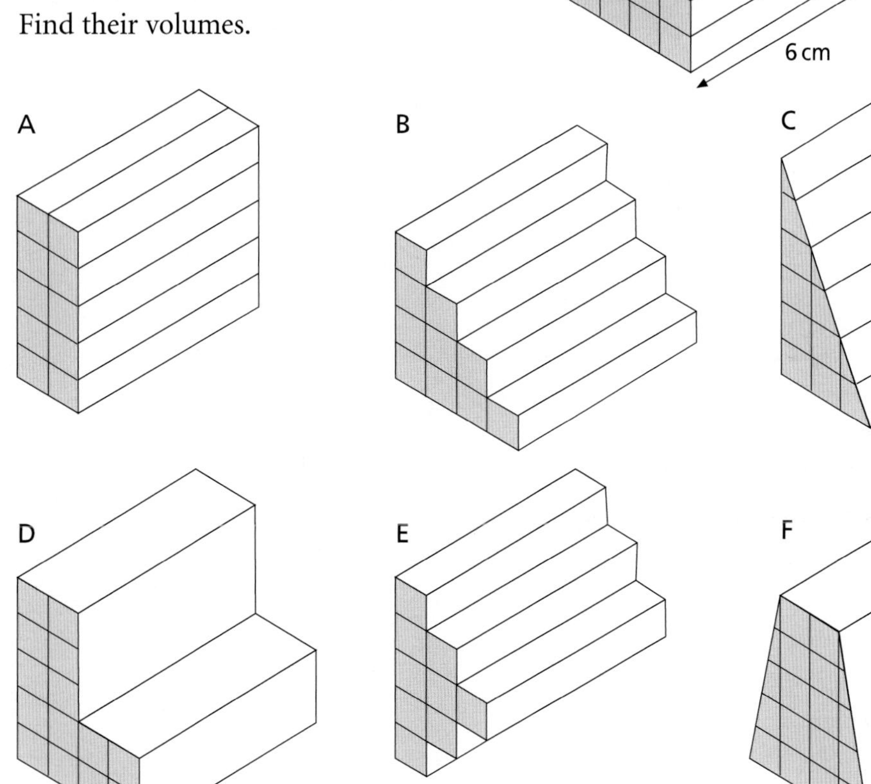

B1 Find the volume of each of these prisms.

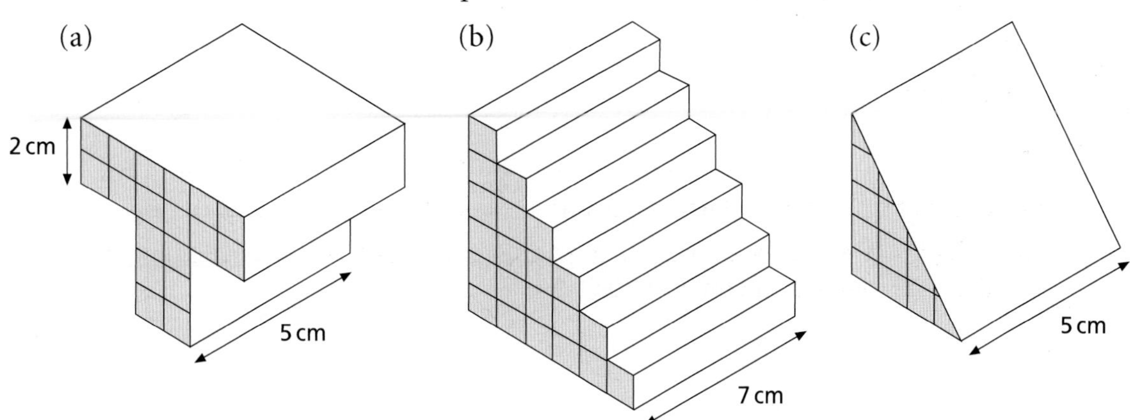

Volume of a prism

A prism has the same cross-section throughout its length.
The volume of a prism is found by
volume = area of cross-section × length

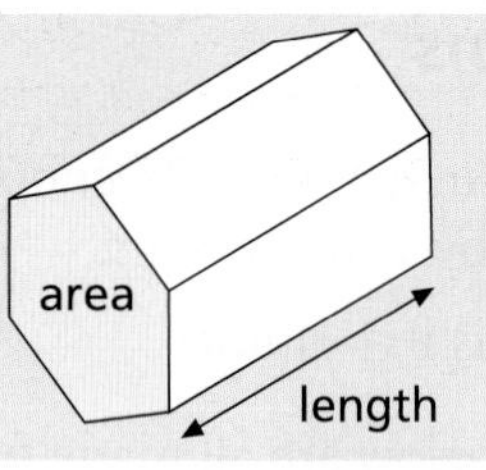

B2 Calculate the volume of these prisms. (Sketching the cross-section may help.)

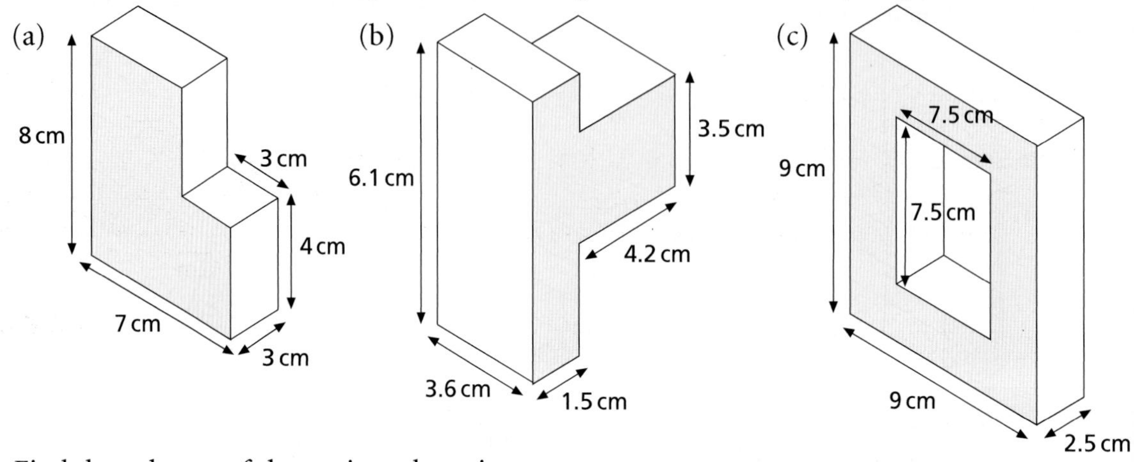

B3 Find the volumes of these triangular prisms.

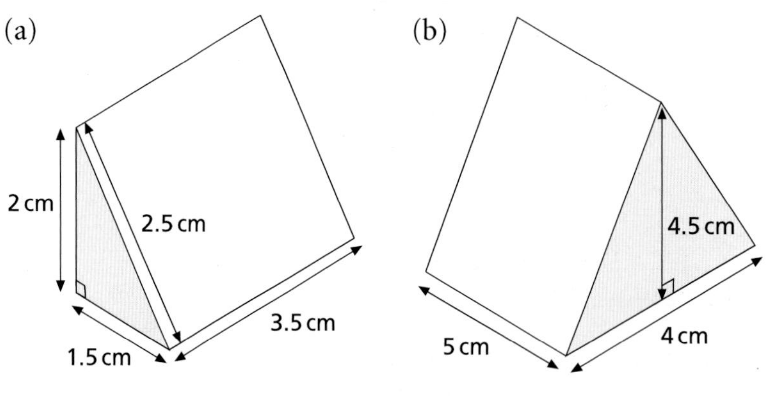

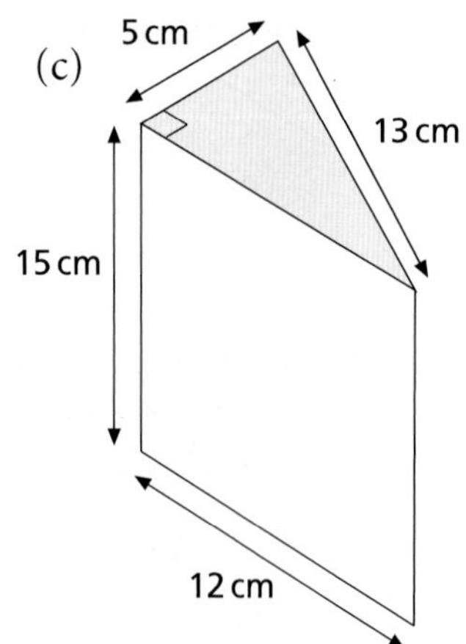

B4 Find the volumes of these prisms.

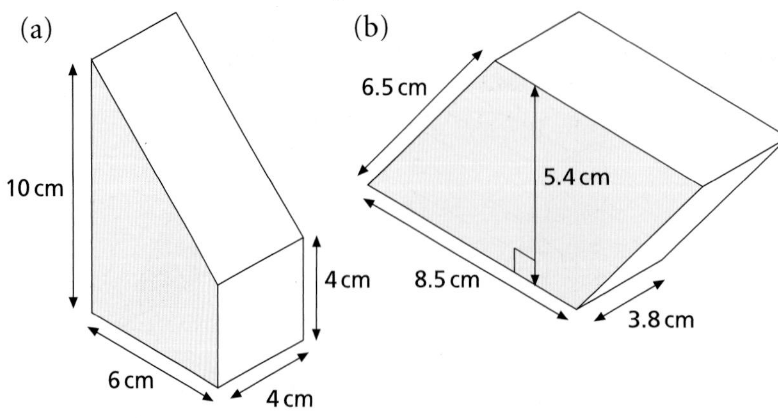

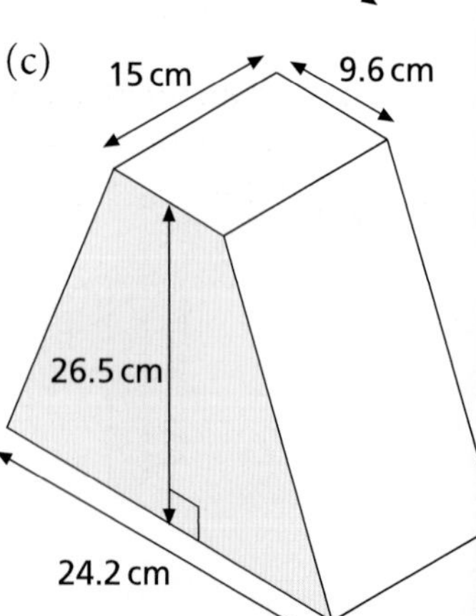

B5 A rubbish skip is made in the shape of a prism whose cross-section is a trapezium.
Find the volume of this skip.

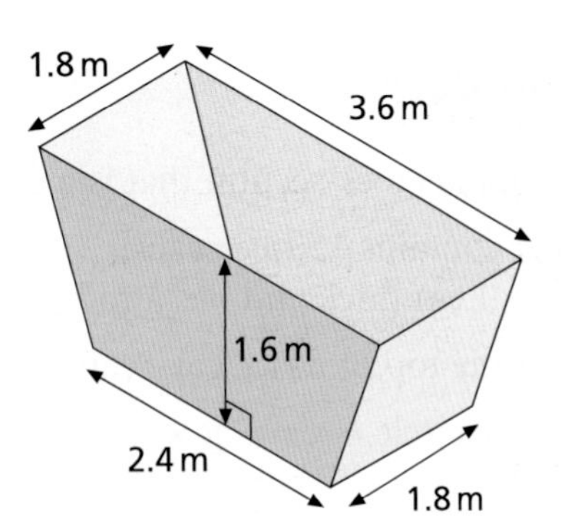

B6 Ice cream is sold in a box that is the shape of a prism.
The ends are parallelograms.
The size of the parallelograms is shown in the diagram.
The length of the prism is 12 cm.
Calculate the volume of the ice cream in the box.

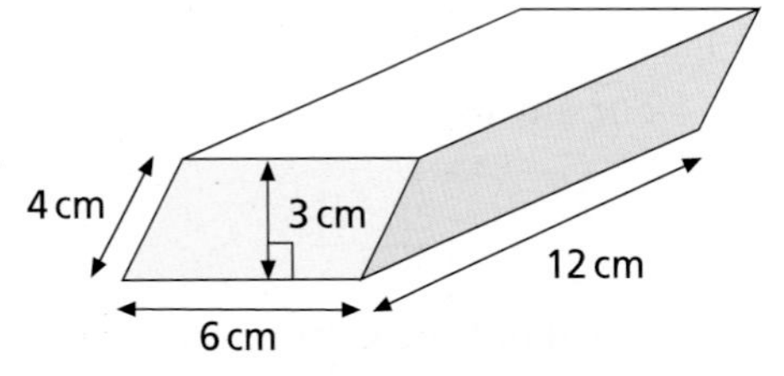

AQA(NEAB) 1998

B7 This prism has a right-angled triangular cross-section.
The volume of the prism is 66 cm^3.
Find the length L.

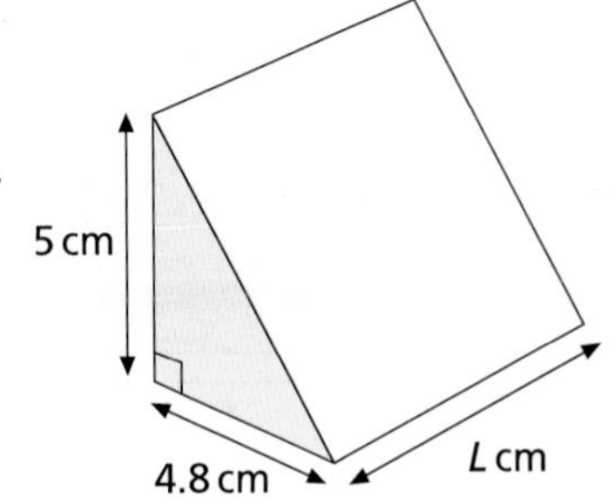

B8 A building site has area 150 m^2.
The topsoil on the site is 0.8 m deep throughout.
What is the volume of topsoil on the site?

B9 A block of glass is a cube measuring 15 cm on each side.
The glass is melted into a sheet which is 0.5 cm thick.
What will be the area of the sheet of glass?

B10 A concrete base is needed to cover a rectangular area 5 m by 3.6 m.
A cement mixer contains 4.5 m^3 of concrete.
How thick will the concrete be if it is spread evenly over the area?

C Cylinders

A cylinder has a cross-section that is a circle.

This packet contains 15 rice cakes.
Each cake is 1 cm thick and has a radius of 5 cm.

The area of the top of a rice cake can be found by

area of the circle = $\pi r^2 = \pi \times (5 \times 5) = 78.5398\ldots \text{ cm}^2$.

Since the rice cakes are 1 cm thick they have volume $1 \times 78.53\ldots = 78.53\ldots \text{ cm}^3$.

The whole packet of 15 cakes has volume $15 \times 78.53\ldots = 1178.097\ldots = 1178.1 \text{ cm}^3$ (1 d.p.).

For any cylinder, volume = area of the circle × height

$= \pi r^2 h$

C1 Find the volumes of these cylinders to one decimal place.

(a) (b) (c)

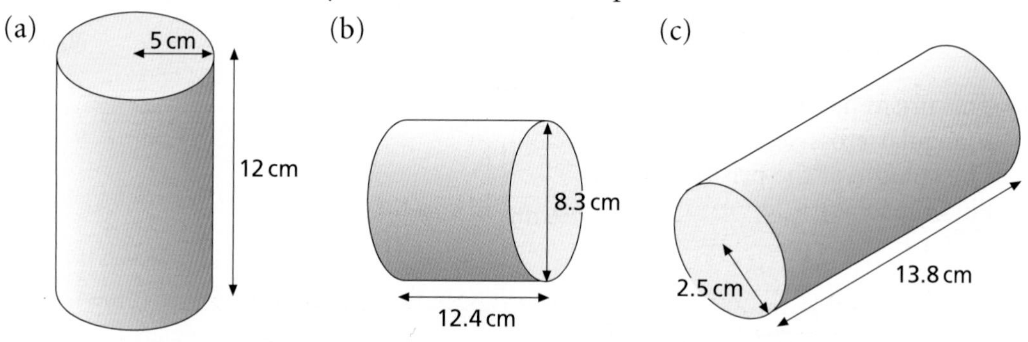

C2 (a) A circle has a diameter of 7 cm.

(i) Calculate the circumference of this circle.

(ii) Calculate the area of this circle.

(b) A plastic beaker has a height of 10 cm and a circular base of diameter 7 cm.
Calculate the volume of the beaker.

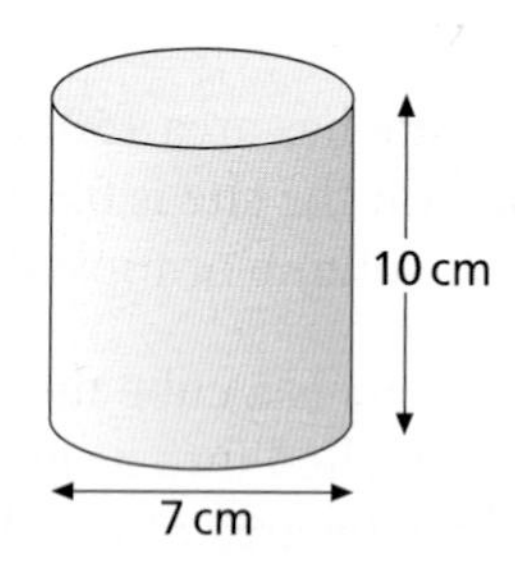

AQA(NEAB) 1997

C3 Becca buys a large tin of coffee.
It is a cylinder with radius 7.5 cm.
It is filled to a depth of 14 cm.

Work out the volume of coffee in the tin.
State clearly the units of your answer.

OCR

Appropriate accuracy

A calculator often gives an answer with several figures after the decimal point.

For example a factory wants to make a cylindrical can with volume 400 cm^3.
The radius of the can is to be 3.2 cm and they want to know how high the can must be.

The height is $400 \div (\pi \times 3.2^2) = 12.433\,979\,929\,1$ cm (from a calculator)

This is clearly far too accurate for practical purposes.
A suitable answer is *Height = 12.433... = 12.4 cm (to one decimal place)*

It has been rounded to one decimal place because the radius was given to one decimal place.
This appears to be the degree of accuracy that the factory uses.

However... in November 2000 the Gateshead Millenium Bridge was put into place.
Although the bridge was made 126 m long it had to be made accurate to
within 3 mm if it was to fit into place when lowered in.

C4 Ranjit has made a new circular fish pond in his garden.
The radius of the pond is 1.5 m.

(a) Calculate the circumference of the pond.

(b) The sides of the pond are vertical.
The water in the pond is 0.7 m deep.
Calculate the volume of the water in the pond.
Give your units in the answer. OCR

C5 A gardener keeps rainwater in a cylindrical butt 1.5 m high with radius 50 cm.

(a) What volume of water does the butt contain in cm^3 when it is full?

(b) A litre is 1000 cm^3.
How many 5-litre watering cans could the gardener fill from a full butt?

C6 Water is poured from a kettle containing half a litre (500 cm^3) into a cup.
The cup has a radius of 4 cm.
How high up the cup will the water come?

C7 A cylinder is 20 cm high and holds 1000 cm^3 of water.
Find the radius of the cylinder.

Capacity

On bottles and cans measurements are often given in millilitres (ml).
A millilitre is one thousandth of a litre and is a liquid measure the same as 1 cm^3.

Carefully measure some different size cans in centimetres.
Calculate the volume of these cans.

How do these volumes compare with the amount they are supposed to contain?

D *Surface area*

The surface area of an object is the total area of all its faces.
The net of an object clearly shows the areas that have to be calculated.

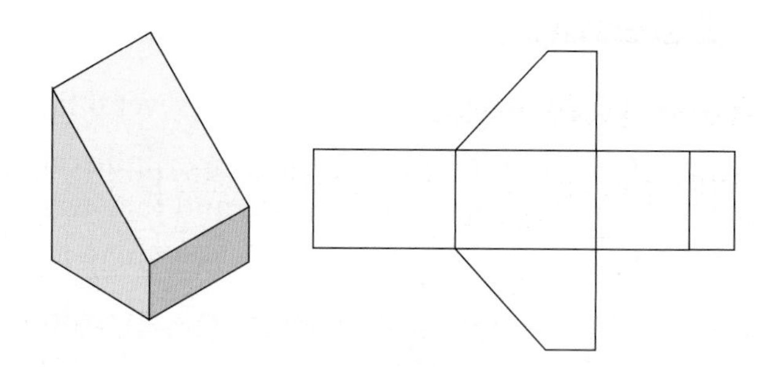

D1 For each of the objects below (i) sketch the net adding any measurements you know
(ii) find the surface area of the object

(a)

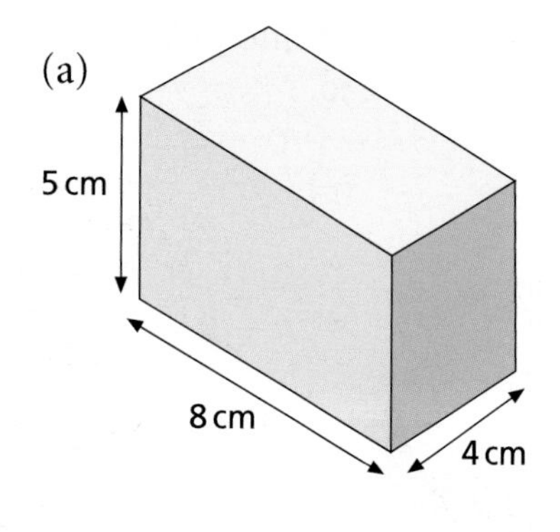

(b)

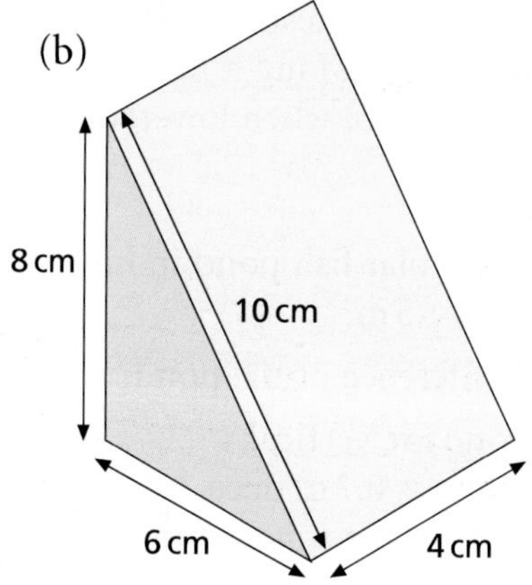

(c)

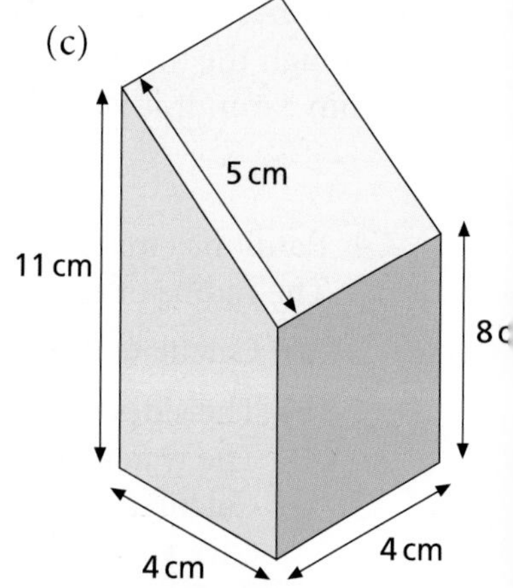

D2 (a) What is the circumference of the circle at each end of this cylinder?

(b) Find the area of one of the circular ends.

(c) Sketch the curved surface of the cylinder laid flat. Add the dimensions of this shape. Find the area of the curved surface of this cylinder.

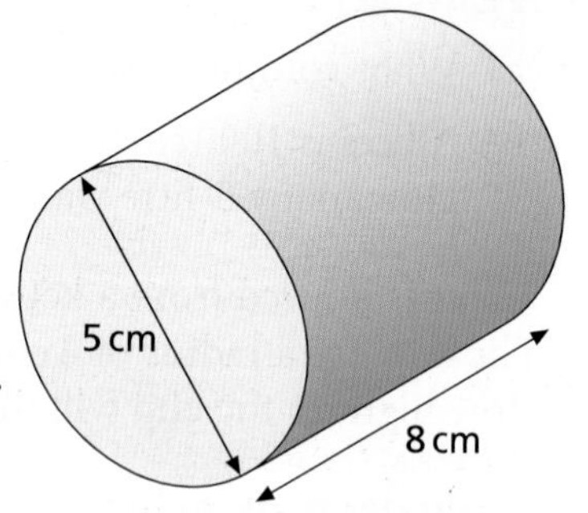

Carrying the can

A cylindrical can with a volume of 1000 cm^3 (1 litre) has radius 5 cm.
How high is it?
What would be the total surface area of material used to make this can?

Find the heights of 1 litre cans with radius (a) 3 cm (b) 4 cm (c) 6 cm (d) 7 cm
Find the surface area of each of these cans.

What should be the radius of a 1 litre can in order to use the least amount of material?

You may find a spreadsheet useful.

E Density

Watching your weights

Paul's grandfather asks him this question.
Do you know the answer?

Which weighs more, a tonne of feathers or a tonne of stones?

The stones clearly have a much greater **density** than the feathers.
Density is usually given as as g/cm^3. (Lead has density 11.4 g/cm^3.)

Weigh some solid objects whose volume you can easily find, such as a brick or a block of polystyrene.
Find their density.

$$\text{Density} = \frac{\text{Weight}}{\text{Volume}}$$

E1 Find the density of these objects.

(a)

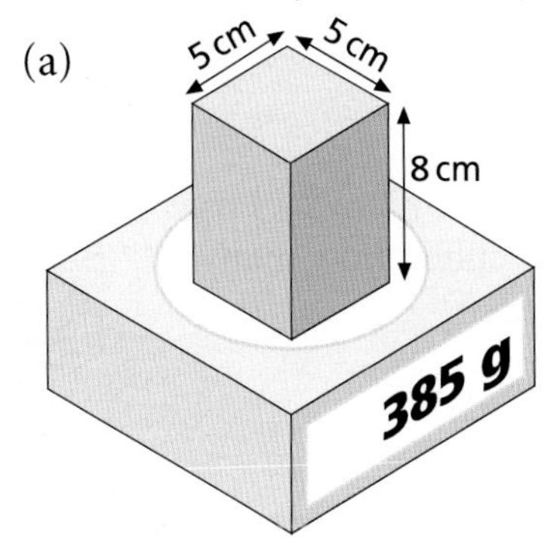

(b)

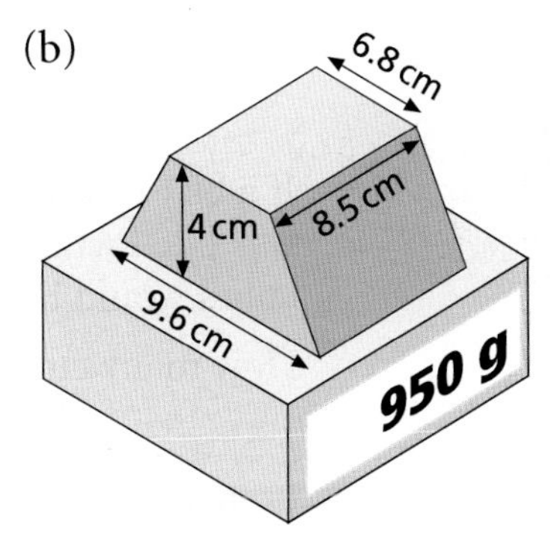

(c)

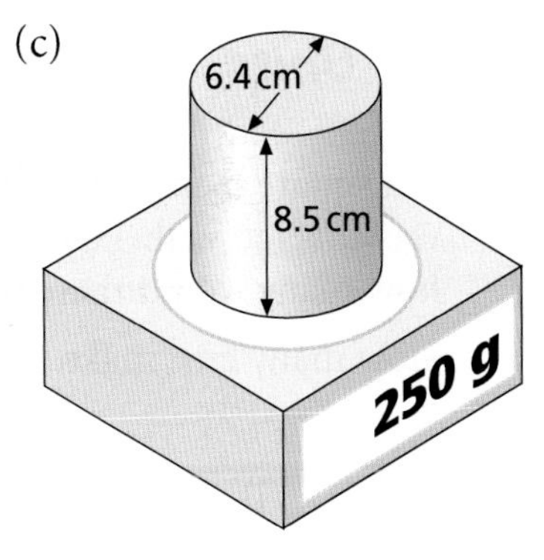

E2 Use the table on the right to work out the weight of these objects.

(a) A stone with volume 92 cm^3

(b) A wooden cuboid 22 cm by 18 cm by 11 cm

(c) The water in a cylindrical container with radius 40 cm and height 140 cm

Material	Density
Wood	0.7 g/cm^3
Stone	3.0 g/cm^3
Water	1.0 g/cm^3

E3 Density can help identify metals.

One of these ingots below is platinum, one is gold, one is silver and one is fake gold.

Work out the density of each ingot and use this table to say what each ingot is made of.

Material	Density
Platinum	21.5 g/cm^3
Gold	19.3 g/cm^3
Silver	10.5 g/cm^3
Fake gold	9.8 g/cm^3

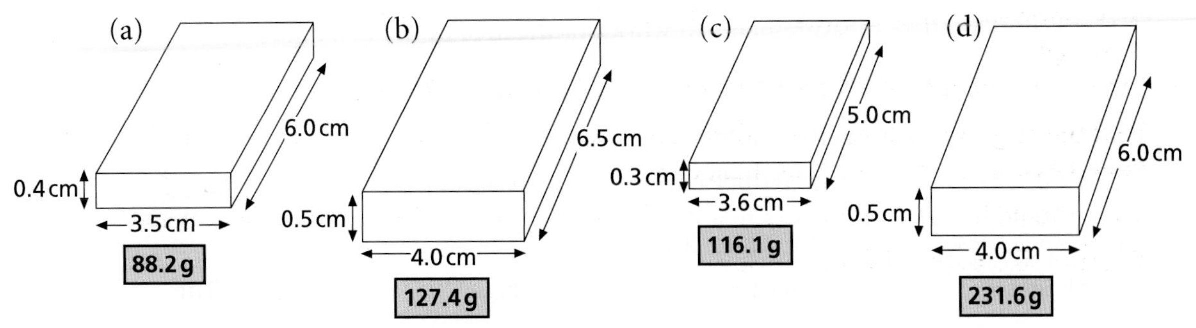

E4 This diagram shows a prism.
The cross-section of the prism is a trapezium.
The lengths of the parallel sides of the trapezium are 8 cm and 6 cm.
The distance between the parallel sides of the trapezium is 5 cm.
The length of the prism is 20 cm.

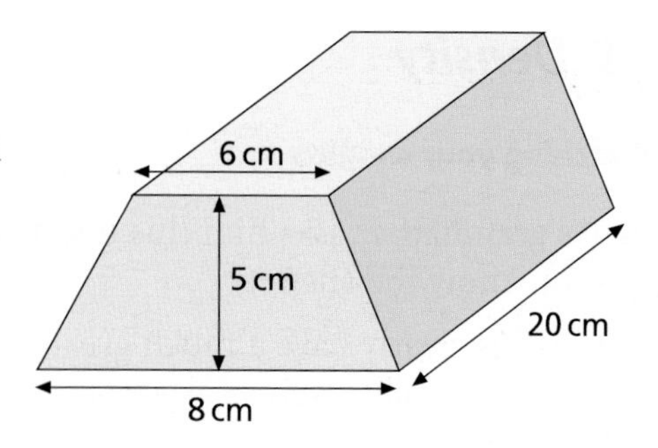

(a) Work out the volume of the prism.

The prism is made out of gold.
Gold has a density of 19.3 grams per cm^3.

(b) Work out the mass of the prism.
Give your answer in kilograms.

Edexcel

F Units

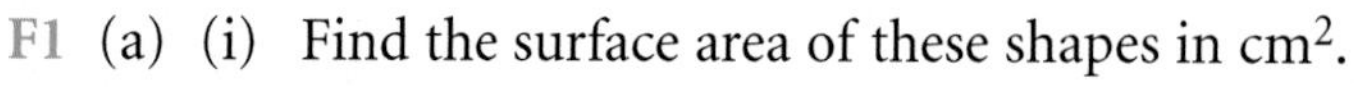

If a square measuring 1 m by 1 m was covered with 1 cm squares, how many would there be?

How many cm^2 make a m^2 ?

If a box measuring 1 m by 1 m by 1 m was filled with 1 cm cubes, how many cubes would be needed?

How many cm^3 make a m^3 ?

F1 (a) (i) Find the surface area of these shapes in cm^2.
(ii) Convert these answers into m^2.
(b) (i) Find the volume of these shapes in cm^3.
(ii) Convert these answers into m^3.

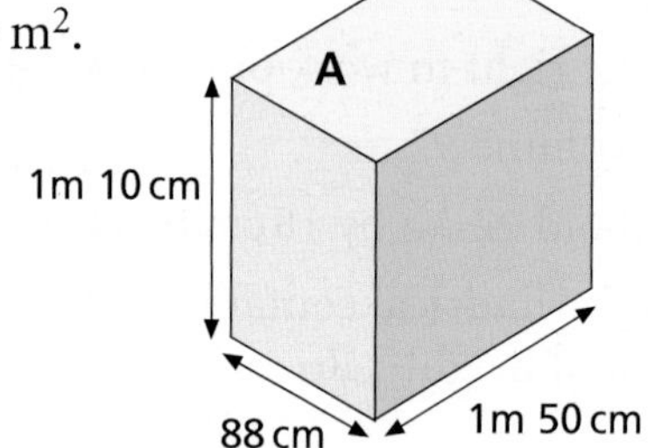

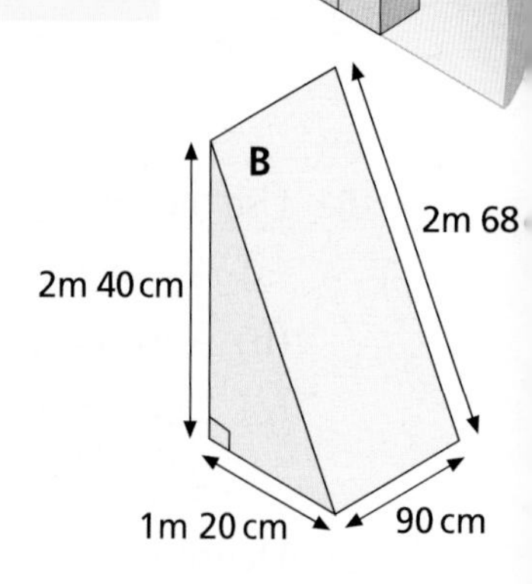

F2 A rectangle has a length of 1.2 m and a width of 0.7 m.
(a) (i) Work out the area of the rectangle in m^2.
(ii) Convert this into cm^2.
(b) (i) Write the length and width of the rectangle in cm.
(ii) Use these measurements to work out the area of the rectangle in cm^2.
(iii) Check your answer agrees with (a) (ii).

F3 Change these areas in cm^2 into m^2.
(a) 6 500 000 cm^2 (b) 480 000 cm^2 (c) 50 000 cm^2 (d) 500 cm^2

F4 Change these volumes in m^3 into cm^3.
(a) 25 m^3 (b) 0.6 m^3 (c) 200 m^3 (d) 0.0008 m^3

Test yourself

T1 Find the volume of these objects.

(a) A cuboid

(b) A triangular prism

(c) A cylinder

7.5 cm, 5 cm, 9 cm

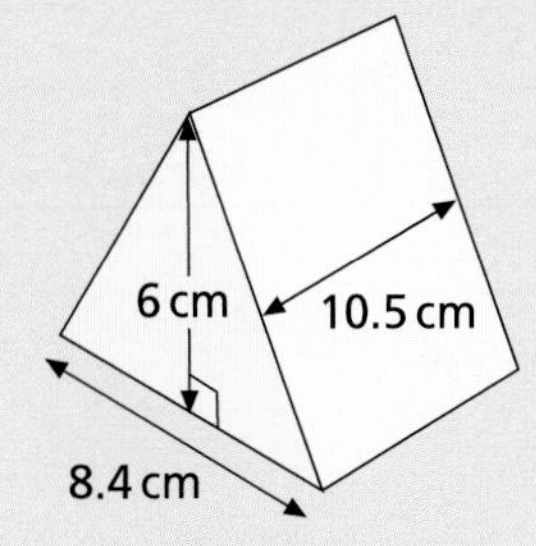

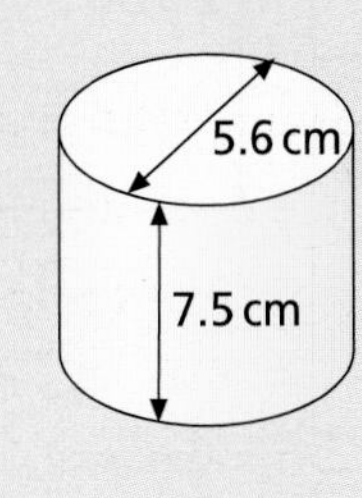

T2 Chocomint is made in blocks as shown in the diagram.

The block is a prism and its cross-section is a trapezium.

(a) Calculate the volume of a block of Chocomint.

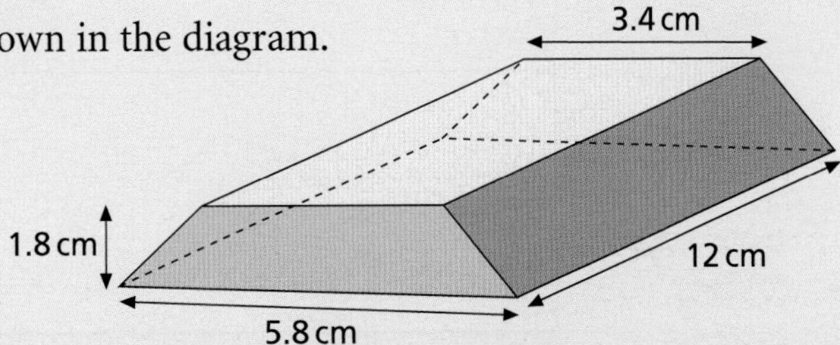

Chocorock is made in cylindrical sticks as shown in the diagram.

The radius of the circular end is 1.2 cm.
The volume of the cylinder is 50 cm^3.

1.2 cm

(b) Find the length of a stick of Chocorock.
Give your answer to a sensible degree of accuracy.

OCR

T3 A skip is in the shape of a prism with cross-section ABCD.
AD = 2.3 m, DC = 1.3 m and BC = 1.7 m.
The width of the skip is 1.5 m.

(a) Calculate the area of the shape ABCD.

(b) Calculate the volume of the skip.

The weight of an empty skip is 650 kg.
The skip is full to the top with sand.
1 m^3 of sand weighs 4300 kg.

(c) Calculate the total weight of skip and sand.

2.3 m, A, D, 1.3 m, 1.5 m, B, 1.7 m, C

Edexcel

T4 This net will fold to make a three-dimensional shape.

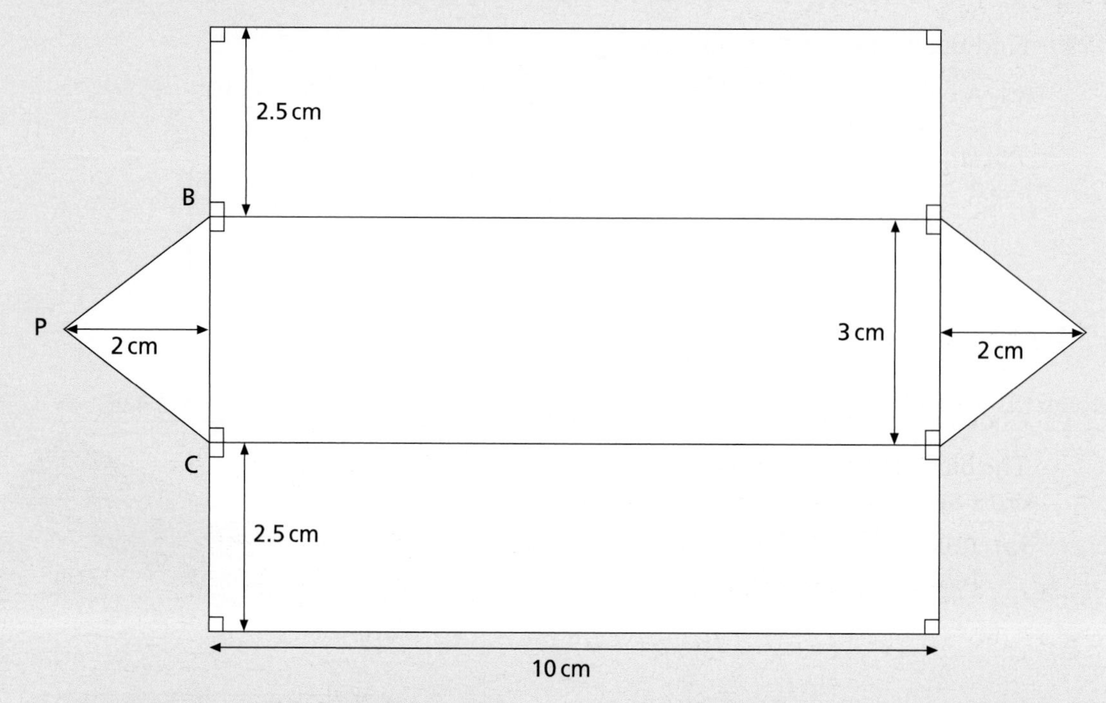

(a) Measure the size of the angle BPC.

(b) Calculate the area of the net.
(Remember to state the units in your answer)

(c) (i) Draw a sketch of the shape it makes when folded.

(ii) What is the mathematical name of this shape?

(iii) Calculate the volume of this shape.
(Remember to state the units in your answer.)

AQA 1997

T5 This brass cuboid weighs 533 grams.
Work out the density of brass,
correct to 2 d.p.

7 cm
3 cm
5 cm

T6 This iron rod has circular ends.
Iron has a density of 7.86 g/cm^3.

What is the weight of the rod?

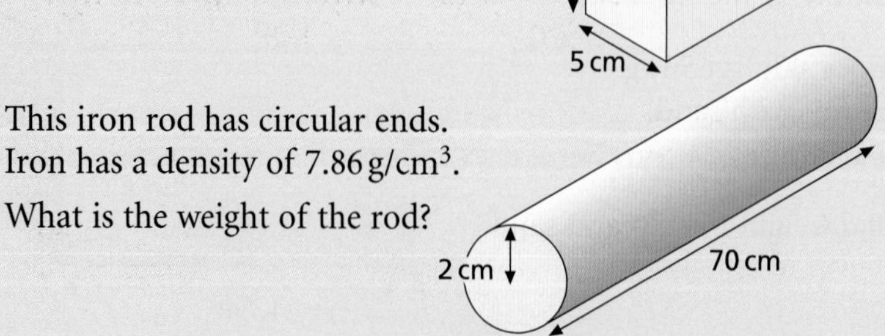

T7 A water container in the shape of a cuboid has a length of 250 cm, a width of 140 cm and a depth of 90 cm.
Calculate the capacity of the tank in cubic metres.

17 Fractions 2

You will revise calculating a fraction of a number

This work will help you

- multiply a fraction by an integer (whole number)
- multiply fractions

A Fractions review

Fractions from dice

Roll a dice twice (or roll two dice).
The first score is the numerator of a fraction.
The second is the denominator.

Roll the dice to make a fraction. Is it

- a proper fraction or an improper fraction?
- equivalent to a whole number?
- a fraction that can be simplified?
- a fraction that gives a recurring decimal?

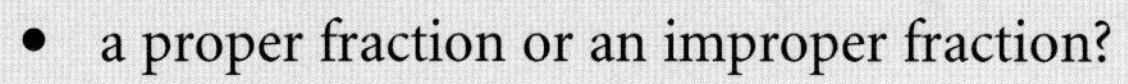

Repeat for other fractions you can make with the dice.

Challenge!

How many different fractions do the dice give?

A1 Errol has to calculate three quarters of 52.

He knows he has to do something with 3 and 4 but doesn't know what.
Explain briefly what he has to do.

A2 Calculate these in your head.

(a) $\frac{1}{7}$ of 28 (b) $\frac{2}{7}$ of 28 (c) $\frac{3}{7}$ of 28 (d) $\frac{1}{9}$ of 72 (e) $\frac{4}{9}$ of 72
(f) $\frac{3}{5}$ of 45 (g) $\frac{4}{5}$ of 30 (h) $\frac{3}{8}$ of 32 (i) $\frac{2}{9}$ of 180 (j) $\frac{5}{6}$ of 420

A3 Write each of these fractions in its simplest form.
(Some are already in their simplest form.)

(a) $\frac{20}{30}$ (b) $\frac{12}{20}$ (c) $\frac{18}{40}$ (d) $\frac{15}{40}$ (e) $\frac{12}{35}$
(f) $\frac{16}{21}$ (g) $\frac{18}{21}$ (h) $\frac{24}{60}$ (i) $\frac{14}{42}$ (j) $\frac{75}{360}$

TG

B *Multiplying a fraction by a whole number*

This picture shows 8 lots of $\frac{1}{2}$.

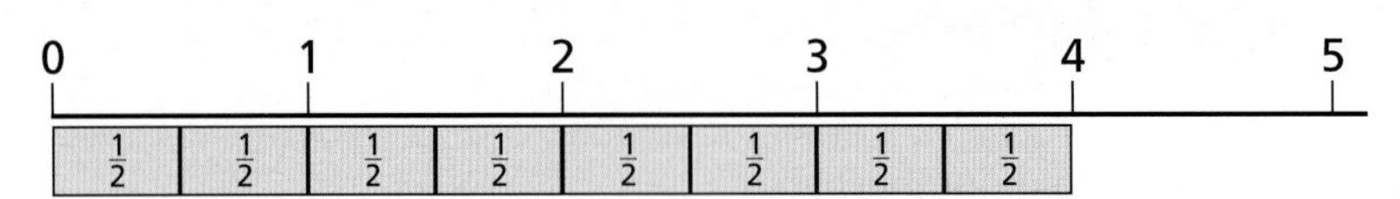

$8 \times \frac{1}{2} = 4 \qquad \frac{1}{2} \times 8 = 4$

This picture shows 7 lots of $\frac{3}{4}$.

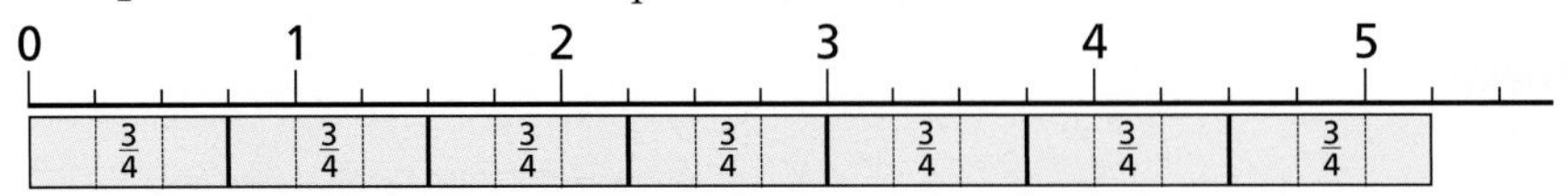

21 quarters = 5 whole ones and 1 quarter

$7 \times \frac{3}{4} = \frac{21}{4} = 5\frac{1}{4}$

Cancelling common factors

$$8 \times \frac{3}{4} = \overset{2}{\cancel{8}} \times \frac{3}{\underset{1}{\cancel{4}}} = 6 \qquad 12 \times \frac{5}{8} = \overset{3}{\cancel{12}} \times \frac{5}{\underset{2}{\cancel{8}}} = \frac{15}{2} = 7\frac{1}{2}$$

B1 Work these out. The answers are all whole numbers.

(a) $\frac{1}{4} \times 12$ (b) $15 \times \frac{1}{3}$ (c) $\frac{1}{5} \times 20$ (d) $24 \times \frac{1}{8}$ (e) $32 \times \frac{1}{2}$

B2 Work these out. The answers are all whole numbers.

(a) $\frac{3}{4} \times 8$ (b) $12 \times \frac{2}{3}$ (c) $\frac{4}{5} \times 10$ (d) $16 \times \frac{1}{8}$ (e) $32 \times \frac{5}{8}$

B3 Janice has 9 glasses of juice that each contain $\frac{1}{4}$ litre of juice.
How many litres of juice does Janice have?

B4 It takes Prakesh $\frac{3}{4}$ hour to paint a window frame.
How many hours will it take him to paint 5 window frames?

B5 Dylan does a health run of $\frac{2}{3}$ mile every day.
How far does he run altogether in 7 days?

B6 Work these out.

(a) $\frac{1}{4} \times 15$ (b) $8 \times \frac{1}{3}$ (c) $\frac{1}{5} \times 12$ (d) $14 \times \frac{1}{8}$ (e) $17 \times \frac{1}{2}$

B7 Work these out.

(a) $\frac{3}{4} \times 9$ (b) $10 \times \frac{2}{3}$ (c) $\frac{4}{5} \times 6$ (d) $6 \times \frac{3}{8}$ (e) $5 \times \frac{4}{5}$

B8 Copy and complete these multiplications.

(a) $\frac{1}{10} \times ■ = \frac{1}{2}$ (b) $■ \times 5 = \frac{1}{3}$ (c) $■ \times 6 = 4$

C 'Of' and multiply

$\frac{1}{2}$ of 8 = 4 $\quad \frac{1}{2} \times 8 = 4$

of and × give the same result

$\frac{3}{4}$ of 12 = 9 $\quad \frac{3}{4} \times 12 = 9$

C1 Copy this: $\frac{\square}{\square}$ of $\square = \square$ Put the digits 3, 4, 6, 8 in the boxes to make the calculation correct.

C2 Put the given digits in the boxes to make each calculation correct.

(a) $\frac{\square}{\square} \times \square = \square$ 2, 3, 4, 6

(b) $\square\square \times \frac{\square}{\square} = \square$ 0, 1, 2, 4, 5

(c) $\frac{\square}{\square}$ of $\square\square = \square$ 0, 1, 4, 5, 8

(d) $\frac{\square}{\square}$ of $\square\square = \square\square$ 0, 1, 2, 3, 4, 5

C3 Use the fact that $\frac{2}{3}$ of $8 = \frac{2}{3} \times 8$ to work out $\frac{2}{3}$ of 8. Write the answer as a mixed number.

C4 Work these out. (a) $\frac{1}{4}$ of 7 (b) $\frac{3}{4}$ of 15 (c) $\frac{2}{3}$ of 10 (d) $\frac{2}{5}$ of 14

D Dividing a fraction by a whole number

This is $\frac{1}{2}$

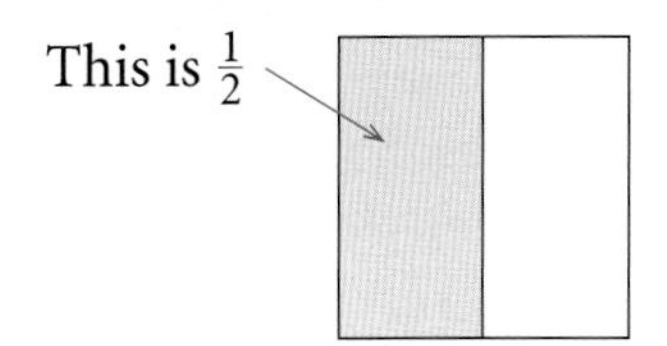

and this is $\frac{1}{2} \div 3$

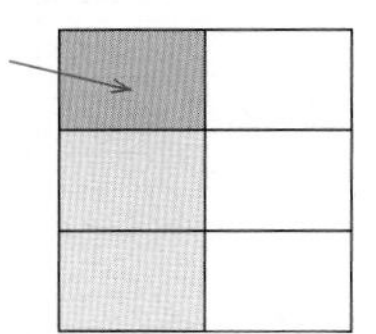

What fraction is $\frac{1}{2} \div 3$?

This is $\frac{2}{3}$

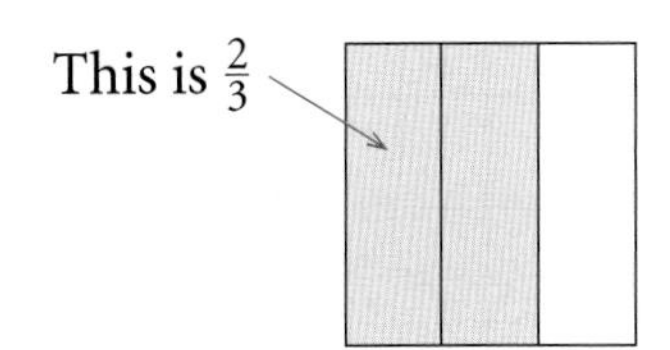

and this is $\frac{2}{3} \div 5$

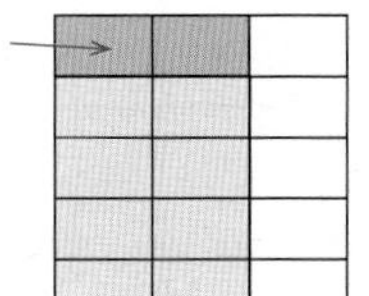

What fraction is $\frac{2}{3} \div 5$?

D1 Work these out.

(a) $\frac{1}{4} \div 2$ (b) $\frac{1}{3} \div 2$ (c) $\frac{1}{3} \div 3$ (d) $\frac{1}{2} \div 5$ (e) $\frac{1}{5} \div 4$

D2 Work these out.

(a) $\frac{3}{4} \div 2$ (b) $\frac{2}{3} \div 2$ (c) $\frac{2}{5} \div 3$ (d) $\frac{3}{4} \div 5$ (e) $\frac{4}{5} \div 4$

D3 Work these out.

(a) $\frac{3}{5} \times 3$ (b) $\frac{2}{3} \div 5$ (c) $\frac{2}{5} \times 7$ (d) $\frac{3}{8} \div 2$ (e) $\frac{4}{5} \times 6$

E *Fractions of fractions*

This square represents 1 unit.

First it is split vertically into **quarters**.

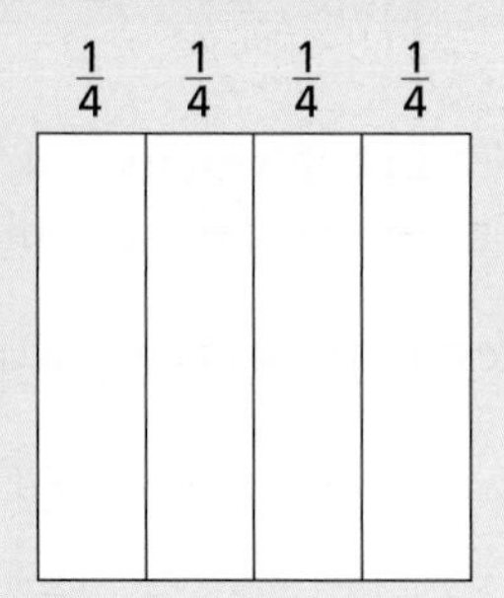

Then split horizontally into **thirds**.

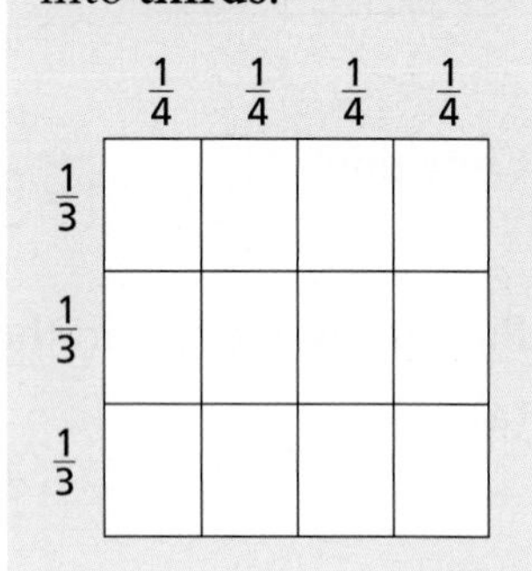

Lightly shade $\frac{1}{4}$.

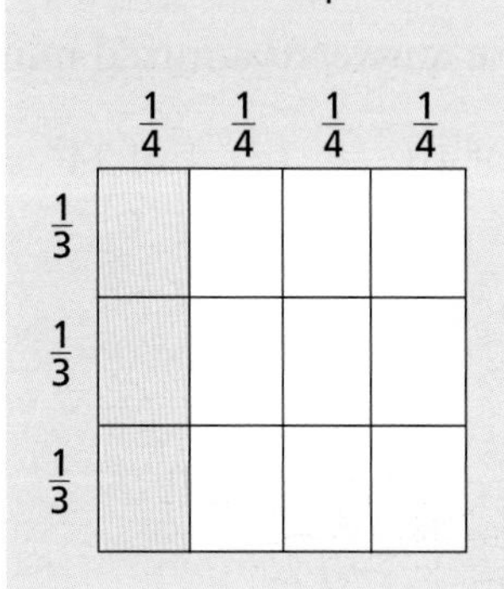

Then heavily shade $\frac{1}{3}$ of $\frac{1}{4}$.

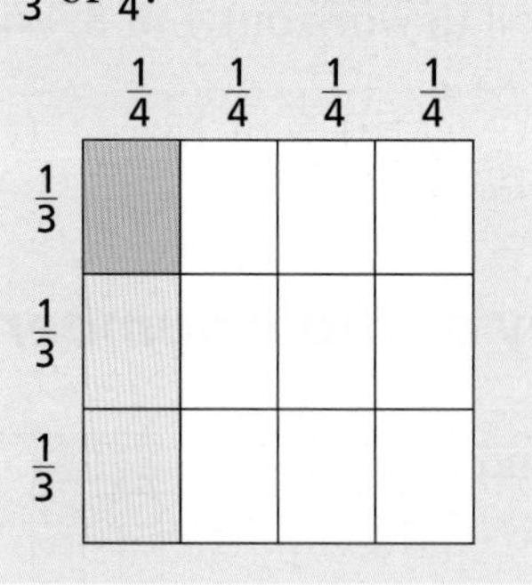

What fraction of the square is $\frac{1}{3}$ of $\frac{1}{4}$?

- What does each of these diagrams show?

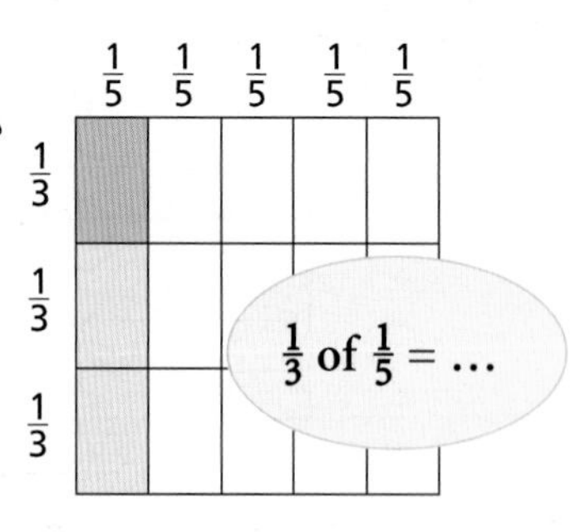

… of … = …

E1 What does each of these diagrams show?

(a)

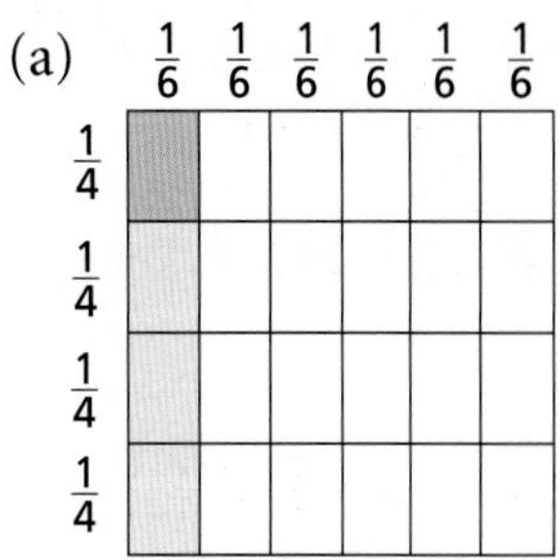

(b)

(c)

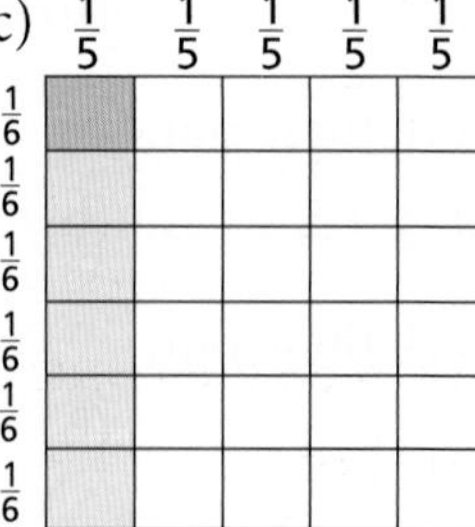

E2 'I lightly shade $\frac{3}{4}$, and heavily shade $\frac{2}{3}$ of $\frac{3}{4}$.'

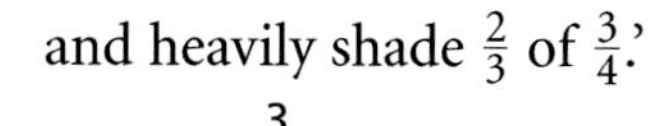

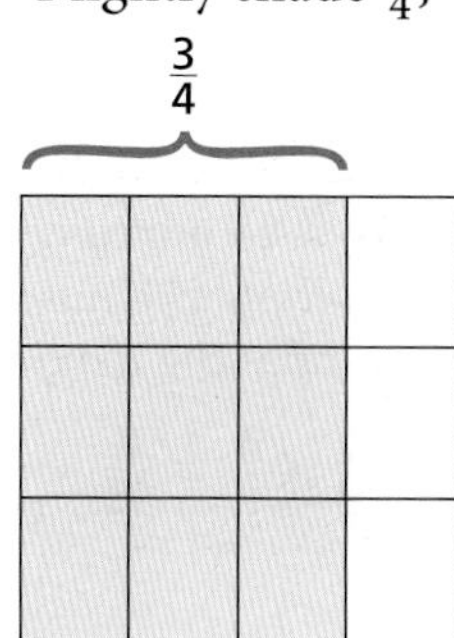

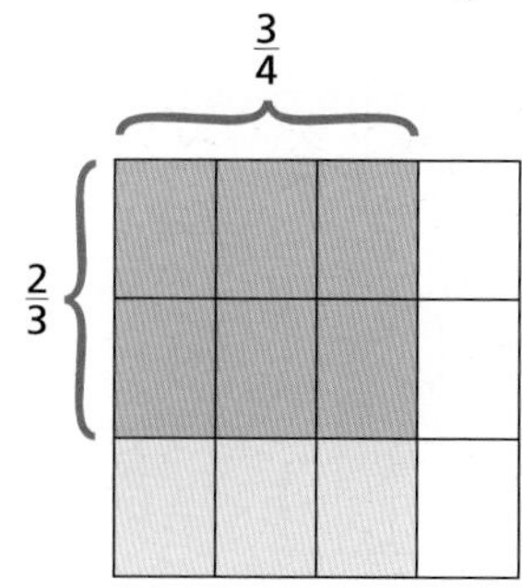

What fraction of the square is $\frac{2}{3}$ of $\frac{3}{4}$?

E3 'I lightly shade $\frac{3}{5}$, and heavily shade $\frac{3}{4}$ of $\frac{3}{5}$.'

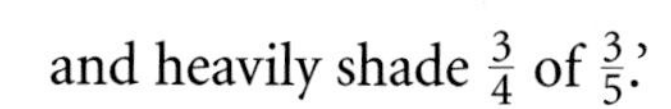

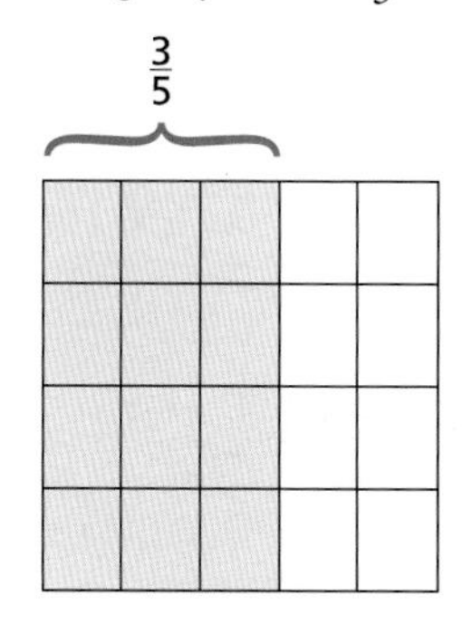

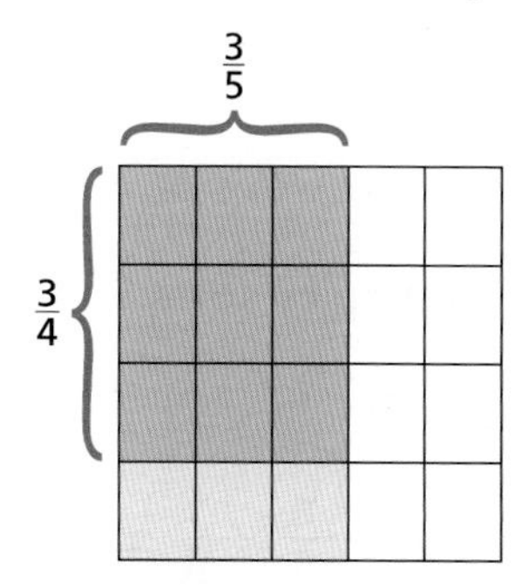

What fraction of the square is $\frac{3}{4}$ of $\frac{3}{5}$?

E4 What does each of these diagrams show?

(a)

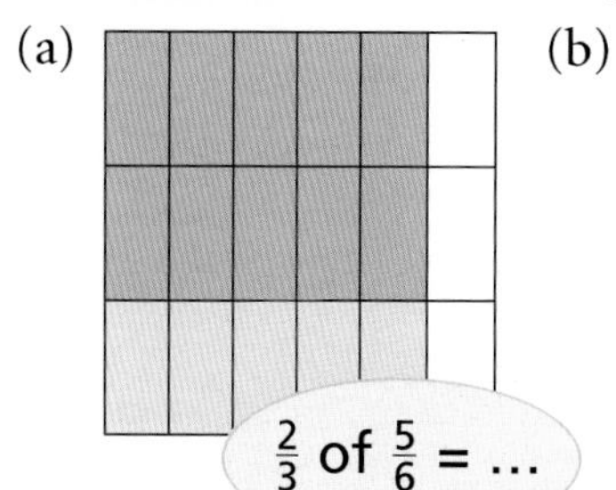

(b)

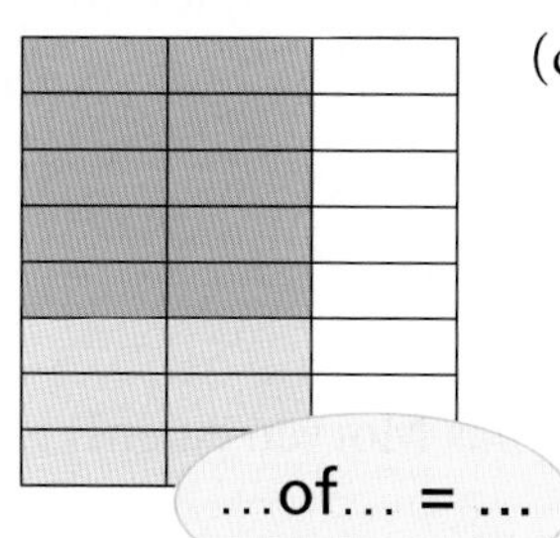

(c)

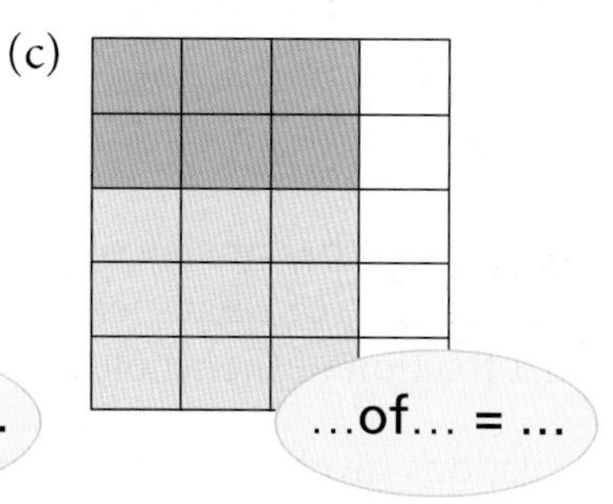

E5 Draw this diagram.

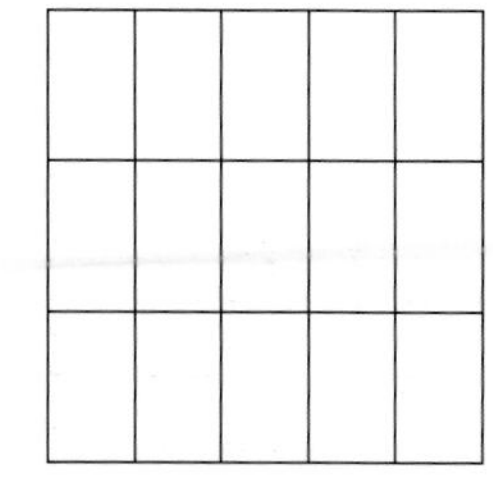

By light and dark shading, show some different fractions of fractions (at least three).

Here is one to start you off.

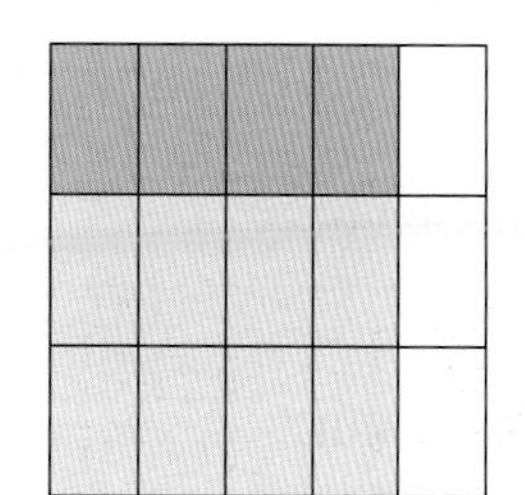

$\frac{1}{3}$ of $\frac{4}{5}$ = ...

E6 Try to do these without drawing diagrams.

(a) $\frac{1}{2}$ of $\frac{1}{4}$ (b) $\frac{1}{3}$ of $\frac{1}{7}$ (c) $\frac{3}{4}$ of $\frac{1}{2}$ (d) $\frac{2}{3}$ of $\frac{3}{5}$

F *Multiplying fractions*

$\frac{1}{2} \times \frac{1}{4}$ and $\frac{1}{2}$ of $\frac{1}{4}$ mean the same.

$\frac{1}{2} \times \frac{1}{4} = \frac{1}{8}$

$\frac{1}{4}$ $\frac{1}{2}$ $\frac{1}{8}$

This diagram shows that $\frac{2}{3} \times \frac{4}{5} = \frac{8}{15}$

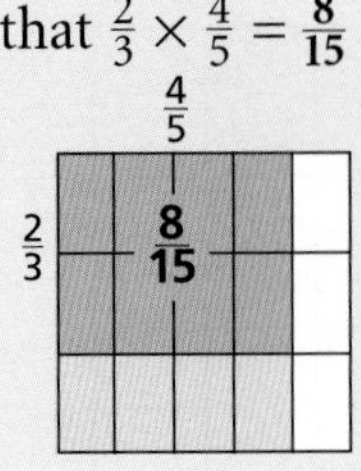

Notice that to multiply fractions, you multiply the numerators and multiply the denominators.

$\frac{2}{3} \times \frac{4}{5} = \frac{8}{15}$

F1 Work these out.

(a) $\frac{1}{2} \times \frac{1}{3}$ (b) $\frac{1}{3} \times \frac{1}{4}$ (c) $\frac{2}{3} \times \frac{1}{5}$ (d) $\frac{2}{3} \times \frac{4}{5}$ (e) $\frac{3}{4} \times \frac{3}{5}$

F2 Copy and complete these.

(a) $\frac{1}{2} \times \blacksquare = \frac{1}{12}$ (b) $\blacksquare \times \frac{1}{5} = \frac{1}{15}$ (c) $\frac{2}{3} \times \blacksquare = \frac{2}{15}$ (d) $\blacksquare \times \frac{5}{8} = \frac{15}{56}$

F3 Work these out, giving each result in its simplest form.

(a) $\frac{2}{3} \times \frac{1}{4}$ (b) $\frac{4}{5} \times \frac{3}{8}$ (c) $\frac{3}{4} \times \frac{5}{6}$ (d) $\frac{2}{3} \times \frac{3}{8}$

Sometimes you can **cancel** common factors first: $\frac{\cancel{4}^{1}}{5} \times \frac{1}{\cancel{8}_{2}} = \frac{1}{10}$

F4 Work these out, giving each result in its simplest form.

(a) $\frac{1}{3} \times \frac{3}{4}$ (b) $\frac{2}{3} \times \frac{5}{6}$ (c) $\frac{2}{3} \times \frac{5}{8}$ (d) $\frac{4}{5} \times \frac{7}{8}$ (e) $\frac{4}{5} \times \frac{5}{8}$

(f) $\frac{1}{8} \times \frac{4}{5}$ (g) $\frac{5}{8} \times \frac{3}{10}$ (h) $\frac{4}{5} \times \frac{7}{10}$ (i) $\frac{2}{3} \times \frac{6}{7}$ (j) $\frac{3}{4} \times \frac{4}{3}$

F5 Jill eats $\frac{1}{3}$ of a bar of chocolate.
Morven eats $\frac{1}{4}$ of what's left.
What fraction of the whole bar has Morven eaten?

For calculations involving **mixed numbers**, it is often a good idea to change any mixed numbers to improper fractions.

For example, $2\frac{2}{3} \times \frac{1}{7} = \frac{8}{3} \times \frac{1}{7}$
$= \frac{8}{21}$

F6 Work these out.

(a) $2\frac{1}{2} \times \frac{1}{3}$ (b) $\frac{1}{4} \times 3\frac{1}{2}$ (c) $2\frac{1}{3} \times \frac{2}{3}$ (d) $\frac{3}{4} \times 1\frac{1}{5}$

F7 Work these out.

(a) $1\frac{1}{2} \times 1\frac{1}{3}$ (b) $1\frac{1}{4} \times 2\frac{1}{2}$ (c) $2\frac{1}{3} \times 1\frac{2}{3}$ (d) $1\frac{2}{3} \times 2\frac{1}{2}$

***F8** Copy and complete these calculations.

(a) $\frac{1}{2} \times \blacksquare = \frac{1}{5}$ (b) $\frac{3}{4}$ of $\blacksquare = \frac{1}{2}$ (c) $\frac{2}{3} \times \blacksquare = 1$ (d) $\blacksquare$ of $2\frac{1}{4} = 1\frac{1}{2}$

G *Mixed questions*

These questions cover all the work on fractions done so far.

G1 (a) What numbers are missing here? (i) $\frac{1}{4} = \frac{■}{12}$ (ii) $\frac{1}{3} = \frac{■}{12}$

(b) Use the answers to (a) to work out $\frac{1}{4} + \frac{1}{3}$. (c) Work out $1\frac{1}{4} + 2\frac{1}{3}$.

(d) Work out $\frac{1}{3} - \frac{1}{4}$. (e) Work out $2\frac{1}{3} - 1\frac{1}{4}$. (f) Work out $3\frac{1}{4} - 1\frac{1}{3}$.

G2 Work these out. (a) $\frac{1}{2} + \frac{1}{3}$ (b) $\frac{3}{4} + \frac{1}{8}$ (c) $\frac{5}{6} - \frac{1}{4}$ (d) $\frac{3}{5} + \frac{3}{4}$

G3 Marty has a jug which holds $1\frac{1}{4}$ litres. He finds that 7 jugfuls will just fill his fish tank. How many litres does his fish tank hold?

G4 Work these out.

(a) $9 \times \frac{3}{4}$ (b) $\frac{1}{3}$ of 20 (c) $\frac{2}{3} \times 10$ (d) $\frac{3}{4}$ of 22 (e) $7 \times \frac{2}{5}$

G5 Work these out.

(a) $\frac{1}{3} \div 2$ (b) $\frac{1}{2} \div 4$ (c) $\frac{2}{3} \div 3$ (d) $\frac{3}{4} \div 3$ (e) $\frac{3}{5} \div 6$

G6 Work these out.

(a) $\frac{1}{3} \times \frac{3}{4}$ (b) $\frac{1}{2} \times \frac{2}{3}$ (c) $\frac{2}{3} \times \frac{3}{4}$ (d) $\frac{3}{4} \times \frac{3}{4}$ (e) $\frac{3}{5} \times \frac{2}{3}$

G7 Work these out.

(a) $1\frac{1}{3} + \frac{3}{4}$ (b) $1\frac{1}{5} \times \frac{2}{3}$ (c) $\frac{5}{6} - \frac{2}{3}$ (d) $\frac{3}{4} \times 1\frac{3}{8}$ (e) $1\frac{3}{5} + 2\frac{2}{3}$

Test yourself

T1 Jim said 'I've got three quarters of a tin of paint'.
Mary said 'I've got four sixths of a tin of paint and my tin of paint is the same size as yours'.

Who has the most paint, Mary or Jim? Explain your answer.

Edexcel

T2 Two rods are fastened together.
The total length is $3\frac{1}{3}$ inches.
The length of rod B is $1\frac{3}{4}$ inches.

Find the length of rod A.

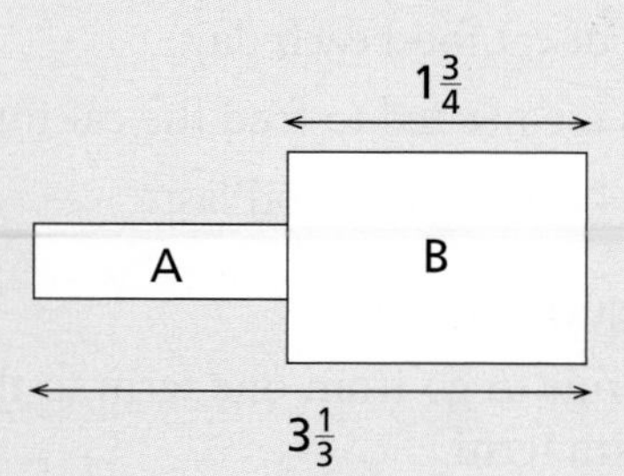

Edexcel

T3 Work out the following.
Give your answers as simply as possible.

(a) $\frac{2}{3} + \frac{4}{5}$ (b) $2\frac{2}{5} \times \frac{5}{6}$

OCR

Review 3

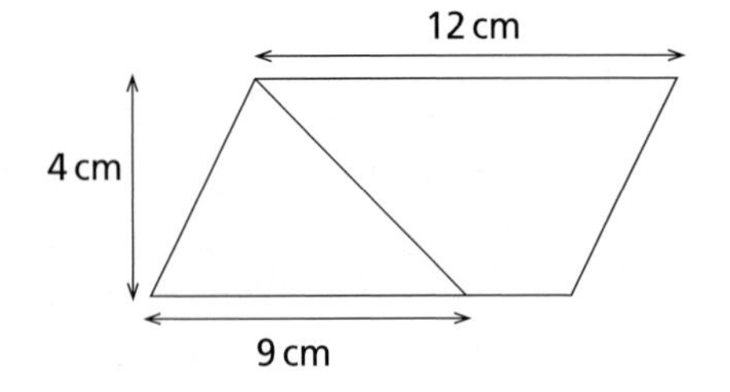

1 (a) What is the area of the whole parallelogram?
(b) Find the area of the triangle.
(c) (i) Write the area of the triangle as a fraction of the area of the parallelogram. Write it in its lowest terms.
(ii) Write this fraction as a decimal.

2 (a) What is the highest common factor of 36 and 27?
(b) (i) What is the lowest common multiple of 15 and 9?
(ii) Which is larger, $\frac{5}{9}$ or $\frac{7}{15}$?
(iii) Calculate $\frac{4}{9} - \frac{2}{15}$.

3 What is the value of $\dfrac{3n^2}{2}$ when $n = 4$?

4 What is the value of $a + b + c$ when $a = \frac{1}{2}$, $b = \frac{2}{5}$ and $c = \frac{7}{10}$?
Write your answer as a mixed number in its lowest terms.

5 There are 30 students in a class.
40% of the students are boys.
20% of the students wear glasses.
2 girls wear glasses.
How many boys do not wear glasses?

6 Work these out.

(a) $\frac{1}{7} \times 35$ (b) $48 \times \frac{1}{4}$ (c) $\frac{4}{5} \times 35$ (d) $84 \times \frac{3}{4}$ (e) $\frac{1}{4} \times 11$
(f) $17 \times \frac{2}{3}$ (g) $\frac{1}{6} \div 4$ (h) $\frac{2}{3} \div 5$ (i) $\frac{3}{5} \times \frac{5}{6}$ (j) $\frac{1}{3} + \frac{1}{5}$

7 A cat eats $\frac{2}{3}$ of a can of cat food each day.
(a) How many cans are needed to feed the cat for 12 days?
(b) How long will 14 cans of cat food last?

8 For each of these sequences,
- describe a rule to go from one term to the next
- find the sixth term

(a) 2, 9, 16, 23, 30, … (b) 0.6, 1.8, 5.4, 16.2, 48.6, … (c) 1, 3, 7, 15, 31, …

9 Joan is paid £117.88 for 14 hours' work.
How much will she be paid for 25 hours' work at the same rate?

10 A factory producing computers recorded this information over several weeks.

Week number	1	2	3	4	5	6
Number of computers made	2030	2289	3982	2847	4021	3109
Number of computers faulty	124	109	154	61	62	47

(a) Use percentages to comment on whether the quality of production is improving or getting worse.

(b) The managers plan to produce 3700 computers in week 7 and want at least 99% of them to be fault-free.
How many fault-free computers is that?

11 The nth term of a series is $\frac{12}{n+1}$.

Calculate the first six terms of the series, correct to two decimal places.

12 A row of 11 one-pound coins is 24.6 cm long.
How long is a row of 7 one-pound coins (to the nearest 0.1 cm)?

13 A box in the shape of a cuboid measures 30 cm by 50 cm by 90 cm.

(a) Work out the volume of the box in cm^3.

(b) Write the volume in m^3.

14 For each of these linear sequences,

- find an expression for the nth term
- use your expression to work out the 100th term

(a) 5, 8, 11, 14, 17, ... (b) 20, 18, 16, 14, 12, ... (c) $\frac{1}{2}$, $1\frac{1}{4}$, 2, $2\frac{3}{4}$, $3\frac{1}{2}$, ...

15 A tin of treacle has these dimensions.

(a) Calculate the volume of treacle it contains when full.

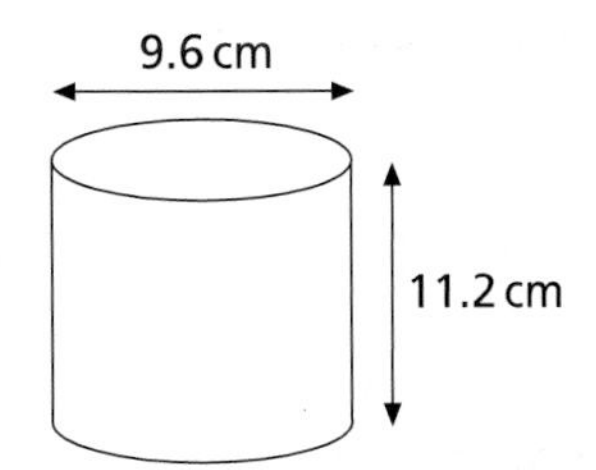

(b) A full tin of treacle is accidentally spilled on a kitchen floor.
The treacle spreads out until it is a puddle 3 mm thick.
What is the area of the puddle in square centimetres?

16 The instructions for some soluble lawn food say
'450 grams of lawn food is enough to feed 100 m^2 of lawn'.

How much lawn food is needed for a rectangular lawn 18 m by 15 m ?

17 Find the volume of each prism.
Give your answers in cm^3 correct to two significant figures.

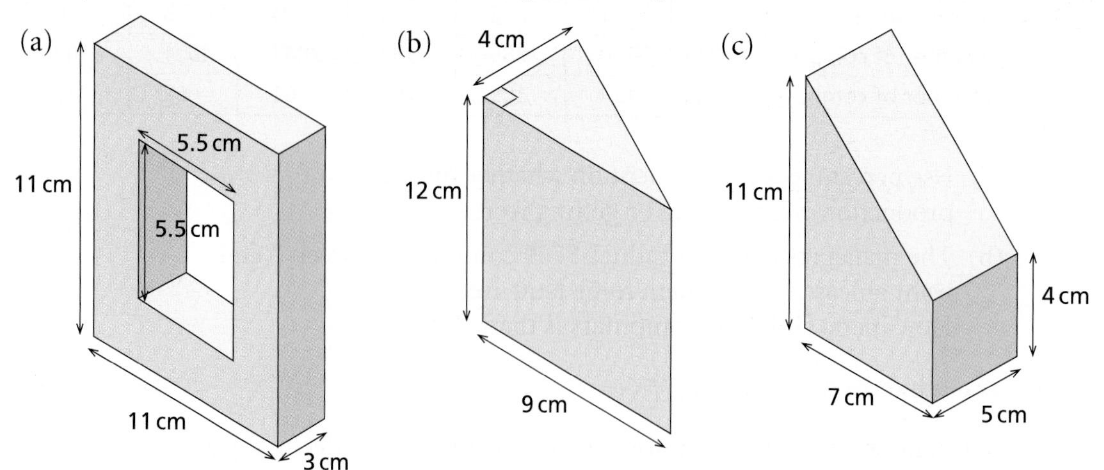

18 A pint is approximately 0.57 of a litre.
A supermarket sells milk at 78p for a two-pint carton.
How much is this per litre?

19 The volume of a square based pyramid is given by the formula

$$V = \tfrac{1}{3}b^2h$$

where V is the volume, b is the edge length of the square base and h is the height.
Find the volume of a square based pyramid where $b = 4.5$ cm and $h = 9.8$ cm.

20 Matchsticks are used to make these designs.

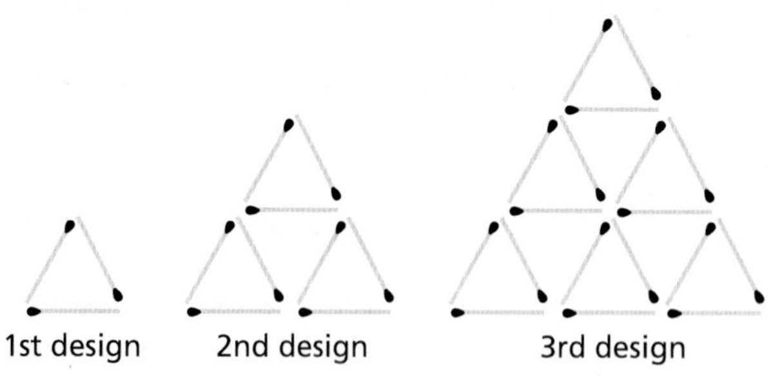

(a) Draw the 4th design.
How many matchsticks are needed for it?

(b) The number of matchsticks in each design gives the sequence 3, 9, 18, …
Write down the first six terms of this sequence.
Is the sequence linear or non-linear?

(c) Describe a rule to go from one term to the next for the sequence.

(d) How is the sequence 3, 9, 18, … related to the sequence of triangle numbers?
What it is about the designs that makes these sequences related in this way?
(Use a sketch to help your explanation if you need to).

18 Pie charts

You will revise how to work with fractions and percentages.

This work will help you

- read information from a pie chart
- draw a pie chart from data

A *Fractions, percentages and angles*

A1 Find these. (a) $\frac{1}{4}$ of 360 (b) $\frac{2}{5}$ of 120 (c) $\frac{2}{3}$ of 240 (d) $\frac{7}{10}$ of 180

A2 Write these fractions in their simplest form.

(a) $\frac{72}{120}$ (b) $\frac{100}{360}$ (c) $\frac{42}{90}$ (d) $\frac{125}{360}$ (e) $\frac{324}{360}$

A3 In a class $\frac{1}{2}$ of the students walk to school, $\frac{1}{3}$ of them cycle and the rest come by bus.

(a) What fraction come by bus?

(b) If there are 30 students in the class, how many come by bus?

A4 In this circle what fraction, in its simplest form, is shaded each of these colours.

(a) Pink (b) Yellow (c) Green

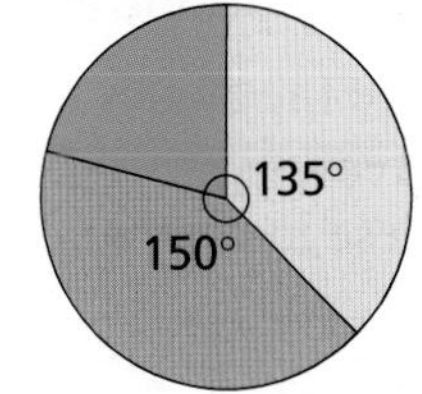

A5 Write these fractions as percentages.

(a) $\frac{1}{2}$ (b) $\frac{3}{4}$ (c) $\frac{8}{10}$ (d) $\frac{3}{5}$ (e) $\frac{11}{20}$

A6 Calculate these. (a) 25% of 180 (b) 20% of 360 (c) 35% of 360

A7 Write down the decimal equivalents of each of these.

(a) 32.5% (b) 68.4% (c) 60.4% (d) 2.4% (e) 0.8%

A8 Write each of these as a percentage.

(a) 0.452 (b) 0.884 (c) 0.703 (d) 0.012 (e) 0.005

A9 Work out to one decimal place (a) 39% of 180 (b) 2% of 360 (c) 72% of 73 (d) 35.6% of 180 (e) 20.4% of 80 (f) 4.5% of 73

A10 Write these as a percentage, correct to 1 d.p.

(a) 124 out of 360 (b) 95 out of 250 (c) 624 out of of 2527

A11 Find these, correct to 1 d.p. (a) $\frac{21}{70}$ of 360 (b) $\frac{74}{360} \times 80$ (c) $\frac{29}{50} \times 132$

B *Reading pie charts*

B1 This chart shows sales of ice-creams at a school fete.

The total number of ice-creams sold was 600.

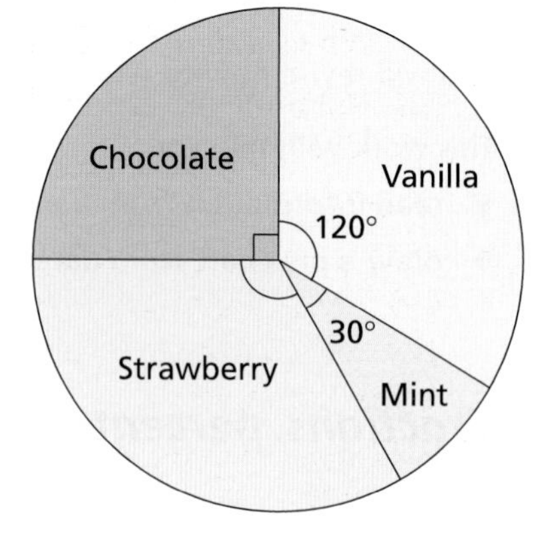

(a) What fraction of the ice-creams sold were chocolate?

(b) How many ice-creams sold were chocolate?

(c) What fraction of the ice-creams were vanilla?

(d) How many vanilla ice-creams were sold?

(e) How many strawberry ice-creams were sold?

(f) How many mint ice-creams were sold?

B2 In a survey in a magazine people were asked what was the main reason for choosing a particular holiday destination. This pie chart shows the replies of 270 people.

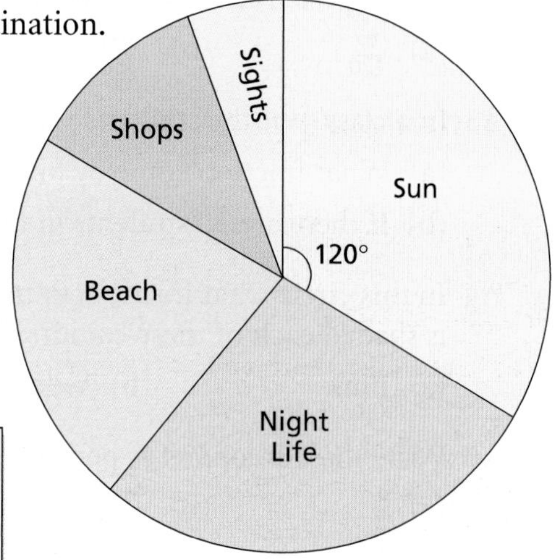

(a) What fraction of people gave 'sun' as their reason? Write this in simplest form.

(b) How many people gave 'sun' as their reason?

(c) Measure the angles for each of the other reasons. Use these to copy and complete this table.

Reason	Angle	Fraction	Number
Sun	120°		
Sights			
Shops			

B3 A store records how many CDs of different types of music they sold in one week. They show the results in a pie chart. There were 25 classical CDs sold and these had an angle of 45° on the pie chart.

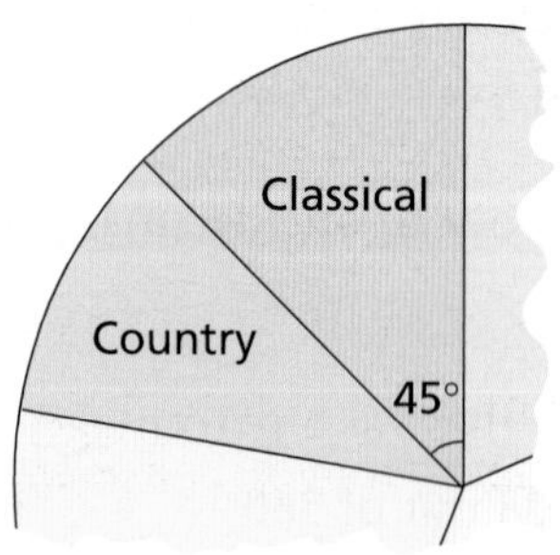

(a) What fraction, in its simplest form, of CDs sold were classical?

(b) How many CDs were sold altogether that week?

(c) There were 75 pop CDs sold that week. What angle would be used on the pie chart to show sales of pop CDs?

B4 (a) The pie chart shows information about the milk sold in a supermarket one day.

(i) Which type of milk is the mode?

(ii) 160 pints of skimmed milk are sold. How many pints of semi-skimmed milk are sold?

(b) Each week the supermarket sells 6480 pints of milk. Two fifths of the milk is sold in 4-pint containers.

How many 4-pint containers of milk are sold?

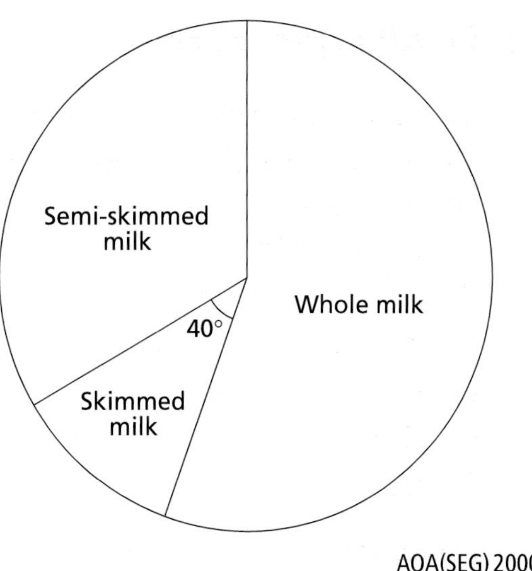

AQA(SEG) 2000

C *Using percentages*

Pie charts are often labelled with the percentages for each category.

Computer programs which draw pie charts can usually be made to show percentages.

This pie chart has been produced on a computer to show the school uniform colour choice of 28 students in a class.

How many people chose black?
35% of 28 = $0.35 \times 28 = 9.8$ so 10 people.

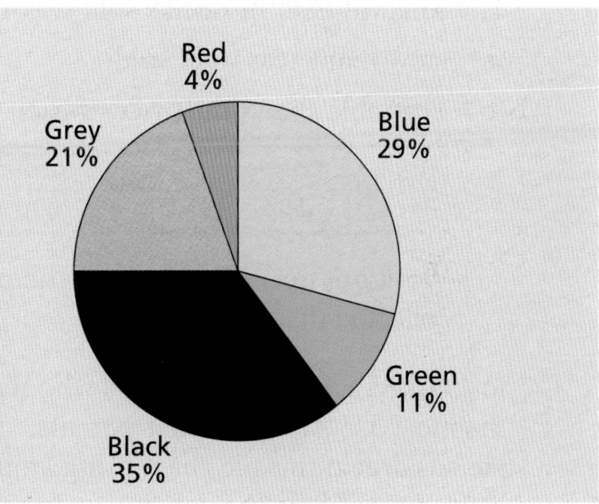

TG

C1 A group of 80 students were asked what was the main carbohydrate in their evening meal main last night. This pie chart shows the results.

(a) How many of the students said chips?

(b) How many students said pizza?

(c) How many students had something other than chips or potatoes?

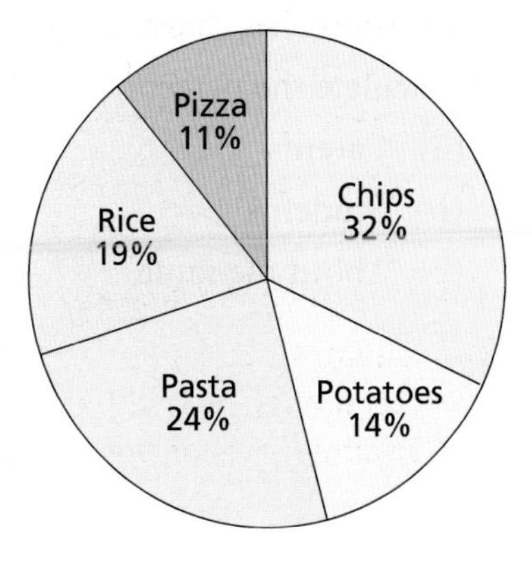

C2 The 55 students in a school year group each entered a piece for a local Art Exhibition.
The pieces that were exhibited were awarded Commendation, Merit or Distinction certificates.
This pie chart shows the awards.

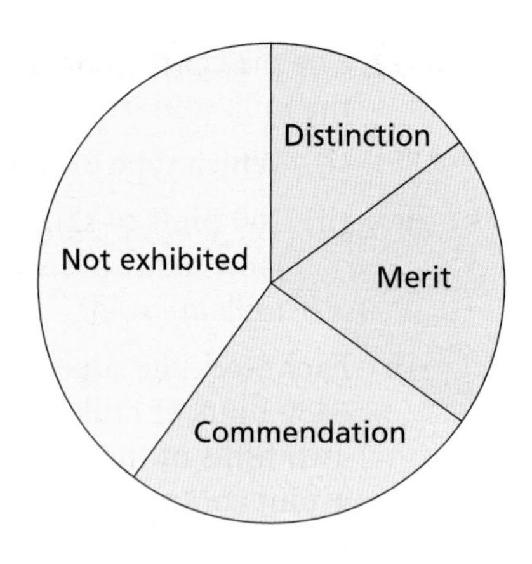

(a) Use a pie chart scale to find the percentage of students whose work was not exhibited.

(b) How many students gained a Distinction?

(c) Schools were given points for those students who exhibited.

Distinction 5 points
Merit 3 points
Commendation 1 point.

Calculate the total points scored by this year group.

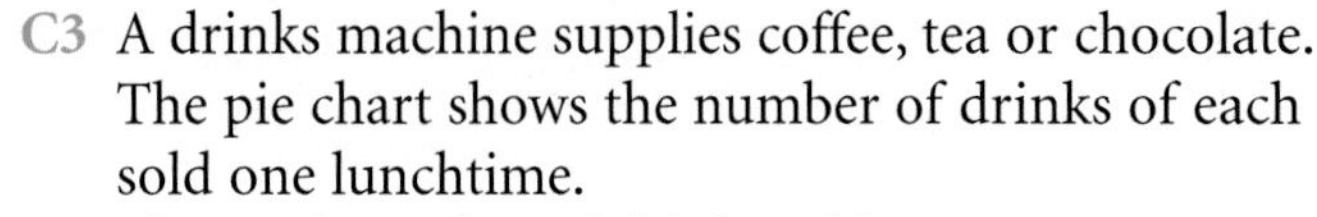

C3 A drinks machine supplies coffee, tea or chocolate.
The pie chart shows the number of drinks of each sold one lunchtime.
The total number of drinks sold was 160.

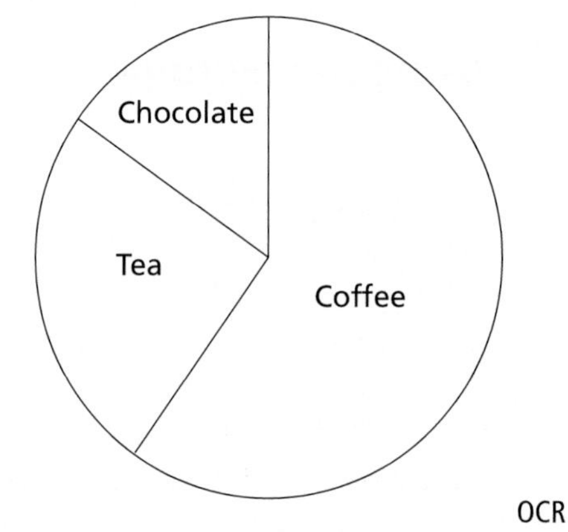

(a) How many teas were sold?

(b) The table shows the price of each drink.

Drink	Coffee	Tea	Chocolate
Price	50p	45p	60p

Work out how much money the machine collected that lunchtime.

OCR

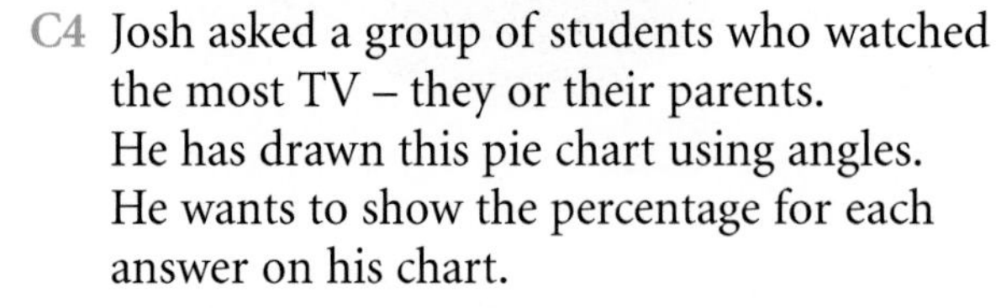

C4 Josh asked a group of students who watched the most TV – they or their parents.
He has drawn this pie chart using angles.
He wants to show the percentage for each answer on his chart.

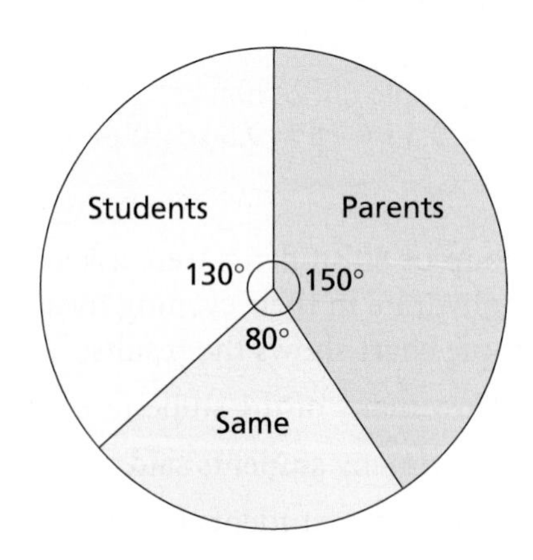

Calculate the percentages who said

(a) 'Parents'

(b) 'Students'

(c) 'About the same'

D Drawing pie charts: angles

Are you a veggie?

Sarah asks a sample of people whether they are vegan, vegetarian or eat meat.
This table shows her results.

She thinks that a pie chart is the best way to show her results.

Reply	*Tally*	*Frequency*
Vegan	*//*	*2*
Vegetarian	*//// //// /*	*11*
Vegetarian - but eat fish	*//// ///*	*8*
Meat eater	*//// //// //// ////*	*19*
Total		***40***

First she works out what angle is used to show a single person.

÷ 40 — 40 people are shown by 360° — ÷ 40
1 person is shown by 9°

So the angle in the pie chart needed for vegan is $2 \times 9° = 18°$

- Work out the angles for the other responses.
  Use these to draw a pie chart.

Reply	Frequency	Angle
Vegan	2	18°
Vegetarian		

D1 In a survey 120 people were asked how they learned to use a computer.
The results are to be shown in a pie chart.
The results were:

How I learnt	Frequency
Self-taught	49
Learned at school	31
Learned at work	28
Taught by family/friend	7
Other	5
Total	120

(a) What angle will be used to show each person in the pie chart?

(b) What angle will represent the people who were self taught?

(c) Draw a pie chart, with radius 5 cm, to show the information in this table.

D2 Pali asked 180 boys what was their favourite sport.
Here are his results.

Sport	Soccer	Rugby	Cricket	Basketball	Other
Number of boys	74	25	18	37	26

(a) Draw a pie chart for these results.
Use a circle of radius 6 cm.

Pali also asked 90 girls about their favourite sport.
In a pie chart showing the results, the angle for Tennis was 84°.

(b) How many of the girls said that Tennis was their favourite sport? OCR

D3 Swimmers taking a survival test can achieve a gold, silver or bronze award.
Last month 240 swimmers took the test.
The results are shown in the table.

Award	Number of swimmers
Gold	30
Silver	80
Bronze	120
Failed	10
Total	240

Draw a pie chart to illustrate this information.
Use a radius of 5 cm.

AQA(SEG) 2000

TG

Tricky numbers

In this survey the total number of people interviewed was 420.
To find out what angle represents one person the calculation is 360° ÷ 420. A calculator gives

0.857142857

This could be rounded but it is more accurate to store this in full in your calculator memory to use each time.

Should the UK adopt the Euro?

Response	*Frequency*
Not at any time	*154*
As soon as possible	*126*
When the time is right	*105*
Don't know	*35*
Total	*420*

D4 Draw a pie chart to illustrate the results from the Euro survey above.
Use a radius of 5 cm.

D5 A council is looking at the causes of road accidents in its area last year.
This table shows the data collected.

Draw a pie chart to illustrate these results.
Use a radius of 5 cm.

Cause of accident	Number of accidents
Speeding	96
Driver error	75
Weather conditions	42
Mechanical failure	30
Other	27
Total	270

D6 In a survey the eye colours of the 540 students in a school were recorded.
The table shows the information.

Eye colour	Number of students
Green	
Blue	123
Grey	
Brown	243
Total	540

This information can be shown in a pie chart.
The pie chart on sheet G112 is incomplete.
Complete the pie chart.

Edexcel

E *Drawing pie charts: percentages*

This table shows the results of a survey of 125 students on what they think of school uniform.

Response	Frequency
Should be compulsory	35
Compulsory but more choice	50
Should not be compulsory	25
Don't know	15
Total	125

To find the percentage who said 'should be compulsory',

35 ÷ 125 = 0.28 which is the decimal equivalent of 28%

- What percentage of the total gave each of the other responses?

A percentage pie chart scale can be used to draw the pie chart.

E1 Keith records the eye colour of the people in his class.

Colour	Frequency
Brown	13
Blue	8
Green	3
Grey	1

(a) How many people are in his class?

(b) What percentage of the class has blue eyes?

(c) Work out all the percentages and draw the pie chart. Label each sector.

E2 Paul asked 50 boys what was their favourite fruit.
Here are his results.

Fruit	Apple	Orange	Banana	Grapes	Other
Number of boys	8	6	20	9	7

(a) Draw a pie chart to show these results.

Paul also asked some girls about their favourite fruit.
This pie chart shows the results.

(b) State one way in which the girls' and boys' results are similar.

(c) State one way in which the girls' results are different from the boys' results.

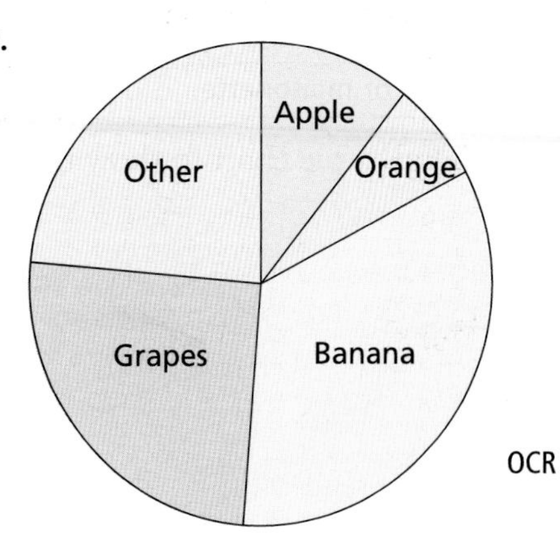

OCR

E3 A school canteen sells 150 packets of crisps one lunchtime.
The table shows the number of each flavour sold.

Flavour	Plain	Salt and vinegar	Cheese and onion	Other
Packets sold	21	57	66	6

(a) What percentage of the crisps sold were plain?

(b) Draw a pie chart to show the sales of the different flavours of crisps.

F *Handling real data*

In these examples the angles or percentages that need to be used are not always whole numbers.
Round such numbers off to whole numbers but check that the total angle is 360°, or the total percentage is 100%.

F1 In a survey, a total of 2975 families with dependent children were asked who looked after the children.
Here are the results.

Main carers	Number of families
Couple	2352
Widowed, divorced or separated mother	357
Single mother	208
Lone father	58

Draw a pie chart to show these results.

F2 In a survey, a total of 9128 people were asked what type of home they lived in.
Here are the results.

Type of home	Frequency
Detached house	1917
Semi-detached house	2921
Terraced house	2465
Flat or maisonette	1825

Draw a pie chart to show these results.

Test yourself

T1 Karen did a survey to find the most popular cereal.

(a) The results for the **adults** are shown in a table.

Cereal	Muesli	Weeta Bites	Cornflakes	Other cereals
Number of adults	20	15	30	25

Draw a clearly labelled pie chart to illustrate this information.

(b) The results for the **children** are shown in this pie chart.

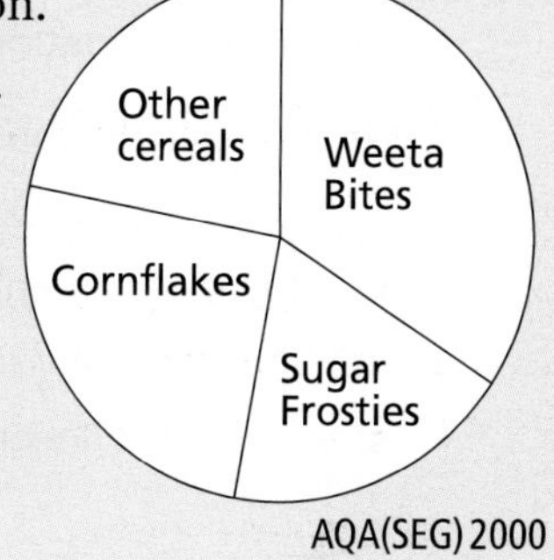

A third of the children eat Weeta Bites.
A quarter of the children eat Cornflakes.
Weeta Bites are eaten by 40 children,
How many children eat Cornflakes?

AQA(SEG) 2000

T2 The pie chart shows the results of a survey about the takeaway foods students like best.

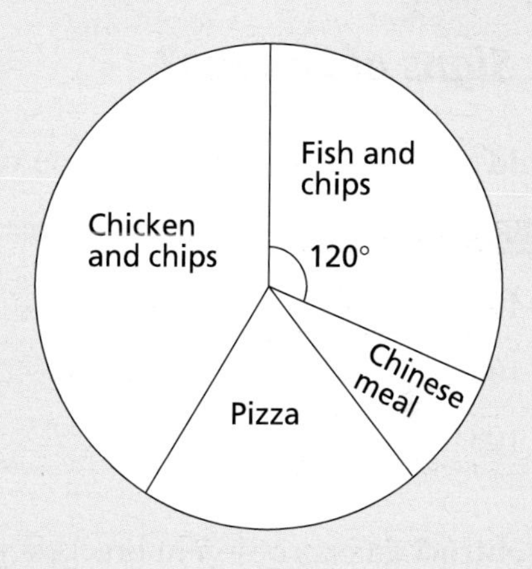

(a) Fish and chips is liked best by 80 students. How many students like Pizza best?

(b) The table shows the results of a survey about the takeaway foods liked best by 100 pensioners.

Takeaway food	Frequency
Fish and chips	40
Chicken and chips	43
Pizza	9
Chinese meal	8

Do these surveys support the hypothesis:

'More pensioners than students like fish and chips.'

Explain your answer.

AQA 2003 Specimen

T3 The table gives information about the times 60 teachers take to travel to school.

Time in minutes	Frequency	Angle
Less than 10	5	
Between 10 and 15	15	
Between 15 and 20	12	
More than 20	28	

Draw a pie chart to show this information.

19 Brackets and equations

You should know how to

- simplify an expression such as $1 - 2x + 6 - 3x$ to give $7 - 5x$
- multiply out brackets such as $2(3x + 4)$ to give $6x + 8$
- simplify divisions such as $\frac{8n - 2}{2}$ to give $4n - 1$
- solve linear equations such as $6 + 3x = 10 - x$

This work will help you

- add and subtract expressions in brackets such as $(5 + 4x) - (3x + 4)$
- simplify more complex expressions such as $4(3x - 5) - 2(4x - 1)$
- use algebra to prove statements like 'The result for this puzzle will always be 4.'
- solve complex linear equations

A *Signs of change?*

TG

To **add** an expression in brackets you can remove the brackets and then simplify.

Examples

$100 + (6 + 2)$	$100 + (6 - 2)$	$6 + (2p + 1)$	$(3n + 5) + (n - 6)$
$= 100 + 6 + 2$	$= 100 + 6 - 2$	$= 6 + 2p + 1$	$= 3n + 5 + n - 6$
$= 108$	$= 104$	$= 7 + 2p$	$= 4n - 1$

To **subtract** an expression in brackets you need to be careful with signs.

Examples

$100 - (6 + 2)$	$100 - (6 - 2)$	$6 - (2p + 1)$	$(3n + 5) - (n - 6)$
$= 100 - 6 - 2$	$= 100 - 6 + 2$	$= 6 - 2p - 1$	$= 3n + 5 - n + 6$
[illegible]	$= 96$	$= 5 - 2p$	$= 2n + 11$

...ng expressions.

(b) $(y + 5) + (2y - 1)$ (c) $(3x + 2) + (x - 6)$

...$w)$ (e) $(2v - 1) + (5v - 3)$ (f) $(6 - u) + (2 - 3u)$

...xpressions.

(b) $10 - (s - 1)$ (c) $3r - (5 + 2r)$

(e) $(8p + 6) - (5 + 3p)$ (f) $(2n + 1) - (9 - 2n)$

A3 Find four pairs of equivalent expressions.

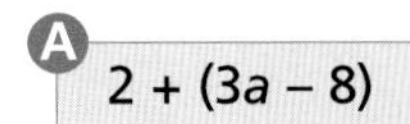

B $4a - (3a + 6)$

C $(2a + 1) + (a - 9)$

D $(6a - 8) + (2 - 5a)$

E $4a - (6 - 3a)$

F $(8a - 7) + (1 - a)$

G $2a - (8 - a)$

H $5a - (6 + 2a)$

A4 Simplify the following expressions.

(a) $(m + 3) + (5m - 9)$ (b) $10k - (3k - 8)$ (c) $(6j + 9) - (4j + 5)$

(d) $(7h - 3) + (5 - 2h)$ (e) $(7g - 3) - (5 - 2g)$ (f) $(f + 2) - (5 - f)$

(g) $(9 - 3e) - (7 + 8e)$ (h) $(5d - 6) - (3d - 5)$ (i) $(5c - 6) + (3c - 5)$

(j) $(10 - 5b) + (2 - 3b)$ (k) $(10 - 5a) - (2 - 3a)$ (l) $(6x + 3) - (7x + 1)$

A5 Solve the puzzle on sheet G113.

*A6 (a) Try some numbers for this puzzle and describe what happens.

(b) Copy and complete the algebra box to explain how the puzzle works.

Puzzle

Think of a number

- Add 5
- Subtract **from** 30
- Add the number you first thought of

What is the result?

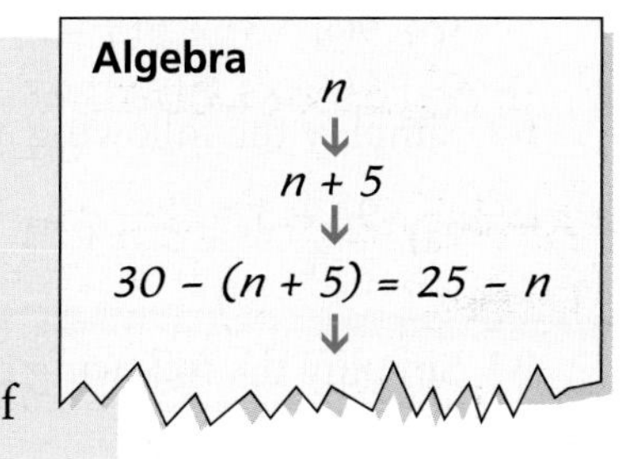

*A7 For each puzzle below,

(a) try some numbers and describe what happens

(b) use algebra to explain how the puzzle works

1

Think of a number

- Multiply by 3
- Add 9
- Subtract from 12
- Divide by 3
- Add the number you first thought of

What is the result?

2

Think of a number

- Subtract from 20
- Multiply by 2
- Subtract from 100
- Divide by 2
- Subtract 30

What is the result?

3

Think of a number

- Subtract 1
- Multiply by 4
- Subtract from 40
- Divide by 4
- Add the number you first thought of

What is the result?

B *Further simplifying*

It is often a good idea to multiply out any brackets and simplify divisions before sorting out any signs.

Examples

$(3n + 5) - 2(n + 6)$
$= (3n + 5) - (2n + 12)$
$= 3n + 5 - 2n - 12$
$= n - 7$

$2(5n - 4) - 3(2n - 6)$
$= (10n - 8) - (6n - 18)$
$= 10n - 8 - 6n + 18$
$= 4n + 10$

$\frac{3n + 6}{3} + 2(n + 5)$
$= \frac{3n}{3} + \frac{6}{3} + (2n + 10)$
$= n + 2 + 2n + 10$
$= 3n + 12$

B1 Simplify the following expressions.

(a) $6n + 7(n + 1)$ (b) $(3n + 5) + 2(2n - 1)$ (c) $2(n + 3) + 6(2n - 3)$
(d) $9(n - 3) + 5(3 - n)$ (e) $2(2n + 1) + 4(3 - n)$ (f) $3(n - 2) + 6(n + 1)$

B2 Simplify the following expressions.

(a) $\frac{9n + 3}{3} + 5(n + 2)$ (b) $\frac{10n + 8}{2} + 3(5n - 2)$ (c) $\frac{6n + 9}{3} + 2(5 - n)$

B3 Simplify the following expressions.

(a) $12 - 2(x + 3)$ (b) $(7x + 5) - 3(x + 1)$ (c) $5(3x + 3) - 4(2x - 3)$
(d) $7(x - 3) - 3(3 + x)$ (e) $10x - 3(2x - 5)$ (f) $4(2x + 3) - 6(2 - x)$

B4 Simplify the following expressions.

(a) $\frac{20x + 8}{4} - 3(2 + x)$ (b) $\frac{14x + 21}{7} - 3(6 - 2x)$ (c) $\frac{10x - 14}{2} - 2(5 - x)$

B5 Simplify the following expressions.

(a) $5p + 2(5 - 4p)$ (b) $(10p - 3) - 6(p + 2)$ (c) $2(5p + 3) - 9(p - 2)$
(d) $\frac{1}{4}(8p - 20) + 2(6 - p)$ (e) $\frac{45p + 40}{5} - 2(3 + 2p)$ (f) $\frac{12p + 36}{6} - 3(2 - 3p)$

***B6** Copy and complete each statement.

(a) $2(3x + 1) + ■(x - ■) = 11x - 13$
(b) $■ - 3(2 - p) = 13p - 6$
(c) $2(3m - ■) - ■(2m - 5) = 13$
(d) $\frac{8h - 12}{■} - 3(■ - h) = 5h - 6$

C Equations

Example

$$10x - 2(x + 5) = 3(15 - x)$$ [multiply out brackets]
$$10x - (2x + 10) = 45 - 3x$$ [simplify]
$$8x - 10 = 45 - 3x$$ [+ 3x]
$$11x - 10 = 45$$ [+ 10]
$$11x = 55$$ [÷ 11]
$$x = 5$$

C1 (a) Simplify the expression $5n + 3(n - 5)$.
(b) Use the result of part (a) to solve the equation $5n + 3(n - 5) = 1$.

C2 (a) Simplify the expression $10 - (5 - c)$.
(b) Use the result of part (a) to solve the equation $10 - (5 - c) = 20$.

C3 (a) Simplify the expression $12 - 3(1 + e)$.
(b) Use the result of part (a) to solve the equation $12 - 3(1 + e) = 21$.

C4 Solve these equations.
(a) $17 + 5(c - 4) = 47$ (b) $16 - 2(d + 3) = 7$ (c) $6f - 3(2 - f) = 12$
(d) $5 - (g - 6) = 1$ (e) $h + 3(h - 1) = 3$ (f) $25 - 5(3k + 4) = 20$
(g) $3m - 5(2 - m) = 10$ (h) $2(3 - 2n) + 5(n + 1) = 8$ (i) $3(p + 1) - 2(1 - 4p) = 34$

C5 Solve these equations.
(a) $12 - (3 + q) = q - 1$ (b) $5r + 2(6 + r) = 3r + 8$
(c) $10s - 3(2s - 1) = 6(s - 1)$ (d) $6(t - 2) - 5(1 - 3t) = 2(t + 1)$

Test yourself

T1 Simplify these expressions.
(a) $10 - (4 + 5x)$ (b) $2(n + 3) + 5(n - 6)$ (c) $4(3m - 2) + 3(2m - 1)$
(d) $\frac{4n + 16}{4} - 3n$ (e) $10k - 3(1 - 2k)$ (f) $5(3x - 4) - 7(2x - 5)$

T2 Solve these equations.
(a) $6m + 2(m - 3) = 58$ (b) $2(c + 6) + 3(c - 1) = 4$
(c) $n - 3(2 - n) = 4$ (d) $3(2k - 5) + 5(3k + 1) = 179$

T3 Solve these equations.
(a) $5s + 2(8 - s) = 17(s - 4)$ (b) $2(x + 1) - 3(x - 5) = 5(x + 7)$

20 Using a calculator

You should know

- what brackets mean in a calculation
- how to round to a number of decimal places or significant figures

This work will help you

- use a calculator for complex calculations
- work with squares, square roots and negative numbers

A Brackets and punctuation

Four add two, multiplied by three

Four, add two multiplied by three

The position of the comma alters the calculation.

Brackets make the calculations clear.

$(4 + 2) \times 3$

$4 + (2 \times 3)$

Scientific calculators do not need the brackets in the second calculation.
They automatically multiply or divide before they add or subtract.

$4 + 2 \times 3 = 4 + 6 = 10$

A1 For each of the calculations below

(i) predict what the result will be without using a calculator

(ii) then check with a calculator

(a) $7 + 5 \times 4$ (b) $5 \times (6 - 2)$ (c) $20 - (6 - 2)$ (d) $20 + 12 \times 4$

(e) $5 \times 6 + 3$ (f) $5 \times 3 + 7 \times 4$ (g) $5 \times (3 + 7) \times 4$ (h) $4 + 2 \times 8 + 3$

A2 Do these on a calculator.
Round each answer to 2 decimal places.

(a) $(4.82 + 2.94) \times 6.5$ (b) $4.82 + 2.94 \times 6.5$

(c) $3.74 \times 2.81 - 1.66$ (d) $12.65 - 2.91 \times 0.36$

(e) $8.64 + 2.37 \times 1.08 - 2.67$ (f) $0.85 \times (3.47 + 1.26) - 2.55$

(g) $4.22 \times 3.14 + 0.88 \times 2.57$

A3 Do these on a calculator.
Round each answer to 3 significant figures.

(a) $2.62 + 3.91 \times 4.5$ (b) $(1.82 + 4.94) \times 2.5$

(c) $40.4 \times (17.31 - 8.86)$ (d) $665 - 16.1 \times 13.2$

(e) $7.14 - 1.47 \times 1.13 + 4.61$ (f) $0.65 \times (3.52 - 1.46) + 3.58$

(g) $8.12 \times 0.64 - 0.92 \times 3.82$

B *Division*

In written calculations, a bar is often used for division.

Written	On calculator	
$6 + \frac{24}{3}$	6 + 24 ÷ 3	Brackets are not needed here. The calculator automatically does 24 ÷ 3 first.
$\frac{6 + 24}{3}$	(6 + 24) ÷ 3	The division bar does a similar job to brackets.
$\frac{24}{7 + 3}$	24 ÷ (7 + 3)	
$\frac{6 + 24}{7 + 3}$	(6 + 24) ÷ (7 + 3)	

B1 Do these on your calculator.
All the answers should be whole numbers.

(a) $\frac{8.71 - 3.01}{1.9}$ (b) $\frac{130.9}{18.7} + 5$ (c) $(6.5 + 5.5) \times 1.5$

(d) $4.95 + 2.5 \times 2.02$ (e) $2.8 + \frac{2.88}{2.4}$ (f) $\frac{109.8}{4.4 + 1.7}$

(g) $\frac{17.38 + 2.22}{6.13 - 1.23}$ (h) $\frac{22.4}{0.76 + 0.64}$ (i) $\frac{14.08 - 6.93}{0.88 + 0.55}$

B2 Match each written calculation to a calculation on a calculator.

Written

A $5 + \frac{8}{2} + 3$ B $\frac{5}{8 + 2 + 3}$ C $\frac{5 + 8 + 2}{3}$ D $\frac{5 + 8}{2 + 3}$

E $5 + \frac{8 + 2}{3}$ F $\frac{5}{8 + 2} + 3$ G $\frac{5 + 8}{2} + 3$

Calculator

T 5 ÷ (8 + 2) + 3 U 5 ÷ (8 + 2 + 3) V 5 + 8 ÷ 2 + 3 W (5 + 8) ÷ 2 + 3

X (5 + 8) ÷ (2 + 3) Y (5 + 8 + 2) ÷ 3 Z 5 + (8 + 2) ÷ 3

B3 Calculate each of these, giving the result to 2 decimal places.

(a) $\frac{4.75 - 1.08}{2.03}$ (b) $0.68 + \frac{2.95}{1.07}$ (c) $\frac{4.86}{2.57 - 1.08}$

(d) $\frac{4.18 - 1.92}{7.15 - 3.28}$ (e) $\frac{115.4}{8.76 - 2.54}$ (f) $\frac{9.08 + 7.12}{6.48 - 3.25}$

C Using the memory

The memory on a calculator can sometimes be used instead of brackets.
Memory keys may be labelled 'Min', 'Mout' or 'Store', 'Recall' (and many other ways).
For example, here are two ways to calculate $\frac{10.98}{4.4 + 1.7}$.

Using brackets *10.98 ÷ (4.4 + 1.7)*

Using memory *Do 4.4 + 1.7 first. Put the result in the memory.* 4 . 4 + 1 . 7 = Min

Then divide 10.98 by the number in the memory. 1 0 . 9 8 ÷ Mout =

Some calculators have an 'ANS' key which recalls the last answer: 4 . 4 + 1 . 7 =
1 0 . 9 8 ÷ ANS =

C1 Do these calculations, giving each answer correct to three significant figures.

(a) $\frac{44.2}{3.84 - 1.67}$ (b) $6.73 - (2.95 - 1.08)$ (c) $\frac{3.06}{5.13 \times 0.96}$

(d) $\frac{12.74 - 8.87}{8.54 + 1.66}$ (e) $\frac{14.31 + 10.84}{2.56 \times 1.42}$ (f) $\frac{352 - 187}{4.53 - 2.86}$

D Checking by rough estimates

D1 Amber had to calculate $\frac{21.39 + 37.78}{4.85}$. She got the answer 29.18, which is wrong.

She should have checked her answer by making a rough estimate:

21.39 is roughly 20, 37.78 is roughly 40 and 4.85 is roughly 5.

(a) Use these numbers to get a rough estimate of the answer to the calculation.

(b) Do the actual calculation on your calculator.

D2 Pat wants to get a rough estimate for $\frac{0.49 \times 216}{3.88}$.

(a) Write down a calculation Pat could do to get a rough estimate.

(b) Work out the rough estimate without using a calculator.

(c) Use a calculator to work out $\frac{0.49 \times 216}{3.88}$ and compare the result with your estimate.

D3 For each calculation below

(i) work out a rough estimate (ii) calculate the result, to three significant figures

(a) $\frac{57.2}{9.13 - 2.78}$ (b) $4.13 \times (38.5 - 18.8)$ (c) $\frac{41.4}{0.97 \times 7.89}$

(d) $\frac{207.4 \times 0.48}{28.4 - 9.7}$ (e) $\frac{77.31 + 38.84}{5.86 \times 9.75}$ (f) $\frac{286 - 18.7}{47.9 + 18.8}$

E *Other keys*

Negative numbers

Most calculators have a 'change sign' key [+/–] for entering negative numbers.

This key is usually pressed after the number: to enter $^-5$ press [5] [+/–].

Squaring

The squaring key is often labelled [x^2]. To do 4^2, press [4] [x^2].

Square root

On some calculators, the square root key is pressed before the number.

On others it is pressed after. So $\sqrt{9}$ may be [$\sqrt{\ }$] [9] or [9] [$\sqrt{\ }$].

E1 Do each of these first without a calculator.
Then use a calculator to check your answer.

(a) $7 + {}^-2$ (b) $^-1 + {}^-4$ (c) $^-7 + 3$ (d) $^-5 - {}^-5$ (e) $^-3 \times {}^-4$

(f) $^-2 \times 5$ (g) $^-10 \div 2$ (h) $^-10 \div {}^-5$ (i) $3 - {}^-1$ (j) $^-1 + {}^-2.5$

E2 (a) Without a calculator, work out $(^-3)^2$.
Then use a calculator to check your answer.

(b) Use a calculator for these.

(i) $(^-4.3)^2$ (ii) $3.2^2 - 2.7^2$ (iii) $(7.19 - 4.42)^2$ (iv) $7.19 - 4.42^2$ (v) $(3.2 - 6.7)^2$

E3 Use a calculator to work these out.
Give each answer correct to two decimal places.

(a) $\sqrt{19}$ (b) $6 \times \sqrt{19}$ (c) $\sqrt{6 \times 19}$ (d) $\dfrac{\sqrt{19}}{6}$ (e) $\sqrt{\dfrac{19}{6}}$

E4 Use a calculator for each of these.
Give each answer correct to two decimal places.
Estimate each answer roughly first.

(a) $16.7 - \sqrt{8.91}$ (b) $(2.83 - 1.64)^2$ (c) $4.67 + \left(\dfrac{2.56}{3.2}\right)^2$

(d) $\dfrac{4.94 - 1.8^2}{2.5}$ (e) $3.28 + \dfrac{\sqrt{7.29}}{1.03}$ (f) $\dfrac{4.86}{2.57 - \sqrt{1.69}}$

(g) $\sqrt{4.4^2 + 1.9^2}$ (h) $\dfrac{13.4}{\sqrt{5.76 - 1.54}}$ (i) $\sqrt{\dfrac{9.8 + 7.2}{6.8 - 3.5}}$

Test yourself

T1 Calculate the value of $\dfrac{21.7 \times 32.1}{16.20 - 2.19}$.

Give your answer correct to three significant figures. Edexcel

T2 (a) Calculate $\dfrac{89.6 \times 10.3}{19.7 + 9.8}$.

(b) Do not use your calculator in this part of the question.

By using approximations show that your answer to (a) is about right.
You must show all your working. AQA(SEG)1999

T3 (a) Work out $\dfrac{4.7 \times 20.1}{5.6 - 1.8}$.

Write down your full calculator display.

(b) Use estimation to check your answer.
Show each step of your working. AQA(NEAB)1998

T4 (a) Estimate the value of

$$S = \frac{738 \times 19}{593 + 392}.$$

Do not use your calculator.
Show all your approximations and working.

(b) Now use your calculator to work out the value of S.

(i) Write down all the figures in your calculator display.

(ii) Write your answer correct to three significant figures. OCR

T5 Use your calculator to work out the value of $\dfrac{\sqrt{12.3^2 + 7.9}}{1.8 \times 0.17}$.

Give your answer correct to one decimal place. Edexcel

T6 (a) Use your calculator to find the value of $3.2^2 - \sqrt{4.84}$.

(b) (i) Use your calculator to find the value of $\dfrac{3.9^2 + 0.53}{3.9 \times 0.53}$.

Write down all the figures on your calculator display.

(ii) Round your answer to (i) to two decimal places.

(iii) Write down a calculation you can do in your head to check your answer to (i).

Write down your answer to this calculation. OCR

T7 Use your calculator to work out the exact value of $\dfrac{14.82 \times (17.4 - 9.25)}{(54.3 + 23.7) \times 3.8}$. Edexcel

21 Graphs

You should know how to

- work out a table of values and use it to plot a straight-line graph
- read values from a graph
- form a formula from a practical situation
- interpret a graph of a practical situation

This work will help you

- substitute into and interpret quadratic functions
- draw the graphs of quadratic equations and use them to solve simple problems
- use quadratic graphs and straight lines to solve related equations

A *Straight lines review*

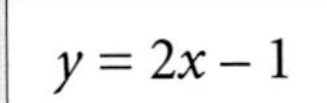

x	$^-2$	0	2
$2x - 1$	$^-5$	$^-1$	3

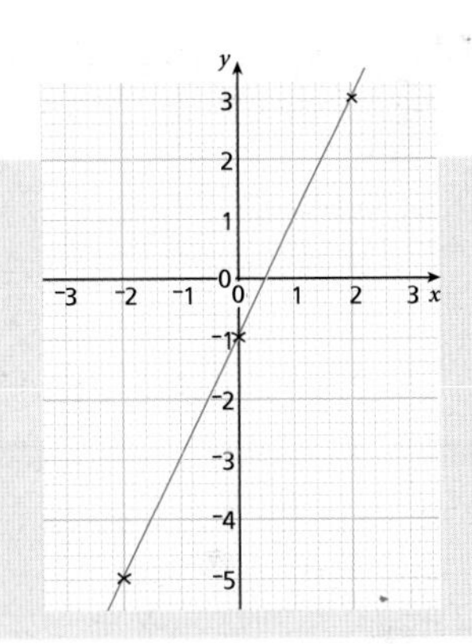

A1 A **linear** equation is one whose graph is a straight line.
Which of these are linear equations?

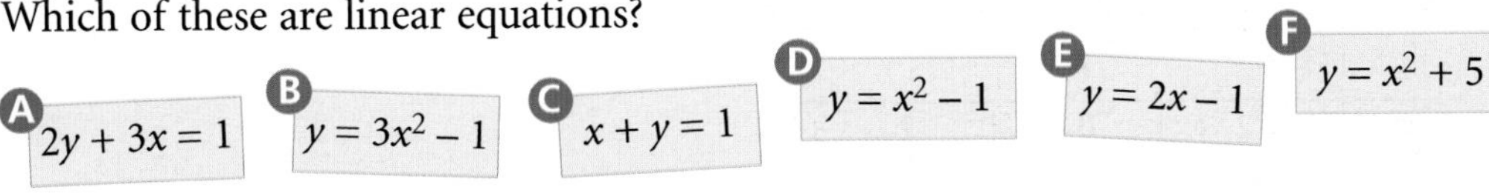

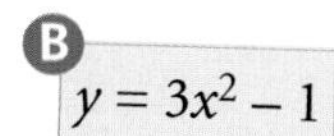

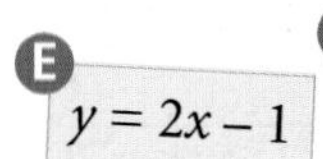

A2 (a) Copy and complete this table for $y = 2x + 3$.

(b) On graph paper, draw axes with x from $^-3$ to 3 and y from $^-4$ to 10.
Draw and label the graph of $y = 2x + 3$.

x	$^-2$	0	2
$2x + 3$			

A3 (a) Copy and complete this table for $y = 6 - 2x$.

(b) On graph paper, draw axes with x from $^-1$ to 5 and y from $^-4$ to 8.
Draw and label the graph of $y = 6 - 2x$.

x	0	2	4
$6 - 2x$			

A4 This question is on sheet G116.

A5 (a) Copy and complete this table of values for $y = \frac{1}{2}x - 2$.

x	$^-2$	0	2
$\frac{1}{2}x - 2$	$^-3$		

(b) On graph paper, draw axes with x from $^-2$ to 5 and y from $^-4$ to 4. Draw and label the graph of $y = \frac{1}{2}x - 2$.

A6 (a) Copy and complete this table of values for $y = 3$.

x	$^-3$	$^-2$	$^-1$	0	1	2	3
y	3	3	3				

(b) Draw and label the graph of $y = 3$. Choose your own values on the axes.

A7 The diagram shows the graphs of four equations, $x = 3$, $x = {^-1}$, $y = 3$ and $y = {^-1}$.
Which line goes with which equation?

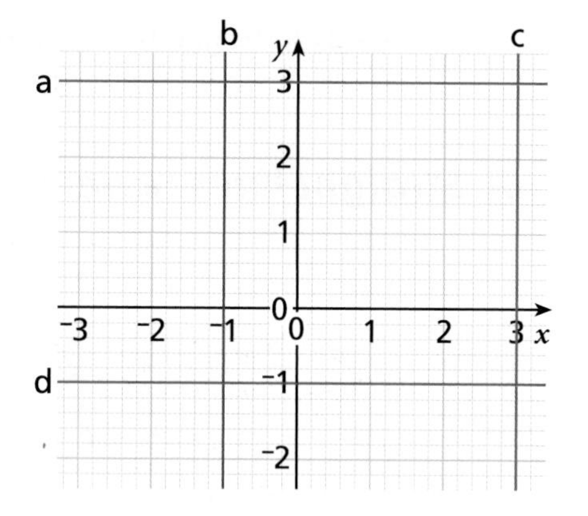

A8

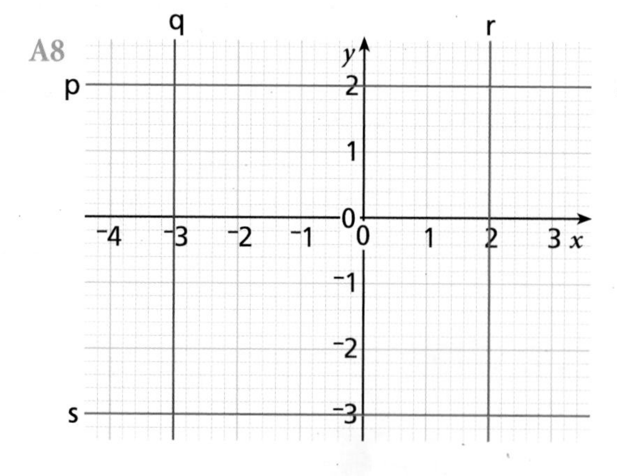

The diagram shows four straight lines.
Write down the equation of each line.

A9 Choosing your own scales on the axes, draw and label the graphs of these equations.

(a) $y = 4$ (b) $y = {^-4}$

(c) $x = 4$ (d) $x = {^-4}$

To draw the graph of $x + 2y = 12$ you need to find points that fit the equation.

- Can you spot any values of x and y that fit?
- When x is 4, what value of y fits the equation? (You need to find y so that $4 + 2y = 12$.)
- Check that when $x = 0, y = 6$.
- Copy and complete this table.
- On graph paper draw axes with both x and y going from 0 to 12.
- Plot your points and draw the line $x + 2y = 12$.

x	0	2	4	6	8	10	12
y	6						

A10 (a) To draw the line $x + y = 5$, we need to find some points that fit the equation $x + y = 5$.
When x is 3 the equation becomes $3 + y = 5$.
What is the value of y when $x = 3$?

(b) Work out the value of y when x is 0.

(c) What is the value of $\mathbf{x}$ when $\mathbf{y} = 0$?

(d) Copy and complete this table for $x + y = 5$.

x	0	3	
y			0

(e) On graph paper, draw axes with x from $^-2$ to 7 and suitable values of y.
Draw the graph of $x + y = 5$.

(f) From your graph, what is the value of y when $x = {}^-0.8$?

A11 (a) Copy and complete this table for $3x + y = 6$.

x	0	1	
y			0

(b) On graph paper, draw axes with x from $^-1$ to 3 and suitable values of y.
On your axes draw the graph of $3x + y = 6$.

A12 (a) Copy and complete this table for $3x + 2y = 12$.

x	0	2	
y			0

(b) Draw axes with x from $^-1$ to 5 and suitable values of y.
On your axes draw the graph of $3x + 2y = 12$.

(c) From your graph, what is the value of y when $x = 2.5$?
(Give your answer to one decimal place.)

A13

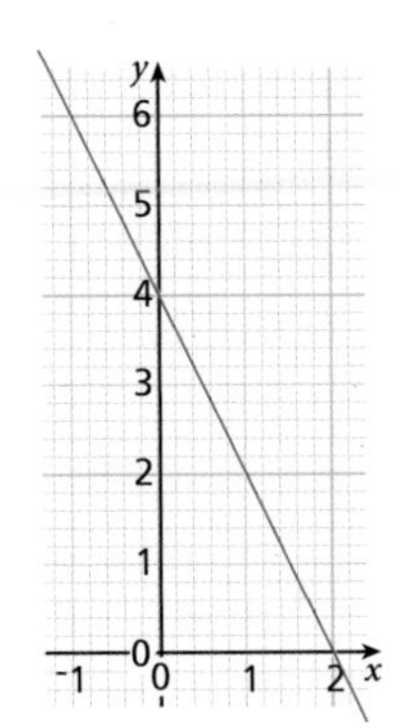

Look at the straight-line graph on the left.

(a) Check that when $x = 0, y = 4$.

(b) Copy and complete this table of values for the line.

x	y
0	4
1	
2	

(c) Which of the equations below is the equation of the straight line?

P $y = x + 1$ Q $y = 2x - 1$ R $x + y = 4$

S $2x + y = 4$ T $x + y = 2$ U $x + 2y = 4$

B *Problem review*

B1 You can put an advertisement into the *Evening News*.
The paper charges £25 to typeset the advert,
and then £4 for each centimetre of depth.

(a) What would the total cost be for this advert?

(b) How much would an advert 20 cm deep cost?

(c) Copy and complete this table for adverts.

Depth (d)	5	10	20
Cost in £(c)			

(d) On graph paper, draw axes with d going across from 0 to 20 and with c going up from 0 to 110.
Plot the points from your table and join them.

(e) Sue spends £75 on an advert.
What is the depth of her advert in cm?

B2 Mendip Mushrooms supply mushroom compost to gardeners.
They charge £35 delivery and then £6 per tonne of compost.

(a) How much would 4 tonnes of compost cost delivered to your door?

(b) How much would 1 tonne cost?

(c) Copy and complete this table for deliveries of Mendip Mushrooms compost.

Weight (w)	1	4	6
Cost in £(c)			

(d) Draw axes with w going across from 0 to 8 and c going up from 0 to 90.
Plot the points from your table and join them.

(e) Dave asks for £55 worth of compost to be delivered.
How much will he get, to the nearest $\frac{1}{10}$th of a tonne?

(f) Find a formula that connects w (the weight delivered in tonnes) and c (the cost in £).

B3 Fuming Fertilisers also supply compost.
The formula they use for working out the cost of a delivery is $c = 10 + 10w$.
c is the cost in £, w is the weight in tonnes.

(a) Copy and complete the table on the right for Fuming Fertilisers' prices.

Weight (w)	1	4	7
Cost in £(c)			

(b) On the same axes you used for B2, draw the graph of $c = 10 + 10w$.

(c) What do Fuming Fertilisers charge for a delivery of 5.5 tonnes of compost?

(d) Use the graph to say which company would be cheaper for 10 tonnes of compost.
Explain your answer carefully.

C *Quadratic graphs*

$y = x^2$

x	−2	−1.5	−1	−0.5	0	0.5	1	1.5	2
x^2	4								

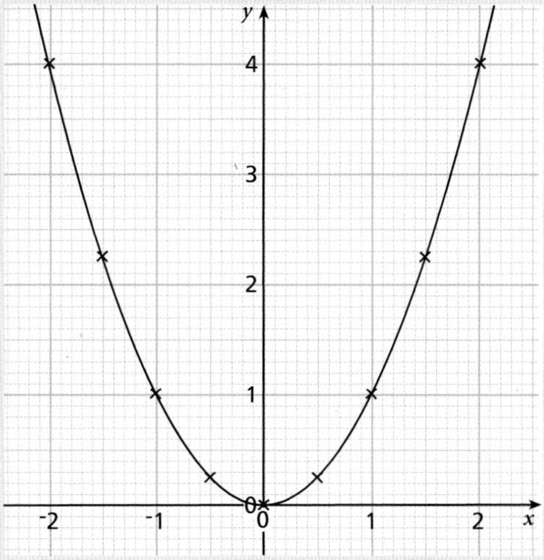

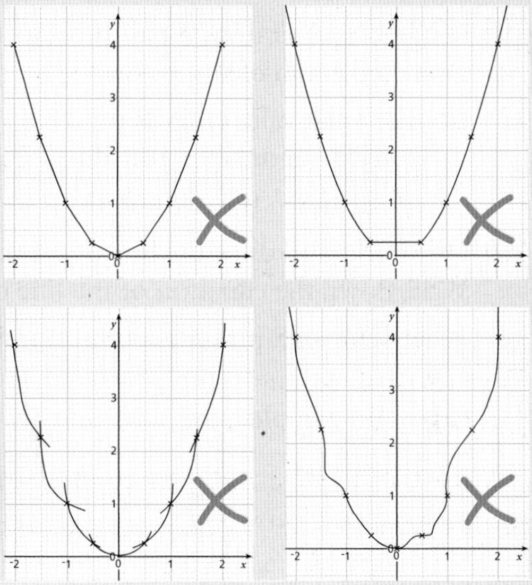

C1 (a) Copy and complete this table of values for $y = x^2 - 2$.

x	−2	−1	0	1	2
x^2	4	1			
$x^2 - 2$	2	−1			

(b) On graph paper draw a pair of axes with x from −2 to 2, and y from −2 to 2.
Draw the graph of $y = x^2 - 2$.

(c) (i) At what values of x does the graph meet the x-axis?
(Give your answers to 1 d.p.)

(ii) Write down the two solutions to the equation $x^2 - 2 = 0$.

(d) What value of x makes y smallest (a **minimum**)?

C2 (a) Copy and complete this table for $y = x^2 + x$.

x	$^-2$	$^-1$	0	1	2
x^2	4				
x^2+x	2				

(b) On graph paper draw a pair of axes.
Draw the graph of $y = x^2 + x$.

(c) (i) For what values of x is $y = 1$?
(Give your answers to 1 d.p.)

(ii) Write down the two solutions to the equation $x^2 + x = 1$.

(d) On your graph draw the line of symmetry of $y = x^2 + x$.
Write down the equation of the line of symmetry.

(e) What value of x makes y a minimum?

C3 (a) Copy and complete this table for $y = 6 - x^2$.

x	$^-3$	$^-2$	$^-1$	0	1	2	3
x^2		4					9
$6 - x^2$		2					$^-3$

(b) On graph paper draw a pair of axes with x from $^-3$ to 3 and y from $^-4$ to 6.
On your axes, draw the graph of $y = 6 - x^2$.
Label the graph with its equation.

(c) Use your graph to solve the equation $6 - x^2 = 3$.

(d) What value of x makes y a **maximum**?

C4 (a) Copy and complete the table below for $y = 2x^2 - 7$.

x	$^-3$	$^-2$	$^-1$	0	1	2	3
x^2	9	4					
$2x^2$	18	8					
$^-7$	$^-7$	$^-7$	$^-7$	$^-7$	$^-7$	$^-7$	$^-7$
$y=2x^2-7$	11	1					

(b) Draw axes with x from $^-3$ to 3, and y from $^-8$ to 12.
Draw the graph of $y = 2x^2 - 7$ on your axes.

(c) (i) What values of x make $2x^2 - 7$ equal to 4?

(ii) Write down the solutions to the equation $2x^2 - 7 = 4$.

(d) Use your graph to solve the equation $2x^2 - 7 = 0$.

C5 This question is on sheet G117. OCR

C6 (a) Copy and complete the following table of values for $y = x^2 + 2x - 4$.

x	$^-4$	$^-3$	$^-2$	$^-1$	0	1	2	3
x^2								
$2x$								
$^-4$	$^-4$	$^-4$	$^-4$	$^-4$	$^-4$	$^-4$	$^-4$	$^-4$
$y = x^2 + 2x - 4$								

(b) On suitable axes, draw the graph of $y = x^2 + 2x - 4$.

(c) What is the minimum value of $x^2 + 2x - 4$?

(d) Use your graph to solve the equation $x^2 + 2x - 4 = 0$.

(e) Solve the equation $x^2 + 2x - 4 = 1$.

C7 Julia throws a stone from the top of a cliff, as shown.

The equation of the path of the stone is $y = 50 - \frac{x^2}{2}$.
(x and y are measured in metres.)

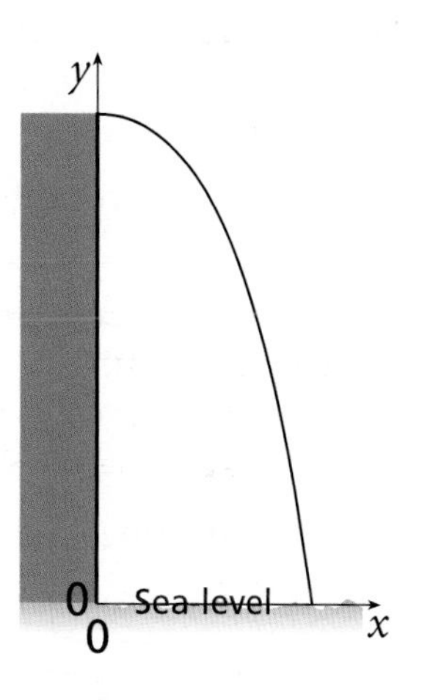

(a) Copy and complete this table for $y = 50 - \frac{x^2}{2}$.

x	0	2	4	6	8	10	12
x^2	0	4	16	36			
$\frac{1}{2}x^2$	0	2	8	18			
$y = 50 - \frac{1}{2}x^2$	50	48	42	32			

(b) On graph paper, draw axes for x from 0 to 12 and for y from $^-30$ to 50. Plot the graph.

(c) What is the height of the cliff?

(d) How far from the bottom of the cliff does the stone hit the sea?

(e) From the graph, what is the value of y when x is 5? What does this tell you?

(f) Use the equation to work out the value of y when x is 16. Why is this information meaningless in this case?

D *Fairground graphs*

TG

At Jeff's stall you can win a goldfish.
The goldfish are in different shaped bowls.

Jeff fills the bowls with water before he puts the goldfish in.
He uses a hose-pipe, from which water flows at a steady rate.

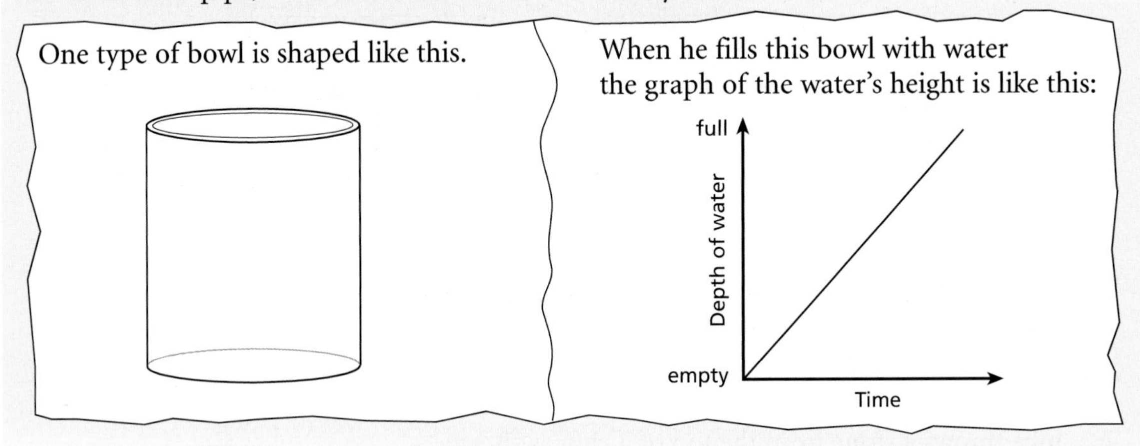

D1 Here are three different shaped bowls.

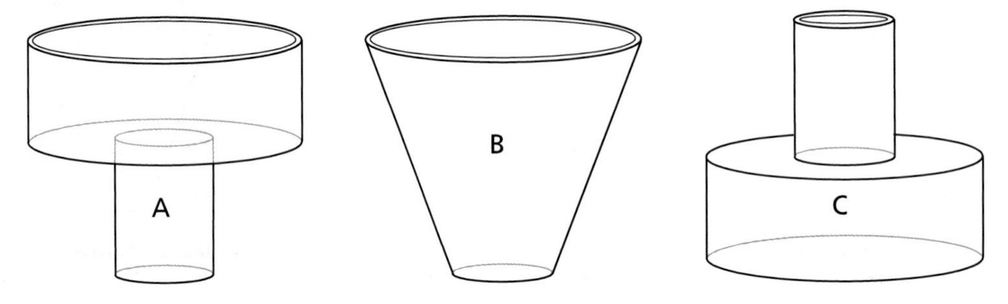

(a) Which description of filling the bowls with water goes with which bowl?

P *The water level goes up fast at first and then suddenly goes up more slowly.*

Q *The water level goes up slowly at first, then changes to go up more quickly.*

R *The water level starts by going up quickly, but gets slower and slower.*

(b) Which graph goes with which bowl?

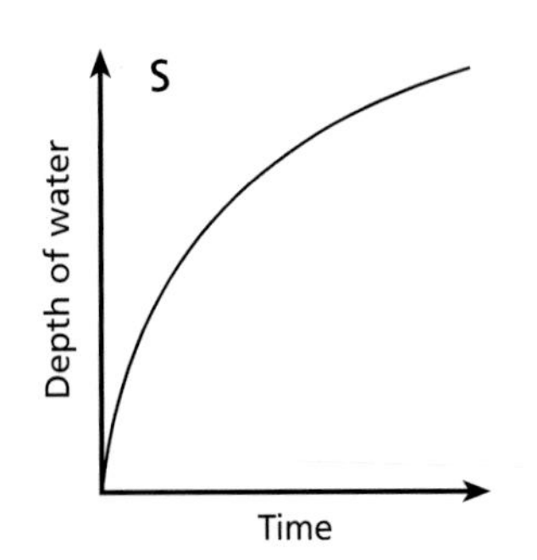

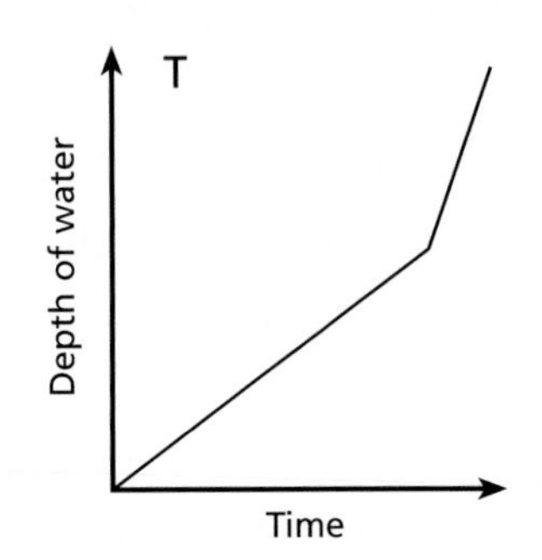

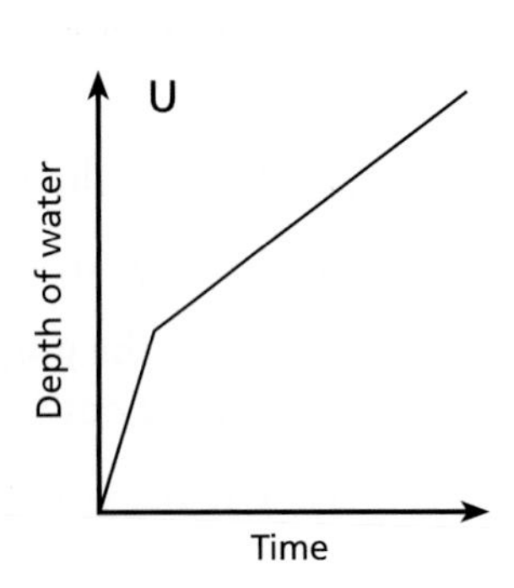

D2 Here are three more bowls.
For each one, sketch a graph showing how it fills up with water.

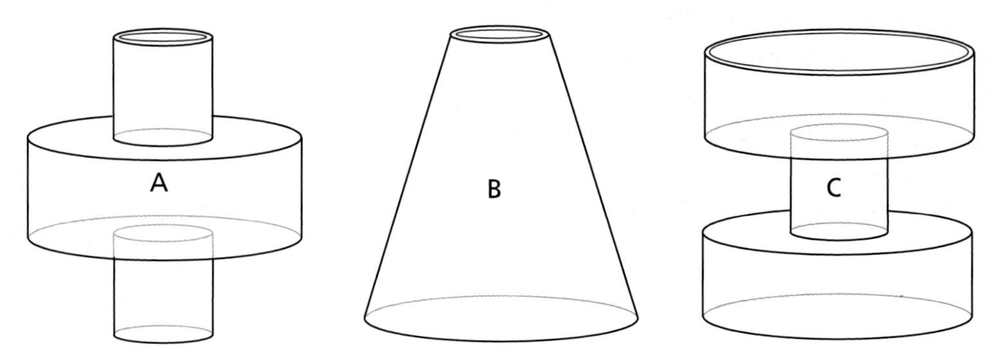

D3 The graph shows the number of people (customers and workers) in the fairground one evening.

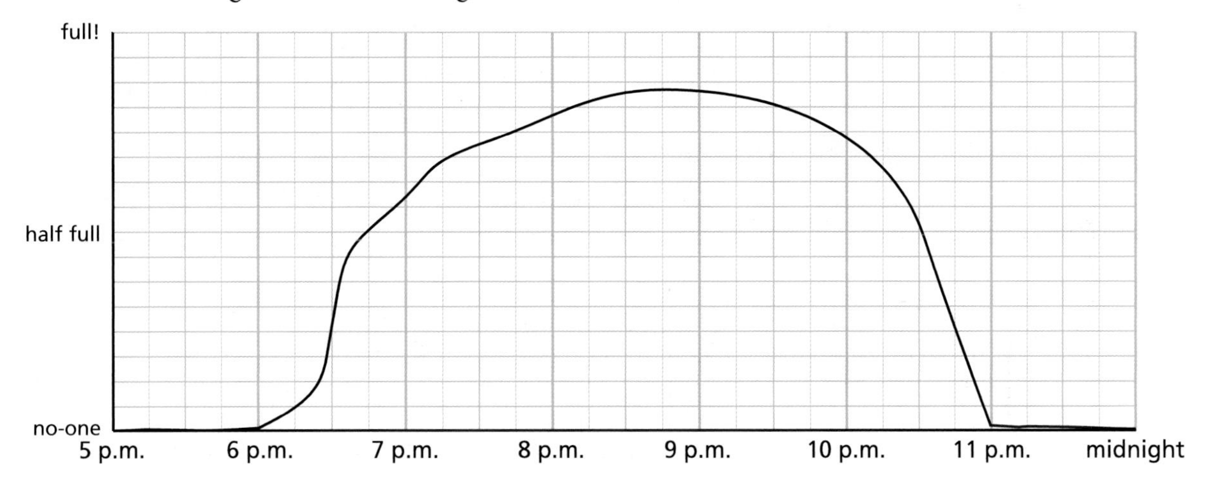

(a) At what time were there most people in the fairground?

(b) When do you think the fair opened?

(c) What time do you think the fair closed?

(d) At what time were most people arriving?

(e) Jeff is happy when the fair is more than half full.
For about how long was Jeff happy this evening?

D4 Look at the graphs at the bottom of the page.
Some of the graphs describe these four situations at the fairground.
Which graph describes which situation?

(Two graphs don't describe anything!)

A The speed (y) of a person against time (x) as they come down the helter-skelter.

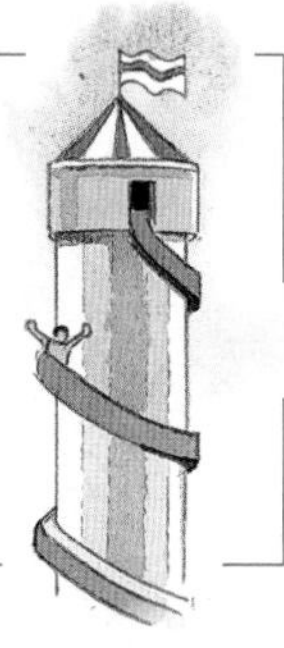

B The height (y) of a horse against time (x) as the roundabout goes round.

C The height (y) of the pinger on the 'try-your-strength' machine against time (x) when someone tries their strength.

D The total amount of money taken (y) against time (x) on Jeff's stall.

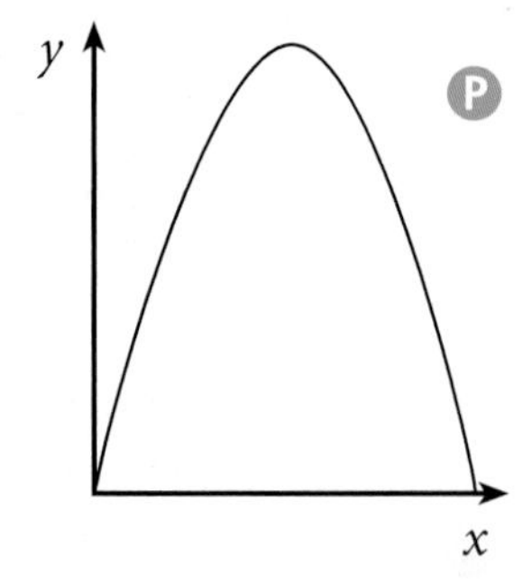

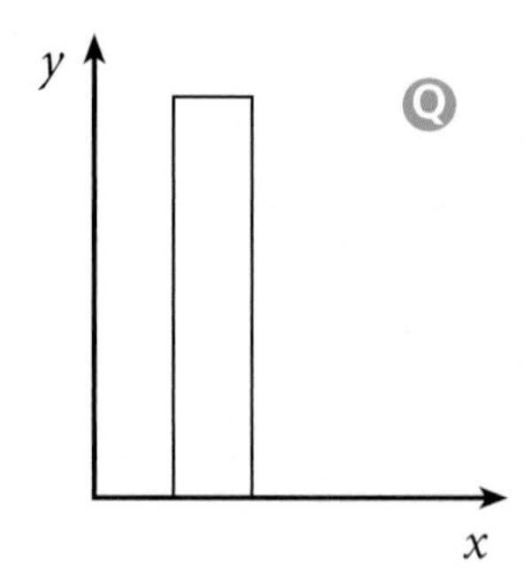

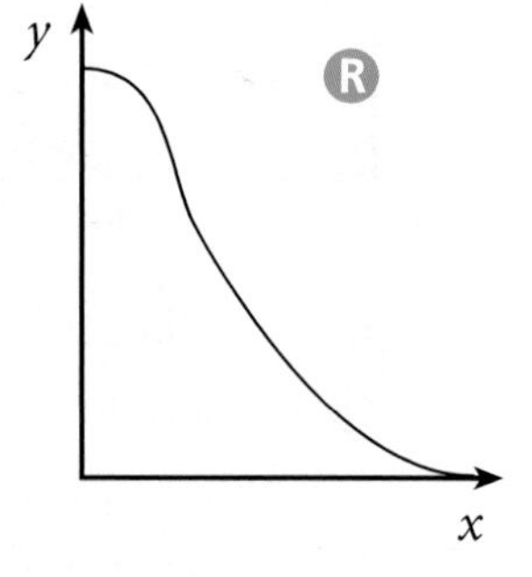

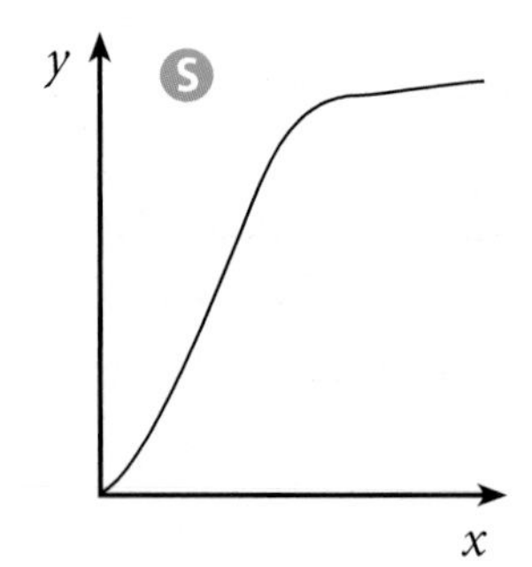

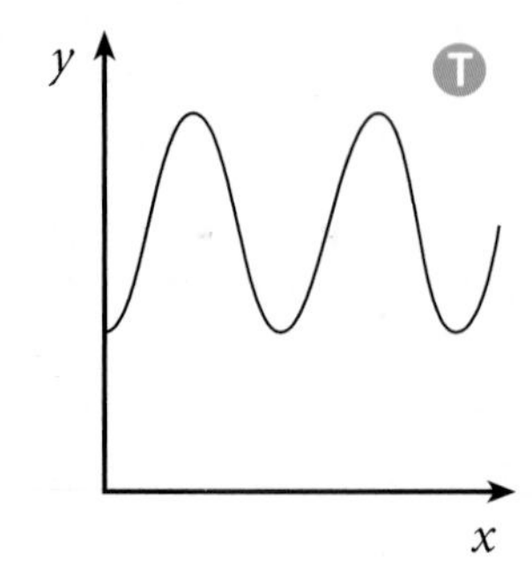

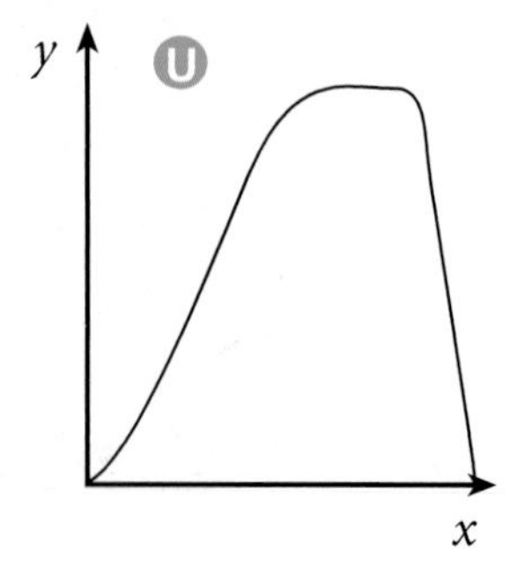

D5 Sketch a graph for each of these situations.
For each graph, write a short explanation of why it looks as you have drawn it.

(a) A dodgem car is going round the track at constant speed.
(Draw the dodgem car's speed on the y-axis against time on the x-axis.)

(b) A dart is thrown and then hits the dart board, 2 metres away.
(Draw the dart's speed (y) against time (x).)

(c) The big wheel goes round twice at constant speed.
(Draw the height of a person on the wheel (y) against time (x).)

Test yourself

T1 (a) Copy and complete this table for $y = 2x - 2$.

x	$^-1$	0	3
$2x - 2$			

(b) On graph paper, draw axes with x from $^-3$ to 3 and y from $^-4$ to 4.
Draw the graph of $y = 2x - 2$.

T2

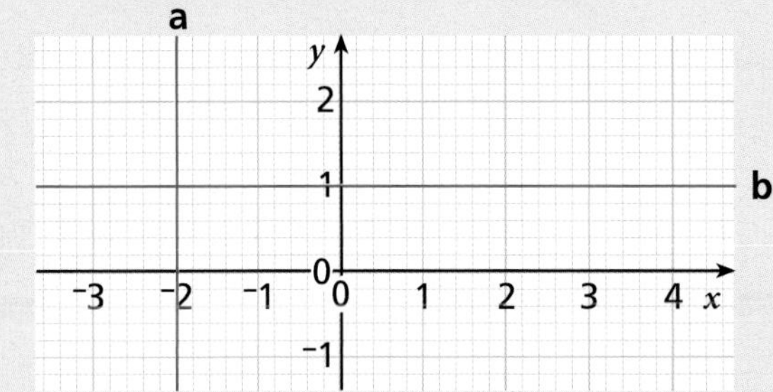

(a) Write down the equation of line **a**.

(b) What is the equation of line **b**?

T3 (a) Copy and complete this table for $y = x^2 - 3x$.

x	$^-1$	0	1	2	3	4
x^2	1	0		4	9	
^-3x	3	0		$^-6$	$^-9$	
$x^2 - 3x$	4	0		-2		

(b) On graph paper draw a pair of axes with x from $^-1$ to 4 and y from $^-3$ to 5.
Draw the graph of $y = x^2 - 3x$.

(c) Use your graph to solve these equations. (i) $x^2 - 3x = 0$ (ii) $x^2 - 3x = 1$

(d) What value of x makes y a minimum?

T4 Draw sketch graphs for each of these situations.
For each graph, write a short explanation of why it looks as you have drawn it.

A A cyclist travels at a steady speed, then goes up a steep hill and stops at the top.
(Draw the cyclist's speed (y) against time (x).)

B The distance travelled on a motorway by a car going at constant speed.
(Draw the car's distance (y) against time (x).)

C The temperature of a saucepan of water that is heated up on a stove, and then left boiling for a short while.
(Draw the pan's temperature (y) against time (x).)

22 Paired data

You will revise

- how to draw scatter diagrams using pairs of data
- how to recognise the different types of correlation

This work will help you

- draw a line of best fit on a scatter diagram
- use a line of best fit to estimate results

A Connections

TG

Sheet G42 has a database about a selection of different models of cars.
This is a scatter diagram showing the engine size and top speed of these cars.

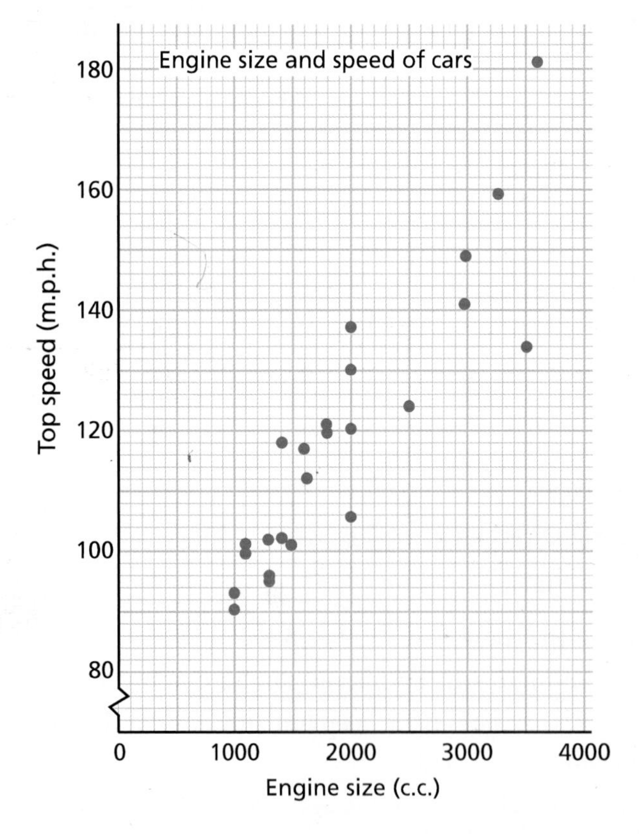

- Describe the relationship between the engine size and top speed of these cars.
- Are there any cars that have a low top speed for the size of their engine?
- Are there any cars that have a high top speed for the size of their engine?

Use the sheet G42 to answer these questions.

A1 (a) Draw a scatter diagram with engine size on the horizontal scale and power on the vertical scale.

(b) Is there any correlation between the power and the engine size? If so, what type of correlation is this?

A2 (a) Draw a scatter diagram with engine size on the horizontal scale and fuel economy (m.p.g.) on the vertical scale.

(b) Describe any correlation between the fuel economy and the engine size.

(c) Why do you think these two variables are related in this way?

A3 (a) Draw a scatter diagram with height on the horizontal axis and fuel economy on the vertical axis. Use a jagged line on the horizontal scale to show the scale does not start at zero.

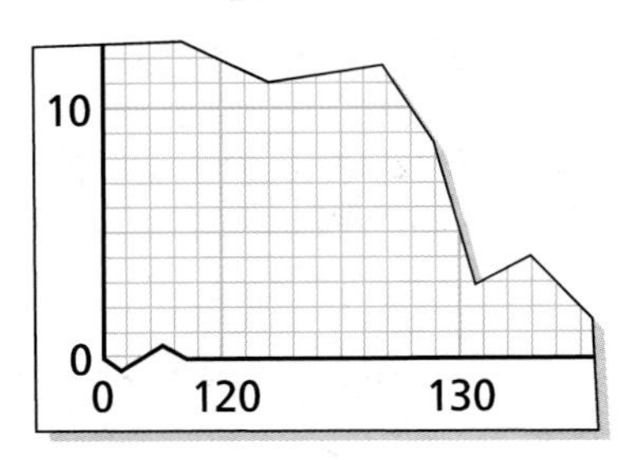

(b) Describe the relationship between the heights of the cars and their fuel economy.

A4 (a) Draw a scatter diagram with the length of the car on the horizontal axis and the size of the boot on the vertical scale. Use these scales.

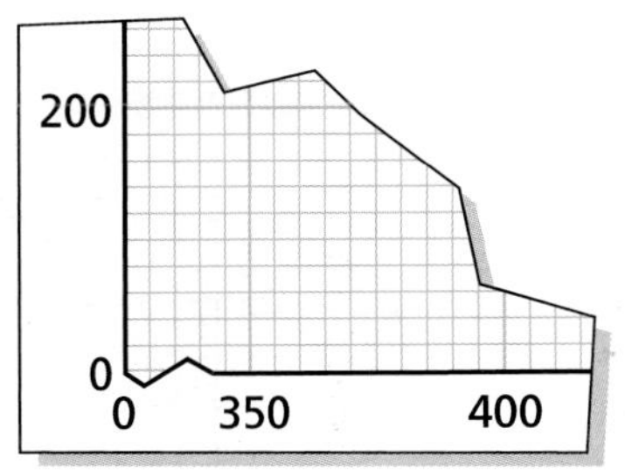

(b) Describe any correlation shown by the scatter diagram.

(c) Does the diagram support a statement in a magazine that longer cars usually have bigger boots?

Finding connections

Use the database on the sheet to investigate any other connections between the facts for the different cars.
You may find a computer spreadsheet or a graphic calculator useful.

The information in the database was found on the internet.
You could update it or add to it.

Create a database on a topic of your own.

B *Lines of best fit*

TG

Forensic scientists sometimes have to decide what someone looked like by examining individual bones.

This scatter diagram shows the heights of some males and the length of their femur (thigh bone).

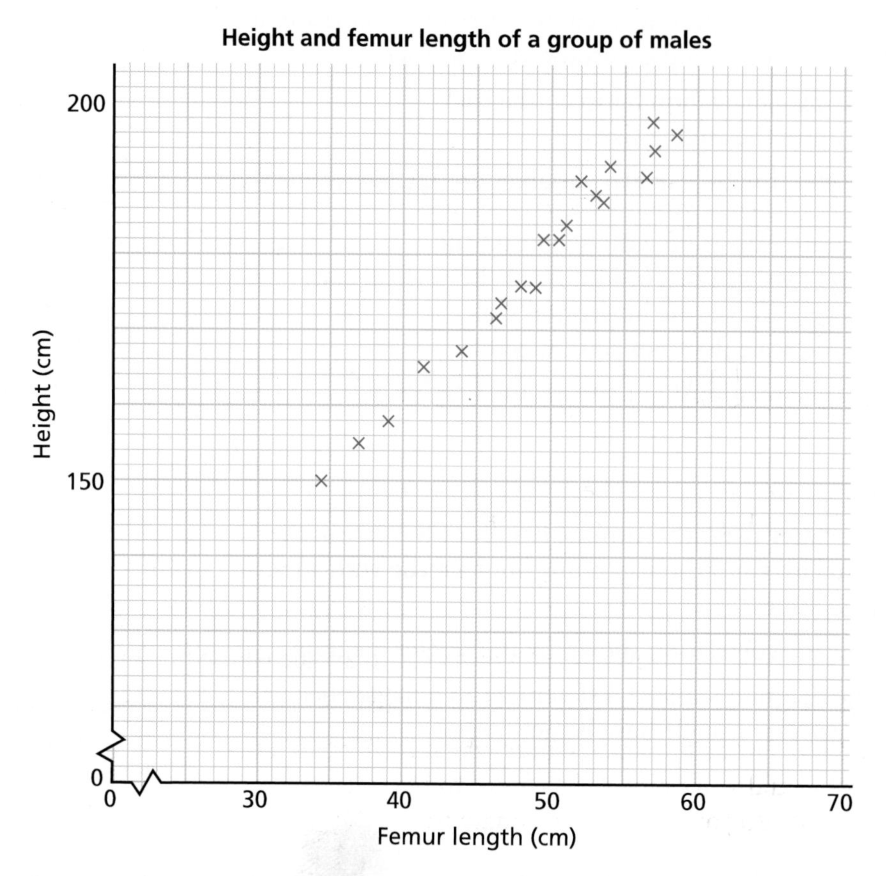

- What correlation is there between femur length and height?
- Roughly how long would you expect a femur to be on a male who is 180 cm tall? How accurate do you think your estimate is?
- Police find a male femur in a pit. It is 42 cm long. How tall would you estimate its owner was? How accurate do you think your estimate is?
- What would you estimate the height of a male to be if his femur is 65 cm long? How accurate do you think this estimate is?

When points on a scatter diagram show strong correlation, it can be useful to draw a straight line through them.
This is called a **line of best fit**.

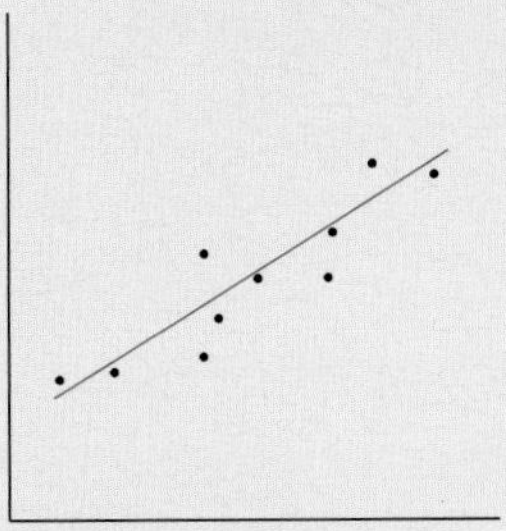

Strong positive correlation – worth drawing a line of best fit

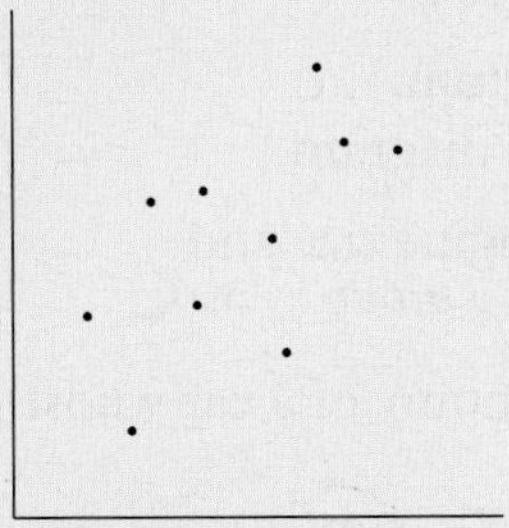

Weak positive correlation – **not** worth drawing a line of best fit

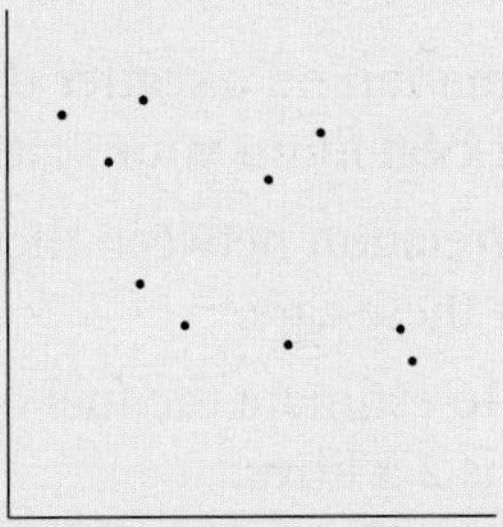

Weak negative correlation – **not** worth drawing a line of best fit

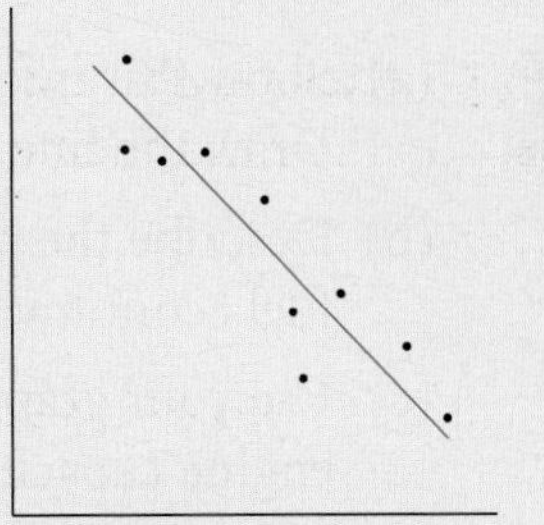

Strong negative correlation – worth drawing a line of best fit

You should draw a line of best fit to look like a 'spine' for the points, with roughly the same number of points on each side.

The line can be used to estimate new values. But extending the line beyond the given points to estimate values is less reliable.

B1 (a) On sheet G40 is a copy of the graph opposite.
Draw a line of best fit on this copy of the graph.

(b) Use your line to estimate the height of a male with a femur this long.

(i) 45 cm (ii) 55 cm (iii) 60 cm (iv) 30 cm

(c) Use your line to estimate the length of femur in a male whose height was

(i) 190 cm (ii) 161 cm (iii) 200 cm (iv) 140 cm

(d) Archeologists unearth a male femur which is 67 cm long.
How tall would you estimate its owner to have been?
How reliable do you think this estimate is?

B2 A park has an outdoor swimming pool.
The scatter graph on sheet G119 shows the maximum temperature and the number of people who used the pool on ten Saturdays in summer.

(a) Describe the correlation between the maximum temperature and the number of people who used the pool.

(b) Draw a line of best fit on the scatter graph.

The weather forecast for the next Saturday gives a maximum temperature of 27°C.

(c) Use your line of best fit to estimate the number of people who will use the pool.

Edexcel

B3 This data shows the engine size and the fuel economy of a range of petrol cars.

Engine size (litres)	4.0	3.5	3.0	2.0	1.7	1.6	1.4	1.3	1.2	1.1	1.0
Fuel economy (m.p.g.)	18	25	32	34	35	37	41	44	43	46	49

(a) Show this information on a scatter diagram.
Draw the line of best fit on your scatter diagram.

(b) Describe the correlation between the engine size and fuel economy of these cars.

(c) Use your graph to estimate the fuel economy of a car whose engine capacity is 2.5 litres.

(d) What capacity engine would you estimate would be needed to obtain a fuel economy of more than 50 m.p.g?

(e) A Lamborghini Diablo has a 5.7 litre engine.
What fuel economy would you expect from this car?
How reliable do you think this estimate is?

In an experiment some students add weights to a strong elastic band.
They measure the length of the elastic band with each weight.
These are their results.

Weight (g)	50	100	150	200	250	300	350	400
Length (cm)	15.6	21.8	23.8	28.5	30.8	36.6	39.7	46.1

Since the weights are controlled by the person doing the experiment, correlation does not apply.
A line of best fit can still be drawn for this data and used to estimate results.

B4 (a) Plot the data for weights and lengths on a graph.
Add a line of best fit.

(b) Estimate the length of the elastic band if a weight of 225 g was used.

(c) Estimate the length of the elastic band before any weight was added.

(d) Estimate the length if a weight of 450 g was used.

(e) If your graph was large enough could you reliably estimate the length of the elastic band if a 1 kg weight was used?

C *Drawing conclusions*

This data shows the weight in kilograms and the top speed of the cars in the database.

- What type of correlation is there between the top speed and weight of these cars?
- It has been suggested that lighter cars go faster. Does this graph support this hypothesis?
- Can you suggest an explanation for the correlation here?

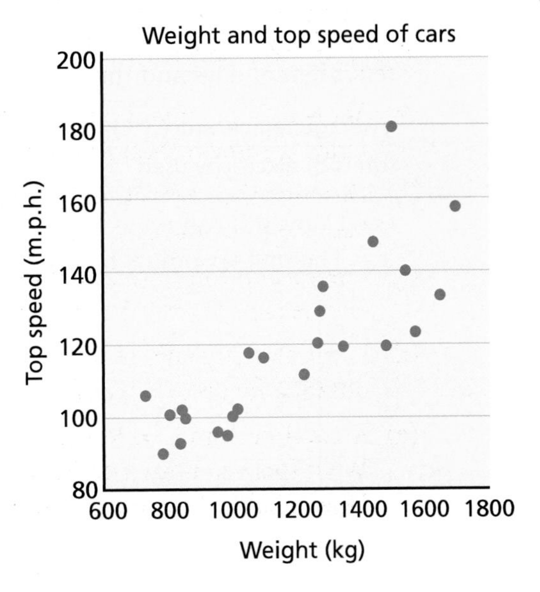

TG

C1 (a) Draw a scatter diagram using the data on sheet G42, with the tank size on the horizontal axis and the top speed on the vertical axis.
The horizontal scale should go from 30 to 100.
The vertical scale should go from 80 to 200.

(b) Describe any correlation shown by the graph.
What might explain it?

C2 This data shows the age and shoulder height of 20 bull elephants from a game reserve in Kenya.

Age (years)	41	9	19	38	3	6	55	10	2	27	1	29	21	15	12	17	5	33	32	10
Height (cm)	293	215	257	287	135	165	317	227	108	272	95	287	260	218	237	238	168	270	290	201

(a) Plot this data on a scatter diagram.

(b) Can you use the graph to estimate the height of a 50 year old bull elephant?

(c) Describe how age and height are related.
Would it be sensible to draw a line of best fit in this case?
Give your reasons.

A likely story!

In a survey in Sweden a researcher found there was a good positive correlation between the number of storks nesting in a village and the number of babies born in the village.

What might explain this?

Test yourself

T1 The table shows the number of units of electricity used in heating a house on ten different days and the average temperature for each day.

Average temperature (°C)	6	2	0	6	3	5	10	8	9	12
Units of electricity used	28	38	41	34	31	31	22	25	23	22

(a) Copy and complete the scatter graph to show the information in the table. The first six points have been plotted for you.

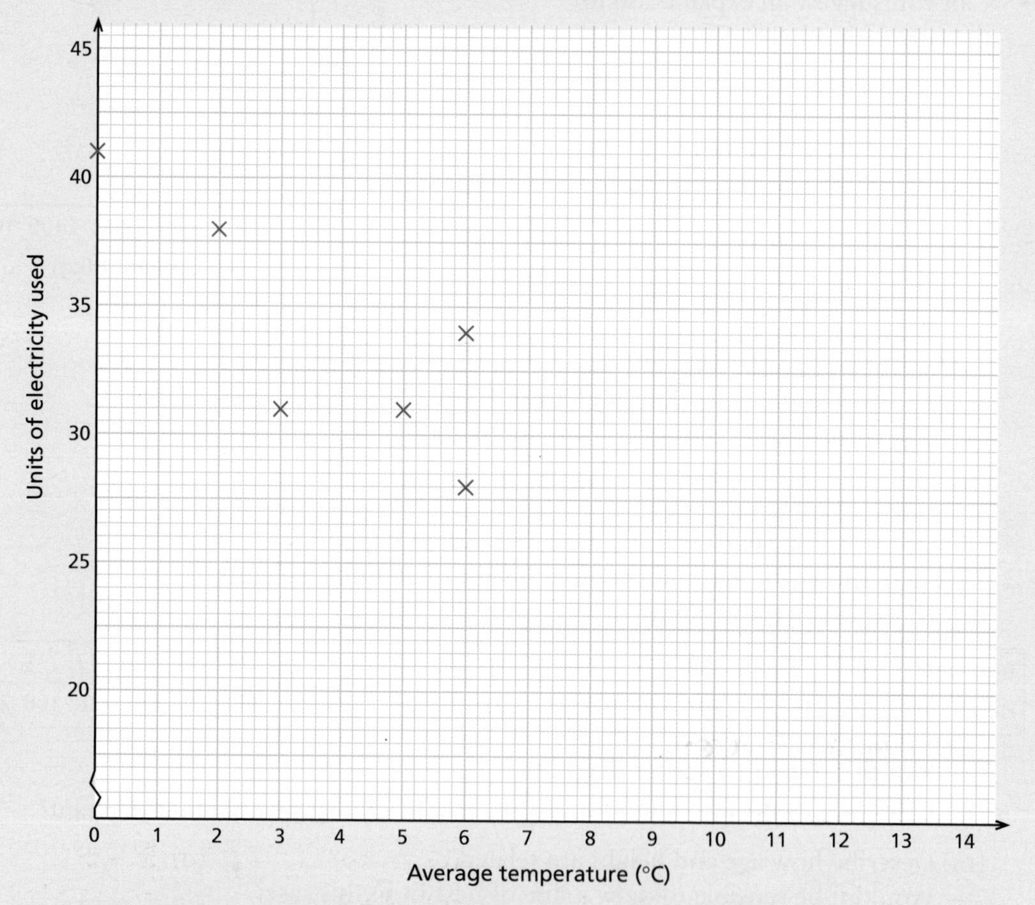

(b) Describe the **correlation** between the number of units of electricity used and the average daily temperature.

(c) Draw a line of best fit on your scatter graph.

(d) Use your line of best fit to estimate

(i) the average temperature if 35 units of electricity are used

(ii) the units of electricity used if the average temperature is 7°C

Edexcel

23 Indices

You should know how to work out the value of powers such as 4^3 (4 to the power 3).

This work will help you

- work with negative indices (and evaluate, say, 7^0)
- use the rules for multiplying and dividing powers of the same number
- use the rules for indices to simplify algebraic expressions

A Reptoids

Each 'active end' of a reptoid produces a small reptoid each day.

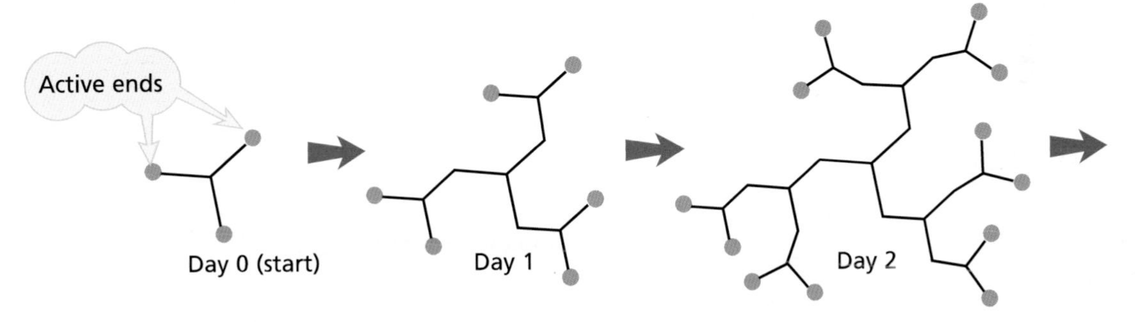

- How many active ends will this reptoid have on day 3, day 4, … ?
- What about day n?
- Investigate for other reptoids.

B Evaluating powers

B1 Evaluate these.

(a) $2^4 + 5$ (b) 3×2^3 (c) $3^2 \times 3^0$ (d) $5^2 + 2^5$
(e) 10×3^4 (f) $10^2 \div 5$ (g) $3^3 \div 9$ (h) $5^1 \times 4^2$

B2 Find the missing number in these statements.

(a) $6^{■} = 36$ (b) $■^3 = 125$ (c) $7^{■} = 7$ (d) $3^{■} = 1$

B3 Work out the value of $2^n + 1$ when

(a) $n = 3$ (b) $n = 5$ (c) $n = 0$ (d) $n = 1$

B4 For each of the following write down the value of n.

(a) $3^n = 81$ (b) $6^n = 6$ (c) $n^3 = 64$ (d) $n^7 = 1$
(e) $10^n = 100$ (f) $3^n = 243$ (g) $10^n = 100\,000$ (h) $n^3 = 125$

B5 Work out the missing number in these statements.

(a) $3^{\blacksquare} + 5 = 14$ (b) $\blacksquare^3 \div 4 = 16$ (c) $5^{\blacksquare} + 4 = 5$

(d) $\blacksquare^3 - 18 = 9$ (e) $2^{\blacksquare} \times 3 = 48$ (f) $8^{\blacksquare} \times 2 = 16$

B6 Work out the value of k in these statements.

(a) $2^k + 9 = 17$ (b) $6 \times 10^k = 600\,000$ (c) $k \times 5^2 = 150$

(d) $3^3 + 2^k = 29$ (e) $3^k \times 2 = 162$ (f) $5^3 - 4^k = 121$

B7 Work out the value of these expressions when $n = 3$.

(a) $n^2 \times n^2$ (b) $2n^2$ (c) $n^2 + n^2$

(d) $n^2 \times n$ (e) $n^2 + n^2 + n^2 + n^2$ (f) n^4

(g) $n^2 + n^1$ (h) n^3 (i) $4n^2$

$n^0 = 1$

For example, $1^0 = 1,\ 2^0 = 1,\ 3^0 = 1,\ 4^0 = 1, \ldots$

C Multiplying

To **multiply** powers of the same number, **add** the indices.

Examples

$10^3 \times 10^2$

$= (10 \times 10 \times 10) \times (10 \times 10)$
$= 10 \times 10 \times 10 \times 10 \times 10$
$= 10^5$

$= 10^{3+2}$
$= 10^5$

$a^4 \times a^3$

$= (a \times a \times a \times a) \times (a \times a \times a)$
$= a \times a \times a \times a \times a \times a \times a$
$= a^7$

$= a^{4+3}$
$= a^7$

C1 Find four pairs of equivalent expressions.

A $3^5 \times 3^2$ B 3×3^7 C 3^7 D 3^{10}

E 3^9 F $3^3 \times 3^7$ G 3^8 H $3^5 \times 3^4$

C2 Copy and complete these statements.

(a) $4^3 \times 4^2 = 4^{\blacksquare}$ (b) $5^6 \times 5^3 = 5^{\blacksquare}$ (c) $3^4 \times 3^{\blacksquare} = 3^{11}$

(d) $8^2 \times 8^{\blacksquare} = 8^7$ (e) $7^{\blacksquare} \times 7^3 = 7^4$ (f) $9 \times 9^2 \times 9^5 = 9^{\blacksquare}$

C3 Write the answers to these using indices.

(a) $6^2 \times 6^7$ (b) $2^4 \times 2^9$ (c) $10^5 \times 10^7$ (d) $5^6 \times 5$

(e) $3^4 \times 3^2 \times 3^5$ (f) $8 \times 8^6 \times 8^2$ (g) $9^3 \times 9 \times 9^3$ (h) $2^4 \times 2^5 \times 2^3$

C4 This table shows some powers of 7.

7^2	7^3	7^4	7^5	7^6	7^7	7^8
49	343	2401	16 807	117 649	823 543	5 764 801

Use the results in the table to evaluate these.

(a) 49×343 (b) $343 \times 16\,807$ (c) 2401×343 (d) $823\,543 \times 7$

C5 In this wall, each expression is written as a power and is found by **multiplying** the two powers on the bricks below.

What should be on the top brick?

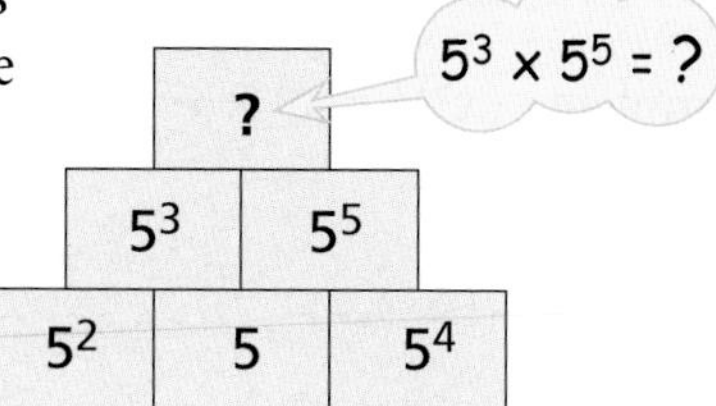

C6 Copy and complete these multiplication walls.

(a)

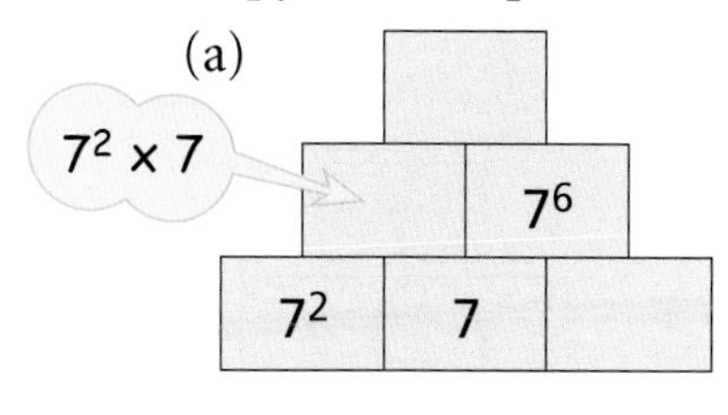

(b)

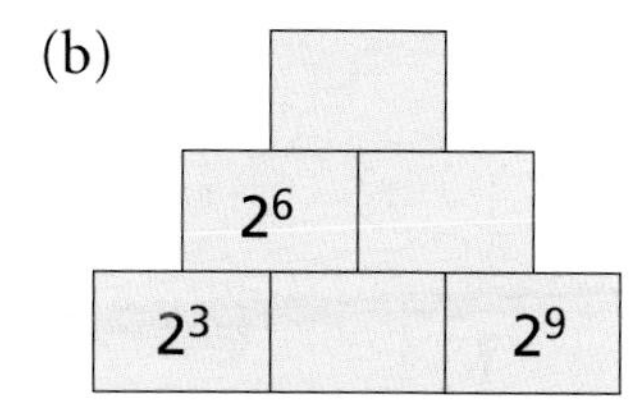

(c)

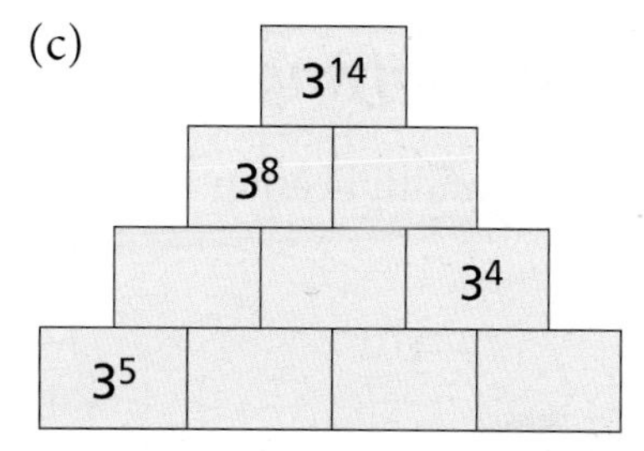

C7 Simplify each of these.

(a) $b \times b \times b \times b$ (b) $h^3 \times h^2$ (c) $a^4 \times a^5$ (d) $k \times k^5$

(e) $d^7 \times d$ (f) $m^2 \times m^4 \times m^6$ (g) $p \times p^9 \times p^3$ (h) $n \times n^7 \times n$

C8 Copy and complete these statements.

(a) $y^5 \times y^3 = y^{\blacksquare}$ (b) $n^2 \times n^{\blacksquare} = n^6$ (c) $h^{\blacksquare} \times h^2 \times h^5 = h^{11}$

(d) $k \times k^{\blacksquare} = k^6$ (e) $b^{\blacksquare} \times b^3 = b^3$ (f) $p^4 \times p^{\blacksquare} \times p^3 = p^{24}$

C9 Copy and complete these multiplication walls.

(a)

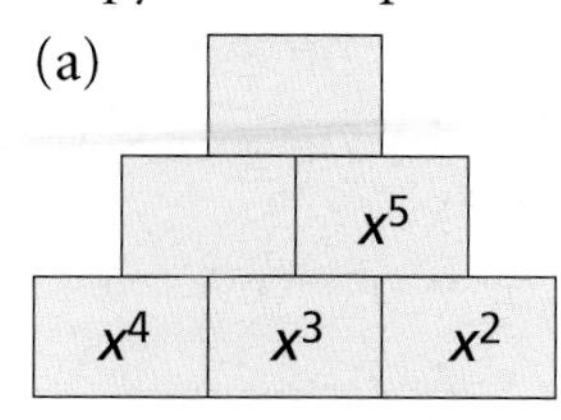

(b)

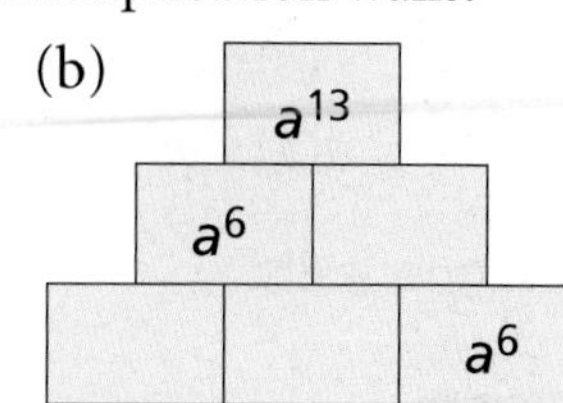

(c)

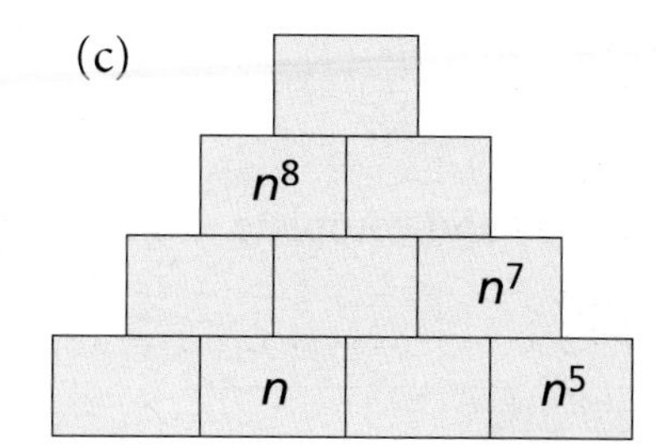

C10 Decide if each statement is true or false.

(a) $(2^3)^2 = 2^3 \times 2^3$ (b) $(2^3)^2 = 2^3 + 2^3$ (c) $(4^2)^3 = 4^2 + 4^2 + 4^2$

(d) $(4^2)^3 = 4^2 \times 4^2 \times 4^2$ (e) $(5^4)^2 = 5^4 \times 5^4$ (f) $(5^4)^2 = 5^4 + 5^4$

C11 Copy and complete these statements.

(a) $(7^3)^2 = 7^3 \times 7^3 = 7^{\blacksquare}$ (b) $(2^4)^3 = 2^4 \times 2^4 \times 2^4 = 2^{\blacksquare}$

C12 Simplify these.

(a) $(3^3)^2$ (b) $(2^3)^3$ (c) $(4^5)^2$ (d) $(3^4)^3$

C13 Copy and complete $(x^5)^2 = x^5 \times x^5 = x^{\blacksquare}$

C14 Simplify these.

(a) $(p^4)^2$ (b) $(x^2)^2$ (c) $(k^0)^4$ (d) $(n^5)^3$

C15 Copy and complete these statements.

(a) $(5^2)^{\blacksquare} = 5^8$ (b) $(10^{\blacksquare})^3 = 10^{12}$ (c) $(n^5)^{\blacksquare} = n^{10}$ (d) $(x^{\blacksquare})^7 = x^{14}$

D *Multiplying further*

These are multiplication walls.

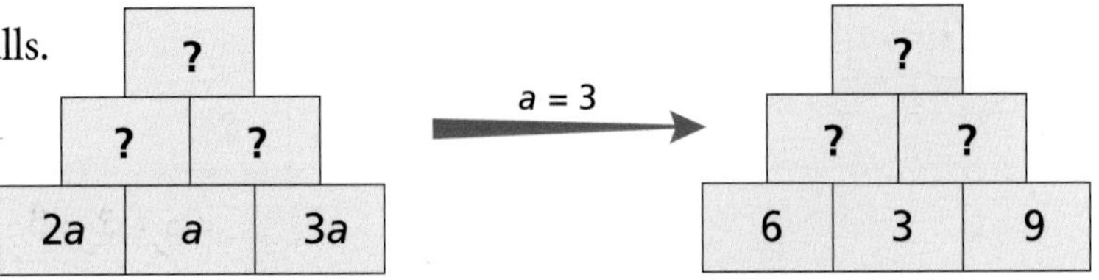

D1 (a) Find four pairs of matching expressions.

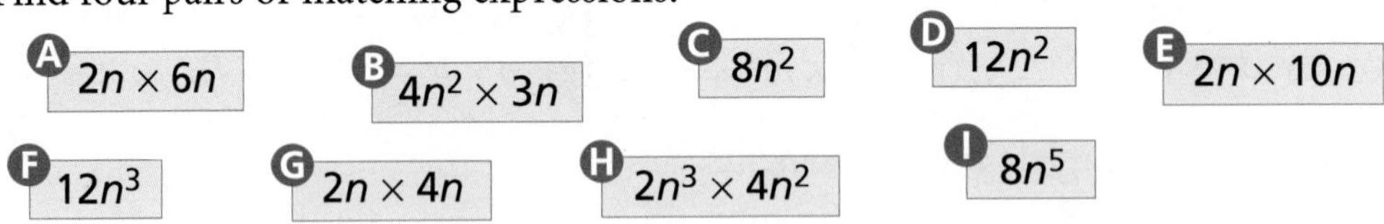

(b) Which is the odd one out?

D2 Simplify these.

(a) $3p \times 5p$ (b) $n \times 2n$ (c) $2m^2 \times 9m$ (d) $7d^3 \times d^4$

(e) $2h^5 \times 3h^2$ (f) $4x^3 \times 5x^3$ (g) $3n^2 \times n^4 \times 7n^3$ (h) $2n^3 \times 2n \times 2n^5$

D3 Copy and complete these multiplication walls.

(a)

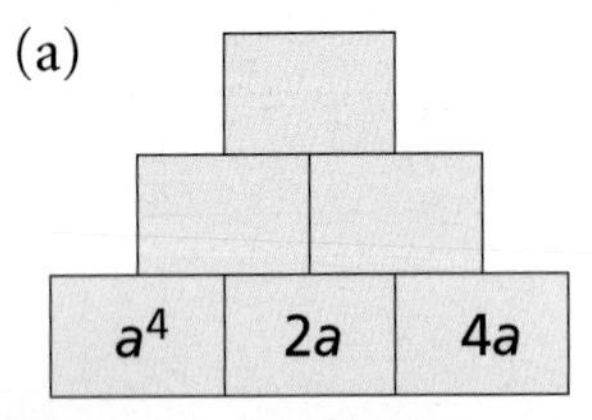

(b)

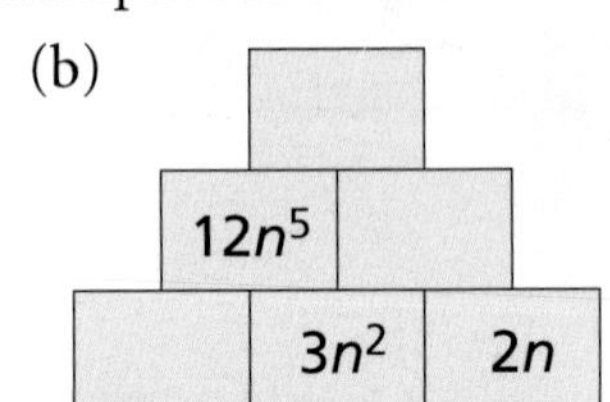

(c)

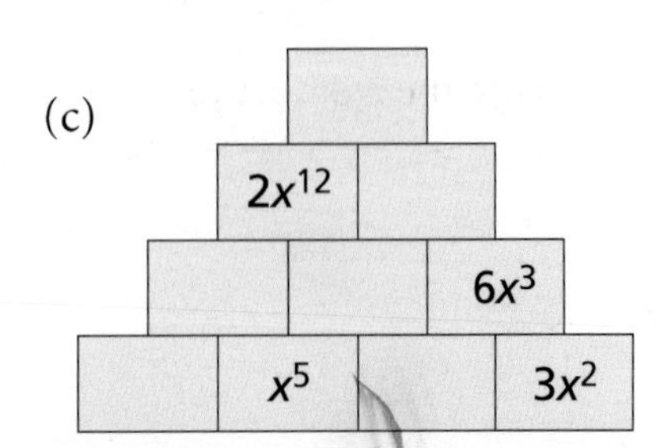

D4 Copy and complete these statements.

(a) $\blacksquare \times 4p = 8p^2$ (b) $7m^2 \times \blacksquare = 7m^3$ (c) $\blacksquare \times 4d = 12d^3$

(d) $3h^5 \times \blacksquare = 6h^{10}$ (e) $\blacksquare \times 3h^6 = 18h^7$ (f) $5p^4 \times \blacksquare = 15p^{12}$

D5 Solve the 'cover-up' puzzle on sheet G123.

D6 (a) Copy and complete $(2p)^3 = 2p \times 2p \times 2p = \blacksquare$

(b) Copy and complete $(3n^3)^2 = 3n^3 \times 3n^3 = \blacksquare$

D7 Simplify these.

(a) $(2y)^3$ (b) $(3n)^2$ (c) $(2p^5)^2$ (d) $(4m^3)^3$

Examples of multiplying expressions

$5a \times 3a = 5 \times a \times 3 \times a$
$= 5 \times 3 \times a \times a$
$= 15a^2$

$2p^2 \times 3p^5 = 2 \times p^2 \times 3 \times p^5$
$= 2 \times 3 \times p^2 \times p^5$
$= 6p^7$

$(5q^3)^2 = 5q^3 \times 5q^3$
$= 5 \times q^3 \times 5 \times q^3$
$= 5 \times 5 \times q^3 \times q^3$
$= 25q^6$

E *Dividing*

$5^6 \div 5^4 = \frac{5^6}{5^4}$
$= \frac{5 \times 5 \times 5 \times 5 \times 5 \times 5}{5 \times 5 \times 5 \times 5}$
$= \frac{5 \times 5 \times \cancel{5}^1 \times \cancel{5}^1 \times \cancel{5}^1 \times \cancel{5}^1}{\cancel{5}_1 \times \cancel{5}_1 \times \cancel{5}_1 \times \cancel{5}_1}$
$= 5 \times 5$
$= 5^2$

$3^7 \div 3^3 = \frac{3^7}{3^3}$
$= \frac{3 \times 3 \times 3 \times 3 \times 3 \times 3 \times 3}{3 \times 3 \times 3}$
$= \frac{3 \times 3 \times 3 \times 3 \times \cancel{3} \times \cancel{3} \times \cancel{3}}{\cancel{3} \times \cancel{3} \times \cancel{3}}$
$= 3 \times 3 \times 3 \times 3$
$= 3^4$

We usually leave out 1s as multiplying or dividing by 1 doesn't affect a number.

- Can you see a rule for dividing powers?

E1 (a) Find four pairs of equivalent expressions.

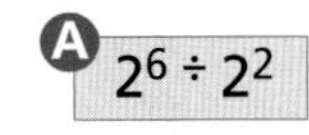

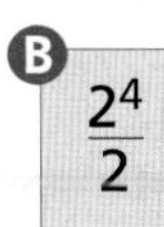

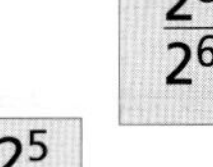

H $2^{10} \div 2^5$

(b) Which is the odd one out?

E2 Write the answers to these using indices.

(a) $7^{10} \div 7^2$ (b) $2^9 \div 2^4$ (c) $10^7 \div 10^2$ (d) $5^6 \div 5$

(e) $\frac{3^9}{3^7}$ (f) $\frac{8^6}{8}$ (g) $\frac{10^{12}}{10^3}$ (h) $\frac{5^4}{5^4}$

E3 Find the value of n in each statement.

(a) $5^8 \div 5^2 = 5^n$ (b) $6^9 \div 6^n = 6^2$ (c) $9^n \div 9^8 = 9^3$ (d) $3^n \div 3^2 = 3^{12}$

(e) $\frac{9^{16}}{9^n} = 9^2$ (f) $\frac{2^n}{2} = 2^5$ (g) $\frac{7^7}{7^n} = 7^3$ (h) $\frac{3^n}{3^8} = 3^0$

E4 Write the answers to these using indices.

(a) $6^3 \times 6^5$ (b) $\frac{7^5}{7^3}$ (c) $\frac{2^5 \times 2^4}{2^3}$ (d) $\frac{3^5 \times 3^6}{3^9}$

(e) $\frac{(5^4)^2}{5^5}$ (f) $\frac{2^8}{2 \times 2^4}$ (g) $\frac{7 \times 7^6}{7^2 \times 7^3}$ (h) $\frac{8^3 \times 8^4}{8^2 \times 8^3}$

E5 Work out $\frac{2^6 \times 2^2}{2^3 \times 2^5}$.

E6 This table shows some powers of 8.

8^2	8^3	8^4	8^5	8^6	8^7	8^8
64	512	4096	32 768	262 144	2097 152	16 777 216

Use the results in the table to evaluate these.

(a) $\frac{32\,768}{512}$ (b) $\frac{262\,144}{512}$ (c) $\frac{16\,777\,216}{2097\,152}$ (d) $\frac{64 \times 262\,144}{16\,777\,216}$

E7 Find the missing number in each statement.

(a) $\frac{p^5}{p^3} = p^{■}$ (b) $\frac{x^7}{x^2} = x^{■}$ (c) $\frac{n^{12}}{n^9} = n^{■}$ (d) $\frac{a^{10}}{a} = a^{■}$

E8 Write the answers to these using indices.

(a) $\frac{h^7}{h^3}$ (b) $\frac{n^9}{n^4}$ (c) $\frac{x^4}{x}$ (d) $\frac{d^{12}}{d^3}$ (e) $\frac{a^5}{a^4}$

E9 Find the missing number in each statement.

(a) $\frac{b^7}{b^{■}} = b^5$ (b) $\frac{k^{10}}{k^{■}} = k^2$ (c) $\frac{m^{■}}{m} = m^3$ (d) $\frac{h^{■}}{h^6} = h$

E10 Work out the value of each expression when $n = 3$.

(a) $\frac{n^4}{n^3}$ (b) $\frac{n^8}{n^6}$ (c) $\frac{n^{10}}{n^9}$ (d) $\frac{n^{14}}{n^{12}}$ (e) $\frac{n^6}{n^3}$

E11 Simplify these.

(a) $g^3 \times g^5$ (b) $\frac{w^6}{w^2}$ (c) $\frac{p^5 \times p}{p^2}$ (d) $\frac{h^5 \times h^6}{h^{10}}$

(e) $\frac{(y^3)^2}{y}$ (f) $\frac{h^8}{h \times h^3}$ (g) $\frac{q \times q^9}{q^3 \times q^4}$ (h) $\frac{z^5 \times z^3}{z^4 \times z^4}$

To **divide** powers of the same number, you can **subtract** the indices.

Examples

$\frac{10^9}{10^7} = 10^{9-7}$
$= 10^2$

$\frac{8^6}{8^5} = 8^{6-5}$
$= 8^1$
$= 8$

$\frac{m^{13}}{m^9} = m^{13-9}$
$= m^4$

F *Dividing further*

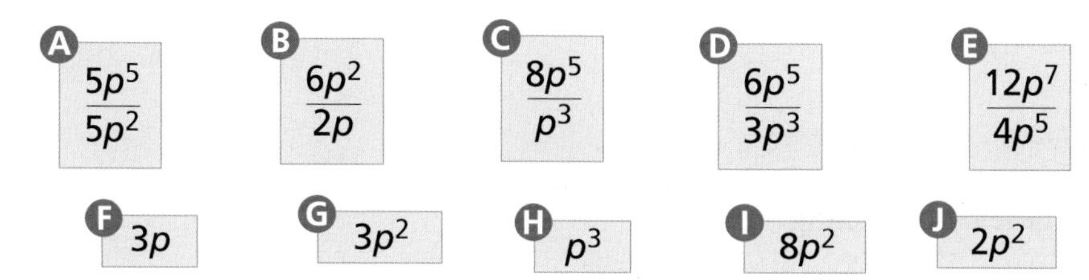

- Can you find five pairs of equivalent expressions?

F1 Simplify these.

(a) $\frac{5p^3}{p^2}$ (b) $\frac{8a^6}{4a^2}$ (c) $\frac{12y^4}{3y^3}$ (d) $\frac{8m^9}{8m^7}$ (e) $\frac{16n^7}{4n}$

F2 What are the missing numbers from each statement?

(a) $\frac{3p^4}{3p^{■}} = p$ (b) $\frac{10x^9}{■x^3} = 5x^6$ (c) $\frac{14n^{■}}{7n^2} = 2n^3$ (d) $\frac{■k^7}{3k^{■}} = 9k$

F3 Copy and complete each grid.
Each space should contain an expression, × or ÷.

Each row (from left to right) and each column (from top to bottom) should show a true statement.

(a)

	×	$6a^6$	=	
×	■	÷	■	
$2a^5$	×		=	$6a^6$
=	■	=	■	=
	÷		=	$5a^3$

(b)

$24n^6$	÷		=	
÷	■	÷	■	÷
	÷		=	$3n^2$
=	■	=	■	=
$8n^3$		$2n$	=	

G *Even further*

One way to simplify divisions is to **cancel** common factors.

Examples

$$\frac{3^2}{3^4} = \frac{3 \times 3}{3 \times 3 \times 3 \times 3} = \frac{{}^1\cancel{3} \times {}^1\cancel{3}}{\cancel{3}_1 \times \cancel{3}_1 \times 3 \times 3} = \frac{1}{3 \times 3} = \frac{1}{3^2}$$

$$\frac{10p^2}{5p^5} = \frac{10 \times p \times p}{5 \times p \times p \times p \times p \times p} = \frac{{}^2\cancel{10} \times \cancel{p} \times \cancel{p}}{\cancel{5} \times \cancel{p} \times \cancel{p} \times p \times p \times p} = \frac{2}{p \times p \times p} = \frac{2}{p^3}$$

$$\frac{6a^3}{10a^4} = \frac{6 \times a \times a \times a}{10 \times a \times a \times a \times a} = \frac{{}^3\cancel{6} \times \cancel{a} \times \cancel{a} \times \cancel{a}}{{}^5\cancel{10} \times \cancel{a} \times \cancel{a} \times \cancel{a} \times a} = \frac{3}{5 \times a} = \frac{3}{5a}$$

G1 Simplify these by cancelling.

(a) $\frac{5^2}{5^6}$ (b) $\frac{7^3}{7^8}$ (c) $\frac{2^9}{2^{10}}$ (d) $\frac{5^6}{5^{12}}$ (e) $\frac{3}{3^5}$

(f) $\frac{p^2}{p^9}$ (g) $\frac{k^3}{k^7}$ (h) $\frac{n^3}{n^{12}}$ (i) $\frac{x^9}{x^{10}}$ (j) $\frac{y}{y^8}$

G2 Simplify these by cancelling.

(a) $\frac{3p^4}{p^7}$ (b) $\frac{10b^2}{5b^6}$ (c) $\frac{9x^3}{3x^8}$ (d) $\frac{m^8}{5m^5}$ (e) $\frac{a^{10}}{7a^9}$

(f) $\frac{12y^3}{24y^2}$ (g) $\frac{3n^7}{15n^5}$ (h) $\frac{30b^4}{3b^7}$ (i) $\frac{3x^7}{21x^{11}}$ (j) $\frac{6x^6}{18x^7}$

G3 Simplify these by cancelling.

(a) $\frac{8a^4}{6a^5}$ (b) $\frac{6n^7}{15n^5}$ (c) $\frac{12p^2}{28p^3}$ (d) $\frac{4x}{18x^3}$ (e) $\frac{15k^7}{25k^{10}}$

H *Negative indices*

A 'doublebug' doubles in length each day.

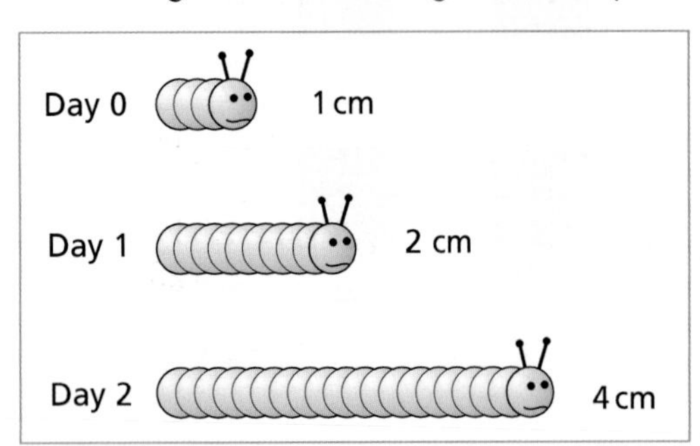

- How long will it be on day 3?
- How long was it on day $^-1$?
- What about day $^-2$, day $^-3$ … ?

H1 (a) Find three matching pairs.

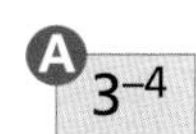 **A** 3^{-4} **B** 3^{-2}  **C** 2^{-3} **D** 4^{-3}  **E** $\frac{1}{4^3}$ **F** $\frac{1}{2^3}$ **G** $\frac{1}{3^4}$

(b) Which is the odd one out?

H2 (a) Find four matching pairs.

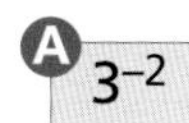 **A** 3^{-2} **B** 2^{-3}  **C** 4^{-4} 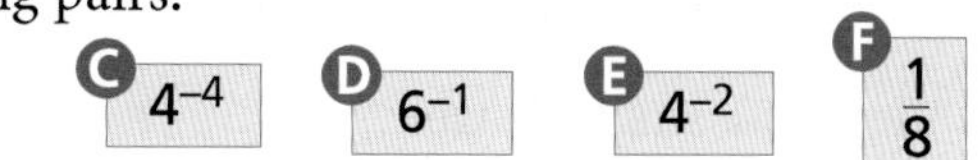 **D** 6^{-1} **E** 4^{-2} **F** $\frac{1}{8}$ 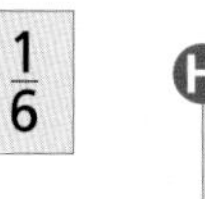 **G** $\frac{1}{6}$ **H** $\frac{1}{16}$ **I** $\frac{1}{9}$

(b) Which is the odd one out?

H3 2^{-4} is equivalent to the fraction $\frac{1}{16}$.
Write these as fractions.

(a) 3^{-3} (b) 7^{-1} (c) 9^{-2} (d) 4^{-3} (e) 11^{-1}

H4 (a) Find four matching pairs.

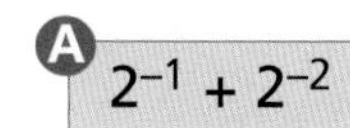 **A** $2^{-1} + 2^{-2}$ **B** $5^0 - 5^{-1}$  **E** $\frac{3}{4}$ **F** $\frac{1}{8}$  **G** $\frac{-1}{5}$ **H** 1 **I** $\frac{4}{5}$

 **C** $8^{-1} \times 8^0$ **D** 4×2^{-2}

(b) Which is the odd one out?

H5 $2^{-2} = \frac{1}{2^2} = \frac{1}{4} = 0.25$ as a decimal.

Work out the decimal value of these.

(a) 2^{-1} (b) 4^{-1} (c) 2^{-2} (d) 10^{-2} (e) 5^{-1}

H6 Write $5^{-1} + 5^0$ as a decimal.

H7 Write $10^{-1} + 10^{-3}$ as a decimal.

H8 a^{-2} is equivalent to $\frac{1}{a^2}$ in fractional form.
Write these in fractional form.

(a) x^{-3} (b) g^{-1} (c) n^{-2} (d) k^{-3} (e) p^{-1}

H9 Find the missing number in each statement below.

(a) $12^{■} = \frac{1}{12}$ (b) $10^{■} = 1$ (c) $2^{■} = \frac{1}{4}$ (d) $4^{■} = 0.25$

(e) $10^{■} = 0.01$ (f) $5^{■} = \frac{1}{25}$ (g) $■^{-2} = \frac{1}{49}$ (h) $■^{-3} = \frac{1}{125}$

$a^{-m} = \frac{1}{a^m}$

For example, $2^{-4} = \frac{1}{2^4}$ $3^{-5} = \frac{1}{3^5}$ $5^{-1} = \frac{1}{5}$

I More multiplying and dividing

A $3^5 \times 3^{-2} = ?$ **B** $2^{-5} \times 2^3 = ?$ **C** $2^{-3} \times 2^3 = ?$ **D** $2^{-1} \times 2^{-2} = ?$

E $10^2 \div 10^4 = ?$ **F** $\frac{3^3}{3^5} = ?$ **G** $\frac{7^2}{7^2} = ?$ **H** $\frac{2^3}{2^4} = ?$

I1 Write the answers to these as a single power.

(a) $3^4 \times 3^{-3}$ (b) $10^{-2} \times 10^5$ (c) $8^{-4} \times 8^4$ (d) $3^{-5} \times 3^3$

(e) $2^2 \times 2^{-7}$ (e) 9×9^{-2} (e) $2^{-4} \times 2^{-1}$ (e) $7^{-2} \times 7^9 \times 7^{-4}$

I2 Write the answers to these as a single power.

(a) $3^2 \div 3^4$ (b) $5^3 \div 5^6$ (c) $2^4 \div 2^5$ (d) $9 \div 9^6$

(e) $\frac{4^5}{4^7}$ (f) $\frac{7^3}{7^9}$ (g) $\frac{6^7}{6^8}$ (h) $\frac{10}{10^7}$

I3 Write the answers to these as a single power.

(a) $5^4 \times 5^{-2}$ (b) $2^3 \div 2^8$ (c) $7^{-9} \times 7^5$ (d) $6 \div 6^8$

(e) $7^{-3} \times 7^{-2}$ (f) $\frac{4^3}{4^7}$ (g) $2^9 \times 2^{-9}$ (h) $\frac{5^2}{5^3}$

I4 Simplify each of these.

(a) $p^4 \times p^{-5}$ (b) $q^3 \times q^{-3}$ (c) $r^{-7} \times r^9$ (d) $s^{-3} \times s$

(e) $\frac{w^2}{w^7}$ (f) $\frac{x^3}{x^6}$ (g) $\frac{y^8}{y^8}$ (h) $\frac{z}{z^5}$

I5 Simplify each of these.

(a) 11×11^{-7} (b) $2^6 \div 2^3$ (c) $a^{-4} \times a^3$ (d) $6 \div 6^4$

(e) $13^{-2} \times 13^{-5}$ (f) $\frac{b^8}{b^6}$ (g) $3^4 \times 3^{-4}$ (h) $\frac{2^3}{2^9}$

J Mixed questions

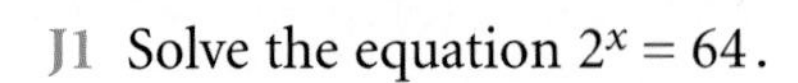

J1 Solve the equation $2^x = 64$.

J2 Work out the value of 5^n when $n = 0$.

J3 Write $2^4 \times 2 \times 2^8$ as a single power of 2.

J4 Simplify these.

(a) $p^2 \times p \times p^5$ (b) $5x \times 2x^3$ (c) $6a^3 \times 3a^2$ (d) $(2k)^4$

J5 Write each of these as a fraction.

(a) 2^{-3} (b) 4^{-1} (c) 3^{-2} (d) 10^{-5}

J6 Write each of these as a single power of 3.

(a) $3^5 \div 3^2$ (b) $\dfrac{3^8}{3^4}$ (c) $\dfrac{3^7}{3^{10}}$ (d) $\dfrac{3^9}{3^8}$

J7 Simplify these.

(a) $\dfrac{15x^5}{5x^3}$ (b) $\dfrac{4a^6}{8a^3}$ (c) $\dfrac{10b^2}{2b^7}$ (d) $\dfrac{4c^7}{12c^9}$

J8 Simplify these.

(a) $p^{-3} \times p^{-2}$ (b) $p^{-1} \times p^8$ (c) $p^5 \times p^{-9}$ (d) $p^5 \div p^7$

J9 Simplify these.

(a) $4n^{-1} \times 2n^{-2}$ (b) $\dfrac{x^5}{x^{-2}}$ (c) $\dfrac{5p^2}{p^6}$ (d) $\dfrac{12a}{6a^3}$

Test yourself

T1 For each of the following equations, write down the value of n.

(a) $2^n = 32$ (b) $n^3 = 125$ (c) $8^n = 8$

AQA(NEAB)1998

T2 Write the answers to these using indices.

(a) $5^3 \times 5^2$ (b) $\dfrac{4^8}{4^5}$ (c) $\dfrac{2^3 \times 2^4}{2^5}$

T3 Simplify these.

(a) $h^3 \times h^2$ (b) $\dfrac{m^7}{m^5}$ (c) $\dfrac{n^5 \times n^6}{n}$

T4 Evaluate these.

(a) 3^3 (b) 2^{-3} (c) 7^0

T5 Write these as single powers.

(a) $7^9 \times 7^{-2}$ (b) $\dfrac{6^3}{6^9}$ (c) $\dfrac{3 \times 3^4}{3^{10}}$

T6 Find the value of p when $2^p \times 5 = 40$.

T7 Simplify these.

(a) $h \times 8h$ (b) $3b^2 \times 2b^6$ (c) $k^3 \times k^{-1}$

T8 Simplify these.

(a) $(2x^4)^3$ (b) $\dfrac{12m^6}{3m}$ (c) $\dfrac{8h^2}{4h^6}$

24 Surveys and experiments

This work will help you plan and carry out a project in data handling. You will need to be able to make frequency tables, draw bar charts or pie charts and use scatter diagrams.

You will learn how to

- write an effective questionnaire
- carry out experiments to get data

A The data handling cycle

TG

Specifying the question	The starting point is a **question** or an area of interest, for example: • If the local library can be open for only ten hours a week, at what times would it be best to open? • Do people remember words better than numbers?
Collecting data	To answer the question, we need to decide what information or data we need. We have to plan how to **collect** it and how we will use it to help answer our question. If we have to collect the data ourselves, for example by asking people questions or by counting or measuring something, then the data is called **primary data.** If the data has already been collected by someone else, it is called **secondary data.**
Processing and representing the data	To help answer the question, the data has to be **processed** (for example, by working out percentages, finding frequencies, calculating means, and so on). It is often helpful to **represent** the data in pictorial form (for example, frequency chart, scatter diagram, pie chart).
Interpreting the data to answer the question	Processing and representing the data allows us to **interpret** it to help answer the question we started with. The result may suggest that some more data needs to be collected. It might also suggest other questions which need answering. So we may go back to an earlier stage of the cycle and repeat.

Primary data and secondary data

Primary data is data which you collect yourself.
For example, you are collecting primary data when you give people questionnaires to fill in. You are also collecting primary data when you make measurements in an experiment.

Height	152 cm	172 cm
Weight	57 kg	78 kg
Pulse rate before exercise	89 b.p.m.	75 b.p.m.
Pulse rate after exercise	127 b.p.m.	133 b.p.m.

Secondary data is data which someone else has collected and organised.
For example, data about crime which is published by the government is secondary data.

Vandalism, per 10 000 households			
Year	1981	1993	1995
Cases	1481	1638	1614

Sometimes data does not fit easily into either type.
For example, suppose you collect information about the prices of secondhand cars from newspaper adverts. Is this primary or secondary data?
It feels more like primary data because although it's written by someone else, it isn't organised in any way.

Ford Fiesta 1.4, 1992, 65000 miles. Blue vgc. MOT. £1250 ono.
Ford Sierra 2.0LX, J reg, 1992, 34000 miles. Red. One owner. FSH. MOT, taxed to Aug. £2600.
Ford Sierra 1.8 estate, 1994, Grey. No rust. Recent service. £2900 ono.

TG

B *Surveys*

<u>School uniform</u> <u>Report by Chris and Melanie</u>

The school council discussed changing the school uniform. Some people didn't like the colour and some wanted sweatshirts instead of blazers. A lot of pupils thought that there shouldn't be a uniform at all.

We decided to find out what other students felt about the uniform. We thought that boys and girls might feel differently and so might different year groups. We wrote a questionnaire and we decided to give it to some students in every year group. (There are about 180 in each year.)

Here is our questionnaire.

1 What year group are you in? (Please tick.) Y7 Y8 Y9 Y10 Y11

2 Are you male or female? Male Female

3 Do you think there should be a school uniform? Yes No

4 If there has to be a uniform, would you prefer blazer sweatshirt

5 What colours would you like the uniform to be?

6 'Students should be allowed to wear jewellery.' What do you think?

Strongly agree Agree Not sure Disagree Strongly disagree

Questions for discussion

- What do you think of the questions? Are they easy to answer?
  Are they clear – will they mean the same to everyone who answers them?
  Will the responses be easy to analyse?
- Who would you give the questionnaire to?
  How would you collect their responses?
  How many people would you give it to?

The report continues like this.

Our teacher told us it was a good idea to pilot a questionnaire. This means giving it to a few people to see if there are any 'bugs' (problems).

We gave it to 10 people. Some of them thought there should be a question about ties. Two people said that 'jewellery' was too vague: ordinary rings could be allowed but not nose rings.

We also found that everybody had written different colours that they liked, sometimes three or four colours, e.g. dark blue, red, yellow. It would be difficult to analyse the answers to this question.

- Look back at the questionnaire.
  How could you improve it to avoid these problems?

In their report, Chris and Melanie made tables of the replies they got to the questions in their questionnaire.

This table shows the replies we got to the question 'Would you prefer blazer or sweatshirt?'

Year		7	8	9	10	11
Boys	Blazer	7	7	4	3	3
	Sweatshirt	8	11	12	11	13
Girls	Blazer	7	7	6	6	7
	Sweatshirt	5	8	9	10	9

B1 Draw a chart, or charts, to illustrate this data.
Explain why you chose your type of chart.

B2 What conclusions would you draw about the preferences?

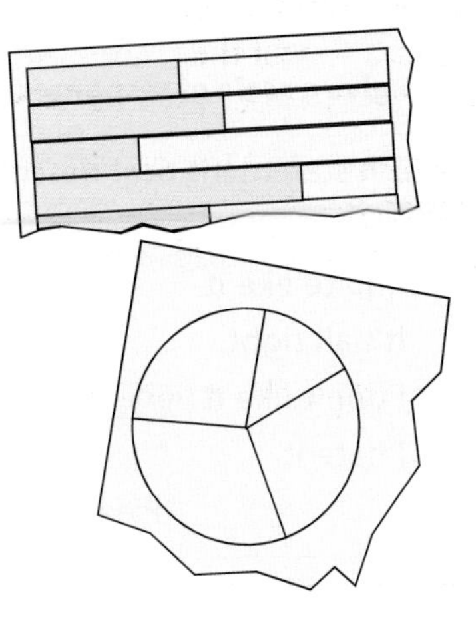

Question types

Here are some types of question you could use in a questionnaire. Questions which ask for boxes to be ticked (or letters to be ringed) make it easier to collect all the data together afterwards.

Yes/no questions

A

> Have you passed the driving test? YES ☐ NO ☐

The question must have a clear 'yes' or 'no' answer. (If you think someone might not know the answer, then you could include DON'T KNOW ☐).

Multiple-choice questions

B

> Which age group are you in?
>
> 0–19 ☐ 20–39 ☐ 40–59 ☐ 60–79 ☐ 80 or over ☐

C

> Which of these statements best describes how you plan what you will watch on TV?
>
> **A** I plan days ahead.
> **B** I decide on the day.
> **C** I just flick around to see what's on.
>
> Please ring A B C

In examples B and C above, the person chooses one response. In example D below, they can choose more than one.

D

> Which of these languages do you study for GCSE?
>
> French ☐ German ☐ Spanish ☐ Gujerati ☐ Latin ☐

Questions which give a scale of responses

E

> Which statement best describes how you feel about maths?
> A I like it a lot.
> B I quite like it.
> C It's all right.
> D I don't like it very much.
> E I hate it.
>
> Please ring A B C D E

Questions which ask for a number

F | How many subjects are you taking at GCSE? Number ....

If you don't need to know the number exactly, then it is better to give groups (as in example B).

Questions which ask for an order of preference

G | What kind of music do you prefer?
Put in order of priority (1 for your favourite, 5 for your least).
Hard rock ☐ Pop ☐ Jazz ☐ Easy listening ☐ Classical ☐

Open questions

H | What do you think about school lunches?

This kind of question is good for finding out people's own ideas, but it is hard to summarise the answers.

Things to avoid!

- Don't ask questions which could be embarrassing. ('How old are you?')
- Don't ask questions which try to lead people to answer in one way. ('Would you like to see the safety of our children improved by banning traffic from the road in front of the school?') These are called **leading questions.**
- Don't ask questions which are difficult to answer precisely. ('How many hours of TV do you usually watch each week?')

B3 Criticise these questions and try to improve them.

How much do you earn? £...............

How many are there in your family? ....

Where do you shop? Please tick. Asda ☐ Sainsbury's ☐ Safeway ☐ Tesco ☐

How much do you spend a week on food? £...............

How do you think supermarket fruit and vegetables compare with the real fruit and vegetables you buy direct from a farm?

Carrying out a survey

1. Be clear about the purpose of your survey.
2. Write a draft questionnaire.
3. Pilot your draft questionnaire with a small number of people.
4. Improve the questions if necessary.
5. Decide who to give the questionnaire to, and how many people to ask.
6. Decide whether you will see people and ask the questions, or give them the questionnaire to fill in.
7. Collect all the responses together, analyse them and write a **report**.

In your report

- State the purpose of your survey. Describe how you carried it out, any difficulties you had to overcome and any changes of plan.
- Include your final questionnaire.
- Say how many people responded.
- Summarise the responses to each question. Use tables and charts where appropriate.

  If you are comparing the responses of different groups (e.g. boys and girls), summarise them **separately**. You could use a table something like this.

Hours of TV	0-9	10-19	20-29	30+
Girls	17	12	15	9
Boys	12	10	19	10

- Write a conclusion.

Points for discussion

Music charts

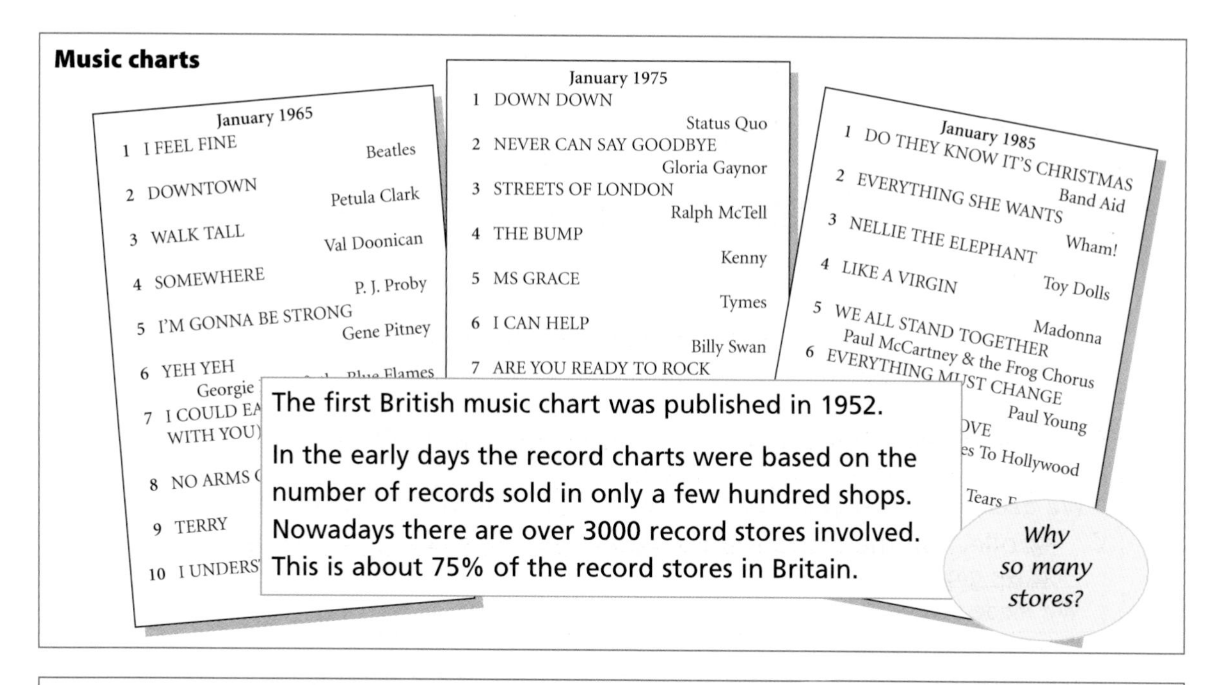

The first British music chart was published in 1952.

In the early days the record charts were based on the number of records sold in only a few hundred shops. Nowadays there are over 3000 record stores involved. This is about 75% of the record stores in Britain.

Why so many stores?

US elections

Surveys got a bad name in 1936. In that year the US Presidential elections were held. There were two candidates, Landon (who represented the better off) and Roosevelt (for the less well off).
A magazine did a postal survey on who people would vote for. They obtained the names and addresses from telephone directories and car registrations.
Over 2 million of the 10 million sent questionnaires replied.
These predicted a massive victory for Landon.
In fact Roosevelt won by a massive majority!

Why do you think the result was so different?

Honest!

About 60 years ago, an American survey contained the question

What do you think of of the new metallic Metals Law?

The option boxes included 'I don't know' as an option, but fewer than 25% ticked it. Everyone else ticked an opinion.

In fact the 'new metallic Metals Law' was completely fictitious!

Why did over 75% of people express an opinion?

C *Experiments*

Priya and Ben decided to investigate how good people are at remembering words, numbers and pictures.
They wrote a report on their findings.

Remembering words, pictures and numbers
by Priya and Ben

We wanted to see if there was any difference between how good young people are at remembering words, pictures and numbers.

We both thought it would be easiest to remember pictures.

We decided to test years 10 to 13, who are mostly between 14 and 18 years old.

<u>How we got our results</u>
We made up some experiments.

We chose:
- 10 words – we tried to make sure there were no links between them (like 'pencil' and 'paper')
- 10 pictures
- 10 numbers between 1 and 100

We showed our class the 10 words for 30 seconds and gave them 60 seconds to write down as many as they could remember. The order didn't matter.

We did the same with the pictures and the numbers.

Each correct word, picture or number scored 1 point.

Each student had three scores out of 10 and wrote them on a slip of paper. Our class is in year 10 and we wanted results from years 10 to 13. We couldn't use year 11 because they were on exam leave so we asked our teacher Mr Cassell to do the same experiment on his year 12 and 13 mathematics groups.

Our results
We collected all the slips of paper and chose 10 at random from each year so that we had the results for 30 students.

Here are some questions for discussion.
Explain each of your answers as fully as you can.

C1 Did you find Priya's and Ben's description of their memory experiments easy to follow?

C2 They made up a list of 10 words for one experiment.
Why do you think they tried to have no links between their words?

C3 Why do you think they used the same number of words, numbers and pictures in their experiments?

C4 Was it a good idea for Mr Cassell to collect the data from his year 12 and 13 mathematics groups?

C5 Why do you think they chose 10 students at random from each year?
Do you think this was a good idea?

We made a table for each year but we analysed all the results together.
W stands for Words; P stands for Pictures; N stands for Numbers.

Year 10		
W	P	N
8	7	5
5	6	6
5	3	7
7	7	5
8	7	7
10	10	8
9	10	8
10	10	9
10	9	10
9	8	6

Year 12		
W	P	N
8	9	6
9	10	9
10	10	8
9	9	9
7	9	8
10	10	7
7	8	4
7	8	10
8	7	8
9	10	7

Year 13		
W	P	N
10	**10**	**9**
9	9	6
9	10	10
7	9	4
8	10	7
8	9	5
8	10	4
8	8	4
8	8	6
10	10	6

Each row shows the scores for one student.
For example, the first row in the year 13 table shows that a student correctly remembered 10 words, 10 pictures and 9 numbers.

Analysing our results

We drew bar charts for our results.

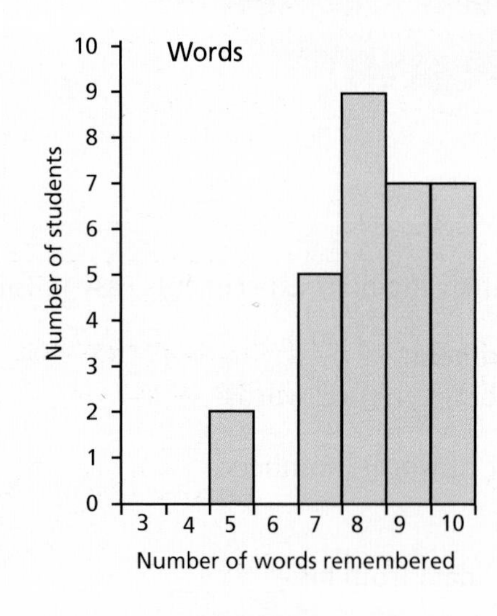

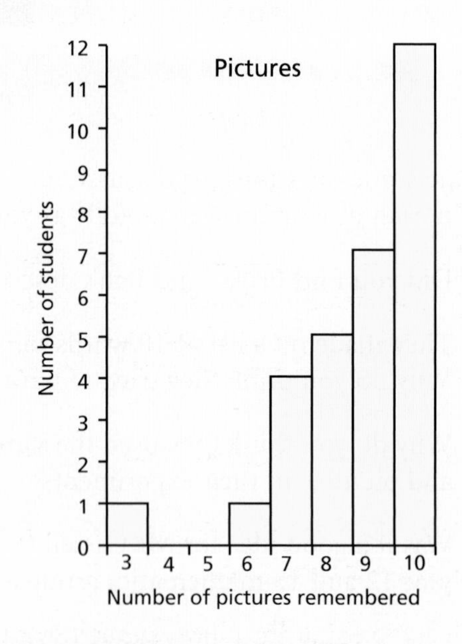

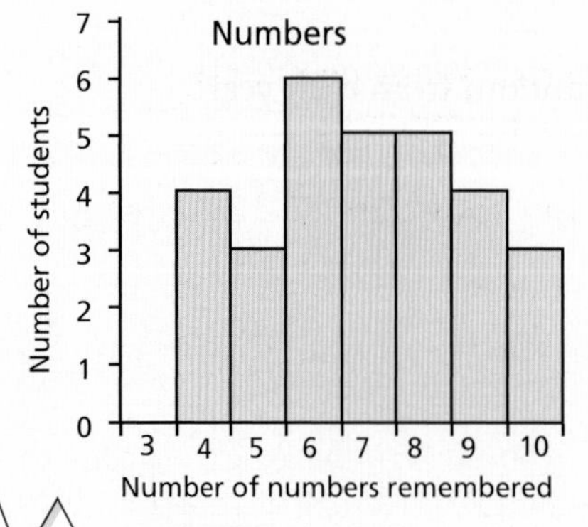

Conclusion

From the shape of our charts, we think that young people are best at remembering pictures, then words and then numbers. We expected that people would be best at remembering pictures.

For this sample:

C6 One student remembered only 3 pictures.
How many words and numbers did this person remember?

C7 How many students in year 13 remembered all 10 pictures?

C8 How many students from all three years remembered fewer than 7 pictures?

C9 How many students from all three years remembered more than 8 words?

C10 Do you think that the bar charts show that the students are best at remembering pictures, then words and then numbers ?

We then decided to calculate the mean, median and range for each set of results.

	Words	Pictures	Numbers
Mean	250 ÷ 30 ≈ **8.3** words	260 ÷ 30 ≈ **8.7** pictures	208 ÷ 30 ≈ **6.9** numbers
Median	**8** words	**9** pictures	**7** numbers
Range	10 – 5 = **5** words	10 – 3 = **7** pictures	10 – 4 = **6** numbers

The means and medians show that our conclusion is correct.
Young people are best at remembering pictures, then words and then numbers.
The ranges show that the results for the pictures are more spread out.

C11 Why do they think that the values for the means and medians show that their conclusion is correct ?

C12 Do you think they have enough evidence to say that young people are best at remembering pictures, then words and then numbers ?

C13 Why do you think they did not compare students from years 10, 12 and 13 ?

Extension
We then investigated if there was a link between our memory for words and for numbers.

We drew a scatter diagram for our results.

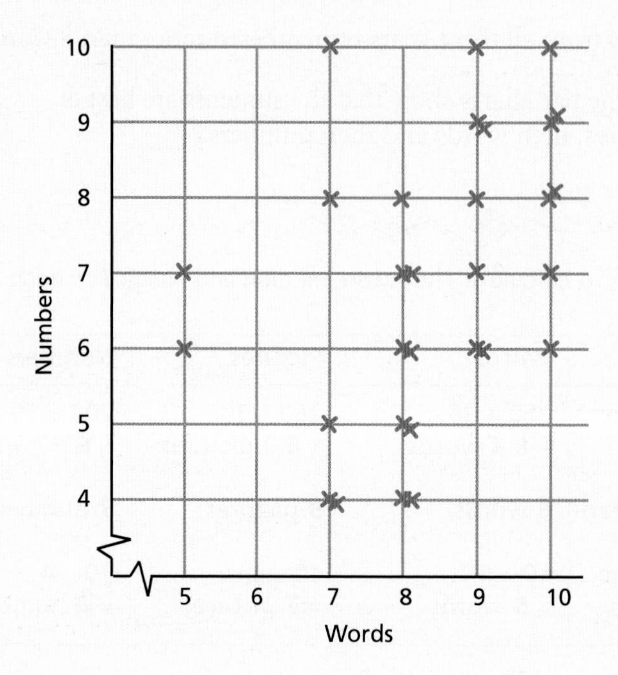

Conclusion
The crosses are quite spread out.
We don't think this shows a link between our memory for words and for numbers.

Possible further work
If we had more time we would have tried to find if there was a link between our memory for words and for pictures and also for numbers and pictures.

We also think that we would like to do the experiments again with more than 10 words, pictures and numbers. A lot of people scored 10 in at least one experiment.

Next week we are going to ask our class how many of the words, pictures and numbers they can remember (but we haven't told them this). We want to see how good they are at remembering these things after a week has passed.

C14 Do you agree with Priya and Ben that the scatter diagram shows there is no link between our memory for words and for numbers?

C15 For the students in Priya's and Ben's investigation, draw a scatter diagram to decide if there is a link between their memory for words and for pictures.

C16 Why do you think Priya and Ben want to repeat their experiments with more than 10 numbers, words and pictures?

C17 Investigate to see if you come to the same conclusions as Priya and Ben for students in your school. (There are 10 pictures on sheet G12 that you can use.)

D *Ideas for primary data projects*

These projects are described in more detail on sheets G124 to G132.

Remember, remember ...

Investigate aspects of memory, such as whether age affects memory or whether background music makes it easier to remember.

Food for thought

Investigate aspects of healthy and unhealthy eating.

First names

Investigate aspects of people's first names, such as popularity or length.

Lunchtime menu

Carry out a survey of people's eating habits in order to decide what to include in the lunchtime menu of a café.

Groovers

Investigate people's preferences for different styles of music, for example to programme the output of a radio station.

Computer games

Investigate opinions about computer games and their popularity.

Wine gums

Compare different makes of wine gum: cost, taste, and so on.

Town and country houses

Use the information given in estate agents' adverts to investigate aspects of houses, such as how their value varies from place to place.

Helicopter seeds

Some trees have seeds with wings that rotate in the wind as the seed falls. Investigate how these seeds fly by making simple paper models.

25 Parallel lines and angles

You will revise vertically opposite angles and angles made with parallel lines.

This work will help you work out angles and explain your reasoning.

A Parallel lines crossing

Draw two sets of parallel lines like this.

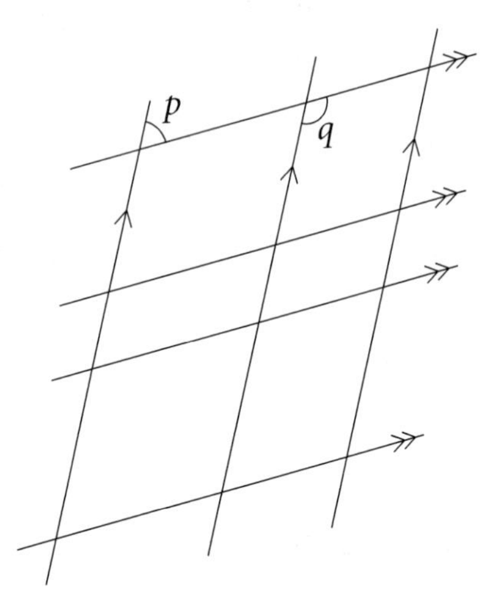

Mark two **different-sized** angles on your diagram and label them p and q.

- Mark with a p every angle that equals angle p.
- Mark with a q every angle that equals angle q.
- If you know the size of p, how do you work out q?

A1 Here are two more sets of parallel lines.
If this angle is 50°, what will each angle marked with a letter be?

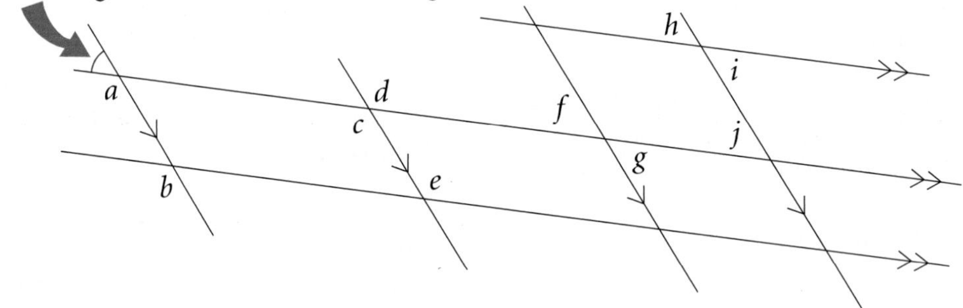

A2 Here are another two sets of parallel lines.
If this angle is 110°, what will each angle marked with a letter be?

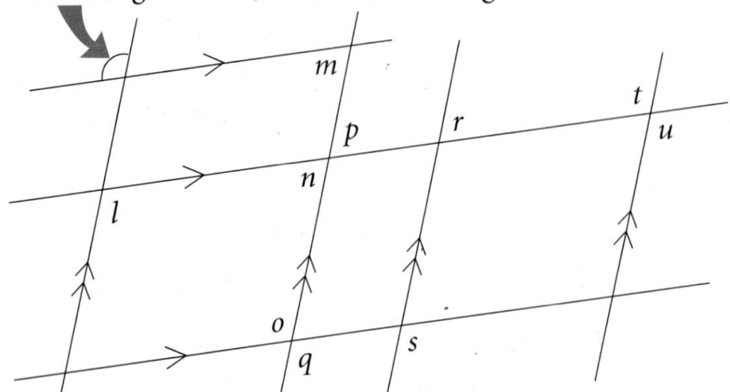

Vertically opposite angles are equal angles like this 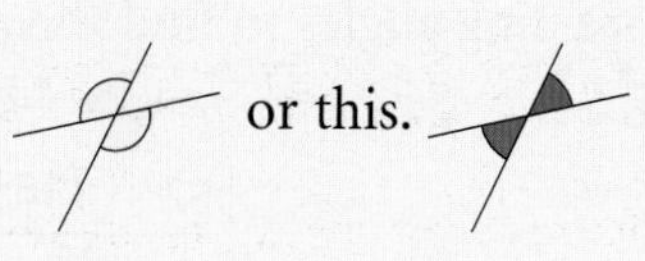 or this.

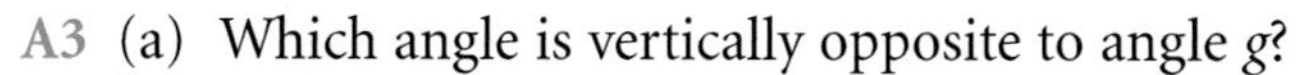

A3 (a) Which angle is vertically opposite to angle g?

(b) Which angle is vertically opposite to angle b?

(c) Give the letters for two more pairs of vertically opposite angles.

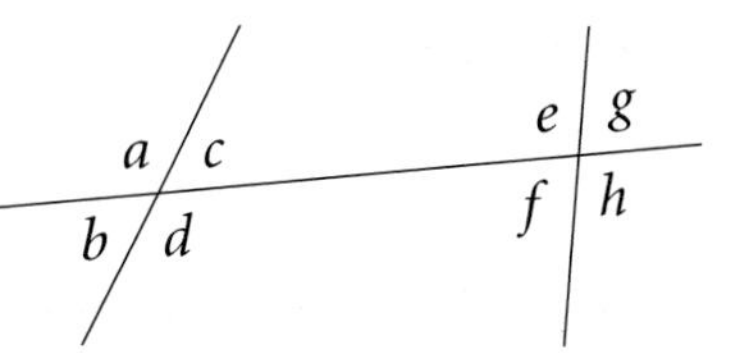

A4 (a) Give the letters for three pairs of vertically opposite angles in the diagram for A1.

(b) Give the letters for three pairs of vertically opposite angles in the diagram for A2.

A5 Use vertically opposite angles to find the angles marked with letters here.

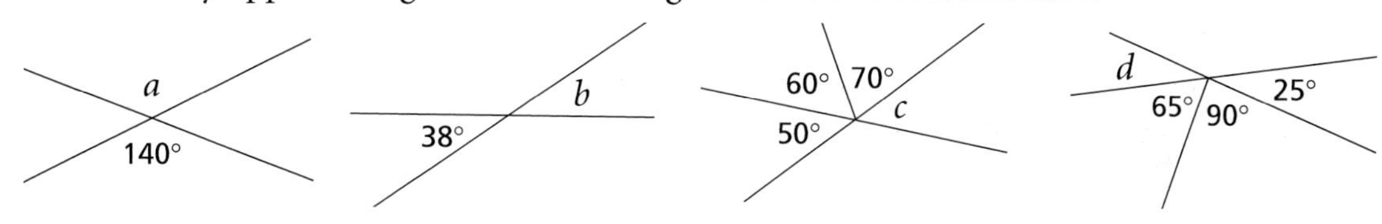

Corresponding angles are equal angles like these.

You can trace an F or a reverse F over them.

To see how corresponding angles work, think of two pencils in a straight line.

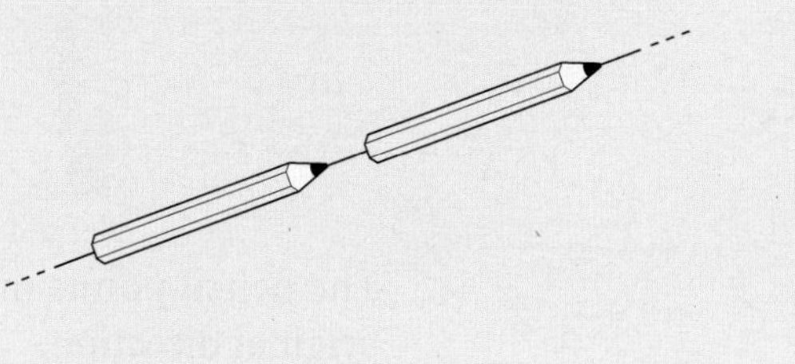

Now both pencils rotate 70° clockwise about their ends.

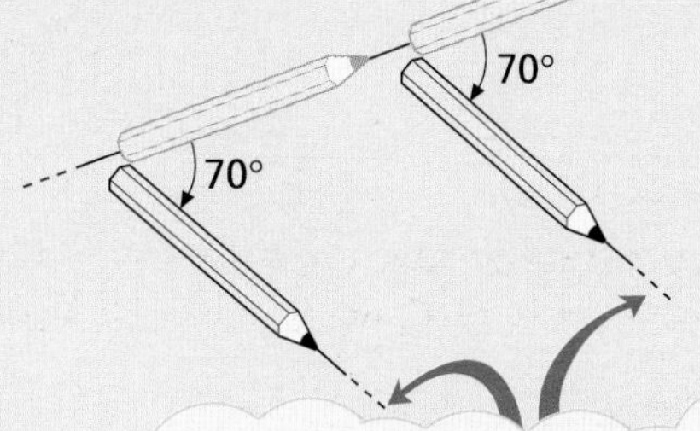

The pencils point in the same direction, so these lines are parallel.

A6 Give the missing letters for these.

(a) Angles p and ___ are corresponding angles.

(b) Angles ___ and t are corresponding angles.

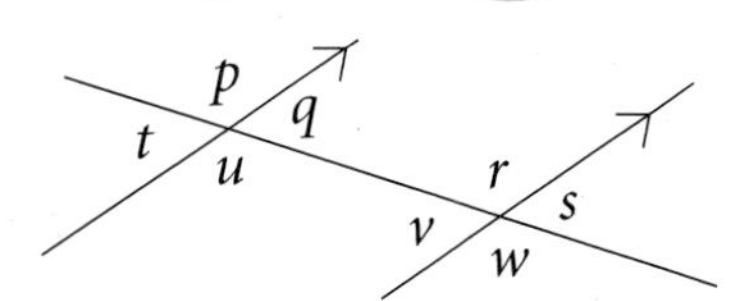

A7 (a) Give the letters for four pairs of corresponding angles in the diagram for A1.

(b) Give the letters for four pairs of corresponding angles in the diagram for A2.

A8 Use corresponding angles to find the angles marked with letters here.

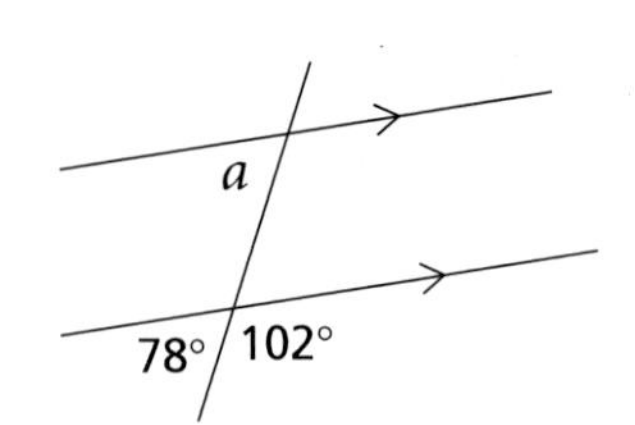

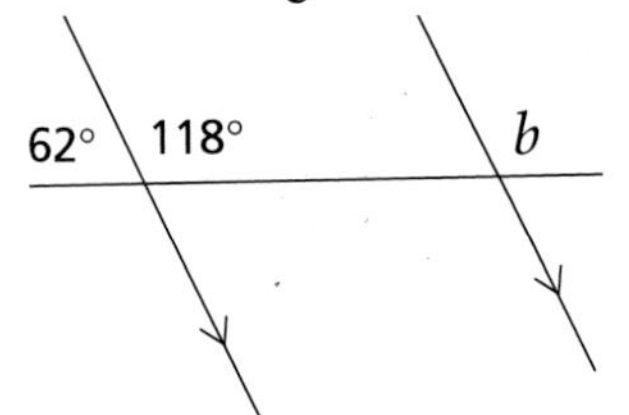

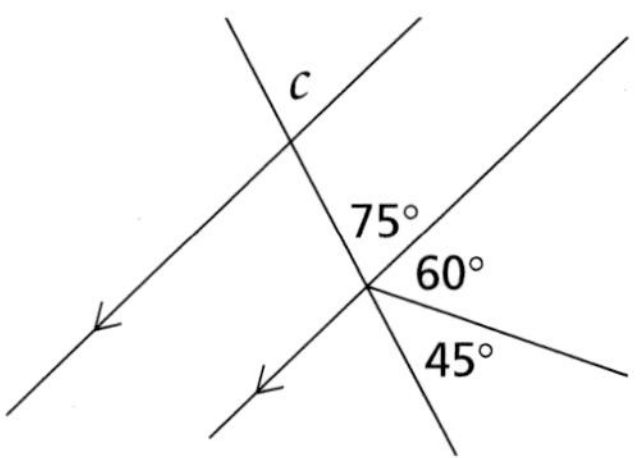

A9 Give the missing letters for these.

(a) Angles a and ___ are corresponding angles.

(b) Angles h and ___ are corresponding angles.

(c) Angles ___ and i are corresponding angles.

(d) Angles ___ and j are corresponding angles.

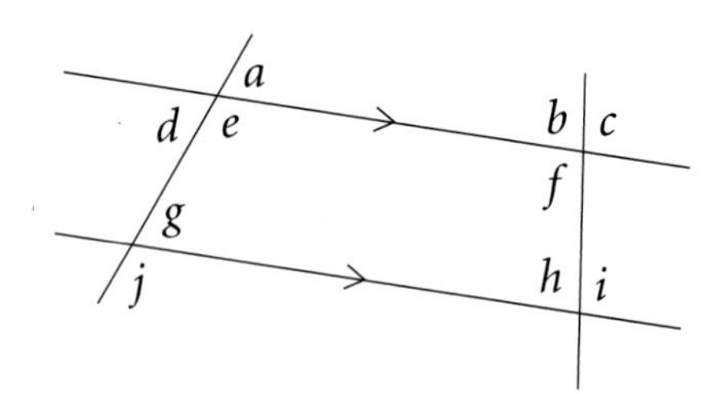

Alternate angles are equal angles like these.

You can trace a Z or a reverse Z over them.

To understand alternate angles, think of one pencil.

It rotates 70° clockwise about its end ...

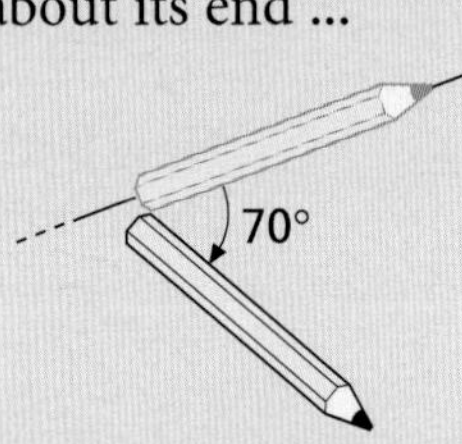

... then 70° anticlockwise about its point.

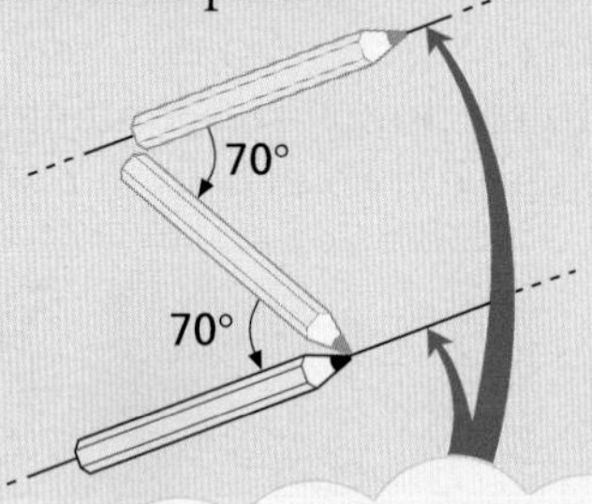

The pencil points in its original direction, so these lines are parallel.

A10 Give the missing letters for these.

(a) Angles c and ___ are alternate angles.

(b) Angles f and ___ are alternate angles.

(c) Angles ___ and h are alternate angles.

(d) Angles ___ and a are alternate angles.

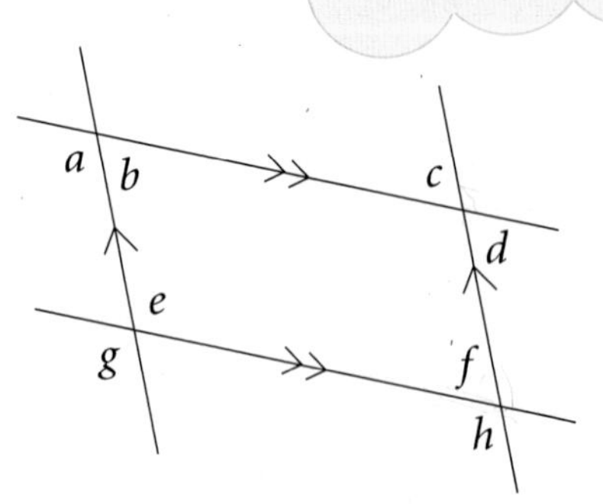

A11 Use alternate angles to find the angles marked with letters here.

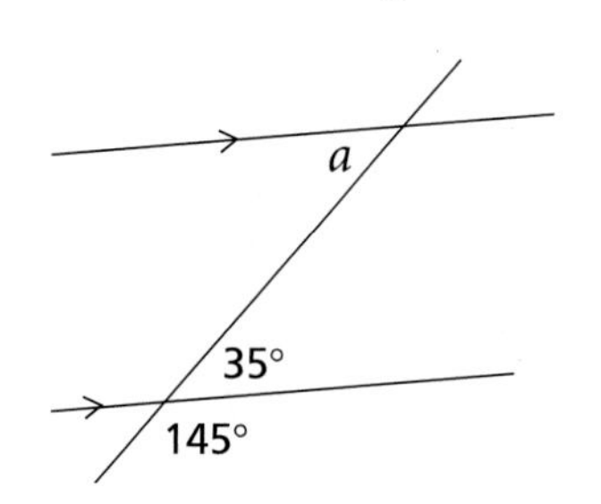

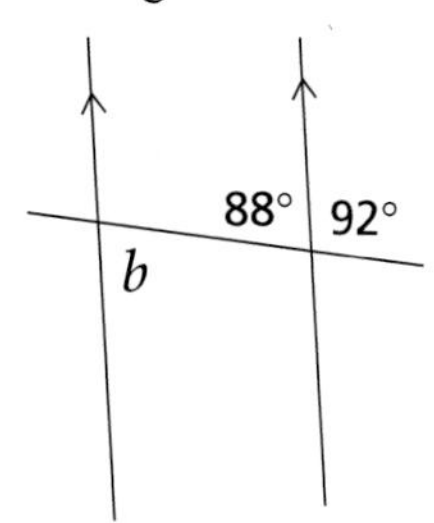

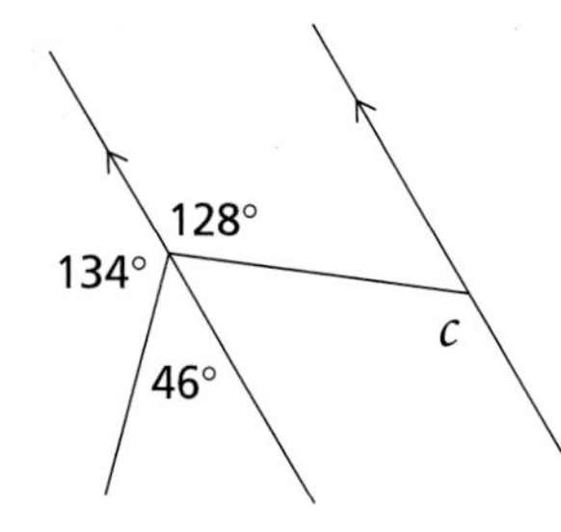

A12 Find four pairs of alternate angles in this diagram. Give their letters.

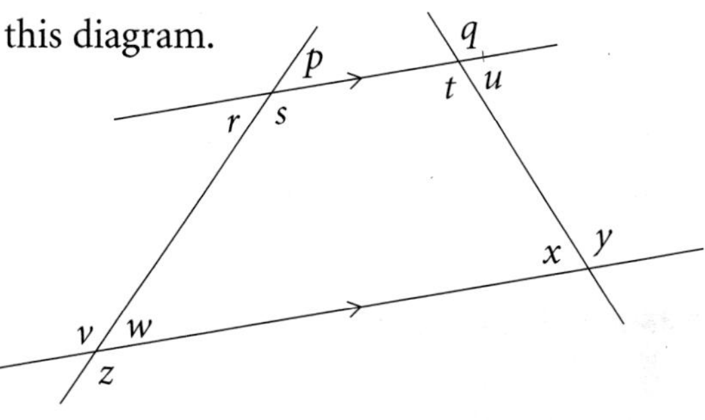

Supplementary angles add up to 180°.

You get supplementary angles on a straight line

or between parallel lines like this or this.

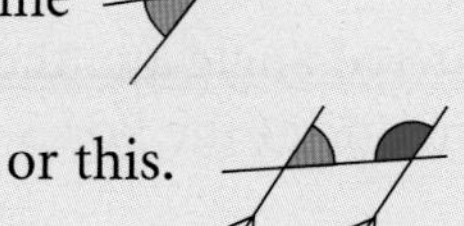

A13 (a) Give the missing letters for these.

(i) Angles ___ and d are supplementary angles on a straight line.

(ii) Angles g and ___ are supplementary angles between parallel lines.

(b) Find one more pair of supplementary angles on a straight line. Give their letters.

(c) Find one more pair of supplementary angles between parallel lines. Give their letters.

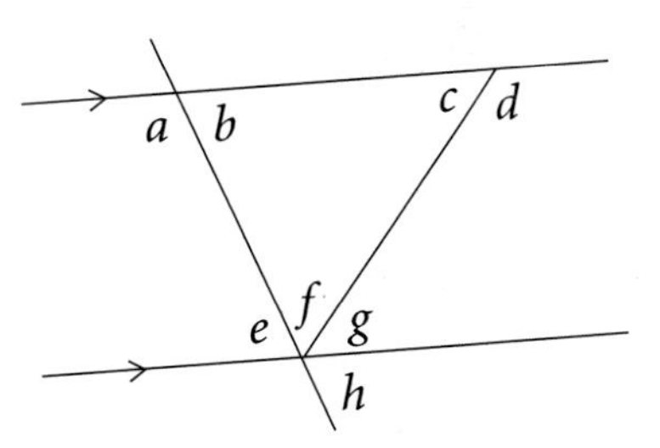

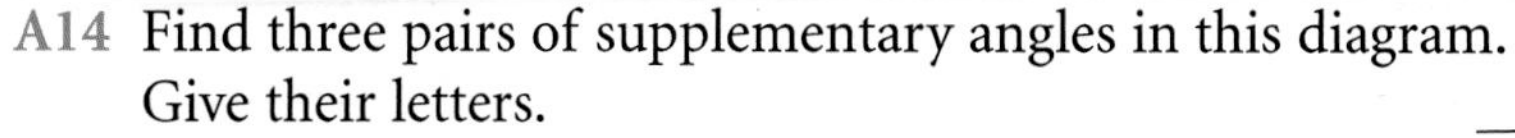

A14 Find three pairs of supplementary angles in this diagram. Give their letters.

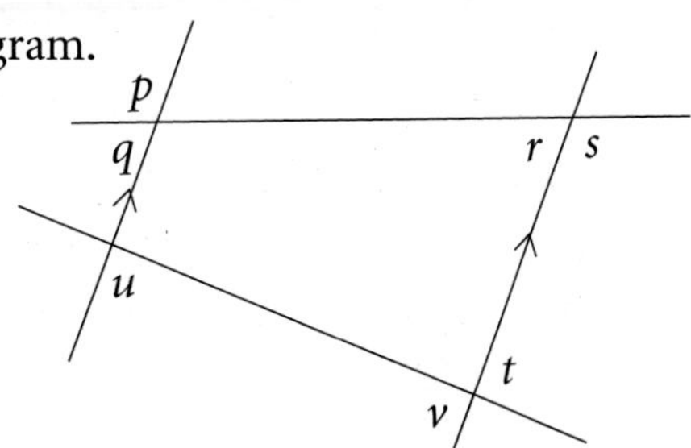

A15 Use supplementary angles to find the angles marked with letters here.

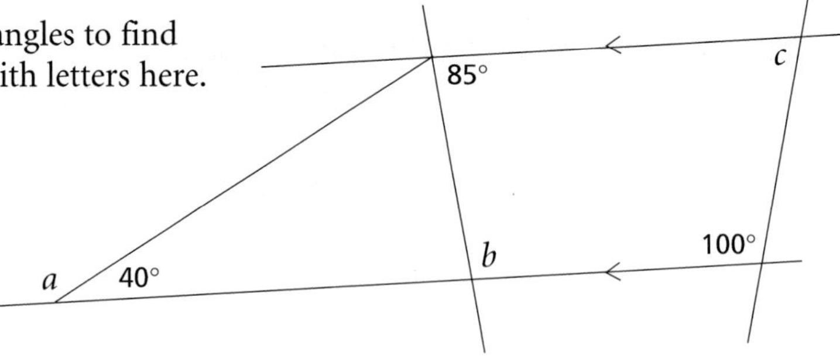

A16 Describe each of these pairs of angles. Choose from these boxes.

(a) Angles b and d
(b) Angles b and f
(c) Angles c and g
(d) Angles a and b
(e) Angles e and f
(f) Angles c and e
(g) Angles e and g
(h) Angles a and e
(i) Angles d and g

Vertically opposite angles

Corresponding angles (F)

Alternate angles (Z)

Supplementary angles on a straight line

Supplementary angles between parallel lines

A17 Give the value of each lettered angle and the reason you know the angle. (Choose each reason from one of the boxes in A16.)

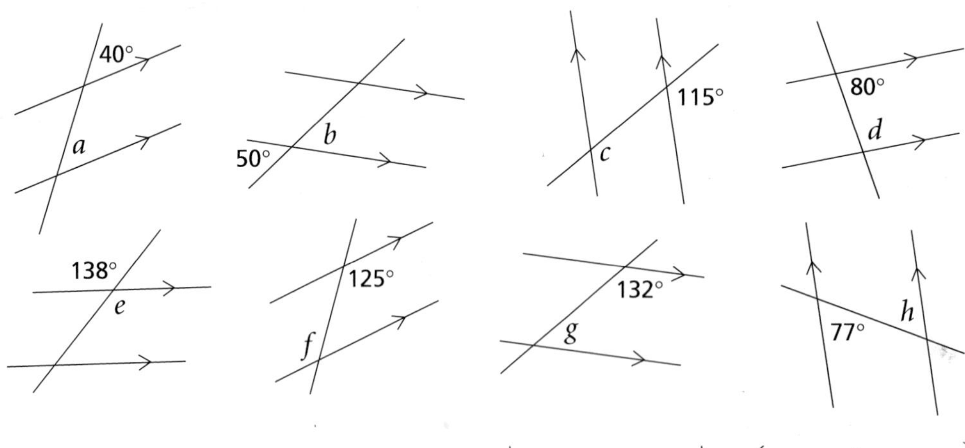

A18 Find the size of each lettered angle, giving a reason.

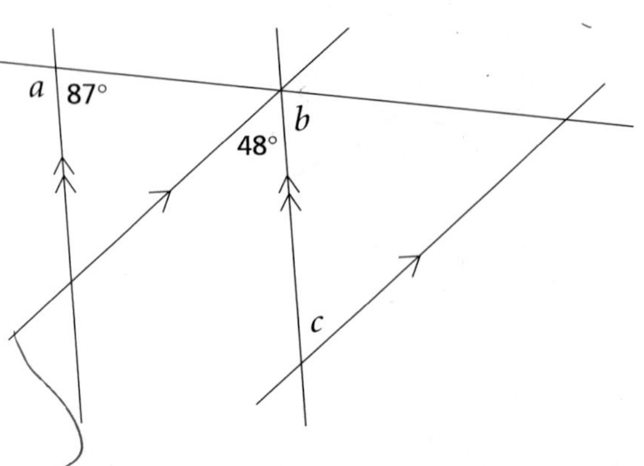

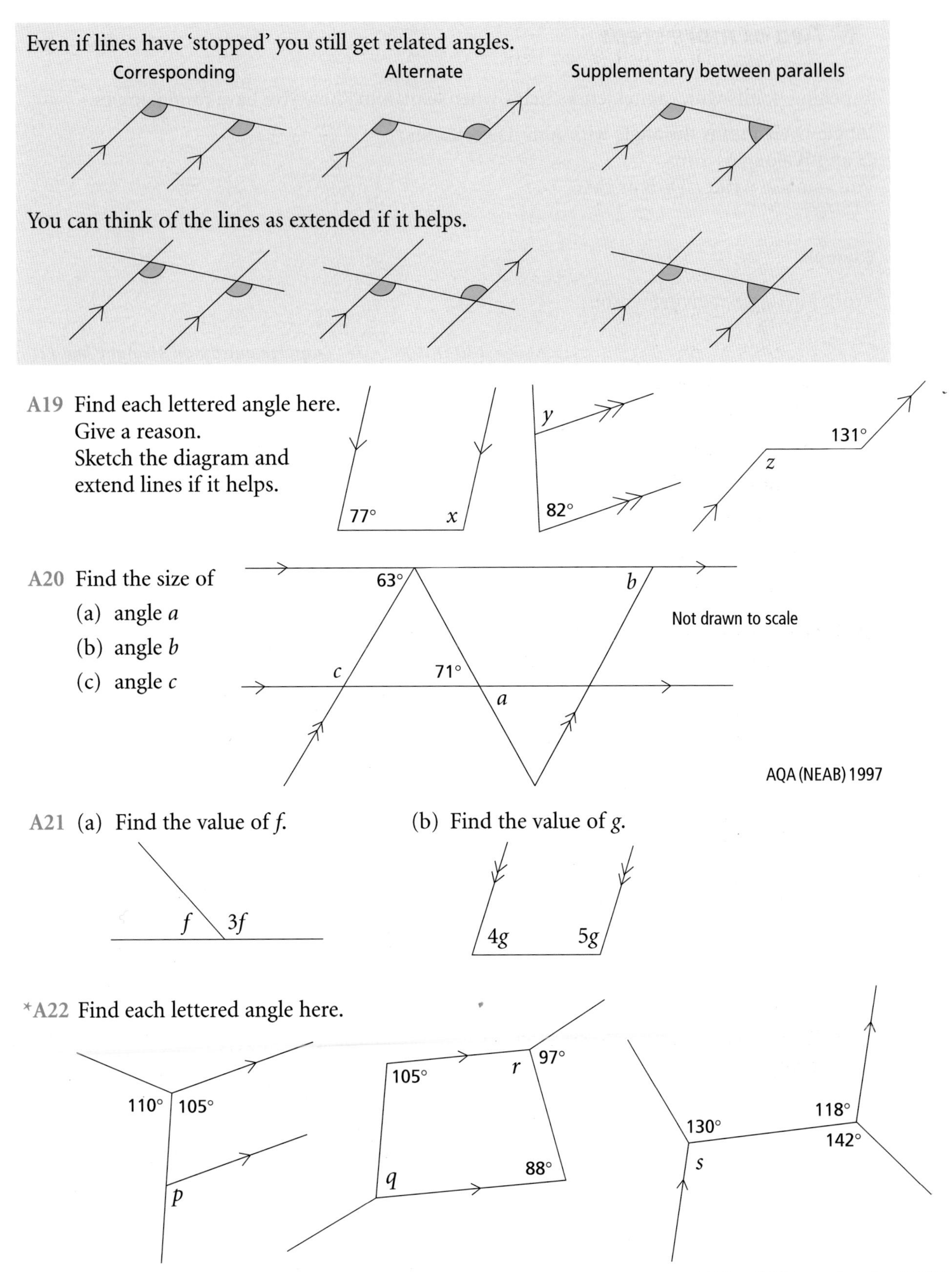

Even if lines have 'stopped' you still get related angles.

You can think of the lines as extended if it helps.

A19 Find each lettered angle here.
Give a reason.
Sketch the diagram and extend lines if it helps.

A20 Find the size of

(a) angle a

(b) angle b

(c) angle c

AQA (NEAB) 1997

A21 (a) Find the value of f.

(b) Find the value of g.

***A22** Find each lettered angle here.

B *Two or more steps*

Labelling points with capital letters helps when explaining how you have found angles.

'Angle DAB' means the angle with A at its vertex and D and B along its arms.
You can also write $\angle DAB$ or $\widehat{DAB}$.

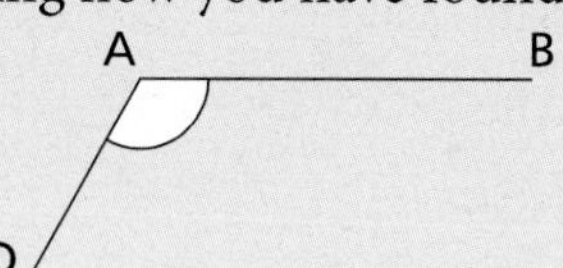

Example

Work out angle x, giving reasons.

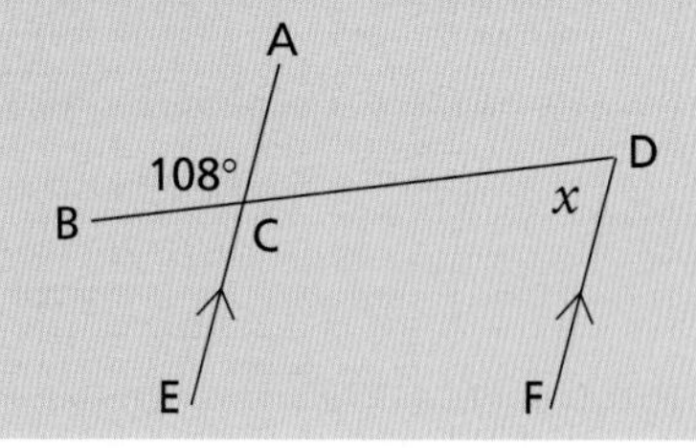

$\angle ACD = 180° - 108° = 72°$ (supplementary on straight line BD)
$\angle CDF = \angle ACD = 72°$ (alternate), so $x = 72°$

OR

$\angle BCE = 180° - 108° = 72°$ (supplementary on straight line AE)
$\angle CDF = \angle BCE = 72°$ (corresponding), so $x = 72°$

B1 Work out the angles marked in blue, explaining your reasoning.

(a)

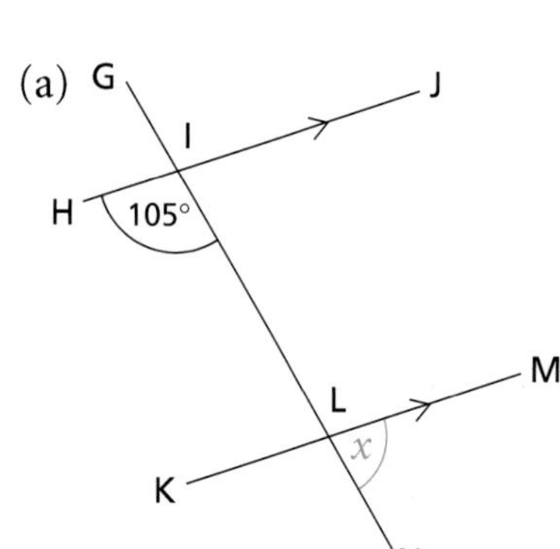

(b)

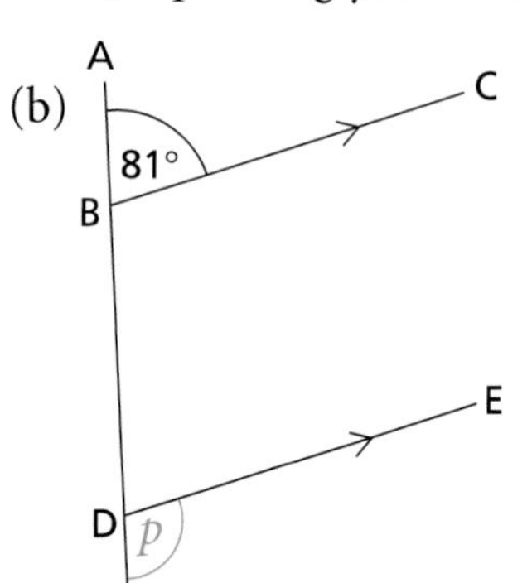

(c)

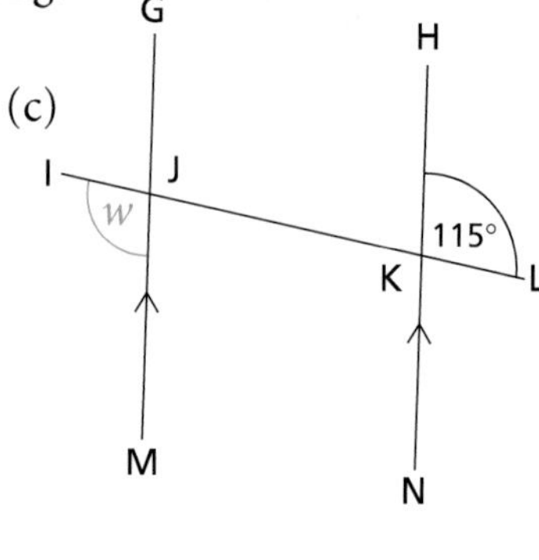

(d)

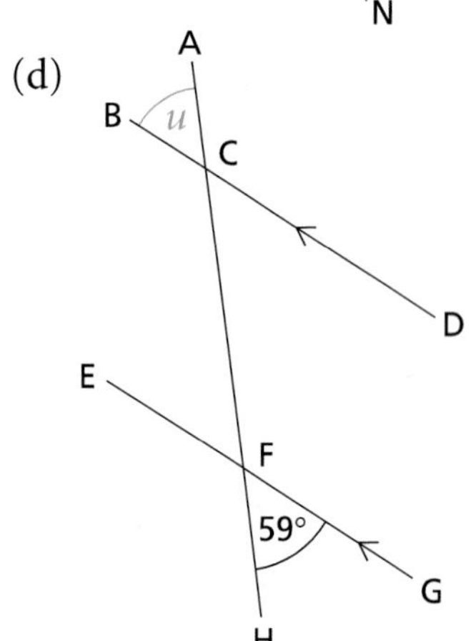

(e)

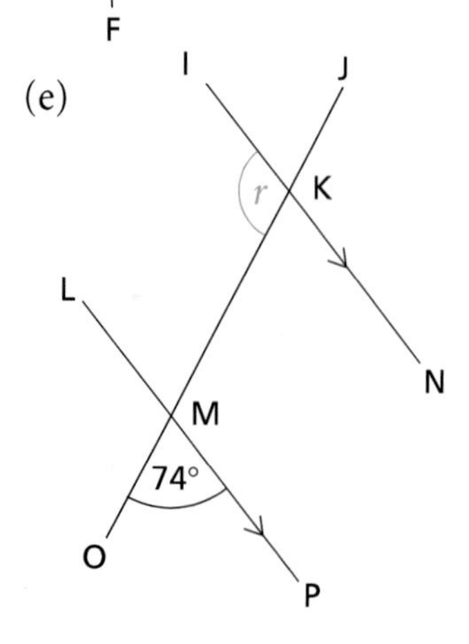

(f)

When solving angle problems you may need to know the following facts as well as those you have just been using.

- The sum of the angles of a triangle is 180°.
- The sum of the angles round a point is 360°.
- The symmetry of an isosceles triangle gives a pair of equal angles.

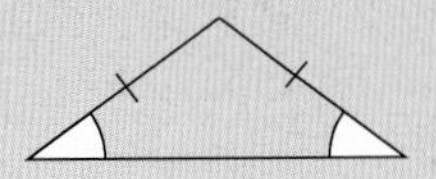

B2 The diagram shows a rectangle.
Work out the sizes of angles x, y and z.

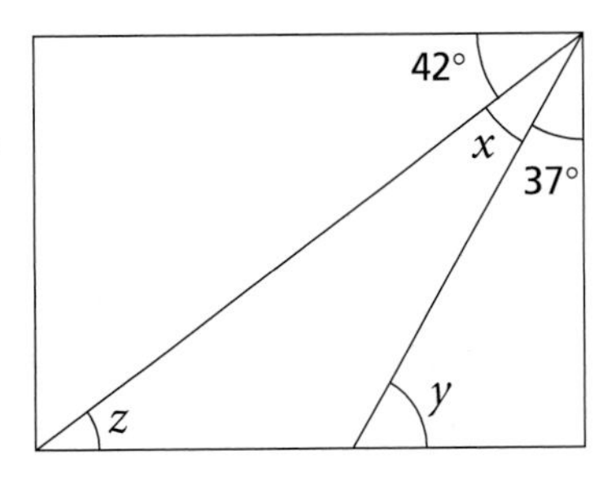

Not to scale

AQA(SEG) 2000

B3 In the diagram, BA is parallel to CE.
Angle BAC = 97° and angle ECD = 35°.
Calculate the size of angle x.
You **must** show your working.

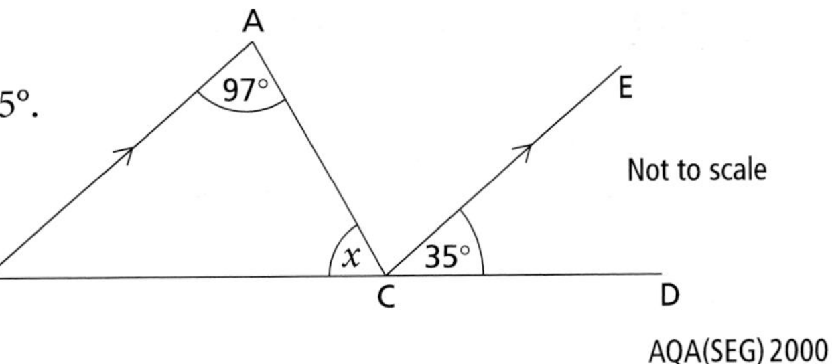

AQA(SEG) 2000

B4 (a) Triangle ABC is isosceles.
AB = AC.
Work out the size of angle x.

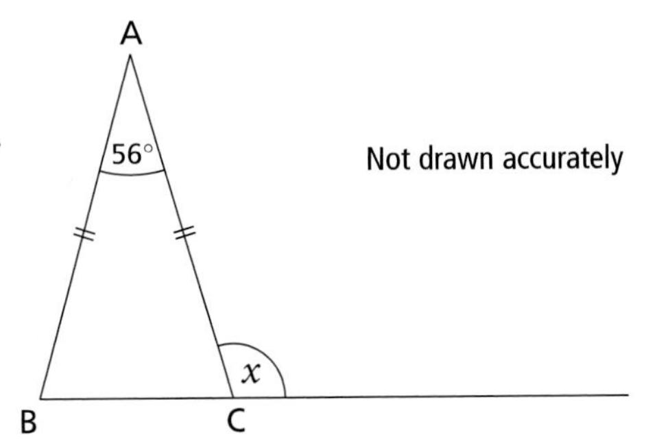

(b) BE is parallel to CD.

(i) Write down the size of angle p.

(ii) Write down the size of angle q.

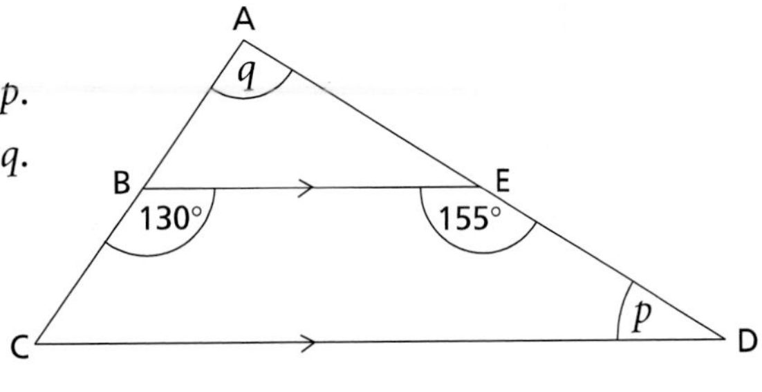

AQA(NEAB) 2000

*B5 Work out the angles marked in blue, explaining your reasoning.

(a)

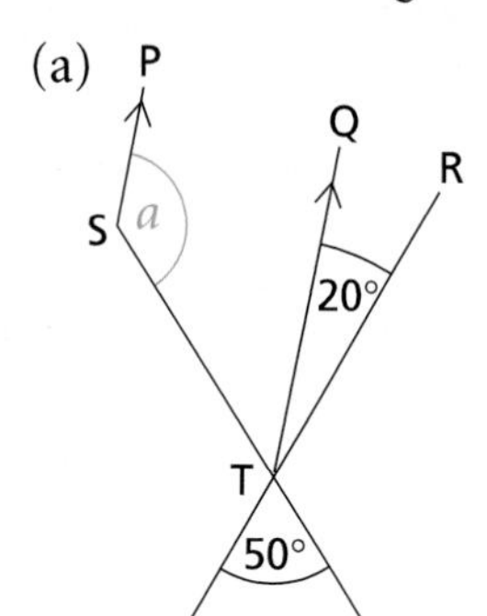

(b)

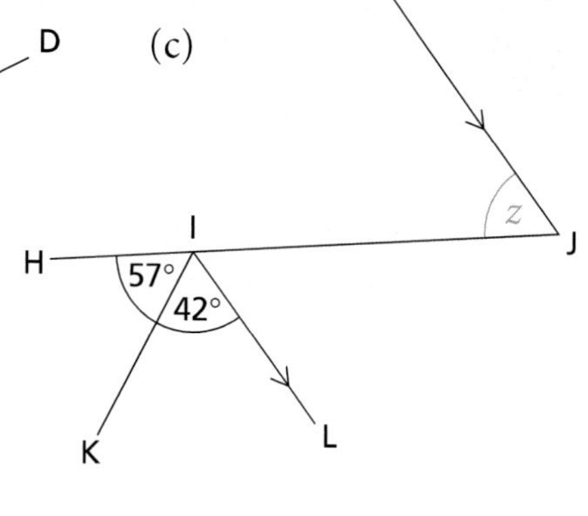

(c)

*B6 Work out the angles marked in blue.
If you need to, copy the diagram and draw any extra lines you need.
Explain your reasoning.

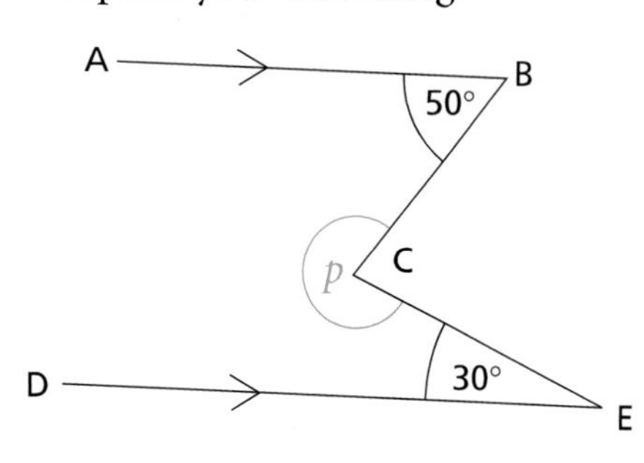

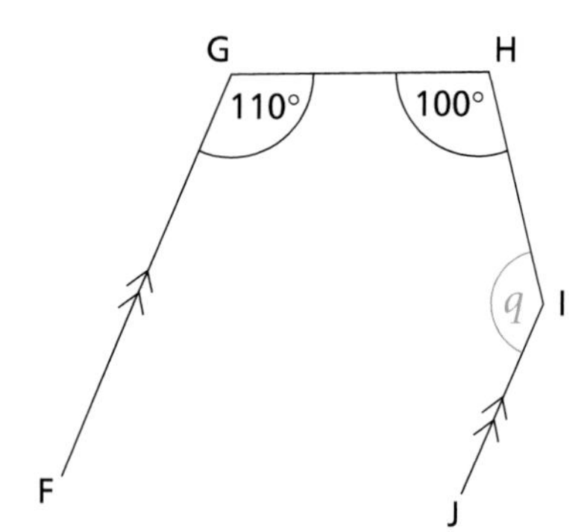

Test yourself

T1 Find four pairs of alternate angles in this diagram. Give their letters.

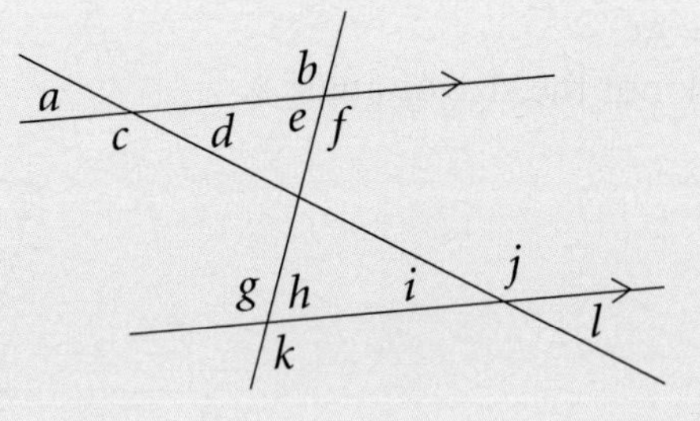

T2 Write down the values of the lettered angles. Give a reason.

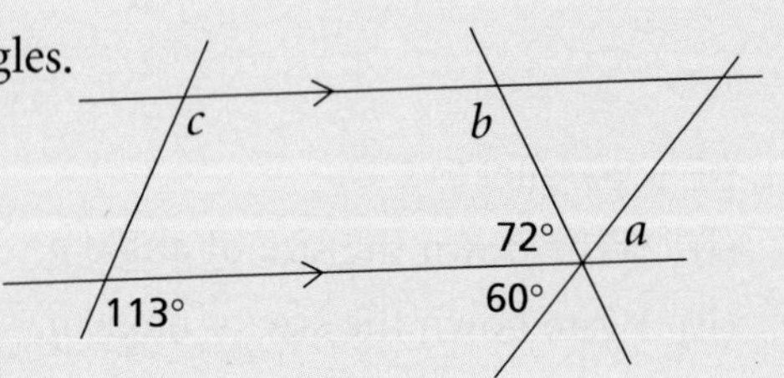

T3 Work out the angle marked x, explaining your reasons.

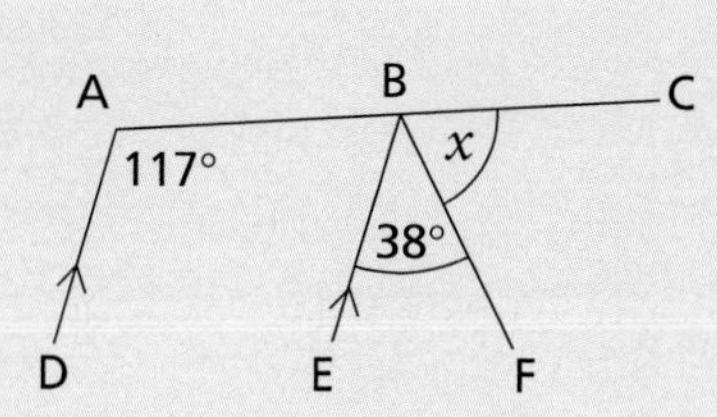

Review 4

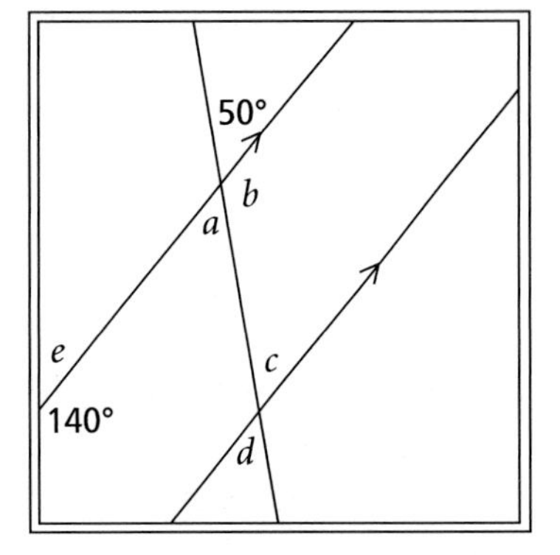

1 This diagram shows a design for a square patchwork cushion.

(a) Copy and complete
'Angles *a* and ___ are alternate angles.'

(b) Find a pair of angles that are vertically opposite.

(c) Work out the size of each lettered angle.
Give a reason each time.

2 Find the value of each of these.

(a) $(4^3)^2$ (b) $(3^2)^2$ (c) $(6^2)^1$ (d) $(3^5)^0$

3 The table on the right shows the heights and weights of some runners.

(a) Show this information on a scatter diagram.

(b) Describe the correlation between the height and weight of the runners.

(c) Draw the line of best fit on your diagram.

(d) Use your graph to estimate the weight of a runner who is 1.9 m tall.

Height (cm)	Weight (kg)
165	45
164	55
159	49
170	62
168	58
161	47
180	69
174	55
197	77
165	55
177	68
167	58
178	58
162	48
155	40
200	82
180	65
168	50
174	60
186	71

4 (a) Use rough estimates to decide on these.

(i) Which calculation gives the greatest result?

(ii) Which gives the smallest result?

(b) Now use your calculator to work out the answers, correct to three significant figures.

P $\dfrac{7.82}{2.08} - 1.81$

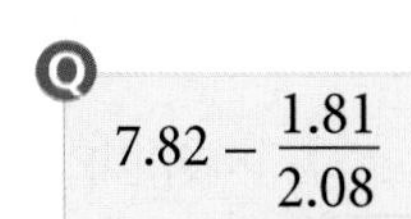

Q $7.82 - \dfrac{1.81}{2.08}$

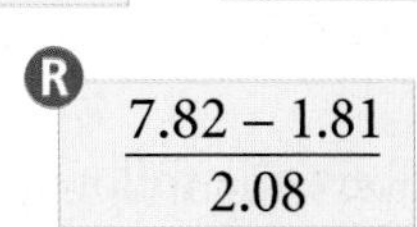

R $\dfrac{7.82 - 1.81}{2.08}$

5 The table gives information about the favourite breakfast drinks of 60 students.

Tea	Coffee	Hot chocolate	Orange	Other
16	24	5	12	3

Draw a pie chart to show this information.

6 Simplify the following expressions.

(a) $4w - (9 + 2w)$ (b) $8b - 7 - (3 + 2b)$ (c) $(5x + 3) - (6x + 1)$

(d) $6q + 3(4 - 5q)$ (e) $11x - 4(3x - 2)$ (f) $2(6a + 4) - 10(2a - 3)$

7 Which expression below gives the size of the angle marked with a dot, in degrees?

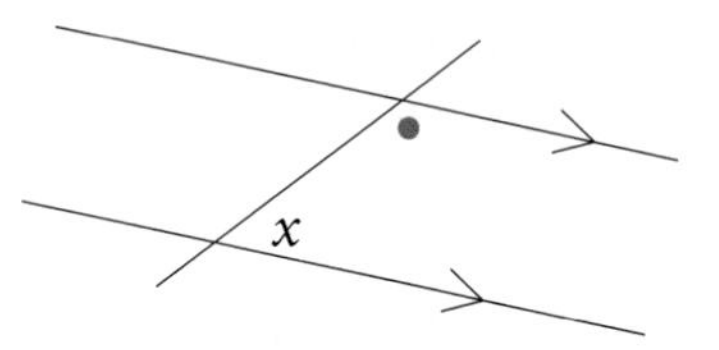

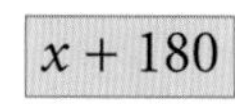

$x - 180$ $180 - x$ $x + 90$

8 Work these out on a calculator, giving your answers to two decimal places.

(a) $(5.71 + 3.82) \times 6.7$ (b) $4.45 - 1.82 \times 1.42$ (c) $\dfrac{6.31}{8.22 - 7.46}$

(d) $\sqrt{7.6 \times (4.2 + 8.1)}$ (e) $(4.2 - 8.9)^2$ (f) $\dfrac{4.3^2 + 0.62}{4.3 + 0.62^2}$

9 For each of these, write down a value of n.

(a) $n^2 = 16$ (b) $9^n = 9$ (c) $5^n = 1$ (d) $n^{-2} = 0.01$

10 This metal tray has a square base x cm by x cm.

(a) Write an expression for the area of the base in cm^2.

The metal sides of the tray are 2 cm high.

(b) Write an expression for the area of one side.

(c) Write an expression for the total area of all four sides.

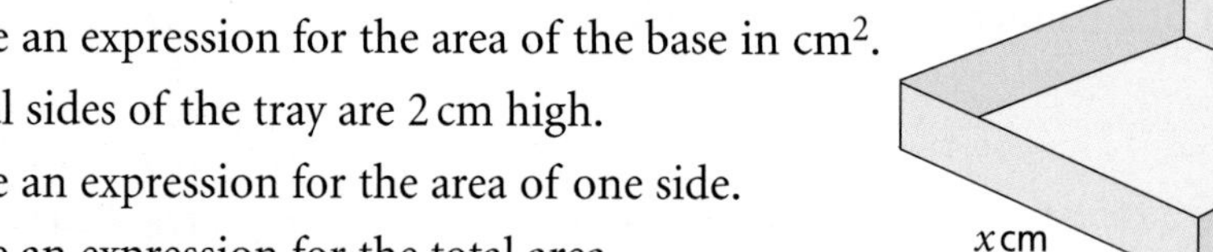

(d) Show that the formula for the total area, y cm^2, of metal used for the tray is

$$y = x^2 + 8x.$$

(e) On graph paper, draw a graph of this equation for values of x from 0 to 6.

(f) Use your graph to find the length of the tray's base if the total area of metal is to be

(i) 40 cm^2 (ii) 25 cm^2 (iii) 80 cm^2

11 Simplify each of these.

(a) $m^2 \times m^3$ (b) $2x^2 \times 3x$ (c) $\dfrac{w^8}{w^3}$ (d) $\dfrac{15a^4}{5a}$ (e) $\dfrac{10b^2}{4b^5}$

12 Solve the following equations.

(a) $5a + 3(7 - a) = 7a - 4$ (b) $3(x - 1) - 4(x - 6) = 5(x - 3)$

26 Money problems

You will revise calculation with money.

This work will help you deal with simple shopping and personal finance problems.

A Shopping

A1 How many 37p stamps can you buy with a £5 note?

A2 Ian paid £4.70 for a melon and some avocados.
Melons cost £1.75 each and avocados cost 59p each.
How many avocados did he buy?

A3 Pluto bars cost 18p each.
A special Christmas tin contains 24 bars and costs £4.99.
How much is the customer paying for the tin?

A4 Twenty-four cakes and twelve pasties cost £19.20.
The pasties cost 46p each. Find the cost of a cake. WJEC

A5 Here is the menu at Carol's snack bar.

Burger	£1.85
Frankfurter	£1.55
Doughnut	54p

Dave bought 3 burgers, 2 frankfurters and some doughnuts. He paid £11.89.

(a) How much did the burgers and frankfurters cost altogether?

(b) How many doughnuts did Dave buy?

A6 These are the ticket prices for an adventure park.

Thrillscape
Admission

Adult	£14.95
Senior citizen	£10.50
Child	£8.95
'Family' ticket	£49.50

(up to 2 adults and up to 4 children)

For each of these groups of visitors, say what is the cheapest way of buying tickets and give the total cost.

(a) 2 adults and 1 child

(b) 1 adult and 4 children

(c) 2 adults and 2 children

(d) 1 adult, 1 senior citizen and 3 children

A7 Becki bought 0.8 kg of pears at £1.60 per kilogram and 0.5 kg of apples.
The total cost was £1.98. What was the price per kilogram of the apples?

A8 When Lizzy uses her car on a business trip she is allowed to claim 46p per mile for the first 50 miles travelled and 27p per mile for the rest of the journey.

(a) How much can she claim for an 80 mile journey?

*(b) On one occasion she claimed £43.25. How far did she travel?

B *Personal finance*

Here are some terms used when talking about personal finance.

Gross pay What you earn before tax, national insurance and other things are taken off (deducted). The money that's left is called your **take-home pay**.

Inflation The tendency for prices to rise as time passes. Inflation is measured by choosing a representative set of things that people spend money on (food, clothing and so on), then calculating the percentage increase in the total cost of those things over a year.

Interest What a bank or building society pays you for leaving (depositing) your savings with them. 'Interest of 4% per annum' means each year you get an amount equal to 4% of what you have deposited. You also pay interest when you borrow money.

Quarter A quarter of the year (three months). Bills for gas, electricity and fixed phones are usually for one quarter.

Standing charge A fixed amount you have to pay for having a service available, however much you use the service. For example, many electricity bills have a standing charge as well as a charge for the amount of electricity you have used. Sometimes called a service charge.

Time-and-a-half A higher rate of pay (1.5 times the normal amount) that some people are paid when they work **overtime** (extra work outside their normal working hours). Some jobs pay **double time** (twice the normal amount) for working on a Sunday and some pay **triple time** for working on Christmas Day.

Unit (of electricity) The measure of energy used by an electricity meter and then for calculating bills. One unit is what a 1-kilowatt appliance uses in 1 hour (or, for example, what a 100-watt light bulb uses in 10 hours).

VAT Value Added Tax, a government tax that is included in the price or added on when you pay for goods and services. VAT has a different percentage rate for different things and the government can change the rates when they choose to. Some things have no VAT added on.

B1 Stewart is paid monthly by his employer.
In a normal month, his gross pay is £1438.00, but he has £162.03 tax, £98.06 national insurance and £78.66 pension contribution deducted.
Work out his take-home pay.

B2 Sam has £550 in a building society account for a year.
At the end of the year he is paid 4% interest.
How much money is that?

B3 A health club puts up its annual subscription from £480 to £495.
At the time, the rate of inflation is 2.8%.
Is the increase more or less than the rate of inflation?

B4 An electricity company makes a standing charge of £11.50 each quarter and charges customers 7.2p for every unit of electricity they use. VAT is charged on the whole amount at 5%.

Ann uses 545 units of electricity in a particular quarter.

(a) Calculate the cost of the units Ann has used.

(b) Add on the standing charge.

(c) Work out the VAT to the nearest penny on the total in (b) and add it on to get the amount Ann has to pay.

B5 Carol is paid a basic rate of £7.25 per hour for a 35-hour week. One week she also works 4 hours at time-and-a-half. Work out her gross pay.

B6 Ruth gets her electricity bill for the 3-month period July–September 2000. The details are as follows.

Previous meter reading	46583
Present meter reading	49468
Charge per unit	6.65 pence
Service charge	£10.56
VAT	5%

Write out the details of the cost of electricity for this period and find the total bill including VAT. WJEC

***B7** After keeping an amount of money in a building society account for a whole year, Di earned £84.00 interest. The interest rate was 3.5%. What was the amount of money that had been in the account?

Test yourself

T1 Mandy sends her son to post 7 identical parcels. She gives him a £20 note and he comes back with £3.55 change. How much did each parcel cost to post?

T2 Luke often travels to London by train. An ordinary return ticket costs £17.25. A network card costs £35.00. If he has one, the return ticket is only £11.50.

If he buys a network card, how many return trips to London must he make for the total cost to be less than for ordinary tickets?

T3 A second-hand car is advertised at a cash price of £8950. Alternatively a customer can pay a deposit of £1800 followed by 24 monthly instalments of £380. How much more expensive is this than the cash price?

27 Cumulative frequency

You should know how to describe an interval using inequalities, for example $3 < w \leq 4$.

This work will help you

- make a cumulative frequency table and draw a cumulative frequency graph
- find and interpret the median, quartiles and interquartile range
- interpret and draw a box-and-whisker plot

A *Hold your breath!*

TG

How long can you hold your breath?

As well as affecting your ability to swim under water, your ability to hold your breath could be a lifesaver in many situations.

Measure how long people in your class can hold their breath for.

Suppose that in a fire training exercise advisers want to be able to evacuate a building in a time for which 90% of all people could hold their breath. How long do you think this would be?

B *Cumulative frequency tables*

This table shows the distribution of the birth weights of some babies.

Altogether there are 15 babies who weigh up to and including 2 kg.

Weight (w kg)	Frequency
$0 < w \leq 1$	2
$1 < w \leq 2$	13
$2 < w \leq 3$	20
$3 < w \leq 4$	16
$4 < w \leq 5$	9

15 babies weigh up to 2 kg.

This table is called a **cumulative frequency table.**

Weight (w kg)	Cumulative frequency
$w \leq 1$	2
$w \leq 2$	15
$w \leq 3$	35
$w \leq 4$	
$w \leq 5$	

This is another way of writing 'weights up to and including 3 kg'.

35 babies weighed up to 3 kg.

B1 (a) What are the two numbers missing from the cumulative frequency table above?

(b) What does the last number in the cumulative frequency column tell you?

B2 This table shows the distribution of the lengths of some snakes.

Length (l cm)	Frequency
$0 < l \leq 50$	4
$50 < l \leq 100$	10
$100 < l \leq 150$	17
$150 < l \leq 200$	14
$200 < l \leq 250$	5
$250 < l \leq 300$	2

(a) How many snakes have lengths up to 150 cm?

(b) How many have lengths up to 200 cm?

(c) How many have lengths up to 250 cm?

(d) How many were measured altogether?

(e) How many snakes are over 150 cm long?

(f) How many are over 200 cm long?

B3 (a) This table shows the distribution of the heights of children at a playgroup.

Height (h cm)	Frequency
$60 < h \leq 65$	2
$65 < h \leq 70$	9
$70 < h \leq 75$	12
$75 < h \leq 80$	6
$80 < h \leq 85$	4

Copy and complete this cumulative frequency table.

Height (h cm)	Cumulative frequency
$h \leq 65$	2
$h \leq 70$	11
$h \leq 75$	

(b) How many children are between 65 and 70 cm tall?

(c) How many are of height 75 cm or less?

(d) How many are between 65 cm and 75 cm tall?

(e) How many are over 70 cm tall?

B4 Make a cumulative frequency table for each of these.

(a)

Age (a years)	Frequency
$10 < a \leq 20$	4
$20 < a \leq 30$	5
$30 < a \leq 40$	10
$40 < a \leq 50$	7
$50 < a \leq 60$	2

(b)

Height (h cm)	Frequency
$140 < h \leq 150$	3
$150 < h \leq 160$	7
$160 < h \leq 170$	14
$170 < h \leq 180$	20
$180 < h \leq 190$	12

C *Cumulative frequency graphs*

These tables give information about the breath-holding times of a group of people.

Time (t seconds)	Frequency
$30 < t \leq 40$	4
$40 < t \leq 50$	8
$50 < t \leq 60$	12
$60 < t \leq 70$	14
$70 < t \leq 80$	2

Time (t seconds)	Cumulative frequency
$t \leq 40$	4
$t \leq 50$	12
$t \leq 60$	24
$t \leq 70$	38
$t \leq 80$	40

We can use the numbers in the cumulative frequency table to draw a **cumulative frequency graph.**

The graph starts here because the frequency table tells us that nobody holds their breath for less than 30 seconds.

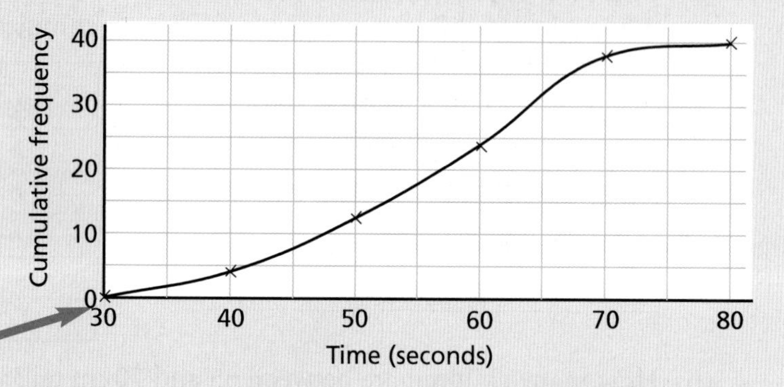

C1 Use the cumulative frequency graph above to estimate how many people can hold their breath for up to

(a) 45 seconds (b) 55 seconds (c) 65 seconds (d) 75 seconds

C2 Use the graph to estimate the number of people who can hold their breath for between 45 and 65 seconds.

C3 Use the graph to estimate the number of people who can hold their breath for more than 55 seconds.

C4 Estimate the percentage of the people who can hold their breath for more than 65 seconds.

C5 Copy and complete this statement.

90% of the people can hold their breath for more than ____ seconds.

C6 This table gives information about the waist measurements of a group of boys.

(a) Make a table of cumulative frequencies.

(b) Draw a cumulative frequency graph.

(c) Estimate the number of boys with waists up to 77 cm.

Waist (w cm)	Frequency
$60 < w \leq 65$	12
$65 < w \leq 70$	20
$70 < w \leq 75$	28
$75 < w \leq 80$	12
$80 < w \leq 85$	8

C6 This table gives information about the weekly milk yields of a herd of cows.

Yield (y litres)	Cumulative frequency
$y \le 260$	30
$y \le 270$	80
$y \le 280$	150
$y \le 290$	220
$y \le 300$	250

(a) How many cows are there in the herd?

(b) Draw a cumulative frequency graph. Start it at (250, 0).

(c) Use the graph to estimate how many cows have milk yields

(i) up to 285 litres (ii) over 265 litres

(d) Estimate how many cows have milk yields between 265 and 295 litres.

C7 This table shows the distribution of marks in an examination.

Number of marks, m	Frequency
$0 < m \le 10$	4
$10 < m \le 20$	7
$20 < m \le 30$	12
$30 < m \le 40$	23
$40 < m \le 50$	38
$50 < m \le 60$	46
$60 < m \le 70$	20
$70 < m \le 80$	16
$80 < m \le 90$	11
$90 < m \le 100$	3

(a) Make a cumulative frequency table.

(b) Draw a cumulative frequency graph.

(c) Estimate the number of people who scored 75 marks or more.

(d) The pass mark was 55.
Estimate the number who passed.

D *Median, quartiles and interquartile range*

Here is the cumulative frequency graph of the heights of a group of boys.

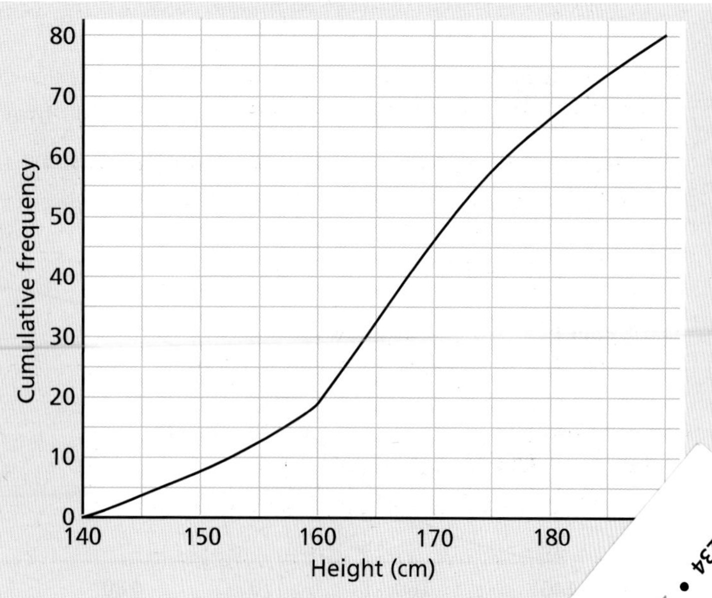

- How can you use the graph to estimate the median height of the group?

TG

This is a cumulative frequency graph of the armspans of a group of 200 girls in year 10.

The **median** armspan is such that 50% of the group are above it and 50% below it.

The **lower quartile** is the armspan that is a quarter of the way up the group: 25% are below it and 75% above.

The **upper quartile** is the armspan that is three quarters of the way up the group: 75% are below it and 25% above.

The 'middle half' of the group have armspans between the lower and upper quartiles.

The difference between the two quartiles is called the **interquartile range**.
For this data its value is

$$180 - 163 = \mathbf{17\,cm}$$

The interquartile range is often used as a measure of how spread out the data is.

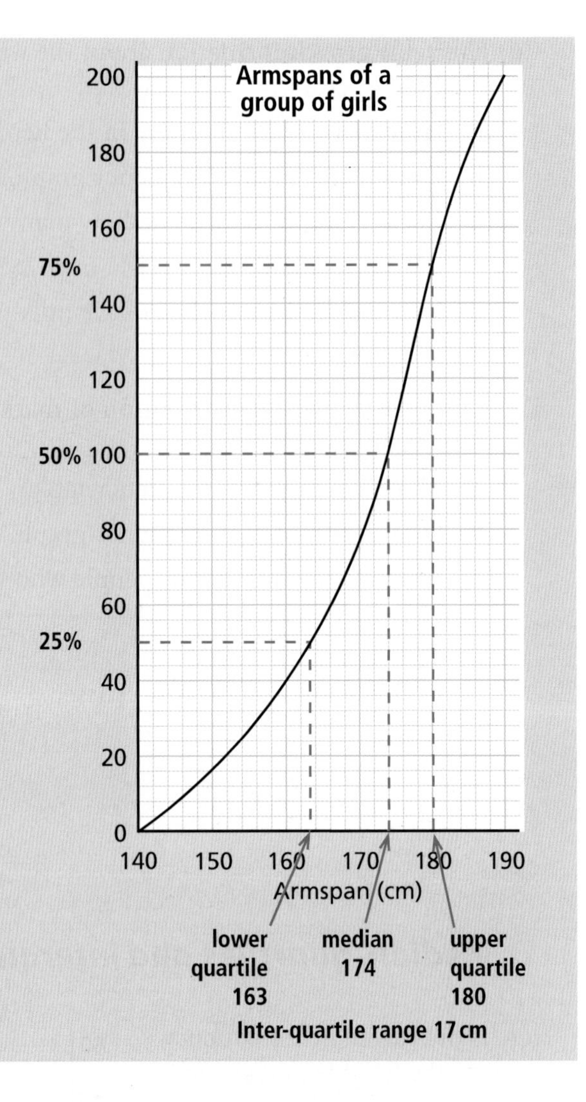

D1 The graph below is based on the armspans of 400 fifteen-year-old boys.

Estimate from the graph (a) the median armspan (b) the lower quartile
(c) the upper quartile (d) the interquartile range

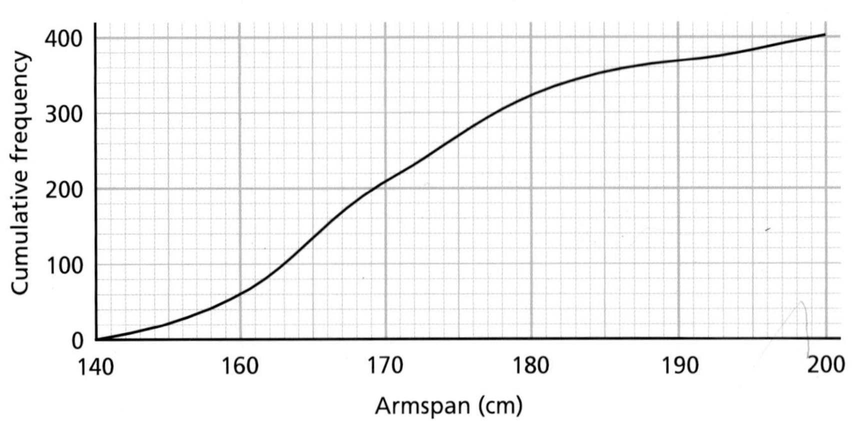

ive frequency

D2 Using your answers to D1, copy and complete these statements.

(a) 25% of the boys have an armspan below …

(b) 50% of the boys have an armspan below …

(c) 75% of the boys have an armspan below …

(d) 25% of the boys have an armspan above …

D3 A firm making light bulbs tested 500 of them to see how long they lasted.
The results are summarised in this frequency table.

Lifetime (x hours)	Frequency
$0 < x \leq 500$	20
$500 < x \leq 1000$	80
$1000 < x \leq 1500$	140
$1500 < x \leq 2000$	180
$2000 < x \leq 2500$	50
$2500 < x \leq 3000$	30

(a) Make a cumulative frequency table for the data.

(b) Draw a cumulative frequency graph.

(c) Estimate

(i) the median lifetime

(ii) the lower quartile

(iii) the upper quartile

(iv) the interquartile range

(v) the percentage of the bulbs that lasted longer than 2200 hours

D4 This table shows the distribution of the birth weights of babies born in a hospital.

Draw a cumulative frequency graph for the data and use it to estimate the median, quartiles and interquartile range.

Weight (w kg)	Frequency
$0 < w \leq 1$	6
$1 < w \leq 2$	18
$2 < w \leq 3$	48
$3 < w \leq 4$	36
$4 < w \leq 5$	12

D5 This table shows the distribution of the weights of the apples picked from a tree.

The frequencies have been given as percentages of the total number of apples.

Weight (w g)	Percentage
$50 < w \leq 60$	8%
$60 < w \leq 70$	13%
$70 < w \leq 80$	24%
$80 < w \leq 90$	27%
$90 < w \leq 100$	16%
$100 < w \leq 110$	9%
$110 < w \leq 120$	3%

(a) Make a cumulative percentage table (like a cumulative frequency table, but with percentages).

(b) Draw a cumulative percentage graph.

(c) Estimate the median weight, the upper and lower quartiles and the interquartile range.

E *Box-and-whisker plots*

TG

This **box-and-whisker plot** displays information about the heights of the year 10 girls in a school.

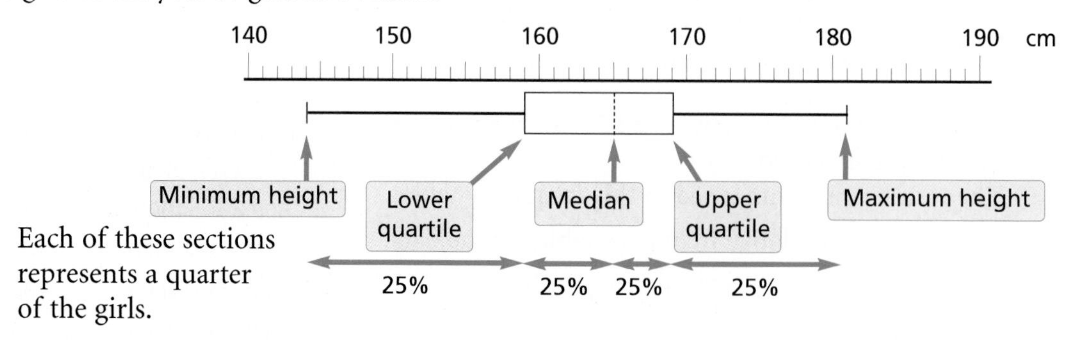

Each of these sections represents a quarter of the girls.

- How high is the tallest girl?
- What is the median height of these girls?
- What percentage of the girls are over 169 cm tall?
- What percentage are between 159 cm and 169 cm tall?

E1 Mark a scale like this on graph paper

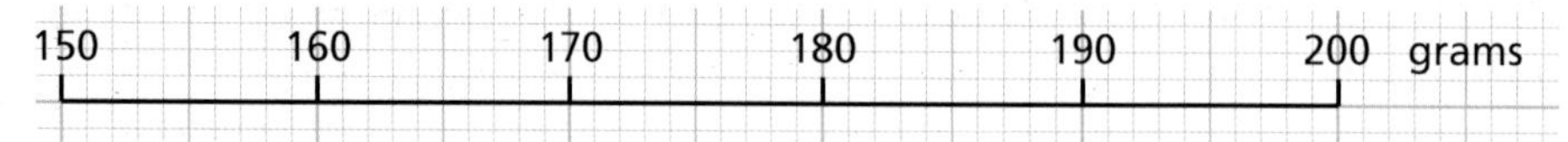

Below your scale, draw a box-and-whisker plot for this information about the weights of apples collected from a tree.

Minimum	Lower quartile	Median	Upper quartile	Maximum
153 g	166 g	174 g	186 g	198 g

E2 These two box-and-whisker plots show the distributions of the ages of the people living in two towns, A and B.

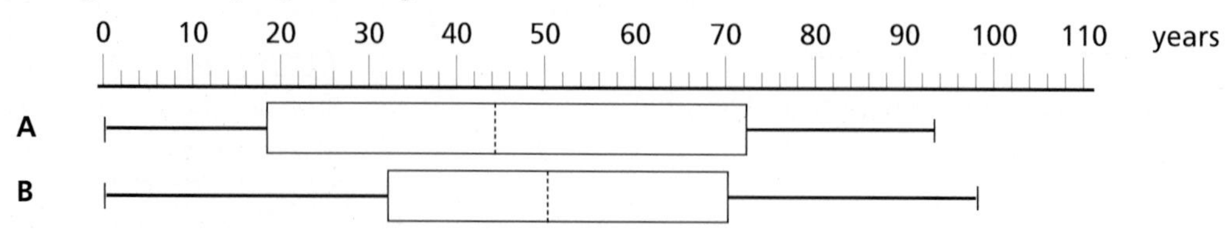

(a) What is the median age of town A's population?

(b) What is the lower quartile of the ages of the people in town B?

(c) What percentage of the population of town B are over 50?

(d) In which town are people older on the whole? Explain your answer.

(e) In which town is the interquartile range of the ages greater?
How can you tell this easily from the box-and-whisker plots?
What does this tell you about the two populations?

E3 These box-and-whisker plots show the distributions of the handspans of year 10 boys and girls.

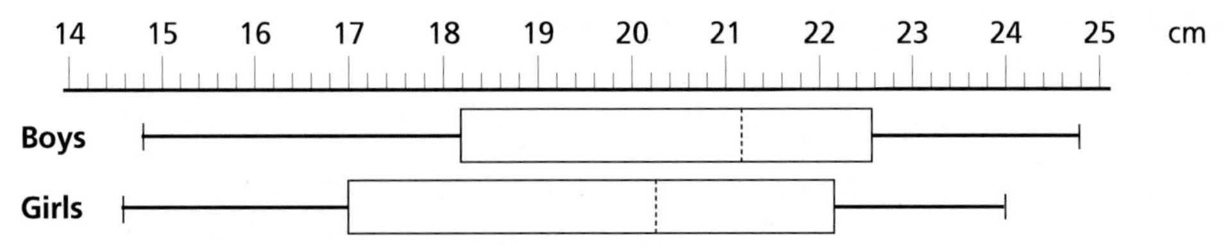

Write a couple of sentences comparing the boys' and girls' handspans.

E4 (a) Draw a box-and-whisker plot to show this information about a group of men.

A quarter of the men weigh 60 kg or less, the lightest being 52 kg.
A quarter weigh 75 kg or more, the heaviest being 93 kg.
The median weight is 66 kg.

(b) What is the interquartile range for the weights?

E5 These box-and whisker plots show the distributions of the salaries in five companies.

(a) In which company are the salaries highest on the whole?
Explain the reasons for your answer.

(b) In which company is there the greatest variation in salaries?
Explain your answer.

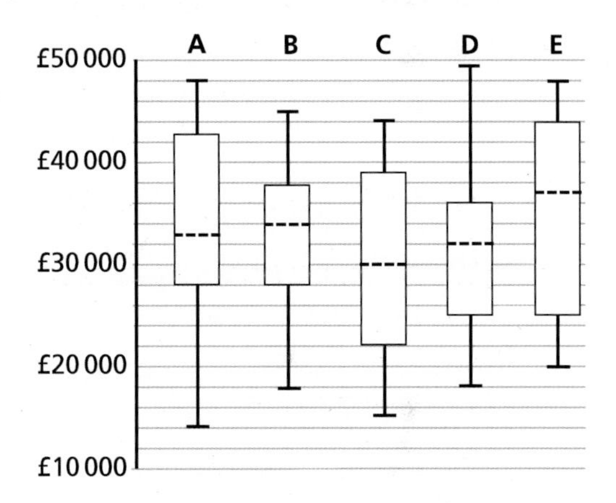

E6 These graphs show the distribution of the lengths of two groups of worms.

(a) Find the median and quartiles of the lengths of each group.

(b) Draw two box-and-whisker plots, one for each group.

(c) Write down the interquartile range for each group.

(d) Write a couple of sentences comparing the two groups.

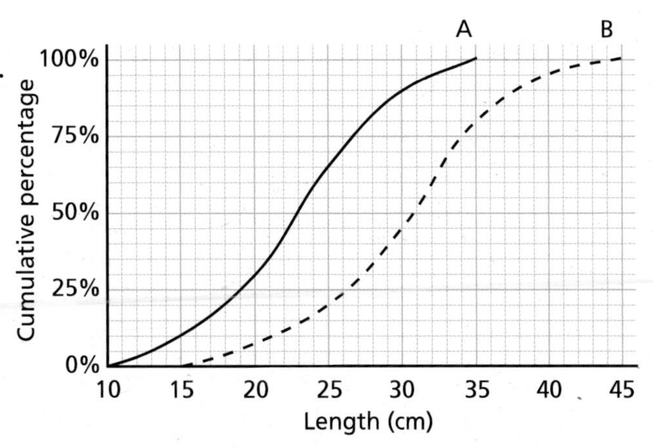

Test yourself

T1 This table shows the distribution of the weights of a group of boys.

Weight (w kg)	Frequency
$40 < w \le 50$	15
$50 < w \le 60$	22
$60 < w \le 70$	48
$70 < w \le 80$	25
$80 < w \le 90$	10

(a) Make a cumulative frequency table.

(b) Draw a cumulative frequency graph.

(c) Use the graph to estimate the median weight of the group.

(d) Estimate the lower and upper quartiles, and the interquartile range.

(e) Draw a box-and-whisker plot for the data.

T2 Here are summaries of the data obtained from measuring the weights of two varieties of apple.

Variety A	
Minimum	131 g
Lower quartile	142 g
Median	155 g
Upper quartile	171 g
Maximum	185 g

Variety B	
Minimum	139 g
Lower quartile	150 g
Median	160 g
Upper quartile	173 g
Maximum	182 g

(a) What percentage of the apples of variety A weigh up to 142 g?

(b) What percentage of the apples of variety B weigh over 173 g?

(c) Use the information in the two tables to compare the weights of the two varieties.

T3 This was the money received by the charity Megalife each week for a year.

Money received (£x)	Frequency
$0 < x \le 50$	32
$50 < x \le 100$	12
$100 < x \le 150$	4
$150 < x \le 200$	2
$200 < x \le 250$	1
$250 < x \le 300$	0
$300 < x \le 350$	1

(a) Calculate an estimate of the mean amount received each week.

(b) Copy and complete the cumulative frequency table below and draw the cumulative frequency graph of the distribution.

Money received (£)	≤ 0	≤ 50	≤ 100	≤ 150	≤ 200	≤ 250	≤ 300	≤ 350
Cumulative frequency	0							

(c) Use your graph to find the median and quartiles of the distribution. Show your method clearly.

(d) A spokesperson for Megalife said 'The weekly average was nearly £60'. Comment on this statement.

OCR

28 *Looking at expressions*

You should know how to

- multiply out brackets such as $4(2x - 3)$
- simplify expressions such as $4n^3 \times 2n$ and $4n^3 \div 2n$

This work will help you

- gather like terms in expressions involving powers
- multiply and divide expressions such as $4ab^3$ and $2ab$
- multiply out complex brackets such as $4x(xy + 3x)$
- factorise expressions such as $6x^2y - 9xy^2$
- form and simplify formulas

A *Gathering like terms*

A $3^2 + 3^2$ **B** 6×3^2 **C** 3^4 **D** $8 \times 3^2 - 2 \times 3^2$

E $2 \times 3^2 + 5 \times 3^2$ **F** 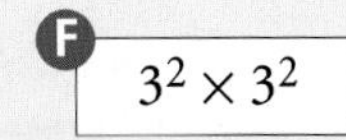

G 7×3^2 **H** 2×3^2

- Can you find four pairs of equivalent expressions?

A $x^2 + x^2$ **B** $3x^4 - 2x^4$ **C** $3x^3 + x$ **D** $2x^2 - x$

E $x^2 + 2x + x^2 - 3x$ **F** $2x^3 + 2x + x^3 - x$ **G** x^4 **H** $2x^2$

- Can you find four pairs of equivalent expressions?

A1 Simplify the following by collecting like terms.

(a) $8 + 3n - 7 + 2n$ (b) $7p + 6 - 5p - 9$ (c) $5k - 7 - 9k + 12$

A2 Simplify the following by collecting like terms.

(a) $n^2 + 3n + n^2 + 2n$ (b) $3a^2 + 5a - a^2$ (c) $k^2 - k + 2k^2 + 6k$

(d) $7m + 4m^2 - 5m + 2$ (e) $g^2 + g^3 + 4g^2 + g^3$ (f) $5h^2 + 2h - 3h^2 - 5h$

(g) $2x + 5x^2 - 3x + 2x^2$ (h) $y^2 + y + y^2 - 7y + 3$

A3 Find the value of each expression when $n = 5$.

(a) $n^2 + n^2 + n^2 + n^2 - 2$ (b) $n^3 + 8n - n^3$

(c) $8n^2 - 7n^2 + n + 1$ (d) $2n^2 + 3n - n^2 - 4n$

A4

A $a - a^2$　　**B** $a^2 + 2a$　　**C** $3a^2 - a + 6$

D $a^2 + 2a - 1$　　**E** $3 - 2a$

(a) Find pairs of the above expressions that add to give these.

(i) $2a^2 + 4a - 1$　　(ii) $a^2 + 3$　　(iii) $2a^2 + 6$

(iv) $4a^2 + a + 5$　　(v) $3a - 1$　　(vi) $a^2 + 2$

(b) Find three of the above expressions that add to give $a + 2$.

B *Multiplying*

Examples

$p(p - 3) = p \times p - p \times 3$	$2n(5 + n^2) = 2n \times 5 + 2n \times n^2$	$3b(2b - 5) = 3b \times 2b - 3b \times 5$
$= p^2 - 3p$	$= 10n + 2n^3$	$= 6b^2 - 15b$

B1 Multiply out the brackets in these expressions.

(a) $n(n + 7)$　　(b) $m(3 + m)$　　(c) $3(2a - 5)$　　(d) $h(h - 9)$

(e) $k(10 - k)$　　(f) $2w(w + 7)$　　(g) $3x(x - 6)$　　(h) $6n(2 - n)$

B2 Find the missing expressions in these statements.

(a) $d(\blacksquare) = d^2 + 5d$　　(b) $2n(\blacksquare) = 2n^2 - 8n$

(c) $3p(\blacksquare) = 15p - 3p^2$　　(d) $5k(\blacksquare) = 20k + 5k^2$

B3 Find five pairs of matching expressions.

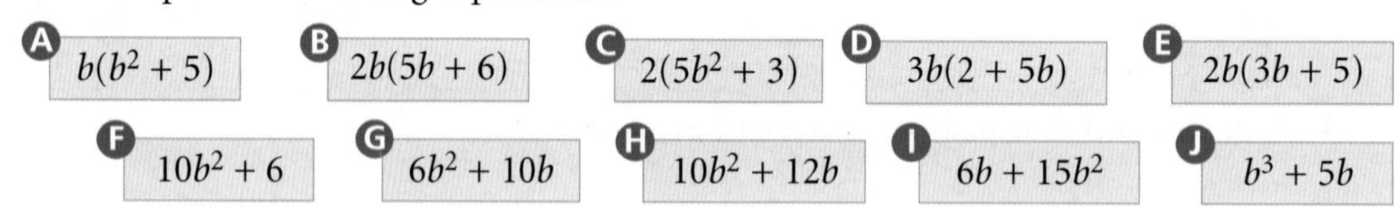

B4 Multiply out the brackets in these expressions.

(a) $2h(7h - 5)$　　(b) $3a(a^2 - 4)$　　(c) $n^2(n^3 - 5)$　　(d) $3k(4k + 5)$

(e) $5d(3 - 2d^2)$　　(f) $7p(3 - 4p)$　　(g) $2b^2(3b + 1)$　　(h) $3w^2(1 + 2w^2)$

B5 3　　x　　$2x$　　$5x$　　x^2　　$2x + 5$　　$x + 1$

Find pairs of the above expressions that multiply to give these.

(a) $6x + 15$　　(b) $x^2 + x$　　(c) $2x^2 + 5x$　　(d) $2x^2 + 2x$

(e) $10x^2$　　(f) $2x^3 + 5x^2$　　(g) $10x^2 + 25x$　　(h) $5x^2 + 5x$

C Factorising

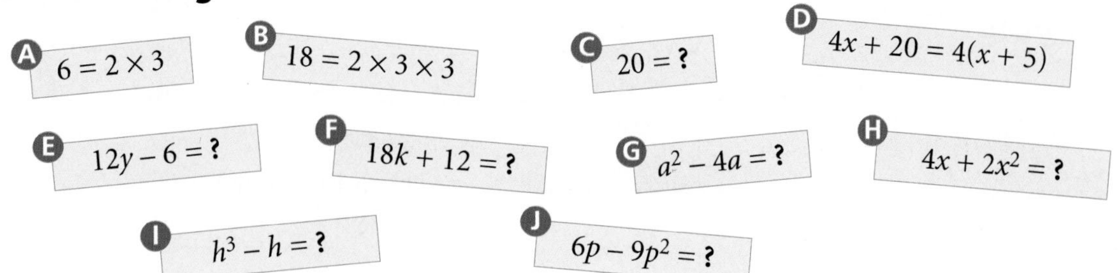

C1 Factorise these expressions.

(a) $3m + 12$ (b) $4n - 6$ (c) $15 - 10p$ (d) $8q - 4$

(e) $9a^2 - 6$ (f) $b^2 + 3b$ (g) $5c + c^2$ (h) $d^2 - 7d$

(i) $11x - x^2$ (j) $y^2 + y$ (k) $w^3 - 2w$ (l) $7h^3 + h$

C2 Find the missing expressions in these statements.

(a) $2k(\blacksquare) = 2k^2 + 6k$ (b) $3p(\blacksquare) = 3p^2 - 6p$

(c) $5n(\blacksquare) = 20n^2 + 5n$ (d) $2x(\blacksquare) = 6x^2 + 4x$

(e) $h^2(\blacksquare) = h^3 + 2h^2$ (f) $y^2(\blacksquare) = 2y^3 + 3y^2$

C3 Factorise these expressions completely.

(a) $3b^2 + 6b$ (b) $10a + 2a^2$ (c) $5d^2 - 15d$ (d) $21c + 7c^2$

(e) $6k^2 + 8k$ (f) $9h + 6h^2$ (g) $9x^2 - 3x$ (h) $2y + 10y^2$

C4

E	L	R	G	U	A	S	B	W	D	H	O
5	7	n	$2n$	$3n$	$n + 1$	$n - 1$	$2n + 3$	$2n - 3$	$3n + 2$	$n^2 + 2$	$n^2 - 2$

Fully factorise each expression below as the product of two factors.
Use the code above to find a letter for each factor.

Rearrange the letters in each part to spell an animal.

(a) $7n + 7$ $2n^2 - 3n$ $3n^2 - 3n$

(b) $14n - 21$ $5n - 5$ $5n + 5$

(c) $10n + 15$ $2n^2 + 2n$ $3n^2 + 2n$

(d) $5n^2 + 10$ $15n + 10$ $2n^3 + 4n$ $2n^3 - 4n$

C5 Factorise these expressions completely.

(a) $n^3 + 4n^2$ (b) $6n^5 - n^3$ (c) $5n^3 + 7n^2$ (d) $2n^3 + 2n^2$

*__C6__ (a) Factorise $3n + 6$.

(b) Explain how the factorisation tells you that $3n + 6$ will be a multiple of 3 for any integer n.

When factorising an expression, remember to factorise completely.

Examples

$3a - 12 = 3(a - 4)$

$8k + 2k^2 = 2(4k + k^2)$
$= 2k(4 + k)$

This is unfinished because $4k + k^2 = k(4 + k)$.

$6x - 15x^2 = 3x(2 - 5x)$

D *More than one letter*

Examples of substitution

Find the value of $3a^2b + b$ when $a = 4$ and $b = 5$.

$$\begin{aligned} 3a^2b + b &= 3 \times a^2 \times b + b \\ &= 3 \times 4^2 \times 5 + 5 \\ &= 3 \times 16 \times 5 + 5 \\ &= 240 + 5 \\ &= 245 \end{aligned}$$

Find the value of $5xy^2 - 2x$ when $x = 3$ and $y = 2$.

$$\begin{aligned} 5xy^2 - 2x &= 5 \times x \times y^2 - 2 \times x \\ &= 5 \times 3 \times 2^2 - 2 \times 3 \\ &= 5 \times 3 \times 4 - 2 \times 3 \\ &= 60 - 6 \\ &= 54 \end{aligned}$$

D1 Find the value of each expression when $a = 2$ and $b = 5$.

(a) $2ab + a$ (b) $5a^2 - b$ (c) $a^2 + b^2 - 1$

(d) $3a + 2b^2 - 5b$ (e) $3ab + b^2 - a^2$ (f) $(ab)^2$

(g) a^2b (h) ab^2 (i) $a^3 + b$

D2 Find the value of each expression when $x = 3$, $y = 4$ and $z = 6$.

(a) $x + y + z$ (b) $xy + yz$ (c) $3xy - z^2$

(d) $x^2 + 2x - y$ (e) $xy^2 - 3y + z$ (f) $\frac{xy}{z}$

D3 Solve the puzzles on sheet G133.

Examples of collecting like terms

$$\begin{aligned} 3x + 2y + 7x - 5y &= 3x + 7x + 2y - 5y \\ &= 10x - 3y \end{aligned}$$

$$\begin{aligned} ab + 4a^2 + 4ab - b - 7a^2 &= ab + 4ab + 4a^2 - 7a^2 - b \\ &= 5ab - 3a^2 - b \end{aligned}$$

Neither of these can be simplified any further.

D4 Simplify the following expressions by collecting like terms.

(a) $2a + b + 3a - 5b$ (b) $ab + b^2 + 5ab + 3b^2 + 2$

(c) $a^2 + 5a + 2 - 8a$ (d) $8b - a^2 + 2b + 3a^2 - 7$

D5 A $x^2 - x$

B 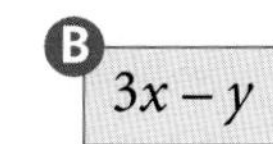

C 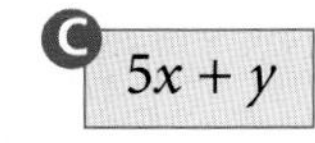

D $y^2 + x^2$

E $5y - y^2$

Find pairs of the above expressions that add to give these.

(a) $y^2 + 2x^2 - x$ (b) $5y + x^2$ (c) $x^2 + 2x - y$

(d) $x^2 + 4x + y$ (e) $8x$ (f) $5x + 6y - y^2$

Examples of multiplying

$$3a \times 4b = 3 \times a \times 4 \times b$$
$$= 3 \times 4 \times a \times b$$
$$= 12ab$$

$$5zy \times 3z^2 = 5 \times z \times y \times 3 \times z \times z$$
$$= 5 \times 3 \times z \times z \times z \times y$$
$$= 15z^3y$$

D6 Find the result of each multiplication in its simplest form.

(a) $b \times 2a$ (b) $2x \times 3y$ (c) $4p \times 3q$

(d) $5c \times d$ (e) $5m \times 4n$ (f) $3v \times 5w$

D7 Find the result of each multiplication in its simplest form.

(a) $2a^2 \times 3b$ (b) $3xy \times 4x$ (c) $2pq \times 3pq$

(d) $4cd \times 5c^2$ (e) $2m^2n^2 \times 7mn^2$ (f) $4vw^4 \times 6v^3w^2$

D8 Find the missing expression in each statement.

(a) $5p \times ■ = 10pq$ (b) $■ \times 7n = 21mn$ (c) $3a^2 \times ■ = 9a^2b$

(d) $■ \times 2y^2 = 10x^2y^2$ (e) $3cd^2 \times ■ = 15c^3d^2$ (f) $■ \times 7vw^3 = 28v^3w^4$

D9 $2a$ $3b$ $5ab$ $3a^2$ $2b^2$ $5a^2b$ ab^3

Find pairs of the above expressions that multiply to give these.

(a) $6ab$ (b) $10ab^3$ (c) $15a^4b$

(d) $9a^2b$ (e) $2ab^5$ (f) $25a^3b^2$

D10 Solve the 'cover-up' puzzle on sheet G134.

Powers

$$(2pq)^3 = 2pq \times 2pq \times 2pq$$
$$= 2 \times p \times q \times 2 \times p \times q \times 2 \times p \times q$$
$$= 2 \times 2 \times 2 \times p \times p \times p \times q \times q \times q$$
$$= 8p^3q^3$$

D11 Expand these expressions and simplify them.

(a) $(3pq)^2$ (b) $(2vw)^3$ (c) $(5x^2y)^2$ (d) $(2a^2b^3)^4$

Examples of division

$$\frac{8ab}{2b} = \frac{8 \times a \times b}{2 \times b} = \frac{\overset{4}{\cancel{8}} \times a \times \cancel{b}}{\cancel{2} \times \cancel{b}} = 4a$$

$$\frac{12a^2b}{4ab} = \frac{12 \times a \times a \times b}{4 \times a \times b} = \frac{\overset{3}{\cancel{12}} \times a \times \cancel{a} \times \cancel{b}}{\cancel{4} \times \cancel{a} \times \cancel{b}} = 3a$$

$$\frac{a^5b^3}{a^2b^4c} = \frac{a \times a \times a \times a \times a \times b \times b \times b}{a \times a \times b \times b \times b \times b \times c} = \frac{a \times a \times a \times \cancel{a} \times \cancel{a} \times \cancel{b} \times \cancel{b} \times \cancel{b}}{\cancel{a} \times \cancel{a} \times b \times \cancel{b} \times \cancel{b} \times \cancel{b} \times c} = \frac{a \times a \times a}{b \times c} = \frac{a^3}{bc}$$

D12 Simplify these expressions.

(a) $\frac{10pq}{2p}$ (b) $\frac{12xy}{6y}$ (c) $\frac{18mn}{6m}$ (d) $\frac{8ab^2}{2a}$

(e) $\frac{6p^2q}{2p}$ (f) $\frac{8x^2y}{4xy}$ (g) $\frac{12m^2n}{3mn}$ (h) $\frac{16a^3b^2}{4a^2b^2}$

D13

A	E	G	L	M	N	O	P	R
$2b$	$4bc$	bc^2	$4d$	cd	$2b^2$	$3bd$	$3c$	$2b^2d$

Simplify each expression below as far as you can.
Use the code above to find a letter for each expression.

Rearrange each set of letters to spell a fruit.

(a) $\frac{8cd}{2c}$ $\frac{12bc}{3}$ $\frac{15cd}{5d}$ $\frac{4bc}{2c}$ $\frac{9c^2b}{3cb}$

(b) $\frac{18b^2d}{6b}$ $\frac{10ab^2}{5a}$ $\frac{20b^2c^2}{5bc}$ $\frac{12cd^5}{3cd^4}$ $\frac{5c^2d}{5c}$

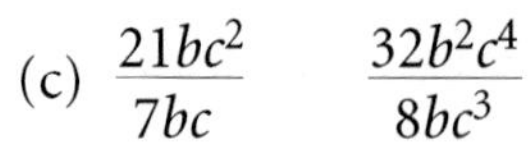

(c) $\frac{21bc^2}{7bc}$ $\frac{32b^2c^4}{8bc^3}$ $\frac{14bcd}{7cd}$ $\frac{6b^5d}{3b^3}$ $\frac{7b^5c^3}{7b^4c}$

(d) $\frac{5b^6c^7}{5b^5c^5}$ $\frac{16b^5d^2}{8b^3d}$ $\frac{8b^6c^3}{4b^5c^3}$ $\frac{2db^5}{b^3d}$ $\frac{6b^2d^7}{2bd^6}$ $\frac{20b^2c^2d}{5bcd}$

D14 Simplify these expressions.

(a) $\frac{ab}{bc}$ (b) $\frac{ab}{6b}$ (c) $\frac{6xy}{y^2}$ (d) $\frac{16mn^2}{8mn^3}$

(e) $\frac{p^6q^4}{p^3q^6}$ (f) $\frac{10ab^2c}{15abc}$ (g) $\frac{3a}{9a^2b}$ (h) $\frac{4gh^2}{8g^2h^2}$

D15 Simplify these expressions.

(a) $\frac{2hk \times 6hk^2}{3h}$ (b) $\frac{4m^2n \times 5mn^2}{10m^3}$ (c) $\frac{4x^3y \times 3xz^3}{6x^2y}$

E *Expanding and factorising*

Examples

Expand $3a(b+a)$.

$3a(b+a) = 3a \times b + 3a \times a$
$= 3ab + 3a^2$

Factorise completely $6a^2 - 9ab$.

$6a^2 - 9ab = a(6a - 9b)$
$= 3a(2a - 3b)$

This is unfinished because $6a - 9b = 3(2a - 3b)$.

E1 Expand these expressions.

(a) $4(a+b)$ (b) $3(x-y)$ (c) $5(m+2n)$ (d) $4(3a-5b)$
(e) $h(k+1)$ (f) $p(p-q)$ (g) $b(3a+5)$ (h) $c(2d+3c)$

E2 Factorise these expressions.

(a) $3p+3q$ (b) $5k-5h$ (c) $2a+6b$ (d) $6n-9m$
(e) $ab+a$ (f) x^2-xy (g) $7pq+9p$ (h) $4ab+5a^2$

E3 Expand these expressions.

(a) $2a(b-a)$ (b) $3x(2y+5)$ (c) $5m(n+2m)$ (d) $xy(y-1)$
(e) $ab(5a+3b)$ (f) $p^2(3p-1)$ (g) $3xy(2x+9)$ (h) $2y^2(5x-1)$

E4 Factorise these expressions completely.

(a) $3m^2-3mn$ (b) $2x^2+4xy$ (c) $3p^2-6pq$ (d) $10mn+15m^2$
(e) ab^2+3ab (f) x^2y-xy (g) $6y^2z+10y^2$ (h) $10k^2h-5k^2$
(i) $2x^2y+2xy^2$ (j) $3a^2b-15ab$ (k) $8hk+4hk^2$ (l) $10p^2q+5pq^2$

E5

E	H	P	S	O	A	I	L	G	R	T	U	N
5	$2a$	$3a$	$2b$	$7b$	a^2	ab	$3b^2$	$a+b$	$a-5b$	$2a-b$	$ab+1$	$2a+3b$

Fully factorise each expression below as the product of two factors.
Use the code above to find a letter for each factor.

Rearrange each set of letters to spell a bird.

(a) $3a^2-15ab$ $2a^3-a^2b$ $7ab-35b^2$
(b) $4a^2-2ab$ $2a^2b+2a$ $2ab-10b^2$
(c) $7ab+7b^2$ $5a-25b$ $2ab^2+2b$
(d) $4ab-2b^2$ $3b^2a+3b^3$ a^3-5a^2b $2a^2b+3ab^2$

E6 Factorise these expressions completely.

(a) $a^3b+2a^2b^2$ (b) $7m^2n^2+mn^2$ (c) $6x^2y^2-2xy^3$ (d) $3p^4q+12p^2q^2$

F *Formulas*

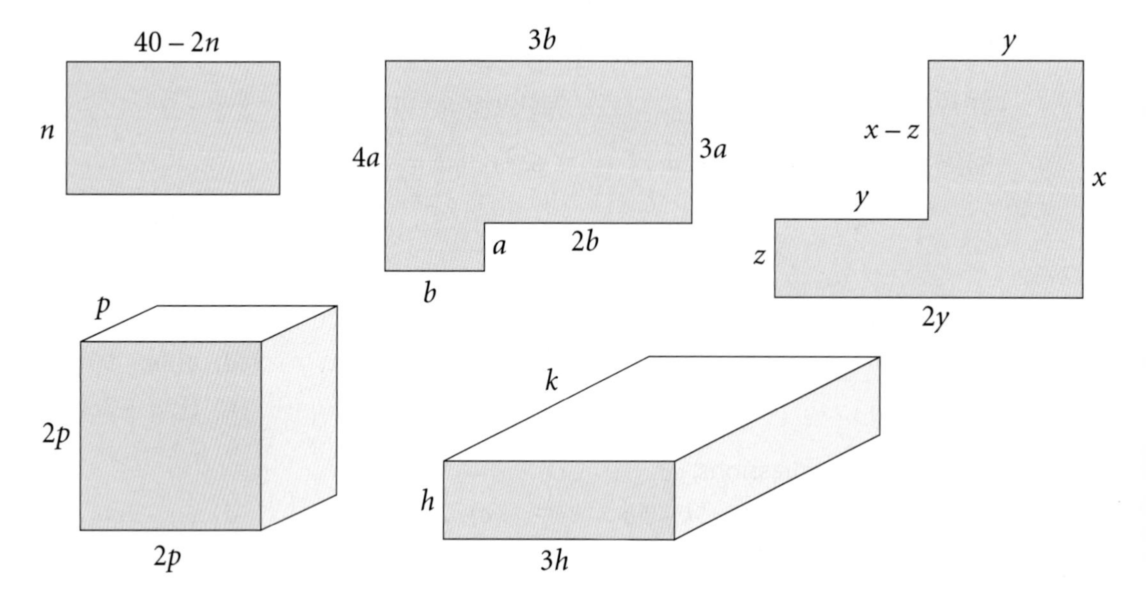

F1 (a) Find a formula for the perimeter of each shape below.
Use P to stand for the perimeter each time. (Each formula begins $P = \dots$.)

(b) Find a formula for the area of each shape.
Use A to stand for the area each time.

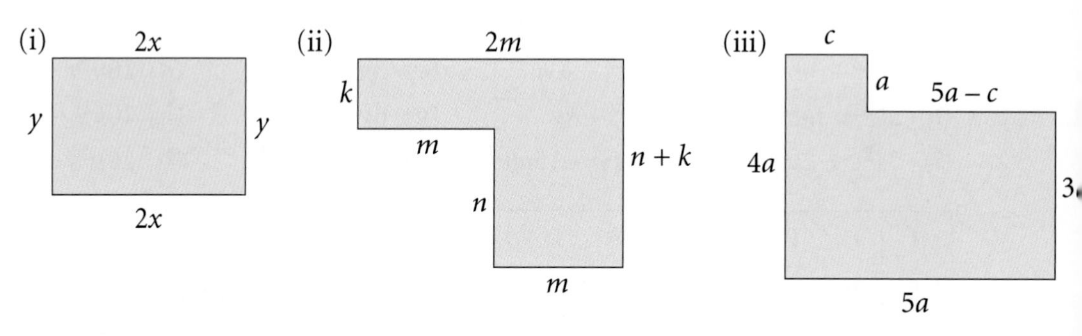

F2 Find a formula for the volume of each prism.
Use V to stand for the volume each time.

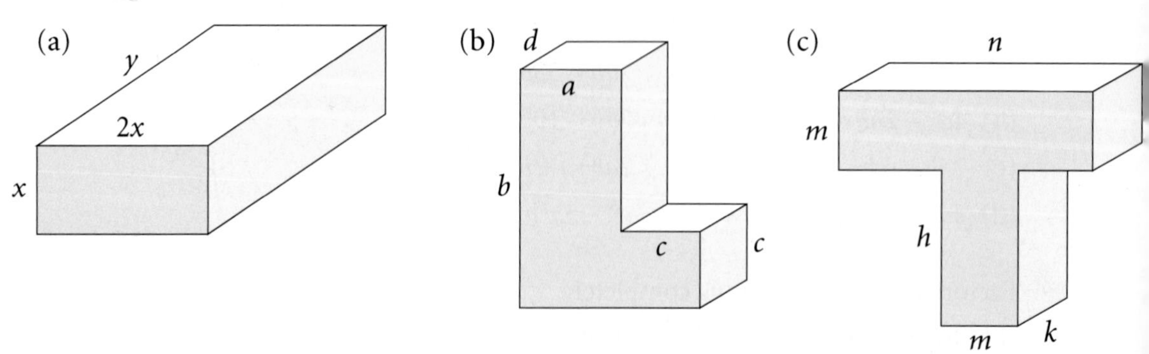

*F3 (a) Find a formula for the volume of each prism.
Use V to stand for the volume each time.

(b) Find a formula for the surface area of each prism.
Use S to stand for the surface area each time.

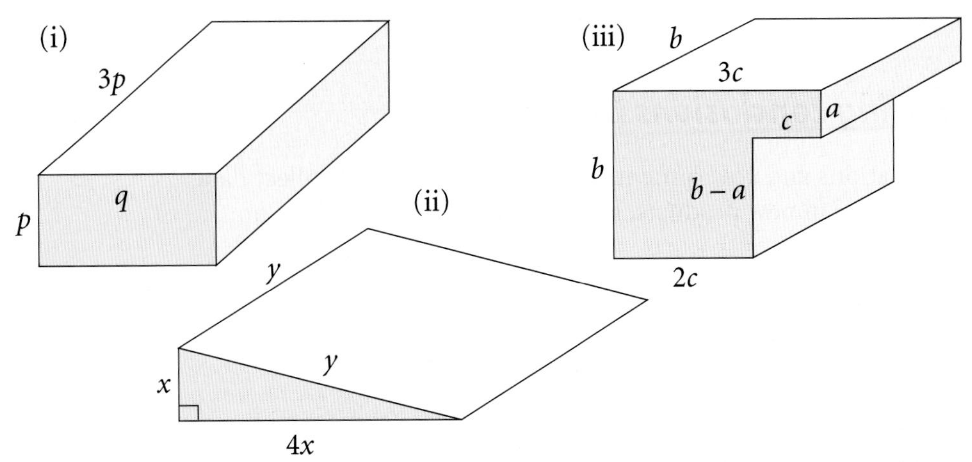

Test yourself

T1 Write an expression, as simply as possible, for the perimeter of this shape.

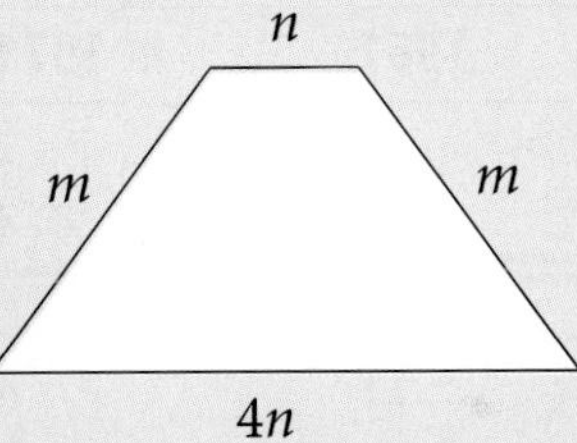

T2 Simplify these expressions.

(a) $4x + 2y + 3x - 6y$ (b) $a^2 - 4a - 1 + 3a - 2$

(c) $3h \times 5k$ (d) $3a^2b \times 2ab$

T3 Multiply out these expressions.

(a) $2(p + q)$ (b) $x(x - 2)$ (c) $p^2(3p - p^4)$ (d) $5h(2h - k)$

T4 Factorise these expressions completely.

(a) $2a + 6b$ (b) $8x - 2xy$ (c) $x^2 + 6x$

(d) $3p^2 + 9pq$ (e) $4n^2 - 8n$ (f) $7a^2b + 21ab^4$

T5 (a) Expand $x(5x^2 + 1)$. (b) Simplify $2a^3y^2 \times 5ay^4$.

(c) Factorise completely $6x^2y - 9xy^2$.

AQA(NEAB)1998

T6 Simplify $\frac{a^6c^4}{a^2c^5}$.

T7 Simplify $\frac{3x^5y^3}{6xy^2}$.

29 Handling secondary data

This work will help you interpret tabulated secondary data.

A Drawing conclusions from data

Many organisations and governments carry out surveys and collect data.
It helps them to plan new products, housing, medical care and so on.

Some of this data is published and may be used by other people.
For them it becomes secondary data, because they did not collect it themselves.

For example, this table gives the distances travelled by different modes of transport in Great Britain.

Distance travelled: by mode

Billion passenger kilometres

	1961	1971	1981	1991	1995
Road					
Car and van[1]	157	313	394	584	594
Bus and coach	76	60	49	44	43
Pedal cycle	11	4	5	5	5
Motorcycle	11	4	10	6	4
All road	**255**	**381**	**458**	**639**	**646**
Rail[2]	39	36	34	38	37
Air[3]	1	2	3	5	6
All modes	**295**	**419**	**495**	**682**	**688**

Source: *Department of Transport*

[1] Includes taxis [2] Data relates to financial years [3] Includes Northern Ireland and Channel Islands

Units

A 'passenger kilometre' is one passenger travelling one kilometre.
So if a family of 3 travelled 20 km, this would be 60 passenger kilometres.

A1 What was the total distance travelled by road in 1961?

A2 Which number below gives the distance travelled by motorcycle in 1991?

6 000 000 km 6 km 6 000 km 6 000 000 000 km

Comparing

A3 Which modes of transport were used less in 1995 than in 1961?

A4 Can you say for certain that more people were flying in 1995 than in 1991? Explain your answer carefully.

A5 (a) There were about 50 million people in Great Britain in 1961. Calculate, approximately, the average distance travelled by a person in that year. (A billion is 1000 million.)

(b) Repeat for 1995, assuming the population was about 60 million.

A6 Between 1961 and 1995, the distance travelled by rail didn't change much. But travel as a whole increased.

(a) What percentage of all travel was by rail in

(i) 1961 (ii) 1995

(b) What happened to the percentage between 1961 and 1995?

A7 Between 1961 and 1995, what happened to the percentage of travel that was by road?

A8 Between 1961 and 1995, what happened to the percentage of road travel that was by bus or coach?

A9 The data in the table came from a survey by the United Nations.

'Brazil is better off for doctors than either Egypt or Kenya.'

Country	Population (millions)	Number of doctors
Brazil	153.3	13 030
Egypt	54.7	10 010
Kenya	25.9	2330

Would you agree with this?
If not, how would you compare the three countries?

A10 Here is part of the British Crime Survey for England and Wales, giving estimates about vandalism.

Vandalism, British Crime Survey estimates: England and Wales

per 10 000 households

Year	1981	1993	1995
Cases of criminal damage (vandalism)	1481	1638	1614

(a) What do these figures tell you about vandalism between 1981 and 1995?

(b) What other information would you need in order to find the number of cases of vandalism in 1995?

B *Percentages from two-way tables*

This two-way table shows gender and age breakdowns for the population of a small town.

Many different percentages can be found using this data. Examples are given below.

	Age 0–59	Age 60+	Total
Males	358	82	440
Females	309	112	421
Total	667	194	861

What percentage of the whole population are male?

The whole population is 861, of whom 440 are male.

$\frac{440}{861} = 0.511$ (to 3 d.p.), so the percentage who are males is 51.1% (to 1 d.p.).

What percentage of the females are aged 60+?

The number of females is 421, of whom 112 are aged 60+.

$\frac{112}{421} = 0.266$ (to 3 d.p.), so the percentage of the females who are aged 60+ is 26.6% (to 1 d.p.)

What percentage of the people aged 60+ are male?

The number of people aged 60+ is 194, of whom 82 are male.

$\frac{82}{194} = 0.423$ (to 3 d.p.), so the percentage of the 60+ group who are male is 42.3% (to 1 d.p.).

B1 What percentage of the whole population are females aged 60+?

B2 What percentage of the people aged 0–59 are female?

B3 What percentage of the males are aged 0–59?

B4 What percentage of the whole population are aged 60+?

B5 This table gives information about the people who work for a company.

	Full-time	Part-time
Men	42	28
Women	33	57

Use the data to compare the proportions of part-time workers among the men and among the women.

B6 A researcher examined data relating to car accidents.
She found that in only 25% of accidents the driver had been drinking and in 75% the driver had not been drinking.

She drew the conclusion that driving was more dangerous if the driver had not been drinking.
Was she correct? If not, why not?

C *Getting the story right*

Here is some data published by the Home Office.

Selected offences recorded by the police: England and Wales

thousands

	1971	1982	1983
Fraud and forgery	99.8	123.1	121.8
Criminal damage (vandalism)	27.0	417.8[a]	443.3
Other offences	5.6	3.8[b]	8.7[b]

Source: *Criminal Statistics, Home Office*

[a] Before 1982 vandalism causing less than £20 of damage was not recorded.

[b] The offence of 'abstracting electricity', of which there were 5688 in 1983, was included among 'other offences' in 1971 and 'theft' in 1982 and 1983.

This data was used for a newspaper article. Here is part of the article.

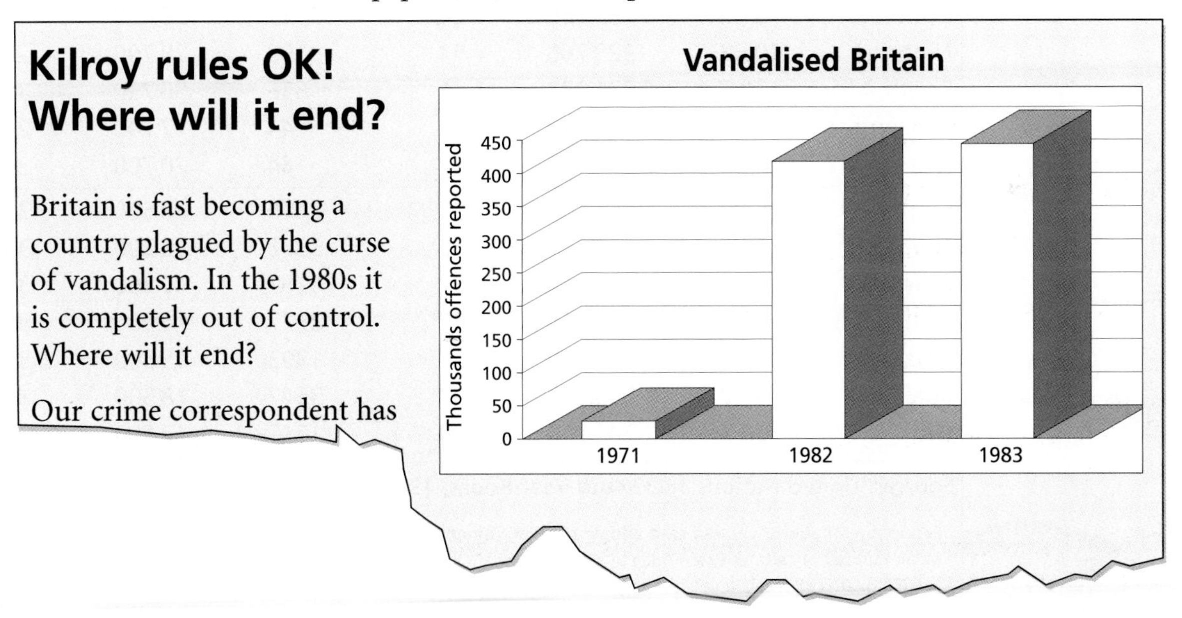

Kilroy rules OK! Where will it end?

Britain is fast becoming a country plagued by the curse of vandalism. In the 1980s it is completely out of control. Where will it end?

Our crime correspondent has

C1 Does the article give an accurate account of the Home Office data?

C2 'When writing a report you should give the source of the data.'
Why do you think this is?

D *Investigating a large data set*

Data is collected in order to answer questions.
But some large collections of data suggest interesting questions to ask.

This data about countries was collected by the United Nations.

Information on twenty-one countries of the World (from So

	Population (million)	Area (square km)	Literacy[1] (%)	Doctors per million[2]	Main roads[3] (km)	Calories p person[4]
Argentina	33.8	2 780 400	94	2506	36 930	3075
Brazil	146.9	8 511 965	80	85	15 050	2723
Chile	15.2	756 626	94	760	10 300	2481
Columbia	34.0	1 138 914	88	778	25 600	2492
Ecuador	11.0	283 561	87	1082	6400	2410
Peru	22.5	1 285 216	81	856	7460	1890
Venezuela	20.8	912 050	90	1282	35 110	2741
Algeria	26.7	2 381 741	50	380	23 700	2989
Egypt	56.5	1 001 449	46	183	17 400	3318
Ethiopia	51.9	1 133 886	24	11	18 490	1694
Nigeria	105.3	923 768	51	108	29 700	2147
South Africa	39.7	1 221 037	76	656	50 730	3158
Tanzania	28.1	883 749	90	44	17 740	2181
Zaire	41.2	2 344 858	72	64	20 700	2094
France	57.4	551 500	99	2485	28 500	3618
Germany	81.2	356 733	100	3356	53 200	3500
Italy	57.1	301 268	97	4267	45 800	3484
Netherlands	15.3	40 844	100	2517	2060	3024
Poland	38.6	323 250	99	1993	45 300	3351
Spain	39.2	505 992	97	3547	18 500	3494
UK	58.3	244 100	100	1615	12 500	3282

Sources: United Nations 38/39/40th Year Books, 1998 World Almanac

[1] Percentage of adults who can read and write several simple sentences
[2] Number of doctors for one million peo
[4] Mean number of calories eaten daily by each person
[5] Gross Domestic Product per person – th total value of goods produced and services provided per person in a year
[7] Annual deaths of under one year old per 1000 live births

merica, Africa and Europe)

GDP per person[5] ($)	Life expectancy[6] men	women	Infant deaths[7]	Primary schools (thousands)
6912	65	73	25	21.7
2238	62	68	63	206.5
3030	68	75	17	8.6
1300	63	69	40	41.0
1142	63	68	63	15.0
1991	63	67	110	26.3
2994	67	73	23	15.8
1743	62	63	74	13.1
746	58	60	43	15.9
52	42	46	137	8.4
256	49	52	105	35.4
2882	58	64	72	–
98	51	55	106	10.4
93	50	54	83	10.8
23 149	73	81	6	42.2
24 157	73	79	6	19.8
21 177	73	80	7	22.9
21 130	74	80	5	8.5
2356	67	75	12	17.9
14 697	73	80	6	19.3
18 182	72	78	6	24.1

Total length of good (A or B) roads – No data available
Mean life-time in years

D1 How could you compare countries by how crowded they are?
Give examples of countries which are relatively uncrowded and examples of those which are relatively crowded.

D2 'Brazil is better off for main roads than the UK.'
Is this hypothesis true? Explain your answer.

*D3 Imagine that Ecuador and Peru were combined into a single country.
Are these statements correct? If not, say why not.

(a) There would be 13 860 km of main roads.
(b) There would be 1938 doctors per million people.
(c) Literacy would be 84%.

D4 'Larger countries have larger populations.'
Draw a scatter diagram to decide whether or not this hypothesis is true.

D5 Investigate one or more of these hypotheses.

A Smaller countries have less roads.
B People in rich countries live longer.
C People live longer in countries with a greater proportion of doctors.
D Richer nations have higher literacy rates.
E Countries where people have less to eat have high infant death rates.

E *Using more than one table*

Sometimes you need to use more than one table to answer a question.

For example, these tables give you some information about the population of the UK from 1901 onwards.

UK population 1901–91: numbers in millions

Year	Males	Females	Total
1901	18.49	19.75	38.24
1921	21.03	22.99	44.03
1941	23.22	24.95	48.22
1961	25.48	27.23	52.81
1981	27.10	28.74	56.35
1991	27.34	29.12	57.80

Source: *Pocket Britain in figures 1997*

UK population 1910–94: percentage in each age group

Year	0–14	15–34	35–64	65+
1910	32.3	35.6	27.2	4.9
1921	28.0	32.8	33.2	6.1
1941	21.0	32.4	37.5	9.2
1961	23.5	25.9	38.9	11.8
1981	20.6	30.2	34.2	15.0
1991	19.2	29.9	35.1	15.7
1994	19.5	29.0	35.8	17.7

Source: *Pocket Britain in figures 1997*

E1 These questions can be answered using one or both of the tables above.

A What percentage of the UK population in 1991 were female?

B How many people aged 15–34 were there in the UK in 1921?

C What percentage of the UK population in 1941 were under 65?

D How many people aged 65 or over were there in the UK in 1991?

(a) Answer each question.

(b) Which questions did you need both tables to answer?

E2 How many people aged over 34 were there in the UK in 1921?

E3 Can you use these tables to find out the number of males aged 65 and above in the UK in 1961? If not, why not?

Titanic

On 5 April 1912, the ocean liner *Titanic* hit an iceberg and many people died.

The number of people who died that night has never been known exactly but figures were published in a British Board of Trade enquiry report. These tables are based on data available on a website.

Males and females

Class	Numbers on board			Number of deaths		
	Male	Female	Both	Male	Female	Both
First class	180	145	325	118	4	122
Second class	179	106	285	154	13	167
Steerage	510	196	706	422	106	528
Crew	862	23	885	670	3	673
Total	**1731**	**470**	**2201**	**1364**	**126**	**1490**

Adults and children

Class	Numbers on board			Number of deaths		
	Adult	Child	Both	Adult	Child	Both
First class	319	6	325	122	0	122
Second class	261	24	285	167	0	167
Steerage	627	79	706	476	52	528
Crew	885	0	885	673	0	673
Total	**2092**	**109**	**2201**	**1438**	**52**	**1490**

E4 Use the data to answer these questions.

(a) (i) How many people were on board?

(ii) How many died?

(b) (i) How many children were on board?

(ii) Roughly, what percentage of the children died?

(c) Roughly what fraction of the men on board were crew?

(d) What percentage of the crew died?

(e) What percentage of children in steerage class died?

E5 Use the data to investigate one or more of these hypotheses.

A 'Women and children were placed in lifeboats first so were more likely to survive.'

B 'First class passengers were more likely to survive than other people on board.'

C 'Loss of life was greatest amongst the crew.'

F *Taking A-level mathematics – girls and boys*

The data on these two pages is from a secondary school in England.

All the students in a year 11 group are shown.
The table gives their sex, their GCSE mathematics grade and whether they chose AS/A-level mathematics in the sixth form (Y = yes).

To be qualified to do AS/A-level mathematics, a student needs to have achieved at least a grade C at GCSE.

- What conclusions can you draw from this data?

Reference number	Sex	GCSE mathematics	A level mathematics
1	M	A	
2	M	E	
3	F	C	
4	F	E	
5	M	A	Y
6	M	B	
7	M	C	
8	F	B	
9	F	B	
10	F	B	
11	M	B	
12	F	A	Y
13	F	B	
14	F	A*	
15	M	A	Y
16	M	C	
17	M	C	
18	M	C	Y
19	M	G	
20	M	A	Y
21	M	D	
22	M	D	
23	M	A*	Y
24	M	E	
25	M	D	
26	M	F	
27	F	B	
28	F	B	
29	F	B	
30	F	A*	Y
31	F	A	
32	F	E	
33	M	D	
34	M	B	
35	M	E	
36	F	A*	Y
37	F	B	Y
38	F	F	
39	M	B	Y
40	M	D	
41	M	B	
42	M	C	
43	F	A	
44	F	B	
45	M	C	
46	M		
47	M	C	
48	F	B	
49	M	E	
50	M	C	
51	M	C	
52	M	C	
53	F	C	
54	F	C	
55	F	A	
56	F	C	
57	F	B	
58	M	D	
59	M	C	
60	M	A*	Y
61	M	F	
62	M	F	
63	M	D	
64	M	A	Y
65	M	B	
66	F	D	
67	M	D	
68	F	E	
69	F	B	
70	F	D	
71	M	F	
72	M	C	
73	M	E	
74	M	E	
75	F	B	
76	F	A	
77	F	C	
78	F	B	
79	F	B	
80	F	C	
81	F	B	
82	F	B	
83	F	D	
84	F	C	
85	F	A	
86	F	C	
87	F	A	
88	F	A	
89	M	B	
90	F	A	Y
91	M	A*	Y
92	F	D	
93	F	D	
94	F	B	
95	F	E	
96	F	E	
97	F	B	
98	F	B	
99	F	B	
100	F	C	

101	F	C	
102	F	C	
103	F	B	
104	F	A	Y
105	F	E	
106	M	B	
107	M	A	Y
108	M	C	
109	F	E	
110	M	E	
111	M	B	
112	M	C	
113	M	E	
114	M	B	Y
115	M	A*	Y
116	M	E	
117	M	E	
118	M	D	
119	M	B	Y
120	M	B	Y
121	M	F	
122	M	C	
123	M	F	
124	F	D	
125	F	C	
126	F	A*	
127	F	E	
128	M	D	
129	F	B	
130	F	B	
131	F	D	
132	F	B	
133	F	A*	
134	F	E	
135	F	A	
136	M	D	
137	M	A	Y
138	M	A	Y
139	M	A*	
140	M	A	
141	F	C	
142	M	D	
143	F	E	
144	M	A	Y
145	M	D	
146	M	B	Y

147	F	A	
148	F	E	
149	F	B	
150	F	B	
151	F	B	
152	F	E	
153	M	E	
154	F	E	
155	F	C	
156	F	D	
157	F	C	
158	F	G	
159	F	A*	Y
160	F	D	
161	F	D	
162	F	A	Y
163	F	D	
164	M	D	
165	F	B	
166	F	D	
167	M	F	
168	M	E	
169	M	A	Y
170	F	G	
171	F	A	Y
172	F	C	
173	F	B	
174	F	F	
175	F	B	
176	F	C	
177	F	C	
178	F	A	Y
179	F	F	
180	M	C	
181	M	C	
182	M	B	
183	M	D	
184	M	C	
185	M	D	
186	M	A*	Y
187	M	B	
188	F	D	
189	M	D	
190	M	D	
191	M	B	
192	M	B	

193	M	B	Y
194	M	A	
195	F	E	
196	M	G	
197	F	C	
198	F	C	
199	M	A	
200	M	B	
201	F	C	
202	F	A	Y
203	M	C	
204	M	A	
205	M	B	
206	M	E	
207	M	A	
208	M	C	
209	M	A	Y
210	M		
211	F	B	
212	F	B	
213	F	E	
214	M	B	Y
215	F	A	
216	F	B	
217	F	A	
218	F	C	
219	F	B	Y
220	F	D	
221	F	B	
222	F	D	
223	F	C	
224	F	C	
225	F	C	
226	M	C	
227	M	B	Y
228	M	A	Y
229	M	D	
230	M	C	
231	F	E	
232	M	E	
233	F	A	Y
234	F	F	
235	M	C	
236	M	E	
237	F	A	Y
238	M	E	

239	F	D	
240	M	C	
241	F	A	Y
242	F	B	
243	F	E	
244	F	A	Y
245	F	A	
246	M	B	
247	F	B	
248	F	C	
249	F	D	
250	F	E	
251	F	C	
252	M	D	
253	M	D	
254	F	F	
255	M	F	
256	F	B	Y
257	M	D	
258	F	D	
259	F	B	
260	F	E	
261	M		
262	M	U	
263	M	D	
264	M	D	
265	M		
266	M	D	
267	M	G	
268	M	D	
269	F	B	
270	M	D	
271	M	A	Y
272	M	B	Y
273	F	E	
274	M	B	
275	M	D	
276	M	E	
277	M	F	
278	F	A	
279	F	A	
280	F	A	Y
281	F	D	
282	M	A	Y
283	F	A	Y

30 3-D vision

You will revise

- how to draw three-dimensional objects
- how to make nets for three-dimensional objects
- show 3-D objects in 2D using plans and views
- recognise reflections of shapes and reflection symmetry in 3-D

A *The Soma Cube*

This photograph shows the pieces of a Soma Cube.
These pieces fit together to make a large cube.

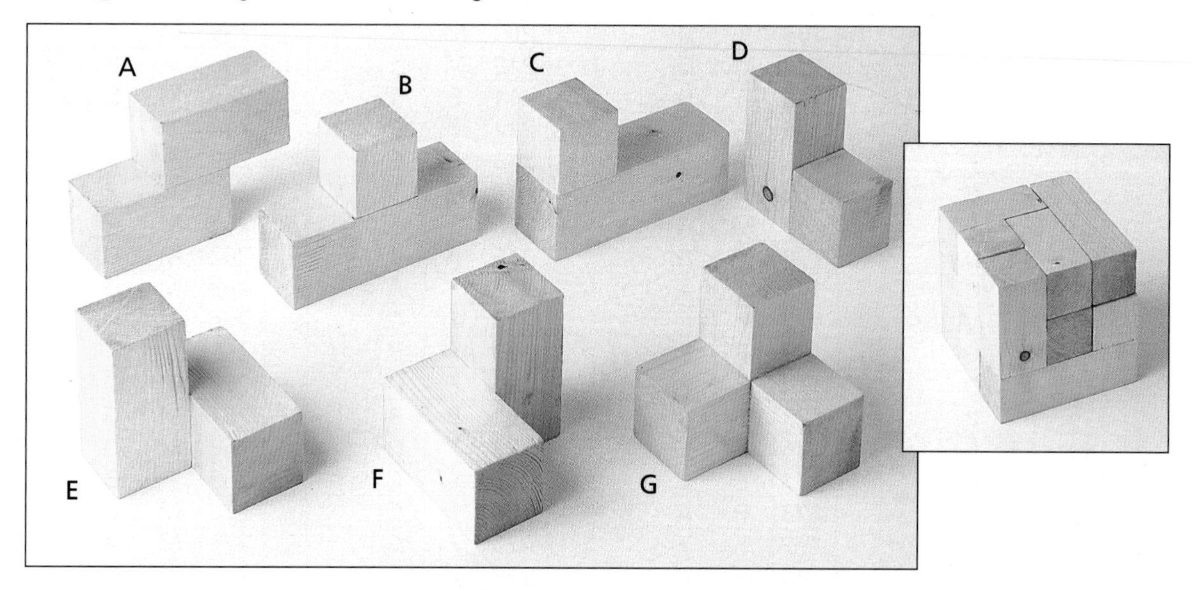

All of these seven pieces can be constructed using cubes.

A1 How many cubes would be needed to make each of these pieces?

A2 Which pieces have the same volume?

A3 This diagram shows one of the pieces drawn on triangular dotty paper.

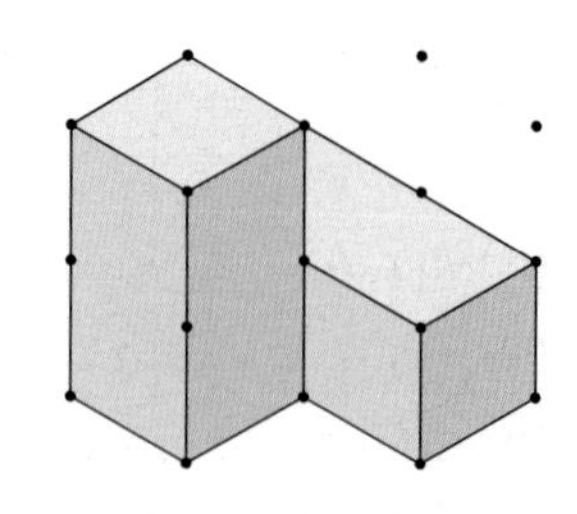

- Draw the rest of the pieces on triangular dotty paper.
- Shade sides which face the same direction in the same way to help show the object more clearly.

B *Nets*

Any pattern which makes a complete shape is called a **net** for that shape. This is a net for a cube.

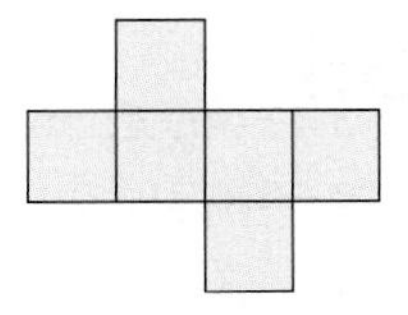

B1 Which of these are possible nets for a cube?

A

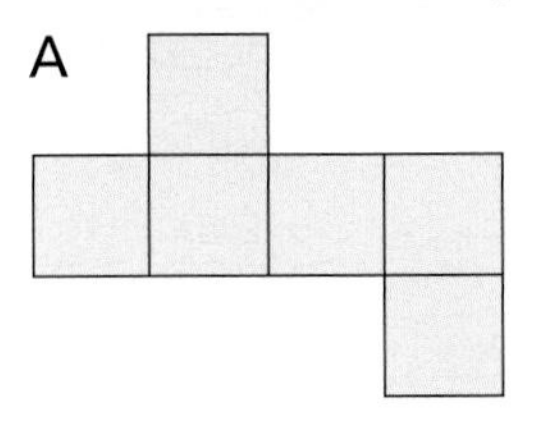

B

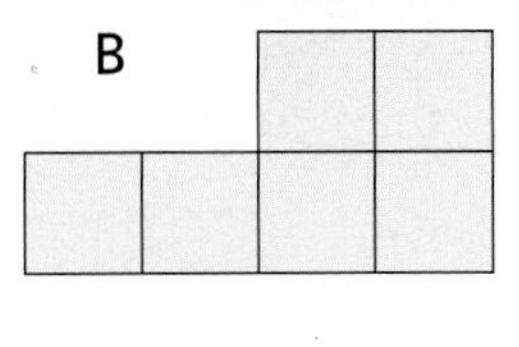

C

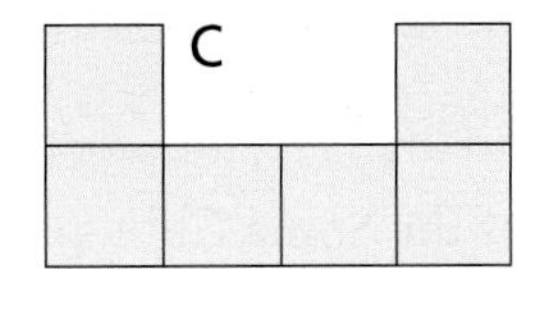

B2 There are 12 possible different nets of a cube.
Draw 4 of them on squared paper.

B3 This is a regular tetrahedron.
All of the triangular faces are equilateral.
Use triangular dotty paper to draw a net for this tetrahedron.

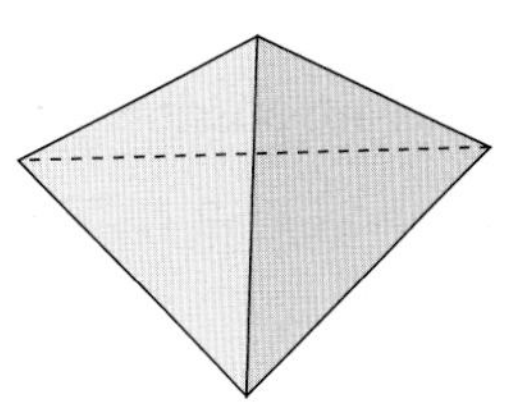

What different nets for a tetrahedron can you find?

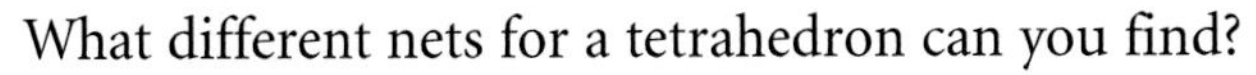

B4 This is a net for a regular octahedron.
It has eight faces all of which are equilateral triangles.

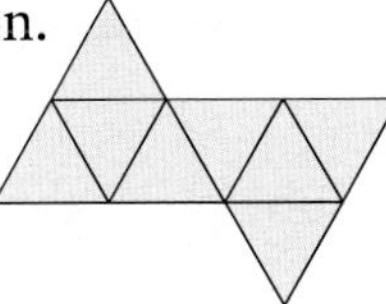

Which of these are nets for an octahedron?

A

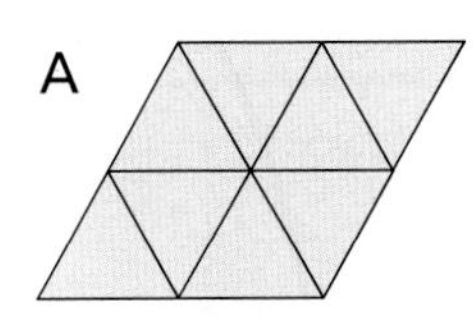

B

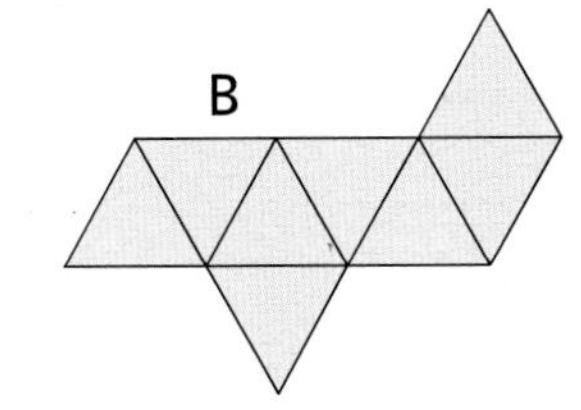

C

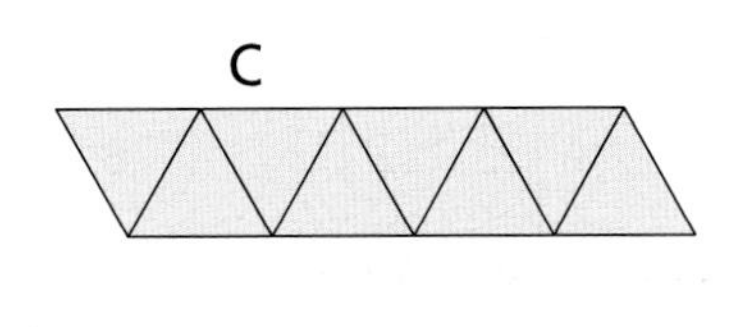

B5 The diagram shows a pyramid with a square base.
The base of the pyramid is a square with edges of length 6 cm.
The length of each sloping edge of the pyramid is 5 cm.

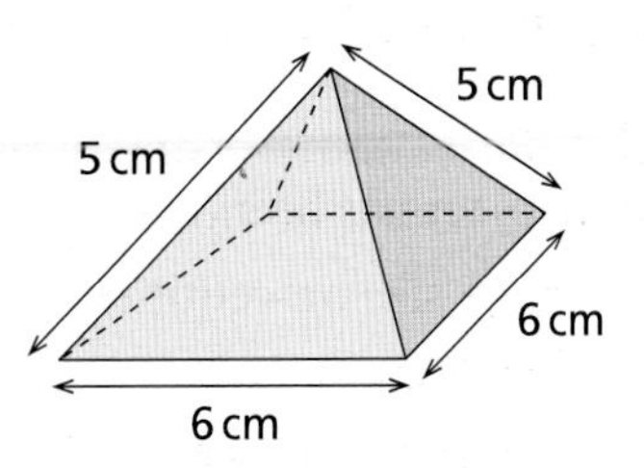

(a) Make a sketch of a suitable net for the pyramid.

(b) Make an accurate full size drawing of one of the triangular faces of the pyramid.

Edexcel

C *Views*

Another way of showing a 3-D object on paper is to draw the view from three different directions:

- a plan view
- a side view
- a front view

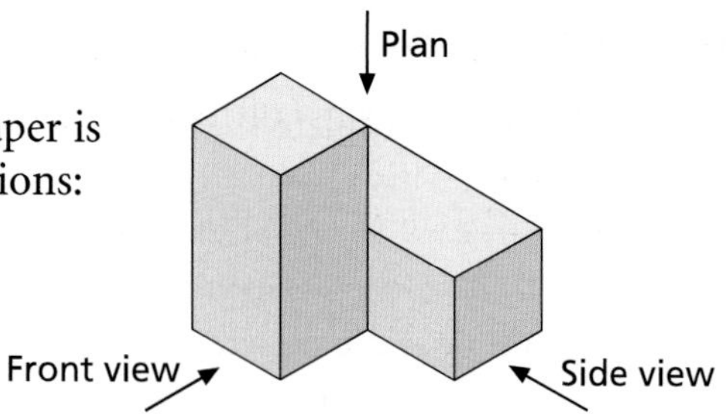

This is a front view of the Soma Cube piece above.

This line is dotted because it is hidden from this view.

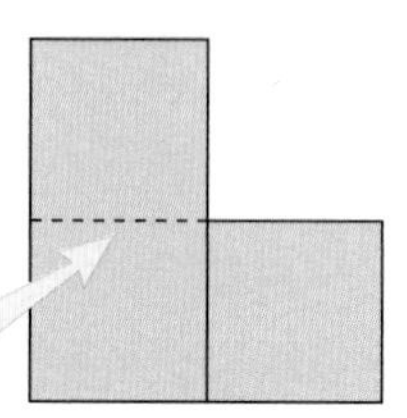

C1 Which of these are possible plan views of the Soma Cube piece above?

A

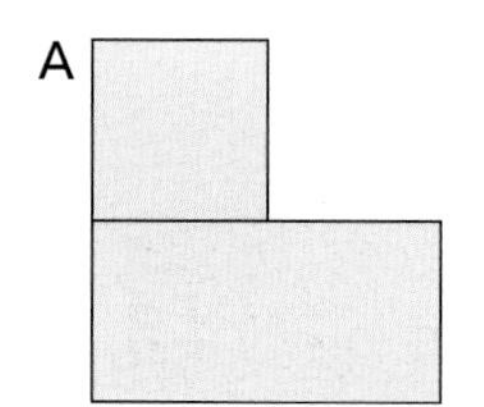

B

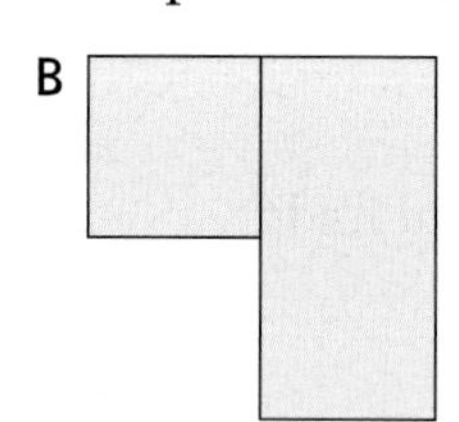

C

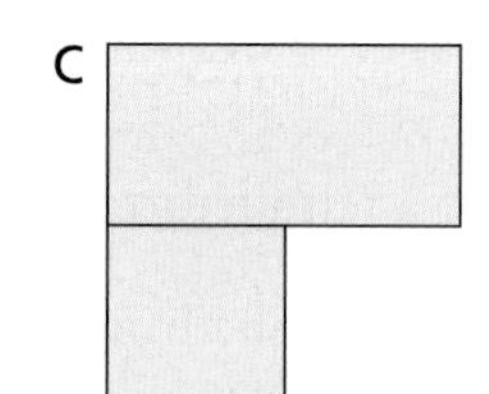

D

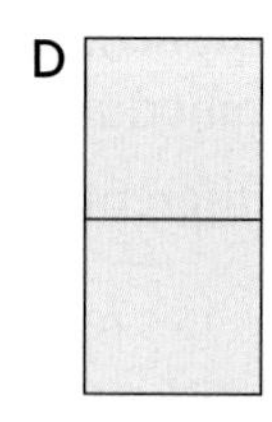

C2 Draw the side view of the Soma Cube piece above.

C3 This is a plan view of one of the Soma Cube pieces.
Which of these is the front view?

A

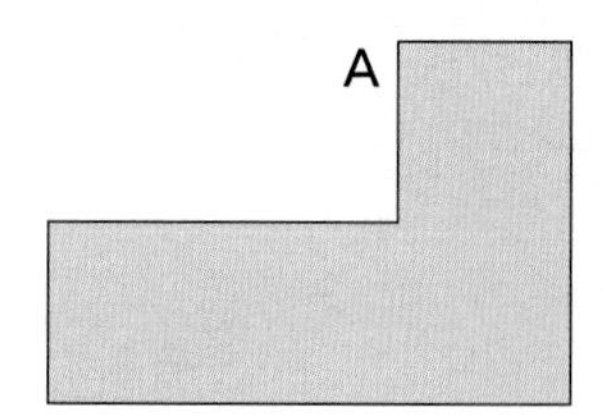

B

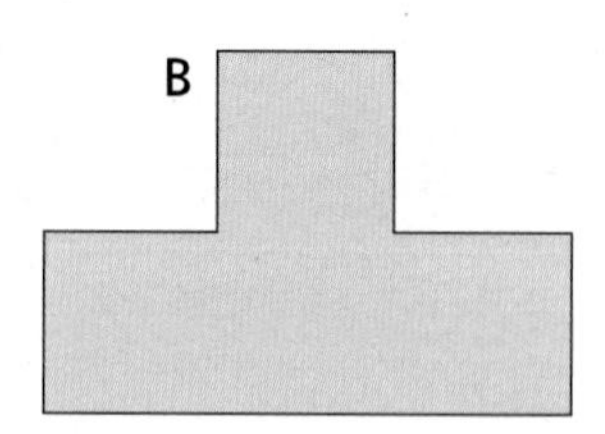

C

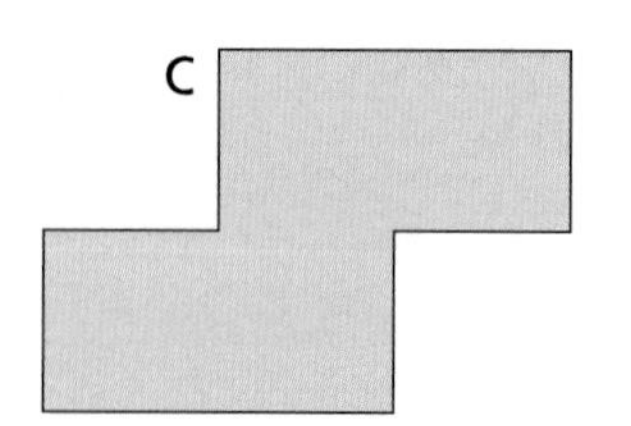

C4 Choose another Soma Cube piece and draw the three views of it.

C5 This object has been made from seven centimetre cubes.
Draw full-size on centimetre squared paper

(a) a plan view
(b) a side view
(c) a front view

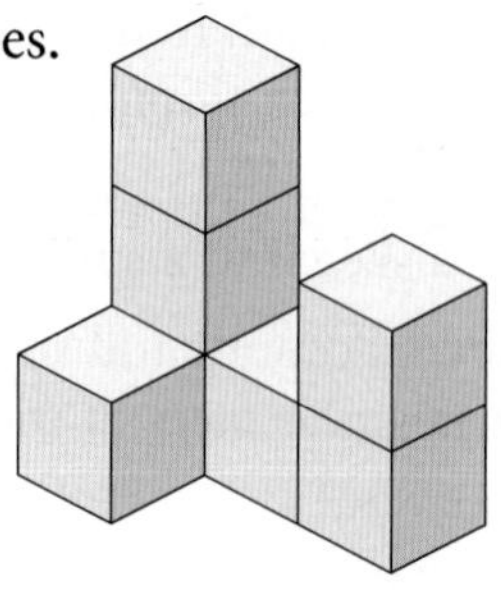

C6 (a) Draw a full-size plan view of this shape.
(b) Draw a full-size side view of this shape from direction S. Show any hidden edges with dotted lines.
(c) Use your drawings to measure the length of the sloping edge AB.

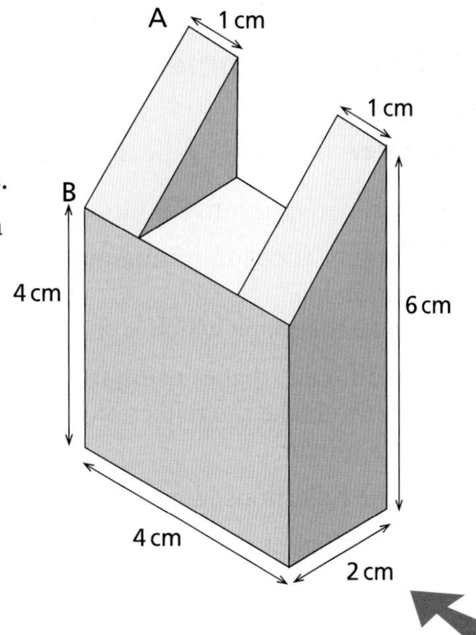

C7 The drawing shows a cuboid with a prism removed. The measurements are in centimetres.

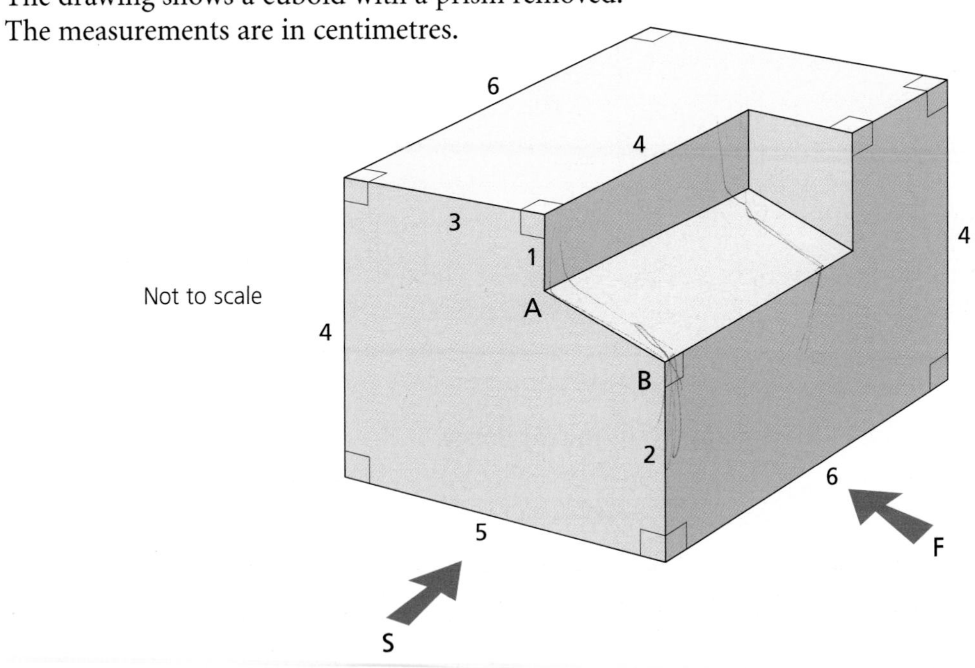

(a) On centimetre squared paper, draw full size the front (F) and the side (S) elevations.
(b) What is the length of the sloping edge marked AB on the drawing?

OCR

D *Reflection symmetry*

Mirror images

This shape is made from five multilink cubes.

What would the reflection of this shape in the mirror look like?
Can you make the shape which is the reflection?

Make some different shapes using five multilink cubes.
Ask a partner to make the reflection of your shape.
Check with a mirror.

Are any of the reflections identical to the original shape?

Do you get a different shape if you put the mirror in a different position?

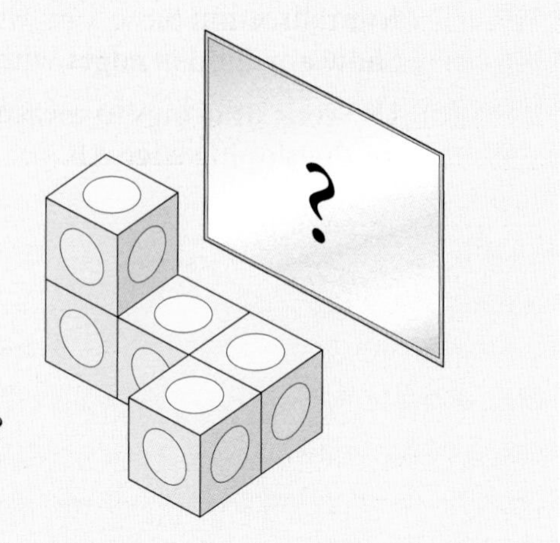

D1 This shape is made from five multilink cubes. Which of the shapes below is a mirror image of this shape?

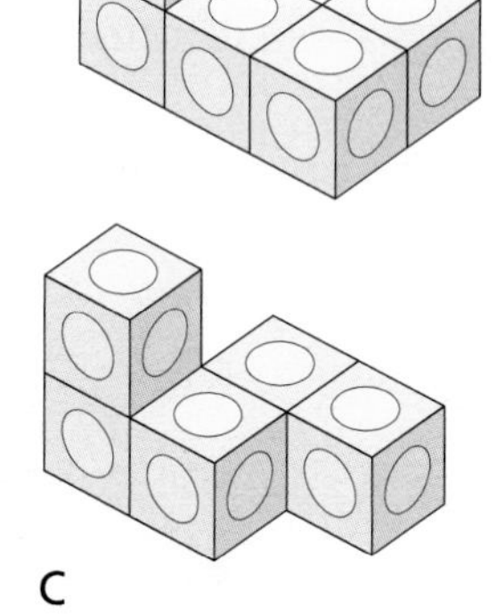

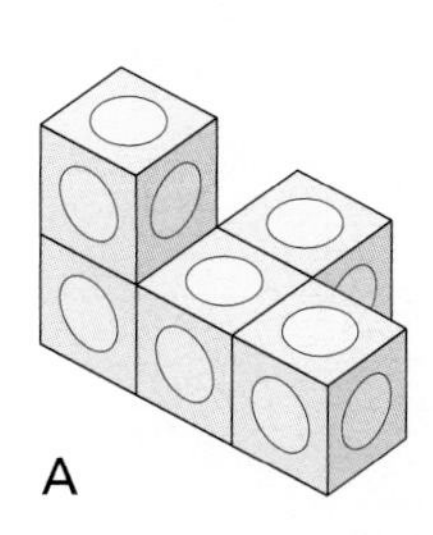

A

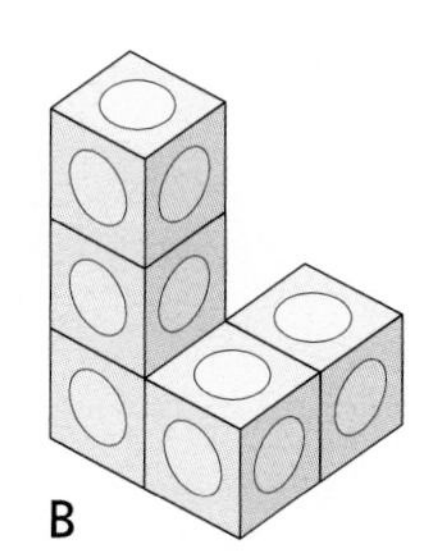

B

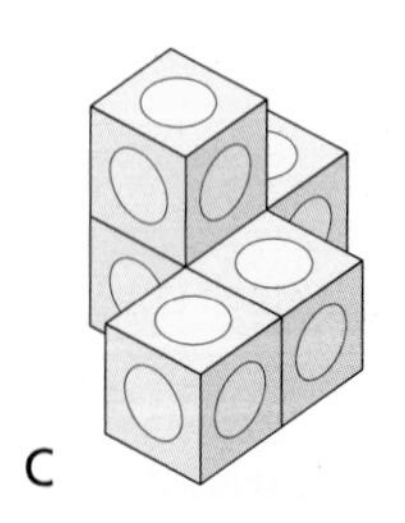

C

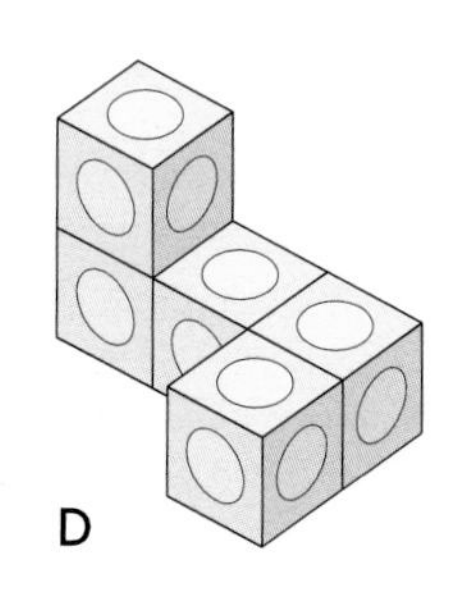

D

D2 Match each of these shapes to its mirror image.

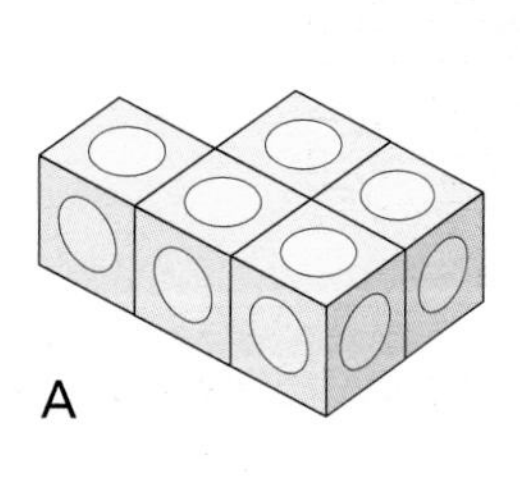

A

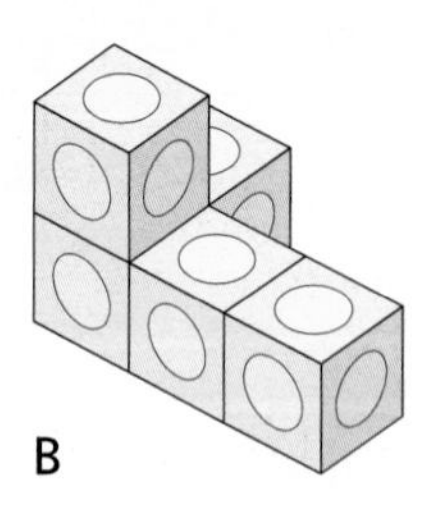

B

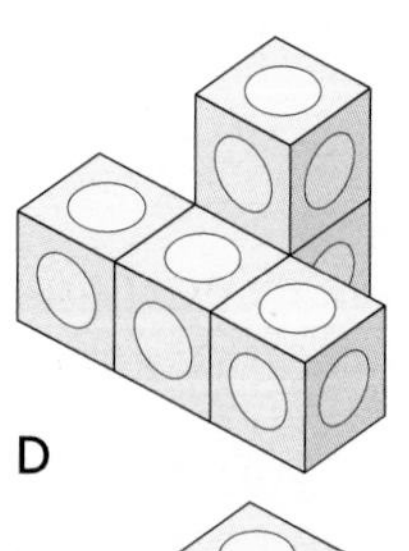

C

D

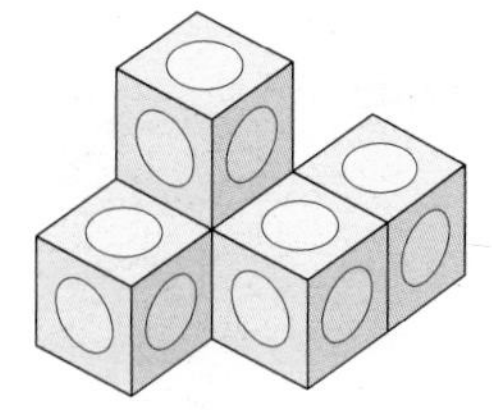

E

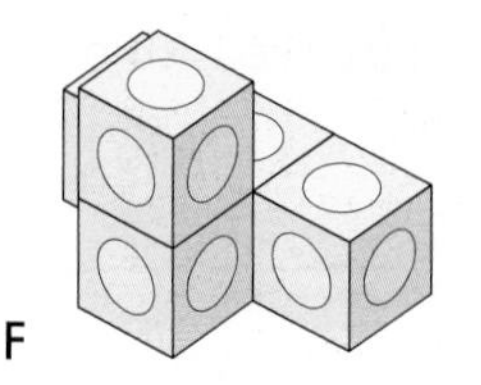

F

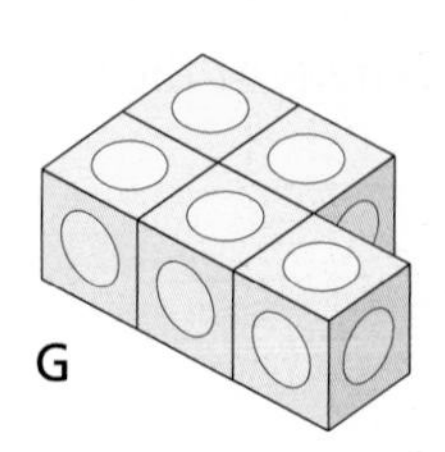

G

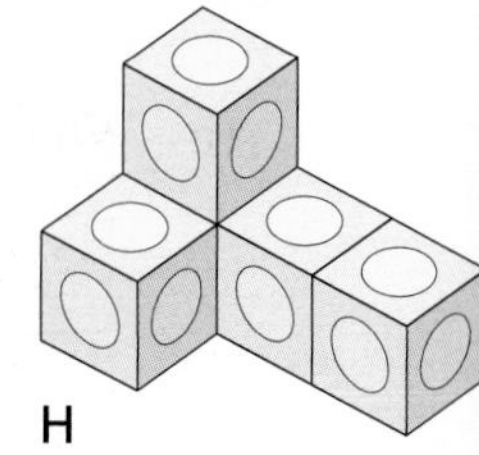

H

This Soma Cube piece has been cut in half and placed against a mirror.

The reflection makes the piece look whole again. This shape has **reflection symmetry.**

Is there any other way this piece could be cut in half and placed against a mirror to give the full shape?

A mirror which cuts a shape in half like this is a **plane of symmetry**.

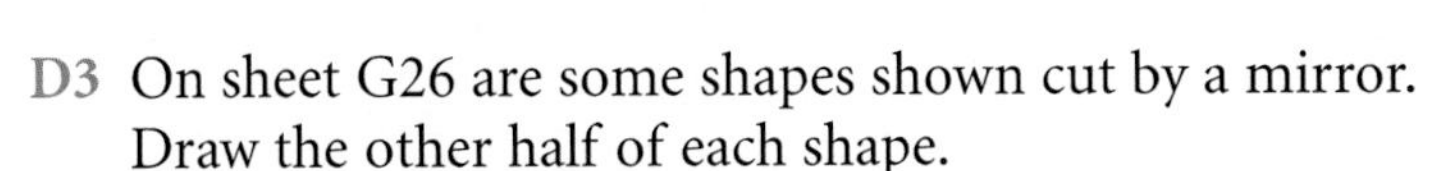

D3 On sheet G26 are some shapes shown cut by a mirror. Draw the other half of each shape.

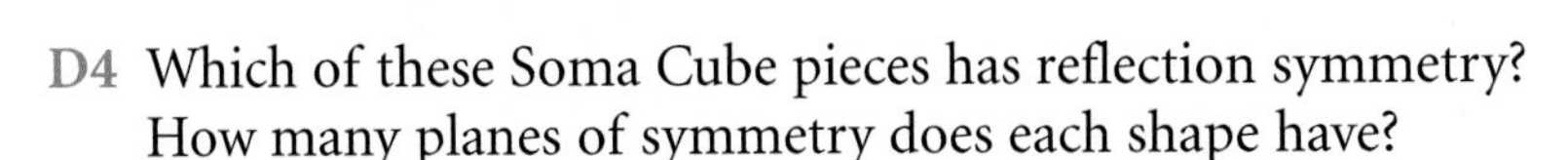

D4 Which of these Soma Cube pieces has reflection symmetry? How many planes of symmetry does each shape have?

(a)

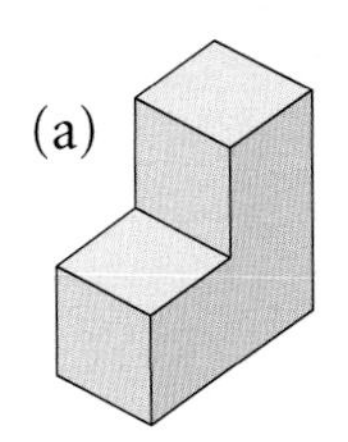

(b)

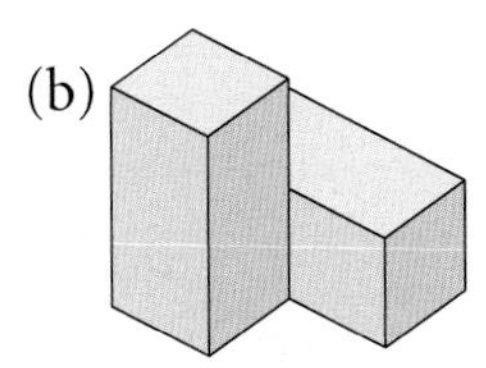

(c)

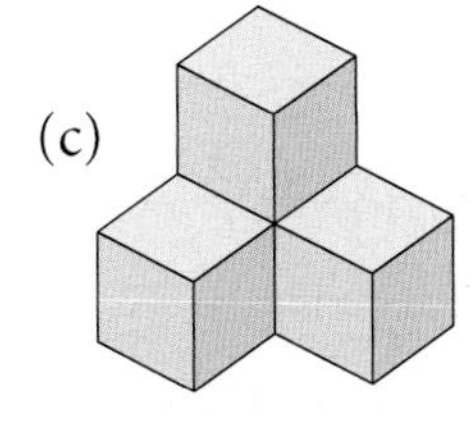

(d)

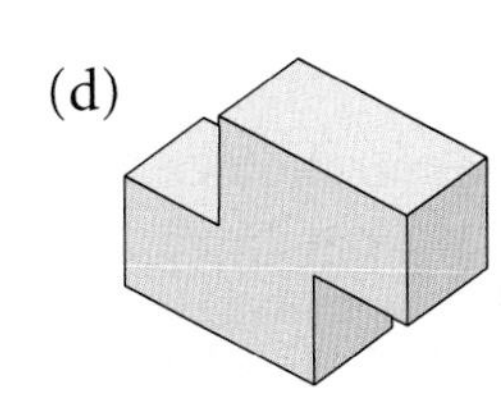

D5 This shape has been made from multilink cubes. It has no planes of symmetry.

(a) Make this shape from multilink cubes.

(b) Add one cube to give it reflection symmetry.

(c) Sketch your shape on triangular dotty paper.

Make up some puzzles like these to try on a partner.

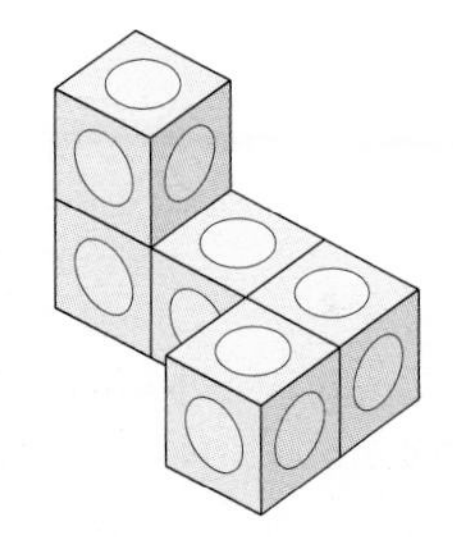

***D6** This is a cube made up from 27 small cubes.

(a) How many planes of symmetry does it have? (Take care not to count the same one twice!)

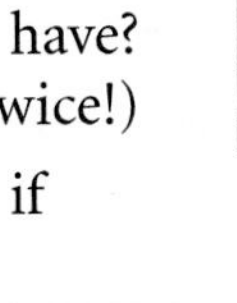

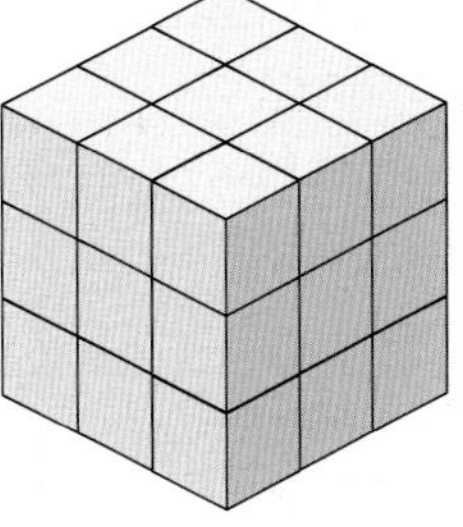

How many planes of symmetry will it have if you remove

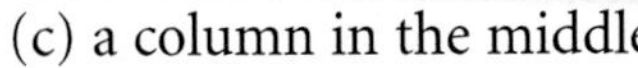

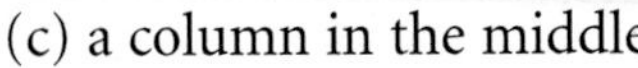

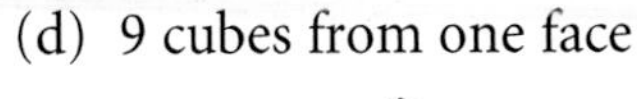

(b) one cube at the corner

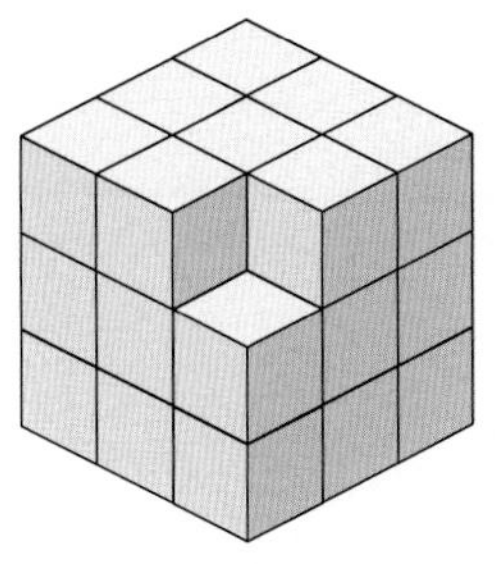

(c) a column in the middle

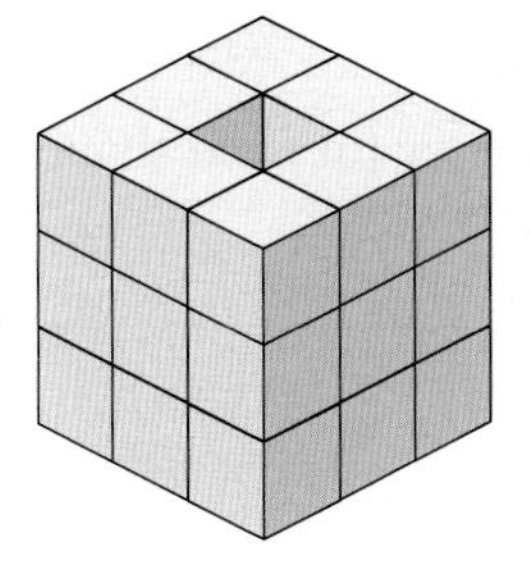

(d) 9 cubes from one face

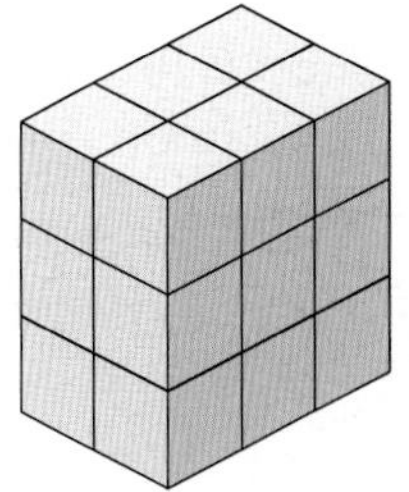

The Soma Cube

The Soma Cube was discovered by Danish mathematician Piet Hein in 1929.
There are many interesting websites which have ideas for other shapes you can make with the pieces and other similar puzzles.
See what you can find out.

Test yourself

T1 The diagram shows a solid cuboid.

(a) Work out the volume of the cuboid.

(b) On a sheet of triangular dotty paper, make an accurate full size drawing of the cuboid.

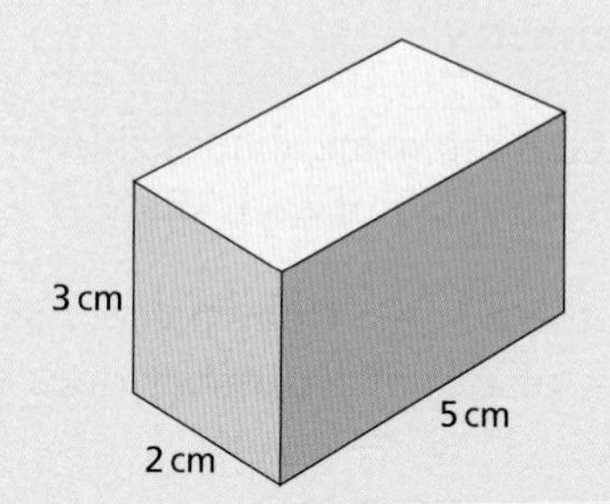

Edexcel

T2 This diagram shows a triangular prism.

(a) Draw a full-size net for this prism.

(b) Use your net to find the perpendicular height (h) of this prism.

(c) Calculate the total surface area of the prism.

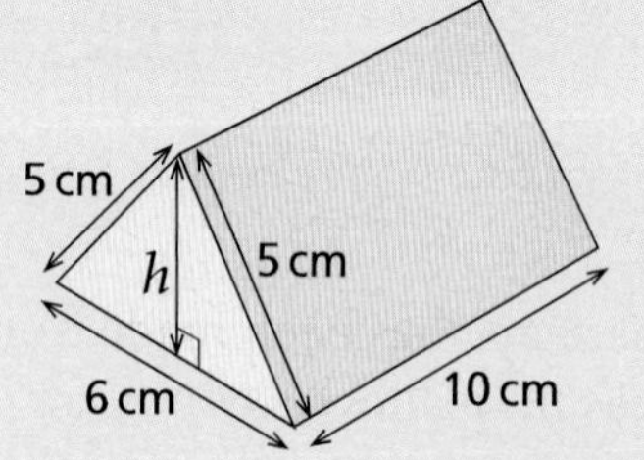

T3 This is a sketch of a house.
Sheet G136 shows the front elevation of this house drawn to a scale of 1 cm to 1 m.

(a) On the sheet draw an accurate plan view of the house.

(b) On the sheet draw an accurate side view of the house.

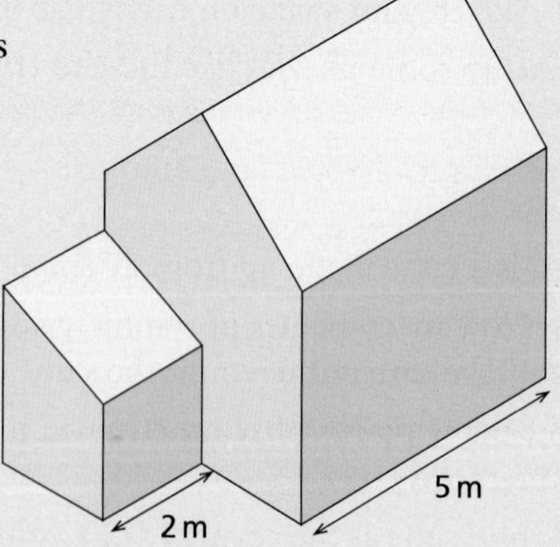

T4 Sheet G28 shows two shapes.
Draw in one plane of symmetry for each shape.

Edexcel

Review 5

1 The cumulative frequency graph shows the distribution of marks (out of 100) scored by 200 students in a test.

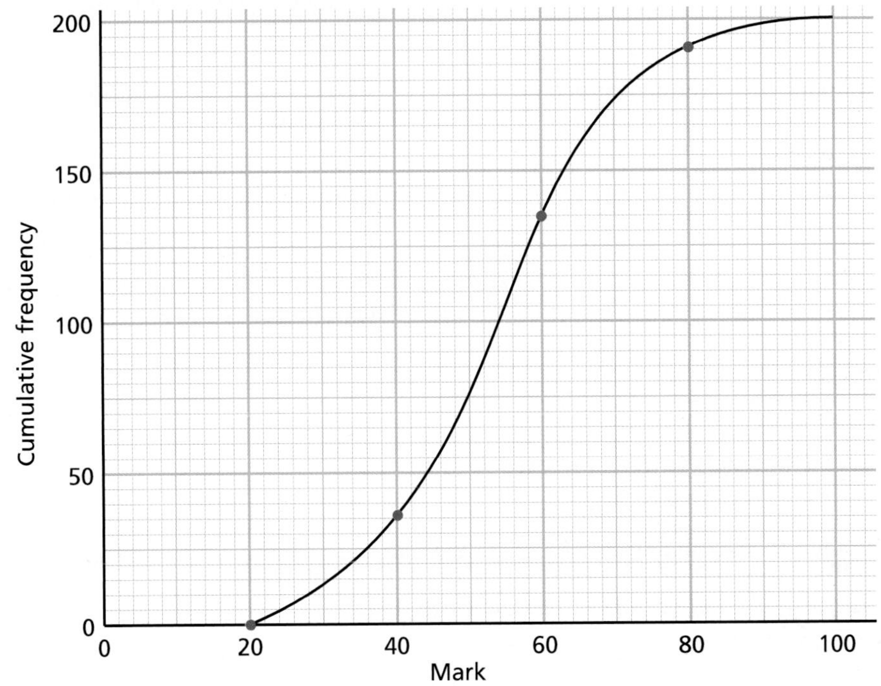

(a) Estimate how many students got fewer than 50 marks in this test.

(b) Estimate the percentage of students who scored more than 54.

(c) What is the median mark?

(d) Estimate the lower and upper quartiles.

(e) Estimate the percentage of students who will pass the test if the pass mark is 40.

2 Look at these shapes.

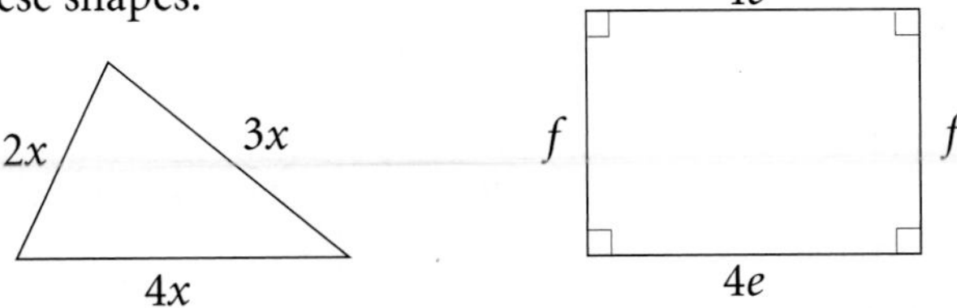

Write as simply as possible an expression for

(a) the perimeter of the triangle

(b) the perimeter of the rectangle

(c) the area of the rectangle

OCR

3 Seven sausage rolls and five pies cost £9.30.
The sausage rolls cost 65p each.
Find the cost of a pie.

4 Simplify these expressions.

(a) $2p \times 3pq$ (b) $mn^2 \times 9mn^3$ (c) $\frac{18q^2r^5}{3qr^2}$ (d) $\frac{2kw^4 \times 2k^3w^5}{8k^7w^7}$

5 A survey asked people how many hours of television they watched in a week.
These are the results.

Number of hours (h)	Number of people
$0 \le h \le 5$	2
$5 < h \le 10$	5
$10 < h \le 15$	14
$15 < h \le 20$	18
$20 < h \le 25$	32
$25 < h \le 30$	15
$30 < h \le 35$	3
$35 < h \le 40$	1

(a) Make a cumulative frequency table for the data.

(b) Draw a cumulative frequency graph to show the results of the survey.

(c) Use your graph to estimate the median number of hours of TV watched in a week.

6 Multiply out the brackets from these expressions.

(a) $5(2a + b)$ (b) $a(a - 5b)$ (c) $n^2(2nk + n^3)$ (d) $2h(7h - 4h^2k)$

7 Joanne is paid a basic rate of £6.95 per hour for a 38-hour week.
One week she also works 3 hours at double time.
Work out her gross pay.

8 For this shape,

(a) find a formula for the perimeter ($P = \ldots$)

(b) find a formula for the area ($A = \ldots$)

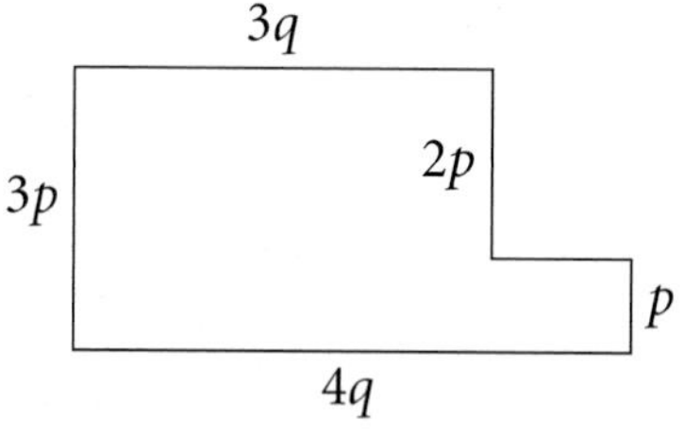

9 Factorise these expressions completely.

(a) $8a + 6b$ (b) $x^2 - 8x$ (c) $4k^2 - 8k$ (d) $8h^3k + 12h^2k^2$

10 The diagram shows a triangular prism.

(a) How many planes of symmetry does this prism have?

(b) Calculate the perpendicular height (h) of the prism.

(c) Find the volume of the prism.

(d) Draw these full size.

(i) A plan view (ii) A side view (iii) A front view

(e) Draw a full size net and calculate the surface area of the prism.

31 Understanding inequalities

This work will help you

- understand, use and combine inequalities
- convert statements in words to inequalities in symbols

A Single inequalities

- Decide which of the following are true.

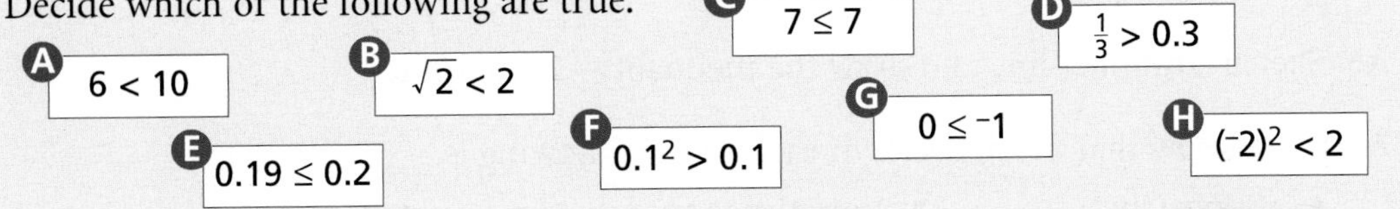

- Find as many matching pairs as you can.

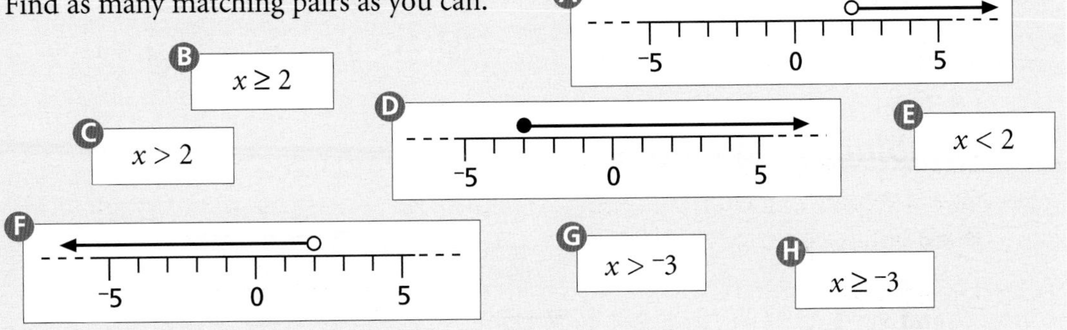

A1 Decide if each of the following is true or false.

(a) $2 > 1$ (b) $\frac{1}{3} < \frac{1}{4}$ (c) $\sqrt{26} \geq 5$ (d) $11^2 \leq 121$

A2 (a) For the set of values $x \leq 1$, which of the numbers in the bubble are values of x?

(b) Which are values of n for the set $n > 3$?

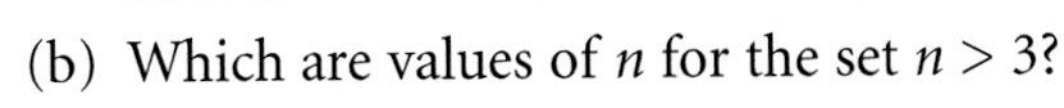

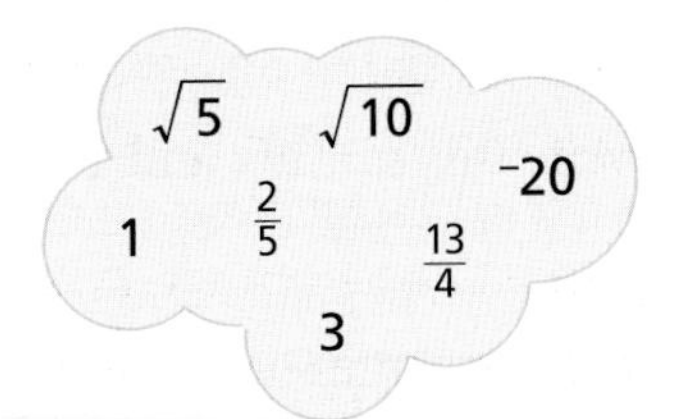

A3 Write inequalities for each of the following diagrams.

(a)

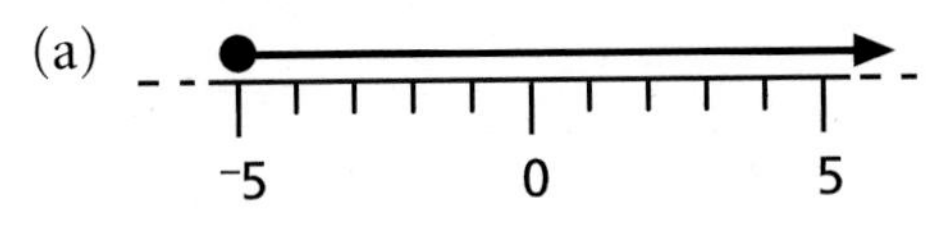

(b)

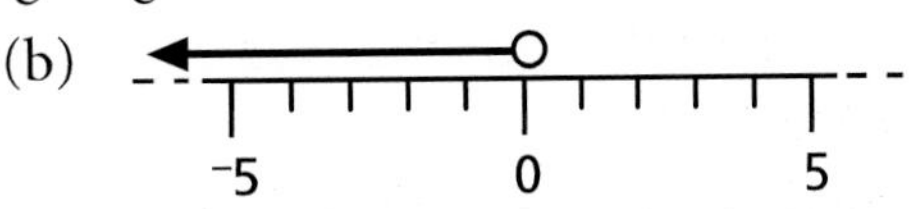

(c)

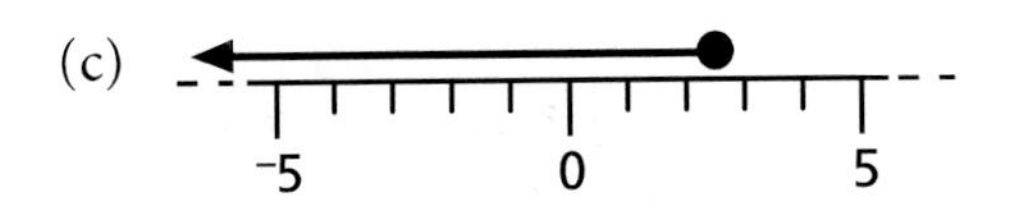

(d)

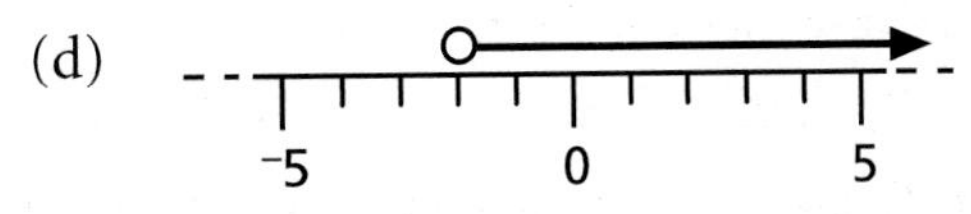

A4 For each of these, sketch a number line and draw the inequality on it.

(a) $x < 4$ (b) $n \geq {}^-1$ (c) $p < 5\frac{1}{2}$ (d) $y \geq {}^-4$

'10 is greater than 6'
means the same as
'6 is less than 10'
so '**10 > 6**' is equivalent to '**6 < 10**'.

'x is less than 3'
means the same as
'3 is greater than x'
so '$\boldsymbol{x < 3}$' is equivalent to '$\boldsymbol{3 > x}$'.

A5 Find three pairs of equivalent inequalities.

$n < 4$ $4 < n$ $n \leq 4$ $n > 4$ $4 \geq n$ $4 > n$

A6 Sketch a number line and draw the inequality $2 \leq x$ on it.

***A7** If we know that $x > 3$, decide if each of the following is

- **always** true or
- **sometimes** true or
- **never** true

(a) $x > 4$ (b) $x > 2$ (c) $x > {}^-1$ (d) $x < 1$

(e) $x + 5 > 8$ (f) $x - 1 < 4$ (g) $2x > 3$ (h) $\frac{x}{2} < 1$

B *Combined inequalities*

TG

If $x \geq 1$ ... $x \geq 1$

... **and** $x < 4$ ... $x < 4$

... then x lies between 1 and 4 (including 1 but not 4).

We can write this as $1 \leq x$ and $x < 4$ or as the combined inequality $\boldsymbol{1 \leq x < 4}$.

A

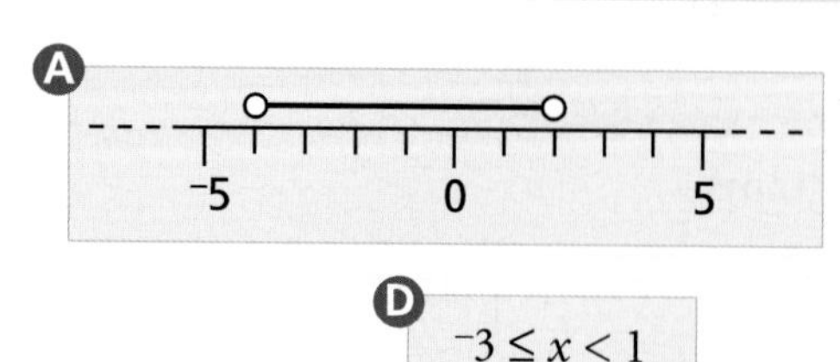

B ${}^-4 \leq x \leq 2$

C ${}^-3 < x \leq 1$

E

D

${}^-3 \leq x < 1$

F

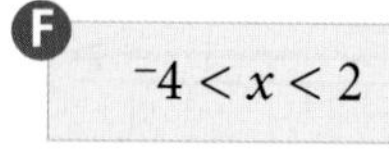

${}^-4 < x < 2$

G

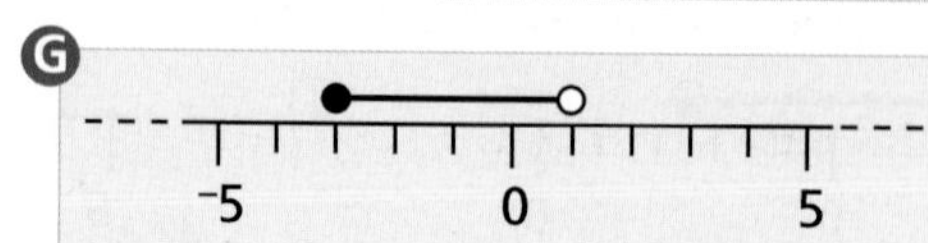

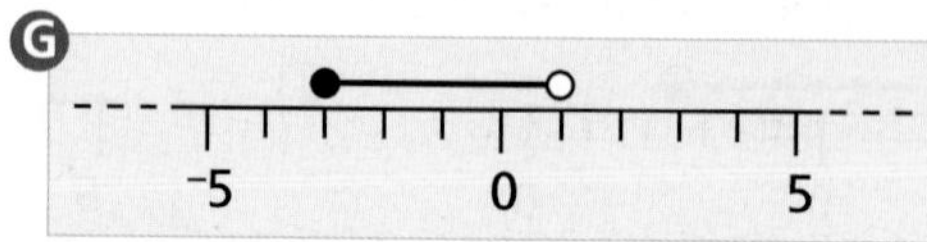

H ${}^-3 \leq x \leq 1$

B1 For each of these, sketch a number line to represent the inequality.

(a) $2 \leq x \leq 4$ (b) $^{-}3 < x \leq 1$ (c) $0 \leq n < 6$ (d) $1 \leq n < 10$

B2 (a) Which of the numbers in the bubble are in the set of values of x given by $0 < x \leq 5$?

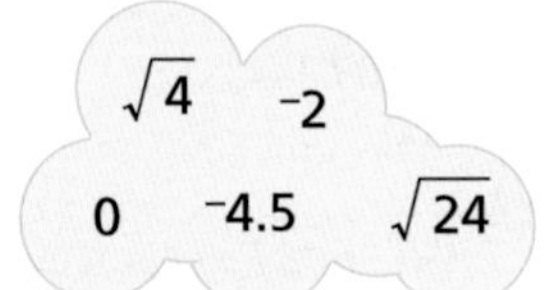

(b) Which are in the set of values of n given by $^{-}3 \leq n \leq 2$?

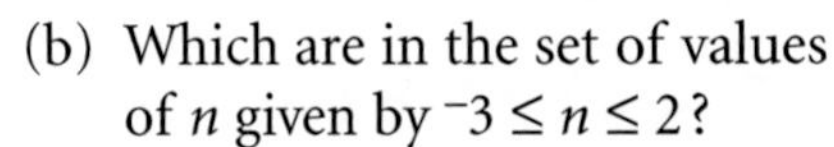

B3 Write inequalities for each of the following diagrams.

(a)

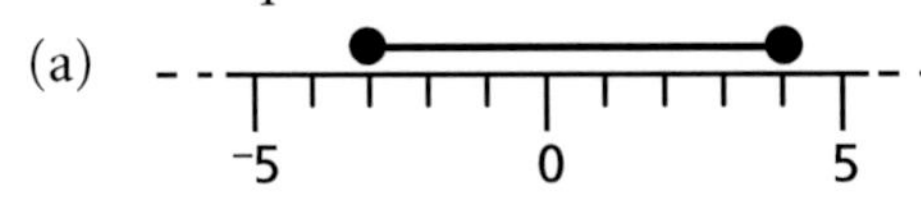

(b)

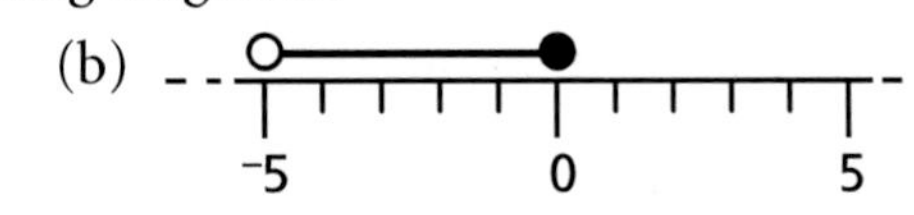

(c)

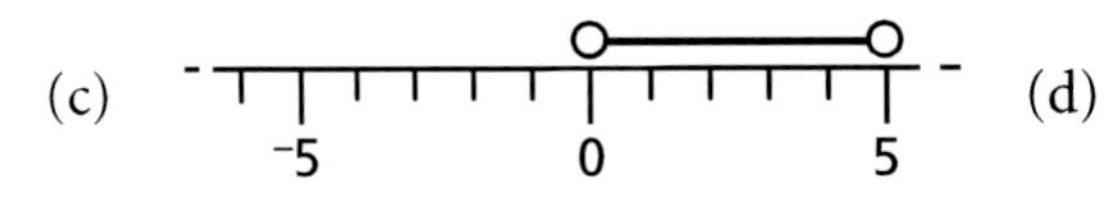

(d)

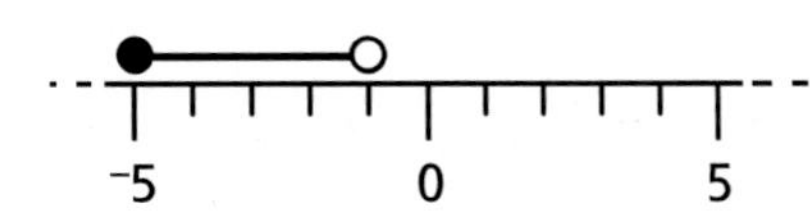

B4 We say that the values of x that make an inequality true **satisfy** the inequality.
Which of these values of x satisfy $^{-}2 < x < 3$?

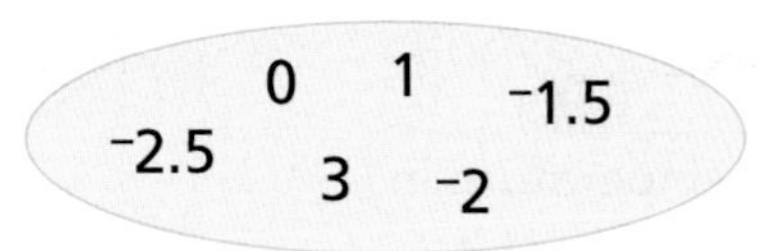

B5 Write down four whole numbers that satisfy the inequality $0 \leq x \leq 3$.

B6 List five different values of n that satisfy $^{-}1 \leq n < 2$.

B7 Find two prime numbers p so that $20 < p < 30$.

B8 m is a multiple of 3.
Find three values of m so that $10 \leq m \leq 20$.

B9 Calculate the value of a^2 when $a = 3$.
Does this value of a satisfy the inequality $a^2 > 8$?

B10 Calculate the value of x^2 when $x = {}^{-}5$.
Does this value of x satisfy the inequality $x^2 \leq 20$?

B11 Which of the numbers n, below, satisfy $n^2 < 100$?

20 10.5 9 $^{-}7$ $^{-}11$ 10 0

B12 **Integers** are positive and negative whole numbers, including zero.
Find all the integers, n, so that $n^2 < 20$.
(There are nine of these integers altogether.)

B13 Find two integers x so that $10 < x^2 < 17$.

B14 List three whole numbers n that satisfy $4 \leq 2n \leq 12$.

B15 List three different integers p so that $9 \leq 2p \leq 23$.

*B16 List all the values of n, where n is an integer, such that $4 \leq n + 5 < 7$.

C *In words and symbols*

TG

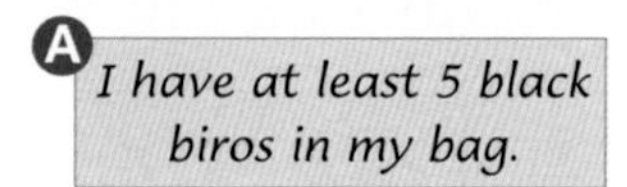

B *There are at most 5 people with black hair in the room.*

C *I'm sure I did not even get 5 marks in my biology test.*

D *Jane has more than five budgerigars.*

$b < 5$ $\quad$ $b \le 5$ $\quad$ $b \ge 5$ $\quad$ $b > 5$

C1 Write each of these as a mathematical statement.
For each one, use t to stand for the temperature in °C.

(a)

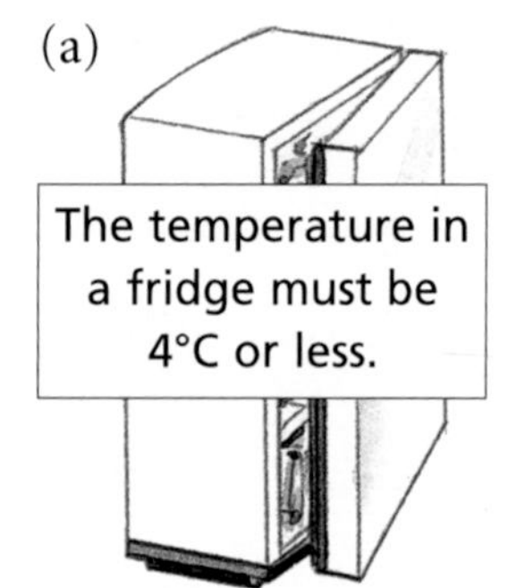

(b)

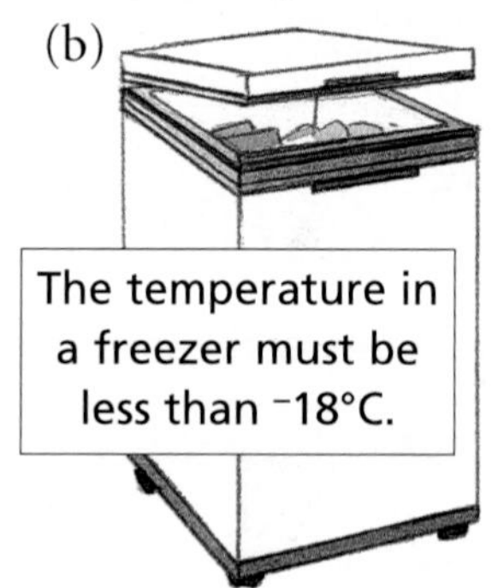

(c)

The temperature in this fish tank must not fall below 24°C.

C2 Translate this statement into mathematics.
Use w to stand for the weight of hand baggage in kg.

IMPORTANT NOTICE
Hand baggage must not weigh more than 7 kilos.

C3 Write each of the following statements using mathematical symbols.

(a)

(Use n for the number of pupils.)

(b)

New Stadium holds at most 35000!

"Scandal" says Jo Bloggs, Mayor of Bigsville, speaking at this year's bingo binge bash.

(Use s for the number of people the stadium holds.)

C4 Make up a sentence for each of these. Say what the letters stand for.

(a) $n \le 35$ $\quad$ (b) $p > 100$ $\quad$ (c) $m < 20$

Test yourself

T1 State whether each of the following is true or false.

(a) $9 \geq 10$ (b) $9 \leq 9$ (c) $(^-3)^2 < 2$ (d) $0.29 \leq 0.3$ (e) $^-2 > ^-6$

T2 Write down an inequality for each of these diagrams.

(a) (b)

(c) (d)

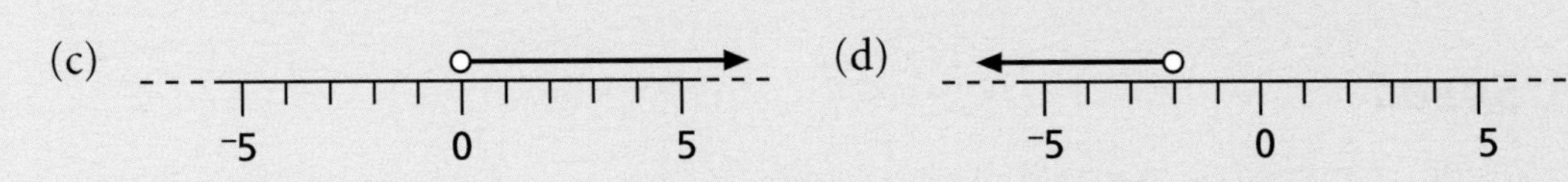
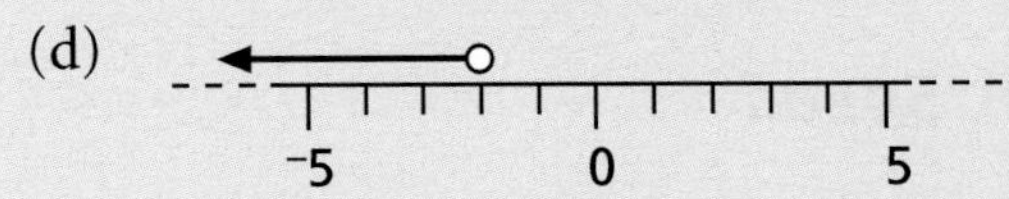

T3 Sketch a number line for each of these inequalities.

(a) $n \geq ^-1$ (b) $4 \geq x$ (c) $^-3 \leq m < 1$ (d) $1 < g < 2$

T4 Write down an inequality for each of these diagrams.

(a) (b)

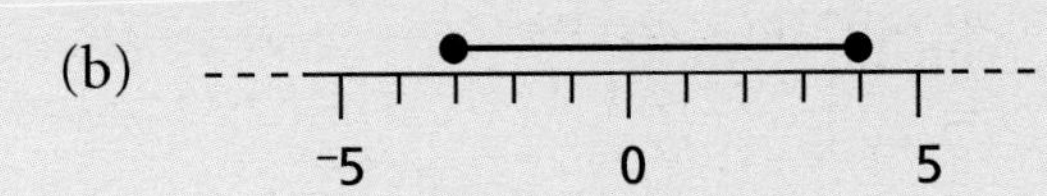

(c) (d)

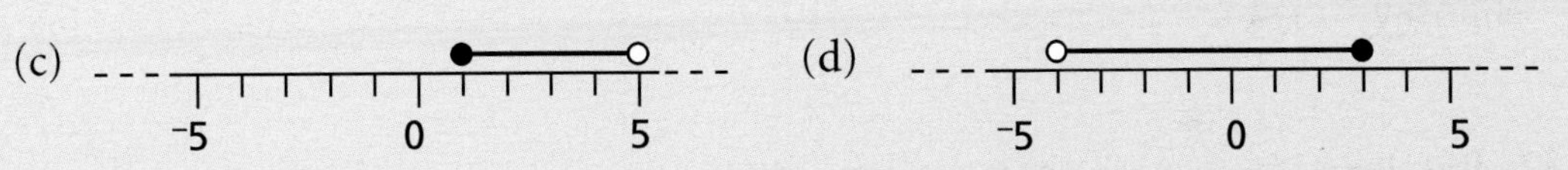
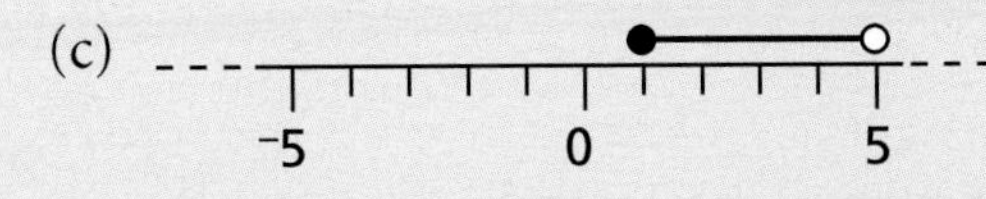

T5 List the values of x, where x is a whole number and $1 < x < 6$.

T6 n is an integer.
Write down the values of n that satisfy the inequality $^-2 < n \leq 3$. Edexcel

T7 List the values of n, where n is an integer, such that $3 \leq 3n < 18$. AQA 2003

T8 Write down five integers, n, for which $n^2 < 10$.

T9 Write down all the integers that satisfy the inequality $4 < n^2 < 25$.

T10 Write each of these as a mathematical statement using symbols.

(a) Maximum number of passengers 25. (Use p for the number of passengers.)

(b) Cost now exceeds £20 000 000. (Use c for the cost in £.)

(c) Win £50 000 or more! (Use x for the amount you can win in £.)

(d) New bike weighs less than 5 kg. (Use w for the weight of the bike in kg.)

32 Speed, distance, time

Before you start, you need to be able to do problems like
'If you need 120 g of flour to make 4 buns, how much do you need to make 15 buns?'

This work will help you

- calculate speeds, distances and times
- read and draw travel graphs

A Speed

24 cm in 4 minutes

Blitz

35 cm in 7 minutes

Which snail is fastest?
Which is slowest?

33 cm in 5 minutes

39 cm in 6 minutes

A1 A cyclist going at a constant speed travels 48 metres in 6 seconds.
Calculate her speed in metres per second (m/s).

A2 Four pigeons are released together.
These are the distances they fly and the times taken.

Pigeon	A	B	C	D
Distance flown (km)	100	90	174	144
Time taken (hours)	4	3	6	3

Calculate the average speed of each pigeon in km per hour (km/h).

A3 Calculate the average speed of each of the following.
Write the units as part of your answer (for example, km/h).

(a) A train that goes 140 km in 2 hours

(b) A man who runs 150 m in 15 seconds

(c) An aircraft that takes 3 hours to fly 840 miles

(d) A coach that travels 20 miles in half an hour

Rocket

Worked example

What is the average speed, in m.p.h., of a ship which travels 15 miles in 2.5 hours?

First method

15 miles in 2.5 hours

= 30 miles in 5 hours (doubling)

= 6 miles in 1 hour (dividing by 5)

So speed = **6 m.p.h.**

Second method

$$\text{Speed in m.p.h.} = \frac{\text{Distance in miles}}{\text{Time in hours}}$$

$$= \frac{15}{2.5} = \frac{30}{5} = \mathbf{6\ m.p.h.}$$

A4 Calculate the average speed of each of these, stating the units.

(a) A car that goes 65 miles in 2 hours

(b) A ship that takes 5 hours to sail 75 km

(c) A plane that flies 210 km in $\frac{1}{2}$ hour

(d) A horse that runs 300 m in 20 seconds

A5 A ferry crosses an estuary, which is 18 miles wide, in $1\frac{1}{2}$ hours.
Calculate its average speed.

A6 A plane flying at a constant speed flies 200 miles in $1\frac{1}{4}$ hours.

(a) How far would it fly in $2\frac{1}{2}$ hours?

(b) How far in 5 hours at this speed?

(c) What is the speed of the plane, in m.p.h.?

A7 A coach takes $3\frac{1}{2}$ hours to travel from Hull to Birmingham, a distance of 140 miles.
Calculate the average speed of the coach.

A8 At the start of a journey, the mileometer on Sharmila's car reads 24 752 miles.
At the end of the journey the mileometer reads 24 941 miles.
The journey took $4\frac{1}{2}$ hours.
Calculate the average speed for the journey.

A9 A non-stop flight of 5625 miles takes 12.5 hours.
Calculate the average speed of the aircraft.

*A10 A train leaves London at 08:15 and travels non-stop to York, arriving at 10:00.
The distance from London to York is 189 miles.

(a) Work out the time taken for the journey, in hours.

(b) Calculate the average speed of the train.

B *Travel graphs*

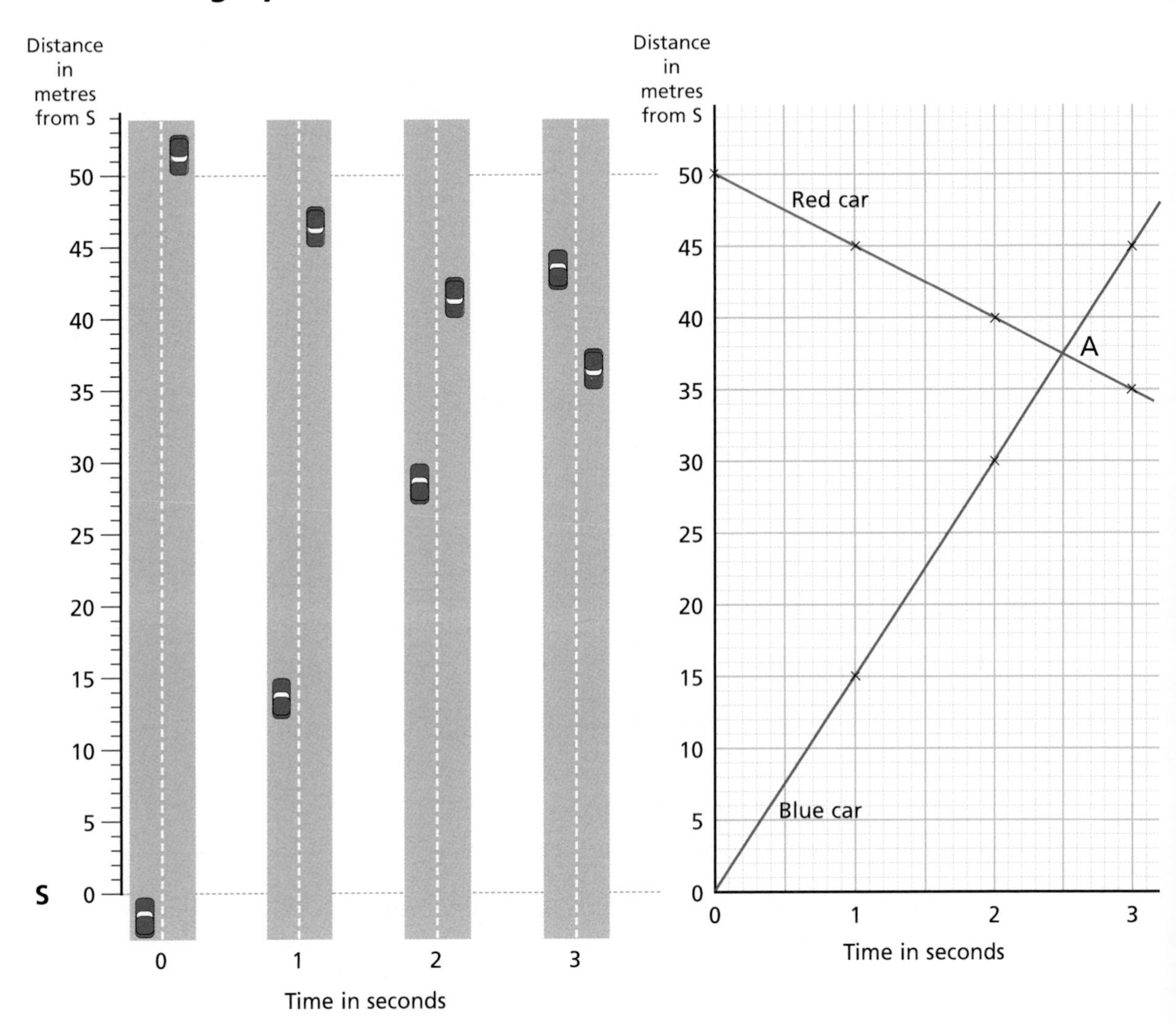

The red car and the blue car are travelling in different directions.

1 What is the speed of the blue car?

2 What is the speed of the red car?

3 What does the point A on the graph show?

4 How far apart are the cars after 1.5 seconds?

5 How far apart are they after 3 seconds?

6 When will the red car reach the point where the blue car was to start with?

B1 Each graph below represents a journey.

Describe each journey fully.

For example, on graph A,

Stage 1: 20 miles in 1 hour = 20 m.p.h.

Stage 2: Stopped for 1 hour

Stage 3:

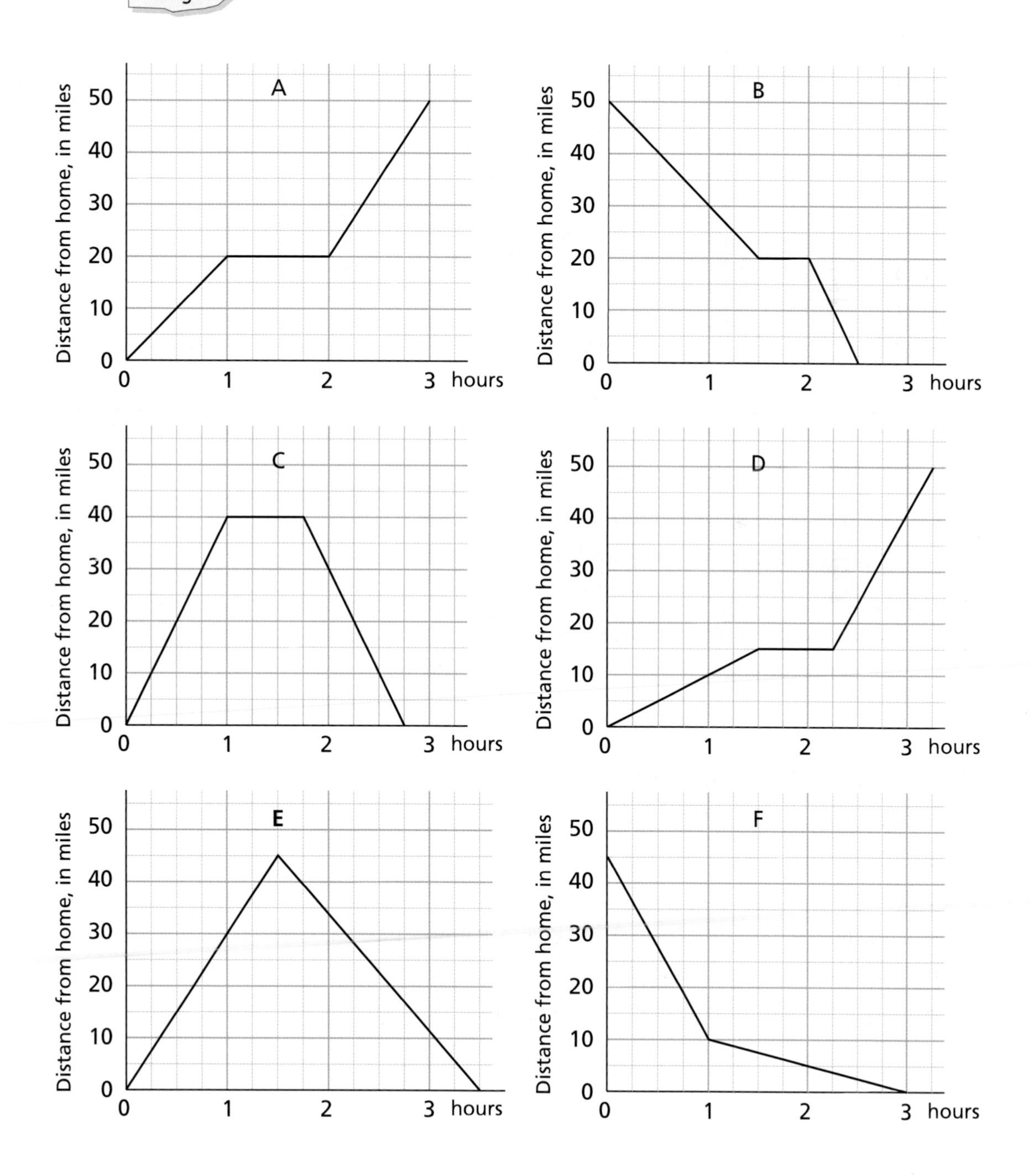

B2 Edward catches a bus from Ashbridge to Benmouth.
Julie does the same journey by car.
This graph shows their journeys.

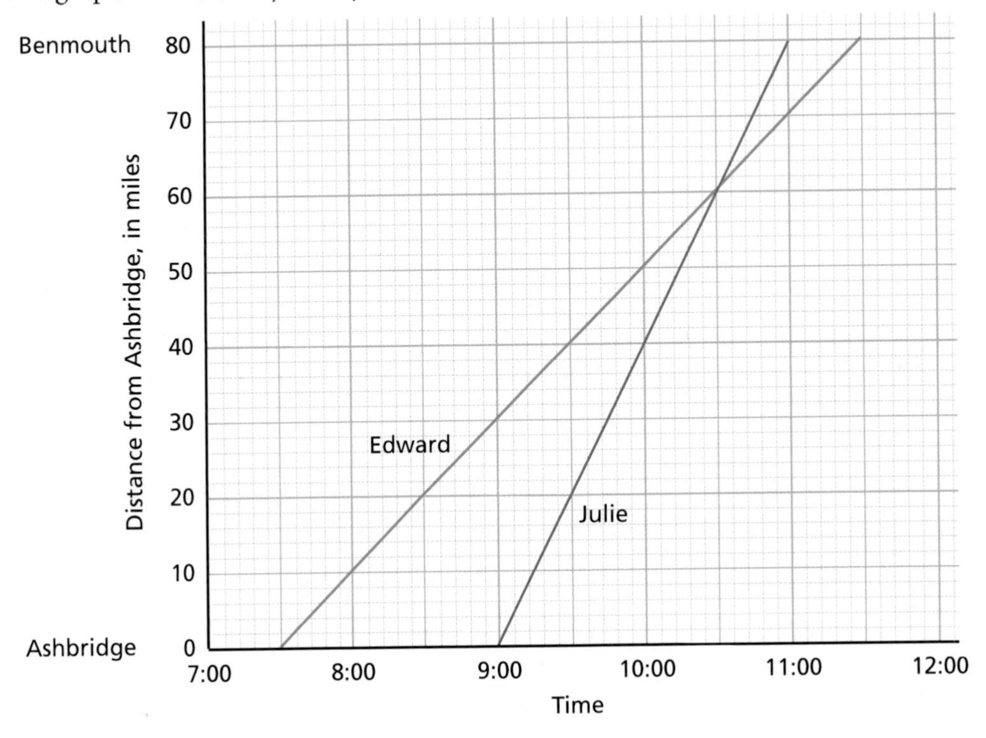

(a) How far is it from Ashbridge to Benmouth?

(b) At what time does Edward leave Ashbridge?

(c) How far apart are Edward and Julie at 9:30?

(d) When does Julie overtake Edward?

(e) What is the speed of (i) the car (ii) the bus

B3 Make a copy of the axes above on graph paper.

(a) Roger leaves Ashbridge at 8:00 and travels to Benmouth at 30 m.p.h.
Draw and label the graph of his journey.

(b) Sally leaves Benmouth at 8:00 and travels to Ashbridge at 20 m.p.h.
Draw and label the graph of her journey.

(c) Roger and Sally pass each other.
How far are they from Ashbridge when they pass?

(d) At what time do they pass?
(First work out how many minutes one small grid square stands for.)

B4

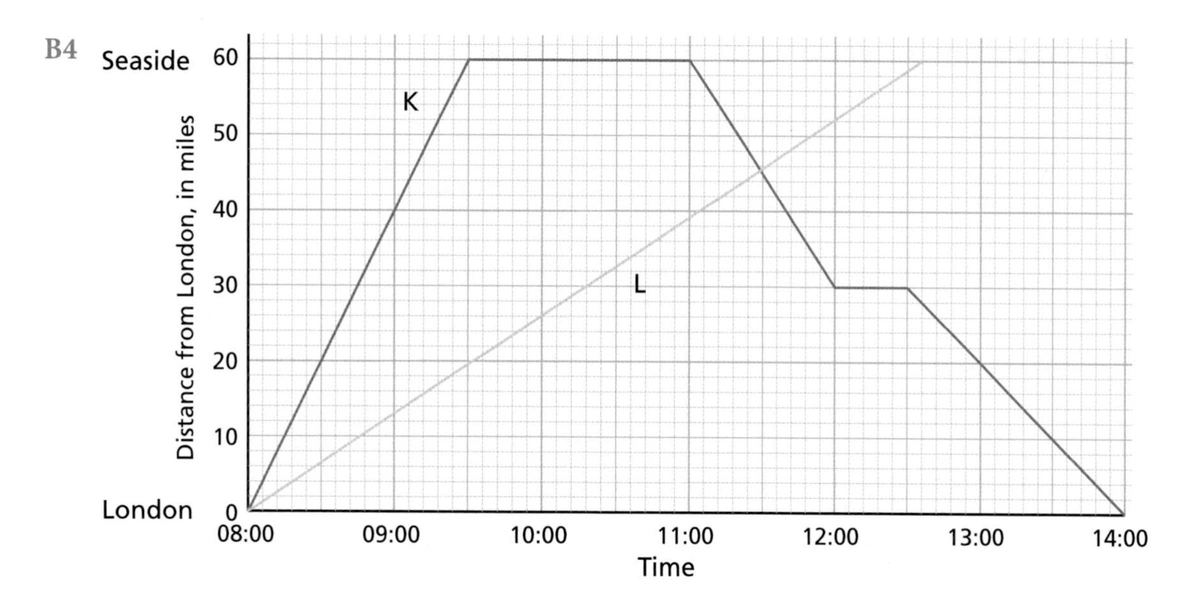

Kylie drives from London to the seaside and back. Graph K shows her journey.

(a) At what time did Kylie leave London?

(b) How long did it take her to reach the seaside?

(c) At what speed did she travel to the seaside?

(d) How long did she spend at the seaside?

(e) On the way home, Kylie stopped for a meal. For how long did she stop?

(f) At what speed was she travelling before she stopped for a meal?

(g) What was her speed for the last part of the journey home?

Kylie's brother Lee drives an old car.
Graph L shows his journey to the seaside.

(h) At what time did Kylie and Lee pass each other?

(i) How far were they from London when this happened?

(j) At what time did Lee get to the seaside?

B5 Make a copy of the axes above on graph paper.

(a) Rajesh leaves London at 8:00 and cycles towards the seaside.
He travels at 10 m.p.h. for 2 hours and stops for an hour's rest.
He decides to return and arrives home at 14:00.
Draw and label the graph of his journey.

(b) Nina leaves the seaside at 11:00 and drives towards London at 40 m.p.h.
Draw and label the graph of her journey.

(c) At what time does Nina pass the place where Rajesh stopped for a rest?

(d) At what time does Nina overtake Rajesh?

C *Calculating distances*

A car travelling at 12 metres per second goes …

$12 \times 1 =$ **12 metres** in 1 second

$12 \times 3 =$ **36 metres** in 3 seconds

Speed in m/s	×	**Time** in seconds	=	**Distance** in metres

C1 Patrick rides his bike at 6 m/s for 15 seconds. How far does he travel?

C2 Henry flies his plane at 240 m.p.h. for 3 hours. How far does he travel?

C3 A slug crawls across a path at a speed of 0.5 cm per second.
How far does it move in

(a) 10 seconds (b) 25 seconds (c) 1 **minute** (d) $2\frac{1}{2}$ minutes

C4 A coach leaves London at 4:00 p.m. and travels at 55 m.p.h.
How far has it travelled at 7:00 p.m.?

C5 A ferry which travels at 12 m.p.h. leaves at 12:30 and arrives at 14:00.
How far does it travel in this time?

C6 A plane flies at 250 m.p.h.
How far does it travel in (a) 4 hours (b) $4\frac{1}{2}$ hours (c) 7 hours

D *Mixing units*

Worked example

A train travels 12 miles in 6 minutes.
Calculate its average speed in m.p.h.

First method

To get from 6 minutes to 60 minutes,
I must multiply by 10.

12 miles in 6 minutes

12 × 10 miles in 60 minutes

120 m.p.h.

Second method

In 6 minutes it goes 12 miles.

So in 1 minute it goes $\frac{12}{6} = 2$ miles.

So in 60 minutes it goes 2 × 60 = 120 miles.

Speed = **120 m.p.h.**

D1 A car travels 8 miles in 15 minutes.
Calculate its average speed in miles per hour.

D2 A boat takes 5 minutes to travel 2 miles. Calculate its speed in m.p.h.

D3 A horse runs at a speed of 10 metres per second.
How far does it run in (a) 1 minute (b) 5 minutes (c) 15 minutes

D4 A jet fighter plane flies at 600 m.p.h.
How far does it travel in (a) 15 minutes (b) 1 minute (c) 30 seconds

D5 Carla drove 3.5 miles in 10 minutes. Work out her average speed in m.p.h.

D6 If your speed is 30 kilometres per hour, how far do you travel in
(a) 20 minutes (b) 5 minutes (c) 40 minutes (d) 45 minutes

E *Hours and minutes on a calculator*

When you use these formulas, …

$$\text{Speed} = \frac{\text{Distance}}{\text{Time}}$$

$$\text{Distance} = \text{Speed} \times \text{Time}$$

… you must be careful about **units**.

Distance	Time	Speed
miles	hours	miles per hour
metres	seconds	metres per second
kilometres	minutes	kilometres per minute

Worked example

A ship travels 37 miles in 1 hour 25 minutes. Calculate its average speed in m.p.h.

First change 25 minutes to **hours** by dividing by 60. $\frac{25}{60} = 0.416\,66...$

So 1 hour 25 minutes = 1.416 66... hours

Average speed = $\frac{\text{Distance}}{\text{Time}} = \frac{37}{1.416\,66...}$ = **26.1 m.p.h.** (to 1 decimal place)

Give answers to these questions to one decimal place.

E1 Calculate the average speed of a cyclist who covers 26 miles in 1 hour 35 minutes.

E2 Find the average speed of a swimmer who takes 2 hours 10 minutes to swim 11 miles.

E3 A long distance walker walks for 1 hour 12 minutes at a constant speed of 5.5 m.p.h.
How far does he walk in this time?

E4 A coach travels a distance of 25 miles in 35 minutes.
Calculate the average speed of the coach in m.p.h., to one decimal place.

E5 Calculate the average speed, in m.p.h., of a cyclist who covers 12 miles in 50 minutes.

E6 A train is travelling at 75 m.p.h. How far does it go in 25 minutes?

F *Calculating times*

Worked example

A canal boat travels at 5 kilometres per hour.
How long does it take to travel 30 kilometres?

First method

Imagine the distance the boat has to travel.

30 km

In each hour it travels 5 km.

1 hour
5 km

So find how many 5s are in 30. $\frac{30}{5}$ = **6 hours**

Second method

First find how long it takes to travel **1 km**.

5 km takes 1 hour.

So 1 km takes $\frac{1}{5}$ hour.

So 30 km takes 30 × $\frac{1}{5}$ = **6 hours**

Notice that time = $\frac{\text{distance}}{\text{speed}}$

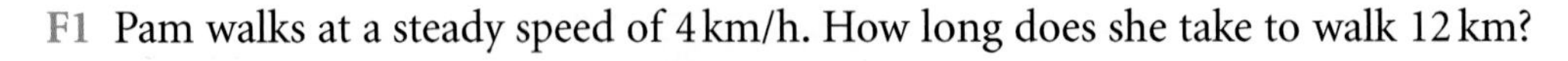

F1 Pam walks at a steady speed of 4 km/h. How long does she take to walk 12 km?

F2 Alvin's speedboat travels at 20 m.p.h. How long does it take to travel 80 miles?

F3 Jim drives at a steady speed of 25 m.p.h. How long does he take to travel 150 miles?

F4 How long does it take to walk 5 miles at a steady speed of 2 m.p.h.?

F5 A boat is 6 miles from the coast and drifting at $1\frac{1}{2}$ m.p.h. towards the coast.
How long will it take the boat to reach the coast?

F6 How long does it take to travel 100 miles at a steady speed of 40 m.p.h.?

Using a calculator

Worked example

A lifeboat travels at 35 kilometres per hour.
How long does it take to reach a ship in danger 48 kilometres away?

Use the formula Time = $\frac{\text{Distance}}{\text{Speed}}$. Time taken = $\frac{48}{35}$ = **1.3714... hours.**

Change the decimal of an hour to minutes by multiplying by 60:
0.3714... x 60 = **22 minutes** (to nearest minute)

So the time taken is **1 hour 22 minutes**.

F7 A train travels at 55 m.p.h.
How long, in hours and minutes, does it take to travel 128 miles?

F8 A motorway coach travels at a steady speed of 85 km/h.
How long, in hours and minutes, does it take to travel 205 km?

F9 The distance between two Channel ports is 42 km.
How long will the journey take

(a) in a ferry travelling at 18 km/h (b) in a hydrofoil travelling at 50 km/h

F10 A plane flies a distance of 254 miles at a speed of 320 m.p.h.
How long, in minutes, does the journey take?
Give your answer to the nearest minute.

G *Mixed questions*

G1 Calculate the missing entries in this table.

Distance	Time	Average speed
50 miles	4 hours	(a)
(b)	3 hours 30 minutes	42 m.p.h.
64 km	(c)	40 km/h
48 km	1 hour 15 minutes	(d)
35 miles	(e)	50 m.p.h.

G2 A lift in a tall office block travels non-stop between the ground floor and the 30th floor, a distance of 92 metres.

The lift travels at 5 metres per second.
How long does the journey take, to the nearest second?

G3 Boris ran 800 metres in 1 minute 45 seconds.
Calculate his average speed in metres per second, to one decimal place.

Test yourself

T1 (a) A train takes 3 hours to travel 150 miles.
What is its average speed?

(b) Another train travels 50 miles at an average speed of 37.5 m.p.h.
How long does the journey take?
Give your answer in hours and minutes. AQA(NEAB) 1998

T2 The travel graph shows the journey of a cyclist from the town of Selby.

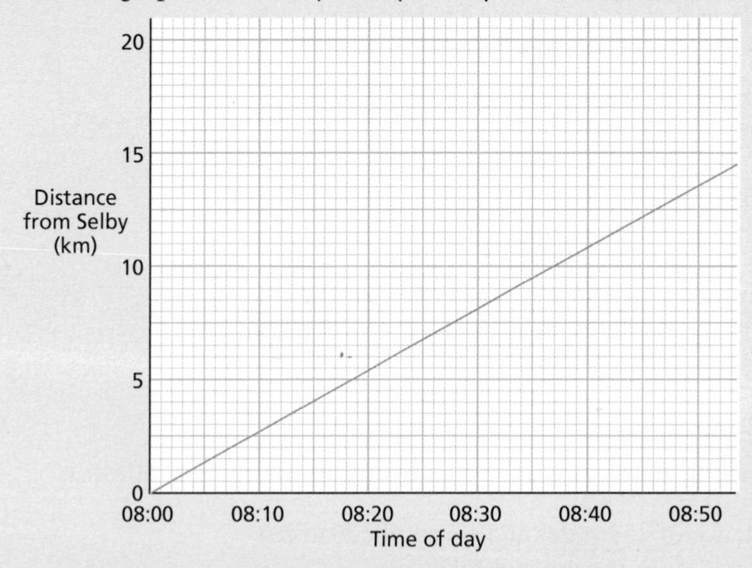

(a) What is the average speed of the cyclist in kilometres per hour?

A motorist is driving towards Selby along the same road as the cyclist. At 08:20 the motorist is 20 km from Selby and travelling at a uniform speed of 60 km/h.

(b) (i) Copy the graph above and draw a second graph on the same axes to show the journey of the motorist to Selby.

(ii) At what time does the motorist pass the cyclist? AQA(SEG) 2000

T3 In the College Games, Michael Jackson won the 200 metres race in a time of 20.32 seconds.
Calculate his average speed in metres per second.
Give your answer correct to 1 decimal place. Edexcel

T4 (a) The train from London to Manchester takes 2 hours 30 minutes.
This train travels at an average speed of 80 miles per hour.
What is the distance from London to Manchester?

(b) The railway company is going to buy some faster trains.
These new trains will have an average speed of 100 miles per hour.
How much time will be saved on the journey from London to Manchester?
AQA(NEAB) 1998

33 *Fractions 3*

You will revise multiplying fractions.

This work will help you

- understand what 'reciprocal' means
- divide by a fraction

A *Multiplying fractions: review*

A1 Copy and complete the statement below each diagram.

(a)

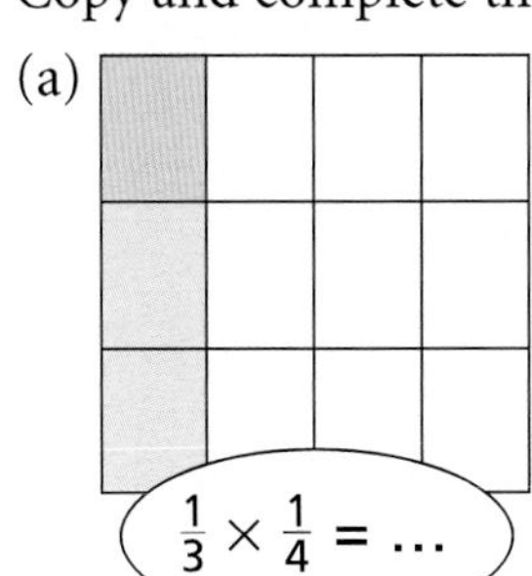

(b)

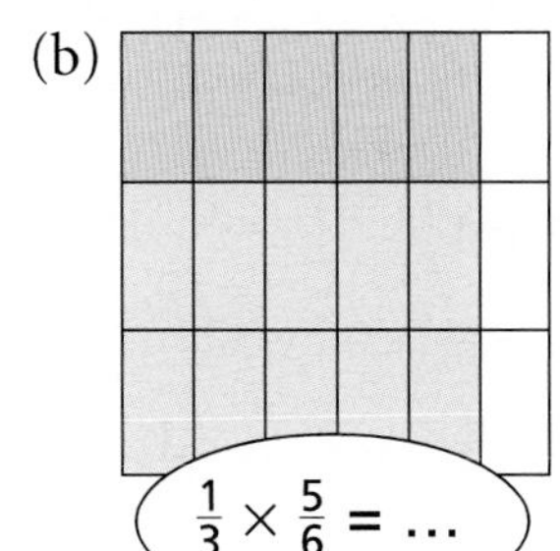

(c)

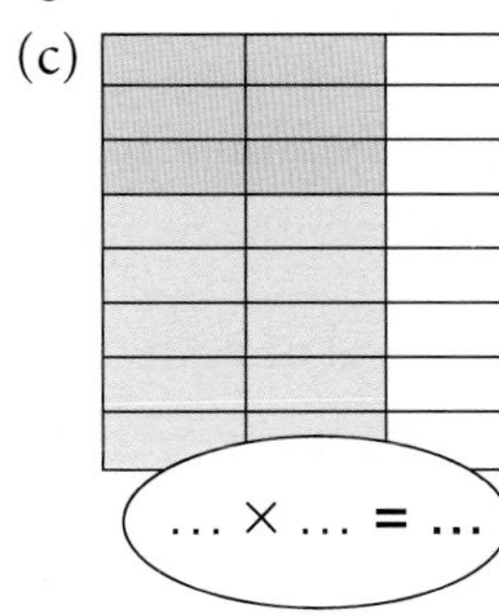

(d)

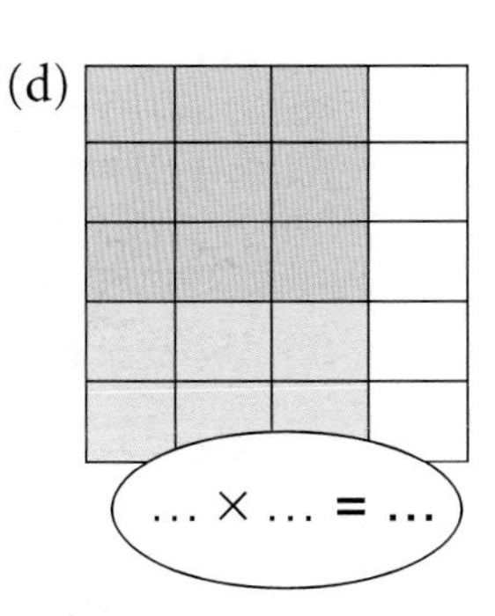

Cancelling common factors – a reminder

Cancel common factors before you multiply.

$$\frac{\overset{1}{\cancel{3}}}{5} \times \frac{1}{\underset{2}{\cancel{6}}} = \frac{1}{10}$$

A2 Work these out.

(a) $\frac{2}{3} \times \frac{3}{4}$ (b) $\frac{4}{5} \times \frac{3}{8}$ (c) $\frac{5}{6} \times \frac{3}{4}$ (d) $\frac{1}{3} \times \frac{4}{5}$ (e) $\frac{4}{5} \times \frac{3}{10}$

Multiplying mixed numbers – a reminder

Change mixed numbers to improper fractions.

$$1\tfrac{1}{4} \times 2\tfrac{2}{3} = \frac{5}{4} \times \frac{8}{3} = \frac{5}{\underset{1}{\cancel{4}}} \times \frac{\overset{2}{\cancel{8}}}{3} = \frac{\mathbf{10}}{\mathbf{3}} = \mathbf{3\tfrac{1}{3}}$$

A3 Work these out.

(a) $1\frac{1}{2} \times \frac{3}{4}$ (b) $\frac{2}{3} \times 1\frac{1}{3}$ (c) $1\frac{1}{2} \times 1\frac{1}{3}$ (d) $\frac{3}{4} \times 2\frac{1}{2}$ (e) $2\frac{1}{2} \times 1\frac{1}{2}$

A4 Work these out.

(a) $2 \times \frac{1}{2}$ (b) $\frac{1}{3} \times 3$ (c) $5 \times \frac{1}{5}$ (d) $\frac{2}{3} \times \frac{3}{2}$ (e) $\frac{3}{4} \times \frac{4}{3}$

B *Reciprocals*

If two numbers multiply to give 1, each is called the **reciprocal** of the other.

$2 \times \frac{1}{2} = 1$	$\frac{3}{4} \times \frac{4}{3} = 1$
$\frac{1}{2}$ is the reciprocal of 2	$\frac{4}{3}$ is the reciprocal of $\frac{3}{4}$
2 is the reciprocal of $\frac{1}{2}$	$\frac{3}{4}$ is the reciprocal of $\frac{4}{3}$

B1 Write down the reciprocal of each of these.

(a) 3 (b) $\frac{1}{3}$ (c) 5 (d) $\frac{2}{5}$ (e) $\frac{5}{6}$

(f) $\frac{1}{8}$ (g) $\frac{5}{7}$ (h) $\frac{5}{4}$ (i) 8 (j) 1

B2 (a) Write $1\frac{1}{2}$ as an improper fraction.

(b) Hence write down the reciprocal of $1\frac{1}{2}$.

B3 What is the reciprocal of each of these?

(a) $3\frac{1}{2}$ (b) $1\frac{1}{3}$ (c) $2\frac{1}{4}$ (d) $1\frac{2}{5}$ (e) $2\frac{2}{3}$

C *Dividing a whole number by a fraction*

$3 \div \frac{1}{4}$

can mean 'how many $\frac{1}{4}$s make 3 whole ones?'

The answer is 12.

Notice that $3 \div \frac{1}{4} = 3 \times 4$

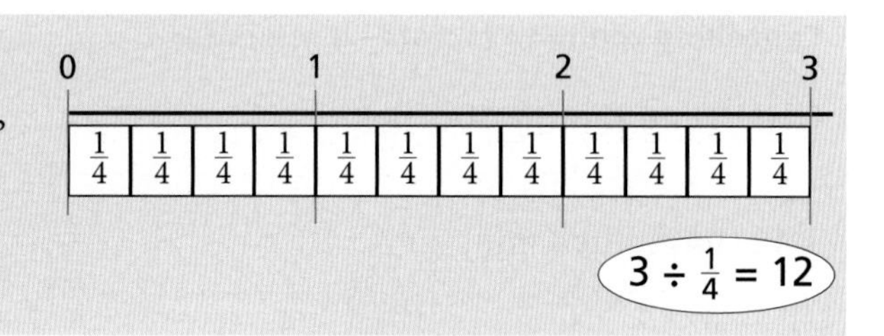

C1 What is $3 \div \frac{1}{3}$?
This diagram may help.

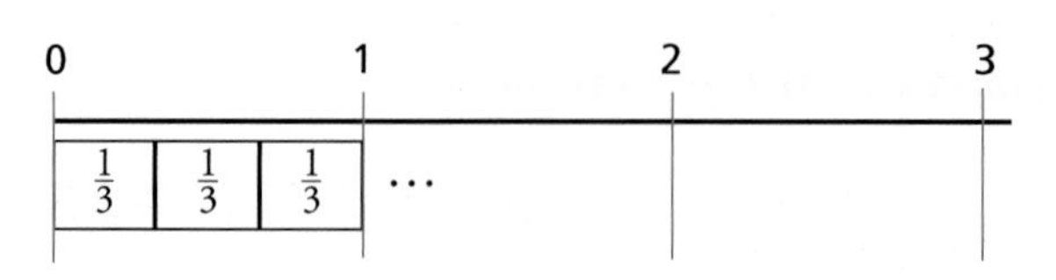

C2 What is $4 \div \frac{1}{6}$?

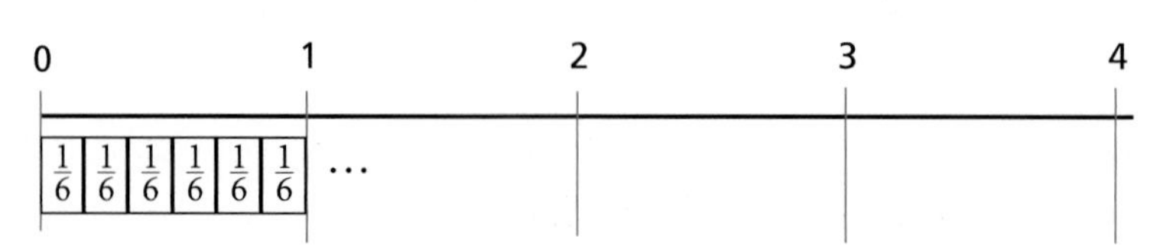

C3 Work these out. Imagine a diagram like those above if it helps.

(a) $4 \div \frac{1}{2}$ (b) $3 \div \frac{1}{5}$ (c) $2 \div \frac{1}{8}$ (d) $5 \div \frac{1}{4}$ (e) $6 \div \frac{1}{3}$

In every case so far, dividing by a fraction is the same as multiplying by its reciprocal.
We shall see if this is true for dividing by, say, $\frac{2}{3}$.

$4 \div \frac{1}{3} = 4 \times 3 = 12$

$4 \div \frac{2}{3} = 6$ (half of 12)

So $\boxed{4 \div \frac{2}{3}}$ is the same as $\boxed{4 \times \frac{3}{2}}$

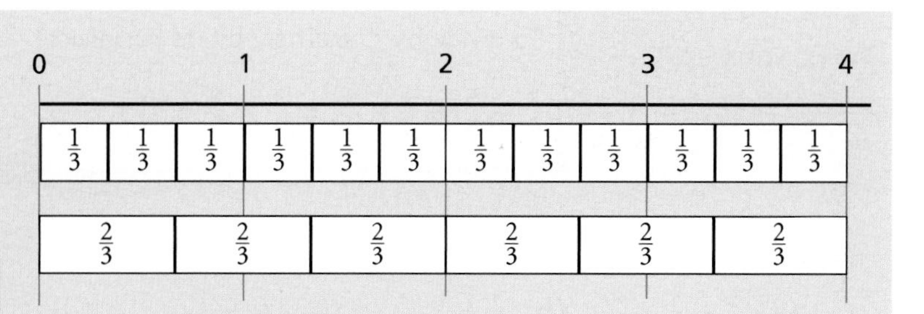

Dividing by a fraction is the same as multiplying by its reciprocal.

C4 (a) Work out $2 \div \frac{1}{5}$. Check from the diagram.
(b) Work out $2 \div \frac{2}{5}$. Check from the diagram.

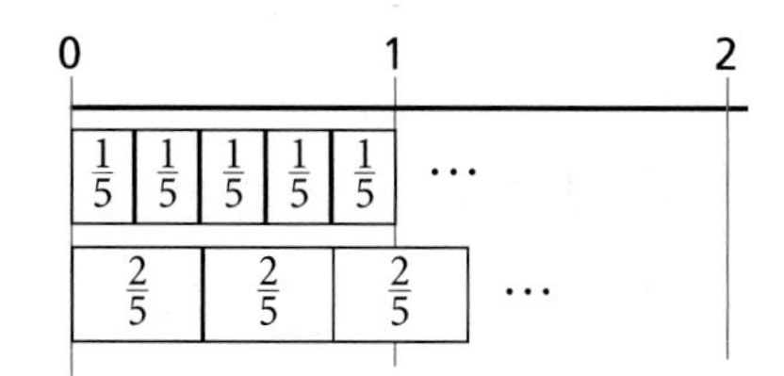

C5 Work these out.

(a) $6 \div \frac{1}{4}$ (b) $6 \div \frac{3}{4}$ (c) $6 \div \frac{1}{3}$ (d) $6 \div \frac{2}{3}$ (e) $4 \div \frac{2}{5}$

C6 Work these out.

(a) $5 \div \frac{2}{3}$ (b) $2 \div \frac{3}{4}$ (c) $4 \div \frac{3}{5}$ (d) $1 \div \frac{3}{4}$ (e) $8 \div \frac{3}{5}$

C7 (a) Ashish's kitten eats $\frac{1}{3}$ of a tin of cat food each day.
Find how many days 8 tins will last the kitten, by dividing 8 by $\frac{1}{3}$.
(b) The kitten's mother eats $\frac{2}{3}$ of a tin each day.
Find how many days 8 tins will last the mother, by dividing 8 by $\frac{2}{3}$.

C8 Max's ox pulls a heavy cart at $\frac{3}{4}$ m.p.h.
How long will it take the cart to travel 6 miles?

C9 Only $\frac{4}{5}$ of the weight of apples is usable for making puddings, because the peel and core are thrown away.
What weight do you need to start with in order to have 20 kg usable?

Here is another way to see why dividing is the same as multiplying by the reciprocal.

to multiply by $\frac{3}{4}$, multiply by 3 and divide by 4 → $\times 3$ → $\div 4$ →

Division is the **inverse** operation, so

to divide by $\frac{3}{4}$, multiply by 4 and divide by 3 ← $\div 3$ ← $\times 4$ ←

D *Dividing a fraction by a fraction*

Worked example

Work out $\frac{3}{4} \div \frac{5}{8}$.

To divide by $\frac{5}{8}$, multiply by its reciprocal, $\frac{8}{5}$.

$\frac{3}{4} \div \frac{5}{8} = \frac{3}{4} \times \frac{8}{5} = \frac{3}{{}_1\not{4}} \times \frac{\not{8}^2}{5} = \frac{6}{5}$

D1 Work these out.

(a) $\frac{5}{6} \div \frac{3}{4}$ (b) $\frac{5}{6} \div \frac{1}{4}$ (c) $\frac{2}{3} \div \frac{3}{4}$ (d) $\frac{1}{2} \div \frac{2}{3}$ (e) $\frac{3}{4} \div \frac{5}{8}$

D2 Work these out.

(a) $\frac{5}{8} \div \frac{3}{4}$ (b) $\frac{1}{6} \div \frac{3}{4}$ (c) $\frac{2}{5} \div \frac{3}{4}$ (d) $\frac{2}{3} \div \frac{3}{5}$ (e) $\frac{3}{8} \div \frac{1}{3}$

E *Substituting into algebraic expressions*

E1 If $a = \frac{1}{2}$ and $b = \frac{1}{3}$, find the value of each of these.

(a) $4a$ (b) $9b$ (c) $3a + 1$ (d) $6b - 2$ (e) $7 - 5a$

(f) ab (g) $6 \div a$ (h) $4 \div b$ (i) $a \div b$ (j) $b \div a$

E2 If $s = \frac{2}{3}$ and $t = \frac{3}{4}$, find the value of each of these.

(a) $6s$ (b) $8t$ (c) $3s - 1$ (d) $6t - 2$ (e) $2 - 2s$

(f) st (g) $1 \div s$ (h) $1 \div t$ (i) $s \div t$ (j) $t \div s$

E3 If $x = \frac{4}{5}$ and $y = \frac{1}{2}$, find the value of each of these.

(a) $x + y$ (b) $x - y$ (c) xy (d) $\frac{x}{y}$ $(= x \div y)$ (e) $\frac{y}{x}$

Test yourself

T1 Write down the reciprocal of each of these.

(a) 4 (b) $\frac{1}{5}$ (c) $\frac{2}{3}$ (d) $\frac{8}{5}$

T2 Work these out.

(a) $3 \div \frac{1}{6}$ (b) $3 \div \frac{5}{6}$ (c) $\frac{2}{3} \div \frac{1}{6}$ (d) $\frac{2}{3} \div \frac{5}{6}$ (e) $\frac{3}{8} \div \frac{2}{5}$

34 Finding probabilities

This work will help you

- estimate probabilities as relative frequencies
- calculate probabilities as fractions using equally likely outcomes
- find all equally likely outcomes by systematically listing or using a grid

A Relative frequency

Going potty

If you hold up a cottage cheese or similar shaped carton at nose height and drop it, it can land in one of three ways.

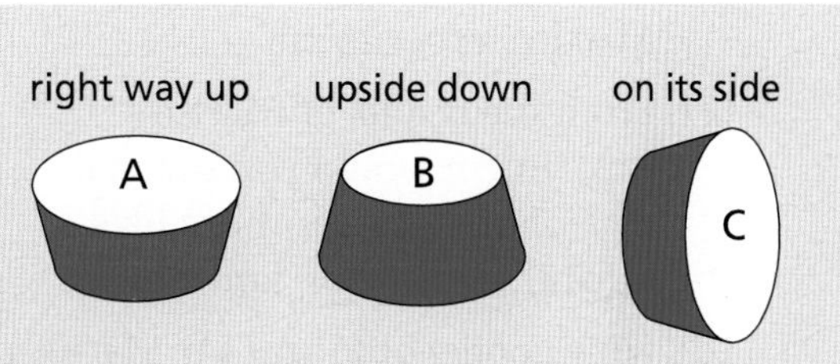

Which way do you think it is most likely to land?

How likely do you think it is to land the right way up?

TG

Trash

In a game show the winning contestant is shown three closed doors.
The host tells the contestant that behind one door is a new car, but behind the other two doors are trash cans.
The host knows where the car is.

The contestant is told to choose one door and they will win the prize behind it.

However, once the contestant has chosen, the host opens one of the **other** doors to reveal a trash can.

He then gives the contestant the choice of sticking with the original door they chose or changing to the other unopened door.

What should the contestant do?

The **relative frequency** of an event happening in a probability experiment is

$$\frac{\text{the number of times the event occurs}}{\text{the total number of trials}}$$

It gives an estimate of the probability of the event happening.

For example, a yoghurt carton was dropped 120 times and it landed on its side 90 times.

The relative frequency of the carton landing on its side $= \frac{90}{120} = 0.75$

So the relative frequency of the carton **not** landing on its side is $1 - 0.75 = 0.25$

A1 Martin carries out an experiment dropping pieces of toast to see if they land 'jam-up' or 'jam-down'.

Here are the results of his experiment.

Total number of trials	*10*	*20*	*30*	*40*	*50*	*60*	*70*	*80*	*90*	*100*
Total number of 'jam-up's	*3*	*8*	*12*	*18*	*23*	*27*	*32*	*36*	*40*	*45*
Relative frequency	$\frac{3}{10} = 0.3$									

(a) Copy and complete the table above for Martin's experiment.

(b) Copy and complete this graph for the relative frequencies in Martin's experiment.

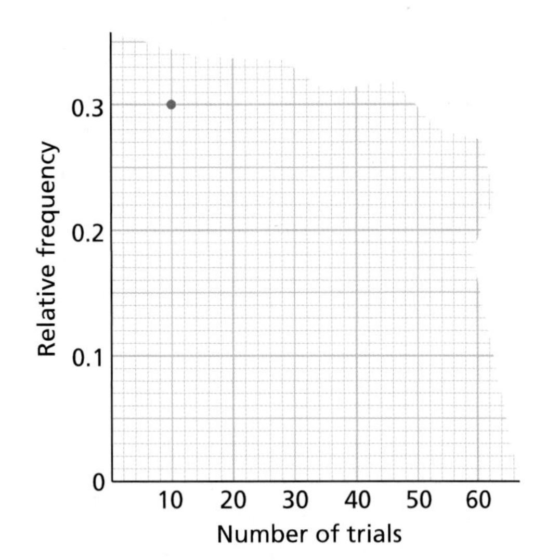

(c) From the results of Martin's experiment would you say that a piece of toast was more likely to land 'jam-up' or 'jam-down'?

(d) How good would you say Martin's estimate of the probability of a piece of toast landing 'jam-up' is after 100 trials?

(e) Estimate the probability of a piece of Martin's toast landing 'jam-down'.

A2 Kay is recording which direction cars go when they reach a road junction near her school. She writes right (R) or left (L) for each car and groups her results in tens.

Here are her results:

R R L R L R R L L L
R R R L L R L R L R
L R L L R R R R R L
L R L R L R R R L R
R L R R R L L R R R

(a) From Kay's results, what is the relative frequency of cars turning right after

(i) 20 results (ii) 40 results (iii) 50 results

(b) If 800 cars a week drive over this junction, roughly how many would you expect to go right?

(c) How reliable do you think Kay's estimate of the probability of going right is?

A3 A cuboctahedron was rolled 400 times.
It landed with a square face on top 340 times.

As a decimal, estimate the probability that it will land with a square face on top.

A4 Steve has a spinner.
He spins it 140 times and it shows red 49 times.

(a) Estimate the probability that it shows red.

(b) What is the probability that it will not show red?

(c) Estimate the number of times it will show red in 200 spins.

A5 Britalite is a company that make light bulbs.
They tested 250 of their bulbs to see how long they lasted.

24 bulbs lasted less that 1000 hours.
208 lasted between 1000 and 2000 hours.
The rest lasted over 2000 hours.

(a) Estimate the probability that a Britalite bulb lasts

(i) less than 1000 hours (ii) over 2000 hours

(b) A company orders 2000 light bulbs.
Estimate how many of them will last 1000 hours or over.

B *Equally likely outcomes*

In working out probabilities it is often necessary to assume that different possibilities or **outcomes** are all equally likely.

The probability of an event happening is $\dfrac{\text{the number of 'successful' outcomes}}{\text{the total number of equally likely outcomes}}$

For example, a bag holds 3 red and 5 black beads and each bead is equally likely to be chosen.

Probability of choosing red = $\frac{3}{8}$

Probability of **not** choosing red = $1 - \frac{3}{8} = \frac{5}{8}$

Be careful about assuming that outcomes are equally likely.
In families we might assume that each child is equally likely to be a boy or girl.
In reality the probability of a child being born a boy is about $\frac{52}{100}$ or 0.52.

B1 In which of these are the possible outcomes equally likely?

A A card from a pack being of a particular suit (clubs, diamonds, hearts, spades)

B The next car to pass your window being of a particular colour (red, black, blue, ...)

C A particular Lottery ball coming up first (1, 2, 3, 4, ..., 49)

D Having a birthday in a particular month, (Jan, Feb, March, ...)

B2 Sharmila takes a cube and writes these numbers on its six faces.

1 1 2 2 2 3

She rolls the cube.
What is the probability, as a fraction, that the number on top is

(a) 1 (b) 2 (c) 3 (d) 4

B3 This fair spinner is spun.

What is the probability that the spinner lands on

(a) yellow (b) red (c) blue

B4 An ordinary dice is rolled.
What is the probability that the number rolled is

(a) a six (b) even (c) odd (d) a multiple of 3

B5 A set of 12 discs have the numbers 1 to 12 marked on them.
One disc is chosen at random.
What is the probability the number on the disc is

(a) a factor of 12 (b) a square number (c) a prime number

B6 A pack of 24 cards have the numbers 1 to 24 marked on them.
The pack is shuffled and one card is chosen from the pack.
What is the probability the number on the card is

(a) even (b) a square number (c) a triangle number
(d) 5 or less (e) a prime number (f) not a prime number

B7 A box contains 3 red buttons, 4 blue buttons and 5 gold buttons.
A button is chosen at random.

(a) How many buttons are in the box?
(b) Find the probability that a button chosen is
 (i) red (ii) gold (ii) not blue

B8 Ben has some coloured cubes in a bag.
The table shows the number of cubes of each colour.

Red	Blue	Yellow	Brown
7	4	8	6

Ben is going to take one cube at random from the bag.
Write down the probability that Ben

(a) will take a yellow cube (b) will **not** take a brown cube

Edexcel

B9 A fair six-sided dice has its faces painted red, white or blue.
The dice is thrown 36 times.
Here are the results.

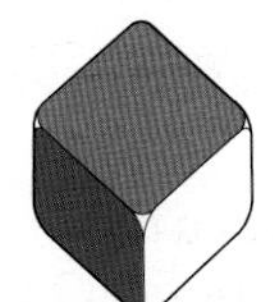

Colour	Frequency
Red	7
White	11
Blue	18

Based on the results, how many faces do you think are painted each colour?

B10 Ken has two spinners, each numbered 1 to 4.
Only one of them is a fair spinner.
These tables show the results of spinning each spinner 80 times.

A

Score	Frequency
1	19
2	22
3	21
4	18

B

Score	Frequency
1	15
2	18
3	15
4	32

Which spinner do you think is fair, spinner A or spinner B?
Explain your decision.

B11 The diagram shows some cakes.

(a) Copy and complete the table to show the number of cakes in each category.

	Pink	White
Cherry		
No cherry		

(b) One of the cakes in the diagram is chosen at random.
Write down the probability that the cake will have

(i) white icing and a cherry (ii) a cherry (ii) pink icing

(c) If all the cakes with pink icing are put in a box and one is chosen at random, what is the probability that it has a cherry?

B12 This table shows information about a group of children.

	Boys	Girls
Blue eyes	3	6
Brown eyes	12	9

(a) How many children are in the group altogether?

(b) If a child is chosen from the group at random what is the probability of that child

(i) having blue eyes (ii) being a boy?

(c) If a boy is chosen from the group what is the probability that he has blue eyes?

C *Listing outcomes*

In many situations, a **list** of equally likely possible outcomes is helpful.

Example

A coin is flipped and an ordinary dice rolled.
What is the probability of getting a head and a number greater than 4?

The outcomes can be listed:

H1	H2	H3	H4	(H5)	(H6)
T1	T2	T3	T4	T5	T6

There are 12 equally likely outcomes altogether.
Two of these outcomes give a head and a number greater than 4 (ringed).
So the probability of flipping a head and rolling a number greater than 4 $= \frac{2}{12} = \frac{1}{6}$.

C1 If a coin is flipped and an ordinary dice is rolled, what is the probability of getting

(a) a tail and a number less than 5

(b) a head and an even number

(c) a tail and a number other than 1

(d) a head and an even number or a tail and an odd number

C2 (a) Copy and complete this table to list all the outcomes when three different coins are flipped.

Coin 1	Coin 2	Coin 3
H	H	H

(b) How many outcomes are there altogether?

(c) What is the probability of all 3 coins showing a head?

(d) What is the probability of all 3 coins showing the same face?

(e) What is the probability of 2 or more coins showing a tail?

(f) What is the probability that there are more heads than tails showing?

C3 Tim writes the 3 letters of his name on pieces of card.
He turns the cards over and shuffles them.
He then turns them face up in a row.

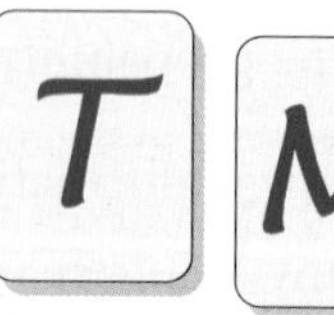

(a) List all the possible outcomes.

(b) What is the probability the cards spell his name?

C4 Kate writes the letters E, A and P on pieces of card.
She turns the cards over and shuffles them.
She then turns them face up in a row.
What is the probability the cards spell a word?

C5 A and B are two fair spinners.

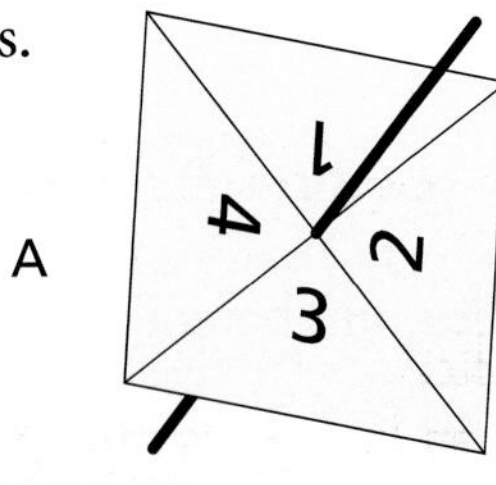

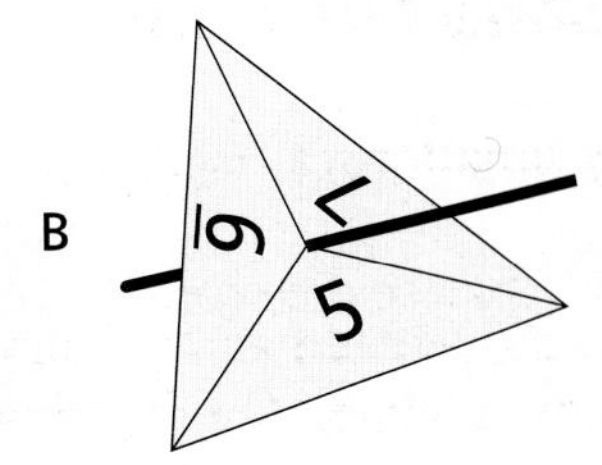

Jane spins the two spinners together at once.

(a) Copy the table below and show all the possible results and the total scores.

Spinner A	Spinner B	Total score

(b) Use your table to find the probability that Jane will get a total score of 7.

Tom spins the two spinners together 60 times.

(c) Work out the number of times you would expect Tom to get a total score of 7.

Edexcel

C6 Credit cards often have a PIN (Personal Identification Number) for security. These usually consist of 4-digit numbers.

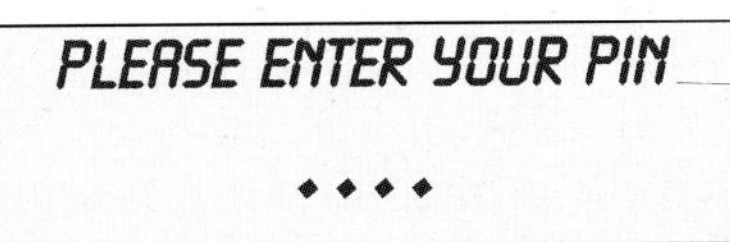

(a) Sarah knows that her PIN uses 1, 9, 6, 7 but cannot remember the correct order. Copy and complete this list of the possible PINs that she might have.

1679 6179 7169
1697 6197
1769

(b) If Sarah tries to guess her number by using the numbers 1, 9, 6, 7 at random, what is the probability she guesses right first time?

(c) Elizabeth cannot remember her number either, but she knows it contains the digits 8, 3, 5, 5.

If Elizabeth tries to guess her number by putting in the digits 8, 3, 5, 5 in a random order, what is the probability she will be right?

D *Using grids*

TG

Chinese dice

A set of Chinese dice consists of three dice numbered:

(A) 6 6 2 2 2 2 (B) 5 5 5 5 1 1 (C) 4 4 4 3 3 3

Two players play with one of these dice each.
Both players roll their dice and the highest score wins.

Which dice will give you the best chance of winning?

Grids can be a useful way of showing all the outcomes in probability situations.

For the Chinese dice all the possible outcomes can be shown in a grid.
For dice A playing dice B the grid would look like this.

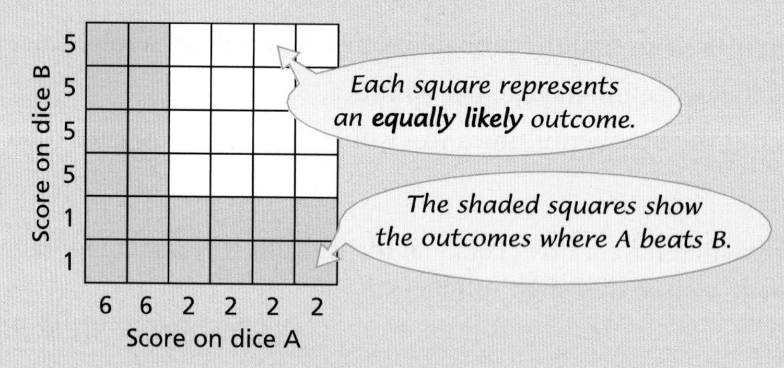

This shows that the probability of A beating B is $\frac{20}{36} = \frac{5}{9}$
The probability of B beating A $= 1 - \frac{5}{9} = \frac{4}{9}$

- Draw grids and work out the probabilities for dice B playing C and dice C playing A.

D1 A game is played with two hexagonal prisms.
Each prism has 1 star, 2 apples and 3 bananas on the faces.
The prisms are rolled and the outcome is
what the two faces on top are showing.

(a) Use a grid to show all the outcomes of rolling the two prisms.

(b) Use your grid to help you calculate the probability of

(i) both top faces showing a star

(ii) only one of the top faces showing a star

(iii) both top faces showing the same symbol

(iv) both faces showing a piece of fruit

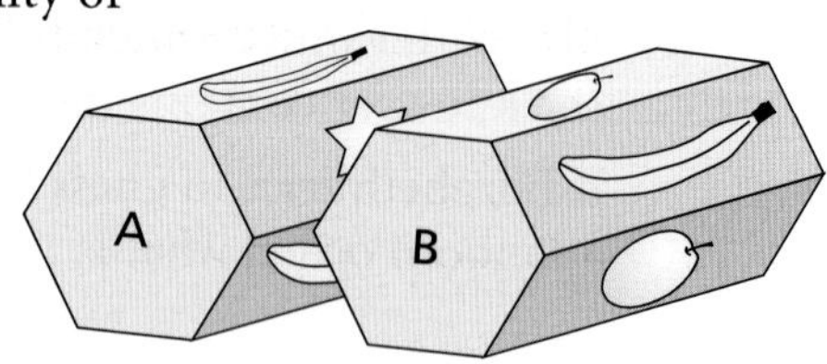

D2 A bag contains five discs that are numbered 1, 2, 3, 4 and 5.

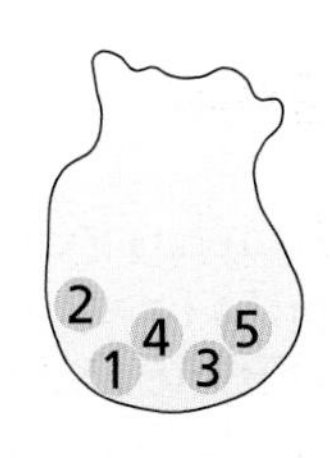

Rachel takes a disc at random from the bag.
She notes the number and puts the disc back.

She shakes the bag and picks again.
She adds this number to the first number.

(a) Copy and complete the table to show all the possible totals.

First number (columns); Second number (rows)

+	1	2	3	4	5
1	**2**				
2					
3				**7**	
4					
5					

(b) Find the probability that Rachel's total is

(i) 10 (ii) 1 (iii) 3 or 4

OCR 2000

D3 Jenny has two ordinary dice, one red and one blue.
She rolls them and finds the **difference** between the two scores.

(a) Copy and complete the grid, to show all the possible outcomes of the two rolls of the dice.

(b) What is the probability that the difference between the two dice scores is

(i) 3 (ii) less than 3 (iii) 2 or more

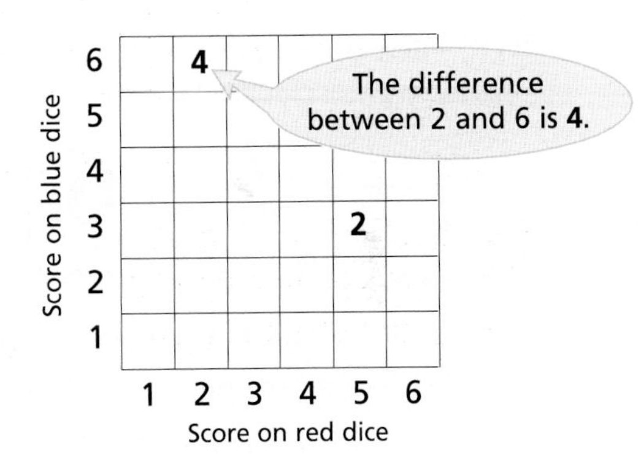

D4 Karl has two fair spinners, numbered as shown.

He spins them and finds the **product** of the two scores.

(a) Copy and complete the grid, to show all possible outcomes of the two spins.

(b) What is the probability that the product is

(i) 12 (ii) greater than 10 (iii) a multiple of 3

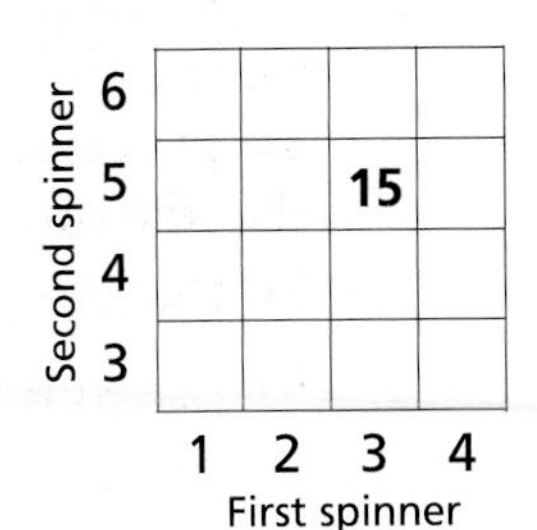

Test yourself

T1 (a) Graham has 9 cards numbered 1, 2, 3, 4, 5, 6, 7, 8, 9.
He picks one at random.
What is the probability that he picks

(i) 5 (ii) 10 (iii) a multiple of 4

(b) Kira has 3 cards, numbered 1, 2, 3.
She shuffles them, then turns them over one by one.

(i) List the different orders in which the three cards can appear.

(ii) What is the probability that the three cards do **not** appear in the order 1, 2, 3?

T2 Lyra made a spinner with three colours, yellow, blue and red.
She tested it by spinning it 500 times.
Her results were:

yellow	234
blue	167
red	99

(a) Estimate the probability of the spinner landing on yellow.

(b) She then spun the spinner 100 times.
About how many times would you expect the spinner to land on yellow?

T3 These are two sets of cards.

SET P 3 6 8 SET Q 2 4 7

A card is taken at random from set P and another from set Q.

(a) List all the possible outcomes.

(b) What is the probability of getting two even numbers?

(c) What is the probability of getting two consecutive numbers?

T4 These two fair spinners are used for a game.
The score is the **difference** of the numbers the spinners land on.

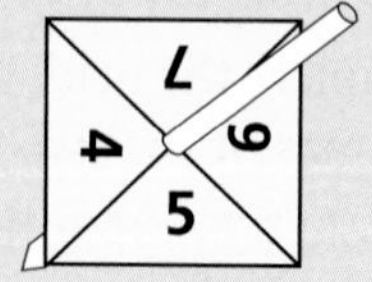

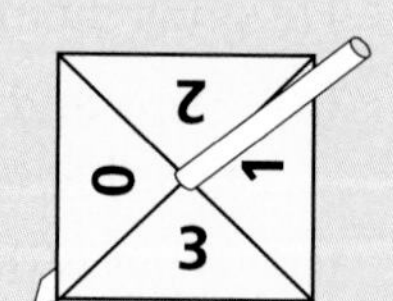

(a) Copy and complete this table to show all the possible scores for the two spinners.

(b) What is the probability of the score being an odd number?

	4	5	6	7
0				
1	3			
2			4	
3				

35 Gradient

This work will help you

- calculate positive and negative gradients
- interpret gradients as rates

A How steep?

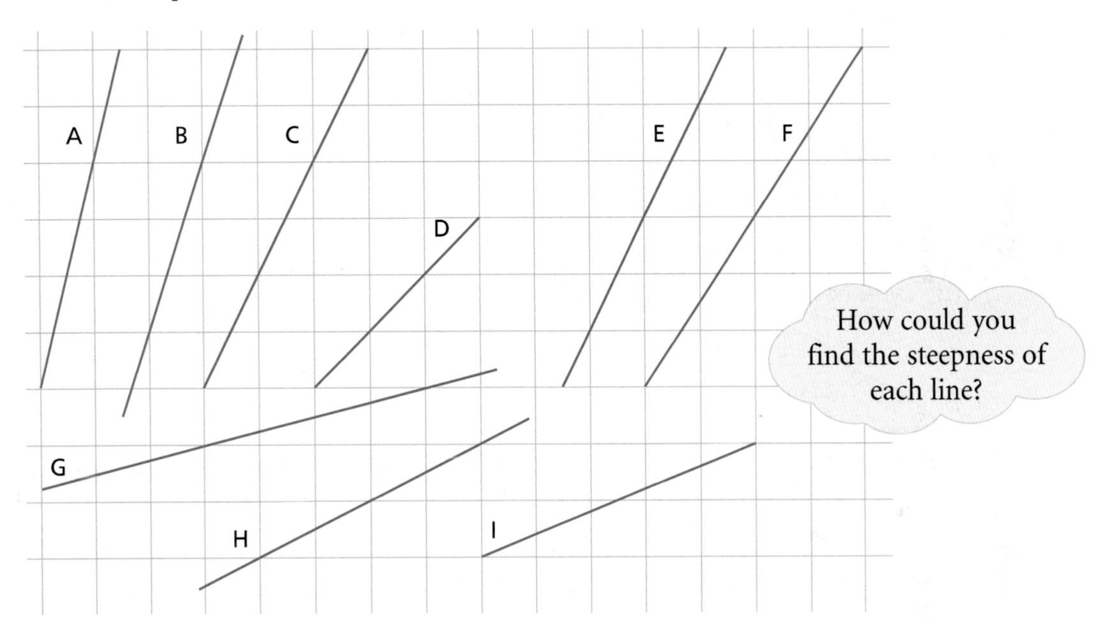

A1 Find the gradient of each line in the diagram below.

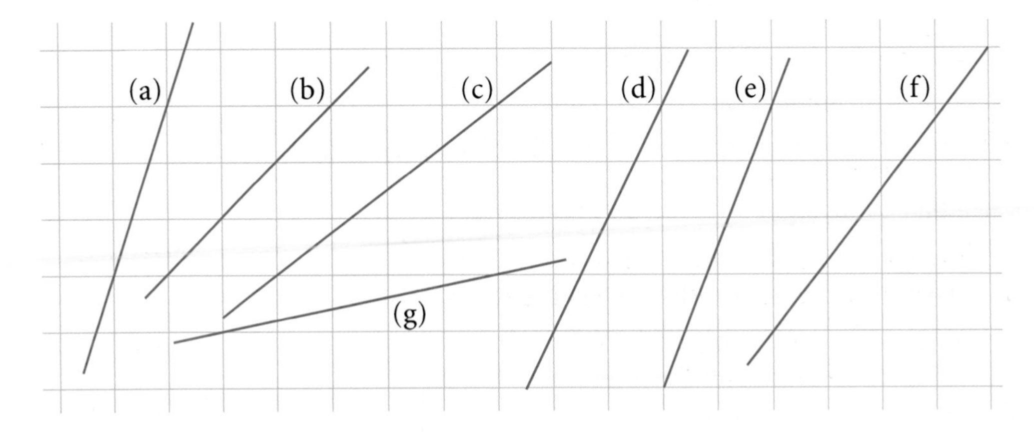

A2 Find the gradient of the line joining the points with coordinates (1, 1) and (6, 4).

A3 A county council uses the rule that the gradient of a wheelchair ramp must not be above 0.083.
Which of these ramps would be suitable for wheelchairs?

These sketches are not to scale.

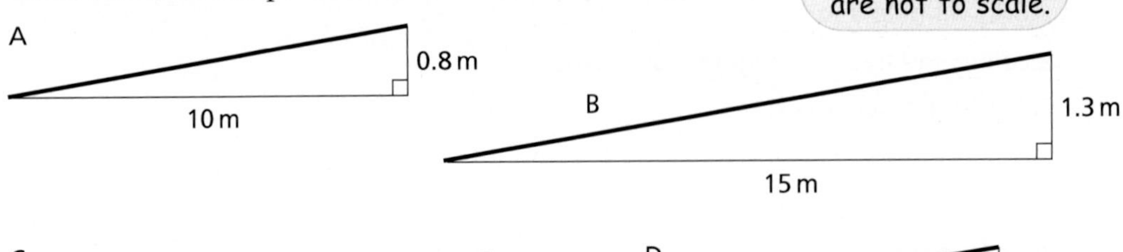

A4 Peter and Vicky are planning some walks.
They draw a sketch for each hill.
The gradient of each dotted line is the average gradient for each hill.

(a) Find the average gradient of each hill, correct to 3 decimal places.

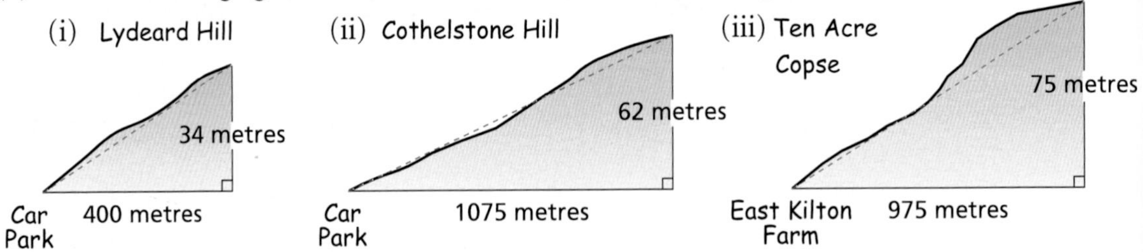

(b) Which hill has the highest average gradient?

A5 Stac Pollaidh is a mountain in Scotland.
The peak is 613 m above sea level.

Stephen and Carol are going to climb it starting at the car park at the foot of the mountain (90 m above sea level).

According to the map, the horizontal distance is 1050 m.

(a) What is the total height of their climb?

(b) What is the average gradient of the climb as a decimal?

A6 Scafell Pike is the highest mountain in England.
It is 977 m above sea level.

Becky and Ian are going to climb it starting at the car park at Wast Water (80 m above sea level).

According to the map, the horizontal distance is 3800 m.

What is the average gradient of the climb as a decimal? OCR

B *Gradient and rates*

Water is added to a container over a period of 8 minutes.
Water flows in at a slow steady rate.

This graph shows the volume of water in the container during these 8 minutes.

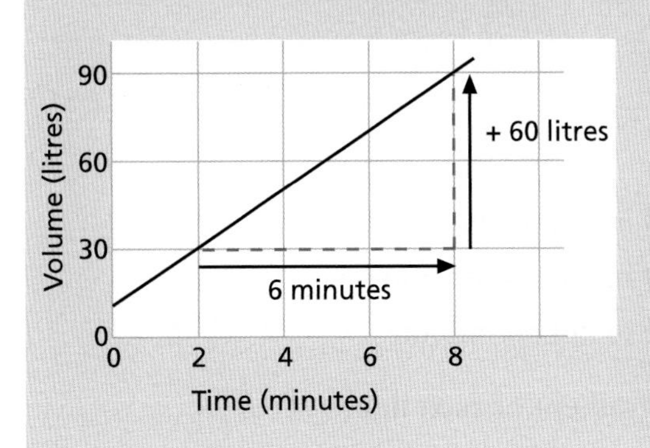

For a horizontal **increase** of 6 minutes there is a vertical **increase** of 60 litres.

The **gradient** is $\frac{60}{6} = 10$

60 **litres** and
6 **minutes** so
10 **litres per minute.**

So the rate of flow of the water is **10 litres per minute.**

B1 What rates of flow are shown by the following graphs?

(a)

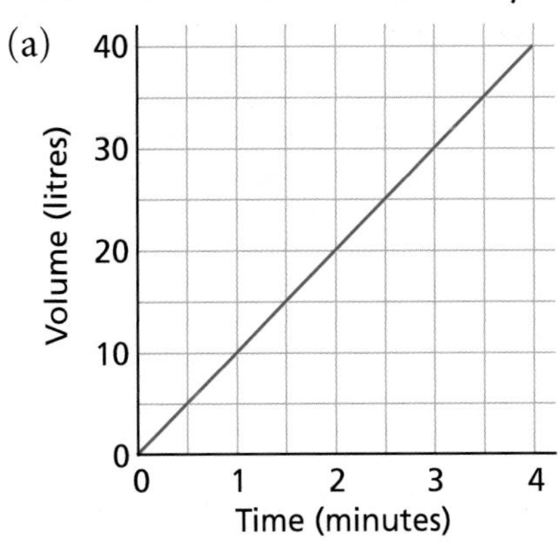

(b)

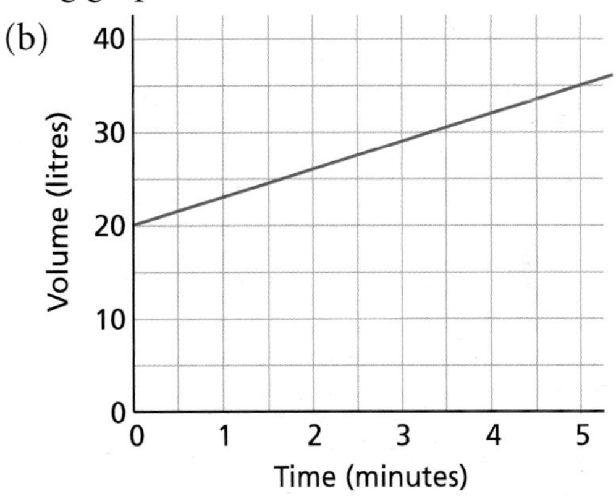

(c)

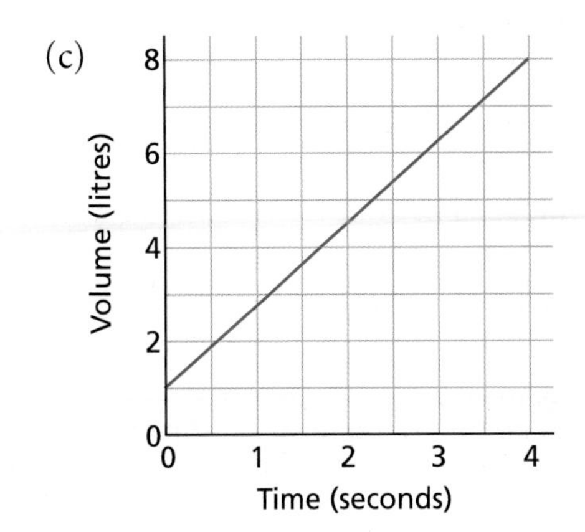

(d)

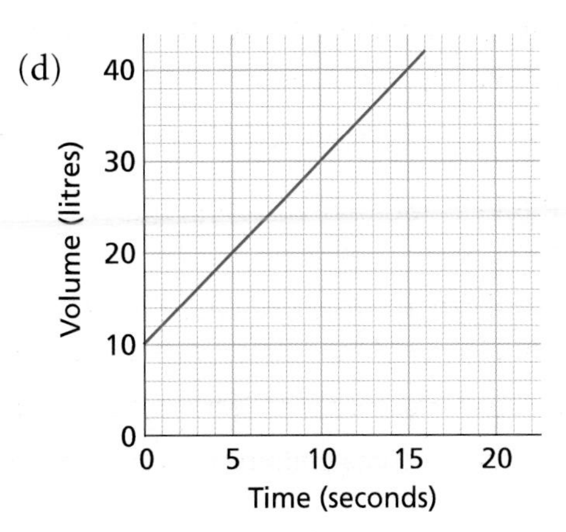

B2 This graph shows the distance Jamie cycled in the first 24 minutes of his journey.

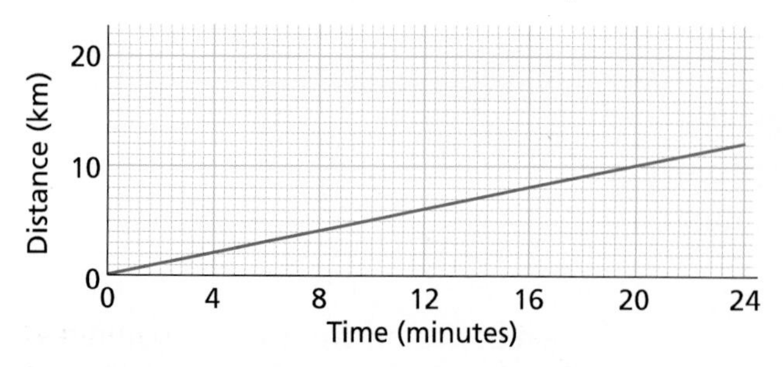

(a) Work out the gradient of this line.

(b) Which of these statements is true?

A The gradient represents the speed in km per hour.

B The gradient represents the speed in metres per minute.

C The gradient represents the speed in km per minute.

B3 (a) For the graphs below, work out the gradient of each line.

(b) What does each gradient represent?

(i) Sue's swimming graph

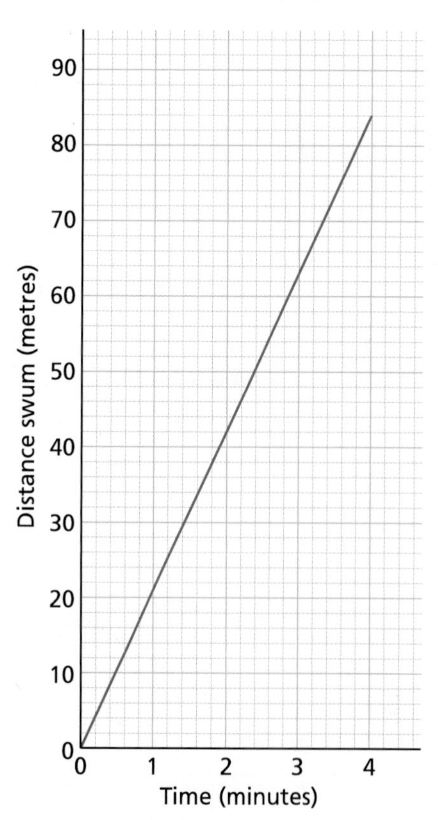

(ii) Mike's cycling graph

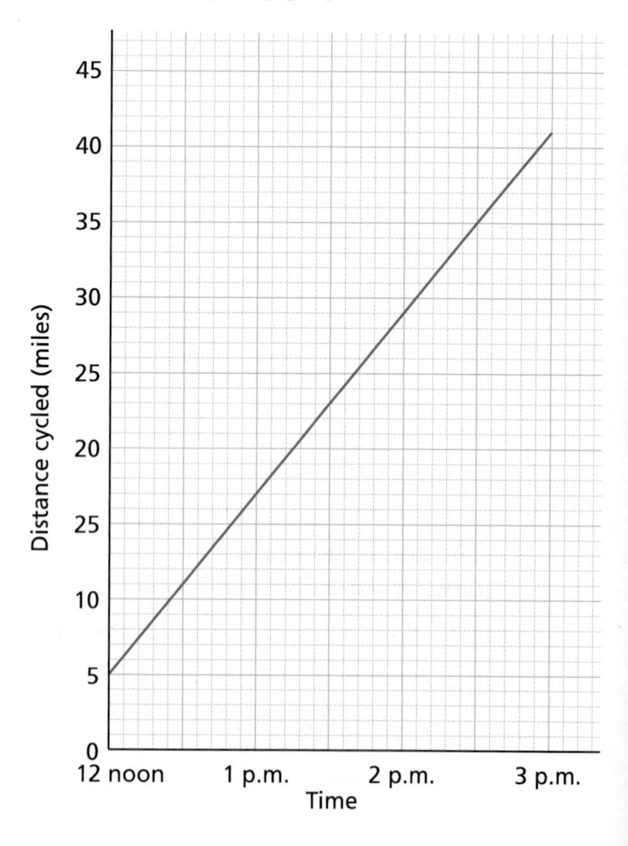

B4 (a) Work out the gradient of each line, correct to 1 d.p.

(b) What does each gradient represent?

(i)

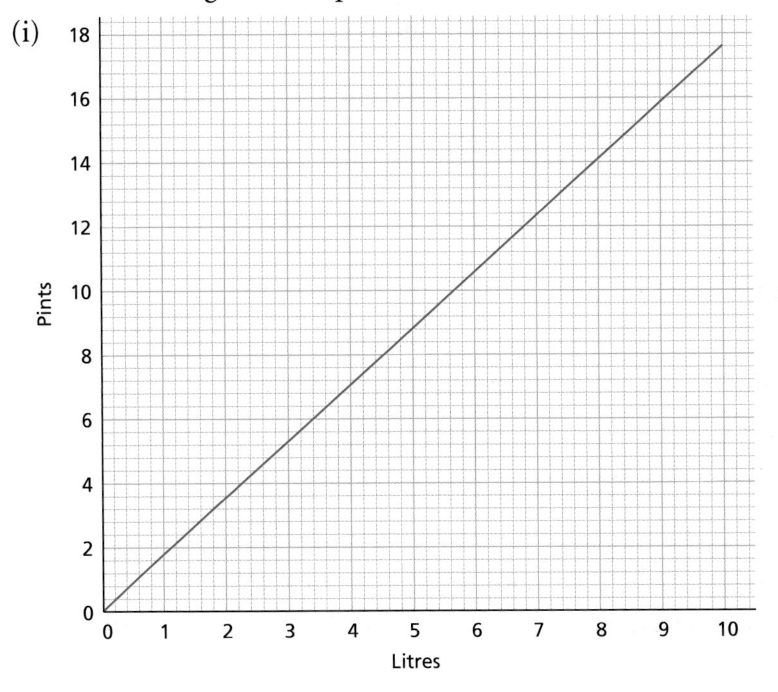

(ii)

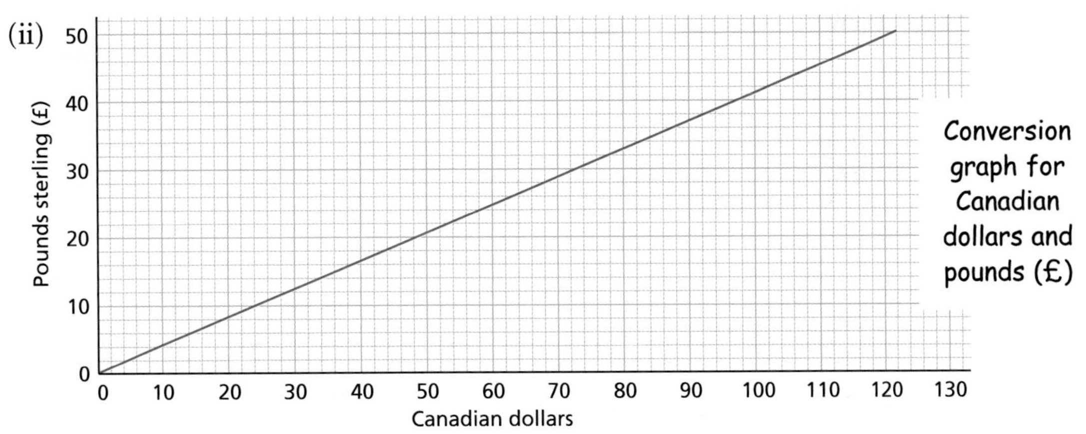

B5 The graph shows the speed of a marble rolling down a slope during a 5 second period.

(a) Work out the gradient of the line.

(b) What does the gradient of the line represent?

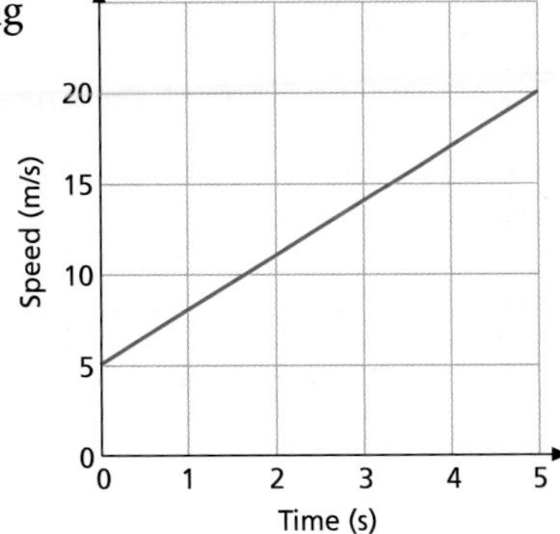

OCR

C *Positive and negative gradients*

The gradient of a straight line is $\dfrac{\text{vertical change}}{\text{horizontal change}}$.

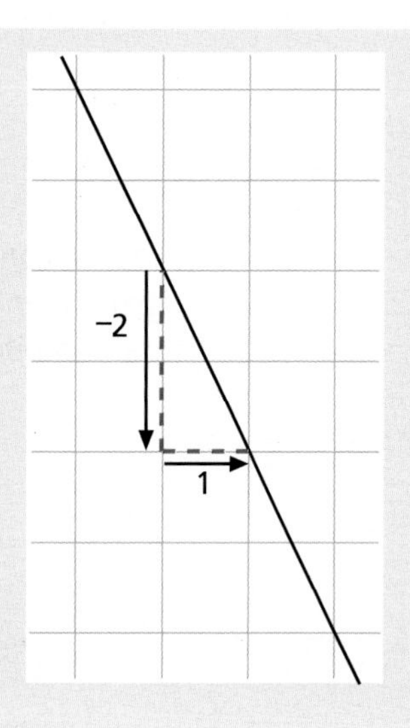

For a horizontal **increase** of 1 there is a vertical **decrease** of 2.

So **gradient** is $\frac{^-2}{1} = {}^-2$.

This sketch shows the volume of water in a tank.

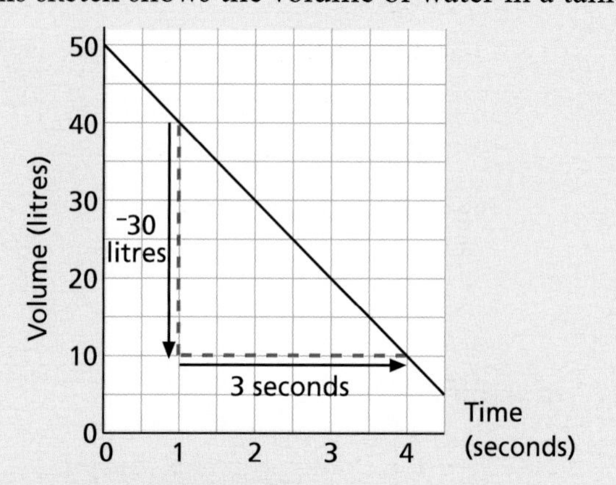

For a horizontal **increase** of 3 seconds there is a vertical **decrease** of 30 litres.

So **gradient** is $\frac{^-30}{3} = {}^-10$.

So the rate of flow is ⁻10 litres per second.

The volume of water is **decreasing**.

C1 Find the gradient of each line in the diagram on the right.

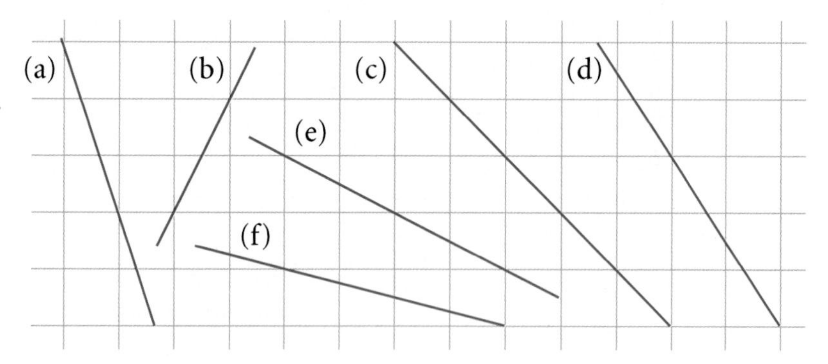

C2 This graph shows the volume of oil in a tank.

(a) Calculate the gradient of the line.

(b) What happens to the oil in the tank during these 5 minutes?

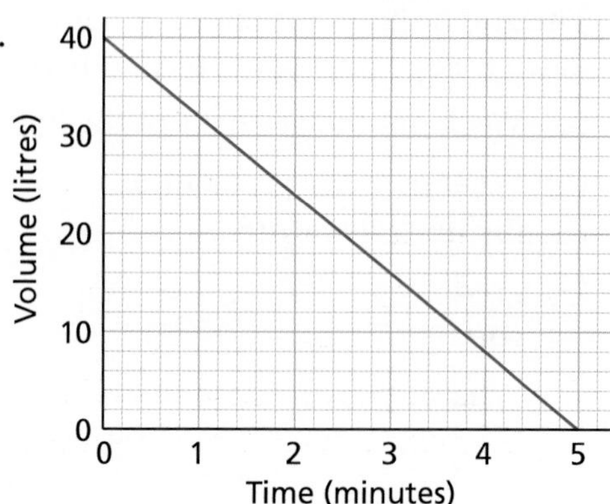

C3 This graph shows the volume of water in a tank.

(a) Find the gradient of each straight-line segment A, B, C and D.

(b) What do you think happened at

(i) 5 minutes from the start

(ii) 15 minutes from the start

(iii) 25 minutes from the start

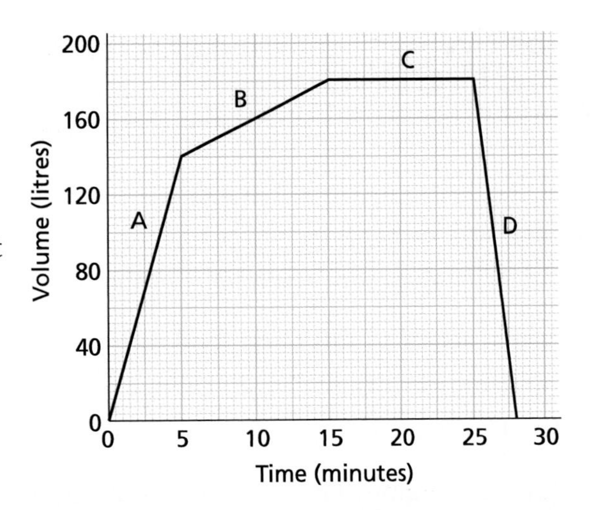

Test yourself

T1 (a) Find the gradient of this ramp (to 2 d.p.).

(b) A fork-lift truck can safely climb a ramp with a gradient of less than 0.17.
Can the fork-lift truck safely use this ramp?

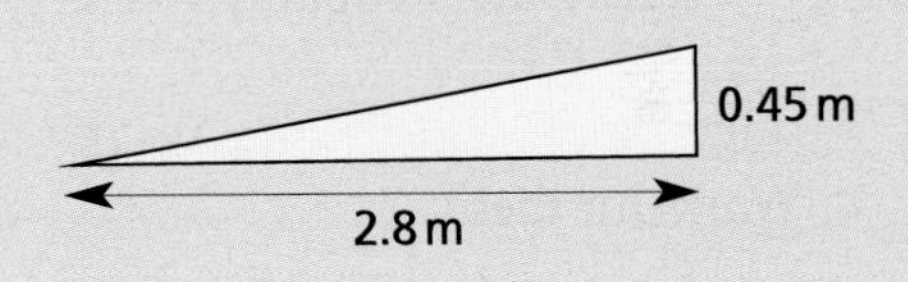

T2 Find the gradient of the line through the points A and B.

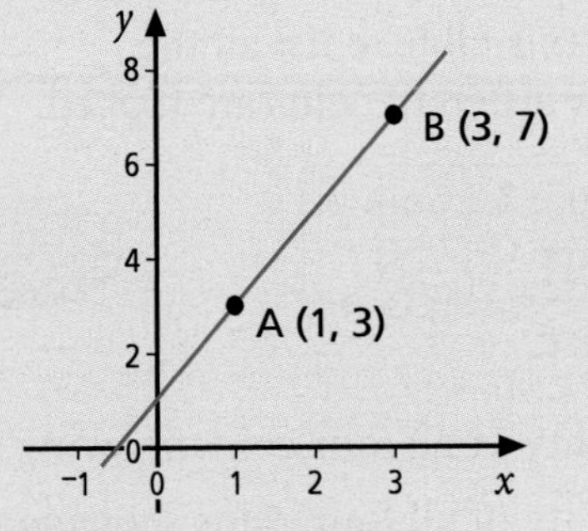

T3 This graph shows the volume of water in a container during 6 seconds.

(a) Find the gradient of the line.

(b) What does the gradient represent?

T4 This graph shows the volume of oil in a tank during 6 minutes.

(a) Find the gradient of the line, correct to 1 d.p.

(b) What is happening to the oil in the tank during these 6 minutes?

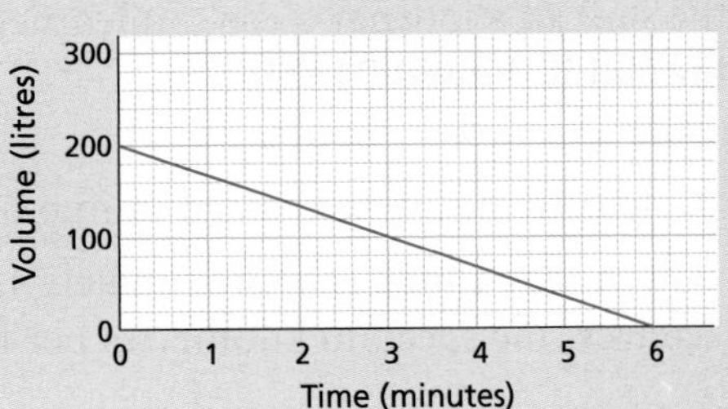

Review 6

1 (a) Work out $1\frac{1}{4} \times \frac{4}{5}$.

(b) What does your result tell you about $1\frac{1}{4}$ and $\frac{4}{5}$?

2 May's cats eat $1\frac{1}{2}$ tins of cat food each day.

(a) How many tins will they eat in a week?

(b) How long will 24 cans of food last them?

3 (a) On a number line, show the set of values of n that satisfy the inequality $1 \le n < 4$.

(b) What values in the bubble satisfy the inequality $1 \le n < 4$?

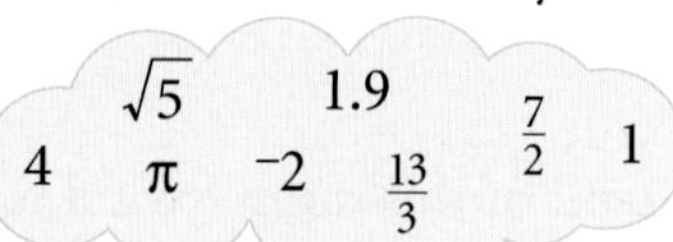

4 Work out these.

(a) $5 \div \frac{1}{2}$ (b) $10 \div \frac{2}{5}$ (c) $\frac{1}{3} \div \frac{1}{6}$ (d) $3\frac{1}{2} \div \frac{1}{4}$ (e) $\frac{2}{3} \div \frac{5}{6}$

5 (a) Copy and complete this table to list all the outcomes when four different coins are flipped.

Coin 1	Coin 2	Coin 3	Coin 4
H	H	H	H

(b) What is the probability of all four coins showing a head?

(c) What is the probability of all four coins showing the same face?

(d) What is the probability of three or more coins showing a head?

(e) What is the probability that there are more tails than heads showing?

6 (a) Find the gradient of this ramp (to 2 d.p.).

(b) A digger can safely climb a ramp with a gradient of less than 0.16. Can the digger safely use this ramp?

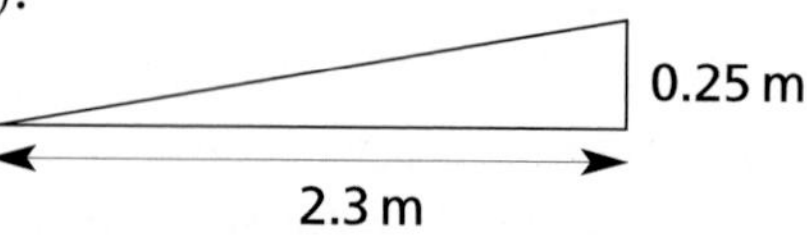

7 At the start of a journey a car's mileometer showed 042786.
At the end it showed 042938.
The journey took $3\frac{3}{4}$ hours.

(a) Calculate the average speed in m.p.h, correct to one decimal place.

(b) Given that 1 mile is approximately 1.6 kilometres, convert the speed to kilometres per hour, correct to one decimal place.

8 A manufacturer keeps records of the number of fridges breaking down during their one-year guarantee period.

Fridge model	Icefresh	Arctic chill	Coolmate
Number sold	57 897	236 745	186 772
Number breaking down	131	1047	550

(a) For each fridge model, calculate, to 3 d.p., an estimate of the probability of a breakdown under guarantee.

(b) On this basis, which model seems the most reliable?

9 Write inequalities to describe the following number line diagrams.

(a)

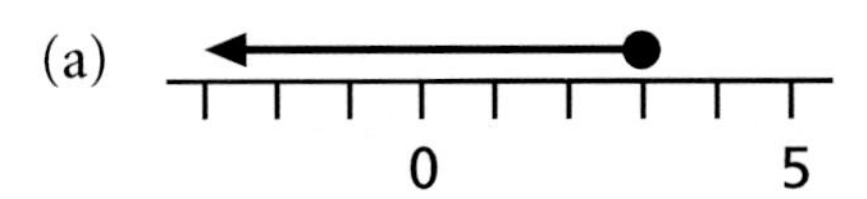

(b)

10 Justin has two six-sided dice, A and B.
Dice A has the numbers 1, 1, 1, 2, 6, 6 on it.
Dice B has the numbers 1, 2, 2, 2, 2, 6 on it.

The two dice are thrown together and their numbers are compared.
Find the probability (as a fraction) that

(a) A beats B (b) B beats A (c) the numbers are the same (a draw)

11 Children are allowed in a play area if they are at least 3 feet tall but under $4\frac{1}{4}$ feet tall.
Using h for the height of a child in feet, write this statement using symbols.

12 This graph shows Karen's journey to school. She walks to a bus stop, waits for a bus, then a bus takes her the rest of the way to school.

(a) How far does Karen walk from home to the bus stop?

(b) At what speed does she walk?

(c) How long does she wait at the bus stop?

(d) How far does the bus take her?

(e) At what speed does the bus go?

(f) Karen's brother leaves home 12 minutes after she does. At what speed must he run in order to catch the same bus as her?

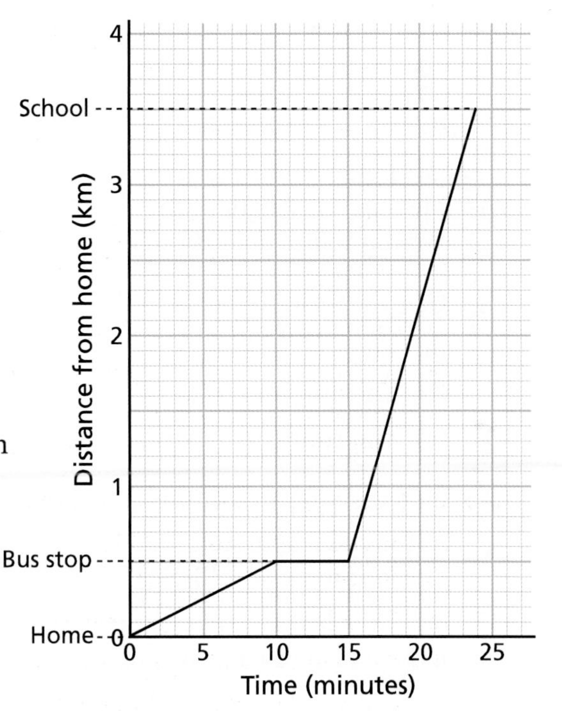

13 A train travels at 65 m.p.h.
How long, in hours and minutes does it take to travel 148 miles?

36 Maps and plans

You will revise how to

- use simple scales
- use bearings

This work will help you

- use four-figure grid references
- use different scales on maps

A Working to plans

This is a plan of a classroom.

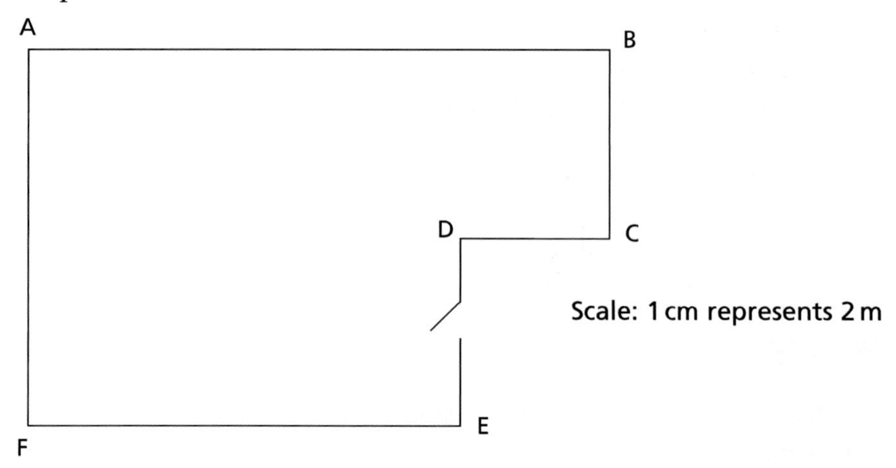

A1 Measure the length of the wall AB on this plan.
What distance does this represent in the real room?

A2 Give the measurements in the real room for these.

(a) The wall from A to F

(b) The wall from B to C

(c) The approximate distance from the door to corner A

A3 Find the total area of this classroom in m^2.

A4 If the door is 1 m wide, calculate the total amount of skirting board that would be needed to go round the edge of this classroom.

A5 Draw a plan of your own classroom on the same scale as the plan above.

B *Grid references*

Map A on sheet G137 is part of an Ordnance Survey map.
Part of it is shown here.

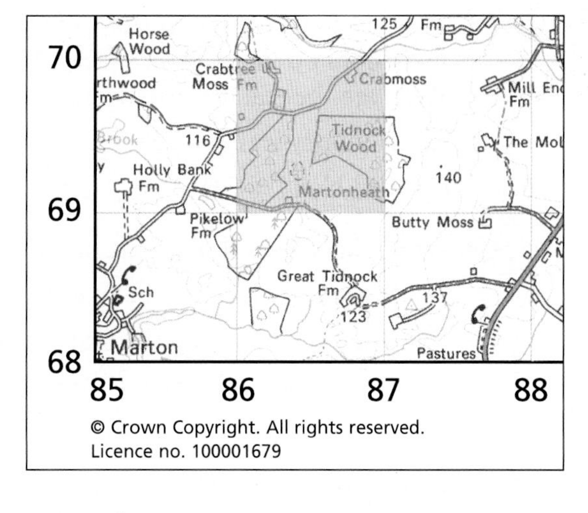

A place can be located by giving the **grid reference** of the square it is in.

A square is described by giving the number on the grid line to the left of it, then the number on the grid line below it.

The shaded square on this piece of map is 86 69.
Martonheath is in grid square 86 69.

As with coordinates, the horizontal reference is always given first.

B1 Look at the part of the map shown above.
In which grid square is each of these?

(a) Holly Bank Farm (b) Great Tidnock Farm

B2 Use sheet G137 to answer these questions.

(a) What is the name of the wood in 87 72?

(b) What disused (dis) features are in 93 69?

(c) What is the name of the hill in 87 76?

(d) What is the name of the hall in 90 75?

C *Scales*

The scale of the map on sheet G137 is given as 1 : 50 000.
This means that 1 cm on the map represents 50 000 cm in real life.

C1 (a) What does 1 cm on the map represent in real life in metres?

(b) What does 1 cm on the map represent in real life in kilometres?

(c) Copy and complete this statement.

On the map .... cm represents 1 km.

(d) How far apart on the map are the gridlines and what distance does this represent in real life?

C2 Measuring a distance 'as the crow flies' means measuring in a straight line.
Fallibroome School is in grid square 89 74. Find this on your map.

(a) Measure the distance on the map as the crow flies from Fallibroome School to The Mount (87 74) to the nearest centimetre.

(b) What is this distance in kilometres?

C3 Measure the distances as the crow flies to these places from the school on the map on sheet G137 to the nearest centimetre.
What are the real life distances in kilometres of these places from the school?

(a) Henbury Hall (86 72) (b) Walnut Tree Farm (89 75)
(c) Old Hall (86 74) (d) Home Farm (87 73)

C4 Map B on sheet G138 is part of an Ordnance Survey 1:25 000 map.

(a) What does 1 cm on the map represent in real life in centimetres?
(b) What does 1 cm on the map represent in real life in metres?
(c) How long on the map is a real life distance of 1 km?

C5 Use map B to find the distances, in kilometres, as the crow flies, from the school (A) to

(a) Big Wood (B) (b) Highlees Wood (C) (c) Hocker Lane Farm (D)
(d) Lower Yew Tree (E) (e) Birchtree Farm (F) (f) the Hospital (G)

C6 The school wants to give free travel to anyone who lives more than 2 km from the school as the crow flies.
Which of these places are more than 2 km from the school?

Fir Tree Farm Whirley Hall Harebarrow Farm Withinlee Farm

C7 Some students measure the distance from the school to Fleets Farm in real life as 720 m.

(a) How far is this distance in real life in centimetres?
(b) Using map C on sheet G138, measure the distance from the School (A) to Fleets Farm (M) on the map.
(c) How many centimetres in real life is represented by 1 cm on map C?
(d) Write the scale of map C in the form $1:n$.

C8 Use map C to find the distance in metres from the school (A) to

(a) the sand pit (N) (b) Windmill Farm (O)
(c) The Mount Farm (P) (d) Whirley Hall (Q)

C9 On map D on sheet G139 the scale is given as 1:250 000.

(a) What distance, in kilometres, does 1 cm on the map represent?
(b) Find the distance in kilometres of these places from the school (A):
  (i) Swan Green (S) (ii) Hoo Green (T)
  (iii) Shutlingslow (U) (iv) Thorns Green (V)

C10 Which scale map, of those you have met in this section, would be the best to use for:

(a) finding a friend's house in town
(b) planning a car journey from London to Manchester
(c) going hill-walking?

D *Bearings*

Bearings tell you which direction to go towards a given point.

Bearings are always measured clockwise from North.
Vertical lines on maps usually point to North.

Bearings are always given as three figures, for example 065°.

Use sheet G137 to answer these questions.
The map is drawn to a scale of 2 cm represents 1 km.

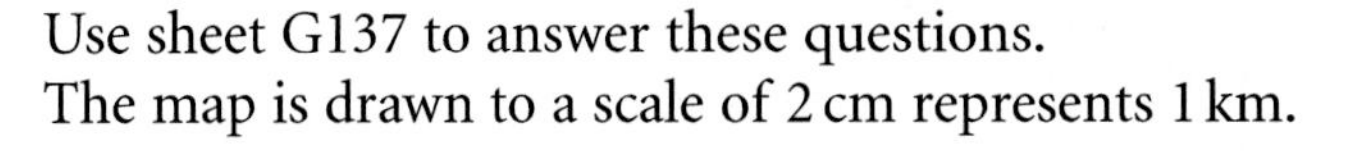

D1 Find the bearing from Fallibroome School (89 74) to these places.

(a) Moat Hall Farm (93 76) (b) Croker (92 69)
(c) Sandbach Farm (86 72) (d) Clock House Farm (86 77)

D2 Find the places which are these distances and bearings from the school.

(a) 3.5 km on a bearing of 050° (b) 3.5 km on a bearing of 309°
(c) 4 km on a bearing of 127° (d) 3.9 km on a bearing of 104°
(e) 4 km on a bearing of 343° (f) 6 km on a bearing of 205°

D3 A hot air balloon leaves the school and travels on a bearing of 217° to land near a farm 5.5 km away.

(a) Which hall will the balloon fly over?
(b) Which farm is nearest to the landing point?

D4 A helicopter sets out from the hill (marked 140 on the map) at 87 69.
It sets off on a bearing of 059° and flies to a point 6 km away.
It then changes course to fly on a bearing of 302° for 7.5 km where it lands.

(a) On sheet G137 show the helicopter's journey.
(b) What is the nearest farm to the landing point?
(c) On what bearing would the helicopter have to fly to return to the hill where the journey started?
(d) How far would this return journey be?

Magnetic variation

The North used on the map is called True North and points to the North Pole.
However, a compass points to Magnetic North which is
currently somewhere over Northern Canada, but changes slightly every year.
An Ordnance Survey map usually tells you what the difference is between
True and Magnetic North in the area it covers.

D5 Sheet G140 shows the Summer Islands on the north-west coast of Scotland. There are two good viewpoints at A (98 09) and B (01 05).

(a) Angus is at point A and spots a kayaker on a bearing of 150°.
Bob is at point B and sees the same kayaker on a bearing of 300°.
Draw lines at a bearing of 150° from A and 300° from B.
Mark the point where the kayaker is with a K.

(b) A ferry is seen at a bearing of 200° from A and 250° from B.
Mark on the map the point where the ferry is with an F.

(c) A yacht has run aground at point C (01 00).

(i) Measure the bearing of point B **from** point C.

(ii) On what bearing would someone at point B have to look to see the yacht at C?

(iii) Measure the bearing of point A from point C.

(iv) On what bearing would someone at point A have to look to see the yacht at C?

D6 The diagram represents the positions of Wigan and Manchester.

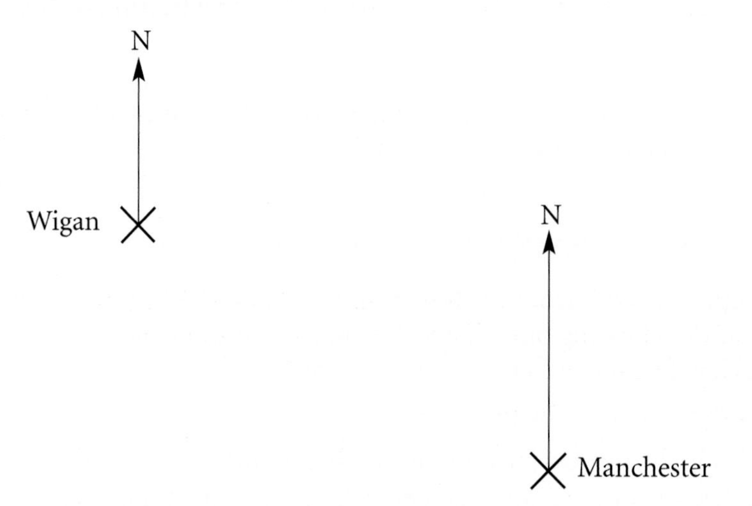

(a) Measure and write down the bearing of Manchester from Wigan.

(b) Find the bearing of Wigan from Manchester. Edexcel

Test yourself

T1 (a) On the map of the Summer Isles on sheet G140 measure the distance from the pier on Tanera Mor (99 06) to the memorial on the mainland (01 08) to the nearest centimetre.

(b) What is the actual distance in kilometres from the pier to the memorial?

(c) On what bearing would a boat leaving the beach by the memorial have to sail to reach the pier on Tanera Mor?

T2 This map shows an island in a bay.
A boat sails from L, on the island, to the harbour H.

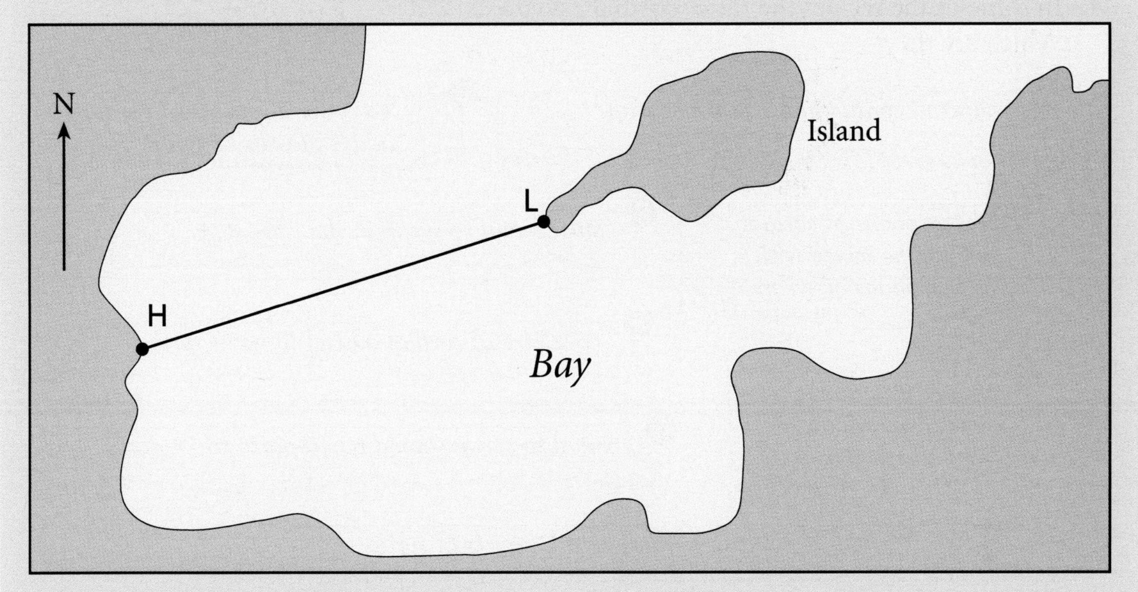

Scale: 1 cm represents 0.5 km

(a) (i) Measure the bearing on which the boat sails from L.

(ii) What is the actual distance from H to L?

(b) The boat then sails on a bearing of 140° from H.
Draw its path on the copy of this map on sheet G157.

AQA(NEAB) 1997

37 Ratio

You will revise using ratios given in the form $a:b$ and $a:b:c$.

This work will help you divide a quantity in a given ratio.

A *Recipes and ratios*

TG

Here are some recipes for fruit drinks, using cordial and sugar syrup.

- In some of the recipes the ratio **cordial : syrup** is **2:3**.
  Which are they?

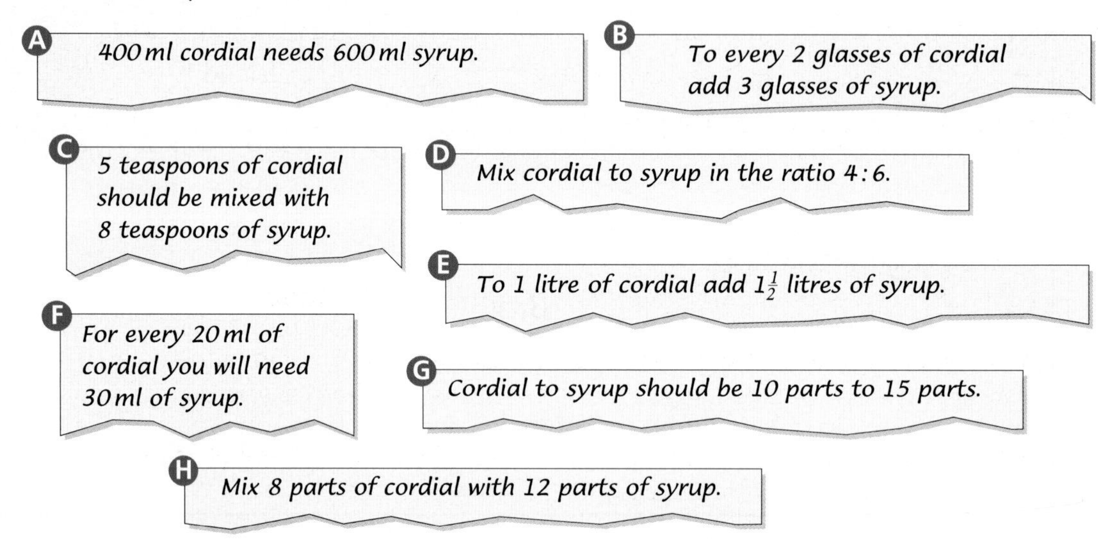

A1 Match up these ratios in pairs.

1:4   6:10   150:200   20:80   3:4   25:75   3:5   2:6

A2 A recipe requires 250 g flour and 100 g sugar.

(a) Write the ratio of flour to sugar in its simplest form.

(b) Write the ratio of sugar to flour in its simplest form.

A3 Write each of these ratios in its simplest form.

(a) 4:16	(b) 5:15	(c) 6:8	(d) 20:25	(e) 12:6
(f) 45:50	(g) 18:12	(h) 40:25	(i) 21:14	(j) 21:15
(k) 48:16	(l) 30:35	(m) 12:32	(n) 100:40	(o) 18:42

A4 Simplify these ratios as far as possible.

(a) 200 g : 500 g (b) 10 m : 25 m (c) 8 cm : 20 cm

A5 A plank of wood is 10 centimetres wide and 5 metres long.
Dean says the ratio of width to length is 2 : 1.

(a) Why is his answer wrong? (b) Write down the correct ratio.

A6 Simplify these ratios as far as possible.

(a) 20 cm : 1 m (b) 300 g : 1 kg (c) 40 cm : 2 m (d) 8 mm : 3 cm
(e) 3 kg : 250 g (f) 5 km : 500 m (g) 2 m : 10 cm (h) 6 cm : 5 mm

Ratios of the form *a* : *b* : *c*

A recipe for blackberry and apple jam needs 8 kg blackberries, 2 kg apples and 6 kg sugar.
The ratio **blackberries : apples : sugar** is 8 : 2 : 6.
This can be simplified (by dividing by 2) as **4 : 1 : 3**.

A7 A recipe for orange and grapefruit marmalade needs 15 kg oranges, 5 kg grapefruit and 10 kg sugar.
Write the ratio oranges : grapefruit : sugar in its simplest form.

A8 A salad recipe needs 1 kg potatoes, 200 g cucumber and 250 g tomatoes.
Write the ratio potatoes : cucumber : tomatoes in its simplest form.

A9 Joan mixes 2 litres of white paint with 500 ml of blue and 200 ml of yellow.
Write the ratio white : blue : yellow in its simplest form.

A10 Steve is making cakes.
He mixes 1.5 kg sultanas with 250 g cherries and 100 g candied peel.
Write the ratio sultanas : cherries : candied peel in its simplest form.

A11 Write each of these ratios in its simplest form.

(a) 3 : 12 : 18 (b) 10 : 15 : 25 (c) 40 : 60 : 100 (d) 48 : 36 : 24

A12 The length of this cuboid is 18 cm.
Its width is 9 cm and its height 6 cm.

6 cm
18 cm
9 cm

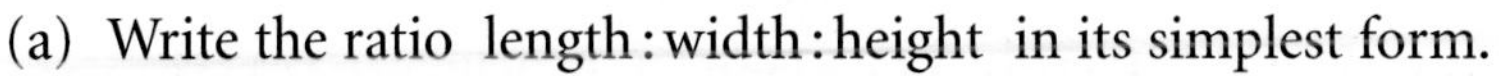

(a) Write the ratio length : width : height in its simplest form.

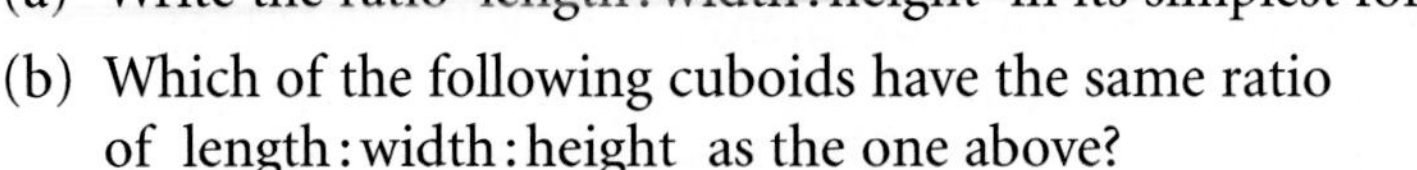

(b) Which of the following cuboids have the same ratio of length : width : height as the one above?

A length 3 m, width 1.5 m, height 1 m

B length 90 cm, width 45 cm, height 20 cm

C length 1.2 m, width 60 cm, height 40 cm

B *Mixtures*

Worked example

A general purpose concrete needs 2 parts of cement to 5 parts of sand.
If 80 kg of cement is used, how much sand will be needed?

Method 1

cement : sand
= 2 : 5

(Multiply both numbers by 40, to make 2 become 80.)

= 80 : **200**

So **200 kg** sand is needed.

Method 2

Cement is 2 parts.

2 parts is 80 kg.
So 1 part is 40 kg.

Sand is 5 parts = 5×40 kg
= **200 kg**

Method 3

2 kg cement needs 5 kg sand.

So 1 kg cement needs 2.5 kg sand.

So 80 kg cement needs 80×2.5
= **200 kg** sand.

B1 Rose pink paint is made by mixing red and white in the ratio 1 : 3.
Copy and complete this mixing table.

Red (1 part)	White (3 parts)
2 litres	
	9 litres
0.5 litre	
	12 litres

B2 Panther pink is made by mixing red and white in the ratio 2 : 3.
Copy and complete this mixing table.

Red (2 parts)	White (3 parts)
6 litres	
	15 litres
8 litres	
	1.5 litres

B3 Tracy knew that she had to mix 2 parts of yellow paint with 5 parts of blue to get the shade of green she liked.

(a) If she had 1 litre of yellow paint, how much blue paint would she need?

(b) If she had 250 ml of blue paint, how much yellow paint would she need?

B4 On a school trip, the ratio of adults to children is one to eight.

(a) If 5 adults are going on the trip, how many children can go?

(b) If 200 children want to go on the trip, how many adults will be needed?

B5 The ratio of sailing dinghies to motor cruisers moored in a harbour is 4 : 1.
If there are 24 dinghies in the harbour, how many motor cruisers are there?

B6 In a herd, the ratio of male to female animals is 5 : 8.
There are 40 males. How many females are there?

B7 A tea blender mixes Indian and African teas in the ratio 3 : 5.

(a) How much African tea does she mix with 15 kg Indian tea?

(b) How much Indian tea does she mix with 20 kg African tea?

B8 Copy and complete the quantities in this table.

Ratio	Quantities
1 : 5	15 kg : ... kg
2 : 3	50 g : ... g
5 : 4	20 m : ... m
3 : 8	... g : 320 g

B9 Bob is 7 years old and his sister Hayley is 11 years old.
Their Nan gives them some money in the ratio of their ages.

(a) If Bob gets £2.10, how much does Hayley get?

(b) If Hayley gets £5.50, how much does Bob get?

B10 In a new housing development, the ratio of starter homes to family homes is 3 to 5.

(a) If 48 starter homes are built, how many family homes will there be?

(b) If 25 family homes are built, how many starter homes will there be?

B11 When choosing tiles for a bathroom floor, Pat wants 2 patterned tiles for every 15 plain tiles.
If he buys 120 plain tiles, how many patterned tiles will he need?

B12 Karen makes purple paint by mixing red and blue in the ratio 2 : 3.
How much blue paint does she mix with 5 litres of red?

B13 Sophie mixes orange juice and pineapple juice in the ratio 4 : 5.
How much pineapple juice does she mix with 10 litres of orange juice?

B14 To make 'Pago fizz' you mix pineapple juice, mango juice and fizzy water in the ratio 5 : 2 : 3.

(a) You have 120 ml of pineapple juice.
How much mango juice and how much fizzy water do you need?

(b) You have 150 ml of fizzy water.
How much pineapple juice and how much mango juice do you need?

B15 The animals on a farm consist of sheep, cows and pigs in the ratio 9 : 5 : 2.
There are 162 sheep.
How many cows and how many pigs are there?

B16 On another farm the sheep, cows and pigs are in the ratio 3 : 8 : 1.
There are 112 cows.
How many animals are there altogether?

C *Dividing in a given ratio*

Worked example

Ali and Ben share a pizza which weighs 450 g.
The ratio of Ali's piece to Ben's piece is 2 : 3.
How much does each person get?

Ali gets 2 parts and Ben 3.
That's 5 parts altogether.

Each part is 450 g ÷ 5 = 90 g

So Ali gets 2 × 90 g = **180 g**
and Ben gets 3 × 90 g = **270 g**

Check: the two shares add up to 450 g.

C1 Colin and Dilip share £200 in the ratio 1 : 3.
How much does each of them get?

C2 Emma and Farnaz share £160 in the ratio 3 : 5.
How much does each of them get?

C3 Sharon makes a drink by mixing pineapple juice and mango juice in the ratio 3 : 2.
She wants to make 1 litre of the drink.

(a) How much pineapple juice will she need?

(b) How much mango juice will she need?

C4 An alloy using 9 parts of silver to 1 part of copper is often used for jewellery.
A chain of mass 50 g is made out of this alloy.

(a) What mass of silver does it contain? (b) What mass of copper does it contain?

C5 (a) Divide £12 in the ratio 1 : 3. (b) Share £35 in the ratio 2 : 5.

(c) Divide 60 kg in the ratio 3 : 7. (d) Divide £4.50 in the ratio 7 : 2.

C6 Paula has a collection of stamps.
She has twice as many foreign stamps as British stamps.

(a) What is the ratio of foreign to British stamps in her collection?

(b) If she has 480 stamps altogether, how many of them are foreign?

C7 Some material is woven from cotton and polyester mixed in the ratio 7 to 3.
How many grams of cotton are there in 2 kg of the material?

C8 Paul, Steph and Ronnie share £24 in the ratio 1 : 2 : 3.
How much does each get?

C9 2 litres of aquamarine paint is mixed using blue, yellow and white paint in the ratio 1 : 3 : 4.

How much of each colour is needed?

C10 A biscuit tin contains chocolate, cream and plain biscuits in the ratio 2 : 2 : 3.
If there are 35 biscuits altogether, how many of each kind are there?

C11 A silver coloured alloy is made using copper, nickel and zinc in the ratio 2 : 2 : 1.
How much of each metal is needed to make a candlestick weighing 350 g?

D *Ratios, fractions and percentages*

Worked example

A packet contains round balloons and long balloons in the ratio 3 : 1.
What fraction of all the balloons are round?

Drawing a picture helps.

There are 3 round balloons for every 1 long balloon: 

Out of every 4 balloons, 3 are round. So $\frac{3}{4}$ of all the balloons are round.

D1 A bag of chocolates contains milk and dark chocolates in the ratio 4 milk to 1 dark.
What fraction of all the chocolates are dark chocolates?

D2 The ratio of male fish to female fish in a tank is 1 : 7.
What fraction of the fish are (a) male (b) female

D3 The ratio of girls to boys in a choir is 3 : 2.

(a) What fraction of the choir are girls?

(b) What percentage are girls?

D4 In a primary school class, $\frac{1}{2}$ the children are boys.
Is the ratio of boys to girls 1 : 2, 2 : 1, 1 : 1, or none of these?

D5 In a pet shop, $\frac{1}{3}$ of the kittens are male.
What is the ratio of male to female kittens?

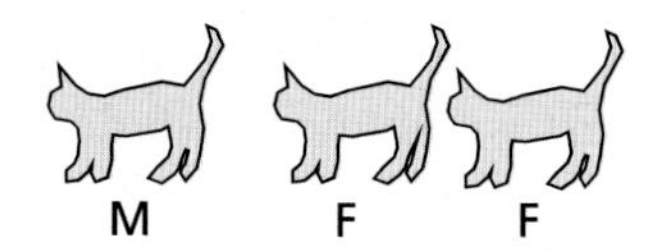

D6 In the pet shop, $\frac{1}{4}$ of the rabbits are male.
What is the ratio of male to female rabbits?

D7 In the pet shop, $\frac{1}{6}$ of the guinea pigs are male.
What is the ratio of male to female guinea pigs?

D8 In the pet shop, $\frac{3}{5}$ of the puppies are male.
What is the ratio of male to female puppies?

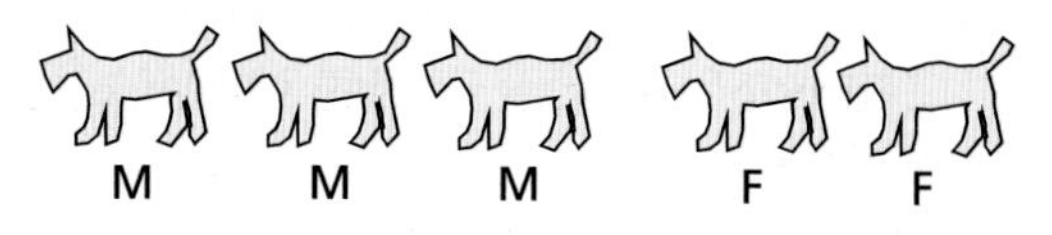

D9 Put these statements into pairs so that the statements in each pair say the same thing.

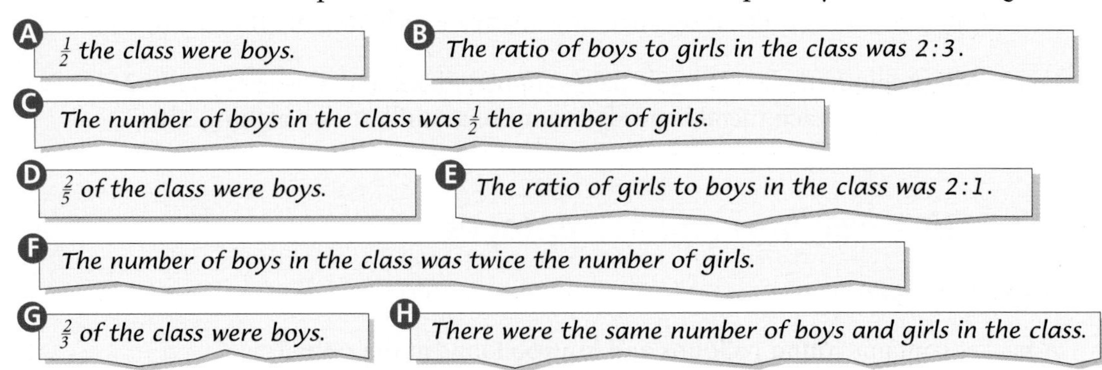

D10 A box of chocolates contains soft centres and hard centres in the ratio 3 : 2.

(a) What fraction of the chocolates are soft centres?

(b) What percentage of the chocolates are soft centres?

D11 (a) Find two pairs of matching statements here.

(b) Write your own statement that matches the odd one.

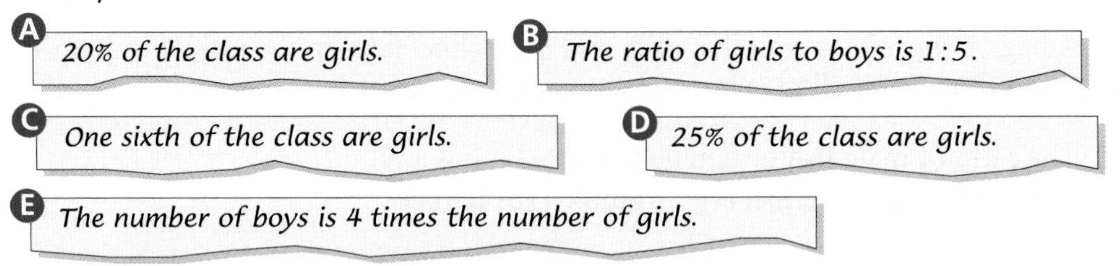

D12 An alloy is made from copper and nickel.
If 20% of the alloy is nickel, what is the ratio of copper to nickel?

E *k* : 1 and 1 : *k*

It is often convenient to use ratios where one of the parts is 1, even if the other part is then not a whole number.

Example

A school with 1560 pupils has 100 teachers.
The ratio pupils : teachers is 1560 : 100.

If we divide both numbers by 100, we get **15.6 : 1** (15.6 pupils for every teacher).

This ratio could be compared with other schools.

E1 To make orange paint, red and yellow are mixed in the ratio 3 : 2.
How much red is needed to mix with 1 litre of yellow?

E2 Write each of the following ratios in the form $k:1$.

(a) 7:2 (b) 10:4 (c) 250:200 (d) 33:10 (e) 2:5

E3 By dividing both parts by 2, write the ratio 2:11 in the form $1:k$.

E4 Write each of the following ratios in the form $1:k$.

(a) 2:5 (b) 10:35 (c) 4:18 (d) 10:7 (e) 4:3

E5 Fat makes up 5% of the ingredients of some biscuits.
Write the ratio of fat to the other ingredients in the form $1:k$.

E6 One Saturday afternoon at a cinema there are 7 children for every 2 adults.
Write the ratio children:adults in the form $k:1$.

E7 Sterling-silver contains silver and copper in the ratio 23:2.

(a) Write this ratio in the form $k:1$.

(b) How much silver needs to be mixed with 50 g of copper?

Test yourself

T1 Rashid has 35 sweets.
He shares them in the ratio 4:3 with his sister.
Rashid keeps the larger share.
How many sweets does Rashid keep? Edexcel

T2 There were 1200 fans at the game between City and United.

(a) The ratio of City fans to United fans was 3:2.
How many fans of each team were there?

150 of the fans attending were women and children.

(b) What fraction of the fans were women and children?
Give your answer in its simplest form. OCR

T3 Wayne shares £360 between his children, Sharon and Liam, in the ratio of their ages.
Sharon is 13 years old and Liam is 7 years old.

(a) Work out how much each child receives.

(b) What percentage of the £360 does Sharon receive? Edexcel

T4 Anna, Beth and Cheryl share the total cost of a holiday in the ratio 6:5:4.
Anna pays £294.

(a) Work out the total cost of the holiday.

(b) Work out how much Cheryl pays. Edexcel

38 *Similar shapes*

You will revise how to recognise and make scaled copies of shapes.

This work will help you

- deal with decimal scale factors
- understand similar shapes and deal with ratios within shapes

A *Scaling*

TG

A graphic artist has designed a logo for a company.

He is asked to make a copy double the size.
But he isn't happy with his drawing.

What is wrong with it?

Original

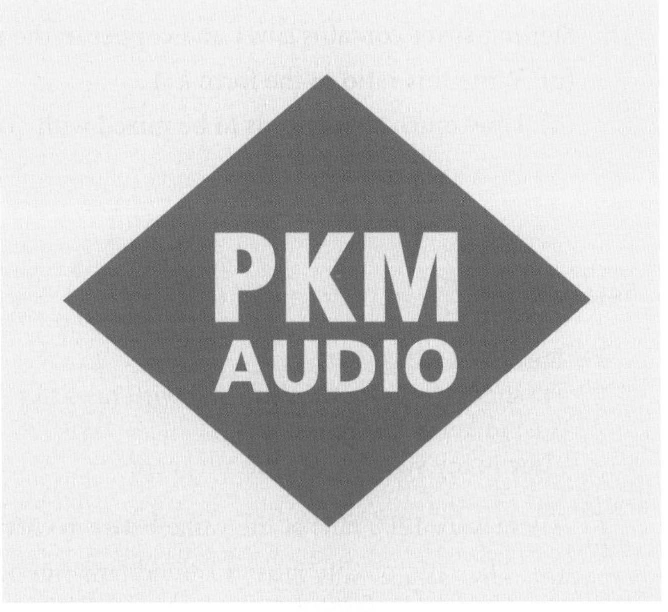

Copy

Here is part of another copy of the original logo.
This one is correctly scaled.
How high is the complete copy?

?

A1 Which of these are scaled copies of the original shape?
Give the scale factor for those that are.

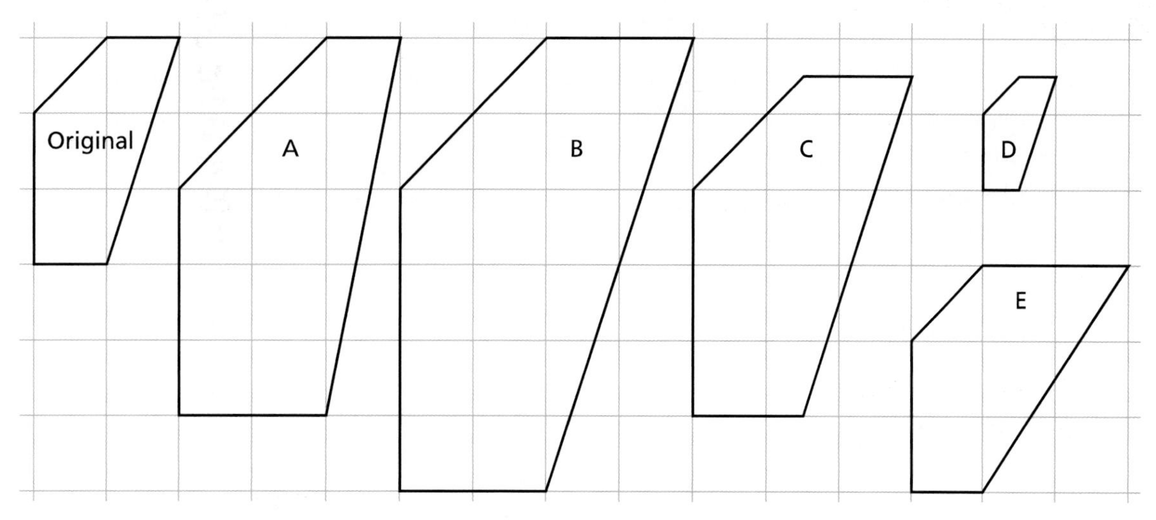

A2 (a) Copy the original shape above on to squared paper.
Draw a scaled copy of it using a scale factor of 3.

(b) Draw another scaled copy using a scale factor of 2.5.

A3 The larger picture here is meant to be a scaled copy of the original.

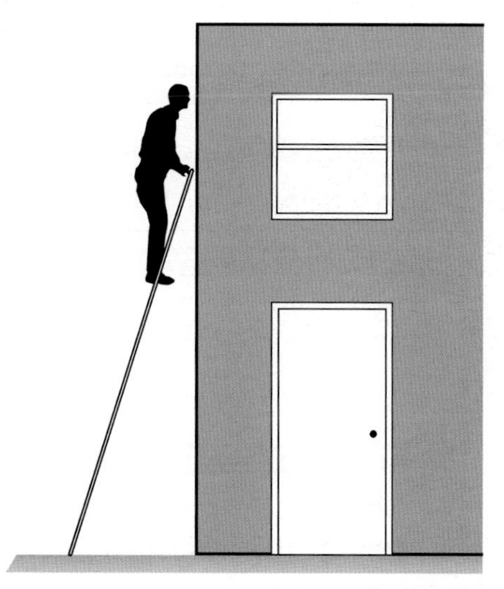

(a) Copy and complete this table of measurements and work out each multiplier.

Measurement	Original length	$\times ?$ →	Length in copy
Height of building			
Length of ladder			
Height of door			
Width of door			

(b) What is the scale factor of the enlargement?

(c) Measure the angle between the ladder and the ground in the original and the copy. What do you find?

A4 A picture shows a house, a car and a hedge.
This table compares measurements in the original picture and a scaled copy.
Copy the table and fill in the missing values.

	Original length	Scale factor	Copy length
Width of picture	10 cm		25 cm
Height of picture	6 cm		
Height of house	3 cm		
Length of car			5 cm
Length of hedge			20 cm

You can use a scale factor that is a decimal.

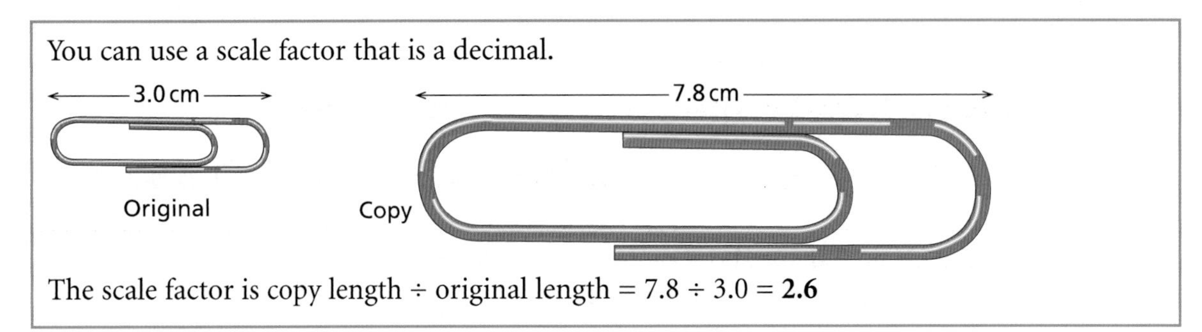

The scale factor is copy length ÷ original length = 7.8 ÷ 3.0 = **2.6**

A5 Find the scale factor for each of these copies of the original paperclip.

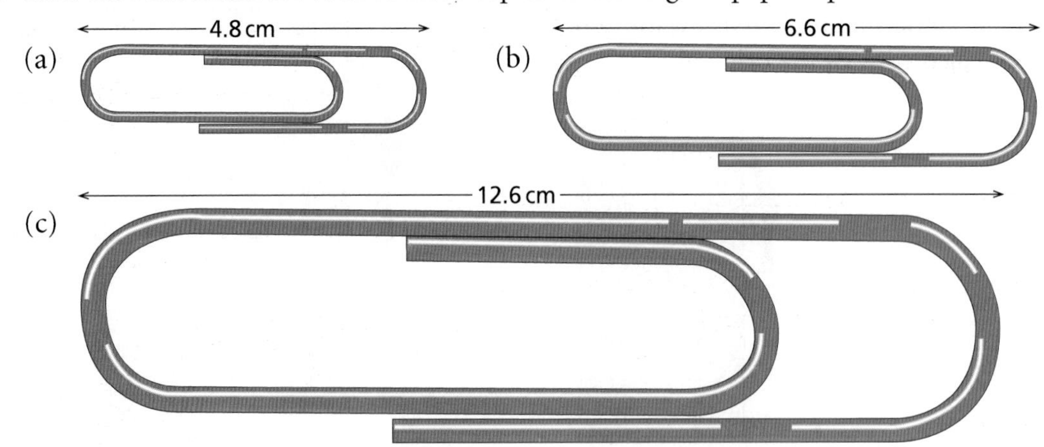

A6 Copy and complete this table for a picture that has been enlarged.

	Original length	Scale factor	Copy length
Width of picture	15.0 cm		54.0 cm
Height of picture	10.0 cm		
Length of bike	13.5 cm		
Height of saddle			27.0 cm
Diameter of wheel			16.2 cm

A7 Bella has a rectangular photo 125 mm by 80 mm.
The photo is enlarged. The longer side of the copy is 350 mm long.
Calculate the length of the shorter side of the copy.

B *Scaling down*

This pencil is life size.

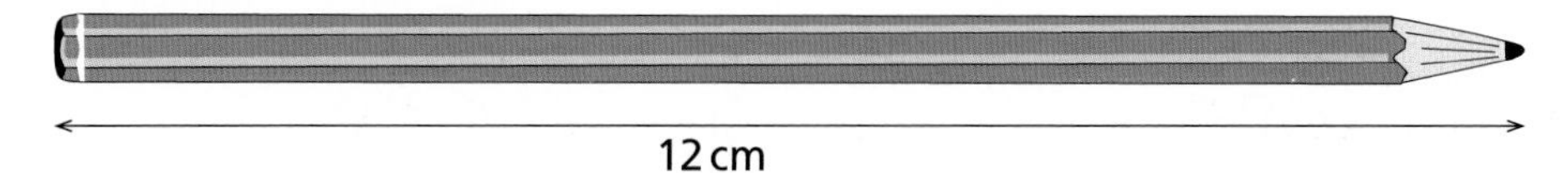

In the copy below it is $\frac{1}{4}$ of its original size. The scale factor is $\frac{1}{4}$.

3 cm

B1 What is the scale factor of each of these copies?

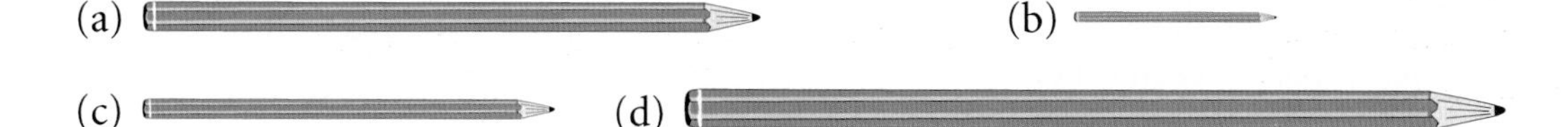

Sometimes it is easier to use decimals.

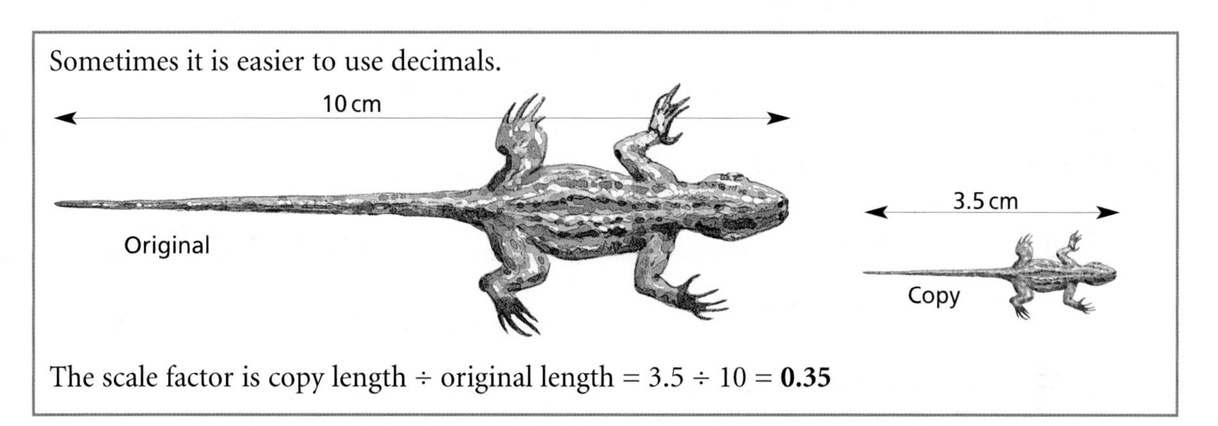

The scale factor is copy length ÷ original length = 3.5 ÷ 10 = **0.35**

B2 Find the scale factor for each of these copies of the original lizard.

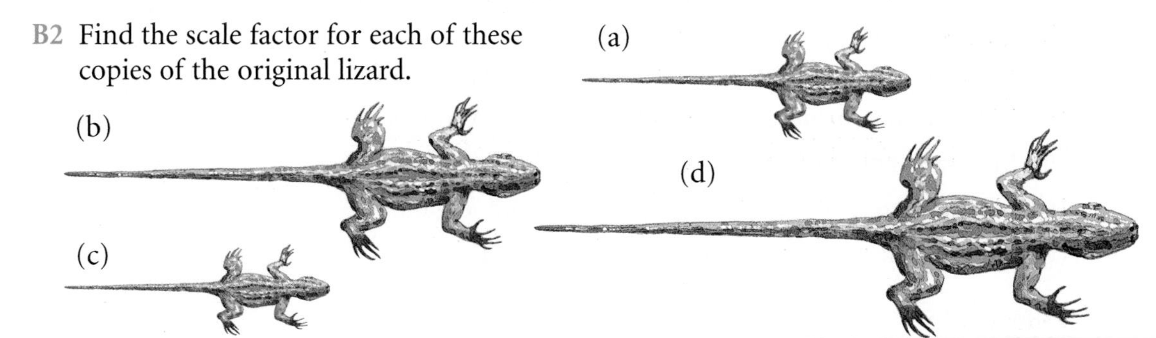

B3 Copy and complete this table for a picture that has been copied.

	Original length	Scale factor	Copy length
Width of picture	8 cm		4.8 cm
Height of picture	5 cm		
Height of tree	3 cm		
Length of pond			4.5 cm
Length of fence			5.4 cm

C *Similar triangles*

TG

Each of these triangles is an exact scaled copy of the other.

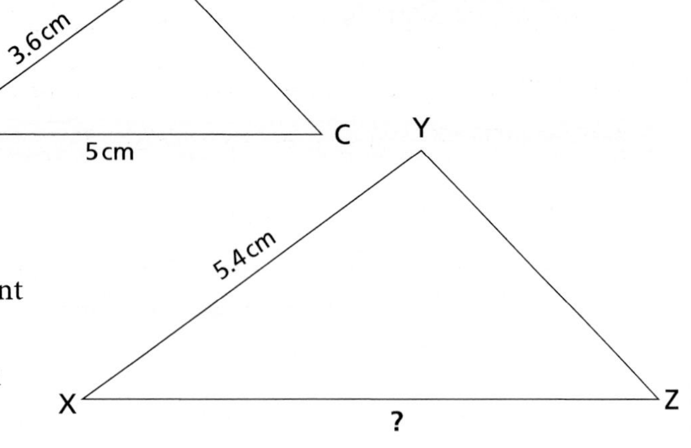

- What is the scale factor of enlargement of ABC to XYZ?
- What is length XZ?

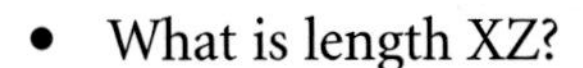

- What is the scale factor of enlargement of length BC to YZ?
- What can you say about the angles in the two triangles?

C1 These two triangles are scaled copies of each other.

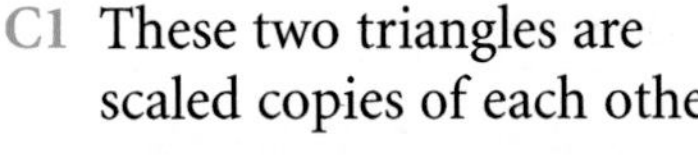

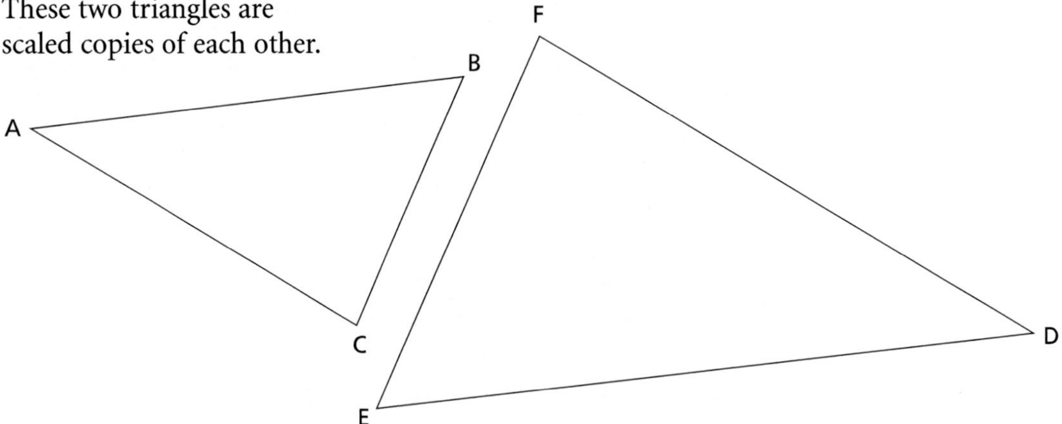

(a) Measure the lengths of AB and DE.
Use these lengths to find the scale factor of enlargement of DE from AB.

(b) Measure the lengths of BC and EF.
What is the scale factor of enlargement of EF from BC?

(c) Without measuring give the scale factor of CA to FD.

(d) Measure angle ABC. What can you say about angle DEF?

(e) Measure angle BCA. What can you say about angle EFD?

(f) Without measuring find angles CAB and FDE.

C2 These triangles are all scaled copies of each other.
Find the lettered angles.

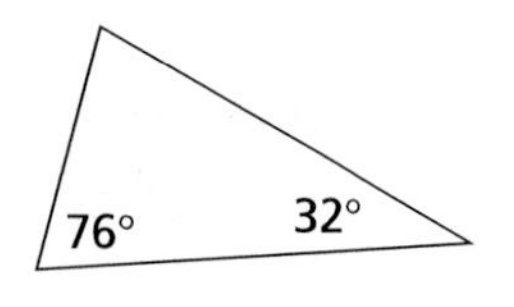

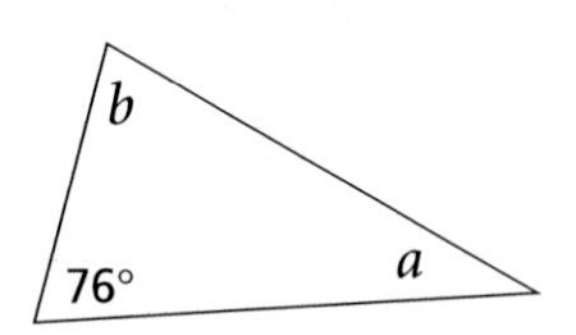

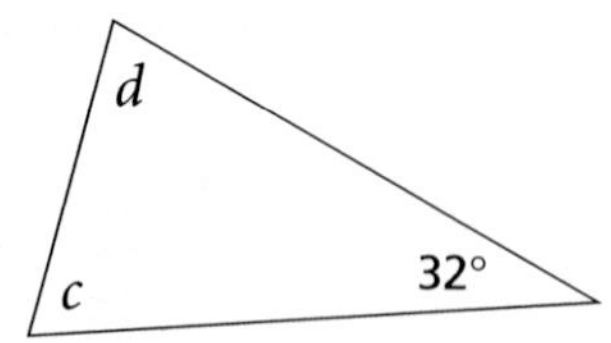

If two triangles are exact scaled copies of each other they are called **similar** triangles.
If the same scale factor is used to enlarge each corresponding side of two triangles then the triangles are similar.
Any two triangles with all the same angles must be similar.

C3 These triangles are all similar right-angled triangles. For each triangle,

(i) from the side given find the scale factor used to enlarge the original triangle

(ii) find the missing lengths

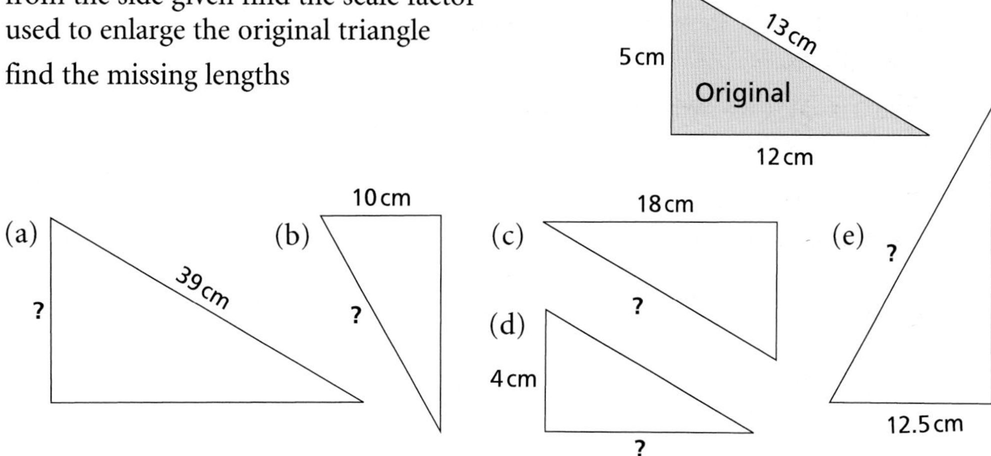

C4 Which of the triangles below are similar to this triangle?

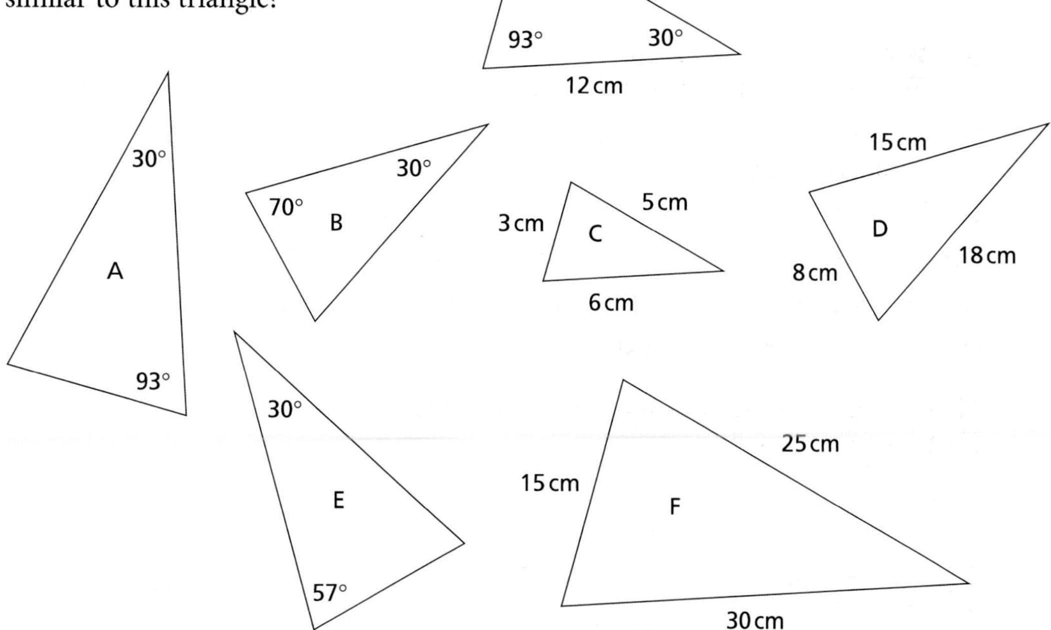

C5 These triangles are all similar.
Find the missing angles.

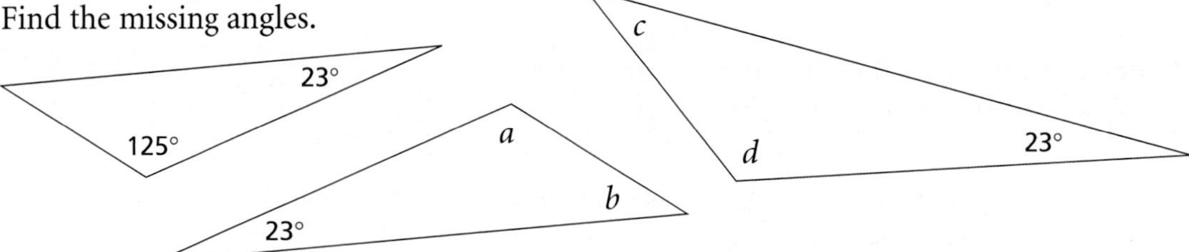

C6 These triangles are similar.

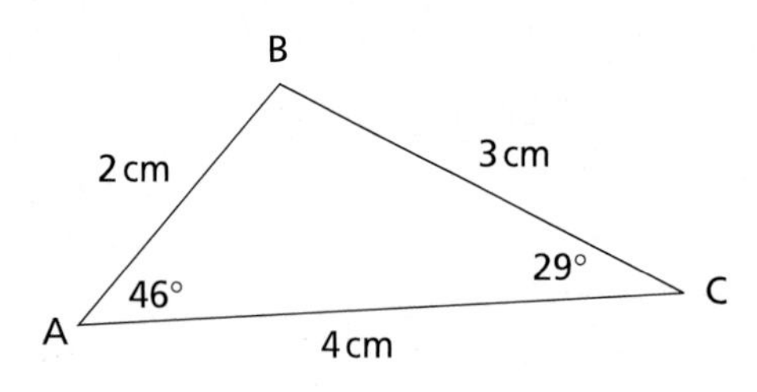

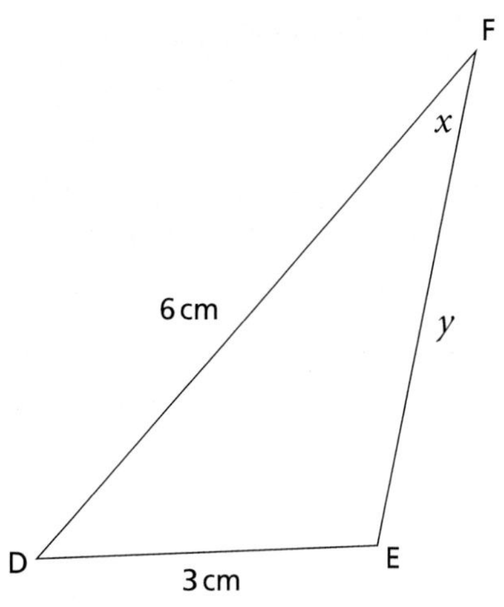

(a) What is the size of angle x?

(b) Calculate the length of y.

AQA(SEG)1997

C7 In this diagram lines AB and DE are parallel.
DE = 7 cm
DC = 4 cm
BC = 6 cm
Angle DEC = 43°

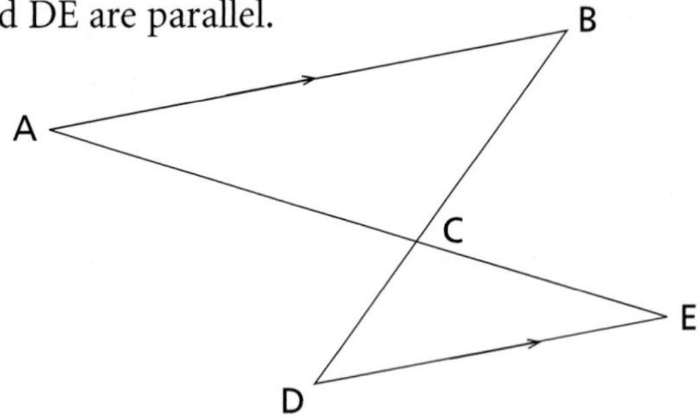

(a) Find angle BAC.

(b) Explain why triangles ABC and DEC must be similar.

(c) What is the scale factor of enlargement of triangle DEC to triangle ABC?

(d) Calculate length AB.

D *Proportions*

Paper sizes

You need some A2 paper, broadsheet newspaper pages, metre rule.

You will often have used A4 paper. This is a standard metric size. Newspapers, however, use a different system.

- Measure the lengths of the sides of the A2 sheet and of the broadsheet.
- Fold each sheet in half, by halving the longer side. Measure the sides of the new sheet.
- Repeat this another three times for each sheet.
- Record your results in a table and calculate the ratio $\frac{\text{long side}}{\text{short side}}$ each time.

	Metric sizes					Newspaper sizes				
	A2	A3	A4	A5	A6	Broadsheet	Tabloid	2T	4T	8T
long side										
short side										
$\frac{\text{long side}}{\text{short side}}$										

- What rule applies to the A sizes? Does the same rule apply to the newspaper sizes?
- What advantage does the A system have over the newspaper sizes?

A ratio is used to compare two quantities.

For example, if the height of a window is 3 times its width, we can write

$$\text{height} = 3 \times \text{width}$$

or $$\frac{\text{height}}{\text{width}} = 3$$

We say 'the ratio of height to width is 3 (or 3 : 1)'.

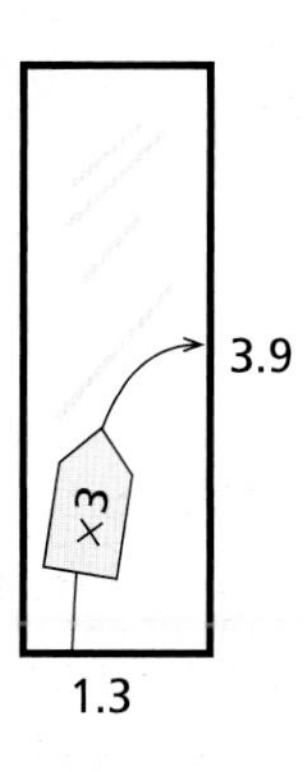

For this window, the height is 0.4 times the width,

so the ratio $\frac{\text{height}}{\text{width}} = 0.4$

D1 All the pictures below are scaled copies of this original.

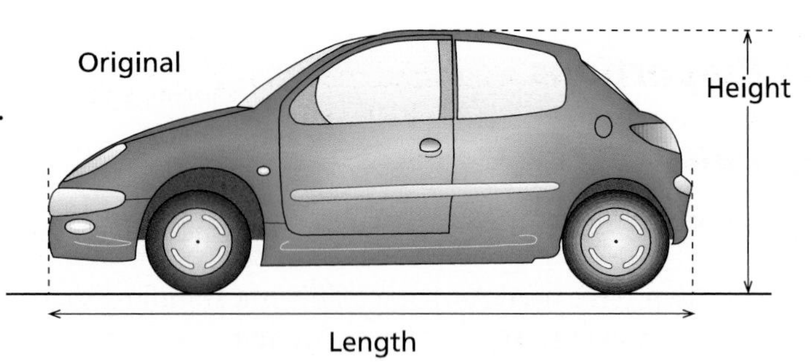

(a) Measure in cm

(i) the height of the car in the original picture

(ii) the length of the car in the original picture

(b) What is the ratio $\frac{\text{length}}{\text{height}}$ for this car?

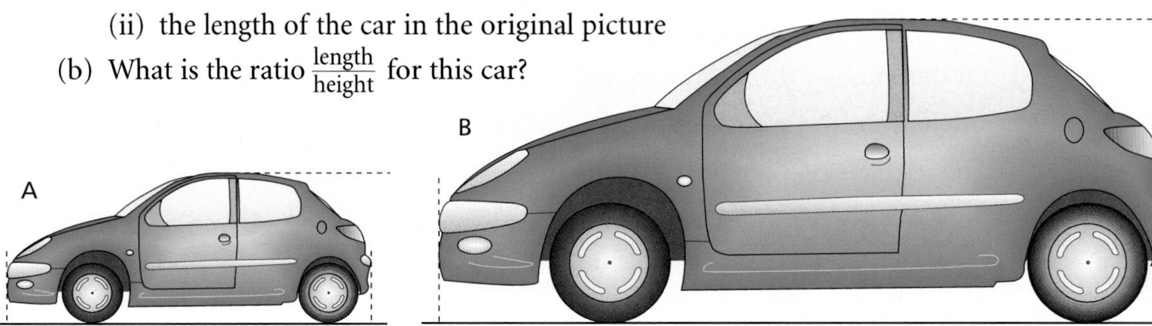

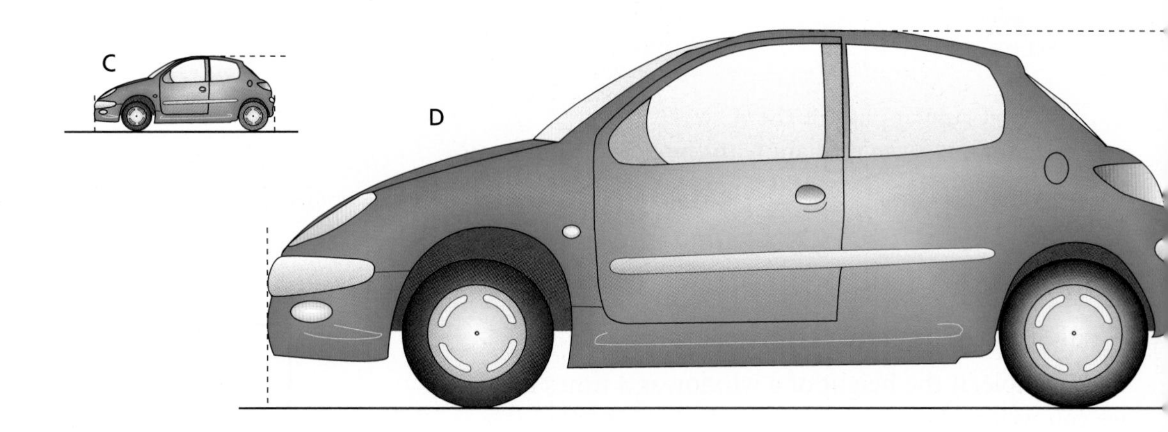

(c) Copy and complete this table for the scaled copies.

Copy	A	B	C	D
Length of car				
Height of car				
Ratio $\frac{\text{length}}{\text{height}}$				

(d) What do you notice about the ratio each time?

(e) A car is now drawn 7 cm high. How long should it be?

(f) How high would a car 20 cm long be if it were a scaled copy?

D2 For each of these cards find the ratio $\frac{\text{longest side}}{\text{shortest side}}$.
Use this to make pairs which are copies from the same original.

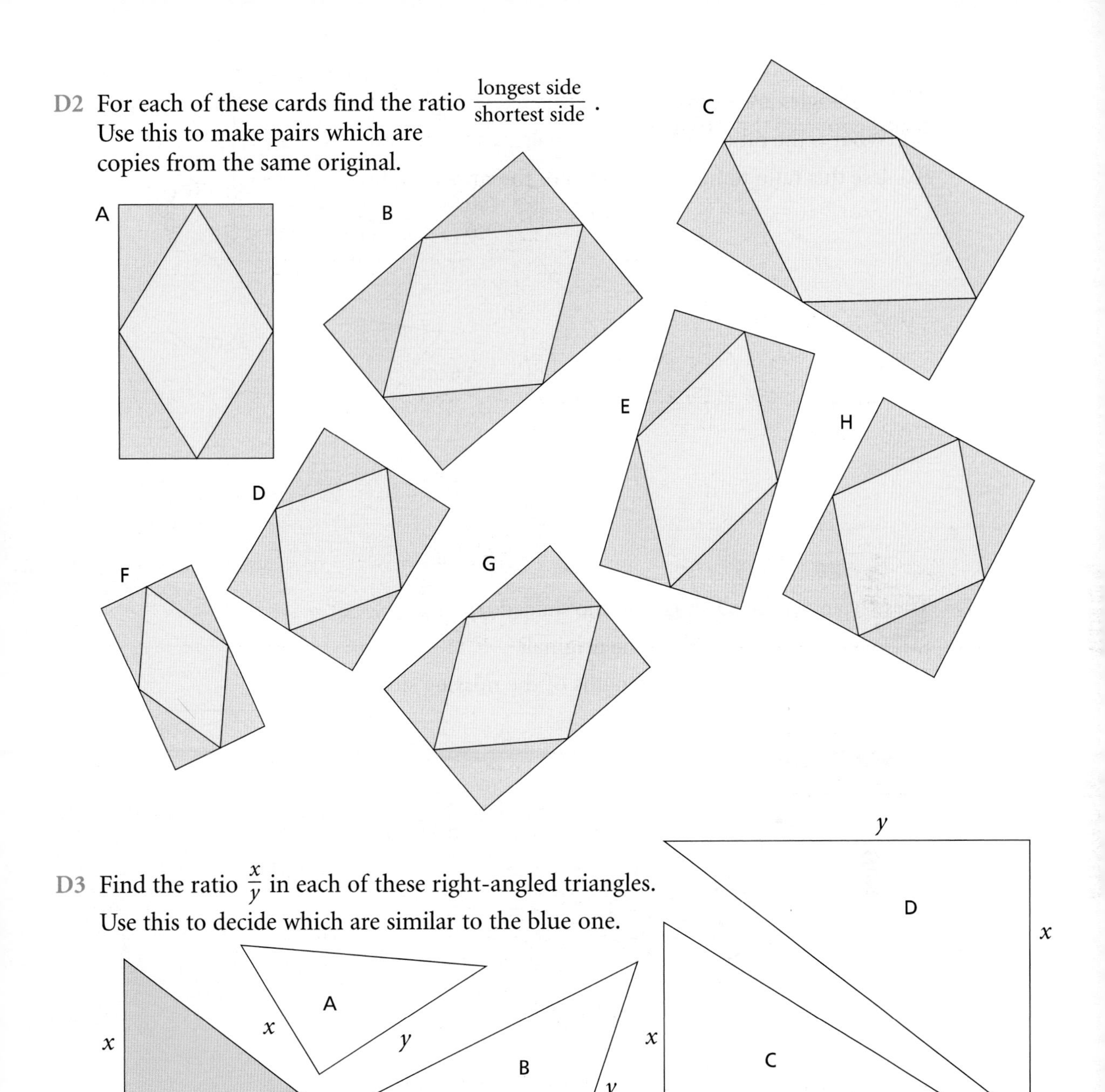

D3 Find the ratio $\frac{x}{y}$ in each of these right-angled triangles.
Use this to decide which are similar to the blue one.

Worked example

The **internal ratio** can be used to find missing sides in similar triangles.
These three triangles are similar.

The internal ratio $\frac{x}{y} = 3 \div 8 = 0.375$.
So $a = 14 \times 0.375 = 5.25\,\text{cm}$
and $b = 1.8 \div 0.375 = 4.8\,\text{cm}$

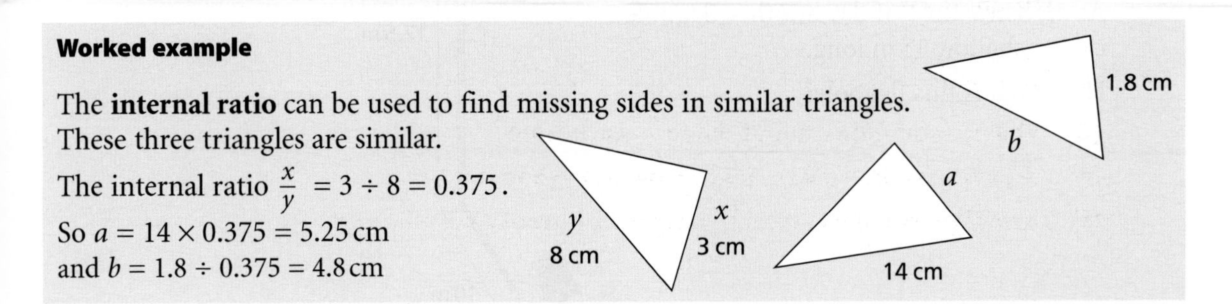

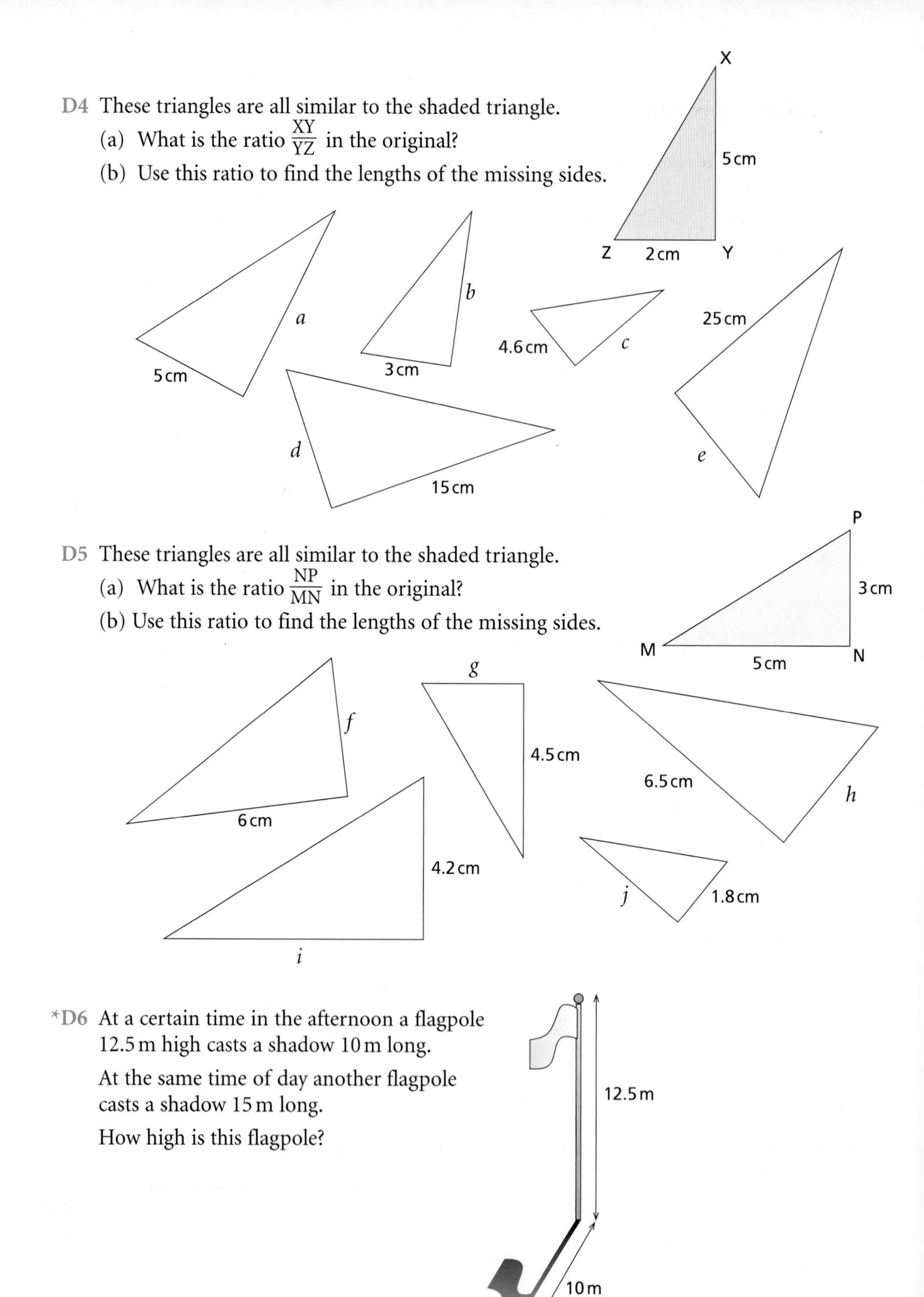

D4 These triangles are all similar to the shaded triangle.

(a) What is the ratio $\frac{XY}{YZ}$ in the original?

(b) Use this ratio to find the lengths of the missing sides.

D5 These triangles are all similar to the shaded triangle.

(a) What is the ratio $\frac{NP}{MN}$ in the original?

(b) Use this ratio to find the lengths of the missing sides.

***D6** At a certain time in the afternoon a flagpole 12.5 m high casts a shadow 10 m long.

At the same time of day another flagpole casts a shadow 15 m long.

How high is this flagpole?

E *Solving problems*

E1 In this diagram BC is parallel to DE.
AB = 8 cm BD = 4 cm
DE = 9 cm Angle ACB = 42°

(a) What is angle CED?
(b) Explain why triangles ABC and ADE must be similar.
(c) What is length AD?
(d) What is the scale factor of enlargement from triangle ABC to ADE?
(e) Find the length BC.

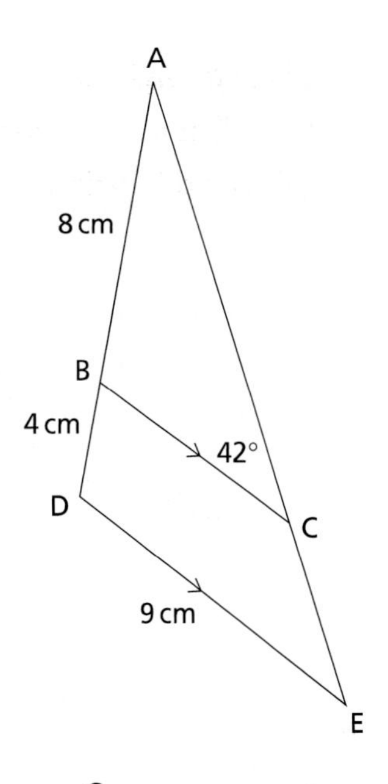

E2 In this diagram PQ is parallel to ST.
PQ = 15cm QR = 8 cm
RS = 12 cm RT = 18 cm

(a) Explain why PQR and RST must be similar triangles.
(b) Calculate length ST.
(c) Calculate length PR.

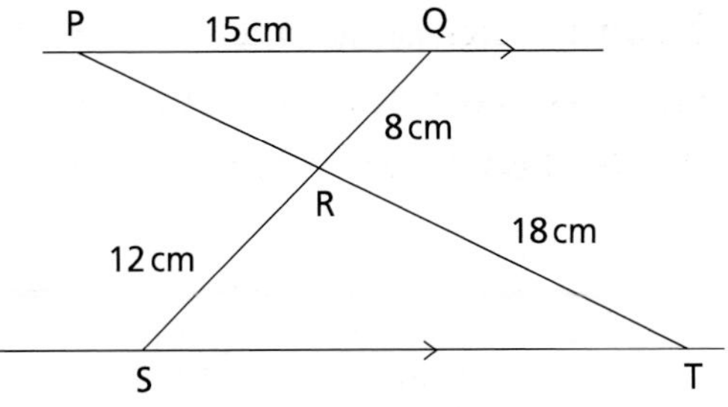

E3 BC is parallel to DE.
AB is twice as long as BD.
AD = 36 cm and AC = 27 cm

(a) Work out the length of AB.
(b) Work out the length of AE.

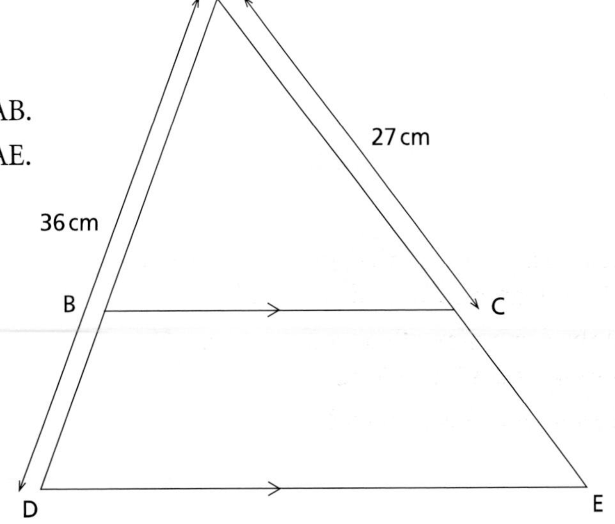

Edexcel

Test yourself

T1 What scale factor in this diagram has been used to copy

(a) shape A to B

(b) shape C to B

(c) shape A to C

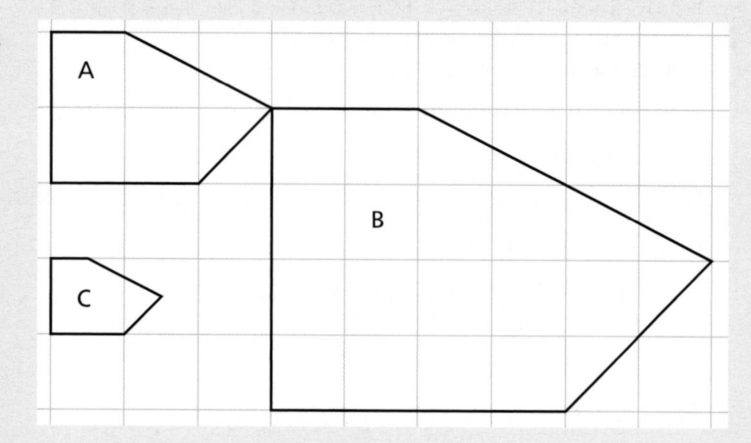

T2 In the diagram, AB is parallel to DE.

(a) Explain how you know that triangle ABC is similar to triangle DEC.

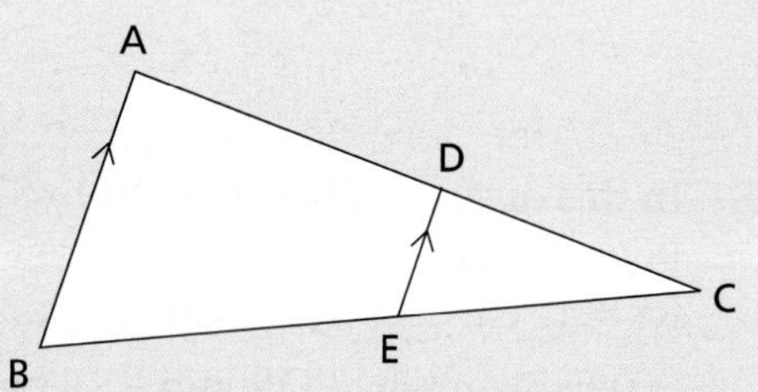

Length BE is 15 cm and length EC is 9 cm.
Length AB is 8 cm.

(b) Calculate length DE.

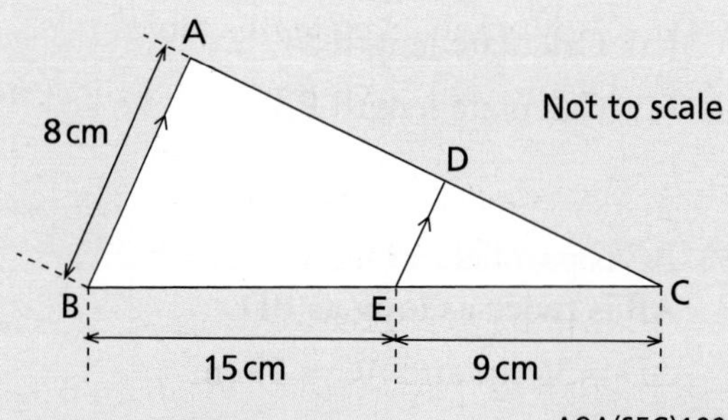

AQA(SEG)1998

T3 In the triangle ABC, AB = 10 cm, AC = 24 cm, BC = 26 cm.

Angle BAC = 90°.
D is the midpoint of AB.
DE is perpendicular to BC.

Use similar triangles to calculate the distance DE.

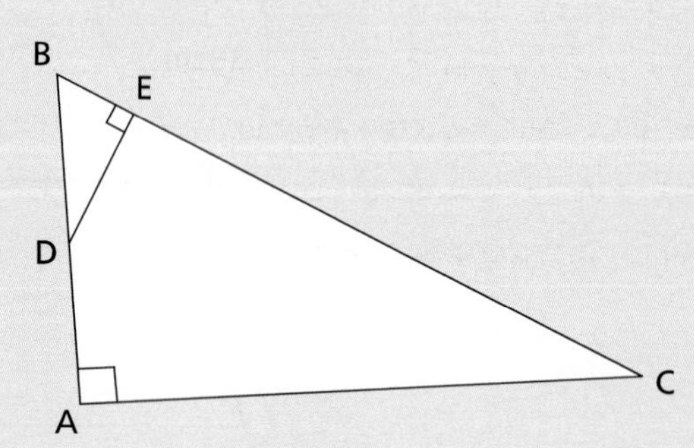

AQA(NEAB)1997

39 Gradients and equations

You should know

- how to plot points and draw the graph of a straight line, given its equation
- how to rearrange simple formulas

This work will help you

- find the equation of any straight line
- decide when two straight lines are parallel

A Straight lines and equations

A1 (a) Copy and complete this table.

(b) On the same set of axes, plot the graphs of $y = x$, $y = 2x$, $y = 3x$, and $y = {}^-4x$ for values of x between $^-1$ and 3.

(c) What is the gradient of each line?

(d) What do you notice? Can you explain it?

x	$^-1$	0	1	2	3
$2x$					
$3x$					
^-4x					

A2 (a) Copy and complete this table.

(b) On the same set of axes, plot the graphs of $y = x + 1$, $y = 4 + x$ and $y = x - 2$ for values of x between $^-1$ and 3.

(c) What is the gradient of each line?

(d) Where does each line cross the y-axis?

(e) What do you notice? Can you explain it?

x	$^-1$	0	1	2	3
$x + 1$					
$4 + x$					
$x - 2$					

A3 Use sheet G141 for this question.

(a) For each set of equations on the right,

(i) draw the graphs on the same set of axes

(ii) find the gradient of each line

(iii) write down where each line crosses the y-axis

(b) Briefly summarise your results.

A: $y = x + 3$, $y = 3 + 2x$, $y = 3x + 3$

B: $y = 2x + 5$, $y = 2x - 1$, $y = 2x + 2$

C: $y = {}^-x + 1$, $y = {}^-x + 5$, $y = {}^-x - 3$

D: $y = {}^-2x + 1$, $y = {}^-2x + 2$, $y = {}^-2x - 1$

A4 (a) Where do you think the line with equation $y = 2x + 1$ crosses the y-axis?

(b) What do you think is the gradient of the line with equation $y = 2x + 1$?

B *Finding equations*

The equation of a straight line can be written in the form $y = mx + c$.

m is the gradient and c is the y-intercept.

The y-intercept is wh
the line cuts the y-ax

Examples

A

The gradient is $\frac{3}{1} = 3$.

The y-intercept is $^{-}2$.

So the equation of the line is $y = 3x - 2$.

B

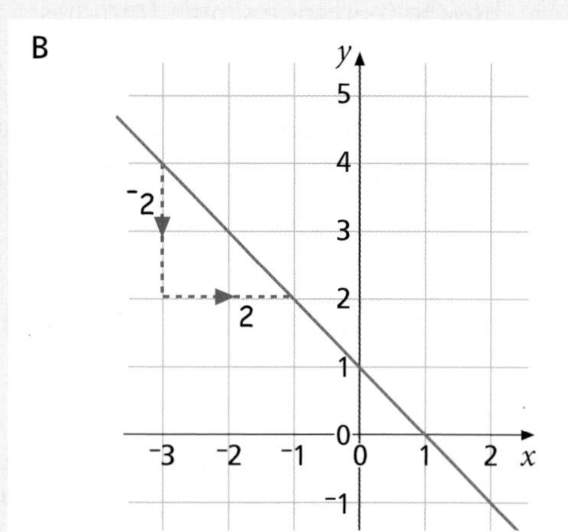

The gradient is $\frac{^{-}2}{2} = {}^{-}1$.

The y-intercept is 1.

So the equation of the line is $y = {}^{-}1x + 1$.

We usually write this as $y = {}^{-}x + 1$ or $y = 1 - x$.

B1 For each line below, (a) find the gradient and y-intercept
(b) write down its equation

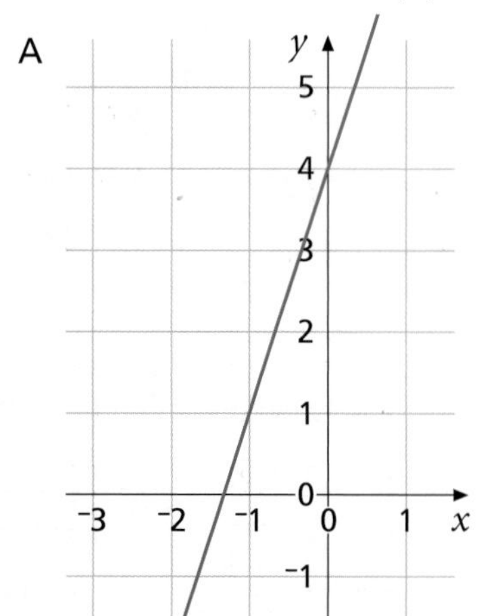

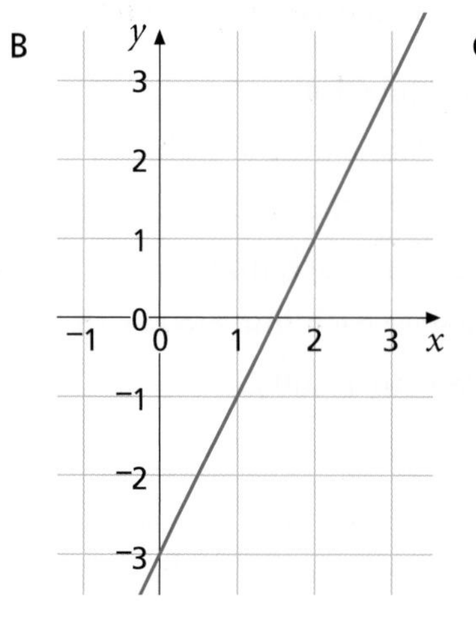

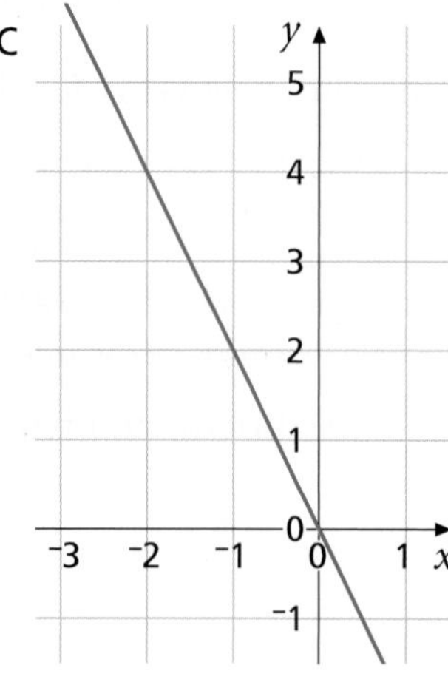

B2 (a) Plot the points $(^{-}2, {}^{-}9)$ and $(3, 11)$ on a set of axes.

(b) Join the points and find the equation of this line.

B3 For each line,

(a) find the gradient and write it as a decimal

(b) find its equation

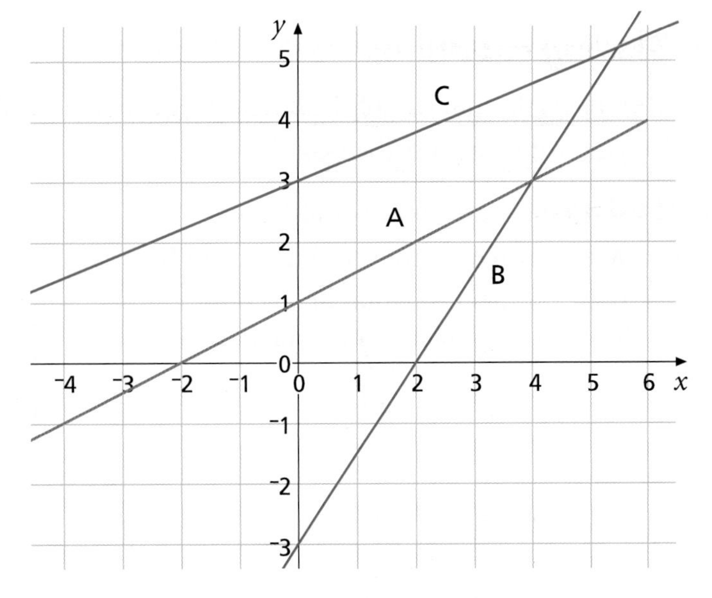

B4 (a) Plot the points (−5, −6) and (5, 2) on a set of axes.

(b) Join the points and find the equation of this line.

B5 Find the equation of each line below.

(a)

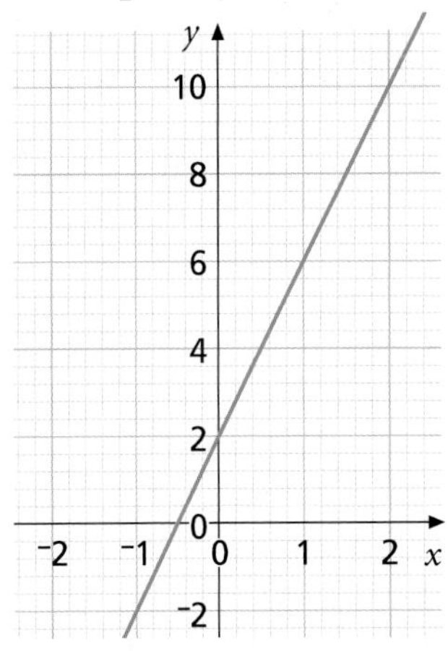

(b)

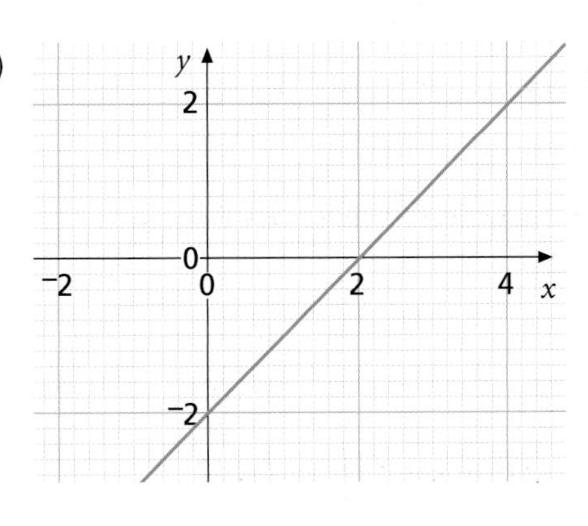

(c)

(d)

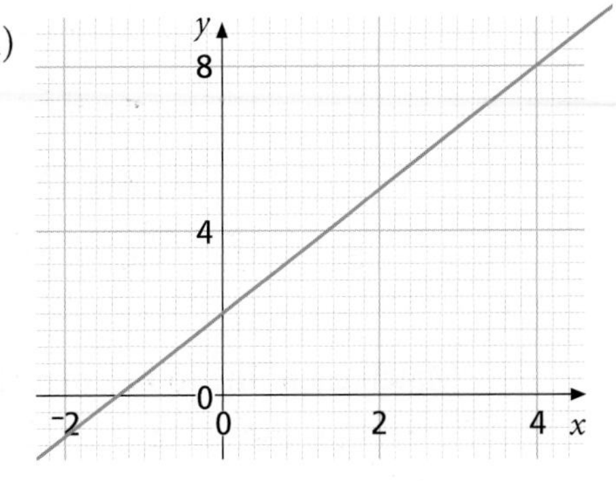

B6 Write down the equation of the line with gradient 8 that crosses the y-axis at (0, 10).

B7 (a) What is the gradient of the line with equation $y = 4x - 9$?

(b) Where does it cross the y-axis?

B8 This diagram shows three parallel lines.

(a) Write down equations for lines A and B.

(b) Write down an equation of any other line that is parallel to these three.

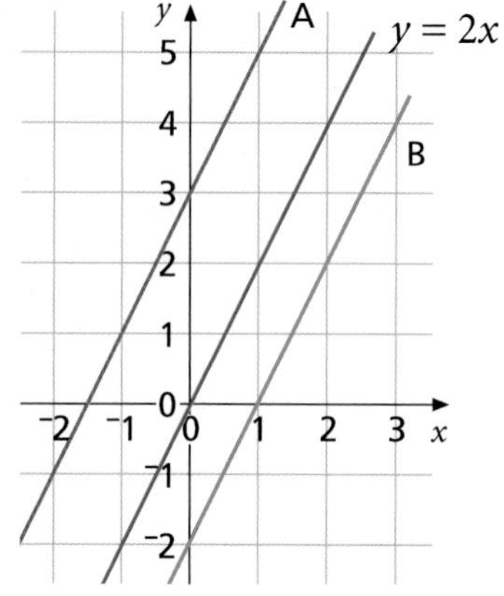

B9 What is the equation of the line parallel to $y = 3x + 2$ that crosses the y-axis at (0, –1)?

B10 The lines labelled A to C match these equations.

$y = 2x + 5$

$y = x + 5$

$y = x - 2$

Match each line to its correct equation.

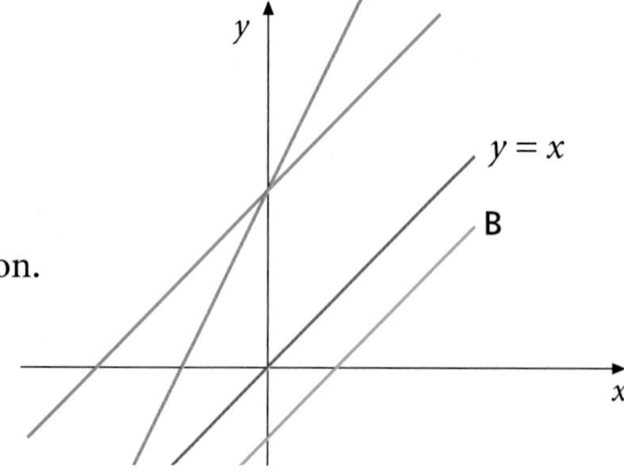

B11 This question is on sheet G142.

***B12** The lines labelled P to T match these equations.

$y = 2x + 1$

$y = x - 6$

$y = 0.5x - 6$

$y = {}^{-}3x - 2$

$y = 0.5x + 1$

Match each line to its correct equation.

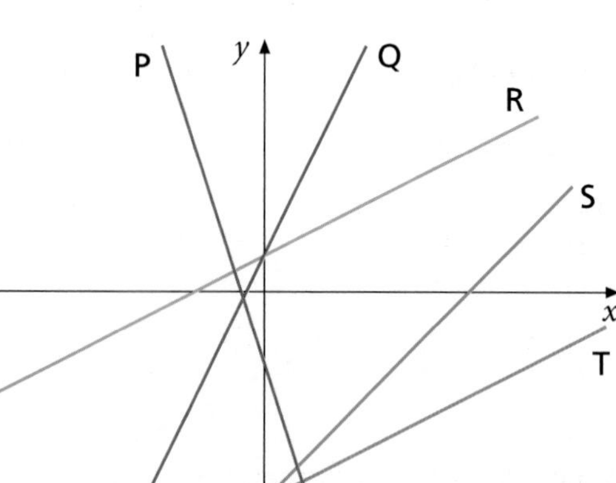

C *Including fractions*

Sometimes the gradient of a line is a fraction that cannot be written as a simple decimal.

Example

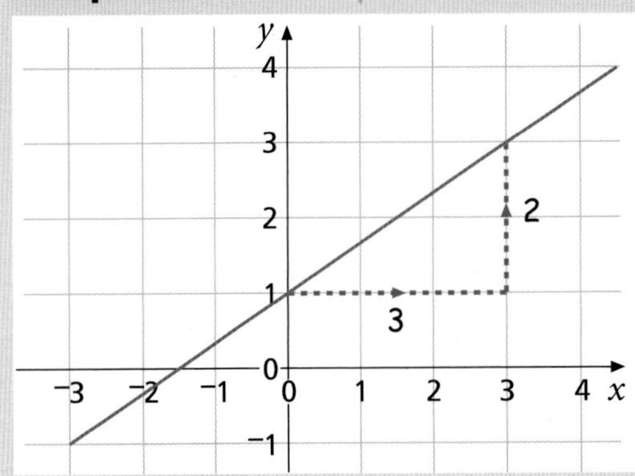

The gradient of this line is $\frac{2}{3}$.
The y-intercept is 1.
So the equation can be written
$y = \frac{2}{3}x + 1$ or $y = \frac{2x}{3} + 1$.

As a decimal $\frac{2}{3} = 0.6666\ldots$ or $0.\dot{6}$.

We don't usually write recurring decimals in equations.

C1 For each line on the right,
  (a) find the gradient as a fraction
  (b) find the y-intercept
  (c) write down its equation

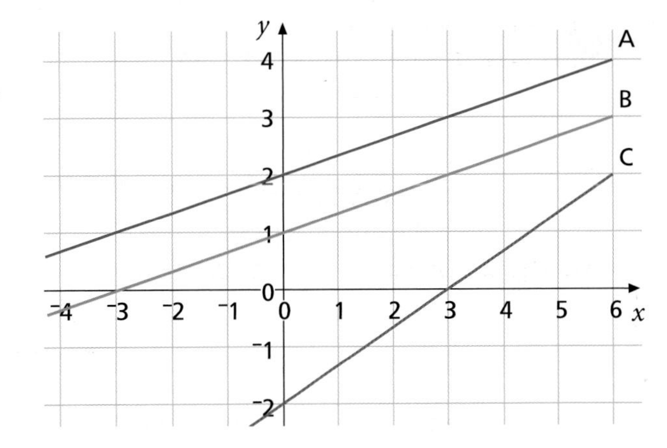

C2 Which of these lines is steeper, $y = \frac{3}{4}x - 2$ or $y = \frac{1}{4}x + 5$?

C3 What is the equation of the line joining (0, 4) to (3, 0)?

C4 (a) Match the equations below to give four pairs of parallel lines.

A $y = \frac{1}{2}x + 1$

B $y = \frac{1}{3}x + 5$

C $y = ^{-}\frac{3}{4}x + 3$

D $y = \frac{x}{5} - 1$

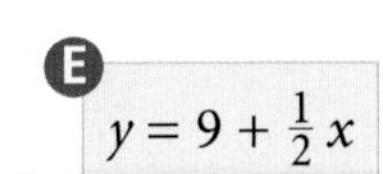

E $y = 9 + \frac{1}{2}x$

F $y = \frac{x}{3} - 2$

G $y = \frac{1}{5}x + 3$

H $y = \frac{4}{3}x + 2$

I $y = 1 - \frac{3}{4}x$

(b) Which equation is the odd one out?

C5 What is the gradient of the line with equation $y = \frac{x}{6} + 5$?

D *Rearranging*

TG

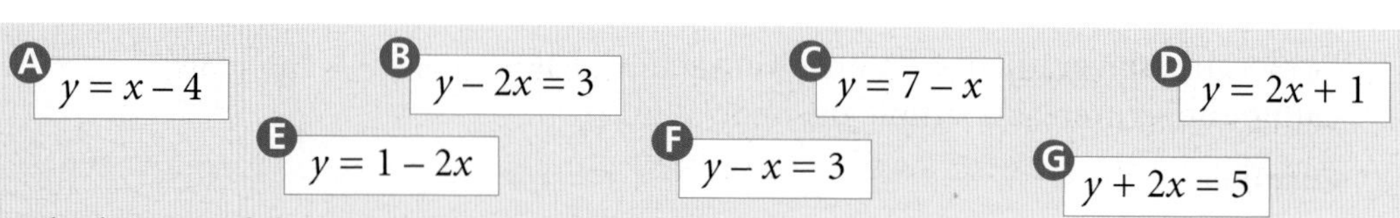

- Which pairs of these equations give parallel lines?

D1 Find the gradient of each of these lines.

(a) $y - x = 5$ (b) $y - 2x = 4$ (c) $3x + y = 6$ (d) $2x = y + 3$

D2 Match the equations below to give four pairs of parallel lines.

A $y - x = 2$ B $y - 3x = 8$ C $y = 5 - 3x$ D $y + 3x = 1$

E $y = 4x - 2$ F $y = x - 6$ G $y - 4x = 5$ H $y = 5 + 3x$

Sometimes you must **divide** the equation of a straight line to give it in the form $y = mx + c$.

Examples

A line has equation $2y = 4x - 8$.

$$2y = 4x - 8 \quad [\div 2]$$
$$y = 2x - 4$$

So the gradient is 2 and the y-intercept is $^-4$.

A line has equation $3y + 15x = 3$.

$$3y + 15x = 3 \quad [\div 3]$$
$$y + 5x = 1 \quad [\text{rearrange}]$$
$$y = 1 - 5x \quad [\text{rearrange}]$$
$$y = {}^-5x + 1$$

So the gradient is $^-5$ and the y-intercept is 1.

D3 Find the gradient of each of these lines.

(a) $2y = 4x + 10$ (b) $3y = 9 - 12x$ (c) $2y - 8x = 12$ (d) $4y + 12x = 8$

D4 Match the equations below to give four pairs of parallel lines.

A $3y = 3x + 21$ B $4y = 8x - 4$ C $2y - 6x = 10$ D $y = {}^-x + 3$

E $y = 2x - 3$ F $y = x + 5$ G $5y + 5x = 10$ H $y = 1 + 3x$

D5 Find the gradients and y-intercepts of each of these lines.

(a) $2y = x + 6$ (b) $3y = x$ (c) $4y = x + 8$

D6 Which two of these lines are parallel to $y = \frac{1}{2}x - 3$?

A $2y = x + 2$ B $2x = y + 10$ C $2y + 8 = x$ D $y - 2x = 9$

***D7** Show that $5x = y - 1$ and $6y - 30x = 6$ are equations for the same line.

E *Lines of best fit*

A pan of water was heated and the temperature measured at various intervals.
The results were plotted and a line of best fit drawn.
How can we find the equation of the line of best fit?

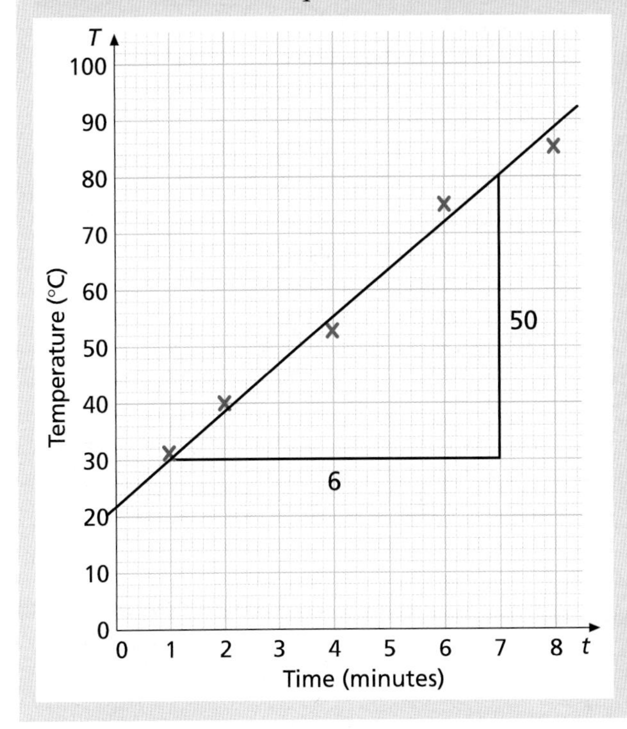

- Choose two convenient points on the line and use them to find the gradient:

$$\frac{50}{6} = 8.3 \text{ (to 1 d.p.)}$$

- Find where it cuts the vertical axis:

The line cuts this axis at about 22.

- So the equation of the line of best fit is approximately

$$T = 8.3t + 22$$

where T is the temperature in °C and t is the time in minutes.

E1 Nigel lit a small candle.
He put a beaker upside down over the candle and counted how many seconds it took for the flame to go out.

He repeated the experiment with larger containers and plotted his results on a graph (on sheet G143).

(a) Draw the line of best fit on the graph.

(b) Choose two points **on your line** and use them to find the gradient, correct to 2 d.p.

(c) Find where the line of best fit cuts the vertical axis.

(d) Hence find an approximate equation for the line of best fit.

(e) Use your equation to estimate how long it would take for the flame to go out in a beaker with volume 1200 ml.

E2 Some more sets of points are shown on sheet G144 and G145.

Follow the instructions below each graph.

Test yourself

T1 (a) Find the gradient of this line.

(b) Write down the equation of the line.

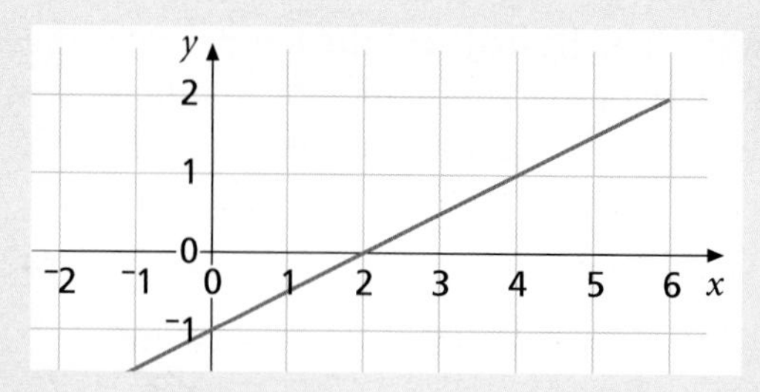

T2 (a) Plot the points (0, 5) and (4, 13) on a set of axes.

(b) Find the equation of the line through these points.

T3 A is the point (0, 3) and B is the point (3, 9).

(a) Calculate the gradient of the line AB.

(b) Write down the equation of the line AB.

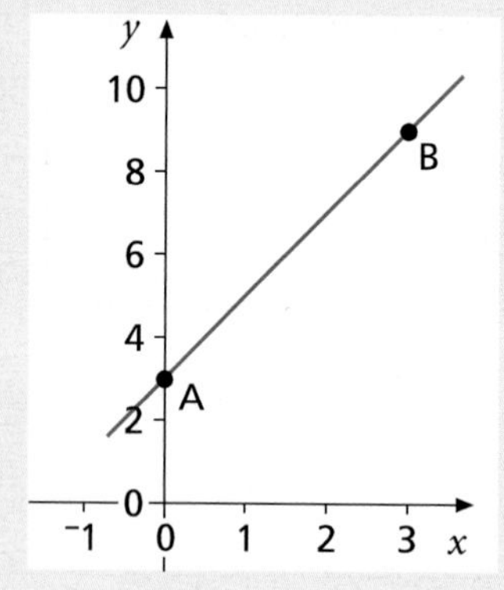

AQA(NEAB)1997

T4 A graph of the equation $y = ax + b$ is shown. Find the values of a and b.

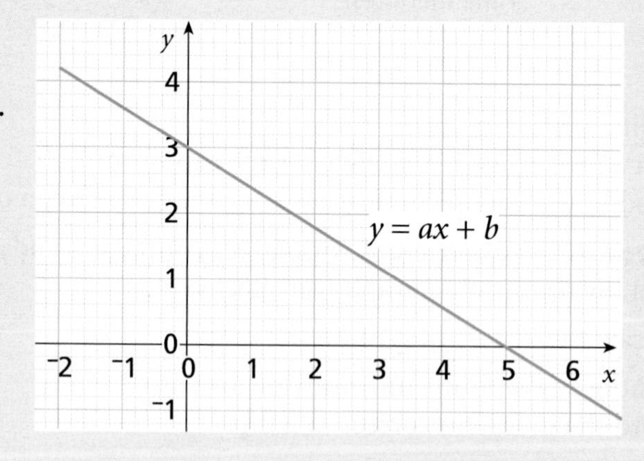

AQA(SEG)1998

T5 Here are the equations of five straight lines. They are labelled from A to E.

Which two lines are parallel?

A $y = 2x + 1$
B $y = 1 - 2x$
C $2y = x - 1$
D $2x - y = 1$
E $x + 2y = 1$

Edexcel

Review 7

1 There are 24 girls and 6 boys in a class.

(a) What is the ratio of girls to boys in its simplest form?

(b) What percentage of the class are boys?

2 (a) Write down the gradient of the line with equation $y = 4x - 7$.

(b) Where does it cross the y-axis?

3 This key is drawn to its exact size.

What scale factor has been used to produce each of these copies?

(a)

(b)

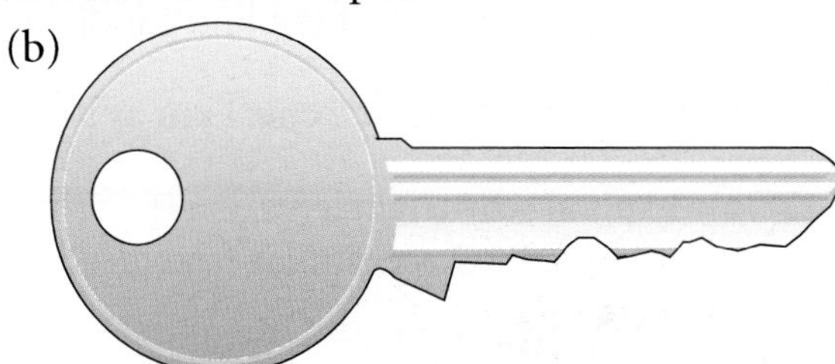

4 What is the equation of the line with a gradient of $\frac{3}{4}$ that crosses the y-axis at $(0, 5)$?

5 Grace is 5 years old, Bob is 8 years old and Hayley is 12 years old.
Their gran gives them £500 to share in the ratio of their ages.

(a) How much does Bob receive?

(b) What percentage of the money does Hayley receive?

6 This is a sketch of a bedroom.

(a) Draw an accurate scale drawing of the room using a scale of 2 cm represents 1 m.

(b) Use your scale drawing to estimate the length XY in the real room.

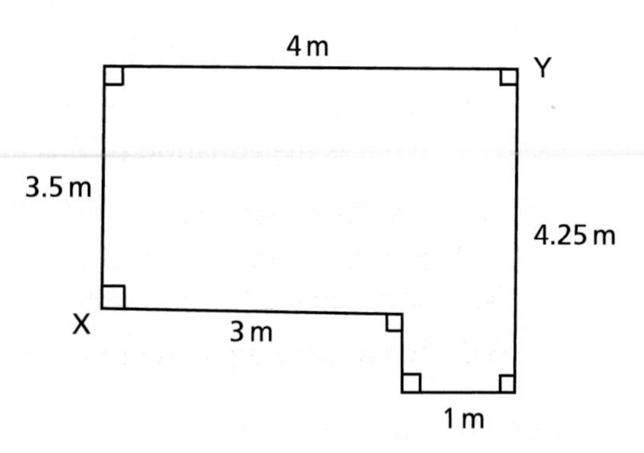

7 Use the map on sheet G146.

(a) How far apart in kilometres are the two lighthouses?

(b) What is the bearing of

(i) Needle Rock from lighthouse A (ii) Needle Rock from lighthouse B

(c) A boat is on a bearing of 105° from lighthouse A and on a bearing of 230° from lighthouse B.

(i) Mark the position of the boat.

(ii) How far is the boat from Needle Rock?

8 A photographic shop offers these sizes of colour prints.

100 mm by 150 mm
125 mm by 175 mm
150 mm by 225 mm
175 mm by 250 mm

Are any of the rectangles similar to one another? Explain how you decided.

9 Sue's recipe for Dry Martinis mixes vermouth and gin in the ratio 1 : 6.

(a) How much gin would Sue mix with 50 ml of vermouth?

(b) How much vermouth would she mix with 180 ml of gin?

10 What is the equation of the line parallel to $y = 4x + 5$ that crosses the y-axis at $(0, {}^{-}2)$?

11 Write the map scale of 2 cm : 1 km as a ratio in the form $1 : n$.

12 (a) Explain why triangle PTS and triangle PRQ are similar triangles.

(b) Calculate the length QR.

(c) If the length QP is 28 cm, work out the length of SP.

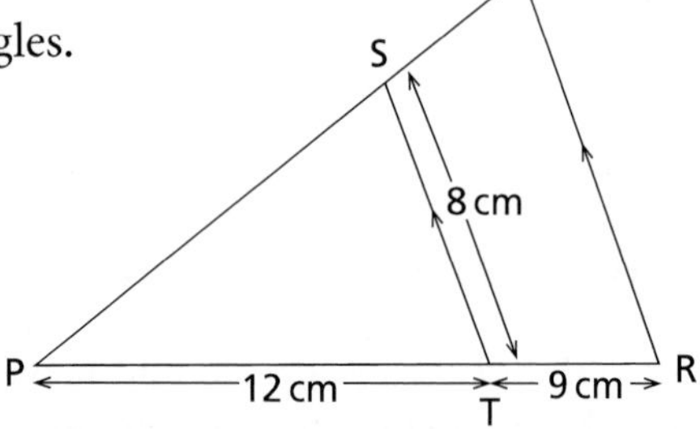

13 (a) Draw a pair of axes, each numbered from $^{-}10$ to 10. Plot and join the points A (1, 9) and B ($^{-}2$, 3).

(b) (i) What is the gradient of the straight line through A and B?

(ii) Find the equation of this straight line.

(c) Draw a line through the point C (4, 0) parallel to the line BA. What is the equation of this line?

(d) Draw the straight line through B and C. Find the equation of this line.

(e) Plot the point D so that ABCD is a square. Give the coordinates of this point.

(f) What is the equation of the straight line through A and D?

14 Draw a scalene triangle. Divide it into four congruent triangles that are similar to it.

40 Large and small numbers

You need to know

- how to multiply and divide by 10, 100, 1000, …
- how to evaluate powers such as 10^2 and 10^{-3}
- how to simplify multiplications and divisions such as $10^2 \times 10^{-3}$ and $\frac{10^9}{10^7}$

This work will help you

- work with numbers written in different ways such as 2.4 billion
- change large and small numbers to and from standard form
- calculate with numbers in standard form, with and without a calculator

A *Powers of ten*

How old will you be one billion seconds from now?

What were you doing a million hours ago?

If you travelled a million metres north of London, where would you be?

How high is a pile of one million 1p pieces?

If you spend £1000 each day, how long will it take you to spend a billion pounds?

TG

A1 Write these as powers of ten.

(a) $10 \times 10 \times 10$ (b) $10 \times 10 \times 10 \times 10 \times 10$

A2 Evaluate each of these.

(a) 10^2 (b) 10^5 (c) 10^4 (d) 10^8

A3 What is the value of the letter in each statement?

(a) $10^x = 1\,000\,000\,000$ (b) $10^y = 100\,000\,000\,000\,000$

A4 Sort these numbers into six matching pairs.

A one thousand

B 10^5

C 100 000 000 000

D ten thousand

E $10 \times 10 \times 10 \times 10$

F 

G $10 \times 10 \times 10 \times 10 \times 10 \times 10 \times 10$

H 

I one billion

J ten million

K 10^3

L one hundred thousand

A5 Write these as single powers of ten.

(a) $10^2 \times 10^3$ (b) $10^4 \times 10^5$ (c) $\frac{10^8}{10^5}$ (d) $\frac{10^9}{10^3}$

A6 Sort these into four matching pairs.

A $4 \times 10\,000$ **B** $4.7 \times 10\,000\,000$ **C**

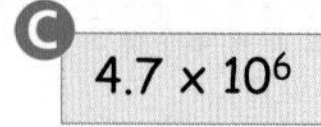

D $47 \times 100\,000$

E

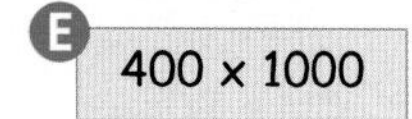

F 40×10^3 **G** 0.47×10^8 **H** 4×10^5

A7 Evaluate the following.

(a) $6 \times 10\,000\,000$ (b) $23 \times 10\,000$ (c) $50 \times 100\,000$

(d) 13×10^6 (e) 207×10^8 (f) 400×10^3

A8 Evaluate the following.

(a) 1.2×100 (b) $51.6 \times 1\,000\,000$ (c) $2.09 \times 10\,000$

(d) 6.3×10^4 (e) 29.4×10^7 (f) 7.62×10^9

B *Writing large numbers*

Large numbers can be written in different ways.

2.3 thousand	20 million	5.49 billion
= 2.3 × 1000	= 20 × 1 000 000	= 5.49 × 1 000 000 000
= 2300	= 20 000 000	= 5 490 000 000

B1 The St. Lawrence river in Canada is 3130 km long.
Which of these is a way to write its length?

A 31.3 thousand km   **B** 3.13 million km

C 3.13 thousand km   **D** 313 thousand km

B2 This table shows the lengths of five well known rivers.

River	km (thousands)
Nile	6.67
Yangtze-Kiang	6.3
Zaire	4.7
Danube	2.84
Seine	0.78

(a) In kilometres, the length of the Nile is 6670 km.
Write the lengths of the other rivers in kilometres.

(b) What is the missing number in this statement:
'The length of the Zaire is about … times the length of the Seine.'

B3 The total fish population of the world's oceans has been estimated at about 10^{14} individual fish.

How many billion fish is this?

B4 Here are some estimates of the world population for different years.

1900	1630 million
1950	2520 million
1960	3 billion
1970	3.7×10^9
1980	4.5 billion
1990	$53 \times 100\,000\,000$
1995	5 690 000 000

(a) Copy and complete this table to show these figures as ordinary numbers and in billions.

Year	Population	Billions
1900	1 630 000 000	1.63
1950		
1960		
1970		
1980		
19		

(b) What is the missing number in this statement?

'The world population in 1990 was about … times the population in 1950.'

B5 The total surface area of land on Earth is 149 200 000 square kilometres. About 35.3 million square kilometres is desert.

Which of these statements is correct?

A 'Desert is about $\frac{1}{2}$ of the total land area of the Earth.'

B 'Desert is about $\frac{1}{10}$ of the total land area of the Earth.'

C 'Desert is about $\frac{1}{4}$ of the total land area of the Earth.'

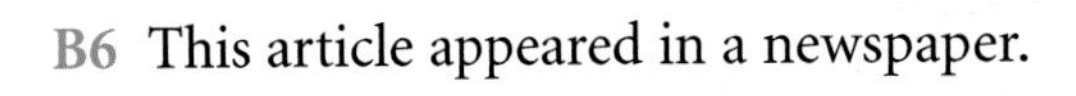

B6 This article appeared in a newspaper.

> The most popular way to unwind these days is by enjoying a biscuit with a cup of tea or coffee.
>
> - 230 billion biscuits are eaten every year in the UK.
> - Over the year these biscuits cost £4.2 billion.
> - On average every UK home spends £3.50 each week on biscuits.

One billion is a thousand million.

From the figures given in the article,

(a) show that the average price of a biscuit is approximately 2p

(b) show that there are approximately 20 million homes in the UK

AQA(NEAB) 1997

C *Standard form*

In 2000, the assets of Queen Beatrix of Holland, Europe's richest royal, were £3 100 000 000. We say 3 100 000 000 is written in **ordinary form**.

All of these are ways to write this number …

- 3100 million
- 3.1 billion
- $3\,100\,000 \times 1000$
- 31×10^8
- 3.1×10^9

… but only 3.1×10^9 is in **standard form** (or **standard index form**).

3.1×10^9

In standard form, this number is between 1 and 10 …

… and this number is a power of 10 written in index form.

C1 Which of these numbers are written in standard form?

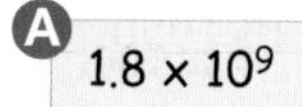

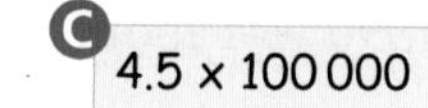

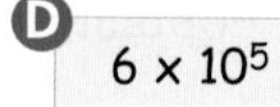

E 2.3×2^4

C2 Write these numbers in ordinary form.

(a) 3×10^4 (b) 2×10^7 (c) 8×10^{11}

(d) 4.2×10^5 (e) 8.1×10^8 (f) 5.3×10^6

(g) 9.37×10^2 (h) 7.04×10^6 (i) 5.89×10^9

C3 Write these numbers in standard form.

(a) 90 000 (b) 50 000 000

(c) 800 000 000 000 (d) 2 000 000 000 000 000

(e) 6 million (f) 3 billion

C4 Write these numbers in standard form.

(a) 63 000 (b) 9 100 000 000

(c) 76 000 000 000 000 (d) 329 000 000

(e) 573 000 000 000 000 000 (f) 127 800 000 000 000

C5 The distance between the Earth and the Moon is about 384 000 km.
Write this distance in standard form.

C6 A light year is a distance of about 9.46×10^{12} km.
Write this distance in ordinary form.

A light year is the distance light travels in a year.

C7 This table shows the most common languages spoken in the world in 1996.

(a) Write each number of speakers in ordinary form.

Language	Number of speakers (approx)
1 Chinese (Mandarin)	1.093×10^9
2 English	4.5×10^8
3 Hindi	3.67×10^8
4 Spanish	3.52×10^8
5 Russian	2.04×10^8

(b) What is wrong with this statement?

'In 1996, the number of Mandarin speakers was about half the number of Russian speakers.'

C8 This table shows the organised religions with most members in 1997.

(a) Write each number in standard form, correct to two significant figures.

(b) Write the religions in order of membership, from the most members to the least members.

Religion	Number of members
Baha'ism	5 835 000
Buddhism	338 600 000
Christianity	1 900 000 000
Confucianism	63 340 000
Hinduism	7 640 000 000
Islam	1 033 000 000
Jainism	3 987 000
Judaism	135 000 000
Shintoism	3 388 000
Sikhism	20 200 000

C9 In 1996, 0.4 million tonnes of fish were caught in the Antarctic. Write this figure in standard form.

D *Using a calculator*

$p = 20\,000\,000$
$q = 1.2 \times 10^{14}$
$a = 5 \times 10^{17}$
$b = 2.96 \times 10^5$

Can you find the value of each expression?

p^2 $\quad q^2$ $\quad pq$

a^2 $\quad ab$ $\quad a + q$ $\quad p + q$

$\frac{a}{b}$ $\quad \frac{q}{b}$ $\quad \frac{1}{2}b^2p$

D1 Write the answer to each calculation in standard form.

(a) $2\,000\,000 \times 30\,000\,000$

(b) $4\,000\,000^2$

(c) $\dfrac{6\,200\,000}{0.0005}$

(d) $5\,000\,000^2 + 70\,000\,000^2$

D2 Write the answer to each calculation in standard form, correct to 3 significant figures.

(a) $61\,920\,000^2$ (b) $82\,543\,000 \div 0.0024$

D3 Give the answer to each calculation in standard form.

(a) $(2.31 \times 10^7) + (1.5 \times 10^6)$ (b) $(8.35 \times 10^6) \times (2.6 \times 10^8)$

(c) $\dfrac{4.2 \times 10^{19}}{8.4 \times 10^8}$ (d) $\dfrac{9.72 \times 10^9}{1.8 \times 10^3}$

D4 Write the answer to each calculation in standard form, correct to 2 significant figures.

(a) $(3.26 \times 10^9) \times 294$ (b) $\dfrac{1.47 \times 10^{13}}{5.39}$

(c) $(6.35 \times 10^6) \times (1.03 \times 10^7)$ (d) $(2.06 \times 10^9)^2$

D5 Give the answer to each calculation as an ordinary number, correct to 2 significant figures.

(a) $\dfrac{4.2 \times 10^{19}}{8.1 \times 10^8}$ (b) $\sqrt{9.5 \times 10^{12}}$ (c) $56\,000 \times 394\,000$

D6 Find the value of each expression when

$p = 2.3 \times 10^9$ and $q = 8.5 \times 10^8$.

Give each answer in standard form.

(a) $p + q$ (b) pq (c) $2p + 5q$

D7 You are given the formula $S = \frac{1}{2}ab^2$.

Find the value of S when

$a = 3.6 \times 10^7$ and $b = 0.5$.

Give your answer in standard form.

D8 You are given the formula $P = \dfrac{xy}{x - y}$

Find the value of P when

$x = 4.9 \times 10^{12}$ and $y = 2.8 \times 10^{11}$.

Give your answer in standard form, correct to three significant figures.

D9 What is the difference in value between 2×10^4 and 2^4?

D10 In 1991 an estimated 1.6×10^7 kg of oil entered the sea each day.
Estimate how much oil entered the sea during 1991.
Give your answer in standard form, correct to two significant figures.

D11 Until it became illegal in 1990, an estimated 6×10^9 kg of rubbish was dumped from ships each year.
Estimate the weight of rubbish that was dumped each day.
Give your answer in ordinary form, correct to one significant figure.

E *Negative powers*

Negative powers of ten are all **less than 1**.

…	10^3	10^2	10^1	10^0	10^{-1}	10^{-2}	10^{-3}	…
…	1000	100	10	1	$\frac{1}{10^1}$	$\frac{1}{10^2}$	$\frac{1}{10^3}$	…

They can be written as a **fraction** or **decimal**, for example

$$10^{-2} = \frac{1}{10^2} = \frac{1}{100} = 0.01$$

So 10^{-2} can be written as a fraction $\left(\frac{1}{100}\right)$ or a decimal (0.01).

E1 Sort these into five matching pairs.

B 10^{-4}

D 10^{-1}

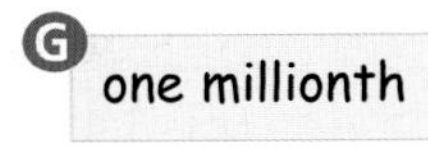

H $\frac{1}{10^5}$

I $\frac{1}{10000}$

J one tenth

E2 Write these as fractions.

(a) 10^{-1} (b) 10^{-3} (c) 10^{-5}

E3 Evaluate these as decimals.

(a) 10^{-4} (b) 10^{-5} (c) 10^{-1} (d) 10^{-6}

When a number is multiplied by a negative power of ten, it gets smaller.

Example

$$5.3 \times 10^{-2} = 5.3 \times \frac{1}{10^2} = 5.3 \times \frac{1}{100} = 5.3 \div 100 = 0.053$$

E4 Evaluate the following.

(a) 600×10^{-1} (b) $410\,000 \times 10^{-2}$ (c) $59\,000\,000 \times 10^{-6}$

(d) 56×10^{-1} (e) $88\,200 \times 10^{-3}$ (f) $45\,100 \times 10^{-5}$

(g) 3.9×10^{-1} (h) 4.67×10^{-1} (i) 39.5×10^{-2}

(j) 6.3×10^{-2} (k) 3×10^{-5} (l) 7×10^{-8}

E5 What is the value of the letter in each statement?

(a) $7\,800\,000 \times 10^a = 7.8$ (b) $5.4 \times 10^b = 0.000\,000\,54$

E6 Write these as single powers of ten.

(a) $10^5 \times 10^{-3}$ (b) $10^4 \times 10^{-7}$ (c) $10^{-6} \times 10^7$ (d) $10^{-2} \times 10^{-3}$

(e) $\frac{10^5}{10^7}$ (f) $\frac{10^3}{10^4}$ (g) $\frac{10^2}{10^8}$ (h) $\frac{10^3}{10^{-2}}$

F *Writing small numbers*

Standard form can be used for very small numbers.

$$\vdots$$
$$3 \times 10^2 = 3 \times 100 = 300$$
$$3 \times 10^1 = 3 \times 10 = 30$$
$$3 \times 10^0 = 3 \times 1 = 3$$
$$3 \times 10^{-1} = 3 \times \frac{1}{10} = \frac{3}{10} = 0.3$$
$$3 \times 10^{-2} = 3 \times \frac{1}{10^2} = \frac{3}{100} = 0.03$$
$$3 \times 10^{-3} = 3 \times \frac{1}{10^3} = \frac{3}{1000} = 0.003$$
$$\vdots$$

$$\vdots$$
$$426 = 4.26 \times 100 = 4.26 \times 10^2$$
$$42.6 = 4.26 \times 10 = 4.26 \times 10^1$$
$$4.26 = 4.26 \times 1 = 4.26 \times 10^0$$
$$0.426 = \frac{4.26}{10} = 4.26 \times \frac{1}{10^1} = 4.26 \times 10^{-1}$$
$$0.0426 = \frac{4.26}{100} = 4.26 \times \frac{1}{10^2} = 4.26 \times 10^{-2}$$
$$0.004\,26 = \frac{4.26}{1000} = 4.26 \times \frac{1}{10^3} = 4.26 \times 10^{-3}$$
$$\vdots$$

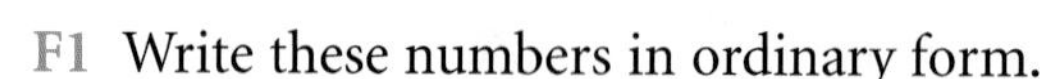

F1 Write these numbers in ordinary form.

(a) 9.1×10^{-3} (b) 6.21×10^{-2} (c) 3.4×10^{-4}
(d) 5.3×10^{-5} (e) 1.92×10^{-7} (f) 6.9×10^{-10}

F2 Write these numbers in ordinary form.

(a) 2×10^{-2} (b) 6×10^{-4} (c) 5×10^{-3}
(d) 4×10^{-5} (e) 3×10^{-6} (f) 2×10^{-11}

F3 Write these numbers in standard form.

(a) 0.002 9 (b) 0.000 048 (c) 0.092 3
(d) 0.000 006 45 (e) 0.000 000 001 9 (f) 0.000 000 000 082
(g) 0.000 3 (h) 0.000 000 7 (i) 0.000 000 000 009

F4 A jawa is a coin that was used in Nepal.
It is the smallest coin ever issued and weighed 0.000 014 kilograms.
Write the weight of this coin in standard form.

F5 The patu marplesi spider is the smallest in the world.
It is found in Samoa and is 4.3×10^{-4} metres long.
Write the length of this spider in ordinary form.

F6 The weights of some living creatures are given below.
Put them in order, heaviest first.

Pygmy shrew: 1.5×10^{-3} kg

House mouse: 1.2×10^{-2} kg

House spider: 1×10^{-4} kg

Helena's hummingbird: 2×10^{-3} kg

Kitti's hog-nosed bat: 1.7×10^{-3} kg

Bee hummingbird: 0.0016 kg

G *Small numbers on your calculator*

A molecule of water has a mass of about 3×10^{-23} grams.
What is the mass of eight million water molecules, written in standard form?

Eight million is 8 000 000 so the mass of these water molecules is:

$3 \times 10^{-23} \times 8\,000\,000 = 2.4 \times 10^{-16}$ grams

Make sure you can work this out on **your** calculator.

G1 Write the answer to each calculation in standard form.

(a) 0.0034^2 (b) 0.0005×0.00042 (c) $4.8 \div 3\,000\,000$

G2 Write the answer to each calculation in standard form, correct to 2 significant figures.

(a) $\sqrt{0.000005}$ (b) $3 \div 98\,261$

(c) $(2.4 \times 10^{-6}) \times (1.56 \times 10^{2})$ (d) $(5.3 \times 10^{-9}) \times (4.82 \times 10^{-3})$

(e) $\dfrac{6.8 \times 10^{-8}}{2.3 \times 10^{-2}}$ (f) $\dfrac{(7.8 \times 10^{-5})^2}{300}$

G3 Give each answer in ordinary form, correct to 3 significant figures.

(a) $\sqrt{9.7 \times 10^{-4}}$ (b) $(4.1562 \times 10^{-3}) + (5.9238 \times 10^{-4})$

G4 Find the value of the expression $\sqrt{\dfrac{GV}{M}}$ when

$G = 4.3 \times 10^{-3}$, $V = 8.5 \times 10^{-2}$ and $M = 5 \times 10^{4}$.

Give your answer in standard form.

H *Calculating without a calculator*

Examples

$(6.4 \times 10^5) \times (2 \times 10^3)$

$= 6.4 \times 2 \times 10^5 \times 10^3$

$= 12.8 \times 10^8$ ← Not yet in standard form.

$= 1.28 \times 10 \times 10^8$

$= 1.28 \times 10^9$

$\dfrac{3 \times 10^7}{6 \times 10^2}$

$= \dfrac{3}{6} \times \dfrac{10^7}{10^2}$

$= 0.5 \times 10^5$

$= 5 \times 10^{-1} \times 10^5$

$= 5 \times 10^4$

H1 Write each of these in **standard form**.

(a) 300×10^6 (b) 26×10^4 (c) 14.9×10^8 (d) 0.5×10^7

H2 Calculate the following, giving your answers in standard form.

(a) $(2 \times 10^6) \times (4 \times 10^4)$ (b) $(3 \times 10^5) \times (3 \times 10^2)$

(c) $(6 \times 10^5) \times 30$ (d) $(5 \times 10^2) \times (7 \times 10^7)$

H3 Calculate the following, giving your answers in standard form.

(a) $\frac{8 \times 10^9}{2 \times 10^7}$ (b) $\frac{9 \times 10^{12}}{2 \times 10^5}$ (c) $\frac{2 \times 10^8}{4 \times 10^6}$

H4 Copy and complete the following and write the answer in **ordinary form.**

$(2 \times 10^4) + (5 \times 10^3) = 20\,000 +$ .... = ...

H5 Calculate the following, giving your answers in ordinary form.

(a) $(4 \times 10^4) + (2 \times 10^5)$ (b) $(5 \times 10^4) - (2 \times 10^4)$

(c) $\frac{8 \times 10^6}{4 \times 10^5}$ (d) $\frac{3 \times 10^4}{6 \times 10^4}$ (e) $\frac{2 \times 10^8}{8 \times 10^6}$

H6 Calculate $(2.3 \times 10^{20}) + (1.5 \times 10^{20})$, giving your answer in standard form.

H7 Write each of these in standard form.

(a) $500\,000 \times 10^{-2}$ (b) $30\,000 \times 10^{-3}$ (c) 63×10^{-5} (d) 0.5×10^{-4}

H8 Calculate the following, giving your answers in standard form.

(a) $(3 \times 10^4) \times (2 \times 10^{-1})$ (b) $(1.2 \times 10^{-2}) \times (4 \times 10^{-3})$

(c) $5000 \times (4 \times 10^{-6})$ (d) $\frac{7 \times 10^2}{2 \times 10^5}$ (d) $\frac{5.2 \times 10^3}{4 \times 10^7}$

H9 The mass of an atom of uranium is 4×10^{-25} kg.

Calculate the mass of 3 000 000 atoms of uranium.
Give your answer in standard form.

Edexcel

I *Mixed problems*

I1 A light year is a distance of about 9.46×10^{12} km.

(a) The Andromeda Spiral Galaxy is about 2 200 000 light years away from Earth.

(i) Which of these calculations gives this distance in kilometres?

A $(9.46 \times 10^{12}) \times 2\,200\,000$

B $\frac{9.46 \times 10^{12}}{2\,200\,000}$

C $\frac{2\,200\,000}{9.46 \times 10^{12}}$

(ii) Calculate the distance and give your answer in standard form.

(b) The star Arcturus is about 3.217×10^{14} km away from Earth.

(i) Which of these calculations gives this distance in light years?

A $(9.46 \times 10^{12}) \times (3.217 \times 10^{14})$

B $\frac{9.46 \times 10^{12}}{3.217 \times 10^{14}}$

C $\frac{3.217 \times 10^{14}}{9.46 \times 10^{12}}$

(ii) Calculate this distance to the nearest light year.

I2 Last year the population of the United Kingdom was approximately 5.3×10^7.

(a) An average of £680 per person was spent on food last year in the United Kingdom.
What was the total amount spent on food?
Give your answer in standard form.

(b) Last year there were 1.4×10^7 car drivers in the United Kingdom.
They spent a total of £1.5×10^{10} on their cars.
What was the average amount spent by each car driver?
Give your answer in standard form. AQA(NEAB) 1998

I3 The total surface area of land on Earth is 1.492×10^8 square kilometres.
About 3.9×10^7 square kilometres is forest.
What percentage of land on Earth is forest?

I4 The mass of one electron is

0.000 000 000 000 000 000 000 000 000 91 grams.

(a) Write 0.000 000 000 000 000 000 000 000 000 91 in standard form.

(b) Calculate the mass of five million electrons.
Give your answer in grams in standard form. Edexcel

I5 (a) The mass of the Earth is 5.98×10^{24} kg.
Calculate the mass of the Earth in tonnes, giving your answer in standard form.

(b) The mass of the moon is 7.34×10^{22} kg.
The mass of the Earth is N times the mass of the moon.
Find the value of N correct to the nearest whole number.

(c) The radius of the Earth is 6.37×10^3 km.
Calculate the cube of this radius, giving your answer in standard form. WJEC

I6 The contents of books and newspapers can be stored on microfilm.
ABCD is one rectangular frame of this microfilm.

AB = 4.5×10^{-3} centimetres and
BC = 6.2×10^{-4} centimetres.

(a) Calculate the area of the rectangle. Give your answer in standard form.
Remember to state the units in your answer.

(b) Calculate the perimeter of the rectangle.
Give your answer in standard form.
Remember to state the units in your answer. AQA(NEAB) 1997

I7 A speed radar sends out a beam of radio waves at
a frequency of 24 thousand million vibrations per second.

(a) Write this number in standard form.

(b) How many vibrations is this in an hour?
Give your answer is standard form. OCR(MEG)

Test yourself

T1 (a) In 1991 the population of the UK was 57 800 000.
Write this population in standard form.

(b) The area of the UK is about 2.45×10^5 square kilometres.
Calculate the average number of people per square kilometre in the UK in 1991.

T2 The earliest dinosaurs existed on Earth 2.05×10^8 years ago.
Dinosaurs became extinct 6.5×10^7 years ago.
For how long did dinosaurs exist on Earth? OCR

T3 $p = 1.65 \times 10^7$, $q = 4.82 \times 10^6$ and $r = 6.17 \times 10^{-2}$
Calculate the value of the following.
Give your answers in standard form.

(a) $2p + 3q$ (b) $p \div r$ AQA(NEAB) 1997

T4 A packet of paper contains 5×10^2 sheets.

(a) The thickness of a sheet of paper is 9.6×10^{-3} cm.
What is the thickness of the packet?

(b) The packet of paper weighs 2.9×10^3 grams.
Calculate the weight of a sheet of paper in grams. AQA(SEG) 1998

T5 Halley's Comet visits Earth every 76 years.
At its furthest point, it is 35 Astronomical Units from Earth.
An Astronomical Unit is 1.496×10^{11} m.

(a) What is this maximum distance from Earth?
Give your answer in metres, using standard index form.

(b) Light travels at 2.998×10^8 m/s.
How far does it travel in one year?
Give your answer in metres, using standard index form.

(c) The distance in (b) is one light year.
Give your answer to (a) in light years, using standard index form. OCR

T6 Write these as ordinary numbers.

(a) 2.53×10^7 (b) 5.2×10^{-5}

T7 $p = 8 \times 10^3$
$q = 2 \times 10^4$

(a) Find the value of $p \times q$.
Give your answer in **standard form.**

(b) Find the value of $p + q$.
Give your answer as an **ordinary number.** Edexcel

41 Forming and solving equations

You will revise how to solve straightforward equations with the unknown on one side or both sides.

The work will help you

- solve more complicated equations
- form equations from problems and solve them

A Review: unknown on one side

Worked examples

$3x - 5 = 13$ [+ 5]
$3x = 18$ [÷ 3]
$x = 6$

$11 - 2x = 3$ [+ 2x]
$11 = 3 + 2x$ [− 3]
$8 = 2x$ [÷ 2]
$x = 4$

$\frac{x+4}{2} = 3$ [× 2]
$x + 4 = 6$ [− 4]
$x = 2$

A1 (a) Solve the equation $x + 4 = 10$.

(b) Substitute your answer for x back into the left-hand side. Check that it makes $x + 4$ equal to 10.

A2 Solve each of these equations. Check each answer works.

(a) $5x = 20$ (b) $x + 10 = 32$ (c) $\frac{x}{2} = 16$ (d) $x - 10 = 25$

A3 Solve each of these equations. Check your solution for each one.

(a) $3n + 5 = 23$ (b) $2n - 3 = 7$ (c) $4n - 1 = 1$

A4 Solve these equations.

(a) $2x + 3 = 8$ (b) $4y - 3 = 15$ (c) $\frac{1}{5}z + 4 = 6$
(d) $2n + 8 = 2$ (e) $3m + 18 = 0$ (f) $2p + 2 = {}^{-}4$

A5 Solve these equations.

(a) $10 = 2x - 4$ (b) $5 = 15 - y$ (c) $2 = 12 - 2x$

A6 Solve these equations.

(a) $2x - 0.5 = 0.3$ (b) $0.5 = 1 - x$ (c) $0.1x = 2$
(d) $0.5x + 0.2 = 1.5$ (e) $0.2 = 0.5 - 3x$ (f) $10x - 7 = 1$

A7 Solve these equations.

(a) $\frac{f-3}{2} = 5$ (b) $\frac{3e-2}{5} = 2$ (c) $\frac{4f+1}{3} = 7$

B Review: unknown on both sides

Worked examples

$$\begin{aligned} 4x - 3 &= 11 + 2x & [-2x] \\ 2x - 3 &= 11 & [+3] \\ 2x &= 14 & [\div 2] \\ x &= 7 \end{aligned}$$

$$\begin{aligned} 4 + x &= 10 - 2x & [+2x] \\ 4 + 3x &= 10 & [-4] \\ 3x &= 6 & [\div 3] \\ x &= 2 \end{aligned}$$

$$\begin{aligned} 8 + 3x &= 14 + 5x & [-3x] \\ 8 &= 14 + 2x & [-14] \\ ^{-}6 &= 2x & [\div 2] \\ x &= ^{-}3 \end{aligned}$$

B1 Solve these equations.

(a) $2x + 3 = 8 + x$ (b) $4x - 3 = 2x + 5$ (c) $6x + 4 = 3x + 16$

(d) $4x + 8 = 2 + 7x$ (e) $3x + 12 = 5x$ (f) $2x - 2 = 4 + x$

B2 Solve these equations.

(a) $2n + 2 = 7 + n$ (b) $n + 1 = 7 - 2n$ (c) $21 - 2n = 3n + 6$

(d) $4 + 8n = 22 - n$ (e) $3n = 14 - n$ (f) $110 - n = 100 + 4n$

B3 Solve these equations.

(a) $2p + 5 = 1$ (b) $3k + 3 = 1 - k$ (c) $0.1x + 3 = 5 - 0.4x$

(d) $1.4 + f = 2.6 - 2f$ (e) $2.2 - 2h = 1 + h$ (f) $8 - 3r = 2r + 8$

B4 Solve these equations.

(a) $\frac{1}{2}d + 5 = 8$ (b) $\frac{1}{2}d + 1 = 4 - \frac{1}{2}d$ (c) $10 + d = \frac{1}{2}d + 12$

B5 Solve these equations.

(a) $\frac{4j - 3}{3} = j$ (b) $\frac{11f + 3}{5} = 2f$ (c) $\frac{27 - h}{4} = 2h$

C Equations from shapes

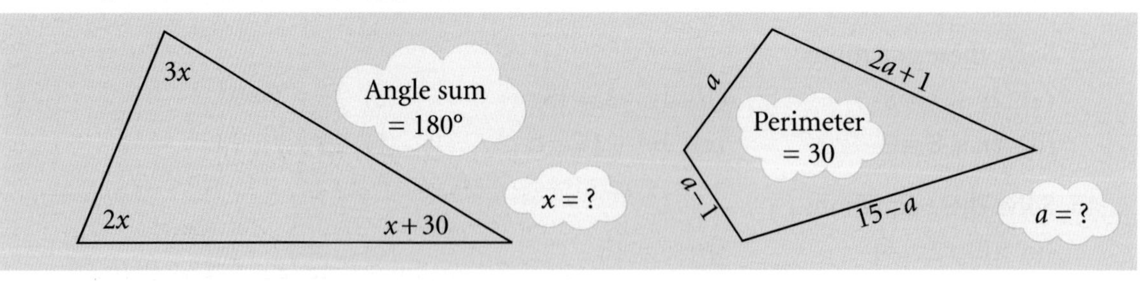

C1 Find each angle in these triangles.

(a)

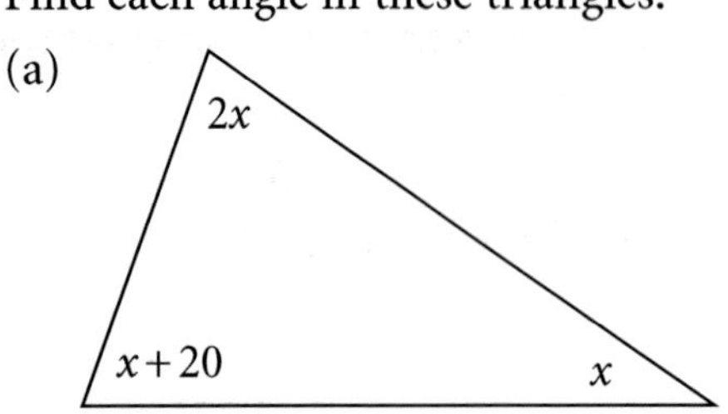

(b)

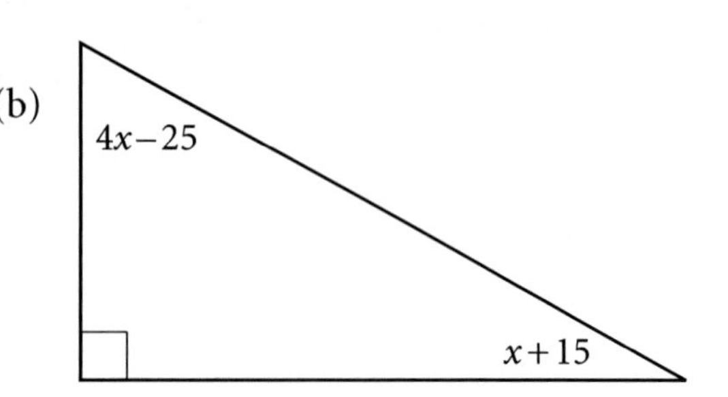

C2 The angles of a triangle are $2x°$, $3x°$ and $4x°$.

(a) Write an expression, in terms of x, for the sum of the angles. Give your answer in its simplest form.

(b) By forming an equation, find the value of x.

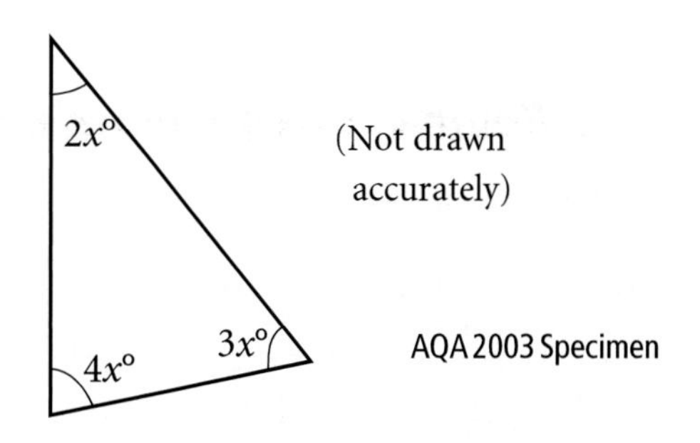

(Not drawn accurately)

AQA 2003 Specimen

C3 The perimeter of each of these shapes is 100. Find the length of each side.

(a)

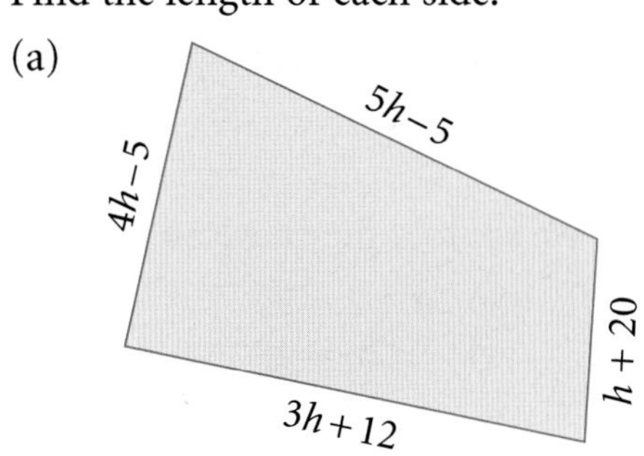

(b)

$5x - 10$

20

C4 The perimeter of the pentagon is 200 cm. Work out the value of x.

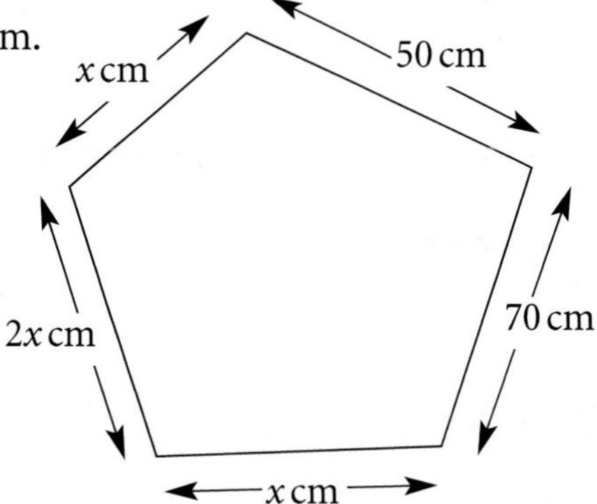

Edexcel

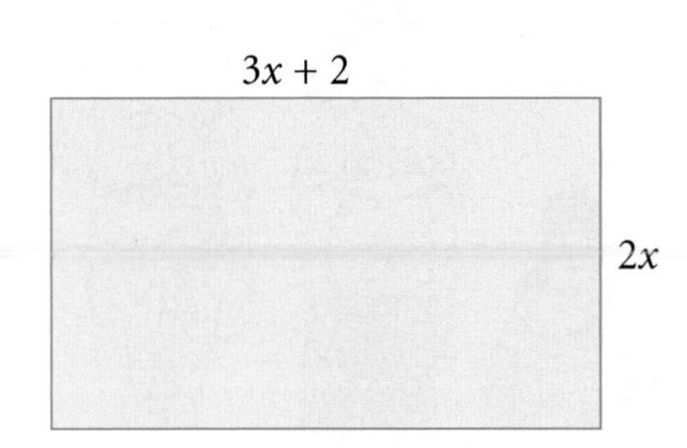

C5 The diagram shows a rectangle with length $3x + 2$ and width $2x$. All measurements are given in centimetres.

The perimeter of the rectangle is P centimetres. The area of the rectangle is A square centimetres.

(a) Write down an expression in its simplest form, in terms of x, for

(i) P (ii) A

(b) $P = 44$. Work out the value of A.

Edexcel

D *Equations from words*

Jan has some pencils. Mary has 2 more pencils than Jan.
Altogether they have 50 pencils. How many do they have each?

Let $\boldsymbol{n}$ stand for the number of pencils that Jan has.

Then Mary has $\boldsymbol{n + 2}$ pencils.

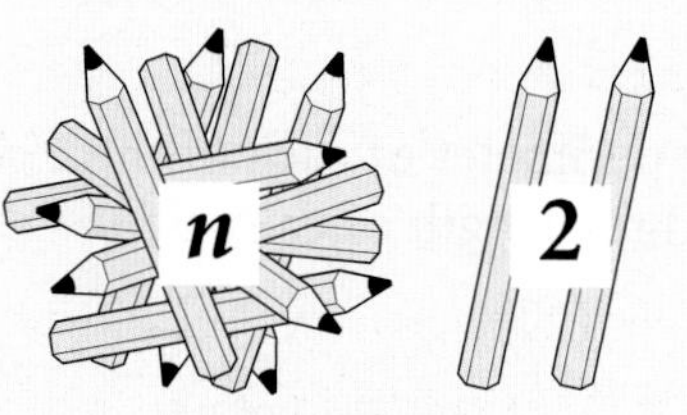

Altogether they have $\boldsymbol{2n + 2}$ **pencils.**

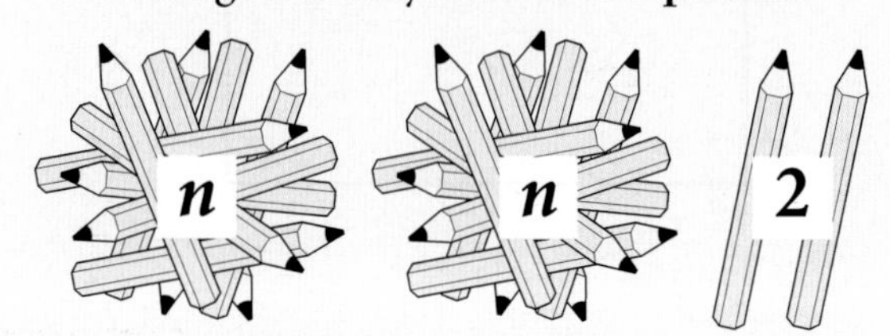

We are told they have **50 pencils.**

So $2n + 2 = 50$
$2n = 48$
$n = 24$

Jan has 24 pencils and Mary has 26.

D1 Alan has some DVDs. Beth has 8 fewer than Alan.

Let n stand for the number of DVDs that Alan has.

(a) Write an expression for the number of DVDs that Beth has.

(b) Write an expression, in terms of n, for the number of DVDs they have altogether.

(c) Altogether they have 100 DVDs.
Use your expression from (b) to form an equation in n.
Solve your equation and write down how many DVDs they have each.

D2 Chloe has two sisters, Becky and Emily.
Becky is 4 years younger than Chloe.
Emily is twice as old as Chloe.

Let y stand for Chloe's age, in years.

(a) How old is Becky, in terms of y?

(b) How old is Emily, in terms of y?

(c) Write an expression for the sum of the three ages.

(d) Their ages add up to 24.
Form an equation in y and solve it.
How old is each of the girls?

D3 Maria buys two chocolate bars costing x pence each and one packet of sweets costing $(x + 2)$ pence.
She spends a total of 56 pence.

(a) Write down an equation in x.

(b) Solve your equation. OCR

D4 An apple costs y pence.
An orange costs 5 pence more than an apple.

(a) Write down an expression, in terms of y, for the cost of one orange.

(b) Write down an expression, in terms of y, for the total cost of three apples and one orange.

(c) The total cost of three apples and one orange is 61 pence.
Form an equation in terms of y and solve it to find the cost of one apple. OCR

D5 Sarah weighs x kilograms. Her mother weighs $2x$ kilograms.
Her father weighs 21 kilograms more than her mother.

(a) Write an expression, in terms of x, for the weight of her father.

The sum of all their weights is 171 kg.

(b) Form an equation and find the value of x. AQA(SEG) 1998

D6 (a) Which of the equations on the right corresponds to this number puzzle?

I think of a number.
I multiply it by 2. I add 12.
My answer is three times my starting number.
What number did I start with?

$2n + 12 = 3$ | $12n + 2 = 3n$ | $2n + 12 = 3n$

(b) Use the correct equation to solve the number puzzle.
Check your solution works.

D7

Think of a number.
Multiply it by three.
Now add seven.

Teacher

My answer is 94.

Abel

What is the number Abel thinks of?

AQA(NEAB) 1998

D8 Solve each of these number puzzles. In each part, let n stand for the number I start with.

(a) *I think of a number.*
I multiply it by 3.
I take off 20.
My answer is twice my starting number.
What was my number?

(b) *I think of a number.*
I double it and add 3.
My answer is 10 more than the number I started with.
What was my number?

(c) *I think of a number.*
I divide it by 2.
I add 14.
My answer is the same as my starting number.
What was my number?

E *Using brackets*

It is often useful to multiply out brackets first when solving an equation.

Worked examples

$3(x+2) = x+18$	
$3x+6 = x+18$	[multiply out brackets]
$2x+6 = 18$	$[-x]$
$2x = 12$	$[-6]$
$x = 6$	$[\div 2]$

$2(3x+2) = 4(x-1)$	
$6x+4 = 4x-4$	[multiply out brackets]
$2x+4 = {}^-4$	$[-4x]$
$2x = {}^-8$	$[-4]$
$x = {}^-4$	$[\div 2]$

E1 Solve each of these equations.

(a) $3(n-2) = n$ (b) $2(m+3) = 24$ (c) $2(x-3) = 1$

(d) $4(d+2) = 2d-7$ (e) $3f+5 = 4(f-3)$ (f) $2(4x-5) = 4(x+1)$

E2 Solve each of these equations.

(a) $2(1-a) = 3a-18$ (b) $3(2-v) = 8(v-2)$ (c) $11(2y-5) = 0$

(d) $4(2x+3) = 3(3x-5)$ (e) $u-8 = 2(1-2u)$ (f) $4(2r+1) = 3(3r+5)$

E3 Solve this equation $5(2x+7) = 11+4x$. OCR

E4 Solve the equation $3x-14 = 5(6-x)$. WJEC

E5 Solve these equations.

(a) $3a-2 = 10$ (b) $5(2x-1)+6x = 7-8x$ OCR

E6 Solve these equations.

(a) $4a+3 = 9$ (b) $5b-7 = 2b+5$ (c) $3(c-6) = 10-2c$ Edexcel

E7

I think of a number.
I take off 5.
I multiply the result by 3.
My answer is 21.
What was my number?

Choose the equation below that you would use to solve this number puzzle.
Then solve the puzzle using the equation.

$3n-5 = 21$ $3(n-5) = 21$ $n-5\times 3 = 21$

E8 Solve each of these number puzzles. In each part, let n stand for the number I start with.

(a)
I think of a number.
I add 7.
I multiply the result by 2.
My answer is 40.
What was my number?

(b)
I think of a number.
I take off 9.
I multiply the result by 3.
My answer is double the number I started with.
What was my number?

(c)
I think of a number.
I take off 6.
I multiply the result by 5.
My answer is 2 more than the number I started with.
What was my number?

E9 Copy and complete this working to solve $3(x-4)+2(3x+2)=19$.

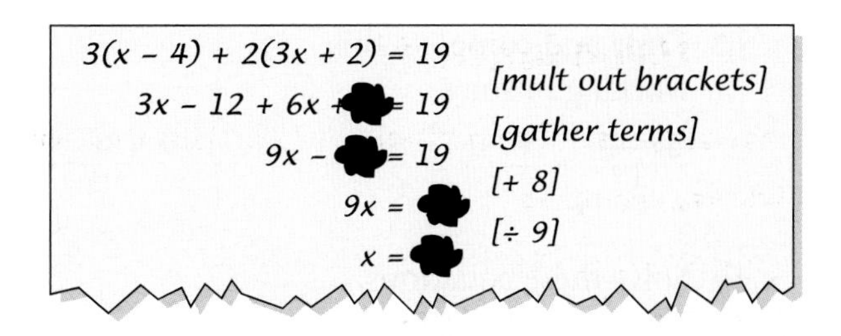

E10 Solve each of these equations.

(a) $2(2n+2)+3(n-1)=15$

(b) $3(4m-10)+5(2m-12)=20$

(c) $4(3k+7)+3(2k+5)=25$

(d) $3(2h-1)+4(3h-2)=5(3h-1)$

***E11** Copy and complete this working to solve $2(3x+2)-2(2x-1)=8$.

$2(3x+2)-2(2x-1)=8$
[mult out brackets]
$(6x+4)-(4x-2)=8$

***E12** Solve these equations.

(a) $5(x+7)-3(2x+1)=35$

(b) $6(5-x)-2(3x-1)=2$

F *Further fractions*

It is often useful to multiply through to get rid of fractions first.

Worked examples

$$\frac{6x-3}{4}=\frac{3}{2}$$
[× 4]
$$\frac{4(6x-3)}{4}=\frac{4\times 3}{2}$$
[cancel fractions]
$$6x-3=6$$
[+ 3]
$$6x=9$$
[÷ 6]
$$x=1\tfrac{1}{2}$$

$$\frac{4x-1}{2}=\frac{5x+1}{3}$$
6 is a multiple of 2 and 3, so × by 6
[× 6]
$$\frac{6(4x-1)}{2}=\frac{6(5x+1)}{3}$$
[cancel fractions]
$$3(4x-1)=2(5x+1)$$
[mult out brackets]
$$12x-3=10x+2$$
[– 10x]
$$2x-3=2$$
[+ 3]
$$2x=5$$
[÷ 2]
$$x=2\tfrac{1}{2}$$

F1 Solve each of these equations.

(a) $\frac{x+1}{3}=\frac{x-1}{2}$

(b) $\frac{2x+1}{3}=\frac{1}{2}$

(c) $\frac{3x+5}{4}=\frac{x}{2}$

(d) $\frac{3x}{4}=\frac{4x-1}{5}$

(e) $\frac{1}{2}(3x+1)=\frac{1}{3}(5x+3)$

(f) $\frac{4x+1}{5}=\frac{7x-2}{8}$

F2 Solve these equations.

(a) $\frac{x-7}{5}=2$

(b) $5x+6=24-10x$

AQA 2000

F3 Copy and complete this working to solve

$$\frac{2x-7}{3} + \frac{x-2}{4} = \frac{5}{6}.$$

$$\frac{2x-7}{3} + \frac{x-2}{4} = \frac{5}{6}$$

12 is a multiple of 3, 4 and 6 so × by 12.

[× 12]

$$\frac{12(2x-7)}{3} + \frac{12(x-2)}{4} = \frac{12 \times 5}{6}$$

[cancel fractions]

F4 Solve these equations.

(a) $\frac{x+1}{2} + \frac{x-1}{4} = 4$ (b) $\frac{2x+1}{3} + \frac{x-4}{2} = \frac{2}{3}$ (c) $\frac{2x+1}{4} - \frac{4x-7}{6} = \frac{1}{4}$

F5 Solve the equation $\frac{2x-3}{6} + \frac{x+2}{3} = \frac{5}{2}$.

WJEC

Test yourself

T1 Solve these equations.

(a) $3a + 16 = 100$ (b) $6b - 4 = 38$ (c) $\frac{1}{3}c + 4 = 2$

(d) $4d + 7 = 25$ (e) $5e - 3 = 0$ (f) $2f - 2 = ^-4$

T2 Solve these equations.

(a) $2n + 1 = 6 + n$ (b) $3g + 5 = 5g - 3$ (c) $5t - 2 = 2t + 10$

(d) $5u + 10 = 4 + 8u$ (e) $5s + 18 = 7s$ (f) $3e - 3 = 3 + 2e$

T3 Solve these equations.

(a) $4x + 1 = 13$ (b) $5x - 2 = 3x + 9$

OCR

T4 Find the size of each angle in these triangles.

(a)

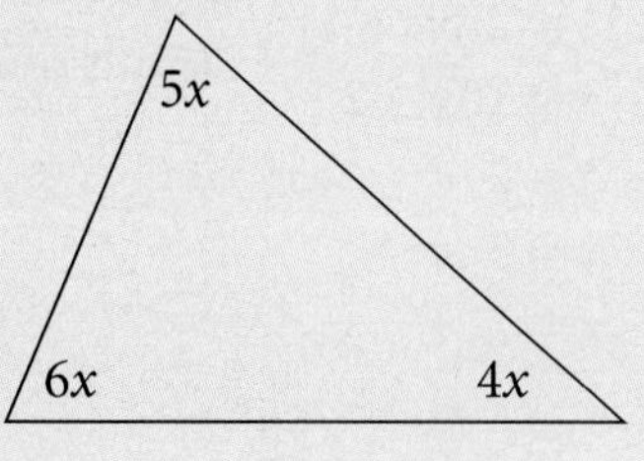

(b)

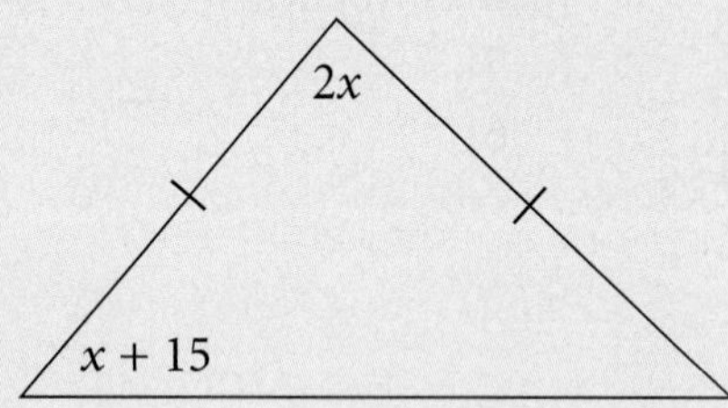

T5 The angles of a triangle are $(2x-3)°$, $(x+4)°$ and $(x+19)°$.

(a) Write an expression, in terms of x, for the sum of the angles. Write your answer in its simplest form.

The sum of the angles is 180°.

(b) (i) Write down an equation in x.

(ii) Solve your equation to find the size of the **smallest** angle in the triangle.

$(2x-3)°$ (Not to scale)

$(x+19)°$

$(x+4)°$

AQA(SEG) 1998

T6 The base of an isosceles triangle is x cm long.
Each of the other sides is 4 cm longer than the base.

The perimeter of the triangle is 24.5 cm.
Form an equation in x and solve it to find the length of the base.

← x cm →

AQA(SEG) 2000

T7 A brick weighs x kilograms.

(a) Write an expression, in terms of x, for the weight of 500 bricks.

(b) A builder orders 500 bricks and 2 bags of cement.
The order weighs 1250 kg. A bag of cement weighs 25 kg.
By forming an equation in terms of x, find the weight of a brick. AQA(SEG) 2000

T8 Solve these equations.

(a) $2(a - 3) = a$ (b) $3(b - 5) = 18$ (c) $2(3g - 10) = 4$

(d) $4(x + 3) = 3(x - 5)$ (e) $3(2c + 1) = 7(2c - 3)$ (f) $8y + 6 = 4(3y + 1)$

T9 Solve these equations.

(a) $\frac{4n - 6}{3} = n$ (b) $\frac{5n - 3}{2} = 3n$ (c) $\frac{n + 1}{2} = \frac{2n - 1}{3}$

(d) $\frac{4n - 3}{2} = 1 + n$ (e) $\frac{3n - 2}{2} + \frac{5n + 3}{4} = 8$ (f) $\frac{3n - 1}{3} + \frac{n + 2}{6} = \frac{7}{6}$

T10 Solve these equations. OCR

(a) $4(x - 2) = 18$ (b) $\frac{1}{3}x + \frac{1}{2}x = 10$ (c) $7x - 4 = 2x + 11$

T11 (a) Simplify $7t + 3s - 5t + s$. Edexcel

(b) Expand and simplify $3(2m + 2) - 2(m - 3)$.

Solve these equations.

(c) $2q + 7 = {}^{-}1$ (d) $12a + 2 = 2a - 6$ (e) $\frac{2h - 1}{3} + \frac{h + 6}{2} = \frac{5}{6}$

42 The tangent function

For this work you need to know that the ratio $\frac{b}{a}$ is the multiplier from a to b.

You will be doing your first work in trigonometry, which is about the relationship between lengths and angles.

A Finding an 'opposite' side

TG

Draw this right-angled triangle accurately.

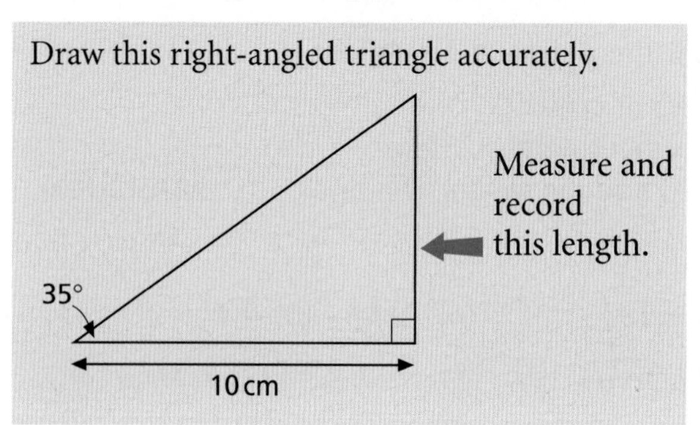

If you draw another vertical line 5 cm from the 35° vertex, how long should it be? Draw and measure to check.

Add vertical lines, 1 cm, 2 cm, 3 cm, ... from the 35° vertex. Work out how long each of them should be. Then check by measuring.

A1 Use your results to work out the missing lengths here.

(a)

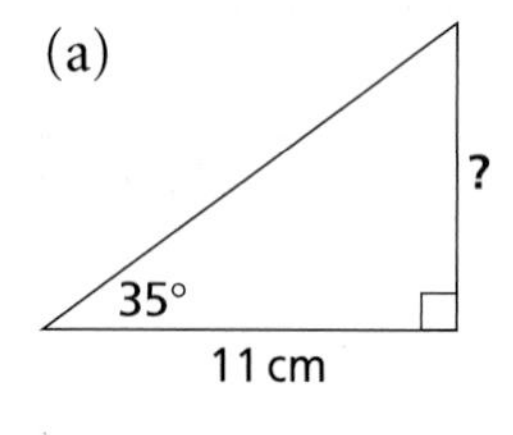

(b)

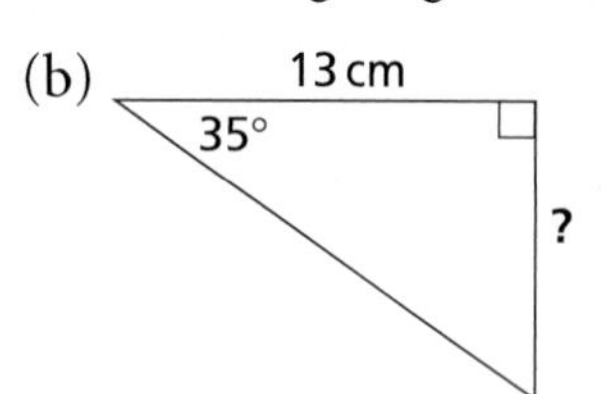

(c)

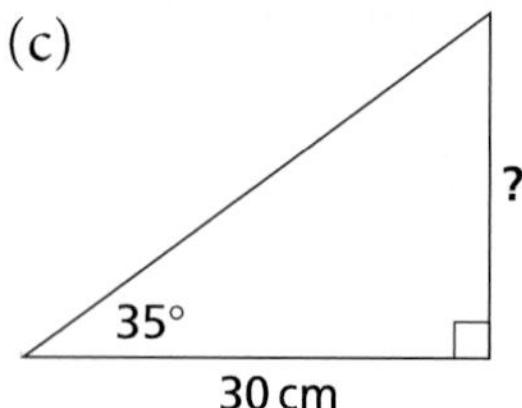

(d)

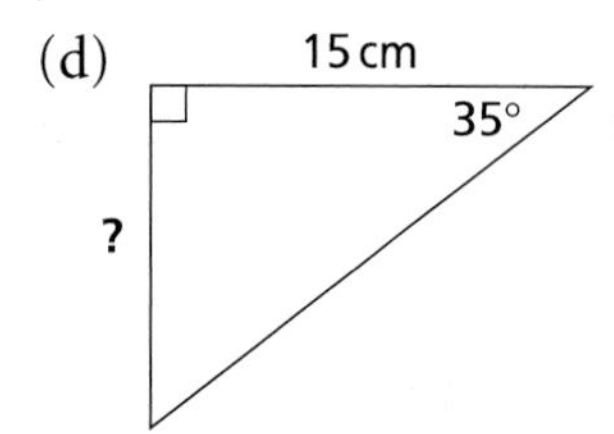

(e)

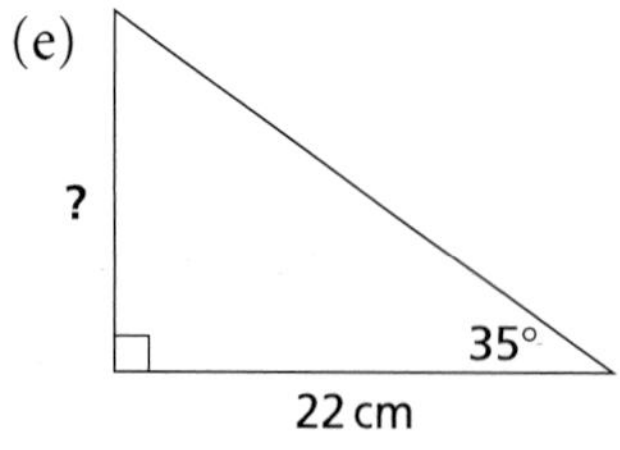

(f)

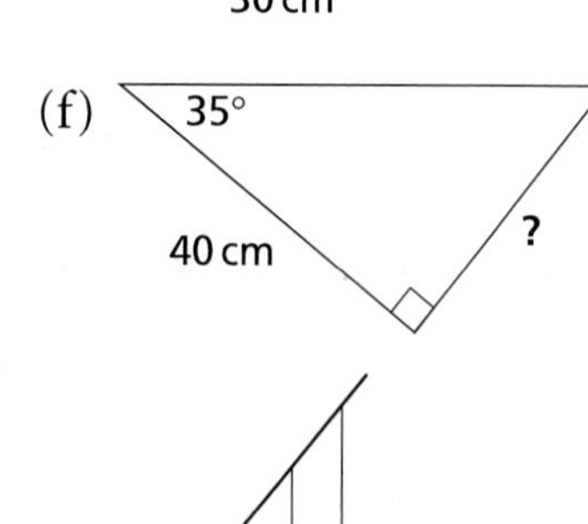

A2 Do a drawing experiment as above but using an angle of 50°.

A3 Use what you discovered in A2 to find the missing lengths here.

(a)

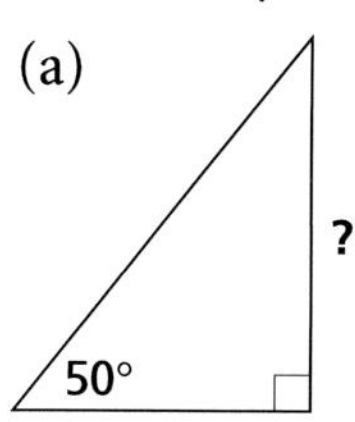

(b)

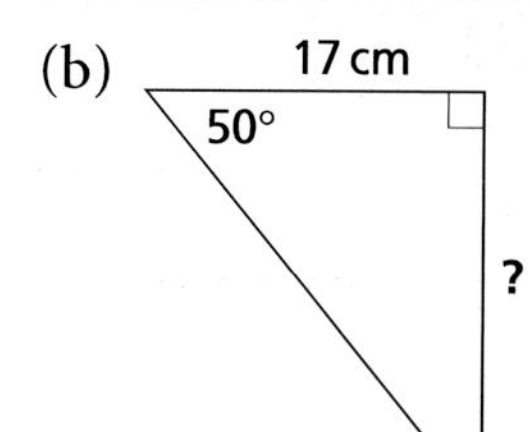

(c)

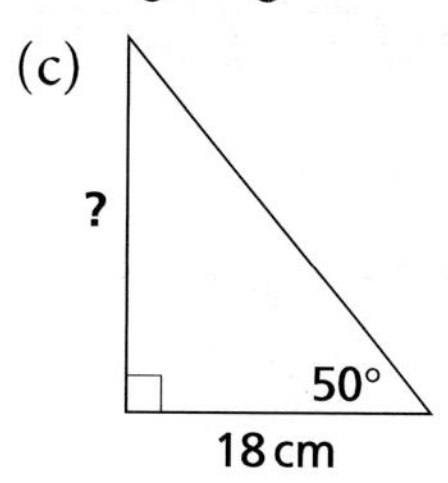

(d)

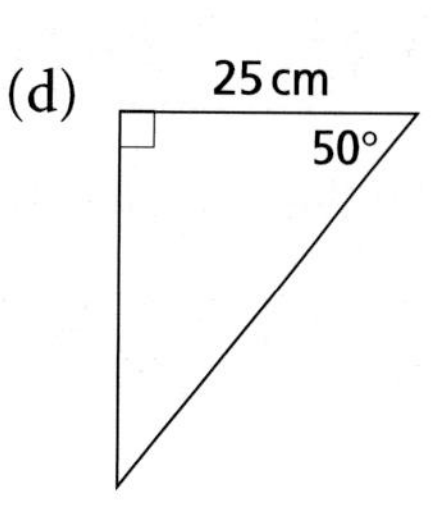

In a right-angled triangle like this,

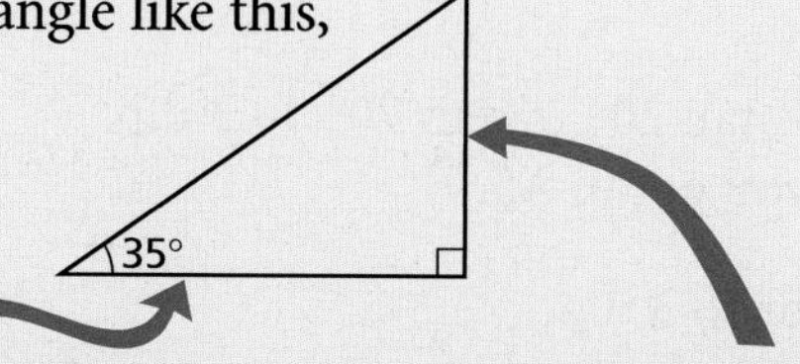

we say this side is **adjacent** to the 35° angle and this side is **opposite** to the 35° angle.

When the angle is 35° you can use the rule: adjacent side —[× 0.7]→ opposite side

This is another way of stating the rule: $\frac{\text{opposite side}}{\text{adjacent side}} = 0.7$

A4 Write a rule in each of these ways for the angle 50°.

A5 Do this drawing experiment to find rules for other angles.

Draw a horizontal line 10 cm long with a vertical line at the right hand end of it.

10 cm

Draw angles of 10°, 20°, 30°, …, 60°, 70°.

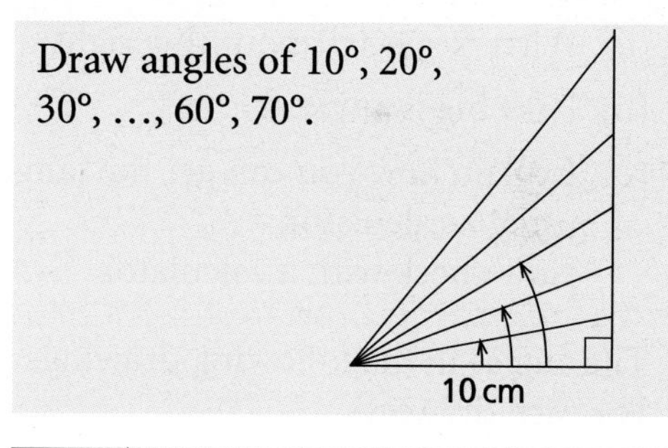

Measure the opposite side for each triangle and record your results in a table like this.

Angle	Adjacent side	× ?	Opposite side
10°	10 cm		
20°	10 cm		
30°	10 cm		
40°	10 cm		

Work out the numbers that go in here and write them in your table.

A6 Use results from your table to find the missing lengths here.

(a)

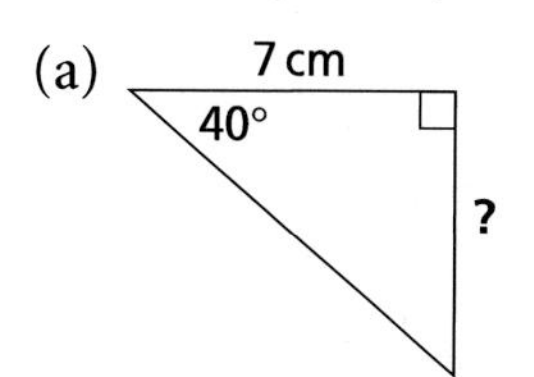

(b)

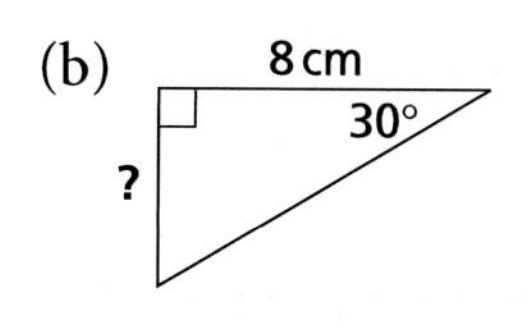

(c)

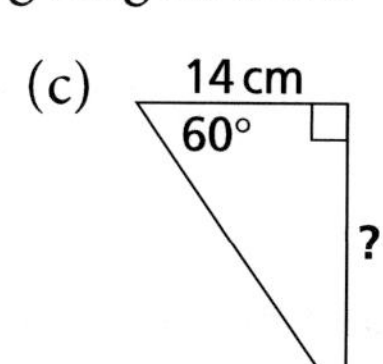

(d)

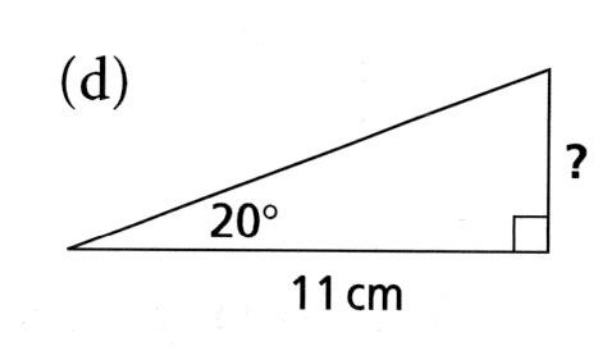

The number you multiply the adjacent side by to get the opposite side is called the **tangent** of the angle.

So the tangent of 35° is about 0.7
and the tangent of 50° is about 1.2.

'tan' is short for tangent, so we can say tan 35° = 0.7
and tan 50° = 1.2 .

A scientific calculator gives very accurate values of tangents.

Try keying in [3] [5] [tan] or [tan] [3] [5]. Is 0.7 close to what you get?

A7 Use your calculator to find tan 10°, tan 20°, ..., tan 70°, to 3 d.p.
Compare these results with what you got in A5.

A8 (a) Find tan 65° on your calculator to 3 d.p.

Use this result to find the missing lengths here.

(b)

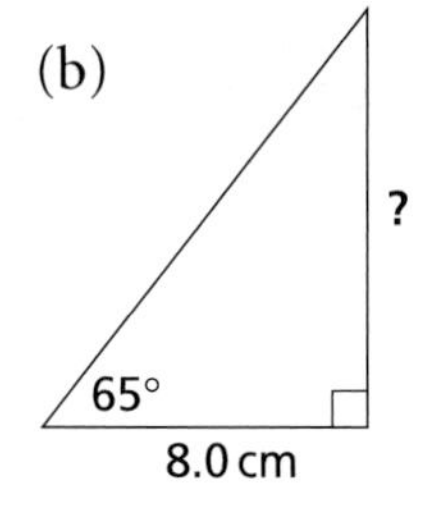

(c)

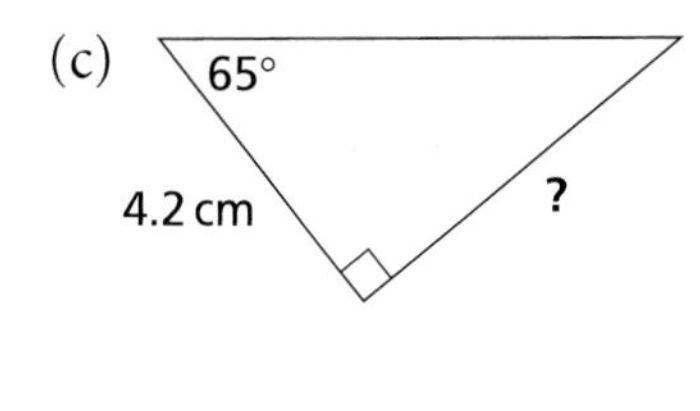

(d)

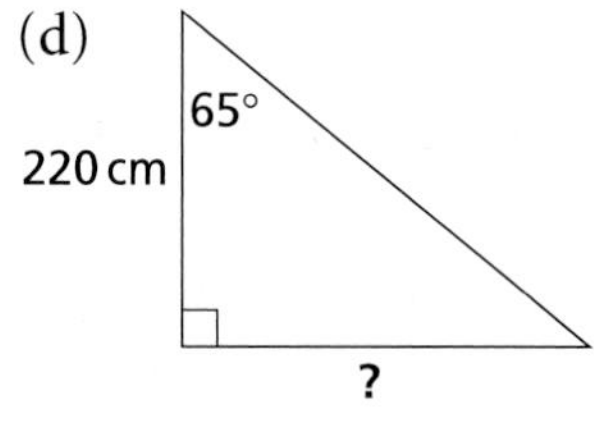

A9 (a) What is special about this right-angled triangle?

(b) How big is angle a?

(c) Explain how you can get the tangent of a without using a calculator.
Now check with a calculator.

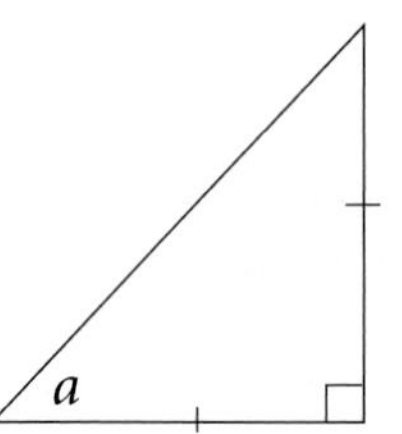

A10 The angles in the following drawings have been drawn accurately.
For each drawing,

(i) write an estimate of the missing length

(ii) then use the tangent button on your calculator to get an answer to 1 d.p.

(a)

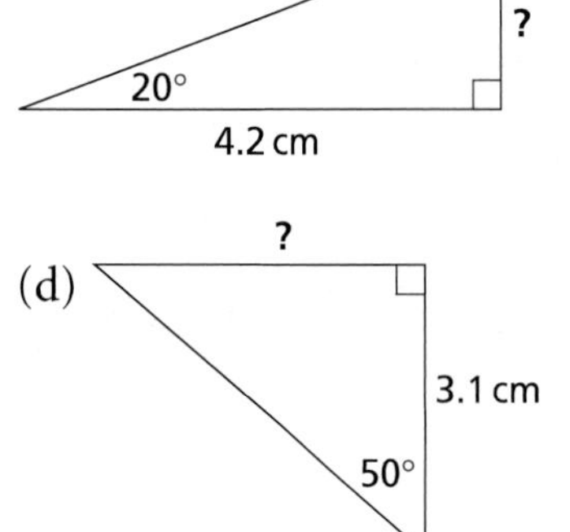

(b)

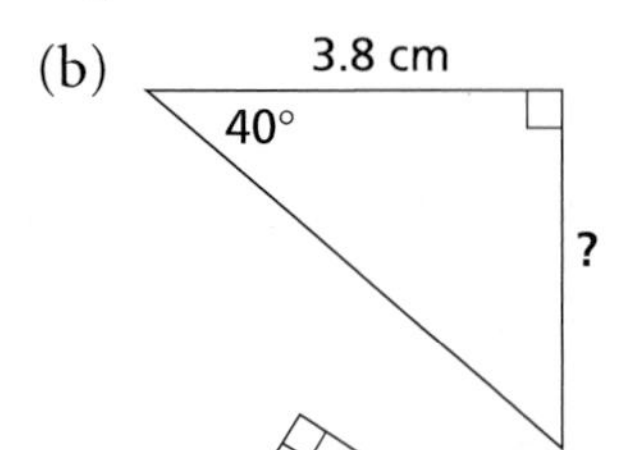

(c)

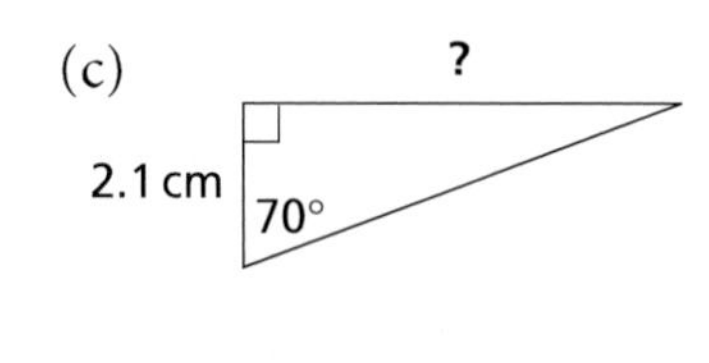

(d)

(e)

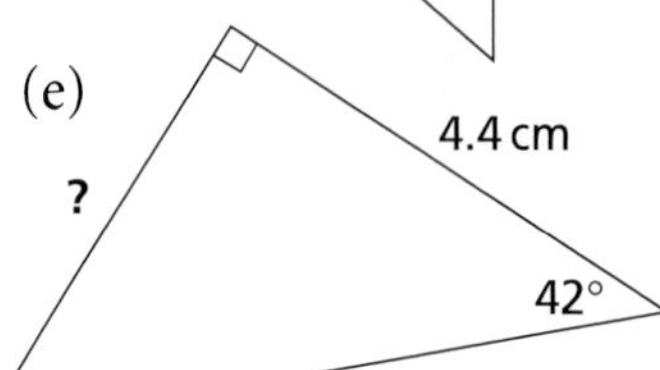

(f)

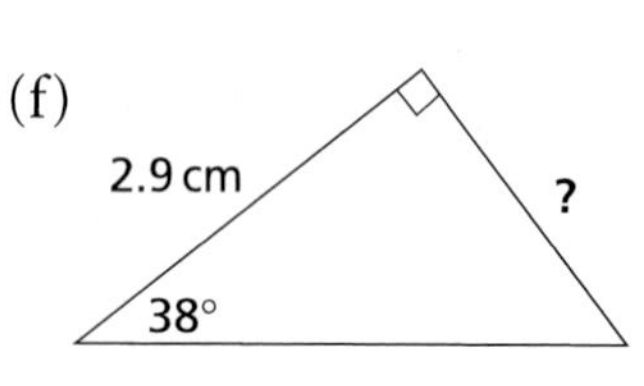

B *Finding an adjacent side*

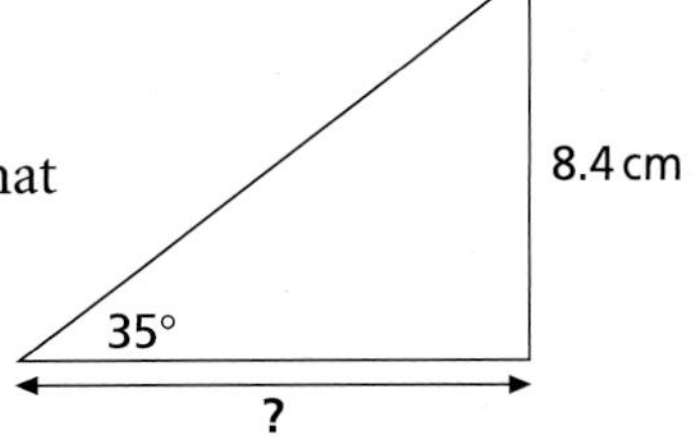

Earlier you found that tan 35° is about 0.7 and that you could use this to find an opposite side.

How long is the **adjacent** side here?

B1 Find each of these adjacent sides, using tan 35° = 0.7.

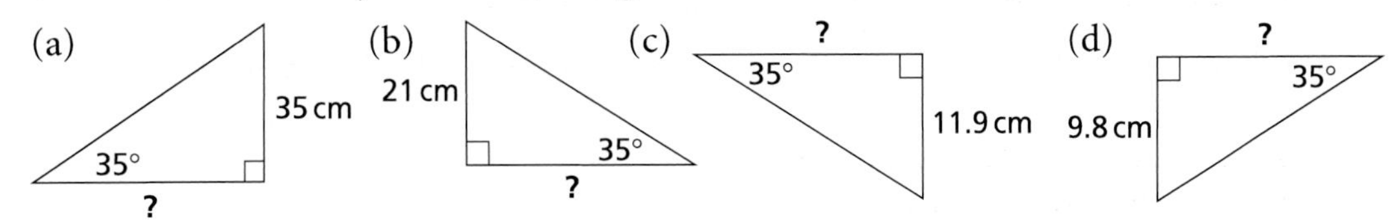

B2 Find each of these adjacent sides, using tan 50° = 1.2.

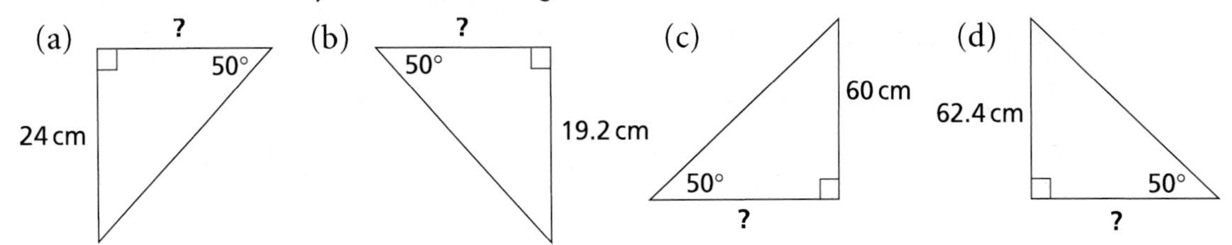

B3 The angles in the following drawings have been drawn accurately.
For each one,

(i) write an estimate of the length of the missing adjacent side

(ii) then find its length to 1 d.p. using the calculator's value of the tangent

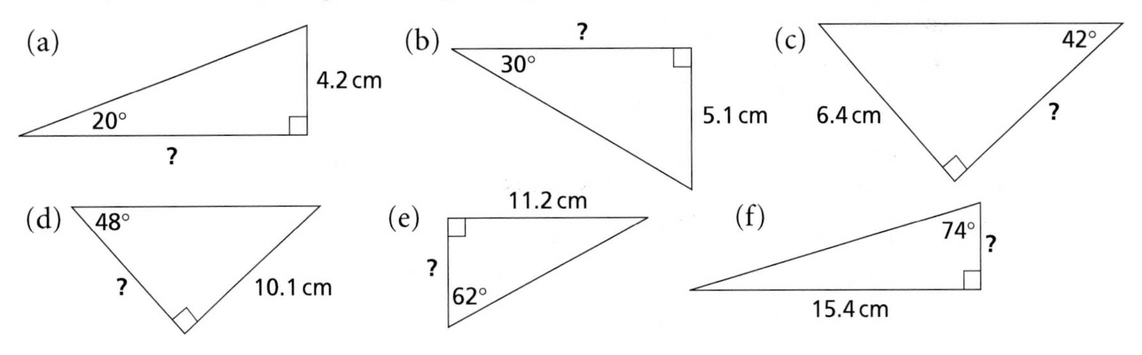

B4 Find the missing sides here to 1 d.p., using a calculator.
Be careful: some are opposite sides and some are adjacent sides.

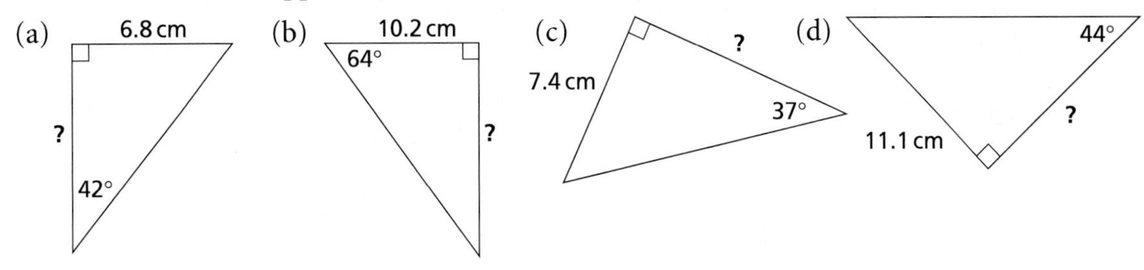

C *Finding an angle*

Before there were calculators, people used tables of tangents.

This simple table gives tangents to 2 d.p.

a	tan a	a	tan a	a	tan a	a	tan a	a	tan a	a	tan a	a	tan a	a	tan a	a	tan a
1	0.02	11	0.19	21	0.38	31	0.60	41	0.87	51	1.23	61	1.80	71	2.90	81	6.31
2	0.03	12	0.21	22	0.40	32	0.62	42	0.90	52	1.28	62	1.88	72	3.08	82	7.12
3	0.05	13	0.23	23	0.42	33	0.65	43	0.93	53	1.33	63	1.96	73	3.27	83	8.14
4	0.07	14	0.25	24	0.45	34	0.67	44	0.97	54	1.38	64	2.05	74	3.49	84	9.51
5	0.09	15	0.27	25	0.47	35	0.70	45	1.00	55	1.43	65	2.14	75	3.73	85	11.43
6	0.11	16	0.29	26	0.49	36	0.73	46	1.04	56	1.48	66	2.25	76	4.01	86	14.30
7	0.12	17	0.31	27	0.51	37	0.75	47	1.07	57	1.54	67	2.36	77	4.33	87	19.08
8	0.14	18	0.32	28	0.53	38	0.78	48	1.11	58	1.60	68	2.48	78	4.70	88	28.64
9	0.16	19	0.34	29	0.55	39	0.81	49	1.15	59	1.66	69	2.61	79	5.14	89	57.29
10	0.18	20	0.36	30	0.58	40	0.84	50	1.19	60	1.73	70	2.75	80	5.67	90	?

C1 Find these in the table.

(a) tan 23° (b) The angle whose tangent is 0.78 (c) tan 52°

(d) The angle whose tangent is 4.01 (e) The angle whose tangent is 0.29

(f) tan 6° (g) The angle whose tangent is 0.05 (h) tan 86°

(i) The angle whose tangent is 0.97 (j) The angle whose tangent is 28.64

C2 (a) Work out the tangent of angle a here.

(b) Use the table to find the angle with this tangent.
(In other words, find angle a.)

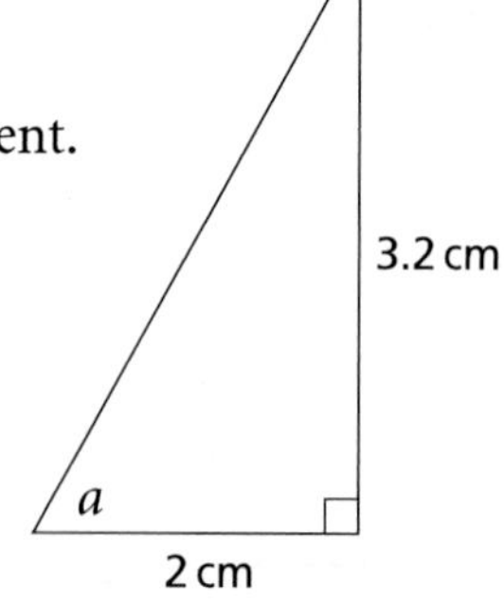

C3 What happens in the table of tangents as the angle a gets closer to 90°?
Why?

C4 For each of these, work out the tangent of the angle, then use the table to find the angle.

(a)

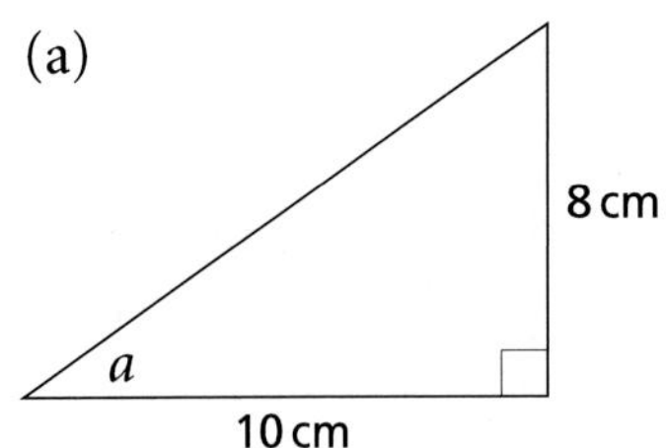

(b)

(d)

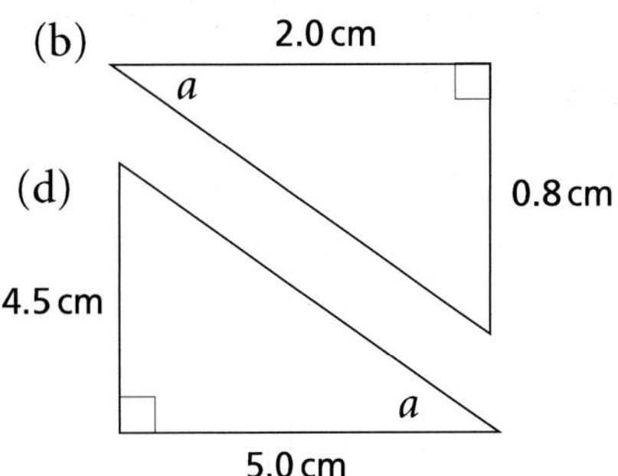

(c)

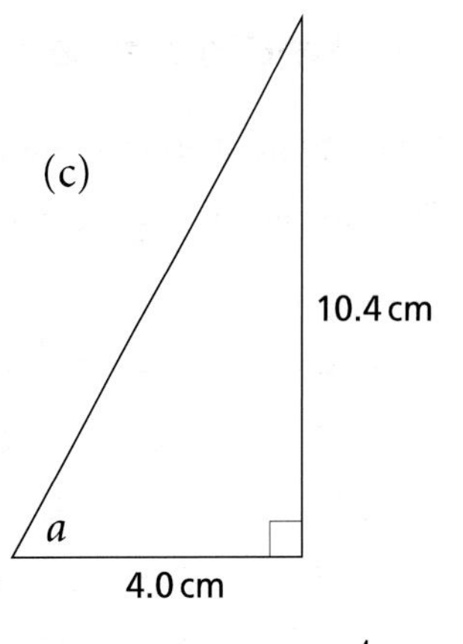

C5 For each of these, work out the tangent of the angle, then use the table to find the angle.

(a)

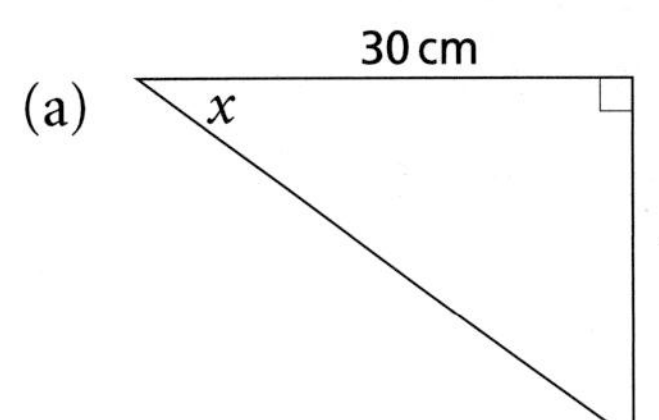

(b)

20 cm

x

11 cm

(c)

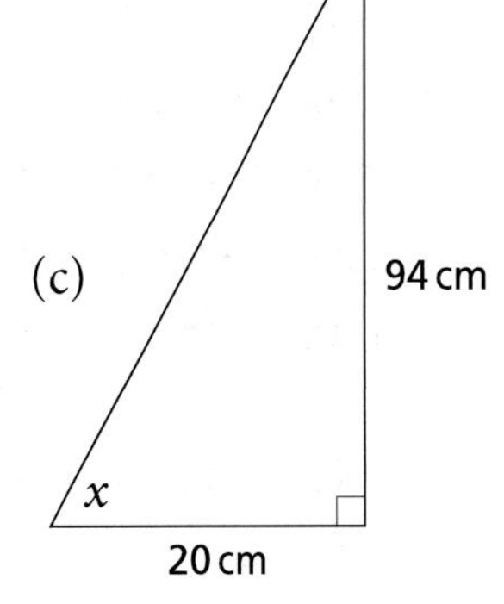

You can find 'the angle whose tangent is …' very accurately on a scientific calculator. The key sequence you use depends on the type of calculator.

Find out how to find 'the angle whose tangent is...' on your calculator.
Experiment with different values.
Use the table opposite to see whether your method makes sense.

C6 Use your calculator to find the angles in C4 and C5 more accurately. Give the angles to 2 d.p.

C7 For each of these, work out the tangent of the angle, then use your calculator to find the angle to 2 d.p.

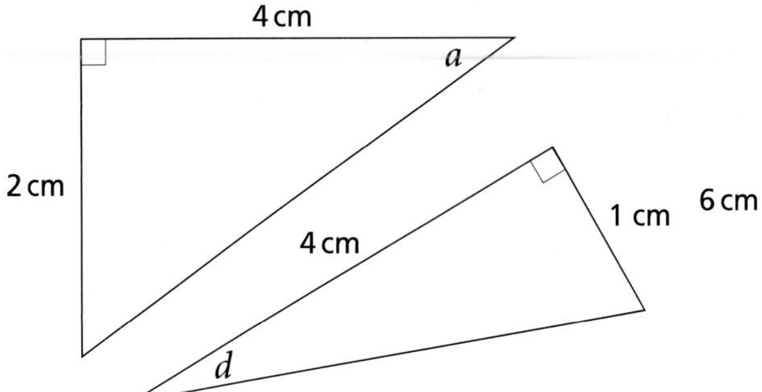

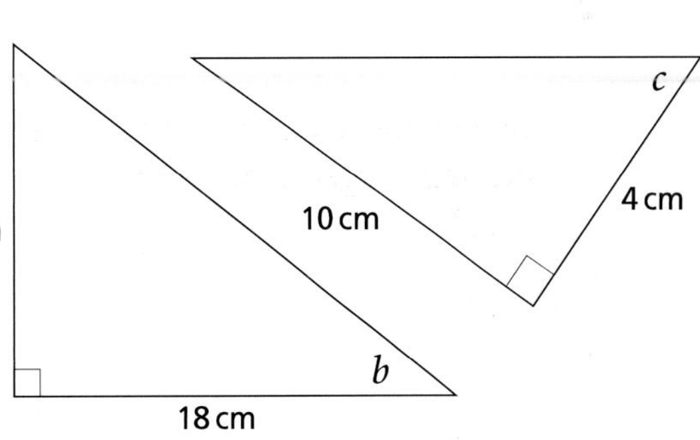

C8 For each of these, write down an estimate of the angle.
Then work out the angle to 2 d.p. using your calculator.
Write down all the stages of your working.

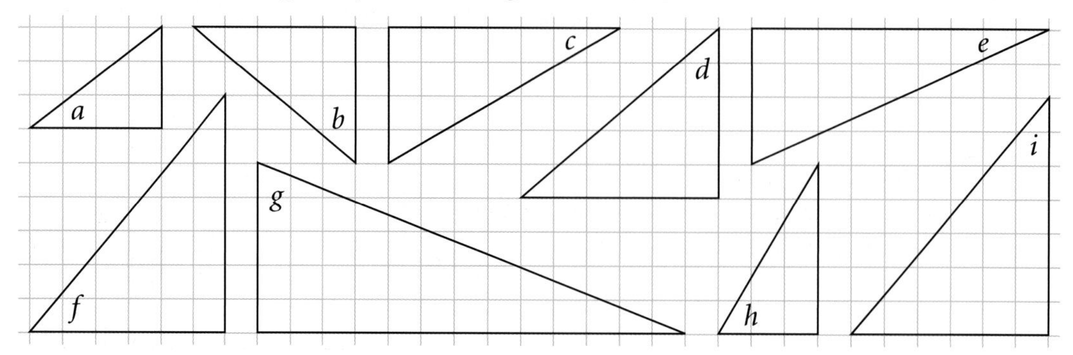

C9 Work out these angles to 2 d.p. using your calculator.
Write down all the stages of your working.

7.5 cm
5.2 cm
a
7.4 cm
6.1 cm
b
6.8 cm
c
10.1 cm
9.4 cm
7.1 cm
4.0 cm
8.4 cm
e
6.8 cm
f
4.5 cm
9.8 cm
5.1
g

D *Mixed questions and problems*

D1 Find the missing lengths and angles here.

(a)
31°
11.5 cm
?
(b)
14.4 cm
37°
?
(c)
13.0 cm
18.2 cm
?

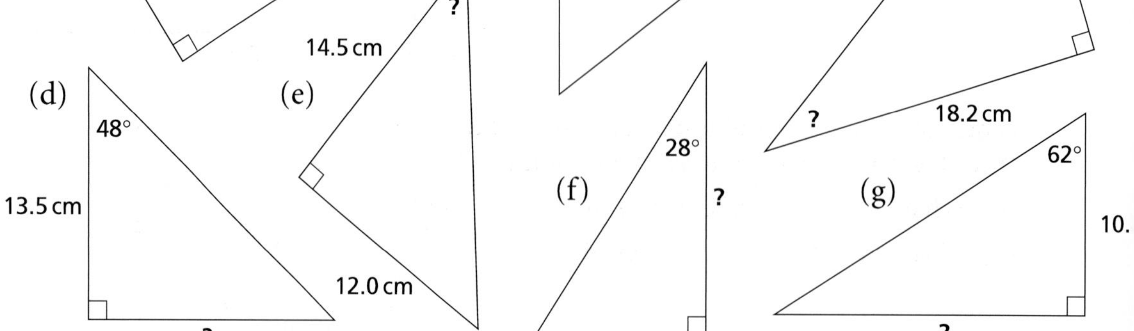

D2 This is the symmetrical end wall of a house.
Calculate, to the nearest degree, the angle a that the roof makes with the horizontal.

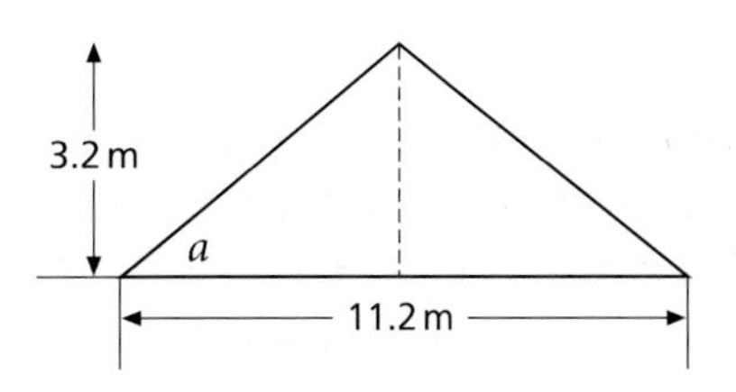

D3 This is the end wall of a shed.
Calculate, to the nearest degree, the angle that the roof makes with the horizontal.

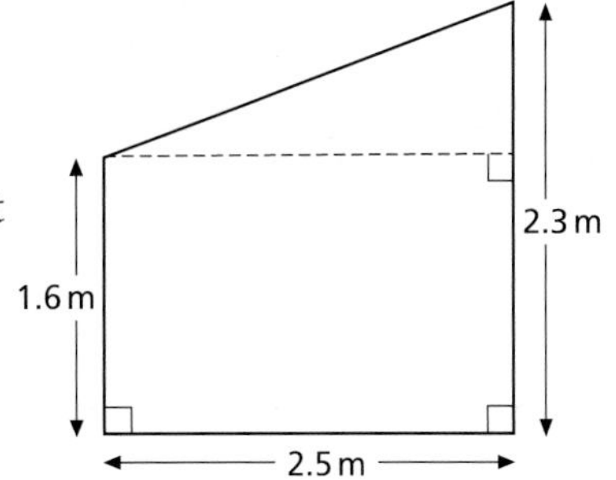

D4 It is possible to get from a farmhouse, F, to a windmill, W, by going 5.3 km north then 6.6 km east.

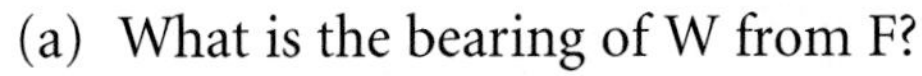

(a) What is the bearing of W from F?

(b) What is the bearing of F from W?

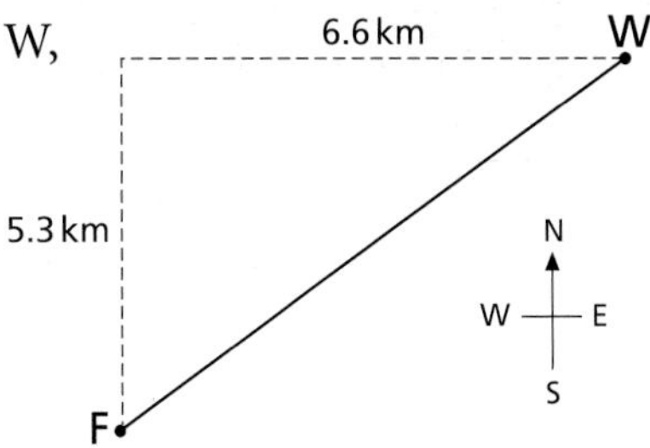

D5 This is the end wall of a shed.
Calculate the missing height to the nearest 0.1 m.

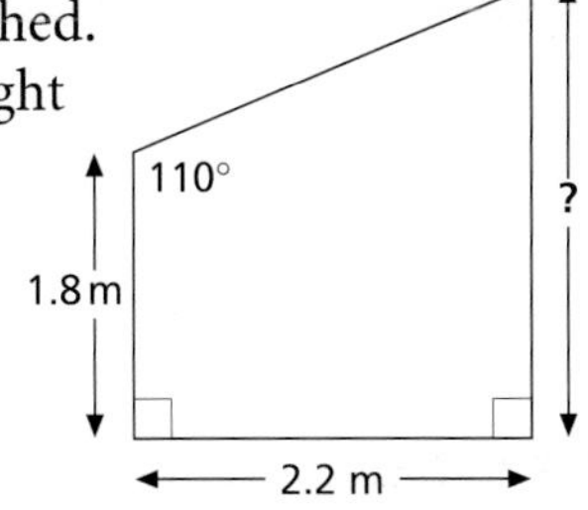

D6 A person at point P is 50 m away from a TV mast.
The angle between the horizontal and a line from P to the top of the mast is 25° (This is called the **angle of elevation**.)
Find the height of the mast.

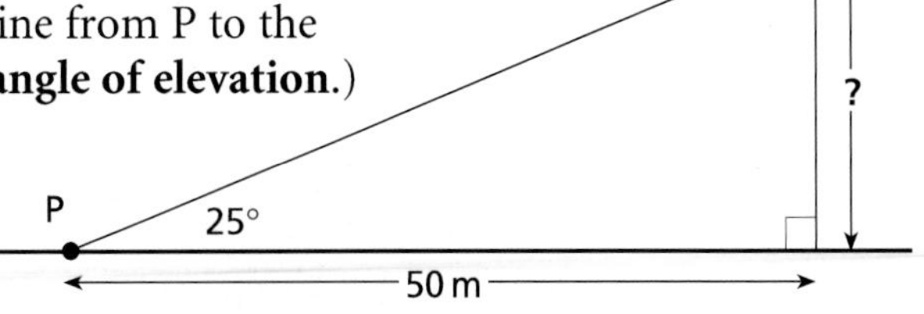

D7 A helicopter starts at point A, flies west 4.2 km, then flies north 5.0 km and lands at point B.

(a) What is the bearing of B from A?

(b) What is the bearing of A from B?

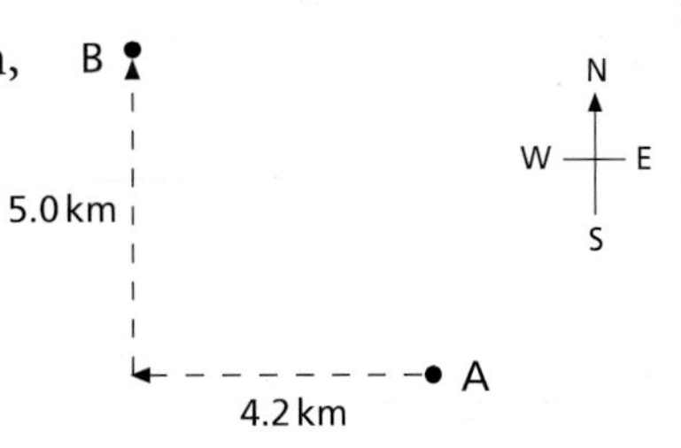

D8 A fisherman, F, at sea in a small boat, looks at a vertical cliff.
The angle of elevation to the top of the cliff is 18°.
The fisherman knows the cliff is 23 m high.
How far is his boat from the foot of the cliff?

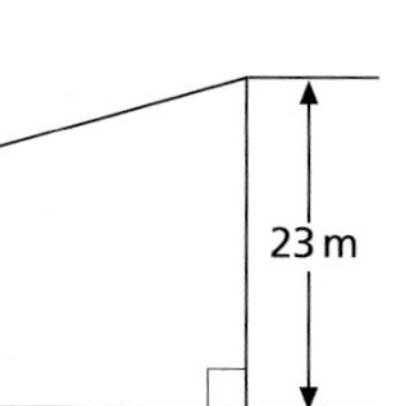

D9 This is an isosceles triangle.
Find the missing length.

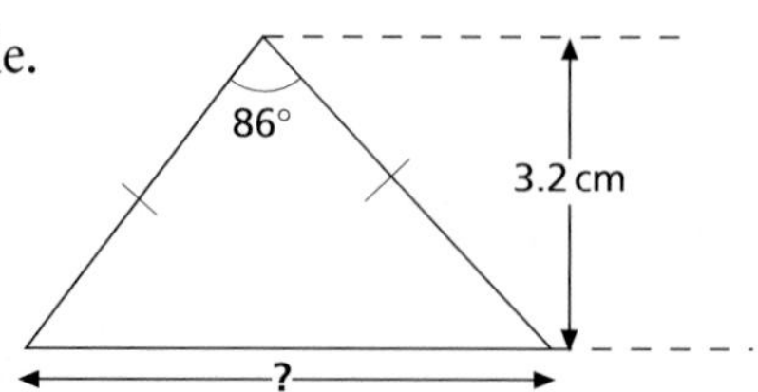

D10 This is a symmetrical trapezium.
Calculate the angle marked b,
to the nearest 0.1°.

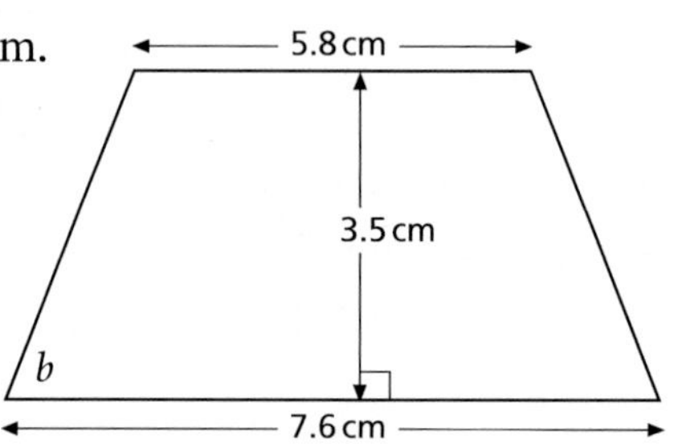

D11 The diagonals of rectangle ABCD cross at O
Find the angles x and y.

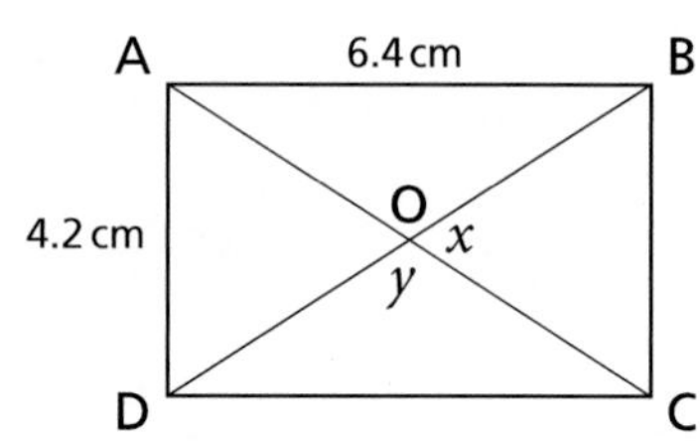

D12 The lengths of the diagonals of this rhombus are shown.
Calculate the angles at the vertices of the rhombus
(to the nearest 0.1°).

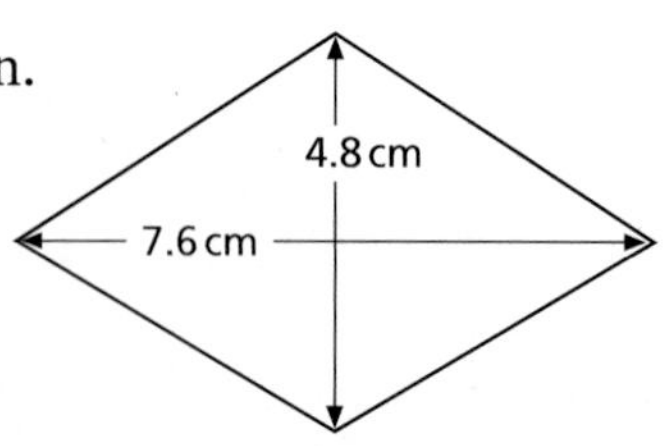

D13 This is an equilateral triangle.

(a) How long is the dotted line (to 2 d.p.)?

(b) What is the area of the equilateral triangle (to 2 d.p.)?

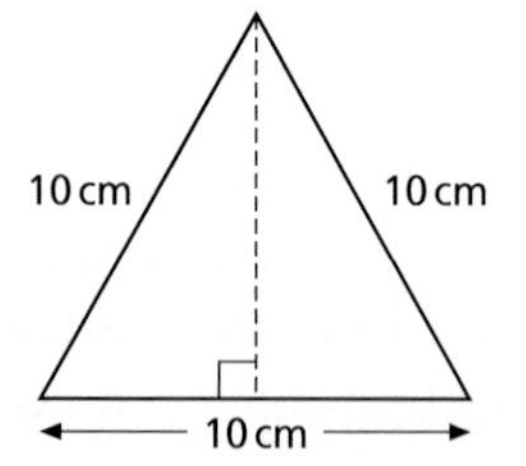

Summary

The tangent of an angle can be thought of as a multiplier ...

... or as a ratio: $\tan a = \dfrac{\text{opposite}}{\text{adjacent}}$

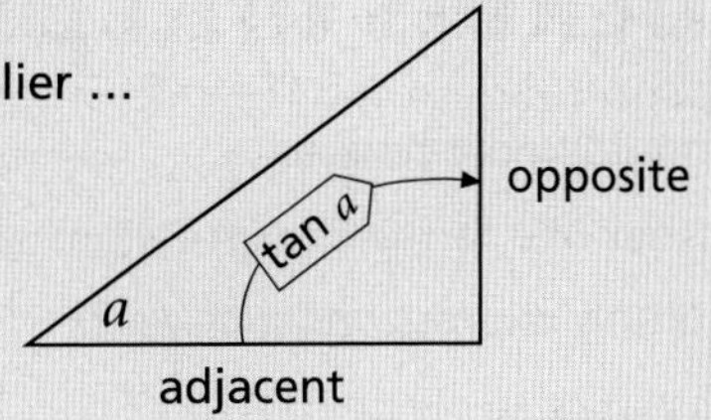

Test yourself

T1 Which is the opposite side to angle a in each of these triangles?

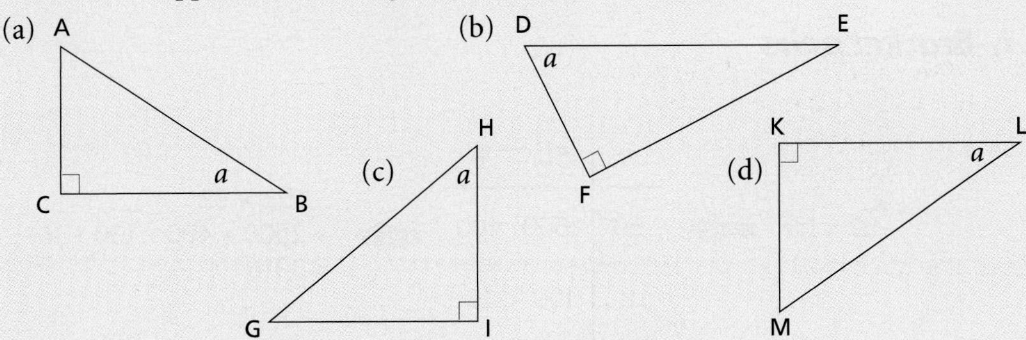

T2 Which is the adjacent side in each of the triangles in T1?

T3 Find the missing quantity in each of these. Give each answer to 1 d.p.

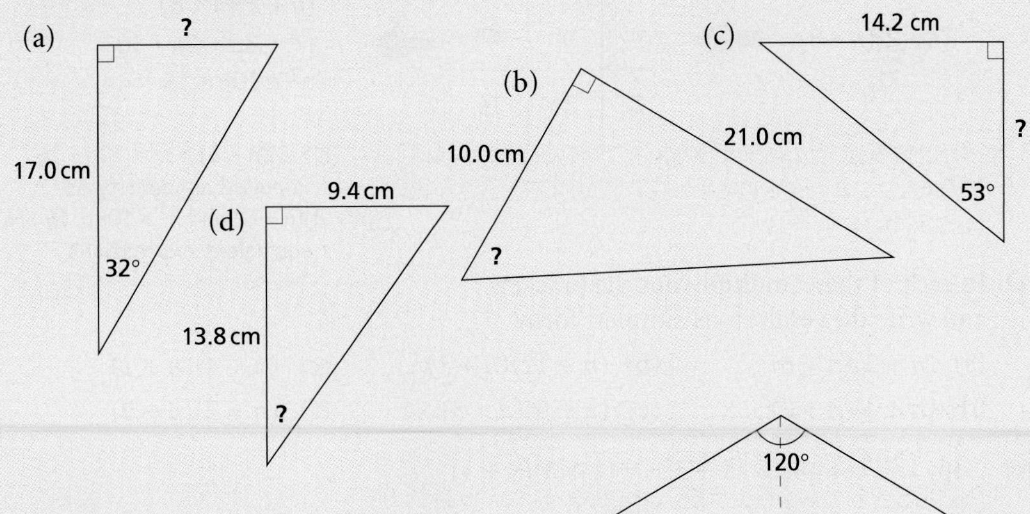

T4 The shorter diagonal of this rhombus is 10 cm long.
How long is the longer diagonal?

120°
60°
60°
120°

43 Brackets and proof

You should know how to

- gather like terms in expressions such as $2x^2 + 5x - 8x - 2$
- multiply expressions such as $2x \times 3x$ and $3x \times 2y$

This work will help you

- multiply out brackets such as $(x + 1)(x - 3)$ and $(4x + 1)(2x - 3)$
- use algebra to prove simple general statements

A Bracket pairs

TG

52×58 →

×	50	8
50	2500	400
2	100	16

→ 52×58
$= 2500 + 400 + 100 + 16$
$= 3016$

$(n + 2)(n + 8)$ →

×	n	8
n	n^2	8n
2	2n	16

→ $(n + 2)(n + 8)$
$= n^2 + 8n + 2n + 16$
$= n^2 + 10n + 16$

$(n + 2)(n + 8) = n^2 + 10n + 16$ is called an identity as $(n + 2)(n + 8)$ and $n^2 + 10n + 16$ are equivalent expressions.

A1 In each of these, multiply out the brackets and write the result in its simplest form.

(a) $(n + 2)(n + 6)$ (b) $(n + 12)(n + 1)$ (c) $(n + 4)(n + 1)$
(d) $(n + 4)(n + 2)$ (e) $(n + 6)(n + 3)$ (f) $(n + 2)(n + 9)$

A2 Copy and complete $(x + 3)^2 = (x + 3)(x + 3)$
$= \ldots\ldots\ldots\ldots\ldots$
Simplify your result.

A3 Multiply out each expression and write the result in its simplest form.

(a) $(x + 4)^2$ (b) $(x + 5)^2$ (c) $(x + 1)^2$

A4 Show that the area of this rectangle is $x^2 + 8x + 15$.

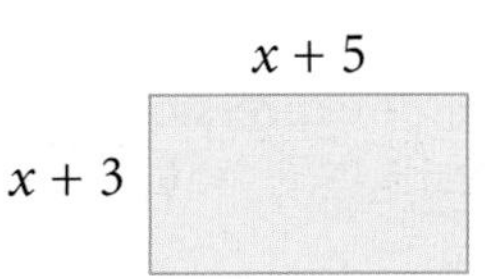

A5 Write an expression for the area of each rectangle below

- with brackets, for example $(x + 2)(x + 8)$
- without brackets, for example $x^2 + 10x + 16$

(a) $x + 4$ by $x + 3$ (b) $x + 8$ by $x + 1$ (c) $x + 2$ by $x + 2$

A6 Find pairs of expressions from the loop that multiply to give each of these.

(a) $n^2 + 7n + 12$ (b) $n^2 + 6n + 5$
(c) $n^2 + 7n + 6$ (d) $n^2 + 5n + 6$

$n + 2$ $n + 1$ $n + 3$ $n + 4$ $n + 5$ $n + 6$

A7 Find pairs of expressions from the loop that multiply to give each of these.

(a) $n^2 + 9n + 8$ (b) $n^2 + 9n + 20$
(c) $n^2 + 14n + 40$ (d) $n^2 + 13n + 40$

$n + 1$ $n + 2$ $n + 4$ $n + 5$ $n + 8$ $n + 10$

B *Including subtraction*

A $(x - 4)(x + 5) = ?$

B $(x - 6)(x + 3) = ?$

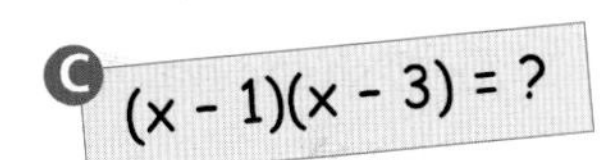

B1 Multiply out the brackets from each expression and write the result in its simplest form.

(a) $(n - 2)(n + 5)$ (b) $(n + 9)(n - 1)$ (c) $(n - 6)(n + 2)$
(d) $(n + 2)(n - 7)$ (e) $(n - 3)(n - 4)$ (f) $(n - 5)(n - 3)$
(g) $(n - 1)(n - 7)$ (h) $(n - 10)(n + 9)$ (i) $(n - 4)(n + 4)$
(j) $(n + 2)(n - 2)$ (k) $(n - 5)(n + 5)$ (l) $(n + 1)(n - 1)$

B2 Show that the area of this rectangle is equivalent to $x^2 + 4x - 12$.

B3 Copy and complete $(x - 4)^2 = (x - 4)(x - 4)$
$= \dots\dots\dots\dots$

Simplify your result.

B4 Multiply out each expression and write the result in its simplest form.

(a) $(x - 3)^2$ (b) $(x - 1)^2$ (c) $(x - 6)^2$

B5 Find pairs of expressions from the loop that multiply to give each of these.

(a) $n^2 + 2n - 3$ (b) $n^2 - n - 2$

(c) $n^2 - 5n + 6$ (d) $n^2 - 4n + 3$

(e) $n^2 - 4$ (f) $n^2 - 9$

$n + 2$ $n + 1$ $n + 3$

$n - 1$ $n - 2$ $n - 3$

Multiplying out brackets involving subtraction

(n + 2)(n - 8) →

×	n	⁻8
n	n^2	⁻8n
2	2n	⁻16

→ (n + 2)(n - 8)
= n^2 - 8n + 2n - 16
= n^2 - 6n - 16

(n - 2)(n - 8) →

×	n	⁻8
n	n^2	⁻8n
⁻2	⁻2n	16

→ (n x 2)(n - 8)
= n^2 - 8n - 2n + 16
= n^2 - 10n + 16

C *Grid totals*

C1 This grid of numbers has ten columns.
An L-shape outlines some numbers.

1	2	3	4	5	6	7	8	9	10
11	12	13	14	15	16	17	18	19	20
21	22	23	24	25	26	27	28	29	30
31	32	33	34	35	36	37	38	39	40

(a) What is the total of the numbers in this L-shape?

(b) Find totals for the L-shape in different positions on the grid.

(c) Suppose the grid is continued downwards.

(i) Copy and complete this L-shape for the grid above.

(ii) What is its total?

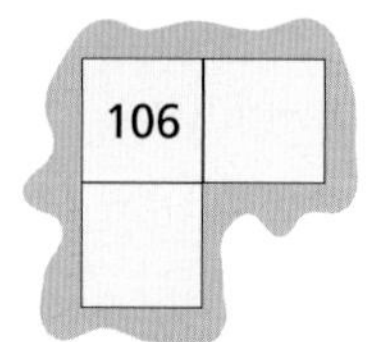

(d) (i) Copy and complete this L-shape for the grid above.

(ii) Find an expression for the total.

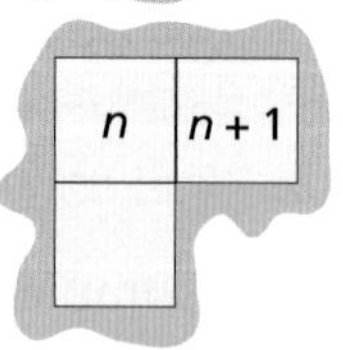

(e) What numbers are in the L-shape that has a total of 614 on this grid?

(f) Explain why you can't have an L-shape with a total of 154 on this grid.

C2 This grid of numbers has ten columns.

A T-shape outlines some numbers.

(a) What is the total of the numbers in this T-shape?

(b) Find totals for the T-shape in different positions on the grid.

1	2	3	4	5	6	7	8	9	10
11	12	13	14	15	16	17	18	19	20
21	22	23		25	26	27	28	29	30
31	32	33	34	35	36	37	38	39	40
		43	44	45	46	47	48		

(c) Suppose the grid is continued downwards.

(i) Copy and complete this T-shape for the grid above.

(ii) What is its total?

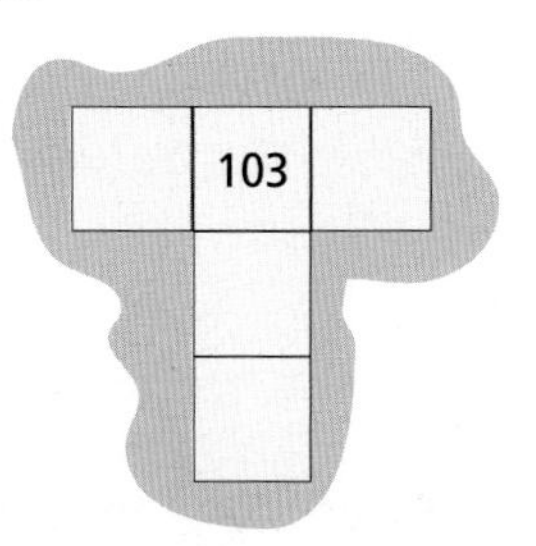

(d) (i) Copy and complete this T-shape for the grid above.

(ii) Find an expression for the total.

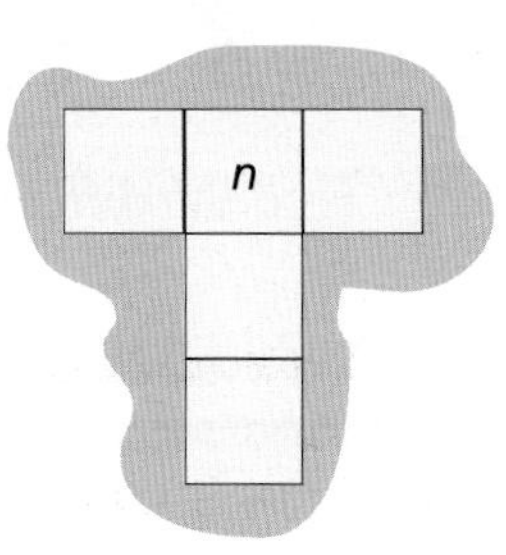

(e) Draw the T-shape that has a total of 1020 on this grid.

(f) Explain why you can't have a T-shape with a total of 231 on this grid.

C3 Another grid of numbers has six columns.

1	2	3	4	5	6
7	8	9	10	11	12
13	14	15	16	17	18
19	20	21	22	23	24
			28	29	

(a) (i) Copy and complete this T-shape for the six-column grid.

(ii) Find an expression for the total.

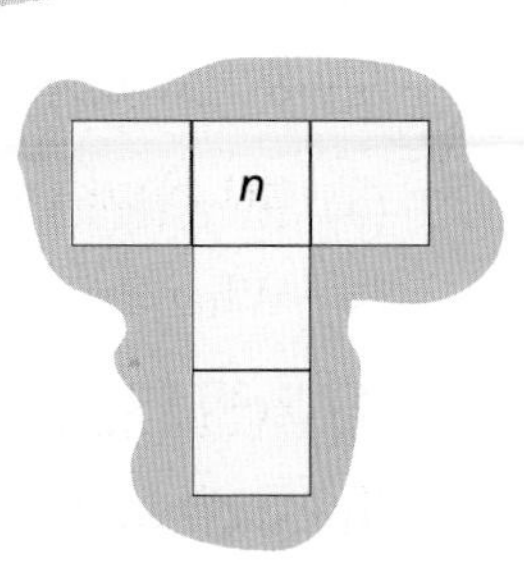

(b) Investigate T-shape totals for grids with different numbers of columns.

D *Opposite corners*

This grid of numbers has ten columns.
A 3 by 3 square outlines some numbers.

1	2	3	4	5	6	7	8	9	10
11	12	13	14	15	16	17	18	19	20
21	22	23	24	25	26	27	28	29	30
31	32	33	34	35	36	37	38	39	40
41		43	44	45	46	47	48		

14	15	16
24	25	26
34	35	36

- Multiply the numbers in opposite corners. $14 \times 36 = 504$, $16 \times 34 = 544$
- Find the difference between the results. $544 - 504 = 40$
- Let's call this the 'opposite corners number'. The 'opposite corners number' for this square is **40**.

D1 Find the 'opposite corners number' for some 3 by 3 squares in different positions on this grid.
What do you think is true about these 'opposite corners numbers'?

D2 (a) Copy this square for the grid above.
Fill in the corner squares.

(b) Find and simplify an expression for the 'opposite corners number' for this square.

(c) What does this prove?

D3 (a) Investigate for 2 by 2 squares on this grid.

(b) What do you think is true about the 'opposite corners number' this time?

(c) Can you prove your result?

D4 Investigate for squares of different size on this grid.

***D5** Investigate for grids with different numbers of columns.

E *Consecutive numbers*

E1 Helen said,

'When you add three consecutive whole numbers, the answer will always be divisible by 3. For example, 9 + 10 + 11 = 30, and 30 divides by 3 without a remainder.'

The **second** of three consecutive numbers is x.

$$\ldots\ldots\ldots,\ x,\ \ldots\ldots\ldots$$

(a) Write an expression for each of the other two numbers in terms of x.

(b) Write an expression for the sum of all three consecutive numbers in terms of x. Write your expression as simply as possible.

(c) Use your answer to (b) to explain whether Helen's statement is correct. AQA(SEG) 1998

E2 (a) (i) Write down any three whole consecutive numbers.

(ii) Multiply the first and the last numbers together.

(iii) Square the middle number.

(b) (i) Repeat (a) with some more sets of three consecutive numbers.

(ii) What do you notice?

(iii) Can you prove your result?

E3 Simon said,

'When you add five consecutive whole numbers, the answer will always be 5 times the middle number. For example, 7 + 8 + 9 + 10 + 11 = 45, and 45 = 5 × 9.'

Prove Simon's result.

E4 Here are the first three lines of a number pattern.

Line 1	$2 \times 3 - 1 \times 4$
Line 2	$3 \times 4 - 2 \times 5$
Line 3	$4 \times 5 - 3 \times 6$

(a) Write down the 10th line of this pattern.

(b) (i) Copy and complete the expression below for the nth line of this pattern.

$$(n + 1)(\ldots\ldots) - n(\ldots\ldots)$$

(ii) Expand and simplify this expression. What does this prove about the pattern?

***E5** (a) Work these out.

(i) $4^2 - 3^2$ (ii) $9^2 - 8^2$ (iii) $10^2 - 9^2$

(b) Prove that the difference between two consecutive square numbers is always odd.

F More brackets

$(2n - 5)(3n + 1)$ →

×	3n	1
2n	$6n^2$	2n
-5	-15n	-5

→ $(2n - 5)(3n + 1)$
$= 6n^2 + 2n - 15n - 5$
$= 6n^2 - 13n - 5$

F1 Multiply out and simplify.

(a) $(2x + 1)(x + 3)$ (b) $(x + 2)(3x + 1)$ (c) $(4x + 3)(x + 2)$
(d) $(x + 5)(3x - 2)$ (e) $(2x - 3)(x + 1)$ (f) $(x + 4)(5x - 2)$
(g) $(2x - 5)(x - 5)$ (h) $(x - 1)(3x - 2)$ (i) $(5x - 2)(x - 2)$

F2 Expand and simplify.

(a) $(2n + 1)(3n + 4)$ (b) $(3n + 2)(3n + 1)$ (c) $(3n + 2)(5n + 4)$
(d) $(5n + 1)(5n + 2)$ (e) $(4n + 5)(2n - 1)$ (f) $(3n - 4)(2n + 1)$
(g) $(2n + 3)(5n - 2)$ (h) $(2n - 1)(2n + 1)$ (i) $(2n - 3)(3n - 5)$
(j) $(5n - 1)(2n - 3)$ (k) $(7n - 2)(2n - 3)$ (l) $(6n - 5)(4n - 3)$

F3 Expand and simplify.

(a) $(2b + 1)^2$ (b) $(3k + 2)^2$ (c) $(5h - 2)^2$

F4 The diagram shows a rectangular paved patio and a square pond. Lengths are in metres.

Show that the expression for the paved area, is $2x^2 + 8x + 4$.

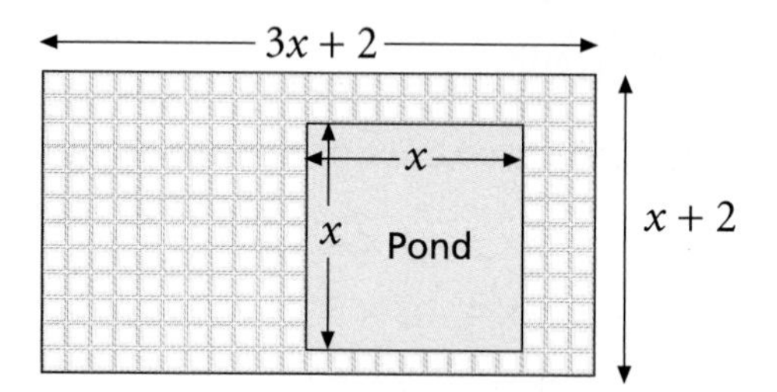

$(2x + y)(3x - 2y)$ →

×	3x	-2y
2x	$6x^2$	-4xy
y	3xy	$-2y^2$

→ $(2x + y)(3x - 2y)$
$= 6x^2 - 4xy + 3xy - 2y^2$
$= 6x^2 - xy - 2y^2$

F5 Expand and simplify where possible.

(a) $(x + y)(2x + 3y)$ (b) $(x + 2y)(2x + y)$ (c) $(x + 3)(y + 2)$
(d) $(3x + y)(x - 2y)$ (e) $(2x - 1)(x + y)$ (f) $(2x - 3y)(x + 5y)$
(g) $(x - y)(2x - y)$ (h) $(2y - x)(x - 3y)$ (i) $(4x + 5)(4 - y)$
(j) $(5x + 2y)(5x - 2y)$ (k) $(2y + x)^2$ (l) $(2y - 3x)^2$

Test yourself

T1 Multiply out and simplify.

(a) $(x + 1)(x + 2)$ (b) $(n + 4)(n + 5)$ (c) $(a + 5)(a - 3)$

(d) $(y - 6)(y + 1)$ (e) $(k - 4)(k - 2)$ (f) $(x + 6)(x - 6)$

(g) $(n + 6)^2$ (h) $(m - 2)^2$ (i) $(p - 5)^2$

T2 Multiply out and simplify.

(a) $(2a - 1)(a + 3)$ (b) $(3x - 2)(x + 5)$ (c) $(2n + 1)(n - 3)$

(d) $(3m + 2)(m - 4)$ (e) $(2x - 1)(x - 3)$ (f) $(2b + 5)(3b - 4)$

(g) $(2x + 1)(3x - 2)$ (h) $(5n - 1)(2n + 3)$ (i) $(3k + 2)^2$

T3 Part of a number grid is shown below.

1	2	3	4	5	6	7	8
9	10	11	12	13	14	15	16
17	18	19	20	21	22	23	24
25	26	27	28	29	30	31	32
33	34	35	36	37	38	39	40

The shaded cross has the number 10 at its centre and is called $\mathbf{C}_{10}$.
The sum of the numbers in the cross is 50.

(a) Calculate the sum of the numbers in $\mathbf{C}_{23}$.

(b) Copy this diagram for $\mathbf{C}_n$ and fill in the empty squares.

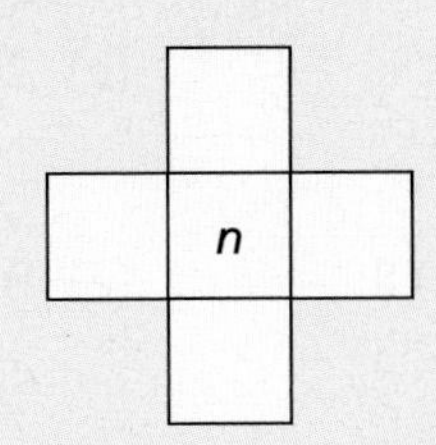

(c) Find the sum of all the numbers in $\mathbf{C}_n$, in terms of n.
Give your answer in its simplest form.

(d) Explain why you cannot find a value of n for which $\mathbf{C}_n = 134$. AQA(SEG) 1998

T4 Multiply out and simplify.

(a) $(2x + y)(x - 2y)$ (b) $(3x - 5y)(2x + y)$ (c) $(3x + y)^2$

***T5** Prove that the sum of two consecutive whole numbers is always odd.

44 Percentage 2

For this work you need to know how to

- convert between decimals and percentages
- find a percentage of a quantity

This work will help you

- calculate an amount after a percentage increase or decrease
- calculate a percentage increase or decrease

A Review

A1 Jason receives £60 as a birthday present.
He spends 25% of his money on a book.

(a) How much is the book?

(b) What percentage of his money does he have left?

A2 In a class of 30 students, 20% have fair hair.
How many students have fair hair?

A3 Work these out.

(a) 75% of £80 (b) 10% of £60 (c) 30% of £50 (d) 5% of £200

A4 Out of 90 pencils in a drawer, 40% of them needed to be sharpened.
How many needed to be sharpened?

A5 Write down the decimal equivalent of these.

(a) 25% (b) 72% (c) 60% (d) 7% (e) 2%

A6 Write each of these as a percentage.

(a) 0.94 (b) 0.54 (c) 0.08 (d) 0.8 (e) 0.01

A7 52% of Ruth's bar of chocolate is sugar.
The bar weighs 120 grams.

How much sugar is in this bar of chocolate?

A8 Work these out.

(a) 28% of £35 (b) 89% of £40 (c) 3% of 2300 (d) 56% of 360

A9 In a town of 26 000 households, 72% own a microwave oven.

(a) What percentage of the households in this town do not own a microwave?

(b) To the nearest hundred, how many households do not own a microwave in this town?

A10 Work these out to the nearest penny.

(a) 47% of £2.65 (b) 38% of £6.82 (c) 69% of £26.60 (d) 81% of £1.80

A11 Write down the decimal equivalent of each of these.

(a) 26.5% (b) 63.8% (c) 50.2% (d) 1.3% (e) 5.8%

A12 Write each of these as a percentage.

(a) 0.437 (b) 0.514 (c) 0.609 (d) 0.052 (e) 0.029

A13 Work these out to one decimal place.

(a) 25.3% of 62 kg (b) 93.8% of 53 m (c) 6.5% of 38

B *Increasing and decreasing*

B1 David has a discount card for his local outdoor shop.
It gives him a 10% reduction on the price of everything in the shop.

(a) What reduction will he get on a pair of boots that cost £60?

(b) What will he pay for these boots?

B2 Peter weighed 4 kg at birth.
After six weeks his weight had increased by 25%.

(a) How much weight did he gain?

(b) What was his new weight?

B3 A machine sorts 2000 letters per hour at normal speed.
At high speed it sorts 15% more letters per hour.
How many letters per hour does it sort at high speed? AQA 2003 Specimen

B4 Joe weighed 80 kg.
He was ill for a while and lost 20% of his body weight.
What was his weight after his illness?

B5 Apples cost 80p per kilogram.
Pears cost 15% per kilogram more than apples.
How much per kilogram are pears? AQA(SEG) 2003 Specimen

B6 It needs 20 litres of orange drink to fill 50 cups.

(a) Work out how many litres of orange drink are needed to fill 60 cups.

The total cost of orange drink for 50 cups is £7.50.
Each cup of drink is sold at a 20% profit.

(b) Work out the price at which each cup of orange drink is sold. Edexcel

C *Increasing using multipliers*

Fares up by 25%

Commuters will be hit again in the new year as the train companies raise fares by 25%. Promises of better punctuali... greater comfort and faster journ...

If fares go up by 25%, this mean 25% of the old fare is added on to make the new fare.

25% or $\frac{25}{100}$ of the old fare is added on.
So the new fare is $1\frac{25}{100}$ or 1.25 times the old fare.

To increase by 25%, you can multiply by 1..

C1 Calculate the new fare after a 25% increase for each of these old fares.
(a) £42.60 (b) £6.80 (c) £25 (d) £35.40 (e) £2.20

C2 If bus fares go up by 12%, what number should you multiply by to get the new fare?

C3 To the nearest penny, calculate the new fare after a 12% increase for these old fares.
(a) £2.90 (b) £38.60 (c) £60 (d) £15.90 (e) £36.75

C4 A shop buys coffee for £2.50 per kilogram.
It sells the coffee to make a profit of 55%.
What is the selling price of one kilogram of coffee in this shop?

C5 In 2001, Mary had 140 budgies.
During the year the number of budgies went up by 35%.
How many budgies did Mary have at the end of the year?

C6 A population in a town is expected to rise by 8%.
(a) Tina says you should multiply the present population by 1.8.
Tim says you should multiply by 1.08.
Who is right?
(b) If the present population is 56 000, what will the population be after a rise of 8%?

C7 The puffin population on a small island is estimated to be 1500 birds.
One year the population is expected to rise by 6%.
What would the new puffin population be after a rise of 6%?

C8 In 1997 Mrs Patel earned £16 640 for a 52-week year.
At the start of 1998 she was given a rise of 3%.
Calculate how much she will earn **per week** in 1998? OCR(MEG)

A computer costs £950 plus VAT at $17\frac{1}{2}$%.
What is the cost of buying the computer, including the VAT?

$17\frac{1}{2}\% = 17.5\% = 0.175$ so multiply by 1.175.

$950 \times 1.175 = 1116.25$

So the total cost is £1116.25.

C9 The cost of a camera is £286 plus VAT.
The rate of VAT is $17\frac{1}{2}$%.
Calculate the cost of the camera. Edexcel

C10 In January Ella earns £1250 but in February she earns 15.6% more.
How much does she earn in February?

C11 One year, workers in a factory receive a pay rise of 4.8%.
Calculate a worker's new weekly pay if their old weekly pay is £300.

C12 (a) Increase £540 by 12.2% (b) Increase £600 by 68.4%
(c) Increase £15 by 2.5% (d) Increase £3.60 by 6.7%

D *Decreasing using multipliers*

Sale!
Massive **reductions!**
All prices down by **15%**

If prices are reduced by 15%, this means 15% of the old price is taken off to make the new price.

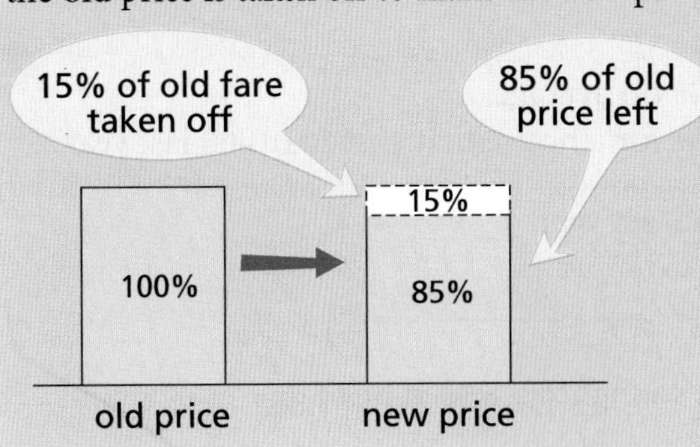

15% of the old price is taken off.
That leaves 85% or $\frac{85}{100}$ of the old price.

So the new price is $\frac{85}{100}$ or 0.85 times the old price.

old price → × 0.85 → new price

To decrease by 15%, you can multiply by 0.85

D1 Reduce each of these prices by 15%.
(a) £16.80 (b) £5.60 (c) £90 (d) £3.40 (e) £0.20

D2 What number should you multiply by to reduce prices by 35%?

D3 In a sale, prices are reduced by 35%.
Calculate the sale prices of skirts with these original prices.
(a) £25 (b) £29.60 (c) £50 (d) £16.99 (e) £39.99

D4 Reduce each of these prices by 16%.

(a) £4.80 (b) £6.30 (c) £19.99 (d) £35.50 (e) £280

D5 What number should you multiply by to reduce prices by 9%?

D6 Reduce each of these prices by 9%.

(a) £1240 (b) £680 (c) £9.50 (d) £0.64 (e) £14.70

D7 What should you multiply by to reduce prices by these percentages

(a) 72% (b) 23% (c) 30% (d) 5% (e) 2%

D8 Reduce

(a) £240 by 13% (b) £620 by 82% (c) £2.95 by 22% (d) £430 by 8%

D9 Sally is interested in buying a car that is priced at £6200.
She is offered a 7% reduction in the price if she pays cash.
How much would the car cost her?

D10 Every percentage increase or decrease corresponds to a multiplier.
Match these percentage changes to their multipliers.

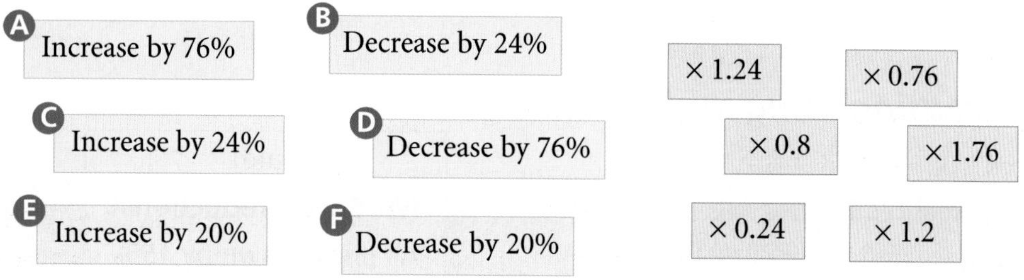

D11 Last year the price of houses increased by 9% on average.
How much would you expect to pay this year for a house that cost £110 000 last year?

D12 The value of a car decreased by 18% over the last year.
The car was worth £4500 a year ago.
How much is the car worth now?

D13 Between the ages of five and ten years, Mike's weight increased by 66%.
When he was five years old he weighed 18 kg.
How heavy was he when he was ten, correct to the nearest kg?

D14 Between 1990 and 2000, the number of school age children in a town went down by 23%.
The number of children in this town in 1990 was 9560.
How many children were living in this town in 2000, correct to the nearest 10?

E *Finding an increase as a percentage*

On an island the number of great skuas goes up from 39 to 54 birds one year.
What is the percentage increase in the number of birds?

You need to find the multiplier from 39 to 54. 39 → × ? → 54

To find the multiplier **divide** 54 by 39. → 54 ÷ 39 = 1.38 (to 2 d.p.)

e multiplier 1.38 corresponds to an increase of 38%. → So the percentage increase is 38%.

E1 The price of a camera goes up from £250 to £270.
Calculate the percentage increase.

E2 Calculate the percentage increase in each case below.

(a) From £25 to £28.50 (b) From £150 to £247.50

(c) From 69 kg to 117.3 kg (d) From 2 metres to 2.14 metres

E3 Jake buys a painting for £400 and sells it for £520.
What is his percentage profit?

E4 Meena sells a book for £22.20 that she bought for only £12.
What is her percentage profit?

E5 From 1975 to 1994, the number of UK public libraries increased from 3714 to 4499.
What was the percentage increase in the number of libraries, correct to the nearest 1%?

E6 In 1994 the number of registered heroin addicts in the UK was 22 313.
In 1992 the number was 16 964.
Find the percentage increase in the number of registered addicts between 1992 and 1994.

E7 The table shows the average price of a UK dwelling in 1985, 1990 and 1995.

1985	1990	1995
£31 103	£59 785	£65 079

Find the percentage increase in price between

(a) 1985 and 1990 (b) 1990 and 1995

E8 The table shows the populations of England and Scotland in 1931 and 1991.
From 1931 to 1991, find the percentage increase in the population in each country.

	1931	1991
England	37 358 000	48 209 000
Scotland	4 843 000	5 100 000

***E9** In 1980 there were 2556 km of motorway in the UK.
By 1994 there were 3168 km of motorway.
Find the percentage increase, correct to one decimal place.

F *Finding a decrease as a percentage*

On an island the number of arctic skuas goes down from 78 to 64 birds one year.
What is the percentage decrease in the number of birds?

You need to find the multiplier from 78 to 64.

78 → × ? → 64

To find the multiplier **divide** 64 by 78.

$64 \div 78 = 0.82$ (to 2 d.p.)

The multiplier 0.82 corresponds to an decrease of 18%.

So the percentage decrease is 18%.

F1 In a sale, the price of a jumper is cut from £42 to £27.30.
Calculate the percentage decrease in the price.

F2 Calculate the percentage decrease in each case below.

(a) From £75 to £57
(b) From £8.50 to £3.23
(c) From 84 kg to 58.8 kg
(d) From 6.5 metres to 6.24 metres

F3 Between 1981 and 1991, the population of Sheffield fell from 538 000 to 503 000.
What was the percentage decrease in the population, correct to the nearest 1%?

F4 Sanjay is buying a car that is priced at £6450.
The saleswoman reduces the price to £5700 as Sanjay is paying cash.
What percentage discount is this?

F5 In 1984 the number of deaths through road accidents in the UK was 5599.
In 1994 the number of deaths had gone down to 3650.
Find the percentage decrease in the number of deaths between 1984 and 1994.

F6 Calculate the percentage change in each case below, correct to the nearest 1%.
Say whether it is an increase or a decrease.

(a) From £560 to £476
(b) From 20 kg to 28.6 kg
(c) From 58 kg to 75.2 kg
(d) From 82 m to 60 m
(e) From £150 to £90
(f) From 40 kg to 43.6 kg
(g) From 1200 to 1176
(h) From 60 to 64

F7 The table shows the numbers of men and women in employment in the UK in 1970 and 1995.

	Men	Women
1970	13 952 000	8 450 000
1995	11 047 000	10 842 000

Between 1970 and 1995, what was the percentage change in the number employed in the UK for

(a) men
(b) women

Say if it is an increase or decrease each time.

F8 Copy and complete this table to show estimates of the percentage changes in our consumption of different foodstuffs between 1965 and 1994.

Estimated consumption in grams per person per week			
	1965	1994	% change
Cheese	91	106	16% increase
Beef and veal	229	131	
Fish	164	145	
Fresh green veg	406	245	
Fresh fruit	533	645	
Instant coffee	7	13	

Just show the first and last columns in your answer.

G *Mixed questions*

G1 Sam wants to buy a Hooper washing machine.
Hooper washing machines are sold in three different shops.

Washing Power	**Whytes**	**Clean Up**
$\frac{1}{4}$ OFF usual price of £330	20% OFF usual price of £320	£210 plus VAT at $17\frac{1}{2}$%

(a) Work out the cost of the washing machine in the Washing Power shop.
(b) Work out the cost of the washing machine in the Whytes shop.
(c) Work out the cost of the washing machine in the Clean Up shop. Edexcel

G2

London – Paris by plane
Normal price: £91
Special offer: 15% discount

An airline company has flights from London to Paris for £91.
They offer a 15% discount.
Calculate the cost of the flight after the discount. AQA 1999

G3 In Scotland there were about 72 900 grey seals in 1989.
By 1990 the number of grey seals had risen to 78 200.
Calculate the percentage increase in numbers of seals to the nearest 1%.

G4 (a) A year ago Martin was 1.60 m tall.
He is now 4% taller.
Calculate his height now.
Give your answer in centimetres.

(b) Martin now weighs 58 kg.
A year ago he weighed 51 kg.
Calculate the percentage increase in his weight.
Give your answer to an appropriate degree of accuracy.

AQA(SEG) 1998

G5 In 1981 there were 855 000 tonnes of cod in the North Sea.
By 1996, this had fallen to 438 000 tonnes.
Calculate the percentage decrease in the cod stocks.

Test yourself

T1 Out of a year group of 180 students, 25% walk to school.
How many of these students walk to school?

T2 Karen sees an advertisement for a suede jacket.
Calculate the final cost of the suede jacket.

Our Price
30% off Recommended
Price of £130

AQA(SEG) 2000

T3 In one year a plant's height increased by 24%.
It was 1.75 m tall at the beginning of the year.
How tall was it at the end of the year?

T4 323 child pedestrians died in road accidents in 1985.
Between 1985 and 1995, the number of child pedestrians killed in road accidents decreased by 59%.
How many child pedestrians died in road accidents in 1995?

T5 Between 1950 and 1995, the number of self-employed people in the UK rose by 80.5%.
In 1950, there were 1 802 000 self-employed people.
How many self-employed people were there in 1995, correct to the nearest thousand?

T6 A shop increases the price of a television from £480 to £648.
What is the percentage increase in price?

T7 A shop sells millennium mugs at £4.49 each.
When Krishna goes to buy five, he finds that the shop has a special offer – 'Buy 5 for only £20.'
What percentage discount is this?

AQA(SEG) 2000

45 *Triangles and polygons*

You will revise the names and properties of special types of triangles and quadrilaterals.

This work will help you understand and use angle properties of triangles, quadrilaterals and other polygons.

A *Describing shapes*

A1 This regular hexagon has been split into two trapeziums.

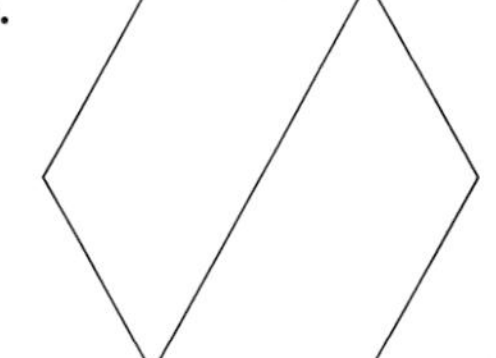

Draw sketches to show how a regular hexagon can be split into each of the following. Use triangular dotty paper if you like.

(a) Three rhombuses

(b) Six equilateral triangles

(c) Four trapeziums

(d) A kite and two isosceles triangles

(e) A rectangle and two isosceles triangles

(f) An equilateral triangle and three isosceles triangles

(g) An isosceles triangle and two trapeziums

A2 This square has been divided into two right-angled triangles and a parallelogram.

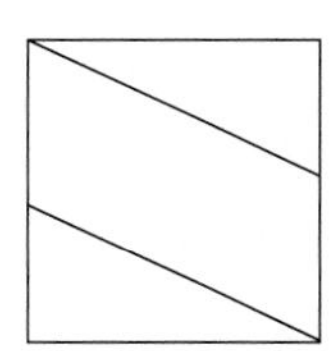

Draw sketches to show how a square can be split into each of the following. Use square dotty paper if you like.

(a) Two right-angled triangles

(b) Three right-angled triangles

(c) Two isosceles triangles and two trapeziums

(d) A kite and two right-angled triangles

(e) An isosceles triangle and two right-angled triangles

(f) Two trapeziums

(g) A square and four right-angled triangles

A3 A quadrilateral has rotation symmetry of order 4.

(a) What is the name of the quadrilateral?

(b) Describe some other special properties that it has.

B *Angle properties – a reminder*

Angles on a line add up to 180°.

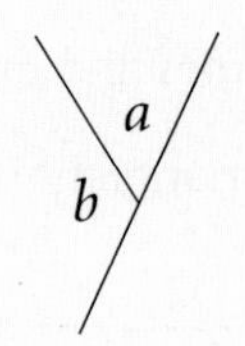

$a + b = 180°$

Angles round a point add up to 360°.

$c + d + e = 360°$

Vertically opposite angles are equal.

$f = g$ and $h = i$

Corresponding angles (made with parallel lines) are equal.

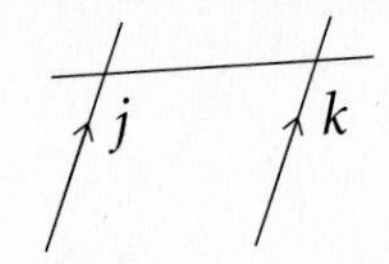

$j = k$

Alternate angles (made with parallel lines) are equal.

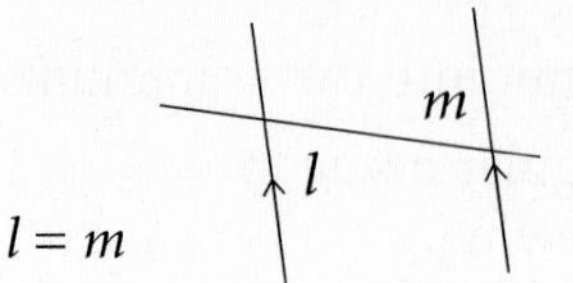

$l = m$

Angles between parallel lines, on the same side of a line crossing them, add up to 180°.

$n + o = 180°$

B1 Find the angles marked with letters.

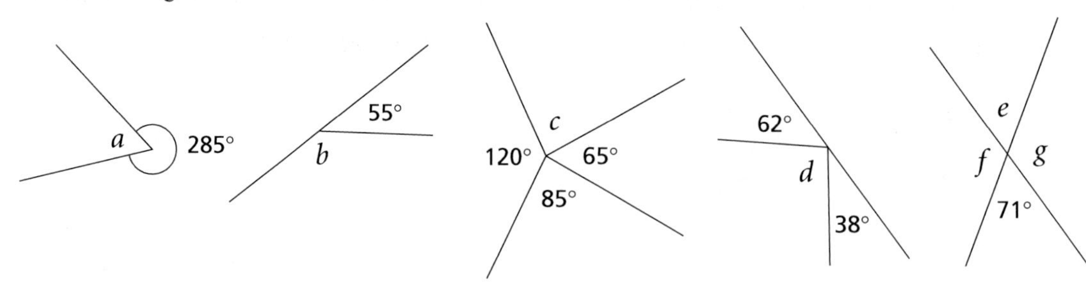

B2 Find the angles marked with letters.

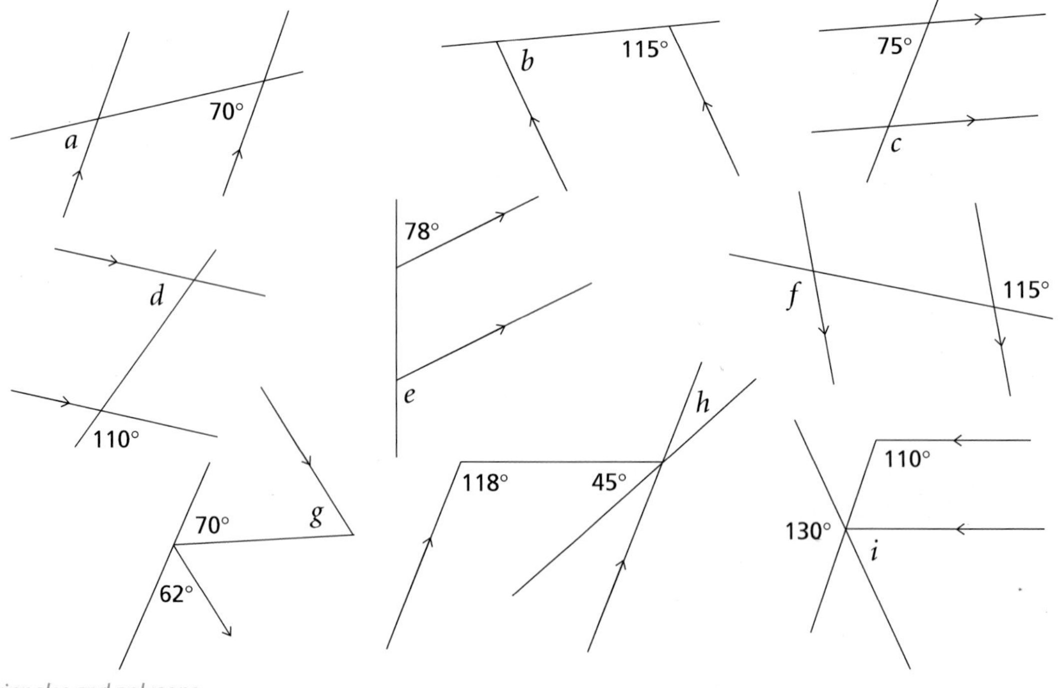

C Angles of a triangle

Angle ACD is an **exterior angle** of triangle ABC.

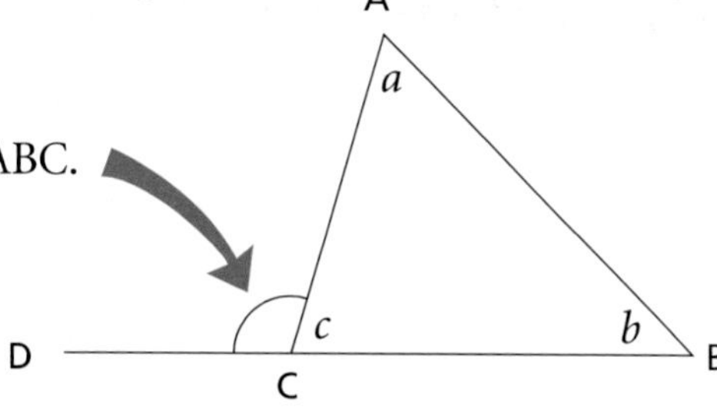

The line CE has been drawn parallel to AB.

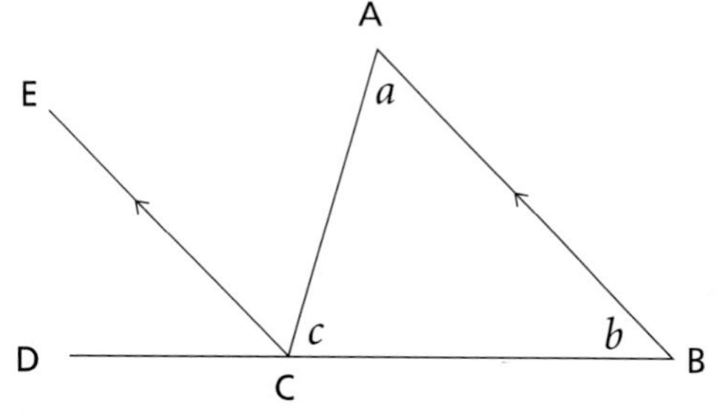

- What is the value of angle ECD? Why?
- What is the value of angle ACE? Why?
- What does the following statement mean and why is it true?

  An exterior angle of a triangle is equal to the sum of the other two interior angles.
- How does this show that **the angles of a triangle add up to 180°**?

C1 Work out the missing angles.

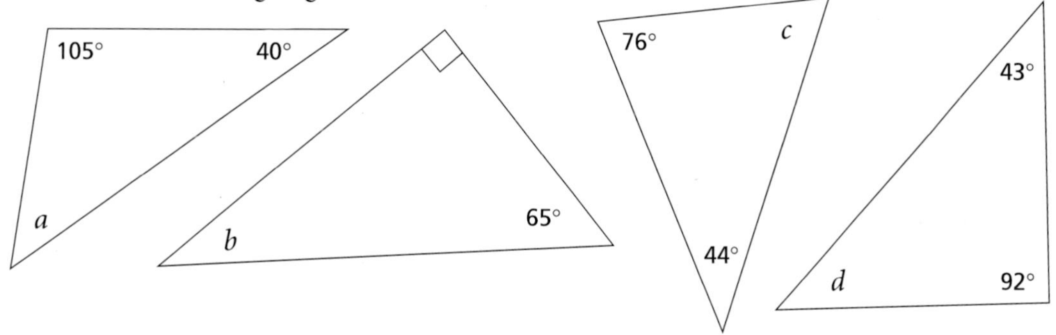

C2 Work out the missing angles in these isosceles triangles.

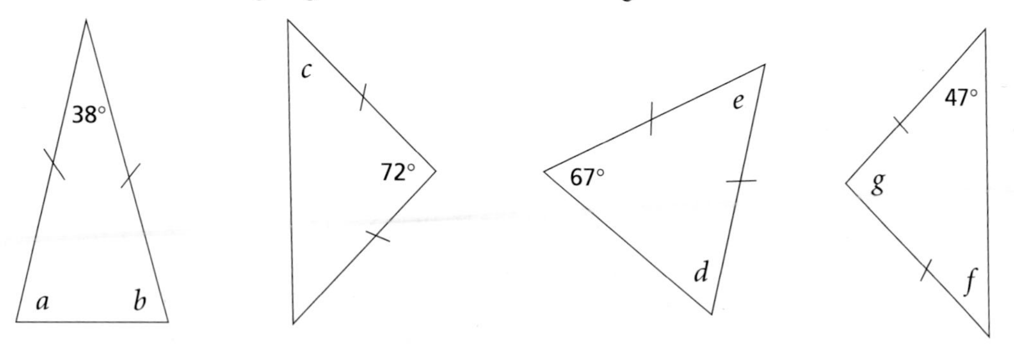

C3 Work out the angles marked with small letters.
Explain how you worked out each angle.

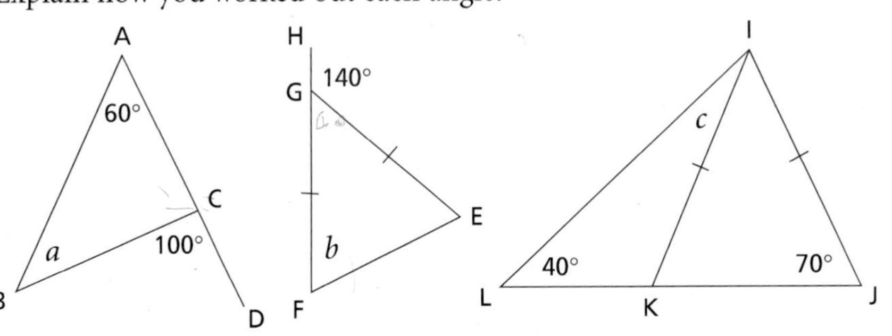

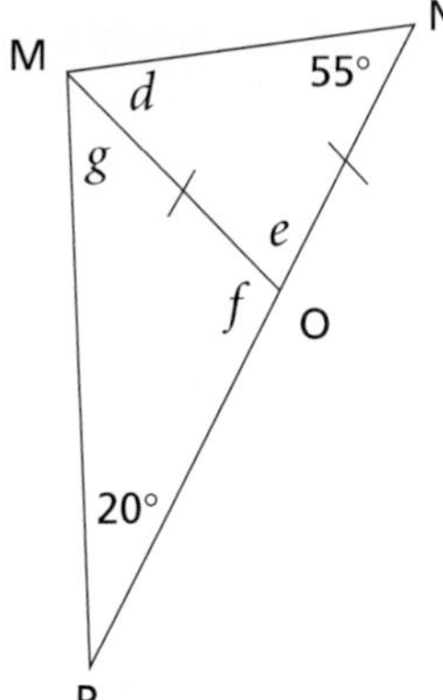

D Polygons

D1 You can split a quadrilateral into two triangles like this.

(a) What is the sum of the 'black' angles?

(b) What is the sum of the 'white' angles?

(c) What is the sum of the interior angles of a quadrilateral?

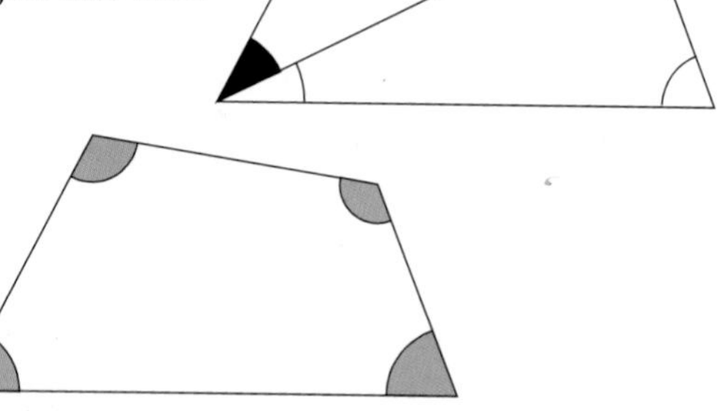

D2 Find the angles marked with letters.
Explain how you worked out each angle.

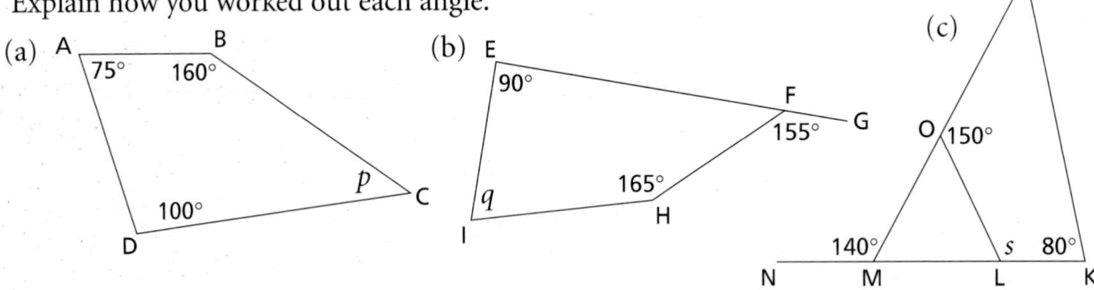

D3 (a) Draw any polygon and record how many sides it has.

Choose a vertex. Draw straight lines from it to all the other vertices.

(b) How many triangles have you made?

(c) What is the total of all the angles in the triangles?

(d) From your answer to (c) write the total of all the interior angles of your polygon.

(e) Do (a) to (d) again, for a polygon with a different number of sides.

(f) Suppose the polygon you start with has n sides.
Go through (a) to (d) again to find a formula for the total of the interior angles.

The sum of the interior angles of a polygon with n sides is $180(n-2)°$.

D4 What is the sum of the interior angles of an 11-sided polygon?

D5 For each of these polygons,

(i) record the number of sides

(ii) work out the sum of the interior angles

(iii) work out the missing angle

(a)

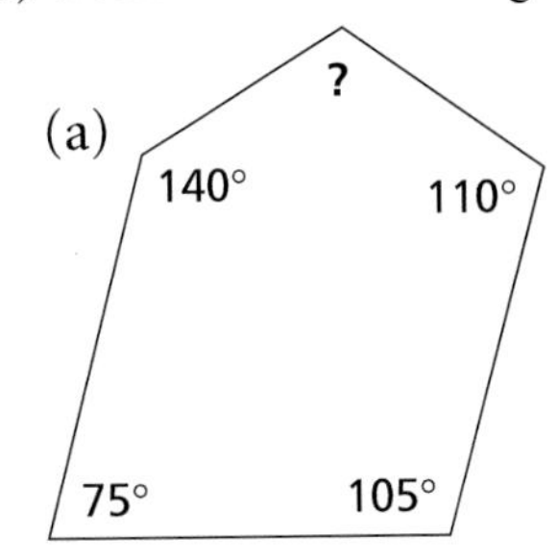

(b)

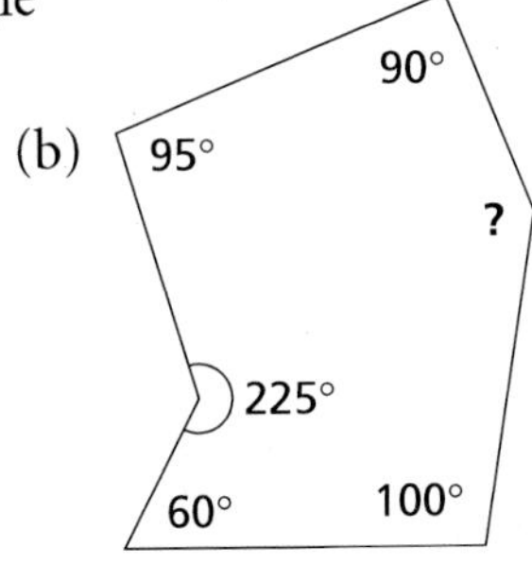

(c)

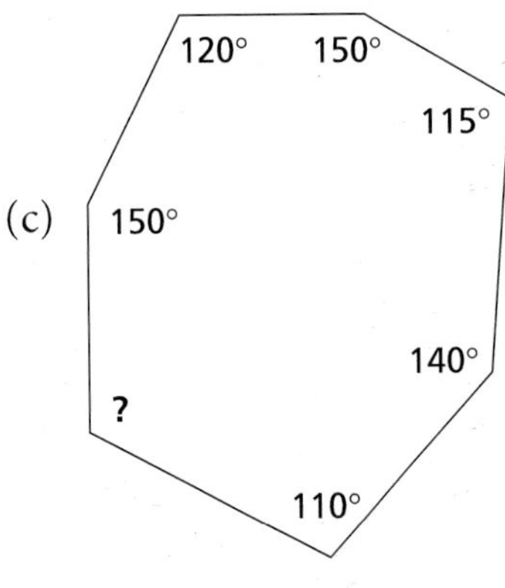

D6 Each of these polygons has one line of reflection symmetry.
Work out the missing angles.

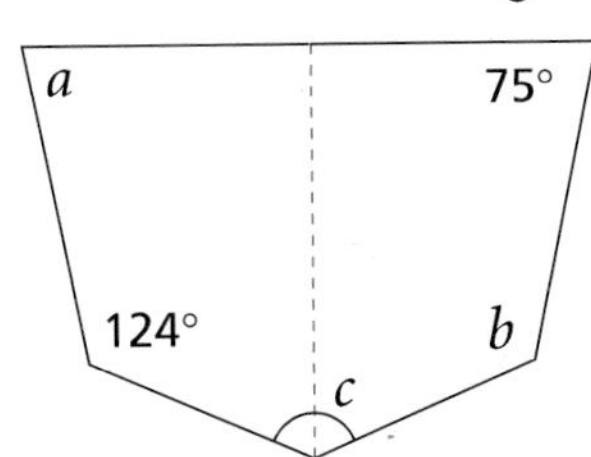

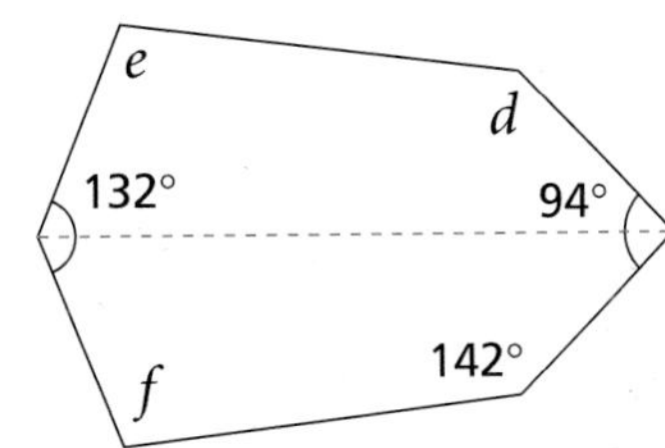

A **regular** polygon has all its sides equal and all its angles equal.

D7 Find the size of each interior angle of

(a) a regular hexagon

(b) a regular nonagon (nine sides)

As with a triangle, if you extend a side of a polygon, the angle made is called an **exterior angle.**

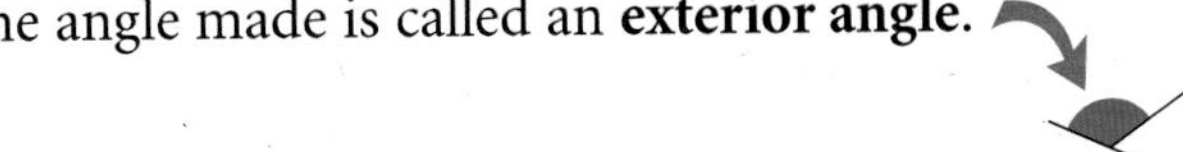

D8 If a pencil is moved around the sides of a polygon, at each vertex it turns through the exterior angle.

(a) When the pencil gets back to where it started from, it will be pointing in the same direction as before. What angle has it turned through?

(b) What is the sum of the exterior angles of a polygon?

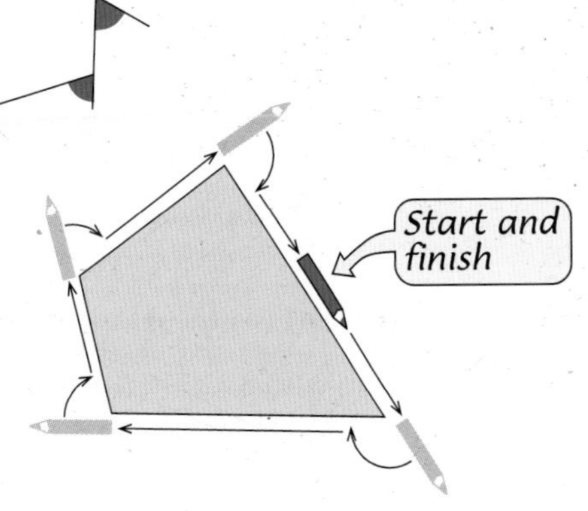

The sum of the exterior angles of a polygon is 360°.
This is true however many sides it has.

D9 For each of these polygons,

(i) find the missing exterior angle or angles

(ii) work out the interior angle at each vertex

(iii) work out the total of the interior angles.
Use the formula from D3 to check whether this total agrees with the number of sides of the polygon.

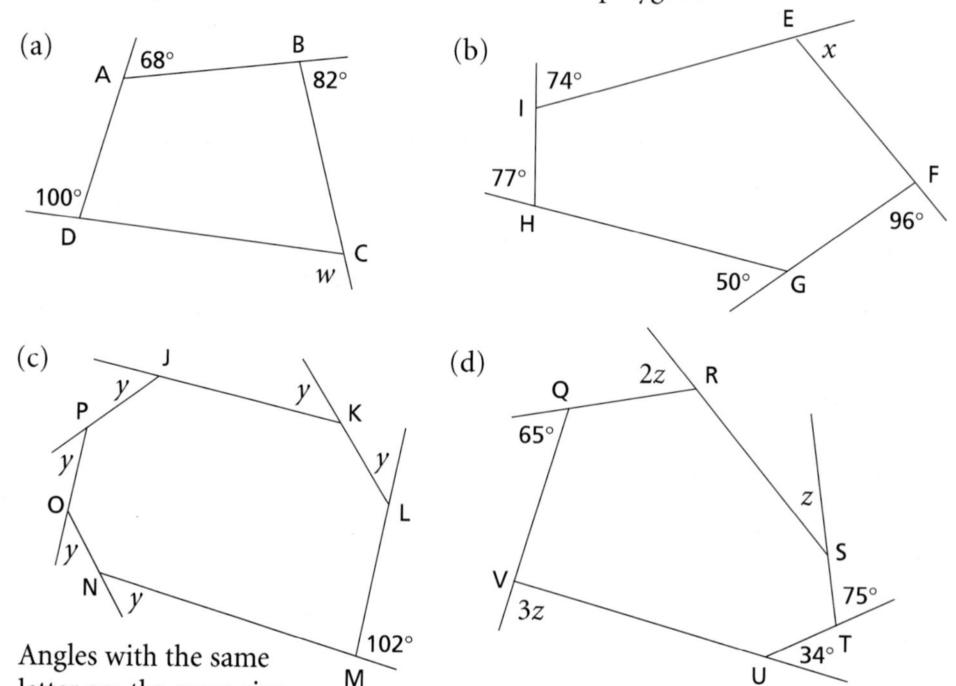

D10 This is a regular 10-sided polygon (a decagon).
Each angle is marked e.

Calculate the size of e.

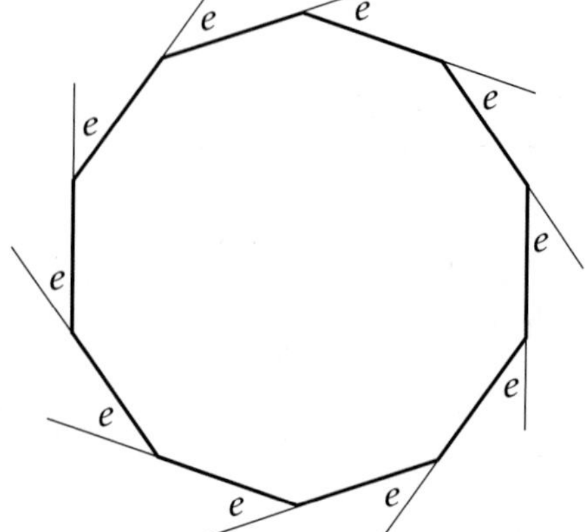

D11 Calculate the size of each exterior angle of a regular polygon with

(a) 18 sides (b) 24 sides (c) 30 sides (d) 45 sides

D12 This is a close-up a vertex of the decagon in D10.
What is the size of the interior angle, i ?

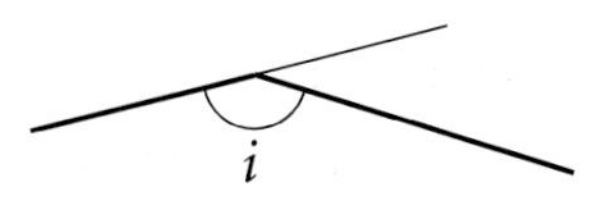

D13 Calculate the interior angle for each regular polygon in D11.

D14 Each exterior angle of a certain regular polygon is 30°.
How many sides must this polygon have?

D15 How many sides does a regular polygon have if each exterior angle is

(a) 9° (b) 24° (c) 10° (d) 18°

D16 How many sides does a regular polygon have if each interior angle is

(a) 135° (b) 108° (c) 175° (d) 174°

D17 A regular polygon has n sides. Write an expression in n for

(a) the size of an exterior angle (b) the size of an interior angle

E *Mixed questions*

When you do questions of this kind, it is a good idea to sketch the diagram and mark the values of angles on it as you work them out.

E1 GHIJ is a rectangle.
JILK is a kite.
GI and JL are parallel.
HL is a straight line.

(a) Find the size of angle KJL.

(b) Find the size of angle KLI.

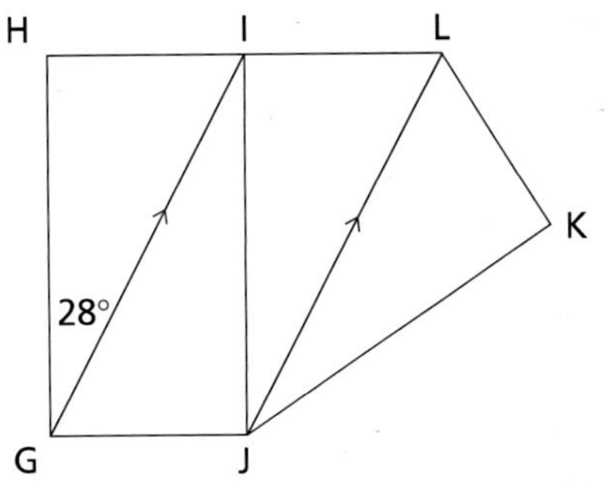

E2 This is a regular nonagon.

(a) Triangle ADG is equilateral.
Calculate angle x.

(b) Calculate angles y and z.

(c) Explain how you know that AG is parallel to IH.

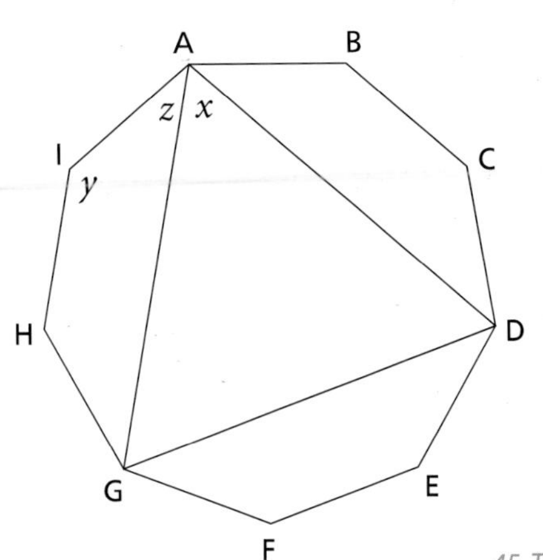

*E3 (a) Calculate angle CAK.

(b) What value must angle AHK have for HK to be parallel to AB?

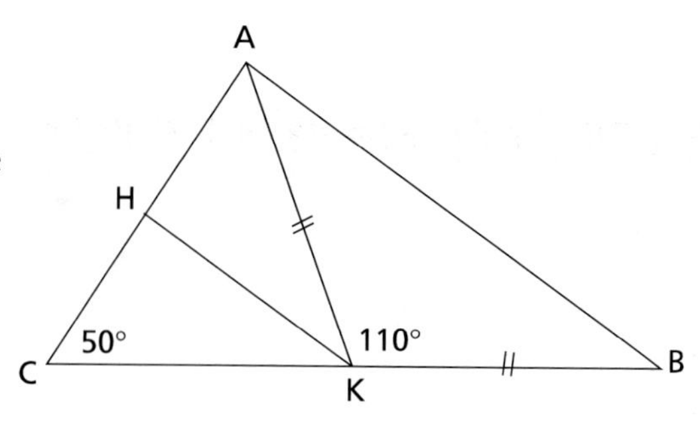

Test yourself

T1 Calculate the lettered angles.

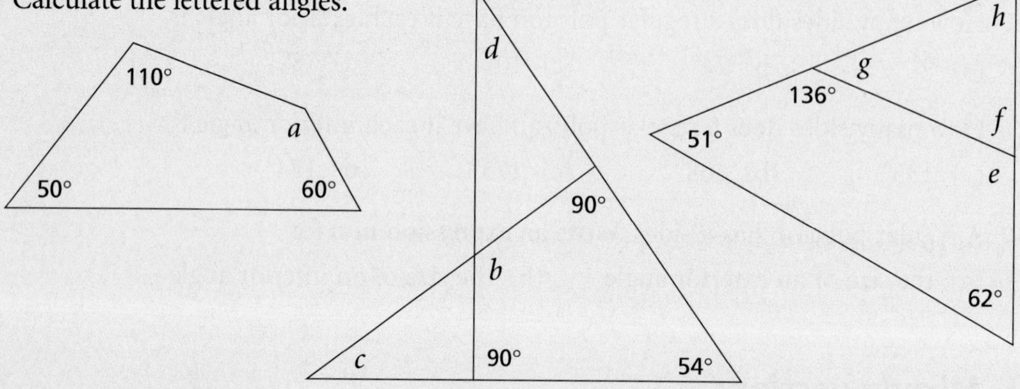

T2 Sketch these diagrams.
Fill in the sizes of all the angles.

(a)

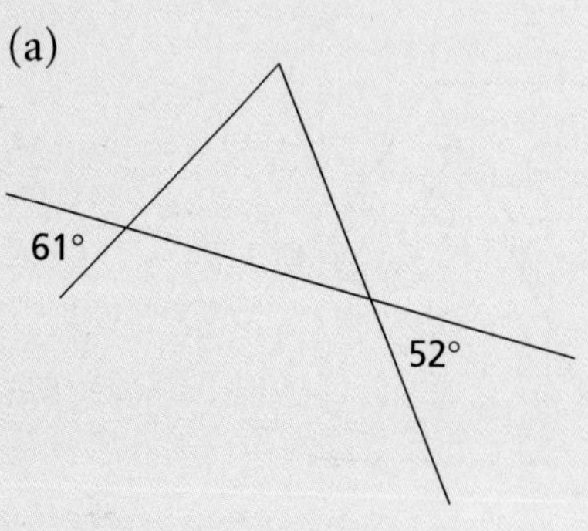

(b)

124°

62°

43°

T3 Find the missing angle.

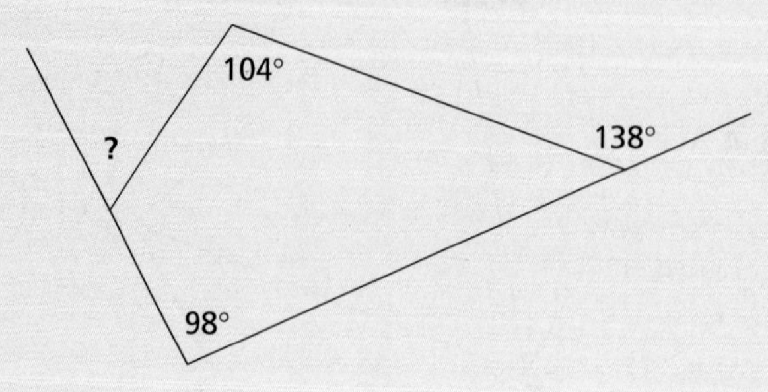

46 *Simultaneous equations*

You should know how to

- simplify expressions such as $2x + 5y + 8x - 5y$
- find the value of expressions such as $2x + 5y$, given the values of x and y
- solve equations such as $2x - 8 = 10$
- draw the graph of a straight line given its equation

This work will help you

- solve simultaneous equations using algebra
- solve problems by forming and solving simultaneous equations
- interpret the solution of simultaneous equations as the point of intersection of two graphs

A *What's the difference?*

A1 All weights in these balance pictures are in grams.

(a) Find the weight of an apple.

(b) What is the weight of a strawberry?

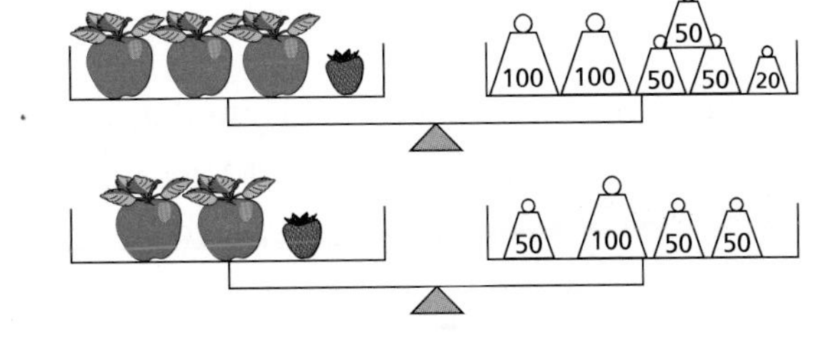

A2 All weights in these balance pictures are in grams.

(a) Find the weight of a cherry.

(b) What is the weight of a pear?

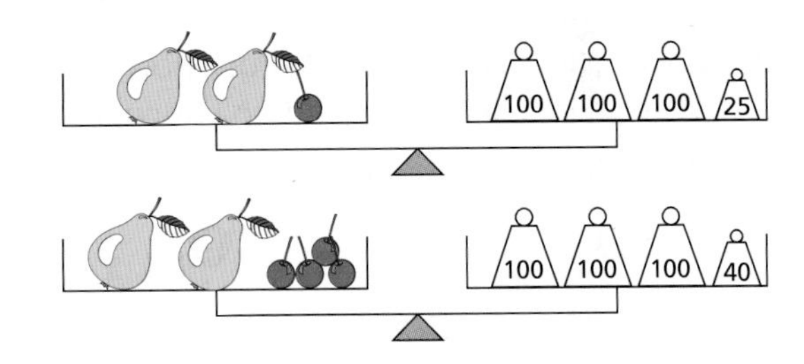

A3 Ayesha and Zoe buy some flowers.

Ayesha buys a rose and a lily.
These cost her £5.35.
Zoe buys a rose and 3 lilies.
These cost her £7.25.

What is the cost of a lily?

AQA(SEG) 2000

A4 In a cafe, two teas and a bun cost £1.90.
Two teas and five buns cost £3.10.
How much is a bun and how much is a tea?

*A5 In this puzzle, each different symbol stands for a number.
What does each symbol stand for?

■ + ♥ + ■ + ♥ + ♥ = 34
♥ + ■ + ◆ + ◆ = 14
♥ + ■ + ■ = 14

B *Solving equations*

TG

Can you find the values of a and b that fit these equations?

$4a + 2b = 460$

$a + 2b = 220$

You can think of these equations as shorthand for a balance problem.

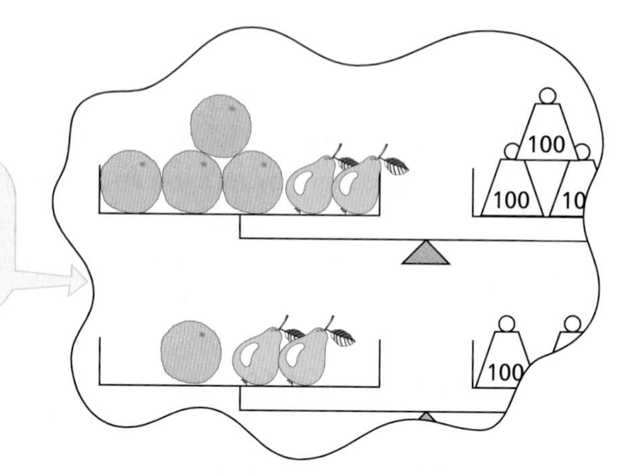

B1 Solve the following pairs of simultaneous equations to find the values of a and b.

(a) $5a + b = 21$
$3a + b = 13$

(b) $6a + 3b = 21$
$4a + 3b = 19$

(c) $3a + 2b = 10$
$4a + 2b = 12$

(d) $a + 7b = 24$
$a + 3b = 12$

(e) $2a + b = 27$
$2a + 6b = 62$

(f) $3a + 8b = 79$
$3a + 2b = 31$

B2 Three chocolate bars and four chocolate eggs weigh 465 grams.
Three chocolate bars and two chocolate eggs weigh 315 grams.

(a) Which of these pairs of equations are correct for the chocolate bars and eggs?

A
$3b + 2e = 465$
$3b + 4e = 315$

B
$b + 4e = 465$
$b + 2e = 315$

C
$3b + 4e = 465$
$3b + 2e = 315$

(b) Solve the pair of simultaneous equations that is correct to find the values of b and e.

B3 Solve the following pairs of simultaneous equations.

(a) $2c + 3d = 10$
$2c + 2d = 7$

(b) $3h + 4k = 12$
$3h + 2k = 9$

(c) $4p + 2q = 9$
$p + 2q = 6$

B4 Solve the following pairs of simultaneous equations.

(a) $4a + b = 7$
$2a + b = 3$

(b) $5p + 2q = 18$
$p + 2q = 2$

(c) $4x + 2y = 12$
$4x + y = 2$

(d) $5g + 3h = 23$
$2g + 3h = 11$

(e) $m + 6n = 15$
$m + 2n = 3$

(f) $2c + d = 4$
$2c + 4d = 19$

B5 Solve the following pairs of simultaneous equations.

(a) $5a + b = 2$
$3a + b = 4$

(b) $5x + 3y = 2$
$2x + 3y = 8$

(c) $3k + h = 9$
$3k + 4h = 0$

C Shall I compare thee ... ?

C1 Here is a pair of equations.

$$a + 2b = 7$$
$$3a + 5b = 19$$

(a) Multiply both sides of the first equation by 3.

(b) Find the values of a and b.

C2 Here is a pair of equations.

$$11x + 4y = 42$$
$$3x + 2y = 16$$

(a) Multiply both sides of the second equation by 2.

(b) Find the values of x and y.

C3 Solve the following pairs of simultaneous equations.

(a) $a + 3b = 7$
$2a + 5b = 13$

(b) $p + 3q = 12$
$3p + 2q = 22$

(c) $4x + y = 10$
$3x + 4y = 14$

(d) $2g + 3h = 5$
$4g + 5h = 9$

(e) $3m + 2n = 10$
$7m + 6n = 24$

(f) $2c + 9d = 1$
$5c + 3d = 22$

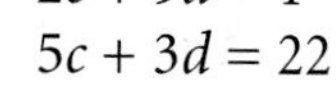

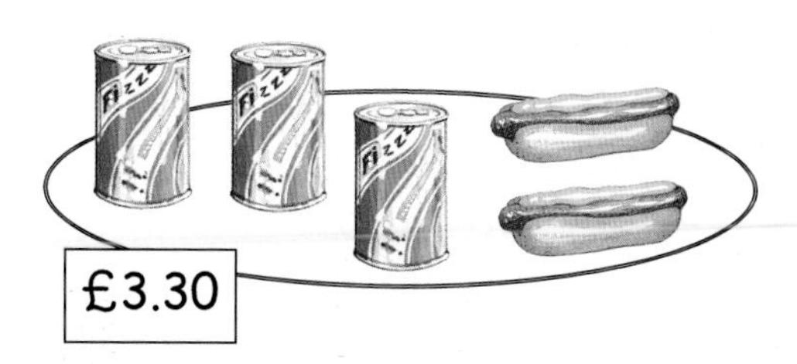

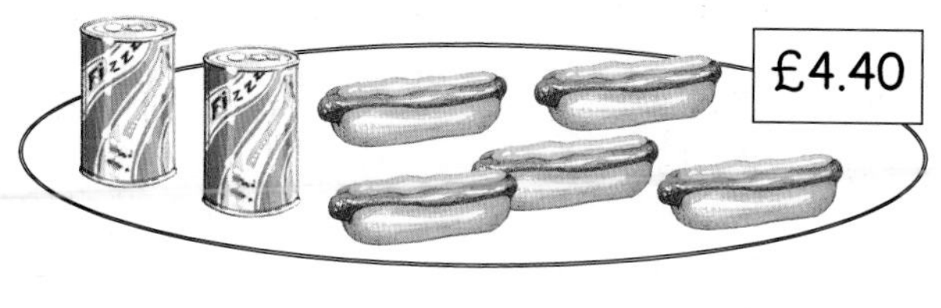

Example

Solve this pair of simultaneous equations.

(A) $2x + 3y = 14$
(B) $5x + 2y = 13$

(A) $\times 5$ $\quad 10x + 15y = 70$
(B) $\times 2$ $\quad 10x + 4y = 26$

So $11y = 44$

$y = 4$

You could start by multiplying the first equation by 2 and the second equation by 3.

(A) $\times 2$ $\quad 4x + 6y = 28$
(B) $\times 3$ $\quad 15x + 6y = 39$

Substitute in equation (A) to give $2x + 12 = 14$

$2x = 2$

so $x = 1$

So the solution is $x = 1, y = 4$

You could substitute in equation (B) instead.

Substitute in equation (B) to check. $5x + 2y = 5 \times 1 + 2 \times 4 = 13$ ✓

C4 Here is a pair of equations.

$2m + 5n = 9$
$3m + 2n = 8$

(a) Multiply both sides of the first equation by 3.

(b) Multiply both sides of the second equation by 2.

(c) Find the values of m and n.

C5 Here is a pair of equations.

$2x + 5y = 14$
$3x + 2y = 10$

(a) Multiply both sides of the first equation by 2.

(b) Multiply both sides of the second equation by 5.

(c) Find the values of x and y.

C6 Solve each pair of simultaneous equations.

(a) $2v + 3w = 8$
$3v + 4w = 12$

(b) $3p + 7q = 19$
$4p + 2q = 18$

(c) $2m + 9n = 11$
$5m + 2n = 7$

(d) $7k + 3h = 37$
$2k + 5h = 23$

(e) $5y + 3x = 31$
$5x + 3y = 25$

(f) $7a + 2b = 23$
$11b + 2a = 17$

C7 Solve each pair of simultaneous equations.

(a) $2v + w = 1$
$3v + 5w = 19$

(b) $3p + 5q = 1$
$7p + 2q = 12$

(c) $5m + 2n = 6$
$10m + 3n = 4$

D *Forming and solving equations*

D1 Jake has some green and yellow rods.

The length of a green rod is g cm.

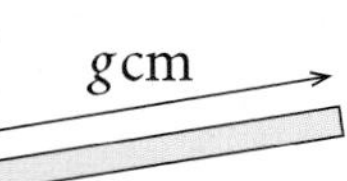

The length of a yellow rod is y cm.

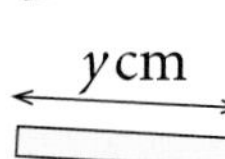

(a) The total length of 2 green rods and 3 yellow rods is 33 cm.

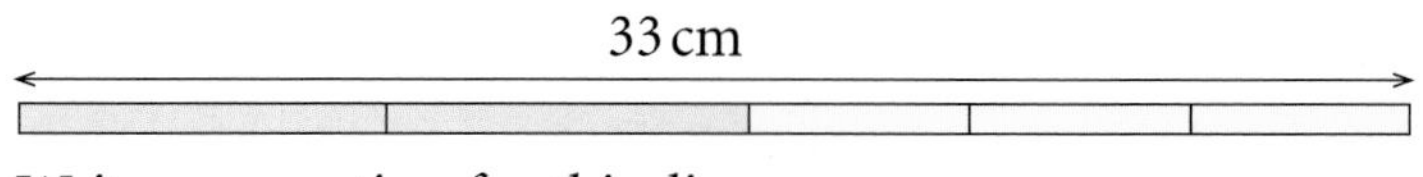

Write an equation for this diagram.

(b) The total length of 4 green rods and 2 yellow rods is 46 cm.

Write an equation for this diagram.

(c) Solve your equations simultaneously to find the values of g and y.
Show all your working clearly.

(d) What is the total length of 1 green rod and 5 yellow rods?

D2 The weight of a blue brick is b grams.
The weight of a red brick is r grams.

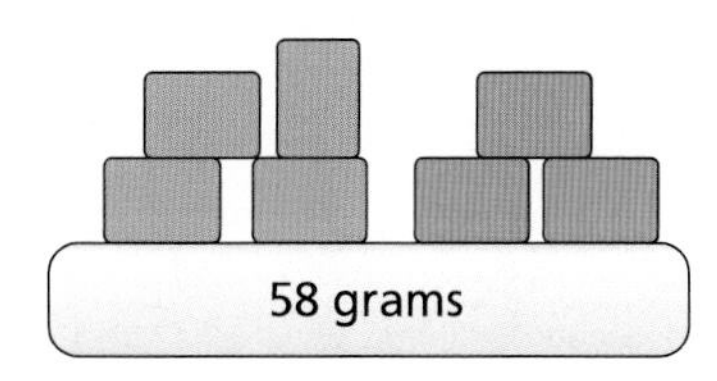

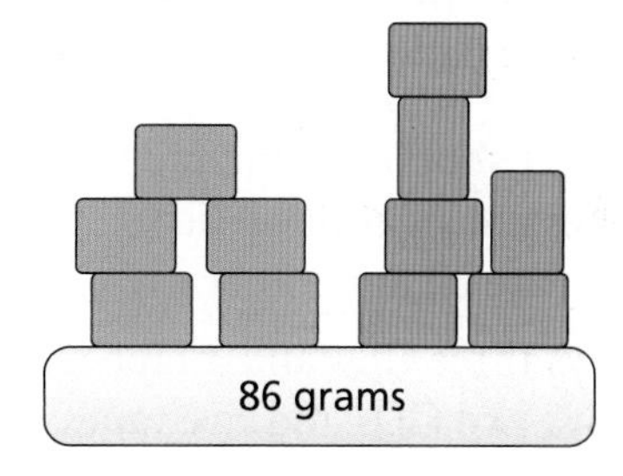

4 blue bricks and 3 red bricks weigh 58 grams.
5 blue bricks and 6 red bricks weigh 86 grams.

(a) (i) Write an equation for the first diagram.

(ii) Write an equation for the second diagram.

(b) Find the weight of a blue brick and the weight of a red brick.

(c) What is the total weight of 2 blue bricks and 5 red bricks?

D3 Janet is buying bushes for her garden.
Laurel bushes cost £x each.
Holly bushes cost £y each.
If Janet buys 8 laurel bushes and 2 holly bushes, she will pay £19.

(a) Use this information to write down an equation in x and y.

If she buys 4 laurel bushes and 6 holly bushes, she will pay £22.

(b) Write down a second equation in x and y.

(c) Solve your equations simultaneously to find the values of x and y.
You **must** show all your working.

AQA(SEG) 2000

D4 Julie and Rosa buy some candy bars and ice creams.

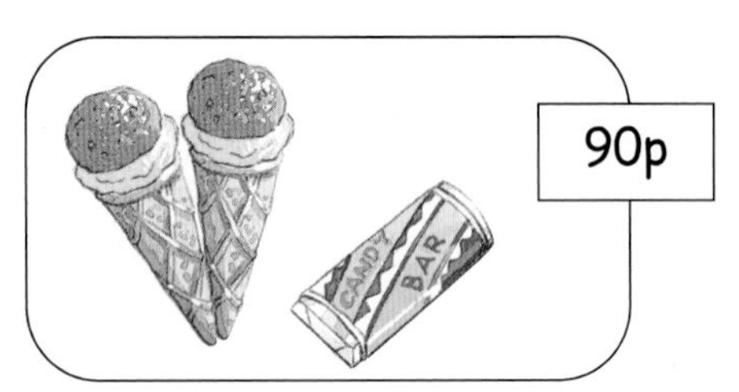

Julie spends 90p on two ice creams and a candy bar.
Rosa spends 95p on one ice cream and three candy bars.

With the cost of an ice cream p pence and the cost of a candy bar q pence, form two equations and solve them to find the cost of a candy bar.

D5 A discount shop is selling tapes and CDs.
The tapes are all at one price.
The CDs are all at another price.

Jane buys three CDs and a tape and pays £8.92.
Paul buys two CDs and five tapes and pays £12.23.

How much does one CD cost?
Show your equations and working clearly.

OCR(MEG)

D6 Three geese and five golden eggs weigh 14 kg.
Five geese and three golden eggs weigh 18 kg.
Find the weight of a golden egg and the weight of a goose.

D7 Greg sold 40 tickets for a concert.

He sold x tickets at £2.00 each and y tickets at £3.50 each.
He collected £92.00.

Write down two equations connecting x and y.
Solve these simultaneous equations to find how many of each kind of ticket he sold.

AQA(NEAB) 2000

E *It all adds up*

Sometimes it's simpler to solve a pair of simultaneous equations by **adding**.

Example

Solve this pair of simultaneous equations.

(A) $4x + 3y = 27$
(B) $x - 3y = 3$

We can see that **adding** will remove the terms that involve y.

If we add everything on the left and everything on the right, the results will be equal.

(A) $4x + 3y = 27$
(B) $x - 3y = 3$ Add

$5x = 30$

so $x = 6$

Adding the left hand sides gives $4x + 3y + x - 3y$ which simplifies to give $5x$.

Substitute in equation (A) to give $24 + 3y = 27$

$3y = 3$

$y = 1$

So the solution is $x = 6, y = 1$

Substitute in equation (B) to check. $x - 3y = 6 - 3 \times 1 = 3$ ✓

E1 Solve each pair of simultaneous equations.

(a) $3p + q = 13$
$2p - q = 2$

(b) $2a - 3b = 1$
$7a + 3b = 44$

(c) $2c + d = 4$
$2c - d = 2$

(d) $x + 2y = 9$
$4x - 2y = 16$

(e) $h - 4k = 1$
$h + 4k = 21$

(f) $3m - 5n = 8$
$m + 5n = 6$

E2 Ahmet and Baljeet each think of a number.

Adding twice Baljeet's number to Ahmet's gives 11.
Subtracting twice Baljeet's number from Ahmet's gives 3.

Let Ahmet's number be a.
Let Baljeet's number be b.

Form two equations and solve them to find the values of a and b.

E3 Solve each pair of simultaneous equations.

(a) $3p + 2q = 10$
$4p - 2q = 18$

(b) $2a + 3b = 2$
$4a - 3b = 22$

(c) $3c - 4d = 17$
$c + 4d = 3$

F *Multiply to eliminate*

Examples

Solve this pair of simultaneous equations.

(A) $x - y = 2$
(B) $4x + 3y = 29$

Multiply both sides of equation (A) by 3 so the numbers in front of y will be the same size.

$$\begin{array}{lrl} (A) \times 3 & 3x - 3y = 6 & \\ (B) & 4x + 3y = 29 & \text{Add} \\ \hline & 7x = 35 & \end{array}$$

so $x = 5$

Substitute in equation (A) to give

$$5 - y = 2$$
$$y = 3$$

So the solution is $x = 5$, $y = 3$

Substitute in equation (B) to check.

$4x + 3y = 4 \times 5 + 3 \times 3 = 29$ ✓

Solve this pair of simultaneous equations.

(A) $2x - 3y = 5$
(B) $5x + 2y = 22$

Multiply both sides of equation (A) by 2 and both sides of equation (B) by 3 so the numbers in front of y will be the same size.

$$\begin{array}{lrl} (A) \times 2 & 4x - 6y = 10 & \\ (B) \times 3 & 15x + 6y = 66 & \text{Add} \\ \hline & 19x = 76 & \end{array}$$

so $x = 4$

Substitute in equation (B) to give

$$20 + 2y = 22$$
$$2y = 2$$
$$\text{so } y = 1$$

So the solution is $x = 4$, $y = 1$

Substitute in equation (A) to check.

$2x - 3y = 2 \times 4 - 3 \times 1 = 5$ ✓

F1 Here is a pair of equations.

$$2x - y = 2$$
$$3x + 2y = 17$$

(a) Multiply both sides of the first equation by 2.

(b) Find the values of x and y.

F2 Here is a pair of equations.

$$7a - 6b = 9$$
$$3a + 2b = 13$$

(a) Multiply both sides of the second equation by 3.

(b) Find the values of a and b.

F3 Solve each pair of simultaneous equations.

(a) $3v + w = 18$
$2v - 3w = 1$

(b) $p + 3q = 29$
$2p - q = 23$

(c) $m + 2n = 4$
$3m - 4n = 7$

(d) $3k - 2h = 8$
$k + 4h = 5$

(e) $2x + y = 9$
$x - 2y = 7$

(f) $a + 8b = 5$
$3a - 4b = 8$

F4 Here is a pair of equations.

$$x - 2y = 2$$
$$2x + 5y = 22$$

(a) Multiply both sides of the first equation by 5.

(b) Multiply both sides of the second equation by 2.

(c) Find the values of x and y.

F5 Solve each pair of simultaneous equations.

(a) $p + 2q = 3$
$5p - 3q = 2$

(b) $5a - 2b = 11$
$3a + 5b = 19$

(c) $5c - 4d = 19$
$2c + 3d = 3$

(d) $2x + 3y = 5$
$3x - 2y = 14$

(e) $4h - 5k = {}^-6$
$h + 2k = 5$

(f) $3m + 5n = 24$
$m - 3n = 1$

G *Mixed problems*

G1 Solve these simultaneous equations algebraically. Show your working.

$$2x + y = 14$$
$$3x + 2y = 22$$

OCR

G2 Solve the simultaneous equations.

$$4x + 3y = 6$$
$$2x - y = 8$$

AQA(SEG) 2000

G3 Solve the simultaneous equations.

$$2x + 5y = 3$$
$$x - 3y = 7$$

OCR

G4 Solve each pair of simultaneous equations.

(a) $x + 3y = 5$
$x - y = 3$

(b) $2a + 3b = 1$
$5a + 2b = 8$

(c) $c + 8d = 6$
$3c - 4d = 11$

(d) $2x + 3y = 1$
$2x + y = 5$

(e) $3h + k = {}^-5$
$h - 4k = 7$

(f) $3m - 2n = 7$
$m + 2n = 4$

H *To solve or not to solve?*

Use the equations below to form pairs of simultaneous equations.

A $x + 2y = 9$ **B** $2x + 2y = 10$ **C** $x + y = 5$ **D** $x + y = 2$

Can you solve them?

TG

Graphs and simultaneous equations

When a pair of simultaneous equations has a solution, it can be found from the point of intersection of the graphs for the equations.

For example, a pair of equations and their graphs are shown below.

$$4x + 2y = 32$$
$$3x + 5y = 31$$

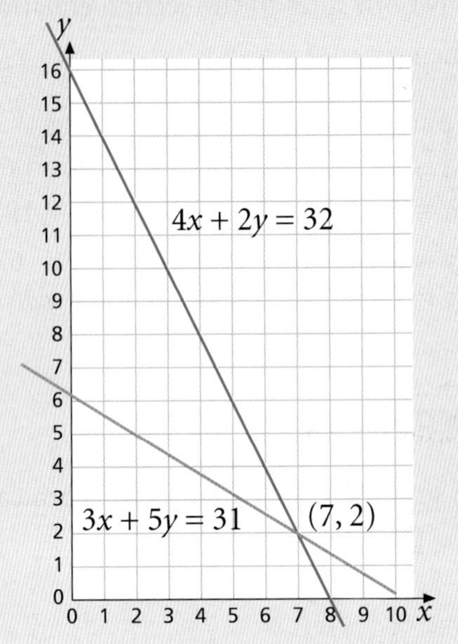

The point of intersection is (7, 2) so the solution is $x = 7, y = 2$.

Check by substituting in each equation.

$4x + 2y = 4 \times 7 + 2 \times 2 = 32$ ✓
$3x + 5y = 3 \times 7 + 5 \times 2 = 31$ ✓

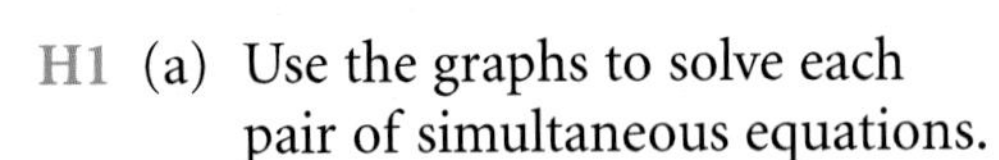

H1 (a) Use the graphs to solve each pair of simultaneous equations.

(i) $y - 2x = 1$, $x + y = 4$ (ii) $y - 2x = 4$, $x + y = 4$

Check each solution by substituting into the equations.

(b) How do you know there is no solution to the following pair of simultaneous equations?

$$y - 2x = 4$$
$$y - 2x = 1$$

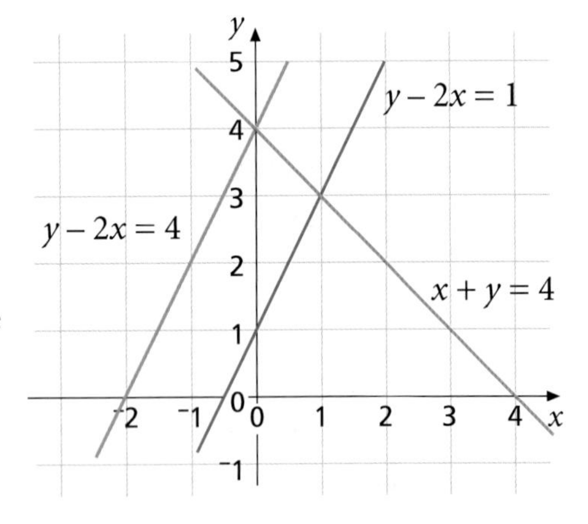

H2 Use graphs to solve each pair of simultaneous equations.

(a) $x + y = 6$, $x - y = 2$

Draw axes for x and y from $^-3$ to 7.

(b) $y + 2x = 5$, $x - y = 1$

Draw axes for x and y from $^-2$ to 6.

Check each solution by substituting into the equations.

H3

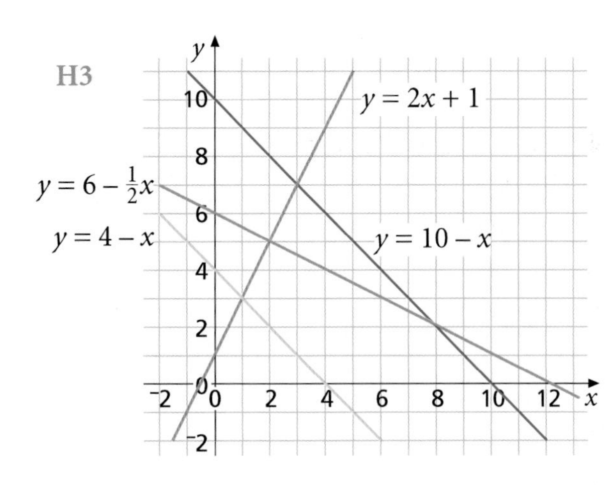

(a) Use the graphs to solve each pair of simultaneous equations.

(i) $y = 2x + 1$
$y = 10 - x$

(ii) $y = 2x + 1$
$y = 6 - \frac{1}{2}x$

(iii) $y = 2x + 1$
$y = 4 - x$

(iv) $y = 10 - x$
$y = 6 - \frac{1}{2}x$

(b) How do you know there is no solution to these simultaneous equations?
$y = 10 - x$
$y = 4 - x$

H4 Use graphs to solve each pair of simultaneous equations.

(a) $y = 5 - x$
$y = 2 + x$
Draw axes for x and y from 0 to 7.

(b) $y = 2x + 3$
$y = 3x - 1$
Draw axes for x and y from $^{-}2$ to 12.

I *Further solving*

How would you solve these pairs of simultaneous equations?

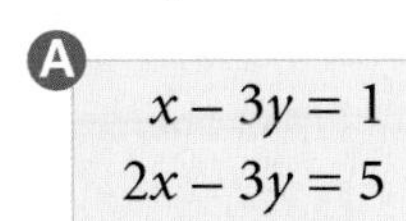

B $p - q = 8$
$p - 4q = 2$

C $2a - 3b = 3$
$5a - b = 14$

D $3h - 2k = 9$
$2h - 3k = 1$

I1 Solve each pair of simultaneous equations.

(a) $4p - q = 11$
$p - q = 2$

(b) $3a - 2b = 2$
$5a - 2b = 4$

(c) $c - d = 1$
$3c - 2d = 8$

(d) $x - y = 5$
$2x - 5y = 1$

(e) $3h - 4k = 10$
$3h - k = 7$

(f) $5m - 2n = 16$
$3m - 5n = 2$

I2 (a) Which of these equations is equivalent to $y = x + 4$?

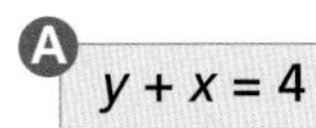

B $y + 4 = x$

C $y - x = 4$

D $x - y = 4$

(b) Use the result of (a) to solve the simultaneous equations

$y = x + 4$
$2y + x = 17$

I3 Solve each pair of simultaneous equations.

(a) $p = q + 5$
$3p + q = 19$

(b) $a = 2b + 1$
$5a + 2b = 29$

(c) $c = 19 - 4d$
$c - 2d = 1$

Test yourself

T1 In a cafe, two coffees and a tea cost £1.90.
Five coffees and a tea cost £4.00.

(a) What is the cost of a coffee?

(b) What is the cost of a tea?

T2 Solve the simultaneous equations.

$$5x + 4y = 13$$
$$3x + 8y = 5$$

OCR

T3 Solve these simultaneous equations algebraically.
Show your working.

$$4x + y = 1$$
$$6x + 5y = 12$$

OCR

T4 Two small mugs and one large mug weigh 758 grams.
Four small mugs and three large mugs weigh 1882 grams.

The weight of a small mug is s grams and the weight of a large mug is l grams.

Write down two equations connecting s and l.
Solve these simultaneous equations to find the weight of each size of mug.

T5 Two people were in front of me in the queue for ice cream.
The man bought 5 cones and 7 tubs for £6.70.
The woman bought 3 cones and 5 tubs for £4.50.

How much will it cost me for my cone?

T6 Solve the simultaneous equations.

$$5x + y = 23$$
$$4x - 2y = 3$$

Do not use a trial and improvement method.

AQA 1999

T7 Solve the simultaneous equations.

$$3x + 4y = 5$$
$$5x - 2y = 17$$

Edexcel

T8

$$4x + 3y = 6$$
$$3x - 2y = 13$$

Solve these simultaneous equations algebraically.
Show your method clearly.

OCR

T9 Solve the simultaneous equations.

$$2x + 5y = {}^{-}1$$
$$6x - y = 5$$

Edexcel

Review 8

1 Out of 30 students, 9 walk to school.
What percentage of the students walk to school?

2 Solve these equations.

(a) $2x + 3 = 4x - 7$ (b) $n + 12 = 6 - 2n$ (c) $13 - 3x = 5x + 1$

3 A shop reduces all its prices by 25%.
What is the sale price of a jumper priced at £16.99 before the sale?

4 In Berlin in September 1923, a loaf of bread cost 1 512 000 marks.
By November the price has risen to 201 000 000 000 marks.
Write each of these prices in standard form.

5 (a) Write and simplify an expression for the sum in degrees of the four angles marked in the sectors below.

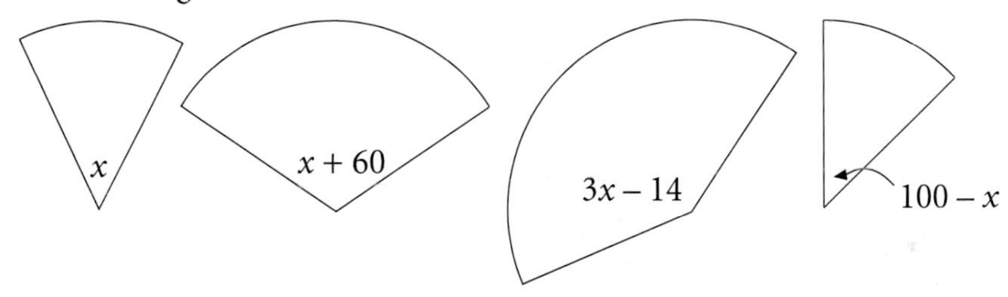

(b) These four sectors fit together to make a complete circle.
Form and solve an equation to find the value of x.

6 A garage increases its prices by 4%.
A car cost £7500 before the price increase.
What is its new price?

7 A white blood cell has a diameter of 7.1×10^{-4} cm.
Write this length as an ordinary number.

8 Show that the area of the rectangle below is given by the expression $x^2 + 9x + 14$.

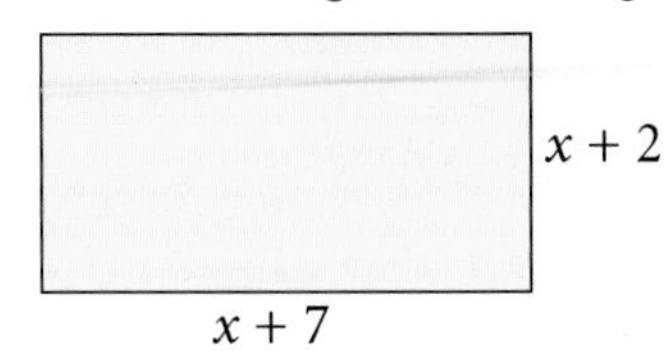

9 Solve $4(c - 5) = 3c - 13$

10 The value of Mike's car decreased by 17% over the past year.
The car was worth £5600 a year ago.
How much is the car worth now?

11 The mass of 3×10^{24} atoms of copper is about 317 grams.
Find the mass in grams of one atom of copper.
Give your answer in standard form correct to 2 significant figures.

12 In this rectangle, the length is 8 cm more than the width.
The perimeter is 28 cm.

length

x cm

(a) Form an equation and solve it to find the width of the rectangle.

(b) What is the area of the rectangle in cm²?

13 Each exterior angle of a regular polygon is 15°.
How many sides will this polygon have?

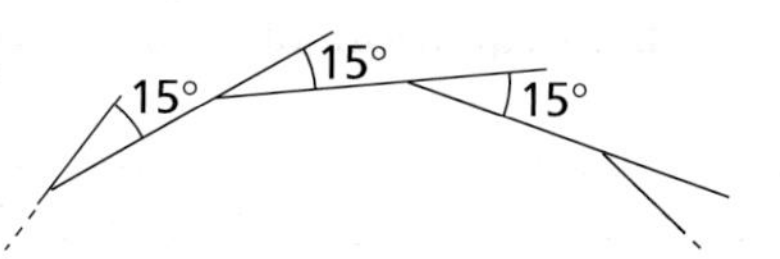

14 Solve these pairs of simultaneous equations.

(a) $3x + 5y = 18$
$6x + 11y = 39$

(b) $2x + 3y = 1$
$5x + 2y = 8$

(c) $6x + y = 28$
$x - 3y = 11$

15 The price of a rail ticket goes up from £89 to £92.
What is the percentage increase in the price?

16 Multiply out the brackets from each expression and write the result in its simplest form.

(a) $(n + 1)(n + 5)$ (b) $(x - 2)(x + 4)$ (c) $(a - 5)^2$

17 Calculate the sides and angles marked with letters.

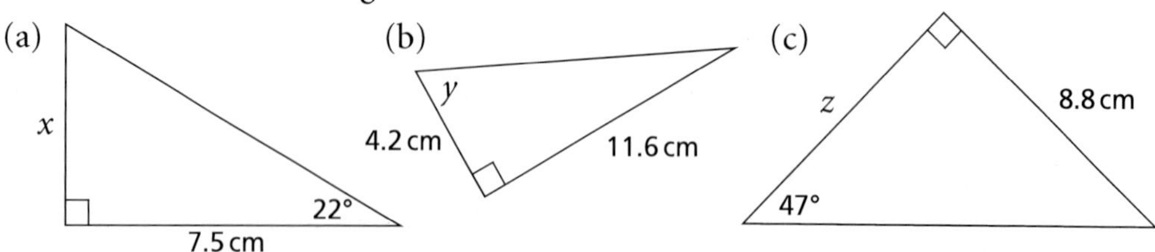

18 The cost of a printer is £250 plus VAT.
The rate of VAT is $17\frac{1}{2}$%.
Calculate the cost of the printer.

19 Solve $\dfrac{n+1}{4} + \dfrac{n+4}{12} = \dfrac{11}{12}$.

20 A group of three adults and one child pay £12 altogether for concert tickets.
Another group of two adults and four children pay £13 altogether.

Form a pair of simultaneous equations.
Solve them to find the cost of an adult ticket and the cost of a child ticket.

21 The total area of land on Earth is about 1.5×10^8 km^2.
The total area covered by forests is 3.9×10^7 km^2
What percentage of land on Earth is covered by forests?

22 A bag contains a mixture of large and small marbles.

The weight of a small marble is n grams.
A large marble weighs 3 grams more than a small one.

(a) Write an expression for the weight of a large marble.

(b) The bag contains 10 small marbles and 15 large marbles.
The total weight of the marbles in the bag is 95 grams.
Form an equation and solve it to find the weight of a small marble.

23 The membership of a badminton club falls from 58 to 47 members over a year.
What is the percentage decrease in the number of members over the year?

24 This is part of a 'ring' made by alternating squares and regular pentagons.

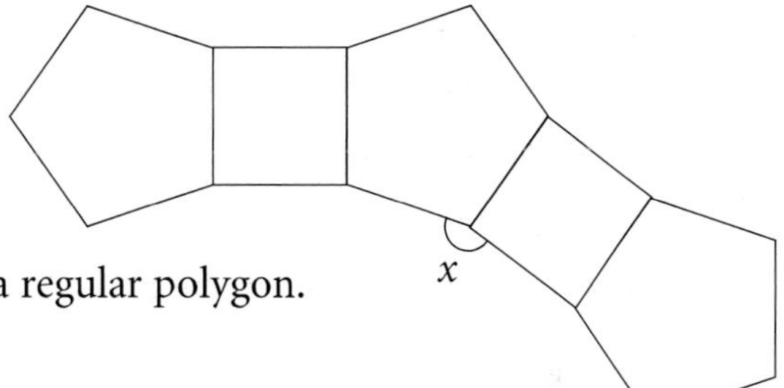

(a) Calculate the angle x.

(b) The inside of the completed ring forms a regular polygon.
How many sides does it have?

(c) Can a ring be made in the same way by

(i) alternating squares and regular hexagons

(ii) alternating squares and regular nonagons (nine-sided polygons)

Describe what happens in each case.

25 Prove the sum of three consecutive numbers is always three times the middle number.

26 $x = 8 \times 10^7$ and $y = 4 \times 10^3$

Calculate the following, giving your answers in standard form. Show all your working.

(a) xy (b) $\frac{x}{y}$ (c) $\frac{y}{x}$

27 Calculate the size of each angle in this isosceles triangle.

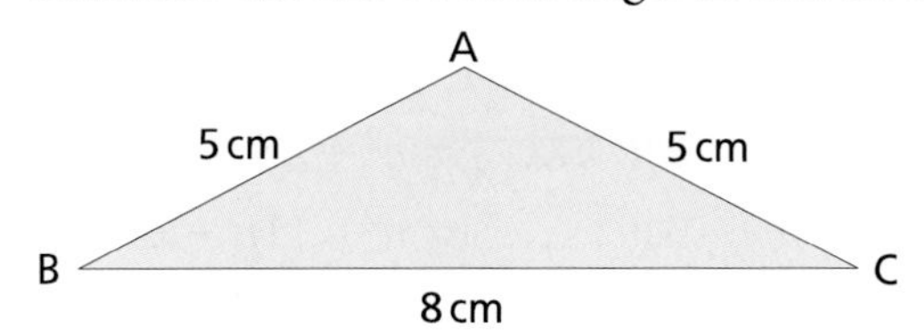

47 Factorising, solving and simplifying

You should know how to multiply out brackets such as $(x + 1)(x - 3)$ and $(4x + 1)(2x - 3)$.

This work will help you

- factorise quadratic expressions
- solve quadratic equations by factorising
- simplify algebraic fractions by factorising

A Review

$n(n + 8)$ →

×	n	8
n	n^2	8n

→ $n(n + 8)$
$= n^2 + 8n$

$(n - 2)(n + 8)$ →

×	n	8
n	n^2	8n
-2	^-2n	$^-16$

→ $(n - 2)(n + 8)$
$= n^2 + 8n - 2n - 16$
$= n^2 + 6n - 16$

A1 Multiply out the brackets from these.

(a) $3(n - 7)$ (b) $n(n + 5)$ (c) $n(n - 1)$

A2 Multiply out the brackets from each expression and write the result in its simplest form.

(a) $(n + 2)(n + 3)$ (b) $(n + 1)(n + 5)$ (c) $(n + 4)(n + 2)$
(d) $(n + 3)^2$ (e) $(n + 5)(n - 2)$ (f) $(n - 1)(n + 3)$
(g) $(n + 2)(n - 4)$ (h) $(n - 3)(n + 1)$ (i) $(n - 3)(n - 5)$
(j) $(n - 1)(n - 2)$ (k) $(n - 2)^2$ (l) $(n - 5)^2$

A3 Show that the area of this rectangle is $x^2 + 7x + 6$.

$x + 1$

$x + 6$

A4 Copy and complete each identity.

(a) $(n + 3)(\ldots\ldots) = n^2 + 4n + 3$ (b) $(n + 2)(\ldots\ldots) = n^2 + 11n + 18$
(c) $(n + 4)(\ldots\ldots) = n^2 + 8n + 16$ (d) $(n - 2)(\ldots\ldots) = n^2 + 4n - 12$
(e) $(n + 7)(\ldots\ldots) = n^2 + 6n - 7$ (f) $(n - 3)(\ldots\ldots) = n^2 - 11n + 24$

B *Factorising*

Can you factorise these?

A $n^2 + 5n + 6 = ?$

B $n^2 + 10n + 16 = ?$

C $n^2 + 10n + 25 = ?$

D $n^2 + 10n + 5 = ?$

E $n^2 - 7n + 10 = ?$

F $n^2 - 8n + 16 = ?$

G $n^2 + 5n - 14 = ?$

H $n^2 - 8n - 20 = ?$

B1 Factorise these.

(a) $n^2 + 3n + 2$ (b) $n^2 + 7n + 12$ (c) $n^2 + 5n + 4$

(d) $n^2 + 4n + 4$ (e) $n^2 + 10n + 21$ (f) $n^2 + 8n + 15$

(g) $n^2 + 11n + 10$ (h) $n^2 + 6n + 9$ (i) $n^2 + 11n + 30$

B2 Find pairs of expressions from the loop that multiply to give these.

(a) $n^2 - 8n + 15$ (b) $n^2 - 9n + 18$

(c) $n^2 - 8n + 12$ (d) $n^2 - 7n + 12$

(e) $n^2 - 7n + 6$ (f) $n^2 - 5n + 6$

$n - 2$ $n - 3$ $n - 1$ $n - 5$ $n - 4$ $n - 6$

B3 Factorise these.

(a) $n^2 - 4n + 3$ (b) $n^2 - 6n + 8$ (c) $n^2 - 9n + 14$

(d) $n^2 - 12n + 32$ (e) $n^2 - 6n + 9$ (f) $n^2 - 10n + 25$

B4 Find pairs of expressions from the loop that multiply to give these.

(a) $n^2 + 2n - 15$ (b) $n^2 - 2n - 8$

(c) $n^2 - 5n - 6$ (d) $n^2 - n - 6$

(e) $n^2 - 4n - 12$ (f) $n^2 + n - 20$

$n + 2$ $n - 3$ $n + 1$ $n + 5$ $n - 4$ $n - 6$

B5 Factorise these.

(a) $n^2 + 4n - 5$ (b) $n^2 - 4n - 5$ (c) $n^2 + 3n - 10$

(d) $n^2 - 3n - 10$ (e) $n^2 + 9n - 10$ (f) $n^2 + 9n - 22$

(g) $n^2 - 3n - 18$ (h) $n^2 - 11n - 12$ (i) $n^2 + n - 12$

B6 Factorise these.

(a) $n^2 + 6n + 5$ (b) $n^2 + 12n + 36$ (c) $n^2 - 9n + 20$

(d) $n^2 + 6n + 8$ (e) $n^2 + 3n$ (f) $n^2 + 2n - 3$

(g) $n^2 - 7n - 8$ (h) $n^2 - 8n$ (i) $n^2 - 2n + 1$

(j) $n^2 + 3n - 18$ (k) $n^2 - 5n - 14$ (l) $n^2 - n - 20$

B7 Multiply out and simplify these expressions.

(a) $(n + 3)(n - 3)$ (b) $(n - 4)(n + 4)$ (c) $(n - 8)(n + 8)$

Comment on your results.

B8 Factorise these expressions.

(a) $n^2 - 36$ (b) $n^2 - 4$ (c) $n^2 - 81$ (d) $n^2 - 25$

It can be easier to use a quadratic expression in its factorised form (if factorising is possible).

Example

Find the value of $x^2 + 8x + 12$ when $x = 14$.

Factorising gives $x^2 + 8x + 12 = (x + 6)(x + 2)$

When $x = 14$, $(x + 6)(x + 2) = (14 + 6)(14 + 2)$

$= 20 \times 16$

$= 320$

B9 (a) Factorise $n^2 + 7n + 10$.

(b) Hence find the value of $n^2 + 7n + 10$ when

(i) $n = 8$ (ii) $n = 3$ (iii) $n = {}^-2$ (iv) $n = {}^-5$

B10 (a) Factorise $n^2 + 3n - 4$.

(b) Hence find the value of $n^2 + 3n - 4$ when

(i) $n = 6$ (ii) $n = 1$ (iii) $n = {}^-4$ (iv) $n = 21$

***B11** (a) Factorise $x^2 - 1$.

(b) Hence find the value of these.

(i) $29^2 - 1$ (ii) $41^2 - 1$ (iii) 61^2

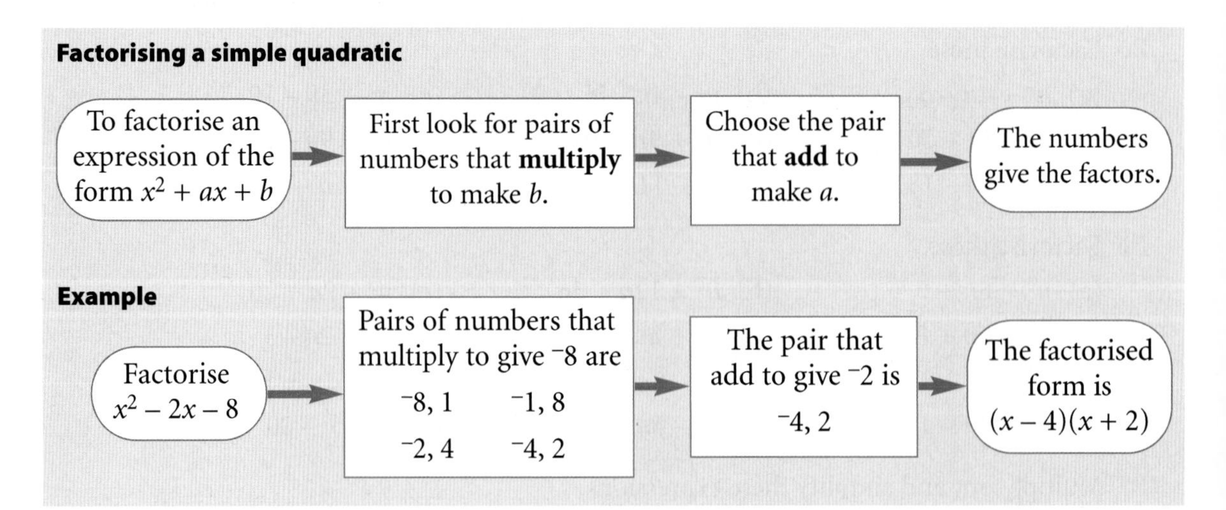

C *Solving quadratic equations*

A curve with this shape is called a ***parabola****.*

The graph of every quadratic expression is a parabola.

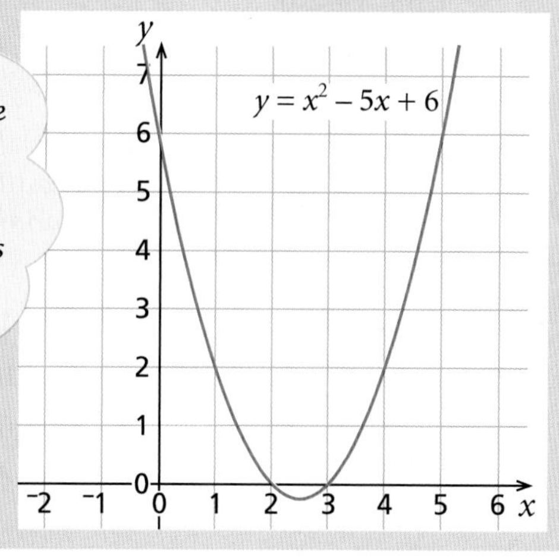

- Can you use the graph to solve the equation $x^2 - 5x + 6 = 0$?
- Can you solve the equation $(x - 2)(x - 3) = 0$?
- What are the links between these equations?

TG

C1 Solve each of these equations.

(a) $(x - 5)(x - 4) = 0$ (b) $(x + 1)(x - 10) = 0$ (c) $x(x + 6) = 0$

C2 Three parabolas are shown here.

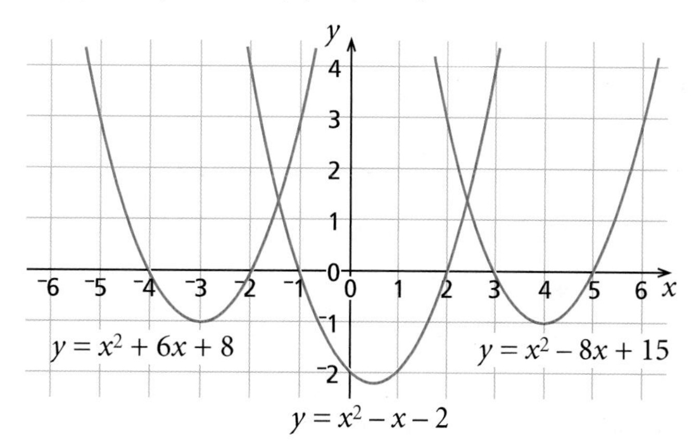

Use the graphs above to solve the following equations (each has two solutions).

(a) $x^2 - 8x + 15 = 0$ (b) $x^2 + 6x + 8 = 0$ (c) $x^2 - x - 2 = 0$

C3 Factorise each expression in C2.

Describe the link between your factorised expressions and your answers to C2.

C4 (a) Solve the equation $(x - 4)(x - 7) = 0$.

(b) Which of the screens below shows the graph of $y = (x - 4)(x - 7)$?

A

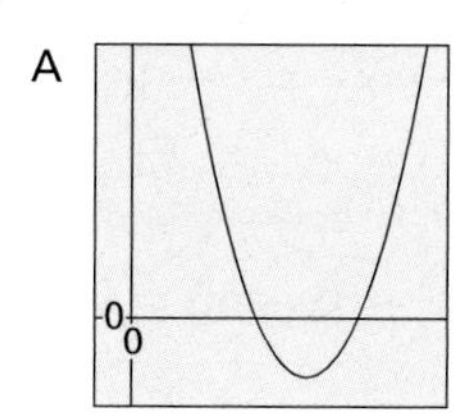

B

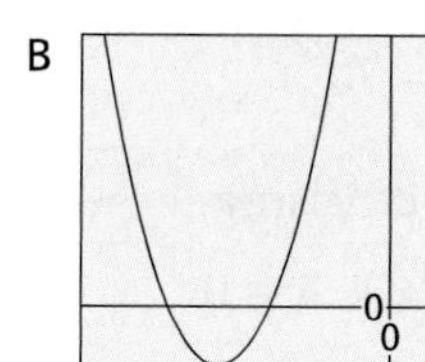

C

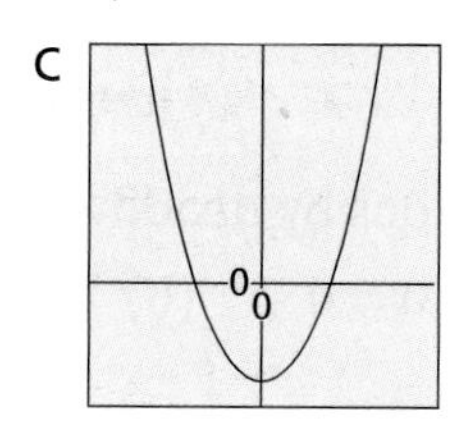

Example

Solve $n^2 + 3n - 4 = 0$.

$$n^2 + 3n - 4 = 0$$
$$(n - 1)(n + 4) = 0$$
Either $(n - 1) = 0$ or $(n + 4) = 0$
So $n = 1$ or $n = {}^{-}4$

You can check your solutions by substituting them in the original equation.

C5 Solve the following by factorising.

(a) $x^2 + 6x + 5 = 0$ (b) $x^2 - 7x + 12 = 0$ (c) $x^2 + 3x - 18 = 0$
(d) $x^2 + 7x + 12 = 0$ (e) $x^2 + 11x = 0$ (f) $x^2 - 9x - 10 = 0$
(g) $x^2 - 3x - 4 = 0$ (h) $x^2 + 6x + 9 = 0$ (i) $x^2 - 5x = 0$
(j) $x^2 - 13x + 40 = 0$ (k) $x^2 + x - 12 = 0$ (l) $x^2 - 4x + 4 = 0$

C6 This is the graph of $y = x^2 + 2x - 15$.
What are the coordinates of points A and B?

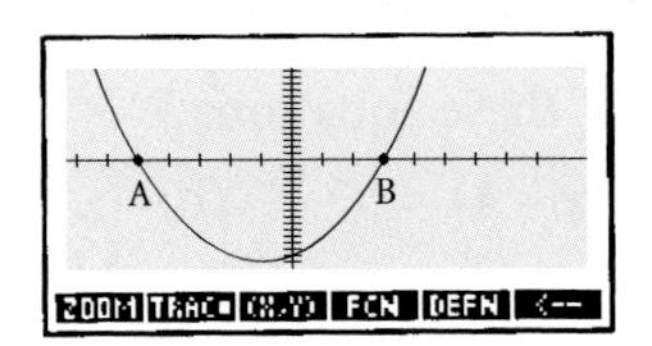

D *Further solving*

Sometimes you need to rearrange the equation to get 0 on one side.

Example

Solve $k^2 - 14k + 40 = 16$.

Subtract 16 from both sides.

$$k^2 - 14k + 40 = 16$$
$$k^2 - 14k + 24 = 0$$
$$(k - 2)(k - 12) = 0$$
So $k = 2$ or $k = 12$

Sometimes you can divide both sides to simplify the problem.

Example

Solve $3k^2 + 3k - 18 = 0$.

Divide bot sides by 3

$$3k^2 + 3k - 18 = 0$$
$$k^2 + k - 6 = 0$$
$$(k + 3)(k - 2) = 0$$
So $k = {}^{-}3$ or $k = 2$

D1 Solve these equations by rearranging and factorising.

(a) $x^2 + 7x + 10 = 4$ (b) $x^2 - 10x + 26 = 5$ (c) $x^2 - 2x - 12 = 3$
(d) $x^2 + 3x + 2 = 30$ (e) $x^2 - 6x + 19 = 10$ (f) $x^2 - 5x = 24$
(g) $x^2 + 7x = 18$ (h) $x^2 - 3x = 70$ (i) $x^2 + 8x + 3 = 36$

D2 Solve these equations by dividing and factorising.

(a) $2x^2 + 18x + 40 = 0$ (b) $4x^2 - 12x + 8 = 0$ (c) $3x^2 - 3x - 36 = 0$

D3 Solve these equations by rearranging and factorising.

(a) $x^2 + 7x - 6 = 2x$ (b) $x^2 + 5x = 3x$ (c) $x^2 + 5 = 5x + 1$

Sometimes you need to expand brackets and then rearrange the equation to get 0 on one side.

Example

Solve $(x + 5)(x - 2) = 8$

$(x + 5)(x - 2) = 8$ — *Expand brackets*

$x^2 + 3x - 10 = 8$ — *Subtract 8 from both sides.*

$x^2 + 3x - 18 = 0$

$(x + 6)(x - 3) = 0$

So $x = {}^-6$ or $x = 3$

D4 Solve these equations by expanding, rearranging and factorising.

(a) $(x + 2)(x + 3) = 2$ (b) $(x - 3)(x - 1) = 24$ (c) $(x - 4)(x - 1) = 4$

(d) $x(x - 2) = 3$ (e) $(x - 2)(x - 3) = 20$ (f) $(x + 2)(x + 1) = 2$

E *Solving problems*

Example

The area of this rectangle is 18 cm^2.
Find the dimensions of the rectangle.

$(x + 4)$ cm

$(x - 3)$ cm

The area of the rectangle is $(x + 4)(x - 3)\text{ cm}^2$.

The area is 18 cm^2 so $(x + 4)(x - 3) = 18$

$x^2 + x - 12 = 18$

$x^2 + x - 30 = 0$

$(x + 6)(x - 5) = 0$

So $x = {}^-6$ *or* $x = 5$

But a length cannot be negative so $x = 5$ and the rectangle measures 2 cm by 9 cm.

E1 The area of this rectangle is 7 cm^2.

$(x + 4)$ cm

$(x - 2)$ cm

(a) Form an equation, in terms of x, and show that it can be written as

$$x^2 + 2x - 15 = 0.$$

(b) Solve this equation to find the dimensions of the rectangle.

E2

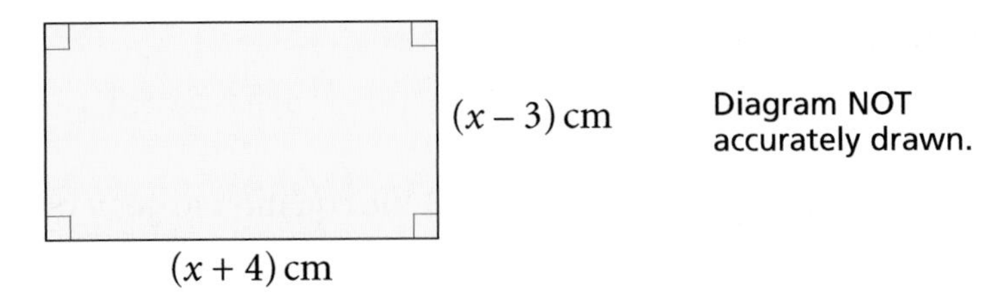

Diagram NOT accurately drawn.

The length of a rectangle is $(x + 4)$ cm.
The width is $(x - 3)$ cm.
The area of the rectangle is $78\,\text{cm}^2$.

(a) Use this information to write down an equation in terms of x.

(b) (i) Show that your equation in (a) can be written as

$$x^2 + x - 90 = 0$$

(ii) Find the values of x which are the solutions of the equation

$$x^2 + x - 90 = 0$$

(iii) Write down the length and width of the rectangle.

Edexcel

E3 The diagram shows a shape, in which all the corners are right angles.

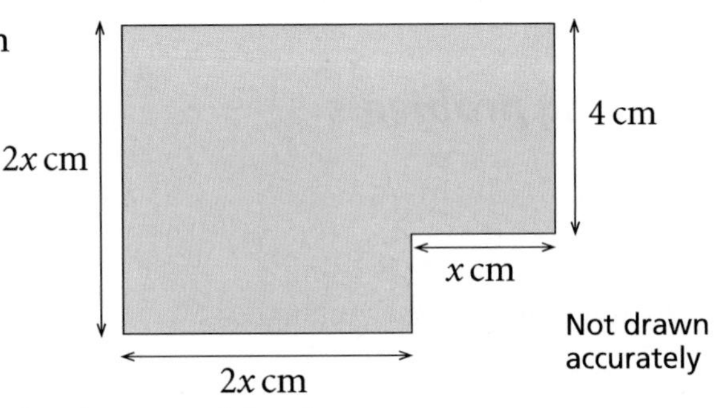

Not drawn accurately

The area of the shape is $48\,\text{cm}^2$.

(a) Form an equation, in terms of x, for the area of the shape.
Show that the equation can be simplified to $x^2 + x - 12 = 0$.

(b) Solve the equation $x^2 + x - 12 = 0$ and hence calculate the perimeter of the shape.

AQA 2003 Specimen

E4 A rectangular garden is made up of a square lawn of side x m and 2 paths 1.5 m wide, as shown in the diagram.

The total area of the garden is $88\,\text{m}^2$.

Write down an equation in x and solve it to find the dimensions of the lawn.

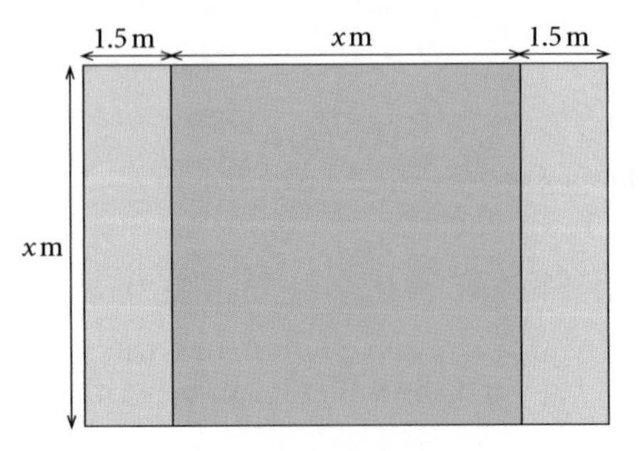

OCR

E5 These two rectangles have the same area.

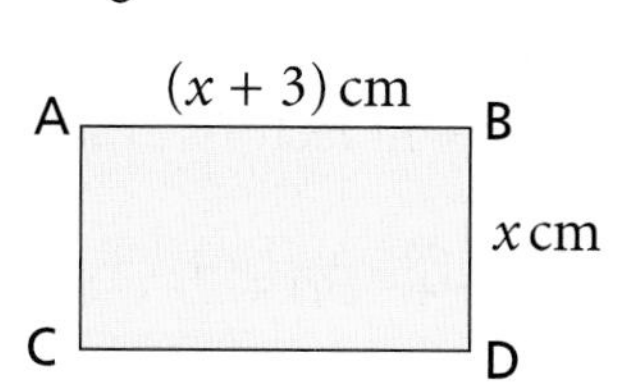

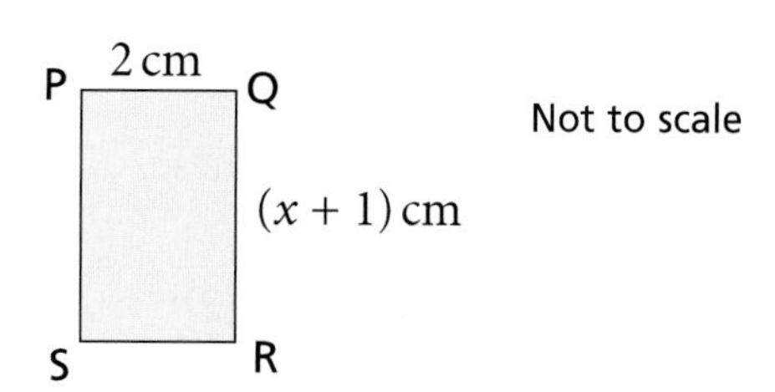

(a) Form an equation in x and show that it can be simplified to $x^2 + x - 2 = 0$.

(b) Solve the equation $x^2 + x - 2 = 0$ to find the length of BD. AQA(SEG)2003 Specimen

F *Simplifying fractions*

We know that, for example, $\frac{27}{15} = \frac{9 \times 3}{5 \times 3} = \frac{9}{5}$.

We can cancel algebraic fractions in the same way.

For example:

- $\frac{3n^3}{n^2} = \frac{3n \times n^2}{n^2} = 3n$
- $\frac{4x - 12}{x - 3} = \frac{4(x - 3)}{x - 3} = 4$
- $\frac{(3x + 1)(x + 2)}{5x + 10} = \frac{(3x + 1)(x + 2)}{5(x + 2)} = \frac{3x + 1}{5}$

F1 Cancel the following fractions as far as possible.

(a) $\frac{12}{3}$ (b) $\frac{35}{14}$ (c) $\frac{3}{36}$ (d) $\frac{30}{12}$ (e) $\frac{9}{27}$

F2 Simplify the following by cancelling.

(a) $\frac{2x}{3x}$ (b) $\frac{7y}{14}$ (c) $\frac{5x^2}{x}$ (d) $\frac{9x^2}{3x}$ (e) $\frac{4p}{8p^2}$

F3 Simplify the following by factorising and cancelling.

(a) $\frac{2x + 12}{x + 6}$ (b) $\frac{3n - 12}{n - 4}$ (c) $\frac{6x - 12}{3x - 6}$ (d) $\frac{2k + 10}{3k + 15}$

F4 Simplify the following.

(a) $\frac{(x-1)(x+3)}{x+3}$ (b) $\frac{2(y+3)(y-9)}{y+3}$ (c) $\frac{2(x-5)^2}{x-5}$ (d) $\frac{4p(p+6)}{2(p+6)}$

F5 Simplify the following by factorising and cancelling.

(a) $\frac{z^2 + 8z + 7}{z + 1}$ (b) $\frac{s^2 - 6s + 9}{s - 3}$ (c) $\frac{n^2 + n - 12}{n + 4}$ (d) $\frac{x^2 + 7x}{x}$

(e) $\frac{a^2 - 64}{a + 8}$ (f) $\frac{2(x + 3)}{x^2 + 8x + 15}$ (g) $\frac{2(y-2)}{y^2 - 4}$ (h) $\frac{n + 9}{n^2 + 18n + 81}$

G *Further examples*

TG

- Multiply out the brackets from these.

A $(2n + 1)(n + 3)$

B $(n - 2)(2n + 5)$

C $(3n - 2)(n + 4)$

D $(n - 5)(5n - 2)$

E $(2n + 3)(3n - 2)$

- Can you factorise these?

A $2n^2 + 15n + 7$

B $3n^2 + 2n - 5$

C $5n^2 - 16n + 3$

D $2n^2 + n - 6$

E $8n^2 - 6n - 9$

G1 Multiply out the brackets from each expression and write the result in its simplest form.

(a) $(2n + 3)(n + 1)$ (b) $(n + 4)(5n + 2)$ (c) $(7n - 3)(n + 2)$
(d) $(n - 2)(3n + 7)$ (e) $(2n - 3)(2n - 1)$ (f) $(2n - 3)(3n + 1)$
(g) $(4n - 3)(2n - 3)$ (h) $(3n + 1)(3n - 1)$ (i) $(2n - 3)(2n + 3)$

G2 Copy and complete each identity.

(a) $(n + 5)(\ \dots\dots\ ) = 2n^2 + 11n + 5$ (b) $(3n + 2)(\ \dots\dots\ ) = 3n^2 + 17n + 10$
(c) $(2n - 5)(\ \dots\dots\ ) = 2n^2 + n - 15$ (d) $(3n + 1)(\ \dots\dots\ ) = 6n^2 - 7n - 3$
(e) $(5n - 2)(\ \dots\dots\ ) = 5n^2 - 17n + 6$ (f) $(2n + 5)(\ \dots\dots\ ) = 4n^2 - 25$

G3 Factorise these expressions.

(a) $2n^2 + 7n + 5$ (b) $3n^2 + 10n + 3$ (c) $5n^2 + 27n + 10$
(d) $2n^2 + n - 3$ (e) $3n^2 + 10n - 8$ (f) $5n^2 - 11n + 6$
(g) $4n^2 + 8n - 5$ (h) $6n^2 - 23n + 15$ (i) $9n^2 - 4$

G4 Simplify the following by factorising and cancelling.

(a) $\dfrac{2z^2 + 13z + 11}{z + 1}$ (b) $\dfrac{2s^2 + 11s + 15}{2s + 5}$ (c) $\dfrac{8n^2 + 14n - 15}{4n - 3}$ (d) $\dfrac{2x^2 + 6x}{x + 3}$

Example of solving a harder quadratic equation

Solve $2n^2 + 5n - 12 = 0$.

$$2n^2 + 5n - 12 = 0$$
$$(2n - 3)(n + 4) = 0$$
Either $(2n - 3) = 0$ or $(n + 4) = 0$

So $n = 1.5$ or $n = {}^-4$

G5 Solve the following by factorising.

(a) $2x^2 - 11x + 5 = 0$ (b) $2x^2 + 27x + 13 = 0$ (c) $2x^2 + 15x - 8 = 0$
(d) $5x^2 - 17x + 6 = 0$ (e) $4x^2 - 15x - 4 = 0$ (f) $4x^2 - 1 = 0$

Test yourself

T1 Factorise these expressions.

(a) $n^2 + 4n + 3$ (b) $n^2 + 7n + 6$ (c) $n^2 + 8n + 15$

T2 Factorise $x^2 - 9x + 18$.

Edexcel

T3 Factorise $p^2 + p - 12$.

AQA 2003 Specimen

T4 Factorise

(a) $x^2 - 16$ (b) $x^2 - 6x - 16$

OCR

T5 (a) Solve the equation $x^2 + 3x = 0$.

(b) Factorise $x^2 - 7x + 12$.

OCR

T6 (a) Factorise the expression

$x^2 + 8x + 15$.

(b) Hence solve the equation

$x^2 + 8x + 15 = 0$.

AQA(NEAB) 1998

T7 Solve the equation $x^2 - 3x - 10 = 0$.

Edexcel

T8 Solve the equation $x^2 + 2x - 15 = 0$.

OCR

T9 Solve the equation $x^2 - 8x + 15 = 0$.

OCR

T10 The diagram shows a square ABCD and a rectangle RBPQ.

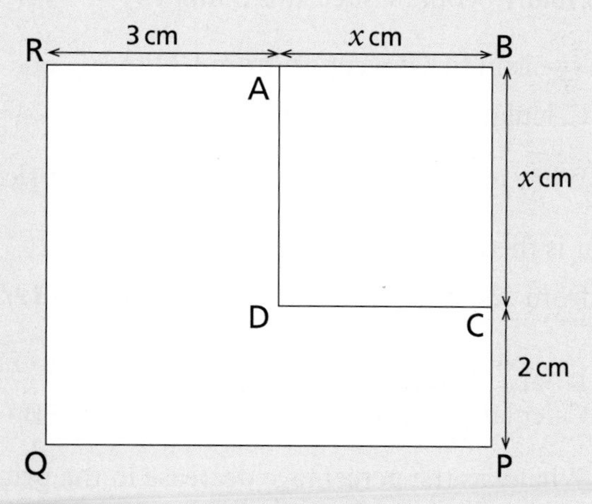

CP = 2 cm and RA = 3 cm.
The length of the side of square ABCD is x cm.
The rectangle RBPQ has an area of 42 cm^2.

(a) Form an equation, in terms of x, for the area of the rectangle.
Show that it can be written in the form $x^2 + 5x - 36 = 0$.

(b) Solve $x^2 + 5x - 36 = 0$, and hence calculate the area of the square ABCD.

AQA(SEG) 1999

48 Percentage 3

You will revise percentage increase and decrease.

This work will help you

- find the result of two or more percentage changes (including compound interest)
- calculate an original value given the value after a percentage change

A *Increase and decrease: review*

A1 What do you multiply by to do these?

(a) Increase a quantity by 6% (b) Increase a quantity by 11.5%
(c) Decrease a quantity by 8% (d) Decrease a quantity by 6.6%

A2 (a) Increase £60 by 12%. (b) Decrease £82 by 11%.

A3 The prices of items are reduced by 15% in a sale.
What is the new price of an item whose price before the sale was

(a) £60 (b) £84 (c) £48.80 (d) £99.60

A4 Last Sunday there were 425 customers visiting a garden centre.
An advert appeared in the local paper and this Sunday the number went up by 4%.
How many people visited this Sunday?

A5 Lara's season ticket went up from £24 to £27.60.

(a) Calculate the multiplier here. £24 → ×? → £27.60

(b) What was the percentage increase in the price of the ticket?

A6 What is the percentage increase

(a) from £30 to £39.60 (b) from £42 to £49.56 (c) from £58.40 to £78.84

A7 The price of a dress went down from £27.50 to £25.30.

(a) Calculate the multiplier here. £27.50 → ×? → £25.30

(b) What was the percentage decrease in the price of the dress?

A8 What is the percentage decrease

(a) from £20 to £18.40 (b) from £35 to £28.70 (c) from £19.60 to £12.74

B *Successive percentage changes*

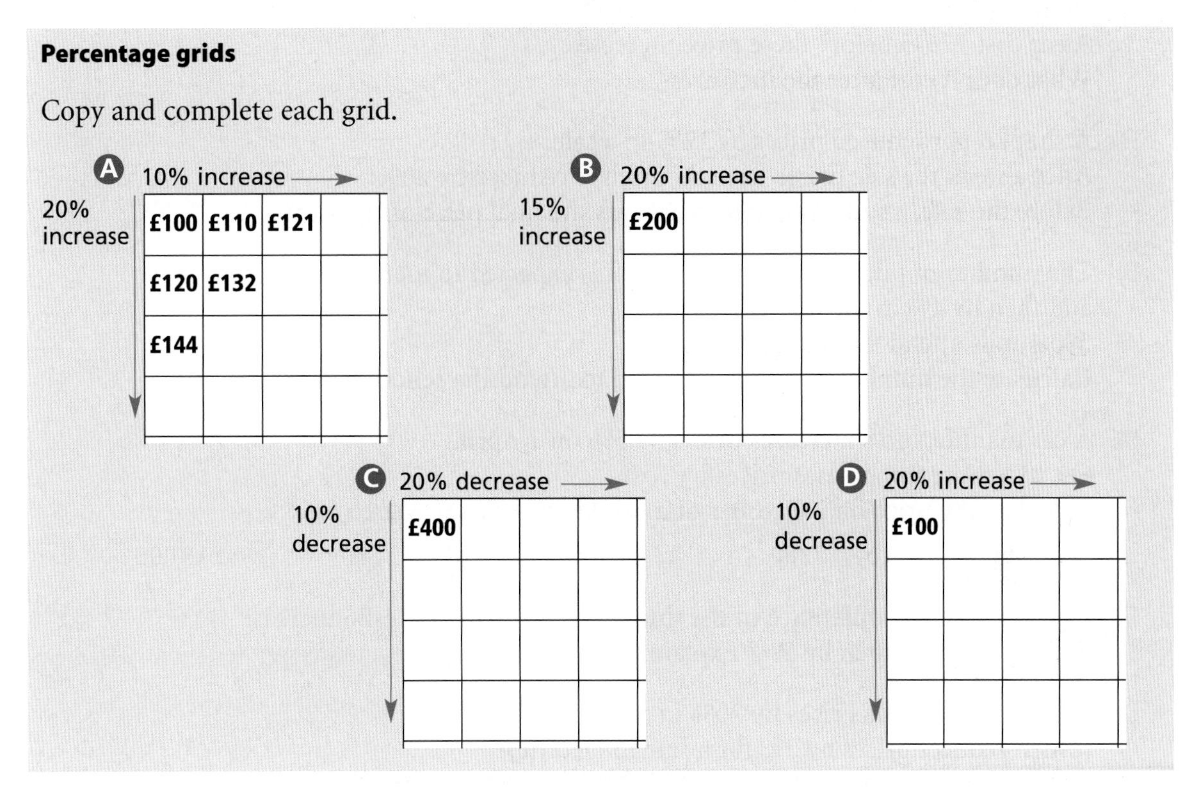

B1 The price of a rail ticket will increase by 12% next month and then by 15% six months later.
The ticket costs £40 now.

This is shown in a flow diagram:

12% increase, 15% increase

£40 → × ? → × ? →

(a) What is the multiplier for a 12% increase?

(b) What is the multiplier for a 15% increase?

(c) Calculate the price of the ticket after both increases.

B2 The value of a house is expected to fall by 6% next year and then by 4% in the year after that. The value now is £80 000.

This is shown in a flow diagram:

6% decrease, 4% decrease

£80 000 → × ? → × ? →

(a) What is the multiplier for a 6% decrease?

(b) What is the multiplier for a 4% decrease?

(c) Calculate the value of the house after both decreases.

B3 A garage increases its prices by 4% in September.
In the following January, prices go up by 6%.
A car cost £7645 before these price increases.
What does it cost after the increases?

B4 A shopkeeper reduced prices by 12% in a sale.
After a week the sale prices were themselves reduced by 20%.
Before the sale, a suit cost £150. What was the final price of the suit?

B5 The number of pupils attending a school is expected to increase by 5% next year and then by 4% in the following year.
500 pupils attend the school at present.
Calculate the number of pupils expected to attend the school in two years' time.

B6 A car manufacturer increases prices by 5% on 1 April.
On 1 October it increases prices by 10%.
Calculate the price on 2 October of a car whose price in March is

(a) £5600 (b) £7200 (c) £10 500 (d) £12 550 (e) £18 000

B7 Does it make any difference to the final price if the prices in B6 increase first by 10% and then by 5%? Explain your answer.

B8 A shop increases its prices by 20% in September.
It then reduces prices by 5% for a sale in December.

(a) What number is missing in this diagram?

price before September → × 1.20 → price in September → × ? → price in December

(b) Calculate the December price of an article whose price before September was

(i) £60 (ii) £55 (iii) £8.80 (iv) £18.50 (v) £405

B9 Calculate the final prices in this table. Round to the nearest penny if necessary.

	Starting price	First percentage change	Second percentage change	Final price
(a)	£80	up by 15%	up by 30%	
(b)	£140	down by 20%	down by 5%	
(c)	£350	down by 6%	up by 45%	
(d)	£8.20	up by 32%	down by 18%	
(e)	£8.20	down by 18.5%	up by 32.5%	

B10 The number of fish in Karl's pond goes up by 10% in the first year and then by 10% in the second year.
Karl says that in two years the population must go up by 20%.
Is he right? If not, why not?

C *Compound interest*

TG

Aunt Ethel wanted to save some money to give to her favourite niece in 10 years' time. She considered three ways of saving the money.

A Put £1000 in a jar on the mantelpiece and at the end of each year put in an extra £100.

B Put £1000 into a bank account earning 8% interest every year.

C Put £1000 in a safe, and add £1 after one year, £2 after two years, £4 after three years, £8 after four years, … doubling the amount each year.

What would Aunt Ethel's niece like her to do?

C1 Rajesh puts £500 into a building society account which pays 5% interest per annum (p.a.).
Copy and complete this table, which shows the amount in the account at the end of each year for 4 years. (Round up to the nearest penny.)

Number of years	Amount
0	£ 500.00
1	£ 525.00
2	
3	
4	

C2 Calculate the final amount for these.

(a) £800 invested at 7% p.a. for 3 years
(b) £650 invested at 4% p.a. for 5 years
(c) £1200 invested at 2.5% for 4 years
(d) £800 invested at 3.75% p.a. for 3 years

Using the power key on a calculator

If £400 is invested at 6% p.a. for 5 years, the final amount can be calculated like this:

$$400 \times 1.06 \times 1.06 \times 1.06 \times 1.06 \times 1.06 = 400 \times 1.06^5$$

Do 1.06 x^y 5 or 1.06 ^ 5

C3 Calculate the final amount for these.

(a) £400 invested at 3% p.a. for 8 years
(b) £750 invested at 8% p.a. for 9 years
(c) £1500 invested at 4.5% p.a. for 10 years
(d) £300 invested at 5.5% p.a. for 7 years

C4 Jacqui invests £2000 in an account which pays interest at 4% p.a.
Find how many complete years she will have to leave the money in the account for it to become at least £2500.

C5 £5000 is invested in an account paying 6% p.a. interest.
For how many complete years will it have to be left to become at least

(a) £5500
(b) £6000
(c) £10 000

D Percentage in reverse

TG

Percentage grids again

- What goes in the first box if, after a 10% increase, the result is £154?

A 10% increase →

?	£154	

- What goes in the first box in each of these? How do you work it out?

B 20% increase →

?	£276	

C 25% increase →

?	£300	

D 6% increase →

?	£371	

Worked examples

(a) A rail fare goes up by 8%. The new fare is £37.80.
What was the old fare?

The old fare is multiplied by 1.08 to get the new fare.

? → × 1.08 → £37.80

So the new fare has to be divided by 1.08
to get the old fare.

£35 ← ÷ 1.08 ← £37.80

Old fare = £37.80 ÷ 1.08 = **£35**

(b) The price of a coat goes down by 16%. The new price is £46.20.
What was the old price?

The old price is multiplied by 0.84 to get the new price.

? → × 0.84 → £46.20

So the new price has to be divided by 0.84
to get the old price.

£55 ← ÷ 0.84 ← £46.20

Old price = £46.20 ÷ 0.84 = **£55**

D1 The price of a theatre ticket goes up by 6% to £13.25.
What was it before the increase?

D2 The cost of hiring a digger goes up by 15% to £96.60.
What was it before?

D3 A restaurant adds a 12.5% service charge to customers' bills.
The total cost of a meal, including the service charge, is £18.90.
What did the meal cost before the service charge was added?

D4 The price of a coat goes down by 14% to £27.95. What was it before?

D5 Calculate the original price of an article which costs

(a) £29.50 after an 18% increase

(b) £39.60 after a 12% reduction

(c) £88.80 after a 7.5% reduction

(d) £50.50 after a 37.5% reduction

D6 The rate of VAT (value added tax) in 2002 was 17.5%.
In some catalogues, prices are shown without VAT but the customer has to pay the full price including VAT.

The price of a computer is '£450 plus VAT'.

(a) What is the multiplier for a 17.5% increase?

(b) What is the price, including VAT, of the computer?

(c) The price of a printer, including VAT, is £103.40.
Calculate the price excluding VAT.

D7 Given that the rate of VAT is 17.5%, calculate these.

(a) The price, including VAT, of a camera whose price is '£280 plus VAT'

(b) The price, excluding VAT, of an amplifier whose price is '£423 including VAT'

D8 Given that the rate of VAT is 17.5%, copy and complete this table.

Price excluding VAT	Price including VAT
£1430	
	£564
£740	
	£2996.25

E *Mixed questions*

E1 Alice has some money in a building society account.
Every year the amount increases by 4%.

At present there is £1352 in the account.

(a) How much will there be in the account in two years' time?

(b) How much was there in the account a year ago? Edexcel

E2 Sam wants to buy a Hooper washing machine.
Hooper washing machines are sold in four different shops.

Washing Power	Whytes	Clean Up
$\frac{1}{4}$ off	15% off	£240
usual price of £370	usual price of £370	plus VAT at $17\frac{1}{2}$%

(a) Find the difference between the maximum and minimum prices Sam could pay for a washing machine.

The price of the washing machine in the Homeworld shop is £293.75.

This includes VAT at $17\frac{1}{2}$%.

Homeworld
£293.75
including VAT

(b) Work out the cost of the washing machine **before** VAT is added. Edexcel

E3 Calculate, to the nearest penny, the compound interest earned when £800 is invested for 3 years at 6% per annum. WJEC

Test yourself

T1 (a) Kelly invested £450 for 3 years at a rate of 6% per year compound interest. Calculate the total amount that the investment is worth at the end of the 3 years.

(b) Kelly decides to buy a television. After a reduction of 15% in the sale, the one she bought cost her £319.60. What was the original price of the television? OCR

T2 (a) A computer costs £699 plus VAT. VAT is charged at $17\frac{1}{2}$%. What is the total cost of the computer?

(b) Another computer is advertised at £1116.25 including $17\frac{1}{2}$% VAT. How much is the computer before VAT is added? AQA 2000

T3 The price of a new television is £423. This price includes value added tax (VAT) at $17\frac{1}{2}$%.

(a) Work out the cost of the television **before** VAT was added.

By the end of each year, the value of a television has fallen by 12% of its value at the start of that year. The value of a television was £423 at the start of the first year.

(b) Work out the value of the television at the end of the **third** year. Give your answer to the nearest penny. Edexcel

T4 The weight of a special offer bar of Milk Chocolate is 200 g. The special offer bar is 60% heavier than the usual bar.

What is the weight of the usual bar? AQA(SEG) 2000

T5 In a sale all the prices are reduced by 30%. The sale price of a jacket is £28.

Work out the price of the jacket before the sale. Edexcel

T6 Joe put £5000 in building society savings account. Compound interest at 4.8% was added at the end of each year.

(a) Calculate the total amount of money in Joe's savings account at the end of 3 years. Give your answer to the nearest penny.

Sarah also put a sum of money in a building society savings account. Compound interest at 5% was added at the end of each year.

(b) Work out the number by which Sarah has to multiply her sum of money to find the total amount she will have after 3 years. Edexcel

49 Sine and cosine

You will revise the use of the tangent function.

This work will help you use sine and cosine to find sides and angles in right-angled triangles.

A The tangent function – a reminder

The work you did earlier on tangents is part of a branch of mathematics called trigonometry.
Trigonometry is about relationships between lengths and angles.

Remember, you can think of the tangent of an angle as a multiplier …

... or as a ratio: $\tan a = \dfrac{\text{opposite}}{\text{adjacent}}$

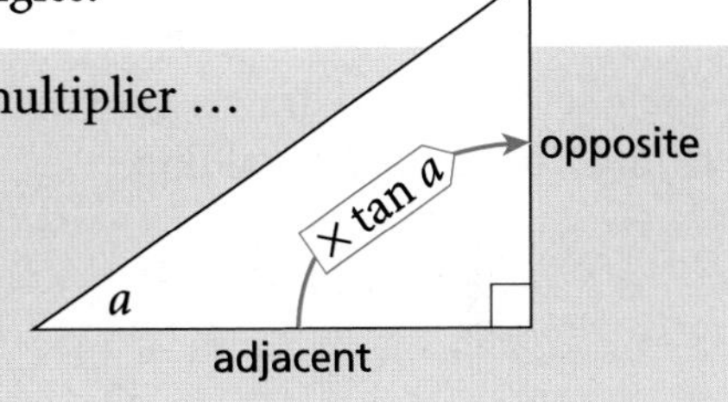

A1 Work out the missing lengths (to 1 d.p.).

(a)

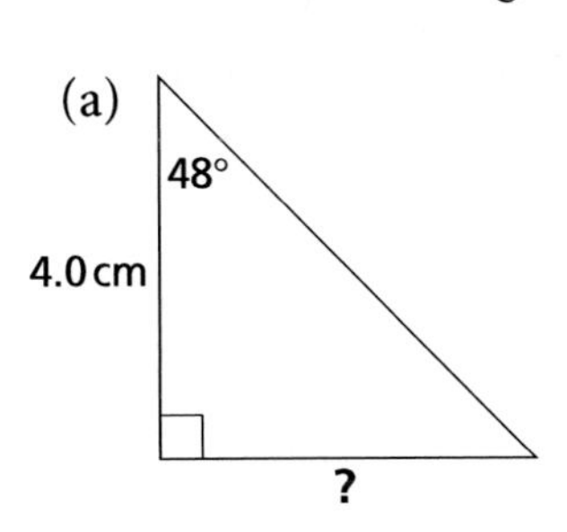

(b)

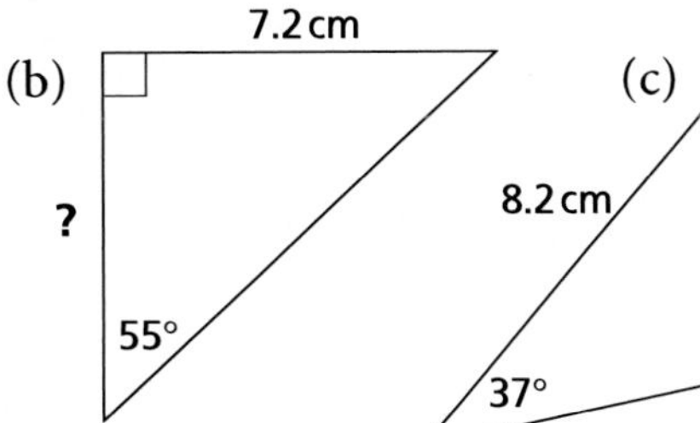

(c)

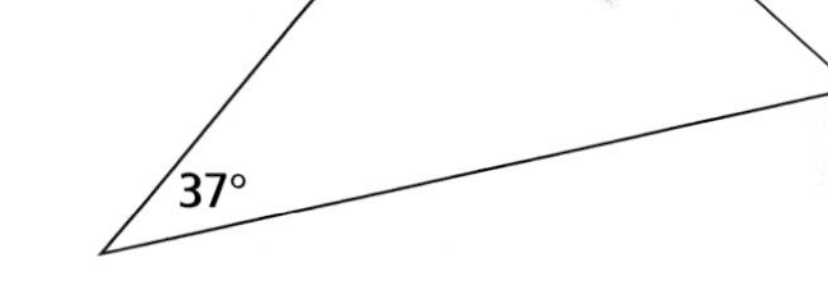

A2 Use your calculator to find the angle whose tangent is 1.666 (to 1 d.p.).

A3 Work out the missing angles (to 1 d.p.).

(a) (b)

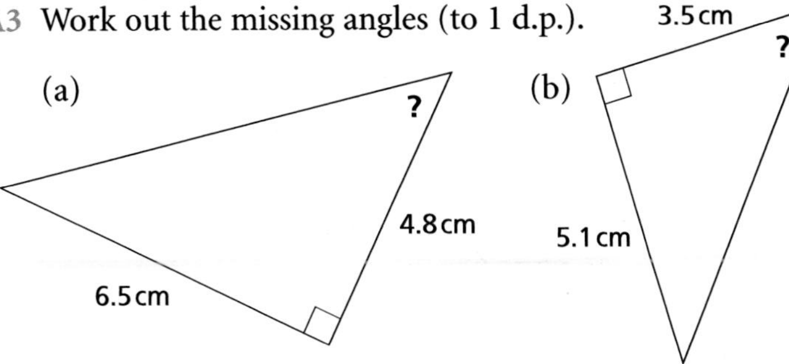

(c)

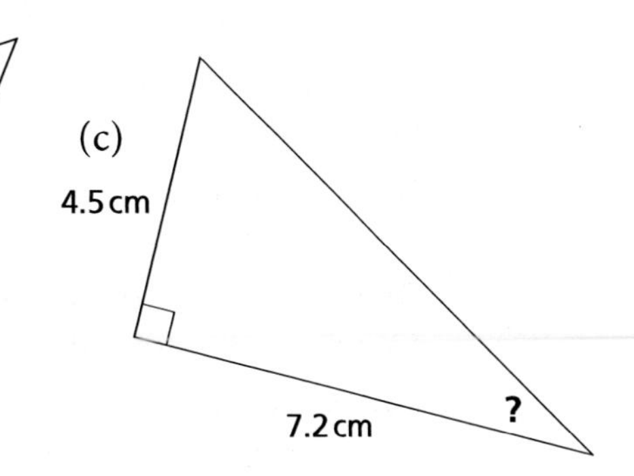

- Could you use the tangent function to work out the missing length here?

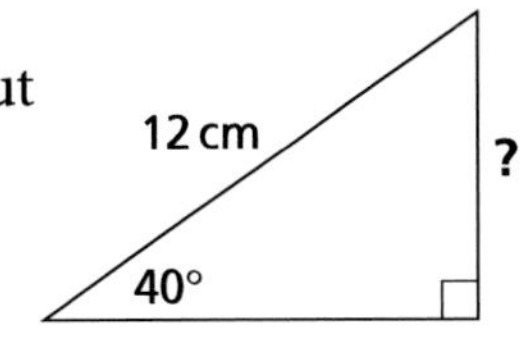

TG

B *The sine function*

TG

Draw a horizontal line.
Draw a quarter circle of radius 10 cm with its centre on the line.

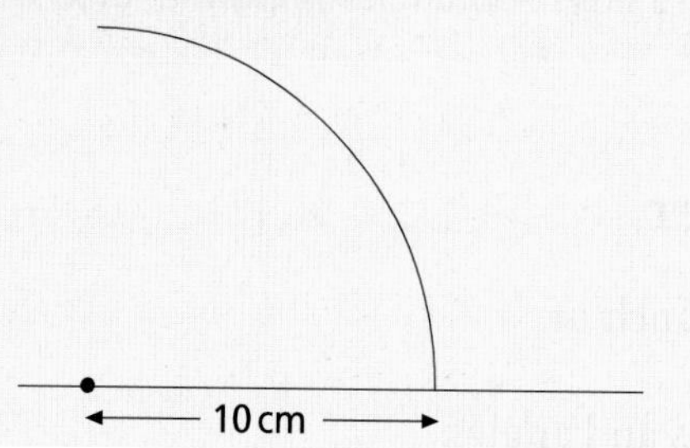

Draw a line 40° to the horizontal line.
Label this point P.

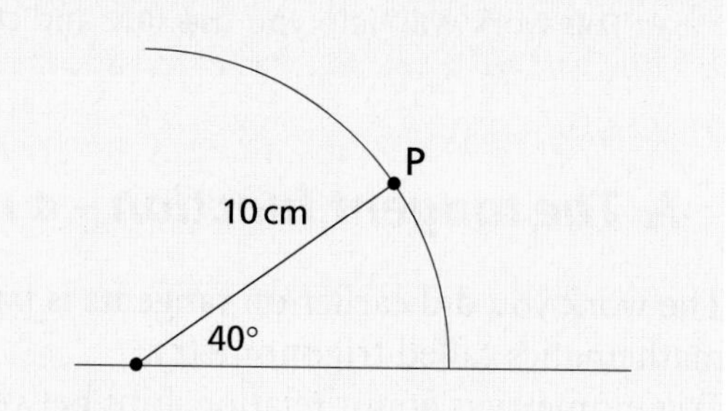

Use a set-square to draw a perpendicular from P to the horizontal line.

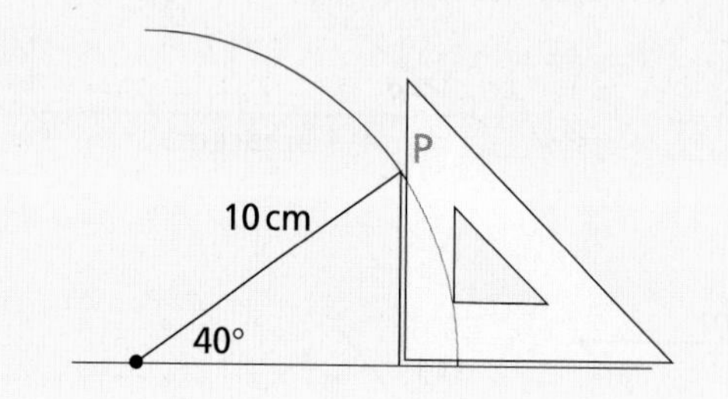

Measure and record this length.

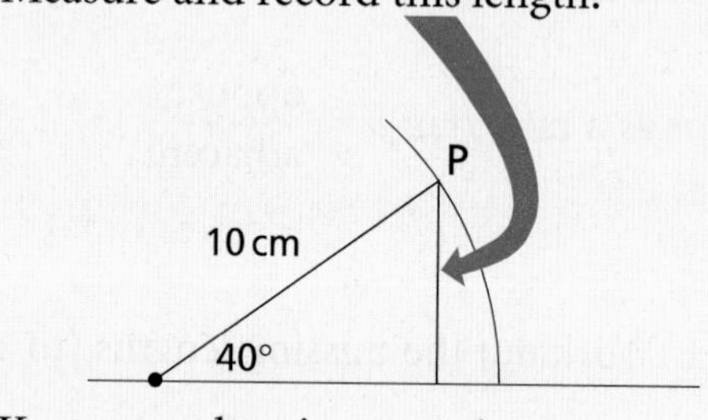

Keep your drawing experiment.

B1 Use your result to find the missing lengths here.

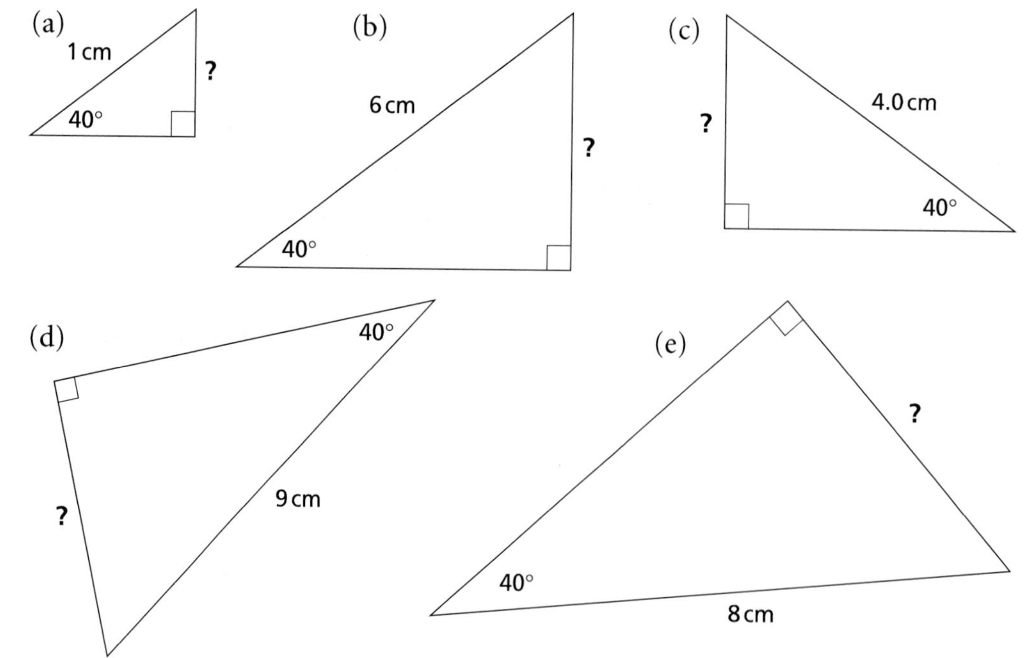

In a right-angled triangle like this, this side is the **hypotenuse** …

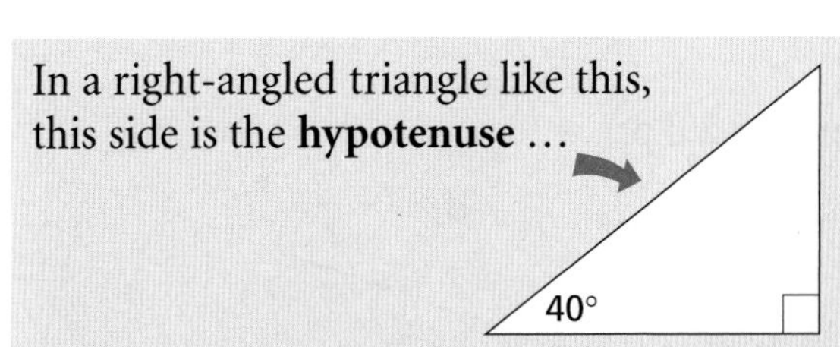

and this is the side **opposite** to the 40° angle.

When the angle is 40° you can use the rule: hypotenuse —[× 0.64]→ opposite side

This is another way of stating the rule: $\dfrac{\text{opposite side}}{\text{hypotenuse}} = 0.64$

The number you multiply the hypotenuse by to get the opposite side is called the **sine** of the angle.

So the sine of 40° is about 0.64.

B2 Continue your drawing experiment to find the sines of other angles.

Draw lines at 10°, 20°, 30°, …, 80° to the horizontal line, going through the centre of the arc.
Label them with their angles where they cross the arc.

40°
30°
20°
10°

Draw a perpendicular from each crossing point down to the horizontal line.

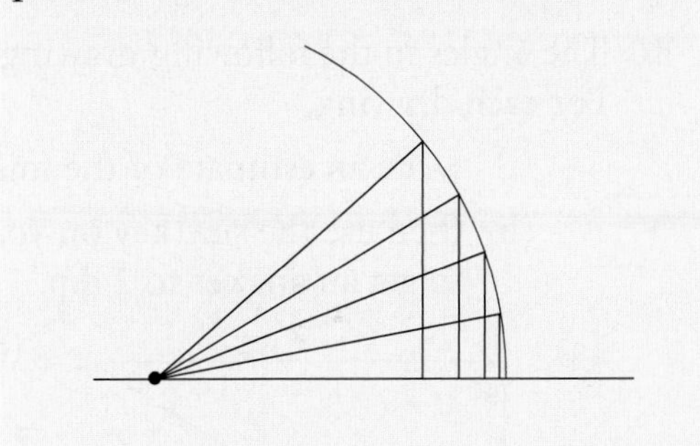

Measure the opposite side for each triangle and record your results in a table like this.

Angle	Hypotenuse	—[×?]→	Opposite side
10°	10 cm		
20°	10 cm		
30°	10 cm		
40°	10 cm		

Work out the numbers that go in here and write them in your table.

'sin' is a short way to write sine (though we still pronounce it sine when written this way).

So we can write sin 40° = 0.64.

A scientific calculator gives very accurate values of sines.

Try keying in [4] [0] [sin] or [sin] [4] [0]. Is 0.64 close to what you get?

B3 Use your calculator to find sin 10°, sin 20°, sin 30° … sin 80°.
Compare these results with what you got in B2.

B4 (a) Find sin 75° on your calculator.

Use this result to find the missing lengths here (to 2 d.p.).

(b)

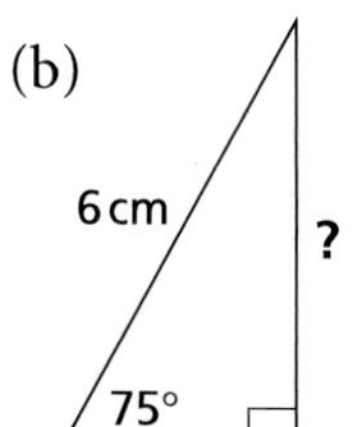

(c)

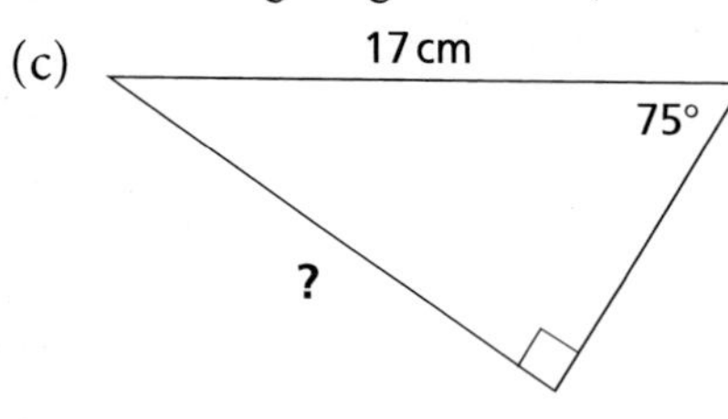

(d)

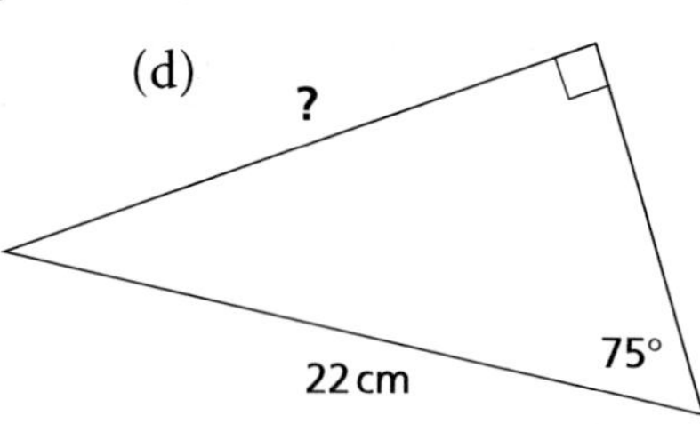

B5 (a) Find sin 28° on your calculator.

Use this result to find the missing lengths here (to 2 d.p.).

(b)

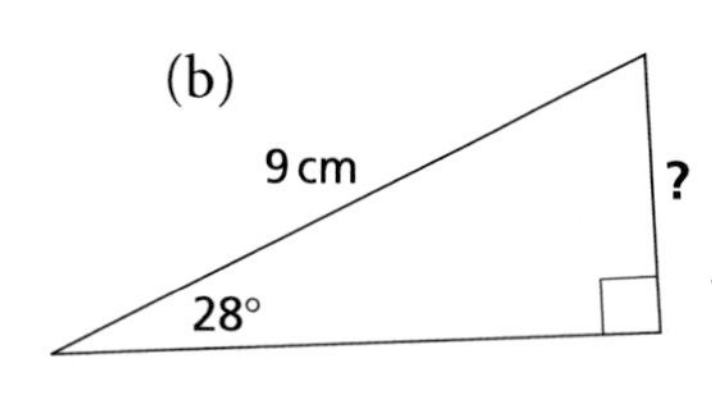

(c)

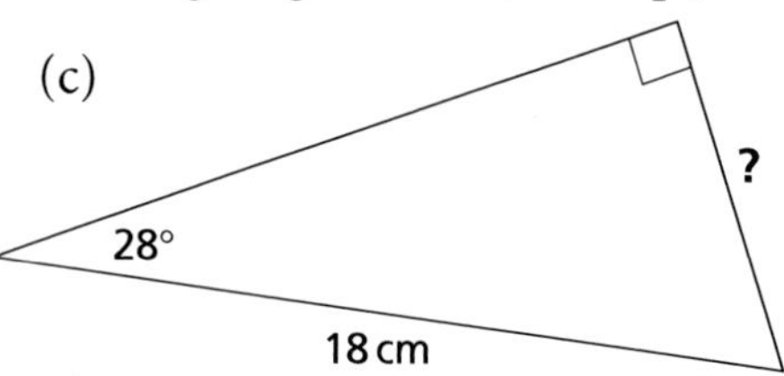

(d)

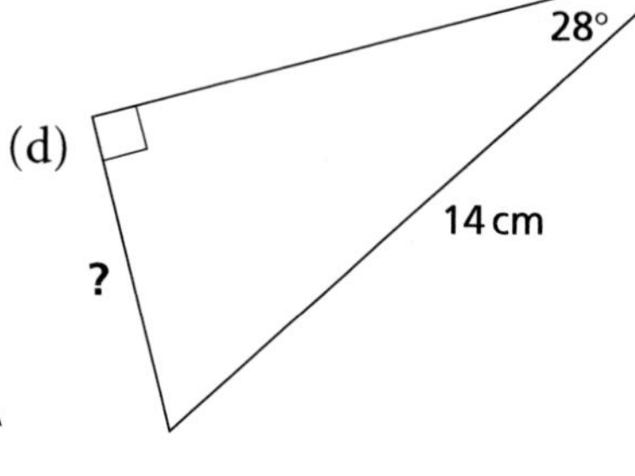

B6 The angles in the following drawings have been drawn accurately.
For each drawing,

(i) write an estimate of the missing length

(ii) then use the sine key on your calculator to get an answer to 2 d.p.

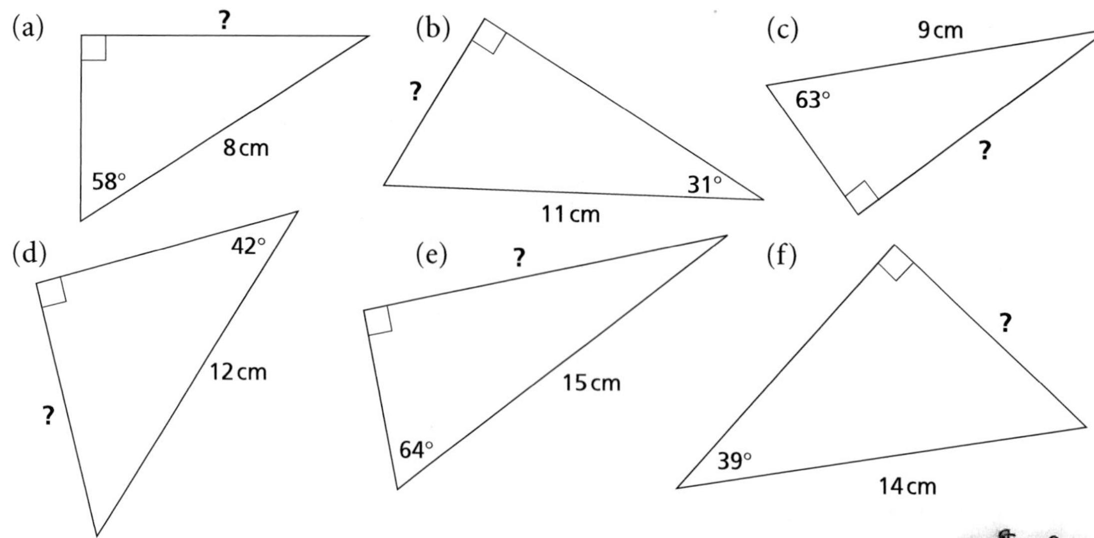

B7 The sloping section of this escalator is 12 metres long.
It slopes at an angle of 35° to the horizontal.

How high is the top of the escalator above the bottom (to the nearest 0.1 m)?

12 m

35°

B8 A ladder 6.4 metres long leans against a vertical wall and makes an angle of 67° with the ground.

How far is the top of the ladder from the bottom of the wall, to the nearest 0.1 m?

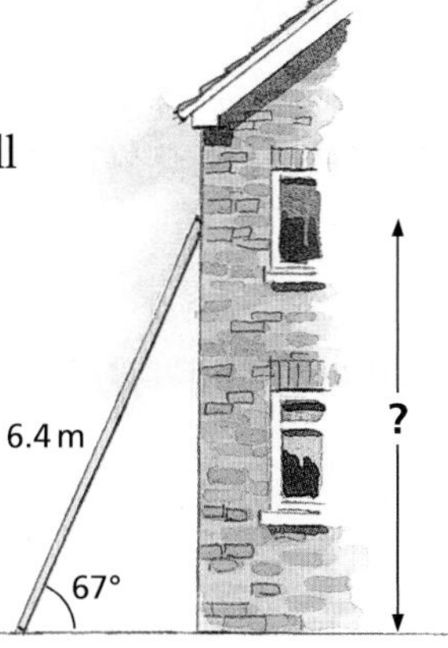

B9 A ship travels 20 km from A to B on a bearing of 042°. How far east has it gone?

(Copy this diagram and complete the triangle that you will need for the calculation.)

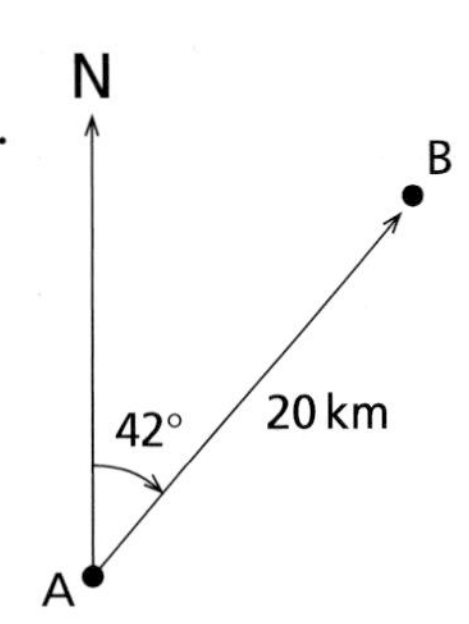

B10 A helicopter travels 93 km from P to Q on a bearing of 082°. Draw a diagram and calculate how far east it has gone.

B11 A plane travels 108 km from T to U on a bearing of 037°. Draw a diagram and calculate how far **north** it has gone.

B12 This is the end wall of a garden shed. Find the missing height.

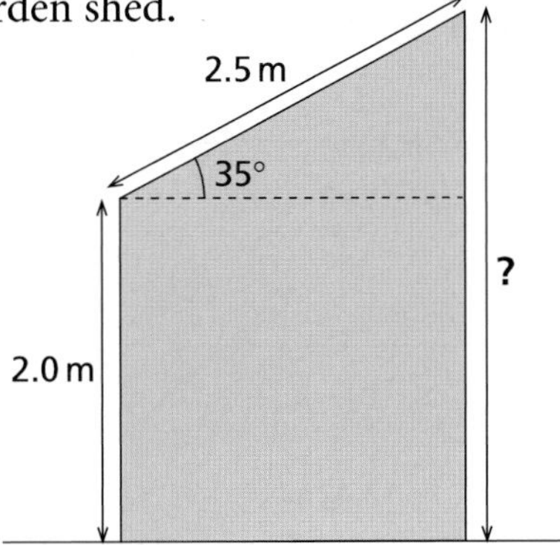

B13 This is a parallelogram.

(a) Work out the length of the perpendicular AQ, showing how you did the calculation.

(b) What is the area of the parallelogram (to the nearest 0.1 cm^2)?

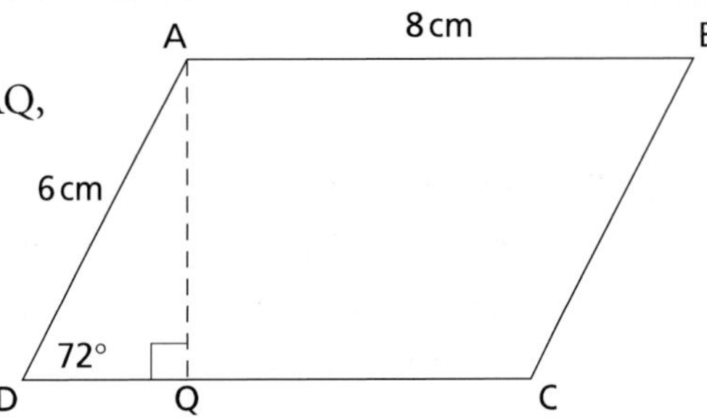

C *Using sine to find the hypotenuse*

sin 53° is about 0.8.

How long is the hypotenuse here?

C1 Make a sketch of each of these.
Find each hypotenuse using sin 53° = 0.8, and mark it on your sketch.

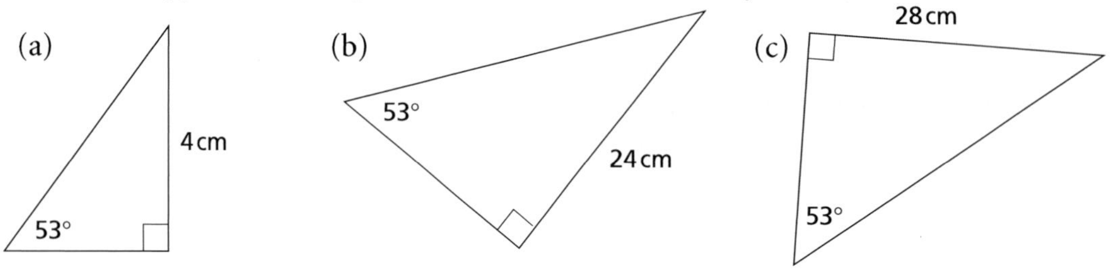

C2 The angles in the following drawings have been drawn accurately.
For each drawing,

(i) write an estimate of the length of the missing hypotenuse

(ii) then find its length to 1 d.p. using the calculator's value of the sine

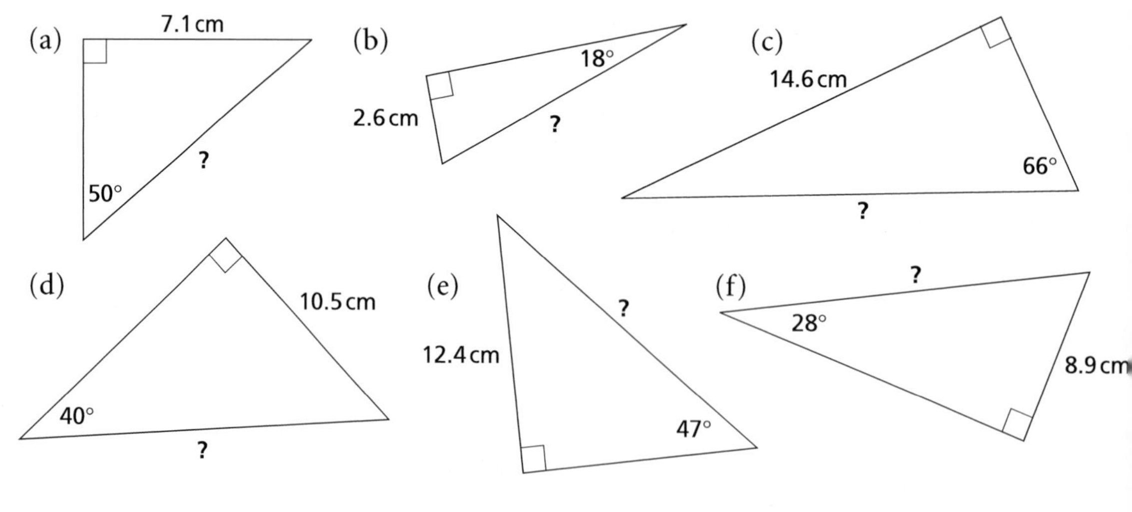

C3 Write a formula for finding h if you know x and p.

$h = \ldots$

D *Finding an angle*

D1 This table shows approximate values of the sines of angles every 10°.

a	$\sin a$
10	0.17
20	0.34
30	0.50
40	0.64
50	0.77
60	0.87
70	0.94
80	0.98

Use the table to **estimate** these.

(a) The angle whose sine is 0.7

(b) The angle whose sine is 0.9

(c) The angle whose sine is 0.2

Now use the $\sin^{-1}$ function on your calculator to find these angles. Your calculator will work the way it did for $\tan^{-1}$.

D2 (a) Work out the sine of angle a here.

(b) Now use your calculator to find the angle whose sine is this value (in other words find a).

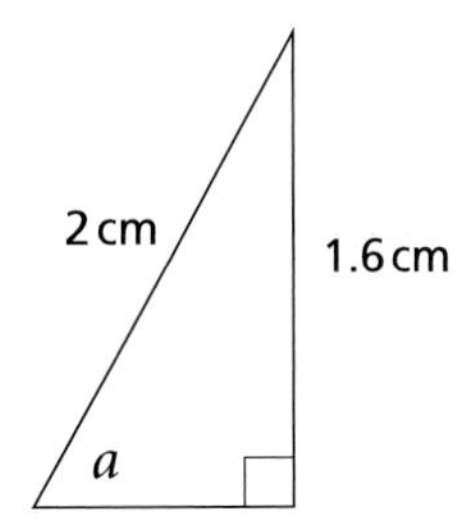

D3 For each of these, work out the sine of the angle. Then use your calculator to find the angle to 1 d.p.

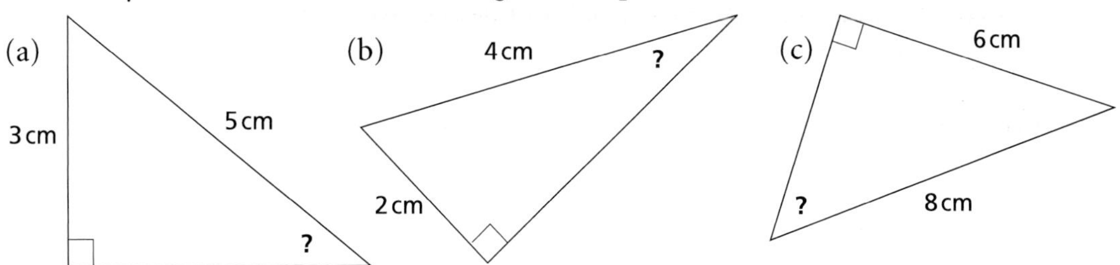

D4 Work out these angles to 1 d.p.

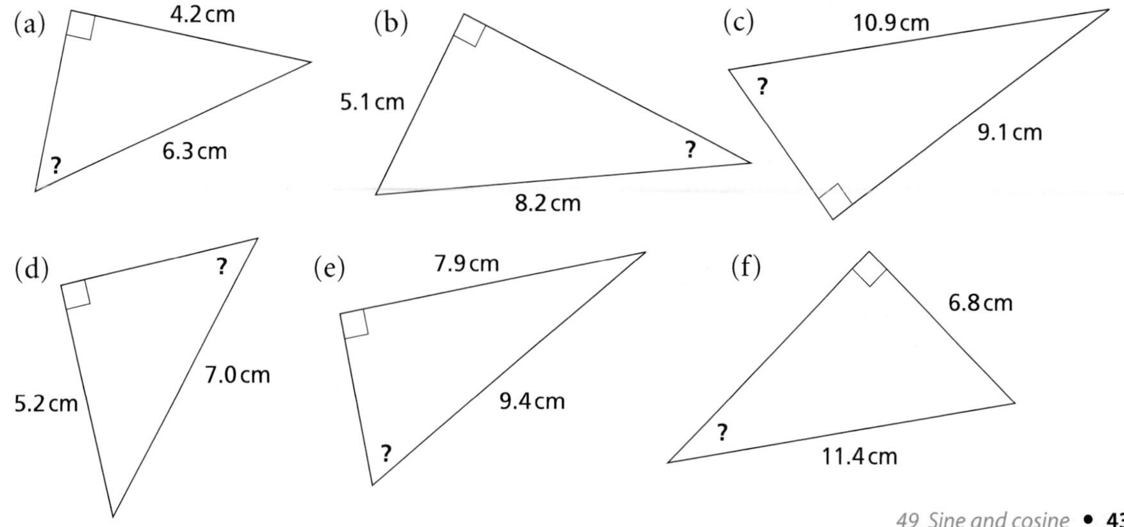

D5 What angle, to the nearest degree, does this bridge make with the horizontal when point P is 3.8 metres above road level?

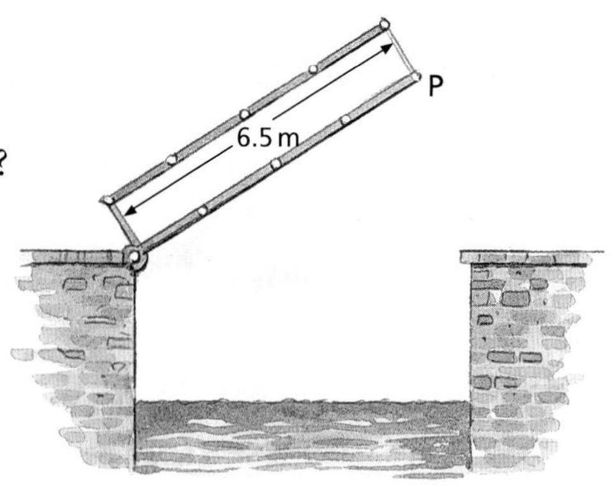

D6 A ladder 4.2 m long is placed against a vertical wall. The top of the ladder is 4.0 m above the ground. The ground is horizontal.

What angle does the ladder make with the ground?

E *The cosine function*

The cosine function ('cos' for short) involves the hypotenuse again but relates it to the side **adjacent** to the angle.

The cosine of an angle can be thought of as a multiplier …

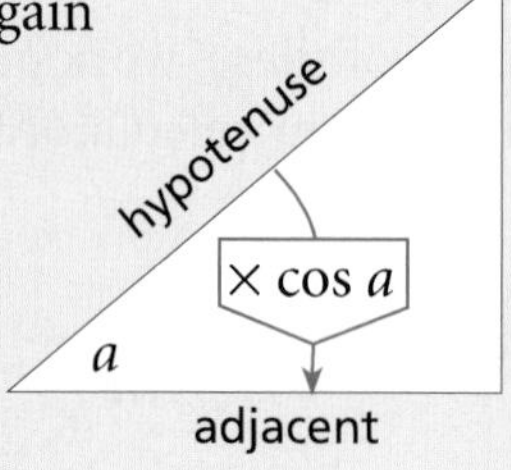

… or as a ratio: $\cos a = \dfrac{\text{adjacent}}{\text{hypotenuse}}$

E1 (a) Copy this table.

x	10	20	30	40	50	60	70	80
$\cos x°$								

Use the cosine function on your calculator to fill in the missing values (to 2 d.p.).

(b) What do you think the cosine of 90° is? Does your calculator agree?

(c) What do you think the cosine of 0° is?

(d) On graph paper, draw axes with x from 0 to 90 and y from 0 to 1.

Use your answers to (a), (b) and (c) to plot points for the graph of $y = \cos x°$.

Join your points with a smooth curve.

(e) Describe carefully what happens to $\cos x°$ as x increases from 0 to 90.

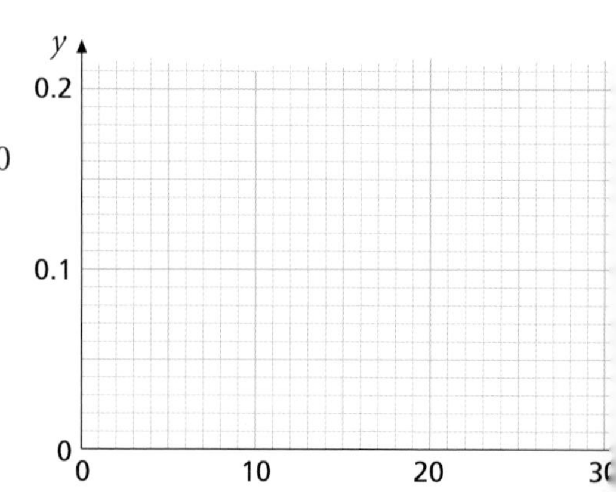

E2 Work out the length of the adjacent side to 1 d.p. in each of these triangles.

(a)

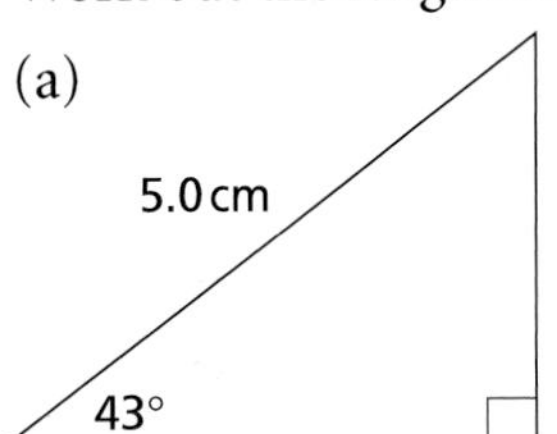

(b) (c)

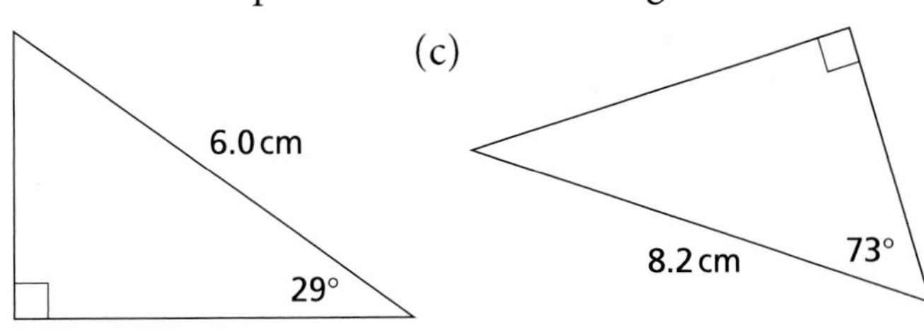

cos 66° is about 0.4 .

How long is the hypotenuse here?

?

66°

8 cm

E3 Copy each sketch.
Find each hypotenuse using cos 66° = 0.4 .
Write your answer on your diagram.

(a)

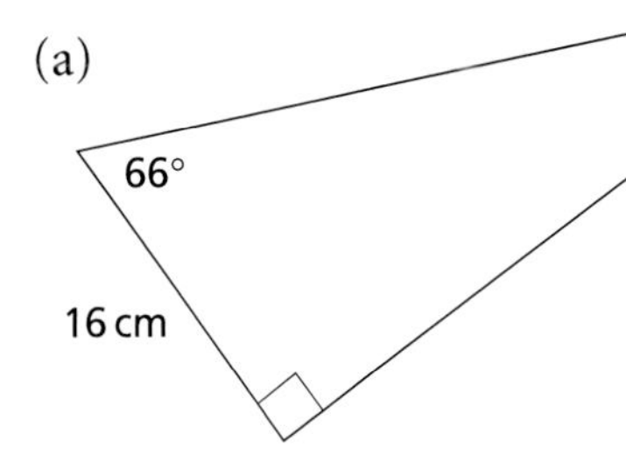

(b) (c)

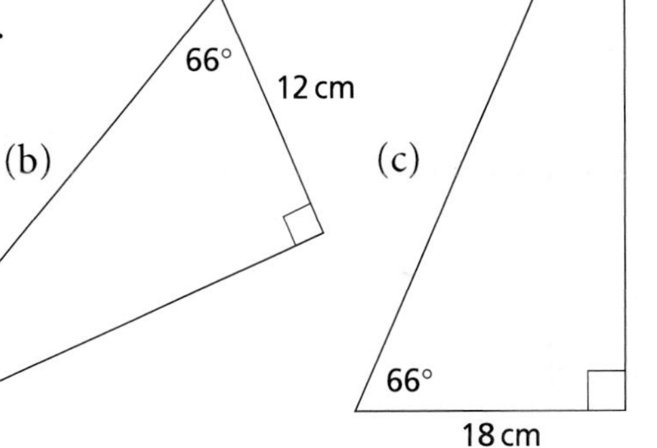

E4 The angles in the following drawings have been drawn accurately.
for each drawing,

(i) write an estimate of the length of the missing hypotenuse

(ii) then find its length to 1 d.p. using the calculator's value of the cosine

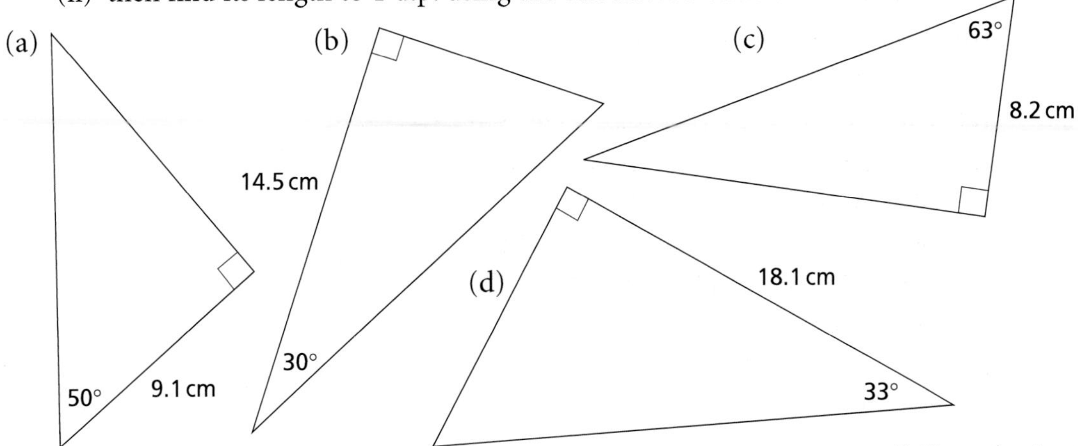

E5 Work out the length of the hypotenuse in each of these.

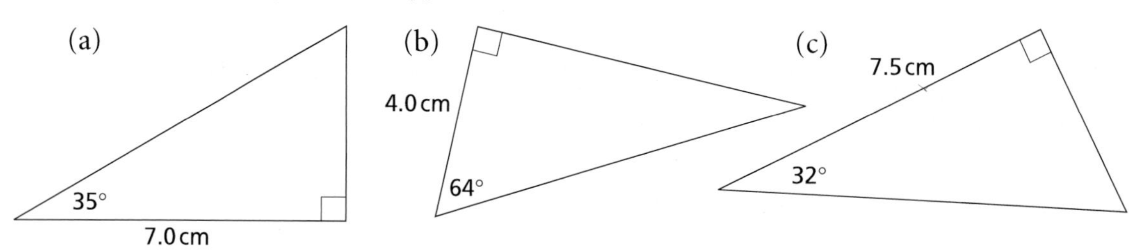

E6 Work out the missing lengths.

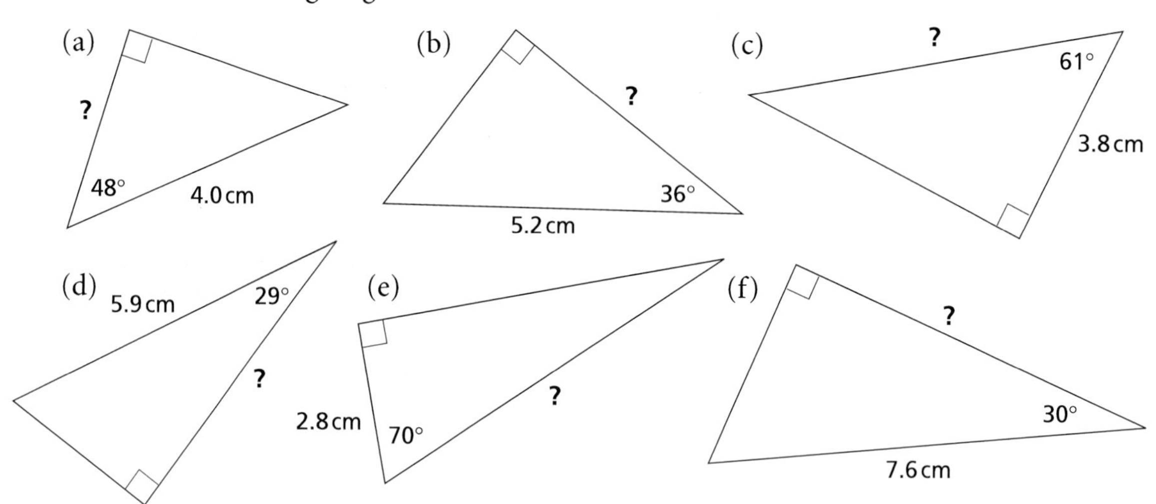

E7 Work out the missing angles.

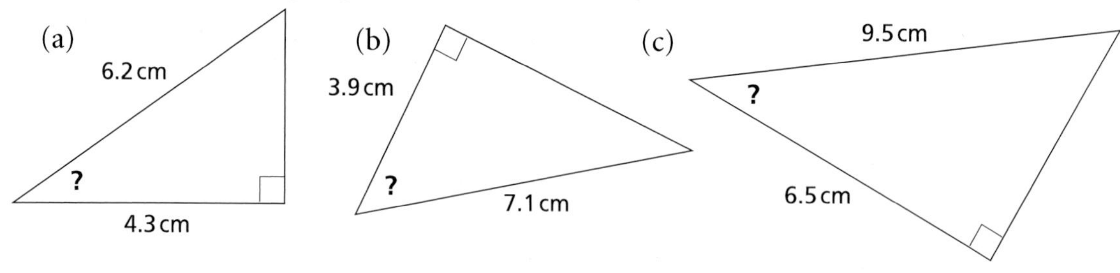

E8 Calculate the width (marked w) of this building.

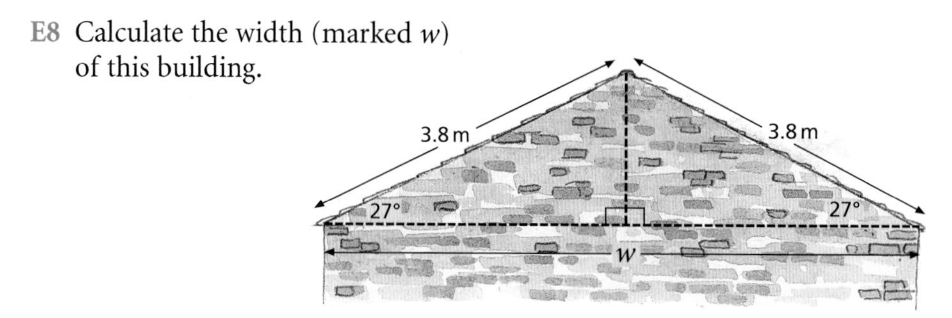

F *Mixed questions*

To decide whether to use sine, cosine or tangent, make a sketch and label the sides
hyp (hypotenuse)
opp (opposite the angle that is given or required)
adj (adjacent to the angle that is given or required)

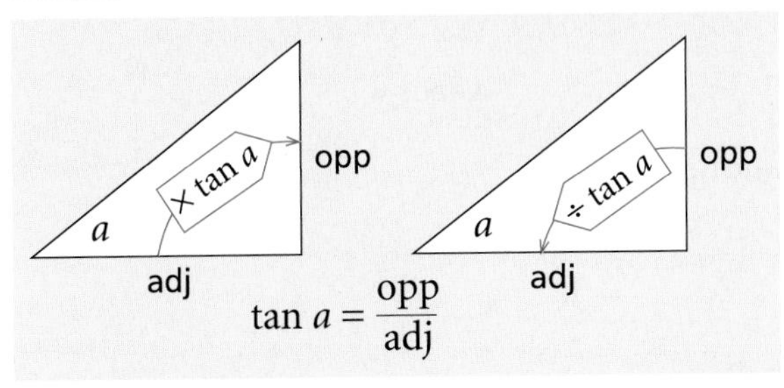

$\tan a = \frac{\text{opp}}{\text{adj}}$

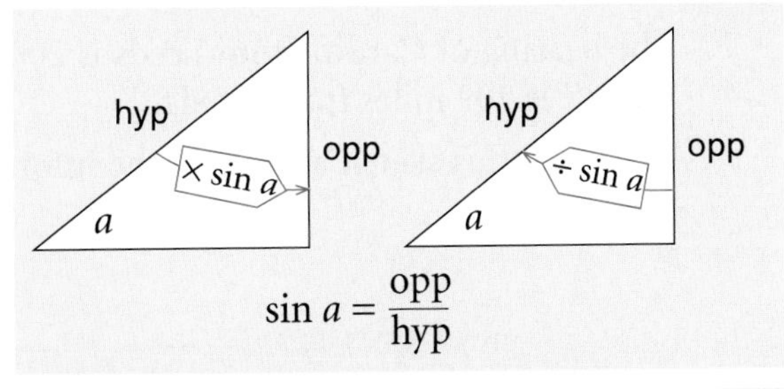

$\sin a = \frac{\text{opp}}{\text{hyp}}$

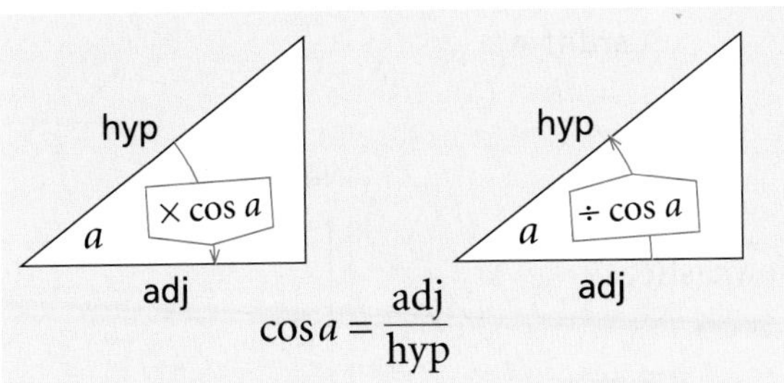

$\cos a = \frac{\text{adj}}{\text{hyp}}$

Sometimes Pythagoras' rule is useful in work where you are using trigonometry.

$\text{hyp}^2 = \text{adj}^2 + \text{opp}^2$

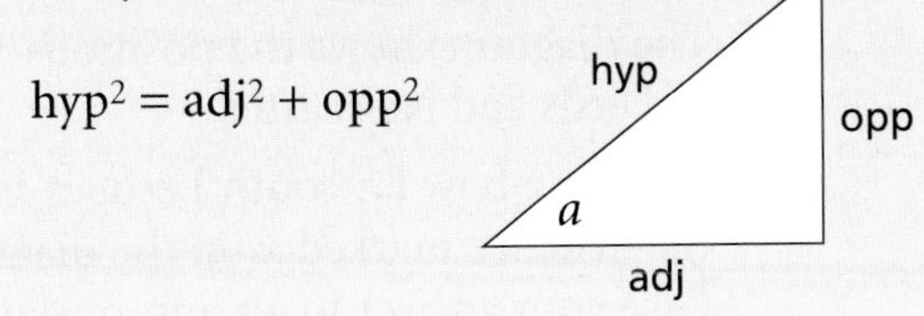

F1 Find the missing lengths and angles here.

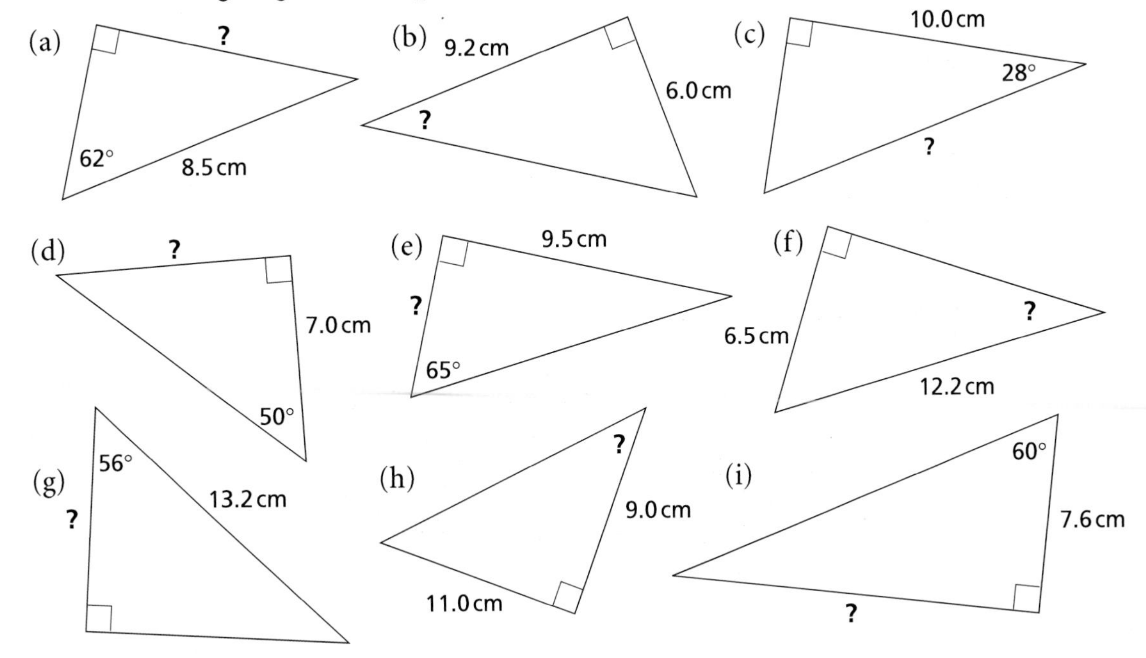

F2 (a) Work out the lengths of sides AC and BC in this triangle. Give your results to 2 d.p.

(b) Use Pythagoras to find AB from the lengths AC and BC. Show your working. Do you get 7 cm, as shown in the diagram?

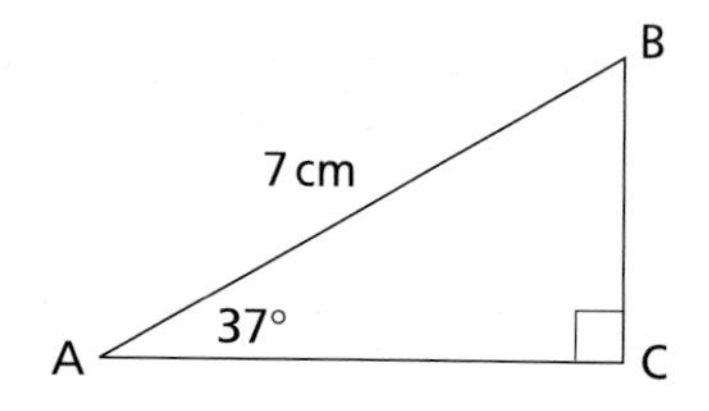

F3 Repeat F2 choosing your own angle at vertex A and your own length AB. Does the same thing happen as before?

F4 The bearing of Cardiff from Leeds is 200°. Cardiff is 209 miles from Leeds.

(a) Copy this sketch and show the information.

Leeds •

N

Cardiff •

(b) The diagram shows the positions of Leeds and Newcastle.

Calculate how far south Leeds is from Newcastle, the distance marked x on the diagram. Give your answer to an appropriate degree of accuracy.

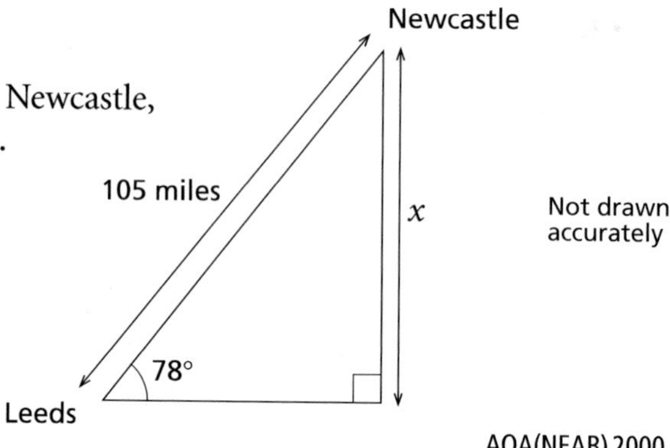

AQA(NEAB) 2000

F5 A glider travels for 8 km on a bearing of 065°.

(a) How much further north is it from when it started?

(b) How much further east has it travelled?

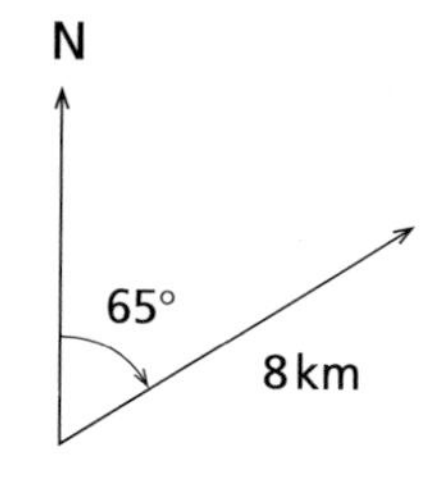

F6 A helicopter travels for 78 km on a bearing of 206°.

(a) How much further south is it from when it started?

(b) How much further west has it travelled?

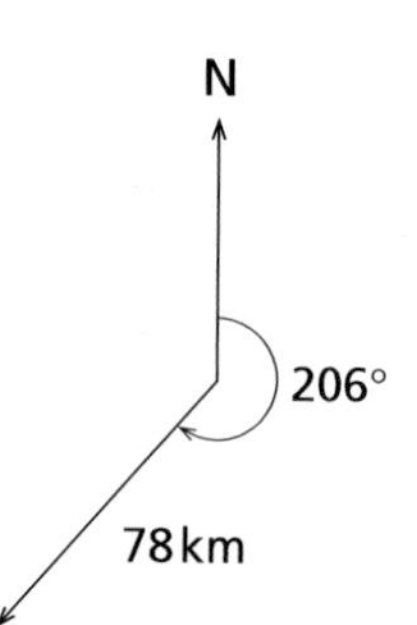

F7 Starting from point A a helicopter flies 20 km south and then flies 32 km west, finishing at point B. Then it flies from B back to A in a straight line.

Draw a sketch and calculate these.

(a) The length of the return journey from B to A

(b) The bearing of the return journey

F8 ABCD is a quadrilateral.

Angle BDA = 90°, angle BCD = 90°, angle BAD = 40°.
BC = 6 cm, BD = 8 cm.

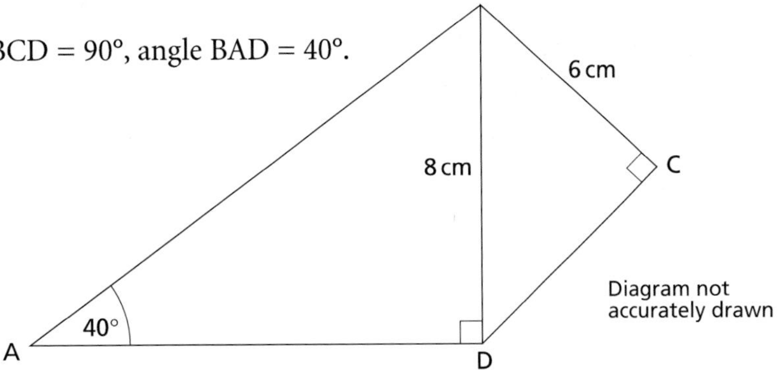

(a) Calculate the length of DC.
Give your answer correct to three significant figures.

(b) Calculate the size of angle DBC.
Give your answer correct to three significant figures.

(c) Calculate the length of AB.
Give your answer correct to three significant figures.

Edexcel

F9 This nonagon has been drawn by spacing 9 dots equally around a circle with radius 7 cm.

(a) What is the size of angle AOB?

(b) What is the size of angle AOM?

(c) Calculate the length of AM to 4 s.f.

(d) What is the length of side AB?

(e) What is the total perimeter of the nonagon, to 3 s.f.?

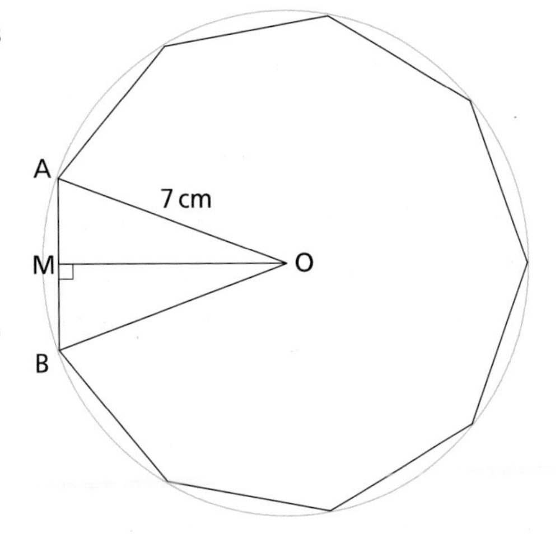

F10 A pentagon is drawn by spacing 5 dots equally around a circle with radius 4 cm.
Show this with a clear sketch.
Calculate the perimeter of the pentagon to three significant figures.

Test yourself

T1 Use your calculator to find the value of these to 3 d.p.

(a) sin 16° (b) tan 8° (c) cos 57° (d) tan 29° (e) sin 1°

T2 Find the values of these to 1 d.p.

(a) The angle whose tangent is 0.04
(b) The angle whose sine is 0.56
(c) The angle whose cosine is 0.82
(d) The angle whose tangent is 156

T3 Find the missing angles.

(a)

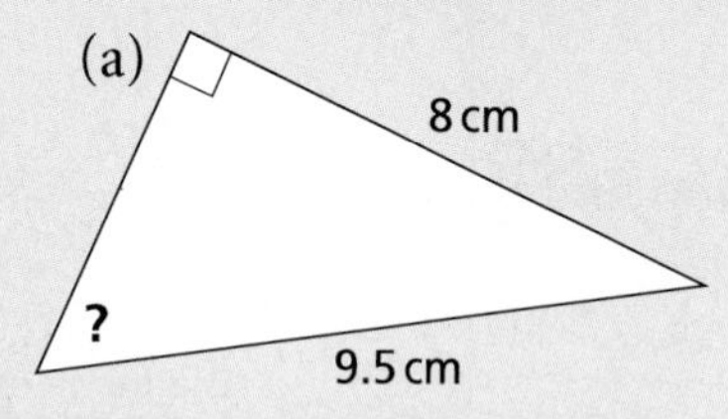

(b) (c)

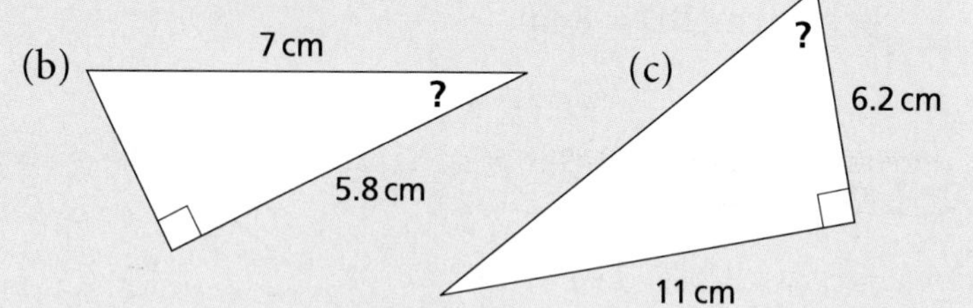

T4 Find the missing lengths.

(a) (b)

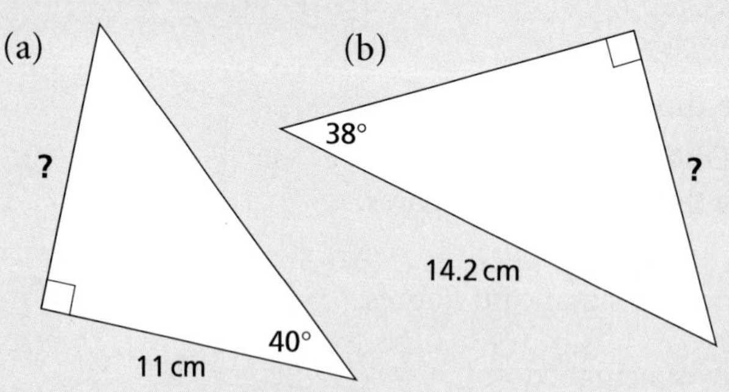

(c) (d)

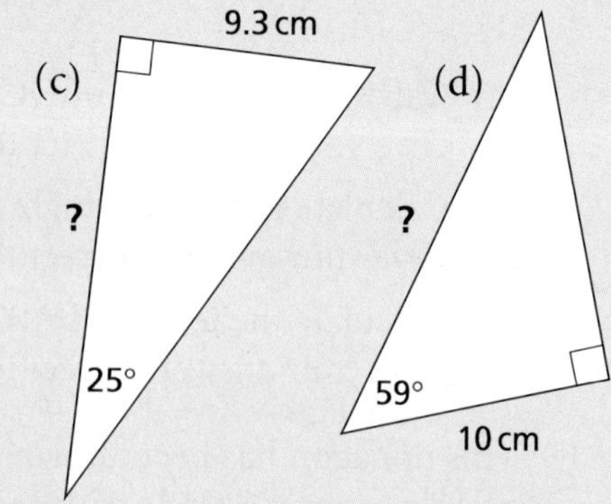

T5 Calculate the heights of the points A, B, C above the ground, each to the nearest 0.1 m.

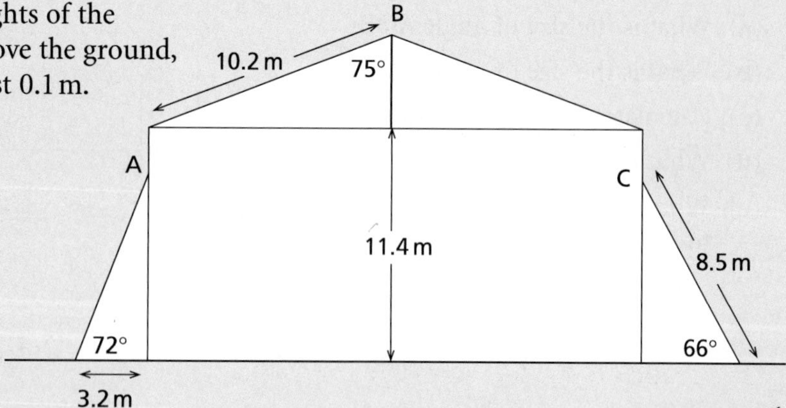

T6 A tree 2.50 metres tall casts a shadow 4.36 metres long. Calculate the angle of elevation of the sun to the nearest degree. (The angle is marked *a* in the diagram.)

50 Changing the subject 2

You will revise how to change the subject of a formula such as $a = 2b + 3$ or $a = 2b - 3$.

This work will help you

- change the subject of a formula with several letters in it
- rearrange a formula where the new subject appears twice

A Review

There are three sets of three equivalent formulas here. Can you find them?

$a = 3b - 10$ $b = \frac{a + 10}{3}$ $a - 3b = 10$ $3a = b + 10$ $a = 3b + 10$

$3a - b = 10$ $a + 10 = 3b$ $3a - 10 = b$ $b = \frac{a - 10}{3}$

TG

A1 Which of the following is a correct rearrangement of $p = 2q - 4$?
There may be more than one correct answer.

R $q = \frac{p - 4}{2}$ **S** $q = \frac{p - 2}{4}$ **T** $q = \frac{p + 4}{2}$ **U** $q = \frac{4p}{2}$ **V** $q = \frac{4 + p}{2}$

A2 Rearrange each of these formulas to make the bold letter the subject.

(a) $4\mathbf{v} = u$ (b) $f = \mathbf{g} + 6$ (c) $v = 2\mathbf{g} + 10$

(d) $v = 2\mathbf{g} - 10$ (e) $10 + 5\mathbf{j} = k$ (f) $5\mathbf{j} - 12 = 3k$

A3 Find three sets of three equivalent formulas here.

$x = \frac{y - 3}{2}$ $2x + 3 = y$ $x = 2y + 3$ $y = \frac{x + 3}{2}$ $y = \frac{x - 3}{2}$

$x = 2y - 3$ $x - 3 = 2y$ $2x = y - 3$ $x + 3 = 2y$

A4 The equation of the line shown is $x = y - 2$.

(a) Rearrange the equation into the form $y = \ldots$

(b) What is the gradient of the line?

(c) What is the y-intercept of the line?

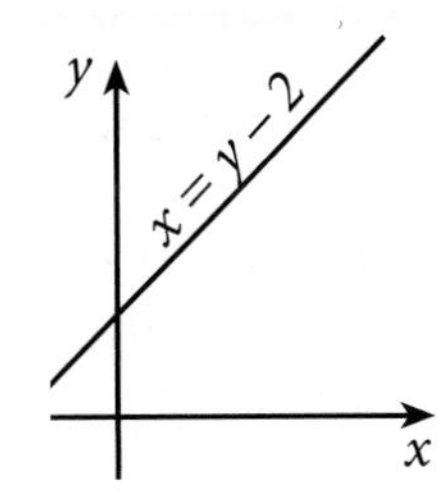

B *Give and take*

Sometimes we need to rearrange formulas with brackets in them.

Rearrange $t = 3(s + 5)$ to give s in terms of t.

$$t = 3(s + 5) \quad \text{[Multiply out brackets]}$$
$$t = 3s + 15 \quad \text{[Take 15 from both sides]}$$
$$t - 15 = 3s \quad \text{[Divide both sides by 3]}$$
$$s = \frac{t - 15}{3}$$

B1 Copy and complete this working to give x in terms of y.

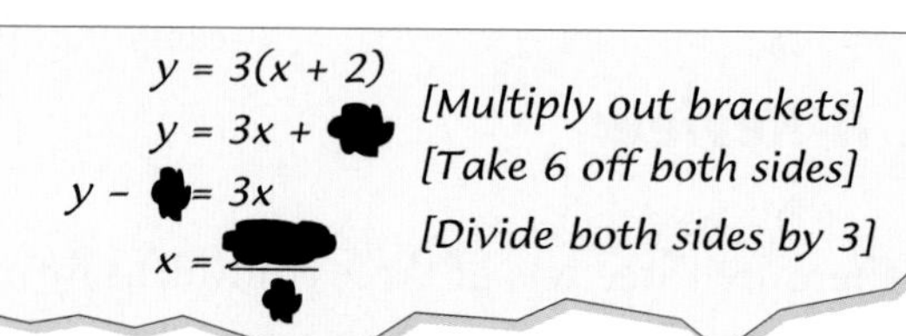

B2 Rearrange each of these formulas so that the bold letter is the subject.

(a) $w = 5(\boldsymbol{u} + 1)$ (b) $a = 3(\boldsymbol{b} - 5)$ (c) $y = 2(\boldsymbol{x} + 7)$

(d) $h = 2(3\boldsymbol{j} + 1)$ (e) $g = 3(4\boldsymbol{f} - 3)$ (f) $s = 5(2\boldsymbol{t} + 1)$

The letter you wish to make into the new subject might be subtracted.

Make s the subject of $t = 12 - 2s$.

$$t = 12 - 2s \quad \text{[Add 2s to both sides]}$$
$$t + 2s = 12 \quad \text{[Take t from both sides]}$$
$$2s = 12 - t \quad \text{[Divide both sides by 2]}$$
$$s = \frac{12 - t}{2}$$

B3 Copy and complete this working to make b the subject of the formula $a = 8 - 2b$.

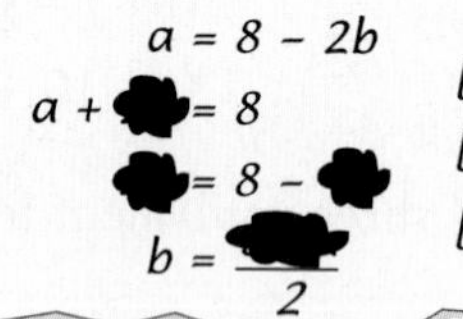

B4 Here are two formulas. **A** $h = 6 - 3k$ **B** $h = 3 - 6k$

Which of the formulas below is equivalent to A? Which is equivalent to B?

$k = \frac{6-h}{3}$ $k = \frac{h-3}{6}$ $k = \frac{h-6}{3}$ $k = \frac{3-h}{6}$

B5 Rearrange each of these formulas so that the bold letter is the subject.

(a) $y = 8 - \boldsymbol{x}$ (b) $s = 2 - 4\boldsymbol{t}$ (c) $x + 3\boldsymbol{y} = 12$

(d) $3 - 2\boldsymbol{f} = g$ (e) $2(\boldsymbol{u} - 3) = w$ (f) $z = 3 + 6\boldsymbol{p}$

(g) $s = 4\boldsymbol{t} - 2$ (h) $r = 3(4 - \boldsymbol{u})$ (i) $2(1 - \boldsymbol{h}) = j$

B6 Copy and complete this working to make f the subject of $e = \frac{6 - f}{3}$.

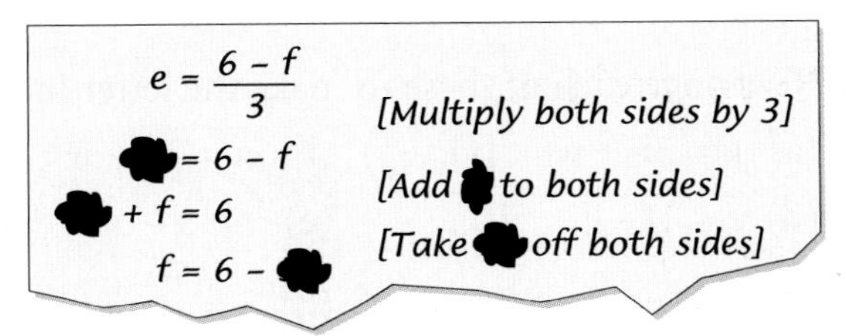

B7 By first multiplying both sides by 5, make b the subject of $a = \frac{4 - b}{5}$.

B8 Make the bold letter the subject in each of these.

(a) $h = \frac{10 - \boldsymbol{k}}{5}$ (b) $h = \frac{10 + \boldsymbol{k}}{5}$ (c) $m = \frac{\boldsymbol{n}}{2} - 5$

C *Three letters*

Some formulas have more than two letters in them, for example $V = IR$.
We can rearrange formulas containing more letters just as before.

Suppose we wish to make R the subject of $V = IR$.

We would rearrange $V = 8R$ like this.

$V = 8R$ [Divide both sides by 8]

$\frac{V}{8} = R$

We rearrange $V = IR$ like this:

$V = IR$ [Divide both sides by I]

$\frac{V}{I} = R$

C1 Rearrange the formula $V = IR$ to make I the subject.

C2 Rearrange $s = a + b$ to make a the subject.

C3 Make k the subject of $h = k - l$.

C4 Which of these are correct rearrangements of $z = x - y$?

A $x = y + z$ **B** $x = z + y$ **C** $y = z - x$ **D** $y = x - z$

C5 Rearrange each of these to make the letter in square brackets the subject.

(a) $a = bc$ [b] (b) $p = q + t$ [t] (c) $u = vw$ [w]

(d) $f = g - h$ [g] (e) $f = g - h$ [h] (f) $y = xz$ [z]

C6 Copy and complete this working to make C the subject of $A = B + 2C$.

$A = B + 2C$ [Take B off both sides]

$A - \blacksquare = 2C$ [Divide both sides by $\blacksquare$]

$\frac{A - \blacksquare}{\blacksquare} = C$

C7 Which of these formulas are equivalent to $y = 5x - k$?

A $k = 5x - y$ **B** $k = y + 5x$ **C** $x = \frac{y - k}{5}$ **D** $x = \frac{y}{5} + k$

C8 Rearrange each of these to make the letter in square brackets the subject.

(a) $u = 3v + w$ [v] (b) $u = 3v + w$ [w] (c) $e = 4f - g$ [g]

(d) $e = 4f - g$ [f] (e) $r = s - 3t$ [s] (f) $r = s - 3t$ [t]

(g) $a = \frac{b - c}{3}$ [b] (h) $a = \frac{b - c}{3}$ [c] (i) $j = \frac{k + m}{10}$ [m]

D *More letters*

Some formulas have more letters in them, for example $p = q + rs$.
You can change the subject of these just as before.

Suppose we wish to make s the subject of $p = q + rs$.

We would rearrange $p = 8 + 5s$ like this.

$p = 8 + 5s$ [Take 8 from both sides]

$p - 8 = 5s$ [Divide both sides by 5]

$s = \frac{p - 8}{5}$

We rearrange $p = q + rs$ like this.

$p = q + rs$ [Take q from both sides]

$p - q = rs$ [Divide both sides by r]

$s = \frac{p - q}{r}$

D1 Rearrange the formula $p = q + rs$ to make r the subject.

D2 Copy and complete each of these to make m the subject.

(a)

$s = 4m - 6$ [Add ■ to both sides]

$s + ■ = 4m$ [Divide both sides by ■]

$\frac{s + ■}{■} = m$

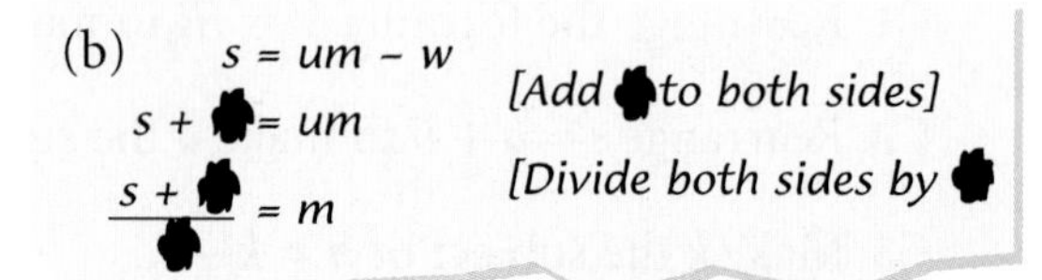

D3 Make the bold letter the subject of each of these.

(a) $t = u\mathbf{v} + w$ (b) $r = \mathbf{s}t + p$ (c) $h = e\mathbf{f} - g$ (d) $s = f - g\mathbf{h}$

(e) $k = d\mathbf{s} - et$ (f) $k = ds - e\mathbf{t}$ (g) $4f = \mathbf{a}b - cd$ (h) $4f = ab - \mathbf{c}d$

D4 Copy and complete this working to make r the subject of the formula $s = \frac{6}{r}$.

$s = \frac{6}{r}$ [Multiply both sides by ■]

$rs = 6$ [Divide both sides by s]

$r = $ ■

D5 Make the bold letter the subject of each of these.

(a) $v = \frac{8}{\mathbf{t}}$ (b) $q = \frac{12}{\mathbf{h}}$ (c) $t = \frac{2 + w}{\mathbf{d}}$ (d) $y = \frac{6 - x}{\mathbf{z}}$

D6 Multiply both sides by a to make d the subject of $b = \frac{d}{a}$.

D7 Make the bold letter the subject of each of these.

(a) $h = \frac{\mathbf{a}}{s}$ (b) $h = \frac{a}{\mathbf{s}}$ (c) $z = \frac{\mathbf{x} - y}{a}$ (d) $z = \frac{x - \mathbf{y}}{a}$

(e) $r = \frac{x + y}{\mathbf{k}}$ (f) $r = \frac{\mathbf{s}}{l} + m$ (g) $u = m - \frac{\mathbf{t}}{k}$ (h) $t = \frac{ef - kl}{\mathbf{h}}$

D8 By dividing both sides by $2f$, make g the subject of $s = 2fg$.

D9 Make n the subject of each of these formulas.

(a) $f = 6mn$ (b) $t = abn$ (c) $r = 2an - d$ (d) $ab = 15 - 4pn$

E *Squares and square roots*

The area, A, of a circle with radius r is given by the formula $A = \pi r^2$. If you know the areas of several circles and want to know their radii it may be useful to rearrange the formula to make r the subject.

$A = \pi r^2$

$\frac{A}{\pi} = r^2$ [Divide both sides by π]

[Take the square root of both sides]

$\sqrt{\frac{A}{\pi}} = r$

E1 A cube has edges of length x.
Each square face has an area of x^2.
So the total surface area, A, is $6x^2$.

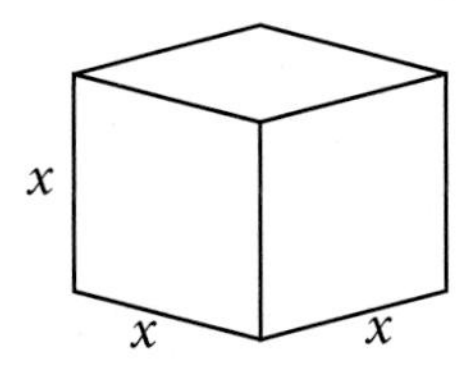

Copy and complete this working to make x the subject of $A = 6x^2$.

$A = 6x^2$

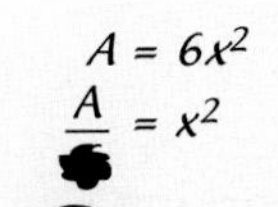

$\frac{A}{\ } = x^2$ [Divide both sides by]

[Take square root of both sides]

$= x$

E2 A cube has a total surface area of $20\,\text{cm}^2$.
Use the result of E1 to work out the length of one edge.

E3 Rearrange each of these to make the bold letter the subject.

(a) $y = 2\mathbf{x}^2$ (b) $a = 25\mathbf{b}^2$ (c) $h = \frac{\mathbf{k}^2}{10}$ (d) $m = \frac{3\mathbf{n}^2}{10}$

E4 Make x the subject of each of these formulas.

(a) $x^2 = 2b$ (b) $y = x + c^2$ (c) $3x^2 = y$ (d) $5x^2 = 6y^2$ (e) $x^2 + k = 25$

E5 Make b the subject of $a = \sqrt{5b}$. (Hint: square each side first.)

E6 Make q the subject of each of these formulas.

(a) $h = \sqrt{pq}$ (b) $k = \sqrt{5pq}$ (c) $5l = \sqrt{6q}$ (d) $t = \sqrt{\frac{q}{2}}$ (e) $r = \sqrt{\frac{aq}{s}}$

E7 You are given the formula $V = \sqrt{PR}$.
Rearrange the formula to give P in terms of V and R. AQA 2003 Specimen

E8 Make n the subject of each of these formulas.

(a) $m = n^2 + 4$ (b) $m^2 = n^2 - 25$ (c) $m = 2(n^2 - 1)$

(d) $m^2 + n^2 = 36$ (e) $m = \dfrac{n^2 - 1}{5}$ (f) $m = \dfrac{1 - n^2}{16}$

E9 Rearrange the formula $v^2 = u^2 + 2as$ to make u the subject. OCR

F *Now appearing twice*

Sometimes the new subject appears twice in the formula.
You need to first manipulate the letters so that it only appears once.

Make a the subject of $4a + 2b = 2(a - b)$.

$4a - 2b = 2(a + b)$

$4a - 2b = 2a + 2b$ [Multiply out brackets]

$4a = 2a + 4b$ [Add 2b]

$2a = 4b$ [Subtract 2a]

$a = 2b$ [Divide by 2]

F1 Make n the subject in each of these.

(a) $21f = 2n + 5n$ (b) $n + 8s = 3n$ (c) $a - 2n = n$ (d) $2n = 3(n - e)$

F2 Make f the subject of each of these.

(a) $8f = 5(f + h)$ (b) $3(f + u) = 5(f - u)$

(c) $2(2f + k) = 3(k - f)$ (d) $2(f - t) = 3(2t - f)$

F3 Copy and complete this working to make k the subject of $4 = \dfrac{k + a}{k}$.

$4 = \dfrac{k + a}{k}$

$\bullet = k + a$ [Multiply both sides by k]

$\bullet = a$ [Subtract k]

$k = \dfrac{\bullet}{\bullet}$ [Divide by 3]

F4 Make k the subject of each of these.

(a) $5 = \dfrac{k + 2l}{k}$ (b) $2 = \dfrac{h - k}{k}$ (c) $1 = \dfrac{3k + d}{4k}$ (d) $3 = \dfrac{4p + 3k}{2k}$

F5 By first multiplying out the brackets, make w the subject of the formula $2w + 7 = 5(w + b)$.

F6 By first multiplying both sides by $(k + 1)$, make k the subject of $2 = \dfrac{5w + 3k}{k + 1}$.

☒ **F7** Make a the subject of the formula $6(a + 2b) = 4a + 7$. OCR

G Forming and changing

Find a formula for the perimeter, P, of a rectangle given its area, A, and the length, l, of one side.

First jot down what you know.
Draw a sketch if it helps.

We know the area and one of the sides.

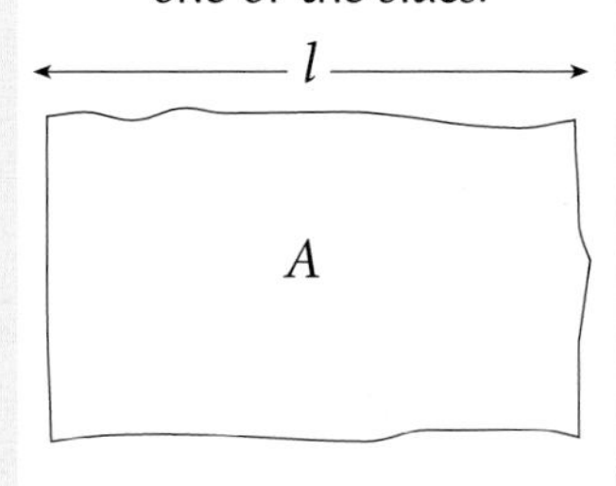

Can you work out anything else from what you are given?
Mark it on the sketch.

Since you get the area of a rectangle by multiplying two of the sides, the unknown side must be equal to $\frac{A}{l}$.

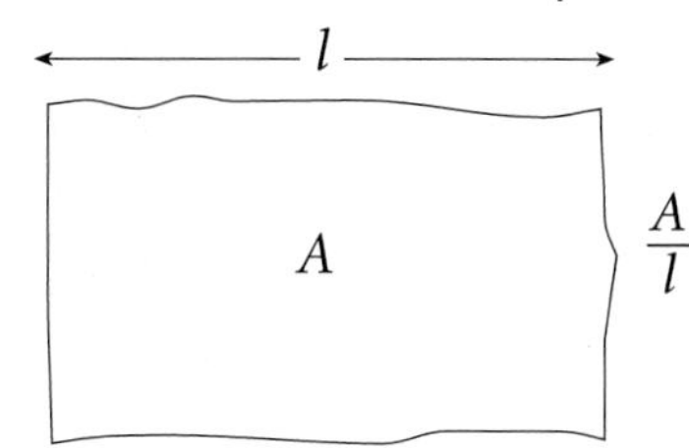

Can you now work out what you need?
Simplify your answer if possible.

We can see that the perimeter is

$$\frac{A}{l} + \frac{A}{l} + l + l$$

$$= 2\left(\frac{A}{l} + l\right)$$

G1 This rectangle has sides $2x$ cm and $3x$ cm long.

(a) Show that the area, A cm^2, is given by the formula $A = 6x^2$.

(b) Rearrange this formula to make x the subject.

(c) Use the rearranged formula to work out the length of the sides when $A = 96$.

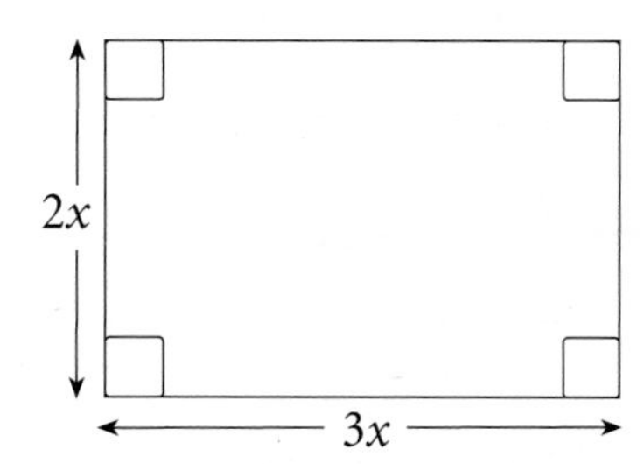

G2

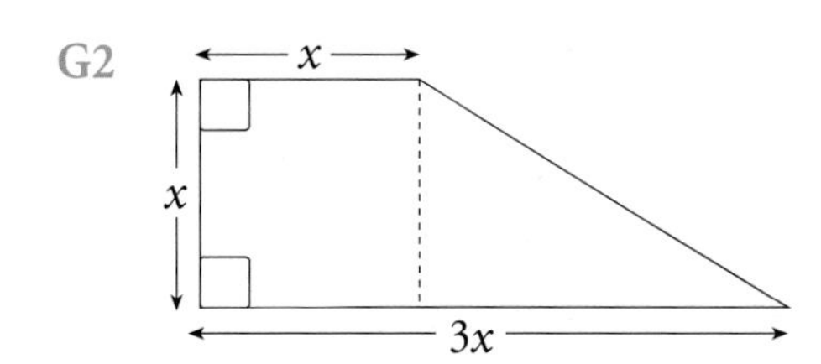

The diagram shows a trapezium.

(a) Show that the area, A, of the trapezium is given by $A = 2x^2$.

(b) Rearrange this formula to make x the subject.

(c) Find the value of x for a trapezium of area 20 cm^2.

G3 This doorway is formed by a semi-circle on top of a square.

(a) Show that a formula for the perimeter , P, of the doorway can be written $P = \pi r + 6r$.

(b) Make r the subject of this formula.

(c) What is the height of a doorway with a perimeter of 10 metres?

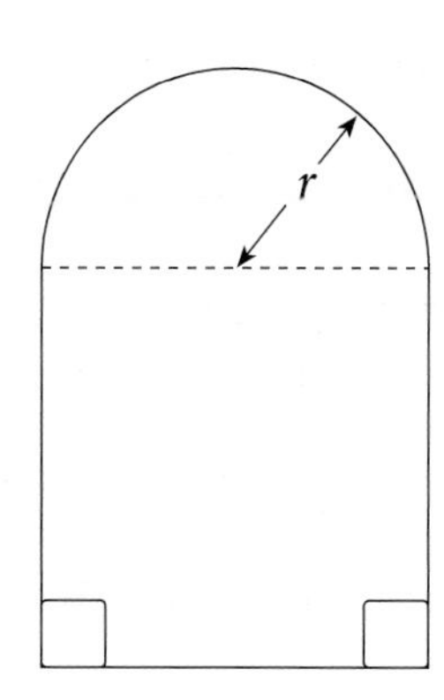

G4 This box is a cuboid, with edges of lengths a, $2a$ and b.

(a) Show that the surface area, A, of the box is given by the formula $A = 4a^2 + 6ab$.

(b) Rearrange this formula to make b the subject.

(c) Work out the value of b for a box with surface area 100 and $a = 2$.

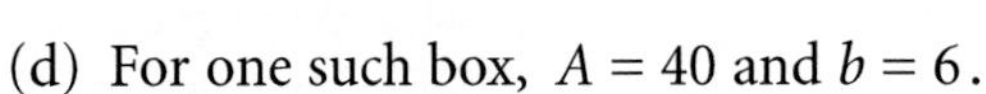

(d) For one such box, $A = 40$ and $b = 6$.

(i) Show that $a^2 + 9a - 10 = 0$.

(ii) Solve the equation and thus write down the dimensions of this box.

a

2a

b

G5 The diagram shows a cuboid.

The end of the cuboid is a square of side x centimetres.

The length of the cuboid is y centimetres.

The surface area of the cuboid is $80\,\text{cm}^2$.

Show that $y = \dfrac{40 - x^2}{2x}$.

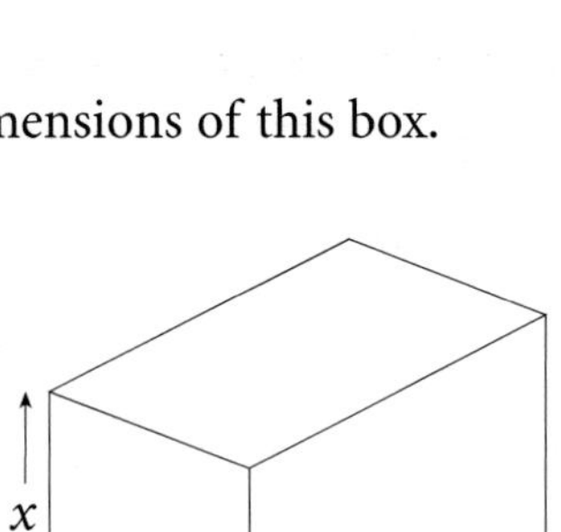

AQA 2003 Specimen

H *Many letters*

Many formulas involve several letters. When rearranging these formulas, you can usually treat several letters as a single item.

Make r the subject of $V = 12\pi r^2 h$.

$$V = 12\pi r^2 h$$

$$\frac{V}{12\pi h} = r^2 \qquad \text{[Divide by } 12\pi h\text{]}$$

$$\sqrt{\frac{V}{12\pi h}} = r \qquad \text{[Take square root]}$$

H1 Make r the subject of $C = 2\pi r$.

H2 Make l the subject of $A = \pi r^2 + \pi rl$.

H3 Make the bold letter the subject in each of these formulas.

(a) $A = \dfrac{\pi \boldsymbol{d}^2}{4}$ (b) $V = \dfrac{\pi \boldsymbol{r}^2 h}{3}$ (c) $A = 2\boldsymbol{p}r + \pi r^2$

(d) $H = 2\pi a^2 + 2\pi \boldsymbol{b}^2$ (e) $p = 4abh - 3\pi \boldsymbol{j}$ (f) $3h = \dfrac{\boldsymbol{b}^2}{2\pi a}$

H4 Rearrange the formula $A = 2\pi rh + \pi r^2$ to make h the subject. OCR

Test yourself

T1 A formula is given as $t = 7p - 50$.
Rearrange the formula to make p the subject. AQA(NEAB) 1998

☒ **T2** A formula which connects the number of sides and the sum of the angles of a polygon is $S = 180n - 360$.
Rearrange the formula to make n the subject. OCR

T3 Rearrange each of these formulas so that the bold letter is the subject.

(a) $g = 2 + 6\mathbf{j}$ (b) $m = 2(3 - \mathbf{n})$ (c) $t = 12 - 3\mathbf{f}$ (d) $y + 2\mathbf{z} = 10$

(e) $f = 2(3\mathbf{g} - 4)$ (f) $r = 3\mathbf{s} - 2$ (g) $w = \dfrac{8 + 2\mathbf{d}}{3}$ (h) $f = \dfrac{\mathbf{a}}{3} - 4$

T4 Make y the subject of the formula $x = 40 - 8y$. AQA 1999

☒ **T5** Make p the subject of the formula $\dfrac{4(p + 3)}{7} = r$. AQA 2000

T6 You are given that $v = u + at$. AQA 1999

(a) Make t the subject of this formula.

(b) Find the value of t when $a = ^{-}10$, $u = 12$ and $v = ^{-}18$.

☒ **T7** Rearrange this formula to make r the subject, $L = 2\pi r + 6$. OCR

T8 Rearrange each of these formulas so that the bold letter is the subject.

(a) $h = s + a\mathbf{k}$ (b) $q = 2(e - \mathbf{f})$ (c) $t = 2r - w\mathbf{d}$ (d) $ax + b\mathbf{z} = cy$

(e) $e = j(3\mathbf{w} - t)$ (f) $R = ps - fg$ (g) $q = \dfrac{u + a\mathbf{v}}{g}$ (h) $j = \dfrac{\mathbf{k}}{l} - h$

T9 Make v the subject of the formula $E = \frac{1}{2}mv^2$. AQA(SEG) 2000

☒ **T10** Make x the subject of the formula $y = \dfrac{x^2 + 4}{5}$. Edexcel

T11 Make x the subject of each of these formulas.

(a) $y = x^2 + 9$ (b) $y^2 = x^2 - a^2$ (c) $y = 4(x^2 - 2)$

(d) $y^2 + x^2 = 100$ (e) $y = \dfrac{x^2 - a^2}{b^2}$ (f) $y = \dfrac{a^2 - x^2}{100}$

T12 Make r the subject of each of these formulas.

(a) $3(a - r) = 2(r + a)$ (b) $20a - r = 4r + 3$ (c) $3 = \dfrac{4b + r}{2r - 10}$

51 *Roots*

You will revise

- squares and square roots
- cubes and cube roots
- positive indices

This work will help you evaluate expressions that use fractional indices.

A *Squares and cubes*

- 6 squared (or the square of 6) $= 6^2 = 6 \times 6 = 36$ so 36 is a **square** number.
- 2 cubed (or the cube of 2) $= 2^3 = 2 \times 2 \times 2 = 8$ so 8 is a **cube** (or cubic) number.

A1 Which of the following numbers are square numbers?

8, 4, 121, 80, 49, 13, 1

A2 (a) Find a square number between 160 and 170.

(b) Is there a square number between 170 and 180?

A3 Which of the following numbers are cube numbers?

9, 16, 27, 1, 30, 64, 1000

A4 Find a cube number between 100 and 200.

A5 Evaluate these.

(a) 3 squared (b) The cube of 4 (c) 5^2 (d) 3^3

A6 Find two square numbers that add to make 29.

A7 Hannah makes patchwork quilts.
She has 150 identical square pieces.

She wants to use these pieces to make
the largest **square** quilt she can.

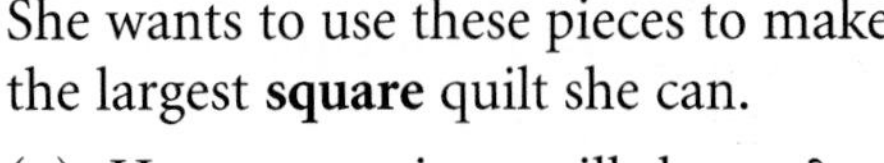

(a) How many pieces will she use?

(b) If each piece is 20 cm by 20 cm, how long will each edge of the quilt be?

A8 125 sugar cubes fit exactly into a cube-shaped box.
How many sugar cubes touch the bottom of the box?

A9 (a) Copy and complete this 'number spiral' using numbers from 1 to 100.

(b) Circle all the square numbers.
What do you notice?
Can you explain this?

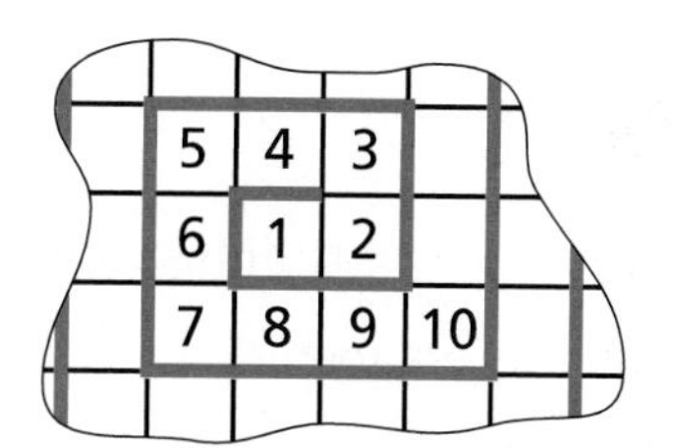

B *Square and cube roots*

B1 Evaluate these.

(a) $(^{-}5)^2$ (b) 5^2 (c) $(^{-}10)^2$ (d) 2^3 (e) $(^{-}2)^3$

3 squared is $3^2 = 3 \times 3 = 9$ so the **positive square root** of 9 is 3.

($^{-}3$) squared is $(^{-}3)^2 = {^{-}3} \times {^{-}3} = 9$ so the **negative square root** of 9 is $^{-}3$.

B2 (a) Write down the positive square root of 100.

(b) Write down the negative square root of 100.

B3 What is the negative square root of 36?

B4 Find two numbers that fit each statement.

(a) $■^2 = 49$ (b) $■^2 = 4$ (c) $■^2 = 1$ (d) $■^2 = 81$

B5 What are the square roots of 121?

6 cubed is $6^3 = 6 \times 6 \times 6 = 216$ so the **cube root** of 216 is 6.

($^{-}2$) cubed is $(^{-}2)^3 = {^{-}2} \times {^{-}2} \times {^{-}2} = {^{-}8}$ so the **cube root** of $^{-}8$ is $^{-}2$.

B6 Find the cube root of these.

(a) 8 (b) 27 (c) 1 (d) 64 (e) $^{-}27$

B7 (a) A cube has a volume of 125 cm³.
What is the length of one edge?

(b) What is the cube root of 125?

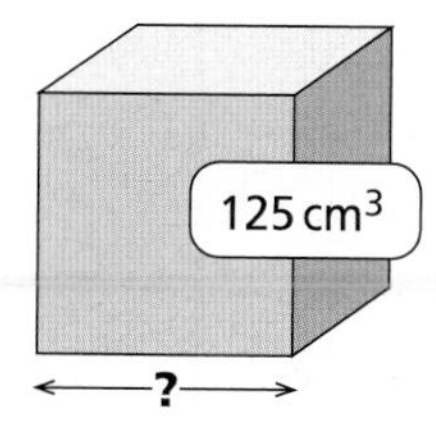

B8 Solve these equations.

(a) $n^2 = 16$ (b) $m^2 = 144$ (c) $x^3 = 216$

(d) $2n^2 = 32$ (e) $5k^3 = 40$ (f) $4n^3 = 4$

*B9 Explain why a number cannot have more than **one** cube root.

C *Graphs*

TG

Part of the graph of $y = x^2$ is shown below.

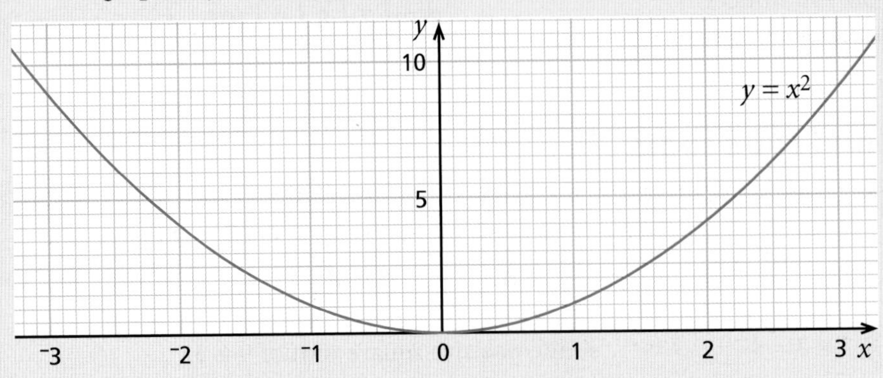

Part of the graph of $y = x^3$ is shown below.

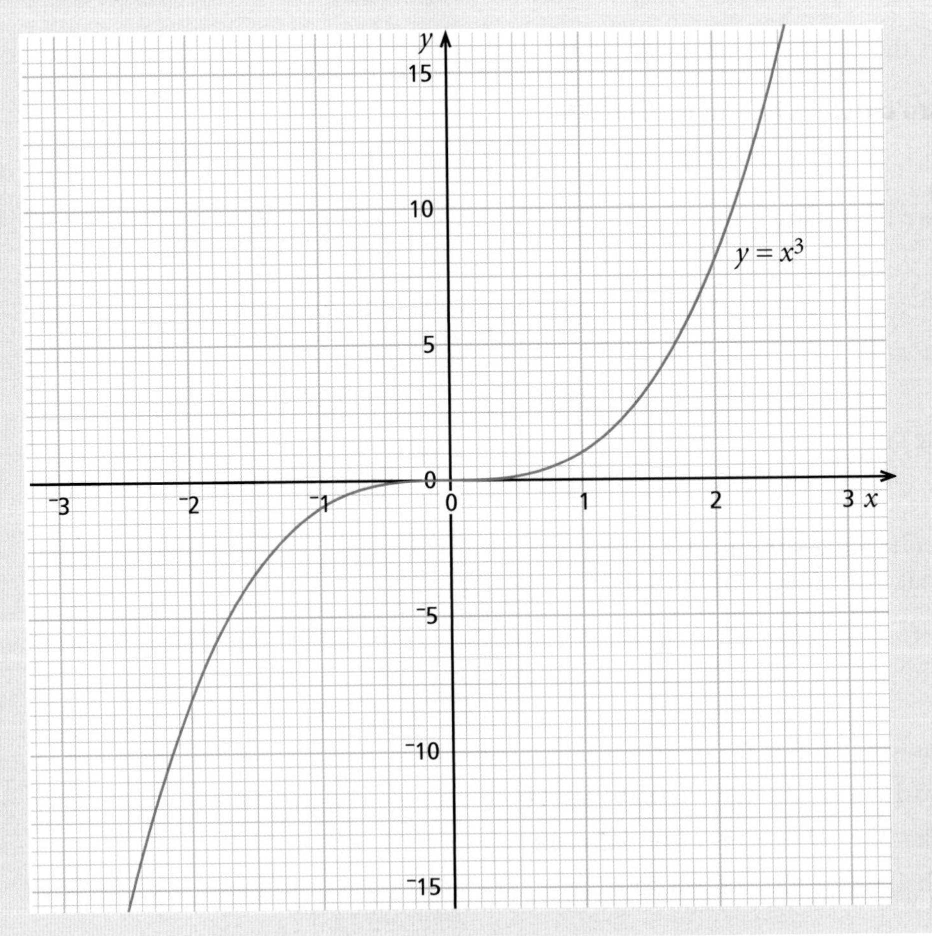

C1 (a) Use the first graph to estimate these.

(i) The square of 2.5 (ii) The square of $^{-}1.4$ (iii) $(^{-}2.8)^2$

(b) Check your results to (a) with a calculator.

C2 (a) Use the graph to estimate these.

(i) The positive square root of 3 (ii) The negative square root of 7

(b) Check your results to (a) by using the square root key on a calculator.

C3 (a) Use the graph to estimate the positive square root of 10.

(b) Use a calculator to find the positive square root of 10 correct to 2 d.p.

(c) What is the negative square root of 10 correct to 2 d.p.?

C4 (a) Use the second graph to estimate these.

(i) The cube of 1.5 (ii) $(^{-}1.8)^3$ (iii) $(2.3)^3$

(b) Check your results to (a) with a calculator.

C5 Use the graph to estimate the cube root of these.

(a) 10 (b) $^{-}10$ (c) 5 (d) $^{-}5$ (e) 7.5

D *Cube roots on a calculator*

The cube root of 20 can be written as $\sqrt[3]{20}$.

Your calculator may have a $\boxed{\sqrt[3]{}}$ key which is the cube root key.

D1 Evaluate these. (a) $\sqrt[3]{2197}$ (b) $\sqrt[3]{^{-}2744}$ (c) $\sqrt[3]{3.375}$

D2 Check your results to C5 by using the cube root key on a calculator.

D3 Use the appropriate graph to estimate the solution to $x^3 = 3$, correct to 1 d.p.
Use your calculator to find the solution correct to 3 d.p.

D4 Evaluate these, correct to 2 d.p.

(a) $\sqrt[3]{30}$ (b) $\sqrt[3]{14 + 28}$ (c) $\sqrt[3]{\frac{25}{3}}$ (d) $\sqrt[3]{\frac{20}{\pi}}$

D5 A formula to find the radius of a sphere is

$$r = \sqrt[3]{\frac{0.75V}{\pi}}$$

where r is the radius and V is the volume.

(a) When $V = 800$, what is the value of r correct to 2 d.p?

(b) A ball uses 1000 cm³ of rubber.
What is the radius of the ball, correct to the nearest 0.1 cm?

E *Fractional indices and roots*

In an expression like 2^5, the raised number '5' is called the **index**.

The value of 2^5 is $2 \times 2 \times 2 \times 2 \times 2 = 32$.

We say 2^5 as 'two to the **power** of five'.

E1 What is the value of 'three to the power of four'?

E2 Write these using index notation.

(a) $2 \times 2 \times 2 \times 2$ (b) $3 \times 3 \times 3$ (c) $5 \times 5 \times 5 \times 5 \times 5 \times 5 \times 5$

E3 Evaluate these. (a) 2^5 (b) 1^6 (c) 10^4 (d) 2^7

E4 Find the missing number in each statement.

(a) $2^3 \times 2^4 = 2^{\blacksquare}$ (b) $3^2 \times 3^8 = 3^{\blacksquare}$ (c) $5 \times 5^5 = 5^{\blacksquare}$

(d) $7^{\blacksquare} \times 7^2 = 7^5$ (e) $6 \times 6^{\blacksquare} = 6^3$ (f) $9^{\blacksquare} \times 9^7 = 9^{12}$

E5 Find the missing number in each statement.

(a) $2^3 \times 2^3 \times 2^3 = 2^{\blacksquare}$ (b) $3^2 \times 3^3 \times 3^{\blacksquare} = 3^{10}$ (c) $11 \times 11^{\blacksquare} \times 11^7 = 11^{11}$

E6 Evaluate these. (a) 2^1 (b) 5^1 (c) 17^1 (d) 239^1

Fractional indices and roots

Using the rules to multiply powers $8^{\frac{1}{3}} \times 8^{\frac{1}{3}} \times 8^{\frac{1}{3}} = 8^{(\frac{1}{3} + \frac{1}{3} + \frac{1}{3})}$

$= 8^1$

$= 8$

It is also true that $2 \times 2 \times 2 = 8$

So $8^{\frac{1}{3}} = 2$ (and $8^{\frac{1}{3}} = \sqrt[3]{8}$)

E7 (a) Copy and complete $9^{\frac{1}{2}} \times 9^{\frac{1}{2}} = 9^{\blacksquare}$.

(b) Hence evaluate $9^{\frac{1}{2}}$.

E8 (a) Copy and complete $25^{\frac{1}{2}} \times 25^{\frac{1}{2}} = 25^{\blacksquare}$.

(b) Hence evaluate $25^{\frac{1}{2}}$.

E9 Which of these expressions is equivalent to $100^{\frac{1}{2}}$?

$\frac{100}{2}$ $\sqrt[3]{100}$ $\sqrt{100}$ $\frac{1}{2}$ of 100

E10 (a) Copy and complete $27^{\frac{1}{3}} \times 27^{\frac{1}{3}} \times 27^{\frac{1}{3}} = 27^{\blacksquare}$.

(b) Hence evaluate $27^{\frac{1}{3}}$.

E11 Evaluate these. (a) $36^{\frac{1}{2}}$ (b) $81^{\frac{1}{2}}$ (c) $64^{\frac{1}{3}}$ (d) $1^{\frac{1}{3}}$

E12 (a) Copy and complete: $8^{\frac{2}{3}} \times 8^{\frac{2}{3}} \times 8^{\frac{2}{3}} = 8^{■} = ■$.
(b) Hence evaluate $8^{\frac{2}{3}}$.

E13 (a) Copy and complete: $16^{\frac{1}{4}} \times 16^{\frac{1}{4}} \times 16^{\frac{1}{4}} \times 16^{\frac{1}{4}} = 16^{■}$.
(b) Hence evaluate $16^{\frac{1}{4}}$.

Test yourself

T1 Work these out. (a) The cube of 5 (b) 2^6 AQA(NEAB) 1998

T2 Copy and complete this number pattern.

$1^3 = 1 = 1^2$
$1^3 + 2^3 = 9 = 3^2$
$1^3 + 2^3 + 3^3 = ... = ...$
$1^3 + 2^3 + 3^3 + 4^3 = ... = ...$
.... = ... = ...

T3 (a) Calculate the cube of 3.7. (b) Calculate the square root of 8.41. Edexcel

T4 Evaluate the following, rounding your answer to three significant figures.

$$\sqrt[3]{\frac{300}{4\pi}}$$

OCR

T5

2, 9, 18, 25, 30, 45, 81, 88

Which of the numbers in the box are square numbers?

T6 (a) This is a number machine.
You start with 36.
What number will go in the answer box?

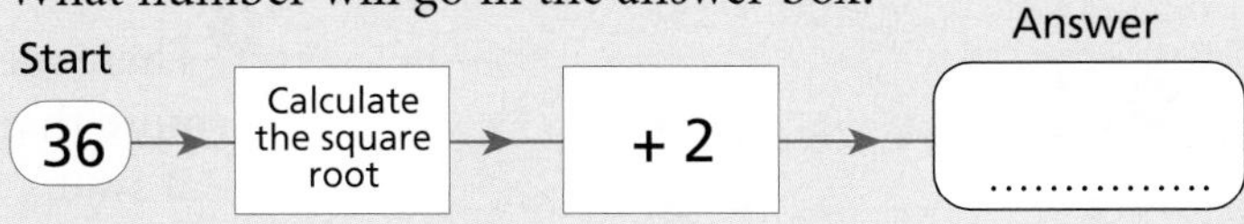

(b) This is a different number machine.
You start with 27.
What number will go in the answer box?

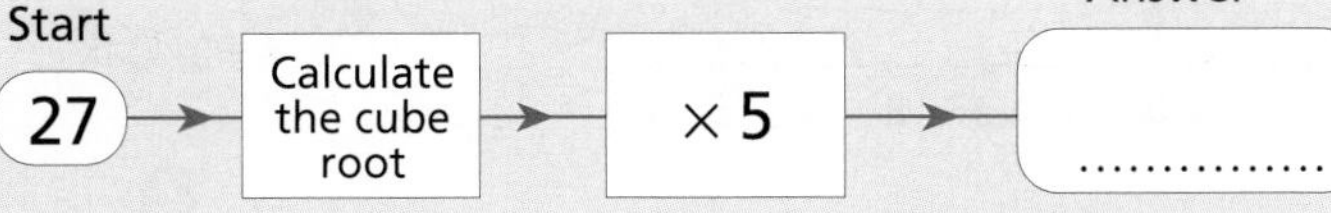

AQA 2000

T7 Evaluate $16^{\frac{1}{2}}$. Edexcel

52 Graphs and inequalities

You should know

- how to draw the graph of a straight line given its equation
- that < stands for 'is less than' and ≤ stands for 'is less than or equal to'
- that > stands for 'is greater than' and ≥ stands for 'is greater than or equal to'

This work will help you interpret inequalities as regions on graphs

A *Animal magic*

Some ducks and swans share a pond in a park.
There are never more than five of each.

This point represents 2 ducks and 1 swan.

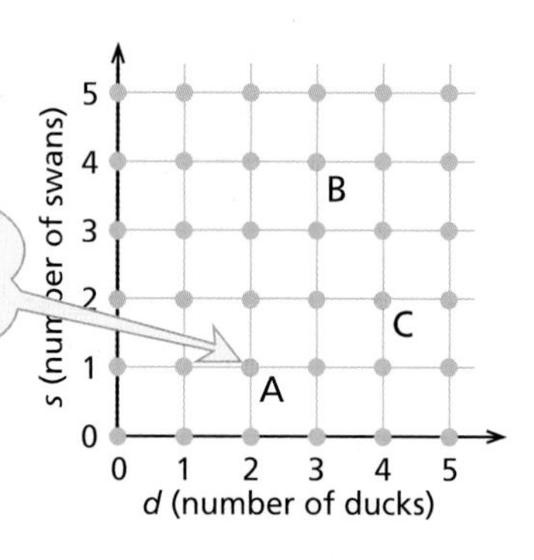

Match up each set of orange points with two statements.

1

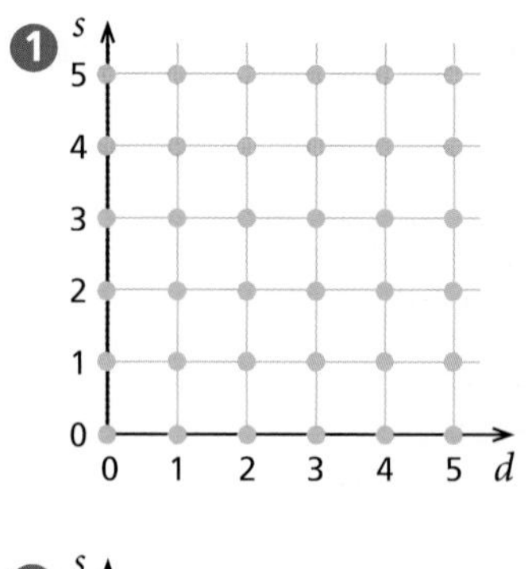

2

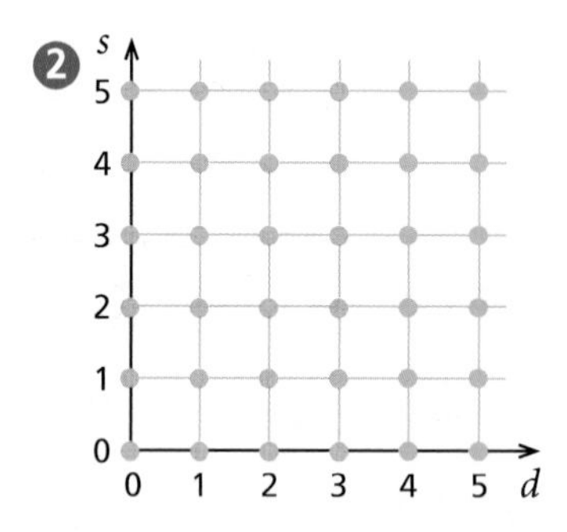

3

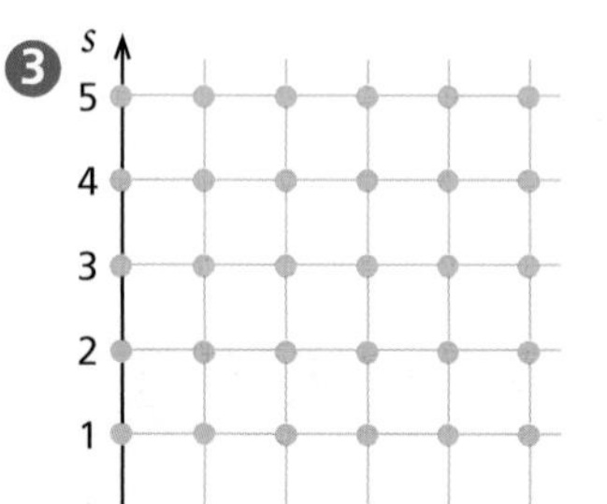

4

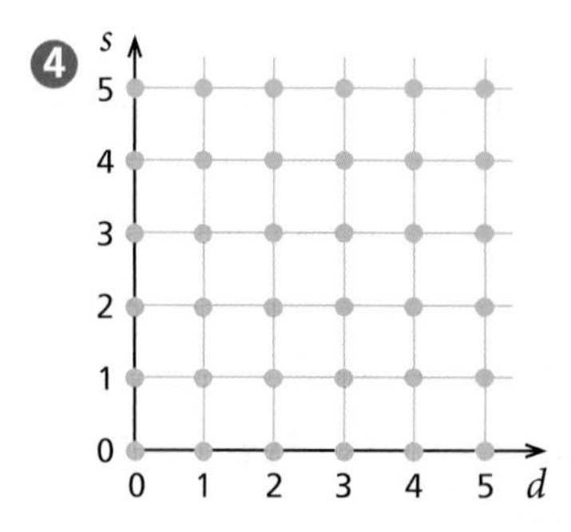

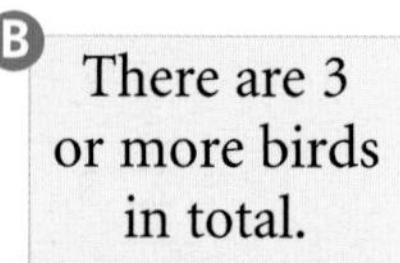

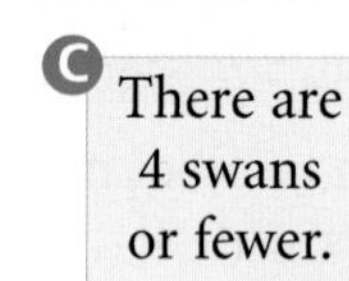

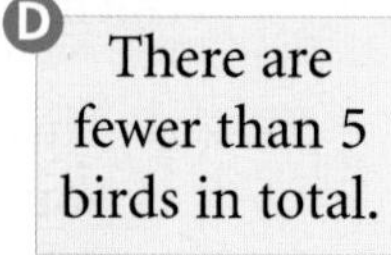

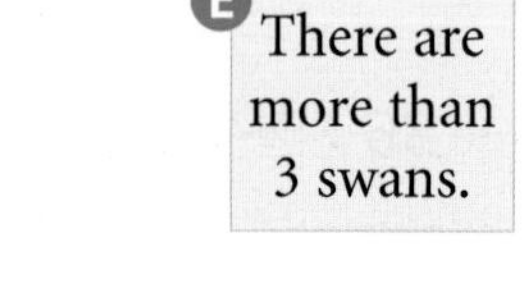

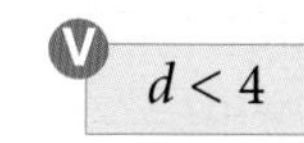

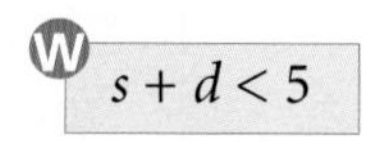

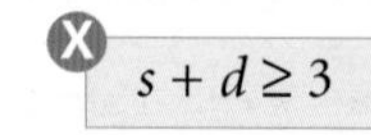

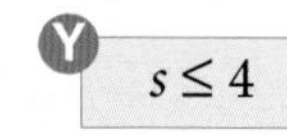

In a game park, hippos and rhinos share the same enclosure.
There are never more than six of each kind of animal.

A1 Which two statements below fit the set of orange points on the right.

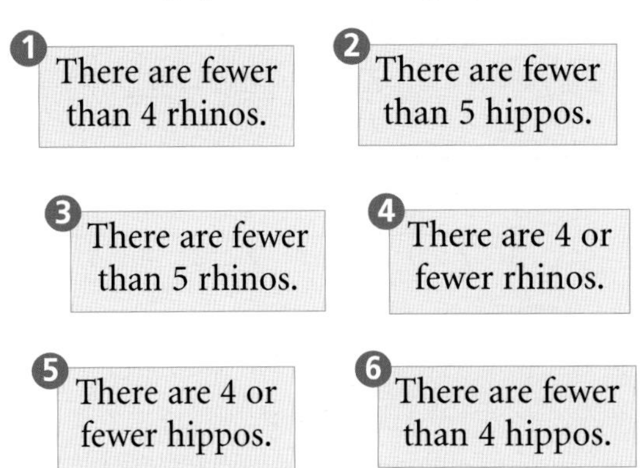

1. There are fewer than 4 rhinos.
2. There are fewer than 5 hippos.
3. There are fewer than 5 rhinos.
4. There are 4 or fewer rhinos.
5. There are 4 or fewer hippos.
6. There are fewer than 4 hippos.

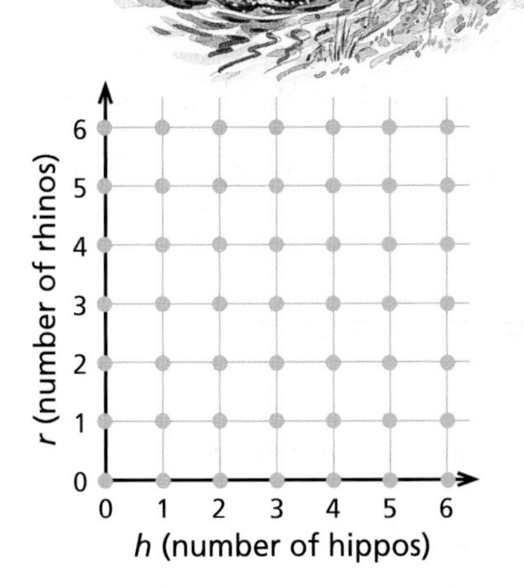

A2 Match each set of orange points below to one of the inequalities.

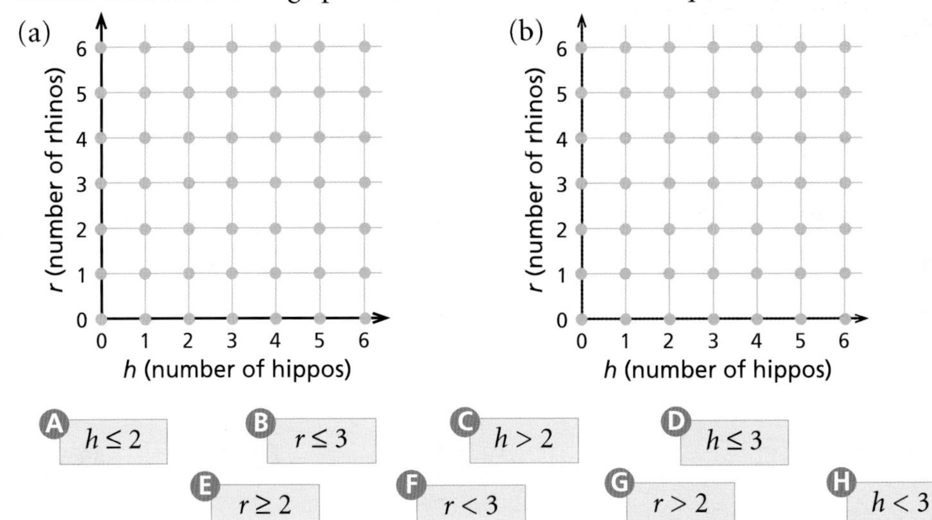

A: $h \leq 2$ B: $r \leq 3$ C: $h > 2$ D: $h \leq 3$

E: $r \geq 2$ F: $r < 3$ G: $r > 2$ H: $h < 3$

A3 Hippos and rhinos live quite happily in a new enclosure as long as the total number of animals is 6 or less.

(a) Which of these inequalities fits this statement?

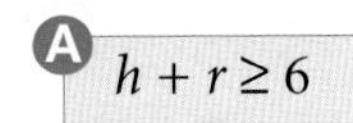
A: $h + r \geq 6$

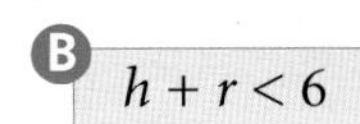
B: $h + r < 6$

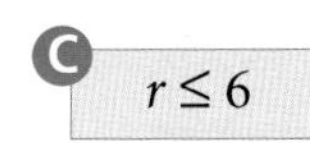
C: $r \leq 6$

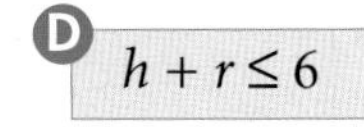
D: $h + r \leq 6$

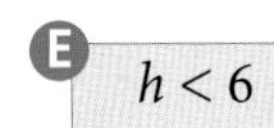
E: $h < 6$

(b) Draw a diagram for the hippos and the rhinos and colour the points that fit this statement.

A4 Draw diagrams for these inequalities in the game park.

(a) $r \leq 3$ (b) $h \geq 2$ (c) $r \geq 1$ (d) $h \leq 5$ (e) $h + r \geq 4$

B *Not just integers*

$x \le 3$?

(2, 0) (0, 5) (4, 1)

(3, 4) (5, 4) (3, 5)

(6, 3) ($^-1$, 6) (3, $^-2$)

($^-2$, $^-1$) (2.5, 2) (3.1, 4.2)

$y \ge 4$?

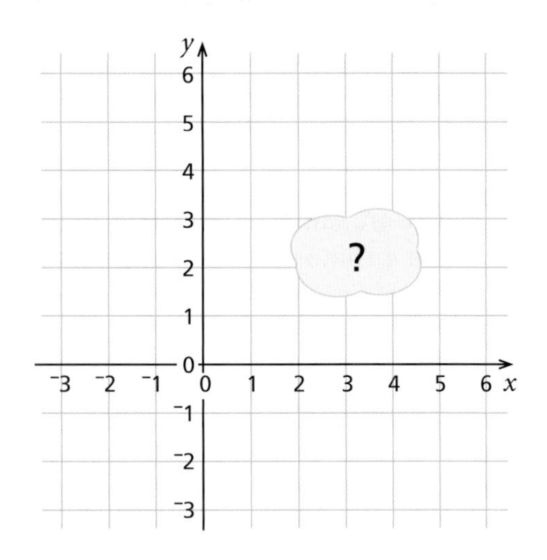

B1 Match each shaded region with one of the inequalities below.

(a)

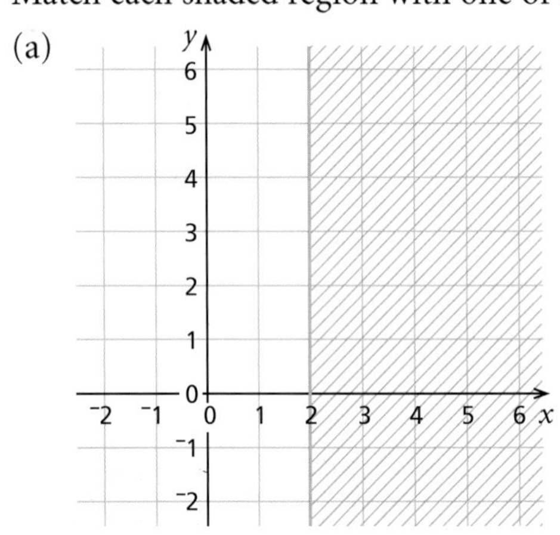

(b)

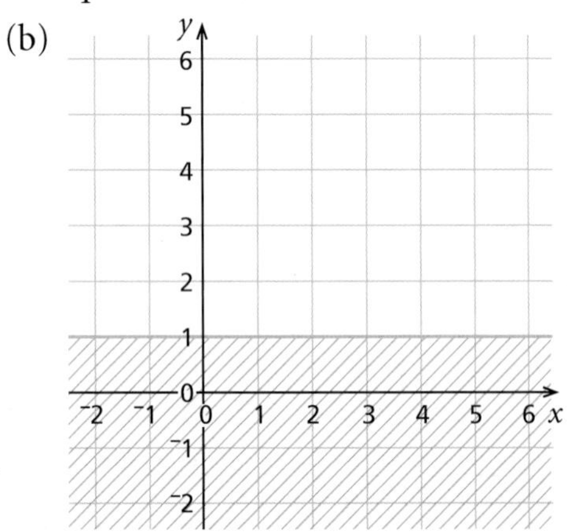

(c)

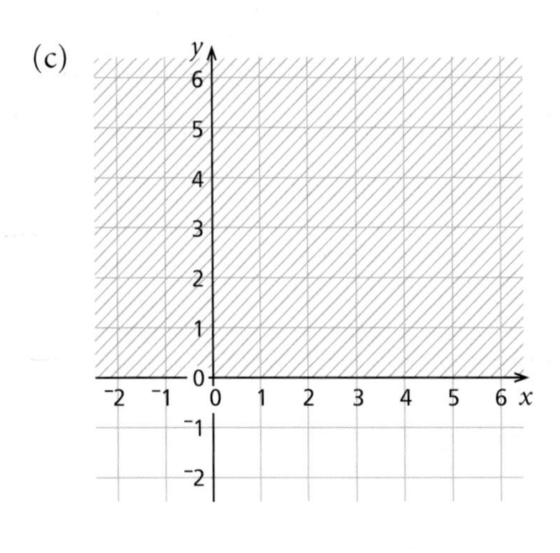

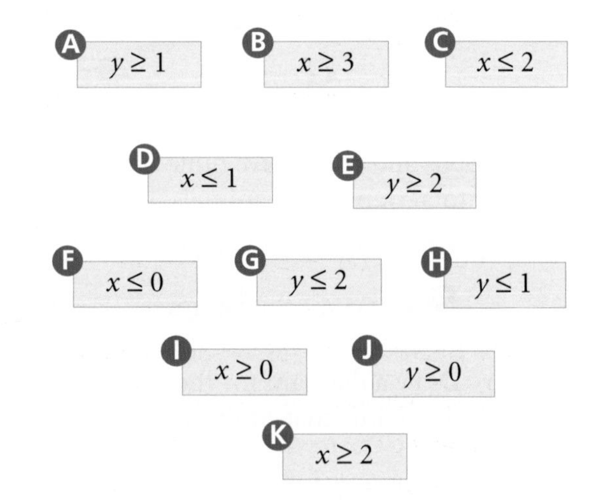

B2 Write an inequality for each shaded region.

(a)

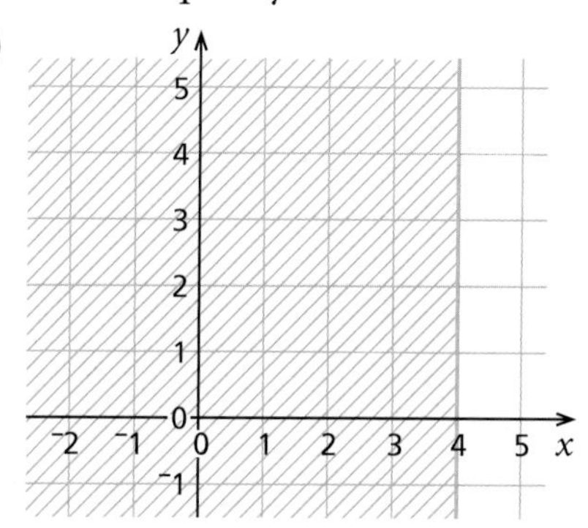

(b)

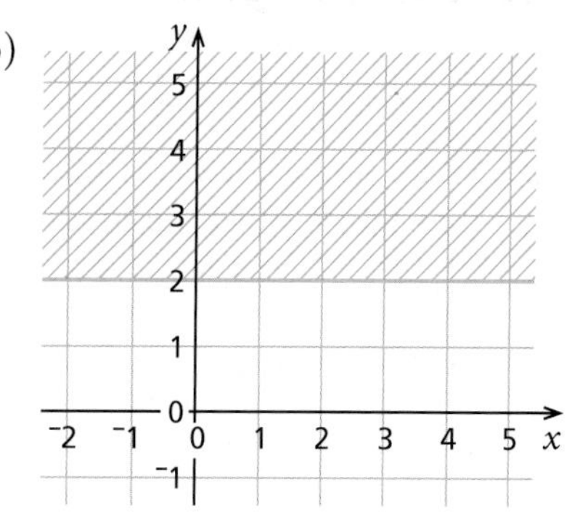

(c)

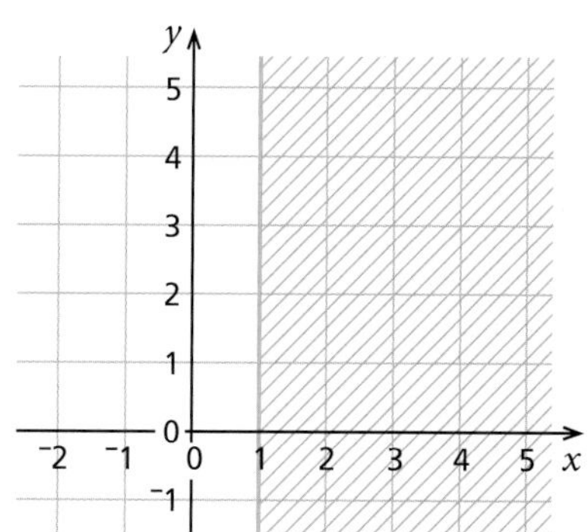

(d)

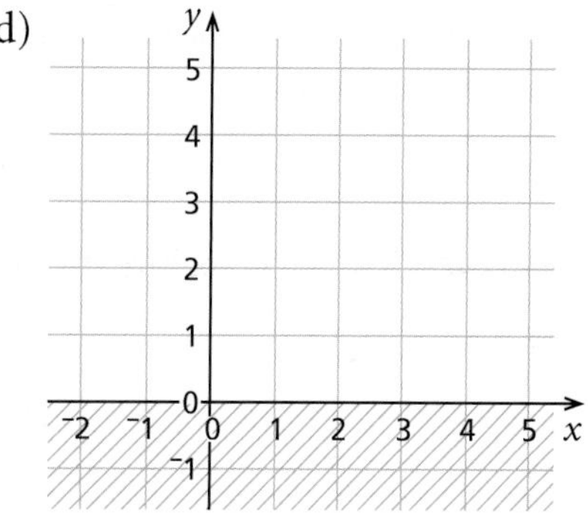

B3 Draw a diagram for the region given by each inequality.

(a) $x \geq 4$ (b) $y \leq 2$ (c) $x \geq 0$ (d) $y \geq {}^{-}1$

B4 Write an inequality for each shaded region.

(a)

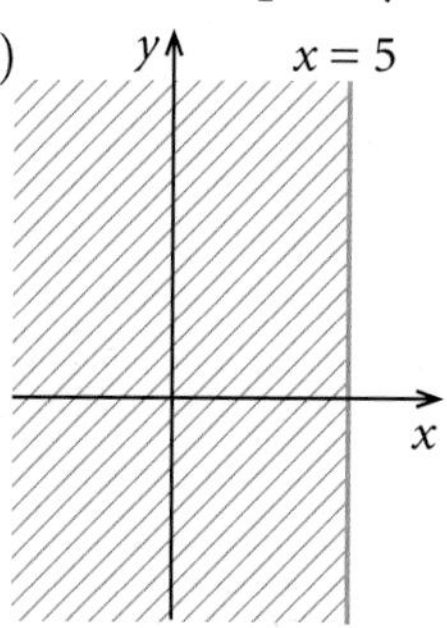

(b)

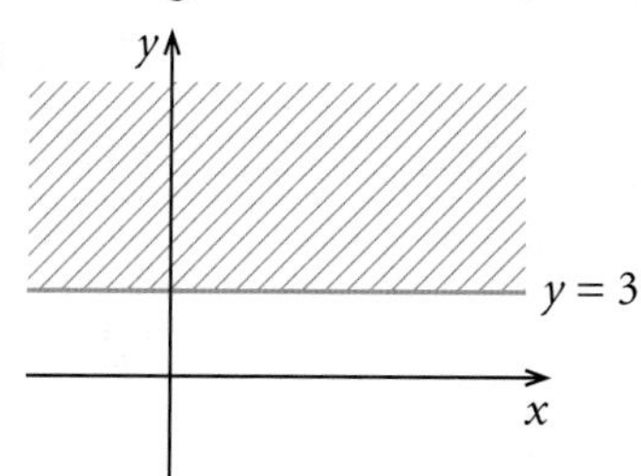

(c)

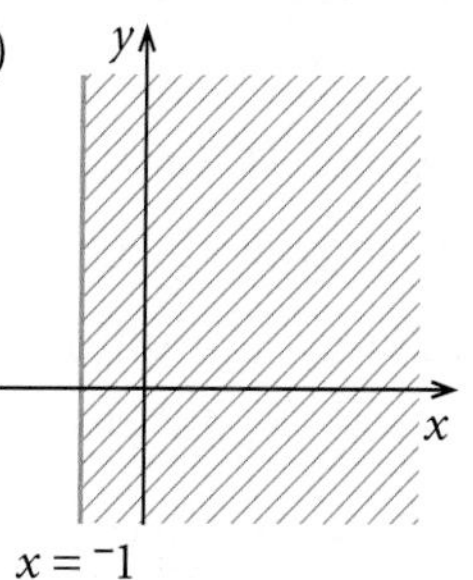

B5 (a) Draw a set of axes, each numbered from 0 to 8.

(b) Draw the line with equation $x = 3$.

(c) Shade the region described by $x \geq 3$.

(d) On the same set of axes, draw the line with equation $y = 5$.

(e) Shade the region described by $y \leq 5$.

(f) Show clearly the region described by both $x \geq 3$ **and** $y \leq 5$.

B6 (a) Which of the four regions A, B, C or D satisfies **both** these inequalities?

$x \leq 2 \qquad y \geq 1$

(b) Write down the coordinates of two points that satisfy both the inequalities above.

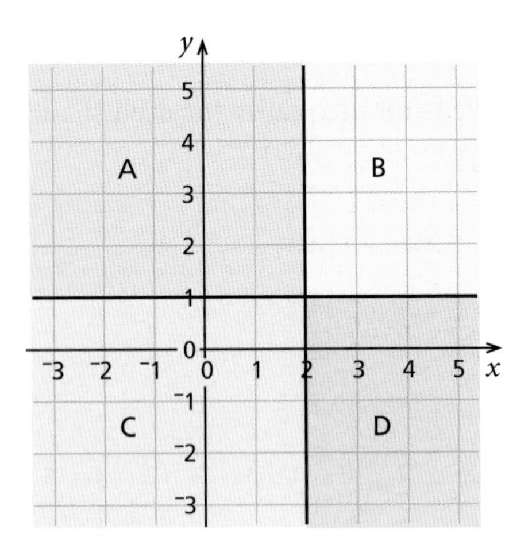

B7 The shaded region below can be defined by four inequalities. One of these is $x \geq 1$.

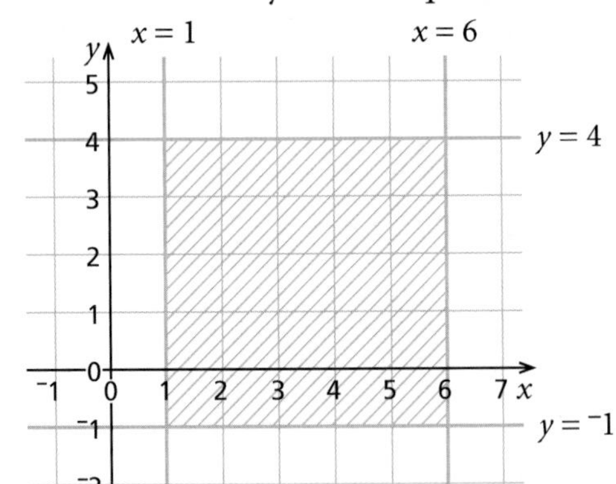

Write down the other three inequalities.

C *Inclined to go further*

TG

Draw the region satisfied by the inequality $y \leq 2x + 1$.

- First draw the boundary line $y = 2x + 1$.
- Choose a point on one side of the line.

  For example, (3, 2)
- Check the inequality for your point.

  $y = 2$ and

  $2x + 1 = 2 \times 3 + 1 = 7$

  As $2 \leq 7$, then $y \leq 2x + 1$ is true for this point.
- Shade the correct region.

  The inequality is true for (3, 2) so shade the region that includes this point.

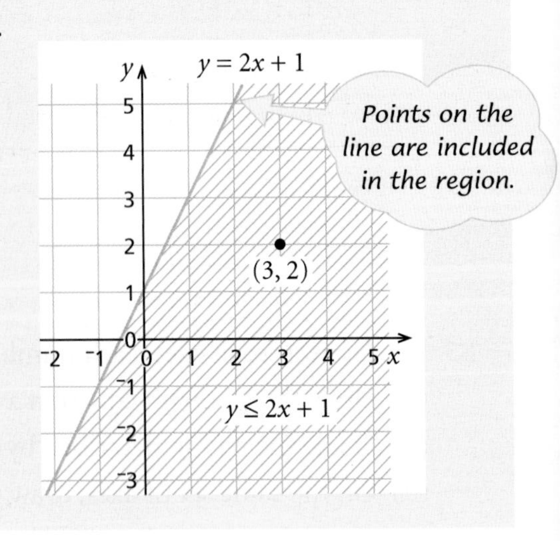

C1 One of these diagrams shows the region defined by $y \geq x + 2$.

Which is it, A or B?
Explain how you decided.

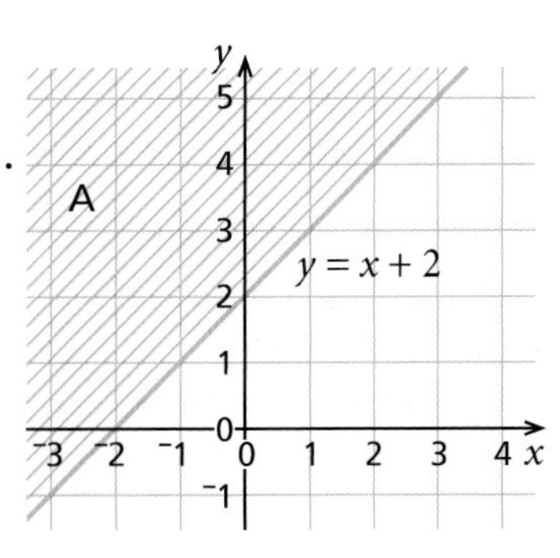

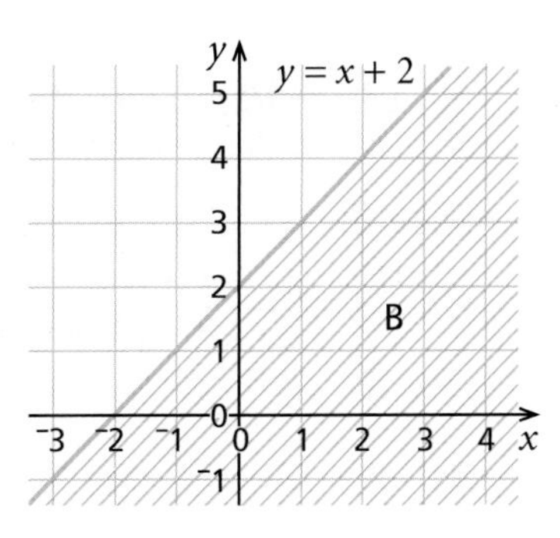

C2 Write an inequality for each shaded region.

(a)

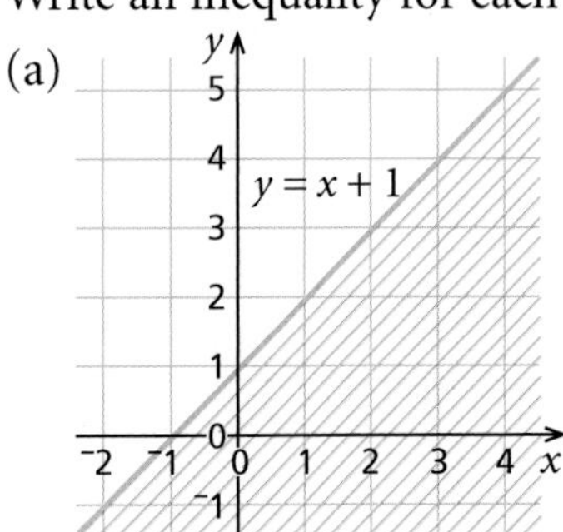

(b)

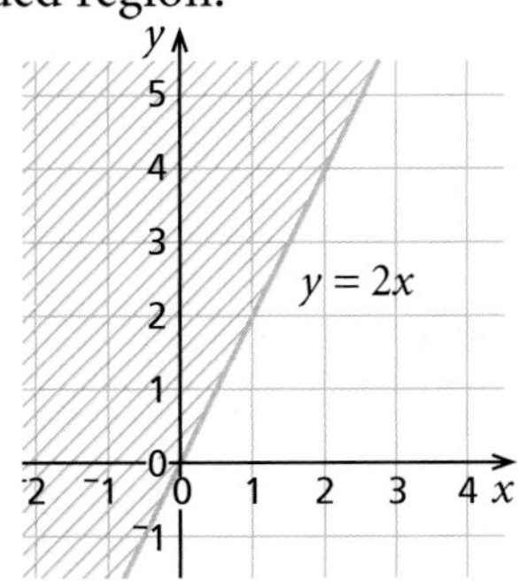

(c)

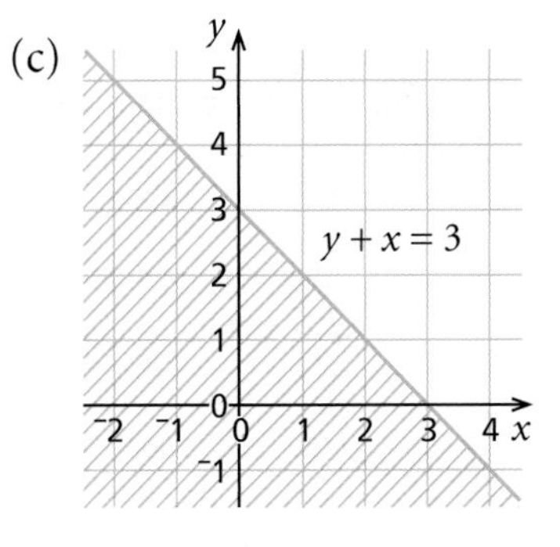

C3 (a) Draw a set of axes and number each axis from $^-2$ to 7.

(b) Draw the line with equation $y = x + 3$.

(c) Shade the region described by $y \geq x + 3$.

(d) Write down the coordinates of two points that satisfy the inequality $y \geq x + 3$.

C4 Draw a diagram for the region given by each inequality.
Number each axis from $^-2$ to 7.

(a) $y \geq x - 1$ (b) $y \leq 3x + 1$ (c) $y \leq x$ (d) $x + y \geq 3$ (e) $y \leq 6 - x$

C5 For each diagram, find the equation of the line and write the inequality for the shaded region.

(a)

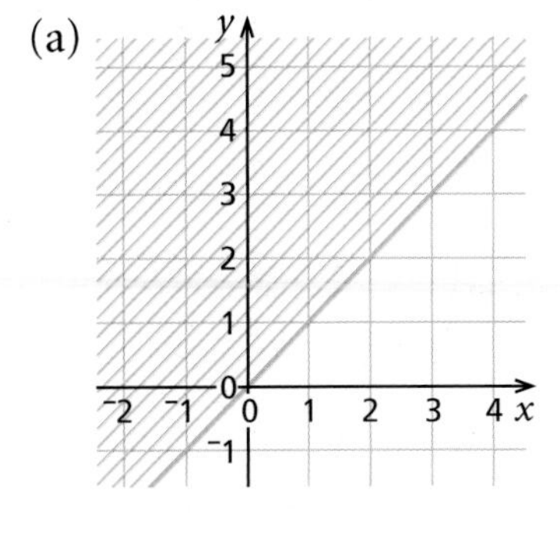

(b)

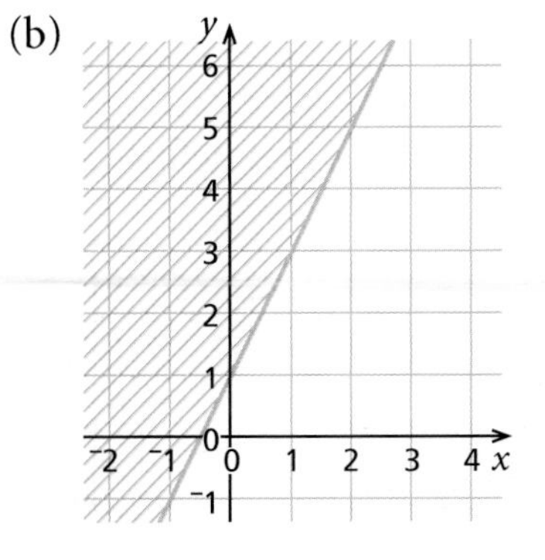

(c)

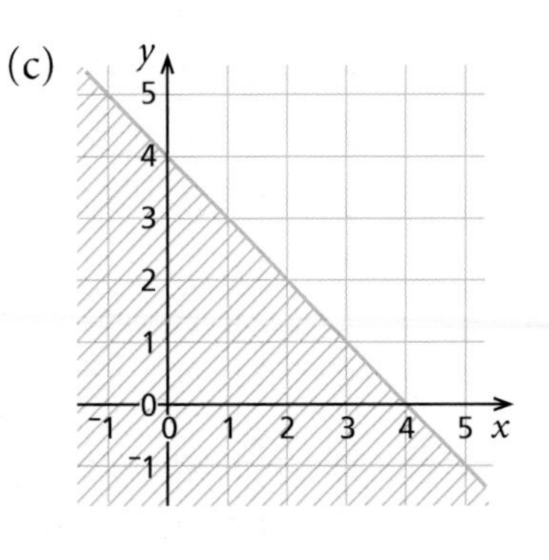

D *Overlapping regions*

TG

Shade the region satisfied by all the inequalities $x \geq 1$ $y \geq 0$ $x + y \leq 4$

- Shade the three different regions on the same set of axes.
- Where the shading overlaps defines the region where **all** the inequalities are satisfied.

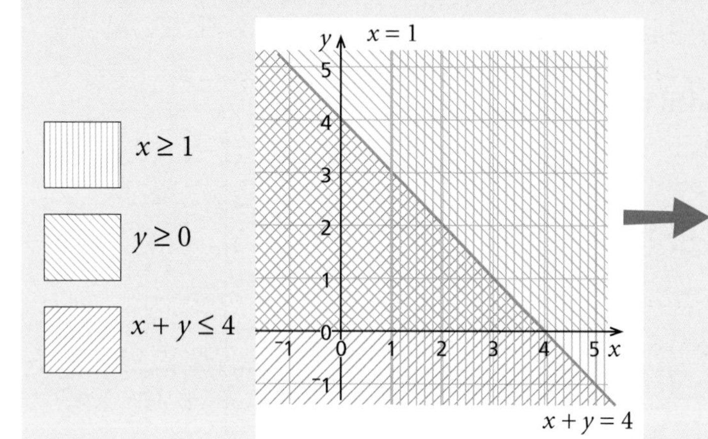

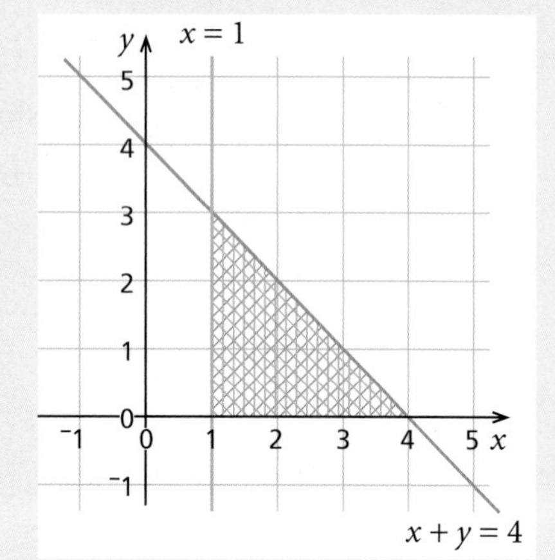

D1

(a) Which region A or B is satisfied by the three inequalities?

$y \leq 6$ $x \geq 0$ $y \geq x + 1$

Write down the coordinates of three points that satisfy **all** these inequalities.

(b) Write down the three inequalities that fully describe the other region.

D2 Write down the three inequalities that define each shaded region.

(a)

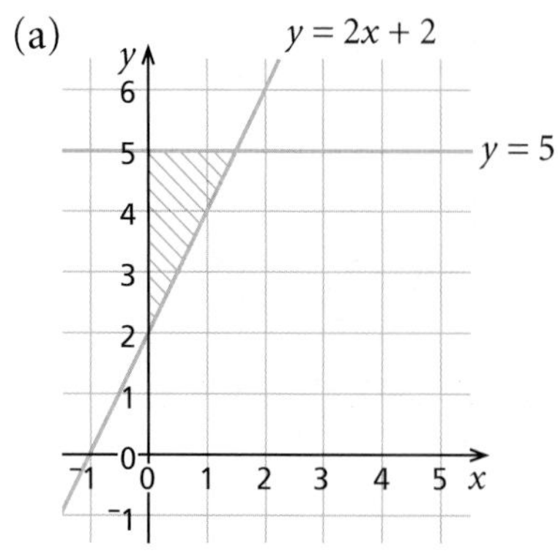

(b)

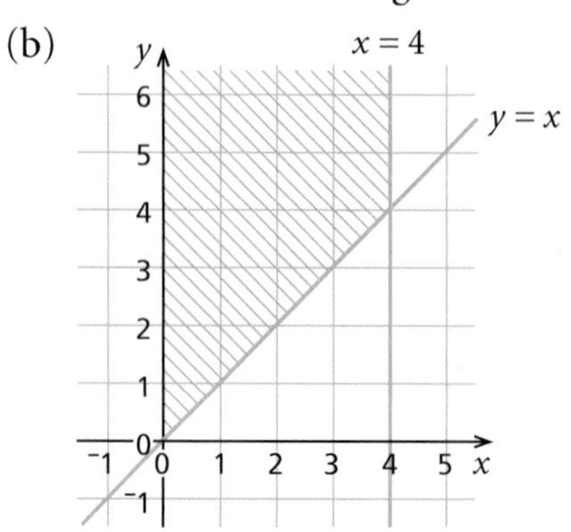

D3 (a) Draw a set of axes, numbered from 0 to 8 on each.
Draw and label the lines with equations $x = 3$, $y = 6$ and $y = x$.

(b) (i) Show clearly the single region that is satisfied by all of these inequalities.

$x \geq 3 \quad y \leq 6 \quad y \leq x$

(ii) Write down the coordinates of two points that satisfy all these inequalities.

D4 (a) Draw a set of axes, numbered from $^-3$ to 6 on each.
Draw and label the line with equation $y = x + 3$.

(b) Show clearly the single region that is satisfied by all of these inequalities.

$x \leq 0 \quad y \geq 0 \quad y \leq x + 3$

Label this region Q.

D5 (a) Draw a set of axes, numbered from $^-3$ to 8 on the x-axis and from 0 to 7 on the y-axis.
On the diagram draw and label the lines $y = 3$ and $x + y = 5$.

(b) Show clearly on the diagram the single region that is satisfied by all of these inequalities.

$x \geq 0, \quad y \geq 3 \quad$ and $\quad x + y \leq 5$

Label this region R.

AQA(SEG) 1998

D6 The shaded region can be defined by three inequalities.
One of these is $y \geq 2$.

Write down the other two inequalities.

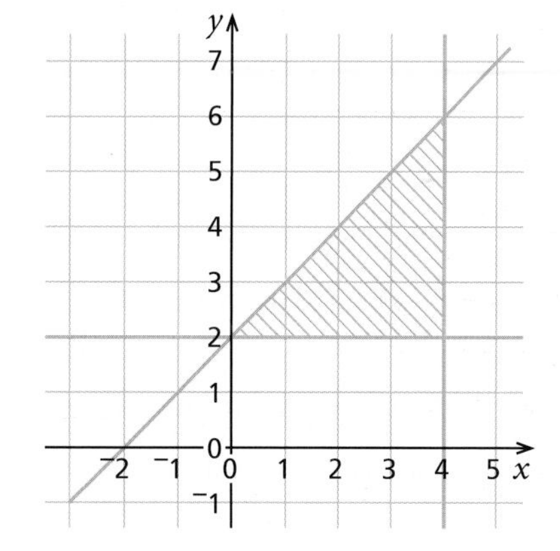

D7 Write down the three inequalities that define each region.

(a)

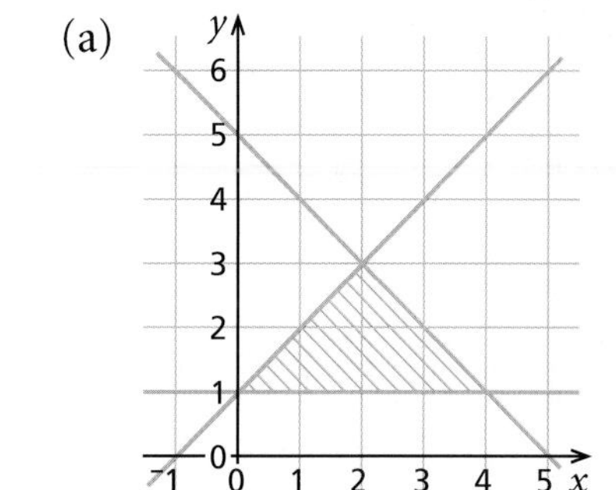

(b)

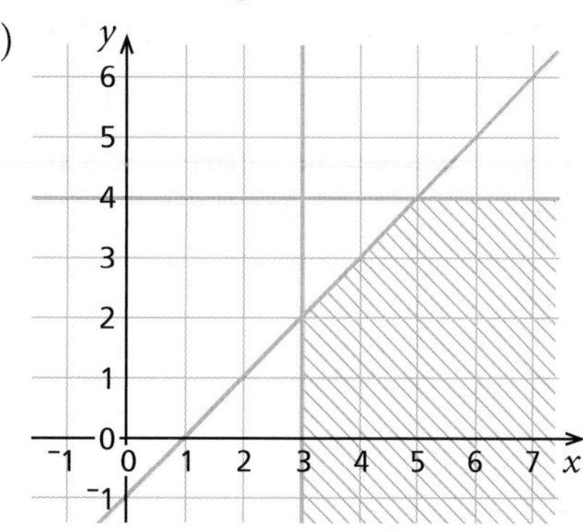

E *Boundaries*

An inequality such as $y < 2x + 1$ does not include values for which $y = 2x + 1$.

So points on the boundary line are **not** included in the region defined by $y < 2x + 1$.

One way to show this is to draw a **dotted** boundary line, as shown in the diagram.

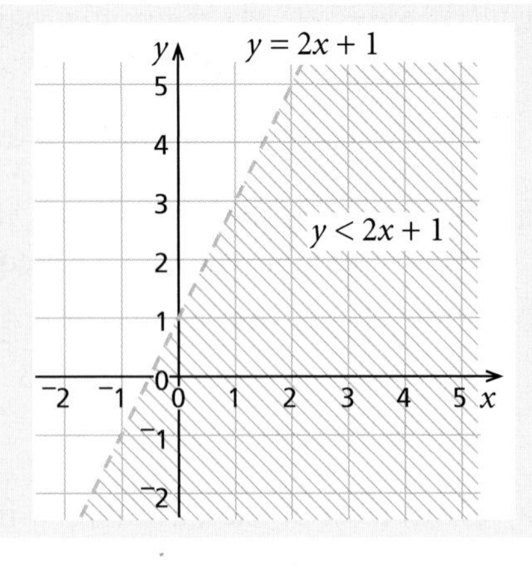

E1 Write an inequality for each region.

(a)

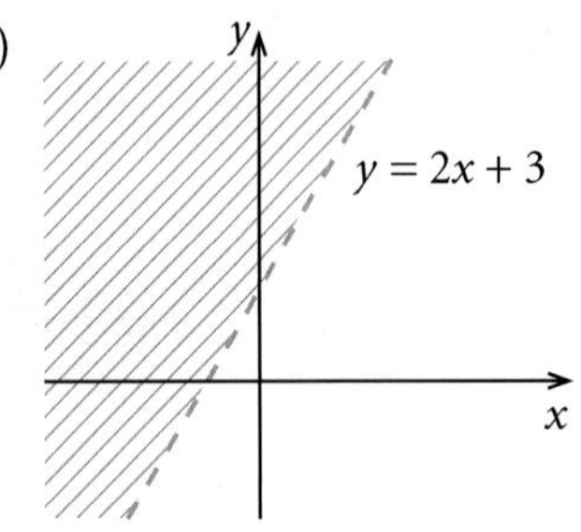

(b)

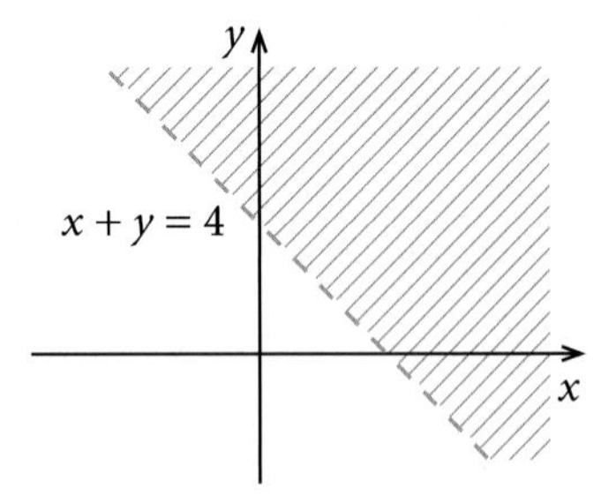

E2 (a) (i) Write the coordinates of a point that is on the line $y = x + 1$.

(ii) Draw a set of axes, numbered from $^-3$ to 6 on both axes. Draw the line $y = x + 1$ on these axes.

(b) On the same diagram shade the region described by the inequalities

$x < 0, \quad y > 0 \quad$ and $\quad y < x + 1$.

AQA(SEG) 1998

E3 The graph shows the x-axis, the y-axis and the straight lines $y = x - 1$ and $x + y = 5$.

Write down which points in the loop below are in the region defined by the inequalities

$x + y < 5, \quad y > x - 1 \quad$ and $\quad x > 0$.

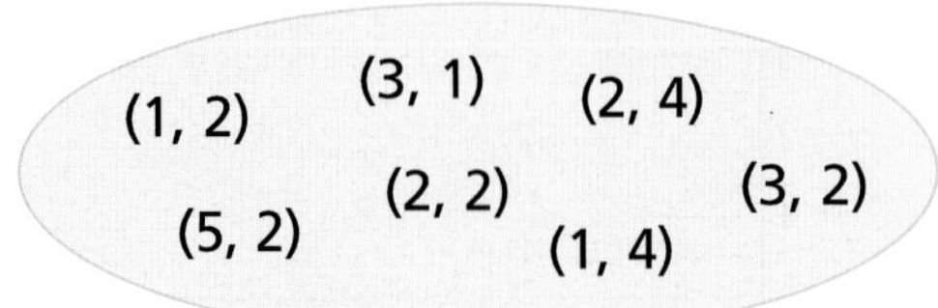

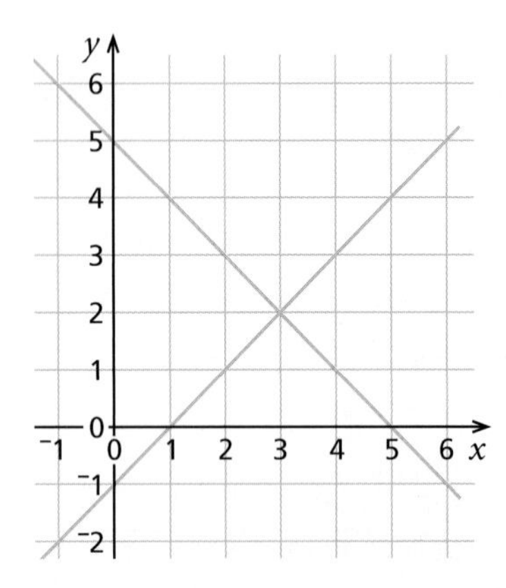

Test yourself

T1 (a) Write down the three inequalities that define the shaded region on the right.

(b) On a similar set of axes, show clearly the region that is satisfied by all of these inequalities.

$$x \le 4, \; y \ge 1, \; y \le x + 2$$

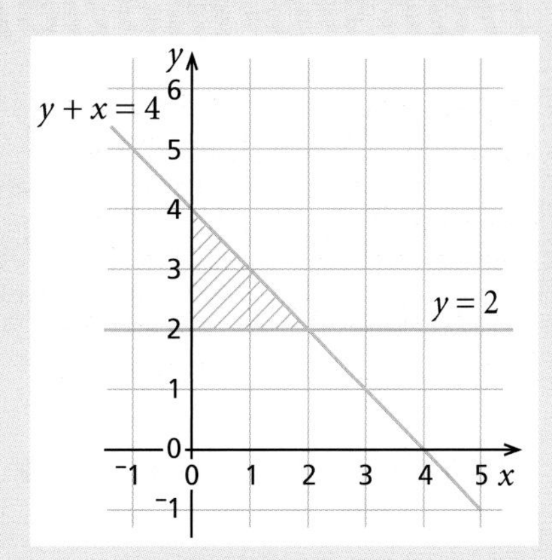

T2

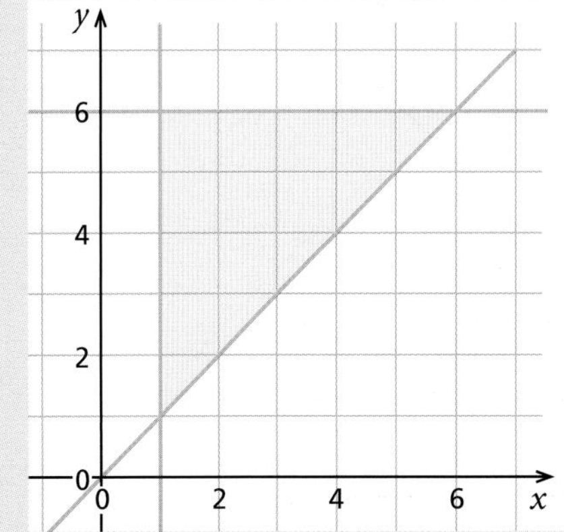

The shaded region can be defined by three inequalities.
One of these is $x \ge 1$.

Write down the other two inequalities.

OCR

T3 The graph shows the x-axis, the y-axis and the straight lines

$$y = x, \quad x + y = 10, \quad x = 10 \quad \text{and} \quad y = 10.$$

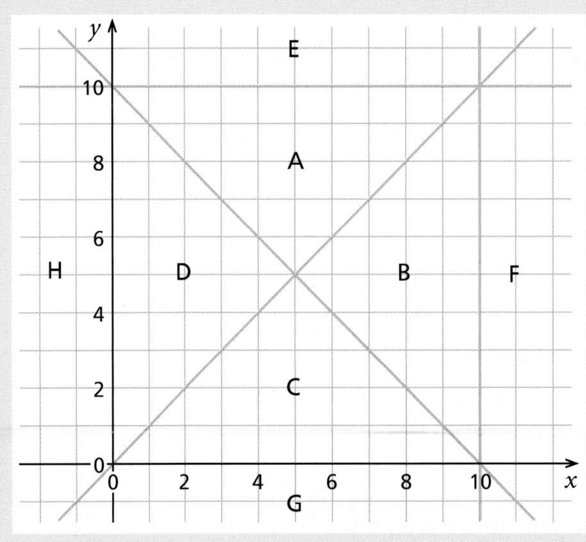

(a) One letter is in the region described by the inequality $y > 10$.
Which letter is it?

(b) Write down the three inequalities which fully describe region A. AQA(SEG) 1998

53 Transformations

This work will help you

- transform points and shapes using translation, reflection, rotation, enlargement or a combination of these
- describe clearly how shapes have been transformed

A Transformations review

TG

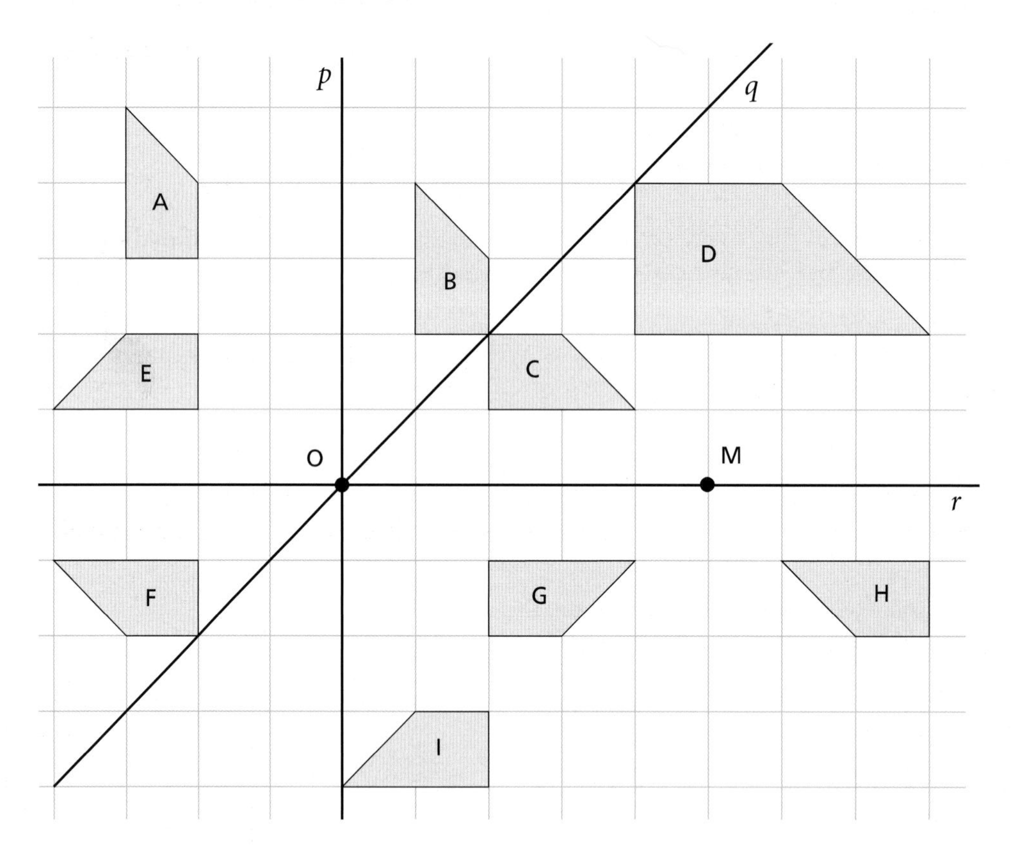

- Which trapezium is the reflection of trapezium C in line r?
- Which trapezium is a 180° rotation of trapezium H with centre point M?
- Trapezium D is an enlargement of trapezium C.
  What is the scale factor? What is the centre of this enlargement?
- Describe the transformation of shape A on to shape B.
- Describe the transformation of shape B on to shape C.
- Describe the transformation of shape B on to shape E.

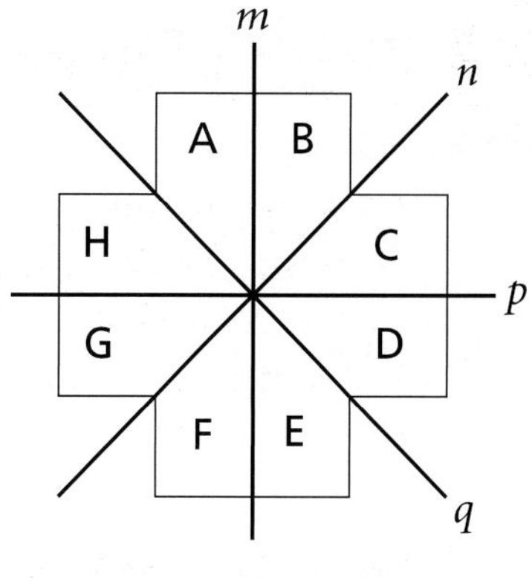

A1 In this diagram what will be the images after reflecting

(a) shape C in line p (b) shape H in line m

(c) shape E in line q (d) shape A in line n

A2 What mirror line is used to reflect

(a) F on to E (b) A on to F

(c) H on to A (d) G on to B

A3 (a) Is it possible to reflect shape H on to D?

(b) What transformation could be used to map shape F on to shape B?

(c) Is it possible to **translate** any of the shapes in the diagram on to another shape?

A4 This diagram shows some trapeziums and four points m, n, p and q.

(a) What shape is the image of shape C after a 90° rotation clockwise, centre n?

(b) What shape is the image of shape E after a translation of 2 right and 2 up?

(c) Describe how to transform

(i) D on to B (ii) B on to H (iii) G on to J

(iv) F on to H (v) B on to E (vi) F on to C

(d) Is it possible to **reflect** any of the shapes in the diagram on to another shape?

A5 These shapes are drawn on a coordinate grid. Describe the transformation that maps

(a) shape A on to shape B

(b) shape A on to shape C

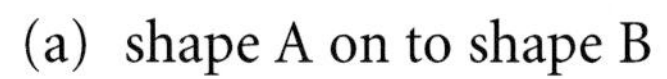

Draw a coordinate grid with both axes numbered from $^{-}5$ to 8.

Copy shape A on to your grid.

(c) Draw the shape which is a reflection of A in the y-axis. Label this D.

(d) Draw the shape which is a reflection of A in the line $y = x$. Label this E.

(e) Draw the shape which is an enlargement scale factor 2 of A, centre (0, 0). Label this F.

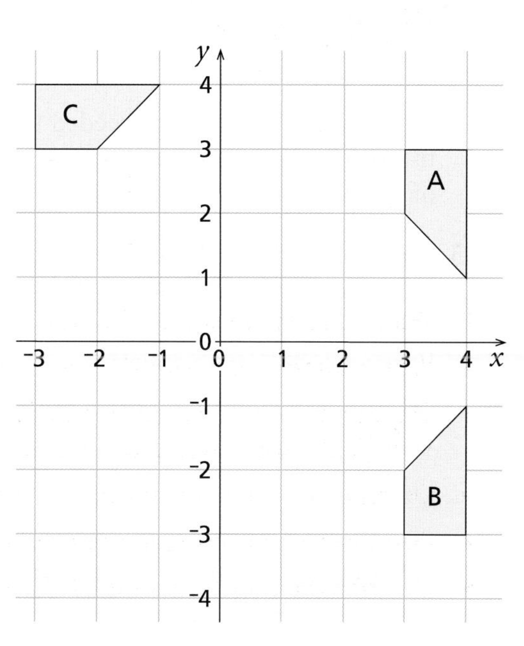

B *Translations*

TG

Using vectors

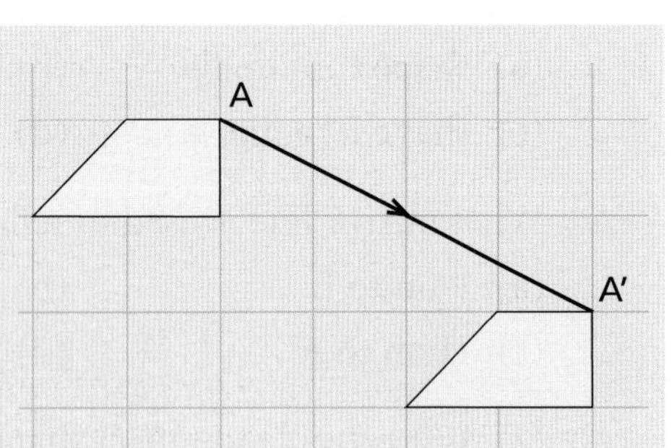

A vector describes a movement from one point to another.

The **vector** $\begin{bmatrix}3\\2\end{bmatrix}$ means 'move 3 units right and 2 units up'.

- What vector has been used to move point A to A′?
- What vectors have been used to move the other points of the trapezium?

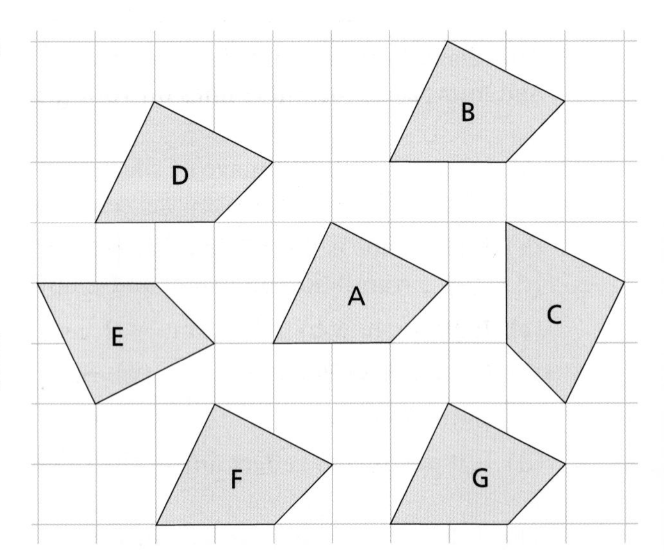

B1 In this diagram what vector describes the translation that maps
(a) A on to B (b) D on to G
(c) F on to G (d) B on to D.

B2 What will be the image of
(a) shape F after a translation of $\begin{bmatrix}2\\3\end{bmatrix}$
(b) shape B after a translation of $\begin{bmatrix}-4\\-6\end{bmatrix}$

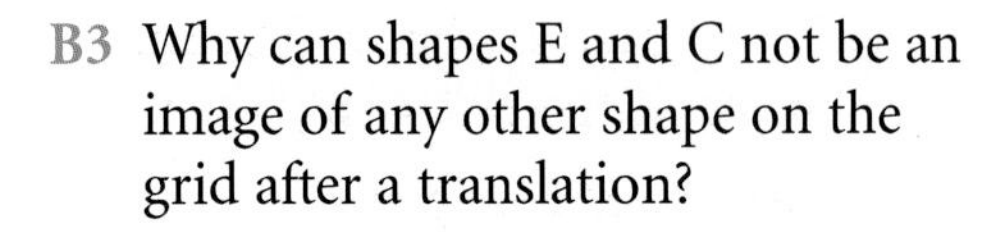

B3 Why can shapes E and C not be an image of any other shape on the grid after a translation?

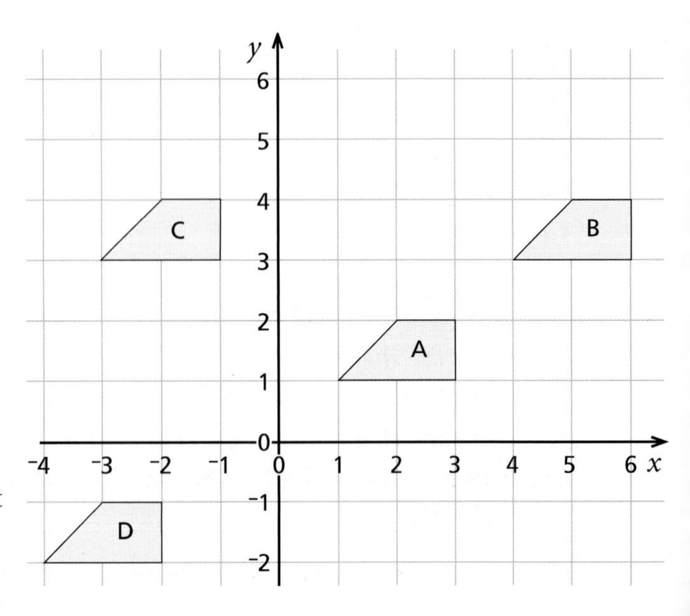

B4 Describe the translations needed to transform the shape A on to each of the other shapes on this grid.

B5 Copy the grid and shape A. Show the image of the shape A after a translation using each of these vectors.
(a) $\begin{bmatrix}2\\3\end{bmatrix}$ (b) $\begin{bmatrix}2\\-4\end{bmatrix}$
(c) $\begin{bmatrix}-6\\-3\end{bmatrix}$

***B6** What will be the image of the point (6, 8) after a translation of $\begin{bmatrix}3\\-2\end{bmatrix}$?

C Reflections

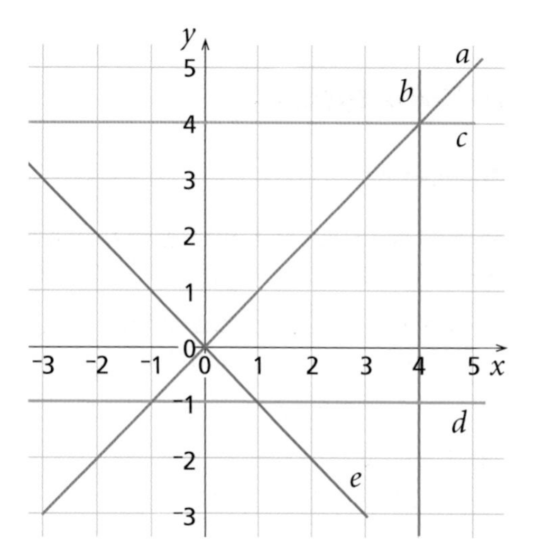

Line a on this graph has the equation $y = x$.

- What are the equations of the other lines on this coordinate grid?
- What equation can be used to describe the x-axis?

The equations of lines on a coordinate grid are useful in describing mirror lines in reflections.

C1 Draw a coordinate grid with both axes numbered from $^-5$ to 8.
On your grid draw and label shape A with corners at (2, 1), (4, 1), (3, 3) and (2, 2).

(a) Draw and label these lines on your grid.

(i) $y = x$ (ii) $x = 1$ (iii) $y = 4$ (iv) $y = {^-1}$

(b) Reflect shape A in the line $y = x$. Label this image B.

(c) Reflect shape A in the line $x = 1$. Label this image C.

(d) Reflect shape A in the line $y = 4$. Label this image D.

(e) Reflect shape A in the line $y = {^-1}$. Label this image E.

(f) What transformation would map shape E on to shape D?

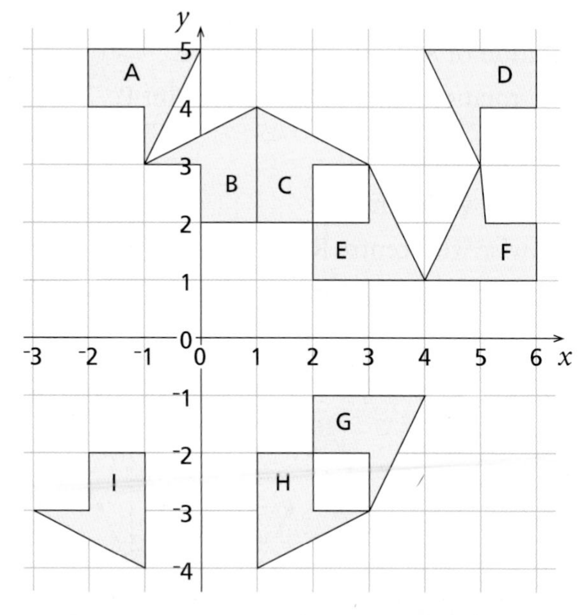

C2 On this grid, what will be the images after reflecting

(a) shape D in $y = 3$

(b) shape C in $y = x$

(c) shape I in the y-axis

(d) shape E in $x = 4$

C3 Give the equation of the mirror line used to reflect

(a) A on to D

(b) H on to G

(c) C on to H

(d) C on to B

C4 (a) To what point will (7, 2) be mapped after a reflection in $y = x$?

(b) Describe what happens to coordinates after reflection in $y = x$.

(c) Describe what happens to coordinates after reflection in the x-axis.

D Rotations

TG

The L method

When rotating a shape on a grid it helps to rotate each corner using an 'L'.
Here is how you rotate a shape through 90° anticlockwise about point P.

Draw an 'L', using the grid, from the centre P to a corner of the shape.

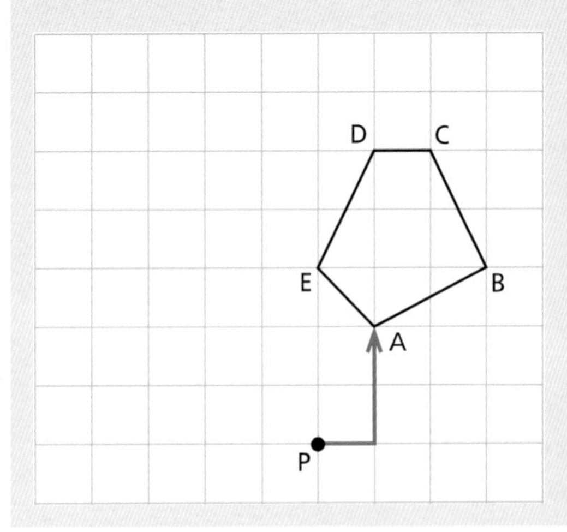

Rotate the L 90° anticlockwise. The end of the L marks the new position of the corner. Repeat for every corner until you can draw the shape.

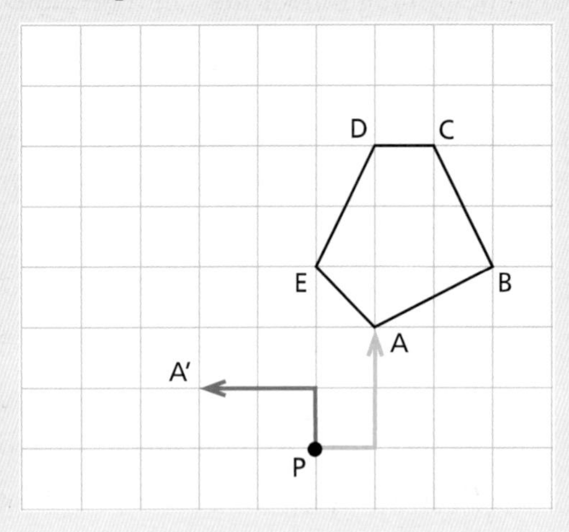

D1 (a) Copy the shape ABCDE above and point P on centimetre squared paper. Complete the 90° anticlockwise rotation of ABCDE about point P.

(b) On the same diagram draw the 180° rotation of ABCDE about point P.

D2 On sheet G104 use the L method to draw the image of

(a) shape B after a rotation of 90° clockwise with centre Q

(b) shape C after a rotation of 90° clockwise with centre R

(c) shape D after a rotation of 90° anticlockwise with centre S

(d) shape E after a rotation of 180° with centre T

D3 This pattern has been drawn on triangular dotty paper by rotating about the centre of the pattern.

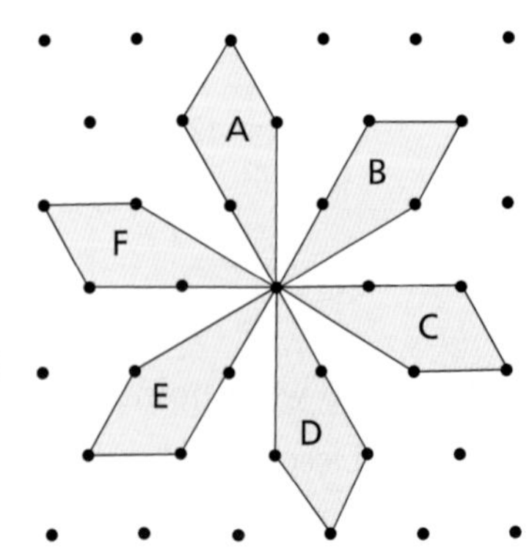

(a) What shape is the image after rotating

(i) shape F by 180° (ii) shape D by 60° clockwise

(iii) shape B by 120° anticlockwise

(b) What is the angle and direction of rotation that maps

(i) B to A (ii) E to C (iii) F to A

D4 On this diagram what is the image of

(a) shape F after a 90° anticlockwise rotation, centre (0, 0)

(b) shape A after a 180° rotation, centre (3, 2)

(c) shape D after a 90° clockwise rotation, centre (5, 0)

(d) shape F after a 180° rotation, centre $(2\frac{1}{2}, {}^{-}2\frac{1}{2})$

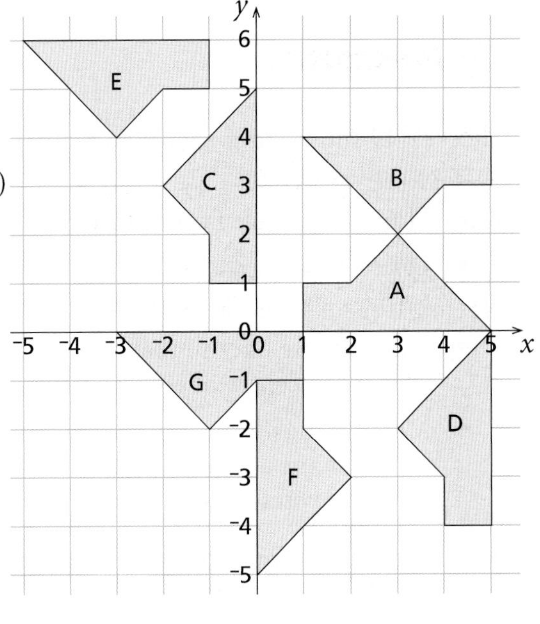

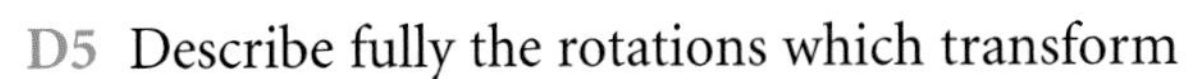

D5 Describe fully the rotations which transform

(a) C on to F (b) A on to C

(c) G on to A (d) E on to C

D6 Draw a coordinate grid with both axes numbered from ⁻5 to 8.
Draw the shape with corners at (3, 1), (4, 1), (4, 3) and (2, 2).
Label it P.

(a) Draw the image of P after a 90° clockwise rotation with centre (0, 0).
Label it Q.

(b) Draw the image of P after a 180° rotation with centre (5, 0).
Label it R.

(c) Draw the image of P after a 90° anticlockwise rotation with centre (4, 4).
Label it S.

(d) Describe fully the transformation which maps shape Q on to shape S.

D7 (a) Describe fully the single transformation that maps triangle P on to triangle Q.

(b) On a copy of this diagram, rotate shape P 90° anticlockwise about the point A(1, 1).

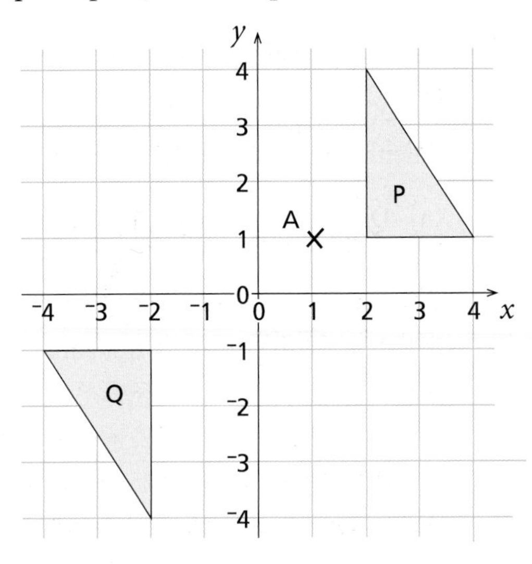

Edexcel

E *Enlargement*

Sheet G149 shows three shapes A, B and C, and enlargements of them.

- What is the scale factor of each enlargement?
- For each of the shapes A, B, C, draw lines between their vertices and the corresponding points on their images.
- Extend these lines so that they all meet at a point. This is the **centre of enlargement.**
- Measure the distance from this centre to each point on the shape and to its image. What do you notice?

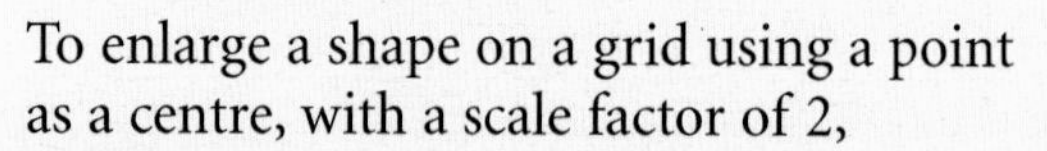

To enlarge a shape on a grid using a point as a centre, with a scale factor of 2,

- draw an L from the centre to a vertex of the shape
- add an identical L to find the image of the vertex
- repeat for each vertex

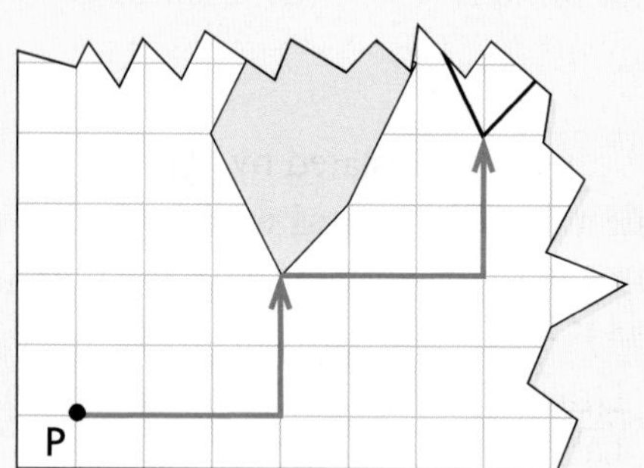

E1 On sheet G149 draw an enlargement of shape D scale factor 2 using point P as the centre.

E2 Sheet G150 has a shaded shape and three enlargements of it. For each enlargement give

(i) the scale factor

(ii) the coordinates of the centre of enlargement

E3 On sheet G150 show the image of the shaded shape after an enlargement scale factor 3 with centre (0, 5).

E4 (a) Draw a coordinate grid with both axes numbered from 0 to 12. Draw the shape with vertices at A (2, 1), B (4, 1), C (4, 2) and D (3, 3).

(b) Draw the image of the shape after an enlargement of scale factor 2 with centre (0, 0).

(c) Copy and complete this table.

vertex	Image
A (2, 1)	(,)
B (4, 1)	(,)
C (4, 2)	(,)
D (3, 3)	(,)

(d) What would be the image of the point (12, 18) after an enlargement scale factor 2 with centre (0, 0)? Explain how you know.

E5 Write down what you think the coordinates of the image of the shape on your grid will be after a scale factor 3 enlargement with centre (0, 0). Draw the image on the grid and check you are right.

E6 Write down what you think the coordinates of the image of the shape on your grid will be after a scale factor $\frac{1}{2}$ enlargement with centre (0, 0). Draw the image on the grid and check you are right.

F *All together*

F1 What is the image on this grid after

(a) shape C is reflected in the line $y = 0$

(b) shape E is rotated 90° clockwise about centre (2, 1)

(c) shape J is translated by $\begin{bmatrix}1\\3\end{bmatrix}$

(d) shape C is reflected in the line $y = x$

F2 Describe fully the transformations that map

(a) D on to F

(b) G on to H

(c) A on to C

(d) I on to J

(e) I on to G

(f) A on to B

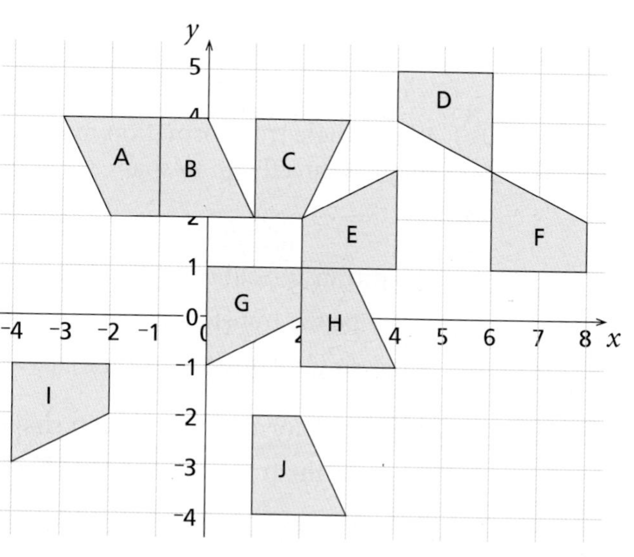

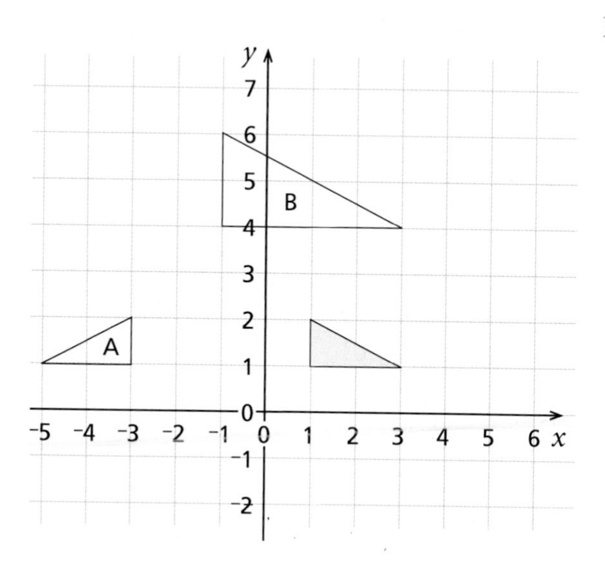

F3 Copy this diagram on centimetre squared paper.

(a) Describe the transformation that maps the shaded triangle on to shape A.

(b) Give the scale factor and centre of the enlargement that maps the shaded triangle on to triangle B.

(c) Show the image of the shaded shape after a reflection in $y = 0$. Label this triangle C.

(d) Show the image of the shaded shape after an enlargement scale factor 2 with centre (1, 1). Label this triangle D.

(e) Describe fully the transformation that maps shape A on to shape C.

(f) Describe fully the transformation that maps shape B on to shape D.

F4 Look at this diagram.

(a) What transformation will map shape A on to shape E?

(b) Describe the transformation that will map shape E on to shape F.

(c) What **single** transformation maps shape A directly on to shape F?

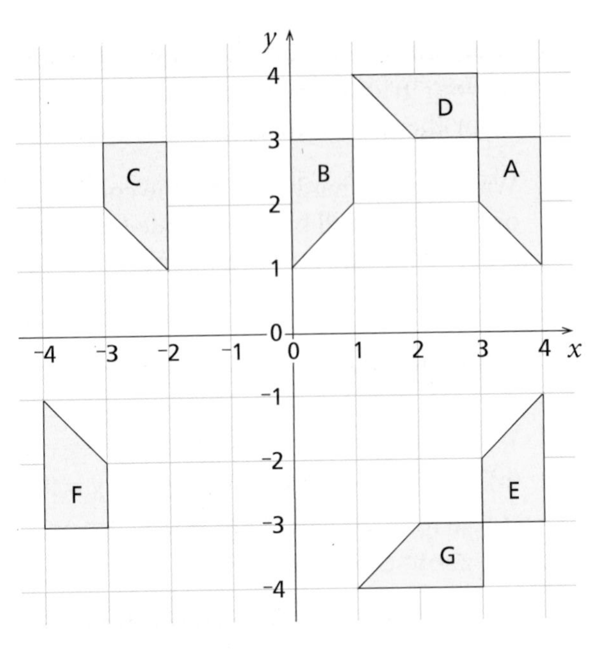

F5 (a) What transformation will map shape A on to shape B?

(b) Describe the transformation that will map shape B on to shape C.

(c) What **single** transformation maps shape A directly on to shape C?

F6 (a) What transformation will map shape A on to shape G?

(b) Describe the transformation that maps shape G on to shape D.

(c) What **single** transformation maps shape A on to shape D?

F7 (a) What transformation will map shape E on to shape F?

(b) Describe the transformation that maps shape F on to shape C.

(c) Is there a **single** transformation that maps shape E on to shape C?

F8 Draw a coordinate grid with both axes numbered from $^{-}4$ to 4.
Draw shape K with corners at (2, 1), (4, 1), (4, 2) and (3, 3).

(a) Draw the reflection of shape K in the line $y = x$.
Label this image L.

(b) Rotate shape L 90° anticlockwise with centre (0, 0).
Label this image M.

(c) Describe the **single** transformation that maps shape K on to shape M.

F9 Draw another coordinate grid with shape K as in F8.

(a) Draw the image of shape K after a translation of $\begin{bmatrix} 0 \\ ^{-}4 \end{bmatrix}$.
Label this image N.

(b) Rotate shape N 180° with centre (0, 0).
Label this image O.

(c) Describe the **single** transformation that maps shape K on to shape O.

F10 Diagram A on sheet G151 shows shapes Q and R, which are transformations of shape P.

(a) Describe the **single** transformation which takes P on to R.

(b) Describe the **single** transformation which takes P on to Q.

(c) On the diagram, draw an enlargement of shape P with scale factor 2, centre (3, 2).

AQA 2003 Specimen

F11 The triangle P has been drawn on diagram B on sheet G151.

(a) Reflect the triangle P in the line $x = 2$.
Label the image Q.

(b) Rotate triangle Q through 90° clockwise about (2, 1).
Label this image R.

(c) Describe fully the single transformation which maps triangle P on to triangle R.

Edexcel

F12 (a) For these triangles, describe fully the single transformation that maps

(i) A on to B

(ii) A on to C

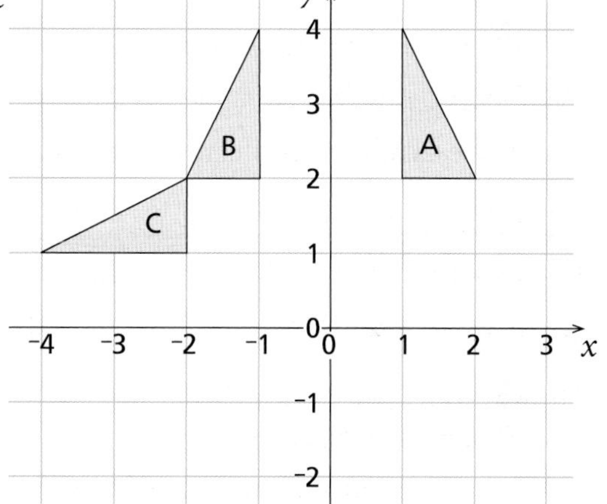

(b) For these quadrilaterals, describe fully the transformation that maps Q on to R.

(c) Q is reflected in $x = 4$, and then in $y = 1$. Describe fully the single transformation that is equivalent to these two transformations.

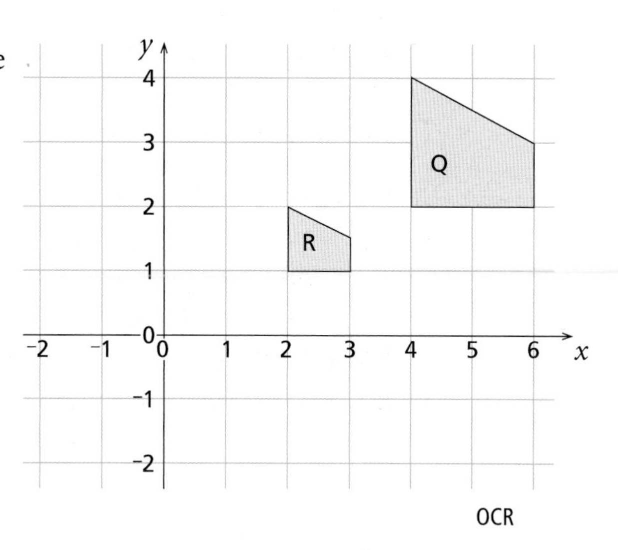

OCR

Test yourself

T1 The star ABCDEFGHIJKL is made up of 12 equilateral triangles.

(a) Which triangle will be covered if

(i) triangle BCD is rotated by 60° clockwise about the point O

(ii) triangle BCD is enlarged by a scale factor of 2 from the point C

(b) Describe two different single transformations that take the black triangle to the grey triangle.

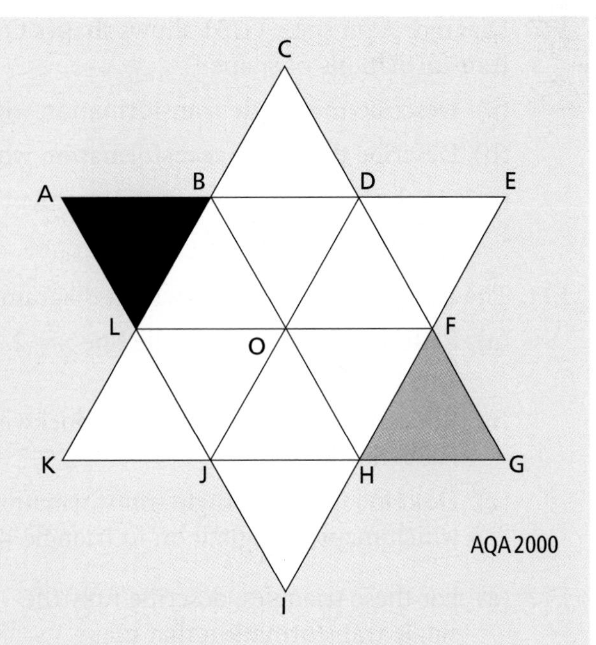

AQA 2000

T2 The diagram shows the position of a shape labelled R.
Copy the diagram onto centimetre squared paper.

Draw the y-axis up to 9.

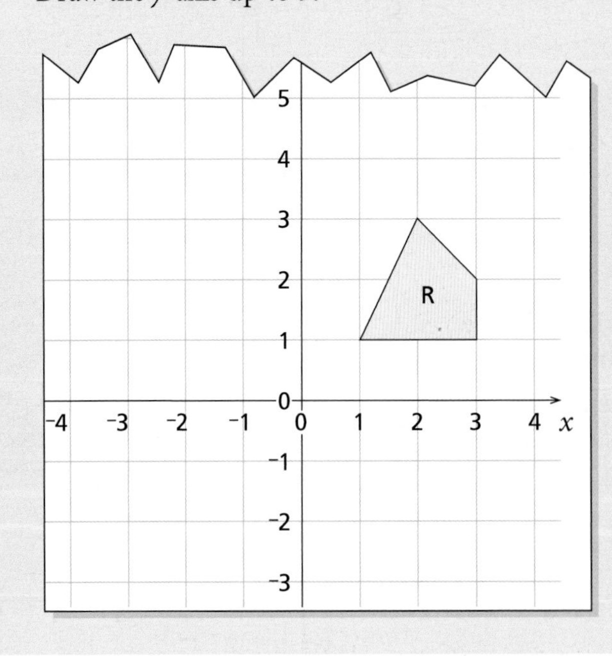

(a) R is mapped on to S by a reflection in the y-axis. Draw and label S.

(b) S is mapped on to T by a reflection in the line $y = 4$. Draw and label T.

(c) Describe fully the single transformation which maps T on to R.

AQA(SEG) 2000

Review 9

1 Rajeev invested £250 at a rate of 4% per annum compound interest.
How much will the investment be worth at the end of 3 years?

2 Work out

(a) the cube of 6 (b) the cube root of $^-64$ (c) $36^{\frac{1}{2}}$

3 (a) A CD player costs £129.99 + VAT. VAT is charged at $17\frac{1}{2}$%.
What is the total cost of the CD player including VAT?

(b) A video recorder cost £289.99 including VAT at $17\frac{1}{2}$%.
What was its cost before VAT was added?

4 Draw a a set of axes, each numbered from $^-6$ to 6.
Plot and join the points (1, 2), (1, 4), (3, 3) and (2, 2). Label the shape P.

(a) (i) Draw the image of P after reflection in the x-axis.
Label it Q.

(ii) Draw the image of Q after a rotation of 90° anticlockwise about O.
Label it R.

(b) What single transformation maps shape R back onto shape P?

(c) Draw the image of Q after translation $\begin{bmatrix} 0 \\ 2 \end{bmatrix}$.
Label the image S.

(d) Describe fully the single transformation that maps shape R to shape S.

5 This diagram shows a vertical mast XY, supported by two wires AC and BX.

(a) Find the angle marked x, to the nearest degree.

(b) Calculate to 2 d.p. the length CY.

(c) Calculate to 2 d.p. the height, XY, of the mast.

(d) Hence find the length CX.

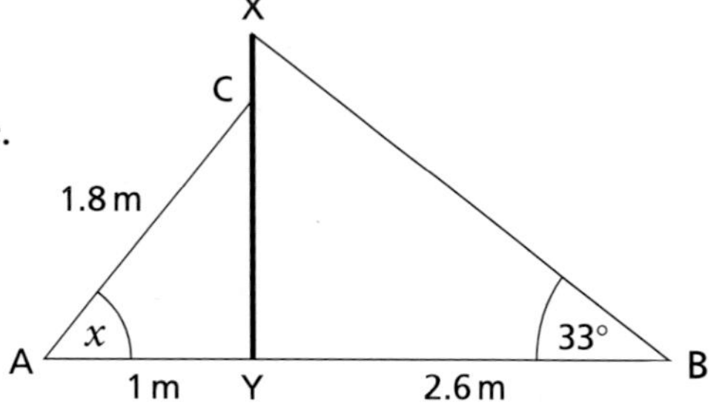

6 (a) Factorise (i) $x^2 - 9x + 20$ (ii) $x^2 - 25$

(b) Simplify (i) $\dfrac{3a+12}{a+4}$ (ii) $\dfrac{c-2}{c^2-4}$

7 Make x the subject of each of these formulas.

(a) $4x - 2a = 3(x + a)$ (b) $\dfrac{5(x-3)}{2} = c$ (c) $3y - 2x = 9$

(d) $5a + 7x = x + 9$ (e) $n = x^2 - 4$ (f) $k^2 = 5(x^2 + 3)$

8 Work out $\sqrt[3]{\dfrac{360}{\pi}}$ giving your answer correct to three significant figures.

9 Solve the equations

(a) $x^2 + 8x = 0$ (b) $x^2 + 5x - 14 = 0$ (c) $2x^2 + 11x - 6 = 0$

10 In a sale, the cost of a dress is reduced by 15%.
The sale price is £25.50.
What was the cost of the dress before it was reduced?

11 (a) Write down the equation of the line L.

(b) Write down three inequalities that describe the pink region.

(c) On a similar diagram, show clearly the region that is satisfied by these three inequalities.

$$x + y \geq 2, \quad y \leq x \quad \text{and} \quad x \leq 2$$

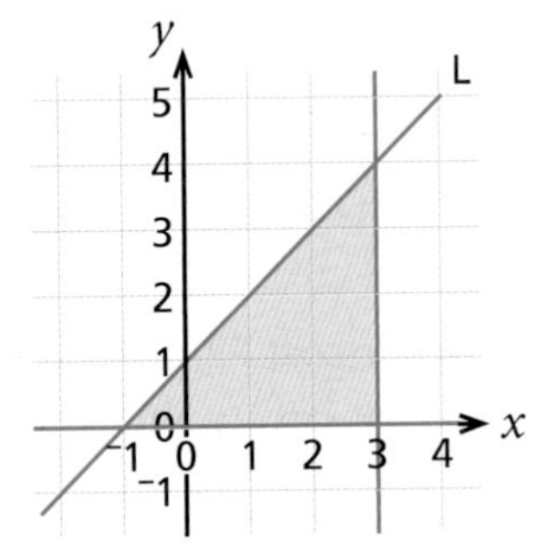

12 The diagram shows a cuboid.

(a) Find an expression for the volume of the cuboid.

(b) The volume of the cuboid is $100\,\text{cm}^3$.
Work out the area of the largest face, correct to 1 d.p.

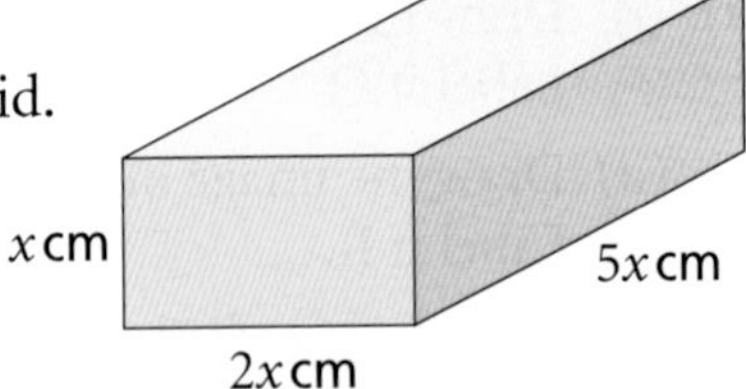

13 The diagram shows a rectangular garden containing a square flower bed of side length x m.

Surrounding the flower bed is a lawn of width 5 m.
The area of the garden is $300\,\text{m}^2$.

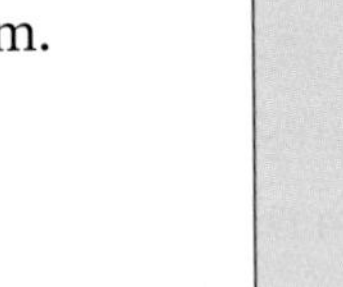

(a) Write down expressions for the length and width of the rectangular garden.

(b) Use the area of the garden to form an equation in x.

(c) Show that the equation can be written $x^2 + 15x - 250 = 0$.

(d) Solve the equation to find x.

(e) Hence find the dimensions of the rectangle.

14 The diagram shows a prism.

(a) Find an expression for the volume of the prism.

(b) Show that the surface area, S, of the prism is given by the formula

$$S = 2a(3a + 4b)$$

(c) Rearrange this formula to make b the subject.

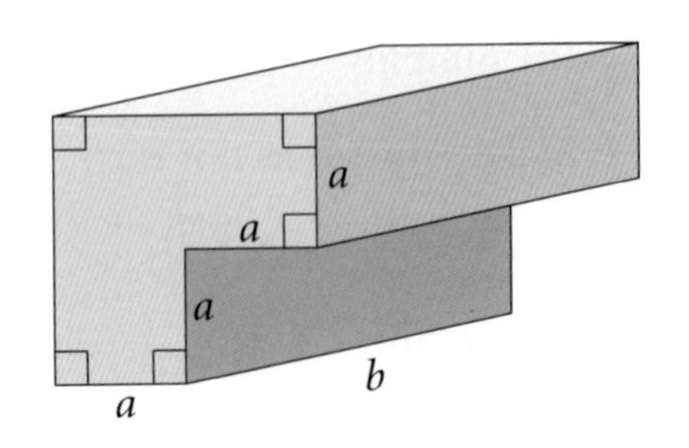

54 Loci and constructions

You will revise drawing and identifying a simple locus (a set of points obeying a certain rule).

This work will help you

- draw other loci
- do formal constructions using a straight edge and compasses only

A Seeing and being seen

This is a plan view.
A fence has 8 posts, lettered A to H on the plan.
There is a tall wall between Ian and the fence.

- Which posts can Ian see?
- What area between the wall and the fence can he **not** see?

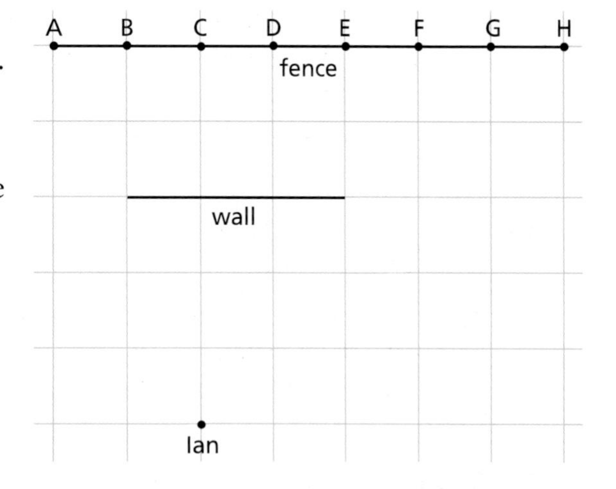

TG

A1 This side view shows two flagpoles and two walls. There is an ant at point A.

(a) Can the ant see the top of flagpole G?

(b) If not, how far to the left or right must it crawl in order to do so?

(c) Looking from point A, what fraction of flagpole F can the ant see?

(d) There is a bee on the top of flagpole F. What fraction of flagpole G can it see?

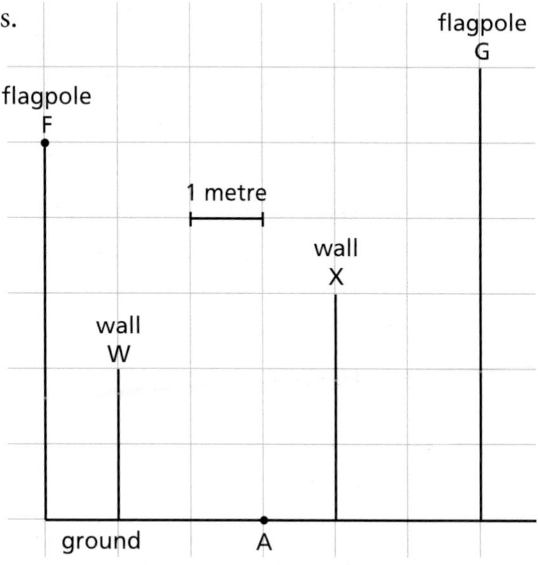

A2 Answer this on sheet G152.

B *Being a certain distance from a point or line*

- A mark has to be made 5 cm away from point P.
  Where could it go? Consider **all** the possible places.
- Now a mark has to be made **5 cm or more** away from P.
  Consider all the possible places it could go.

P

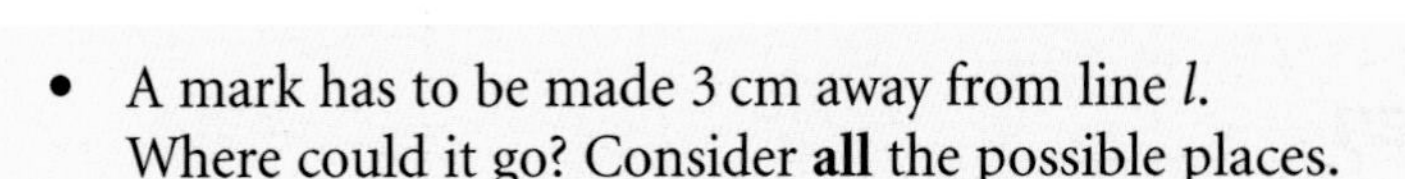

- A mark has to be made 3 cm away from line *l*.
  Where could it go? Consider **all** the possible places.
- Now a mark has to be made **3 cm or less** away from *l*.
  Consider all the possible places it could go.

l

B1 Mark a point Q on paper.

Draw accurately the locus of all points 4 cm away from Q. Label it (a).

Shade the locus of points 4 cm or less away from Q. Label it (b).

B2 Draw a line m on paper.

Draw accurately the locus of all points 2 cm away from m. Label it (a).

Shade the locus of points 2 cm or more away from m. Label it (b).

B3 Mark a point R on paper.

Mark a point X that is more than 5 cm away from R but is less than 7 cm away from R.

Now shade the locus of points that are more than 5 cm away from R and less than 7 cm away from R.

B4 The grass in this garden must be at least 2 m away from the tree and at least 1 m from the surrounding fence.

Draw the plan to scale and shade the grass.

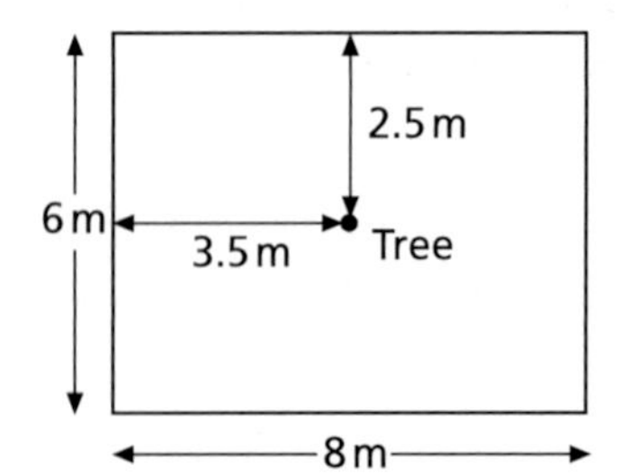

B5 A goat in a field is attached to a rope 3 metres long. On the other end of the rope is a ring that can slide along a horizontal bar 5 metres long.

Draw a plan view to a scale of 1 centimetre to 1 metre, representing the bar by a straight line. Shade where the goat can graze, showing the boundary clearly.

B6 

A monkey can reach out 50 cm from the bars that go all round its cage.

Draw the plan of the cage to scale. Shade the ground outside the cage that the monkey can reach.

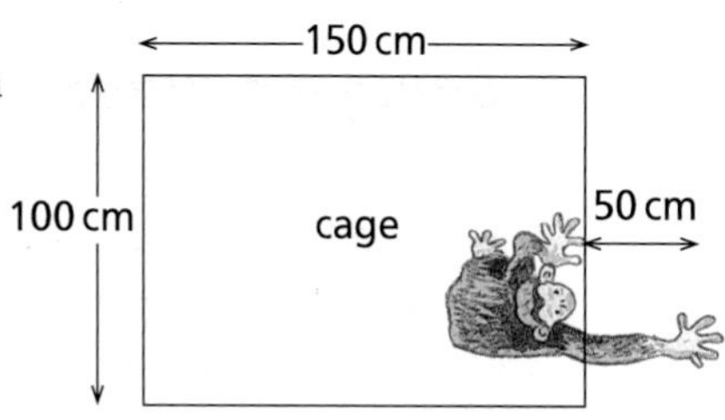

B7 Draw a line k on paper.
Mark a point P, 5 cm from line k.

(a) Draw the locus of points 4 cm from point P.

(b) Draw the locus of points 3 cm from line k.

(c) Shade the locus of points that are less than 4 cm from P and less than 3 cm from k.

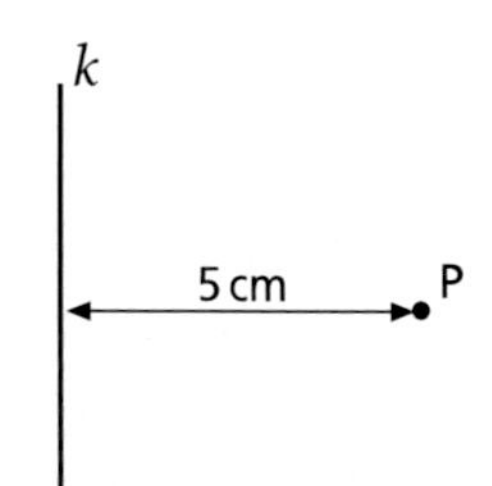

B8 These shaded loci are drawn on centimetre squares.
Describe each one, referring to the lettered points.

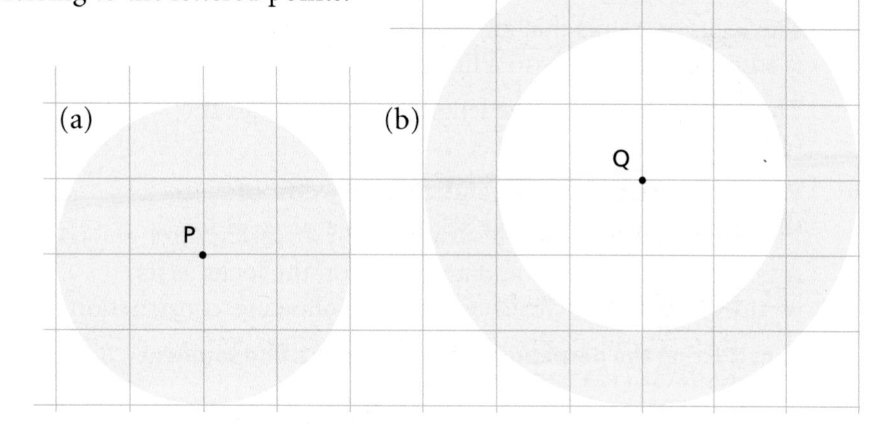

***B9** Describe these loci, referring to the lettered points or line.

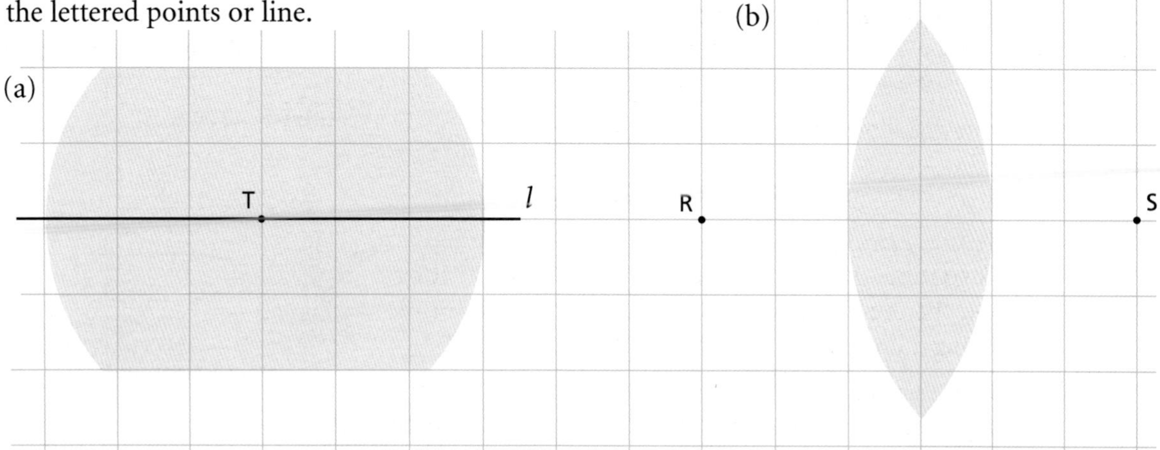

C *Being the same distance from two points*

- A and B are two girls. A third girl, C, has to walk so she is always the same distance from B as she is from A. Where can she walk? (We say C is always **equidistant** from A and B.)

• B

A •

- If A and B are two points marked on tracing paper and the paper is folded so A and B match up, what do you notice about the fold line?

C1 (a) Use Pythagoras's theorem to show that AP is 5 units long. How many units long is BP?

(b) Use Pythagoras to find the lengths AQ and BQ. Leave your answers in the form $\sqrt{n}$.

(c) How long are AR and BR?

(d) How long are AS and BS?

(e) What can you say about the line that P, Q, R, and S are on?

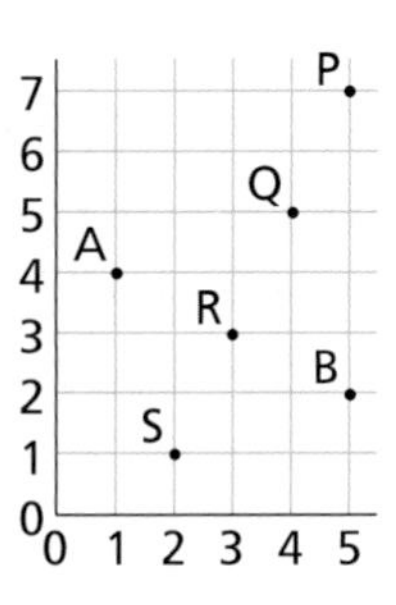

The locus of points that are equidistant from points A and B is a line at right angles to a line between A and B.

This locus also **bisects** the length between A and B (cuts it exactly in half).

We call this locus the **perpendicular bisector of the line segment AB** (a line segment is a piece of line).

A triangle that has A, B and any point on the locus as its vertices is isosceles. This is used in the following 'construction'.

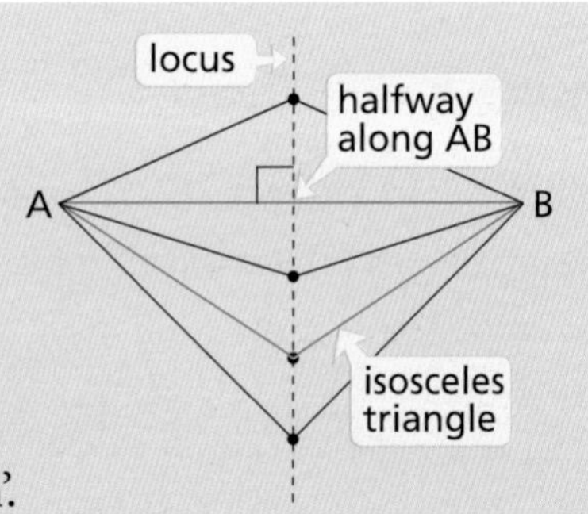

Constructing the perpendicular bisector of a line segment

1 Draw a line segment. Draw an arc about this big with its centre at one end of the segment.

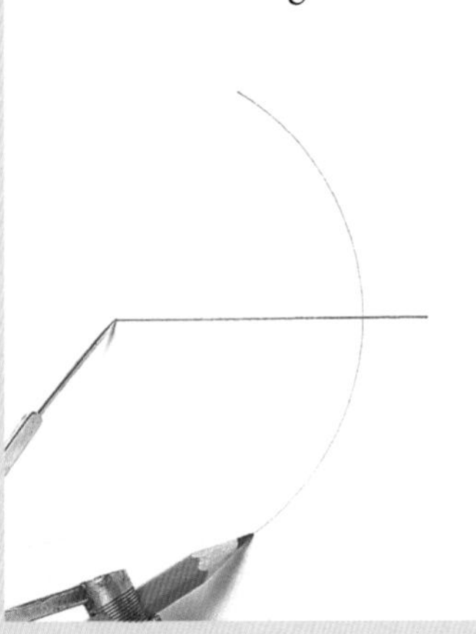

2 Keep your compasses the same radius. Draw an arc with its centre at the other end of the segment.

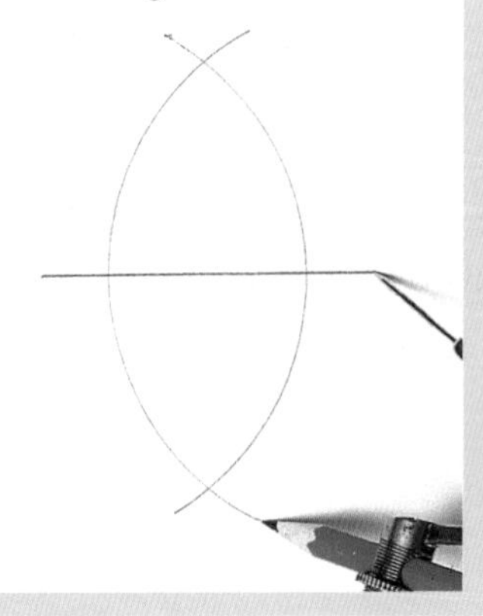

3 Draw a line through the points where the the two arcs cross. This is the perpendicular bisector of the original segment.

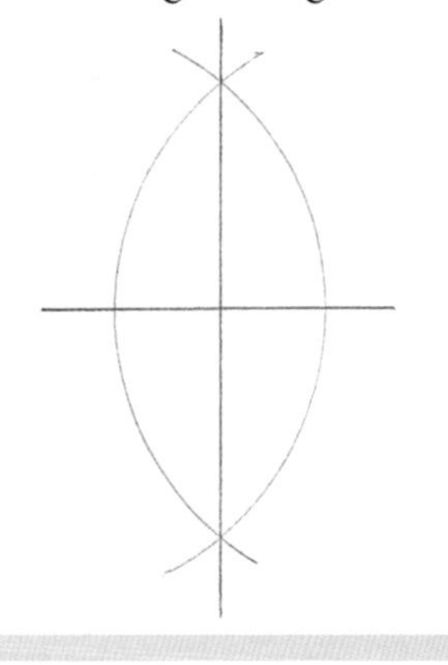

C2 Draw this rectangle accurately.
Construct the perpendicular bisector of the line AC using ruler and compasses only.
Show, by shading, the locus of points within the rectangle that are closer to point A than to point C.

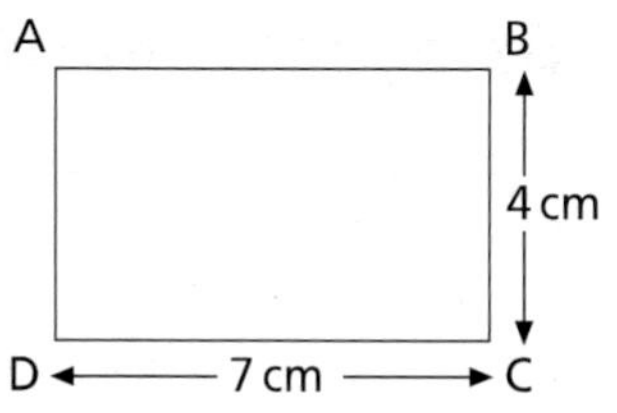

C3 Draw a circle and mark two points U and V inside it.
Show how to find a point on the circle equidistant from U and V.
How many such points are there?

C4 Construct accurately the triangle sketched here.

Show the following loci by shading, using only a ruler and compasses to find the boundaries.

(a) The set of points within the triangle that are closer to C than to A, but are less than 3 cm from A.

(b) The set of points within the triangle that are closer to A than to C, but are less than 7 cm from B.

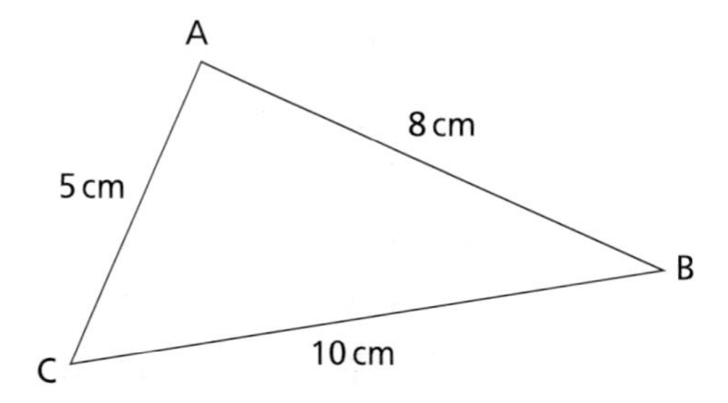

Triangle investigation 1

Draw a scalene triangle in the middle of a piece of paper.

Draw the perpendicular bisector of one side.

Now do the same for the other two sides.

What happens? Does it happen for other people's triangles?

C5 In 'Triangle investigation 1' the three bisectors you drew should have all met at one point.

Using that point as the centre, draw a circle that goes through one of the vertices of the triangle.

What happens?

C6 There are two dangerous rocks, P and Q, in the ocean.
The bearing of P from Q is 290°.

A ship going between P and Q, with P on its left-hand side, has to ensure that it is always equidistant from the two rocks.

Draw a sketch of the situation, showing the ship's course.

What is the bearing of its course?

D *Going to a line by the shortest route*

The shortest route from a point to a line is at right angles to the line.

This seems obvious when the line is horizontal … … or vertical.

It is less obvious (but still true) when the line is at some other angle.

D1 Copy these axes and lines carefully on to squared paper (centimetre squares are best).

Use a set square to draw the shortest route from point A to the line BC.

From where you met BC, draw the shortest route to line AB.

From where you met AB, draw the shortest route to BC.

From where you are now, draw the shortest route to AB.

Write the coordinates of the point you have reached.

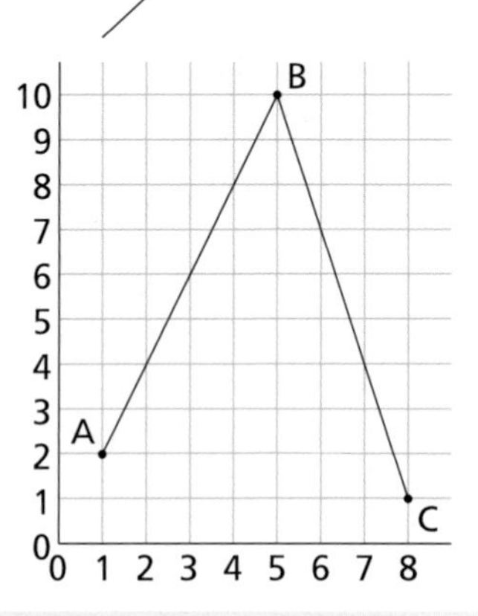

Constructing a perpendicular from a point to a line

1 Suppose you have been given a point P and a line *l*.
Draw an arc with its centre at P, crossing line *l*.

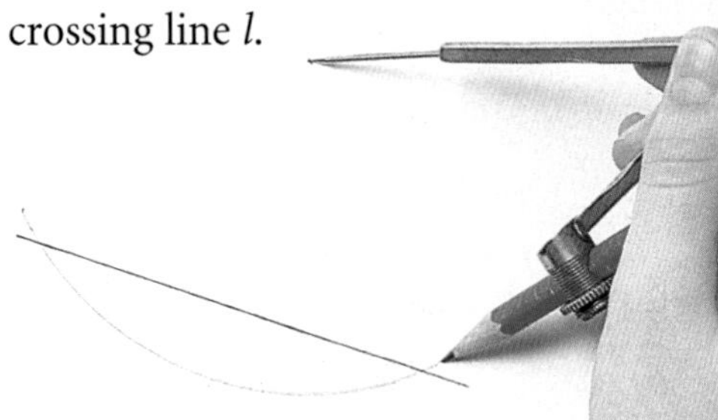

2 Put the point of the compasses at one of the points where your arc crosses line *l*.

Draw an arc below the line.
You need not use the same radius as before.

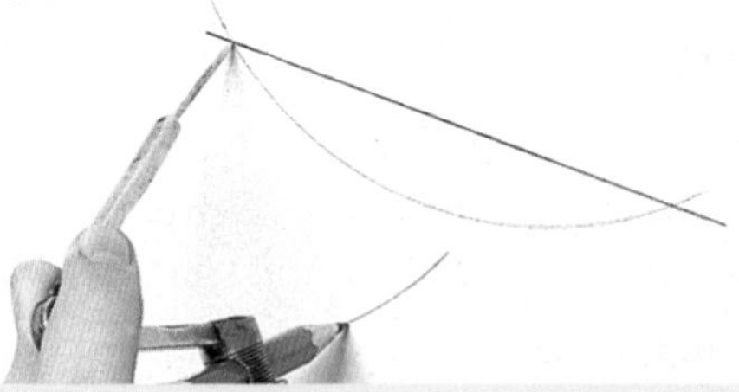

3 Do not alter the radius.
Draw another arc like this.

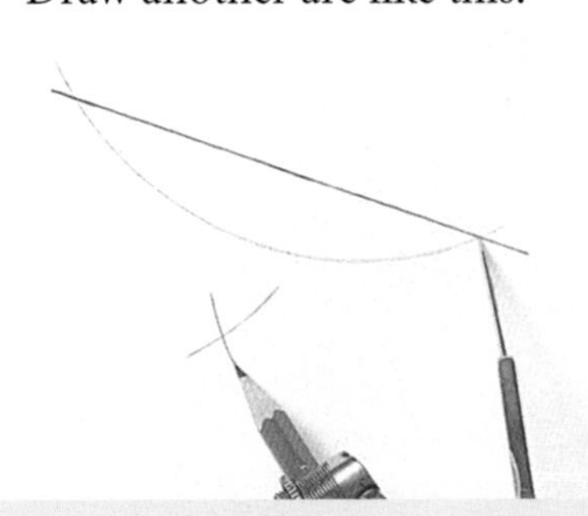

4 The line from P to where the last pair of arcs cross is perpendicular to line *l*.

Can you explain why?

D2 Use the construction shown on the previous page to answer the questions on sheet G153.

Triangle investigation 2

In the middle of a piece of A4 paper, draw a scalene triangle with sides between 8 and 16 cm long and all its angles acute. Label its vertices A, B and C.

Using a ruler and compasses, construct

- a line from A perpendicular to BC
- a line from B perpendicular to AC
- a line from C perpendicular to AB

What do you notice about these three lines?
Did what you notice happen with other people's triangles?

What happens when you try to do this for a triangle with one obtuse angle?

D3 A walker is somewhere on a moor.
She knows that a straight road to the north of the moor goes from town A on a bearing of 120° to town B.

Draw a sketch of the situation.

What bearing should she walk on to get to this road by the shortest route?

E *Being the same distance from two lines*

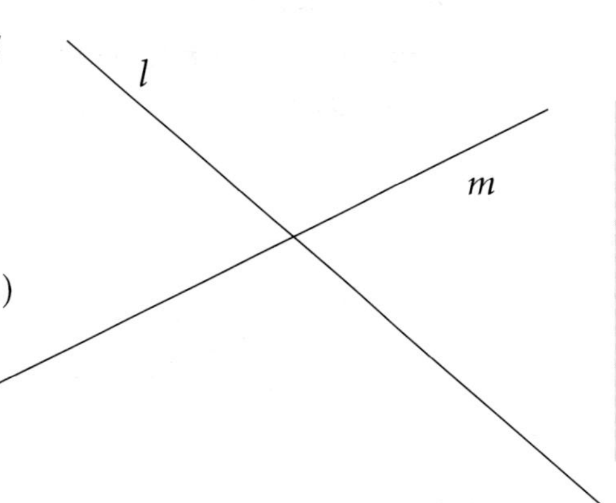

- Two lines, l and m are drawn on the floor.
A boy, P, has to walk so he is always the same distance from line l as he is from line m.
Where can he walk?
(We say P is always **equidistant** from line l and line m.)
- If lines l and m are marked on tracing paper and the paper is folded so l and m match up, what can you say about the fold line?

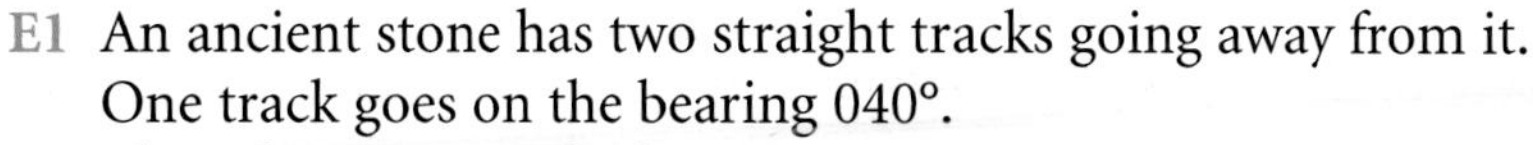

E1 An ancient stone has two straight tracks going away from it.
One track goes on the bearing 040°.
The other goes on the bearing 080°.
There is open moorland between the two tracks.

A walker wants to start at the stone and walk on the moor so that he is always the same distance from the two tracks.

Draw a sketch of the situation.

Work out the bearing that the walker should walk on.

The locus of points equidistant from two lines is
the line that bisects the angle between the two points.
('Bisect' means cut exactly in half.)

Bisecting an angle

1 Draw an arc with its centre at the vertex of the angle.

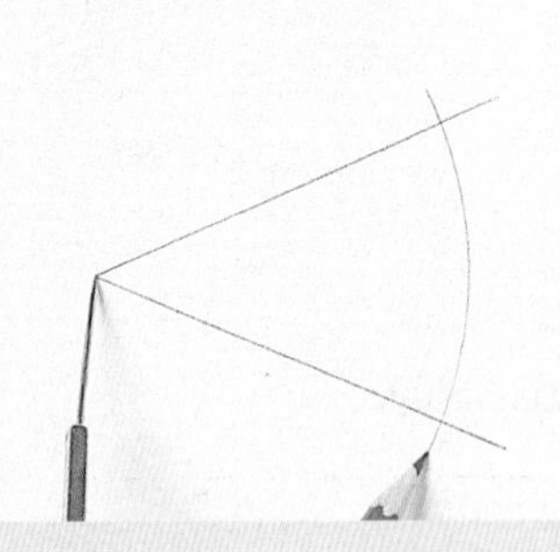

2 Draw two arcs with the same radius from the points where your first arc crosses the arms of the angle.

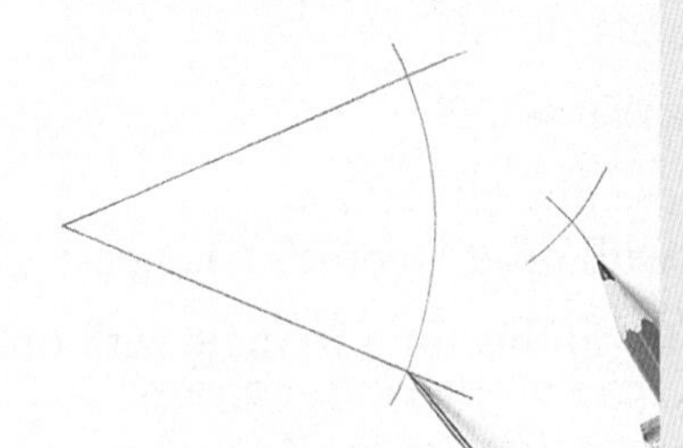

3 Draw the line that bisects the angle. (Can you explain why it bisects the angle?)

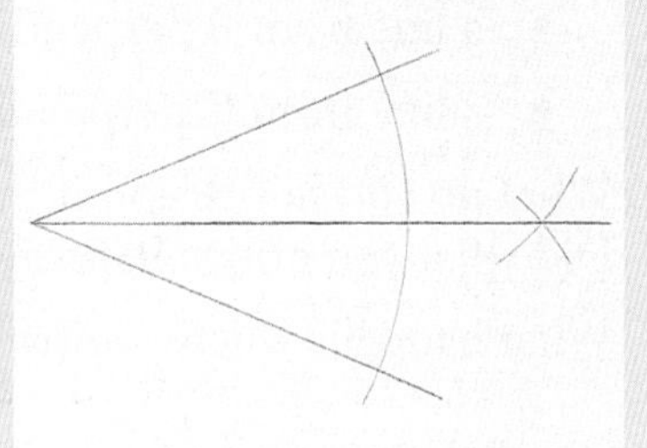

E2 Construct an angle of 45° by

(a) constructing a perpendicular from a point to a line

(b) bisecting the right angle

E3 Construct an angle of 30° by

(a) constructing an equilateral triangle with compasses to get angles of 60°

(b) bisecting one of the 60° angles

E4 Construct an angle of 75°.
Do not rub out the stages of your construction.

Triangle investigation 3

Draw a large scalene triangle on A4 paper.

Draw the bisector of one angle of the triangle.
Now do the same for the other two angles.

What happens? Does it happen for other people's triangles?

E5 In 'Triangle investigation 3' the three bisectors you drew should have all met at one point.

Using that point as the centre, draw a circle that just touches one side of the triangle. What happens?

E6 Copy this diagram using the lengths shown.

Shade the region containing points that satisfy all three of these conditions.

- They must be more than 4 cm from line BA.
- They must be less than 7 cm from A.
- They must be closer to line BC than line BA.

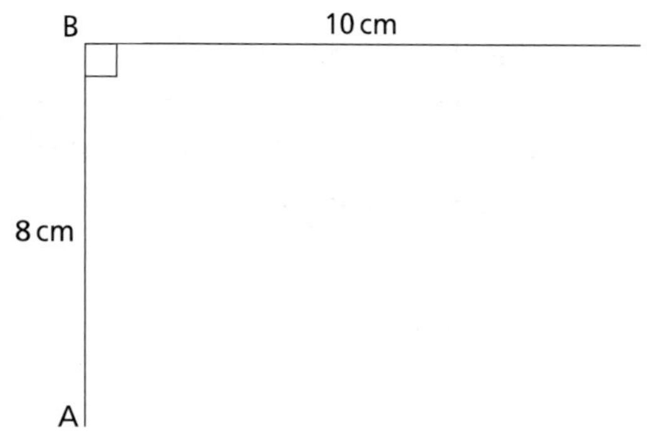

E7 Ceri and Diane want to find how far away a tower, T, is on the other side of a river.

To do this they mark out a base line, AB, 100 metres long as shown in the diagram.

Next they measure the angles at the ends A and B between the base line and the lines of sight of the tower. These angles are 30° and 60°.

(a) **Use ruler and compasses only** to make a scale drawing of the situation.
Use a scale of 1 cm to represent 10 m.
Show clearly all your construction lines.

(b) Find the shortest distance of the tower, T, from the base line AB.

AQA 2000 Specimen

F *The perpendicular from a point on a line*

P is a point on line *l*. Follow this construction to draw a line from P perpendicular to *l*.

1 Draw arcs with centre P and the same radius.

2 Draw two arcs with equal radius from the points where your first arcs cross line *l*.

3 Join P to the point where the last two arcs cross.

F1 Draw a circle with radius of about 5 cm.

Draw any radius, extending your line beyond the circle.

Construct the perpendicular to this line at the point where it meets the circle.

This perpendicular is called a **tangent** to the circle. It should touch the circle without crossing it.

Draw another radius and construct a tangent where it meets the circle.
Extend the two tangents until they cross.

Measure from where they cross to where each of them touches the circle. What do you notice?

F2 Draw a circle with radius about 5 cm.

From a point A on the circle, draw a line AB which crosses the circle at C.

Construct the perpendicular from C to point D on the circle.

Join AD with a straight line.
What do you notice about this line?
Did the same thing happen with other people's lines?

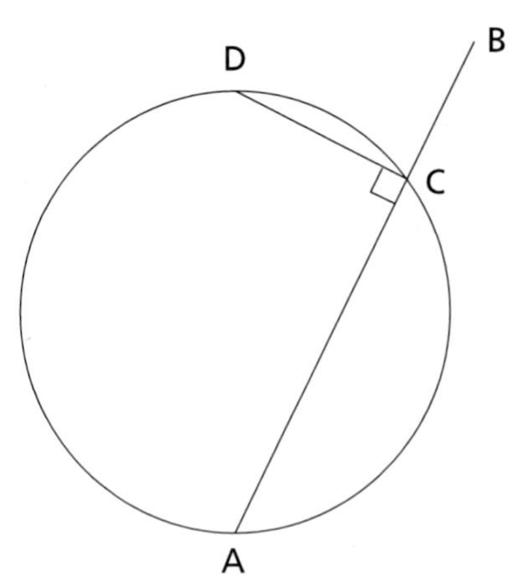

G *Mixed questions*

G1 A square meadow has sides 10 m long.

A goat is tied to a rope 6 m long.
The rope is fastened to a post at one corner of the meadow.

(a) What is the area of the grass the goat can reach?

(b) What percentage of the area of the whole meadow is this?

G2 Do a scale drawing to solve this puzzle and mark the position of the treasure with a cross.

> *The treasure is in a rectangular field ABCD.*
> *Side AB is 11 m long and side BC is 8 m long.*
>
> *The treasure is equidistant from corners A and C.*
> *It is along one of the edges of the field.*
> *It is closer to corner B than to corner D.*

G3 A tree is to be planted in this rectangular garden.
The tree must be equidistant from sides AB and AD.
The tree must also be exactly 3.0 m from corner C.

Draw the plan to scale, showing clearly how you find the position for the tree.

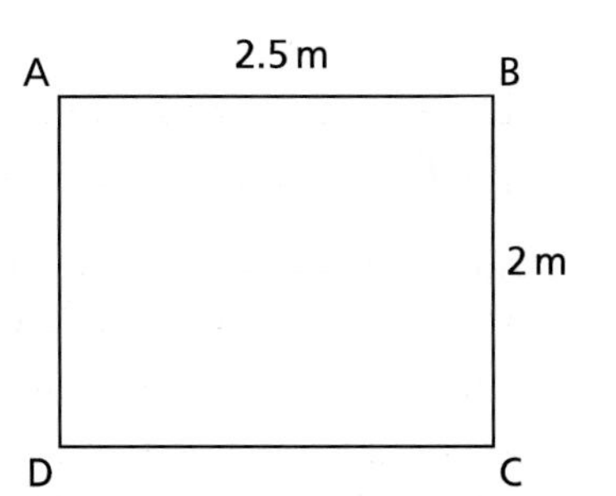

G4 All the angles of this quadrilateral have been bisected. The bisectors have produced another quadrilateral in the middle of the original one.

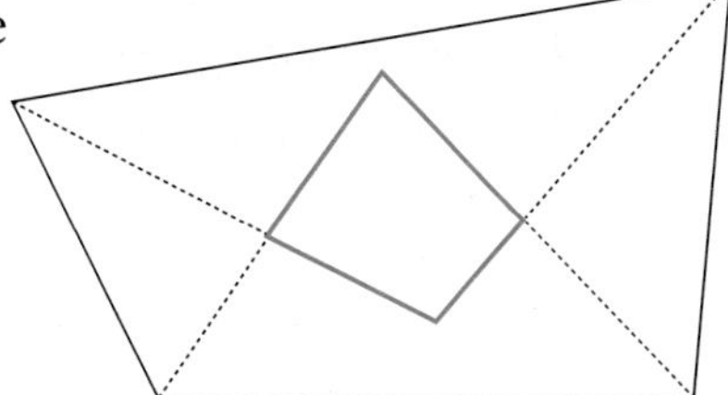

For each special quadrilateral below, if you bisect all its angles, do the bisectors produce another quadrilateral? If so, what sort?

(a) A rectangle that is not a square

(b) A parallelogram that is not a rhombus or rectangle

(c) A rhombus

(d) An isosceles trapezium (one with a line of reflection symmetry)

(e) A kite

Test yourself

T1 This is the plan of a square garden.
The tree is at the centre.

Grass is to be planted. It must be at least 3 m from the tree and at least 4 m from the wall of the house. It can go right up to the edge on the other sides.

Draw the plan to scale and shade the part where the grass goes.

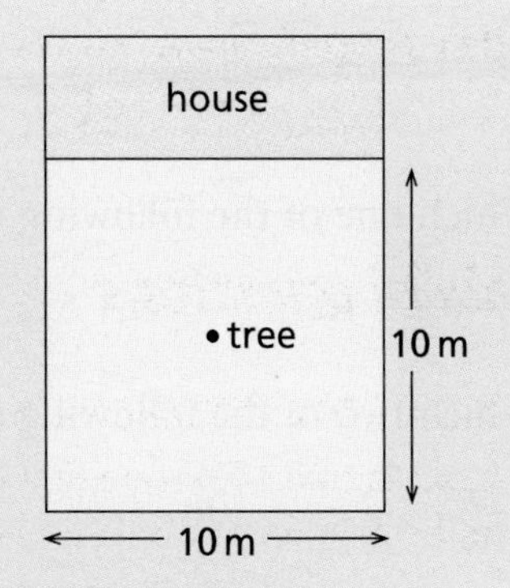

T2 In both parts of this question, do not rub out your construction lines.

(a) Construct accurately triangle ABC when

AB = 8.4 cm, ABC = 74° and AC = 9.7 cm.

(b) Using ruler and compasses only, construct the perpendicular bisector of BC. OCR

T3 Copy this diagram using the lengths shown.

Shade the region containing points that satisfy all three of these conditions.

- They must be more than 4 cm from Y.
- They must be closer to line YX than line YZ.
- They must be closer to Z than X.

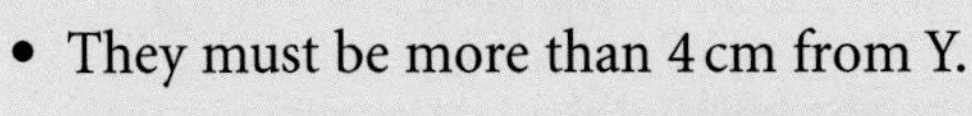

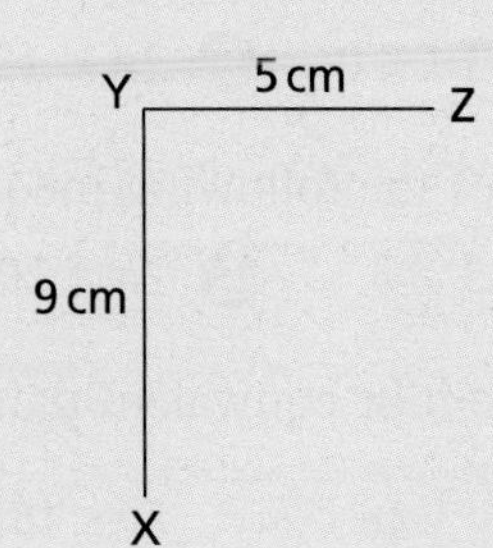

55 Solving inequalities

This work will help you solve inequalities.

A Manipulating inequalities

This diagram shows the set of numbers where $n \leq 4$.

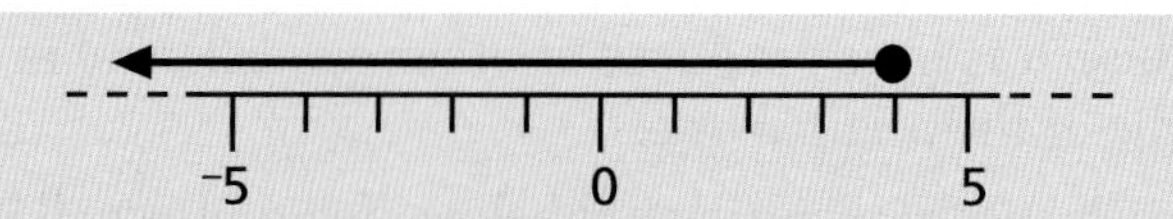

- Which of these inequalities gives the above set of numbers?

$2n \leq 8$ $n + 1 \leq 4$ $n + 1 \leq 5$ $n - 1 \leq 5$ $\frac{n}{2} \leq 3$ $\frac{n}{4} \leq 1$ $3n \leq 10$ $n - 3 \leq 1$

- Match up these inequalities.

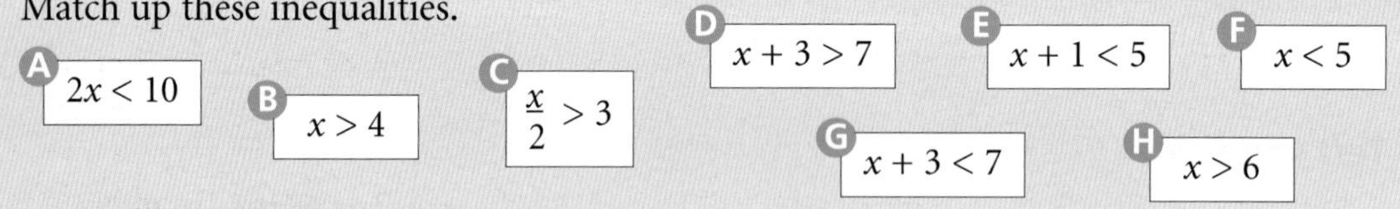

A1 Which one of the following is equivalent to $n \leq 8$?

$n + 2 \leq 16$ $n + 5 \leq 3$ $n + 6 \leq 14$ $n + 4 \leq 2$ $n + 1 \leq 10$

A2 Which two of the following are equivalent to $m > 6$?

$2m > 8$ $\frac{m}{2} > 12$ $3m > 2$ $2m > 12$ $\frac{m}{3} > 2$ $\frac{m}{2} > 4$

A3 Which of the following are equivalent to $n \leq 3$?

A $n + 1 \leq 4$ **B** $3n \leq 6$ **C** $3 \leq n$ **D** $\frac{n}{2} \leq 1\frac{1}{2}$ **E** $2n \leq 6$

A4 Which of the following are equivalent to $p < 10$?

A $p - 10 < 0$ **B** $2p < 12$ **C** $2p < 20$ **D** $\frac{p}{2} < 20$ **E** $p + 10 < 20$

A5 Which of the following inequalities are equivalent to $a \geq 10$?

A $a - 5 \geq 5$ **B** $2a \geq 20$ **C** $a + 5 \geq 5$ **D** $\frac{1}{2}a \geq 5$ **E** $a + \frac{1}{2} \geq 10\frac{1}{2}$

A6 Find the four equivalent pairs in these eight inequalities.

$p \leq 8$ $4p \leq 24$ $2p \leq 18$ $p - 2 \leq 6$ $p \leq 9$ $p + 4 \leq 14$ $3p \leq 18$ $2p \leq 20$

B *Solving simple inequalities*

- If we are given an inequality, we can add or subtract any number on both sides.
  For example, $x \leq 12$ so $x + 1 \leq 13$ (add 1)
  $n + 4 > 9$ so $n > 5$ (subtract 4)

- We can multiply or divide both sides of an inequality by the same **positive** number.
  For example, $\frac{x}{2} \leq 12$ so $x \leq 24$ (multiply by 2)
  $2n > 8$ so $n > 4$ (divide by 2)

- You can **solve** inequalities using the rules above.
  (To solve is to find, in its simplest form, the set of numbers that satisfy the inequality.)
  For example,
  $2x + 17 \geq 25$
  $2x \geq 8$ (take 17 off both sides)
  $x \geq 4$ (divide both sides by 2)

  We can show the solution on a number line.

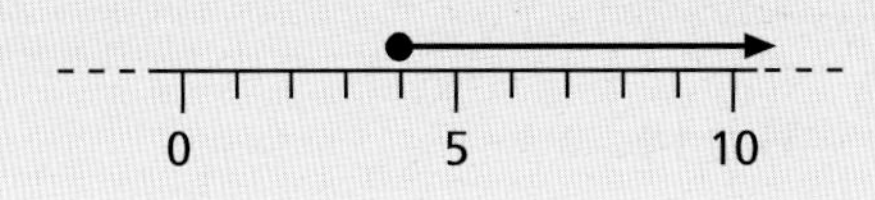

Checking a few values that fit the solution can help you spot mistakes.

For example when $x = 5$,
$2x + 17 = 2 \times 5 + 17$
$= 27$
which **is** greater than or equal to 25.

B1 (a) Solve $x + 4 > 6$.
(b) Write down three numbers that fit your solution. Check they fit the original inequality.
(c) Sketch your solution on a number line.

B2 Solve each of these inequalities.
(a) $n + 5 \leq 11$ (b) $n - 5 \geq 11$ (c) $n - 1 < 6$ (d) $n + 3 < 10$

B3 Solve each of these inequalities.
(a) $2x \leq 12$ (b) $3x > 24$ (c) $\frac{x}{2} \geq 5$ (d) $9 < \frac{x}{3}$

B4 Solve the following inequalities.
(a) $r + 4 \leq 8$ (b) $x - 5 \geq 12$ (c) $3m \leq 45$ (d) $\frac{a}{2} < 12$
(e) $20 \geq 4t$ (f) $2p \geq 7$ (g) $3p > {}^{-}6$ (h) $t + 3 < 2$

B5 Solve each of these inequalities.
(a) $4r + 1 \geq 17$ (b) $2t - 1 \leq 13$ (c) $1 + 2f > 11$ (d) $3d - 2 \leq 10$
(e) $2n + 1 > 10$ (f) $17 \leq 3 + 2z$ (g) $\frac{a}{2} + 4 < 8$ (h) $\frac{s}{3} + 2 \geq 5$

B6 Solve each of these inequalities.
(a) $x + 9 < 5$ (b) $t - 1 \leq {}^{-}6$ (c) $6f + 1 > {}^{-}11$ (d) $5n + 11 \geq 1$

C *Unknown on both sides*

When solving inequalities, sometimes the unknown is on both sides.

For example,

$7 + 3a < 25 + a$
$7 + 2a < 25$ (subtract a from both sides)
$2a < 18$ (subtract 7 from both sides)
$a < 9$ (divide both sides by 2)

C1 Solve each of these.

(a) $2x < x + 7$ (b) $7y \geq 5y + 2$ (c) $9w < 6w + 21$ (d) $4r - 12 \geq 3r$

C2 Solve $5x + 7 > 3x + 19$ by first subtracting $3x$ from both sides.

C3 Solve each of these inequalities.

(a) $4s + 2 < 3s + 12$ (b) $7n + 1 \geq 3n + 29$ (c) $4x + 3 < 4 + x$
(d) $5a - 3 \leq 4a + 1$ (e) $6b - 9 < 6 + b$ (f) $5z - 4 \leq 3z + 7$
(g) $3y - 6 > 2y - 4$ (h) $5y + 7 \leq 2y + 1$ (i) $7t + 1 > 5t - 7$

C4 Multiply the brackets out from $2(x - 3)$.
Use this to help you solve the inequality $2(x - 3) \leq 14$.

C5 Solve these by first multiplying out any brackets.

(a) $2(n + 1) > n + 15$ (b) $3(k - 3) \geq 2(k + 2)$ (c) $5(x - 5) \leq 3(x - 3)$

C6 Solve $2x + 8 \geq 4x + 2$ by first subtracting $2x$ from each side.

C7 Solve each of these inequalities.

(a) $2p + 15 < 5p$ (b) $6t + 11 > 10t + 3$ (c) $10 + 3a < 7a - 6$
(d) $6n < 8n - 18$ (e) $4d - 2 \leq 5d$ (f) $b + 2 \geq 17 + 4b$

C8 Solve each of these inequalities.

(a) $7(n + 1) \leq 3n - 7$ (b) $2(k - 5) < 7k - 15$ (c) $h + 7 \geq 5 + 4h$

D *Avoiding negatives*

5 is the **largest** number that satisfies the inequality $^-2x \geq {}^-10$.
Anything **larger** does not satisfy the inequality so the solution is $x \leq 5$.

Dividing both sides of the inequality by $^-2$ 'turns round' the inequality sign.

$^-2x \geq {}^-10$
$x \leq 5$ (divide both sides by $^-2$ and 'turn round' the sign)

For example, if $x = 6$ then $^-2x = {}^-2 \times 6 = {}^-12$ which is smaller than $^-10$.

Divide or multiply both sides by a *negative* number and the inequality sign 'turns round'.

D1 Solve each of these.

(a) $^-2x \leq {}^-8$ (b) $^-6t \geq 12$ (c) $^-4r < {}^-12$ (d) $-\frac{n}{2} > {}^-7$

Always aim to get a positive number in front of the unknown.
This avoids having to divide or multiply by a negative number.

For example, $8 - 2b < b - 7$

$8 < 3b - 7$ (add $2b$ to both sides)

$15 < 3b$ (add 7 to both sides)

$5 < b$ (divide both sides by 3)

which we usually write as $b > 5$

D2 Solve $6 < 10 - x$ by first adding x to both sides.

D3 Solve $2n + 3 \geq 13 - 3n$ by first adding $3n$ to both sides.

D4 Solve each of these.

(a) $3 > 7 - p$ (b) $7 \leq 13 - 2d$ (c) $2 + f < 20 - 2f$

(d) $6n - 2 \leq 18 - 2n$ (e) $22 - 5w \geq 2w + 1$ (f) $5 - z > 7 - 2z$

(g) $2(n + 3) > 8 - n$ (h) $12 - 2m \leq 3(m + 1)$ (i) $5(k + 1) < 3(9 - 2k)$

E *Further examples*

To solve a combined inequality we can do the same thing to each part.

For example, $5 \leq 2x - 1 < 11$

$6 \leq 2x < 12$ (add 1 to each part)

$3 \leq x < 6$ (divide all parts by 2)

We can show the solution on a number line.

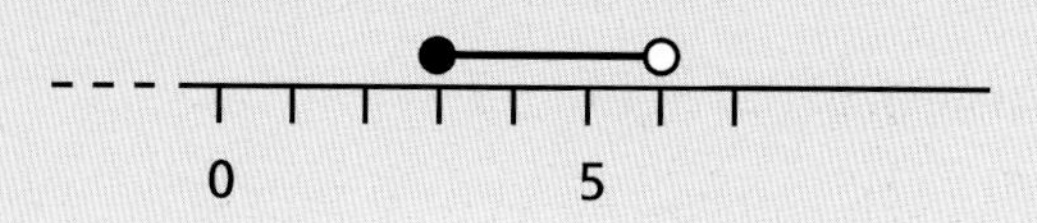

E1 (a) Solve $4 \leq x + 1 < 9$.

(b) Show your solution on a number line.

E2 Solve $6 < 2x \leq 10$ and show your solution on a number line.

E3 Solve these inequalities.

(a) $7 \leq x + 4 < 20$ (b) $0 < n - 2 < 7$ (c) $^-1 \leq x + 2 < 11$

(d) $12 \leq 3z < 24$ (e) $3 \leq \frac{n}{2} \leq 5$ (f) $^-8 \leq 4z < 10$

E4 Solve $10 \leq 3n + 1 \leq 25$ and show your solution on a number line.

E5 Solve these inequalities.

(a) $2 \le 3x - 4 < 8$ (b) $4 < 3x + 1 \le 16$ (c) $^-8 \le 2x + 4 < 7$

E6 (a) Solve $9 \le 2x + 1 < 21$.

(b) List the values of x, where x is an **integer**, such that $9 \le 2x + 1 < 21$.

E7 List the values of n, where n is an integer, such that $1 \le 2n - 3 < 5$. AQA 1999

E8 There are seven integers, n, such that $n^2 \le 9$. List them.

E9 Solve the inequality $x^2 < 25$.
(Hint: the answer is **not** simply $x < 5$.)

E10 Solve the inequality $x^2 < 9$. AQA(NEAB) 1998

Test yourself

T1 Which of the following inequalities are equivalent to $m < 3$?

A $m + 2 < 5$

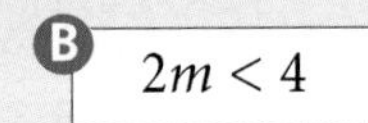

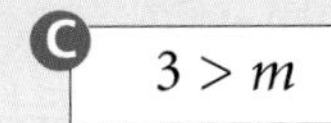

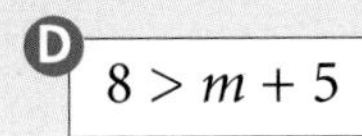

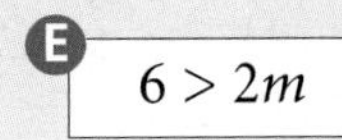

T2 Solve each of these and sketch each solution on a number line.

(a) $4r \le 12$ (b) $h + 2 > 0$ (c) $j - 1 \le 1$ (d) $\frac{a}{2} < 1$

T3 Solve the inequality $3x - 5 \le 16$. AQA 2003 Specimen

T4 Solve $3x + 19 > 4$. OCR

T5 Solve the inequality $12n - 13 \le 7n + 2$.

T6 Solve these inequalities.

(a) $4x - 3 < 7$ (b) $11 + 2x > 5x - 7$ OCR

T7 Solve the inequality $9n + 1 < 14n - 2$. OCR

T8 Solve the following inequality for x.

$4x - 3 > 3x - 2$ AQA(NEAB) 2000 Specimen

T9 Solve the inequality $3(x - 2) < x + 7$. AQA(SEG) 1998 Specimen

T10 Solve these inequalities.

(a) $5 - 2h \le 3h$ (b) $^-1 < \frac{w}{2} - 1$ (c) $3(x + 3) > 2(2 - x)$

T11 Solve the inequality $3 < 2x + 1 < 5$. AQA(SEG) 2000

T12 Solve the inequality $^-1 \le 3x + 2 < 5$. AQA(SEG) 2000 Specimen

T13 Solve $x^2 < 49$. Represent your solution on a number line.

56 *Working with coordinates*

You should know how to

- use vectors
- find the equation of a straight line
- calculate the length of a line segment using Pythagoras' theorem
- calculate areas

This work will help you

- find the mid-point of a line segment
- use coordinates in 3D

A *Shapes on grids*

A1 (a) Draw a pair of axes, each numbered from $^-5$ to 10.
Plot the points P ($^-4$, 3), Q ($^-2$, 7) and R (10, 1). Join P to Q and Q to R.

(b) Plot the point S so that PQRS is a rectangle.
What are the coordinates of S?

(c) Draw the lines of symmetry on the rectangle.
What are the coordinates of the point where the lines of symmetry intersect?

A2 (a) On centimetre squared paper, draw a pair of axes, each numbered from $^-6$ to 6.
Plot the points A (5, 2), B ($^-4$, 5) and C ($^-5$, 2).

(b) Plot the point D so that ABCD is a kite.
What are the coordinates of D?

(c) Work out the area of the kite.

(d) Plot the point E so that ABCE is a rectangle.
What are the coordinates of E?

(e) What is the area of the rectangle?

A3 MNOPQ is a pentagon and three of its points are M (3, 4), N (7, 2) and O (7, $^-3$).

(a) Draw a pair of axes, each numbered from $^-5$ to 8 and plot the points M, N and O.

The line with equation $x = 3$ is a line of symmetry of the pentagon.

(b) Plot the points P and Q and write down their coordinates.

A4 (a) Draw a pair of axes, each numbered from $^-4$ to 7.
Plot the points K ($^-2$, $^-1$), L (2, 1) and M (6, $^-1$).

(b) Plot the point N so that KLMN is a rhombus and write down the coordinates of N.

(c) Draw the lines of symmetry on the rhombus.
Write down the equation of each line.

A **vector** can describe a movement from one point to another.

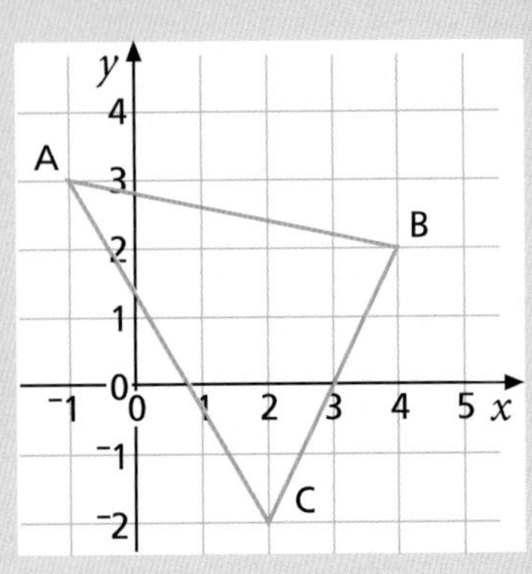

The vector $\overrightarrow{AB}$ can be written as the column vector

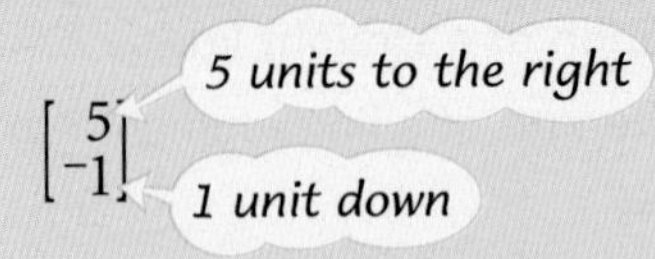

A5 Write down column vectors for $\overrightarrow{AC}$ and $\overrightarrow{BC}$ in the diagram above.

A6 The diagram shows three points D, E and F.

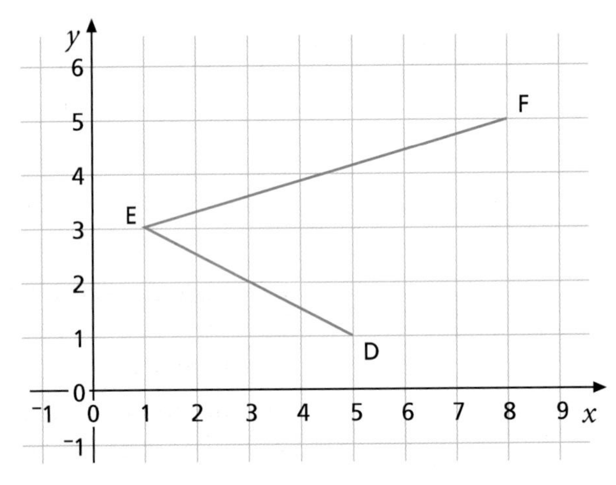

(a) Write down the vector $\overrightarrow{EF}$ as a column vector.

(b) Work out the coordinates of a fourth point G so that DEFG is a parallelogram.

A7 (a) On a coordinate grid, plot and join the points P $(^-4, 5)$, Q $(12, 1)$, R $(4, ^-3)$ and S $(^-4, ^-1)$.

(b) (i) Write down column vectors for $\overrightarrow{PQ}$ and $\overrightarrow{SR}$.

(ii) What is the special name for the quadrilateral PQRS?

(c) Mark the mid-points of each edge of the quadrilateral.
Label these mid-points A, B C and D.
(Work clockwise and begin with the mid-point of PQ.)

(d) (i) Write down column vectors for $\overrightarrow{AB}$, $\overrightarrow{DC}$, $\overrightarrow{DA}$ and $\overrightarrow{CB}$.

(ii) Explain how these vectors show that the shape ABCD is a parallelogram.

B *Mid-points*

This number line shows the line segment with end-points 1 and 9.
The **mid-point** of this line segment is 5.

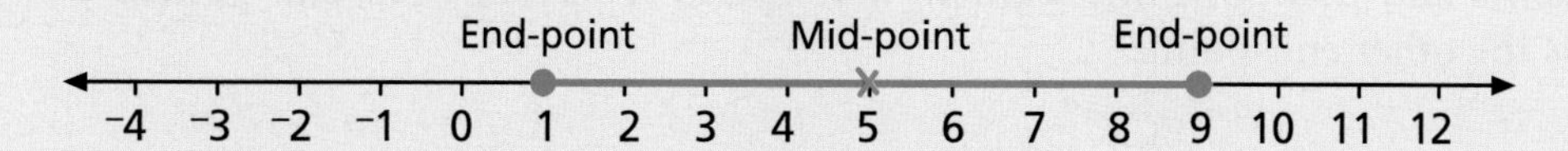

- Investigate the mid-points of different line segments on the number line (Remember to include some negative numbers.)
- Record your results in a table.
- Can you find a rule that links the end-points with the mid-point?

End-points		Mid-point
1	9	5

- What is the mid-point of the line segment with end-points a and b?

This grid shows the line segment with end-points (1, 2) and (7, 5).
The mid-point of this line segment is $(4, 3\frac{1}{2})$.

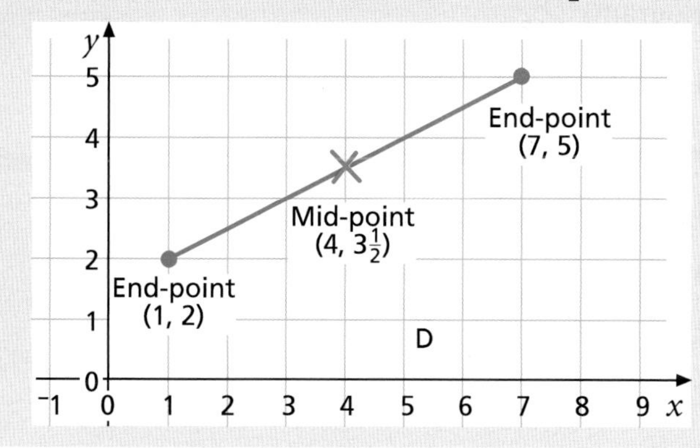

- Investigate the mid-points of different line segments on a coordinate grid.
- Can you find a rule that links the end-points with the mid-point?

B1 Which number is half-way between each of these pairs?

(a) 8 and 12 (b) 3 and 11 (c) 1 and 8 (d) $^-2$ and 6
(e) $1\frac{1}{2}$ and $7\frac{1}{2}$ (f) $^-1$ and 7 (g) $^-4$ and $^-2$ (h) $^-9$ and $^-3$

B2 8 is the mid-point of a line that has 3 as one of its end-points.
What is the other end-point?

B3 What is the mid-point of the line segment AB?

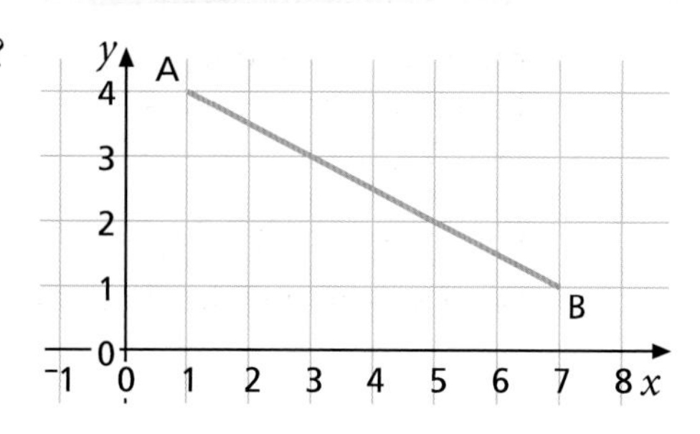

B4 Work out the mid-points of the line segments joining these pairs of points.

(a) (0, 2) and (6, 8) (b) (1, 5) and (11, 7) (c) ($^-$2, 5) and (4, 1)

(d) ($^-$3, 6) and (3, 2) (e) (1, 9) and (8, 1) (f) ($^-$2, 8) and (10, 9)

B5 (2, 3) is the mid-point of a line segment that has (5, $^-$1) as one of its end-points. What is the other end-point?

C *Mixed problems*

In each problem, the coordinates refer to a square centimetre grid.

C1 The line segment AB is one edge of a parallelogram ABCD.
The point A has coordinates (0, 3).
The point B has coordinates (6, 5).
The diagonals of the parallelogram cross at the point (3, 2).

(a) Draw the whole parallelogram.

(b) Write down the coordinates of points C and D.

(c) Calculate the area of the parallelogram.

C2 M is the mid-point of the line segment KL.
The point K has coordinates ($^-$2, $^-$6).
The point L has coordinates (4, 12).

(a) Find the equation of the line through M that is parallel to the y-axis.

(b) Find the equation of the line through M that is parallel to the x-axis.

C3 The line segment XY is the diameter of a circle.
The point X has coordinates ($^-$1, 0).
The point Y has coordinates (5, 8).

(a) What are the coordinates of the centre of the circle?

(b) Use Pythagoras' rule to calculate the length of XY.

(c) Calculate the area of the circle, correct to two decimal places.

C4 (a) Plot and join the points A (5, 9), B (13, 10) and C (1, 2).

(b) (i) Calculate the length of AB.

(ii) Calculate the length of AC.

(iii) What is the special name for triangle ABC?

(c) (i) Plot M, the mid-point of BC, and write down its coordinates.

(ii) Explain how you know that $\angle AMB = 90°$.

(d) Write down the coordinates of D so that shape ABDC is a rhombus.

C5 The diagram shows a triangle PQR.
P, Q and R have coordinates ($^-2$, 4), (5, 3) and ($^-1$, $^-1.5$) respectively.
X is a point on RQ with coordinates (1, 0).

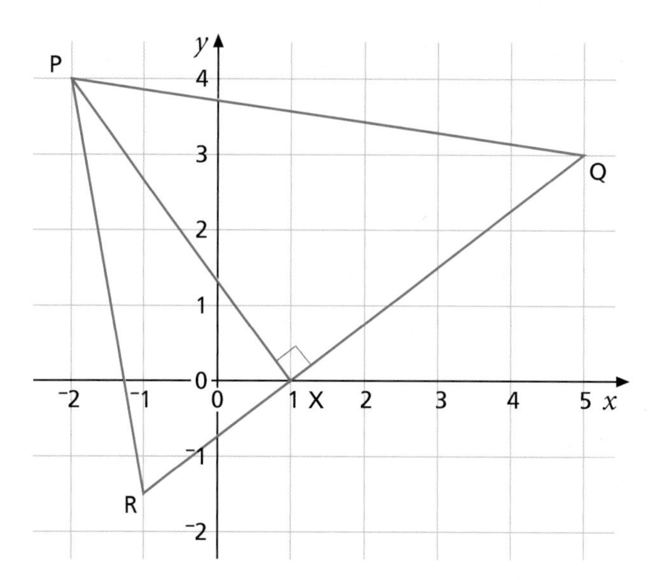

(a) Calculate the length PX.

(b) Calculate the length QR.

(c) Find the area of triangle PQR.

C6 (a) Draw a pair of axes, each numbered from $^-6$ to 8.
Plot and join the points A (1, 2) and B (4, 5).

(b) Find the equation of the straight line through A and B.

A and B are vertices of a square ABCD.
Points C and D are on the line $y = x - 5$.

(c) Draw the line and plot the points C and D.
Give the coordinates of points C and D.

(d) Find the area of the square.

(e) Show all the lines of symmetry of the square.
What is the equation of each line of symmetry?

C7 ABCD is a parallelogram whose vertices are all above the x-axis.

- A and B are points on the line $y = 2x + 1$.
- The point D has coordinates (2, 1).
- The edge AD is parallel to the x-axis.
- The area of the parallelogram is 8 cm^2.

Draw the parallelogram in the correct position on a coordinate grid.

D Points in 3-D

To give the position of a point in 3-D space, a third axis is needed called the **z-axis**. So each point has three coordinates, written in the form (x, y, z).

TG

Making your own grid

- Cut out the 3-D grid from sheet G71 and stick it together. Place it on the desk with the x-axis and the y-axis on the desk and the z-axis pointing upwards.
- Here a rod 3 cm long has been placed on the grid. The bottom of the rod has coordinates (2, 4, 0). What are the coordinates of the top of the rod?

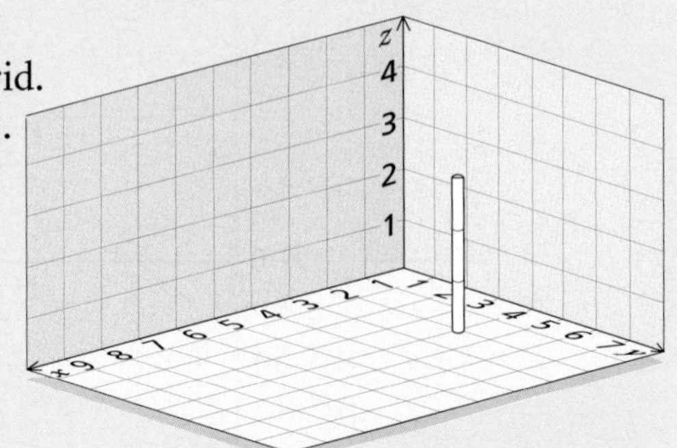

- Cut out the rectangle from sheet G72. Place it on the bottom of the 3-D grid with its x-axis and y-axis matching the grid. What are the 3-D coordinates of P, Q, R and S?
- Lift the rectangle up 3 units. What are the coordinates of P, Q, R and S now?
- Cut out the net for the cuboid from sheet G72 and glue it together. Place the cuboid on the 3-D grid like this (corner B is at (0, 0, 0) and face P is at the bottom). What are the coordinates of each corner that you can see?

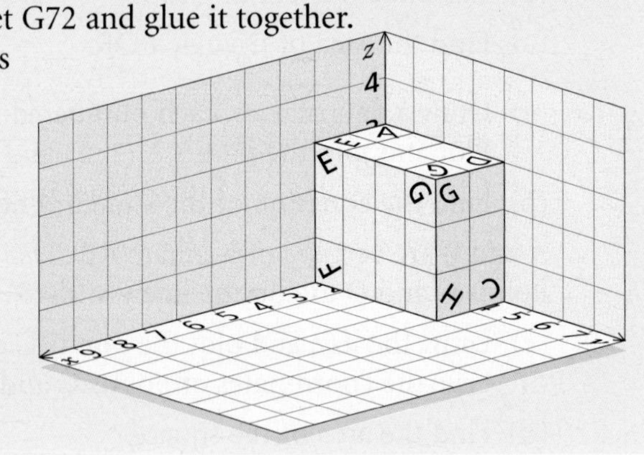

D1 Place the cuboid on the 3-D grid with corner A at (0, 0, 0) and face M at the bottom. Write down the coordinates of these corners.

(a) F (b) C (c) E (d) H

D2 Place the cuboid with corner C at (0, 0, 0) and face N at the bottom. Write down the coordinates of these corners.

(a) B (b) G (c) E (d) A

D3 Place the cuboid with face M at the bottom, corner A at (5, 2, 0) and corner D at (1, 2, 0). Write down the coordinates of these corners.

(a) G (b) B (c) F (d) H

D4 Place the cuboid so that face P is at the bottom, B is at (1, 3, 0) and C is at (1, 7, 0). Write down the coordinates of these points.

(a) H (b) A (c) D (d) G

D5 If the cuboid is placed so that C is at (3, 2, 1), E is at (1, 6, 4) and face P is facing downwards, what are the coordinates of these points?

(a) F (b) B (c) G (d) A

D6 A cube has vertices at (0, 0, 0), (4, 0, 0) and (0, 4, 0). What are the coordinates of the other five vertices?

D7 On this 3-D grid is a shape made from five centimetre cubes.

(a) What letter is at the point (2, 2, 1)?

(b) Write down the 3-D coordinates of the other four labelled points.

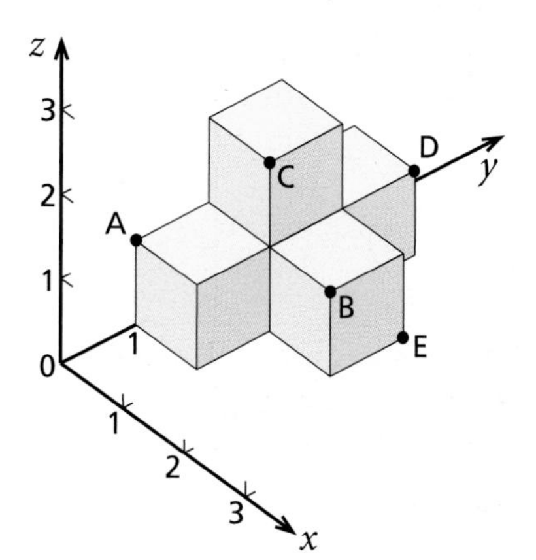

D8 This is a flight of steps with each step the same size. The x, y and z-axes are shown.

Point A is at (6, 0, 0) Point B is at (6, 3, 2)

(a) How high is the flight of stairs?

(b) Write down the coordinates of these points.

(i) C (ii) D

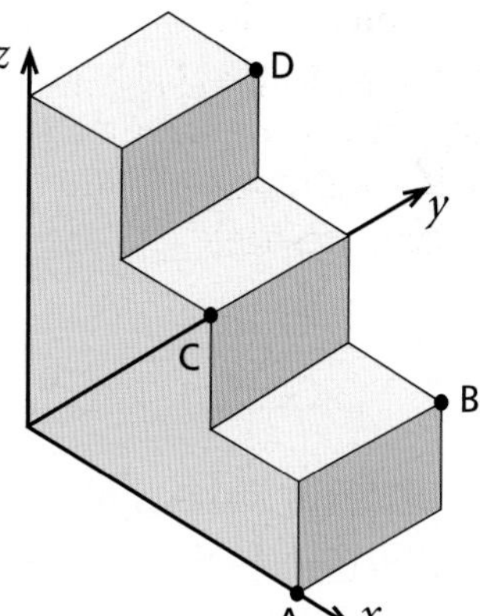

***D9** This shows a 3-D grid and a cube with sides 2 units long. Point A is at (0, 1, 0).

The cube is reflected in the horizontal plane containing the x-axis and y-axis.

What will be the images of these points after the reflection?

(a) A (b) B (c) C

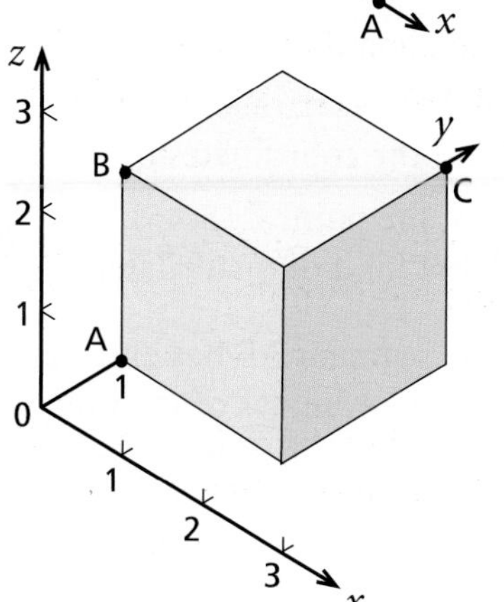

Test yourself

T1 A is the point (4, 2), B is the point (4, 0) and C is the point $(^-1, ^-3)$.

ABCD is a kite.

On a suitable set of axes, draw the kite ABCD and write down the coordinates of D.

T2

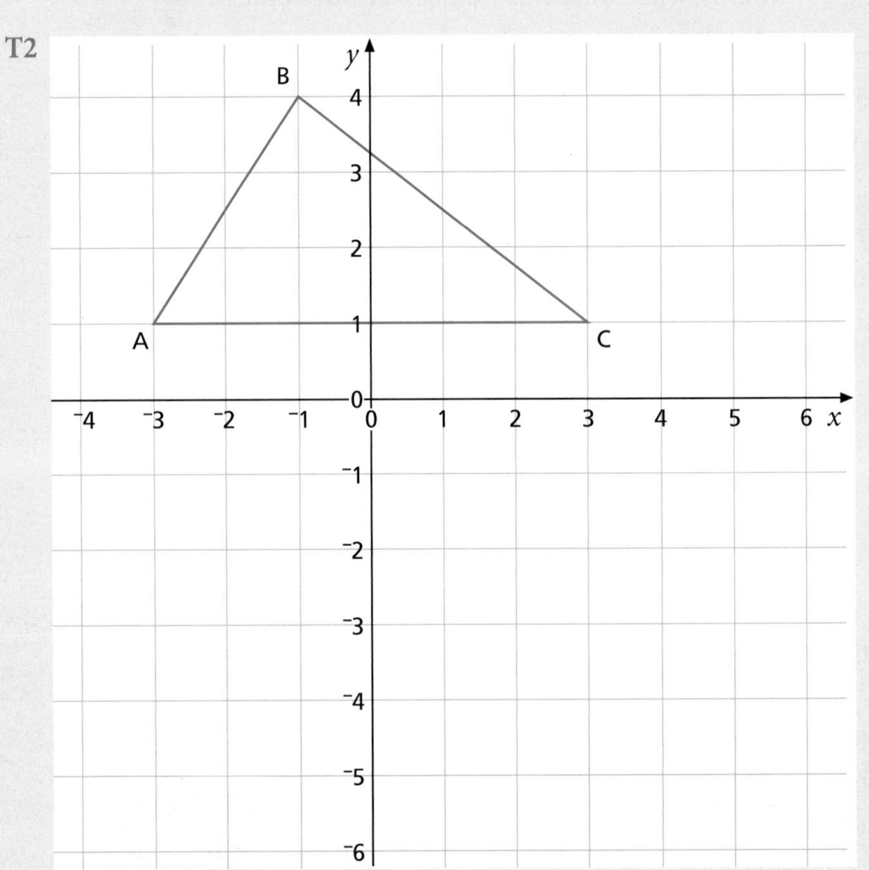

The diagram shows a triangle ABC drawn on a one centimetre grid.

(a) Calculate the area of triangle ABC.

Copy the diagram.

(b) ABCD is a parallelogram.
Find the coordinates of the point D.

(c) Plot the point E $(5, ^-5)$.
What kind of quadrilateral is ABCE? OCR

T3 The line segment AB has end-points A $(^-2, 4)$ and B (6, 1).
Find the coordinates of the mid-point of AB.

T4 Calculate the length of the line joining the points A ($^-3$, 2) and B (6, $^-2$).

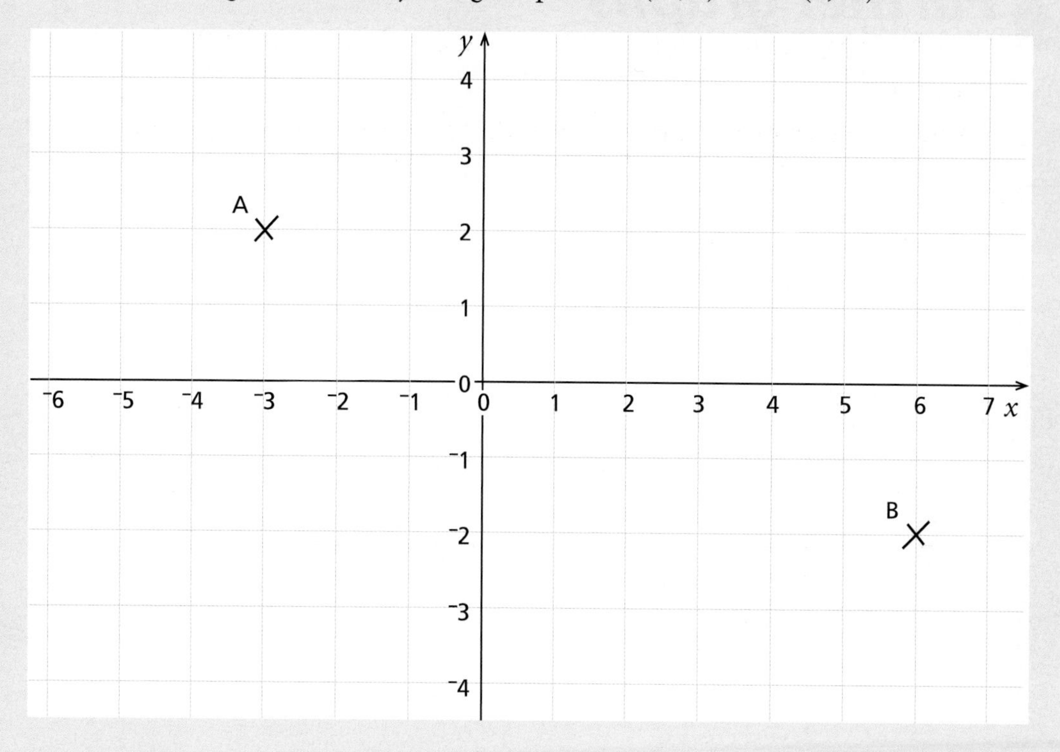

AQA(NEAB) 2000

T5 The diagram shows eight one-centimetre cubes fixed together.

Corner A has coordinates (1, 1, 0).

Write down the coordinates of points B and C.

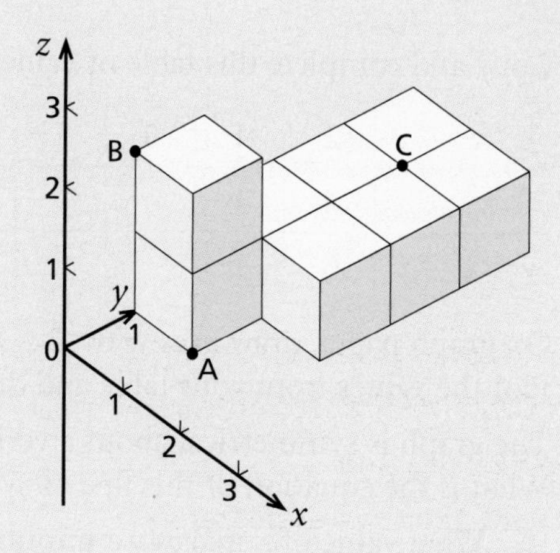

OCR

57 Further graphs

You will revise how to draw quadratic graphs and use them to solve equations

The work will help you

- plot graphs involving x^3 and $\frac{1}{x}$ and recognise a range of graphs
- solve equations by trial and improvement

A Parabolas

TG

Investigate the graphs of families of quadratic equations.

$y = x^2$
$y = x^2 + 1$
$y = x^2 + 2$
$y = x^2 + 3$
...

$y = x^2$
$y = x^2 - 1$
$y = x^2 - 2$
$y = x^2 - 3$
...

$y = x^2$
$y = 2x^2$
$y = 3x^2$
$y = 4x^2$
...

$y = {}^-x^2$
$y = {}^-2x^2$
$y = {}^-3x^2$
$y = {}^-4x^2$
...

B Working with quadratics

B1 (a) Copy and complete this table of values for the equation $y = x^2 - x$.

x	$^-2$	$^-1$	0	1	2	3
x^2	4	1				9
$y = x^2 - x$	6	2				6

(b) On graph paper, draw axes with $^-2 \leq x \leq 3$, and $^-1 \leq y \leq 6$.
Plot the values from your table and draw the graph of $y = x^2 - x$.

(c) The graph is symmetrical about a vertical line.
What is the equation of this line of symmetry?

(d) (i) What value of x makes y a minimum?

(ii) Substitute this value of x into the equation and thus work out the minimum value of y.

(iii) Does this minimum agree with the value shown by your graph?

(e) From the graph, what values of x make $x^2 - x = 3$?

(f) (i) What values of x make $x^2 - x = 0$?

(ii) Factorise the left-hand side of $x^2 - x = 0$.
Use your factorisation to check your answers to (f) (i).

B2 This is the graph of $y = 9 - x^2$.

(a) What is the maximum value of y?

(b) Find the values of x that make $y = 5$.

(c) Use the graph to write down the two solutions to the equation $9 - x^2 = 8$.

(d) Can you solve the equation $9 - x^2 = 10$? Explain your answer.

(e) From the graph what are the solutions of $9 - x^2 = 1$? (Give your answers to one decimal place.)

(f) What are the solutions to $9 - x^2 = 0$?

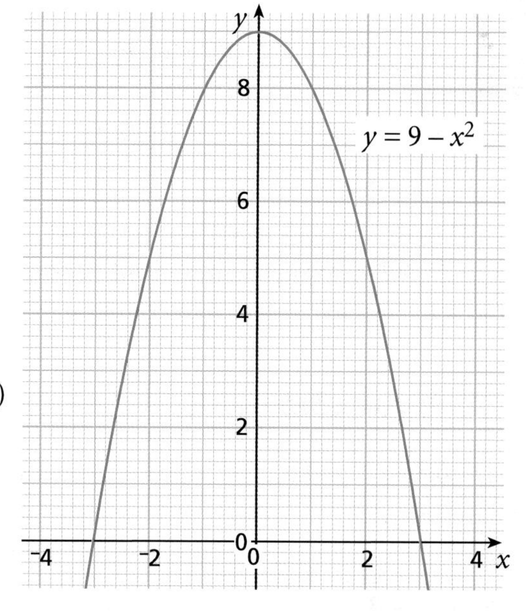

B3 (a) Copy and complete this table for $y = x^2 - 3$.

x	⁻2	⁻1	0	1	2
x^2	4	1			
$y = x^2 - 3$	1	⁻2			

(b) On graph paper draw the graph of $y = x^2 - 3$ for $^-2 \leq x \leq 2$. Use axes where 2 cm stands for 1 unit.

(c) Use your graph to write down

(i) the positive value of x for which $x^2 - 3 = {}^-1$

(ii) the negative value of x for which $x^2 - 3 = {}^-1$

(d) Use your graph to write down to one decimal place

(i) the positive square root of 3

(ii) the negative square root of 3

B4 (a) Copy and complete this table for $y = (x - 2)^2$.

x	⁻1	0	1	2	3	4
$x - 2$	⁻3					
$y = (x - 2)^2$	9					

(b) On graph paper draw the graph of $y = (x - 2)^2$ for $^-1 \leq x \leq 4$. Use axes where 2 cm stands for 1 unit.

(c) Use your graph to write down the values of x for which $(x - 2)^2 = 3$. Give your answers to one decimal place.

(d) What is the solution to $(x - 2)^2 = 0$?

B5 This question is on sheet G154.

B6 (a)

x	$^-3$	$^-2$	$^-1$	0	1	2	3	4
y	...	19	9	3	...	3	9	19

Copy and complete the table of values above and use it to draw the graph of $y = 2x^2 - 4x + 3$ for values of x from $^-3$ to 4.

Use axes as shown here.

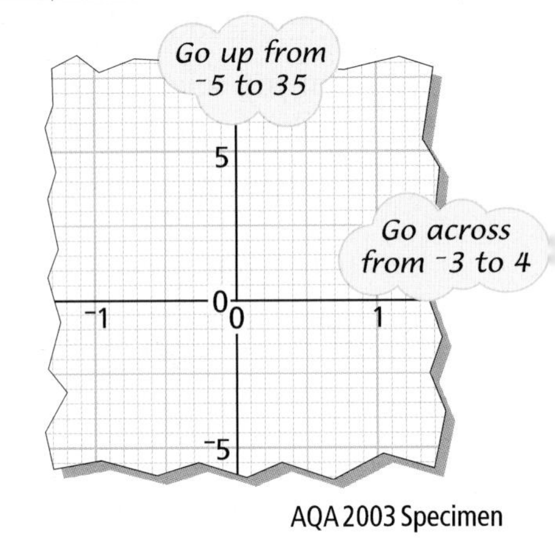

(b) Use your graph to find the value of x when $y = 6$ and $x < 0$.

AQA 2003 Specimen

C Cubics

C1 (a) Copy and complete this table for $y = x^3 - 2x$.

x	$^-2$	$^-1.5$	$^-1$	$^-0.5$	0	0.5	1	1.5	2
x^3	$^-8$	$^-3.38$		$^-0.13$		0.13			
^-2x	4	3		1		$^-1$			
$y = x^3 - 2x$	$^-4$	$^-0.38$		0.87		$^-0.87$			

(b) On graph paper, draw axes like these:

(c) Plot the points from your table. Join them up with a smooth curve to show the graph of $y = x^3 - 2x$.

(d) Describe any symmetry that the graph of $y = x^3 - 2x$ has.

(e) From the graph, write down the three values of x for which $x^3 - 2x = 1$. (Give your answers to one decimal place.)

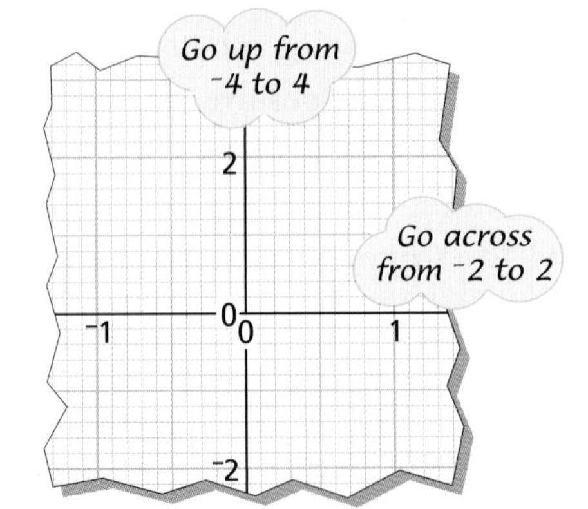

(f) Use the graph to solve (to 1 d.p.) the equation $x^3 - 2x = 3$.

(g) Use the graph to solve $x^3 - 2x = 0$.

C2 This question is on sheet G155.

Investigate the graphs of families of cubic equations.

$y = x^3$
$y = x^3 + 1$
$y = x^3 + 2\ldots$
$y = x^3 - 1$
$y = x^3 - 2\ldots$

$y = x^3$
$y = 2x^3$
$y = 3x^3\ldots$
$y = {}^-2x^3$
$y = {}^-3x^3\ldots$

$y = x^3$
$y = x^3 + x$
$y = x^3 + 2x$
$y = x^3 + 3x$
$y = x^3 + 4x\ldots$

$y = x^3$
$y = x^3 - x$
$y = x^3 - 2x$
$y = x^3 - 3x$
$y = x^3 - 4x\ldots$

D *Trial and improvement*

This sketch shows a small part of $y = x^3 + x - 1$. You can see that there is a root of the equation $x^3 + x - 1 = 0$ between 0 and 1.

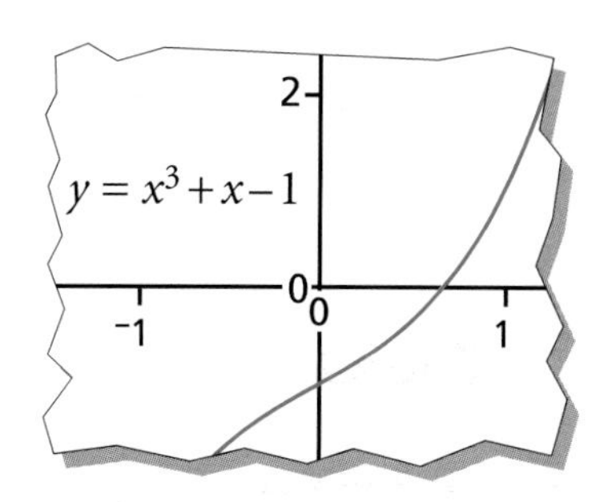

In order to get an accurate root of $x^3 + x - 1 = 0$ we can use trial and improvement, starting with, say, 0.5 as the first trial.

It is best to be systematic and use a table for this.

x	$y = x^3 + x - 1$	y *too high or too low*
0.5	*⁻0.375*	*too low*
0.6	*⁻0.184*	*too low*
0.7	*0.043*	*too high*
0.65	*⁻0.075 375*	*too low*
0.67	*⁻0.029 237*	*too low*
0.68	*⁻0.005 568*	*too low*
0.69	*0.018 509*	*too high*

The value of x must lie between 0.6 and 0.7

So try a number between 0.6 and 0.7, say 0.65

The value of x must lie between 0.68 and 0.69

D1 The root of $x^3 + x - 1 = 0$ lies between 0.68 and 0.69.

(a) Draw a table with the same headings as the one above.
In your table copy the last two lines above (the lines for 0.68 and 0.69).

(b) Take $x = 0.685$ as the next starting point.
Fill in a line of the table for $x = 0.685$.

(c) Is the root closer to 0.68 or 0.69?
Write down the solution of $x^3 + x - 1 = 0$ accurate to two decimal places.
(You can check your answer using a graphical calculator or plotting program.)

D2 (a) Copy and complete this table and draw the graph of $y = x^3 - 7x + 2$ for values of x from $^-3$ to 3.

x	$^-3$	$^-2$	$^-1$	0	1	2	3
y	$^-4$	8				$^-4$	8

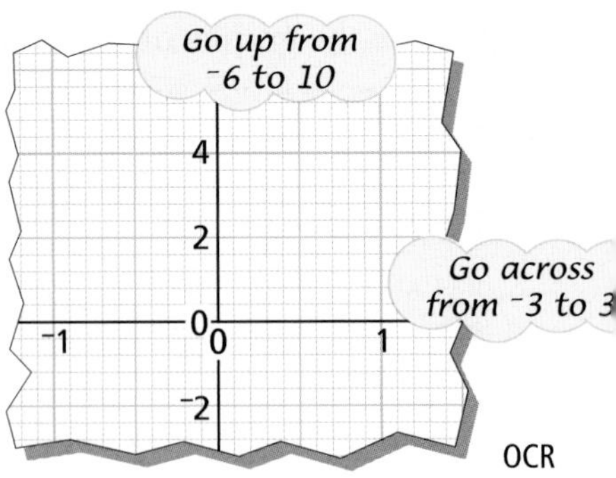

(b) Use trial and improvement to find, correct to 2 decimal places, the solution of $x^3 - 7x + 2 = 0$ which lies between $x = 2$ and $x = 3$.
Show clearly your trials and their outcomes.

OCR

You do not need to draw any graphs for D3 to D5.

D3 A solution to the equation $x^3 + 7x - 40 = 0$ lies between 2 and 3.
Use the method of trial and improvement to find this solution correct to one decimal place.

WJEC

D4 Use trial and improvement to find the positive root of the equation $x^3 + 5x = 10$.
Show all your trials and give your answer to one decimal place.

OCR

D5 The equation $x^3 - 5x = 38$ has a solution between 3.5 and 4.

Use a trial and improvement method to find this solution.
Give your answer correct to one decimal place.
You must show **all** your working.

Edexcel

E *Reciprocals*

Your calculator probably has a reciprocal key on it. 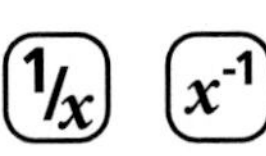

Find the reciprocal key on your calculator. Use it to find the reciprocal of 2.

The reciprocal of a number, n, means simply $1 \div n$, often written as $\frac{1}{n}$.

E1 Use the reciprocal key of your calculator to write down the reciprocal of these.

(a) 5 (b) $^-5$ (c) 4 (d) $^-4$ (e) 10 (f) $^-10$

E2 The reciprocal of 25 is 0.04. What is the reciprocal of $^-25$?

E3 $\frac{1}{40} = 0.025$. Write down the decimal value of $\frac{1}{^-40}$.

E4 Use the reciprocal key of your calculator to write down the reciprocal of these.

(a) 10 (b) 0.1 (c) 8 (d) 0.125 (e) 12.5 (f) 0.08

E5 The reciprocal of 2 is $\frac{1}{2}$. What is the reciprocal of $\frac{1}{2}$?

E6 What is the reciprocal of these? (a) $\frac{1}{4}$ (b) $\frac{1}{6}$ (c) $\frac{1}{8}$

E7 $\frac{1}{32} = 0.03\,125$. Write down the value of $\frac{1}{0.031\,25}$.

E8 Which will be bigger, the reciprocal of 7 or the reciprocal of 70?

E9 (a) $\frac{1}{100} = 0.01$; write down $\frac{1}{0.01}$. (b) $\frac{1}{1000} = 0.001$; write down $\frac{1}{0.001}$.

E10 Which will be bigger $\frac{1}{0.001}$ or $\frac{1}{0.0001}$?

E11 (a) Copy and complete this table for $y = \frac{1}{x}$ using the reciprocal key on your calculator.

x	$^-4$	$^-3$	$^-2$	$^-1$	$^-0.5$	$^-0.25$	0.25	0.5	1	2	3	4
$y = \frac{1}{x}$	$^-0.25$	$^-0.33$				$^-4$	4					

(b) On graph paper, draw axes like these:

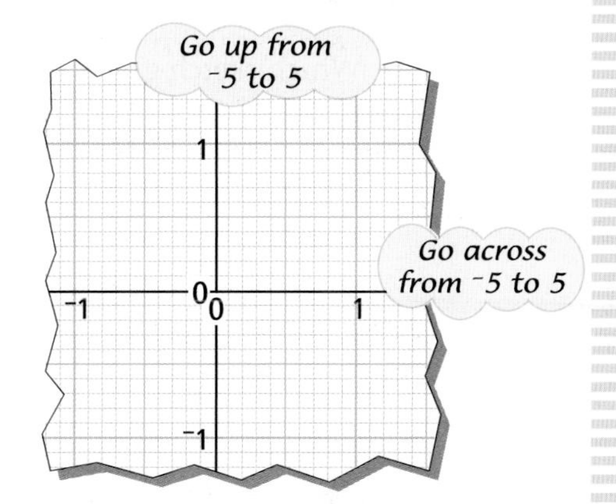

(c) Plot the points from your table on the axes.
Do not join them up yet.

(d) When $x = 0.1$, $y = 10$.

(i) When $x = 0.01$ what is y?

(ii) When $x = 0.001$ what is y?

(ii) Join up the points where $x > 0$.

(e) When $x = ^-0.1$ $y = ^-10$.

(i) When $x = -0.01$ what is y?

(ii) When $x = -0.001$ what is y?

(ii) Join up the points where $x < 0$.

E12 Look at your graph of $y = \frac{1}{x}$.

(a) Does the graph have any reflection symmetry?
If so what are the equations of the mirror lines?

(b) Does the graph have any rotation symmetry?
If so what is the centre and order of rotation symmetry?

F *Graph spotting*

TG

Which sketch graph goes with which equation?

A 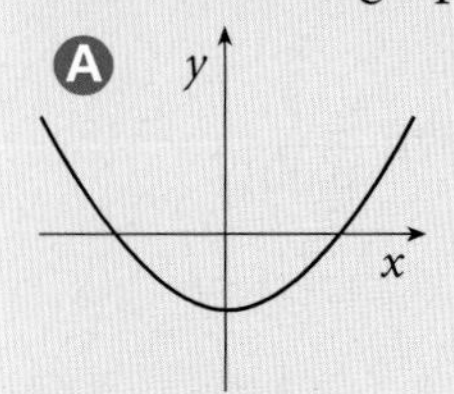

B 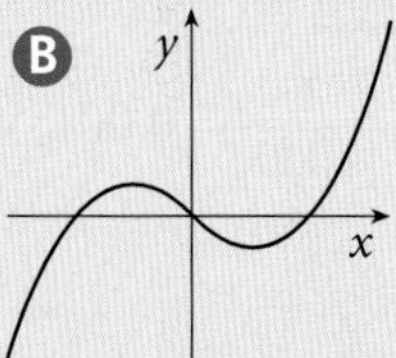

C 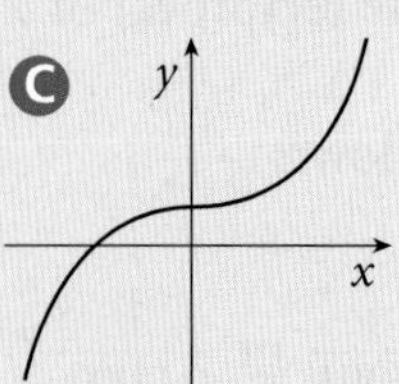

D 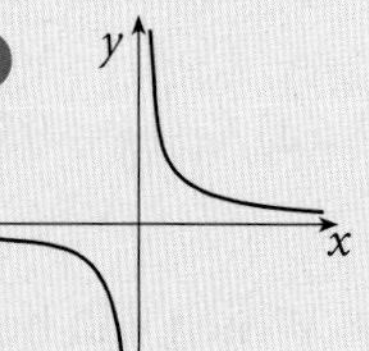

E 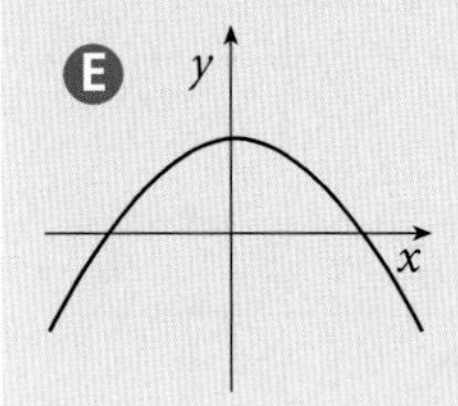

F 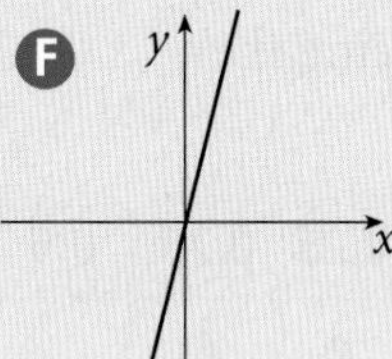

$y = x^2 - 4$

$y = x^3 + 2$

$y = 4 - x^2$

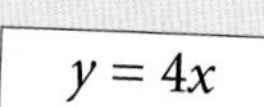

$y = \dfrac{1}{x}$

$y = x^3 - x$

F1 (a) Which sketch graph fits which equation?
(b) Draw a sketch of the missing graph.

A 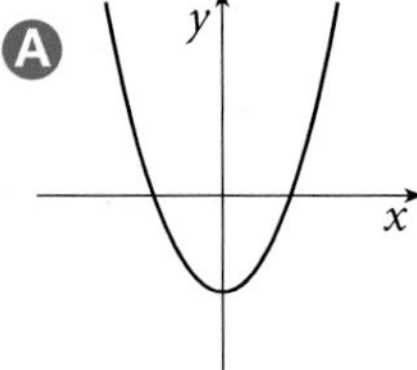

B 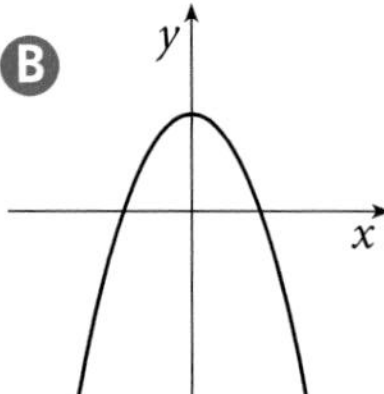

C 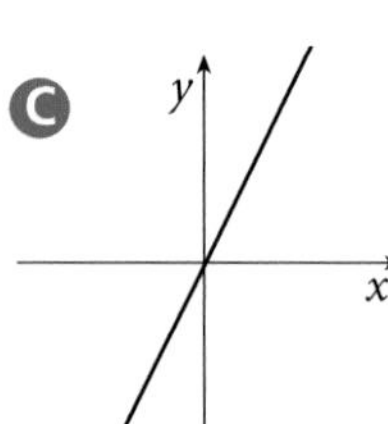

$y = 2x$

$y = x^2 - 2$

$y = 2 - x^2$

$y = x^2 + 2$

F2 Which sketch graph fits which equation?

A 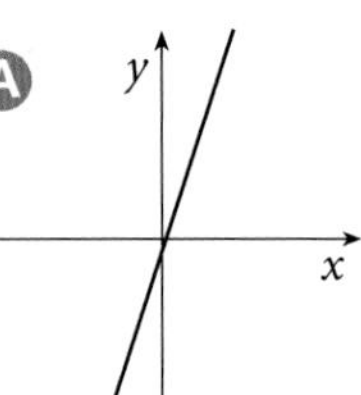

B 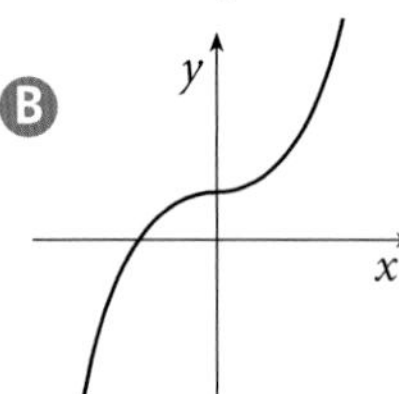

C 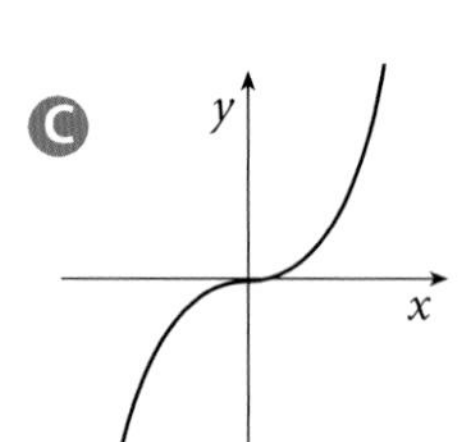

$y = x^3$

$y = 3x$

$y = x^3 + 3$

F3 Match each of the graphs below with one of the equations.
In each equation, k is a positive number.
(One of the equations is not needed.)

A 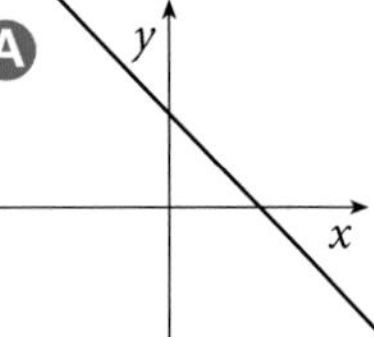

B 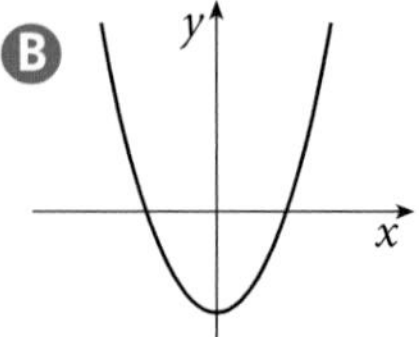

C 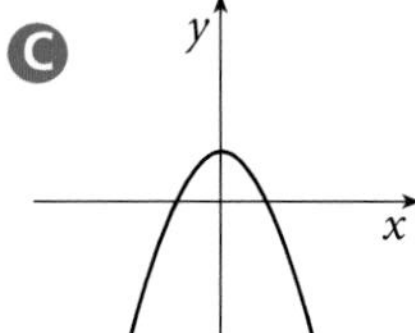

$y = kx$

$y = x^2 - k$

$y = k - x^2$

$y = k - x$

F4 Here are nine equations and nine sketch graphs. Match them up.

A $y = 2x - 1$ **B** $y = {}^{-}2x + 1$ **C** $y = x^2 + 2$

D $y = 2x^2$ **E** $y = x^2 - x$ **F** $y = x^3 + 2$

G $y = 2x^3 + 1$ **H** $x + y = 2$ **I** $y = \frac{1}{x}$

P

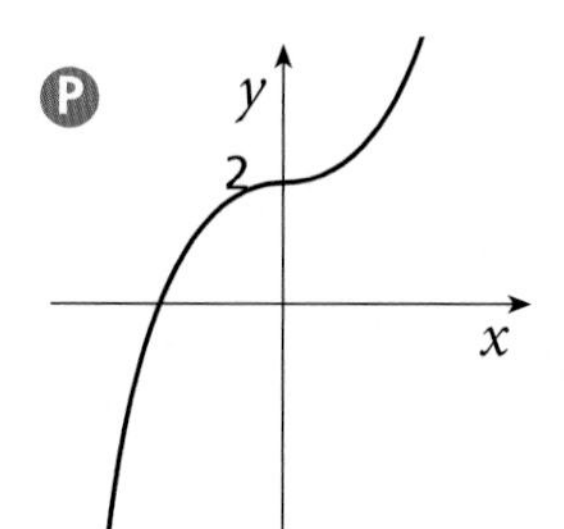

Q

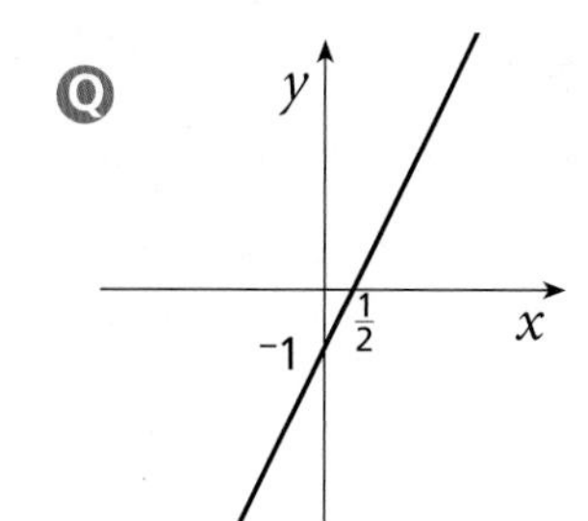

R

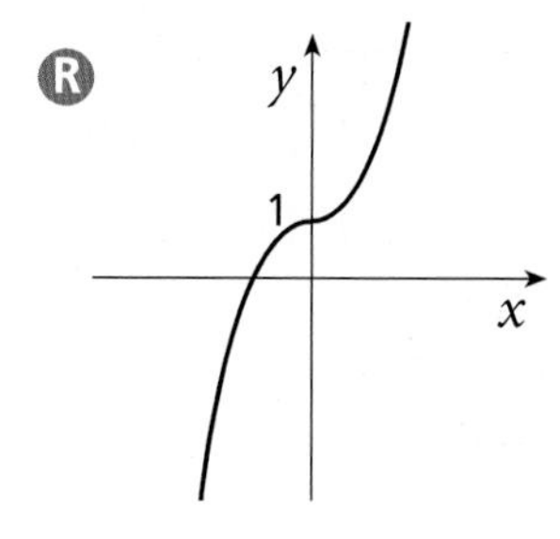

S

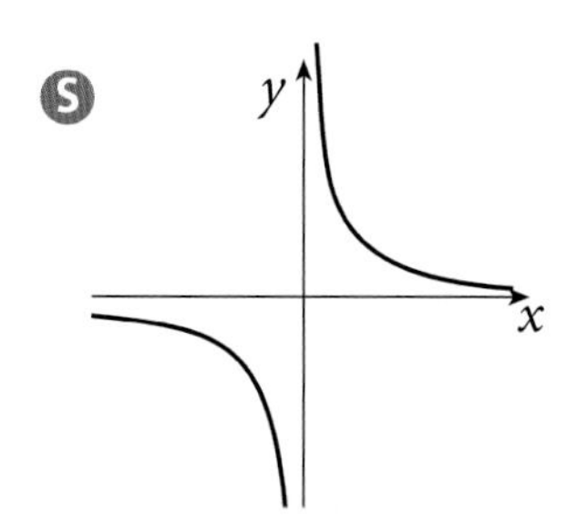

T

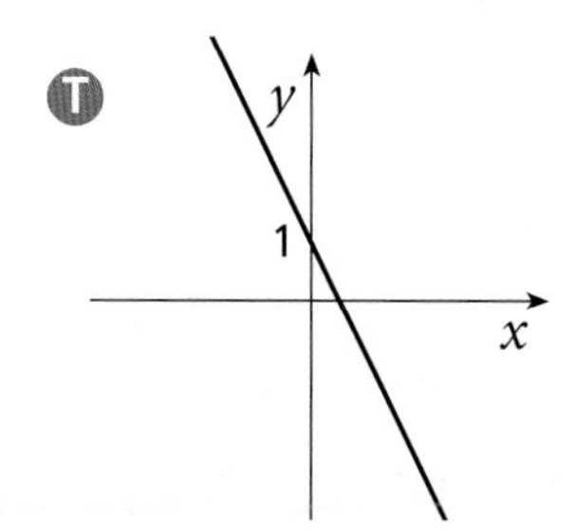

U

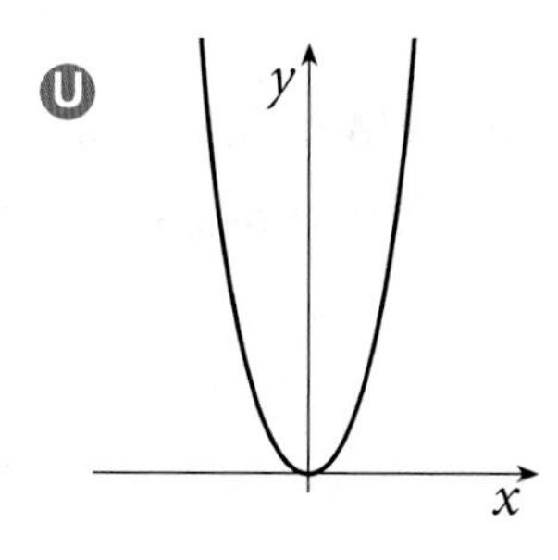

V

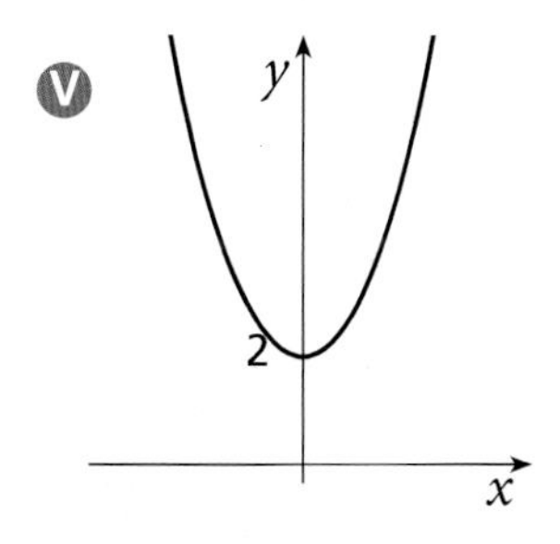

W

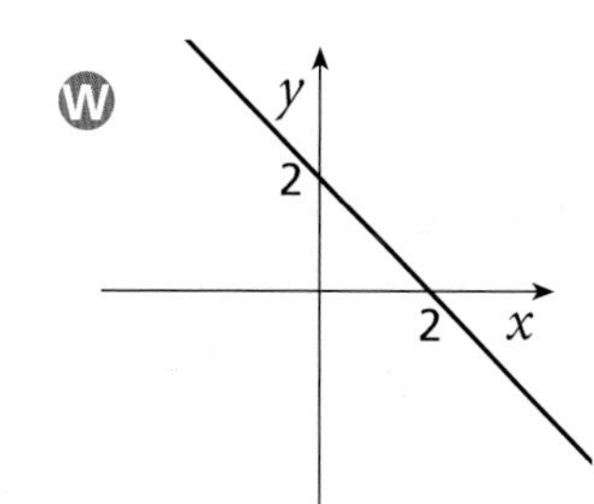

X

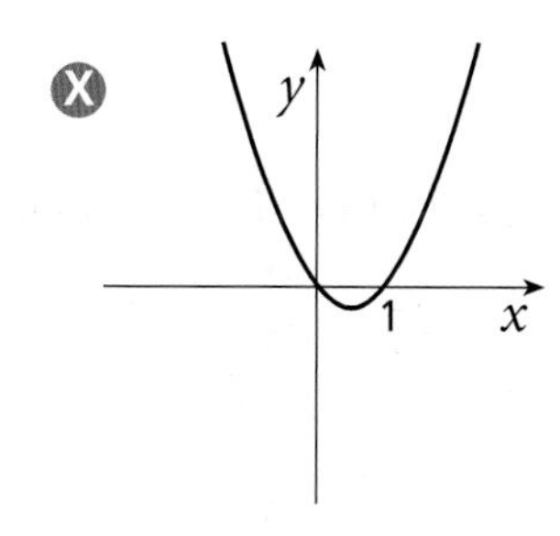

***F5** Match each of the graphs below with one of the equations.

$y = \frac{1}{x} + 2$

$y = \frac{1}{x} - 2$

$y = \frac{2}{x}$

A

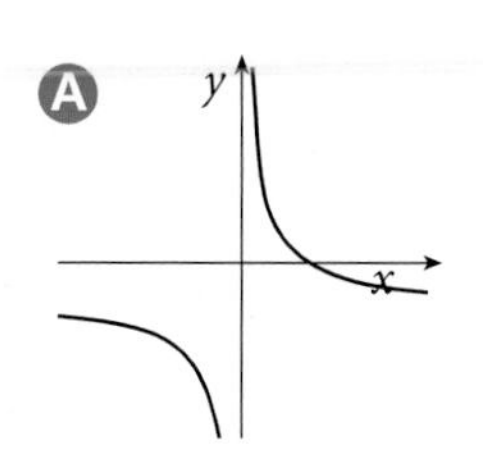

B

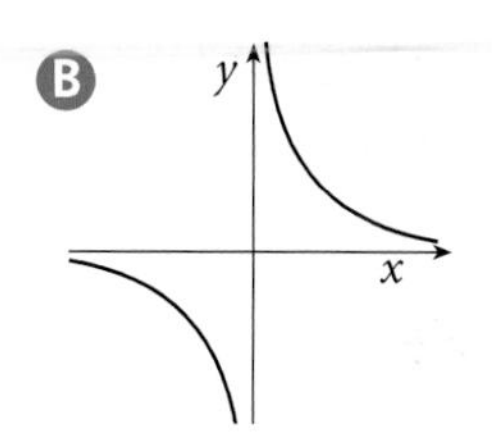

C

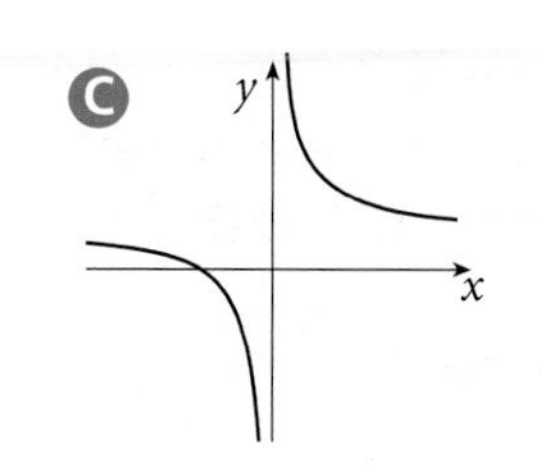

Test yourself

T1 (a) Copy and complete the table of values for $y = 8x - x^2$.

x	0	1	2	3	4	5	6	7	8
y		7	12			15	12	7	0

(b) On axes like these draw the graph of $y = 8x - x^2$.

(c) Use your graph to solve the equation $8x - x^2 = 6$.

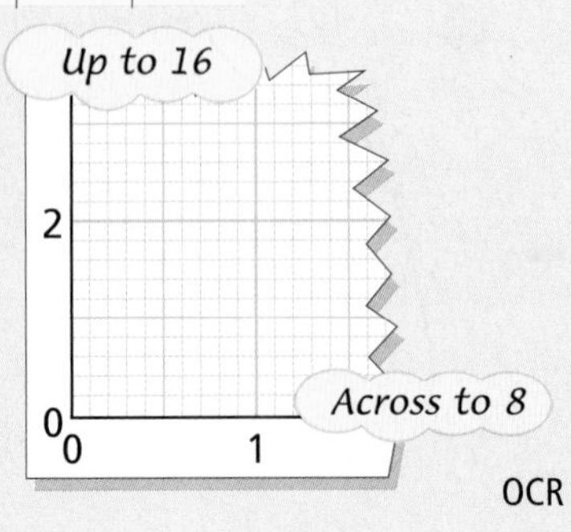

OCR

T2 Write these down.

(a) The positive square root of 36

(b) The negative square root of 81

(c) The values of n that satisfy the equation $n^2 = 25$

T3 (a) Copy and complete the table of values for $y = x^3 + x$.

x	$^-3$	$^-2$	$^-1$	0	1	2	
y		$^-10$		0	2		30

(b) On axes like these draw the graph of $y = x^3 + x$ for values of x from $^-3$ to 3.

(c) Use your graph to solve the equation $x^3 + x = 5$.

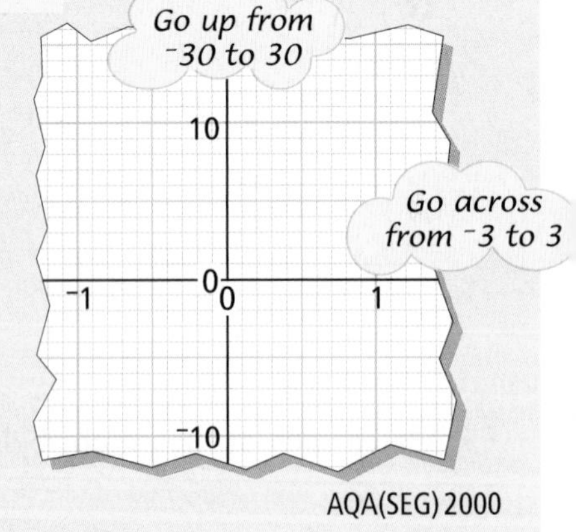

AQA(SEG) 2000

T4 The equation $x^3 + 8x - 40 = 0$ has a solution between 2 and 3. Use trial and improvement to find this solution.

Give your answer correct to two decimal places.
Show clearly the outcome of all your trials.

OCR

T5 This is question A on sheet G156.

T6 This is question B on sheet G156.

58 Combining probabilities

You will revise

- calculating with fractions
- calculating a probability using equally likely outcomes

This work will help you

- understand what is meant by 'independent' events
- calculate probabilities involving independent events
- draw and use tree diagrams for probabilities

A *Calculating with fractions: review*

A1 (a) Write the fraction with denominator 12 that is equivalent to $\frac{1}{6}$.

(b) Write the fraction with denominator 12 that is equivalent to $\frac{3}{4}$.

(c) Use your answers to (a) and (b) to calculate $\frac{1}{6} + \frac{3}{4}$.

(d) Calculate $\frac{3}{4} - \frac{1}{6}$.

A2 Work these out.

(a) $\frac{1}{3} - \frac{1}{4}$ (b) $\frac{1}{2} + \frac{1}{6}$ (c) $\frac{3}{8} + \frac{1}{3}$ (d) $\frac{5}{6} - \frac{1}{4}$ (e) $\frac{4}{5} - \frac{2}{3}$

A3 Aaron, Bharat and Charlotte share a pizza.
Aaron has $\frac{1}{4}$, Bharat has $\frac{1}{3}$ and Charlotte has the rest.

(a) What fraction does Charlotte have?

(b) Who has most pizza? Give the reason for your answer.

A4 Work these out. (a) $\frac{1}{3} \times \frac{1}{4}$ (b) $\frac{2}{3} \times \frac{1}{5}$ (c) $\frac{2}{3} \times \frac{4}{5}$

A5 Work these out.
Write each result in its simplest form.

(a) $\frac{1}{2} \times \frac{1}{5}$ (b) $\frac{1}{3} \times \frac{2}{5}$ (c) $\frac{3}{4} \times \frac{3}{5}$ (d) $\frac{2}{3} \times \frac{3}{4}$ (e) $\frac{4}{5} \times \frac{3}{8}$

A6 Work these out and write each result in its simplest form.

(a) $\frac{1}{3} + \frac{2}{5}$ (b) $\frac{2}{5} \times \frac{3}{5}$ (c) $\frac{3}{4} - \frac{3}{5}$ (d) $\frac{5}{6} \times \frac{3}{4}$ (e) $\frac{5}{6} - \frac{3}{5}$

A7 Work out the missing fraction in each of these.
Write it in its simplest form.

(a) $\frac{3}{8} + \textbf{?} = 1$ (b) $\frac{1}{2} + \frac{1}{3} + \textbf{?} = 1$ (c) $\frac{1}{4} + \frac{3}{5} + \textbf{?} = 1$

(d) $\frac{1}{8} + \frac{1}{4} + \frac{1}{2} + \textbf{?} = 1$ (e) $\frac{1}{6} + \frac{1}{4} + \frac{1}{3} + \textbf{?} = 1$ (f) $\frac{2}{5} + \frac{1}{4} + \frac{1}{10} + \textbf{?} = 1$

B *Events and favourable outcomes*

One shape is to be chosen at random from this set.

Event	Favourable outcomes	Probability of event
The chosen shape is blue.		$\frac{4}{7}$
The chosen shape is red **and** has at least 4 sides.		$\frac{2}{7}$
The chosen shape is either a hexagon **or** a triangle.		$\frac{3}{7}$
The chosen shape is either red **or** a triangle.		$\frac{4}{7}$

B1 A shape is chosen at random from the set shown above.
What is the probability that

(a) the shape is blue and has at least 5 sides

(b) the shape is either a square or a hexagon

(c) the shape is either blue or a pentagon

B2 The diagram shows some shapes.

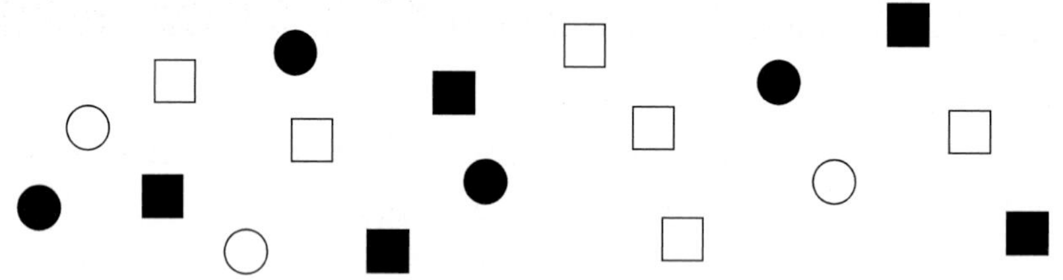

(a) Copy and complete the table to show the number of shapes in each category.

	White	Black
Circle		
Square		

One of the shapes in the diagram is chosen at random.

(b) Write down the probability that the shape will be

(i) a black square (ii) a white square or a black circle

Edexcel

B3 The diagram shows two sets of cards.

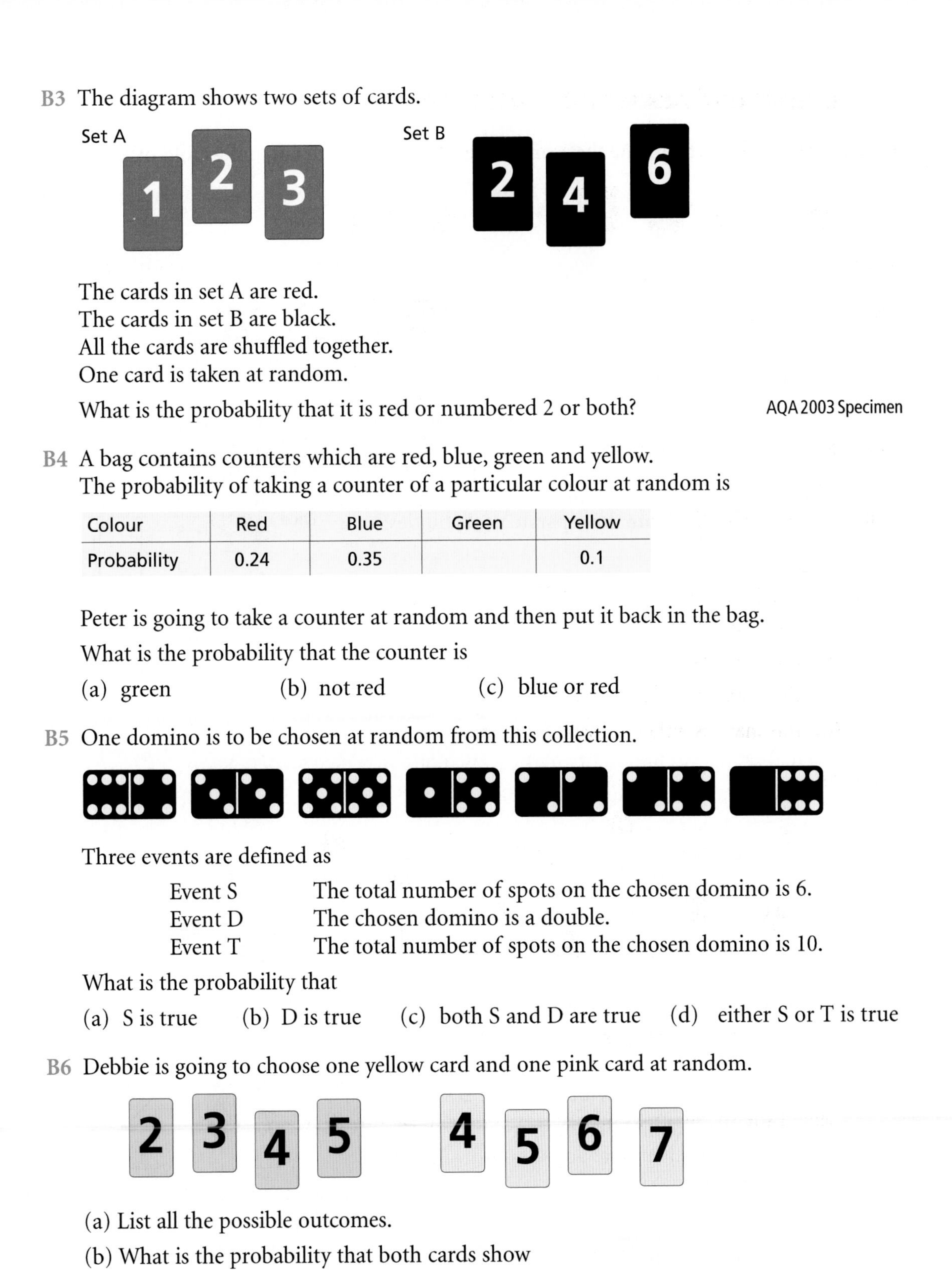

The cards in set A are red.
The cards in set B are black.
All the cards are shuffled together.
One card is taken at random.

What is the probability that it is red or numbered 2 or both? AQA 2003 Specimen

B4 A bag contains counters which are red, blue, green and yellow.
The probability of taking a counter of a particular colour at random is

Colour	Red	Blue	Green	Yellow
Probability	0.24	0.35		0.1

Peter is going to take a counter at random and then put it back in the bag.

What is the probability that the counter is

(a) green (b) not red (c) blue or red

B5 One domino is to be chosen at random from this collection.

Three events are defined as

Event S	The total number of spots on the chosen domino is 6.
Event D	The chosen domino is a double.
Event T	The total number of spots on the chosen domino is 10.

What is the probability that

(a) S is true (b) D is true (c) both S and D are true (d) either S or T is true

B6 Debbie is going to choose one yellow card and one pink card at random.

(a) List all the possible outcomes.

(b) What is the probability that both cards show

(i) the number 4 (ii) the number 6 (iii) the same number

(iv) even numbers (v) factors of 20 (vi) numbers greater than 4

C *Independent events*

For the rest of this unit, assume that coins, dice and spinners are fair, unless told otherwise.

Paul flips a coin 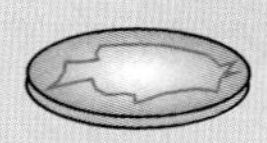 and rolls a dice. 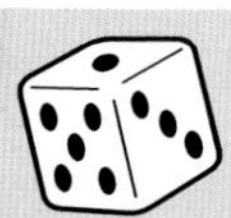

The coin and the dice do not affect each other. Their outcomes are **independent**.

There are 12 equally likely outcomes of the coin and dice. They are shown in this diagram.

The probability of each outcome (for example H, 5) can be found by **multiplying** the separate probabilities:

$$\frac{1}{2} \times \frac{1}{6} = \frac{1}{12}$$

probability of Head × probability of 5 = probability of Head and 5

Dice	H(ead)	T(ail)
6	H, 6	T, 6
5	H, 5	T, 5
4	H, 4	T, 4
3	H, 3	T, 3
2	H, 2	T, 2
1	H, 1	T, 1

Coin

The **multiplication rule for independent events** says

> If two events are independent, the probability that they **both** happen is found by multiplying their probabilities.

C1 (a) What is the probability of getting an even number on the dice?

(b) What is the probability of getting a Head on the coin?

(c) Use the multiplication rule to find the probability of getting an even number on the dice and Head on the coin.

Check from the diagram of outcomes that your result is correct.

C2 (a) What is the probability that spinner A shows red?

(b) What is the probability that spinner B shows red?

(c) Find the probability that both spinners show red.

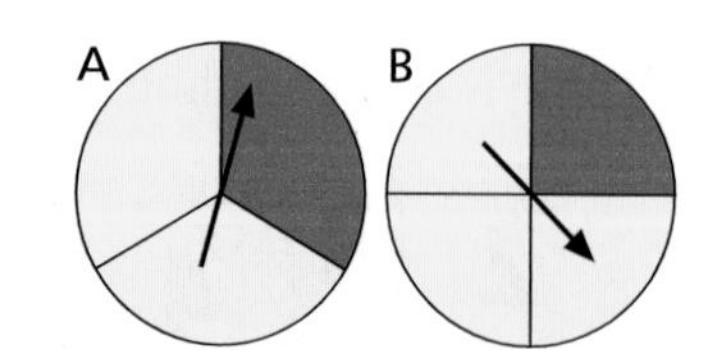

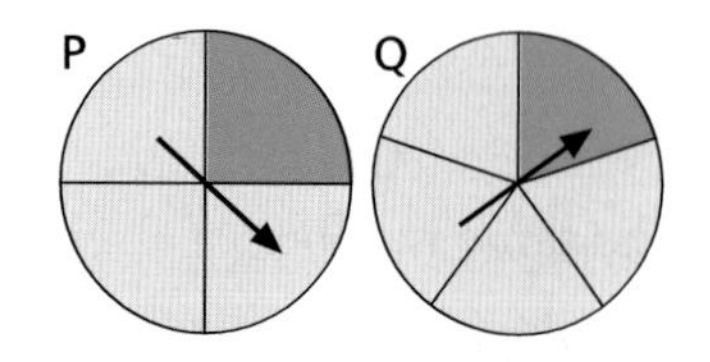

C3 (a) What is the probability that spinner P shows blue?

(b) What is the probability that spinner Q shows blue?

(c) Find the probability that both spinners show blue.

Worked example

These two spinners are spun.
What is the probability that spinner A shows red and spinner B shows white?

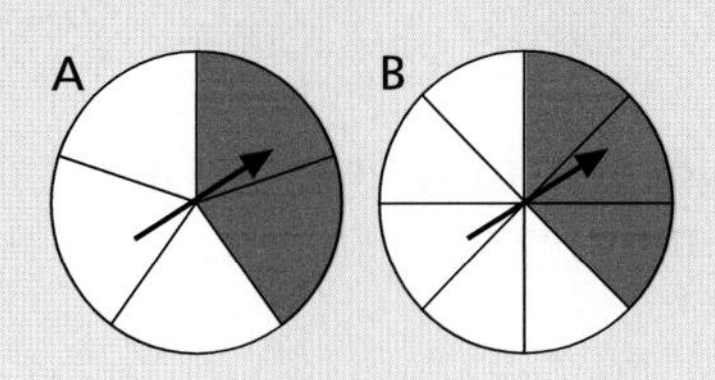

Probability that A shows red = $\frac{2}{5}$

Probability that B shows white = $\frac{5}{8}$

Probability of (A red, B white) = $\frac{2}{5} \times \frac{5}{8} = \frac{10}{40} = \frac{1}{4}$

C4 These spinners are both spun.
Find the probability that

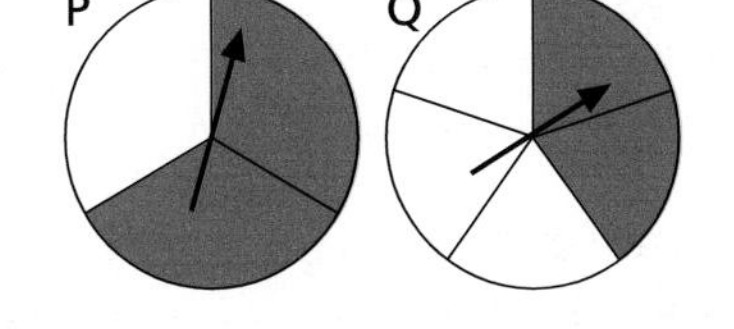

(a) P shows red and Q shows white
(b) P shows white and Q shows red
(c) both spinners show red
(d) both spinners show white

C5 Sharmila takes a card at random from each of these packs.
Find the probability that

Pack A: 1 1 2 2 1 3

Pack B: 2 3 2 1 3 3 1 1

(a) she takes a 1 from pack A and a 2 from pack B
(b) she takes a 2 from pack A and a 3 from pack B
(c) she takes a 3 from both packs

C6 Susie has 2 blue skirts and 3 pink skirts in a drawer.
In another drawer she has 3 blue tops and 4 pink tops.
She takes a skirt at random and a top at random.
Find the probability that the skirt and the top are (a) both blue (b) both pink

C7 Class 1A consists of 10 boys and 15 girls.
Class 1B consists of 18 boys and 12 girls.
One child is picked at random from each class.
What is the probability that the children picked are (a) both boys (b) both girls

C8 A train and a coach go from London to Brighton.
The probability that the train is late is 0.3.
The probability that the coach is late is 0.2.
These two events are independent.

(a) What is the probability that the train is not late?
(b) Find the probability that the coach is late but the train is not late.
(c) Find the probability that both the train and the coach are late.
(d) Find the probability that neither the train nor the coach is late.

D *Tree diagrams*

The possible outcomes when these two spinners are spun can be shown in a **tree diagram**.

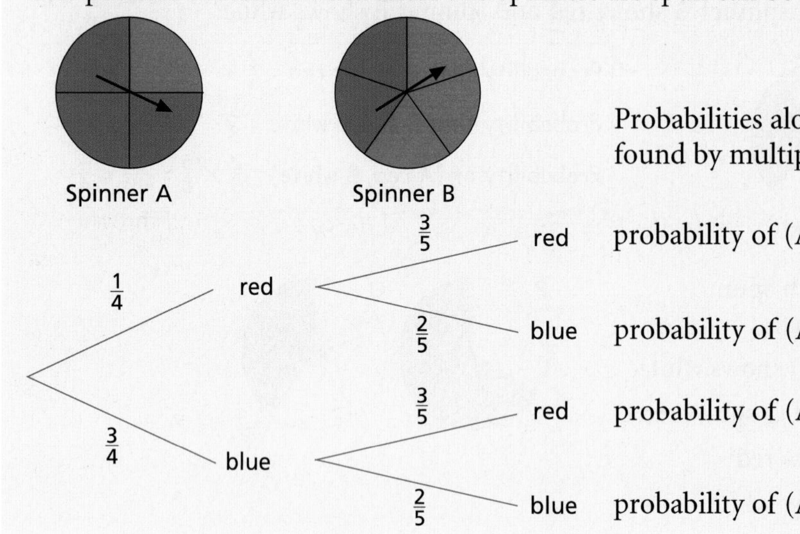

Probabilities along the branches are found by multiplying.

probability of (A red, B red) = $\frac{1}{4} \times \frac{3}{5} = \mathbf{\frac{3}{20}}$

probability of (A red, B blue) = $\frac{1}{4} \times \frac{2}{5} = \mathbf{\frac{2}{20}}$

probability of (A blue, B red) = $\frac{3}{4} \times \frac{3}{5} = \mathbf{\frac{9}{20}}$

probability of (A blue, B blue) = $\frac{3}{4} \times \frac{2}{5} = \mathbf{\frac{6}{20}}$

The probability that both spinners give the same colour is found by adding.

probability of same colour = probability of (A red, B red) + probability of (A blue, B blue)

$$= \frac{3}{20} + \frac{6}{20} = \mathbf{\frac{9}{20}}$$

It is better **not** to simplify the fractions here – it makes them easier to compare and add.

D1 (a) Copy and complete the tree diagram for these two spinners.

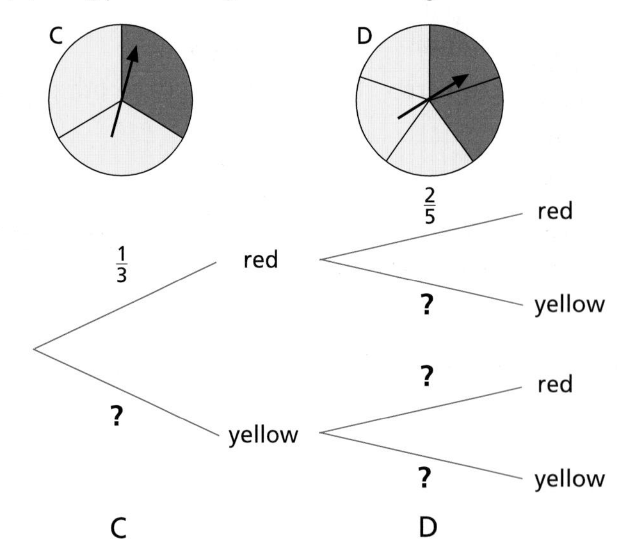

(b) What is the probability that C and D show

(i) the same colour (ii) different colours

D2 A bag contains 4 red beads and 3 blue beads.
A second bag contains 2 red beads and 8 blue beads.
Jahal takes one bead at random from each bag.

(a) Complete the probability tree diagram.

(b) Find the probability that Jahal takes one bead of each colour.

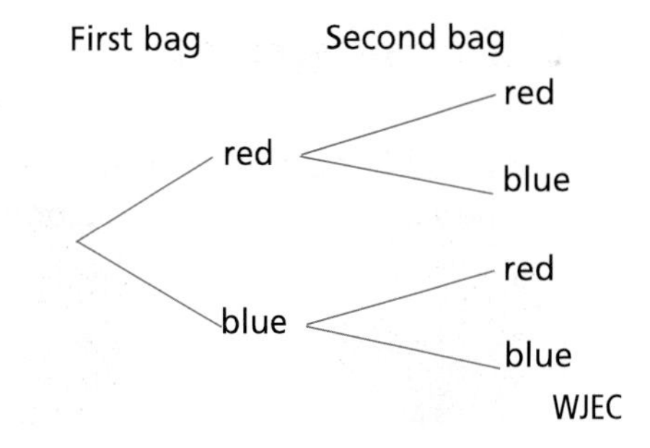

D3 Gill has a coin which is weighted so that the probability that it lands 'head' is $\frac{3}{5}$ and 'tail' $\frac{2}{5}$.

(a) Copy and complete the tree diagram for two throws of the weighted coin.

(b) What is the probability of two heads?

(c) Find the probability of getting one 'head' and one 'tail' (in either order).

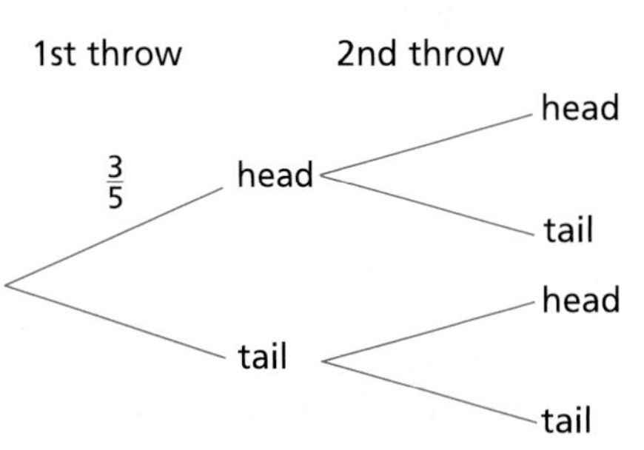

D4 Pauline has a cube with 5 red faces and 1 green face.
She rolls the cube twice.

(a) Copy and complete the tree diagram.

(b) Find the probability that the cube shows the same colour each time.

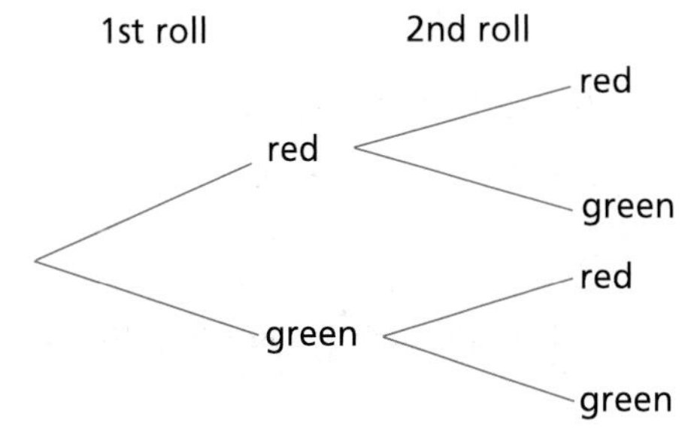

D5 Applicants for a job take two tests, A and B.
Experience has shown that the tests are independent.

The probability of passing test A is 0.3.
The probability of passing test B is 0.8.

(a) Copy and complete the tree diagram.

(b) Find the probability of a person chosen at random

(i) passing both tests

(ii) passing one of the tests and failing the other

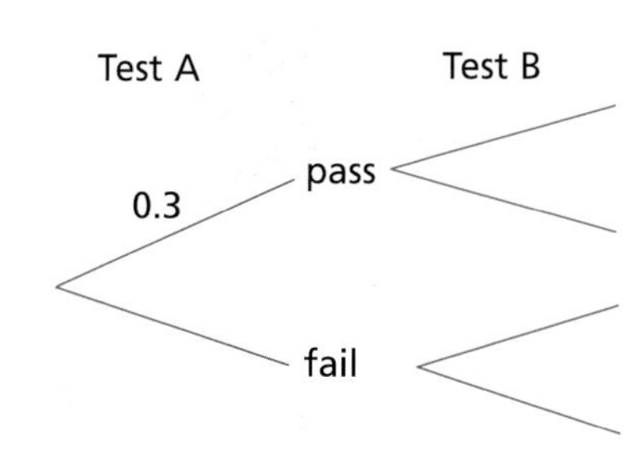

D6 Two trains, A and B, go from London to Reading by different routes.
The probability that train A is late is $\frac{3}{10}$.
The probability that train B is late is $\frac{1}{5}$.
These two events are independent.

(a) What is the probability that train A is not late?

(b) Find the probability that both trains are late.

(c) Find the probability that only one of the two trains is late.

D7 A chicken coup is protected by two alarms A and B.
The alarms are intended to sound when a fox approaches the coup.
The probability of alarm A sounding is 0.9.
The probability of alarm B sounding is 0.8.
These two events are independent.

(a) What is the probability that both alarms fail to sound?

(b) What is the probability that at least one of the alarms sounds when a fox approaches?

(c) A third alarm is installed.
The probability that this new alarm sounds when a fox approaches is 0.7.
It is now more likely or less likely that at least one alarm sounds when a fox approaches?

Test yourself

T1 **One person** is to be chosen at random from four men and two women.

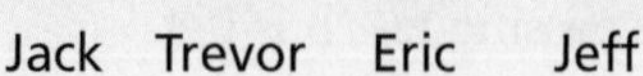

Joan Jill

Four events are defined as

Event J	Someone with a name beginning with J is chosen.
Event M	A man is chosen.
Event N	Someone reading a newspaper is chosen.
Event W	A woman is chosen.

What is the probability that, if **one person** is chosen at random

(a) both J and M are true (b) both J and N are true (c) either N or W is true

AQA 2000

T2 A coin is flipped three times.

(a) What is the probability of getting a head on the first flip?

(b) Find the probability of getting three heads.

T3 Bag A contains 2 blue beads and 3 red beads.
Bag B contains 3 blue beads and 6 red beads.

A bead is picked at random from each bag.
What is the probability that both beads are red?

T4 A bag contains 20 coins.
There are 6 gold coins and the rest are silver.

A coin is taken at random from the bag.
The type of coin is recorded and the coin is then returned to the bag.
A second coin is then taken at random from the bag.

(a) The tree diagram shows all the ways in which two coins can be taken from the bag. Copy the diagram and write the probabilities on it.

(b) Use your tree diagram to calculate the probability that one coin is gold and one coin is silver.

First coin
Second coin
gold
gold
silver
silver
gold
silver

AQA(SEG) 2000

T5 On his way to work, Nick goes through a set of traffic lights and then passes over a level crossing.
Over a period of time, Nick has estimated the probability of stopping at each of these.
The probability that he has to stop at the traffic lights is $\frac{2}{3}$.
The probability that he has to stop at the level crossing is $\frac{1}{5}$.

These probabilities are independent.

(a) Construct a tree diagram to show this information.

(b) Calculate the probability that Nick will not have to stop at either the lights or the level crossing on his way to work.

OCR

T6 An office has two photocopiers, A and B.

On any one day,

the probability that A is working is 0.8,
the probability that B is working is 0.9 .

(a) Calculate the probability that, on any one day, both photocopiers will be working.

(b) Calculate the probability that, on any one day, only one of the photocopiers will be working.

AQA(SEG) 2000

59 Time series

You will revise how to interpret and draw a graph for a time series.

This work will help you calculate a moving average.

A Time series graphs

TG

Temperature in an oven, measured at one minute intervals

Time (minutes)	0	1	2	3	4	5	6	7	8
Temperature (°C)	16	35	53	78	92	113	124	133	134

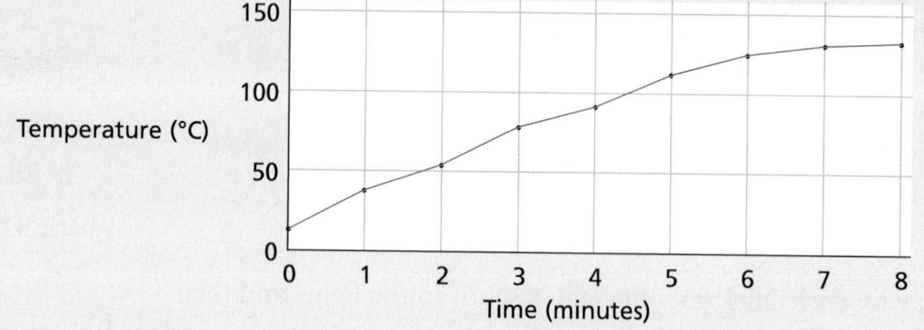

Midday temperatures at Marby-on-Sea for the first 10 days in August

Date in August	1	2	3	4	5	6	7	8	9	10
Midday temperature (°C)	18	14	13	14	17	19	19	18	20	22

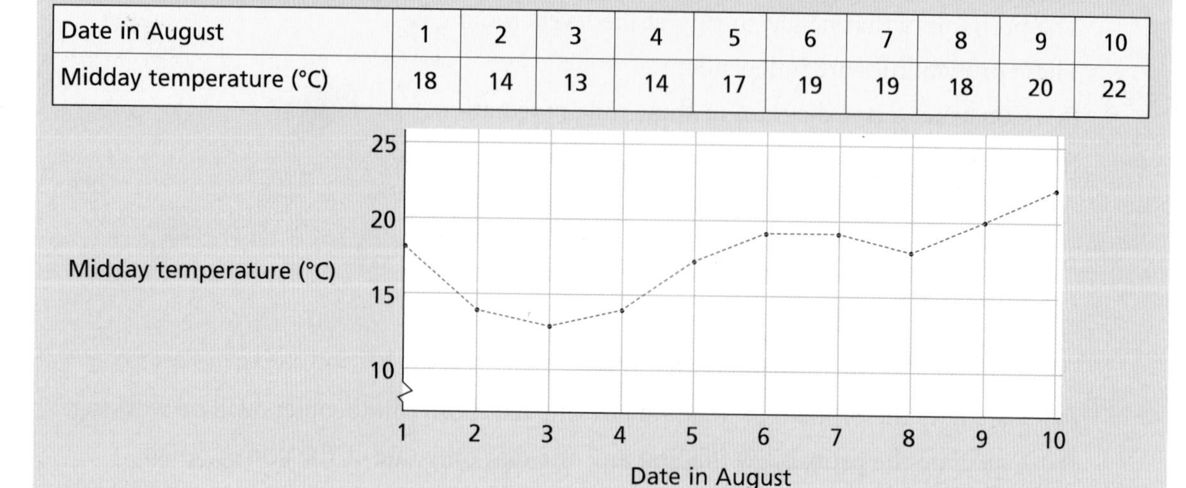

A1 A cinema showed a film for 6 days. The graph shows the number in the audience each day.

Use the graph to answer the questions below, where possible. If the question cannot be answered, write 'not possible'.

(a) When was the audience greatest?

(b) When was the audience 260?

(c) What was the mean number in the audience for the six days?

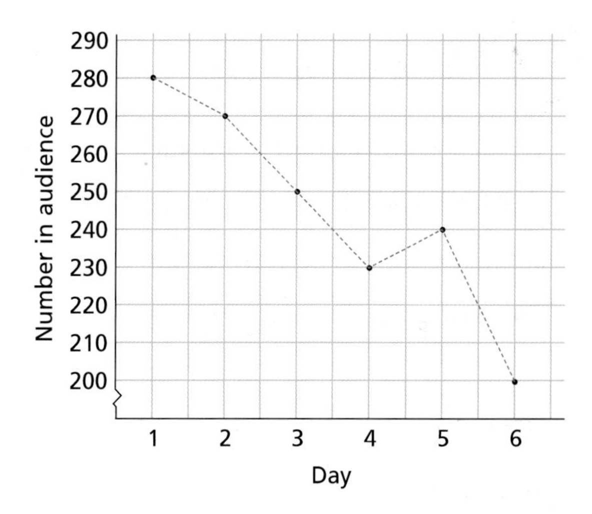

B *Trends*

Saveway profits rise steadily

The profits of supermarket giant Saveway show a steady upward trend over a seven-year period, the company reported yesterday.

'One must be careful about predicting the future from the past,' said a company spokesman, 'but we believe that the trend will

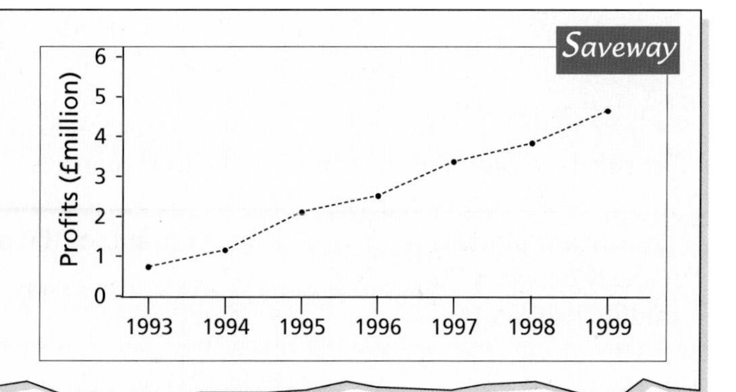

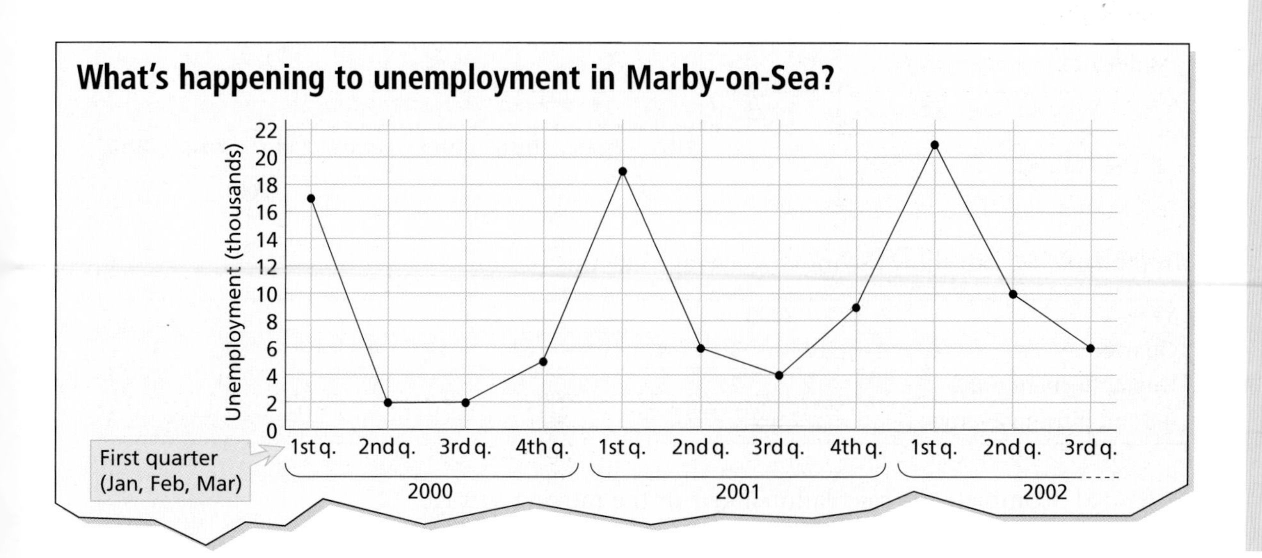

One way to see a trend in the unemployment figures would be to take the mean for each year and see how it changes over time. But we would have to wait for a whole year's figures before we could compare with previous years.

To get a more frequent update we can use a **moving average**. We use overlapping periods of four quarters, like this, and find the mean for each period.

1st	2nd	3rd	4th		
	2nd	3rd	4th	1st	
		3rd	4th	1st	2nd

This is called a **4-point moving average**.

The following example uses the data for the Marby-on-Sea graph.

Year	2000				2001				2002		
Quarter	1	2	3	4	1	2	3	4	1	2	3
Unemployment (000)	17	2	2	5	19	6	4	9	21	10	6

$$\frac{17 + 2 + 2 + 5}{4} = \mathbf{6.5}$$

$$\frac{2 + 2 + 5 + 19}{4} = \mathbf{7}$$ … and so on.

We have to decide how to show the moving average on the graph. The rule is to plot it at the centre of the four quarters it covers.

This means plotting it halfway between the middle two quarters.

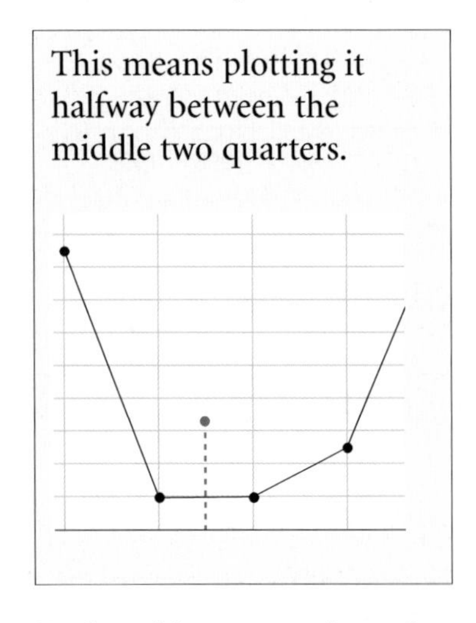

So the graph of the moving average starts like this.

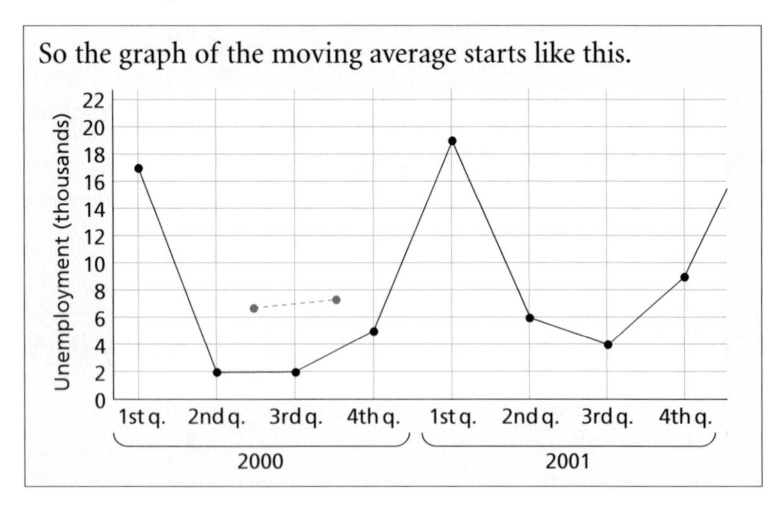

In the table we can show the moving average like this:

Year	2000				2001				2002		
Quarter	1	2	3	4	1	2	3	4	1	2	3
Unemployment (000)	17	2	2	5	19	6	4	9	21	10	6
4-point moving average		6.5		7							

B1 (a) Complete the calculation above of the moving average.

(b) Describe the trend in unemployment.

B2 This table shows the numbers of visitors to a seaside town.

Year	1998			1999				2000	
Quarter	2	3	4	1	2	3	4	1	2
Visitors (000)	16	23	10	7	15	21	11	3	13

(a) Calculate a 4-point moving average and show it, with the original data, on a graph.

(b) Describe the trend.

B3 This table shows the numbers of visitors to a museum.

Year	1998			1999				2000	
Quarter	2	3	4	1	2	3	4	1	2
Visitors (000)	7	9	14	22	10	10	17	25	11

(a) Calculate a 4-point moving average and show it, with the original data, on a graph.

(b) Describe the trend.

B4 This table shows the number of visitors (in thousands) at a tourist attraction each month.

Month	04/99	05/99	06/99	07/99	08/99	09/99	10/99	11/99	12/99	01/00
Number	18	19	29	33	31	23	10	6	9	5

Month	02/00	03/00	04/00	05/00	06/00	07/00	08/00	09/00	10/00	11/00
Number	7	14	20	22	25	28	27	20	12	7

(a) Choose an appropriate moving average and calculate it.

(b) Describe the trend in the data.

Test yourself

T1 The total rainfall figures, in millimetres, for the past 7 years in Egypt are shown below.

27 24 31 30 28 15 29

Find the five-yearly moving averages. OCR

T2 This table shows the quarterly profits of a garden centre.

Year	1998				1999				2000	
Quarter	1	2	3	4	1	2	3	4	1	2
Visitors (000)	32	58	75	41	30	63	77	40	36	65

(a) Calculate a 4-point moving average.

(b) Draw a graph showing the original data and the moving average.

(c) Comment on the trend.

60 Accuracy

You will revise rounding and using sensible accuracy.

This work will help you

- find the lower and upper bounds for a rounded quantity
- find the upper and lower bounds for the result of a simple calculation involving rounded quantities

A Sensible accuracy

TG

- What would be a sensible degree of accuracy in each of these?

A It takes **8 minutes 55.16 seconds** to walk to the station.

B *Tim has been dieting.*
*He has lost **1.5054 kg** in **2 weeks 5 days 7 hours and 4 minutes**.*

C The distance from Amber's house to town is **2 kilometres and 435.54 metres**.

D *Helen has a very big dictionary.*
*It weighs **2.732 kg**.*

E Vijay spent **2 hours 44 minutes** on his homework.

F Tom is going to paint a rectangular wall.
First he measures the wall and calculates its area.

Length 4.125 m
Height 3.452 m

Area = 4.125 × 3.452
= **14.2395 m²**

Big beast isn't he? And believe it or not this skeleton is **70 000 002** years old!

How do you know its age so accurately?

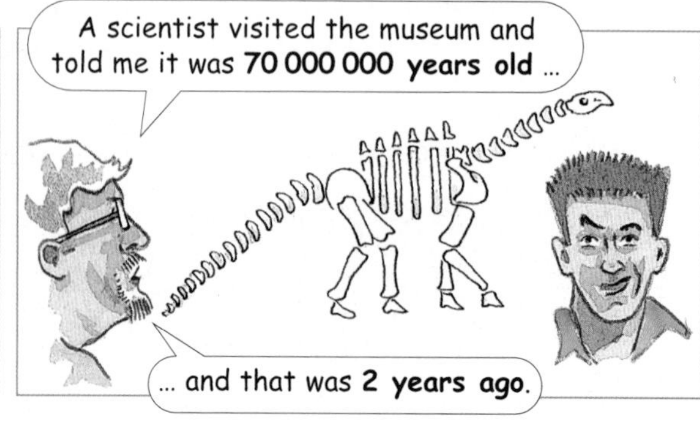

A1 Write each of the quantities in bold to a sensible degree of accuracy. (Some may already be sensible, in which case don't change them!).

*The city of Bunchester is **243.673 km** from the capital. The journey by train takes **2.482** hours.*

*The population of the city is **148 843**, of whom **21.783%** are over the age of sixty.*

*Bunchester covers an area of **11.8643 km²**. It is situated on the River Bunn, which at this point is **186.23 m** wide and is **35.271 km** from the point where it flows into the sea.*

*In the city there are four bridges across the river. The newest of these is a suspension bridge with a span of **144.8 m** and towers of height **58.3 m** above the river bed. Each of the main cables of this bridge is **316.6 mm** in diameter.*

*Bunchester Cathedral dates from **1284** and has a spire of height **87.632 m**. Inside it is a bishop's throne made from solid granite and weighing **18 538.296 kg**.*

*Bunchester is famous for its open air Rock Music Festival. Last year **184 529** people visited the festival and the final concert by The Maniacs could be heard up to a distance of **6.842 km** away.*

A2 Bickerton Rovers and Naggingford United play in a football league. Teams get 4 points for an away win, 3 for a home win, 2 for an away draw and 1 for a home draw.

So far Bickerton have 26 points from 15 games.
Naggingford have 30 points from 18 games.

Calculate the mean number of points per game for each team, to a sensible degree of accuracy. Which team is doing better?

B *Lower and upper bounds*

If you are rounding to the **nearest whole number**,

- which of these numbers will be rounded to 18?

18.63 17.842 17.486 18.33

17.752 17.497 18.761 18.2794

17.741 18.523 18.464 17.503

- What is the **lowest** number you can think of that will be rounded to 18?
- What is the **highest** number you can think of that will be rounded to 18?

(This number line may help.)

17 18 19

TG

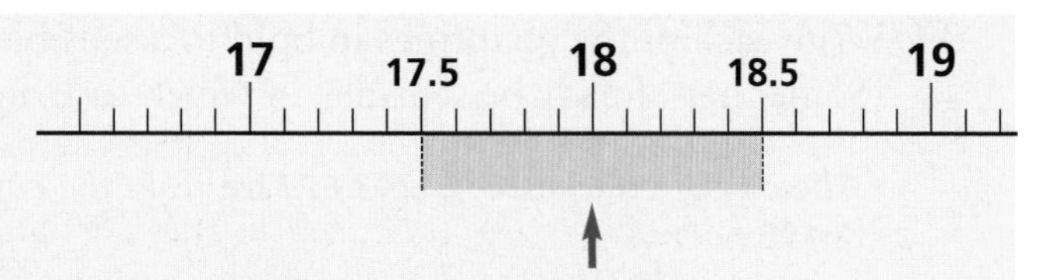

All the numbers for which 18 is the nearest whole number lie in this **interval.**

The **lower bound**, or minimum, of the interval is **17.5**.
The **upper bound**, or maximum, is **18.5**.

(Strictly speaking, if we round up 18.5 itself should not be in the interval, because 18.5 becomes 19. But usually this does not matter.)

B1 You are told that the temperature of some water is 13°C, to the nearest degree.
(a) What is the lowest possible temperature of the water?
(b) What is the highest possible temperature?

B2 The volume of water in a glass is measured as 347 ml, to the nearest ml. What are the lower and upper bounds of the volume of the water?

B3 A man's weight is recorded as 78 kg, correct to the nearest kg. What are the lower and upper bounds of his weight?

B4 The volume of water in a bottle is measured as 170 ml, to the nearest ml. What are the minimum and maximum values of the volume of the water?

B5 Marie's kitchen scales weigh to the **nearest 10 grams.** She weighs some flour and the scales show 270 g.

What are the minimum and maximum possible weights of the flour? (The diagram may help.)

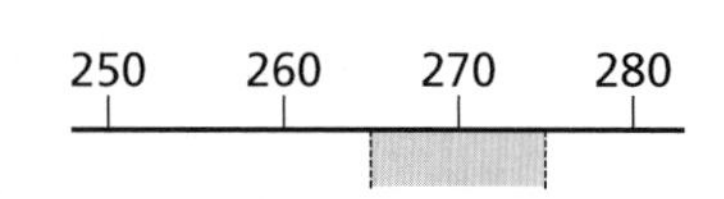

B6 The speed of an aircraft is 420 km/h, correct to the nearest 10 km/h. What are the minimum and maximum possible values of the speed?

B7 The length of a river is given as 3800 km, correct to the **nearest 100 km.** What are the minimum and maximum possible values of the length?

B8 The length of another river is given as 2300 km, but this time the length is correct to the **nearest 10 km.** What are the minimum and maximum values?

Summary

Quantity is given to the nearest ...	Minimum value	Maximum value
whole number	given value – 0.5	given value + 0.5
ten	given value – 5	given value + 5
hundred	given value – 50	given value + 50
thousand	given value – 500	given value + 500

Lower and upper bounds: decimal places

Suppose we are rounding to **one decimal place.**

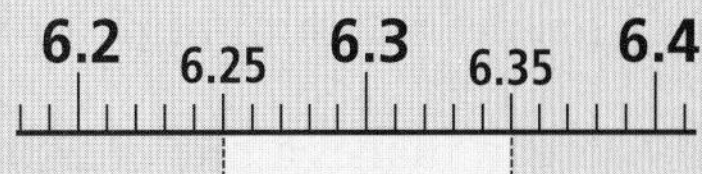

The shaded interval shows the numbers that are rounded to **6.3**.

The lower bound is **6.25** and the upper bound **6.35**.

B9 A baby's weight is recorded as 3.8 kg, to the nearest 0.1 kg.
What are the lower and upper bounds of the baby's weight?

B10 The height of a mobile phone mast is 13.9 m, to the nearest 0.1 m.
What are the minimum and maximum heights of the mast?

B11 The voltage of a battery is given as 1.3 volts, to the nearest 0.1 volt.
What are the lowest and highest possible values of the voltage?

B12 The air temperature on the roof of a building is recorded as $^-7.2$°C, to the nearest 0.1°C.
What are minimum and maximum values of the temperature?

C *Calculating with lower and upper bounds (1)*

Worked examples

A computer weighs 8 kg and a printer 3 kg, both to the nearest kg.
What are the minimum and maximum possible values of the total weight of the computer and printer?

> The computer weighs from 7.5 kg to 8.5 kg.
> The printer weighs from 2.5 kg to 3.5 kg.
>
> So the minimum total weight is 7.5 + 2.5 = **10 kg.**
> The maximum total weight is 8.5 + 3.5 = **12 kg.**

Packs of cheese contain 1.3 kg to the nearest 0.1 kg.
What are the minimum and maximum possible weights of 6 packs?

> One pack weighs from 1.25 kg to 1.35 kg.
>
> So the minimum total weight is 6 x 1.25 = **7.5 kg.**
> The maximum total weight is 6 x 1.35 = **8.1 kg.**

C1 The distances on this map are correct to the nearest km.
What are the minimum and maximum possible values of the distance from A to C?

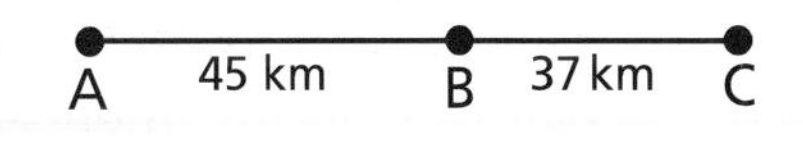

C2 Gordon makes a tower from eight bricks.
Each brick has a height of 9 cm, correct to the nearest cm.
What are the minimum and maximum possible heights of the tower?

C3 A classroom block has five rooms, each with a floor area of 284 m^2, to the nearest m^2.
What are the minimum and maximum possible values of the total area of the rooms?

C4 Morgan makes a pile of 20 tiles each 6 mm thick, to the nearest mm.
What are the minimum and maximum heights of the pile?

C5 A city has three parks.
Their areas, to the nearest 0.1 km^2, are 4.8 km^2, 3.9 km^2 and 5.1 km^2.

What are the minimum and maximum possible values of the total area of the parks?

C6 Kemal jogs round the edge of a field 12 times.
The perimeter of the field is 0.9 km, correct to the nearest 0.1 km.

What are the minimum and maximum possible values, of the distance Kemal jogs?

C7 A photocopier makes copies at the rate of 6.4 per minute, to one decimal place.
What is the minimum number of copies that it will make in 20 minutes?

C8 Ken's bookshelf is 42 cm long, to the nearest cm.
Ken has 8 books, each 5 cm thick, to the nearest cm.
Explain why Ken may not be able to fit all the books on his bookshelf.

Worked example

A rectangular field is 58 m by 41 m, each to the nearest metre.
What are the minimum and maximum possible values of the area of the field?

The length is from 57.5 m to 58.5 m. The width is from 40.5 m to 41.5 mg.

To get the smallest possible area, multiply the smallest length and the smallest width.
So the minimum area is $57.5 \times 40.5 =$ **2328.75 m^2**.

Similarly to get the greatest area, multiply the greatest length and greatest width.
So the maximum area is $58.5 \times 41.5 =$ **2427.75 m^2**,

C9 A games pitch is a rectangle 24 m by 18 m, each correct to the nearest metre.
Calculate the minimum and maximum possible values for the area of the pitch.

C10 A room has a rectangular floor 4.2 m by 2.9 m, each to the nearest 0.1 m.
Calculate the minimum and maximum possible values for the area of the floor.

***C11** A train travels at a constant speed of 56 m.p.h., to the nearest 1 m.p.h.
It travels for 2.4 hours, correct to the nearest 0.1 hour.

(a) What are the minimum and maximum possible values for the speed of the train?

(b) What are the minimum and maximum possible values for the time of travel?

(c) Calculate the minimum and maximum possible values for the distance travelled by the train.

D *Calculating with lower and upper bounds (2)*

Worked example

Saul weighed 85 kg before training and 81 kg afterwards.
Both weights are to the nearest kilogram.
Find the minimum and maximum values for his weight loss.

Before training minimum weight 84.5 kg, maximum weight 85.5 kg
After training minimum weight 80.5 kg, maximum weight 81.5 kg

The sketch below shows these intervals.

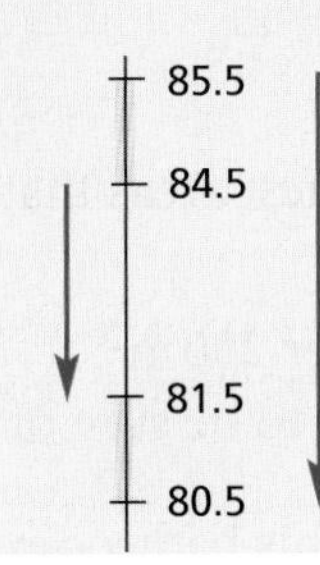

The loss would be smallest if he went from the lowest starting weight to the highest finishing weight.

So the lower bound of his weight loss is 84.5 – 81.5 = **3 kg**

The loss would be biggest if he went from the highest starting weight to the lowest finishing weight.

So the upper bound of his weight loss is 85.5 – 80.5 = **5 kg**

D1 Peter is 167 cm tall, to the nearest centimetre.
His sister Kirsty is 128 cm tall, also to the nearest centimetre.

(a) Write down the minimum and maximum possible values of Peter's height.

(b) Do the same for Kirsty's height.

(c) Work out the minimum difference in height between Peter and Kirsty.

(d) Work out the maximum difference in height between Peter and Kirsty.

D2 A beaker of water weighed 426 g, to the nearest gram.
After the water had been poured out, the beaker weighed 173 g, to the nearest gram.
Find the lower and upper bounds of the weight of the water.

D3 A cheese weighs 8.4 kg, correct to the nearest 0.1 kg.
A piece weighing 2.6 kg, to the nearest 0.1 kg, is cut from the cheese.
Find the minimum and maximum possible weight of the cheese that remains.

***D4** Jan measures two of the angles of a triangle, to the nearest degree.
They are 61° and 46°.

Calculate the minimum and maximum possible values of the size of the third angle.

61° 46°

***D5** Hitesh has a reel of wire.
The wire on the reel is of length 900 cm, to the nearest centimetre.

Hitesh cuts off 20 pieces of wire.
Each piece is of length 35 cm, to the nearest centimetre.

Calculate the minimum and maximum possible values of the length that is left on the reel.

E *Mixed questions*

E1 Here is a conversation.

Roger My road atlas says that the distance from Bristol to Exeter is 134 km.
There are 1000 metres in a kilometre, so the distance is also 134 000 metres.
There are 1000 millimetres in a metre, so the distance is also 134 000 000 mm.

Lucy But you can't measure the distance from Bristol to Exeter in millimetres!
You can't be as accurate as that when you're measuring along roads!

Roger You must be able to do it in millimetres, because I've just worked it out.

Who do you think is right? Why?

E2 (a) What are the smallest and greatest areas that 5 tins of this paint will cover.

(b) Sue needs enough paint to cover 200 m^2.
How many tins should she buy to be sure of having enough?

Stone paint
Covers from
16 m^2 to **18** m^2
depending on surface

E3 Ajit wants to weigh his suitcase on his bathroom scales.
But the case won't balance on the scales, so he weighs himself holding the case and then again without it.

With the case he weighs 102 kg and without it 74 kg. Both weights are to the nearest kg.

Find the minimum and maximum possible weight of the case.

E4 An Egyptian temple is 4300 years old, correct to the nearest 100 years.
What are the minimum and maximum possible ages of the temple?

Test yourself

T1 The length of Martin's hand is 17 cm correct to the nearest centimetre.
What is the minimum length his hand could be? AQA 2003 Specimen

T2 A book on dieting states that one pancake contains 155 calories, correct to the nearest calorie.
Write down the greatest and least number of calories that one pancake could contain.
OCR

T3 A pen is of length 10 cm, measured to the nearest centimetre.
A pen case is of length 10.1 cm, measured to the nearest millimetre.
Explain why it might not be possible for the pen to fit the pen case. Edexcel

T4 Bags of potatoes each weigh 25 kg correct to the nearest kg.
What is the minimum weight of 9 bags of potatoes? AQA 2003 Specimen

T5 John buys 500 g of strawberries.
The weight of the strawberries is correct to the nearest 10 g.
What is the minimum weight of the strawberries? AQA(SEG) 2000

61 Angles in circles

This work will help you

- understand the properties of angles formed with straight lines and circles
- calculate missing angles around circles

A Angles on the circumference

Investigation 1

- Draw two points A and B about 6 cm apart in the centre of an A4 sheet of paper.
- Using the 60° angle of a 60/30/90 set square, place the set square so that the two edges touch A and B. Mark a point at the point of the 60° angle.
- Move the set square to other positions where the two edges touch A and B and mark points at the 60° point.
- What do you notice about the locus of the points?
- Repeat the experiment with the 30° angle of the set-square.
- Try using a 45° set square or other angles cut from card.
- Do you always get a similar locus?

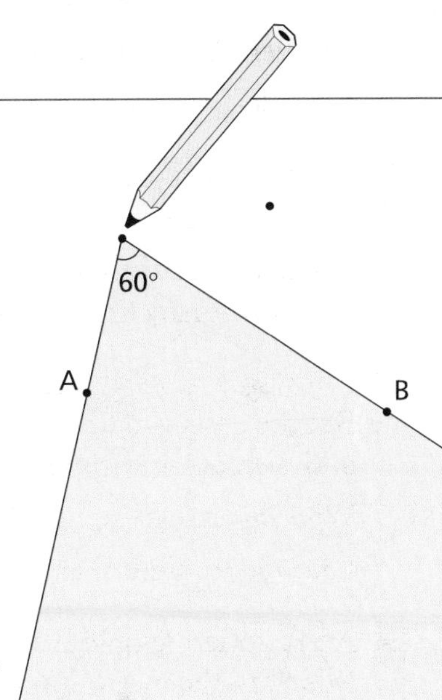

Investigation 2

- Draw a circle with radius about 6 cm on a piece of paper.
- Mark two points A and B anywhere on the edge of this circle.
- Now mark a new point C on the circle. Draw lines from A to C and B to C. Measure angle ACB.
- Now draw lines from A and B to a new point D. Measure angle ADB.
- Using the same A and B repeat for other points around the circle. What angle do you get each time?
- On a new circle repeat the experiment with a different A and B.
- What happens if AB is a diameter?

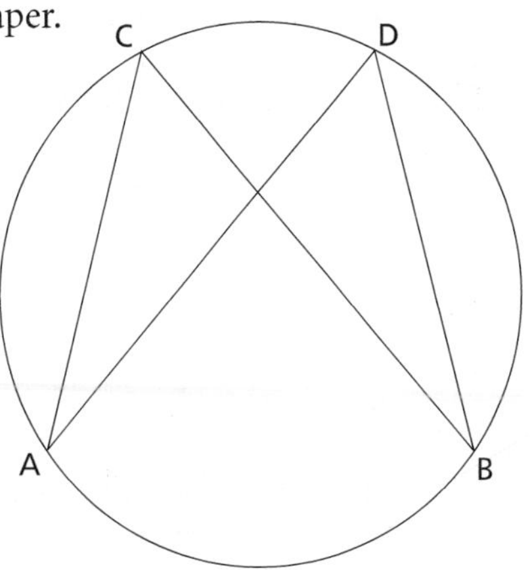

Angles on the circumference

If lines are drawn from two points A and B on the circumference of a circle to any other point on the circumference, the angle at the circumference is always the same.

This only works for points on the same side of chord AB, that is, in the same segment.

If A and B are opposite ends of a diameter and X is on the circumference, then angle AXB will always be 90°.

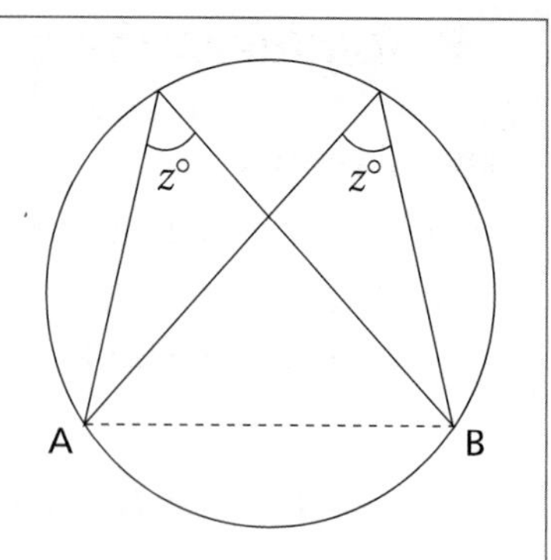

A1 Find the lettered angles in these diagrams.

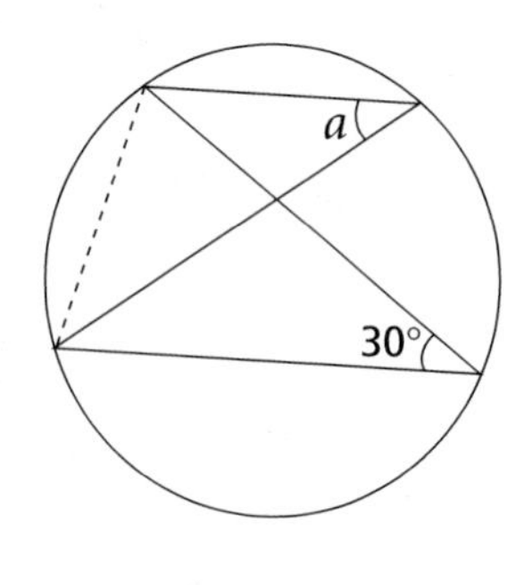

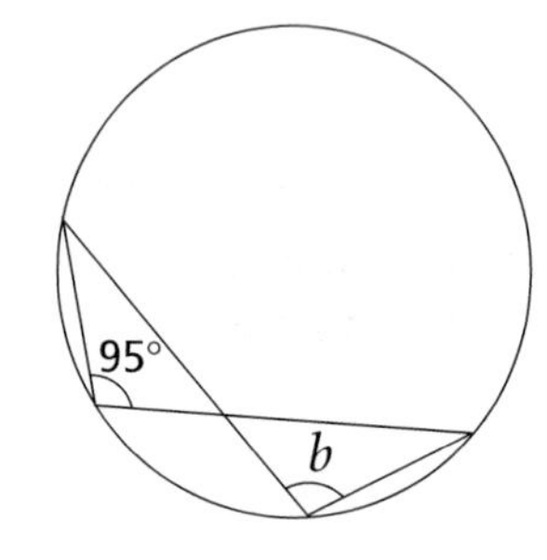

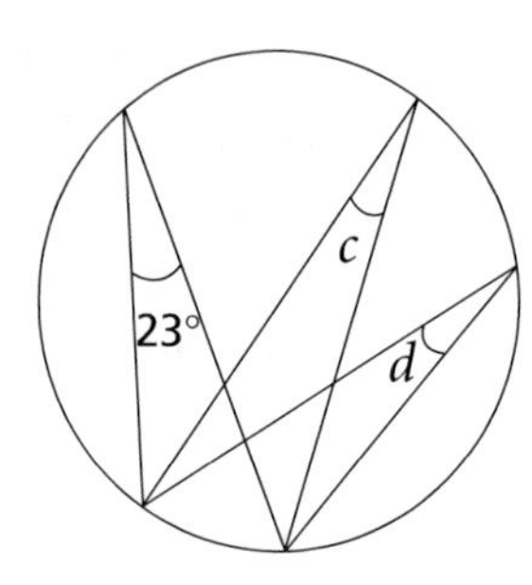

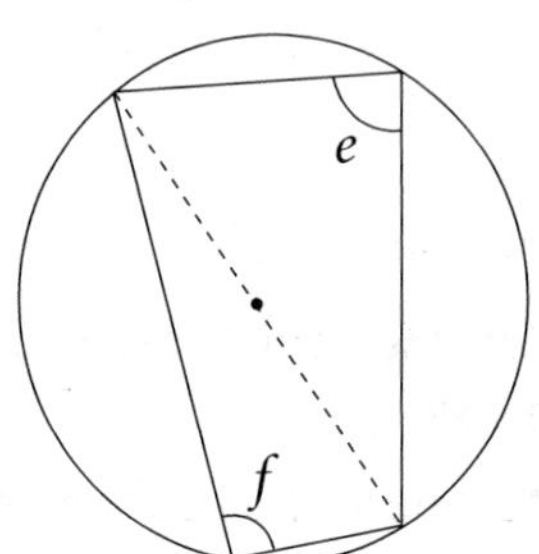

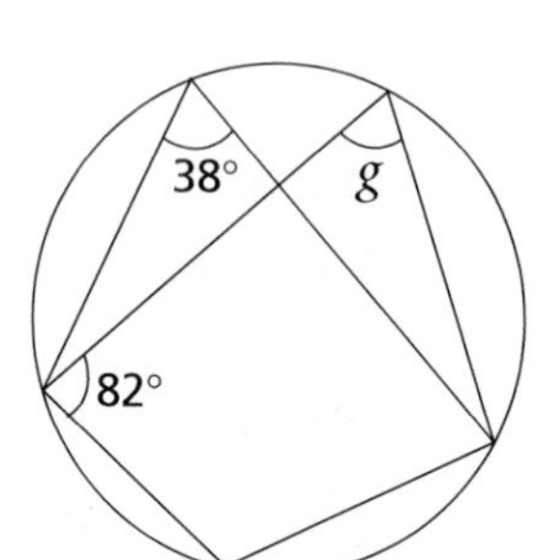

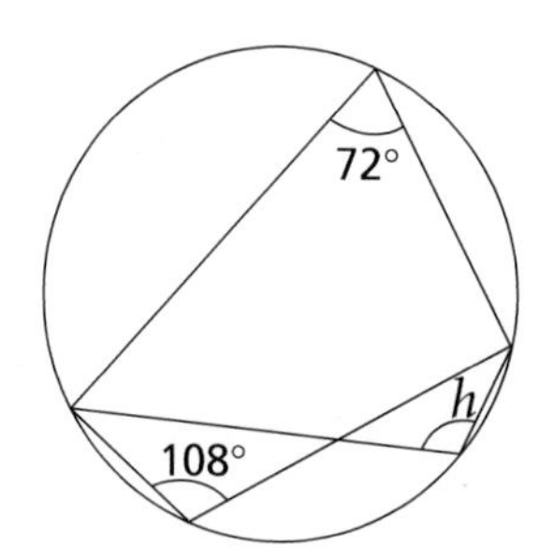

A2 Find the lettered angles in these diagrams.

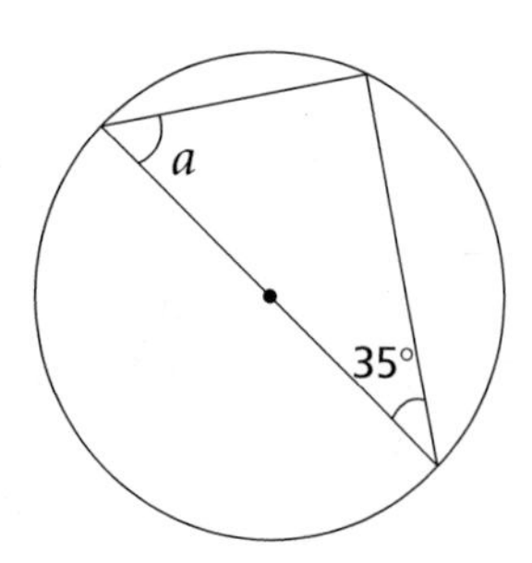

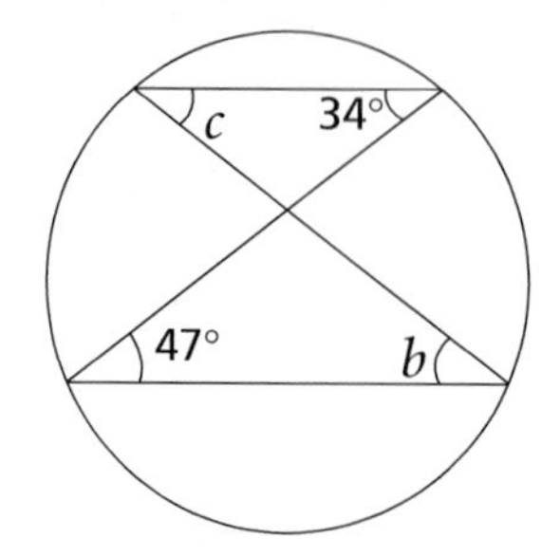

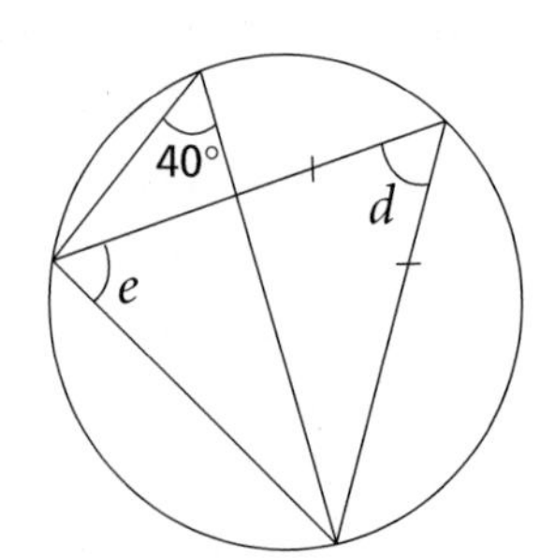

B *Angles at the centre*

Investigation 3

- Draw a circle with radius 6 cm and mark the centre O.
- Mark two points A and B on the circumference of the circle.
- Draw lines from A and B to the centre O.
- Draw lines from A and B to any other point C on the circumference.
- Measure the obtuse angle AOB.
  Measure angle ACB.
  What do you notice?
- Use different points A, B and C.
  What can you say about angles AOB and ACB each time?
- Does your rule still work when A, B and C are all in the same half circle as shown here?

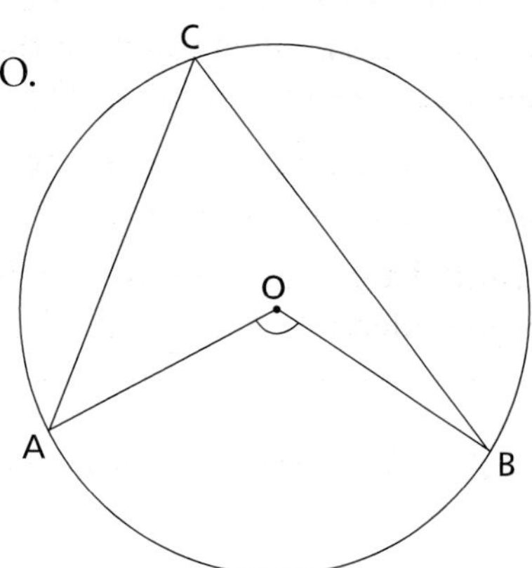

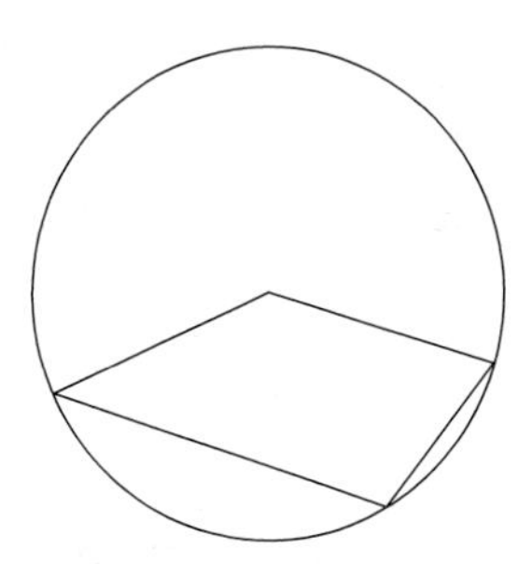

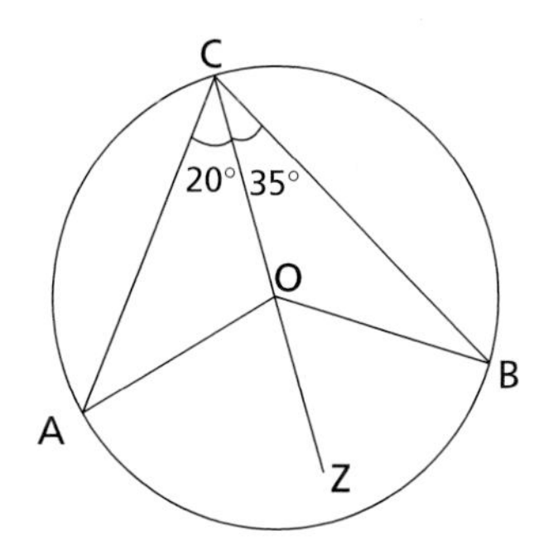

In this diagram,

- What type of triangles are AOC and AOB?
- Use this and any other angle facts to find as many other angles on this diagram as you can.
- Explain how this illustrates the rule you found above.

B1 Use your rule to find the lettered angles in these diagrams.

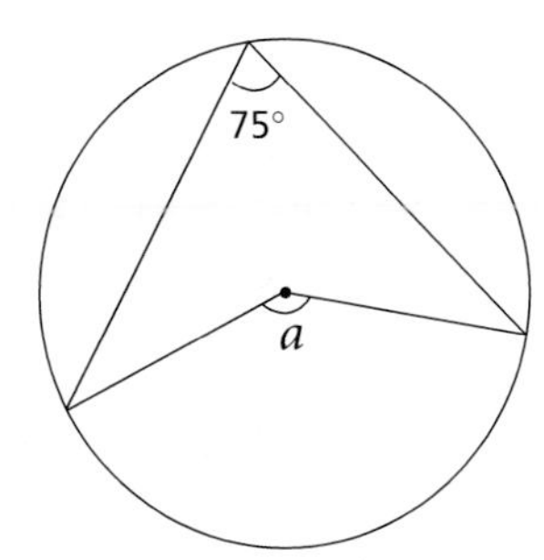

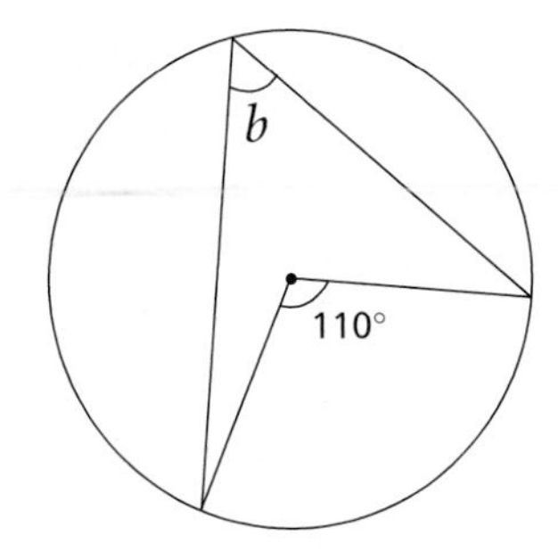

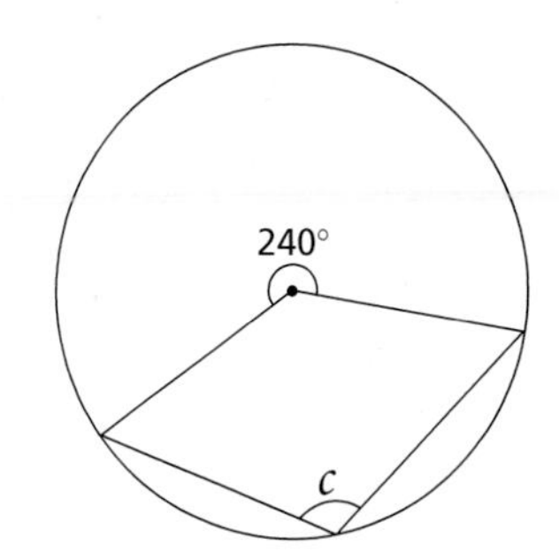

Angles at the centre

If two points, A and B, on the circumference of a circle are joined to the centre of the circle O, and to another point C on the circumference then

angle AOB = $2 \times$ angle ACB

This also proves the result that if AB is a diameter (so AOB = 180°) then ACB must be a right angle.

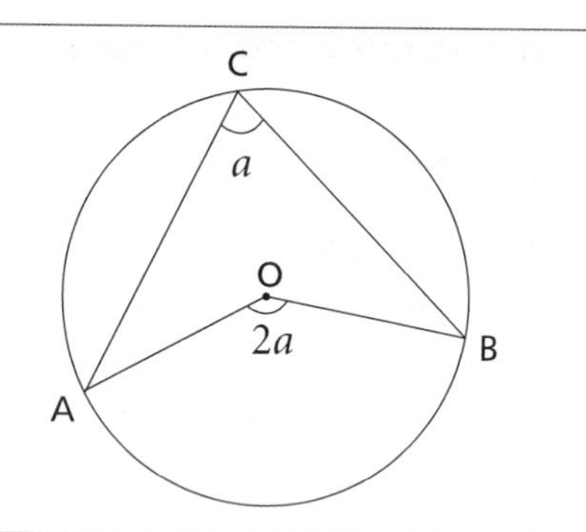

B2 Find the lettered angles in these diagrams.

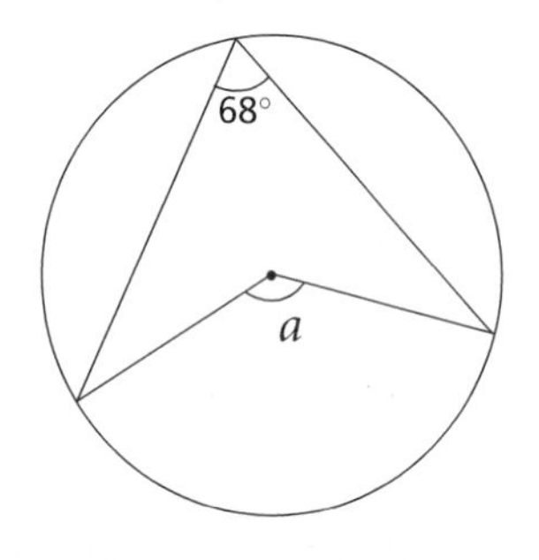

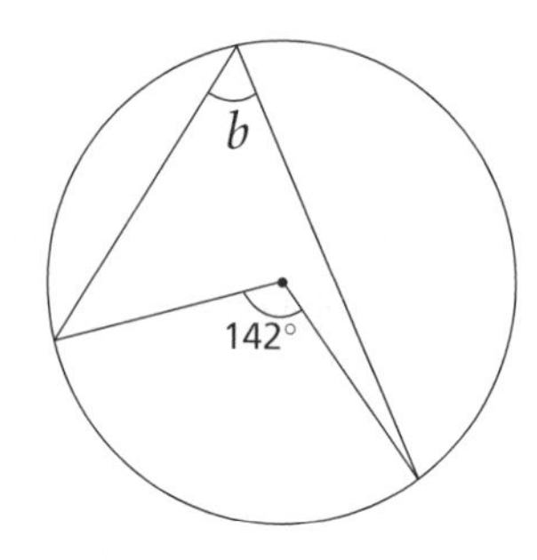

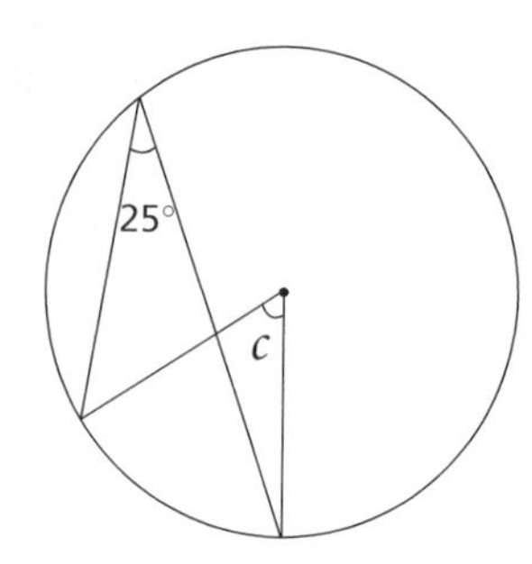

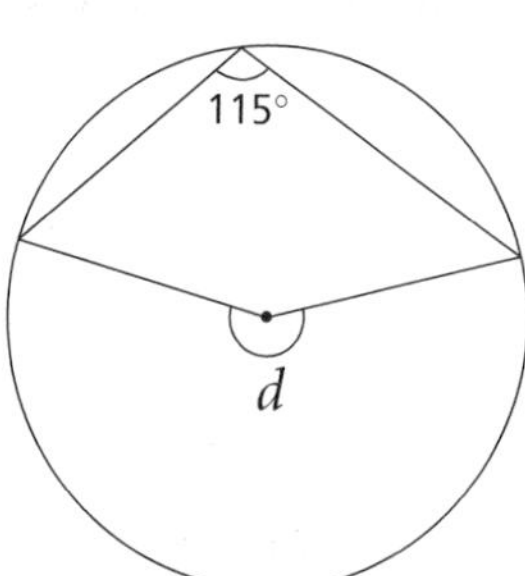

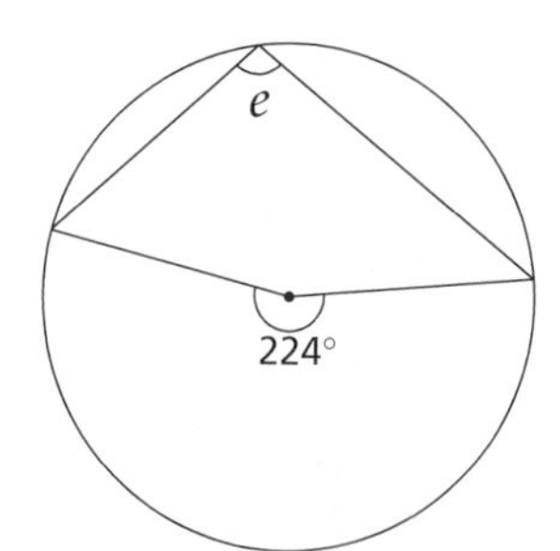

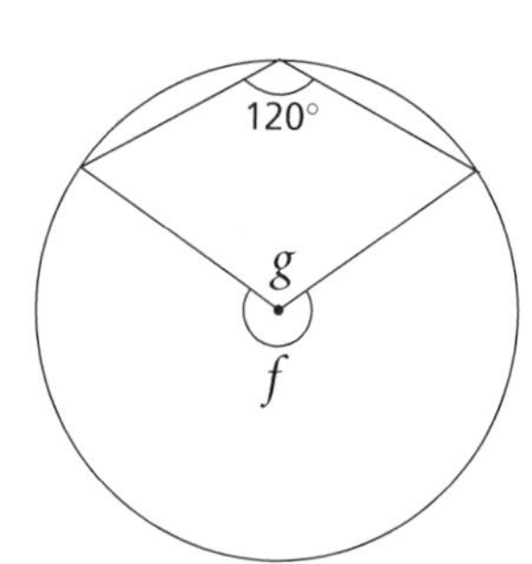

B3 In this diagram O is the centre of the circle. Angle PQR is 74°.

(a) What type of triangle is POR?

(b) Find angle POR.

(c) Find angle ORP.

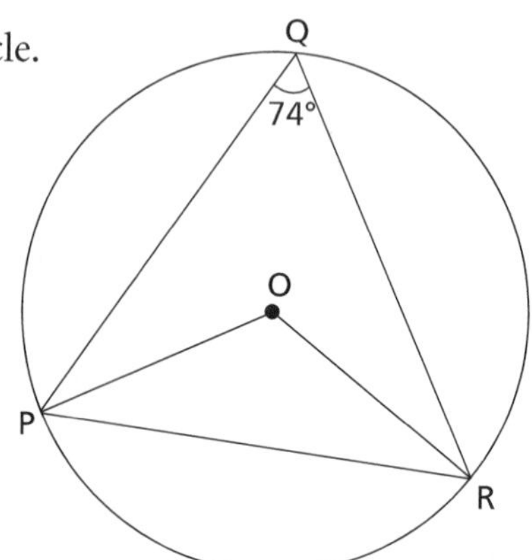

C *Cyclic quadrilaterals*

Investigation 4

Any quadrilateral which has all four corners on the edge of a circle is called a **cyclic quadrilateral**.

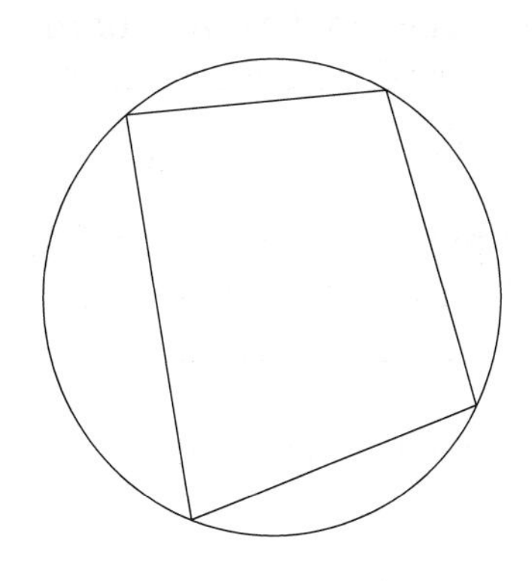

- Draw a circle with radius 6 cm. Draw a cyclic quadrilateral and measure the four angles. What do you notice?
- Investigate the angles in other cyclic quadrilaterals.
- Can a trapezium be cyclic? What special quadrilaterals cannot be cyclic?

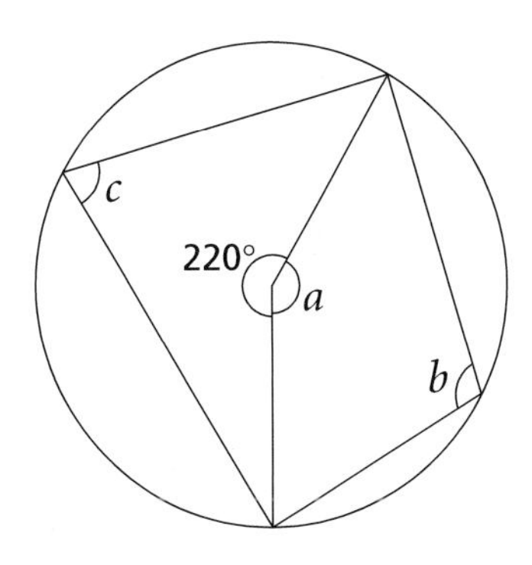

Use this diagram to answer the following.

- Find angle a.
- Use the results of section B to find angles b and c.
- What can you say about angles b and c?
- Explain how this illustrates the rule you found above.

C1 Find the lettered angles in these diagrams.

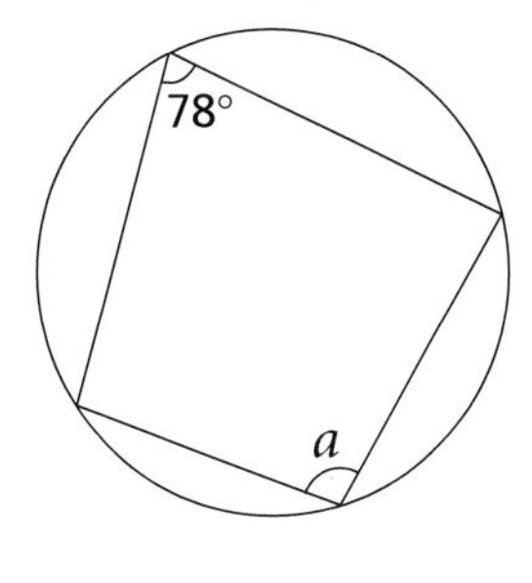

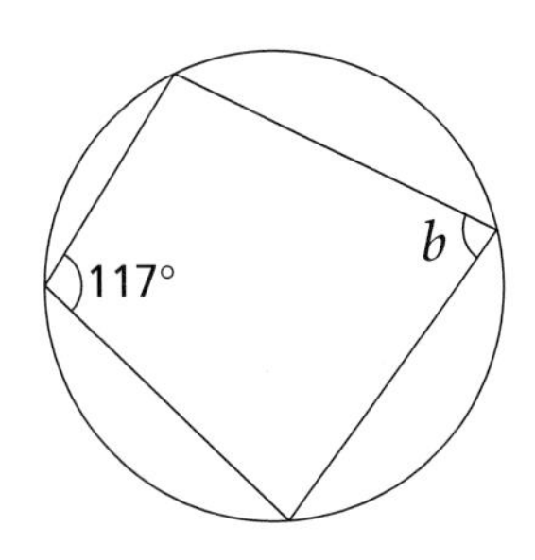

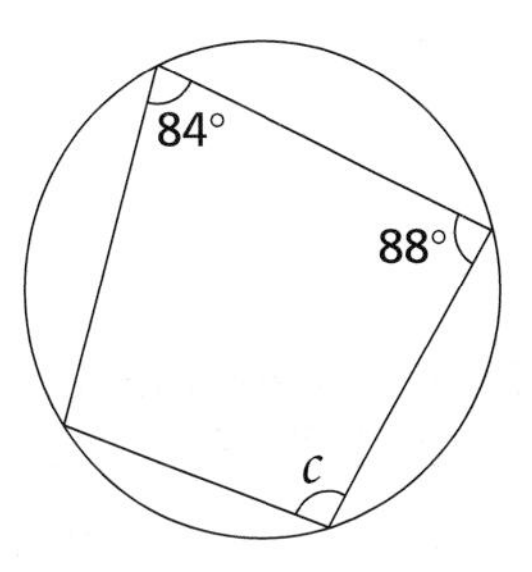

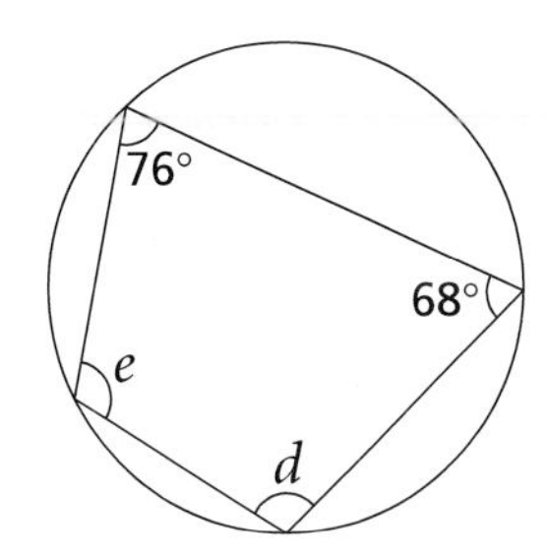

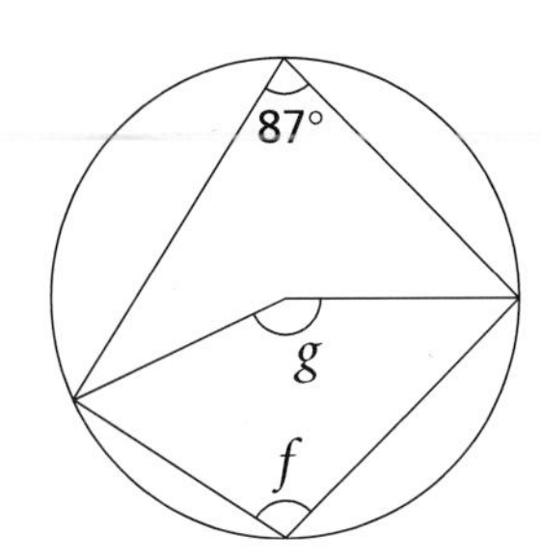

Angles in a cyclic quadrilateral

Opposite angles in a cyclic quadrilateral add up to 180°.

angle ABC + angle CDA = 180°

angle DAB + angle BCD = 180°

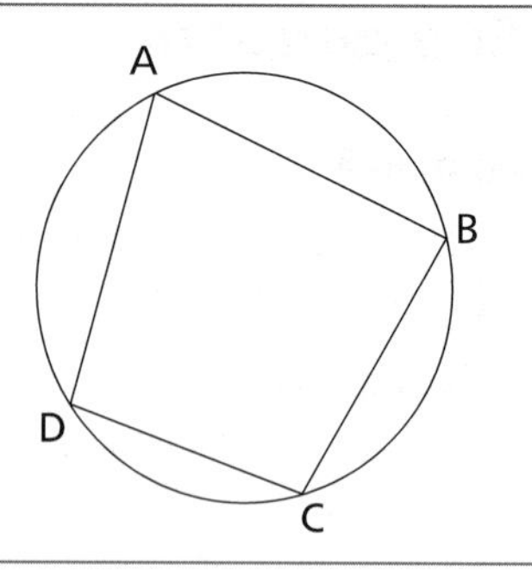

C2 Find the lettered angles in these diagrams.

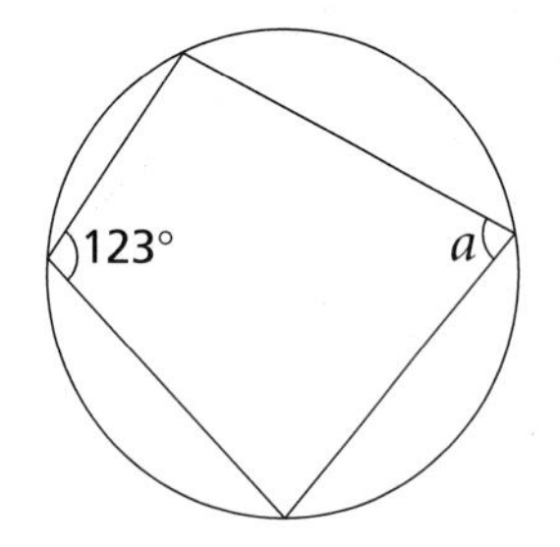

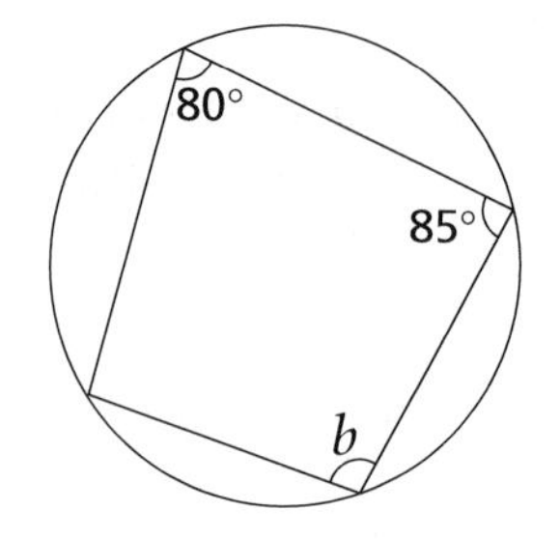

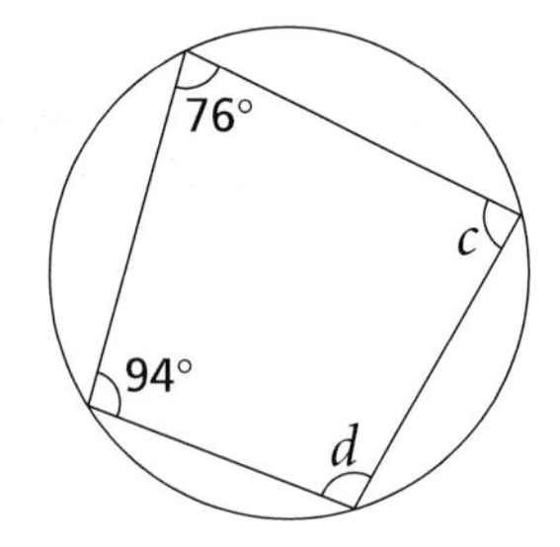

C3 (a) Find angles h and i in this diagram.

(b) What special type of quadrilateral is this?

(c) XY is the one line of symmetry of this shape. How is XY related to the circle?

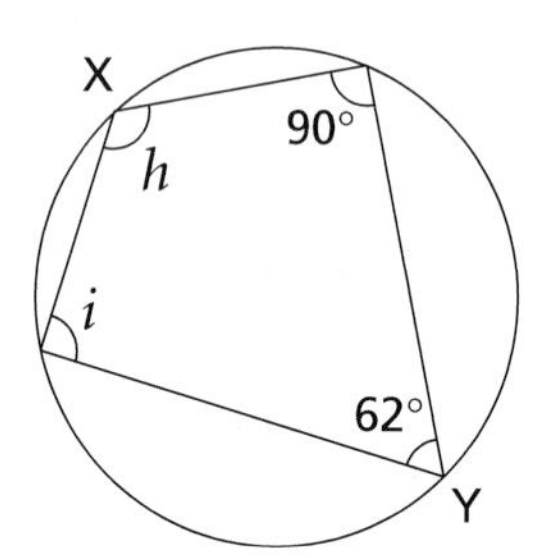

C4 (a) Draw a circle with two diameters on it. Label the ends of the diameters A, B, C, D.

(b) Join A, B, C and D to make a cyclic quadrilateral.

(c) What type of quadrilateral is ABCD? Explain why this must always be true.

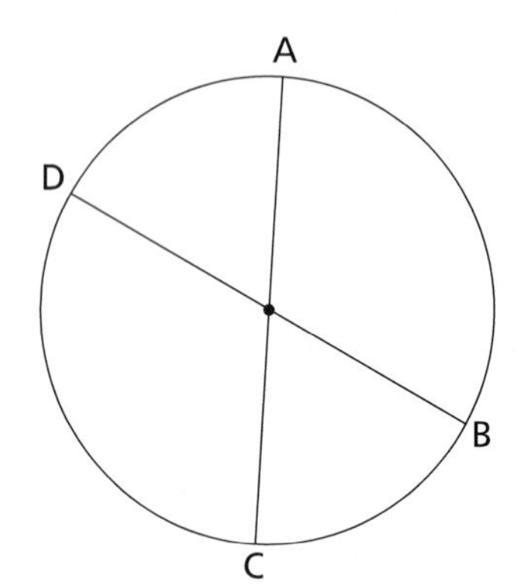

D *At a tangent*

Investigation 5

- Copy this diagram on to paper with point O 5 cm above the horizontal line.
- Mark a point A further along the horizontal line. Draw a straight line from A which just touches the circle at a point B.
- What is angle OBA?
- Investigate what happens to angle OBA when point A is placed in different positions.
- A line which touches a circle is called a tangent. What can you say about a tangent and the radius of a circle at the point where it touches?

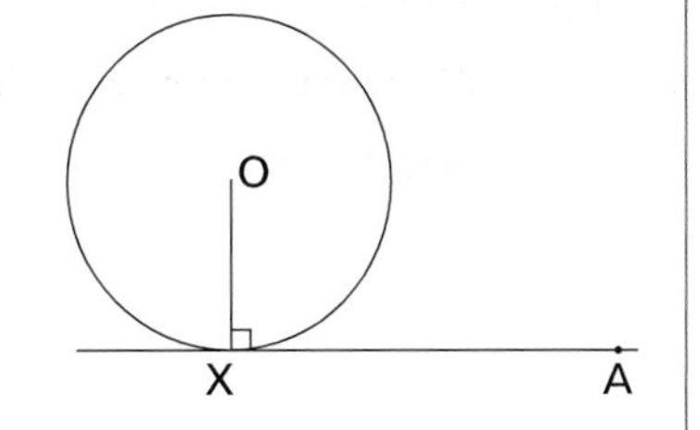

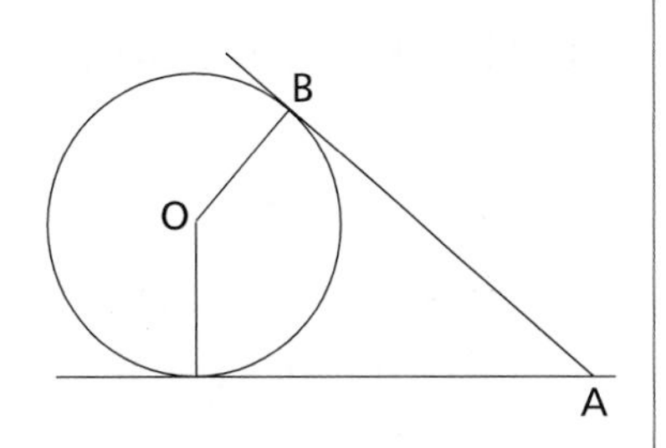

D1 In each of these diagrams the line AB is a tangent to the circle. Point O is the centre of the circle. Find the missing angles in each diagram.

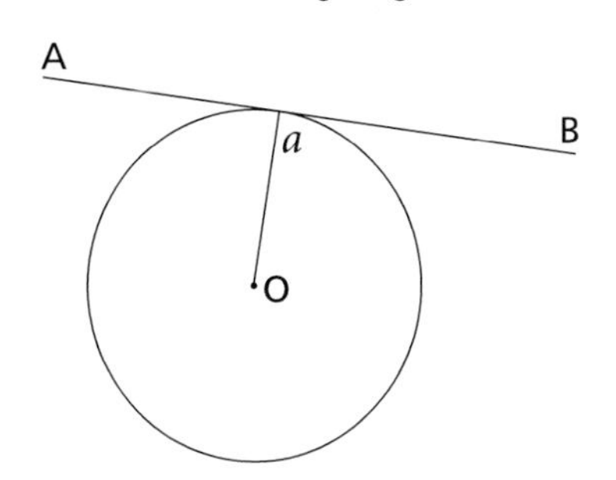

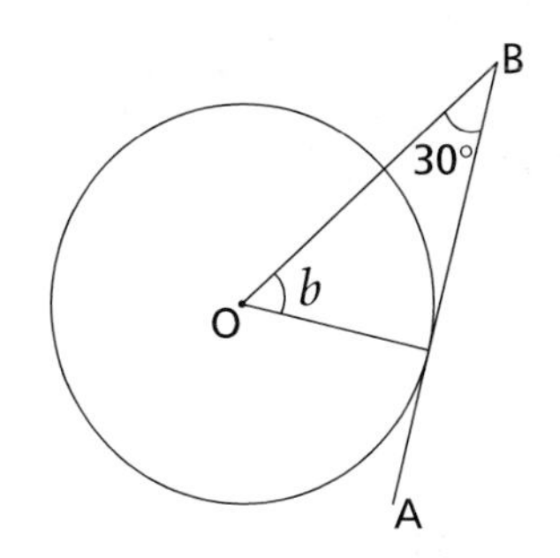

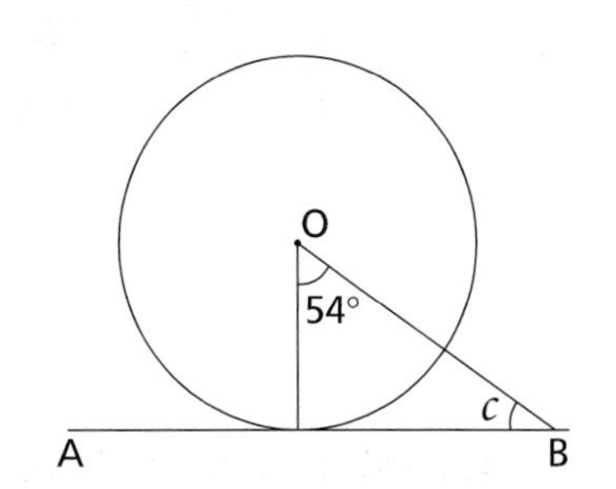

D2 In this diagram AB is a tangent to the circle centre O.

(a) What is angle OCA?

(b) Find these angles.

(i) CDA (ii) CED (iii) ECD

(iv) ACE (v) AEC

(c) What can you say about triangles ACE and CDE?

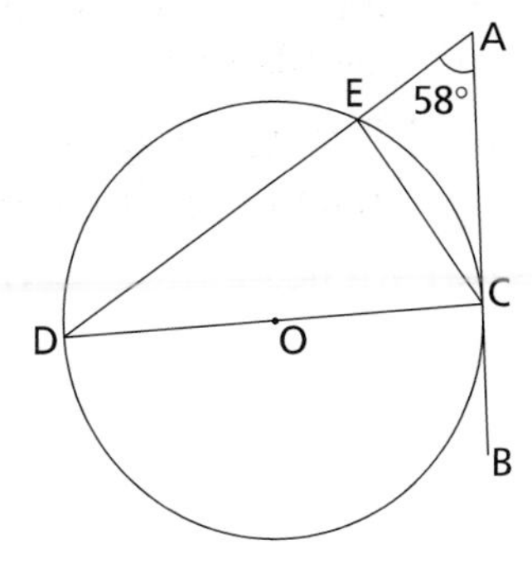

E *Reasons*

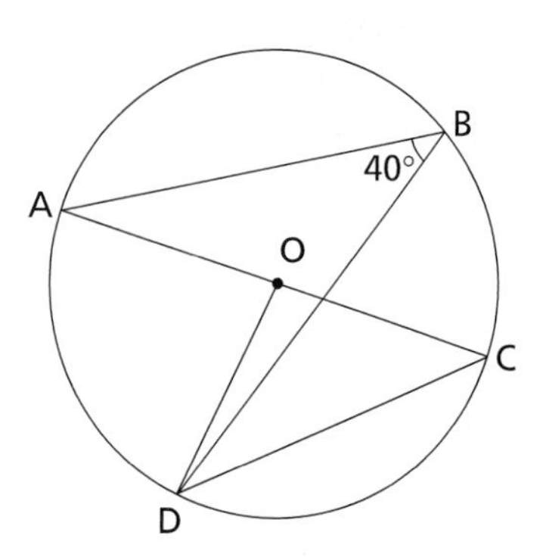

In this diagram there are four points A, B, C and D on the circumference of a circle with centre O.
Angle ABD = 40°

Several other angles can be calculated, for example

∠ACD = 40° (∠ACD = ∠ABD because the angles are made by lines from the same two points on the circumference.)

E1 Answer these questions from the diagram above.

(a) Explain why angle AOD = 80°.

(b) Explain why angle DOC = 100°.

(c) What type of triangle is DOC? Explain your answer.

(d) Find angle ODC.

E2 In this diagram points P, Q, R and S are all on the circumference of a circle centre O.

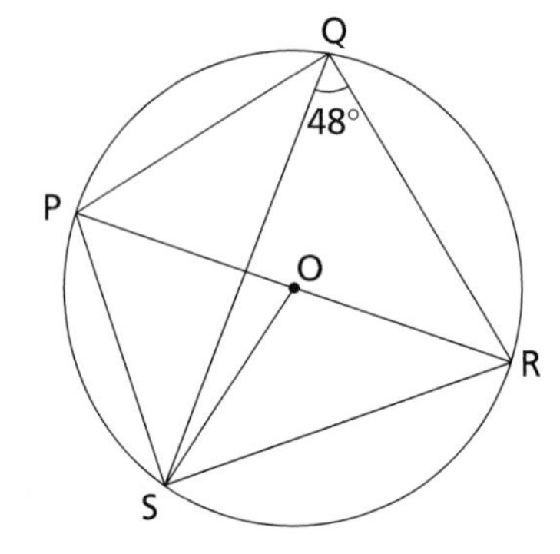

(a) State angle PQR.
Use this to find angle PQS.

(b) Show that angle SOR is 96°.

(c) What type of triangle is SOR?
Use this to find angle ORS.

(d) Find angle SPR.
Give the reasons for your answer.

E3 In this diagram points K, L, M and N lie on a circle with centre O.
MT is a tangent to the circle.
Angle MLK is 75°.
Angle NMT is 30°.

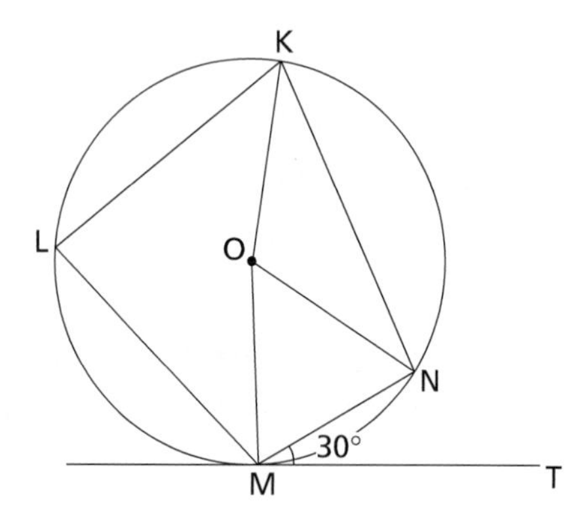

Find these angles, giving your reasons.

(a) MOK (b) KNM

(c) OMN (d) NKO

Test yourself

T1 Find the lettered angles in these diagrams.

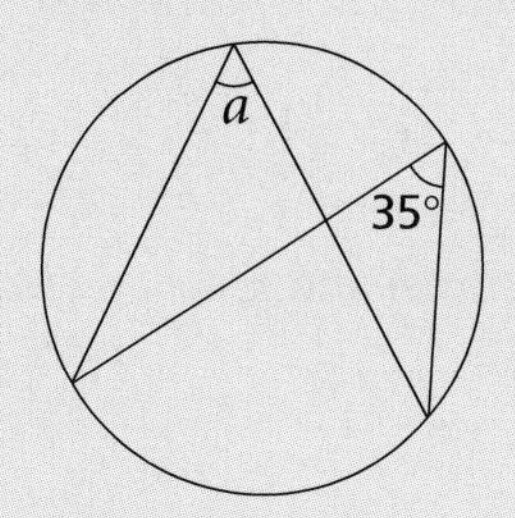

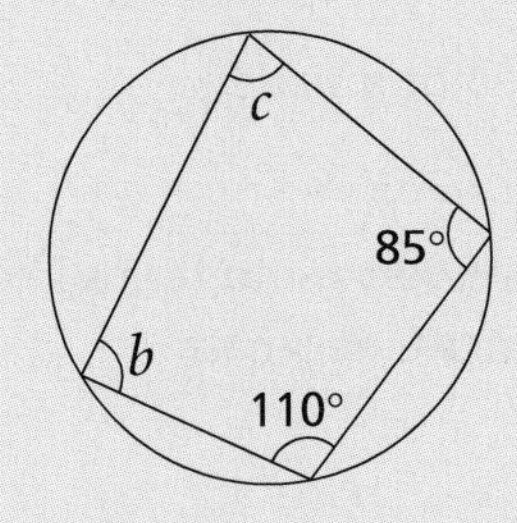

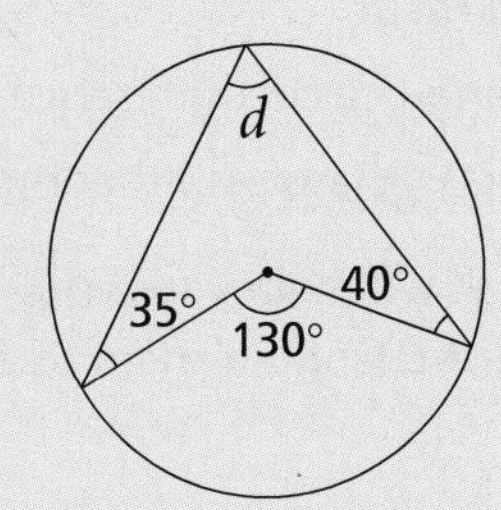

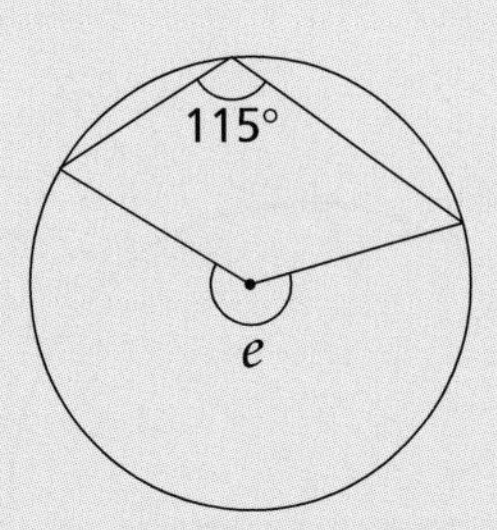

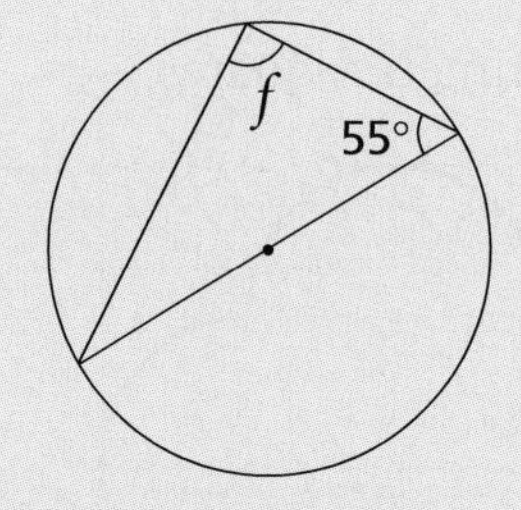

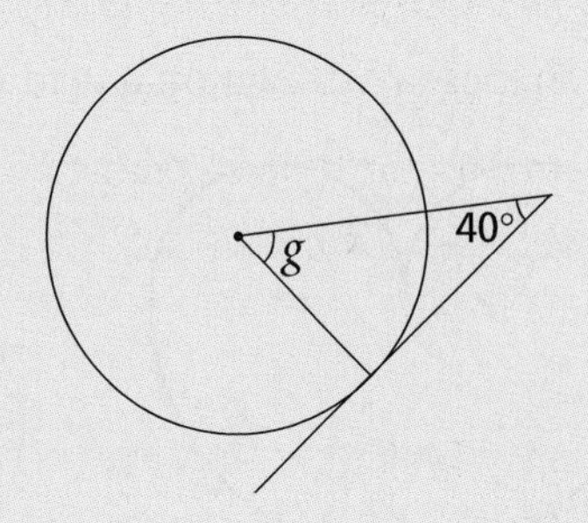

T2 Calculate the lettered angles in these diagrams.
Explain how you got your answers.

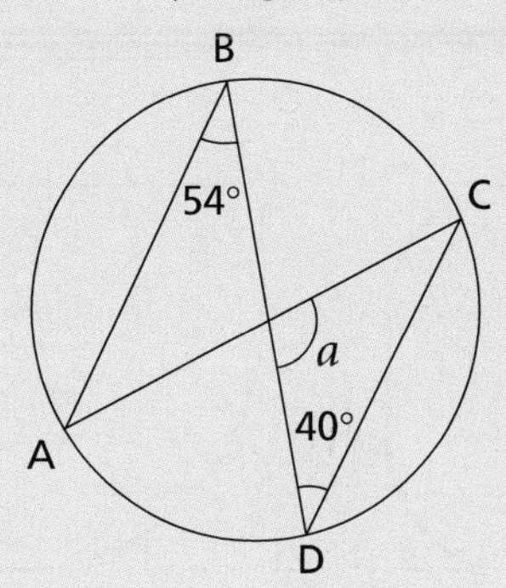

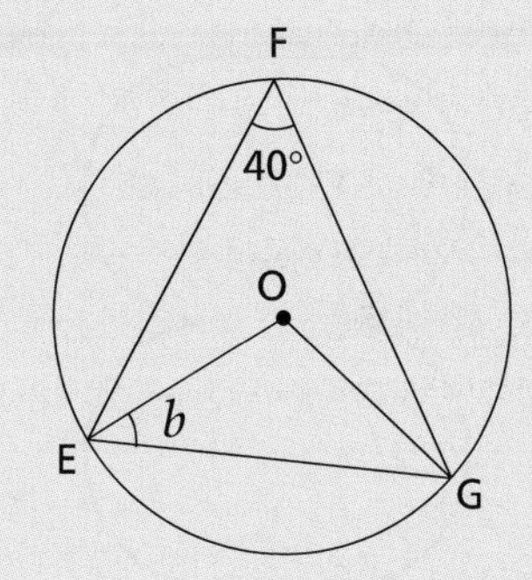

T3 In this diagram, lines ABC and ED are parallel.
EOB is a diameter of the circle, centre O.
Angle OED = 35°.

(a) Find the size of

(i) angle x (ii) angle y

(b) Write down the size of angle z.
Give a reason for your answer.

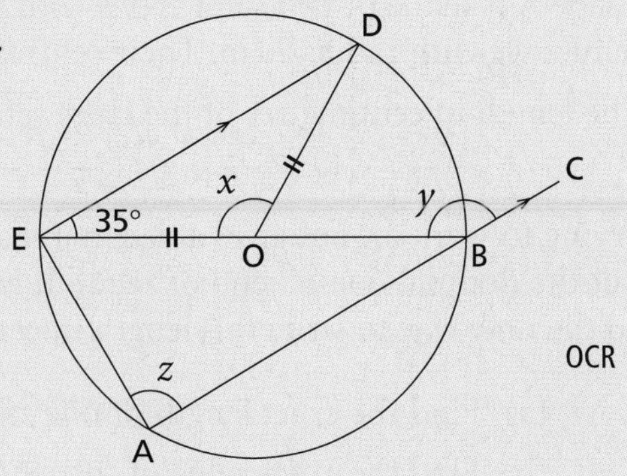

OCR

62 *Exactly so*

You will revise

- finding the circumference and area of a circle
- using Pythagoras's theorem

This work will help you write exact answers using terms like $\sqrt{10}$ (surds) and π, instead of changing them to approximate decimals.

A *Keeping sight of* π

These shapes are drawn on a grid of centimetre squares.

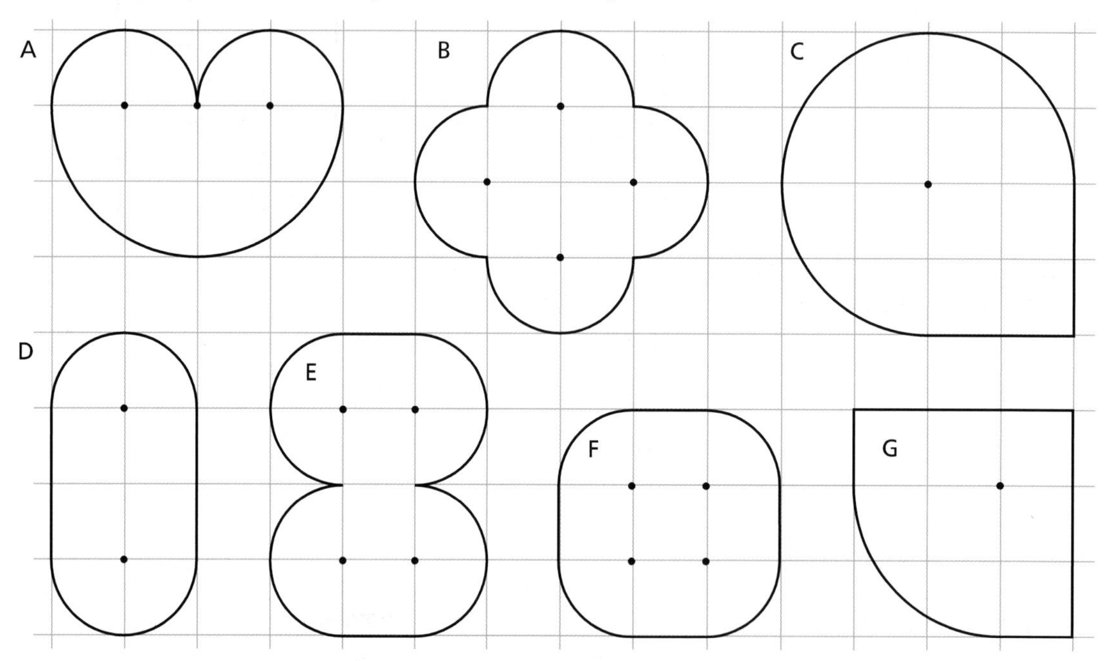

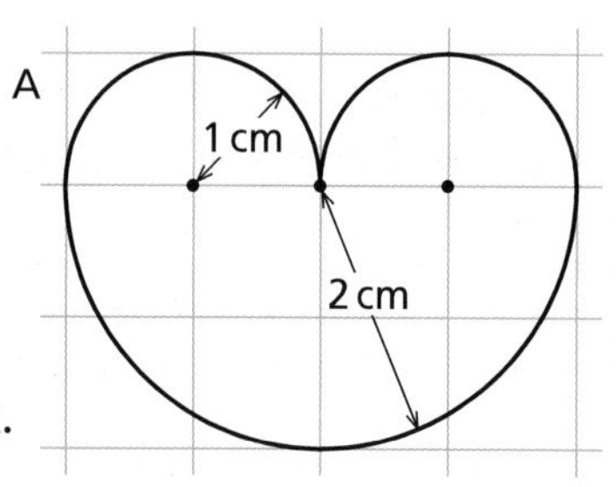

Shape A is made of two semicircles with radius 1 cm and one semicircle with radius 2 cm. Their centres are marked with dots.

The length in centimetres of the large semicircle is

$$\tfrac{1}{2} \times 2\pi r = \tfrac{1}{2} \times 2 \times \pi \times 2 = 2\pi$$

Trying to work 2π out gives a decimal that starts as 6.283 185 307…
But the decimal doesn't end or recur. It isn't equal to an exact fraction.
So the only way to write this length in centimetres **exactly** is 2π.

A1 (a) Find the exact length of one small semicircle in shape A.

(b) Find the exact value of the whole perimeter of shape A.

A2 Find the exact perimeter of each of the other shapes above.

A3 (a) Find the area of one small semicircle in shape A on the opposite page. Give the **exact** answer, with π left in it.

(b) Find the exact area of the large semicircle in in shape A.

(c) Find the exact value of the whole area of shape A.

A4 Find the exact area of all the other shapes on the opposite page.

A5 (a) What is the area of the square with the black outline?

(b) What is the exact area of the quarter circle?

(c) Write an exact expression for the area of the yellow shape.

(d) Write an exact expression for the perimeter of the yellow shape.

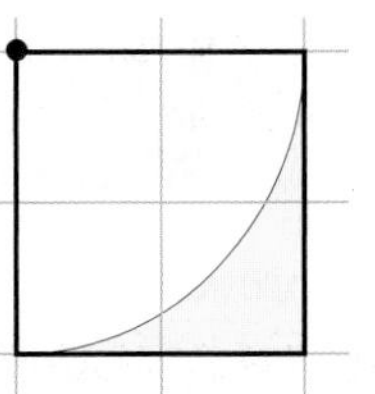

A6 For each of these shapes, find

(i) the exact area

(ii) the exact perimeter

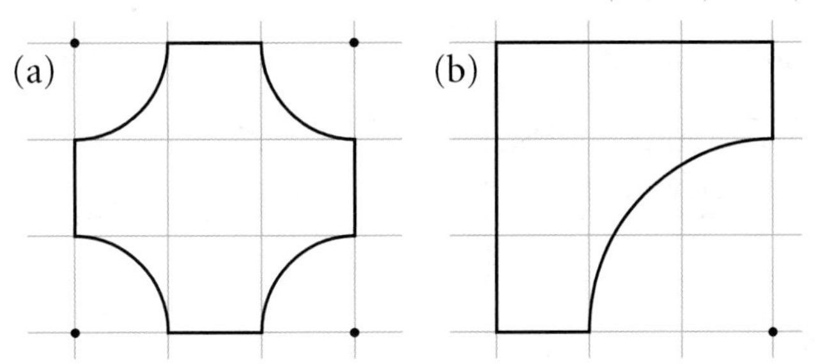

A7 Find the perimeter of this shape, keeping π in your answer.

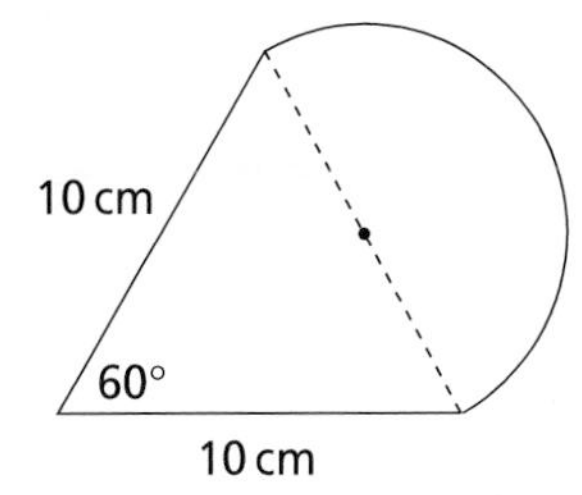

B *Keeping sight of surds*

This is a right-angled triangle.

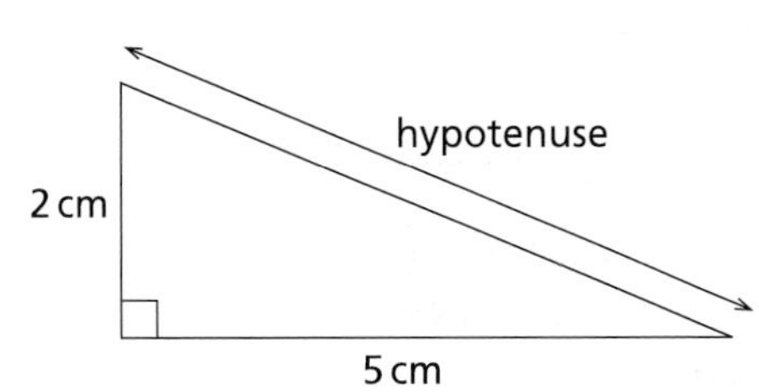

Using Pythagoras's theorem, the length in centimetres of its hypotenuse is $\sqrt{29}$.

Trying to work this out gives a decimal that starts as 5.385 164 807…
But the decimal doesn't end or recur.
So the only way to write this length in centimetres **exactly** is $\sqrt{29}$.

B1 Find the length of each hypotenuse, leaving each answer as an exact value.

(a)

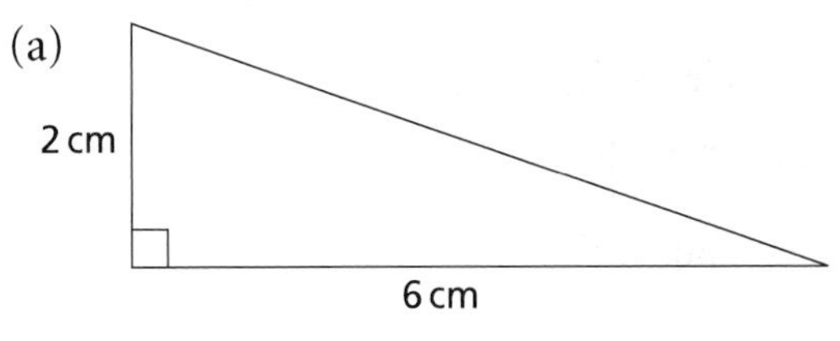

(b)

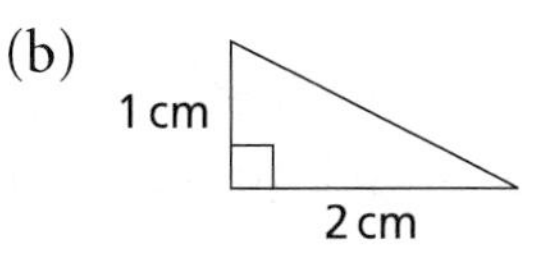

This triangle is drawn on centimetre squares.
In centimetres, the exact length of its hypotenuse is $\sqrt{10}$.
So its perimeter is $1 + 3 + \sqrt{10}$, which you can leave as the exact value $4 + \sqrt{10}$.

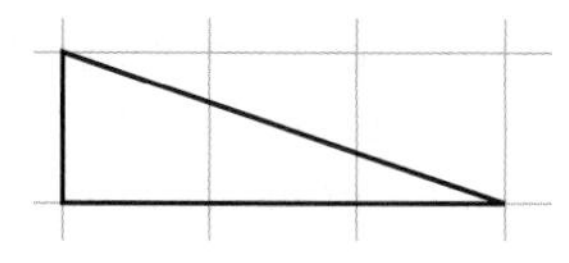

B2 This triangle is on centimetres squares.

(a) How long is AB exactly?

(b) How long is AC exactly?

(c) What is the exact perimeter of the triangle?

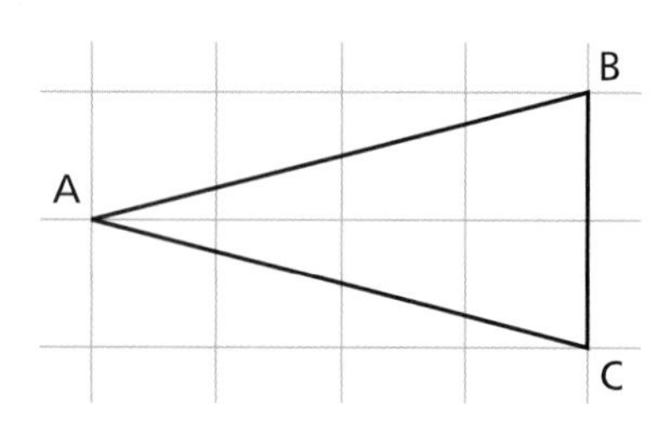

An expression with an exact square root in, like $4 + \sqrt{10}$, is called a surd.
The answers to B1 and B2 are also surds.

B3 Shapes P to W are drawn on centimetre squares.
By working out exact perimeters (keeping your answers as surds), sort them into pairs with the same perimeter.

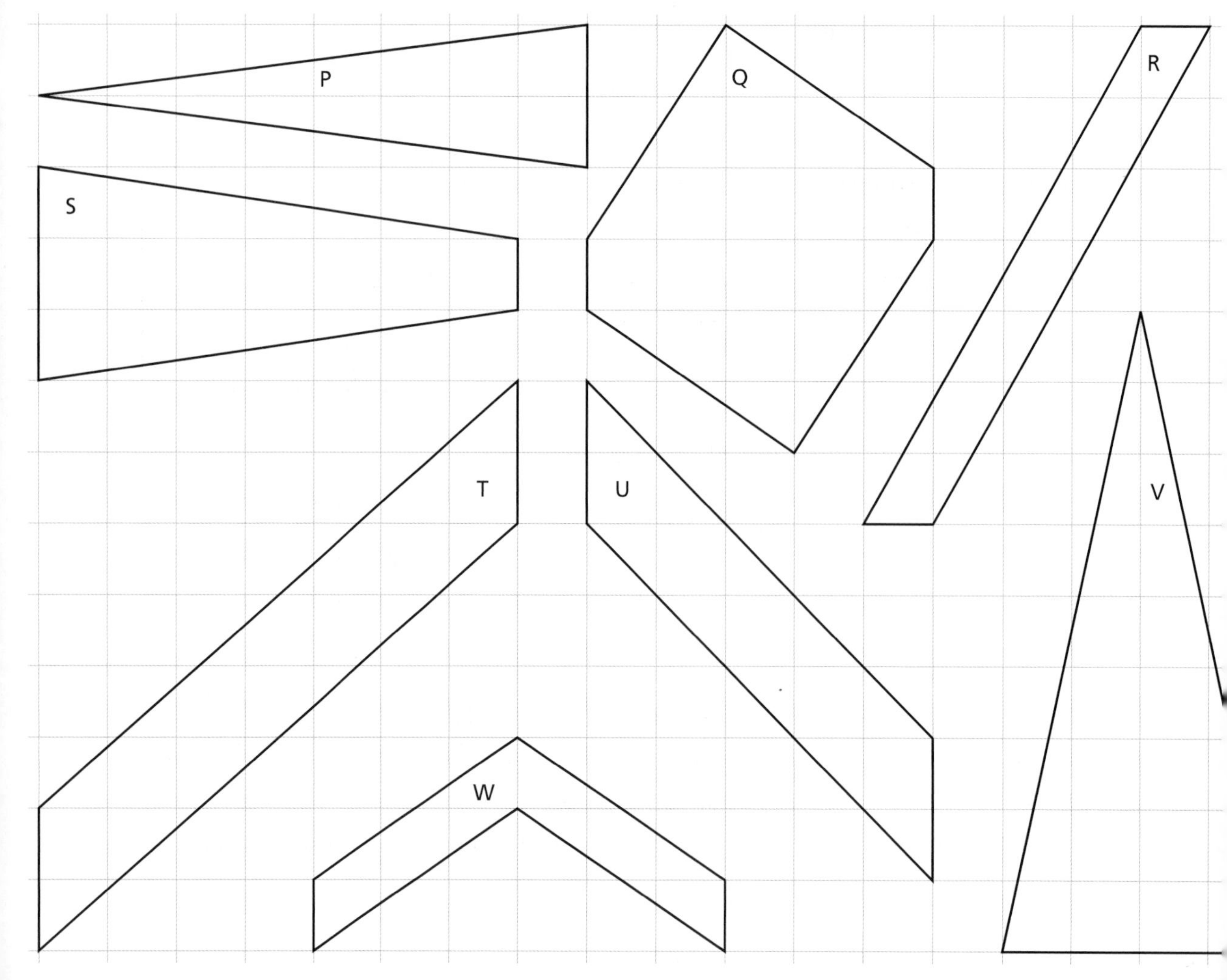

B4 Use Pythagoras to find the missing side in each of these.
They are not drawn accurately.
Leave each answer as an exact value.

(a)

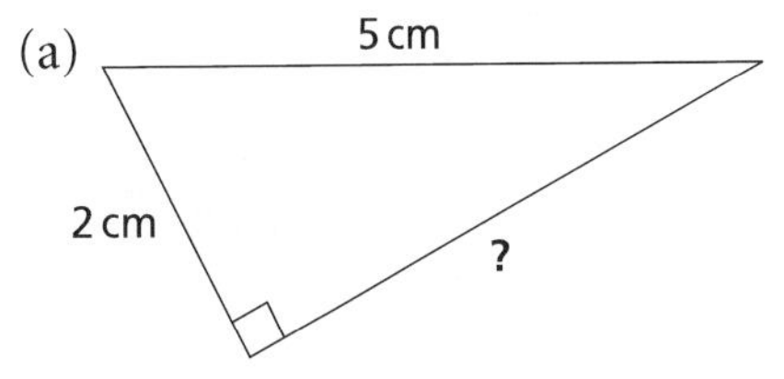

(b)

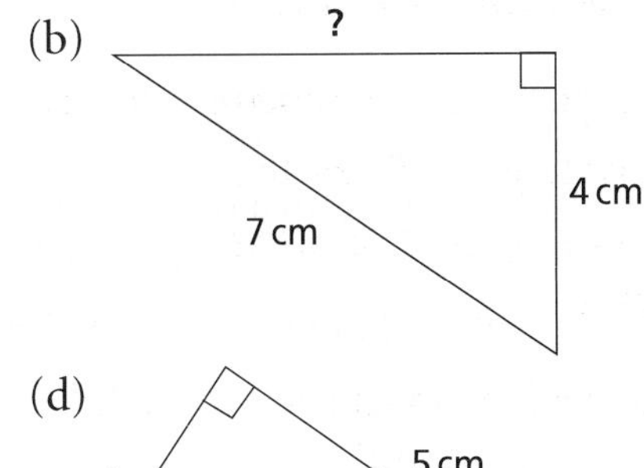

(c)

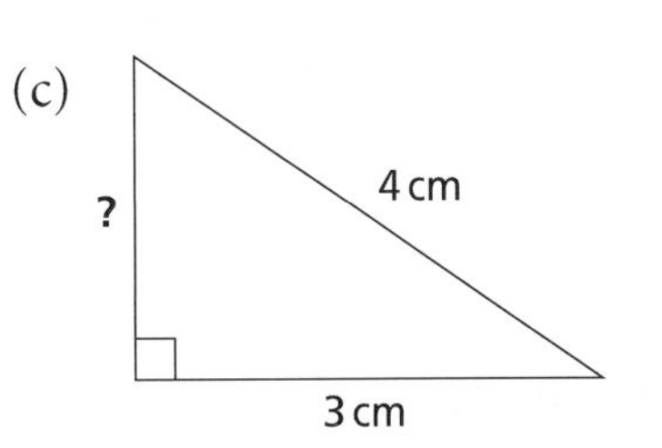

(d)

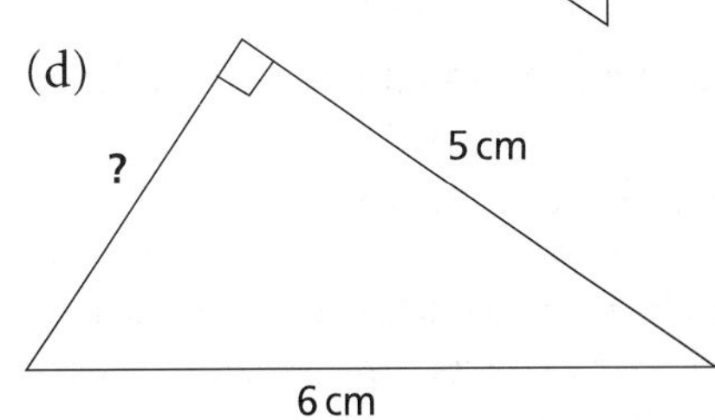

B5 Give the perimeter of each of the triangles in B4, leaving your answers as surds.

B6 Calculate the area of each of the triangles in B4, leaving your answers as exact values.

B7 The length of the hypotenuse of this right-angled triangle is $\sqrt{2}$.
So the sine of 45° is **exactly** $\frac{1}{\sqrt{2}}$.

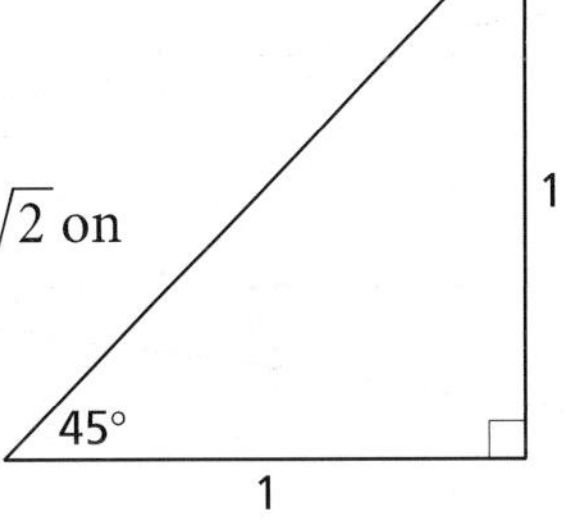

As an approximate check, make sure you can get 0.707… for $1 \div \sqrt{2}$ on a calculator, and that the calculator also gives 0.707… for sin 45°.

Use the triangle to give an exact value for cos 45°.
Do an approximate calculator check for your answers.

***B8** This equilateral triangle has sides 2 units long.
M is the midpoint of side BC.

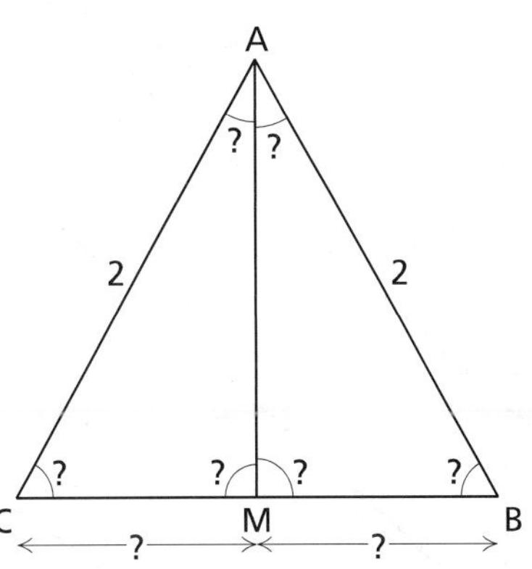

(a) Make a large sketch of the triangle but replace the question marks by values.

(b) How long is the line AM **exactly** (left as a surd)? Mark this on your sketch.

(c) Use the diagram to give these exactly.
(i) sin 60° (ii) cos 60° (iii) tan 60°
(iv) sin 30° (v) cos 30° (vi) tan 30°
Do a calculator check as in B7 for these answers.

(d) Calculate the area of the equilateral triangle, leaving any surds in your answer.

C *Mixed questions*

C1 (a) Calculate the area of a circle of radius 4 cm. Give your answer in terms of π.

(b) A square is drawn inside the circle, as shown in the diagram.

(i) Calculate the area of the square. Remember to state the units in your answer.

(ii) Calculate the area of the shaded segment. Give your answer in terms of π.

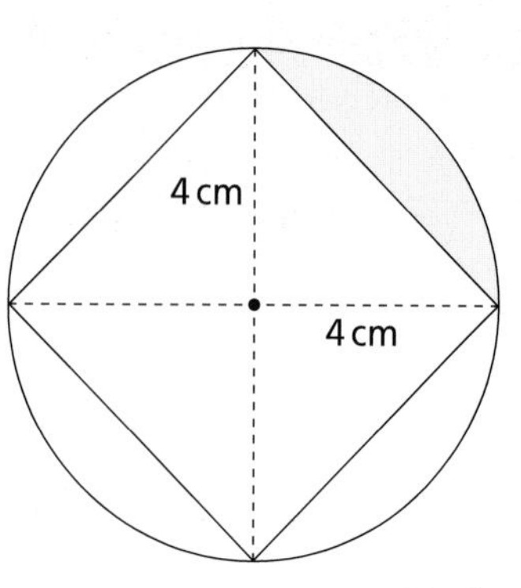

AQA (NEAB) 2000

C2 These shapes are drawn on a centimetre squared grid. Find their areas and perimeters, giving exact values.

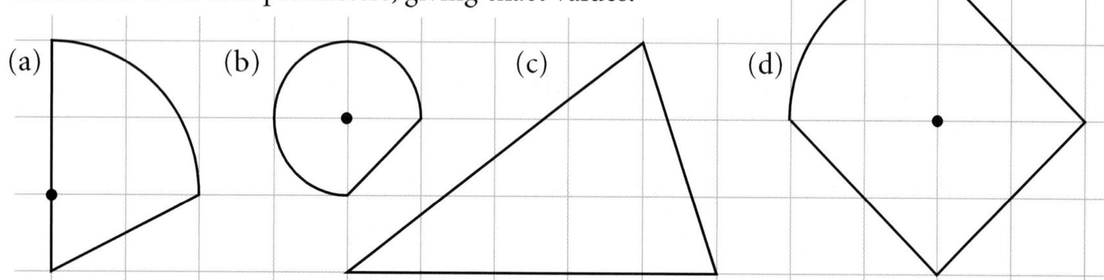

Test yourself

T1 Find the missing lengths, leaving your answers as exact values.

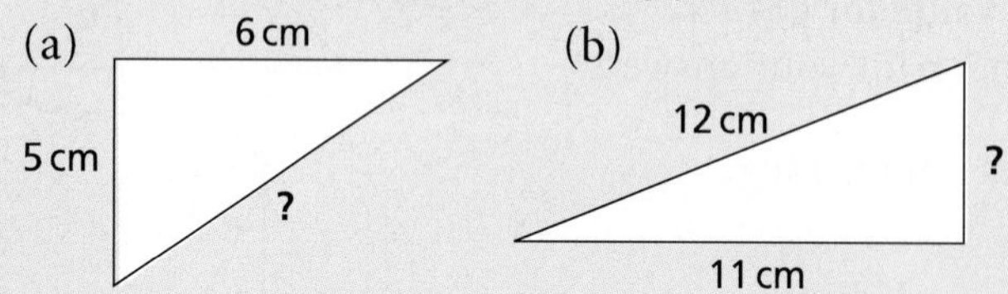

T2 These shapes are drawn on centimetre squares with centres of arcs shown by dots. Find their areas and perimeters, giving exact values.

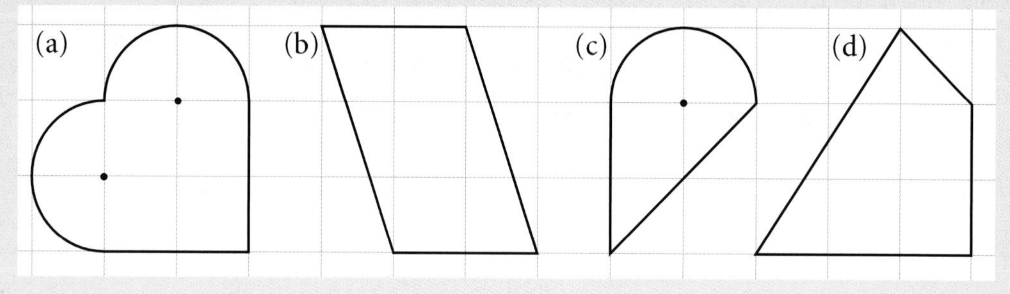

63 Dimensions

This work will help you

- work out the dimension of an expression
- use dimensions to check that an expression is sensible

The area of a triangle is given by $\frac{1}{2}$ **base × height**

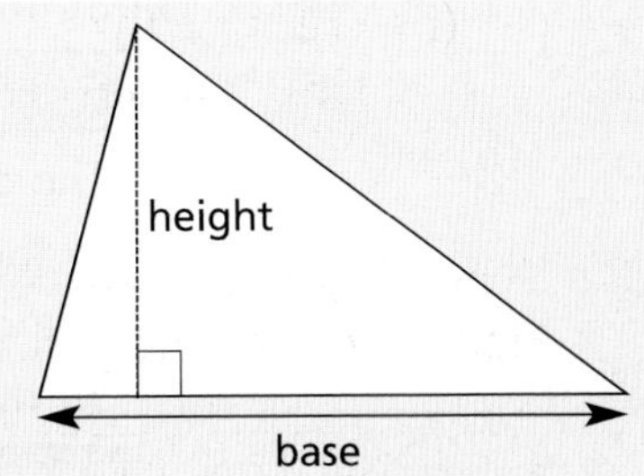

In this expression,

the base is a ***length***

the height is a ***length***

the $\frac{1}{2}$ is a ***pure number***

We say the **dimension** of the area is **[*length*]**^{2} because it is found by multiplying *length* × *length* × *a number.*

(This is also shown by the units, for example cm for length and cm^2 for area.)

A length has dimension [*length*]^1.

A pure number (including, for example, π) has no dimension.

The volume of a cylinder of radius r and height h is $\pi r^2 h$.

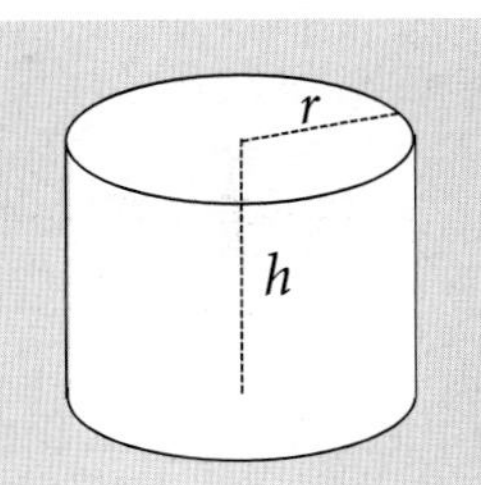

The dimension of the expression $\pi r^2 h$ is **[*length*]**^{3}
because it is found by multiplying *number* × (*length*)^2 × *length*.

- You can add or subtract quantities with the same dimension.

  4 cm + 2 cm = 6 cm

  6 cm^2 + 3 cm^2 = 9 cm^2

  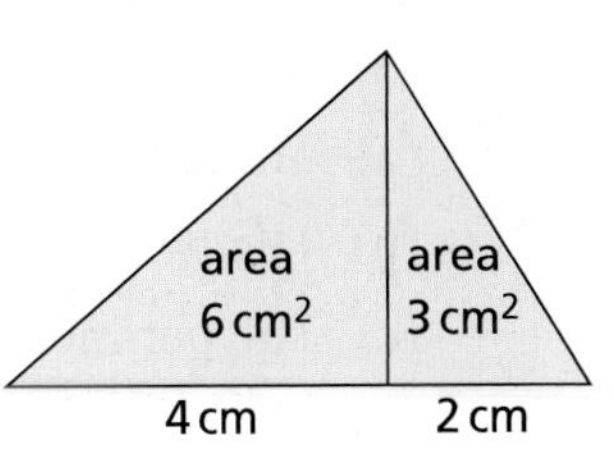

  But it does not make sense to add or subtract quantities with different dimensions.
  For example, you can't add an area of 6 cm^2 to a length of 4 cm.

  6 cm^2 + 4 cm = nonsense!

By checking dimensions we can see whether an expression could represent a length, an area or a volume (or none of these).

Worked examples

Suppose a, b, c represent lengths. What, if anything, could these represent?

(a) $(a+b)^2$

> The dimension of $(a+b)$ is [*length*],
> so the dimension of $(a+b)^2$ is [*length*]^2.
> So the expression could represent an **area**.

(b) $a(b-2c)$

> The dimension of $2c$ is [*length*],
> so the dimension of $(b-2c)$ is also [*length*].
> The dimension of $a(b-2c)$ is [*length*] x [*length*] = [*length*]^2
> So the expression could represent an **area**.

(c) $\frac{a^3b}{c}$

> The dimension of a^3b is [*length*]^3 x [*length*] = [*length*]^4.
> The dimension of $\frac{a^3b}{c}$ is $\frac{[length]^4}{[length]}$ = [*length*]^3
> So the expression could represent a **volume**.

(d) b^2+c

> The dimension of b^2 is [*length*]^2. The dimension of c is [*length*].
> It is impossible to add a length to an area.
> So the expression is **dimensionally inconsistent**.
> It does not represent anything.

In these questions, the letters a, b, c, d, h, r, … represent lengths.

1 Write an expression for each of the following.
Check that your expression is dimensionally correct.

(a) The area of the green rectangle
(b) The perimeter of the green rectangle
(c) The perimeter of the whole coloured rectangle
(d) The total area of the coloured rectangle
(e) The difference between the green and yellow areas

2 What is the dimension of each of these expressions?

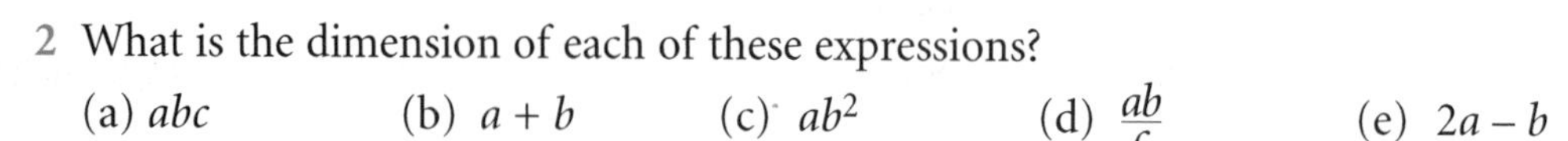

(a) abc (b) $a+b$ (c) ab^2 (d) $\frac{ab}{c}$ (e) $2a-b$

3 One of the expressions below could represent a length, one an area, one a volume and one a pure number. Which is which?

$$a^2b \qquad \frac{ab}{c^2} \qquad 2ab \qquad a + 3b$$

4 What is the dimension of each of these expressions?

(a) $a(b + c)$ (b) $\frac{a - b}{2}$ (c) $\frac{a^2 - b^2}{4}$ (d) $(2a - b)^3$

5 Say whether each of these expressions could represent a length, an area, a volume or a pure number, or whether it is dimensionally inconsistent.

(a) $ab + cd$ (b) $\frac{a^2 + b^2}{c}$ (c) $\frac{abc}{d^3}$ (d) $ab^2 - 4c^3$ (e) $a^2 + 3b$

6 A book on engineering includes the formulas below, which relate to cylinders, cones and spheres.

For each formula, say whether it could represent a length, an area, a volume, or a pure number.

(a) $4\pi r^2$ (b) $\frac{\pi(b^2 - a^2)}{4}$ (c) $2\pi r(r + h)$ (d) $\frac{4\pi r^3}{3}$

(e) $\pi h(a + b)$ (f) $\frac{ah}{b - a}$ (g) $\frac{1}{3}\pi h(a^2 + ab + b^2)$

The length of the hypotenuse of this right-angled triangle is

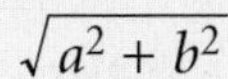

$$\sqrt{a^2 + b^2}$$

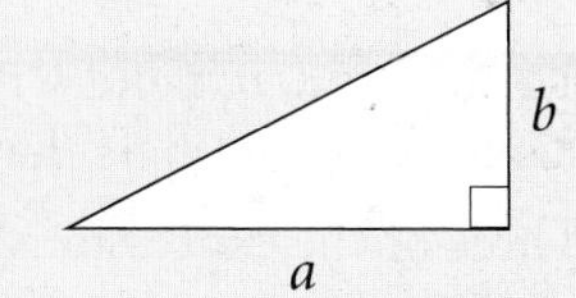

We can check that this expression has the correct dimension.

a^2 and b^2 are both $[length]^2$

So $a^2 + b^2$ is also $[length]^2$

So $\sqrt{a^2 + b^2}$ is $[length]$.

7 What is the dimension of each of these expressions?

(a) $\sqrt{ab}$ (b) $a\sqrt{bc}$ (c) $\sqrt{b^2 - 2c^2}$ (d) $\frac{a^3}{\sqrt{bc}}$ (e) $\frac{2\sqrt{ab}}{c}$

*8 The following formulae represent certain quantities connected with containers, where a, b and c are dimensions.

$$\pi a^2 b \qquad 2\pi a(a + b) \qquad 2a + 2b + 2c \qquad \tfrac{1}{2}(a + b)c \qquad \sqrt{a^2 + b^2}$$

(a) Which of these formulae represent area?

(b) Which of these formulae represent volume?

AQA(SEG) 1999

Test yourself

T1 The diagram shows a prism.

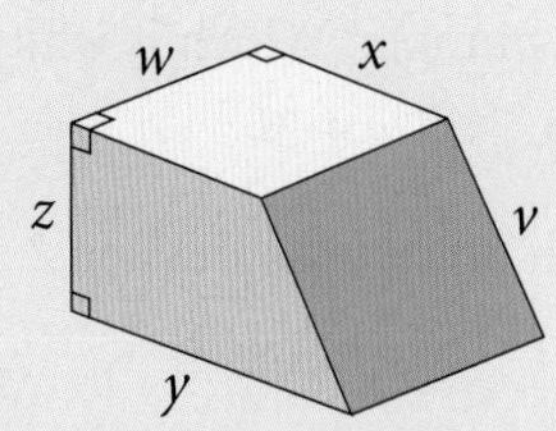

Not to scale

The following formulae represent certain quantities connected with the prism.

$$wx + wy \qquad \tfrac{1}{2}z(x+y)w \qquad \frac{z(x+y)}{2} \qquad 2(v + 2w + x + y + z)$$

(a) Which of these fomulae represents length?

(b) Which of these formulae represents volume? AQA(SEG) 2000

T2 In the following expressions r, a and b represent lengths.
For each expression state whether it represents

a **length** an **area** a **volume** or **none** of these

(a) πab (b) $\pi r^2 a + 2\pi r$ (c) $\dfrac{\pi r a^3}{b}$ AQA 2000

T3 Here are some expressions.

$$\frac{ab}{h} \quad 2\pi b^2 \quad (a+b)ch \quad 2\pi a^3 \quad \pi ab \quad 2(a^2+b^2) \quad \pi a^2 b$$

The letters a, b, c and h represent lengths.
π and 2 are numbers that have no dimensions.
Three of the expressions could represent areas. Which are they? Edexcel

T4 The letters f, g and h all represent lengths.
For each of the following expressions, state whether it could represent a length, an area, a volume or none of these.

(a) $f^2(h+g)$ (b) $\sqrt{h^2 gf}$ (c) $\pi(3f+2g)$ OCR

T5

A	B	C	D
$p^3 + 3q^3$	$p^2 + 2q$	$2p + 3q$	$3p^2 + 2pq$

The boxes A, B, C and D show four expressions.
The letters p and q represent lengths.
2 and 3 are numbers which have no dimension.

(a) Write one of the letters A, B C or D for the expression which represents

(i) an area (ii) a length

The box X shows an expression.
The letters p and q represent lengths. n is a number.
The expression represents a volume.

X
$p^n(p+q)$

(b) Find the value of n. Edexcel

Review 10

1 The number of visitors (in thousands) per year, for the past 8 years, to an historic castle are shown.

19 18 19 17 20 22 19 21

(a) Calculate a 4-yearly moving average.

(b) Describe the trend in the data.

2 Solve each of these inequalities and sketch each solution on a number line.

(a) $2a - 7 \leq 4$ (b) $7c + 3 < 2c + 18$ (c) $5x + 2 \geq 3(x - 2)$

3 (a) An ordinary six-sided dice is rolled once.
What is the probability of rolling an even number?

(b) If this dice is rolled twice, what is the probability of rolling two odd numbers?

4 On the right is a scale diagram of a lawn and two trees.

When a cat appears in the garden, each bird on the lawn flies up to the nearest tree.

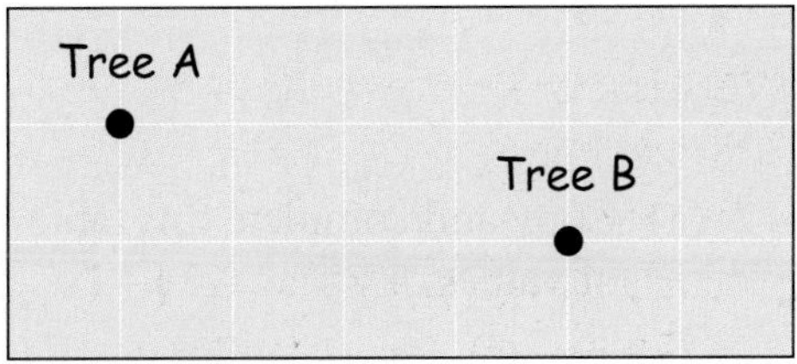

Copy the diagram and shade the area that contains all the points from where birds will fly to Tree A.

5 A cardboard box is 28 cm high, to the nearest centimetre.
What are the greatest and least possible heights of a pile of 5 of these boxes?

6 The diagram shows 5 cubes.
Vertex O is at the origin.
Vertex P has coordinates (0, 2, 1).
Write down the coordinates of vertices A, B and C.

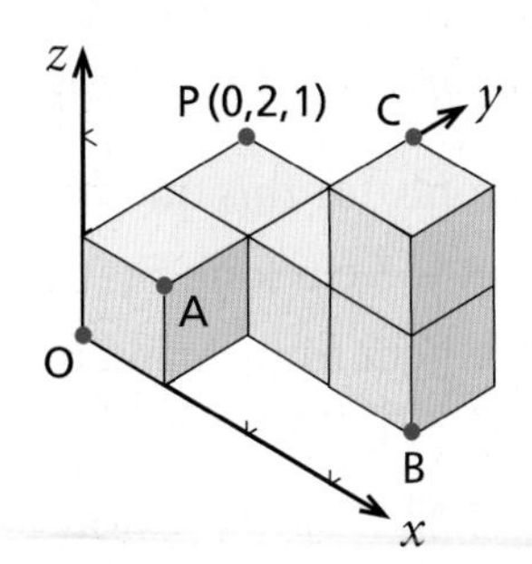

7 Using a ruler and compasses only, construct an angle of 105°.

8 In this diagram P, Q, R and S are points on the circumference of a circle centre O.

Find the sizes of angles x and y, giving reasons for your answers.

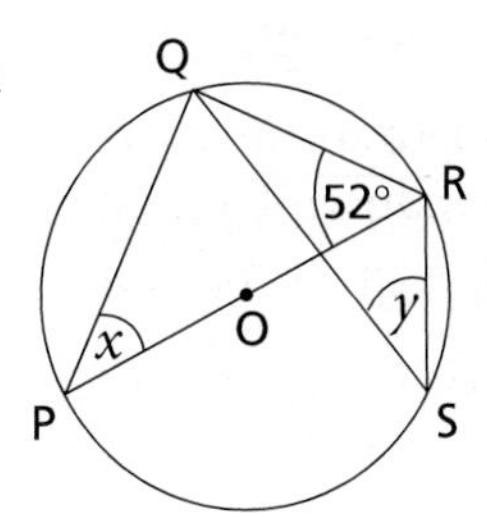

9 Sunil passes two sets of traffic lights on his route into town.
The probability that the first set of lights is green is 0.7.
The probability that the second set of lights is green is 0.4.
These two events are independent.

Work out the probability that (a) both sets of lights are green
(b) neither set of lights is green
(c) only one of the sets of lights is green

10 Marie's suitcase weighs 21.6 kg to the nearest 0.1 kg.
Tom's suitcase weighs 19.4 kg to the nearest 0.1 kg.

(a) What is the minimum possible weight of the two suitcases together?

(b) What is the largest possible difference in the weights of the two suitcases?

11 In this diagram points A, B, C and D lie on a circle centre O.
Find these angles, giving reasons for your answers.

(a) ABC (b) ADC (c) OCA (d) OAB

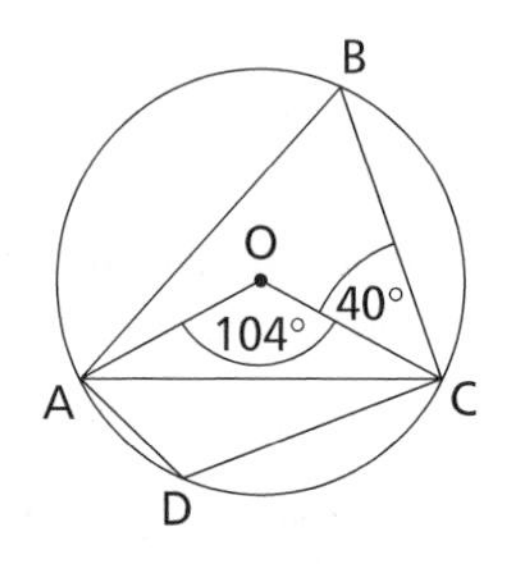

12 (a) Copy and complete this table of values of $y = x^3 - 2x - 1$.

x	⁻3	⁻2	⁻1	0	1	2	3
y	⁻22	⁻5			⁻2		

(b) On graph paper, draw axes with x from ⁻3 to 3 and y from ⁻25 to 25.
Draw the graph of $y = x^3 - 2x - 1$.

(c) Use your graph to find an approximate solution to the equation $x^3 - 2x - 1 = 0$ between 1 and 2.

(d) Now use trial and improvement to find this solution correct to two decimal places.

13 Use a ruler and compasses only for this question.

Draw a straight line AB that is 8 cm long.

Mark a point C so that it is 4 cm from A and 6 cm from B.
The points A, B and C form a triangle ABC.

Construct a perpendicular from C to the side AB.

Measure the length of this line and hence calculate the area of triangle ABC.

14 AB is a diameter of this circle. AB = 12 cm and BC = 7 cm.

(a) Calculate the length of AC correct to 1 d.p.

(b) Use trigonometry to calculate angle CAB to the nearest degree.

(c) Hence find the size of angle APC.

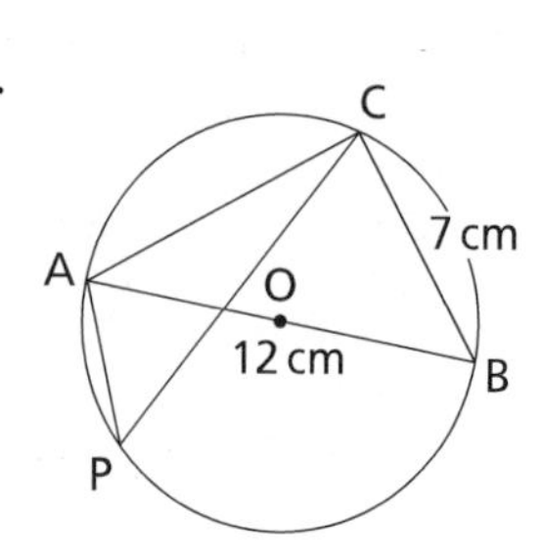

15 Write down the reciprocal of (a) 5 (b) 0.4 (c) 100

16 Give **exact** answers for each of these.

(a) Calculate the length of the line segment joining $(^-3, 5)$ to $(7, 1)$.

(b) Work out the area of a circle with a radius of 6 cm.

(c) Find the circumference of a circle with a diameter of 14 cm.

(d) What is the perimeter of a semicircle with a radius of 10 cm?

17 Solve each of these inequalities and sketch each solution on a number line.

(a) $a^2 \leq 25$ (b) $d^2 + 1 < 17$ (c) $^-1 < 2e - 1 \leq 9$

18 In the following expressions the letters r, s and t all represent lengths.
For each expression state whether it could represent a length, an area, a volume or none of these.

$3r(s + 2t)$ $\quad r^2s + \pi r^2$ $\quad r^2 + s^2$ $\quad 2\pi s(s + t)$ $\quad \frac{1}{3}\pi s^2 t$

19 Chris is going to roll a biased dice.
The probability that he will get a six is 0.09 .

(a) Work out the probability that he will **not** get a six.

Chris is going to roll the dice 30 times.

(b) Work out an estimate for the number of sixes he will get.

Tina is going to roll the same biased dice **twice**.

(c) Work out the probability that she will get
(i) **two** sixes (iii) **exactly one** six

Edexcel

20 Match the sketch graphs with the equations and sketch the missing graph.

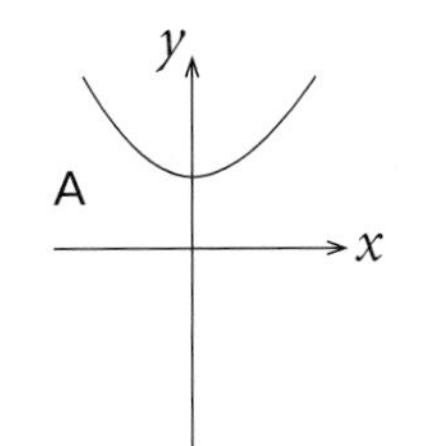

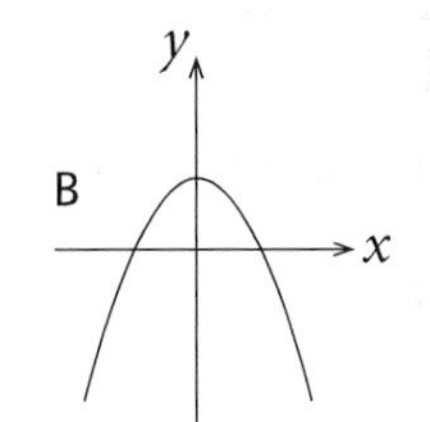

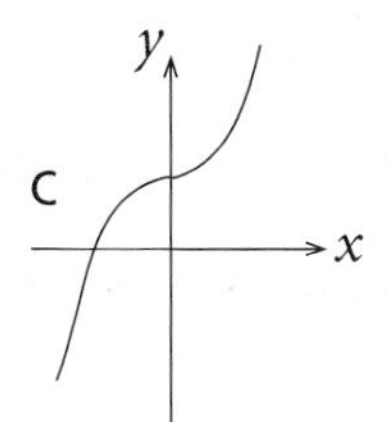

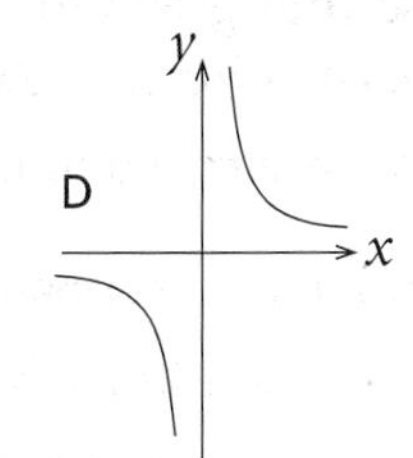

$y = 3 - x^2$

$y = x^2 - 3$

$y = x^3 + 3$

$y = \frac{3}{x}$

$y = x^2 + 3$

21 This solid is a cylinder.

(a) Show that the surface area, S, of the cylinder is given by the formula

$$S = 2\pi r^2 + 2\pi rl$$

where r is the radius of the circle and l is the length of the cylinder.

(b) A prism like this with a radius of 2 cm has a surface area of 80π cm^2.
Without using a calculator, calculate the value of l.

Index